RESTITUTION LAW

Second edition

Cavendish
Publishing
(Australia)
Pty Limited

Sydney • London

RESTITUTION LAW

Second edition

Sharon Erbacher, LLM, LLB, B Com
Solicitor, Senior Lecturer in Law
Deakin University

Cavendish
Publishing
(Australia)
Pty Limited

Sydney • London

Second edition first published in Great Britain 2002 by
Cavendish Publishing Limited, The Glass House,
Wharton Street, London WC1X 9PX, United Kingdom
Telephone: + 44 (0)20 7278 8000   Facsimile: + 44 (0)20 7278 8080
Email: info@cavendishpublishing.com
Website: www.cavendishpublishing.com

Published in the United States by Cavendish Publishing
c/o International Specialized Book Services,
5804 NE Hassalo Street, Portland,
Oregon 97213-3644, USA

Published in Australia by Cavendish Publishing (Australia) Pty Ltd
3/303 Barrenjoey Road, Newport, NSW 2106, Australia
Telephone: (02) 9999 2777   Facsimile: (02) 9999 3688
Email: info@cavendishpublishing.com.au

National Library of Australia Cataloguing in Publication Data
Erbacher, Sharon
Australian Restitution Law 2nd ed
1 Unjust enrichment – Australia 2 Fraudulent conveyances – Australia
3 Restitution – Australia I Title

Library of Congress Cataloguing in Publication Data
Data available

ISBN 1-876905-09-3

1 3 5 7 9 10 8 6 4 2

Printed and bound in Great Britain

PREFACE

The law of restitution, as founded on the principle of unjust enrichment, is now firmly entrenched in Australia as an independent branch of the law of civil obligations, providing additional and alternative relief to that provided by the laws of contract, torts and equity. Since the publication of the first edition of this book in 1998, a large body of restitutionary authority has built up in Australia, with a burgeoning number of cases at first instance and on appeal being decided in accordance with restitutionary principles. Nevertheless, because of its relatively recent origins, the principles of restitution law, and in particular the principle of unjust enrichment upon which restitutionary relief is based, are still relatively unknown in the profession. As such, an urgent need still exists for Australian legal practitioners, as well as law students, to be educated as to the circumstances where the law of restitution applies and the relief it provides. This book, which at the time of writing is the only Australian text containing source materials on restitution law, will hopefully assist in fulfilment of this need as well as being a vital resource for researchers in this area.

There still appears to be a lingering perception amongst Australian practitioners that the law of restitution is largely the creation of legal academics, and that unjust enrichment principles are the result of a forced or creative interpretation of the cases. One of my aims in writing and updating this book is to establish convincingly that restitutionary principles have a strong basis in the case law. Readers will see that I have only occasionally relied upon secondary sources to illustrate important principles, preferring instead to source those principles directly in judicial authorities. It cannot be doubted, however, that the important work in providing a common conceptual basis for apparently disparate lines of authority was the genius of academics and that the views of academics have perhaps an unusually high degree of influence upon the courts when deciding restitutionary cases. As such, the academic contribution in this area is too prominent to be disregarded, prompting me to include a summary of the main academic views on each topic.

There have been some important developments in restitution law since the publication of the first edition. The High Court of Australia in its decision in *Roxborough v Rothmans of Pall Mall Australia Ltd* (2001) 185 ALR 335 examined the principles relating to recovery of payments where the basis for the payments has failed, and established the proposition that money is recoverable on that ground even though the unperformed obligation was not a specific contractual obligation. The House of Lords has also been active in the restitution area, delivering two groundbreaking decisions. In *Kleinwort Benson Ltd v Lincoln City Council* [1999] 2 AC 349, it recognised mistake of law as a ground of recovery in England for the first time, and addressed difficult issues relating to the effect of retrospectivity of judicial decisions on mistake of law claims. In *Attorney-General v Blake* [2001] AC 268, the court recognised for the first time that an account of profits will be available in some circumstances upon a breach of contract. In this second edition I have documented these and other major developments at length, as well as taken advantage of the opportunity to enhance the commentary and analysis throughout the book.

Grateful thanks to the staff at Cavendish Publishing for their cheerful and thorough editorial assistance. Lastly, my thanks and expression of appreciation to my parents, Des and Glenda, for their constant and ongoing support, no matter what.

Sharon Erbacher
School of Law, Deakin University
August 2002

CONTENTS

TABLE OF CASES

TABLE OF LEGISLATION

JOURNAL ABBREVIATIONS

ABLR	Australian Business Law Review
ABR	Australian Bar Review
Adel LR	Adelaide Law Review
ALJ	Australian Law Journal
BCL	Building and Construction Law
Bond LR	Bond Law Review
CLJ	Cambridge Law Journal
CLP	Current Legal Problems
CLQ	Commercial Law Quarterly
Corn LQ	Cornell Law Quarterly
Corp and Bus LJ	Corporate and Business Law Journal
EL Rev	European Law Review
Harv L Rev	Harvard Law Review
JBL	Journal of Banking Law
JCL	Journal of Contract Law
JLS	Journal of Legal Studies
Leg Dec	Legal Decisions Affecting Bankers
LMCLQ	Lloyd's Maritime and Commercial Law Quarterly
LQR	Law Quarterly Review
LS	Legal Studies
MLR	Modern Law Review
Mon ULR	Monash University Law Review
MULR	Melbourne University Law Review
Newc LR	The Newcastle Law Review
NLJ	New Law Journal
NSWLR	New South Wales Law Review
NZLJ	New Zealand Law Journal
NZLR	New Zealand Law Review
OJLS	Oxford Journal of Legal Studies
QUTLJ	Queensland University of Technology Law Journal
RLR	Restitution Law Review
Syd LR	Sydney Law Review
Tort L Rev	Tort Law Review
U of West Ont Law Rev	University of Western Ontario Law Review

UQLJ	University of Queensland Law Journal
UWAL Rev	University of Western Australia Law Review
Yale LJ	Yale Law Journal

CHAPTER 1

THE HISTORY AND BASIS OF
THE LAW OF RESTITUTION

HISTORICAL ANTECEDENTS

**Goff, R, and Jones, G, *The Law of Restitution*, 5th edn, 1998,
London: Sweet & Maxwell, pp 3–4 [footnotes omitted]**

[3] The law of restitution is the law relating to all claims, quasi-contractual or otherwise, which are founded upon the principle of unjust enrichment. Restitutionary claims are to be found in equity as well as at law. But the common law of quasi-contract is the most ancient and significant part of restitution and, for that reason, restitution is more easily understood if approached through that topic.

We understand quasi-contract to be that part of restitution which stems from the common *indebitatus* counts for money had and received and for money paid, and from *quantum meruit* and *quantum valebat* claims. The *action for money had and received* lay to recover money which the plaintiff had paid to the defendant, on the ground that it had been paid under a mistake or compulsion, or for a consideration which had wholly failed. By this action the plaintiff could also recover money which the defendant had received from a third party, as when he was accountable or had attorned to the plaintiff in respect of the money, or the money formed part of the fruits of an office of the plaintiff which the defendant had usurped. The action also lay to recover money which the defendant had acquired from the plaintiff by a tortious act; and, in the rare cases, where the defendant had received money which the plaintiff could identify as his own at the time of receipt and for which the defendant had not given consideration, the plaintiff could assert his claim by means of this action.

The *action for money paid* was the appropriate action when the plaintiff's claim was in respect of money paid, not to the defendant, but to a third party, from which the defendant had derived a benefit. Historically, the plaintiff had to show that the payment was made at the defendant's request; but we shall see that the law was prepared to 'imply' such a request on certain occasions, in particular [4] where the payment was made under compulsion of law or, in limited circumstances, in the course of intervention in an emergency on the defendant's behalf, which we shall call necessitous intervention.

[4] *Quantum meruit* and *quantum valebat* claims lay respectively to recover reasonable remuneration for services and a reasonable price for goods supplied by the plaintiff. Since, like payment to a third party, services can be rendered and goods supplied without the co-operation of the defendant, something more than the mere supply of the services or goods must be shown to make the defendant liable to pay for them. So here, too, the plaintiff had to prove, and indeed must still plead, a request by the defendant. But again the notion of request has been extended. It is now enough that the defendant had freely accepted the services rendered or the goods delivered.

To draw the boundaries of quasi-contract, it is necessary to refer to the limits of these old forms of action. But these limits, though relevant, are not definitive. Not every right enforced by these remedies can be classified as quasi-contractual. Each one of the remedies might be used to enforce purely contractual claims. Thus the action for money had and received was used to compel a contracting party, such as an agent, to account; and the action for money paid lay to enforce the contractual right of indemnity, for example, by a surety against his principal debtor. *Quantum meruit* and *quantum valebat* claims were employed to recover reasonable remuneration for services or a reasonable price for goods which had been rendered or supplied under a contract in which the remuneration or price had not been agreed. Moreover, as we have seen, the action for money had and received also lay in respect of money as property; and the action could be used to recover miscellanea such as statutory penalties and judgment debts, these claims being part of the inheritance which *indebitatus assumpsit* received from *debt* in the 17th century. Historical accident is an unsatisfactory basis for classification and, to arrive at a satisfactory description of quasi-contract, jurists have been forced to search for a predominant principle which will enable them to reject a minority and unify the majority of the claims enforced by these forms of action. This principle is widely accepted to be *unjust enrichment*.

Quasi-contractual claims are, therefore, those which fall within the scope of the actions for money had and received or for money paid, or of *quantum meruit* or *quantum valebat* claims, and which are founded upon the principle of unjust enrichment ...

Commentary

As the extract from Goff and Jones shows, the modern law of restitution includes all claims which used to be described as 'quasi-contractual'. But while the quasi-contractual claims comprise the bulk of the law of restitution, this area of law encompasses any claim which is founded upon the principle of unjust enrichment. Further, apart from the various restitutionary *causes of action*, restitutionary principles also operate purely at the remedial level, providing a 'disgorgement of gain' remedy for certain civil wrongs (see further Chapter 17).

The old forms of action which comprised the law of quasi-contract (money had and received, money paid, *quantum meruit* and *quantum valebat*) have long been abolished, though the terminology is still in frequent use. The High Court of Australia has emphasised, however, that the old forms of action are not to constrain the development of the law of unjust enrichment:[1]

[I]n a modern context where common law and equity are fused with equity prevailing, the artificial constraints imposed by the old forms of action can, unless they reflect coherent principles, be disregarded where they impede the principled enunciation and development of the law. In particular the notions of good conscience, which both the common law and equity recognised as the underlying rationale of the law of unjust enrichment, now dictate that, in applying the relevant doctrines of law and equity, regard be had to matters of substance rather than technical form.

---

1   *Baltic Shipping Co v Dillon* (1993), p 376 *per* Deane and Dawson JJ (see extract, p 286). These sentiments were approved by a majority of the High Court in *Dart Industries Inc v The Decor Corporation Pty Ltd* (1993), p 111.

THE 'IMPLIED CONTRACT' THEORY

The concept of unjust enrichment is now widely recognised as the true basis of the law of restitution.[2] However, the notion that a claim in restitution (or, formerly, quasi-contract) is based upon the injustice of the defendant's retention of the enrichment has had a chequered history in both England and Australia. Although injustice of retention was recognised very early on in *Moses v Macferlan* (1760) (see extract, p 8) as the basis for the money had and received action, for much of the 20th century the orthodox view was that the action was based upon an implied promise to repay the money.[3] Although the implied contract view has now been discarded, it is important to have a general knowledge of the doctrine of implied contract in order to understand many of the earlier authorities which have now been pressed into service in the modern law of restitution.

Sinclair v Brougham [1914] AC 398 House of Lords

The Birkbeck Building Society, an unincorporated body, had for many years been carrying on business as a bank. In 1911 the Society went into insolvency and a question of priority arose between the claims of shareholders and the Society's depositors. The House of Lords held that the carrying on of the banking business was *ultra vires* the objects of the Society, and that the debts owed to the depositors were themselves void as being *ultra vires*. The *ultra vires* depositors claimed that they were entitled to the return of their deposits on two grounds: first, on the basis of a monies had and received claim and, secondly, on the basis that they were able to trace their deposits into the assets of the Society. The House of Lords upheld the tracing claim but rejected the personal claim in quasi-contract.

Viscount Haldane LC: ... [414] In the jurisprudence of England the doctrine of *ultra vires* must now be [415] treated as established in a stringent form by acts of the legislature and decisions of great authority which have interpreted these acts. This is a principle which it appears to me must today be taken as a governing one, not only at law but in equity. I think it excludes from the law of England any *claim in personam* based even on the circumstance that the defendant has been improperly enriched at the expense of the plaintiff by a transaction which is *ultra vires*. All analogies drawn from other systems, such as that of the Roman law, appear to me to be qualified in their application by two considerations. The first is that, broadly speaking, so far as proceedings *in personam* are concerned, the common law of England really recognises (unlike the Roman law) only actions of two classes, those founded on contract and those founded on tort. When it speaks of actions arising *quasi ex contractu* it refers merely to a class of action in theory based on a contract which is imputed to the defendant by a fiction of law. The fiction can only be set up with effect if such a contract would be valid if it really existed ... Consideration of the authorities has led me to the conclusion that the action was in principle one which rested on a promise to pay, either actual or imputed by law. [Viscount Haldane then referred to various authorities, including *Moses v Macferlan* (1760) (see extract, p 8) and continued, at p 417:]

---

2   See, in Australia, *Pavey & Matthews Pty Ltd v Paul* (1987) (see extract, p 15).
3   Due to the influence of *Sinclair v Brougham* (1914) (see following extract).

My Lords, notwithstanding the wide scope of the remedy so described, I think that it must be taken to have been given only, as I have already said, where the law could consistently impute to the defendant at least the fiction of a promise. And it appears to me that as a matter of principle the law of England cannot now, consistently with the interpretation which the courts have placed on the statutes which determine the capacity of statutory societies, impute the fiction of such a promise where it would have been *ultra vires* to give it. The fiction becomes, in other words, inapplicable where substantive law, as distinguished from that of procedure, makes the defendant incapable of undertaking contractual liability. For to impute a fictitious promise is simply to presume the existence of a state of facts, and the presumption can give rise to no higher right than would result if the facts were actual ...

Lord Dunedin: ... [433] Let me ... examine the position where the money is received under a contract to repay and where that contract is found to be *ultra vires*. That there can be no resulting proper contractual obligation is clear from the decisions of this House in *Ashbury Railway Carriage and Iron Co v Riche* (1875) and *Wenlock v River Dee Co* (1887). It is here that the difficulty comes in in extending the action for money had and received to such a case. For, in the first place, if that action lay it would have the effect of bringing in A, who has, *ex hypothesi*, no binding contract to urge against B, *pari passu* with the ordinary creditors of B who have got binding contracts; and in the second, how is it possible to say that there is a fictional contract which is binding in circumstances in which a real contract is not binding? ...

Lord Parker of Waddington: ... [440] It is not ... open to the House to hold that in such a case [an *ultra vires* loan of money] the lender has an action against the company or association for money had and received. *To do so would in effect validate the transaction so far as it embodied a contract to repay the money lent.* The implied promise on which the action for money had and received is based would be precisely that promise which the company or association could not lawfully make. At the same time there seems to be nothing in those decisions which would bind the House, if they were considering whether an action would lie in law or in equity to recover money paid under any *ultra vires* contract which was not a contract of borrowing; for example, money paid to a company or association for the purchase of land which the company had no power to sell and the sale of which was therefore void, or money paid to the company or association by way of subscription for shares which it had no power to issue. In such cases the implied promise on which the action for money had and received depends would form no part of, but would be merely collateral to, the *ultra vires* contract ...

Lord Sumner: ... [452] The depositors' case has been put, first of all, as consisting in a right enforceable in a common law action. It is said that they paid their money under a mistake of fact, or for a consideration that has wholly failed, or that it has been had and received by the society to their use. My Lords, in my opinion no such actions could succeed. To hold otherwise would be indirectly to sanction an *ultra vires* borrowing. All these causes of action are common species of the *genus assumpsit*. All now rest, and long have rested, upon a notional or imputed promise to repay. The law cannot *de jure* impute promises to repay, whether for money had and received or otherwise, which, if made *de facto*, it would inexorably avoid.

To the other difficulties of such claims I will allude shortly. There was no mistake of fact. The facts were fully known so far as was material. The rules and objects of the society were accessible to all. The only mistake made was a mistake as to the law, or that mistake of conduct to which all of us are prone, of doing as others do and chancing the law.

There was no failure of consideration. As Bowen LJ says in the *Guardian* case [*In re Guardian Permanent Building Society* (1883)]:

> Those who deal with a society which professes to have power to borrow have equal means of knowledge with the society itself of the statutory powers of the company; they are put, so to speak, upon inquiry whether the company really can borrow validly or not, and if they choose to lend their money to a company which cannot properly borrow it cannot be said there is a failure of consideration. The company has got their money, it is true, but they must be taken to have known what they bought, and to have been willing to pay their money on the chance ...

[453] In these straits, Lord Mansfield's celebrated account of the action of money had and received in *Moses v Macferlan* (1760) was of course relied upon. It was said that for any one to keep the depositors' money as against them would be unconscientious, while that they should get it back would be eminently *ex quo et bono*, though it appeared also that conscience had nothing to say against payment of the depositors in full at the expense of the shareholders, though all alike must be deemed cognisant of the invalidity of the society's banking business. *Burges and Stock's Case* in *Phoenix Life Assurance Company's Liquidation* (1862), which was relied on, is irrelevant if treated as a case of an *intra vires* borrowing of the amounts of the premiums in question, which seems to have been the *ratio decidendi* of Wood VC. If the decision is supposed to be that in every case where money is paid under a contract which proves to be *ultra vires* it may be recovered as upon a consideration that has wholly failed, I think it goes too far, for the reasons I have already given. There may have been special facts to justify such an opinion in that case, though I think not, for the effect of it must in any view have been to bind the society in fact to a contract which in law was not binding at all. The other cases cited seem to me insufficient to support the appellants' claim to any common law right. The action for money had and received cannot now be extended beyond the principles illustrated in the decided cases, and [454] although it is hard to reduce to one common formula the conditions under which the law will imply a promise to repay money received to the plaintiff's use, I think it is clear that no authority extends them far enough to help the appellants now.

Resort was then had to equity, and, as I understood it, the argument was that the action for money had and received was founded on equity and good conscience, and imported a head of equity (apart altogether from its possibly too limited application at law), namely, that whenever it is *ex quo et bono* for A to repay money which he has received from B, and would be against conscience for A to keep it, then B has an equity to have A decreed to repay it. For this again Lord Mansfield's authority in the same case was invoked.

My Lords, I cannot but think that Lord Mansfield's language has been completely misunderstood. Historically, the action for money had and received was not devised by the Court of Chancery, nor was it applied there either in form or in substance. It was a form of *assumpsit*, already old in Lord Mansfield's time, and his own citation of earlier actions of this sort should be enough to shew, if that were necessary, that he never thought otherwise ...

[455] I think it is evident that Lord Mansfield did not conceive himself to be deciding that this action was one in which the courts of common law administered 'an equity' in the sense in which it was understood in the Court of Chancery (see observations of Farwell LJ in *Baylis v Bishop of London* (1913)) and the cases actually decided shew that the description of the action as being founded in the *æquum et bonum* is very far from being precise. Even the decision in *Moses v Macferlan* (1760), which has since been dissented from, for some time unsettled the law (see *Smith's Leading Cases* [11th edn, p 421], 'Notes to *Marriot v Hampton*' (1797)) and this last mentioned case is one which illustrates the proposition that money is not thus recoverable in all cases where it is unconscientious for the defendant to retain it for no one could doubt that Hampton's retention of the money in that case was very like sharp practice. *Crockford v Winter* (1807) and *Martin v Morgan* (1819) are instances, on the other hand, which shew that Lord Ellenborough and Dallas CJ respectively understood that in that form of action the court strove to do what was just and not to administer equity. With whatever complacency the Court [456] of King's Bench might regard the views expressed in *Moses v Macferlan* (1760), protests were very early made against it in the Common Pleas (*Johnson v Johnson* (1802)) and in *Miller v Atlee* (1849) Pollock CB bluntly declared the notion that the action for money had and received was an equitable action to be 'exploded', and Parke B, sitting by him, did not say him nay. This episode is reported only in 13 Jurist, but it smacks of truth. Since, then, allusions have been made from time to time to the connection between this cause of action and equity or the *æquum et bonum* (though they are not precisely the same things), for example, in *Smith v Jones* (1842), *Tregoning v Attenborough* (1830), *Rogers v Ingham* (1876), *Phillips v London School Board* (1898), and *Lodge v National Union Investment Company* (1907), but I take them all to be merely descriptive of the undoubtedly wide scope of this essentially common law action. There is now no ground left for suggesting as a recognisable 'equity' the right to recover money *in personam* merely because it would be the right and fair thing that it should be refunded to the payer ...

Commentary

The House of Lords in the principal case was unanimous in rejecting the personal claim by the depositors for monies had and received. In their Lordships' view, that claim was based on an implied contract, however, to imply a contract to repay in this case would be to imply a contract to exactly the same effect as the express *ultra vires* contract of loan. Accordingly, any implied contract would itself be void as being *ultra vires*.

The decision in *Sinclair v Brougham* as it related to the personal (quasi-contractual) claim must now be considered to be highly doubtful in England following the House of Lords decision in *Westdeutsche Landesbank Girozentrale v Council of the London Borough of Islington* (1996) (see extract, p 372). Although there was no clear majority in *Westdeutsche* for overruling this aspect of *Sinclair v Brougham*, it was suggested that the application of unjust enrichment principles would have resulted in a successful personal claim by the depositors (p 688 *per* Lord Goff; p 710 *per* Browne-Wilkinson).

The implied contract theory was dutifully adopted by the High Court of Australia in *Hirsch v The Zinc Corp Ltd* (1917) and in *Smith v William Charlick Ltd*

(1924). However, in certain categories of cases recovery was allowed even though this was inconsistent with the implied contract theory. For example, courts allowed a *quantum meruit* for services provided under a void or unenforceable contract even where it was acknowledged that an action to enforce the contract itself would fail.[4] The fictional nature of the implied contract theory is discussed in the following case.

United Australia Ltd v Barclays Bank Ltd [1941] AC 1 House of Lords

The facts are stated at p 501.

Lord Atkin: ... [26] I do not propose to discuss at any length the history of the claim in *indebitatus assumpsit*, and the cases through which that history has been traced. Very much learning has been devoted to this subject, and lawyers are indebted to Professor Ames, Sir William Holdsworth, and Professor Winfield for the light they have thrown upon the subject in well known works: and I should not like to omit the work of Mr RM Jackson on *The History of Quasi-Contract in English Law*, published in 1936 in the *Cambridge Studies in English Legal History*, from which I have derived assistance. There is also what I hope I may respectfully call a valuable contribution to the discussion in the articles recently published by my noble and learned friend Lord Wright on *Sinclair v Brougham* (1914), and a review of the American *Restatement of the Law of Restitution*, pp 1–65 of *Legal Essays and Addresses* published in 1939. I have myself consulted most of the cases referred to in these works with the exception of the cases from the Yearbooks which I have accepted from the authors.

The story starts with the action of debt which was not necessarily based upon the existence of a contract, for it covered claims to recover sums due for customary dues, penalties for breaches of bylaws and the like. The action of debt had its drawbacks, the chief being that the defendant could wage his law. There followed the application of the action on the case of *assumpsit* to debt. 'The defendant being indebted then promised.' At first there must be an express promise; then the courts implied a promise from an executory contract: *Slade's* case (1602). *Slade's* case was not a claim in *indebitatus assumpsit*, but the principle was applied, and it became unnecessary to prove an express promise in those cases. Then the action was allowed in respect of cases where there was no contract, executory or otherwise, as in the cases where debt would have lain for customary fees and the like; and by a final and somewhat [27] forced application to cases where the defendant had received money of the plaintiff to which he was not entitled. These included cases where the plaintiff had intentionally paid money to the defendant, eg, claims for money paid on a consideration that wholly failed and money paid under a mistake: cases where the plaintiff had been deceived into paying money, cases where money had been extorted from the plaintiff by threats or duress of goods. They also included cases where money had not been paid by the plaintiff at all but had been received from third persons, as where the defendant had received fees under colour of holding an office which in fact was held by the plaintiff; and finally cases like the present where the defendant had been wrongfully in possession of the plaintiff's goods, had sold them and was in possession of the

---

4   See, eg, *Ward v Griffiths Bros Ltd* (1928); *Horton v Jones* (1934); *Horton v Jones (No 2)* (1939) (see extract, p 385).

proceeds. Now to find a basis for the actions in any actual contract whether express or to be implied from the conduct of the parties was in many of the instances given obviously impossible. The cheat or the blackmailer does not promise to repay to the person he has wronged the money which he has unlawfully taken. Nor does the thief promise to repay to the owner of the goods stolen the money which he has gained from selling the goods. Nevertheless, if a man so wronged were to recover the money in the hands of the wrongdoer, and it was obviously just that he should be able to do so, it was necessary to create a fictitious contract, for there was no action possible other than debt or *assumpsit* on the one side and action for damages for tort on the other. The action of *indebitatus assumpsit* for money had and received to the use of the plaintiff in the cases I have enumerated was therefore supported by the imputation by the court to the defendant of a promise to repay. The fiction was so obvious that in some cases the judge created a fanciful relation between the plaintiff and the defendant. Thus in cases where the defendant had wrongfully sold the plaintiff's goods and received the proceeds it was suggested in some cases, not in all, that the plaintiff chose to treat the wrongdoer as having sold the goods as his agent and so as being under an implied contract to his principal to repay. Even here in the [28] relatively more recent cases where this explanation is given by Grose J in *King v Leith* (1787) and *Marsh v Keating* (1834) by Park J in delivering the opinion of the judges in the House of Lords the wrongdoer had in fact in both cases purported to sell the goods as the agent of his principal. But the fiction is too transparent. The alleged contract by the blackmailer and the robber never was made and never could be made. The law, in order to do justice, imputed to the wrongdoer a promise which alone as forms of action then existed could give the injured person a reasonable remedy ...

UNJUST ENRICHMENT AS THE BASIS OF RESTITUTION LAW

The orthodox view: unjust enrichment is the sole basis of restitutionary relief

The orthodox view is that the law of restitution is based on the principle of preventing unjust enrichments gained at the expense of the plaintiff.

Moses v Macferlan (1760) 2 Burr 1005; 97 ER 676 King's Bench

A third party, Jacob, issued promissory notes to the plaintiff who endorsed the notes to the defendant so the defendant could recover the sums from Jacob in his own name. The plaintiff and defendant agreed in writing that the defendant would not be able to sue the plaintiff on the notes. Jacob did not pay on the notes and the defendant sued the plaintiff in the Court of Conscience, which awarded the defendant the amounts represented by the notes. The plaintiff then sued the defendant in the present action for the recovery of the money.

Lord Mansfield: ... [1008] *2d objection*. That no *assumpsit* lies, except upon an express or implied contract: but here it is impossible to presume any contract to refund money, which the defendant recovered by an adverse suit.

Answer. If the defendant be under an obligation, from the ties of natural justice, to refund; the law implies a debt, and gives this action, founded in the equity of the plaintiff's case, as it were upon a contract ('*quasi ex contractu*', as the Roman law expresses it).

This species of *assumpsit* ('for money had and received to the plaintiff's use') lies in numberless instances, [1009] for money the defendant has received from a third person; which he claims title to, in opposition to the plaintiff's right; and which he had, by law, authority to receive from such third person.

3d objection. Where money has been recovered by the judgment of a court having competent jurisdiction, the matter can never be brought over again by a new action.

Answer. It is most clear, 'that the merits of a judgment can never be over-haled by an original suit, either at law or in equity'. Till the judgment is set aside, or reversed, it is conclusive, as to the subject matter of it, to all intents and purposes.

But the ground of this action is consistent[5] with the judgment of the Court of Conscience: it admits the commissioners did right. They decreed upon the indorsement of the notes by the plaintiff, which indorsement is not now disputed. The ground upon which this action proceeds, was no defence against that sentence.

It is enough for us, that the commissioners adjudged 'they had no cognisance of such collateral matter'. We cannot correct an error in their proceedings; and ought to suppose what is done by a final jurisdiction, to be right. But we think, 'the commissioners[6] did right, in refusing to go into such collateral matter'. Otherwise, by way of defence against a promissory note for 30s they might go into agreements and transactions of a great value: and if they decreed payment of the note, their judgment might indirectly conclude the balance of a large account.

The ground of this action is not, 'that the judgment was wrong' but, 'that (for a reason which the now plaintiff could not avail himself of against that judgment) the defendant ought not in justice to keep the money'. And at Guildhall, I declared very particularly, 'that the merits of a question, determined by the commissioners, where they had jurisdiction, never could be brought over again, in any shape whatsoever'.

Money may be recovered by a right and legal judgment; and yet the iniquity of keeping that money may be manifest, upon grounds which could not be used by way of defence against the judgment.

---

5   'Qu of this? For how can it be legal for any court of law to give judgment for a plaintiff to recover a sum, which as soon as paid, the defendant hath a legal right to recover back again, and that on the very same facts as in the former suit.'

6   'The commissioners, supposing this judgment right, clearly did wrong, for the reason above mentioned; and also, because the plaintiff below could have no damage by non-payment of money, if he could not keep it. And *vide* 18 Vin 312, pl 5, and the notes: there several cases cited, that are, in effect, contrary to the opinion of the court, as here reported. But if the agreement had not been in writing, the commissioners would have been right in rejecting it. Buller, pp 269, 270. So if Macferlan had indorsed the note over, and the action had been brought by his indorsee, the above reasoning seems to be contradictory to itself, and is really a contradiction in terms: for it is saying, a man has a right, which the moment he has received, the person paying it has a right to recover back; which is a right and no right. Even in real actions, if the demandant is bound to warrant, the tenant may, to prevent circuity, rebut him; yet one estate may be more convenient to the demandant than another, though all money is alike.'

Suppose an indorsee of a promissory note, having received payment from the drawer (or maker) of it, sues and recovers the same money from the indorser who knew nothing of such payment.

Suppose a man recovers upon a policy for a ship presumed to be lost, which afterwards comes home – or upon [1010] the life of a man presumed to be dead, who afterwards appears – or upon a representation of a risque deemed to be fair, which comes out afterwards to be grossly fraudulent.

But there is no occasion to go further; for the admission 'that unquestionably, an action might be brought upon the agreement', is a decisive answer to any objection from the judgment. For it is the same thing, as to the force and validity of the judgment, and it is just equally affected by the action, whether the plaintiff brings it upon the equity of his case arising out of the agreement, that the defendant may refund the money he received; or upon the agreement itself, that besides refunding the money, he may pay the costs and expenses the plaintiff was put to.

This brings the whole to the question saved at *Nisi Prius*, 'viz whether the plaintiff may elect to sue by this form of action, for the money only; or must be turned round, to bring an action upon the agreement'.

One great benefit, which arises to suitors from the nature of this action, is, that the plaintiff need not state the special circumstances from which he concludes 'that, *ex æquo et bono*, the money received by the defendant, ought to be deemed as belonging to him': he may declare generally, 'that the money was received to his use'; and make out his case, at the trial.

This is equally beneficial to the defendant. It is the most favourable way in which he can be sued: he can be liable no further than the money he has received; and against that, may go into every equitable defence, upon the general issue; he may claim every equitable allowance; he may prove a release without pleading it; in short, he may defend himself by every thing which shews that the plaintiff, *ex æquo et bono*, is not entitled to the whole of his demand, or to any part of it.

If the plaintiff elects to proceed in this favourable way, it is a bar to his bringing another action upon the agreement; though he might recover more upon the agreement, then he can by this form of action. And therefore, if the question was open to be argued upon principles at large, there seems to be no reason or utility in confining the plaintiff to an action upon the special agreement only.

But the point has been long settled; and there have been many precedents: I will mention to you only one; which was very solemnly considered. It was the case of *Dutch v Warren*. An action upon the case, for money had and received to the plaintiff's use.

[1011] The case was as follows – upon the 18th of August 1720, on payment of £262 10s by the plaintiff to the defendant, the defendant agreed to transfer him five shares in the Welsh copper mines, at the opening of the books; and for security of his so doing, gave him this note – '18th of August 1720. I do hereby acknowledge to have received from a Philip Dutch, £262 10s as a consideration for the purchase of five shares; which I do hereby promise to transfer to the said Philip Dutch as soon as the books are open; being five shares in the Welsh copper mines. Witness my hand Robert Warren'. The books were opened on the 22nd of the said month of August; when Dutch requested Warren to transfer to him the said five shares; which he refused to do: and told the plaintiff, 'he might take his remedy'. Whereupon the plaintiff brought this action, for the consideration money paid by him. And an objection was taken at the trial, 'that this action upon the case, for money had and received to the plaintiff's use, would not lie; but that the action should have been brought for the non-performance of the contract'. This objection was overruled by the[7] Chief Justice; who notwithstanding left it to the consideration of the jury, whether they would not make the price of the said stock, as it was upon the 22nd of August, when it should have been delivered the measure of the damages; which they did; and gave the plaintiff but £175 damages.

And a case being made for the opinion of the Court of Common Pleas, the action was resolved to be well brought; and that the recovery was right, being not for the whole money paid, but for the damages, in not transferring the stock at the time; which was a loss to the plaintiff, and an advantage to the defendant, who was a receiver of the difference money to the plaintiff's use.

The court said, that the extending those actions depends on the notion of fraud. If one man takes another's money to do a thing, and refuses to do it; it is a fraud: and it is at the election of the party injured, either to affirm the agreement, by bringing an action for the non-performance of it; or to disaffirm the agreement *ab initio*, by reason of the fraud, and bring an action for money had and received to his use.

The damages recovered in that case, shew the liberality with which this kind of action is considered; for though the defendant received from the plaintiff £262 10s yet the difference money only, £175 was retained by him against conscience: and [*Dale v Sollet* (1767)] therefore the plaintiff, *ex æquo et bono*, ought to recover no more; agreeable to the rule of the Roman law – '*Quod condictio indebiti non datur ultra, quam locupletior factus est, qui accepit*'.[8]

[1012] If the five shares had been of much more value, yet the plaintiff could only have recovered the £262 10s by this form of action.

The notion of fraud holds much more strongly in the present case, than in that: for here it is express. The indorsement, which enabled the defendant to recover, was got by fraud and falsehood, for one purpose, and abused to another.

This kind of equitable action, to recover back money, which ought not in justice to be kept, is very beneficial, and therefore much encouraged. It lies only for money which, *ex æquo et bono*, the defendant ought to refund [*Dale v Sollet* (1767)]: it does not lie for money paid by the plaintiff, which is claimed of him as payable in point of honour and honesty, although it could not have been recovered from him by any course of law; as in payment of a debt barred by the Statute of Limitations, or contracted during his infancy, or to the extent of principal and legal interest upon an usurious contract, or, for money fairly lost at play: because in all these cases, the defendant may retain it with a safe conscience, though by positive law he was barred from recovering. But it lies for money paid by mistake; or upon a consideration which happens to fail; or for money got through imposition (express, or implied); or extortion; or oppression; or an undue advantage taken of the plaintiff's situation, contrary to laws made for the protection of persons under those circumstances.

---

7 'Sir Peter King was then LCJ of KB (and qu if the law is not altered by 7 Geo 2, col 8, s 5).'
8 The rule is misapplied; for Warren who received the £262 10s was certainly the richer by that sum; and therefore, if the jury had given the plaintiff that sum it would not have been, *ultra quam locupletior factus est qui accepit*. The reverse of this rule would apply to this case, *condictio indebiti non datur ultra quam pauperior factus est qui solvit*.

In one word, the gist of this kind of action is, that the defendant, upon the circumstances of the case, is obliged by the ties of natural justice and equity to refund the money ...

Commentary

Lord Mansfield's principles were followed in various Australian cases,[9] until the decision in 1914 in *Sinclair v Brougham* (1914) (see extract, p 3) which established the implied contract theory as the basis for the action for money had and received. Despite *Sinclair v Brougham*, however, it was possible to find judicial statements to the effect that the true basis of recovery was unjust enrichment, not implied contract. The most important of those statements was by Lord Wright in the following case.

Fibrosa Spolka Akcyjna v Fairbairn Lawson Combe Barbour
[1943] AC 32 House of Lords

The facts are stated at p 346.

Lord Wright: ... [61] It is clear that any civilised system of law is bound to provide remedies for cases of what has been called unjust enrichment or unjust benefit, that is to prevent a man from retaining the money of or some benefit derived from another which it is against conscience that he should keep. Such remedies in English law are generically different from remedies in contract or in tort, and are now recognised to fall within a third category of the common law which has been called quasi-contract or restitution. The root idea was stated by three Lords of Appeal, Lord Shaw, Lord Sumner and Lord Carson, in *RE Jones Ltd v Waring & Gillow Ltd* (1926), which dealt with a particular species of the category, namely, money paid under a mistake of fact. Lord Sumner referring to *Kelly v Solari* (1841), where money had been paid by an insurance company under the mistaken impression that it was due to an executrix under a policy which had in fact been cancelled, said: 'There was no real intention on the company's part to enrich her.' Payment under a mistake of fact is only one head of this category of the law. Another class is where, as in this case, there is prepayment on account of money to be paid as consideration for the performance of a contract which in the event becomes abortive and is not performed, so that the money never becomes due. There was in such circumstances no intention to enrich the payee. This is the class of claims for the recovery of money paid for a consideration which has failed. Such causes of action have long been familiar and were assumed to be common-place by Holt CJ, in *Holmes v Hall* in 1704. Holt CJ was there concerned only about the proper form of action and took the cause of action as beyond question. He said: 'If A give money to B to pay to C upon C's giving writings, etc, [62] and C will not do it, indebit will life for A against B for so much money received to his use. And many such actions have been maintained for earnests in bargains, when the bargainor would not perform, and for premiums for insurance, when the ship, etc, did not go the voyage.' The Chief Justice is there using earnest as meaning a prepayment on account of the price, not in the modern sense of an irrevocable payment to bind the bargain, and he is recognising that the *indebitatus assumpsit*

---

9   See, eg, *White v Copeland* (1894); *Sargood Bros v The Commonwealth* (1910), p 303; *Campbell v Kitchen & Sons Ltd* (1910), p 531.

had by that time been accepted as the appropriate form of action in place of the procedure which had been used in earlier times to enforce these claims such as debt, account or case.

By 1760 actions for money had and received had increased in number and variety. Lord Mansfield CJ in a familiar passage in *Moses v Macferlan* (1760), sought to rationalise the action for money had and received, and illustrated it by some typical instances. 'It lies,' he said, 'for money paid by mistake; or upon a consideration which happens to fail; or for money got through imposition (express, or implied); or extortion; or oppression; or an undue advantage taken of the plaintiff's situation, contrary to laws made for the protection of persons under those circumstances. In one word the gist of this kind of action is, that the defendant, upon the circumstances of the case, is obliged by the ties of natural justice and equity to refund the money'. Lord Mansfield prefaced this pronouncement by observations which are to be noted. 'If the defendant be under an obligation from the ties of natural justice, to refund; the law implies a debt and gives this action [viz *indebitatus assumpsit*] founded in the equity of the plaintiff's case, as it were, upon a contract ("*quasi ex contractu*" as the Roman law expresses it).' Lord Mansfield does not say that the law implies a promise. The law implies a debt or obligation which is a different thing. In fact he denies that there is a contract; the obligation is as efficacious as if it were upon a contract. The obligation is a creation of the law, just as much as an obligation in tort. The obligation belongs to a third class, distinct from either contract or tort, though it resembles contract rather than tort. This statement of Lord Mansfield has been the basis of the modern law of quasi-contract, notwithstanding the criticisms which have been launched against it. Like all large generalisations, it has needed and received qualifications in practice. There is, for [63] instance, the qualification that an action for money had and received does not lie for money paid under an erroneous judgment or for moneys paid under an illegal or excessive distress. The law has provided other remedies as being more convenient. The standard of what is against conscience in this context has become more or less canalised or defined, but in substance the juristic concept remains as Lord Mansfield left it.

The gist of the action is a debt or obligation implied, or, more accurately, imposed, by law, in much the same way as the law enforces as a debt the obligation to pay a statutory or customary impost. This is important because some confusion seems to have arisen, though perhaps only in recent times when the true nature of the forms of action have become obscured by want of user. If I may borrow from another context the elegant phrase of Viscount Simon LC, in *United Australia Ltd v Barclays Bank Ltd* (1942), p 21, there has sometimes been, as it seems to me, 'a misreading of technical rules, now happily swept away'. The writ of *indebitatus assumpsit* involved at least two averments, the debt or obligation and the *assumpsit*. The former was the basis of the claim and was the real cause of action. The latter was merely fictitious, and could not be traversed, but was necessary to enable the convenient and liberal form of action to be used in such cases. This fictitious *assumpsit* or promise was wiped out by the Common Law Procedure Act 1852. As Bullen and Leake [*Precedents of Pleading*, 3rd edn, 1868, p 36] point out, this Act, by s 3, provided that the plaintiff was no longer required to specify the particular form of action in which he sued, and by s 49 that (*inter alia*) the statement of promises in *indebitatus* counts which there was no need to prove were to be omitted; 'the action of *indebitatus assumpsit*', the authors add, 'is [that is by 1868] virtually become obsolete'. Lord Atkin in the *United Australia* case (1941), after instancing the case of the blackmailer, says: 'The man has my money which I have not delivered to him with any real intention of passing to him the property. I sue him because he has the actual property taken.' He adds: 'These fantastic resemblances of contracts invented in order to meet requirements of the law as to forms of action which have now disappeared should not in these days be allowed to affect actual rights.' Yet the ghosts of the forms of action have been allowed at times to [64] intrude in the ways of the living and impede vital functions of the law. Thus in *Sinclair v Brougham* (1914), Lord Sumner stated, p 452, that 'all these causes of action [for money had and received] are common species of the genus *assumpsit*. All now rest, and long have rested, upon a notional or imputed promise to repay'. This observation, which was not necessary for the decision of the case, obviously does not mean that there is an actual promise of the party. The phrase 'notional or implied promise' is only a way of describing a debt or obligation arising by construction of law. The claim for money had and received always rested on a debt or obligation which the law implied or more accurately imposed, whether the procedure actually in vogue at any time was debt or account or case or *indebitatus assumpsit*. Even the fictitious *assumpsit* disappeared after the Act of 1852. I prefer Lord Sumner's explanation of the cause of action in *Jones's* case (1926), at p 696. This agrees with the words of Lord Atkin which I have just quoted, yet serious legal writers have seemed to say that these words of the great judge in *Sinclair v Brougham* closed the door to any theory of unjust enrichment in English law. I do not understand why or how. It would indeed be a *reductio ad absurdum* of the doctrine of precedents. In fact, the common law still employs the action for money had and received as a practical and useful, if not complete or ideally perfect, instrument to prevent unjust enrichment, aided by the various methods of technical equity which are also available, as they were found to be in *Sinclair v Brougham* ...

Commentary

Despite this persuasive pronouncement, it was not until the House of Lords' decision in *Lipkin Gorman v Karpnale Ltd* (1991)[10] in 1991 that the implied contract theory was authoritatively abandoned in England and unjust enrichment was recognised conclusively as the conceptual basis of the law of restitution. The House of Lords subsequently confirmed unjust enrichment as the foundation of restitutionary actions in *Westdeutsche Landesbank Girozentrale v Council of the London Borough of Islington* (1996) (see extract, p 372) and *Kleinwort Benson Ltd v Glasgow City Council* (1997).

There are judicial statements scattered throughout the early authorities of the High Court of Australia to the effect that the basis of the action for money had and received is unjust enrichment, not implied contract. For example, in *Mason v New South Wales* (1959),[11] Windeyer J rejected the need to imply a contract in a claim for money had and received, stating that:

---

10 See extracts, pp 595 and 654. See also Birks, 'The English recognition of unjust enrichment' [1991] LMCLQ 473.

11 At p 146. See also *Phillips v Ellison Bros Pty Ltd* (1941), p 235; *Burns Philp & Co Ltd v Gillespie Bros Pty Ltd* (1947), p 175 (see extract, p 177).

Provided it be recognised that the action for money had and received is not only the origin of but, as developed, still determines the scope of the English law of quasi-contract, it seems to me not inapt to describe it as a law of 'unjust enrichment' ... I certainly see no need today to look for the implication of a contract or to speak of the fiction of a contract when in reality there was no contract.

The case of *Pavey & Matthews Pty Ltd v Paul* (1987) settled the question for
• Australian law. The High Court abandoned the implied contract theory and held that the obligation to pay for the reasonable value of services is an independent obligation imposed by law in order to prevent unjust enrichment.

Pavey & Matthews Pty Ltd v Paul (1987) 162 CLR 221 High Court of Australia

The appellant builder orally agreed with the respondent to perform building work on premises owned by the respondent. Pursuant to the oral agreement the respondent agreed to pay a reasonable remuneration for the building work, calculated by reference to prevailing rates of payment in the building industry. When the work was done the respondent paid to the appellant $36,000 for the building work, however the appellant claimed that the reasonable value of the work done and materials received was $62,945.50. The appellant sued for the disputed amount of $26,945.50 on a *quantum meruit* claim. The building agreement was unenforceable by the appellant due to the provisions of s 45 of the Builders Licensing Act 1971 (NSW) which provided that:

> A contract (in this section referred to as a 'building contract') under which the holder of a licence undertakes to carry out, by himself or by others, any building work or to vary any building work or the manner of carrying out any building work, specified in a building contract is not enforceable against the other party to the contract unless the contract is in writing signed by each of the parties or his agent in that behalf and sufficiently describes the building work the subject of the contract.

Mason and Wilson JJ: ... [227] The question then is whether the appellant's action on a *quantum meruit* amounts to a direct or an indirect enforcement of the oral contract.

Deane J, whose reasons for judgment we have had the advantage of reading, has concluded that an action on a *quantum meruit*, such as that brought by the appellant, rests, not on implied contract, but on a claim to restitution or one based on unjust enrichment, arising from the respondent's acceptance of the benefits accruing to the respondent from the appellant's performance of the unenforceable oral contract. This conclusion does not accord with the acceptance by Williams, Fullagar and Kitto JJ in *Turner v Bladin* (1951), p 474, of the views expressed by Lord Denning in his articles in the Law Quarterly Review ((1925) 41 LQR 79; (1939) 55 LQR 54), basing such a claim in implied contract. These views were a natural reflection of prevailing legal thinking as it had developed to that time. The members of this court were then unaware that his Lordship had, in his judgment in *James v Thomas H Kent & Co Ltd* (1951), as reported in the authorised reports, discarded his earlier views in favour of the restitution or unjust enrichment theory. Since then the shortcomings of the implied contract theory have been rigorously exposed[12] and the virtues of an approach based on restitution and unjust enrichment, initially advocated by Lord Mansfield and later by Fuller and Perdue,[13] widely appreciated.[14] We are therefore now justified in recognising, as Deane J has done, that the true foundation of the right to recover on a *quantum meruit* does not depend on the existence of an implied contract.

Once the true basis of the action on a *quantum meruit* is established, namely execution of work for which the unenforceable contract provided, and its acceptance by the defendant, it is difficult to regard the action as one by which the plaintiff seeks to enforce the oral contract. True it is that proof of the oral contract may be an indispensable element in the plaintiff's success but that is in order to show that: (a) the benefits were not intended as a gift, and (b) that the [228] defendant has not rendered the promised exchange value.[15] The purpose of proving the contract is not to enforce it but to make out another cause of action having a different foundation in law.

If the effect of bringing an action on a *quantum meruit* was simply to enforce the oral contract in some circumstances only, though not in all the circumstances in which an action on the contract would succeed, it might be persuasively contended that the action on a *quantum meruit* was an indirect means of enforcing the oral contract. So, if all the plaintiff had to prove was that he had fully executed the contract on his part and that he had not been paid the contract price, there would be some force in the suggestion that the proceeding amounted to an indirect enforcement of the contractual cause of action. However, when success in a *quantum meruit* depends, not only on the plaintiff proving that he did the work, but also on the defendant's acceptance of the work without paying the agreed remuneration, it is evident that the court is enforcing against the defendant an obligation that differs in character from the contractual obligation had it been enforceable ...

Brennan J (dissenting): ... [233] The modern lawyer does not need to remember that the action of *indebitatus assumpsit* is founded on a separate and subsequent fictional promise to pay a debt arising out of a contract – a promise which the Statute of Frauds does not touch – but he needs to remember that this category of action of *indebitatus assumpsit* is founded on the debt to which the contract has given rise. As AT Denning (as his Lordship then was) pointed out in an article 'Quantum meruit and the Statute of Frauds' (1925) 41 LQR 79, p 83, when 'in 1677 the Statute of [234] Frauds said "No action shall be brought upon any agreement, etc"; the answer was quite clear "This is not an action upon an agreement, it is an action upon a debt"'. The observation cited from *Turner v Bladin* distinguishes between an action on the contract which is barred by the Statute of Frauds and an action on the debt arising out of the contract which is not ...

[235] An obligation in quasi-contract ... is imposed by law independently of contract and is founded, as Denning LJ said in *James v Thomas H Kent & Co Ltd*

---

12 See Goff and Jones, *The Law of Restitution*, 2nd edn, 1978, pp 5–11.
13 See Fuller and Perdue, 'The reliance interest in contract damages' (1936–37) 46 Yale LJ 52, p 373, especially p 387.
14 Goff and Jones, *op cit*, fn 12, p 15ff; and see *Deglman v Guaranty Trust* (1954), pp 794–95.
15 Fuller and Perdue, *op cit*, fn 13, p 387, n 125.

(1951), p 556, 'not in contract at all, but in restitution'. A claim in quasi-contract is distinct from a claim for money due under a contract. The distinction between a debt arising out of contract – whether a fixed amount or a reasonable [236] amount – and a quasi-contractual pecuniary obligation imposed by law independently of contract has not always been clearly drawn ...

Is it possible to make a quasi-contractual claim in *quantum meruit* and circumvent the operation of the Statute of Frauds on a subsisting contract? ...

[237] The principle is that no quasi-contractual obligation arises when there is a subsisting contractual obligation governing the same subject matter. That principle underlies the general rule established by *Cutter v Powell* (1795), namely, that no action of *indebitatus assumpsit* can be brought for anything done under a subsisting contract while it remains substantially unperformed. The principle inheres in the rule that when a contract providing for special remuneration is performed, no quasi-contractual obligation to pay arises: see *per* Jordan CJ in *Horton v Jones (No 2)* (1939). There is no distinction in principle between a contract which provides for remuneration that is special and a contract which provides for remuneration that is not special. When a subsisting contract provides, expressly or impliedly, for remuneration to be paid, the performance of that contract cannot give rise to a quasi-contractual right to remuneration. Although an action of *indebitatus assumpsit* lies when performance of the contract gives rise to a debt, it does not lie on a cause of action arising *dehors* the contract. If it did, the 'reasonable remuneration' which might be recovered on a quasi-contractual [238] claim would not necessarily be equal to the agreed remuneration whether 'special remuneration' or not.

Where work is done by a plaintiff under a contract which expressly or impliedly provides for the plaintiff's remuneration, there is no ground in restitution or unjust enrichment for imposing an obligation to pay remuneration different from the agreed remuneration. If it were possible to impose a quasi-contractual obligation to pay reasonable remuneration when there is a subsisting unwritten contract which falls within the Statute of Frauds, the imposed obligation would be either inconsistent with the contract or it would duplicate the contractual obligation. An inability to sue on a contract provides no ground for imposing a quasi-contractual obligation inconsistent with the contractual obligation to pay remuneration, and the effect of the Statute on the contractual obligation cannot be circumvented by substituting a corresponding quasi-contractual obligation. A subsisting contract is the source and charter of the rights and obligations of the parties, and the law cannot impose other rights and obligations either to vary the contractual provisions or to negative the effect which the Statute of Frauds has upon them ...

[239] By way of contrast, there is no difficulty in the way of recovery on a quasi-contractual *quantum meruit* when the work is done in performance of what is believed to be, but what is not, a valid contract[16] or when necessaries are supplied to an infant who lacks contractual capacity[17] or when work is done in an expectation that a contract will be made.[18] But when the work is done under a valid and subsisting contract which provides for remuneration to be paid for the

---

16 *Craven-Ellis v Canons Ltd* (1936).
17 *Nash v Inman* (1908), pp 8, 9.
18 *William Lacey (Hounslow) Ltd v Davis* (1957).

work and which falls within the Statute of Frauds, no action of *indebitatus assumpsit* lies save on the debt arising on the contract.

It follows that the only actions which can be brought to enforce a debt arising out of a subsisting unwritten contract falling within s 4 of the Statute of Frauds is an action of *indebitatus assumpsit* or, if the debt arises out of a stipulation for a fixed sum, an action of debt ...

Deane J: ... [250] The basic propositions to be drawn from the ... authorities were identified by Jordan CJ in *Horton v Jones (No 1)* (1934), pp 367–68, in a passage which was subsequently quoted with approval by Williams J in this court.[19] I take the liberty of stating those propositions, with which I respectfully agree, in a different order and in varied words. Omitting all but one of the references cited by Jordan CJ, they are: (1) The 'mere fact that the consideration is executed is not sufficient' to make the Statute of Frauds inapplicable. (2) 'If, however, a person does acts for the benefit of another in the performance of a contract [upon which an action cannot be brought by reason of the Statute of Frauds], and the other so accepts the benefit of those acts, or otherwise behaves in relation to them, that, in the absence of the ... contract, the former could maintain an action ... upon the common money counts, he may sue in *indebitatus* to obtain reasonable remuneration for the executed consideration.' [(1925) 41 LQR 79.] (3) 'The existence of the unenforceable contract prevents a new contract, in respect of which special *assumpsit* could be maintained, from being implied from the acts performed ... and the unenforceable contract may be referred to as evidence, but as evidence only, on the question of amount ...' (4) The appropriate action to obtain such reasonable remuneration is 'an action of debt'. 'In such a case the action is in *indebitatus* only.'

It is clear from the above propositions that the obligation to pay 'reasonable remuneration for the executed consideration' was seen by Jordan CJ as arising independently of any genuine agreement or promise upon which a special count could be framed. The 'existence of the unenforceable contract' prevented any such genuine agreement from being implied. The reference to the 'unenforceable contract' being relevant 'as evidence, but as evidence only, on the question of amount' emphasised the perception that the obligation to pay reasonable remuneration was quite different from liability to make the payments under the 'unenforceable contract'. Plainly enough, his Honour saw that obligation as a liability in debt arising by operation of law upon the circumstances: the 'obligation is imposed by law, and does not depend on an inference of an implied [251] promise': *per* Jordan CJ, Halse Rogers and Owen JJ, *Horton v Jones (No 2)* (1939), p 320.

The 'action of debt' for 'reasonable remuneration' to which Jordan CJ referred was not an action on the old express *quantum meruit* count under which a plaintiff claimed not a liquidated amount payable by the defendant but a nominated sum being 'so much money as he therefore *reasonably deserved* to have'.[20] That being so, his Honour was not concerned to resolve the old conflict about whether the special *quantum meruit* and *quantum valebant* (or *valebat*) counts could lie in debt where the essence of the action was the alleged retention of a liquidated amount which was due: contrast, eg, the views expressed in *Chitty's Treatise on Pleading*, p 375 and in

---

19 See *Phillips v Ellinson Bros Pty Ltd* (1941), p 246.
20 See *Chitty's Treatise on Pleading*, 7th edn, 1844, Vol 1, p 351.

Ames, *Lectures on Legal History*, p 89. It is true that *Horton v Jones (No 1)* was decided at a time when the old forms of action were still alive in New South Wales. The special *quantum meruit* and *quantum valebant* counts had, however, long been obsolete: see, eg, *Chitty*, p 352; *Horton v Jones (No 2)* (1939), p 316. The position was explained by Bullen and Leake [*Precedents of Pleading*, 3rd edn, 1868], in words which were subsequently quoted with approval by Farwell LJ in *Lagos v Grunwaldt* (1910), p 48: '[t]here were also formerly in use counts known as *quantum meruit* and *quantum valebat* counts, which were adopted where there was no fixed price for work done or goods sold, etc.[21] These counts however have fallen into disuse, and have been superseded by the general application of the *indebitatus* counts.' In a case where there was no fixed remuneration or price, the action on one of the ordinary common *indebitatus* counts, which had absorbed the express *quantum meruit* and *quantum valebant* counts, was in substance to recover a '*quantum meruit*' or '*quantum valebant*' in the sense that it was to recover the amount which represented reasonable remuneration. It had, however, long been settled that such an action on an ordinary common *indebitatus* count was to recover the amount payable as a liquidated amount or debt. As Farwell LJ observed in *Lagos v Grunwaldt* (1910), p 48, 'everything that could be sued for under those counts comes within the description of debt or liquidated demand'. That being so, there remained no objection to such an action being brought in debt: see, generally, *Horton v Jones (No 2)* (1939), p 31ff; *Chitty's Treatise on Pleading*, p 352; and, eg, *Gardner v Bowman* (1834).

[252] The impression has sometimes been conveyed by colourful phraseology that the retention of the old forms of action in New South Wales until 1970, when they were abolished by the belated introduction of the Judicature Act system of pleading, meant that the administration of civil justice in that State had lagged behind the 19th century. Such an impression bears little relationship to the reality. Whatever may have been the comparative advantages and disadvantages of the formal system of pleading and the formal separation of law and equity,[22] the substantive common law developed in New South Wales with little real hindrance from the continued observance of them. In a situation where causes of action could be joined, where it had become unnecessary to specify the particular form of action adopted or to plead the fictional promise in an action of *assumpsit* and where 'the same conveniences as to final judgment and the assessment of damages [were] extended to all causes of action to which they can be applied',[23] any real point in distinguishing in the ordinary case between a common *indebitatus* count in debt and one in *assumpsit* had disappeared and the fictional *assumpsit* underlying a common *indebitatus assumpsit* count had become largely forgotten. Indeed, the notion that an action on a common *indebitatus* count for a reasonable remuneration was not an action to recover as a debt the actual liquidated amount payable but was an action for breach of some unmentioned fictional *assumpsit* or promise to pay it would have sounded as bizarre in the ears of a practising New South Wales lawyer at the time *Horton v Jones (No 1)* was decided as in the ears of a practising

---

21 *Ibid.*

22 See, eg, Sir Owen Dixon, 'Concerning judicial method' (1956) 26 ALJ 468, pp 469–70.

23 See Bullen and Leake, *Precedents of Pleading*, 3rd edn, 1868, p 36; Common Law Procedure Act 1853 (NSW), ss 3, 37, 45, 85, 86, 87; Common Law Procedure Act 1899 (NSW), ss 5, 49, 129, 130, 131.

lawyer in a jurisdiction where the old forms of action had been formally interred. In that context, the present significance of Jordan CJ's statement that the relevant action upon a common *indebitatus* count was 'an action of debt' to obtain 'reasonable remuneration' is not that his Honour intended to suggest, for he plainly did not, that an action on a common *indebitatus* count in *assumpsit* would have been unavailable or inappropriate. Its present significance is that, once liability to pay reasonable remuneration is recognised as arising not from the 'unenforceable contract' (which 'may be referred to as evidence, but as evidence only, on the question of amount') but from the operation of law upon the circumstances, there is plainly no need to resort to the fictional promise of *assumpsit* to explain why the Statute of Frauds does not preclude the bringing of an action upon a common *indebitatus* count [253] to recover the amount of that liability as a liquidated sum. The reason for that is that such an action is plainly not brought upon the unenforceable contract regardless of whether it is seen as an action in debt to recover the amount of that reasonable remuneration or as an action in *assumpsit* to recover damages for breach of the fictional *assumpsit* to pay that liquidated amount.

The reference by Jordan CJ to an article in 41 Law Quarterly Review (1925) was to the first of two related articles in that journal in which Mr AT Denning, as his Lordship then was, discussed the availability of an action in a common *indebitatus* count notwithstanding the provisions of the Statute of Frauds (see also (1939) 55 LQR 54). In those articles, Lord Denning propounded a general proposition, based on Tindal CJ's *dictum* in *Souch v Strawbridge* (1846), that 'the Statute of Frauds does not apply when the claim is in substance in *indebitatus assumpsit* on an executed consideration' ((1925) 41 LQR 79, p 85) or, more broadly expressed, 'that once the contract is executed, the Statute of Frauds does not apply' ((1939) 55 LQR 54, p 63). In the context of Professor Ames's celebrated analysis of the development of express and implied *assumpsit*,[24] Lord Denning's essential justification of that general proposition was his then view that an action on a common *indebitatus* count in a case where an unenforceable contract had been executed by the claimant was an action in *assumpsit* on the fictional promise of the other party to the contract to discharge the very debt arising under the executed but unenforceable agreement. Upon analysis, that view, which (as will be seen) Lord Denning was himself subsequently to abandon, conflicts with Jordan CJ's view, with which I have indicated my agreement, that an action on the common *indebitatus* count in such a case is not to recover the agreed amount under the unenforceable agreement but to enforce an obligation to pay 'reasonable remuneration'. It is, however, necessary that particular attention be paid to that earlier view expressed by Lord Denning since his two articles were subsequently cited with approval in the joint judgment of this court in *Turner v Bladin* (1951).

With due respect, there are several related criticisms which can be levelled at Lord Denning's earlier view about why an action on a common *indebitatus* count could be brought upon an executed consideration provided under a contract upon which the Statute of [254] Frauds precluded the bringing of an action. First, that explanation does not lie well with Tindal CJ's judgment in *Souch v Strawbridge* which, far from resting on any fictional promise to pay the debt arising under the

---

24 See the revised reprint of the (1888–89) 2 Harv L Rev articles, pp 1, 53, in Ames, *Lectures on Legal History*, pp 129ff, 149ff.

executed agreement, rests on the same basis as that which can be discerned in subsequent cases, namely, that the obligation which it is sought to enforce is one which arises independently of, and not derivatively from, the unenforceable agreement. Thus, as Tindal CJ explained,[25] '[t]here was evidence enough to shew that the child was placed under the care of the plaintiff at the charge of the defendant, with his assent, and that he had made payments on account of its maintenance. That is equivalent to the proof that is ordinarily given in an action for goods sold and delivered, whence the law implies a promise on the defendant's part to pay for them'. The second criticism is that I see little appeal in logic in the proposition that to sue on a fictional promise to pay the very debt arising under an executed agreement is not to bring an action upon that agreement. The fictional *assumpsit* to pay may have constituted a convenient procedural device for enabling the substance of a dispute to be litigated by acceptable legal procedures. It did not, however, obliterate the reality that an action on an *indebitatus* count to recover the liquidated amount payable under an executed agreement was an action brought upon the agreement regardless of whether, for procedural reasons, the pleader sued directly to recover the debt or indirectly to enforce a fictional promise to pay it. Indeed, to identify the discarded procedural fiction of a promise to pay the debt arising under an executed agreement as the rationale of a substantive juristic concept is to accord to the fiction a significance which it did not enjoy when it was utilised by common lawyers as a live stratagem. As Lord Wright pointed out (*Sinclair v Brougham* (1938), p 317):

> The old common lawyers were a robust people, and if a fiction was convenient under the old rigid forms of pleading they did not worry about its correspondence to reality or to juristic concepts. But it does not follow that they did not realise the true nature of the concept.

The third criticism of the explanation advanced by Lord Denning in his Law Quarterly Review articles is a more fundamental one and is made with the benefit of the hindsight flowing from subsequent elucidation of the law for which Lord Denning is entitled to no small part of the credit. It is that adverted to by Sir Robert (now Lord) [255] Goff and Professor Jones in their landmark work *The Law of Restitution*[26] namely, that the basis of the obligation to make payment for an executed consideration given and received under an unenforceable contract should now be accepted as lying in restitution or unjust enrichment. Indeed, so much was recognised by Professor Ames himself: see Ames, pp 162–66 and *per* Viscount Haldane LC, *Sinclair v Brougham* (1914), p 417. In such a case, the underlying obligation or debt for the work done, goods supplied, or services rendered does not arise from a genuine agreement at all. It is an obligation or debt imposed by operation of law which 'arises from the defendant having taken the benefit of the work done, goods supplied, or services rendered ...'[27] and which can be enforced '*as if* it had a contractual origin' (emphasis added) (*In re Rhodes* (1890), p 107 *per* Lindley LJ) and see, among many other relevant works and cases, Lord Wright, *op cit*, pp 317ff; RM Jackson, *History of Quasi-Contract in English Law* (1936); *Pulbrook v Lawes* (1876) (*per* Blackburn J, pp 290–91) (*per* Lush J); *Fibrosa Spolka*

---

25 (1840) 2 CB 808, p 814; 135 ER 1161, p 1164.
26 2nd edn, 1978, pp 320–21.
27 *Phillips v Ellinson Bros Pty Ltd* (1941), p 235 *per* Starke J.

Akcyjna v Fairbairn Lawson Combe Barbour Ltd (1943), pp 61–62; *Deglman v Guaranty Trust* (1954), pp 788, 794–95; the judgment of Lord Denning himself (then Denning LJ) in *James v Thomas H Kent & Co Ltd* (1951), p 556; and the judgment of the Privy Council, delivered by Lord Denning, in *Kiriri Cotton Co Ltd v Dewani* (1960), pp 204–05.

It is not necessary to pursue here the question whether, now that the common law is released from the controls of the old forms of action, there is a continuing need for or utility in the traditional approach that any claim which would in previous times have been asserted by a common *indebitatus* count must be seen as lying either in contract or quasi-contract.[28] It suffices to say that, even accepting that traditional approach, it is clear that the old common *indebitatus* count could be utilised to accommodate what should be seen as two distinct categories of claim: one to recover a debt arising under a genuine contract, whether express or implied; the other to recover a debt owing in circumstances where the law itself imposed or imputed an obligation or promise to make compensation for a benefit accepted. In the first [256] category of case, the action was brought upon the genuine agreement regardless of whether it took the form of a special or a common count. It follows from what has been said above that the cases in which a claimant has been held entitled to recover in respect of an executed consideration under an agreement upon which the Statute of Frauds precluded the bringing of an action should be seen as falling within the second and not the first category. In that second category of case, the tendency of common lawyers to speak in terms of implied contract rather than in terms of an obligation imposed by law[29] should be recognised as but a reflection of the influence of discarded fictions, buried forms of action and the conventional conviction that, if a common law claim could not properly be framed in tort, it must necessarily be dressed in the language of contract. That tendency should not be allowed to conceal the fact that, in that category of case, the action was not based upon a genuine agreement at all. Indeed, if there was a valid and enforceable agreement governing the claimant's right to compensation, there would be neither occasion nor legal justification for the law to superimpose or impute an obligation or promise to pay a reasonable remuneration. The quasi-contractual obligation to pay fair and just compensation for a benefit which has been accepted will only arise in a case where there is no applicable genuine agreement or where such an agreement is frustrated, avoided or unenforceable. In such a case, it is the very fact that there is no genuine agreement or that the genuine agreement is frustrated, avoided or unenforceable that provides the occasion for (and part of the circumstances giving rise to) the imposition by the law of the obligation to make restitution.

To identify the basis of such actions as restitution and not genuine agreement is not to assert a judicial discretion to do whatever idiosyncratic notions of what is fair and just might dictate. The circumstances in which the common law imposes an enforceable obligation to pay compensation for a benefit accepted under an unenforceable agreement have been explored in the reported cases and in learned writings and are unlikely to be greatly affected by the perception that the basis of such an obligation, when the common law imposes it, is preferably seen as lying in

---

28 See, eg, the discussion of the subject by Lord Wright in *Sinclair v Brougham* (1938) and by Holdsworth, 'Unjustifiable enrichment' (1939) 55 LQR 37.

29 See, eg, *per* Salter J, *Scott v Pattison* (1923), pp 727–28.

restitution rather than in the implication of a genuine agreement where in fact the unenforceable agreement left no room for one. That is not to deny the importance of the concept of unjust enrichment in the law of this country. It constitutes a unifying legal concept which explains [257] why the law recognises, in a variety of distinct categories of case, an obligation on the part of a defendant to make fair and just restitution for a benefit derived at the expense of a plaintiff and which assists in the determination, by the ordinary processes of legal reasoning, of the question whether the law should, in justice, recognise such an obligation in a new or developing category of case.[30] In a category of case where the law recognises an obligation to pay a reasonable remuneration or compensation for a benefit actually or constructively accepted, the general concept of restitution or unjust enrichment is, as is pointed out subsequently in this judgment, also relevant, in a more direct sense, to the identification of the proper basis upon which the quantum of remuneration or compensation should be ascertained in that particular category of case.

The fact that the action which can be brought on a common *indebitatus* count consistently with the Statute of Frauds is founded on an obligation arising independently of the unenforceable contract does not mean that the existence or terms of that contract are necessarily irrelevant. In such an action, it will ordinarily be permissible for the plaintiff to refer to the unenforceable contract as evidence, but as evidence only, on the question whether what was done was done gratuitously. In many cases, such as where the claim is for money lent or paid, the obligation to make restitution will plainly involve the obligation to pay the precise amount advanced or paid. In those cases where a claim for a reasonable remuneration or price is involved, the unenforceable agreement may, as Jordan CJ pointed out in *Horton v Jones (No 1)* (1934), pp 368–69, be referred to as evidence, but again as evidence only, on the question of the appropriate amount of compensation. If the unenforceable contract has not been rescinded by the plaintiff or otherwise terminated, the defendant will be free to rely on it as a defence to the claim for compensation in a case where he is ready and willing to perform his obligations under it.[31] The defendant will also be entitled to rely on the unenforceable contract, if it has been executed but not rescinded, to limit the amount recoverable by the plaintiff to the contractual amount in a case where that amount is less than what would constitute fair and reasonable remuneration.

[Deane J then referred to *Turner v Bladin* (1951) in which the High Court had expressed approval of the implied contract reasoning. Deane J reiterated his view that he saw this reasoning as mistaken, and that the *indebitatus* count was not based on a fictional promise, but on an obligation imposed by law to make fair and just restitution. His Honour continued at p 260:]

It was submitted on behalf of Mrs Paul that the cases establishing the right of a claimant to recover compensation for an executed consideration under an agreement upon which the bringing of an action is precluded by the Statute of Frauds could not be applied, by analogy, to sustain the right of the builder to sue her on a common *indebitatus* count in the present case to recover a liquidated amount representing reasonable remuneration for the work done and materials

---

30 See *Muschinski v Dodds* (1985), pp 619–20; Goff and Jones, *op cit*, fn 12, p 11ff.
31 See *Thomas v Brown* (1876).

provided under the contract which was rendered unenforceable against her by the provisions of s 45 of the Act. The primary basis of this submission was the distinction between a provision precluding the bringing of an action by either party upon an agreement (such as the Statute of Frauds) and a provision that an agreement is not enforceable by a designated party against the other party to it (such as s 45 of the Act).

On the approach accepted in *Bladin*, namely that the action which could be brought consistently with the Statute of Frauds was a common *indebitatus assumpsit* count based on the fictional promise to pay the actual debt arising under the agreement, there was obvious force in this submission since it would not necessarily follow from an acceptance of the view that such an action was not technically brought 'upon' the unenforceable agreement that the action could not properly be seen as none the less brought to enforce it. Once the approach in *Bladin* is rejected, however, the force in the submission disappears. The common *indebitatus* count for compensation does not involve enforcing an agreement which is unenforceable by the builder under s 45 of the Act any more than it involves bringing an action upon an agreement upon which the bringing of an action is precluded by the Statute of Frauds. As has been seen, the basis of such an action lies not in agreement but in restitution and the claim in restitution involves not enforcing the agreement but recovering compensation on the basis that the agreement is unenforceable ...

[Dawson J identified the relevant cause of action by reference to a common count based upon a promise implied in fact and not upon a 'constructive obligation or quasi-contract'.]

Commentary

The majority in the principal case viewed the claim for a *quantum meruit* as resting, not on implied contract, but on a claim to restitution or one based on unjust enrichment.[32] Deane J identified the concept of unjust enrichment as consisting of three elements:

(a) an enrichment to the defendant;

(b) that is gained at the plaintiff's expense;

(c) as a result of an unjust factor.[33]

The onus then shifts to the defendant to displace *prima facie* liability by establishing a defence.[34]

---

32 This decision has been discussed and analysed in numerous articles: see, eg, Ibbetson, 'Implied contracts and restitution: history in the High Court of Australia' (1988) 8 OJLS 312; Jones, 'Restitution: unjust enrichment as a unifying concept in Australia' (1988) 1 JCL 8; Mason, 'Restitution in Australian law', in Finn (ed), *Essays on Restitution*, 1990, Chapter 2; Burrows, 'Understanding the law of restitution: a map through the thicket' (1995) 18 UQLJ 149, pp 152–53.

33 See, eg, McInnes, 'The structures and challenges of unjust enrichment', in *Restitution: Developments in Unjust Enrichment*, 1996, p 18, for a general discussion of these elements.

34 These elements of the unjust enrichment concept have been widely accepted. See, eg, *Roxborough v Rothmans of Pall Mall Australia Ltd* (2001), pp 341, 383; *Commonwealth v SCI Operations Pty Ltd* (1998), p 317; *Woolwich Equitable Building Society v Inland Revenue Commissioners* (1993), p 197; *Portman Building Society v Hamlyn Taylor Neck (A Firm)* (1998), p 206.

The courts in England[35] and Canada[36] have also recognised unjust enrichment as the basis of restitution law.

Australia and New Zealand Banking Group Ltd v Westpac Banking Corporation (1988) 164 CLR 662 High Court of Australia

The facts are stated at p 639.

The court: ... [673] The basis of the common law action of money had and received for recovery of an amount paid under fundamental mistake of fact should now be recognised as lying not in implied contract but in restitution or unjust enrichment.[37] In other words, receipt of a payment which has been made under a fundamental mistake is one of the categories of case in which the facts give rise to a *prima facie* obligation to make restitution, in the sense of compensation for the benefit of unjust enrichment, to the person who has sustained the countervailing detriment.[38] The common law right of action may arise in circumstances which also give rise to a resulting trust of specific property or funds or which would lead a modern court to grant relief by way of constructive trust. However, notwithstanding that the grounds of the action for recovery are framed in the traditional words of trust or use and that contemporary legal principles of restitution or unjust enrichment can be equated with seminal equitable notions of good conscience, the action itself is not for the enforcement of a trust or for tracing or the recovery of specific money or property. It is a common law action for recovery of the value of the unjust enrichment and the fact that specific money or property received can no longer be identified in the hands of the recipient or traced into other specific property which he holds does not of itself constitute an answer in a category of case in which the law imposes a *prima facie* liability to make restitution. Before that *prima facie* liability will be displaced, there must be circumstances (eg, that the payment was made for good consideration such as the discharge of an existing debt or, arguably, that there has been some adverse change of position by the recipient in good faith and in reliance on the payment) which the law recognises would make an order for restitution unjust ...

The dissenting views: unjust enrichment does not provide the sole explanation for restitutionary recovery

This book is largely premised on the so called 'Quadration Thesis' of restitution law, which views unjust enrichment as being the sole basis of the law of

---

35   *Lipkin Gorman v Karpnale Ltd* (1991) (see extracts, pp 595 and 654); *Kleinwort Benson Ltd v Lincoln City Council* (1999) (see extract, p 126).

36   *Deglman v Guaranty Trust Co of Canada* (1954) (see extract, p 359).

37   See generally *Fibrosa Spolka Akcyjna v Fairbairn Lawson Combe Barbour* (1943), pp 61–64; Goff and Jones, *The Law of Restitution*, 3rd edn, 1986, p 5ff; Birks, 'English and Roman learning in *Moses v Macferlan*' (1984) 37 CLP 1.

38   Cf *Pavey & Matthews Pty Ltd v Paul* (1987), pp 227, 254–57, 267.

restitution. According to the Quadration Thesis, 'unjust enrichment logically supports only restitution and restitution logically follows only from unjust enrichment'.[39] Although this theory still has its vigorous supporters,[40] a number of well regarded and influential academic commentators have suggested that a restitutionary response might be triggered by causative events other than unjust enrichment.[41] Many academics would now accept, for example, that the causative event which triggers a restitutionary response in the division of restitution law concerned with restitutionary relief for a wrong[42] is not unjust enrichment, but rather the wrong itself.[43] That is the view adopted in this book.[44]

This book is not the appropriate place to analyse the various commentators' complex theoretical arguments, though it is necessary to refer briefly to a few of the theories that could potentially gain influence in Australia. Peter Birks,[45] for example, has argued that the causative events triggering restitution are not only unjust enrichment and wrongs, but also consent[46] and miscellaneous events such as retention of another's property. Ian Jackman[47] argues that the law of restitution is based on three principles of injustice: the non-voluntary conferral of an incontrovertible benefit;[48] the fulfilment of non-contractual promises;[49] and the need to protect certain facilitative institutions of private law.[50] Joachim Dietrich argues that the law of restitution fulfils an essentially 'gap-filling' role, and argues that there are four broad categories of restitutionary claims: claims

39 McInnes, 'Restitution, unjust enrichment and the perfect quadration thesis' [1999] RLR 118, p 119.

40 See particularly Burrows, 'Quadrating restitution and unjust enrichment: a matter of principle?' [2000] RLR 257; cf McInnes, *ibid*.

41 See, eg, Birks, 'Misnomer', and Virgo, 'What is the law of restitution about?', both in Cornish *et al*, *Restitution: Past, Present and Future*, 1998; Dietrich, *Restitution: A New Perspective*, 1998; Jackman, *The Varieties of Restitution*, 1998; Hedley, 'Unjust enrichment as the basis of restitution – an overworked concept' (1985) 5 Legal Studies 56; Sutton, 'Unjust enrichment' (1981) 5 Otago LR 187; Perillo, 'Restitution in a contractual context' (1973) 73 Col LR 1208.

42 See the discussion of restitution for wrongdoing, Chapter 17.

43 Birks, *An Introduction to the Law of Restitution*, rev edn, 1989, pp 39–44; Birks, *op cit*, fn 41, pp 14–15; cf McInnes, *op cit*, fn 39, pp 120–22; contrast Burrows, *op cit*, fn 40.

44 It is sometimes suggested that the restitution for wrongdoing cases do in fact form part of the law of restitution: see, for example, *Commissioner of State Revenue (Vic) v Royal Insurance Australia Ltd* (1994), p 73 and *Attorney General v Guardian Newspapers Ltd (No 2)* (1990), p 286. However, this author prefers Peter Birks' view that the basis of the cause of action is the commission of the wrong, not unjust enrichment: Birks, *ibid*; cf McInnes, *op cit*, fn 39; contrast Burrows, *op cit*, fn 40.

45 Birks, *op cit*, fn 43; Birks, 'The "law of restitution" at the end of an epoch' (1999) 28 UWALR 1.

46 Birks is here referring to the presumably exceptional situation where it is possible to find a genuine implied promise to repay the money.

47 Jackman, *The Varieties of Restitution*, 1998.

48 This principle is said to explain recovery in mistake, duress, undue influence, necessitous intervention and total failure of consideration claims.

49 This principle is said to be the basis of claims for benefits in kind voluntarily conferred under an ineffective contract, as well as claims based on legal compulsion.

50 This third principle is said to explain, *inter alia*, restitutionary remedies for legal and equitable wrongs such as breach of fiduciary obligation.

based on the conduct of the defendant;[51] claims based on contingencies arising out of a relationship of common interest which have not been provided for;[52] claims based on a plaintiff's unsolicited intervention in the affairs of another; and claims based on unintentional transfers to an innocent defendant.[53]

Whilst acknowledging these and other reformist views of restitution law, the remainder of this book is premised on the conventional theory that the basis of independent restitutionary claims is the prevention of unjust enrichments at the expense of the plaintiff.[54] I am fortified in adopting this (admittedly conservative) view by the fact that unjust enrichment has been accepted as the basis of restitutionary liability by the highest courts in Australia,[55] the United Kingdom[56] and Canada.[57] However, this approach has not secured universal judicial support, as shown by the following extract.

Roxborough v Rothmans of Pall Mall Australia Ltd (2001) 185 ALR 335
High Court of Australia

The facts are stated at p 81.

Gummow J: … [354] Writing extrajudicially, Justice Paul Finn has said of the concept of 'unjust enrichment' that '[a]t a quite visceral level it provides an important catalyst to further legal inquiry', particularly as 'a unifying legal concept'[58] which 'explains why the law recognises an obligation to make restitution in particular contexts'.[59] The conventional view is that it is the unjust enrichment which gives rise to the obligations of restitution. However, Justice Finn expresses concern that the concept of unjust enrichment may 'contrive legal analysis' and continues (in a passage I would adopt):

---

51 Included in this category are claims for money and services rendered under an ineffective contract.

52 This category includes claims for contribution between co-sureties and the division of property upon the breakdown of a *de facto* relationship.

53 Claims that are included in this category are mistaken payments of money and mistaken improvements to land, and the transfer of money or benefits in kind upon a condition that fails.

54 Throughout the book, however, I will identify those categories of case where restitutionary recovery has been permitted but which fit uneasily with the unjust enrichment principle, for example in the case of contracts which fail to materialise (see Chapter 14).

55 *Pavey & Matthews Pty Ltd v Paul* (1987), pp 227, 256–57 (see extract, p 15); *Australia & New Zealand Banking Group Ltd v Westpac Banking Corporation* (1988) (see extract, p 25); *David Securities Pty Ltd v Commonwealth Bank of Australia* (1992), pp 375, 378–79, 389, 406 (see extract, p 30); *Baltic Shipping Co v Dillon* (1993), pp 375, 385 (see extract, p 286); *Commissioner of State Revenue (Vic) v Royal Insurance Australia Ltd* (1994) (see extract, p 120); *Roxborough v Rothmans of Pall Mall Australia Ltd* (2001), pp 341, 383 (see extracts, pp 268 and 273.

56 *Lipkin Gorman v Karpnale Ltd* (1991) (see extracts, pp 595 and 654); *Woolwich Equitable Building Society v Inland Revenue Commissioners* (1993), pp 196–97 (see extract, p 456); *Kleinwort Benson Ltd v Lincoln City Council* (1999), pp 363, 399, 400, 401, 408, 409, 410, 411 (see extract, p 126).

57 *Deglman v Guaranty Trust* (1954) (see extract, p 359); *Pettkus v Becker* (1980).

58 *Pavey & Matthews Pty Ltd v Paul* (1987), pp 256–57; *David Securities Pty Ltd v Commonwealth Bank of Australia* (1992), p 375.

59 Finn, 'Equitable doctrine and discretion in remedies', in Cornish *et al*, *op cit*, fn 41, p 251.

[T]o the extent that it directs attention to outcomes and to the character to be attributed to them, it is capable of concealing rather than revealing why the law would want to attribute a responsibility to one party to provide satisfaction to the other. This is particularly so where, as is so often the case, it is conduct in a relationship or dealing – an expectation created and relied upon; a mistake not corrected; etc – which provides the focus of legal attention and which generates the issue of legal policy for which resolution is required. This, I suspect, provides the reason why 'unconscionable conduct' and not 'unjust enrichment' (a possible effect of that conduct) has achieved the currency it has in Australian law [p 252].

However, in *Baltic Shipping* (1993), Mason CJ said that, in cases of money had and received, the retention of the money in question:

> ... is regarded, in the language of Lord Mansfield, as 'against conscience' or, in the modern terminology, as an unjust enrichment of the defendant because the condition upon which it was paid, namely, performance by the defendant may not have occurred [p 359, footnote omitted].

Nevertheless, reflection will demonstrate that the notion of unjust enrichment cannot be accepted as a modern synonym for a refusal 'against conscience' to pay the money in question. This is because, as Rothmans emphasised in its submissions, the action for money had and received lies against defendants who fail to account but who, on any sensible understanding of the term, have not been enriched. A recent example[60] is the decision of the New Zealand Court of Appeal [355] in *Martin v Pont* (1993).[61] A principal who entrusted money to an agent for the purpose of investing it with a nominated finance company was entitled to recover from the agent when, by reason of a defalcation by an employee of the agent which did not benefit the agent, the purpose was not carried out.

Considerations such as these, together with practical experience, suggest caution in judicial acceptance of any all-embracing theory of restitutionary rights and remedies founded upon a notion of 'unjust enrichment'. To the lawyer whose mind has been moulded by civilian influences, the theory may come first, and the source of the theory may be the writing of jurists not the decisions of judges. However, that is not the way in which a system based on case law develops; over time, general principle is derived from judicial decisions upon particular instances, not the other way around.

In *McGinty v Western Australia* (1996), p 232, McHugh J referred to Judge Posner's description of 'top-down reasoning' by which a theory about an area of law is invented or adopted and then applied to existing decisions to make them conform to the theory and to dictate the outcome in new cases. Judge Posner spoke of the use of the theory by its adherents:[62]

---

60 Earlier authorities include *Parry v Roberts* (1835); cf *The Oriental Bank Corporation v Hewitt* (1862). See also Jackson, *The History of Quasi-Contract in English Law*, 1936, pp 24–26.

61 See also Stoljar, 'Unjust enrichment and unjust sacrifice' (1987) 50 MLR 603, pp 612–13; Kwai-Lian Liew, 'Restitution and contract risk: commentary', in McInnes (ed), *op cit*, fn 33, pp 165–66, 171–75; Grantham and Rickett, *Enrichment and Restitution in New Zealand*, 2000, pp 277–79.

62 'Legal reasoning from the top down and from the bottom up: the question of unenumerated constitutional rights' (1992) 59 U of Chicago L Rev 433, p 433. See also Waters, 'The reception of equity in the Supreme Court of Canada (1875–2000)' (2001) 80 Can Bar Rev 620, p 645.

... to organize, criticize, accept or reject, explain or explain away, distinguish or amplify the existing decisions to make them conform to the theory and generate an outcome in each new case as it arises that will be consistent with the theory and with the canonical cases, that is, the cases accepted as authoritative within the theory.

As it happens, Lord Mansfield favoured the development of legal principle by a journey in the opposite direction. In *Ringsted v Lady Lanesborough* (1783), his Lordship said:

General rules are, however, varied by change of circumstances. Cases arise within the letter, yet not within the reason, of the rule; and exceptions are introduced, which, grafted upon the rule, form a system of law.

Unless, as this court indicated in *David Securities Pty Ltd v Commonwealth Bank of Australia* (1992), pp 378–79, unjust enrichment is seen as a concept rather than a definitive legal principle, substance and dynamism may be restricted by dogma. In turn, the dogma will tend to generate new fictions in order to retain support for its thesis. It also may distort well-settled principles in other fields, including those respecting equitable doctrines and remedies, so that they answer the newly mandated order of things. Then various theories will compete, each to deny the others. There is support in Australasian legal scholarship for [356] considerable scepticism respecting any all-embracing theory in this field, with the treatment of the disparate as no more than species of the one newly discovered genus.[63]

On the other hand, the action to recover the moneys sought by the appellants after the failure of the purpose of funding Rothmans to renew its licence may be illustrative of the gap-filling and auxiliary role of restitutionary remedies.[64] These remedies do not let matters lie where they would fall if the carriage of risk between the parties were left entirely within the limits of their contract. Hence there is some force in the statement by Laycock:[65]

The rules of restitution developed much like the rules of equity. Restitution arose to avoid unjust results in specific cases – as a series of innovations to fill gaps in the rest of the law.

Commentary and questions

Gummow J went on to suggest that the obligation to make restitution in an action for money had and received is founded on general equitable notions, and

---

63   See, eg, Stoljar, 'Unjust enrichment and unjust sacrifice' (1987) 50 MLR 603, pp 610–13; Tilbury, *Civil Remedies*, Vol 1, 1990, at [4003]–[4019]; Tilbury, 'Restitutionary damages' in Carroll (ed), *Civil Remedies: Issues and Developments*, 1996, pp 2–6, 43–47; Glover, *Commercial Equity: Fiduciary Relationships*, 1995, at [5.15]–[5.17]; Dietrich, *Restitution: A New Perspective*, 1998, pp 92–100; Grantham and Rickett, 'Property and unjust enrichment: categorical truths or unnecessary complexity?' [1997] NZLR 668; Grantham and Rickett, *Enrichment and Restitution in New Zealand*, 2000, pp 13–16; Wright, 'Professor Birks and the demise of the remedial constructive trust' (1999) 7 RLR 128, pp 129–36; Doyle and Wright, 'Restitutionary damages – the unnecessary remedy?' (2001) 25 MULR 1, pp 17–20; Kremer, 'The action for money had and received' (2001) 17 JCL 93, pp 94–97. See, further, Jaffey, *The Nature and Scope of Restitution*, 2000, pp 15–26.

64   Dietrich, *Restitution: A New Perspective*, 1998, pp 29–35; Grantham and Rickett, 'On the subsidiarity of unjust enrichment' (2001) 117 LQR 273, pp 289–93.

65   'The scope and significance of restitution' (1989) 67 Tex L Rev 1277, p 1278.

that the obligation to repay money on a consideration that failed is founded on the unconscionability of retention of the money.

Why is Gummow J critical of the development of unjust enrichment theory and of the principle of unjust enrichment as the basis of restitutionary liability? What role does Gummow J see the law of restitution playing in the Australian law of obligations?

NATURE OF THE CONCEPT OF UNJUST ENRICHMENT

David Securities Pty Ltd v Commonwealth Bank of Australia (1992) 175 CLR 353 High Court of Australia

The facts are stated at p 110.

Mason CJ, Deane, Toohey Gaudron and McHugh JJ: ... [378] [T]he respondent argues that a plaintiff should be required to prove that retention of the moneys by the recipient would be unjust in all the circumstances before recovery should be granted; if the circumstances of the case showed that it would not be unjust for the recipient to retain the money, the fact that the plaintiff could point to a causative mistake, whether of fact or law, would not assist the plaintiff. According to the respondent's submissions, moneys paid under a mistake of law could only be recoverable in so far as the recipient has been unjustly enriched at the expense of the payer, such that it would be unconscionable for the recipient not to give restitution to the payer. In support of this approach, the respondent relies, *inter alia*, on the recent decisions of this court in *Westpac Banking Corporation* (1988) and *Pavey & Matthews* (1987) ...

[T]his ... approach ... appears to proceed from the view that in Australian law unjust enrichment is a definitive legal principle according to its own terms and not just a concept.

The two decisions of this court just mentioned reject that approach ... Accordingly, it is not legitimate to determine whether an enrichment is unjust by reference to some subjective evaluation of what is fair or unconscionable. Instead, recovery depends upon the existence of a qualifying or vitiating factor such as mistake, duress or illegality. As this court stated in *Westpac Banking Corporation* (1988):

> In other words, receipt of a payment which has been made under a fundamental mistake is one of the categories of case in which the facts give rise to a *prima facie* obligation to make restitution, in the sense of compensation for the benefit of unjust enrichment, to the person who has sustained the countervailing detriment.

As La Forest J stated in *Air Canada v British Columbia* (1989), the two species of mistake (ie, fact and law) should be 'considered as factors which can make an enrichment at the plaintiff's expense "unjust" or "unjustified"'.

The respondent's submission that the appellants must independently prove 'unjustness' over and above the mistake cannot therefore be sustained. The fact that the payment has been caused by a mistake is sufficient to give rise to a *prima facie* obligation on the part of the respondent to make restitution. Before that *prima facie* liability is displaced, the respondent must point to circumstances which the law recognises would make an order for restitution unjust. There can be no restitution in such circumstances because the law will not provide for recovery except when the enrichment is *unjust*. It follows that the recipient of a payment, which is sought to be recovered on the ground of unjust enrichment, is entitled to raise by way of answer any matter or circumstance which shows that his or her receipt (or retention) of the payment is not unjust ...

Commentary

The High Court in the principal case emphasised that the plaintiff must plead and prove a specific ground of liability, such as mistake or total failure of consideration; in other words a specific unjust factor. It is not sufficient merely to allege an enrichment is unjust as a matter of subjective 'fairness'.[66] The same point was made by Lord Goff in *Lipkin Gorman v Karpnale* (1991) (see extract, p 595):

> I accept that the solicitor's claim in the present case is founded upon the unjust enrichment of the club ... But it does not, in my opinion, follow that the court has carte blanche to reject the solicitors' claim simply because it thinks it unfair or unjust in the circumstances to grant recovery. The recovery of money in restitution is not, as a general rule, a matter of discretion for the court. A claim to recover money at common law is made as a matter of right and even though the underlying principle of recovery is the principle of unjust enrichment, nevertheless where recovery is denied, it is denied on the basis of legal principle.

The specific grounds of liability, or unjust factors, currently recognised in the Australian law of restitution are identified in Chapter 4. Each of the recognised unjust factors is grounded upon a body of rules and principles laid down in previous cases.

Unjust enrichment is not in itself a cause of action;[67] nor even, apparently, is it a 'definitive legal principle according to its own terms'.[68] Nevertheless, as a 'unifying legal concept'[69] it fulfils a number of important functions in the law of restitution:[70]

(1) it provides the conceptual framework that explains the imposition of an obligation to make restitution in recognised categories of case;

(2) it provides the conceptual framework for determining whether the law should recognise an obligation to make restitution in a new or developing category of case;

---

66 See also *Christiani and Nielsen Pty Ltd v Goliath Portland Cement Co Ltd* (1993) 2 Tas R 122 (see extract, p 330).

67 See further discussion below at p 32.

68 *David Securities Pty Ltd v Commonwealth Bank of Australia* (1992), pp 378–79 (see extract, p 30).

69 *Pavey & Matthews Pty Ltd v Paul* (1987), p 256 *per* Deane J (see extract, p 15). See also *Kleinwort Benson Ltd v Lincoln City Council* (1999), p 407 *per* Lord Hope (see extract, p 126).

70 In addition to the principal case, see *Pavey & Matthews Pty Ltd v Paul* (1987), p 257 *per* Deane J (see extract, p 15); *Australia and New Zealand Banking Group Ltd v Westpac Banking Corporation* (1988), p 672 (see extract, p 25); *Kleinwort Benson Ltd v Lincoln City Council* (1999), pp 407–08 *per* Lord Hope (see extract, p 126).

(3) it provides the analytical framework for determining whether a claim in a particular case should succeed; and

(4) it guides the courts as to relevant policy considerations.

PLEADING AN UNJUST ENRICHMENT CLAIM

The High Court has indicated that unjust enrichment is not a cause of action.[71] The exact source of the cause of action for claims in restitution remains unclear, although there are statements in the cases indicating that the cause of action inheres in the unjust factor grounding the claim.[72]

The courts have struck out pleadings that assert merely that an unjust enrichment has occurred or that it would be 'unjust' for the defendant to retain an enrichment. The plaintiff is required to plead specifically the essential facts underlying each element of unjust enrichment; in particular the essential facts supporting the unjust factor(s) on which the claim is based.[73] In *Winterton Constructions Pty Ltd v Hambros Australia Ltd* (1991) Gummow J struck out as embarrassing pleadings that did not:

> ... specify with anything like sufficient clarity what are the material facts upon which [the plaintiff] relies (i) to show enrichment of [the defendant], (ii) at the expense of [the defendant] and (iii) in circumstances demonstrating the necessary element of injustice [pp 375–76].

THE RELATIONSHIP BETWEEN UNJUST ENRICHMENT AND UNCONSCIONABILITY

The relationship between unjust enrichment and the equitable doctrine of unconscionable conduct is uncertain and controversial. The conventional view is that the concept of unconscionability does not have a significant role to play in personal claims in the law of restitution.[74] Restitutionary liability is seen to be

---

71 *David Securities Pty Ltd v Commonwealth Bank of Australia* (1992), pp 378–79, 406 (see extract, p 30).

72 That is, the cause of action lies in mistake, acceptance, total failure of consideration and so on. See *Commissioner of State Revenue (Vic) v Royal Insurance Australia Ltd* (1994), p 65 *per* Mason CJ ('an action for recovery of money paid under a mistake of fact or law') (see extract, p 120); *Torrens Aloha Pty Ltd v Citibank NA* (1997), p 102 ('cause of action for the recovery of money paid under a mistake'). In *Kleinwort Benson Ltd v Lincoln City Council* (1999) (see extract, p 126), the House of Lords appeared to take the view that the plaintiff's cause of action was based on the mistake of law: see in particular Lord Hoffman at p 401 ('claim based on mistake') and Lord Hope at 407 ('mistake provides the cause of action for recovery of the money had and received by the payee').

73 *Marriott Industries Pty Ltd v Mercantile Credits Ltd* (1990), p 238; *Winterton Constructions Pty Ltd v Hambros Australia Ltd* (1991), pp 375–76; *Reed International Books Australia Pty Ltd t/a Butterworths v King & Prior Pty Ltd* (1993); *Griffiths v Commonwealth Bank of Australia* (1994), p 122; *Mick Skorpos Petrol Discount King Pty Ltd v Shell Company of Australia Ltd* (1997).

74 Glover, 'Equity and restitution', in Parkinson (ed), *The Principles of Equity*, 1996, pp 101–02; Byrne, 'Restitution and equity' (1995) 11 QUTLJ 169, p 181.

independent of fault,[75] whereas the quality of the defendant's conduct is central to the concept of unconscionability.[76] However, in *Roxborough v Rothmans of Pall Mall Australia Ltd* (2001) Gummow J suggested that the obligation to make restitution on an action for money had and received is found on general equitable notions (pp 356–64), and more specifically that the obligation to repay money on a consideration that failed is founded on the unconscionability of retention of the money.[77] There is no significant support for these views in the other judgments,[78] though some academics have called for better integration of common law and equitable doctrine in this area.[79]

RESTITUTION FOR WRONGDOING

There are two major divisions of claims that are traditionally discussed under the rubric of restitution law: independent claims in restitution, and claims for a restitutionary remedy for a wrong. An independent claim in restitution refers to those categories of claim based on unjust enrichment by subtraction, where both the cause of action and the remedial response lie in the law of restitution. Restitution for wrongdoing, on the other hand, refers to that category of case where a restitutionary (gain-based) remedy is awarded for the commission of certain legal and equitable wrongs. In this category of case, the cause of action does not lie in the law of restitution, but rather in the area of law that governs the operative wrong, such as torts law, contract law or equity. Although the better view is that such claims do not technically form part of the law of restitution,[80] gain-based remedies are restitutionary in measure (in the sense that they involve restoring to the plaintiff the defendant's gain), and are traditionally included in restitution law courses. For these reasons, restitution for wrongdoing is discussed in Chapter 17. Unless otherwise indicated, however, the remainder of the book deals with the independent action in restitution based on the principle of preventing unjust enrichments gained at the expense of the plaintiff.

---

75 *Air Canada v Ontario (Liquor Control Board)* (1997) (see extract, p 151).

76 Glover, *op cit*, fn 74.

77 At pp 363–64, 365. Justice Gummow analogised with cases such as *Muschinski v Dodds* (1985) (see extract, p 688) which involved the division of property on the breakdown of a *de facto* relationship.

78 Though see the passing reference to the concept of unconscionability of retention and the notion of an 'equitable foundation' of restitutionary claims in the joint judgment of Gleeson CJ, Gaudron and Hayne JJ.

79 Bryan and Ellinghaus, 'Fault lines in the law of obligations: *Roxborough v Rothmans of Pall Mall Australia Ltd*' (2000) 22 Syd LR 636, pp 665–66; Bryan, 'Where the constitutional basis for payment has failed' [2000] RLR 218, pp 228–29.

80 It is sometimes suggested that the restitution for wrongdoing cases does in fact form part of the law of restitution: see, eg, *Commissioner of State Revenue (Vic) v Royal Insurance Australia Ltd* (1994), p 73 and *Attorney General v Guardian Newspapers Ltd (No 2)* (1990), p 286. However, this author prefers Peter Birks' view that the basis of the cause of action is the commission of the wrong, not unjust enrichment: Birks, *op cit*, fn 43; cf McInnes, *op cit*, fn 39; contrast Burrows, *op cit*, fn 40.

CHAPTER 2

IDENTIFICATION AND MEASUREMENT OF ENRICHMENT

INTRODUCTION

Proof of an enrichment to the defendant is an essential requirement of a claim in restitution. The requirement of an enrichment to the defendant distinguishes restitution from tort and contract law, where the primary objective is compensation for loss rather than reversal of an enrichment.

Portman Building Society v Hamlyn Taylor Neck (A Firm)
[1998] 4 All ER 202 English Court of Appeal

The defendant firm of solicitors acted for Biggins in the purchase of a seaside property, and also for the plaintiff building society to which Biggins had applied for finance in the amount of £92,100. The building society offered to provide the finance on the condition that the property would be used solely for Biggins' own use. Biggins in fact intended to use, and did use, the property as a guesthouse. The defendant knew of Biggins' intention, however failed to disclose this to the building society, and confirmed that the conditions of offer had been complied with and that there were no matters affecting the property about which the building society should be advised. The building society advanced the amount of £92,100 to the defendant's client trust account, and the defendant duly paid this amount to the vendor's solicitors. Some years later, Biggins defaulted in making payments under the mortgage and the building society became aware that Biggins had been using the property as a guesthouse. It commenced proceedings against the defendant claiming recovery of £92,100 on the ground of a mistake of fact. The mistake of fact it relied on was the mistaken belief induced by the defendant that the condition contained in the mortgage offer that the property would be used solely for personal occupation was complied with.

Millett LJ: ... [206] The first sentence of the first edition of Goff and Jones's *The Law of Restitution* published in 1965 states: 'The law of restitution is the law of all claims ... which are founded on the principle of unjust enrichment.'

That passage echoes section 1 of the Restatement of the Law of Restitution, published by the American Law Institute in 1937, in which the authors, Professors Warren Seavey and Austin Scott, made the epoch-making assertion: 'A person who has been unjustly enriched at the expense of another is required to make restitution to that other.'

This formulation explains why any claim to restitution raises the questions: (1) has the defendant been enriched? (2) If so, is his enrichment unjust? (3) Is his enrichment at the expense of the plaintiff? There are several factors which make it unjust for a defendant to retain the benefit of his enrichment; mistake is one of them. But a person cannot be unjustly enriched if he has not been enriched at all. That is why it is necessary to ask all three questions and why the fact that a payment may have been made, for example, by mistake, is not by itself sufficient to justify a restitutionary remedy.

In the present case the firm was not enriched by the receipt of the £92,100. The money was trust money, which belonged in equity to the society, and was properly paid by the firm into its client account. The firm never made any claim to the money. It acknowledged that it was the society's money, held to the order of the society and it was applied in accordance with the society's instructions in exchange for a mortgage in favour of the society. The firm did not receive the money for its own use and benefit, but to the society's use. Given that the money was held to the order of the society, the only question is whether the firm obtained a good discharge for the money. It is conceded that it did.

In its argument before us the society relies on three lines of authority. The first is the line of cases which establish that an action lies to recover payments made under a mistake of fact; see for example *Barclays Bank v WJ Simms* (1980), p 695. So it does. In such cases the money is (mistakenly) paid to the defendant for his own use and benefit, [207] or at least for the use and benefit of a third party and not for the use and benefit of the plaintiff himself. But for the mistake, there would be no injustice in the defendant or the third party retaining the benefit of the payment, for that is the common intention of the parties. The effect of the plaintiff's mistake, however, is to make it unjust for the defendant or the third party to retain the benefit of the payment. The action for restitution reverses the unjust enrichment.

But in the present case the society paid the money to the firm to hold to the society's order, that is to say for the society's own use and benefit. The society was entitled to give the firm directions as to the application of the money, and to revoke those directions and demand the repayment of the money if not previously applied in accordance with its unrevoked directions. The society did not need to plead mistake or any other ground of restitution. The firm received the money on terms which made it an accounting party and has never denied its liability to account. The society's difficulty is not in establishing the firm's liability to account, but in showing that anything is due from the firm after it applied the money in accordance with the society's instructions.

Secondly, the society relies on those cases which show that the cause of action for money had and received is complete when the plaintiff's money is received by the defendant. It does not depend on the continued retention of the money by the defendant. Save in strictly limited circumstances it is no defence that the defendant has parted with the money. All that is true. But it is, of course, a defence that he has parted with it by paying it to the *plaintiff or to the plaintiff's order*: see *Holland v Russell* (1861) (affd (1863)). That is what the firm did in the present case.

...

[The third argument Millett LJ addresses is an argument based on the defence of ministerial receipt. This aspect of Millett LJ's judgment is extracted at p 643.]

TRADITIONAL APPROACH TO IDENTIFICATION OF BENEFIT

The traditional approach of the courts to the question of benefit is to identify an objective benefit, and then to determine whether that benefit should be subjectively devalued. The principle of subjective devaluation[1] protects the values of individuality of tastes and economic priorities. Although the defendant may have received something of objective value, the defendant may subjectively devalue the benefit by appeal to the value of freedom of choice; that is, the defendant will be permitted to argue that he or she does not personally value the thing provided, or would not have chosen to allocate their resources to pay for that thing. The notion of subjective devaluation is expressed in the classic statement: 'One cleans another's shoes, what can the other do but put them on?'[2] Recourse to subjective devaluation will be precluded, however, where the benefit is incontrovertible (as in the case of money) or where it has been requested or accepted by the defendant.

OBJECTIVE BENEFIT

An objective benefit means the receipt of something which has a market value. It may be positive in the sense of the receipt of something tangible, or negative in the sense of the saving of an expense which might reasonably have been incurred. Despite the influential arguments of Beatson[3] it is now settled in Australia that the receipt of pure services (services which do not result in a tangible accretion to wealth) which have a market value will be objectively beneficial (at least where the services have been requested by the defendant in the context of a contract that has become ineffective).[4]

The identification of an objective benefit becomes problematic where services have been requested, and the plaintiff has incurred considerable expense in relying on the request, however no part of the end product has been delivered to the defendant at the time the contract became ineffective. This issue is illustrated by the following controversial decision.

Planché v Colburn (1831) 8 Bing 14; 131 ER 305 Common Pleas

The defendant contracted with the plaintiff for the plaintiff to write a volume on costume and ancient armour for the defendant's publication, *The Juvenile Library*. After the plaintiff had commenced researching and writing the work, but before he tendered or delivered any part of it, the defendant abandoned the publication.

Tindal CJ: ... [306] I agree that, when a special contract is in existence and open, the Plaintiff cannot sue on a *quantum meruit*: part of the question here, therefore, was, whether the contract did exist or not. It distinctly appeared that the work was

---

1   The term 'subjective devaluation' was first coined by Peter Birks: *An Introduction to the Law of Restitution*, rev edn, 1989, pp 109–14. For a discussion of the concept of subjective devaluation, see McInnes, 'The structure and challenges of unjust enrichment' in *Restitution: Developments in Unjust Enrichment*, 1996, pp 19–20.

2   Pollock CB in *Taylor v Laird* (1856).

3   Beatson, 'Benefit, reliance and the structure of unjust enrichment' in *The Use and Abuse of Unjust Enrichment*, 1991, Chapter 2.

4   See *Segur v Franklin* (1934); *Brenner v First Artists' Management Pty Ltd* (1993) (see extract, p 39); *Independent Grocers Co-Operative Ltd v Noble Lowndes Superannuation Consultants Ltd* (1993).

finally abandoned; and the jury found that no new contract had been entered into. Under these circumstances the Plaintiff ought not to lose the fruit of his labour ...

Commentary

The principal case was followed by the Full Court of the Supreme Court of Victoria in *Brooks Robinson Pty Ltd v Rothfield* (1951). The defendant requested the plaintiff to construct a cocktail cabinet, but when the cabinet was almost completed, and before any part of it had been delivered, the defendant repudiated the contract and refused to accept the cabinet. The plaintiff's claim for a *quantum meruit* was successful.

Burrows (in *The Law of Restitution*) criticises cases such as *Planché v Colburn* and *Brooks Robinson Pty Ltd v Rothfield* as resulting in an 'unrealistic and overinclusive notion of benefit', arguing that services can be regarded as objectively beneficial only at the time of *receipt* of the services. In the absence of any receipt of services it is fictitious to decide such cases on the basis of a reversal of an unjust enrichment: there is simply no enrichment to reverse. Other commentators express similar views, arguing that recovery in such cases appears to be based upon the conduct of the defendant in requesting the services, and the subsequent reliance by the plaintiff in commencing the work, rather than the receipt of a benefit that it would be unjust to retain.[5]

The need to establish an objective benefit has, however, been questioned by some commentators and members of the judiciary.[6] In *Brenner v First Artists' Management Pty Ltd* (1993) Byrne J attempted to reconcile these decisions with unjust enrichment principles by equating benefit with request:

> ... where a person requests another to do something, it is not unreasonable for the law to conclude that the former sees some benefit in its performance, however wrong this may be on an objective basis and for the law to act upon the perception of the recipient ... I conclude that in a case where the services were requested and accepted, the law will not stop to enquire whether they were, on any other basis, of benefit to the party requesting and accepting them.

Byrne J agreed with an argument by Birks that the focus should be on the services themselves rather than on whether an end product has resulted from those services.[7] Garner[8] has advocated a similar approach based on the concept

---

5   See, eg, Wyvill, 'Enrichment, restitution and the collapsed negotiations cases' (1993) 11(2) ABR 93; Pegoraro, 'Recovery of benefits conferred pursuant to failed anticipated contracts – unjust enrichment, equitable estoppel or unjust sacrifice' (1993) 23 ABLR 117. As to whether the law of restitution can encompass a principle of detrimental reliance or 'unjust sacrifice', see also Stoljar, 'Unjust enrichment and unjust sacrifice' (1987) 50 MLR 603; Muir, 'Unjust sacrifice and the officious intervener' in Finn (ed), *Essays on Restitution*, 1990, Chapter 9; Mason and Carter, *Restitution Law in Australia*, 1995, pp 309–10.

6   The need for an objective benefit has been vigorously debated in the context of cases dealing with expenditure incurred in anticipation of a contract which fails to materialise: see further, below, Chapter 14.

7   See Birks, *op cit*, fn 1, pp 126–27, 232.

8   Garner, 'Benefits – for services rendered: commentary', in McInnes, *op cit*, fn 1, Chapter 6; cf Garner, 'The role of subjective benefit in the law of unjust enrichment' (1990) 10 OJLS 42, pp 129, 232.

of 'subjective revaluation'. In essence Garner argues that a defendant who has acknowledged by conduct that the defendant values the services rendered by the plaintiff (at minimum a request must be shown) should be held to have been enriched by the (full) performance of the services, even if they are objectively valueless.

Where an objective benefit can be found, the defendant will nevertheless be permitted to devalue that objective benefit in the absence of acceptance of the benefit or the benefit amounting to an 'incontrovertible' benefit. The doctrine of acceptance is discussed in the next section. The doctrine of incontrovertible benefit is discussed below (pp 51–66).

REQUEST AND ACCEPTANCE

Introduction

A defendant who (freely) accepts a non-monetary benefit will be precluded from subjectively devaluing that benefit. In *Brenner v First Artists' Management Pty Ltd* (1993) Byrne J held that the recipient of a non-monetary benefit will be taken to have accepted the benefit where the recipient:

> ... as a reasonable person, should have realised that a person in the position of the provider of the services would expect to be paid for them and did not take a reasonable opportunity to reject those services [p 260, quoting Jones, *Restitution in Public and Private Law*, 1992, p 108].

This test of acceptance was also adopted in *Angelopoulos v Sabatino* (1995) (see extract, p 418). On this formulation it is sufficient if the defendant had constructive knowledge of the plaintiff's expectation of payment.[9]

Brenner v First Artists' Management Pty Ltd
[1993] 2 VR 221 Supreme Court of Victoria

In June 1987 the second plaintiff, Fenner, was engaged as manager by the second defendant, Daryl Braithwaite, who wished to revive his career as a pop star. A commission of 15% was agreed between the parties, but the basis on which it was to be calculated was not determined. By the end of 1987 the first defendant, First Artists' Management (FAM), a management company controlled by investors, was set up to manage the artist. The investors and Braithwaite agreed that the proceeds of the artist's professional activities were to be distributed between the investors, FAM and the artist in an agreed manner. In January 1988 the first plaintiff, Brenner, was invited to join in the management arrangement which then existed between Braithwaite and Fenner. At this stage Braithwaite effectively had two sets of managers, Fenner and Brenner, pursuant to the arrangement made in June 1987

---

9   Peter Birks argues, however, that liability should be imposed only where the defendant has *actual* knowledge of the plaintiff's expectation of payment. He argues that the true basis of recovery for acceptance is the unconscientious behaviour of the defendant in failing to reject the benefit knowing that it was not being provided gratuitously: Birks, 'In defence of free acceptance' in Burrows, *Essays on the Law of Restitution*, 1991, esp at pp 128–29 (see extract, p 46).

as modified in January 1988, and FAM which had been appointed by the investors. In order to rationalise the management arrangements, Fenner and Brenner were appointed as directors of FAM and thereafter they, or a company controlled by them, provided managerial and like services as consultant to FAM in anticipation of the finalisation of contractual arrangements which had been agreed on that date. These arrangements were never finalised. On 15 August 1988 management arrangements involving Fenner and Brenner were determined by notice and they were removed as directors of FAM. Brenner and Fenner commenced proceedings against FAM and Braithwaite seeking remuneration for the management services provided by them, claiming in contract or alternatively in restitution for the value of their services. FAM was subsequently dissolved and Fenner and Brenner pursued their remuneration claim against Braithwaite only. Byrne J rejected the claim based on contract, holding that the management arrangement entered into between Braithwaite and Fenner in June 1987, as modified by the inclusion of Brenner in January 1988, was too uncertain to constitute a binding contract. However Byrne J allowed the claim in restitution.

Byrne J: ... [255] *Legal principles as to liability*

Both parties took as their starting point the judgments of the High Court in *Pavey & Matthews Pty Ltd v Paul* (1987). [Byrne J referred to the judgment of Deane J in *Pavey & Matthews Pty Ltd v Paul* (see extract, p 15) and continued at p 256:] An examination of these judgments and the cases referred to make it clear that there are two broad categories of claim which are commonly described as *quantum meruit*. First, the case where the services are performed under an existing and enforceable contract which contains an express or implied term to pay for them a fair and reasonable sum. The second category, that with which their Honours were concerned, is that where it is said that the law imposes on a person an obligation independent of contract to pay a fair and reasonable sum for the services. In the latter case the obligation arises by the application of the law of restitution or unjust enrichment, and not out of contract, express or implied.

It is necessary to emphasise at the outset two matters. First, this claim is one of the second category. The second is that this is a claim arising out of services performed. If different principles apply to different restitution claims such as those for the recovery of money paid or the value of goods delivered, I am not concerned with them. Furthermore, it may be that even within that class of restitution claims which are for recompense for services performed, different principles will apply, or principles will apply differently, to different types of case. For example, services performed under a contract which is valid but unenforceable or avoided through no [257] fault of the plaintiff may be treated differently from services performed where there is no contract at all. The primary case before me is put by the plaintiffs on the basis that there was no contract between Fenner or Brenner on the one hand and Braithwaite on the other.

In such a case, the gist of the claim is that the defendant has actually or constructively accepted the benefit of the plaintiffs' services in circumstances where it would be unjust for that party to do so without making restitution to the plaintiffs: *Pavey's* case (p 227) (*per* Mason and Wilson JJ), and pp 256–57 (*per* Deane J). The circumstances in which the law considers it unjust to accept the benefit without payment are to be discerned from the principles to be extracted from the decided cases. For present purposes these indicate that an obligation will not arise where there is a subsisting enforceable contract between the parties for the performance of the services in question: *Update Constructions Pty Ltd v Rozelle Child Care Centre Ltd* (1990), p 275. The obligation will not arise where the services were provided 'officiously'[10] or where they were volunteered.[11] This means that the plaintiffs in the present case must show that they performed the services in circumstances where the law requires that payment be made.

Counsel for the defendant fastened attention on the essential requirement of benefit. He submitted in respect of many of the services for which payment was sought that they did not confer a benefit upon the defendant. Where a manager attends a meeting with a view to obtaining work for an artist and no work results, he said, the plaintiffs do not demonstrate a benefit. I should state at the outset that I do not accept the two unstated premises in this submission. First, that the failure of the manager to prove that any particular service produced an engagement or other profit or, indeed, some other economic benefit for the artist, means that no benefit was conferred for the purposes of a claim in restitution. It may be that the benefit is something other than a direct consequence of any particular service, as for example the promotion of the artist or advice given to him. Second, that 'benefit' for the purpose of the rule of restitution for services must be an economic benefit: the statements of principle in *Pavey's* case are not so limited.

The defendant's submission, however, exposes a difficulty which arises in different ways in this area of law. Where a person pays money to another it is not difficult to see that a benefit has thereby accrued to the recipient. Services present greater difficulty. If the law of restitution is available to oblige the recipient of the benefit of services to make restitution, it must acknowledge that such benefit may take many forms. It seems to me unlikely that the law would introduce into this area the difficult and somewhat arbitrary distinction which has been drawn in the law of negligence between pure economic loss and physical loss. To take an extreme case, it may be of benefit to an artist simply that it be known that a particular person has accepted the role of his or her manager or that the manager by accepting the artist as a client is then precluded from acting for a competitor of the artist. I have referred to non-economic benefits which may be requested, conferred and accepted. I would need clear authority to deny a claimant the right to restitution for such services when all the other requirements of the cause of action are established. If a landowner requests an architect to [258] prepare a design for a building in circumstances where there is no enforceable contract and the architect undertakes the preparatory work but does not produce any design before the defendant abandons the project, it may be said that no benefit exists which is capable of acceptance. *Planché v Colburn* (1831) is authority against such a conclusion. In my opinion, 'benefit' in this context must be seen from the perspective of the recipient who is, after all, the person to be charged. It may be that for some idiosyncratic reason a defendant seeks the performance of work which another would see as without benefit or, indeed, as a positive dis-benefit. Examples of this are given by Goff J in *BP Exploration Co (Libya) Ltd v Hunt (No 2)* (1979), p 803. But where a person requests another to do something, it is not unreasonable for the law to conclude that the former sees some benefit in its performance, however wrong this view may be on an objective basis and for the law to act upon the perception of the recipient.

---

10   Goff and Jones, *The Law of Restitution,* 3rd edn, 1986, p 42ff.
11   Birks, *op cit*, fn 1, p 100ff.

His Lordship in *BP Exploration Co (Libya) Ltd v Hunt (No 2)* also explored an ambiguity in the concept of 'benefit' which may be of importance. Is the benefit to be seen in the performance of the service, or in the end-product which the service may or may not produce? His Lordship was concerned in that case with the construction of the Law Reform (Frustrated Contracts) Act 1943, s 1(2), and not with a claim in restitution, but he acknowledged that the principle underlying that Act was the principle of unjust enrichment. In that case, his Lordship concluded, as a matter of construction of the statute, that 'benefits' referred to the end-product of the services, not the services themselves. It does not follow that 'benefit' in the law of restitution must be given the same meaning. Indeed, the difficulties exposed by his Lordship from this conclusion (pp 802–03) and the emphasis in *Pavey's* case on the services themselves, suggest to me that the principle of restitution requires me to look there for the necessary benefit. The *BP* case concerned a claim under a frustrated contract for remuneration for prospecting services. These services, like those of a selling broker or an artist's manager, were such that they might bear no proportion to the end product. A mineral prospector might with very little effort discover a rich resource or it may be that the result of considerable effort is no benefit at all. Can it be said in the latter case that no benefit accrues to the person requesting the services? The cases of work done in anticipation of contract are of assistance in this area. In *William Lacey (Hounslow) Ltd v Davis* (1957), the plaintiff was led to believe that it would receive the contract to rebuild certain war damaged premises. The plaintiff carried out estimating work before the defendant sold the premises and the project was abandoned. The plaintiff succeeded on the now discredited basis that a promise to pay was implied from the request to do the work. Barry J was, however, prepared to infer that the defendant had derived some actual benefit from the work inasmuch as it may have produced a greater price on the sale of the premises. Be this as it may, his Lordship's decision in the *William Lacey* case, was in my view, predicated on a wider principle: the expectation of the parties that the work would be paid for. See *Sabemo Pty Ltd v North Sydney Municipal Council* (1977).[12] I conclude that in a case where the services were requested and accepted, the law will not stop to enquire [259] whether they were, on any other basis, of benefit to the party requesting and accepting them. See Goff and Jones, p 18.

Indeed, where the services have been requested by the party to be charged, the main area of interest is likely to be whether the circumstances of the request are such as to give rise to a right of payment. This will involve proof that the services were not provided as a gift: *Pavey's* case (pp 227–28). Furthermore, it will be necessary for the plaintiff to establish, where a certain event has not occurred, that the services were not provided on the basis that they were not to be paid for unless that event came to pass. In this category will fall cases where a tenderer carries out estimating or other work in response to an invitation to tender for a contract. It is understood in such cases that, in general, the tenderer takes the risk that the tender will be unsuccessful and that, as a consequence, the work will be unrewarded. It may be, however, that, even in such a case, an obligation to pay the tenderer will arise where the contract is not entered into by reason of a change of heart on the part of the proprietor: *Sabemo's* case; or where the work done falls outside that

12 At p 902. Compare Beatson, 'Unjust enrichment in the High Court of Australia' (1988) 104 LQR 13, p 16.

normally expected of tenderers: *William Lacey's* case; or where the work performed is of particular benefit to the proprietor: *British Steel Corp v Cleveland Bridge and Engineering Co Ltd* (1984).

In *Watson v Watson* (1953), the plaintiff joined the defendant, his brother, in an enterprise and performed work for the erection of a saw mill in the expectation that it would in due course be conducted by them in partnership. No partnership agreement was entered into and the plaintiff sued for the value of his work upon *quantum meruit*. The judgment was couched in terms of implied contract. The court held that those services which had been performed as prospective partner were not compensable since 'an implied contract to pay for such services would be quite inconsistent with the basis on which the work was done' (p 272). But, after the mill was established and the business was operating without the expected partnership having been made, the pre-existing basis was abandoned by the defendant who 'must be regarded as having accepted the services (which he was under no obligation to do) not exclusively on the basis of a prospective partnership but on the basis that the plaintiff might become a partner but that, if he did not, payment for his services would be made' (p 272). See also *Sinclair v Rankin* (1907). Insofar as these decisions stand for the proposition that a claim in *quantum meruit* without contract cannot be maintained where the services are provided on the basis that they will be covered by a contract which the parties intend to make, I do not think they can survive the analysis of Sheppard J in *Sabemo's* case (with which I respectfully agree), the demise of the implied contract theory for unjust enrichment cases, or the decision of the High Court in *Pavey's* case. Where a person performs work in the expectation that, in due course, payment will be made for it under an anticipated contract, that party ought not be in a worse position than a party who performs work under a contract which is unenforceable (*Pavey's* case) or which proves to be void[13] or bad for uncertainty.[14]

It was submitted on behalf of the defendant that the test was whether each of the parties thought at the relevant time that the work would be recompensed. I think that the court is not concerned with the actual state [260] of mind of the parties or of either of them: *Sabemo's* case (p 900). Moreover, the enquiry must in my view be principally directed to the position of the party to be charged, for the thread running through this area of law is the injustice of the enrichment of that party. In my opinion the appropriate enquiry is whether the recipient of the services, as a reasonable person, should have realised that a person in the position of the provider of the services would expect to be paid for them and did not take a reasonable opportunity to reject those services.[15] Where the services are provided under a contract which turns out to be void or otherwise ineffective or pursuant to a request made in a normal commercial relationship with a person whose business it is to provide those services for reward, this requirement will be satisfied.

Furthermore, I find that the mere fact that Braithwaite had a manager was of benefit to him and that it was of benefit to him that that manager was Fenner and later Nathan Brenner as well. Moreover, he was thereby relieved of the worry of finding another manager. I find too, as will appear, that Fenner and Brenner

---

13   *Craven-Ellis v Canons Ltd* (1936).
14   *Way v Latilla* (1937).
15   Jones, *Restitution in Public and Private Law*, 1992, p 108.

provided Daryl Braithwaite and [Braithwaite's wife] with support and advice which contributed to the production of the album 'Edge' and to the ultimate success of the Braithwaite project.

In the present case where the management services provided by the plaintiffs as professional artists' managers were so provided pursuant to a request accompanied by a discussion as to the mode of payment, the imposition by the law of an obligation to make restitution for the benefit thereby accepted is consonant with the decided authorities and with the notion of justice and fairness which underlies the law relating to restitution. In the present case too the existence of the request serves a further purpose. Unlike those cases to which I have referred, there is in the case before me an issue as to the person for whom the services were rendered: the first defendant, FAM, or the second defendant, Braithwaite. Insofar as I am able to determine the person who requested the services this issue is resolved. Insofar as this situation changed, so too does the solution ...

[261] The claim of the plaintiffs is that they provided services and that the defendant accepted the benefit of them in circumstances giving rise to an obligation to make restitution. In a case such as this, the plaintiffs must show that the defendant accepted the benefit of their services in circumstances where he, as a reasonable person, should realise that the plaintiffs would expect to be paid for them. It is of significance on the facts of this case that it is *the defendant* who accepts the services in these circumstances for it is the defendant from whom restitution is sought. Where, upon a proper analysis of the facts, it cannot be said that it was the defendant who obtained the benefit of the services or, in this case, it was not in the contemplation of the defendant as a reasonable man that the plaintiffs realised that he would be responsible for payment, then the claim against him in respect of those services must fail. Furthermore, the situation may change as circumstances alter from time to time: *Watson v Watson* (1953). When, as I have found in this case, certain of the services were provided at a time when the plaintiffs understood that they would in due course be recompensed by FAM and that it was for FAM that they were providing the services, there can be no room for restitution by the defendant, Braithwaite. The fact that Braithwaite under his contract with FAM and the investors stood to benefit from the income of FAM derived as a result of these services does not impose on him an obligation of the kind contended for by the plaintiffs. This result must follow from the fact that the services were provided at the request of FAM and any recompense in the absence of contract must be sought from that quarter ...

Commentary and questions

According to Byrne J, is it necessary to establish that the defendant has been objectively benefited? Were FAM and Braithwaite objectively benefited by the plaintiffs' management services? Why did the court partially reject the plaintiff's claim?

Byrne J recognises in the principal case that the elements of the test of acceptance will almost always be satisfied where the defendant requested the services pursuant to a commercial contract that has become ineffective.[16]

---

16 *Brenner v First Artists' Management Pty Ltd* (1993), p 260. See also *ABB Power Generation Ltd v Chapple* (2001); *Lopresto v Sam* (2000).

Accordingly, proof of a contractual request for the services is normally[17] sufficient to establish a benefit. For this reason, 'contractual request' can be seen to be a particular instance of acceptance.

Partial performance

There is Australian authority supporting a claim in restitution by a plaintiff who has failed to fully perform the services requested under a contract, in circumstances where completion of the performance was prevented by the repudiation/breach of the contract by the defendant.[18] The defendant in breach is precluded from arguing that he or she did not receive the full benefit requested.[19] The principle is expressed by Mason and Carter as follows:[20] 'where a plaintiff makes a claim for restitution following discharge of a contract based on breach or repudiation by the defendant, acceptance will be deemed to have occurred, on the basis of actual or constructive prevention of performance.' Birks[21] reaches the same result by applying a doctrine he calls 'limited acceptance' the rationale of which is that 'the defendant freely accepted the whole work and, therefore, in a limited sense also accepted that work which would be necessary in order to achieve the complete performance'.

However the position is different where the plaintiff is the party in breach. The fact that the *innocent* defendant requested the services will not of itself be sufficient to establish a benefit.[22] The plaintiff must show an independent act of acceptance by the defendant; that is, that the defendant had a genuine choice whether to accept or reject the incomplete services, and chose to accept.[23] This freedom of choice will be absent where the benefit has become absorbed into the property of the defendant, but will be present where the defendant has taken the benefit of goods which could have been returned specifically.[24]

Acceptance and unsolicited services

Acceptance does not depend on an actual request by the defendant for the benefit. A defendant who did not actually request the benefit, but who encouraged the plaintiff to confer the benefit, or acquiesced in its conferral, will

---

17 However the request for the services will not be sufficient where the plaintiff is the party in breach, as discussed in the next section.

18 *Brooks Robinson Pty Ltd v Rothfield* (1951); *Brenner v First Artists' Management Pty Ltd* (1993), p 263 (see extract, p 39); *Iezzi Constructions Pty Ltd v Currumbin Development Pty Ltd* (1995); *Independent Grocers Co-Operative Ltd v Noble Lowndes Superannuation Consultants Ltd* (1993).

19 Byrne, 'Benefits – for services rendered', in McInnes (ed), *op cit*, fn 1, p 100; cf Garner, *op cit*, fn 8.

20 Mason and Carter, *op cit*, fn 5, p 52.

21 Birks, *op cit*, fn 1, p 232.

22 *Sumpter v Hedges* (1898) (see extract, p 325); *Steele v Tardiani* (1946), pp 402–03 *per* Dixon J (see extract, p 327).

23 Mason and Carter, *op cit*, fn 5, pp 50–52; *Sumpter v Hedges* (1898) (see extract, p 325); *Steele v Tardiani* (1946), pp 402–03 *per* Dixon J (see extract, p 327).

24 *Munro v Butt* (1858); *Pattinson v Luckley* (1875); *Sumpter v Hedges* (1898) (see extract, p 325); *Steele v Tardiani* (1946), pp 402–03 *per* Dixon J (see extract, p 327).

be found to have accepted the benefit.[25] Thus, in *Van den Berg v Giles* (1979) a tenant performed extensive work on premises leased from the defendant, having been led by the defendant to believe that he would have the option of purchasing the house. The tenant was able to recover the cost of the work on the basis the defendant had accepted the work:

> From the commencement of the work on the property the defendant fully understood the need for it, the extent of it, and freely accepted it. I find on [the defendant's] part an active encouragement for it to have been carried out, and the deliberate creation of uncertainty about the possible sale of the house. I do not find on her part any request for the services, but a definite acquiescence and acceptance [p 120].

In *Cooke v Dunn* (1998) the plaintiff (Mr Dunn) lived in a house for a number of years owned by the defendant (Mr Bell). Mr Bell was aware that someone was living in his house and was making improvements to it, but did not object. When Mr Bell reclaimed possession of his house, Mr Dunn was held to be entitled to the reasonable value of the improvements he had made to the property:

> [F]rom 1990, Mr Dunn decided to improve the property and live in it as his own. It is clear on the evidence that this is when the bulk of the work was done. I further note that Mr Bell was aware, from either 1983 or 1985, that someone was living in the property and making various improvements to it. He clearly was happy to be the beneficiary of the improvements, never demurring. Although at least some of the maintenance work carried out during that time was consideration for the licence to occupy the property ... I consider the amount of work done to exceed what would be expected as maintenance in consideration for the right to occupy the property. Certainly, from November 1993, when Mr Bell was aware of Mr Dunn's identity and the fact that he was living in the property, he must have been taken to be freely accepting the benefits of the improvements both then and earlier. Indeed he could throughout the 1980s have had them stopped as well as later and did not.

> So far as the requirement that the benefit conferred must have been done 'non-gratuitously',[26] I consider that this refers to the fact that the recipient should have known that the benefit was not being conferred upon the recipient as a gift. It is inconceivable that Mr Dunn would have expended time, effort and money on the property so as to confer a benefit on the documentary owners of the property as a gift. Certainly, from 1990, I believe he considered, as he stated, that the owners were never going to appear and that he could treat the property as his own.

Birks, P, 'In defence of free acceptance', in Burrows, A (ed), *Essays on the Law of Restitution*, 1991, Oxford: Clarendon Press, pp 128–31[27]

... [128] Where what was received was not incontrovertibly valuable, in what circumstances will the common law hold that it was nevertheless a valuable benefit? The general answer is, wherever the benefit has an objective (ie, market)

---

25 *Angelopoulos v Sabatino* (1995), p 13 (see extract, p 418); *Van den Berg v Giles* (1979), pp 120–23.

26 Birks, *op cit*, fn 1, p 265.

27 Printed by permission of Oxford University Press.

value *and* for some reason the recipient cannot evade that objective valuation by an appeal to the argument from the subjectivity of value (in shorthand, he cannot subjectively devalue). Here we are only concerned with the thesis that one case where the recipient cannot subjectively devalue is that in which he has freely accepted. Just as, in relation to the unjust factor, the phrase 'free acceptance' can only be given meaning in the light of the larger question whether in all the circumstances the defendant's receipt was unconscientious, so here, in relation to the issue of enrichment, its meaning is determined by the larger question whether the court could in all the circumstances reasonably allow the defendant to resort to subjective devaluation. So far as the word 'unconscientious' can be used in both cases, the question *quoad* the unjust factor is whether in the given circumstances it was unconscientious to receive; *quoad* the issue of enrichment it is whether it would be unconscientious to resort to subjective devaluation.

Both Burrows and, even more emphatically, Garner take the view that the law's commitment to the subjectivity of value is such that a valuation in money is only possible if the recipient has manifested a positive desire to have the thing in question at a money price. Burrows observes that the inference from the facts of free acceptance falls short of this. Often one could infer no more than that the recipient did not care whether the work was done or not.[28] Garner calls this 'the indifference argument'.[29] Burrows insists on a request as the foundation for an inference that the recipient wanted and bargained for the benefit,[30] while Garner says, more explicitly, that the plaintiff must show that the defendant wanted the thing, was willing to pay for it, and attached immediate priority to getting it.[31] Both defer to people's freedom of economic choice more than is reasonably required for that freedom to be amply protected. The six propositions which follow seek to secure a less extreme position:

(1) Free acceptance never indicates that the recipient does value the [129] thing in question, much less values it at a particular sum of money.

(2) A free acceptance only settles the enrichment issue by interposing an obstacle to the argument from the subjectivity of value, with the effect that the freely accepting recipient must acknowledge the objective valuation of the benefit.

The first of these propositions accepts the initial step in 'the indifference argument'. The second denies that the inference of indifference leaves the recipient free to evade the market valuation. Indifferent or not, the freely accepting party may be unconscientious in subsequently appealing to the subjectivity of value.

(3) Automatic market valuation of the freely accepted benefit is qualified to the extent that the free acceptance was itself qualified. For example, where a defendant accepted in the belief that the thing with a market value of £20 was being offered at £10, the valuation cannot exceed £10.

This is not a true exception to the previous proposition, the truth being that in such circumstances it is not unconscientious in the defendant to appeal to subjective devaluation to defeat any valuation above £10. A defendant who accepts in the

---

28 Burrows, 'Free acceptance and the law of restitution' (1988) 104 LQR 576, p 580.
29 Garner, 'The role of subjective benefit in the law of unjust enrichment' (1990) 10 OJLS 42, p 50.
30 Burrows, *op cit*, fn 28, esp pp 578–80.
31 Garner, *op cit*, fn 29, especially pp 43–44, 48–52.

belief that the thing is offered as a gift will not be barred from subjective devaluation. A defendant who accepts believing the price of the thing is £10 will not be barred in respect of any sum by which the market valuation exceeds £10. This can create the illusion that acceptance operates other than as an obstacle to the attempt to evade the market valuation.

(4) When the argument from the subjectivity of value (subjective devaluation) is available, it does not consist in an appeal to and proof of the tastes and priorities of the particular recipient but, on the contrary, only requires the recipient to show he made no choice to receive the benefit: 'I did not choose this.' Even hypotheses as to what might have been the tastes and priorities of the recipient are strictly speaking superfluous.[32]

(5) The recipient's argument is none the less called 'subjective devaluation' because, if someone were to ask why it mattered whether he chose or not, the explanation would be in terms of the subjectivity of value. The argument derives its force from the need to protect people generally from the danger implicit in obligatory market valuation, namely that their choices will be dictated to them by their being made to pay for what they themselves do not value.[33]

[130] These two propositions vigorously protect freedom of economic choice. For a party who can conscientiously make the 'I did not choose it' argument thereby evades the market valuation.[34] Vis à vis those whose appeal to that argument would be unconscientious, the law has no reason to deny the objective value of the benefit for which the other seeks to be paid.

(6) A system which, to defend freedom of choice, does accept the possibility of subjective devaluation, and correspondingly does not peremptorily impose objective (market) valuation where subjective devaluation is possible, is bound to produce conclusions which will be very surprising to some or even most people.

In the present state of the debate about the issue of enrichment, this sixth proposition is especially important. The startling nature of some of the results easily distracts the observer from the strength of the logic by which they are dictated. In the eye of a beholder who does subscribe to the demand which creates the market for, say garages, a conclusion that a garage is not valuable will seem perverse. Yet such a conclusion will be reached where the defendant can and does evade the objective devaluation by appeal to the subjectivity of value. And one who does not subscribe to the market in fur-styling for poodles will be affronted in the contrary case. It was no doubt in response to the startling nature of some results that Deane J recently coined the phrase 'constructive enrichment'.[35] The word 'constructive' has an awkward history in this subject and implies 'deemed' or 'fictitious'. Rather than distinguish between actual and constructive, it would be better, while distinguishing money or money's worth, to give a warning that, as the market itself proves, conclusions as to money's worth will reflect the diversity of people's tastes.

---

32 Cf Brett MR in *Leigh v Dickeson* (1884), p 65.

33 This point is well captured in Matthews, 'Freedom, unrequested improvements and Lord Denning' [1981] CLJ 340.

34 It is not clear whether it would be theoretically admissible to argue that the unchosen benefit did have a subjective value.

35 *Foran v Wright* (1989), p 24.

Suppose that a woman returns from abroad to find that a garage has been built beside her house. Let it be given that it has not been built by her spouse. If it had been our example would be located in a statutory exception to the normal deference to subjectivity of value.[36] Suppose the woman's neighbour built it, either thinking the land was his or that the woman would let him have it. Let it also be true that the garage cost £2,000 to build and that the land is now worth £3,000 more on the market than it was without the garage. Is the woman enriched? It would be very difficult to hold that a garage was an incontrovertibly valuable benefit, since very many people with means and space for a garage [131] prefer to have a greenhouse or leave things as they are and use their buying-power to take holidays abroad. So this woman is not enriched. She uses the garage. That changes nothing. 'One man cleans another's shoes, what can the other do but put them on?'[37] Privately she is delighted to have the garage, and it is the case that she might very well have decided to pay for one to be built. Subject to one hitherto unexplored argument which we cannot pursue,[38] that makes no difference either. All she has to show (it not being incontrovertibly valuable) is that in fact she made no choice to have it. She might have wanted to use her money differently. The hypothetical 'might' protects everyone's liberty to arrange priorities according to taste. But the objection will be made that she has an asset which can be sold for more. That too is irrelevant (unless she voluntarily chooses to realise the asset and the excess attributable to the £2,000 input is still identifiable when she does so). She cannot be forced to realise the asset. She might – again merely hypothetically – be fond of the house for non-economic reasons.[39] Once more the hypothetical nature of the observation protects the freedom of choice of all of us. The conclusion is that this woman, returning from abroad and presented with a new garage, has not received a valuable benefit. We were warned by our sixth proposition to expect startling conclusions.

Suppose now that the same woman comes back early and sees the work beginning. Knowing what mistake or misprediction the neighbour has made she decides to withdraw to her country cottage until the work is finished, so as to be able to take advantage of it under the doctrines in the preceding paragraph. She returns when the garage is finished. This time she is enriched. The reason is that she cannot conscientiously assert, 'Oh, but I did not choose to have this garage built'. She had her opportunity to say so earlier. It is not that her neglect of that opportunity affirmatively indicates that she attached value to the garage; it merely makes it impossible for her to get to her appeal to the subjectivity of value. It would be outrageous in the circumstances if she were allowed to evade objective valuation by calling for a defence of the right to freedom of economic choice ...

---

36 Matrimonial Proceedings and Property Act 1970, s 37. The improving spouse acquires an interest without regard to the other's wishes. The trust for sale effects *ipso iure* a notional, and perhaps ultimately actual, realisation in money.

37 *Taylor v Laird* (1856), p 332.

38 There might be a subjective version of incontrovertible value. Cf Garner's concept of 'subjective revaluation', in 'The role of subjective benefit in the law of unjust enrichment' (1990) 10 OJLS 42, p 43 (where the concept is first introduced). In cases of incontrovertible value it is unconscientious to appeal to freedom of choice because it is for practical purposes certain that people so placed would have incurred the expenditure in question. The untested argument would seek to add that it is similarly unconscientious to appeal to freedom of choice when you yourself, given your own tastes and priorities, would have chosen to incur the expenditure if you had had the opportunity to choose.

39 This is contrary to Goff and Jones, *op cit*, fn 10, p 19.

Commentary

There is authority for Birks's view that a request for services is not crucial to a free acceptance claim: *Angelopoulos v Sabatino* (1995) (see extract, p 418); *Van den Berg v Giles* (1979). Both these cases, however, involved a finding that the defendant had actively encouraged the plaintiff to render the services. Whether mere passive acquiescence is sufficient to support a claim is uncertain.[40]

Birks's test of free acceptance is stricter than the test, formulated by Jones, which has been accepted in *Brenner v First Artists' Management Pty Ltd* (1993) (see extract, p 39) and *Angelopoulos v Sabatino* (1995) (see extract, p 418). The 'Jones test' requires only constructive knowledge of the plaintiff's expectation of payment: that is, that a *reasonable person in the recipient's position* would have realised that the plaintiff expected to be paid. In contrast, Birks emphasises that the rationale for adopting free acceptance as an obstacle to subjective devaluation is that a freely accepting defendant cannot as a matter of conscience deny the objective valuation of the benefit. Birks's test probably requires that the defendant has *actual knowledge* of the plaintiff's expectation of payment.[41]

Birks wrote the principal article in response to an attack on free acceptance by Burrows.[42] Burrows argued that free acceptance does no more than indicate indifference to the benefit being received: the defendant may have failed to take advantage of an opportunity to reject the benefit because of indifference as to whether or not the benefit was conferred, rather than because of a positive desire to receive the benefit. Burrows has rejected the notion of free acceptance in favour of what he calls the 'bargained-for' test, which holds that a defendant will be presumed to be benefited where the plaintiff performs what the defendant bargained for.[43] This test excludes from the concept of enrichment services which were provided without a request.

The conduct of the plaintiff must be closely scrutinised where the services were conferred in the absence of a request by the defendant. In such a circumstance the plaintiff runs the risk of being regarded as an officious intervener[44] or of acting in self-interest.[45]

---

40 *Angelopoulos v Sabatino* (1995), p 13 (see extract, p 418). Though see *Cooke v Dunn* [1998] 16 BPR 489.

41 For other differences between the two tests in their role in supplying the unjust factor see McInnes, 'Contract and restitution' (1996) 24(3) ABLR 238.

42 Burrows, *op cit*, fn 28.

43 Burrows, *The Law of Restitution*, 1993, pp 14–15.

44 *J Gadsden Pty Ltd v Strider 1 Ltd, The AES Express* (1990) (see extract, p 63). The recipient of unsolicited goods or services will be excused from liability to pay for those goods or services (unless she has wilfully damaged or lost the unsolicited goods) where the circumstances attract the operation of the Trade Practices Act 1974 (Cth) or the State's fair trading legislation.

45 *Proctor & Gamble Philippine Manufacturing Corp v Peter Cremer GmbH & Co, The Manila* (1988) (see extract, p 61).

INCONTROVERTIBLE BENEFIT

An incontrovertible benefit is a benefit which no reasonable person could deny.[46] It is 'an unquestionable benefit, a benefit which is demonstrably apparent, and not subject to debate and conjecture'.[47] An incontrovertible benefit can take both a positive form (a realised, or possibly realisable, gain to the plaintiff's wealth) or a negative form (the saving of a legally or factually necessary expense). The concept of an incontrovertible benefit has been accepted in a number of Australian decisions, for example *J Gadsden Pty Ltd v Strider 1 Ltd, The AES Express* (1990) (see extract, p 63); *Strang Patrick Stevedoring Pty Ltd v The Owners of the Motor Vessel 'Sletter'* (1992); *Monks v Poynice Pty Ltd* (1987) (see extract, p 53); *McKeown v Cavalier Yachts Pty Ltd* (1988) (see extract, p 157); and *Home Management Maintenance Pty Ltd v Doyle* (1992).

Money

Money is the very measure of value in our society, and as such its receipt is always an incontrovertible benefit.

BP Exploration Co (Libya) Ltd v Hunt (No 2) [1979] 1 WLR 783 Queen's Bench Division

Robert Goff J: ... [799] [I]t is always necessary to bear in mind the difference between awards of restitution in respect of money payments and awards where the benefit conferred by the plaintiff does not consist of a payment of money. Money has the peculiar character of a universal medium of exchange. By its receipt, the recipient is inevitably benefited; and (subject to problems arising from such matters as inflation, change of position and the time value of money) the loss suffered by the plaintiff is generally equal to the defendant's gain, so that no difficulty arises concerning the amount to be repaid. The same cannot be said of other benefits, such as goods or services. By their nature, services cannot be restored; nor in many cases can goods be restored, for example where they have been consumed or transferred to another. Furthermore the identity and value of the resulting benefit to the recipient may be debatable. From the very nature of things, therefore, the problem of restitution in respect of such benefits is more complex than in cases where the benefit takes the form of a money payment ...

Commentary

Occasionally issues will arise regarding the currency in which the enrichment should be assessed. In *Lamesa Holdings BV v Federal Commissioner of Taxation* (1999) the applicant paid US $55 million to the Australian Tax Office in payment of an assessment issued by the Commissioner. The Commissioner subsequently refunded the sum of approximately A $70 million after the Full Federal Court set aside the assessment. The Australian dollar had depreciated between the date of the payment of the money and the date of the refund and at the date of

---

46   Birks, *op cit*, fn 1, pp 116–17.
47   *Peel (Regional Municipality) v Canada* (1992), p 159 *per* McLachlin J (see extract, p 56).

the refund A $70 million was equated to approximately US $50 million. The applicant sought recovery in restitution of the difference. The court rejected the claim, holding that any enrichment to the Commissioner was in Australian, not US currency. When the substance of the transaction was examined, it was clear that the assessment was in Australian currency, and that the applicant was required to discharge its liability under the assessment in that currency.

Realised/realisable gains

A defendant will in some circumstances be incontrovertibly benefited by the receipt of a non-monetary benefit that improves the value of an asset belonging to the defendant. An incontrovertible benefit will have been received where the improvement to the asset has actually been realised prior to the date of trial.[48] It is less clear whether an improvement that can readily be realised in money, but that is not actually realised, is an incontrovertible benefit. The matter is the subject of considerable academic debate.[49] The weight of judicial authority arguably supports the conclusion that realisable benefits are within the concept of incontrovertible benefit.[50] Nevertheless, the plaintiff might be required to prove not only that the benefit was capable of being realised by the defendant, but also that there was some reasonable prospect of the defendant realising the benefit in the foreseeable future.[51]

Legally necessary expenses

The clearest category of a negative incontrovertible benefit is where the plaintiff saves the defendant an expense which the defendant was legally obligated to meet. This is because the defendant has no legal choice whether or not to discharge that obligation. For example, in *Jenkins v Tucker* (1788) (see extract, p 182) the defendant married the plaintiff's daughter, and some time later went to Jamaica, leaving her and an infant child behind. During the defendant's absence his wife died and the plaintiff successfully brought a claim to recover the money he had paid for her funeral. The daughter's husband was under a legal obligation to bury his wife and accordingly was liable to reimburse the plaintiff for the cost of her funeral. Although the issue of enrichment was not

---

48 *Cadorange Pty Ltd (In Liq) v Tanga Holdings Pty Ltd* (1990); *Angelopoulos v Sabatino* (1995), p 13 (see extract, p 418); Mason and Carter, *op cit*, fn 5, pp 47–49, 300; Birks, *op cit*, fn 1, pp 121–24; Burrows, *The Law of Restitution*, 1993, p 10.

49 See, eg, Birks, *op cit*, fn 1, pp 121–24 (only realised benefits should be recognised as incontrovertible benefits); Goff and Jones, *The Law of Restitution*, 5th edn, 1998, p 27 (realisable benefits can be incontrovertible benefits, though never improvements to land); Burrows, *The Law of Restitution*, 1993, p 10 (a benefit is an incontrovertible benefit if it is 'reasonably certain' it will be realised).

50 *Marston v Kigass* (1989); *Home Management Maintenance Pty Ltd v Doyle* (1992); *McKeown v Cavalier Yachts Pty Ltd* (1988) (see extract, p 157); *Countrywide Communications Ltd v ICL Pathway Ltd* (1999) (see extract, p 424).

51 *Republic Resources Ltd v Ballem* (1982), pp 708–09.

directly addressed, the facts establish that the defendant was incontrovertibly benefited by the plaintiff meeting the funeral expenses. The applicable unjust factor would be necessitous intervention.

Similarly, in *County of Carleton v City of Ottawa* (1965) the city annexed, in 1952, certain parts of the township of Gloucester which were within the county. Upon annexation, the city assumed responsibility for the social service obligations of the county to the residents of the areas annexed. By an oversight, the county continued for 12 years to pay for the maintenance of an indigent resident, Nora Baker, who resided in one of the annexed areas and who was thus the city's legal responsibility. The county brought a claim against the city for the cost of care and maintenance of Ms Baker for the 12 year period and was successful. The facts establish that the city was incontrovertibly benefited by the county meeting the city's legal obligation to pay for the maintenance of Nora Baker. Necessitous intervention would be the operative unjust factor.

Factually necessary expenses

The second type of negative incontrovertible benefit is the saving of a factually necessary expense; that is, an expense that the defendant would as a matter of *factual reality* have had no choice but to incur. As the following cases illustrate, claims based on the conferral of a factual incontrovertible benefit are difficult to establish because the defendant will often have available various other options to meet the necessitous situation other than the incurring of the claimed expense. Nevertheless, there are some categories of case where the defendant had no realistic option except to incur the expense claimed, such as the receipt by a company of management services,[52] and the receipt by minors or incapacitated persons of the necessities of life.[53] The following case exemplifies the first of those categories.

Monks v Poynice Pty Ltd (1987) 8 NSWLR 662 Supreme Court of New South Wales

A receiver (the third defendant) was appointed to a company pursuant to a floating charge, but the appointment was subsequently found to be invalid. The receiver lodged a claim for: (a) reasonable remuneration for acting as manager for a period of approximately one month; (b) costs, charges and expenses in acting as manager; and (c) reasonable legal expenses of obtaining advice in relation to the validity of his appointment.

Young J: ... [663] There was no contract between the company and the third defendant appointing the third defendant as the company's agent or receiver, so if there is to be any claim by the third defendant, other than perhaps against the second defendant under some indemnity, it would have to lie in what is nowadays referred to as the law of restitution.

---

52   *Monks v Poynice* (1987); *Sutherland v Take Seven Group Pty Ltd* (1999).
53   See, eg, *Re Rhodes* (1890) 44 Ch D 94 (see extract, p 184).

The law of restitution has developed strongly over the last 50 years and it is still in the stage where it is sometimes difficult to fill in the gaps between the various principles which have been laid down in the rather few decided cases. Helpfully, there are two textbooks of very high renown in the area which give guidance in this area and these are Sir R Goff and G Jones, *Law of Restitution* and P Birks, *Introduction to the Law of Restitution* and I will refer to these later in these reasons.

It seems to me that equity, if not the common law, finds that a person is liable to pay a reasonable sum for services provided to it in at least four [664] circumstances, notwithstanding that there is no contract.

First, it does so where there is a request, expressed or implied, for the performance of the service. This is *quantum meruit* in its most basal form, but even here it is to be noted that the better view seems to be that this is really a doctrine of equity and it was because of Lord Mansfield's work in commingling the principles of law and equity in the late 18th century that it is nowadays classed as a principle of the common law. It seems to me that the analysis of *quantum meruit* by the High Court in *Pavey & Matthews Pty Ltd v Paul* (1987) makes this clear.

The second situation is where the party benefited, accepted or acquiesced in the provision of the service under circumstances where it must have known that the service was not being rendered gratuitously. Examples of this sort of situation occurred in *Sabemo Pty Ltd v North Sydney Municipal Council* (1977), pp 902–03; in *Van den Berg v Giles* (1979) and in a great number of the proprietary estoppel cases. See also Birks [*Introduction*, p 275].

The third class of case, and it may indeed be that these are overlapping categories, and many cases in this third class fall into classes one and two, is where the service that is provided is necessary to be carried out for the protection of the defendant's personal property. Cases of that nature are dealt with in Birks [*Introduction*, pp 119–20].

Fourthly, there is a class of case where the service conferred incontrovertible benefit on the defendant and it would be unconscionable for the defendant to keep the benefit of the service without paying a reasonable sum therefore. This is really the same sort of principle as was dealt with by Deane J in *Muschinski v Dodds* (1985). p 455. Whilst it may be that some of the learned judges who decided the cases would be surprised to know that their decisions were included by me in this fourth category, it would seem to me that some of the cases that are cited in the text books fall into it. These would include *Re Allison Johnson & Foster Ltd ex p Birkenshaw* (1904), where a liquidator was invalidly appointed [639] on a voluntary winding up, but was permitted in a compulsory winding up to prove as a creditor for work done and expenses incurred by him while purporting to act as liquidator. This decision was approved in similar circumstances in Western Australia in *Re Kyra Nominees Pty Ltd* (1980), p 65. Again, the classic case of *Craven-Ellis v Canons Ltd* (1936) may also be put into this category, even though it is quite obvious that the learned judges who decided that case may not themselves have so categorised it. It does not seem to me of over-much assistance to refer to the way in which both Goff and Jones, *op cit*, on the one hand, and Birks on the other, have treated those cases or to refer again to the detailed consideration Shepherd J gave to it in the *Sabemo* case. Whatever the appropriate classification of the *Craven-Ellis* case is, it has been accepted as laying down the correct result, a result which is summed-up in the words of Professor J O'Donovan in his *Company Receivers and Managers* (1981, at p 165) as saying that where, notwithstanding that there has been no acceptance of the service, a company is benefited incontrovertibly by the acts of the claimant, then the claimant has a right against the company to be remunerated ...

[665] That is the principle, it is only necessary now to apply it to the facts in this particular case. So far as claim (a) is concerned, it would seem to me that the acting as a manager may well have been of benefit to the company and, accordingly, the third defendant should be permitted to prove in the winding up, and the liquidator will doubtless allow anything which in his opinion was of incontrovertible benefit to the company and will doubtless consider *Allison's* case by way of analogy. I do not think, however, I should usurp the liquidator's position by working out just what acts were of incontrovertible benefit to the company. It is probable, looking at the affidavit, that the acts of actually managing would, unless they were obviously in the interests of the person appointed or the secured creditors, be allowable and the main question for the liquidator will be one of quantum. I should point out, though, that I agree with Birks that one does not have to find, before a charge is allowable, that the work was 100% for the benefit of the company, nor even that the company would have survived even if the work had not been done.

So far as the costs, charges and expenses in acting as manager are concerned, again these would have to be analysed; there would have to be a proof lodged by the receiver and those costs, charges and expenses as were incontrovertibly beneficial to the company would be allowed and the others not. Some of those costs may be in the nature of overheads and doubtless the liquidator will do the best he can in fairness to apportion these, if he is not allowing the full amount.

The third claim involves reasonable legal expenses for the receiver obtaining advice in relation to the validity of his appointment. I cannot see how any of these can be said to be for the benefit of the company ...

Commentary

The defendant company in the principal case was incontrovertibly benefited by the plaintiff's managerial services as the company (as a legal entity) could not have managed itself. It does not have to be 100% certain that the defendant would have incurred the expense: the court should ignore 'unrealistic or fanciful possibilities' that the defendant would not have incurred it. So, for example, the possibility that the defendant company in the principal case might have chosen to go into liquidation rather than to trade out of its difficulties was rightly not taken into account by the court.[54]

Craven-Ellis v Canons Ltd (1936) (see extract, p 383), referred to in the principal case, involved a claim by a managing director of a company for remuneration for services provided by him to the company. The contract appointing the plaintiff as managing director was void as the directors who purported to enter into the contract on behalf of the company were disqualified. The plaintiff's claim for remuneration was successful. The best explanation of benefit in that case is that the company was incontrovertibly benefited by the services provided by the plaintiff: if the plaintiff had not provided the services

---

54   Birks, *An Introduction to the Law of Restitution*, rev edn, 1989, p 120.

the company would have had to hire someone else.[55] A finding that the company had freely accepted or requested the services would be precluded given the directors were incapable of binding the company.[56]

Peel (Regional Municipality) v Canada [1992] 3 SCR 762 Supreme Court of Canada

Section 20(1) of the Juvenile Delinquents Act RSC 1970 [the 'Act'] conferred upon appropriate judges the jurisdiction to issue a variety of alternative orders upon finding a child had committed an act of delinquency. Section 20(2) of the Act empowered these judges to order that the parents of the child or the relevant municipality contribute to the child's support. Over a period of eight years the Family Court judges in the Peel municipality, purporting to act pursuant to s 20(1), directed that a number of juveniles be placed in 'group homes'. Acting pursuant to s 20(2) of the Act, the judges ordered the municipality to pay the *per diem* rate that each group home charged for the care of the children. The municipality challenged both the authority of the Family Court judges to place children in group homes under s 20(1) and the constitutionality of s 20(2). These challenges were both ultimately upheld and the municipality commenced proceedings against the provincial and federal governments seeking reimbursement of the money paid by the municipality to the group homes over the eight year period pursuant to the invalid orders made under s 20(1) and 20(2) (less certain *ex gratia* payments paid by the provincial government to the municipality).

McLachlin J: ... [155] It seems clear that the municipality in this case made the payments under statutory compulsion. It may also be argued that it did so out of necessity, since someone had to care for the children in question. In some ways payment under an invalid statute may be likened to payment under an ineffective transaction. And if one rejects the compulsion argument, one might argue that the federal and provincial governments requested the payments.

The difficulty lies not in establishing that the plaintiff made payments which might potentially attract the doctrine of unjust enrichment. The difficulty lies rather in establishing that the payments conferred a 'benefit' on the federal and provincial governments which represents an unjust retention or enrichment. As Professors Goff and Jones note: 'In restitution it is not material that the plaintiff has suffered a loss if the defendant has gained no benefit.'[57] As already noted, the concept of restoration of a benefit retained without juristic reason lies at the heart of the doctrine of unjust enrichment. The word 'restitution' implies that something has been given to someone which must be returned or the value of which must be restored by the recipient. The word 'enrichment' similarly connotes a tangible benefit. It follows that without a benefit which has 'enriched' the defendant and which can be restored to the donor *in specie* or by money, no recovery lies for unjust enrichment.

Since the establishment of such a benefit is essential for recovery under any of the traditional categories, as well as under [156] the general test for recovery which this court has adopted, the remainder of these reasons focus on that concept. To date, the cases have recognised two types of benefit. The most common case

---

55 Burrows, *op cit*, fn 49, p 11.
56 See Birks, '*Negotiorum gestio* and the common law' (1971) 24 CLP 110, pp 120–22.
57 See Goff and Jones, *op cit*, fn 10, p 16.

involves the positive conferral of a benefit upon the defendant, for example the payment of money. But a benefit may also be 'negative' in the sense that the benefit conferred upon the defendant is that he or she was spared an expense which he or she would have been required to undertake, ie, the discharge of a legal liability ...

The municipality acknowledges that it cannot meet the test for benefit in the category of payment under compulsion of law, nor indeed, in any of the traditional categories of recovery. The requirement that the plaintiffs have discharged the defendant's *legal* liability is simply not met in the sense required by the [157] traditional tests. There was no constitutional obligation on either the federal or provincial government to provide for the care of these children; as the courts below noted, the power to legislate does not give rise to an obligation to legislate. Nor were the federal or provincial governments under a statutory or *legal* liability to provide for the care of the children. The provincial statutes relied on by the municipality as evidence of the province's obligation generally create a discretion in the province to finance the acquisition or construction of institutions for the care of children and in some cases to finance the operation of these institutions in cooperation with others. The benefit which the federal government is said to have received is the care of 'prisoners' which it might otherwise have had to provide itself (even though they are not obliged to, provincial prisons house many persons convicted of federal offences), and a more general 'political' benefit of having the goals of its legislation furthered. The benefit which the province is said to have received is the discharge of responsibilities which it might have undertaken because conscience required that someone do so. So there was no legal liability on either government as required by the traditional tests.

Unable to meet the traditional tests, the municipality turns to the general principles governing recovery for unjust enrichment enunciated by this court in cases such as *Pettkus v Becker* (1980). It argues that the third condition of the traditional rule has been revised by the Canadian jurisprudence so as to require only that the plaintiff's payments have discharged a political, social or moral responsibility of the defendant, for which the defendant was primarily liable; the plaintiff need not have discharged a liability enforceable at law. Stated otherwise, a defendant may be found to have benefited from the payment of a certain sum even though the defendant had the option of whether or not it wished to incur this expenditure. It is in the failure to accept this proposition that the appellate courts below are said to have erred.

The question thus reduces to this: how should 'benefit' in the general test for recovery for unjust enrichment be defined? More particularly, can it encompass payments which fall short of discharging the defendant's legal liability?

We have been referred to no cases in Canada or the Commonwealth where a 'negative' benefit has been found in the absence of an underlying legal liability on the defendant. The municipality relies on this court's decision in *County of Carleton v City of Ottawa* (1965). But in that case the defendant had assumed legal responsibility for the care of the indigent woman in question ...

[158] Notwithstanding the absence of authority, some scholars (Goff and Jones, Maddaugh and McCamus) perceive a 'whittling away' of the hard and fast rule barring recovery absent proof of a defendant's legal obligation to undertake the expense or perform the act which the plaintiff claims to have accomplished on the

defendant's behalf. They suggest that where the plaintiff has conferred on the defendant an 'incontrovertible benefit' recovery should be available even in the absence of a defendant's legal liability. An 'incontrovertible benefit' is found in the gain of 'a demonstrable financial benefit' or the saving of an 'inevitable expense'. Goff and Jones state (pp 21–22 of *The Law of Restitution*):

> To allow recovery because a defendant has been incontrovertibly benefited is to accept that he must make restitution even though he did not request or freely accept the benefit. In the past, the principle embodied in Bowen LJ's well known *dictum* in *Falcke's* case, that 'liabilities are not to be forced on people behind their backs any more than you can confer a benefit upon a man against his will,' has been regarded as paramount. Free choice must be [159] preserved inviolate. To accept the principle of incontrovertible benefit is to admit a limited and, in our view, desirable exception. *The burden will always be on the plaintiff to show that he did not act officiously, that the particular defendant has gained a demonstrable financial benefit or has been saved an inevitable expense and that it will not be a hardship to the defendant, in the circumstances of the case, to make restitution.* [Emphasis added.]

An 'incontrovertible benefit' is an unquestionable benefit, a benefit which is demonstrably apparent and not subject to debate and conjecture. Where the benefit is not clear and manifest, it would be wrong to make the defendant pay, since he or she might well have preferred to decline the benefit if given the choice. According to Justice Gautreau of the District Court of Ontario, where an unjust benefit is found 'one discharges another's debt that is owed to a third party or discharges another's contractual or statutory duty'.[58] The late Justice Gautreau cites this court's decision in *County of Carleton v City of Ottawa* as an example of such a case but adds the following pertinent remarks (pp 270–71):

> While the principle of freedom of choice is ordinarily important, it loses its force if the benefit is an incontrovertible benefit, *because it only makes sense that the defendant would not have realistically declined the enrichment*. For example, choice is not a real issue if the benefit consists of money paid to the defendant or paid to a third party to satisfy the debt of the defendant that was owing to the third party. In either case there has been an *unquestionable* benefit to the defendant. In the first case, he can return it or repay it if he chooses; in the second, he had no choice but to pay it, the only difference is that the payee has changed. Likewise, the principle of freedom of choice is a spent force if the benefit covers an expense that the defendant would have been put to in any event, and, as an issue, it is weak if the defendant subsequently adopts and capitalises on the enrichment by turning it to account through sale or profitable commercial use.
>
> The principle of incontrovertible benefit is not the antithesis of freedom of choice. It is not in competition with the latter; rather, it exists when freedom of choice as a problem is absent. [Emphasis added.]

Justice Gautreau's comment takes us back to the terms of the traditional test; the discharge of a legal liability creates an 'unquestionable' benefit because the law allowed the defendant no choice. Payment of an amount which the defendant was under no legal obligation to discharge is quite another matter.

---

58   Gautreau, 'When are enrichments unjust?' (1988–89) 10 Adv Q 258.

The same requirement of inevitable expense is reflected in McInnes's discussion of the notion of incontrovertible benefit.[59] He asserts (p 346) that 'restitutionary relief should be available to one who has saved another an inevitable or [160] necessary expense (whether factually or legally based)'. *Arguendo*, he suggests that recovery may lie where one 'has discharged an obligation which the obligee *would likely have paid* another to discharge' [emphasis added]. He goes on (p 347) to caution that 'although otherwise warranted, restitutionary relief should be denied if the benefit was conferred officiously, or if liability would amount to a hardship for the recipient of the benefit'. McInnes concludes (p 362) that the case law provides only theoretical and not express support for the incontrovertible benefit doctrine and suggests that, as such relief is 'somewhat extraordinary', it 'should not be imposed unless the equities of the circumstances demand it'.

It is thus apparent that any relaxation on the traditional requirement of discharge of legal obligation which may be effected through the concept of 'incontrovertible benefit' is limited to situations where it is clear on the facts (on a balance of probabilities) that had the plaintiff not paid, the defendant would have done so. Otherwise, the benefit is not incontrovertible.

While not much discussed by common law authorities to date, it appears that a further feature which the benefit must possess if it is to support a claim for unjust enrichment, is that it be more than an incidental blowby. A secondary collateral benefit will not suffice. To permit recovery for incidental collateral benefits would be to admit of the possibility that a plaintiff could recover twice – once from the person who is the immediate beneficiary of the payment or benefit (the parents of the juveniles placed in group homes in this case), and again from the person who reaped an incidental benefit. See, for example, Fridman and McLeod,[60] Maddaugh and McCamus,[61] and Gautreau.[62] It would also open the doors to claims against an undefined class of persons who, while not the recipients of the payment or work conferred by the plaintiff, indirectly benefit from it. This the courts have declined to do. The cases in which claims for unjust enrichment have been made out generally deal with benefits conferred directly and specifically on the defendant, such as the services rendered for the defendant or money paid to the defendant. This limit is also recognised in other jurisdictions. For example, German restitutionary law confines recovery to cases of direct benefits.[63]

Where does this discussion of 'benefit' in the doctrine of unjust enrichment bring us? Accepting for the purposes of argument that the law of restitution should be extended to incontrovertible [161] benefits, the municipality still falls short of the law's mark. The benefit conferred is not incontrovertible in the sense in which Goff and Jones define that concept; the municipality has not shown that either level of government being sued 'gained a demonstrable financial benefit or has been saved an inevitable expense'. Nor is it 'unquestionable', to use Justice Gautreau's test; the federal and provincial governments were under no legal obligation and their

---

59   McInnes, 'Incontrovertible benefits and the Canadian law of restitution' (1990–91) 12 Adv Q 323.
60   McLeod, *Restitution*, 1982, p 361.
61   Maddaugh and McCamus, *The Law of Restitution*, 1990, p 717.
62   Gautreau, *op cit*, fn 58.
63   Zwiegert and Kötz, *Introduction to Comparative Law*, 2nd edn, 1987, Vol 2, pp 234–35.

contention that they were not benefited at all, or in any event to the value of the payments made, has sufficient merit to require, at the least, serious consideration. It was neither inevitable nor likely, in McInnes's phrase, that in the absence of a scheme which required payment by the municipality the federal or provincial government would have made such payments; an entirely different scheme could have been adopted, for example.

To admit recovery in this case would be to extend the concept of benefit in the law of unjust enrichment much further than contemplated by any of the authorities to date. It would open the door to recovery wherever a payment has been made under compulsion of law which arguably has an incidental beneficial effect of a non-pecuniary nature. In short, it would take the law of unjust enrichment far beyond the concept of restoration of property, money, or services unfairly retained, which lies at its core.

To elaborate, Parliament was clearly aware of *and* relied upon the obligation of parents to support their children, expressly acknowledged in s 16(1) of the (then) Family Law Reform Act, because s 20(2) of the Juvenile Delinquents Act provided that the municipality could recover any expenditures ordered under s 20(2) from the parent or parents responsible. The fact that the municipality's payments can be said to have furthered Canada's general interest in the welfare of its citizens or its more particular interest in the effective administration of its scheme for the regulation of criminal conduct by minors is an insufficient 'correlative link' upon which to found recovery even on the application of the broader 'incontrovertible benefit' doctrine; it falls short of proof of a *'demonstrable financial benefit'* or proof that the federal government was saved an *'inevitable expense'*. The principle of freedom of choice, referred to by Gautreau and Maddaugh and McCamus is not a 'spent force' in this instance – the municipality has failed to establish that its payments covered an expense that the federal government 'would have been put to in any event' nor did it proffer any evidence that the Canadian government 'capitalised' in any direct fashion upon these payments. On close examination, even McInnes's proposition (p 346) that 'restitutionary relief should be available to one who has saved [162] another an inevitable or necessary expense (whether factually or legally based) or, arguably, has discharged an obligation which the obligee would likely have paid another to discharge', does not assist the municipality in this instance. Federal government (financial) support of the juveniles' stay in the group homes in Peel was not 'inevitable'. Neither was this expense 'necessary', first and foremost, given the host of dispositions available to judges under s 20, and second, given the municipality's statutory authority to seek reimbursement from the children's parents. The legislative scheme set up by Parliament is proof positive that Parliament did not believe it had any obligation to provide financial support for the juveniles assigned to group homes; any obligation it had to the provinces in this regard was created by a voluntary federal-provincial agreement to which the appellant was not privy. These facts confirm that any benefit received by the Government of Canada from the municipality's payments was incidental or indirect; the federal government had no greater responsibility for the welfare of these children than did the municipality from whence they came and cannot be found liable in restitution.

The same inability to establish an incontrovertible benefit bedevils the municipality's claim against the province. The fact that the appellant's payments necessarily furthered the province's general interest in the welfare of its citizens or its more specific interest in the protection and supervision of children residing within its boundaries is, for the reasons already outlined, not a sufficient basis upon which to found recovery even if the court were to apply the 'incontrovertible benefit' doctrine.

... I am in agreement with the Ontario Court of Appeal that a ... probable ... order would have placed the juvenile delinquents at issue directly in the custody of a foster home, an order which would *not* necessarily involve any cost to the Government of Ontario, or into the custody [163] of the [Children's Aid Society]. Such an eventuality is, however, still too speculative for proof on the balance of probabilities – the standard which the appellant must meet.

... As with its claim against the respondent federal government, the appellant has failed to establish that its payments to the specified group homes covered an expense that the province 'would have been put to in any event', nor did it lead sufficient evidence by which to establish on a balance of probabilities that the province was saved an *'inevitable or necessary* expense', whether factually or legally based. As found by the Court of Appeal, the appellant [164] has, at most, shown that its payments *may have* relieved the province of some obligation or debt that *might have* arisen ...

Commentary and questions

Does McLachlin J ultimately adopt for Canadian restitution law the proposition that a factually inevitable or necessary expense amounts to an enrichment?

Do you think the municipality would have been successful if it had alternatively sought to establish a benefit based on request/free acceptance? Should it make a difference that the benefit was conferred on a third party, not on the defendant?

McLachlin J suggested that the injustice element in this case is necessitous intervention. This unjust factor is the subject of Chapter 7.

Proctor & Gamble Philippine Manufacturing Corp v Peter Cremer GmbH & Co, The Manila **[1988] 3 All ER 843 Queen's Bench Division**

The sellers agreed to sell two lots of copra cake to the buyers, to be shipped from the Philippines to Rotterdam. Due to the insolvency of the ship's owners the ship was prevented from commencing its voyage after it was loaded. In order to ensure that the vessel made its voyage to Rotterdam the buyers paid additional freight to the ship's owners. Shortly after the vessel arrived in Rotterdam the buyers terminated the contract of sale on the ground that the bills of lading were incorrectly dated. The dispute between the buyers and sellers was referred to arbitration and the arbitrator held that the buyers were contractually entitled to the repayment of the purchase money paid under the contract of sale. The arbitrator also made an order in restitution, directing the sellers to reimburse the buyers for the additional freight paid to the shipowner in order to ensure the vessel was able to sale. The sellers appealed.

Hirst J: ... [854] I now turn to the issue of restitution ... It turns on the conclusions set out in the supplemental award ... as follows:

(i) The owner of *The Manila* was a company called Maritime Company of the Philippines ('MCP').

(ii) After *The Manila* was loaded and after the insurance of the Bills of Lading, MCP was found to be in financial difficulties.

(iii) On 26 April 1984, as a result of *The Manila* failing to sail with its cargo, the cargo interests instructed Recourse and Recovery Bureau MV of Rotterdam (RRB) to conduct an investigation into the reasons for the vessel failing to sail and to consider solutions to the problems as found by them.

(iv) RRB found in its report that the vessel owners, MCP, were hopelessly insolvent and that therefore the ship could not sail. On behalf of the cargo interests, they considered a number of possible alternatives, including local sales of the cargo, and they concluded that the best solution was for the vessel to be sailed to Rotterdam at the expense of the cargo interests and the banks involved.

(v) This course of action was followed with the result that the vessel duly arrived at Rotterdam on 8 July 1984 as above stated.

(vi) The Buyers' contribution as holders of the two Bills of Lading before mentioned amounted to US $28,500.00, which they duly paid.

(vii) We find that this payment by the Buyers which was to enable the holder of the Bills of Lading to obtain the goods in Rotterdam was for the benefit and protection of the holder (whoever he may be) of the Bills of Lading. As we have found by our said award that the Buyers were entitled to reject the Bills of Lading, it follows in our view that the Buyers are entitled to be reimbursed for this sum as it was paid for the benefit of goods which we hold they can now reject and further that as between the Buyers and the Sellers, the Buyers are entitled to be put in the position in which they would have been had they been able to reject the documents on presentation.

(viii) Our award in this respect is on the principle of restitution on the grounds that the payment made by the Buyers under (vi) above was commercially justified and for the benefit of the goods and the holder of the Bills of Lading. Consequently, 'causation and remoteness or foreseeability of damage' do not arise and are not applicable.

It is thus manifest that the supplemental award was based wholly and exclusively on restitution and not at all on common law damages for breach of contract.

The relevant principles are common ground between the two parties, and are conveniently set out in the leading textbook on the law of restitution, Goff and Jones, *The Law of Restitution*, as follows:

> The general principle should be that restitution should always be granted when, as a result of the plaintiff's services, the defendant has gained a financial benefit readily realisable without detriment to himself or has been saved expense which he inevitably must have incurred.

This forms part of a section headed 'Restitutionary Claims; where the defendant has gained an incontrovertible benefit', a neat phrase which in my judgment epitomises the whole doctrine under consideration here.

Counsel for the buyers submits that the board of appeal have found, and rightly found, that the sellers did indeed obtain an incontrovertible benefit, in that, as a result of the buyers' funding the extra freight, they had the advantage of being able to sell the goods in Rotterdam rather than locally, and were saved expense.

In my judgment this is not a proper interpretation of the supplemental award. I am unable to derive any findings from it that an incontrovertible benefit was conferred; at most it amounted to the finding that, in the difficult circumstances of the shipowners' insolvency, RRB, on behalf of the (presumably European) cargo interests collectively, formed the view that, to make the best of a bad job, the most favourable solution all round was for the vessel to sail to Rotterdam. This falls far short even of a general finding of incontrovertible benefit, still less of a finding (which in my judgment would be essential to justify relief under this heading) that the present sellers viewed in isolation received an incontrovertible benefit. It is not surprising that the board of appeal did not focus on this critical point, since the question of restitution was, it seems clear, never argued before them. Nor is there any finding that the sellers were saved any expense which they would 'inevitably have incurred'; indeed it is by no means clear that such was the case, since, as a corporation themselves based in the Philippines, they might well have [856] thought it prudent from their own point of view to withdraw the cargo there in the hope of an upturn in the market. It follows, in my judgment, that there was no proper basis for the award based on restitution ...

Questions

Did Hirst J accept the concept of incontrovertible benefit as being part of the English law of restitution? On what basis did Hirst J deny the restitutionary claim? Was an unjust factor present on the facts of this case?

J Gadsden Pty Ltd v Strider 1 Ltd, The AES Express (1990) 20 NSWLR 57
Supreme Court of New South Wales (Admiralty Division)

The defendant, Strider 1 Ltd (Strider), owned a cargo vessel called *The AES Express*. Strider chartered the vessel to another company (AES). In early 1986 the vessel was scheduled to undertake a voyage from Norfolk in the USA to Auckland, and from there to Sydney and Melbourne. AES agreed to carry on this voyage, cargo belonging to the plaintiff, J Gadsden Pty Ltd (Gadsden), from Norfolk to Melbourne. Gadsden paid the freight in advance. In February 1986, during the course of the voyage, AES advised Strider that it was ceasing business operations and Strider immediately withdrew the vessel from the charter. The vessel reached Auckland on 18 March 1986, discharged certain cargo there, and then continued on to Sydney. It was not until the next day, 19 March, that Gadsden was informed of the termination of the charter by a letter from Strider. The letter stated that Strider would carry Gadsden's cargo to Melbourne only on the basis that Gadsden paid all freight costs incurred by Strider. A few days later Gadsden sent a telex to Strider rejecting any liability to pay for the additional freight costs. The vessel eventually reached Melbourne and Gadsden obtained release of its cargo, but only after depositing into a joint account the amount of $42,587 (representing the freight costs incurred by Strider) pending resolution of the dispute over the freight expenses. Gadsden commenced proceedings claiming a declaration that it was entitled to the deposit in the joint account, and Strider cross-claimed on the basis that it was entitled to the money on restitutionary principles. It was common ground between the parties that there was no request by Gadsden to Strider to carry its cargo to Melbourne after the vessel was withdrawn from the charter.

Carruthers J: ... [Carruthers J held that Strider was under an obligation according to principles of maritime law to carry Gadsden's cargo to Melbourne without payment of any extra freight. However, he then turned to consider what the position would be on the assumption that Strider was entitled to discharge the cargo at Auckland:]

[65] It is Strider's contention ... that its entitlement to remuneration from Gadsden for the carriage of the cargo from Norfolk to Melbourne is to be found in the principle of restitution or unjust enrichment. More specifically, it was argued that there is a principle discernible from the cases that a defendant should make restitution if he has been incontrovertibly benefited by the receipt of services which have been unofficiously rendered by the plaintiff, that is, if the defendant has made thereby an immediate and realisable financial gain or has been saved an expense which he otherwise would necessarily have incurred: see Goff and Jones, *The Law of Restitution*, where the following passage appears:

> To allow recovery because a defendant has been incontrovertibly benefited is to accept that he must make restitution even though he did not request or freely accept the benefit.

In his article 'Restitutionary claims for services rendered' (1977) 93 LQR 273, Professor Jones suggests (at p 295) that the principle should be stated thus:

> ... Where the defendant has neither requested nor freely accepted the services, a restitutionary claim should, however, be recognised only if it can be demonstrated that the defendant has been incontrovertibly benefited *and the equities of the plaintiff's claim are more compelling* [66] *than the defence that the defendant had no opportunity to reject the services rendered*. This principle has been called the principle of incontrovertible benefit. [Emphasis added.]

It has now been authoritatively accepted in this country that the category of cases where the law recognises an obligation to pay a reasonable remuneration or compensation for a benefit actually or constructively accepted does not depend upon the existence of an implied contract but on a claim to restitution or one based on unjust enrichment: see *Pavey and Matthews Pty Ltd v Paul* (1987).

[Carruthers J then referred to the judgments in *China Pacific SA v Food Corporation of India, The Winson* of Lloyd J at first instance (1979) and of Lord Diplock in the House of Lords (1982) (see extract, p 179) and continued at p 70:]

It is significant that in this passage Lord Diplock cited with approval the decision of the Court of Sessions in *Garriock v Walker*, where the cargo owner did not acquiesce in the steps taken by his bailee to preserve the cargo, 'Nevertheless he took the benefit of them by taking delivery of the cargo thus preserved at the conclusion of the voyage' (Goff and Jones at p 21). I should add that the approach which Lord Denning MR took in *Greenwood v Bennett* (1973) was applied in this court by Young J in *McKeown v Cavalier Yachts Pty Ltd* (1988). There is thus, I think, authority for the view that where a defendant has been incontrovertibly benefited, he may be liable to make restitution even though he did not request or freely accept the benefit.

It is well established, however, that a restitutionary claim can be defeated if the claimant has acted officiously: see, eg, *Owen v Tate* (1976), p 412 *per* Scarman LJ, where the plaintiff acted 'behind the backs of the defendants' and despite their protests.

Professor Birks[64] suggests that the word 'officious', common though it is in this particular context, in fact has no work to do which is not capable of being done through 'voluntary' and 'volunteer'. He submits that if the intervener takes the risk of losing his labour without return, then he is a volunteer and his transfer of value is voluntary. To say that he is 'officious' only reaffirms that he took the risk of disappointment.

In challenging Strider's claim for restitution, counsel for Gadsden submitted that the evidence established that the vessel had an obligation to discharge at Auckland, Sydney and Melbourne and to load at Melbourne, which necessitated the vessel travelling to those ports irrespective of any benefit which Strider sought to confer upon Gadsden. I must say that apart from what can be gleaned from the letter dated 13 March 1986, there is no evidence of the basis upon which other cargo was discharged at Auckland, Sydney and Melbourne and upon which cargo was loaded at Melbourne.

Stress was also placed on the fact that Gadsden was denied the opportunity of exercising a commercial choice in relation to the cargo. That is to say, whether it would have preferred the cargo to be discharged at Auckland rather than being carried to Melbourne.

Counsel for Gadsden also referred me to a number of cases to the effect that there is no principle of law which requires a person to contribute to an outlay merely because he has derived a material benefit from it: see for example, *Ruabon Steamship Co Ltd v London Assurance* (1900).

My conclusions upon this matter may be shortly stated. Strider elected of its own motion to carry the subject containers to Melbourne, rather than discharging them, at its own cost, at Auckland. I am prepared to draw the inference that Strider proposed to send the vessel to Melbourne in any event, bearing in mind that cargo was loaded at that port. There is no evidence before me that there would have been any additional costs involved in [71] carrying the subject containers to Melbourne (other than what may be thought to be *de minimis*). The vessel is described in the charter party as being capable of carrying '329 TEU/159 FEU'. Therefore, eight 40 ft containers [Gadsden's cargo] represented a small proportion of her cargo capacity.

One must also take into consideration that if Strider had elected to discharge the subject containers at Auckland, it would have been required to make arrangements for their safekeeping, in accordance with its obligations as a bailee. It is not surprising therefore that it elected to carry the containers to Melbourne in the hope (or anticipation) that it would obtain freight from Gadsden.

It does not seem to me, therefore, that justice requires that Strider be compensated for the carriage of Gadsden's containers to Melbourne under the principle of restitution or unjust enrichment. In other words, the equities of Strider's claim are not more compelling than Gadsden's plea that it did not request or freely accept the services: Goff and Jones (at p 144). I do not overlook, of course, that Gadsden received the benefit of having the cargo carried to Melbourne rather than being required to make its own arrangements to have the cargo carried from Auckland to Melbourne.

---

64   Birks, *op cit*, fn 1, p 103.

However, in the terminology used in this area of the law, I consider that Strider acted officiously or as a volunteer. I do not, of course, use the word 'officiously' in a pejorative sense.

Further, the case is distinguishable from *China Pacific SA v Food Corporation of India, The Winson* and the cases there cited, where the plaintiff was entitled to recover expenditure which it had clearly incurred solely for the benefit of the defendant – in most cases the benefit being the preservation of its goods.

Accordingly, I would also reject Strider's claim upon the basis upon which it was argued before me.

Accordingly, I declare that the plaintiff is entitled to the sum of $42,857.14 ...

Commentary and questions

Was Gadsden incontrovertibly benefited by the actions of Strider in carrying the cargo to Melbourne rather than offloading it in Auckland?

The principal case illustrates that the plaintiff will be denied a restitutionary claim where she acts 'officiously' in conferring what otherwise might be viewed as being an incontrovertible benefit or, alternatively, acted in her own self-interest. Although different definitions of officiousness have been advanced,[65] the underlying idea is that restitution will be denied as a matter of policy to a plaintiff who consciously took the risk of non-payment for the services: *Brenner v First Artists' Management Pty Ltd* (1993), p 275 (see extract, p 39). The element of conscious adoption of the risk of non-payment will be absent where the plaintiff has conferred the services under an operative mistake.

MEASUREMENT OF ENRICHMENT

The measure of enrichment on a personal claim for the recovery of money is usually straightforward: the enrichment equals the amount of money claimed to be unjustly received. Where the claim is for the provision of goods or services the usual basis for measuring the enrichment is the market value of the goods or services,[66] not the amount by which the defendant's assets have been enhanced.[67] However, the ultimate objective is to determine a fair recompense,[68] and the defendant might be permitted to subjectively devalue the

---

65 See, eg, American Law Institute, *Restatement of the Law of Restitution: Quasi-Contract and Constructive Trusts*, 1937, para 2; cf Birks, *op cit*, fn 1, p 103.

66 *Brenner v First Artists' Management Pty Ltd* (1993), p 263 (see extracts, pp 39 and 71); *Bunbury-Harvey Regional Council v Giacci* (2000).

67 *Pavey & Matthews Pty Ltd v Paul* (1987), p 263 per Deane J (see extracts, pp 15 and 70); *Renard Constructions (ME) Pty Ltd v Minister for Public Works* (1992) (see extract, p 322); *Brenner v First Artists' Management Pty Ltd* (1993), p 263 (see extracts, pp 39 and 71); *William Lacey (Hounslow) Ltd v Davis* (1957), p 940 (see extract, p 405). The contract price does not form a cap on recovery: *Renard Constructions (ME) Pty Ltd v Minister for Public Works* (1992) (see extract, p 322); *Pavey & Matthews Pty Ltd v Paul* (1987), p 257 per Deane J (see extract, p 70).

68 *Brenner v First Artists' Management Pty Ltd* (1993), p 263 (see extracts, pp 39 and 71). See generally *Council of City of Sydney v Woodward* (2000).

benefit to an amount lower than the market price for the services.[69] Further, the value which the plaintiff has put on the services in prior correspondence will be relevant (though not determinative) to determining the fair value of the services.[70]

The following case illustrates that the fair value of the services might be different to the recompense contemplated by the parties in the ineffective contract.[71]

Way v Latilla [1937] 3 All ER 759 House of Lords

The appellant, Mr Way, acquired gold mining concessions on behalf of the respondent, Mr Latilla; Mr Way at all times acting at the request of Mr Latilla. Mr Way claimed that he had acted pursuant to an agreement with Mr Latilla to obtain the concessions in consideration for which Mr Latilla would give to Mr Way the customary, or a reasonable, share in the acquired mining concessions. Mr Latilla obtained considerable profits from the concessions, but Mr Way was granted no interest in them. The court held that the alleged agreement was incomplete, and therefore void, as there was no agreement as to the amount of the share of interest that Mr Way was to receive.

Lord Atkin: ... [763] The question now is, what are Mr Way's rights to remuneration? He originally claimed that there was a completed agreement to give him an interest in the concession, which, by custom, or on a reasonable basis, the court was asked to define as one-third. The trial judge accepted this view, holding that he was entitled to assess a reasonable share, and he accordingly awarded him £30,000, as being roughly 3% on the sum of about £1,000,000, which he took to represent Mr Latilla's profits in the transaction. The Court of Appeal rejected this view, and, in my opinion, rightly. There certainly was no concluded contract between the parties as to the amount of the share or interest that Mr Way was to receive, and it appears to me impossible for the court to complete the contract for them ... But, while there is, therefore, no concluded contract as to the remuneration, it is plain that there existed between the parties a contract of employment under which Mr Way was engaged to do work for Mr Latilla in circumstances which clearly indicated that the work was not to be gratuitous. Mr Way, therefore, is entitled to a reasonable remuneration on the implied contract to pay him *quantum meruit*. It is on the assessment of this amount that I believe all your Lordships differ from the Court of Appeal. The members of the court appear to have acted on the view that Mr Way had given no evidence as to the value of his services, that the only evidence before the court was the evidence of one or two consulting mining engineers, in particular that of Colonel Lake, on whom the Court of Appeal relied, and that, following this evidence, the proper reward was a fee of 500 [764] guineas. My Lords, this decision appears to me to ignore the real business position. Services of this kind are no doubt usually the subject of an express contract as to remuneration, which may take the form of a fee, but may also take the form of a commission share of profits, or share of proceeds calculated

---

69   *Bunbury-Harvey Regional Council v Giacci* (2000).
70   *Council of City of Sydney v Woodward* (2000).
71   See also *Deglman v Guaranty Trust* (1954) (see extract, p 359); *Horton v Jones (No 2)* (1939), pp 320–21 (see extract, p 385); *Stinchcombe v Thomas* (1957).

at a percentage, or on some other basis. In the present case, there was no question of fee between the parties from beginning to end. On the contrary, the parties had discussed remuneration on the footing of what may loosely be called a 'participation,' and nothing else. The reference is analogous to the well known distinction between salary and commission. There are many employments the remuneration of which is, by trade usage, invariably fixed on a commission basis. In such cases, if the amount of the commission has not been finally agreed, the *quantum meruit* would be fixed after taking into account what would be a reasonable commission, in the circumstances, and fixing a sum accordingly. This has been an everyday practice in the courts for years. But, if no trade usage assists the court as to the amount of the commission, it appears to me clear that the court may take into account the bargainings between the parties, not with a view to completing the bargain for them, but as evidence of the value which each of them puts upon the services. If the discussion had ranged between 3% on the one side and 5% on the other, all else being agreed, the court would not be likely to depart from somewhere about those figures, and would be wrong in ignoring them altogether and fixing remuneration on an entirely different basis, upon which, possibly, the services would never have been rendered at all. That, in fixing a salary basis, the court may pay regard to the previous conversation of the parties was decided by the Court of Exchequer in 1869, in *Scarisbrick v Parkinson* (1969), where the terms of an agreement, invalid under the Statute of Frauds, were held to be admissible as evidence in a *quantum meruit*. This seems to me to be good law, and to give effect to a principle which has been adopted regularly by the courts not only in fixing remuneration for services but also in fixing prices, sums due for use and occupation, and, indeed, in all cases where the court has to determine what is a reasonable reward for the consideration given by the claimant. As I have said, the rule applied in fixing the amount of the remuneration necessarily applies to the basis on which the amount is to be fixed. I have therefore no hesitation in saying that the basis of remuneration by fee should, in this case, on the evidence of the parties themselves, be rejected, and that Mr Way is entitled to a sum to be calculated on the basis of some reasonable participation.

What this should be is a task primarily to be undertaken by the trial judge. He did make an alternative award, and arrived at the sum of £5,000. I see no reason to differ from this. It is true that there is evidence that Mr Latilla made very large profits. On the other hand, this amount was very favourably affected by this country's financial policy in respect of gold, which was altered some time after the services [765] were rendered. Mr Way does not profess to have discovered the line of reef on which the concessions lay, and some of them at least were in respect of abandoned workings. These concessions had to be financed for some years, and other interests had to be satisfied. Mr Way had no reason to contemplate even a participation based on a percentage of profits. A transfer of a substantial number of shares would have been an adequate satisfaction of any contemplated obligation on Mr Latilla's part. I think that the sum of £5,000 which the judge appears to have arrived at on consideration of all the necessary factors would be a reasonable remuneration in all the circumstances. I therefore think that the judgment of the judge should be varied by entering judgment for the plaintiff for £5,000, instead of for £30,000 ...

Lord Wright: My Lords, I have had the advantage of reading in print the opinion of my noble and learned friend on the woolsack, and agree with it. I add a very few observations, out of respect to the very careful judgments delivered in the Court of Appeal. On the main decision at which the Court of Appeal arrived in reversing the judge, I am in full agreement with the Lords Justices. There was, I think, no justification for making for the parties, as Charles J did, a contract which they did not make themselves. It is, however, clear, on the evidence, that the work was done by the appellant and accepted by the respondent on the basis that some remuneration was to be paid to the appellant by the respondent. There was thus an implied promise by the respondent to pay on a *quantum meruit*, that is, to pay what the services were worth. My difference with the Court of Appeal turns on a narrow issue, which is whether the *quantum meruit* should be determined on the footing of a fee as for professional services, or on some other footing. The Court of Appeal took the former view. I cannot, however, with respect, find, on the whole of the evidence in the case, and, in particular, on the discussions between the parties, any sufficient reason for accepting that view. The services of the appellant were, I [766] think, outside the range of his duties as mining engineer, and were those of an agent for purchase, who suggests to his principal a transaction, and negotiates and completes it for him. While it is not unknown that such services should be remunerated by a fee if it is expressly or impliedly so agreed, this is by no means necessarily, and would not generally be, the case. The idea of such a fee being excluded, it follows that the question of the amount to which the appellant is entitled is left at large, and the court must do the best it can to arrive at a figure which seems to it fair and reasonable to both parties, on all the facts of the case. One aspect of the facts to be considered is found in the communings of the parties while the business was going on. Evidence of this nature is admissible to show what the parties had in mind, however indeterminately, with regard to the basis of remuneration. On those facts, the court may be able to infer, or attribute to the parties, an intention that a certain basis of payment should apply. This evidence seems to me to show quite clearly that the appellant was employed on the basis of receiving a remuneration depending on results. If he had been unsuccessful, he would have been entitled to no more than his expenses, but the respondent had led him to believe that, if the concessions he obtained were valuable, his remuneration would be on the basis of some proportion of their value. The realisation of that value was removed from the actual services by the lapse of time (during which large sums of money were expended and adventured), and by many contingencies, and therefore the proper proportion may be comparatively very small, though the fruits of success were very large. The precise figure can be only a rough estimate. If what the court fixes is either too small or too large, the fault must be ascribed to the parties in leaving this important matter in so nebulous a state. But, forming the best judgment I can, I agree with your Lordships that the figure to be awarded to the appellant should be £5,000, which is what Charles J was prepared to adopt if his judgment were reversed.

Questions

What interest did the parties contemplate that the plaintiff would receive in return for the provision of his services? What award did the court in fact make to the plaintiff?

Pavey & Matthews Pty Ltd v Paul **(1987) 162 CLR 221 High Court of Australia**

The facts are stated at p 15.

Deane J: ... [263] The tendency in some past cases to see the rationale of the right to recover remuneration for a benefit provided and accepted under an unenforceable contract as contract or promise rather than restitution has tended to distract attention from the importance of identifying the basis upon which the quantum of the amount recoverable should be ascertained. What the concept of monetary restitution involves is the payment of an amount which constitutes, in all the relevant circumstances, fair and just compensation for the benefit or 'enrichment' actually or constructively accepted. Ordinarily, that will correspond to the fair value of the benefit provided (eg, remuneration calculated at a reasonable rate for work actually done or the fair market value of materials supplied). In some categories of case, however, it would be to affront rather than satisfy the requirements of good conscience and justice which inspire the concept or principle of restitution or unjust enrichment to determine what constitutes fair and just compensation for a benefit accepted by reference only to what would represent a fair remuneration for the work involved or a fair market value of materials supplied. One such category of case is that in which unsolicited but subsequently accepted work is done in improving property in circumstances where remuneration for the unsolicited work calculated at what was a reasonable rate would far exceed the enhanced value of the property. More relevant for present purposes is the special category of case where restitution is sought by one party for work which he has executed under a contract which has become unenforceable by reason of his failure to comply with the requirements of a statutory provision which was enacted to protect the other party. In that category of case, it would be contrary to the general notions of restitution or unjust enrichment if what constituted fair and just [264] compensation for the benefit accepted by the other party were to be ascertained without regard to any identifiable real detriment sustained by that other party by reason of the failure of the first party to ensure that the requirements of the statutory provision were satisfied. Thus, if it is established on the hearing of the present case that Mrs Paul has sustained an identifiable real detriment by reason of the failure of the builder to ensure that there was a written memorandum of the oral contract which satisfied the requirements of s 45 of the Act, that would be an important factor in determining what constituted fair and just restitution in the circumstances of the case for the work done and materials supplied of which she has accepted the benefit. The mere fact that the reasonable remuneration for the building work done at Mrs Paul's request exceeded Mrs Paul's expectations would not, however, of itself constitute any such identifiable real detriment since it is not necessary for the purposes of s 45 of the Act that a written contract contain either an agreed price for the building work or an estimate of what the cost of it to the building owner will ultimately be ...

Commentary

Deane J recognises that the primary approach to the quantification of non-monetary benefits is to calculate the fair market value of the work done or materials supplied. However, he recognises that there will be exceptional cases where the enhanced value of the property is the appropriate measure of enrichment. It is arguable that one such exceptional case is where the enrichment is established by a positive accretion in the value of assets which are realised or realisable – that is, the defendant has received a positive incontrovertible benefit. In such instances the enhancement in the value of the asset represents the most appropriate valuation measure.[72]

Deane J states that when assessing the benefit, the courts should take into account any detriment sustained due to the plaintiff's non-compliance with the statutory requirements. The court might also make an allowance which adjusts the value of the benefit where the work performed is defective and requires rectification[73] although the loss to the defendant might alternatively be compensated by way of a cross-claim for damages.[74]

Brenner v First Artists' Management Pty Ltd [1993] 2 VR 221 Supreme Court of Victoria

The facts are stated at p 39.

Byrne J: ... [262] *Legal principles as to quantum*

I turn now to the aspect of the case which I have found most difficult, the assessment of the fair and reasonable remuneration for the work of Fenner and Brenner.

... It is convenient at the outset to set out the legal principles which I apply in making the assessment. First, my task is not to assess damages for breach of contract. The claims of the plaintiffs presuppose that no contract existed. Accordingly, I am not concerned to assess the sum which would compensate Fenner and Brenner for the benefits they might have received had they remained as managers of Braithwaite for the full term of the management engagement of June 1987 or that made in January 1988, even if it were possible to determine this, given the infirmities of this engagement.

Second, the fundamental yardstick is what is a fair and reasonable remuneration or compensation for the benefit accepted actually or constructively by Braithwaite. It will be recalled that in the context of liability I drew a distinction between the benefit which is presumed where a person requests another to perform services, and the end-product of those services. Take the case of a selling agent who after one hour's work achieves [263] a sale which earns an enormous profit to the principal. What is in these circumstances the benefit to the principal? In my view the answer to this difficulty is suggested by Deane J in *Pavey's* case (p 263). Where the services have been performed at the request of a defendant or under an ineffective contract, the fair value of the work of the party will ordinarily be the remuneration calculated at a reasonable rate for the work actually done, for the defendant having obtained the benefit of a plaintiff's work ought not be permitted to enjoy this work without having paid for it. The assessment, then, must have regard to what the defendant would have had to pay had the benefits been conferred under a normal commercial arrangement. The enquiry is not primarily

---

72 See *BP Exploration Co (Libya) Ltd v Hunt (No 2)* (1979), p 805; Mason and Carter, *op cit*, fn 5, p 570; *Lexane Highfern Pty Ltd v Highfern Pty Ltd* (1985), p 455; *McKeown v Cavalier Yachts Pty Ltd* (1988), p 313 (see extract, p 157).

73 *Riverside Motors Pty Ltd v Abrahams* (1945) VLR 45, p 53.

74 *Tea Tree Gully Builders Co Pty Ltd v Martin* (1992). See generally Byrne, 'Benefits – for services rendered', in McInnes (ed), *Restitution: Developments in Unjust Enrichment*, 1996, Chapter 5.

directed at the cost to the plaintiff of performing the work since the law is not compensating that party for loss suffered. See *Minister for Public Works v Renard Constructions (ME) Pty Ltd* (1989). Compare *Renard Constructions (ME) Pty Ltd v Minister for Public Works* (1992), p 276. But this is not to ignore these costs for the reasonable remuneration for work must have some regard to the cost of its performance. See *Jennings Construction Ltd v OH & M Birt Pty Ltd* (1988).

Third, where the parties have agreed upon a price for certain services to be performed and those services have in fact been performed, but for some reason their agreement is ineffective or is no longer on foot, the agreed price is evidence of the value that the parties themselves put on the services performed and may be received as evidence of the appropriate remuneration, but is not determinative of it: *Pavey's* case (p 257); *Horton v Jones (No 1)* (1934), p 368. These cases are concerned with contracts which have been performed by the plaintiff, but there seems no reason in principle why the court should not equally have regard to the agreed price in assessing the benefit of services where they are not totally performed. In such a case, however, there may be in particular circumstances difficulties in applying a pro rata basis for the agreed price to incomplete works: see *Jennings's* case. Where the court has regard to the agreed remuneration or the agreed mode of calculating remuneration, it is entitled to modify this to determine what is in all the circumstances a fair recompense. See, for example, *Hansen v Mayfair Trading Co Pty Ltd* (1962).

Fourth, in many cases the appropriate method of assessing the benefit of the work is by applying an hourly rate to the time involved in performing those services. If this procedure is adopted, the court may have regard to the rate of remuneration which is commonly accepted in the industry. But in so doing it should have regard to the standing of the person performing the services, the difficulty of the task, the fact that the services required imagination and creativity which may be difficult to discern in the end product. See also *Graham & Baldwin v Taylor, Son and Davis* (1965); *Hudson's Building & Engineering Contracts* (10th edn, pp 183–85).

Fifth, in the case where the services are of such kind that it is difficult or impossible to assess the number of hours involved or to itemise the precise services, the court is entitled to make a global assessment or to reduce or increase the remuneration which can be proved with some certainty in order to reflect the fair and reasonable value. See *The Commonwealth of Australia* [264] *v Amman Aviation Pty Ltd* (1991), p 83. In such a case the court is simply performing the task of the jury, which would be directed to have regard to all the circumstances and to return a verdict in the proper sum.

Sixth, where it is customary in the industry for the services to be recompensed on a commission basis, the court may have regard to what is a reasonable commission and to apply it where appropriate: *Way v Latilla* (1937), p 764 *per* Lord Atkin. This manner of valuing the services, however, provides difficulties in the case where the event giving rise to the payment of commission has not occurred, as for example where an estate agent is deprived of the right to earn commission because the property is withdrawn from sale. In such a case it cannot be appropriate to treat the benefits to the employer as being the procuring of a sale which has not occurred, nor is it appropriate to value the lost chance of the agent to make this sale, for this is to apply a rule more appropriate for the assessment of damages. But what is the sense of attempting to value the agent's fruitless services performed at the request of the defendant, for the market or current price of those services cannot be realistically assessed in that industry otherwise than by reference to the commission which they might have earned? The researches of counsel and of myself have not disclosed an authority on this point which is central to the assessment in the present case. Accordingly, it is necessary to turn to first principles.

The function of the task of the court is to undertake an assessment of the benefit or the enrichment which has been unjustly accepted by the defendant. The benefit may be looked at first as the benefit of certain services which the estate agent or, as here, the managers were to undertake with the intent and expectation of profit for the employer. It is necessary to bear in mind that these services were not the making of a certain telephone call or the attending at a particular meeting, though they certainly included such things. The services which were requested and which I infer were of value to the artist were the assumption of the role of manager and the performance of the various tasks which this role involved. In this context the benefit to the artist includes the expectation that these services will be performed with the prospect of profit to him and on the basis that in such event he must make payment. Indeed, it is on this assumption that the manner of assessing payment on a commission basis was agreed.

The consequence of this, it seems to me, is that it would be to affront rather than to satisfy the requirements of good justice for the law to ignore, in the case of a commission agent or manager whose services have been provided at the request of an employer in circumstances entitling the former to restitution, the commission which might have accrued had the relationship not been terminated. This is not to say that the benefit conferred by the agent or manager should be valued as equivalent to that commission, for to do this would be to ignore the fact that the employment has been prematurely terminated, and that the agent/manager has been relieved of the burden of completing the task for which he or she was engaged, and the possibility that the success which was achieved after the termination was the product of the efforts of persons other than the agent/manager. The recognition of the role of these factors, together with a predisposition in such a case to fulfil the expectation of the parties at the time of request, may require the adjustment of the commission which might [265] otherwise have been payable in order to cater for the contribution made by the manager to the success of the artist.

These approaches, which may be to a greater or less extent of assistance in a given case, are all subordinate to the basic function of the court – to assess the sum which represents a fair and reasonable value of the benefit of the services performed.

The application of these principles to the case before me presents difficulties. I have been told and I accept that the functions of a manager whose task it is to promote the professional interests of an artist include the placing of the name of the artist before those persons who might be likely to engage him. This involves making efforts in different ways to promote the profile of the artist in areas of likely benefit to him. Fenner, for example, spoke of his efforts at social gatherings in the entertainment industry to promote to agents and others the name of Braithwaite as a star about to be once more in the ascendancy, stating that this was part of the ordinary functions of a manager. The expected consequence of these efforts was that when the opportunity for work arose, the agent might recall what he or she had been told at the social function and at least consider the possibility of engaging that artist. The same might be said in an indirect way of Fenner's efforts to make himself agreeable to well placed executives in the recording industry. It was apparent from the evidence of Karpin that he was pleased to be working with Fenner as a person whom he found to be a pleasant companion and friend. This 'oiling of the wheels' must be an important part of the 'people industry' which is the entertainment world. It would be, to my mind, unrealistic to deny remuneration to a manager for these services simply because it could not be shown that the efforts produced income for the artist. However difficult it may be, I see my task as that of valuing such efforts which I have no doubt provide value and benefit to the artist.

... In this case an important function of the manager was that of developing and maintaining the morale of Braithwaite. Although I accept that he always had confidence in his own ability and prospects, it was evident that there were times when Braithwaite was despondent, or even depressed. The role of the manager in such a case includes the task of lifting the artist's spirits and ensuring that the artist concentrates on the task in hand. These non-tangible services are included in the services which were of benefit to the artist and for which commission was agreed to be paid ...

[Byrne J then assessed the fair value of the services provided by the managers by determining the fair hourly rate appropriate to the standing of the managers and applying this rate to the number of hours proved to have been reasonably engaged.]

Questions

On what basis was the *quantum meruit* calculated in this case? Was it relevant that the plaintiffs could not demonstrate that their efforts had secured a singing engagement for the defendant prior to the cessation of the parties' relationship?

CHAPTER 3

AT THE PLAINTIFF'S EXPENSE

SUBTRACTION FROM THE PLAINTIFF

The purpose of the requirement that the enrichment be 'at the plaintiff's expense' is to identify the proper person to recover the enrichment.[1] The High Court in *Commissioner of State Revenue (Vic) v Royal Insurance Australia Ltd* (1994) has held that the proper plaintiff is normally the person who was the immediate source of the enrichment, in the sense that the enrichment passed from (or was subtracted from) the plaintiff's wealth.[2] On this view, it is the person who paid the money or transferred the property to the defendant who generally has standing to sue. It is irrelevant whether the enrichment was at the plaintiff's expense in the sense that the plaintiff will ultimately incur a loss or suffer a detriment due to the conferral of the enrichment. The objective of restitutionary relief is not to provide compensation for loss but to restore unjust enrichments.[3] Accordingly, the enrichment remains at the plaintiff's expense even if the plaintiff has recouped the value of the enrichment from third parties.[4]

The major cases dealing with the nature of the requirement that the enrichment be at the plaintiff's expense have dealt with a claim for the recovery of money paid. It is unclear how this requirement will operate outside that context. The non-fulfilment of a promise by an insurance company to indemnify a third party beneficiary under a policy of insurance has been suggested to be 'at the expense of' the third party beneficiary.[5] On the other hand, the loss of a bequest under a will due to the negligence of the solicitor drawing up the will has been held not to be 'at the expense of' the disappointed beneficiary.[6]

---

1   *Kleinwort Benson Ltd v Birmingham City Council* (1997), pp 742, 744, 749 (see extract, p 126).
2   At pp 75, 78 *per* Mason CJ, p 90 *per* Brennan J (Toohey and McHugh JJ concurring) (see following extract). See also *Kleinwort Benson Ltd v Birmingham City Council* (1997).
3   *Commissioner of State Revenue v Royal Insurance Australia* (1994), pp 75, 78 *per* Mason CJ (see following extract).
4   *Commissioner of State Revenue v Royal Insurance Australia* (1994), pp 75, 78 *per* Mason CJ, p 90 *per* Brennan J (Toohey and McHugh JJ concurring) (see following extract). See also *Mason v New South Wales* (1959), p 146 *per* Windeyer J; *Kleinwort Benson Ltd v Birmingham City Council* (1997), p 742 *per* Evans LJ, p 749 *per* Morritt LJ.
5   *Trident General Insurance Co Ltd v McNiece Bros Pty Ltd* (1988), p 176 *per* Gaudron J. Gaudron J's classification of the claim for enforcement of the indemnity as a claim in restitution has been criticised extensively: Soh, 'Privity of contract and restitution' (1989) 105 LQR 4; Jackman, 'Contract rights and liabilities of third parties' (1989) 63 ALJ 638; Edgell, 'Privity of contract in Australia: the beginning of the end?' [1989] LMCLQ 139; Jones, 'The law of restitution in the past and the future' in Burrows (ed), *Essays on Restitution*, 1991, p 3; McInnes, 'The plaintiff's expense in restitution: difficulties in the High Court' (1995) 23 ABLR 472, pp 473–74.
6   *Hill v Van Erp* (1997), pp 225–27 *per* Gummow J. For a critique see Tapsell, 'The negligence juggernaut and unjust enrichment' (1997) 16 ABR 70.

Commissioner of State Revenue (Vic) v Royal Insurance Australia Ltd
(1994) 182 CLR 51 High Court of Australia

Royal brought an action against the Commissioner seeking repayment of stamp duty which it had mistakenly paid on premiums received from the holders of certain workers' compensation insurance policies.

The facts are stated in more detail at p 120.

Mason CJ: ... [66] In argument, much attention was directed to the question whether the Commissioner could properly refuse to make a refund on the ground that Royal had charged the duty to its insured and that, as a consequence, the duty had been paid by the insured so that recovery by Royal would result in a windfall to Royal. Here, it seems that Royal charged the duty to its insured, believing it to be payable. Whether the duty formed the subject of a separate charge in addition to the premium does not appear from the materials. Generally, insurers charge duty separately to the insured in premium notices. The insured paid to Royal the duty as well as the premium. Royal then paid the duty to the Commissioner.

According to the Commissioner's counsel, one of the reasons why the Commissioner refused to make a refund was that, if the duty was refunded to Royal, in all probability it would be a windfall because difficulties Royal would face in seeking to refund the duty to its policy holders would be so great as to make it unlikely that it would seek to take that course. The primary judge did not make a finding that these difficulties existed or that it was unlikely that Royal would seek to take that course. Instead, his Honour regarded the possibility that such a situation could arise as a reason for rejecting the proposition that there was an obligation to make a refund whenever an overpayment took place or was found by the Commissioner to have taken place. According to his Honour, the discretion could be exercised adversely to Royal by reference to the possible existence of that situation. I should mention that at no stage of the proceedings did counsel for Royal suggest that Royal was suing for the benefit of the insured who bore the burden of the tax or that it would seek to pass on a refund, if obtained, to them ...

[68] That only brings us to what is a crucial question in this case: was the Commissioner unjustly enriched *at the expense of Royal?*[7] That the Commissioner was unjustly enriched there can be no doubt. The Commissioner received payments to which the State revenue was not entitled under the Act. The question remains whether the enrichment was at the expense of Royal. And here the fact that Royal charged the duty to its insured again becomes significant. The suggestion is that the enrichment of the Commissioner has taken place not at the expense of Royal but at the expense of its policy holders. They are the persons who have suffered a detriment; Royal has suffered no detriment and, if it recovers, it will make a windfall gain.[8] Indeed, it might be said that, if Royal recovers, it will be unjustly enriched. But such an enrichment, if it be unjust, would be at the expense of the policy holders, not at the expense of the Commissioner. The source of any windfall, if windfall there be, was in the excessive charges made by Royal to its policy holders, and the payments which they made to Royal.

---

7   Birks, 'The English recognition of unjust enrichment' [1991] LMCLQ 473, p 507.
8   See Burrows, 'Public authorities, *ultra vires* and restitution', in Burrows, *op cit*, fn 5, pp 59–60.

[Mason CJ discussed the defence of passing on (see extract, p 658) and continued at p 73:]

The United States and European decisions demonstrate that any acceptance of the defence of passing on is fraught with both practical and theoretical difficulties.[9] Indeed, the difficulties are so great that, in my view, the defence should not succeed unless it is established that the defendant's enrichment is not at the expense of the plaintiff but at the expense of some other person or persons.[10] In that event, the plaintiff fails, not because it has passed on the tax or charge, but because the defendant has been enriched by receiving moneys which belonged to or proceeded from someone other than the plaintiff. Take, for example, the case where there is an overpayment of a tax levied on someone other than the plaintiff who collects the tax and pays it to the public authority. In such a case, the plaintiff should not recover unless it is established that the plaintiff will distribute the proceeds to the true taxpayers ...

[75] Restitutionary relief, as it has developed to this point in our law, does not seek to provide compensation for loss. Instead, it operates to restore to the plaintiff what has been transferred from the plaintiff to the defendant whereby the defendant has been unjustly enriched. As in the action for money had and received, the defendant comes under an obligation to account to the plaintiff for money which the defendant has received for the use of the plaintiff. The subtraction from the plaintiff's wealth enables one to say that the defendant's unjust enrichment has been 'at the expense of the plaintiff',[11] notwithstanding that the plaintiff may recoup the outgoing by means of transactions with third parties.

On this approach, it would not matter that the plaintiff is or will be over-compensated because he or she has passed on the tax or charge to someone else. And it seems that there is no recorded instance of a court engaging in the daunting exercise of working out the actual loss sustained by the plaintiff and restricting the amount of an award to that measure.

Nonetheless, in the United States, relief has been denied, on equitable amongst other grounds, to a plaintiff who has passed on the tax or charge, reference being made to coming to court with unclean hands.[12] Why, as between the plaintiff and the defendant, the passing on of the tax to customers of the plaintiff results in conduct which should disentitle the plaintiff in equity from recovery is difficult to understand. The better view is that, if passing on of the tax disentitles the plaintiff, it is because, in the particular circumstances, the defendant's enrichment has not been at the expense of the plaintiff.

---

9   See also Rudden and Bishop, 'Gritz and Quellmehl: pass it on' (1981) 6 EL Rev 243, esp pp 253–56.

10 There is limited support from the textwriters for the view that passing on is not a defence: see Birks, *Restitution – The Future*, 1992, p 75, n 55; Burrows, *The Law of Restitution*, 1993, pp 475–76 (though he favours a mitigation of loss defence in some cases where it is established that the charge has been passed on). But others consider it is a defence: see Palmer, *The Law of Restitution*, 1986 Supp, p 255; see also Goff and Jones, *The Law of Restitution*, 4th edn, 1993, p 553, where it is suggested that 'the burden should, in principle, be on the defendant to show that the plaintiff has suffered no loss'. In *Woolwich Equitable Building Society v Inland Revenue Commissioners (No 2)* [1993] AC 70, p 178, Lord Goff of Chievely commented: '... the point is not without its difficulties; and the availability of the defence may depend upon the nature of the tax.'

11 Birks, *An Introduction to the Law of Restitution*, rev edn, 1989, pp 23–24.

12 *Standard Oil Co v Bollinger* (1929); see also *Richardson Lubricating Co v Kinney* (1929).

That was the way in which the problem was approached by Judge Learned Hand in his dissenting opinion in *123 East Fifty-Fourth Street v United States* (1946). There the court rejected the defence of passing on in circumstances where a restaurant owner, in accordance with advice received from revenue authorities that it was liable to cabaret tax, paid amounts as and for that tax. The court held that the tax was not payable because the restaurant was not a cabaret. The restaurant owner had charged the tax to its patrons so that items on the patrons' bills were actually part of the price paid by them and the money became that of the restaurant owner. The [76] majority considered that this was no bar to recovery by the restaurant owner because the money, when paid to the government, belonged to and was the property of the restaurant owner. However, Judge Learned Hand was prepared to infer that the owner had added the tax as a separate item to the bills and described it as a tax which it must pay and was collecting it from patrons in order to pay it to the Treasury. His Honour regarded as crucial the distinction between passing on the tax in this form and merely including in the bills the amount of the tax without saying anything about it.

Judge Learned Hand went on to say:[14]

> If it said nothing, I should agree ... that the guests had no legally recognisable interest in the money collected, which gave them any claim to it superior to the plaintiff's ... On the other hand, if the plaintiff collected the money under what the guests must have understood to be a statement that it was obliged to pay it as a tax, and that it meant to do so, the money was charged with a constructive trust certainly so long as it remained in the plaintiff's hands.

According to his Honour, the constructive trust attached to the claim for recovery of the money so that if the plaintiff recovered the payments it would hold as trustee for the patrons. That would be no answer to the claim if the plaintiff could and would distribute the recovery to the patrons. But that did not appear to be the case so that in the result, the equities being equal, the legal title should prevail.

In *Decorative Carpets Inc v State Board of Equalisation* (1962) the Supreme Court of California followed the dissenting opinion of Judge Learned Hand. In that case, the plaintiff had overpaid sales tax with respect to transactions combining sales and installation. The plaintiff had collected for each transaction giving rise to a liability to pay sales tax a separately stated amount to cover the tax imposed on it, and had charged to its customers the amounts computed to be payable as sales tax on those transactions. The court held that the plaintiff's mistake of law gave rise to an involuntary trust in favour of the customers and that the plaintiff could recover only if it submitted proof that the refund would be returned to the customers [77] from whom the payments were erroneously collected. Traynor J, with whom Gibson CJ, Peters and White JJ concurred, said:

> To allow the plaintiff a refund without requiring it to repay its customers the amounts erroneously collected from them would sanction a misuse of the sales tax by a retailer for his private gain.

The court considered that, although the defendant would ordinarily, like the plaintiff, become a constructive trustee of the moneys for the plaintiff's customers,

---

14 See also *Wayne County Produce Co v Duffy-Mott Co* (1927), p 669 *per* Cardozo CJ (where Duffy-Mott recovered the tax that it had paid to the federal government but, having charged the tax specifically to its customers in addition to the price of the goods sold, was held liable to account to them for the tax recovered).

adherence to statutory procedures precluded the imposition on the defendant of an obligation to make refunds to the customers. The court did not discuss the question whether the defendant would be unjustly enriched if the plaintiff were unable to offer proof that it could and would refund the sums to its customers.

On the other hand, in *Javor v State Board of Equalisation* (1974), car purchasers sought to recover amounts of sales tax which had been passed on to them by retailers. The amount paid was excessive because of the repeal, with retrospective effect, of a federal manufacturers' excise tax which had been included in the sales tax base. The overpaid tax was in excess of $10 million; however, each customer was owed only a very small amount.[18] Only a retailer could apply for a refund, which was required to be paid over to the customer. Accordingly, a retailer had no particular incentive to request the refund. Sullivan J, with whom Wright CJ, Tobriner, Mosk and Burke JJ concurred, considered that:

> ... the Board is very likely to become enriched at the expense of the customer to whom the amount of the excessive tax actually belongs.

> The integrity of the sales tax requires not only that retailers not be unjustly enriched, but also that the state not be similarly unjustly enriched.

The court found that the customers could compel the retailers to make refund applications, and require the refunded sales tax to be paid into court.

I would accept so much of Judge Learned Hand's analysis in *123 East Fifty-Fourth Street* as leads to the conclusion that the restaurant owner was a constructive trustee of the amount of the tax received from its patrons if the owner charged the separate amount of the tax to its patrons. The tax so received was received by the owner as a [78] fiduciary on the footing that it would apply the money in payment of the tax. If that purpose failed or could not be effected because the tax was not payable then the owner held the moneys for the benefit of the patrons who paid the moneys. The same result would ensue if the owner recovered payments from the revenue authority made as and for tax which was not payable. And, in my view, the patrons who paid the tax to the owner would have a right of recovery, as Judge Learned Hand makes clear, against the revenue authority so long as it retained the payments which it was not entitled to retain.

But does all this require the further conclusion that in the circumstances predicated by Judge Learned Hand – the addition of the tax as a separate item to the bills – the restaurant owner could not recover? I would answer the question in the negative on the footing that the restaurant owner had a legal title to the money immediately before it was paid to the revenue authority. In that respect, the money belonged to the plaintiff even though, if it recovered the money, it would hold as trustee for the patrons. But, in such a case, the plaintiff should be required to satisfy the court, by the giving of an undertaking or other means, that it will distribute the moneys to the patrons from whom they were collected, thereby recognising their beneficial ownership of those moneys.

If, however, the plaintiff did not become the constructive trustee of the moneys by separately charging them as tax to the patrons, I do not see why the plaintiff's claim should be defeated simply because the plaintiff has recouped the outgoing from others. As between the plaintiff and the defendant, the plaintiff having paid

18   For example, the plaintiff, who had purchased a Rolls Royce, was owed $65.72.

away its money by mistake in circumstances in which the defendant has no title to retain the moneys, the plaintiff has the superior claim. The plaintiff's inability to distribute the proceeds to those who recoup the plaintiff was, in my view, an immaterial consideration, as Windeyer J suggested it was in *Mason v New South Wales*. There was in that case the additional element of an unlawful demand but the absence of that element does not mean that, in the situation under consideration, unjust enrichment was otherwise than at the plaintiff's expense ...

Brennan J (Toohey and McHugh JJ concurring): ... [90] The fact that Royal had passed on to its policy holders the burden of the payments made to the Commissioner does not mean that Royal did not pay its own money to the Commissioner. The passing on of the burden of the payments made does not affect the situation that, as between the Commissioner and Royal, the former was enriched at the expense of the latter. It may be that, if Royal recovers the overpayments it made, the policy holders will be entitled themselves to claim a refund from Royal[20] of so much of the overpayments made by Royal to the Commissioner as represents the amount paid to Royal by the policy holder.[21] However that may be, no defence of 'passing on' is available to defeat a claim for moneys paid by A acting on his own behalf to B where B has been unjustly enriched by the payment and the moneys paid had been A's moneys ...[22]

Dawson J: ... [101] The application of the common law would also raise the question whether the principle of unjust enrichment can be invoked when moneys paid under a mistake of fact or law constitute an expense which has been passed on to someone else, as the respondent insurer is said to have passed on the overpayments of stamp duty to its insured in this case. The better view would seem to be that it is the unjust enrichment of the payee rather than loss suffered by the payer which should govern entitlement to restitution, but, having regard to the view which I take [viz that the Commissioner had a statutory duty to refund the overpayments], it is unnecessary to determine that question in these proceedings ...

Commentary

In the principal case Mason CJ advances two qualifications to the rule that the plaintiff can recover provided that the plaintiff paid the money. First, his Honour recognises that the payment would not ordinarily be at the plaintiff's expense where the plaintiff acted merely as a conduit in collecting the tax from customers and paying it over to the government.[23]

---

20 *Mutual Pools & Staff Pty Ltd v The Commonwealth* (1994), pp 177, 191.

21 This was the effect of s 99(8) and (9) of the Act in relation to the particular refunds which the comptroller was directed to make to insurers under s 99. The original sub-sections inserted by the Accident Compensation Act were amended by the Stamps and Business Franchise (Tobacco) (Amendment) Act 1985, s 11(3)(a), (b).

22 *Mason v New South Wales* (1959), pp 136, 146; see also *Woolwich Equitable Building Society v Inland Revenue Commissioners* (1993), pp 177–78 and *Air Canada v British Columbia* (1989) SCR pp 1215–16; DLR pp 167–70 *per* Wilson J (dissenting).

23 Although his Honour does then go on to hold that the plaintiff taxpayer would be allowed to recover provided it undertook to to return the monies to its customers.

Secondly, Mason CJ suggests that a plaintiff who recovers an enrichment in a restitutionary action might in some circumstances be required to account for it to the third party from whom the plaintiff had recouped the expense. His Honour suggests this will be the case where the plaintiff has recouped specifically the enrichment from customers as a separate and identifiable charge.[24] In this circumstance the plaintiff will hold the money as constructive trustee for customers on the basis that the money will be used to pay the tax.[25] If the tax is found not to have been payable, the plaintiff as owner of the legal title to the money, has standing to commence proceedings for recovery, however must undertake to hold the moneys on trust for its customers.[26] On this view, if the plaintiff recovers the amount of the tax, the customers would have a claim under the trust to recover the amount of tax paid by them.[27]

In the following case, *Roxborough v Rothmans of Pall Mall Australia Ltd* (2001), a majority of the High Court affirmed the basic proposition that a payment will be at the plaintiff's expense provided the plaintiff made the payment out of the plaintiff's own funds. The only qualification suggested to this principle is where the plaintiff is paying the money as an agent on behalf of third parties who in fact bear the legal obligation to make the payment (at p 342; Gleeson CJ, Gaudron and Hayne JJ). Thus, there is some support in this decision for Mason CJ's first qualification in *Royal* discussed above. However, there was no support for Mason CJ's view that a plaintiff might, in an action for restitution, be required to give an undertaking to the court to hold an amount recovered on trust where it has been specifically passed on to customers.[30]

Roxborough v Rothmans of Pall Mall Australia Ltd (2001) 185 ALR 335 High Court of Australia

The appellants were retailers of tobacco products and at the material time held retailer's licences under the Business Franchise Licences (Tobacco) Act 1987 (NSW) (the Act). The respondent, Rothmans, sold tobacco products by wholesale to the appellants. The Act imposed an obligation on both wholesalers and retailers to pay licence fees on tobacco products sold by them. Section 41 of the Act in effect exempted retailers from paying fees to the extent that they purchased the products from a licensed wholesaler that paid the applicable licence fee. The contractual arrangement between Rothmans and the retailers was that the retailers paid to Rothmans the amount of the licence fees as part of the purchase price of the products, and Rothmans paid over the licence fees to the government when they fell due. The amount of the purchase price attributable to the licence fees was always separately enumerated in each invoice.

---

24 *Commissioner of State Revenue (Vic) v Royal Insurance Australia Ltd* (1994), pp 77–78 *per* Mason CJ.

25 *Ibid.*

26 *Ibid.* See the further discussion in Chapter 18.

27 Cf *Mutual Pools & Staff Pty Ltd v Commonwealth* (1994), at 177, 191.

30 Cf Gummow J, p 350. Though Kirby J held that such an undertaking would be relevant on an action in equity to recover under a constructive trust: see pp 664 and 696 for extracts of Kirby J's judgment on this point.

In 1997 the High Court decided in *Ha v New South Wales* (1997) 189 CLR 465 that the licence fees imposed by the Act were duties of excise, and thus the Act was beyond the legislative competence of the New South Wales Government and unconstitutional. The retailers commenced proceedings in restitution to recover an amount of licence fees which they had paid to Rothmans but which Rothmans, due to the advent of the decision in *Ha*, had not paid over to the Government. The retailers' claim failed both at first instance and on appeal to the Full Court of the Federal Court of Australia. One of the issues before the High Court was whether the appellants were prevented from recovering the sums representing the licence fees from the respondent by virtue of the fact that they had recouped the cost of the fees from their customers by raising the price of their cigarettes.

Gleeson CJ, Gaudron and Hayne JJ: ... [341] According to the respondent, if the respondent has been enriched, then that has been at the expense, not of the appellants, but of the customers of the appellants, and justice does not require it to make restitution to the appellants.

...

[342] [T]he respondent's objection [is] based upon the fact that, at least in a practical sense, the burden of the tax has been passed on by the appellants to their customers. The factual basis of this objection cannot be refuted. It is in the nature of an indirect tax that it enters into the cost of the goods the subject of the tax and is borne by the consumers of the goods. The conclusion that the character of the tax was that of a tax on tobacco rather than a personal tax on wholesalers and retailers was an important part of the reasoning leading to the decision that it was a duty of excise.

Although the factual basis of the objection is correct, it is necessary to be clear as to its legal frame of reference. It cannot be simply an assertion that the appellants lack merit. In that respect, their position is no worse than that of the respondent. It was put on the basis that any enrichment of the respondent is not at the expense of the appellants and that, in consequence, the equitable foundation for a claim for restitution does not exist. But this, in turn, assumes that, in the circumstances of a case such as the present, it would only be unconscionable of the respondent to withhold repayment of the amounts referable to the tax if the appellants, for their part, were ultimately left impoverished to that extent. It is clear that, in a direct and immediate sense, the payments were made by the appellants, out of their own funds, to the respondent. They did not pay the amounts as agents, on behalf of third parties. The consumers of cigarettes, in an economic sense, bore the burden of the tax, but they were never legally liable as taxpayers. The appellants themselves were taxpayers under the licensing scheme, although if the respondent paid, or became liable to pay, tax in respect of particular tobacco products, the value of those products was disregarded in calculating the appellants' licence fees. And the respondent passed the tax on to the appellants, not merely in an economic sense, but also by the express terms of the dealings between the parties. They dealt on the basis that the appellants would pay to the respondent an amount equal to that part of the respondent's 'tobacco licence fees' referable to the products sold to the appellants.

There having been a failure of a distinct and severable part of the consideration for the net total payments made by the appellants to the respondent, then, as between the parties to the payments, the respondent has no right to retain the amounts in question. If the tobacco products in question remained unsold by the appellants at the time the claims for repayment arose for determination, the [343] respondent's obligation to make restitution would be clear. Why does it make a difference to the conscientiousness of the respondent's retention of the moneys that the products were sold by the appellants at prices that had the practical effect of recouping the expense they bore in paying the 'tobacco licence fees'? The holders of licences were those upon whom the tax was imposed, but they were always intended to pass the tax on to the consumers. As between the licensees, it was the appellants who incurred the expense, in that they were charged, and paid, a severable amount for the purpose of the tax.

The decision of this court in *Commissioner of State Revenue (Vict) v Royal Insurance Australia Ltd* (1994) strongly supports the appellants on this question. That was a case of moneys paid by an insurance company to a revenue authority by mistake, in the form of overpaid stamp duty. The revenue authority was held liable to refund the overpayments, even though the amounts had been passed on to policy holders. That conclusion was reached on general restitutionary principles.

Mason CJ said (p 75):

> Restitutionary relief, as it has developed to this point in our law, does not seek to provide compensation for loss. Instead, it operates to restore to the plaintiff what has been transferred from the plaintiff to the defendant whereby the defendant has been unjustly enriched. As in the action for money had and received, the defendant comes under an obligation to account to the plaintiff for money which the defendant has received for the use of the plaintiff. The subtraction from the plaintiff's wealth enables one to say that the defendant's unjust enrichment has been 'at the expense of the plaintiff', notwithstanding that the plaintiff may recoup the outgoing by means of transactions with third parties.

He also pointed out, in terms equally applicable to the present case, that, as between the parties to the litigation, the defendant having no title to retain the moneys, the plaintiff had the superior claim (p 78). That, in our view, is the critical question. As between the appellants and the respondent, who has the superior claim? The answer lies in the circumstance that there has been a payment of moneys by the appellants to the respondent for a consideration which has failed, and the respondent has no title to retain the moneys.

Brennan J, with whom Toohey J and McHugh J agreed (p 103), said (pp 90–91):

> The fact that Royal had passed on to its policy holders the burden of the payments made to the Commissioner does not mean that Royal did not pay its own money to the Commissioner. The passing on of the burden of the payments made does not affect the situation that, as between the Commissioner and Royal, the former was enriched at the expense of the latter. It may be that, if Royal recovers the overpayments it made, the policy holders will be entitled themselves to claim a refund from Royal … However that may be, no defence of 'passing on' is available to defeat a claim for moneys paid by A acting on his own behalf to B where B has been unjustly enriched by the payment and the moneys paid had been A's moneys.

It is impossible to explain those judgments, or that decision, upon the ground that there is some constitutional reason for treating restitutionary claims [344] against governments differently from claims against private citizens. It may be that the same principle applies with even greater force in the case of claims against governments, but *Royal Insurance* stands as clear authority against the respondent's argument on this question. We see no reason to depart from that recent decision of this court; and every reason in principle to support it ...

Commentary and question

Gummow J in *Roxborough v Rothmans* agreed that the retailers' claim was not defeated by virtue of the fact that they had recouped the licence fees from their customers (pp 353–54). His Honour endorsed the following statement by Windeyer J in *Mason v New South Wales* (1959), p 146 (see extract, p 434):

> The concept of impoverishment as a correlative of enrichment may have some place in some fields of continental law. It is foreign to our law. Even if there were any equity in favour of third parties attaching to the fruits of any judgment the plaintiffs might recover – and there is nothing proved at all remotely suggesting that there is – this circumstance would be quite irrelevant to the present proceedings.

Kirby J accepted that in relation to claims against the government for the recovery of invalid taxes, it is irrelevant that the plaintiff taxpayer has passed on the tax to customers. On the other hand, his Honour considered that in relation to claims between private parties, as in the principal case, the courts were entitled to take into account the fact that the plaintiff had recouped the cost of the tax from its customers. This aspect of Kirby J's judgment is extracted at pp 664 and 696.

Assume that the appellant retailers commenced proceedings in restitution directly against the New South Wales Government to recover licence fees that Rothmans had paid over to it. Would the retailers have been able to establish that the payments of the fees were 'at their expense'?

SUBTRACTION FROM A THIRD PARTY

It has long been established that a plaintiff, who is entitled by virtue of her office to receive certain fees or rents from a third party, may recover the fees or rents from the defendant who has received them in usurpation of the plaintiff's office. Birks views these 'usurpation of office' cases as the central example[39] of the doctrine of 'interceptive subtraction'. Birks argues that the gain will be at the plaintiff's expense even though paid by a third party where 'the wealth in question would certainly have arrived in the plaintiff if it had not been

---

39 Other examples, for which, however, there is a sparsity of authority, are cases of attornment and secret trusts: Birks, *An Introduction to the Law of Restitution*, rev edn, 1989, pp 134–35; Goff and Jones, *The Law of Restitution*, 5th edn, 1998, pp 38–40.

intercepted by the defendant *en route* from the third party'.[40] Other commentators however view the usurpation of office cases as an exception to the requirement of subtraction from the plaintiff.[41]

Boyter v Dodsworth (1796) 6 Term Rep 681; 101 ER 770 King's Bench Division

The plaintiff, who held the offices of belfry sexton and church sexton of the Salisbury Cathedral, was authorised to show people around the Cathedral. The defendant usurped the plaintiff's office by himself showing people around the Cathedral, for which endeavours he received tips from the visitors. The plaintiff brought an action against the defendant seeking recovery of the tips as monies had and received. The plaintiff admitted that there was no regular fee for showing people around the Cathedral, but gave evidence that it was usual for visitors to give gratuities in varying amounts.

Lord Kenyon CJ: [683] There is no ground on which this action can be supported. If there had been certain fees annexed to the discharge of certain duties belonging to this office, and the defendant had received them an assize would have lain; and the action for money had and received to recover fees has always been considered as being substituted in the place of an assize. But there is no pretence to say that an assize will lie for a gratuity, for money given which the party might have refused to give if he had pleased. And with regard to natural justice; the person who performs the duty is in justice entitled to the money given for such duty: here the defendant in fact performed the service, and on principles of natural justice he is entitled to the reward. If there had been regular fees due for the duties performed, and the defendant had intruded into the offices, the plaintiff might either have supported an action for money had and received or for disturbing him in his office.

Ashburt J: This is a *damnum sine injuria*, for which no action will lie; the plaintiff has not been injured, for the defendant had the trouble of shewing the church.

Grose J: The grant only permits the plaintiff to shew the church, but that is not the grant of any office. The sums given for shewing the church are mere gratuities; and the law does not imply any promise by the defendant to restore to the plaintiff the money so received by the former for his own labour. If there were any appropriated fees, the case would be different; but the sums of money paid to the defendant were not fees, but gratuities for the trouble he had taken.

Lawrence J: The argument in support of the rule proceeds on a supposition that the plaintiff would have received the money that the defendant has received: but it depends entirely on the behaviour and civility of the person shewing the church; and *non constat* that anything would have been paid to the plaintiff, if he had shewn it.

Commentary and questions

Why did the court disallow the plaintiff's claim? Did it reject the concept of interceptive subtraction?

---

40 Birks, *An Introduction to the Law of Restitution*, rev edn, 1989, pp 133–34.

41 Smith, 'Three-party restitution: a critique of Birks' theory of interceptive subtraction' (1991) 11 OJLS 481; Burrows, *The Law of Restitution*, 1993, pp 49–51; Goff and Jones, *The Law of Restitution*, 5th edn, 1998, pp 38–40.

One major concern with the concept of interceptive subtraction is that it potentially exposes the defendant to double liability. Using the principal case as an example, the duped visitors would have been able to recover on a restitutionary claim the amount of their tips from the defendant on the basis that they were paid under a mistake of fact. The prospect of double liability would have become a problem had the court also recognised the plaintiff sexton's claim. Accordingly, the doctrine of interceptive subtraction might potentially place the defendant in the position of having to make restitution both to the third party on the basis that the money was immediately subtracted from that party, and to the plaintiff on the basis of interceptive subtraction.

In order to avoid the spectre of double liability, the doctrine of interceptive subtraction should be limited to cases where the third party was under a legal obligation to make the payment to the plaintiff. This is the view taken in the following case.[42] On this view, recovery was properly denied in *Boyter v Dodsworth* where no such legal obligation existed. If payment by the third party to the defendant is recognised as discharging the obligation owed to the plaintiff to make the payment, the third party will have no interest in suing the defendant and the contest becomes one between the plaintiff and defendant.[43] Unfortunately, there is no clear authority to the effect that payment to the defendant discharges the third party's liability to the plaintiff.

Official Custodian for Charities v Mackey (No 2)
[1985] 1 WLR 1308 Chancery Division

The plaintiffs granted a long term lease of a property to a company with a condition entitling re-entry if the company should go into liquidation. The company subleased the property and also raised money by mortgaging the lease. The mortgagees appointed joint receivers under their mortgage who proceeded to collect rents from the sub-lessees and to manage the property. The company went into liquidation and on 20 July 1982 the plaintiffs served a writ on the company seeking forfeiture of the lease. The lease was eventually forfeited by an order of the Court of Appeal on 18 April 1984. The Court of Appeal ordered the company to pay mesne profits (damages for trespass) from 20 July 1982 until the date of the Court of Appeal's order. This judgment for damages was satisfied. The joint receivers continued to collect rents and to manage the property on behalf of the mortgagees. The plaintiffs then commenced proceedings against the receivers and mortgagees seeking injunctions to restrain them from receiving moneys from sub-lessees and managing the property. On the hearing of the motion Scott J, on 15 June 1984, held that the plaintiffs were entitled to the property freed from the lease and mortgages and that the receivers had no right to collect rents or manage the property. The plaintiffs commenced proceedings against the receivers for the difference between the mesne profits and the amount of rent actually received from the sub-lessees for the period from 20 July 1982 until 14 June 1984. The differential between the mesne profits which the receivers paid to the plaintiffs as

---

42 *Official Custodian for Charities v Mackey (No 2)* (1985), p 1314.
43 Goff and Jones, *The Law of Restitution*, 5th edn, 1998, 38–40.

damages, and the actual rent received by the receivers from the sub-lessees, was in the order of £1 million.

Nourse J: [Nourse J held that the receivers were entitled to the rents collected from the sub-lessees, but discussed what the position would have been had the receivers been trespassers who were not entitled to the rents.] [1314] In Goff and Jones, *The Law of Restitution* the case of a person who wrongly collects another's rents is treated as an example of a wider class of case where the defendant, intervening without right between the plaintiff and a third party, renders himself accountable to the plaintiff for the sum which he receives from the third party. It seems to me that it is of the essence of all those cases both that there is a contract or some other current obligation between the third party and the plaintiff on which the defendant intervenes and that the third party is indebted to the plaintiff in the precise amount of the sum [1315] which he pays to the defendant, so that he cannot claim repayment from the defendant in the face of a claim made against the defendant by the plaintiff. It is that which enables the plaintiff to sue the defendant without joining the third party, who no longer has any interest in the subject matter of the suit. It would be a waste of time and money if the plaintiff had to sue the third party and the latter had to sue the defendant. The suit for money had and received avoids circuity of action.

[Counsel for the receivers] submitted that there was no analogy between the wrongful collection of rents and the present case, on the ground that there was here no contract between the subtenants and the plaintiffs for the payment of rent or any other sum. Admittedly the subtenants were liable to pay mesne profits to the plaintiffs, but they are not owed until they are sued for and judgment has been entered. Accordingly, there was no contractual or other current obligation between the subtenants and the plaintiffs and no intervention by the receivers. In my judgment this simple view of the matter is probably conclusive of the point. But there is more to come. I will assume, contrary to the view just expressed, that the receivers could properly be described as persons who, without right, intervened between the subtenants and the plaintiffs. I will also assume that it is immaterial for this purpose that the payments were made and received in the honest belief on both sides that they were rent owed by the subtenants to the receivers. There still remains this difficulty. It cannot be assumed that the amount of mesne profits for which the subtenants were liable to the plaintiffs was the precise equivalent of the sums which they paid to the receivers. Suppose that they exceeded the amount of the mesne profits. It would be most unjust if the plaintiffs were allowed to claim the whole from the receivers. In that event the subtenants would have an interest in the subject matter of the suit between the plaintiffs and the receivers. I conceive that they would be entitled to set up the mistake of fact under which the sums were paid to the receivers and claim repayment of the excess. Circuity of action would be inevitable.

In all the circumstances I am quite unable to see how the plaintiffs could ever have had an action against the receivers for money had and received. Assuming that they could not or did not sue the receivers for mesne profits, their remedy was to sue the subtenants for mesne profits. No doubt the subtenants could then have sued the receivers for the recovery of sums paid under a mistake of fact. But whether that be right or wrong it cannot give the plaintiffs a right to recover the sums paid by the subtenants to the receivers.

On this fundamental ground I hold that the plaintiffs' claim to recover the moneys as moneys had and received fails ...

[Nourse J went on to hold that, in any event, the plaintiffs were estopped from suing the receivers in restitution as they had earlier obtained judgment on the action in tort for mesne profits.]

Questions

According to Nourse J, what circuity of action will result from denying the plaintiff a claim directly against the usurper? Why then were the plaintiffs precluded from bringing a restitutionary claim against the receivers in this case?

CHAPTER 4

THE UNJUST FACTOR

THE NATURE OF THE UNJUST FACTOR

The plaintiff must prove a principled ground of recovery or 'unjust factor'.[1] It is not enough merely to allege the enrichment is unjust 'by reference to some subjective evaluation of what is fair or unconscionable'.[2] The unjust factors grounding recovery are those that have been identified in the case law as a ground for reversing unjust enrichments and for which a body of principle has developed throughout the precedents.[3] In determining whether a new unjust factor should be accepted the court will analogise with existing unjust factors and will evaluate the proposed new unjust factor against the framework of the concept of unjust enrichment.[4]

THE UNJUST FACTORS

Recognised unjust factors

A number of unjust factors have been recognised by the courts in Australia:

(1) mistake (including ignorance);

(2) duress;

(3) colour of office;

(4) legal compulsion;

(5) necessitous intervention;

(6) total failure of consideration;

(7) free acceptance;

(8) illegality;

(9) unauthorised payments out of consolidated revenue;

(10) *ultra vires* demand by a public authority.

---

1   *Pavey & Matthews Pty Ltd v Paul* (1987), pp 256–57 (see extract, p 15); *David Securities Pty Ltd v Commonwealth Bank of Australia* (1992), pp 378–79 (see extract, p 30); *Lipkin Gorman v Karpnale Ltd* (1991), p 578 (see extract, p 595); *Kleinwort Benson Ltd v Lincoln City Council* (1998), p 56 (see extract, p 126).

2   *David Securities Pty Ltd v Commonwealth Bank of Australia* (1992), p 379 (see extract, p 30).

3   *Australia and New Zealand Banking Group Ltd v Westpac Banking Corporation* (1988), p 673 (see extract, p 25).

4   *Pavey & Matthews Pty Ltd v Paul* (1987), p 257 (see extract, p 15).

These factors can be categorised as falling into three main groups: non-intentional transfer, acceptance and policy-motivated factors.[5] Factors (1) to (6) can be categorised as cases of non-intentional transfer. Mistake and the various forms of illegitimate pressure operate to vitiate the plaintiff's intention that the defendant should retain the enrichment. Total failure of consideration also falls within this category. It is based on qualified intent, in that the plaintiff intends the enrichment to be retained only on the condition that the defendant renders the agreed counter-performance. The unjust factor of free acceptance (factor 7) falls into a category of its own; focusing as it does on the defendant's conduct rather than the plaintiff's intent. Factors (8) to (10) are based largely on policy considerations rather than the plaintiff's intent or the defendant's conduct.

CAUSATION

'But for' and causation

As a general rule, the plaintiff must establish on the balance of probabilities that the operative unjust factor was a cause of the defendant's receipt of the benefit. In *David Securities Pty Ltd v Commonwealth Bank of Australia* (1992), pp 377–78 (see extracts, pp 102 and 110), the High Court emphasised that the plaintiff's mistake must have been causative of the enrichment. As with the law of torts, the general test of causation in restitution is the 'but for' test; that is, the plaintiff would not have conferred enrichment on the defendant but for the operation of the unjust factor.[6] These principles are illustrated in the following case.

Holt v Markham [1923] 1 KB 504 English Court of Appeal

The defendant was on the emergency list of the Royal Air Force and was entitled to a gratuity upon demobilisation. The plaintiffs mistakenly paid the defendant his gratuity at a higher rate than he would have been entitled to had he not been on that list. The plaintiffs paid the higher gratuity in ignorance of the fact that the defendant was on the emergency list, but also having forgotten the existence of the regulation providing that officers on that list were to be paid the gratuity at a lower rate. The ignorance of the regulation, and accordingly of the significance of officers being on the emergency list, was a mistake of law which has never been recognised as a ground of recovery in restitution law in England.

Bankes LJ: [510] [Having stated the facts and referred to the correspondence above set out, his Lordship came to the conclusion that the plaintiffs in paying the money to the defendant did not act under any mistake of fact at all. Even if the clerk in the plaintiffs' office who drew up the order for the payment of the gratuity did not know that the defendant was on the emergency list, that was not a mistake which caused the payment to be made, for it appeared clear from the correspondence that the plaintiffs did not until long after that payment appreciate the materiality of an

---

5   See generally Birks, *An Introduction to the Law of Restitution*, rev edn, 1989, Chapter IV.
6   Burrows, *The Law of Restitution*, 1993, pp 25–27; *Marshall v Marshall* (1999), p 178 (see extract, p 394).

officer being on that list. The provisions of Order 263 of 1919 appeared to have been altogether overlooked. The plaintiffs' mistake, if any, was one of law; it resulted from a failure to apply what was now said to be the true construction of the Orders relating to gratuities to the defendant's case. The plaintiffs consequently could not recover.]

Warrington LJ: [511] ... The first question then is: Have the plaintiffs established that this money was paid under a mistake of fact? In my opinion they have not. It seems to me that when the position of this officer and the various and conflicting Orders, which might or might not be applicable to [412] his case, are considered the mistake (if there was any mistake at all, as to which I am not satisfied) was not a mistake of fact, but arose from a misapplication or misconstruction of the Orders having regard to the special circumstances of the case. That the defendant's case was a special one appears from a letter from the Admiralty to the Air Ministry, dated 15 May 1922, in which they say that he should be treated as being upon the emergency list for part of his service and as an officer holding a temporary commission for the rest of his service, and upon the receipt of which letter the Air Ministry agreed to reduce the amount of the disallowance. How, in the face of that admission, that the fact of the defendant having been on the emergency list was left out of consideration, it can be said that his having been on the list gave rise to a mistake of fact inducing the payment of the gratuity, I cannot understand ...

Scrutton LJ: [Scrutton LJ held that the plaintiff was estopped from recovering the money and then turned to consider the question whether there was, in any event, a causative mistake of fact.] [515] But I desire further to say that I am not at all satisfied that there was in this case any mistake of fact in the sense in which that term is used in the cases, such for instance as *Kelly v Solari* (1841), where Parke B thus expresses the principle: 'I think that where money is paid to another under the influence of a mistake, that is, upon the supposition that a specific fact is true, which would entitle the other to the money, but which fact is untrue, and the money would not have been paid if it had been known to the payer that the fact was untrue, an action will lie to recover it back.' It is said here that the specific fact which was supposed to be true, the knowledge of the untruth of which would have prevented the plaintiffs from paying the money, was that the defendant was not on the emergency list. But if they had known that he was on that list that would in my opinion have made no difference, for I am satisfied that at that time no one appreciated what the effect was of an officer being on that list. An officer on the emergency list was a very rare person. We have been furnished with a very long list, containing hundreds of names, of officers transferred from the Navy to the Air Force. I have looked through the whole of the names, under the letters E to M inclusive, and the only name I can find indicated as being on the emergency list is that of the defendant. If therefore those letters fairly represent the [516] rest of the alphabet the defendant's case was a most exceptional one. I come therefore to the conclusion that the mistake of the plaintiffs, which was partly one of fact and partly of construction, was in no respect connected with the payment of the money ...

Commentary

The plaintiff's claim for restitution in the principal case failed as the payment was not caused by a relevant mistake of fact; even had the plaintiff been aware the defendant was on the emergency list it would in any event have still paid the higher gratuity, as it failed to appreciate the materiality of an officer being on that list. As a mistake of law could not found recovery in restitution, the plaintiff could not establish that the payment of the higher amount had been caused by an operative unjust factor. In Australia, now that mistake of law has been recognised as an unjust factor in restitution,[7] the requirement of causation would be satisfied in the circumstances of *Holt v Markham*, as the two sufficient causes of the payment are both recognised unjust factors.[8]

Lack of causation was also one of the reasons for the denial of the mistake claim in *Roxborough v Rothmans of Pall Mall Australia Ltd* (1999) at both first instance and on appeal to the Full Court of the Federal Court. The appellant tobacco retailers bought tobacco products from Rothmans. Both Rothmans and the retailers were liable by legislation to pay licence fees on tobacco products sold by them. The contractual arrangement between Rothmans and the retailers was that the retailers paid to Rothmans the amount of the licence fees as part of the total contract price of the tobacco products, and Rothmans would then pass on those fees to the Government as and when required. The legislation was subsequently held to be unconstitutional[9] and the retailers claimed to be entitled to recover certain of the licence fees on the ground, *inter alia*, that they had been paid under a mistake of law. At first instance and on the appeal to the Full Court of the Federal Court the claim based on mistake was rejected on the basis that, if there was a mistake, the mistake had not caused the payments. The evidence established that the retailers paid the total contract price demanded by Rothmans, including the component representing licence fees, because they could not risk a decision by Rothmans not to supply them with the tobacco products if they withheld the fees. Hill and Lehane JJ in the Full Court put it this way, p 348:

> [A]ll of the retailers were aware, at least, that there was a constitutional challenge to the validity of the Act. And none gave evidence that he would not, but for a mistake, have paid the full amount claimed by the invoices. In the absence of such evidence, to infer that any of the retailers would not have paid the full amount would be a bold step indeed. They could, as they did, continue to pay the full amount in the knowledge that they could recoup it from their own purchasers. The natural inference, in our view, is that this is what they would have done rather than run the risk, at least, of a dispute with Rothmans.

---

7   *David Securities v Commonwealth Bank of Australia* (1992) (see extract, p 110).

8   Burrows, *The Law of Restitution*, 1993, p 25.

9   *Ha v New South Wales* (1997).

This case was appealed to the High Court of Australia, which by majority allowed the retailers' claim on a different ground (see extracts, pp 27 and 81). Kirby J (who dissented) was alone in discussing the mistake claim. His Honour rejected the claim on the basis that the cause of the payments was the obligation of the retailers to pay the money under binding contracts, not any mistake as to the constitutional validity of the legislation.[10]

Cases involving illegitimate pressure

The courts have not insisted on proof of 'but for' causation where the unjust factor is based on illegitimate pressure by the defendant, such as duress. In these cases two principles apply: first, a rebuttable presumption of causation arises once the plaintiff establishes that illegitimate pressure was exercised, and secondly, the plaintiff need only establish that the illegitimate pressure was *one of the reasons* for the plaintiff conferring the enrichment. The claim will not fail even if the evidence shows that the plaintiff would have conferred the enrichment anyway for other, non-restitutionary reasons. These causation principles were stated in *Crescendo Management Pty Ltd v Westpac Banking Corporation* (1988), p 46:[11]

> It is unnecessary ... for the victim to prove that the illegitimate pressure was the sole reason for him entering into the contract. It is sufficient that the illegitimate pressure was one of the reasons for the person entering into the agreement. Once the evidence establishes that the pressure exerted on the victim was illegitimate, the onus lies on the person applying the pressure to show that *it made no contribution to the victim entering into the agreement*. [Emphasis added.]

---

10 At pp 369–70. In this regard Kirby J accepted the arguments advanced in Bryan and Ellinghaus, 'Fault lines in the law of obligations: *Roxborough v Rothmans of Pall Mall Australia Ltd*' (2000) 22 Syd LR 636, p 658. See also Bryan, 'Where the constitutional basis for payment has failed (*Roxborough v Rothmans of Pall Mall Australia*)' [2000] 2 RLR 218, pp 222–23.

11 See also *Barton v Armstrong* (1973) (see extract, p 219) where the majority held that causation had been established despite a finding that the plaintiff would have entered into the contract for commercial reasons, even had the illegitimate pressure not been exerted. Compare *Dimskal Shipping Co SA v International Transport Workers Federation* (1992), p 165 (see extract, p 248) (the illegitimate pressure must be a 'significant cause').

CHAPTER 5

MONEY PAID UNDER A MISTAKE

THE NATURE OF MISTAKES GROUNDING LIABILITY

Mistake and ignorance

The central conception of a 'mistake' is a positive but mistaken belief about a particular factual or legal state of affairs. There is no significant judicial authority on the test to be applied to determine at what point a certain level of suspicion as to the true position will convert the plaintiff's state of mind from a mistaken to a correct one. Perhaps the best approach is that suggested by Andrew Burrows[1] who argues simply that the plaintiff should be held to be acting under a mistake where, although the plaintiff might have some suspicion about or knowledge of, the true position, he or she can nevertheless be said to have been greater than 51% mistaken.[2]

The majority of the High Court in *David Securities v Commonwealth Bank of Australia* (1992) (see extract, p 110) indicated that the notion of mistake includes 'sheer ignorance of something relevant to the transaction in hand' (p 369). In that case the plaintiff was acting under a mistake where it paid withholding tax to the Bank in ignorance of the fact that legislation imposed the obligation to pay withholding tax upon the Bank itself. However a debate still exists as to whether ignorance of the fact *that a transfer of money has taken place at all* should constitute an independent ground of recovery.[5] There is little judicial authority on this question.[6]

---

1 Burrows, *The Law of Restitution*, 1993, pp 101–03.

2 For an example of a case where the plaintiff was not mistaken, see *Lamesa Holding BV v Federal Commissioner of Taxation* (1999), where it was held that a taxpayer had not paid tax under mistake, but only after it had received legal advice and decided to appeal the assessment.

5 An example of such a situation would be if the plaintiff's money was embezzled by a third party and paid to the defendant.

6 Goff J in *Barclays Bank Ltd v Simms* (1980) (see extract, p 99) considered that mistake would encompass a computer malfunction which causes multiple payments of money to be made in error. There is little other judicial authority yet to support this. For a thorough academic analysis of ignorance as an unjust factor see Fitzgerald, 'Tracing at law, the exchange product theory and ignorance as an unjust factor in the law of unjust enrichment' (1994) 13 U Tas Law Rev 116.

Mistake and misprediction

A 'mere misprediction' is not a mistake, and will not ground recovery.[7] A misprediction is a mistaken belief or prediction about whether an event will occur in the future, rather than a mistaken belief about (or lack of awareness of) an existing factual or legal matter.[8] A misprediction is 'nothing but the taking of a risk, an exercise of judgment which turns out badly rather than a judgment vitiated'.[9] Liability for a misprediction will arise only on proof of conduct by the defendant encouraging the plaintiff's expectation of what will occur in the future (that is, free acceptance)[10] or where the money was paid on an understanding that adjustments will take place in the future.[11]

The nature of the mistake is irrelevant

Traditionally, the courts placed restrictions on the type of mistake that could ground a restitutionary claim. Payments made under a mistake of fact were actionable only if the mistake was a 'liability mistake',[12] or alternatively was 'fundamental' to the transaction.[13] Payments made under a mistake of law were not generally recoverable. However modern courts have refused to draw distinctions based upon the nature of the mistake involved.[14] A *prima facie* mistake claim will be established where the plaintiff can show that the mistake (whether of fact or law) caused the payment to the defendant.[15] In recognition of the fact that a greater number of payments will be recoverable under this modern approach, the courts have indicated that they will develop new, or expand existing, defences to place appropriate limitations upon recovery.[16]

---

7   *Commissioner of State Revenue (Vic) v Royal Insurance Australia Ltd* (1994), p 89 *per* Brennan J (see extract, p 120); *Dextra Bank & Trust Company Ltd v Bank of Jamaica* (2001) (see extract, p 623).

8   *Strang Patrick Stevedoring Pty Ltd v The 'Sletter'* (1992), p 524; *Marriott Industries Pty Ltd v Mercantile Credits Ltd* (1990), p 238; *Cadorange Pty Ltd v Tanga Holdings Pty Ltd* (1990), p 32; *Sunstar Fruit Pty Ltd v Cosmo* (1995), p 225.

9   Birks, *An Introduction to the Law of Restitution*, rev edn, 1989, p 278.

10 *Strang Patrick Stevedoring Pty Ltd v The 'Sletter'* (1992), p 524; Birks, *ibid*, pp 147, 278.

11 *Commissioner of State Revenue (Vic) v Royal Insurance Australia Ltd* (1994), p 89 *per* Brennan J (see extract, p 120). The basis of recovery in that circumstance has been variously described as implied contract, estoppel or total failure of the basis of the return: Merralls, 'Restitutionary recovery of taxes after the *Royal Insurance* case', in McInnes (ed), *Restitution: Developments in Unjust Enrichment*, 1996, pp 118, 120); Butler, 'Restitution of overpaid taxes, windfall gains and unjust enrichment: *Commissioner of State Revenue (Vic) v Royal Insurance Australia Ltd*' (1995) 18(2) UQLJ 318.

12 *Aiken v Short* (1856), p 215 *per* Bramwell B (see extract, p 97); *Kelly v Solari* (1841) (see extract, p 139); *Commonwealth Trading Bank v Reno Auto Sales Pty Ltd* (1967).

13 *Porter v Latec Finance (QLD) Ltd* (1964); *Morgan v Ashcroft* (1938), p 66.

14 See, in particular, *Barclays Bank Ltd v Simms* (1980) (see extract, p 99); *David Securities Pty Ltd v Commonwealth Bank of Australia* (1992) (see extract, p 110); *Commissioner of State Revenue (Vic) v Royal Insurance Australia Ltd* (1994) (see extract, p 120); *Kleinwort Benson Ltd v Lincoln City Council* (1999) (see extract, p 126).

15 *David Securities Pty Ltd v Commonwealth Bank of Australia* (1992) (see extract, p 110); *Kleinwort Benson Ltd v Lincoln City Council* (1999) (see extract, p 126).

16 *Barclays Bank Ltd v Simms* (1980) (see extract, p 99); *David Securities Pty Ltd v Commonwealth Bank of Australia* (1992) (see extract, p 110).

The negligence of the plaintiff does not bar recovery

The plaintiff's claim will not be affected by the fact that he or she was negligent in failing to properly investigate the circumstances of the payment.[17] In *Kelly v Solari* (1841) an insurance company negligently paid out a claim under an insurance policy that had lapsed. Its negligence in failing to properly investigate the status of the policy did not prevent recovery:

> [I]f [the money] is paid under the impression of the truth of a fact which is untrue, it may, generally speaking, be recovered back, however careless the party paying may have been, in omitting to use due diligence to inquire into the fact ... [p 59 *per* Parke B].

PAYMENTS MADE UNDER A MISTAKE OF FACT

Traditional position: the 'supposed liability' test

The traditional view was that a mistake of fact could not ground recovery unless it was a 'liability mistake', that is, a mistake as to a fact which, if true, would have given rise to a *legal liability* to make the payment. In other words, the payment must have been made with the intention of discharging a legal obligation.

Aiken v Short (1856) 1 H & N 210; 156 ER 1180 Exchequer Chamber

Short lent to George Carter the sum of £200 which was secured by a bond and by an equitable charge upon property which was later mortgaged to the plaintiff bank. Short died and the executor of his will claimed repayment of the £200 from George Carter, who referred the claim to the bank. The bank paid off the debt in order to remove the charge. It was subsequently discovered that George Carter had no valid title over the property and the bank claimed recovery of the £200 on the ground it had paid it under the mistaken belief that George Carter was the owner of the property.

Bramwell B: ... [1182] In order to entitle a person to recover back money paid under a mistake of fact, the mistake must be as to a fact which, if true, would make the person paying liable to pay the money; not where, if true, it would merely make it desirable that he should pay the money. Here, if the fact was true, the bankers were at liberty to pay or not, as they pleased. But relying on the belief that the defendant had a valid security, they, having a subsequent legal mortgage, chose to pay off the defendant's charge. It is impossible to say this case falls within the rule. The mistake of fact was, that the bank thought that they could sell the estate for a better price. It is true that if the plaintiff could recover back this money from the defendant, there would no difficulty in the way of the defendant suing Carter. In *Pritchard v Hitchcock* (1843) a creditor was held to be at liberty to sue

---

17　*Scottish Equitable plc v Derby* (2001), pp 824–25; *Dextra Bank & Trust Company v Bank of Jamaica* (2001) (see extract, p 636); *Kleinwort Benson Ltd v Lincoln City Council* (1999), p 399 (see extract, p 126); *Tutt v Doyle* (1990), approved on appeal *Tutt v Doyle* (1997), p 13; *Commercial Bank of Australia Ltd v Younis* (1979), p 450.

upon a guarantee of bills, though the bills had been in fact paid, but the money afterwards recovered back by the assignees of the acceptor, as having been paid by way of fraudulent preference. But that does not shew that the plaintiffs can maintain this action, and I am of opinion they cannot, having voluntarily parted with their money to purchase that which the defendant had to sell, though no doubt it turned out to be different to, and of less value than, what they expected ...

Commentary and questions

What do you suppose is the policy rationale underlying this restrictive rule?

The genesis of the 'supposed liability' test was an *obiter* statement by Parke B in the earlier case of *Kelly v Solari* (1841):

> ... where money is paid to another under the influence of a mistake, that is, upon the supposition that a specific fact is true, which would *entitle* the other to the money, but which fact is untrue, and the money would not have been paid if it had been known to the payer that the fact was untrue, an action will lie to recover it back, and it is against conscience to retain it; though a demand may be necessary in those cases in which the party receiving may have been ignorant of the mistake. [Emphasis added; see extract, p 139.]

The courts subsequently developed a number of exceptional categories of case where recovery was permitted despite the mistake not being a 'liability' mistake in terms of the principal case. For example, recovery was permitted where the plaintiff paid money to the defendant under the mistaken belief as to a legal liability to a third party to do so;[18] under a mistaken belief as to a moral obligation to do so;[19] under a mistaken belief that a liability to pay would accrue in the future;[20] and under a mistake as to the identity of the recipient.[21]

A alternative restriction on recovery of payments made under a mistake of fact that was sometimes suggested was that the mistake must have been as to a matter 'fundamental' to the transaction,[22] although the notion of fundamentality was never well defined.[23]

---

18 *Jones Ltd v Waring & Gillow Ltd* (1926).
19 *Larner v London City Council* (1949).
20 *Kerrison v Glyn, Mills, Currie & Co* (1911).
21 *Morgan v Ashcroft* (1938).
22 *Porter v Latec Finance (QLD) Ltd* (1964); *Morgan v Ashcroft* (1938), p 66.
23 *David Securities Pty Ltd v Commonwealth Bank of Australia* (1992), pp 377–78 (see extracts, pp 102 and 110).

Modern position: causative mistake

Modern courts have rejected the requirement that the mistake be a liability mistake and/or fundamental, instead preferring the approach that the plaintiff need only show a mistake that was causative.

Barclays Bank Ltd v WJ Simms, Son & Cooke (Southern) Ltd [1980] 1 QB 677 Queen's Bench

A housing association drew a cheque for £24,000 on its account with the plaintiff bank, Barclays, in favour of a building company. The following day a mortgagee of the company appointed a receiver and the housing association phoned Barclays and instructed it to stop the cheque. Barclays immediately entered that instruction into its computer and the following morning a staff member checked the computer amendment to ensure the stop instruction had been recorded accurately. The housing association subsequently confirmed its telephone instructions in writing to Barclays. The receiver of the building company presented the cheque, and Barclays' paying official paid it, having overlooked the stop instruction. Barclays commenced proceedings against the receiver and the building company claiming an entitlement to be repaid the £24,000 on the basis it had been paid under a mistake of fact.

Robert Goff J: [Robert Goff J discussed previous authorities including *Kelly v Solari* (1841) (see extract, p 139); and *Aiken v Short* (1856) (see extracts, pp 97 and 651); and the House of Lords' decisions of *Kleinwort, Sons & Co v Dunlop Rubber Co* (1907); *Kerrison v Glyn, Mills, Currie & Co* (1911); and *RE Jones Ltd v Waring and Gillow Ltd* (1926) and continued at p 695.] From this formidable line of authority certain simple principles can, in my judgment, be deduced: (1) If a person pays money to another under a mistake of fact which causes him to make the payment, he is *prima facie* entitled to recover it as money paid under a mistake of fact. (2) His claim may however fail if (a) the payer intends that the payee shall have the money at all events, whether the fact be true or false, or is deemed in law so to intend; or (b) the payment is made for good consideration, in particular if the money is paid to discharge, and does discharge, a debt owed to the payee (or a principal on whose behalf he is authorised to receive the payment) by the payer or by a third party by whom he is authorised to discharge the debt; or (c) the payee has changed his position in good faith, or is deemed in law to have done so.

To these simple propositions, I append the following footnotes. (a) Proposition 1: this is founded on the speeches in the three cases in the House of Lords, to which I have referred. It is also consistent with the opinion expressed by Turner J in *Thomas v Houston Corbett & Co* (1969), p 167. Of course, if the money was due under a contract between the payer and the payee, there can be no recovery on this ground unless the contract itself is held void for mistake (as in *Norwich Union Fire Insurance Society Ltd v Wm H Price Ltd*) (1934) or is rescinded by the plaintiff. (b) Proposition 2 (a): this is founded on the *dictum* of Parke B in *Kelly v Solari* (1841). I have felt it necessary to add the words 'or is deemed in law to so intend' to accommodate the decision of the Court of Appeal in *Morgan v Ashcroft* (1938), a case strongly relied on by the defendants in the present case, the effect of which I shall have to consider later in this judgment. (c) Proposition 2 (b): this is founded on the decision in *Aiken v Short* (1856), and upon *dicta* in *Kerrison v Glyn, Mills, Currie & Co* (1912). However, even if the payee has given consideration for the payment, for example by accepting the payment in discharge of a debt owed to him by a third party on whose behalf the payer is authorised to discharge it, that transaction may itself be set aside (and so provide no defence to the claim) if the payer's mistake was induced by the payee, or possibly even where the payee, being aware of the payer's mistake, did not receive the money in good faith: cf *Ward & Co v Wallis* (1900), pp 678–79 *per* Kennedy J. (d) Proposition 2 (c): this is founded on the statement of principle of Lord Loreburn LC in *Kleinwort, Sons & Co v Dunlop Rubber Co* (1907). I have deliberately stated this defence in broad [696] terms, making no reference to the question whether it is dependent on a breach of duty to the plaintiff or a representation by him independent of the payment, because these matters do not arise for decision in the present case. I have however referred to the possibility that the defendant may be deemed in law to have changed his position, because of a line of authorities concerned with negotiable instruments which I shall have to consider later in this judgment, of which the leading case is *Cocks v Masterman* (1829). (e) I have ignored, in stating the principle of recovery, defences of general application in the law of restitution, for example where public policy precludes restitution. (f) The following propositions are inconsistent with the simple principle of recovery established in the authorities: (i) that to ground recovery, the mistake must have induced the payer to believe that he was liable to pay the money to the payee or his principal; (ii) that to ground recovery, the mistake must have been 'as between' the payer and the payee. Rejection of this test has led to its reformulation (notably by Asquith J in *Weld-Blundell v Synott* (1940) and by Windeyer J in *Porter v Latec Finance (Qld) Pty Ltd*) (1964), p 204 in terms which in my judgment mean no more than that the mistake must have caused the payment.

In the case before me, [counsel for the defendants submitted] that I could not proceed on the basis of the simple principles I have stated, because I was precluded from so doing by binding authority, viz the decision of the Court of Appeal in *Morgan v Ashcroft* (1938). That case came on appeal from the county court. The respondent was a bookmaker, with whom the appellant was in the habit of making bets. The respondent claimed that his clerk mistakenly credited the appellant twice over with a sum of £24 2s 1d, and claimed to recover that sum from the appellant as having been paid under a mistake of fact. The county court judge held that the respondent was entitled to recover the money. The Court of Appeal allowed the appeal, holding that the money was not recoverable. The first ground of the court's decision was that, in order to ascertain whether there had been an overpayment, it would be necessary for the court to examine the state of account between the parties, and that the court could not do, by reason of the Gaming Act 1845. However the court also held that the money was in any event not recoverable as having been paid under a mistake of fact. [Counsel for the defendants] relied in particular on a passage in the judgment of Sir Wilfrid Greene MR, in which he stated, p 66:

> ... a person who intends to make a voluntary payment and thinks that he is making one kind of voluntary payment whereas upon the true facts he is making another kind of voluntary payment, does not make the payment under a mistake of fact which can be described as fundamental or basic.

That passage [counsel for the defendants] identified as being the crucial passage in Sir Wilfrid Greene MR's judgment on this point; and he submitted further that the expression 'voluntary payment' must here be understood as a payment made without legal obligation, so that, generally speaking, a person who makes a payment without the intention of discharging a legal obligation cannot recover the money from the payee although it has been paid under [697] a mistake of fact except possibly in circumstances where the mistake can be described as fundamental, for example where the mistake is as to the identity of the payee.

It is legitimate to observe the consequences of [counsel for the defendants'] submission. If he is right, money would be irrecoverable in the following, by no means far-fetched, situations: (1) a man, forgetting that he has already paid his subscription to the National Trust, pays it a second time; (2) a substantial charity uses a computer for the purpose of distributing small benefactions. The computer runs mad, and pays one beneficiary the same gift one hundred times over; (3) a shipowner and a charterer enter into a sterling charterparty for a period of years. Sterling depreciates against other currencies; and the charterer decides, to maintain the goodwill of the shipowner but without obligation, to increase the monthly hire payments. Owing to a mistake in his office, the increase in one monthly hire payment is paid twice over; (4) a Lloyd's syndicate gets into financial difficulties. To maintain the reputation of Lloyd's, other underwriting syndicates decide to make gifts of money to assist the syndicate in difficulties. Due to a mistake, one syndicate makes its gift twice over. It would not be difficult to construct other examples. The consequences of [counsel for the defendants'] submission are therefore so far-reaching that it is necessary to examine the *ratio decidendi* of this part of the decision in *Morgan v Ashcroft* to ascertain whether it produces the result for which counsel contends. [Robert Goff J then discussed the judgments in *Morgan v Ashcroft* and continued at p 698:]

... [I]t is by no means easy to determine the *ratio decidendi* of this part of the case. It may well be found in the opinion of both judges that an overpayment of betting debts by a bookmaker is not made under a mistake of fact sufficiently fundamental to ground recovery, apparently on the basis that the payment is in any event intended to be a purely voluntary gift, because 'the law prevents the plaintiff from saying that he intended anything but a present',[24] and the plaintiff is therefore deemed in law to intend that the payee shall be entitled to retain the money in any event.

That the *ratio decidendi* is not to be found in the passage from Sir Wilfrid Greene MR's judgment on which [counsel for the defendants] relied is shown by the fact that the subsequent decision of the Court of Appeal in *Larner v London County Council* (1949) is, in my judgment, inconsistent with that passage. In that case, the London County Council had resolved to pay all their employees who went to the war the difference between their war service pay and their civil pay until further order. Mr Larner was an ambulance driver employed by the council, who was called up in 1942. As a result of his failure to keep the council accurately informed about changes in his war service pay, the council overpaid the difference. In contending that the overpayment was irrecoverable, Mr Larner's counsel relied on the *dictum* of Bramwell B in *Aiken v Short* (1856). The Court of Appeal however held that the money was recoverable. Denning LJ, who delivered the judgment of the court, declined to follow that *dictum*, because he said, p 688, '... that *dictum*, as Scott, LJ pointed out in *Morgan v Ashcroft*, cannot be regarded as an exhaustive statement of the law'. He pointed out that the council:

---

24 *Morgan v Ashcroft* (1938), p 77 *per* Scott LJ.

... made a promise to the men which they were in honour bound to fulfil. The payments made under that promise were not mere gratuities. They were made as a matter of duty ...

[699] But he went on to state that it was irrelevant that the council's promise was unsupported by consideration or unenforceable by action. It was enough that the council would never have paid the money to Mr Larner had they known the true facts: see p 688 of the report. It is doubtful if the decision in *Larner v London County Council* (1949) is one of which Sir Wilfrid Greene MR would have approved; but, if I may say so with respect, it is entirely consistent with the principles of recovery established in the earlier decisions of the House of Lords to which I have referred. Accordingly it is those principles which I intend to apply in the present case. [Robert Goff J's determination of this case is extracted below.]

Commentary

The general principles which Robert Goff J formulated to govern claims for recovery of money paid under a mistake of fact were approved by the High Court of Australia in the following case.

David Securities Pty Ltd v Commonwealth Bank of Australia (1992) 175 CLR 353

The facts are stated at p 110.

Mason CJ, Deane, Toohey, Gaudron and McHugh JJ: ... [376] The proposition that there should be a *prima facie* entitlement to recover moneys paid when a mistake of fact or law has caused the payment has not been universally accepted. Two alternative formulations of the basis of recovery have been proposed: first, that the person making the mistaken payment must have supposed that he or she was legally liable to make the payment; and, secondly, that the mistake of the person making the payment must have been a fundamental one.[25] The first of these formulations can be subjected to the same criticism levelled at the traditional rule denying recovery in cases of mistake of law, namely, that it is illogical to concentrate upon the type of mistake made when the crucial factor is that the recipient has been enriched. To overturn the traditional rule and then replace it with a proposition incorporating the classic formulations of the liability approach by Parke B [377] in *Kelly v Solari* (1841) and Bramwell B in *Aiken v Short* (1856) would be counter-productive. In *Barclays Bank v WJ Simms Ltd* (1980), Goff J illustrated how existing authority had moved beyond the narrow liability approach. In *Australia & New Zealand Banking Group Ltd v Westpac Banking Corporation* (1988), this court implicitly accepted that view and we see no reason now to doubt that conclusion.

The second alternative formulation asserts that, in addition to being causative, the mistake must also be fundamental. This raises the question expressly left open in *Westpac Banking Corporation*. In that case, the court stated:

... it is unnecessary, for the purposes of the present case, to investigate what constitutes a 'fundamental mistake' for the purposes of the principle that money payable under a fundamental mistake of fact is *prima facie* recoverable

---

25 Beatson, *The Use and Abuse of Unjust Enrichment*, 1991, p 150.

by the payer: see, eg, *Porter v Latec Finance (Qld) Pty Ltd* (1964). It can, however, be said that we can see no reason to doubt the correctness of the view expressed or implicit in the judgments in the courts below to the effect that the notion of 'fundamental mistake' does not require either that the payer's mistake be shared by the payee or that the mistake be as to the existence of a fact which, if it had existed, would have resulted in the payee being under a legal obligation to make the payment: see *Commercial Bank of Australia Ltd v Younis* (1979); *Barclays Bank Ltd v WJ Simms Son & Cooke (Southern) Ltd* (1980); *Bank of New South Wales v Murphett* (1983). That having been said, it is preferable to leave for another day consideration of the question whether the requirement that the mistake be fundamental involves any more than that it appears that, without the mistake on the part of the payer, the payment would not have been made: cf, eg, *Porter* and *Barclays Bank Ltd v WJ Simms Son & Cooke (Southern) Ltd.*

The requirement that the mistake be fundamental as well as causative is not as restrictive as the liability approach considered above, but it has been suggested that the requirement is still a worthwhile precaution against a potential flood of claims and consequent insecurity of receipts.[26] The notion of fundamentality [378] is, however, extremely vague and would seem to add little, if anything, to the requirement that the mistake causes the payment. If the payer has made the payment because of a mistake, his or her intention to transfer the money is vitiated and the recipient has been enriched. There is therefore no place for a further requirement that the causative mistake be fundamental; insistence upon that factor would only serve to focus attention in a non-specific way on the nature of the mistake, rather than the fact of enrichment. If a strict approach is taken towards the issue of mistake so that a plaintiff bears the burden of establishing on the balance of probabilities that a causative mistake has been made, there would also be no need to appeal to the element of fundamentality as a limiting factor.

Commentary

The High Court did not identify the applicable test of causation, however presumably the plaintiff must establish that the mistake was a cause of the payment, in the sense that the plaintiff would not have made the payment had he known of his mistake at the time of payment.[27] A payment made for personal or commercial reasons irrespective of the mistake will be irrecoverable.[28]

---

26 Birks, *An Introduction to the Law of Restitution*, rev edn, 1989, p 159.

27 *Kleinwort Benson Ltd v Lincoln City Council* (1999), Lord Hope, pp 409–11 (see extract, p 126); *Marshall v Marshall* (1999), p 178; *Naomi Cotton Co-operative Ltd v IAMA Agribusiness Pty Ltd* (2001). See also *David Securities Pty Ltd v Commonwealth Bank of Australia* (1992), pp 392, 393 (see extracts, pp 102 and 110); Burrows, *The Law of Restitution*, 1993, p 24; Goff and Jones, *The Law of Restitution*, 5th edn, 1998, pp 191–92.

28 For examples of cases where causation failed see: *Halgido Pty Ltd v DG Capital Company Ltd* (1996); *Roxborough v Rothmans of Pall Mall Australia Ltd* (1999) (Full Court of the Federal Court).

Mistakes in cheque transactions

Barclays Bank Ltd v WJ Simms, Son & Cooke (Southern) Ltd
[1980] 1 QB 677 Queen's Bench

The facts are stated at p 99.

Robert Goff J: [Robert Goff J stated the general principles which should apply to the recovery of payments made under a mistake of fact (see extract, p 99). His Honour continued, at p 699:]

Where a bank pays a cheque drawn on it by a customer of the bank, in what circumstances may the bank recover the payment from the payee on the ground that it was paid under a mistake of fact?

It is a basic obligation owed by a bank to its customer that it will honour on presentation cheques drawn by the customer on the bank, provided that there are sufficient funds in the customer's account to meet the cheque, or the bank has agreed to provide the customer with overdraft facilities sufficient to meet the cheque. Where the bank honours such a cheque, it acts within its mandate, with the result that the bank is entitled to debit the customer's account with the amount of the cheque, and further that the bank's payment is effective to discharge the obligation of the customer to the payee on the cheque, because the bank has paid the cheque with the authority of the customer.

In other circumstances, the bank is under no obligation to honour its customer's cheques. If, however, a customer draws a cheque on the bank without funds in his account or agreed overdraft facilities sufficient to meet it, the cheque on presentation constitutes a request to the bank to provide overdraft facilities sufficient to meet the cheque. The bank has an option whether or not to comply with that request. If it declines to do so, it acts entirely within its rights and no legal consequences follow as between the bank and its customer. If however the bank pays the cheque, it accepts the request and the payment has the same legal consequences as if the payment had been made pursuant to previously agreed overdraft facilities; the payment is made within the bank's mandate, and in particular the bank is entitled to debit the customer's account, and the bank's payment discharges the customer's obligation to the payee on the cheque.

In other cases, however, a bank which pays a cheque drawn or purported to be drawn by its customer pays without mandate. A bank does so if, for example, it overlooks or ignores notice of its customer's death, or if it pays a cheque bearing the forged signature of its customer as drawer, but, more important for present purposes, a bank will pay without mandate if it overlooks or ignores notice of countermand of the customer who has drawn the cheque. In such cases the bank, if it pays the cheque, pays without mandate from its customer; and unless the customer is able to and does ratify the payment, the bank cannot debit the customer's account, nor will its payment be effective to discharge the obligation (if any) of the customer on the cheque, because the bank had no authority to discharge such obligation.

[700] It is against the background of these principles, which were not in dispute before me, that I have to consider the position of a bank which pays a cheque under a mistake of fact. In such a case, the crucial question is, in my judgment, whether the payment was with or without mandate. The two typical situations,

which exemplify payment with or without mandate, arise first where the bank pays in the mistaken belief that there are sufficient funds or overdraft facilities to meet the cheque, and second where the bank overlooks notice of countermand given by the customer. In each case, there is a mistake by the bank which causes the bank to make the payment. But in the first case, the effect of the bank's payment is to accept the customer's request for overdraft facilities; the payment is therefore within the bank's mandate, with the result that not only is the bank entitled to have recourse to its customer, but the customer's obligation to the payee is discharged. It follows that the payee has given consideration for the payment; with the consequence that, although the payment has been caused by the bank's mistake, the money is irrecoverable from the payee unless the transaction of payment is itself set aside. Although the bank is unable to recover the money, it has a right of recourse to its customer. In the second case, however, the bank's payment is without mandate. The bank has no recourse to its customer, and the debt of the customer to the payee on the cheque is not discharged. *Prima facie*, the bank is entitled to recover the money from the payee, unless the payee has changed his position in good faith, or is deemed in law to have done so.

It is relevant to observe that if, in *Chambers v Miller* (1862), the action had, instead of being a claim by the bearer for damages for false imprisonment, taken the form of a claim by the paying bank for recovery of the money as having been paid under a mistake of fact, that claim would, on the foregoing analysis, have failed, because the mistake of the bank in that case was a mistaken belief that there were sufficient funds in the customer's account to meet the cheque. Similarly in *Pollard v Bank of England* (1871) where a bank paid a bill of exchange accepted by one of their customers payable at the bank, in ignorance of the fact that the balance of the credit of the acceptors at the bank was insufficient to meet the bill and indeed that the acceptance had, in the general sense, stopped payment (and so were unable to pay their debts when they fell due), the bank was held to be unable to recover from the payee the money so paid: see p 631 of the report *per* Blackburn J, who delivered the judgment of the court. In both these cases, the bank acted within its mandate; but where the bank's mistake relates not to sufficiency of funds in its customer's account, but arises from ignorance or oversight of a notice of countermand, the bank acts without mandate, and the money is in my judgment *prima facie* recoverable.

[Robert Goff J rejected the argument that it was a defence to the plaintiff's claim that the plaintiff had failed to notify the defendants of its claim for repayment on the day the cheque was paid and continued at p 703:]

Application of the foregoing principles to the present case

In the light of the above principles, it is plain that in the present case Barclays are entitled to succeed in their claim. First, it is clear that the mistake of the bank, in overlooking the drawer's instruction to stop payment of the cheque, caused the bank to pay the cheque. Second, since the drawer had in fact countermanded payment, the bank was acting without mandate and so the payment was not effective to discharge the drawer's obligation on the cheque; from this it follows that the payee gave no consideration for the payment, and the claim cannot be defeated on that ground. Third, there is no evidence of any actual change of position on the part of either of the defendants or on the part of [the mortgagee]; and, since notice of dishonour is not required in a case such as this, the payee is not deemed to have changed his position by reason of lapse of time in notifying them of the plaintiff's error and claiming repayment.

I must confess that I am happy to be able to reach the conclusion that the money is recoverable by the plaintiff bank. If the bank had not failed to overlook its customer's instructions, the cheque would have been returned by it marked 'orders not to pay', and there would have followed a perfectly *bona fide* dispute between the association and the receiver on the question, arising on the terms of the building contract, whether the association was entitled to stop the cheque – which ought to be the real dispute in the case. If the plaintiff bank had been unable to recover the money, not only would that dispute not have been ventilated and resolved on its merits but, in the absence of ratification by the association, the plaintiff bank would have had no recourse to the association. Indeed, if under the terms of the building contract the money had not been due to the company, non-recovery by the plaintiff bank would have meant quite simply a windfall for the preferred creditors of the defendant company at the plaintiff bank's expense. As however I have held that the money is recoverable, the situation is as it should have been; nobody is harmed, and the true dispute between the association and the receiver can be resolved on its merits ...

Commentary and questions

According to Goff J, can a bank that has mistakenly overlooked a countermand on a cheque recover the amount of the mistaken payment from its customer? Can it recover from the payee?

According to Goff J, can a bank that paid out on a cheque mistakenly believing that there were sufficient funds in the customer's account to cover the cheque recover the amount of the mistaken payment from its customer? Can it recover from the payee? Why might it be argued that Goff J is adopting a fiction in concluding that the bank in making the payment is to be regarded as having consented to a request for an overdraft?[29]

There is Australian authority supporting Goff J's view that a bank that pays on a cheque which has been stopped will have a *prima facie* right of recovery against the payee, however this has usually been based on the (now discredited) reasoning that the bank's mistake was fundamental to the payment: *Commercial Bank of Australia Ltd v Younis* (1979); and *Bank of New South Wales v Murphett* (1983),[30] *per* Starke J (but see Crockett J who applied the principles formulated by Robert Goff J in the principal case).

A bank that pays out on a cheque with a forged signature[31] or that has been fraudulently altered in a material respect[32] can recover from the payee.

---

29 Ellinger, EP and Lemnicka, E, *Modern Banking Law* (Oxford: Clarendon Press, 1994), p 415; Mason and Carter, *Restitution Law in Australia*, 1995, pp 133–34.

30 Cf *Griffiths v Commonwealth Bank of Australia* (1994).

31 *National Westminster Bank Ltd v Barclays Bank International Ltd* (1975); *Barclays Bank Ltd v Simms* (1980), pp 701–03. For full discussion of this area see Dow, 'Restitution of payments on cheques with forged drawers' signatures: loss allocation under English law' [1996] 1 RLR 27.

32 *Imperial Bank of Canada v Bank of Hamilton* (1903).

Recovery from the customer would not be permitted as the bank had no mandate to pay out on the cheque.[33]

A number of academic articles have discussed the effect of mistake in cheque transactions.[34]

Mistakenly conferred gifts

The High Court is yet to address the question of mistakenly conferred gifts of money. It seems clear that the principles in *David Securities Pty Ltd v Commonwealth Bank of Australia* (1992) (see extracts, pp 102 and 110), which require merely that the mistake be causative of the payment, will apply where the mistake is about the nature or effect of the gift rather than the motive for making it. Thus, it has been said that a gift paid under a mistake as to the identify of a recipient,[35] or a donation paid to a charity in forgetfulness that it had already been paid,[36] would be recoverable on the basis of mistake. On the other hand, it has been suggested that a mistake which merely falsifies a matter going to motive should not be recoverable:[37]

> If a father, believing that his son has suffered a financial loss, gives him a sum of money, he surely could not claim repayment if he afterwards discovers that no such loss had occurred ... To hold the contrary would almost amount to saying that motive not mistake was the decisive matter.

Post-*David Securities* however the nature of the mistake should be treated as irrelevant[38] so that it arguably should not matter whether the mistake goes to motive or to some other fact; the real question is whether the mistake is causative.[39] There is support for this view in *University of Canterbury v Kent* (1995) where a plaintiff who had transferred shares to a scholarship fund on the mistaken assumption that it required more funds to pay out realistic scholarship awards was successful in recovering the shares. The plaintiff had not simply changed his mind about the donation but had acted on a false assumption that led him to make the transfer (p 81).

---

33   *Barclays Bank Ltd v Simms* (1980), pp 701–03.

34   Goode, 'The bank's right to recover money paid on a stopped cheque' (1981) 97 LQR 254; Nicholson, 'Recovery of money paid under a mistake of fact' (1986) 60 ALJ 459; Dow, 'Restitution of payments on cheques with forged drawers' signatures: loss allocation under English law' [1996] RLR 27.

35   *Morgan v Ashcroft* (1938), p 66.

36   *Barclays Bank Ltd v Simms* (1980), p 697 (see extract, p 99).

37   *Morgan v Ashcroft* (1938), p 66 *per* Sir Wilfrid Greene MR. The academics are in disagreement as to whether this limitation is justified: contrast Mason and Carter, *Restitution Law in Australia*, 1995, pp 125–26 and Goff and Jones, *The Law of Restitution*, 5th edn, 1998, pp 189–91.

38   *David Securities Pty Ltd v Commonwealth Bank of Australia* (1992) (see extracts, pp 102 and 110).

39   Goff and Jones, *The Law of Restitution*, 5th edn, 1998, pp 189–91.

PAYMENTS MADE UNDER A MISTAKE OF LAW

Traditional position: recovery generally not permitted

Brisbane v Dacres (1813) 5 Taunt 143; 128 ER 641 Common Pleas

The plaintiff paid to Admiral Dacres part of the freight money received for the carriage of bullion pursuant to a supposed naval custom, unaware that at the time of payment the custom had been abolished. The plaintiff later discovered his error and commenced proceedings against the Admiral's estate for repayment of the money.

Gibbs J: ... [152] We must take this payment to have been made under a demand of right, and I think that where a man demands money of another as a matter of right, and that other, with a full knowledge of the facts upon which the demand is founded, has paid a sum, he never can recover back the sum he has so voluntarily paid. It may be, that upon a further view he may form a different opinion of the law, and it may be, his subsequent opinion may be the correct one. If we were to hold otherwise, I think many inconveniences may arise; there are many doubtful questions of law: when they arise, the defendant has an option, either to litigate the question, or to submit to the demand, and pay the money. I think, that by submitting to the demand, he that pays the money gives it to the person to whom he pays it, and makes it his, and closes the transaction between them. He who receives it has a right to consider it as his without dispute: he spends it in confidence that it is his; and it would be most mischievous and unjust, [153] if he who has acquiesced in the right by such voluntary payment, should be at liberty, at any time within the statute of limitations, to rip up the matter, and recover back the money. He who received it is not in the same condition: he has spent it in the confidence it was his, and perhaps has no means of repayment. I am aware cases were cited at the bar, in which were *dicta* that sums paid under a mistake of the law might be recovered back, though paid with a knowledge of the facts; but there are none of these cases which may not be supported on a much sounder ground. [Gibbs J discussed the previous authorities, in particular *Farmer v Arundel* (1772); *Lowry v Bourdieu* (1780); *Bize v Dickason* (1786); and *Chatfield v Paxton* and concluded at p 157:] I am therefore of opinion this money cannot be recovered back. I think on principle that money which is paid to a man who claims it as his right, with a knowledge of all the facts, cannot be recovered back. I think it on principle, and I think the weight of the authorities is so, and I think the *dicta* that go beyond it, are not supported or called for by the facts of the cases. *Bilbie v Lumley* (1802), I think, is a decision to that effect; [158] and for these reasons, I am of the opinion, the plaintiff is not entitled to recover.

Chambre J (dissenting): ... As to the freight for the carriage of the public property, I think it stands on a different ground, and that the action is maintainable. The plaintiff had a right to it, and the defendant in conscience ought not to retain it. The rule is, that when he cannot in conscience retain it, he must refund it, if there is nothing illegal in the transaction: the case is different where there is an illegality. I do not think the case of *Chatfield v Paxton* applies much in this view of the question. I never heard of the several parts of that case till now, but I think there are sufficient authorities to say this person has paid this money in his own wrong, and that it may be recovered back. In the case of *Bilbie v Lumley*, there was a letter said to have been concealed, that ought to have been disclosed: this letter was shown to the underwriters, and they, after reading it, thought fit to pay the money. Now there the maxim *volenti non fit injuria* applies: in that case all argument was prevented by a question put by the court to the counsel. I am not aware of any particular danger in extending the law in cases of this sort, for they are for the furtherance of justice; neither do I see the application of the maxim used by Buller J in the case of *Lowry v Bourdieu*, and cited by the court in *Bilbie v Lumley*, [159] *ignorantia juris non excusat*, it applies only to cases of delinquency, where an excuse is to be made. I have searched far, to see if I could find any instance of similar application of this maxim. I have a very large collection of maxims, but can find no instance in which this has been so applied. I cannot see how it applies here ... Now the case against the plaintiff is not so strong as it has been stated. I do not find in the case that any demand was ever made of him, or any question mooted, upon which he thought it better to submit, than to litigate the point. No option ever presented itself to [160] him, and the maxim, *volenti non fit injuria* does not apply. It appears to me that the justice of the case with respect to the freight of the public treasure is entirely with the plaintiff ...

Heath J: ... There are two questions in this case. As to the question whether a payment made in ignorance of the law without ignorance of the facts, will enable a man to recover his money back again it is very difficult to say that there is any evidence of ignorance of the law here; an officer is sent on a profitable service, the admirals are in the habit of receiving a proportion of the officer's recompense, and it is very likely the officer should acquiesce in the demand. He might not like to contest the point with his superior officer ... [161] Lord Eldon, Chancellor in *Bromley v Holland* (1802), approves Lord Kenyon's doctrine [in *Chatfield v Paxton*] and calls it a sound principle, that a payment voluntarily made is not to be recovered back. The plaintiff ought not to recover.

Mansfield CJ: ... I find nothing contrary to *æquum et bonum*, to bring it within the case of *Moses v Macferlan*, in his retaining it. So far from its being contrary to *æquum et bonum*, I think it would be most contrary to *æquum et bonum*, if he were obliged to repay it back. For see how it is! If the sum be large, it probably alters the habits of his life, he increases his expenses, he has spent it over and over again; perhaps he cannot repay it at all, or not without great distress; is he then, five years and eleven months after, to be called on to repay it? [Mansfield CJ discussed authorities such as *Bilbie v Lumley* and concluded that the plaintiff should not be permitted to recover.]

Questions

What were the policy concerns underlying the prohibition on recovery for mistakes of law? Do these policy concerns apply with equal force to claims based on a mistake of fact?

Modern position: causative mistake

The mistake of law bar was eventually overturned by the High Court in 1992 in the following case of *David Securities Pty Ltd v Commonwealth Bank of Australia* (1992). The court there held that mistakes of law should be treated on the same basis as mistakes of fact, and hence would be recoverable provided that causation could be established.

The mistake of law bar has also been judicially overturned in England,[40] Canada[41] and South Africa[42] and has been abolished by legislation in New Zealand.[43]

David Securities Pty Ltd v Commonwealth Bank of Australia (1992) 175 CLR 353 High Court of Australia

The appellants entered into foreign currency loan transactions with the respondent bank. The loan agreements were secured by a mortgage and personal guarantees. Almost immediately upon entering into the loan agreements, adverse fluctuations in exchange rates caused a substantial increase in the amount of interest repayments and resulted in financial losses for the appellants, who subsequently defaulted on the loan transactions. Clause 8(b) of the loan agreements provided that the appellants were to pay additional amounts to the respondent representing the amount of withholding tax payable on the interest on the loan. This provision was an attempt to avoid the operation of Part VI of the Income Tax Assessment Act 1936 (Cwlth) which imposed the liability for paying withholding tax upon the lender. In particular, s 261 of that Act rendered void any provision of a mortgage which purported to impose on the borrowers the liability to pay the withholding tax. The appellants commenced proceedings against the respondent arguing in the Full Court of the Federal Court and in the High Court that s 261 rendered cl 8(b) void and that they could recover the moneys paid by them pursuant to cl 8(b) on the basis that they had made the payments under a mistake as to their legal liability to pay the withholding tax.

Mason CJ, Deane, Toohey, Gaudron and McHugh JJ: [Their Honours held that s 261 of the Act did operate to render void cl 8(b) of the loan agreements and turned to consider whether the appellants were entitled to restitution of the moneys paid under a mistake of law.]

[367] *Second issue: the sufficiency of the finding that there was a mistake of law*

... Notwithstanding that the pleadings did not throw up the specific issue whether the moneys in question were paid under a mistake, whether of fact or law, it is evident that the case was argued on that basis. Hill J [the trial judge] observed, with reference to the payments:

> These payments, if cl 8(b) was, as [a] result of s 261, void, were paid by the borrowers under a mistake of law, the mistake being that cl 8(b) required the payment to be made. So far as appears the payments were not made under protest ... and indeed, it is highly doubtful whether the borrowers' case, as pleaded, claimed at all a recovery of amounts wrongfully paid under the clause. However, I am content to assume that such a case was pleaded.

[368] His Honour went on to hold that money paid under a mistake of law was not recoverable.

---

40 *Kleinwort Benson Ltd v Lincoln City Council* (1999) (see extract, p 126).
41 *Air Canada v British Columbia* (1989).
42 *Wills Faber Enthoven Pty Ltd v Receiver of Revenue* (1992).
43 Judicature Act 1908 (NZ), ss 94A and 94B.

The appellants applied for leave to call evidence that the payments were made under a mistake. That application was evidently made during the course of addresses and was rejected, probably because his Honour was of the opinion that if the moneys were paid under a mistake, the mistake was one of law.

The full court said:

> Counsel for the bank submitted that the appellants had offered no direct evidence to the effect that without the mistake being made on their part, by regarding cl (8)(b) as valid rather than void, they would not have made payments pursuant to that sub-clause. However, in the circumstances of this case, there is sufficient evidence from which one can infer that the appellants would have made no payment but that which they regarded themselves as legally obliged to make pursuant to their contractual and security arrangements with the bank.

Having regard to the way in which the case was conducted at the trial, the issue whether payment was made under a mistake was litigated. Whether there was evidence to support the inference drawn by the full court and the finding that appears to have been made by the primary judge is not an easy question to determine. That is because neither the primary judge nor the full court has identified the evidence which sustains the finding or gives rise to the inference. In the circumstances, we are not satisfied the evidence warrants the drawing of such an inference. Certainly the fact that the bank required the payments to be made does not of itself warrant the drawing of such an inference, the more so since it is arguable that the appellants may have wished to ensure that there was a roll over, whatever their belief as to the existence of an obligation to do so.

But this conclusion does not mean that the appeal should be dismissed. If the court were to conclude that moneys paid under a mistake of law were recoverable, contrary to the views expressed by Hill J and the full court of the Federal Court, the matter should be remitted to the primary judge to enable him to reconsider the appellants' application to call evidence on the issue of mistake. His Honour refused that application in a context where he considered that moneys paid under a mistake of law were not recoverable. If that view be mistaken, then the application should be considered afresh.

[369] *Third issue: if the moneys were paid by the appellants under a mistake, are the appellants entitled to restitution?*

In considering this question, it is necessary to have regard to the nature of the mistake which, it is alleged, was made. In this respect the full court of the Federal Court stated:

> In the present case, the mistake related to the subsistence of the liability itself, and [was] not made simply because of what was or was not stated in the loan agreement or because of the existence of some related circumstance, such as the date on which a payment fell due. The mistake was as to the existence of s 261 and its operation to render void the purported contractual obligation in cl 8(b). This was a mistake of law for the purposes of this particular field of discourse, or at least a mistake as to law mixed with fact.

As Winfield makes clear, mistake not only signifies a positive belief in the existence of something which does not exist but also may include 'sheer ignorance of something relevant to the transaction in hand'.[44] A mistake of this latter kind, and one similar to the mistake allegedly made in this case, was found in *J & S Holdings Pty Ltd v NRMA Insurance Ltd* (1982). In that case, the failure of a money lender to comply with an Australian capital territory ordinance regulating loan contracts meant that the loan contract was void in so far as it provided for payment of a rate of interest higher than 12%. The borrower unsuccessfully sought repayment of the excess interest it had paid in compliance with the contractual provision for interest. The full court (Blackburn, Deane and Ellicott JJ) concluded that the borrower's mistake consisted of its 'ignorance of or inadvertence to the existence or operation of the general statutory provisions contained in s 12 of the ordinance' and denied recovery to the appellants on the basis of the so called traditional rule that restitution is not available in cases of a mistake of law. Their Honours referred to various authorities in other jurisdictions, as well as to textbooks, which reject the rule, but having noted that 'the distinction which has been drawn between mistake of fact and mistake of law has been subjected to much learned criticism and is often difficult to apply', observed that, at least as far as the Federal Court was concerned, the distinction was 'firmly entrenched'. Further, in that case, there was no insistence that the borrower show that it had protested before paying or that duress or involuntariness be proven in order for a [370] finding of mistake to be made, though the court referred to such matters in the context of when money paid under a mistake of law might be recoverable. Thus, in this case, the bank's claim that the appellants paid the additional amounts without protest is of little consequence in itself.

The full court in the present case also applied what was seen as the traditional rule precluding recovery in a case of mistake of law, quoting the statement of Williams J in *York Air Conditioning & Refrigeration (A/asia) Pty Ltd v The Commonwealth* (1949), p 30:

> A mistake in the construction of a contract is a mistake of law and payments made under a mistake of law cannot be recovered in an action for money had and received.

Like the full court in *J & S Holdings*, their Honours noted the criticism which the rule has attracted but nonetheless felt constrained to apply it, observing that it is open only to the High Court to remove the distinction between mistakes of fact and mistakes of law.[45]

The traditional rule

The *Restatement of the Law of Restitution* states:[46]

> Until the 19th century no distinction was made between mistake of fact and mistake of law and restitution was freely granted both in law and in equity to persons who had paid money to another because of a mistake of law.

In *Farmer v Arundel* (1772) De Grey CJ stated:

> When money is paid by one man to another on a mistake either of fact or of law, or by deceit, this action [ie, *assumpsit*] will certainly lie.

---

44 Winfield, 'Mistake of law' (1943) 59 LQR 327.

45 (1990) 23 FCR 33, p 35.

46 American Law Institute, 1937, p 179.

However, in *Bilbie v Lumley* (1802), Lord Ellenborough CJ refused recovery of moneys paid under a mistake of law. An underwriter sought recovery of moneys from a successful insurance claimant whom he had paid, unaware that non-disclosure by the insured of essential facts at the time of entering the insurance contract relieved the insurer from liability. The underwriter was in possession of all the facts which would have allowed him to deny liability. After counsel was unable to name a case in which recovery had been allowed to a plaintiff who was aware of all relevant facts, Lord Ellenborough CJ denied recovery on the basis of a maxim wholly inapplicable to the case, namely, *ignorantia juris non excusat*. [371] This approach appears to have been based on an *obiter dictum* in the judgment of Buller J in *Lowry v Bourdieu* (1780).[47] On its facts, the decision in *Bilbie v Lumley* was probably correct because the payment appears to have been made voluntarily and not under any mistake at all. Only a few years before, in *Cartwright v Rowley* (1799), Lord Kenyon CJ had stated:

> This action cannot be maintained, nor the money recovered back again by it: it has been paid by the plaintiff voluntarily; and where money has been so paid, it must be taken to be properly and legally paid; nor can money be recovered back again by this form of action, unless there are some circumstances to shew that the plaintiff paid it through mistake, or in consequence of coercion.

This was not a case of mistake of law. The plaintiff had employed the defendant, an engine maker, to make engines under the plaintiff's patent. While work was in progress, the plaintiff advanced money to the defendant, which he then sought to recover because the defendant had caused the plaintiff to miss a business opportunity by taking too long to complete the work. The plaintiff's payment was 'voluntary' in the sense that he had known all the relevant circumstances and yet had chosen to pay the defendant rather than withhold payment or dismiss him. A similar concept of voluntariness was adopted by Chambre J, in dissent, in *Brisbane v Dacres* (1813), where he concluded that the plaintiff was entitled to recover money paid under a mistake of law because he could not be said to have waived inquiry and chosen to settle the claim. In the same case, Gibbs J took a similar approach in principle, holding that, if a person paid money in response to a claim when fully aware of all the facts, he or she was deemed to have submitted to the demand.

It is on the basis of such opinions as this that it has been suggested that *Bilbie v Lumley* is authority for the limited proposition that payment made in settlement of an honest claim is irrecoverable.[48] However, rather than being confined to its facts, *Bilbie v Lumley* became recognised as authority for the broad proposition that recovery will not be ordered of moneys paid under a mistake of law. It was followed by the majority in *Brisbane v Dacres* (1813) where Gibbs J said:

> [372] ... where a man demands money of another as a matter of right, and that other, with a full knowledge of the facts upon which the demand is founded, has paid a sum, he never can recover back the sum he has so voluntarily paid.

Bilbie v Lumley was distinguished in *Kelly v Solari* (1841), a case allowing recovery of moneys paid under a mistake of fact. It thereby became entrenched as a decision denying recovery because the mistake of the plaintiff was one of law. Despite its

---

47   Cf the view of Lord Ellenborough adopted in the later case, *Perrott v Perrott* (1811).

48   Goff and Jones, *The Law of Restitution*, 3rd edn, 1986, pp 118–19.

dubious foundation, the principle gained such acceptance that Croom-Johnson J said of it that it was 'beyond argument at this period in our legal history'.[49]

The respondent claims that the principle has also been accepted in this court; however, an examination of the relevant cases, apart from the statement of Williams J in *York Air Conditioning* (1949), p 30, suggests that they may also be reconciled with the narrower principle of voluntary submission. In *Werrin v The Commonwealth* (1938), in which the plaintiff sought recovery of sales tax that he had paid upon second hand goods sold by him, Latham CJ stated:[50]

> The principle appears to me to be quite clear that if a person, instead of contesting a claim, elects to pay money in order to discharge it, he cannot thereafter, because he finds out that he might have successfully contested the claim, recover the money which he so paid merely on the ground that he made a mistake of law.

In *South Australian Cold Stores Ltd v Electricity Trust of South Australia* (1957), the plaintiff made monthly payments to the defendant of electricity charges assessed at an increased rate, then successfully challenged the validity of the minister's order increasing the charges and sought recovery of the excessive charges paid over. Prior to making the monthly payments, the plaintiff had objected to the increased charge and had even declined to pay the extra amount pursuant to the first monthly account. In a unanimous judgment, the court denied recovery. It stated:

> In the present case the only reason why the higher rates were not chargeable was because the formal requirements of the law were not observed by a third party for expressing or giving effect to the decision at which he had actually arrived. Neither he nor the trust were aware of his failure lawfully to exercise his authority. They were unaware because they did not perceive what was required or the true effect of what the document [373] contained. On the side of the company it was simply taken for granted that somehow or other the charges might be lawfully made. This seems to fall outside the reason of the rule under which an action of money had [and] received lies in cases of payment by mistake. Under that rule the action is available when the payee cannot justly retain the money paid to him because it would not have come to his hands if it had not been for a false supposition of fact on the part of the payer causing the latter to believe that he was compellable to make the payment or at all events that he ought to make it. It is to be noticed that Parke B in *Kelly v Solari* defines the requisite mistake as 'the supposition that a specific fact is true, which would entitle the other to the money, but which fact is untrue'.[51] According to the decision of Pilcher J in *Turvey v Dentons (1923) Ltd* (1953) it is too restrictive to say that the fact would if true have entitled the payee to the money; and perhaps the word 'specific' may also be too definite. But here there was nothing but an assumption that in some way or other the increased charge might lawfully be made and a readiness to comply with the payee's demand without more, a demand which but for formal defects in the authorisation would have been enforceable.

---

49   *Sawyer & Vincent v Window Brace Ltd* [1943] KB 32, p 34.
50   At p 159. See also p 168 *per* McTiernan J.
51   (1841) 9 M & W 54, p 58; 152 ER 24 Exchequer, p 26.

More recently, as has been mentioned, the full court of the Federal Court has applied the principle against recovery. In the case of *J & S Holdings* (1982), the full court quoted the above passage from *South Australian Cold Stores* and then stated:

> The insufficiency of mistake of law as the foundation of an action for recovery of money paid is commonly stated as a general principle or rule of law precluding any right of action in a case where the payment was voluntary ... It is preferable to frame the general rule in terms of insufficiency rather than in terms of preclusion. So stated, *the general rule is that a mistake of law does not, on its own,* found an action for the recovery of money paid: see, generally, *Kiriri Cotton Co Ltd v Dewani.*[52] [Emphasis added.]

An important feature of the relevant judgments in these three cases is the emphasis placed on voluntariness or election by the plaintiff. The payment is voluntary or there is an election if the plaintiff chooses to make the payment even though he or she believes a particular law or contractual provision requiring the payment is, or may be, invalid, or is not concerned to query whether payment is legally required; he or she is prepared to assume the validity of the obligation, or is prepared to make the payment [374] irrespective of the validity or invalidity of the obligation, rather than contest the claim for payment. We use the term 'voluntary' therefore to refer to a payment made in satisfaction of an honest claim, rather than a payment not made under any form of compulsion or undue influence. If such qualifying, factual circumstances are considered relevant, the sweeping principle that money paid under a mistake of law is irrecoverable or even the Federal Court's modification of that principle to the effect that mistake of law does not on its own found an action for the recovery of money paid is broader and more preclusive than is necessary. As the authorities cited earlier in explanation of the term 'mistake of law' make clear, the concept includes cases of sheer ignorance as well as cases of positive but incorrect belief. To define 'mistake' as the supposition that a specific fact is true, as Parke B did in *Kelly v Solari* (above), which was a mistake of fact case, leaves out of account many fact situations. A narrower principle, founded firmly on the policy that the law wishes to uphold bargains and enforce compromises freely entered into, would be more accurate and equitable.

The identification and acceptance of such a narrow principle is strongly supported by the difficulty and illogicality of seeking to draw a rigid distinction between cases of mistake of law and mistake of fact. The artificiality of this distinction and the numerous exceptions to it[53] lie behind many of the calls for abolition of the traditional rule. Judge Learned Hand called it 'that most unfortunate doctrine'.[54] The Supreme Court of Canada indicated its willingness to abolish the rule in its recent decision of *Air Canada v British Columbia*, following the 'thorough, scholarly and damning analysis of the mistake of law doctrine'[55] by Dickson J in his dissenting judgment in the earlier case of *Hydro Electric Commission of Nepean v Ontario Hydro* (1982). Western Australia and New Zealand have abolished the rule

---

52 [1960] AC 192, pp 204–05.
53 Goff and Jones, *op cit*, fn 48, pp 124–25.
54 *St Paul Fire & Marine Ins Co v Pure Oil Co* (1933), p 773.
55 (1989) 59 DLR (4th) 161, p 191 *per* La Forest J.

by legislation.[56] The Law Reform Committee of South Australia[57] and the Law Reform [375] Commissions of New South Wales[58] and British Columbia[59] have recommended abolition of the rule, as has most recently the English Law Commission.[60] Also very recently, the House of Lords has had occasion to refer to the strong criticism to which the traditional rule has been subjected.[61]

Commentators have been highly critical of both the fact versus law distinction and the traditional rule precluding recovery. Goff and Jones reject the rule and seek to reconcile the cases with a narrower principle.[62] Palmer is unable to find any reason to support treating restitution in cases of mistake of law any differently from cases of mistake of fact.[63] Birks considers that the old rule cannot be justified and that recovery should be permitted in certain cases where there is a mistake of law.[64] In Canada, the authors of a recent text on the law of restitution condemn the traditional rule and conclude that it is unnecessary to distinguish between mistakes of law and of fact in order to fulfil the policy in favour of the finality of dispute resolution.[65] As the same authors say, it 'would be difficult to identify another private law doctrine which has been so universally condemned'.[66]

The criticism gains added impetus in Australia by virtue of the recognition by this court in *Pavey & Matthews Pty Ltd v Paul* of the 'unifying legal concept' of unjust enrichment (1987).[67] As Dickson J stated in *Ontario Hydro* (1982):

> Once a doctrine of restitution or unjust enrichment is recognised, the distinction as to mistake of law and mistake of fact becomes simply meaningless.

If the ground for ordering recovery is that the defendant has been unjustly enriched, there is no justification for drawing distinctions on the basis of how the enrichment was gained, except in so far as the manner of gaining the enrichment bears upon the justice of the case.

[376] In the light of our view that the decision in *South Australian Cold Stores* can in this court be justified on a narrower basis and that the traditional rule was not necessary to the decision, there is no other decision of this court which constrains us to adopt the traditional rule. For the reasons stated above, the rule precluding

---

56 Property Law Act 1969 (WA), ss 124 and 125 (s 124 was applied in *Inn Leisure v DF McCloy* (1991)); Judicature Act 1908 (NZ), ss 94A and 94B.

57 *Report Relating to the Irrecoverability of Benefits Obtained by Reason of Mistake of Law*, Report LRC 84, 1984.

58 *Restitution of Benefits Conferred Under Mistake of Law*, Report LRC 53, 1987.

59 *Report on Benefits Conferred Under a Mistake of Law*, Report LRC 51, 1981.

60 *Restitution of Payments Made Under a Mistake of Law*, Consultation Paper No 120, 1991.

61 *Woolwich Equitable Building Society v Inland Revenue Commissioners* (1992), pp 153–54 *per* Lord Keith of Kinkel; pp 164–65 *per* Lord Goff of Chieveley; pp 199–200 *per* Lord Slynn of Hadley.

62 Goff and Jones, *op cit*, fn 48, p 119.

63 Palmer, *The Law of Restitution*, 1978, Vol 3, pp 14, 27.

64 Birks, *An Introduction to the Law of Restitution*, rev edn, 1989, pp 166–67.

65 Maddaugh and McCamus, *The Law of Restitution*, 1990, p 255.

66 *Ibid*, p 256.

67 At pp 256–57 *per* Deane J (with whom Mason and Wilson JJ agreed); see also *Australia & New Zealand Banking Group Ltd v Westpac Banking Corporation* (1988), p 673.

recovery of moneys paid under a mistake of law should be held not to form part of the law in Australia. In referring to moneys paid under a mistake of law, we intend to refer to circumstances where the plaintiff pays moneys to a recipient who is not legally entitled to receive them. It would not, for example, extend to a case where the moneys were paid under a mistaken belief that they were legally due and owing under a particular clause of a particular contract when in fact they were legally due and owing to the recipient under another clause or contract.[68]

Having rejected the so called traditional rule denying recovery in cases of payments made under a mistake of law, it is necessary to consider what principle should be put in its place. It would be logical to treat mistakes of law in the same way as mistakes of fact,[69] so that there would be a *prima facie* entitlement to recover moneys paid when a mistake of law or fact has caused the payment. Jurisdictions which have abolished the traditional rule by legislation have done so by stating that recovery should be allowed in cases of mistake of law in the same circumstances as it would be were the mistake one of fact (Western Australia and New Zealand).

[Their Honours then rejected the requirement that the mistake must be a 'liability' or 'fundamental' mistake (see extract, p 102) and continued at 378:]

So, the payer will be entitled *prima facie* to recover moneys paid under a mistake if it appears that the moneys were paid by the payer in the mistaken belief that he or she was under a legal obligation to pay the moneys or that the payee was legally entitled to payment of the moneys. Such a mistake would be causative of the payment ...

[Their Honours considered the question of defences (see extracts, pp 592 and 646) and remitted the matter to the trial judge to determine the issues of mistake and change of position.]

Brennan J: [Brennan J agreed that s 261 rendered cl 8(b) void and that there was insufficient evidence in this case to support a finding of a causative mistake. He then rejected the argument that cases of mistake can be reanalysed as instances of failure of consideration and turned to consider the principles which should govern recovery of payments made under a mistake.]

[391] *Unjust enrichment in cases of payment under a mistake*

... [392] Leaving aside defences that arise from supervening circumstances, the essential condition for an order for restitution of money paid by mistake is that the receipt of the payment by the defendant has unjustly enriched the defendant at the expense of the plaintiff. What is meant by unjust enrichment?

In essence, to say that a defendant has been unjustly enriched by the receipt of a payment is to say that the defendant has no right to receive it. Palmer[70] translates the judgment in an ancient case[71] as holding 'if I pay money in satisfaction of a

---

68 *Barclays Bank Ltd v WJ Simms, Son & Cooke (Southern) Ltd* (1980), p 695 *per* Robert Goff J: 'Of course, if the money was due under a contract between the payer and the payee, there can be no recovery on this ground.'

69 *Barclays Bank v WJ Simms Ltd* (1980); *Australia & New Zealand Banking Group Ltd v Westpac Banking Corporation* (1988).

70 Palmer, *op cit*, fn 63, p 144, para 14.1, n 4.

71 *Bonnel v Foulke* (1657).

duty, and he to whom it is paid has no title to receive it, and so the duty is not satisfied, he to whom the money is paid is thereby indebted to me'. If a defendant has a right to receive a payment, whether under a statute, in discharge of a liability owing to him or pursuant to a contract,[72] a mistake by the plaintiff in making the payment does not convert the receipt into an unjust enrichment.[73] To the extent that a payment satisfies a defendant's right to receive it, the defendant gives good consideration and is not unjustly enriched. If the defendant receives more than his due, he may be unjustly enriched to the extent of the excess and restitution may be ordered *pro tanto*.[74] Apart from cases where a payment is made by mistake to satisfy a defendant's supposed right to receive it, a plaintiff may mistakenly make a payment by way of gift, not intending to acquire a benefit or discharge a liability. If the payer would not have paid the money had the payer known all the relevant circumstances, both legal and factual, the defendant is unjustly enriched by the receipt. In principle, there seems to be no reason – [393] though there are cases to the contrary[75] – why the donor should not be entitled to restitution in such a case. It is not necessary to decide that question now. Again, when a plaintiff has paid money for a consideration that has totally failed, the defendant's unjust enrichment consists in his retaining money which, when the consideration fails, he no longer has any right to retain.[76] Enrichment is unjust because the defendant has no right to receive or, as the case may be, to retain the money or property which the plaintiff has paid or transferred to him.[77]

When a defendant receives a payment which he has no right to receive and which the plaintiff has paid to him by mistake, the injustice of the defendant's enrichment does not depend on the nature of the mistake that caused the payment to be made. Whether the plaintiff made a mistake of law or a mistake of fact, the defendant, having no right to receive the payment, is unjustly enriched by its receipt. Then should the distinction between the two categories of mistake make any difference to a finding of unjust enrichment? In *Hydro Electric Commission of Nepean v Ontario Hydro* (1982)[78] Dickson J, in a notable dissenting judgment, said:

> Once a doctrine of restitution or unjust enrichment is recognised, the distinction as to mistake of law and mistake of fact becomes simply meaningless.

The statement may be too broad but I respectfully agree with the reasons of their Honours in the majority in the present case for rejecting the distinction between a mistake of fact and a mistake of law as critical to the question whether the

---

72 The position of a defendant authorised to receive a payment on behalf of a third person need not now be addressed, but see *Australia & New Zealand Banking Group Ltd v Westpac Banking Corporation* (1988).

73 See *Aiken v Short* (1856), pp 214–15 *per* Pollock CB and Platt B.

74 Eg, *Devaux v Conolly* (1849); *Anglo-Scottish Beet Sugar Corporation v Spalding UDC* (1937); *York Air Conditioning & Refrigeration (A/asia) Pty Ltd v The Commonwealth* (1949).

75 *Aiken v Short* (1856), p 215 *per* Bramwell B; cf *South Australian Cold Stores Ltd v Electricity Trust (SA)* (1957), p 75.

76 *Fibrosa Spolka Akcyjna v Fairbairn Lawson Combe Barbour Ltd* (1943), p 65.

77 Restitution lies when property has passed: *Barclays Bank v WJ Simms Ltd* (1980), p 689. If mistake affects the passing of the property, the plaintiff may be entitled to proprietary remedies.

78 Laskin CJC concurred in the judgment and it commanded the assent of Lamer, Wilson, La Forest and L'Heureux-Dube JJ in *Air Canada v British Columbia* (1989).

defendant has been unjustly enriched. But that is not to say that the distinction is immaterial to the question whether there has been a mistake of the kind which entitles the plaintiff to restitution. The distinction between mistakes of fact and mistakes of law is material to the question whether a payment is 'voluntary' and, on that account, is irrecoverable ...

[395] [A] number of factors have been proposed to limit the cases in which mistake of law will ground recovery. Their Honours in the majority judgment consider and discard two suggested criteria: first, that the mistake should be as to the legal liability of the plaintiff to make the payment; and, second, that the mistake be fundamental. I respectfully agree ...

The term 'fundamental' lacks sufficient specificity to be invoked as a working criterion of mistakes that ground recovery.[79] What is essential to a claim in restitution is that the mistake be a cause of the payment to be recovered. If the payer would have made the payment even if the mistaken fact or mistaken operation of law had [396] been known, the money paid is not recoverable on the ground of that mistake. [Brennan J then rejected the voluntary submission principle which was adopted in the joint judgment in favour of a defence of 'honest claim' (see extract, p 146), though ultimately decided that this defence was not available to the bank.]

[Dawson J agreed with the reasons given in the joint judgment for rejecting the mistake of law bar and also recognised a *prima facie* entitlement to restitution when a mistake of law has caused a payment to be made. The case was subsequently settled.[80]]

Commentary and questions

What explanation is given in the joint judgment for the previous cases where payments made under a mistake of law were said to be irrecoverable?

The court held that a *prima facie* right to recover payments made under a mistake of law arises provided the mistake was causative of the payment. A payment will be irrecoverable, despite proof of a mistake of law, where the plaintiff would have made the payment for personal or commercial reasons irrespective of the mistake. This principle is illustrated well by the decision of the Full Court of the Federal Court in *Roxborough v Rothmans of Pall Mall Australia Ltd* (1999). The facts in outline[81] were that Rothmans sold tobacco products by wholesale to the appellant tobacco retailers. The contractual arrangement between Rothmans and the retailers was that the retailers would pay to Rothmans the amount of state licence fees as part of the total price of purchasing the tobacco products, and Rothmans would pay over the licence fees

---

79 Goff and Jones, *op cit*, fn 48, p 88.

80 This case has been the subject of much academic discussion: see Bryan, 'Mistaken payments and the law of unjust enrichment: *David Securities Pty Ltd v Commonwealth Bank of Australia*' (1993) 15 Syd LR 461; Liew, 'Recovery of moneys paid under a mistake of law: the Australian approach' (1994) 6(2) Corp and Bus LJ 3; McInnes, 'Case comment: *David Securities v Commonwealth Bank of Australia*' [1994] 22 ABLR 437; Birks, 'Modernising the law of restitution' (1993) 109 LQR 164.

81 For a more comprehensive statement of the facts see extract, p 81.

to the State government as the fees fell due. In 1997 the High Court held in separate litigation[82] that the fees were unconstitutional as imposing a duty or duties of excise. The retailers commenced an action to recover the licence fees paid by them to Rothmans which Rothmans had not paid over to the government due to the intervention of the High Court decision. The retailers based their claim, *inter alia*, on mistake. The majority of the Full Court (Hill and Lehane JJ) rejected the mistake claim on the basis that the retailers had failed to establish a causal link between the payment of the fees and the alleged mistaken belief by the retailers that they were legally obliged to pay the fees. The evidence given by the retailers established that they paid the total amount that Rothmans demanded, including the licence fees, because if they didn't Rothmans would refuse to supply the tobacco to them. Further, the retailers never intended to bear the cost of the fees themselves; they always intended to pass on the fees to their customers.[83] This decision was appealed to the High Court, which decided by majority in favour of the retailers on a different ground.[84] Kirby J (who dissented) was alone in discussing the mistake claim. His Honour rejected the claim on the basis that the cause of the payments was the obligation of the retailers to pay the money under binding contracts, not any mistake as to the constitutional validity of the legislation.[85]

Commissioner of State Revenue (Vic) v Royal Insurance Australia Ltd
(1994) 182 CLR 51 High Court of Australia

Royal carried on the business of insurance in Victoria, including workers' compensation insurance. Prior to 1985 premiums on workers' compensation insurance policies had been subject to stamp duty. In 1985 a new regime for workers' compensation came into effect and it was provided by statute that premiums for workers' compensation policies which were taken out or extended after 30 June 1985 were exempt from stamp duty. In 1987 it was realised that this exemption covered 'wages' policies, but did not extend to 'cost-plus' policies. The premiums payable on wages policies were payable in advance and were calculated on an estimate of wages for a year with an adjustment being made at the end of the year based on the actual wages paid for that year. Royal paid stamp duty on the premiums on the wages policies when the premiums were received. The premiums payable on cost-plus policies were paid in arrears and reimbursed the insurer for any amounts paid out in settlement of claims in the antecedent period, plus the administrative cost of handling the claims. Royal would estimate the premiums which were likely to be received during the year on the cost-plus

---

82 *Ha v New South Wales* (1997).

83 For a further discussion of the Full Court decision see Bryan, 'Where the constitutional basis for payment has failed (*Roxborough v Rothmans of Pall Mall Australia*)' [2000] 2 RLR 218; Bryan and Ellinghaus, 'Fault lines in the law of obligations: *Roxborough v Rothmans of Pall Mall Australia Ltd*' (2000) 22 Syd LR 636; Erbacher, 'Recent developments in restitutionary recovery of contractual payments: *Roxborough v Rothmans of Pall Mall Australia Ltd*' (2000) 28 ABLR 226.

84 *Roxborough v Rothmans of Pall Mall Australia Ltd* (2001) (see extracts, pp 268 and 273).

85 *Ibid*, pp 369–70. In this regard Kirby J accepted the arguments advanced in Bryan and Ellinghaus, *op cit*, fn 83, p 658. See also Bryan, *op cit*, fn 83, pp 222–23.

policies and pay stamp duty on the basis of that estimate. On 12 November 1987 a statutory amendment came into effect exempting premiums received on cost-plus policies from stamp duty and this exemption was made retrospective to 30 June 1985. For some reason, Royal was unaware of the granting of the exemptions either in 1985 or 1987 and continued to pay duty on premiums received for its workers' compensation policies until 21 August 1989. Royal claimed to be entitled to a refund of stamp duty overpaid between 30 June 1985 and 21 August 1989, amounting to approximately $1,908,000. The overpayments can be divided into three categories. Category (i) covers duty paid on premiums for wages policies taken out or extended after 30 June 1985. Category (ii) covers duty paid on premiums for cost-plus policies after 30 June 1985 and can be subdivided into: (a) premiums paid between 30 June 1985 and the enactment of the amendment on 12 November 1987; (b) premiums paid after the 1987 amendment came into effect. Category (iii) covers duty paid on premiums for cost-plus policies where Royal overestimated the premiums which would be received by it before 1 July 1985. Royal commenced an action for mandamus, seeking to compel the Commissioner to refund the overpayments of stamp duty pursuant to an alleged duty to refund in accordance with s 111(1) of the Stamps Act 1958 (Vic) (which was incorporated into the Act in 1978):

> Where the Comptroller finds in any case that duty has been overpaid, whether before or after the commencement of the Stamps Act 1978, he may refund to the company, person or firm of persons which or who paid the duty the amount of duty found to be overpaid.

Mason CJ: [Mason CJ held that s 111(1) granted a discretionary power to refund and then went on to consider whether there are any limits on the power to refuse a refund.] [64] The Commissioner argues that there is nothing in the context or the scope and objects of the Act which requires or indicates that the discretion to make a refund must be exercised on any particular occasion. Indeed, the Commissioner points to the use of the word 'may' again in s 111(2) and (3) and the contrasting use of the word 'shall' in s 111(4).[86] But these provisions do no more than support the presumption that in s 111(1) the words 'may refund' are facultative. They do not establish that the discretion is in any sense absolute or unfettered. Nor do they bear upon the question whether the discretion must be exercised in a particular way or upon a particular occasion.

In approaching that question, the first and foremost consideration is that the Act is a taxing Act and that in terms it confers no authority upon the Commissioner to levy, demand or retain any moneys otherwise than in payment of duties and charges imposed by or pursuant to the Act. In that context, there is no persuasive reason why the grant of a positive discretionary power to make a refund, once an overpayment of duty has been found by the Commissioner to have taken place, should be treated as a source of authority in the Commissioner to retain the overpayment in the absence of circumstances disentitling the payer from recovery. Nothing short of very clear words is sufficient to achieve such a remarkable result. The court should be extremely reluctant to adopt any construction of s 111 which would enable the Commissioner by an exercise of discretionary power to defeat a taxpayer's entitlement to recover an overpayment of duty. No reason emerges for

---

86 'The duty paid on a return ... shall be denoted on the return by a cash register receipt imprint.'

thinking that the purpose of the provisions was other than to confer legal authority [65] upon the Commissioner to refund an overpayment found by her to have taken place.

In *R v Tower Hamlets London BC ex p Chetnik Developments Ltd* (1988), the House of Lords dealt with a discretionary power to refund in particular circumstances rates paid when not payable and not recoverable otherwise than by means of an exercise of the discretionary power. Lord Bridge of Harwich expressed the principle invoked by the House of Lords in these terms (p 877):

> Parliament must have intended rating authorities to act in the same high principled way expected by the court of its own officers and not to retain rates paid under a mistake of law ... unless there were, as Parliament must have contemplated there might be in some cases, special circumstances in which a particular overpayment was made such as to justify retention of the whole or part of the amount overpaid.

Much the same comment may be made about s 111.

At the same time, I cannot accept the proposition that, once overpayment has been found to have been made, the discretion must be exercised by making a refund. Assume the State has in good faith changed its position for the worse acting in reliance on the fact that the payment was made and received for duty apparently due and payable under the Act, the regime of monthly returns and payments being one of self-assessment, it could scarcely be suggested that a refusal to make a refund in such a situation could be an erroneous exercise of discretion. In *David Securities Pty Ltd v Commonwealth Bank of Australia* (1992), pp 384–86, it was recognised that, according to the principles of the law of restitution, such a change of position would constitute a good 'defence' to an action for recovery of money paid under a mistake of fact or law. It would be surprising, to say the least of it, if the conferral of a discretion to make a refund was intended to exclude power to refuse a refund when in the circumstances the taxpayer was not entitled to recover under the general law. An action which is time barred is another illustration of circumstances in which refusal to make a refund would be justified.

Royal sought to answer this difficulty by submitting that under s 111 the Commissioner was under a duty to investigate whether there had been an overpayment and that, in the context of a duty to investigate, there was a duty to refund once overpayment was found to have taken place. On the assumption that the section creates a [66] duty to investigate, I do not consider that the existence of such a duty leads to the existence of an obligation to refund once overpayment is established. No doubt there will be circumstances in which it will be a proper response, indeed the only proper response, to refund the overpayment but that will not always be the case ...

Recovery according to restitutionary principles

As I have already indicated, the grant of the discretionary power to refund an overpayment should not be regarded as authority to refuse a refund which a taxpayer is entitled to recover according to the principles of the general law. It is necessary then to ascertain how Royal's claim to recover stands under the law of restitution. We [67] begin with the proposition, accepted in *David Securities*, that mistake of law is no bar to recovery, and in this case there is no question but that Royal made the relevant payments in the mistaken belief that in law it was bound to do so. In one respect, Royal's belief at the time of payment was not mistaken: in the case of the cost-plus policies, payments were made when there was a legal liability to pay them. Only subsequently and retrospectively was an exemption granted. But the retrospective operation of s 2(4) of the 1987 Act enables one to say that, in the light of the law as it was enacted with retrospective effect in 1987, the payments of duty were made under a mistake as to the legal liability to pay them. In *David Securities* it was accepted that:[87] 'the payer will be entitled *prima facie* to recover moneys paid under a mistake if it appears that the moneys were paid by the payer in the mistaken belief that he or she was under a legal obligation to pay the moneys or that the payee was legally entitled to payment of the moneys. Such a mistake would be causative of the payment.' And, *prima facie*, that is all that is required where, as here, the recipient has no legal entitlement to receive or retain the moneys. The recipient has been unjustly enriched. Indeed, it is perhaps possible that the absence of any legitimate basis for retention of the money by the Commissioner might itself ground a claim for unjust enrichment without the need to show any causative mistake on the part of Royal.[88] But there is no occasion to pursue this aspect of the case further.

The belated recognition in *David Securities* that moneys paid away as a result of a causative mistake of law are recoverable, enables us to discard some of the complications associated with the old law governing the recovery of moneys paid as and for taxes which were not due and payable because causative mistake of law was not thought to be a sufficient basis of recovery. Recovery was permitted only in cases in which money was exacted under an unlawful demand by a public authority where the payment was made under a mistake of fact or under compulsion of some kind. The relevant principles have been examined by this court in *Sargood Bros v The Commonwealth* (1910) and *Mason v New South Wales* (1959), and, very recently, by the House of Lords in *Woolwich Equitable Building Society v Inland Revenue Commissioners* (1993). In *Woolwich*, the [68] House of Lords, though unwilling to acknowledge that causative mistake of law is a basis for recovery, reformulated the principles so as to recognise a *prima facie* right of recovery based solely on payment of money pursuant to an *ultra vires* demand by a public authority. With that development in the law of restitution in England we are not presently concerned because, as I have explained, Royal made the relevant payments as a result of a causative mistake of law. In conformity with *David Securities*, payment in these circumstances opens the gateway to recovery where the payment results in the enrichment of the defendant at the expense of the plaintiff ...

[Mason CJ held that no defences were available to the Commissioner (see extract, p 658) and granted mandamus directing that the Commissioner refund the amounts overpaid.]

Brennan J: [Brennan J held that the Commissioner will be under a duty to make a refund pursuant to s 111(1) of the Stamps Act 1958 (Vic) only where there is a legal liability to make the refund, either under statutory provisions other than s 111(1) or under the general law. He continued at p 89.]

Legal liability to refund

---

87   (1992) 175 CLR 353, p 378.
88   *Air Canada v British Columbia* (1989) *per* Wilson J (dissenting).

Some of the moneys overpaid by Royal were paid under a mistake. The amounts in items (i) and (ii)(b) were paid under a mistake as to the existence of a statutory liability to pay; the amount in item (iii) was paid under a mistake as to the quantum of premiums to be received or, alternatively, was paid provisionally pending final determination of the quantum of the premiums actually received. In the case of the amounts in items (i) and (ii)(b), the Comptroller must be taken to have known at all material times that the statutory liability had been repealed and that she had no entitlement to retain these amounts.[89] It would therefore be unjust that the Commissioner should retain these amounts; they were recoverable under the general law of restitution. As the amount in item (iii) was paid on the understanding that the amount paid would be adjusted when the quantum of the premiums on which the payments of stamp duty had been calculated became known, the Comptroller was bound to refund or to allow credit for the amount of the overpayment when ascertained.

However, there was no mistake affecting the payment of the amount in item (ii)(a). When paid, the Comptroller was entitled – indeed, she was bound – to retain it. But, by force of the operation attributed to the 1987 amendment, the Commissioner is retrospectively disentitled to retain what was paid as stamp duty under the Act as it had stood before the 1987 amendment commenced. What effect in law does the 1987 amendment have? If the 1987 amendment is to be effective retrospectively, the rights and liabilities of the Commissioner and those who overpaid money must be so altered as to place them in the same position as they would have been in had the Act not imposed the stamp duty abolished by the 1987 amendment during the period of the retrospective operation of the 1987 amendment. In other words, the Commissioner is bound to refund the amount paid by way of stamp duty exigible under the Act during the period of the retrospective operation of the 1987 amendment. It is only by creating a right to a refund of stamp duty already paid that retrospective effect can be given to the 1987 amendment. The Commissioner's liability thus arises directly from the provisions of the Taxation Acts Amendment Act 1987. I see no reason to treat the Commissioner's liability to refund the amount in item (ii)(a) as other than statutory. There is [90] no occasion to invoke notions of common law restitution in order to discover a cause of action entitling a payer to a refund.[90]

It follows that, *prima facie*, all of the amounts claimed by Royal are recoverable. The Commissioner's liability to refund would have been enforceable by action if it were not for s 111(1) but, as that provision is clearly intended to prescribe the means by which the Commissioner's liabilities should be discharged, mandamus is the appropriate remedy to compel the Commissioner to refund overpayments which she is legally liable to refund ...

Dawson J: [Dawson J held that s 111(1) of the Stamps Act 1958 (Vic) imposed a duty on the Commissioner to refund any overpayment and continued at p 99.] Nor do I think it can be said that s 111(1) confers a discretion which must then be exercised in accordance with the law relating to restitution, for that would be to confer no discretion at all. Clearly the sub-section authorises the making of a

---

89 *David Securities Pty Ltd v Commonwealth Bank of Australia* (1992), p 399.

90 This case is quite different in principle from *Air Canada v British Columbia* (1989), and *Woolwich Equitable Building Society v Inland Revenue Commissioners* (1993), where payments had been made under statutory provisions that were held to be invalid.

refund, and is not confined merely to conferring capacity upon the Comptroller should she otherwise be under a duty to do so. The occasion for the [100] exercise of the authority is identified. The only question which arises is whether the authority must be exercised when the necessary finding of overpayment has been made or whether its exercise is discretionary. If the common law, rather than the sub-section, were to govern the Comptroller's obligation to make a refund, then no doubt a refund would now be required. That would be the result of applying the decision of this court in *David Securities Pty Ltd v Commonwealth Bank of Australia* (1992) where it was held that the principle of restitution upon the basis of unjust enrichment extends to moneys paid under a mistake of law as well as moneys paid under a mistake of fact. However, as the law stood, or at least was believed to have stood, before *David Securities*, moneys paid under a mistake of law were not recoverable and Royal was not entitled to recover upon the basis of a mistake of law. And, if the common law of restitution governed the Comptroller's obligation under s 111(1), that result must have been intended by the legislature, because s 111(1) came into force before the decision in *David Securities* and the legislature cannot be taken to have anticipated that decision.

Moreover, assuming that the common law was intended to govern the Comptroller's obligations under s 111(1) and even assuming that the effect of that sub-section changed following *David Securities*, the bulk of Royal's claim was not paid under a mistake of law or fact. Of the total amount of $1,674,301.94, some $1,370,000 was paid in respect of premiums received for cost-plus policies between 30 June 1985 and the commencement of the retrospective legislation in 1987. That amount of duty was payable according to law at the time it was paid and only became an overpayment when the legislation was retrospectively amended. It does not seem to me that the retrospective amendment converted the payments of duty making up the amount of $1,370,000 into payments made under a mistake of law, however much the amendment retrospectively removed the Comptroller's entitlement or authority to receive those payments. As Deane J observed in *University of Wollongong v Metwally* (1984):

> A parliament may legislate that, for the purposes of the law which it controls, past facts or past laws are to be deemed and treated as having been different to what they were. It cannot, however objectively, expunge the past or 'alter the facts of history'.

It need hardly be added that the legislation in question did not deem [101] the payments made by Royal to have been made under a mistake of fact or law ...

[Toohey and McHugh JJ agreed with Brennan J, thus constituting the majority of the court.]

Commentary and questions

On what basis were the category (i) and (ii)(b) payments held to be recoverable? According to Brennan and Dawson JJ were the category (ii)(a) payments made under a mistake? Did Mason CJ take the same view? Which of these competing views do you prefer?

The categorisation by Mason CJ in *Royal* of the category (iii) payments – that is, duty paid because of overestimations of premiums – as payments made under a mistake has been criticised on the basis that Royal's error was only as to premiums to be received in the future, and hence Royal had made a misprediction only. The majority in *Royal* do not appear to have based recovery of this category of payments on the law of restitution but rather simply on the basis of the parties' previous practice of subsequently adjusting the payments. The precise legal basis for recovery was not elaborated, but it has been variously suggested by commentators to be breach of contract or estoppel.[91] Butler and McInnes alternatively argue that the category (iii) payments were recoverable in restitution on the basis of a failure of consideration or 'failure of the basis of the transaction'.[92]

Payments made in accordance with overturned law

Overturned judicial decisions

An important question that arises in this area of law is whether a payment that was legally due on the state of the law at the date of payment is made under a mistake of law where it is decided in a subsequent decision that payments of that kind were not legally due. This issue arises because, on the traditional declaratory theory of decision making, a judicial decision holding that monies formerly thought payable are not in fact payable does not effect a change in the law, but merely rectifies a previously erroneous view. As will be seen, a majority of the court in the following case held that a payment is made under a mistake when a later decision holds that payments of that type are not payable, even though the settled view of the law at the date of payment was that it *was* legally payable.

Kleinwort Benson Ltd v Lincoln City Council [1999] 2 AC 349 House of Lords

The appellant Bank entered into interest rate swap agreements[93] with four local authorities between 1982 and 1984. Each of the agreements were fully performed by the parties and at the end of the term of the agreements the Bank was in the position where it had made net payments to the authorities of £811,208. In 1991 the House of Lords decided in separate litigation in *Hazell v Hammersmith and Fulham London Borough Council* (1992) that the interest rate swap agreements were *ultra vires* local authorities, and the Bank commenced proceedings to recover the net amount it had paid to the authorities. The Bank was successful in recovering

---

91 Merralls, 'Restitutionary recovery of taxes after the *Royal Insurance* case', in McInnes (ed), *Restitution: Developments in Unjust Enrichment*, 1996, Chapter 7, pp 118, 120; Glover, 'Restitutionary recovery of taxes after the *Royal Insurance* case: commentary', in McInnes (ed), *Restitution: Developments in Unjust Enrichment*, 1996, Chapter 8, p 131.

92 Butler, 'Restitution of overpaid taxes, windfall gains, and unjust enrichment: *Commissioner of State Revenue v Royal Insurance Ltd*' (1995) 18(2) UQLJ 318; McInnes, 'Mistaken payments return to the High Court' (1996) 22(2) Mon ULR 209, pp 220–22; cf Mason and Carter, *Restitution Law in Australia*, 1995, p 118.

93 An interest rate swap agreement is an agreement where each party agrees to pay to the other on a specified date an amount of 'interest' calculated on a notional principal sum. The amount payable by one of the parties is calculated in accordance with a fixed rate of interest, whereas the other party's liability is based on a floating rate of interest. These sums are offset, and the party owing the higher amount pays the difference.

£388,114 which represented payments within six years of the date of issuing the writ. At issue on the appeal was whether the Bank could recover the net payments made outside of the six year period. The Bank claimed that the payments were recoverable as having been paid under a mistaken belief that there was a binding contract between it and the authorities. It relied on s 32(1)(c) of the Limitation Act 1980 (UK) which provided that in an action for mistake the limitation period does not begin to run until the plaintiff 'has discovered the ... mistake ... or could with reasonable diligence have discovered it'.

Lord Browne-Wilkinson (dissenting): ... [357] [T]he majority of your Lordships take the view that when established law is changed by a subsequent decision of the courts, money rightly paid in accordance with the old established law is recoverable as having been paid under a mistake of law. I take the view that the moneys are not recoverable since, at the time of payment, the payer was not labouring under any mistake.

The majority view is that *Hazell v Hammersmith and Fulham London Borough Council* (1992) established that the swaps agreements were void; that although the decision in *Hazell* postdated the last of the payments made by the bank to the local authorities the decision operated [358] retrospectively so that under the law as eventually established the bank were labouring under a mistake at the time they made each payment in thinking that they were liable to make such payment. Therefore, in their view, the bank can recover payments made under a mistake of law. My view, on the other hand, is that although the decision in *Hazell* is retrospective in its effect, retrospection cannot falsify history: if at the date of each payment it was settled law that local authorities had capacity to enter into swap contracts, the bank were not labouring under any mistake of law at that date. The subsequent decision in *Hazell* could not create a mistake where no mistake existed at the time.

There are two questions to be considered. First, when the common law is changed by later judicial decision, have all payments made on the basis of the previous law been made under a mistake of law? Second, in what circumstances can it be said that there was earlier law which was changed by judicial decision? Does there have to be a clear judicial decision overruled by a later judicial decision of a higher court or is it enough that, at the date of payment, there was a generally accepted view of the law which view was upset by the later decision?

Where the law is established by judicial decision subsequently overruled

I will take the case where the law has been established by a single decision of the Court of Appeal made in 1930. In 1990 the payer makes a payment which would only have been due to the payee if the Court of Appeal decision was good law. The payer was advised that the Court of Appeal decision was good law. In 1997 this House overruled the Court of Appeal decision. Is the plaintiff entitled to recover the payment made in 1990 on the ground of mistake of law?

...

The theoretical position has been that judges do not make or change law: they discover and declare the law which is throughout the same. According to this theory, when an earlier decision is overruled the law is not changed: its true nature is disclosed, having existed in that form all along. This theoretical position is, as Lord Reid said in the article 'The judge as law maker' (1972–72) 12 JSPTL (NS) 22 a fairy tale in which no one any longer believes. In truth, judges make and change the law. The whole of the common law is judge-made and only by judicial change in the law is the common law kept relevant in a changing world. But whilst the underlying myth has been rejected, its progeny – the retrospective effect of a change made by judicial decision – remains. As Lord Goff of Chieveley in his speech demonstrates, in the absence of some form of prospective overruling, a judgment overruling an earlier decision is bound to operate to some extent retrospectively: once the higher court in the [359] particular case has stated the changed law, the law as so stated applies not only to that case but also to all cases subsequently coming before the courts for decision, even though the events in question in such cases occurred before the Court of Appeal decision was overruled.

Therefore the precise question is whether the fact that the later overruling decision operates retrospectively so far as the substantive law is concerned also requires it to be assumed (contrary to the facts) that *at the date of each payment* the plaintiff made a mistake as to what the law then was. In my judgment it does not. The main effect of your Lordships' decision in the present case is to abolish the rule that money paid under a mistake of law cannot be recovered, which rule was based on the artificial assumption that a man is presumed to know the law. It would be unfortunate to introduce into the amended law a new artificiality, viz, that a man is making a mistake at the date of payment when he acts on the basis of the law as it is then established. He was not mistaken at the date of payment. He paid on the basis that the then binding Court of Appeal decision stated the law, which it did: the fact that the law was later retrospectively changed cannot alter retrospectively the state of the payer's mind at the time of payment. As Deane J said in the High Court of Australia in *University of Wollongong v Metwally* (1984):

> A parliament may legislate that, for the purposes of the law which it controls, past facts or past laws are to be deemed and treated as having been different to what they were. It cannot, however objectively, expunge the past or 'alter the facts of history'.

If that be true of statutory legislation, the same must *a fortiori* be true of judicial decision. In my judgment, therefore, if a man has made a payment on an understanding of the law which was correct as the law stood at the date of such payment he has not made that payment under a mistake of law if the law is subsequently changed.

I am fortified in that view by considering what will be the effect of your Lordships' decision. A payment which was initially irrecoverable will subsequently become recoverable. Consider the hypothetical case I have put. A payment was made in 1990 when the Court of Appeal decision was still valid. Under the existing law, the claim in restitution should apparently have arisen at the date of such payment: see *Baker v Courage & Co* (1910). Yet at that date there could be no question of any mistake. It would not have been possible to issue a writ claiming restitution on the grounds of mistake of law until the 1997 decision had overruled the 1930 Court of Appeal decision. Therefore a payment which, when made, and for several years thereafter, was entirely valid and irrecoverable would subsequently become recoverable. This result would be subversive of the great public interest in the security of receipts and the closure of transactions. The position is even worse because all your Lordships consider that the claims to recover money paid under a mistake of law are subject to s 32(1)(c) of the Limitation Act 1980, ie that in such a case time will not begin to run until the 'mistake' is discovered. A subsequent overruling of a Court of Appeal decision by the House of Lords could occur many decades after payments have been made on the [360] faith of the Court of Appeal decision: in such a case 'the mistake' would not be discovered until the later overruling. All payments made pursuant to the Court of Appeal ruling would be recoverable subject only to the possible defence of change of position.

...

[362] In my view therefore, if, at the date of payment, the law was settled by clear judicial authority then a payment in accordance with such law was not made under a mistake of law even if the law has subsequently been changed by later judicial decision ...

Settled law in the absence of judicial decision?

It is not suggested in the present case that before the decision of this House in *Hazell's* case there was any judicial decision which established that local authorities had the capacity to enter into swap agreements. What is said is that, even in the absence of such a decision, [363] there was a 'settled view' that local authorities had the necessary capacity and that swap agreements were therefore valid. It is not for your Lordships on these preliminary issues to seek to determine whether in fact there was such a settled view of the law. However, your Lordships do have to decide whether, if at the trial such a settled view is proved to have existed, it would prevent the bank from recovering the moneys paid on the basis of moneys paid under a mistake of law.

Much commercial and property activity occurs on the basis of law which is not laid down by judicial decision. Such 'law' consists of the practice and understanding of lawyers skilled in the field. If, before payment, the payer had sought advice in some cases he would have been told that the law was dubious: if having received such advice he paid over, he must have taken the risk that the law was otherwise and cannot subsequently recover what he has paid. In other cases, he would have been told that the law was clear and he could safely act on it. If in this latter case the payer acted on the law as so advised and subsequently a court held that the law was not as advised, can the payer recover his payment as moneys paid under a mistake of law? In the ordinary case, the payer's adviser will just have given wrong legal advice: as a result the payment will have been paid under a mistake of law and will be recoverable. But in a limited number of cases, of which this may be one, it is not really possible to say that the legal adviser made a mistake in advising as he did. There are areas of the law which are sparsely covered by judicial decision, for example, real property, banking and regulatory law. In such areas the commercial world acts, has to act, on the generally held view of lawyers skilled in the field. In such cases, a payer who sought advice would receive the same advice from everyone skilled in the field. It used to be said that the practice of conveyancers of repute was strong evidence of real property law: see *In re Hollis' Hospital Trustees and Hague's Contract* (1899). As late as the middle of this century, Denning LJ said in *In re Downshire's Settled Estates* (1953): 'The practice of the profession in these cases is the best evidence of what the law is; indeed, it makes law.'

I doubt whether today anyone would claim that a uniform practice of the profession makes the law. But in the present context it does have a significant impact. In holding that money paid under a mistake of law is recoverable, an essential factor is that the retention of the money so paid would constitute an unjust enrichment of the payee. What constitutes the unjust factor is the mistake made by the payer at the date of payment. If, at the date of payment, it was settled law that payment was legally due, I can see nothing unjust in permitting the payee to retain moneys he received at a time when all lawyers skilled in the field would have advised that he was entitled to receive them and the payer was bound to pay them. Again it is critical to establish the position at the time of payment: if, at that date, there was nothing unjust or unmeritorious in the receipt or retention of the moneys by the payee in my judgment it was not an unjust enrichment for him subsequently to retain the moneys just because the law was, in one sense, subsequently changed.

...

[364] My Lords, I ... would therefore have held that the bank would not be entitled to recover on the grounds of mistake of law if at the time of payment the bank [was], or if [it] had sought advice would have been, advised by all lawyers skilled in the field that the swaps agreement were valid.

...

Lord Goff of Chieveley: ... [377] *The declaratory theory of judicial decision*

Historically speaking, the declaratory theory of judicial decisions is to be found in a statement by Sir Matthew Hale over 300 years ago, viz that the decisions of the courts do not constitute the law properly so called, but are evidence of the law and as such 'have a great weight and authority in expounding, declaring and publishing what the law of this Kingdom is': see *Hale's Common Law of England*.[94] To the like effect, *Blackstone Commentaries*[95] stated that 'the decisions of courts are the evidence of what is the common law'. In recent times, however, a more realistic approach has been adopted, as in Sir George Jessel MR's celebrated statement that rules of equity, unlike rules of the common law, are not supposed to have been established since time immemorial, but have been invented, altered, improved and refined from time to time: see *In re Hallett's Estate, Knatchbull v Hallett* (1880). There can be no doubt of the truth of this statement; and we all know that in reality, in the common law as in equity, the law is the subject of development by the judges – normally, of course, by appellate judges. We describe as leading cases the decisions which mark the principal stages in this development, and we have no difficulty in identifying the judges who are primarily responsible. It is universally recognised that judicial development of the common law is inevitable. If it had never taken place, the common law would be the same now as it was in the reign of King Henry II; it is because of it that the common law is a living system of law, reacting to new events and new ideas, and so capable of providing the citizens of this country with a system of practical justice relevant to the times in which they live. The recognition that this is what actually happens requires, however, that we should look at the declaratory theory

94   6th edn, 1820, p 90.
95   6th edn, 1774, pp 88–89.

of judicial decision with open eyes and reinterpret it in the light of the way in which all judges, common law and equity, actually decide cases today.

...

[378] Bearing these matters in mind, the law which the judge then states to be applicable to the case before him is the law which, as so developed, is perceived by him as applying not only to the case before him, but to all other comparable cases, as a congruent part of the body of the law. Moreover when he states the applicable principles of law, the judge is declaring these as constituting the law relevant to his decision. Subject to consideration by appellate tribunals, and (within limits) by judges of equal jurisdiction, what he states to be the law will, generally speaking, be applicable not only to the case before him but, as part of the common law, to other comparable cases which come before the courts, whenever the events which are the subject of those cases in fact occurred.

It is in this context that we have to reinterpret the declaratory theory of judicial decision. We can see that, in fact, it does not presume the existence of an ideal system of the common law, which the judges from time to time reveal in their decisions. The historical theory of judicial decision, though it may in the past have served its purpose, was indeed a fiction. But it does mean that, when the judges state what the law is, their decisions do, in the sense I have described, have a retrospective effect. That [379] is, I believe, inevitable. It is inevitable in relation to the particular case before the court, in which the events must have occurred some time, perhaps some years, before the judge's decision is made. But it is also inevitable in relation to other cases in which the law as so stated will in future fall to be applied. I must confess that I cannot imagine how a common law system, or indeed any legal system, can operate otherwise if the law is be applied equally to all and yet be capable of organic change. This I understand to be the conclusion reached in *Cross and Harris Precedent in English Law*[96] from which I have derived much assistance, when at p 33 they ask the question: 'what can our judges do but make new law and how can they prevent it from having retrospective effect?' ... The only alternative, as I see it, is to adopt a system of prospective overruling. But such a system, although it has occasionally been adopted elsewhere with, I understand, somewhat controversial results, has no place in our legal system ...

Was the bank mistaken when it paid money to the local authorities under interest swap agreements which it believed to be valid?

... This [question] requires that I should consider whether parties in the position of the appellant bank were mistaken when they paid money to local authorities under interest swap agreements which they, like others, understood to be valid but have later been held to be void. To me, it is plain that the money was indeed paid over under a mistake, the mistake being a mistake of law. The payer believed, when he paid the money, that he was bound in law to pay it. He is now told that, on the law as held to be applicable at the date of the payment, he was not bound to pay it. Plainly, therefore, he paid the money under a mistake of law, and accordingly, subject to any applicable defences, he is entitled to recover it. It comes as no surprise to me that, in the swaps litigation, it appears to have been assumed that money paid pursuant to interest rate swap agreements was paid under a

---

96   4th edn, 1991.

mistake which, in *Westdeutsche Landesbank Girozentrale v Islington London Borough Council* (1994), [380] was inevitably held by Hobhouse J to have been a mistake of law and so, on the law as it then stood, irrecoverable on that basis. Not surprisingly, there is very little previous authority on the question whether in such circumstances the money has been paid under a mistake of law; but such authority as there is supports this view.

...

[381] I recognise, of course, that the situation may be different where the law is subject to legislative change. That is because legislation takes effect from the moment when it becomes law, and is only retrospective in its effect to the extent that this is provided for in the legislative instrument. Moreover even where it is retrospective, it has the effect that as from the date of the legislation a new legal provision will apply retrospectively in place of that previously applicable. It follows that retrospective legislative change in the law does not necessarily have the effect that a previous payment was, as a result of the change in the law, made under a mistake of law at the time of payment. (I note in parenthesis that in *Commissioner of State Revenue v Royal Insurance Australia Ltd* (1994), the High Court of Australia was divided on the question whether the retrospective legislation there under consideration had the effect that a previous payment had been made under a mistake of law.) As I have already pointed out, this is not the position in the case of a judicial development of the law. But, for my part, I cannot see why judicial development of the law should, in this respect, be placed on the same footing as legislative change. In this connection, it should not be forgotten that legislation which has an impact on previous transactions can be so drafted as to prevent unjust consequences flowing from it. That option is not, of course, open in the case of judicial decisions.

[Lord Goff then went on to draw a distinction between payments of tax and payments made pursuant to private transactions. His Lordship recognised that a case could be made that taxes paid under a settled understanding of the law should be irrecoverable on the basis that public finances could be seriously affected: see extract, p 483. However, his Lordship refused to apply this principle to payments made from one private party to another. After rejecting certain other arguments against recovery and discussing s 32(1)(c) of the Limitation Act (see extract, p 668), Lord Goff continued at 389:]

I recognise that the effect of s 32(1)(c) [of the Limitation Act] is that the cause of action in a case such as the present may be extended for an indefinite period of time. I realise that this consequence may not have been fully appreciated at the time when this provision was enacted, and further that the recognition of the right at common law to recover money on the ground that it was paid under a mistake of law may call for legislative reform to provide for some time limit to the right of recovery in such cases. The Law Commission may think it desirable, as a result of the decision in the present case, to give consideration to this question indeed they may think it wise to do so as a matter of some urgency. If they do so, they may find it helpful to have regard to the position under other systems of law, notably Scottish and German law. On the section as it stands, however, I can see no answer to the submission of the bank that their claims in the present case, founded upon a mistake of law, fall within the subsection.

Lord Lloyd of Berwick (dissenting): ... [393] An inevitable consequence of determining the law in relation to a particular case is that the same law will apply to other cases as yet undecided, in which the same point arises. This is so whether the transaction in question lies in the past or the future. So again, to that limited extent, it can be said that the decision operates retrospectively. But that, as it seems to me, is the full extent of any retrospective effect. There is no way in which the decision can be applied retrospectively to cases which have already been decided. Nor is there any logical reason why there should be. It is the function of the court to decide what the law is, not what it was. So when the House of Lords overrules a line of Court of Appeal decisions it does not, and cannot, decide those cases again. The law as applied to those cases was the law as decided at the time by the Court of Appeal. The House of Lords can say that the Court of Appeal took a wrong turning. It can say what the law should have been. But it [394] cannot say that the law actually applied by the Court of Appeal was other than what it was. It cannot, in my learned and noble friend Lord Browne-Wilkinson's vivid expression, falsify history.

It follows that in such a case the House of Lords is doing more than develop the law. It is changing the law, as common sense suggests, and as [Counsel for local authorities] was right to concede. If this view of what happens is inconsistent with the declaratory theory of the court's function, then it is time we said so. It always was a fairy tale.

If it is right that the House of Lords can change the law by overruling a previous decision of the Court of Appeal, it must follow that a person relying on the old law was under no mistake at the time, and cannot claim to have been under a mistake *ex post facto* because the law is subsequently changed. This is obviously true where the law is changed by legislation. In my opinion it is equally true when the law is changed by judicial decision.

...

[395] The prospect of transactions being reopened many years after the event by a subsequent decision of the Court of Appeal or House of Lords is not one which the law should favour, especially in the field of commerce. It is true that in many cases the defendant would be able to rely on change of position as a defence. But this would not necessarily be so in every case. Certainty and finality, as has been said so often, are twin policy objectives of the highest importance in formulating legal principles.

...

Even when ... legislation is retrospective, it by no means follows, as Lord Goff points out, that a previous payment will have been made under a mistake of law at the time of payment. My noble and learned friend Lord Hope is of the same opinion. The correct analysis in his view is that there will have been no mistake of law when the payment was made. I respectfully agree. If the retrospective legislation positively requires a transaction to be reopened, the liability to repay will arise, not because the payee's conscience is affected, but by operation of statute: see *Commissioner of State Revenue v Royal Insurance Australia Ltd* (1994), p 89 *per* Brennan J. But if that be so, it is difficult to defend, on policy grounds, a different rule for changes in the law effected by judicial decision. Appellate courts ought to be encouraged to change the law in those rare cases where change is needed. They should not be inhibited by the fear of reopening past transactions.

[Lord Lloyd referred to Lord Goff's conclusion that payments made in accordance with a settled view of the law should be recoverable where that settled view is subsequently overturned. His Lordship continued at 397:]

For the reasons already mentioned, I find [Lord Goff's conclusion] hard to accept. I agree that the payment might be recoverable on some other ground, for example, total failure of consideration, assuming the claim was not time-barred, but not on the grounds of mistake. For if there really was a settled understanding of the law, then that was the law at the time of payment. The payer was not mistaken. The subsequent change in the law could not create a cause of action which, *ex hypothesi*, did not exist at the relevant time. Even if the change were to come very soon after the payment it would make no difference.

...

Lord Hoffman: [398] [I] should say something on the issue which divides your Lordships, because I have to confess that on this point I have changed my mind. At the end of the argument I was of opinion, perhaps not in a very focused way, that a person who pays in accordance with what was then a settled view of the law has not made a mistake. In fact it seemed to me that one could go further and say that if he had acted in accordance with a tenable view of the law, he had not made a mistake. In the first case he was right, and in the second neither right nor wrong, but in both cases his state of mind could be better described as a failure to predict the outcome of some future event (*scilicet*, a decision of this House) than a mistake about the existing state of the law.

On reflection, however, I have come to the conclusion that this theory was wrong, both in its stronger (tenable view) and in its weaker (settled view) form. The reason, I think, is that it looks at the question of what counts as a mistake in too abstract a way, divorced from its setting in the law of unjust enrichment.

The problem arises because (1) the law requires that a mistake should have been as to some existing fact or (on the view which your Lordships now take) the then existing state of the law but (2) a judicial statement of the law operates retrospectively. So the question is whether the retrospectivity of the law-making process enables one to say that holding a contrary view of the law at an earlier stage was a mistake. This question cannot be answered simply by taking a robust, commonsense definition of a mistake and saying that one does not believe in fairy stories. It is easy to understand the expostulation of Lord Coleridge CJ in *Henderson v* [399] *Folkestone Waterworks Co* (1885) at the suggestion that, because his judgment had been reversed by the House of Lords, he had been 'ignorant of the law'. The commonsense notion of a mistake as to an existing state of affairs is that one has got it wrong when, if one had been better informed, one could have got it right. But common sense does not easily accommodate the concept of retrospectivity. This is a legal notion. If the ordinary man was asked whether Lord Coleridge had made a mistake, he would no doubt have said that in the ordinary sense, which might carry some reflection on his competence as a judge, he had not. But if he was asked whether he should be treated for the purposes of some legal rule as having made a mistake, he might say 'I don't know. You tell me that the later decision operated retrospectively, which means that at least for some purposes, it must be assumed to have been the law at the time. Therefore it may be that for some purposes a person who held the contrary view should be treated as having made a mistake. It all depends upon the context. You had better ask a lawyer.'

The lawyer would, I think, start by considering why, in principle, a person who had paid because he held some mistaken belief should be entitled to recover. The answer is that it is *prima facie* unjust for the recipient to retain the money when, if the payer had known the true state of affairs, he would not have paid. It has never been suggested that, in the case of a mistake of fact, he could not recover if everyone would probably have shared the same false belief. On the contrary, there was once a view that he should not be able to recover if a reasonable person in his position would not have shared his false belief, but this was repudiated in *Kelly v Solari* (1841). Since then, it has not mattered whether the person making the payment could have discovered the true state of affairs or not.

The distinction therefore does not turn upon the fact that the person making the payment could not have discovered the true state of affairs about the law any more than about the facts. It turns upon the purely abstract proposition that in principle (and leaving aside the problem of Schrodinger's cat) the truth or falsity of any proposition of existing fact could have been ascertained at the time, whereas the law, as it was subsequently be declared to have been, could not.

One must therefore ask why, in the context of unjust enrichment, this should make a difference. In both cases it has turned out that the state of affairs at the time was not (or was deemed not to have been) what the payer thought. In the case of a mistake of fact, it is because things were actually not what he believed them to be. In the case of a mistake of law, it is by virtue of the retrospectivity of the decision. Does the principle of unjust enrichment require that this retrospectivity should be carried through into the question of whether the payer made a mistake?

In my view, it would be very anomalous if it did not. Imagine a client who has paid under what he thought to be a legal obligation. He had not consulted a lawyer at the time, but seeks advice after a case in the House of Lords which decides that the obligation was void. The lawyer tells him that according to the House of Lords, he need not have paid. He asks whether he can recover his money on the grounds of mistake. On the 'settled view' theory, the lawyer has to say: 'No, because if you had consulted me at the time, I would have told you that you were certainly [400] right to pay. Therefore you made no mistake.' The client asks: 'Does that mean that the obligation was actually valid? If so, what has made it invalid?' The lawyer has to answer: 'No, the House of Lords has told us that it was always void. Nevertheless, you made no mistake. On the other hand, if lawyers had regarded it as a doubtful point, or if any lawyer would have told you then that the obligation was void, so that it would have been extremely foolish of you not to have sought advice, then you would have been able to recover.'

My Lords, it seems to me that the imaginary client would have great difficulty in understanding how these distinctions can arise out of a rule giving a remedy for unjust enrichment. In each case he thought that the obligation was valid and it has subsequently turned out that it was not. In principle, the question should not turn upon what other people might have thought was the law but upon what he thought was the law. And this has turned out to have been wrong, however many lawyers might have agreed with him at the time. So there ought to be a remedy in all cases or none ...

An analogy was drawn in argument between a retrospective decision of a court and a retrospective Act of Parliament. A failure to predict the latter, it was said, could not possibly be a mistake and therefore why should the former. I do not myself see why, in principle, if an Act of Parliament requires that the law be deemed to have been different on an earlier date, it should not follow that a person who acted in accordance with the law as it then was should be deemed to have made a mistake. This was the view of Mason CJ in *Commissioner of State Revenue v Royal Insurance Australia Ltd* (1994) and I respectfully think that in principle he was right. But usually the question will turn upon the construction of the statute: it may provide expressly for the refund of money declared not to be owing, or such an obligation may be implied, or it may be argued that the failure to provide expressly for repayment showed a Parliamentary intention that transactions under the previous law should not be disturbed. I find the analogy of a retrospective Act of Parliament, which can deal with the consequences of its retrospectivity, unhelpful in dealing with a change of law by judicial decision. The judges who change the law can use only the common law to remedy any injustices which compliance with the previous law may have caused.

I therefore do not think that there are any reasons of principle for distinguishing cases in which a subsequent decision changes a settled view of the law, or, for that matter, settles what was previously an unsettled view [401] of the law. The enrichment of the recipient is in each case unjust because he has received money which he would not have received if the payer had known the law to be what it has since been declared to have been.

...

I accept that allowing recovery for mistake of law without qualification, even taking into account the defence of change of position, may be thought to tilt the balance too far against the public interest in the security of transactions. The most obvious problem is the Limitation Act 1980, which as presently drafted is inadequate to deal with the problem of retrospective changes in law by judicial decision. But I think that any measures to redress the balance must be a matter for the legislature. This may suggest that your Lordships should leave the whole question of the abrogation of the mistake of law rule to the legislature, so that the change in the law and the necessary qualifications can be introduced at the same time. There is obviously a strong argument for doing so, but I do not think that it should prevail over the desirability of giving in this case what your Lordships consider to be a just and principled decision.

...

Lord Hope of Craighead: [411] It is [best] to face up to the fact that every decision as to the law by a judge operates retrospectively, and to concentrate ... on the question – which I would regard as the critical question – whether the payer would have made the payment if he had known what he is now being told was the law. It is the state of the law at the time of the payment which will determine whether or not the payment was or was not legally due to be paid, and it is the state of mind of the payer at the time of payment which will determine whether he paid under a mistake. But there seems to me to be no reason in principle why the law of unjust enrichment should insist that that mistake must be capable of being demonstrated at the same time as the time when the payment was made. A mistake of fact may take some time to discover. If there is a dispute about this, the question whether there was a mistake may remain in doubt until the issue has been resolved by a judge. Why should this not be so where the mistake is one of law?

In the present case we have no evidence about the state of the law at the time of the payments other than what can be derived from the agreed facts. But the background, as it can be discovered from the judgment of Hobhouse J in the *Westdeutsche* case (1994) is reasonably clear. He said, at 931E, that the effect of the statutory provisions of which the relevant bank had previously been unaware was subsequently 'declared' by the Divisional Court and the House of Lords in the *Hazell* case (1992). His choice of language seems to me to have been entirely appropriate. There had been no previous judicial decision on the point until the practice in the money markets was challenged for the first time in that case by the district auditor. Nor is it suggested that an opinion had been expressed about it which could be regarded as authoritative in the sense that it was binding on all parties including the auditor. If it were necessary to decide this point, I do not think that it would be right to say that the decision in the *Hazell* case 'changed' the law. What it did was to clarify a point which had been overlooked and was in need of determination by the court. But the situation seems to me to be no different in principle from one where the facts are shown, as a result of inquiries which at the time of the payment were overlooked or not thought to be necessary, to have been different from what they had been thought to be at the time of the payment by the payer. *Prima facie* the bank is entitled to restitution on the ground of mistake.

...

[416] *Limitation*

[Lord Hope held that s 32(1)(c) of the Limitation Act was applicable (see extract, p 668) and continued at 417:]

The objection may be made that time may run on for a very long time before a mistake of law could have been discovered with reasonable diligence, especially where a judicial decision is needed to establish the mistake. It may also be said that in some cases a mistake of law may have affected a very large number of transactions, and that the potential for uncertainty is very great. But I do not think that any concerns which may exist on this ground provide a sound reason for declining to give effect to the section according to its terms. The defence of change of position will be available, and difficulties of proof are likely to increase with the passage of time. I think that the risk of widespread injustice remains to be demonstrated. If the risk is too great that is a matter for the legislature.

...

Commentary and questions

What reasons did the majority give for concluding that payments legally made in accordance with settled law should be recoverable where the law is changed? What is the risk to certainty of transactions and security of receipts if the majority's view is adopted? How did the majority consider that such risks should be dealt with?

Why did Lords Browne-Wilkinson and Lloyd hold in dissent that the Bank could not recover the monies? What pragmatic reasons did their Lordships give to support their views that monies should not be recoverable in this situation?

There is a significant amount of academic comment supporting the minority view in the principal case that a payment should not be recognised as having been made under mistake where it was legally payable according to the settled law at the date of the payment.[97]

The limitations legislation of each Australian jurisdiction, with the exception of South Australia and Western Australia, contain a provision in like terms to s 32(1)(c) of the UK limitations legislation considered in the principal case.[98] Although this legislation could be amended to provide for the limitations period to run from the date of payment where the claim is based on mistake of law, this might not be effective to prevent the recovery of unconstitutional taxes,[99] and would have the undesirable effect of reviving the difficult distinction between mistakes of fact and mistakes of law.

Legislation in New South Wales prohibits recovery of invalid imports that have become recoverable because of a non-legislative change in the law.[100]

Retrospective legislation

In *Commissioner of State Revenue (Vic) v Royal Insurance Australia Ltd* (1994) Brennan and Dawson JJ held that the category (ii)(a) payments – the duty paid on premiums for cost-plus policies during the period of retrospectivity – were not paid under a mistake of law.[101] Dawson J endorsed a statement by Deane J in *University of Wollongong v Metwally* (1984) that retrospective legislation cannot 'expunge the past or alter the facts of history'. Kirby J expressed a similar view in *Commonwealth of Australia v SCI Operations Pty Ltd* (1988) p 323, holding that a deeming provision usually:

> ... without clear language ... does not change the character, for legal purposes, of the payments when originally made so as to pretend that they were made by mistake or unnecessarily.

97　Mason and Carter, *Restitution Law in Australia*, 1995, pp 124–25; Birks, 'Modernising the law of restitution' (1993) 109 LQR 164 at 166; Merralls, 'Restitutionary recovery of taxes after the *Royal Insurance* case', in McInnes (ed), *Restitution: Developments in Unjust Enrichment*, 1996, p 118. For comments on the principal case see: Smith, 'Restitution for mistake of law (*Kleinwort Benson v Lincoln CC*)' [1999] RLR 148; Hudson, 'Assessing mistake of law in derivative transactions: *Kleinwort Benson* and the local authority swaps cases' (1999) 14(3) JIBL 96; Perell, '*Kleinwort Benson v Lincoln CC* and mistake of law and unjust enrichment – the House of Lords starts down a new path' (1999) 21 The Advocates' Quarterly 495.

98　Limitation Act 1985 (ACT), s 34(1); Limitation Act 1969 (NSW), s 56(1); Limitation Act 1981 (NT), s 43(1); Limitation of Actions Act 1974 (QLD), s 38; Limitation Act 1974 (Tas), s 32; Limitations of Actions Act 1958 (Vic), s 27(c). For a discussion of limitation periods that apply to taxes see pp 475–77.

99　As discussed in Chapter 15, statutory provisions which effectively abrogate a right of recovery of unconstitutional taxes will themselves be unconstitutional: *Antill Ranger & Co Pty Ltd v Commissioner for Motor Transport (Vic)* (1995); *Barton v Commissioner of Motor Transport* (1957).

100　Recovery of Imports Act 1963 (NSW), s 3.

101　Contrast Mason CJ who acted on the basis that the payments were made under a mistake.

A majority of the House of Lords in *Kleinwort Benson Ltd v Lincoln City Council* (1999) (see extract, p 126) also took the view that retrospective legislation cannot retrospectively create a mistaken state of mind.[102] Lord Goff in that case distinguished retrospective legislation from judicial changes. Judicial changes were seen as having some retrospective effect in the sense that they will apply to factual events that occurred prior to the date of the decision but which only come before the court after the date of the decision. Legislation, on the other hand, 'takes effect from the moment when it becomes law, and is only retrospective in its effect to the extent that this is provided for in the legislative instrument' (p 381). Thus, it seems that money paid during a period of legislative retrospectivity will be recoverable only where the legislation expressly or impliedly provides a right of refund (p 395 *per* Lord Lloyd).

VOLUNTARY SUBMISSION TO AN HONEST CLAIM

A claim to recover payments on the basis of mistake will be denied where the plaintiff made the payments voluntarily in settlement of an honest claim. However, as will be seen from the following cases, the exact ambit of this defence is still 'somewhat undefined'.[103]

Kelly v Solari (1841) 9 M & W 54; 152 ER 24 Exchequer

The defendant's husband took out a life insurance policy with Argus Assurance Co. By an oversight, a premium was not paid shortly before the death of the defendant's husband. Two of the three directors of Argus were informed by an employee that the policy had lapsed by reason of the non-payment of the premium and one of the directors wrote 'lapsed' on the policy. The defendant claimed under the policy and the claim was paid out by the directors. The third director brought an action to recover the sum paid to the defendant on the basis it had been paid to her by the company under a mistake of fact. The two directors who had been informed of the lapse of the policy gave evidence that at the time of paying the money they had entirely forgotten that the policy in question had lapsed.

Lord Abinger CB: ... [57] I think that the defendant ought to have had the opportunity of taking the opinion of the jury on the question whether in reality the directors had a knowledge of the facts, and therefore that there should be a new trial, and not a verdict for the plaintiff; although I am now prepared to say that I laid down the rule too broadly at the trial, as to the effect of their having had means of knowledge. That is a very vague expression, and it is difficult to say with precision what it amounts to; for example, it may be that the party may have the means of knowledge on a particular subject, only by sending to and obtaining information from a correspondent abroad. In the case of *Bilbie v Lumley*, the argument as to the party having means of knowledge was used by counsel, and adopted by some of the judges; but that was a peculiar case and there can be no question that if the point had been left to the jury, they would have found that the

---

102 At p 359 (Lord Browne-Wilkinson), p 381 (Lord Goff), pp 394, 395 (Lord Lloyd); contrast Lord Hoffman, p 400 (see extract, p 126).
103 *Kleinwort Benson Ltd v Lincoln City Council* (1999), p 385 *per* Lord Goff (see extract, p 126).

plaintiff had actual knowledge. The safest rule however is [58] that if the party makes the payment with full knowledge of the facts, although under ignorance of the law, there being no fraud on the other side, he cannot recover it back again. There may also be cases in which, although he might by investigation learn the state of facts more accurately, he declines to do so, and chooses to pay the money notwithstanding; in that case there can be no doubt that he is equally bound. Then there is a third case, and the most difficult one – where the party had once a full knowledge of the facts, but has since forgotten them. I certainly laid down the rule too widely to the jury, when I told them that if the directors once knew the facts they must be taken still to know them, and could not recover by saying that they had since forgotten them. I think that the knowledge of the facts which disentitles the party from recovering, must mean a knowledge existing in the mind at the time of payment. I have little doubt in this case that the directors had forgotten the fact, otherwise I do not believe they would have brought the action; but as [counsel for the defendant] certainly has a right to have that question submitted to the jury, there must be a new trial.

Parke B: I entirely agree in the opinion just pronounced by my Lord Chief Baron, that there ought to be a new trial. I think that where money is paid to another under the influence of a mistake, that is, on the supposition that a specific fact is true, which would entitle the other to the money, but which fact is untrue, and the money would not have been paid if it had been known to the payer that the fact was untrue, an action will lie to recover it back, and it is against conscience to retain it; though a demand may be necessary in those cases in which the party receiving may have been ignorant of the mistake. The position that a person so paying is precluded from recovering by laches in not availing himself of the means of knowledge in his power, seems, from the cases cited, to [59] have been founded on the *dictum* of Mr Justice Bayley, in the case of *Milnes v Duncan*; and with all respect to that authority, I do not think it can be sustained in point of law. If, indeed, the money is intentionally paid, without reference to the truth or falsehood of the fact, the plaintiff meaning to waive all inquiry into it, and that the person receiving shall have the money at all events, whether the fact be true or false, the latter is certainly entitled to retain it; but if it is paid under the impression of the truth of a fact which is untrue, it may, generally speaking, be recovered back, however careless the party paying may have been, in omitting to use due diligence to inquire into the fact. In such a case the receiver was not entitled to it, nor intended to have it.

Rolfe B: I am of the same opinion. With respect to the argument, that money cannot be recovered back except where it is unconscientious to retain it, it seems to me, that wherever it is paid under a mistake of fact, and the party would not have paid it if the fact had been known to him, it cannot be otherwise than unconscientious to retain it. But I agree that [counsel for the defendant] has a right to go to the jury again, upon two grounds: first, that the jury may possibly find that the directors had not in truth forgotten the fact; and secondly, they may also come to the conclusion, that they had determined that they would not expose the office to unpopularity, and would therefore pay the money at all events; in which case I quite agree that they could not recover it back.

Commentary

According to the principal case, a payment is made voluntarily in submission to a claim where the plaintiff has paid the money in order to close the transaction and consciously waives any right to challenge the validity of the payment. However, the court emphasises that a mistaken payment is not a voluntary payment merely because the plaintiff was negligent in not properly investigating the circumstances of the payment.[104]

David Securities Pty Ltd v Commonwealth Bank of Australia
(1992) 175 CLR 353 High Court of Australia

The facts are stated at p 110.

Mason CJ, Deane, Toohey, Gaudron and McHugh JJ: ... [373] The payment is voluntary or there is an election if the plaintiff chooses to make the payment even though he or she believes a particular law or contractual provision requiring the payment is, or may be, invalid, or is not concerned to query whether payment is legally required; he or she is prepared to assume the validity of the obligation, or is prepared to make the payment [374] irrespective of the validity or invalidity of the obligation, rather than contest the claim for payment. We use the term 'voluntary' therefore to refer to a payment made in satisfaction of an honest claim, rather than a payment not made under any form of compulsion or undue influence ...

Brennan J: ... [394] *Voluntary payments and mistakes of law*

... It is not surprising that payments made under a mistake of law have been treated as a class of voluntary payments. That has been a convenient legal mechanism for holding such payments to be irrecoverable. To admit mistake of law as a ground for restitution in any case in which a mistake of fact would ground such a remedy would render many payments insecure even in cases where both parties expected the payment to be final: the uncertainty of the law and the overruling of decisions by later cases or on appeal would infect many payments with a provisional quality incompatible with orderly commerce. Moreover, while mistakes of fact are specific to particular relationships, the revealing of a mistake of law in one case could throw into uncertainty the finality of payments made in a great variety of cases. Although payments made under a mistake of law should not be excluded entirely from the categories of cases in which restitution may be ordered, something more than a mere mistake of law is required before the remedy is available. As Lord Denning said in *Kiriri Cotton Co Ltd v Dewani* (1960), p 204:

> The true proposition is that money paid under a mistake of law, by itself and without more, cannot be recovered back.

The problem, of course, is to articulate the elements additional to a mere mistake of law that entitle a plaintiff to restitution or preclude recovery of the money paid under a mere mistake of law. That problem, it should be said immediately, does not affect payments [395] made in compromise of contested claims. When a claim

---

104 This principle has been confirmed in a number of subsequent decisions: see, eg, *Commercial Bank of Australia Ltd v Younis* (1979), p 450; *Barclays Bank Ltd v Simms* (1980) (see extract, p 99); *Doyle v Tutt* (1993); *Marook Pty Ltd v Winston Gellard Pty Ltd* (1994); *Kleinwort Benson Ltd v Lincoln City Council* (1999) (see extract, p 126).

is settled by accord and satisfaction, a payment made in satisfaction is made in discharge of an obligation created by the accord: it is unaffected by any mistake as to the validity of the claim compromised ...

[396] Regretfully, I am unable to accept the proposal in the majority judgment that payments made in satisfaction of an honest claim should be classified as 'voluntary' and, on that account, be held to be irrecoverable. Such a definition of irrecoverable payments is at once too broad and too narrow. It is too broad because it is capable of including payments under compulsion or duress and, in cases of mistake of fact, it precludes recovery in cases where it is undoubted that restitution lies. All that the definition requires is that the payee should make a claim honestly and the payment be made in satisfaction of the claim. If the case stated in *Porter v Latec Finance (Qld) Pty Ltd* had been understood as Kitto J understood it (that is, Latec on its own behalf paid Porter the amount required to secure a discharge of the purported mortgage held by Porter and to obtain possession of a clear certificate of title), the payment by Latec to Porter would have been made in satisfaction of Porter's honest claim but Latec would nevertheless have been entitled to recover the money paid under the mistake that Porter held a valid mortgage. 'Voluntary' is a term descriptive of the state of mind of the payer. It is essential to retain the state of mind of the payer as the criterion of voluntariness in order to distinguish voluntary payments from payments made, for example, under compulsion, duress or undue influence. It is inappropriate to define the term by reference to the state of mind of the payee. That is not to say that payments made under a mistake of law in satisfaction of an honest claim should not be protected. To the contrary, they should be protected but, in my respectful opinion, not by characterising such payments as voluntary.

So long as mistake of law was excluded as a ground for recovery of a payment, it was appropriate to use the term 'voluntary' to indicate the state of mind of a payer who, having full knowledge of the material facts, is consciously unaware of the relevant law but chooses to pay a demand honestly made.[105] In that event, as PA Butler points out:[106] 'there is simply no operative mistake forming part of the facts founding recovery; that is, the money is irrecoverable as being paid in the settlement of an honest claim. The principle embodied here may be called the "voluntary settlement" principle.' When such a voluntary settlement is made, the payer consciously abandons any right to impeach the finality of the payment. But, once a mere mistake of law is admitted as a *prima facie* [397] ground for recovery of a payment, the payer has, so to speak, reserved a right to impeach the finality of the payment if it should turn out that the payee had no right to receive it. Of course, if a plaintiff consciously waives any right to impeach a payment if the law should turn out to be different from what the payee assumes it to be and intends to satisfy the payee's honest demand in any event, any mistake of law that emerges is not causative and it is right to describe such a payment as voluntary. But such a case would be exceptional. The ordinary case of payment under a mistake of law arises when the payer and the payee make an erroneous assumption as to the existence of an obligation and the error of law is subsequently revealed to both. It

---

105 See *Kelly v Solari* (1841).
106 'Mistaken payments, change of position and restitution', in Finn (ed), *Essays on Restitution*, 1990, p 95.

would lead to great uncertainty if the payer should be entitled to recover the money paid in every case of that kind. Gibbs J sought to avoid this result in *Brisbane v Dacres* (1813) by bundling all payments under a mistake of law into the class of voluntary submissions to claims:

> We must take this payment to have been made under a demand of right, and I think that where a man demands money of another as a matter of right, and that other, with a full knowledge of the facts upon which the demand is founded, has paid a sum, he never can recover back the sum he has so voluntarily paid. It may be, that upon a further view he may form a different opinion of the law, and it may be, his subsequent opinion may be the correct one. If we were to hold otherwise, I think many inconveniences may arise; there are many doubtful questions of law; when they arise, the defendant has an option, either to litigate the question, or to submit to the demand, and pay the money. I think, that by submitting to the demand, he that pays the money gives it to the person to whom he pays it, and makes it his, and closes the transaction between them.

Latham CJ in *Werrin v The Commonwealth* (1938) stated the principle in similar terms:

> The principle appears to me to be quite clear that if a person, instead of contesting a claim, elects to pay money in order to discharge it, he cannot thereafter, because he finds out that he might have successfully contested the claim, recover the money which he so paid merely on the ground that he made a mistake of law.

The fallacy in this approach is that many payments, without conscious adversion to the relevant law, would not have been made had the payer known the true legal position. Such payments are no more voluntary than payments made under a mistake of fact when the payer does not have full knowledge of the facts when the [398] payment is made. Many cases of payments that turn out to have been made under a mistake of law are made simply by an omission to consider the law: they cannot realistically be treated as payments made in submission to a claim. Professor Birks reminds us that:[107]

> Not only are there many doubtful questions of law, there are also many decent people and institutions whose habit is to meet their liabilities without waiting to be hounded, and necessarily they meet the liabilities they think they see. Mistakes only come out later. Since the law is often misunderstood and even changes under foot, recipients have a special need for security whether they actively claim ... or passively receive.

Dawson J: ... [402] Mason CJ, Deane, Toohey, Gaudron and McHugh JJ point out that the relevant authorities in this court[108] which have denied the recovery of money paid under a mistake of law may, with the exception of a passage in the judgment of Williams J in *York Air Conditioning & Refrigeration (A/asia) Pty Ltd v The Commonwealth* (1949), be explained upon the basis that the payments were made voluntarily and were not recoverable for that reason regardless of any mistake of law. At the same time these cases illustrate the difficulty of establishing that a

---

107 Birks, *op cit*, fn 97, p 166.
108 *Werrin v The Commonwealth* (1938); *South Australian Cold Stores Ltd v Electricity Trust (SA)* (1965), p 247.

payment was made under a mistake of law as opposed to a mistake of fact. Facts tend to be black or white but the law [403] very often is not. Where it is not possible to be completely confident of the relevant law, a person may meet an honest claim in the belief that he is entitled to resist it and yet make the payment voluntarily. That is to say, he may make the payment in the exercise of his judgment, notwithstanding his belief that the law does not require him to do so or relieves him of the obligation of doing so. *A fortiori*, where a person makes a payment with no belief one way or the other about the relevant law, he makes the payment voluntarily even though he is not obliged by law to do so and may not have done so had he known that he was not obliged to do so. In that respect a mistake of law is no different to a mistake of fact. As Parke B said in *Kelly v Solari* (1841):

> If, indeed, the money is intentionally paid, without reference to the truth or falsehood of the fact, the plaintiff meaning to waive all inquiry into it, and that the person receiving shall have the money at all events, whether the fact be true or false, the latter is certainly entitled to retain it; but if it is paid under the impression of the truth of a fact which is untrue, it may, generally speaking, be recovered back, however careless the party paying may have been, in omitting to use due diligence to inquire into the fact.

Those who honour their contractual obligations may or may not do so because they believe them to be legally binding. They may do so simply because they have contracted to do so and not because they have turned their minds to any question of law. A payment made in those circumstances is made voluntarily and even if it turns out that there was no legal obligation to make the payment, it does not seem to me that it can be said that the payment was made under a mistake of law. Indeed, it cannot necessarily be said that, if the payer had turned his mind to the question of law, he would not have made the payment. Some contractual obligations are commonly performed in the knowledge that they are not binding and not every question of law can be answered so clearly or definitely as to warrant the resistance of an honest claim for payment.

Considerations such as these would seem to lie behind the modern tendency to justify the rule that there can be no recovery of money paid under a mistake of law, not upon the basis of presumed knowledge of the law (which is unsupportable), but upon the basis that payments made under a mistake of law are made voluntarily unless they are induced by the behaviour of the payee, for example, by compulsion, extortion or undue influence. This is reflected in the [404] observation of the Federal Court in *J & S Holdings Pty Ltd v NRMA Insurance Ltd* (1982):

> The insufficiency of mistake of law as the foundation of an action for recovery of money paid is commonly stated as a general principle or rule of law precluding any right of action in a case where the payment was voluntary.[109]

It is also reflected in the view of Latham CJ and McTiernan J in *Werrin v The Commonwealth*. In that case the plaintiff resisted the payment of sales tax upon a basis which ultimately proved to be correct. Nevertheless he paid, albeit reluctantly. There was no compulsion, extortion or undue influence or anything of that kind. Latham CJ and McTiernan J held that the payment was made

---

109 See also Goff and Jones, *op cit*, fn 48, pp 118–19; Birks, *op cit*, fn 97, p 164.

voluntarily, albeit under a mistake of law. Latham CJ said that 'if a person, instead of contesting a claim, elects to pay money in order to discharge it, he cannot thereafter, because he finds out that he might have successfully contested the claim, recover the money which he so paid merely on the ground that he made a mistake of law' (p 159). And in *South Australian Cold Stores Ltd v Electricity Trust of South Australia* (1957), the plaintiff was held to have voluntarily paid the higher rates at which electricity was supplied to it by the defendant notwithstanding that it is a fair inference that, had it known that they were not validly imposed, it would not have paid them. There was 'nothing but an assumption that in some way or other the increased charge might lawfully be made and a readiness to comply with the payee's demand without more, a demand which but for formal defects in the authorisation would have been enforceable' (p 75).

But a payment made under a mistake of law is not necessarily voluntary when it is made in the absence of some compulsion or inducement by the payee. Voluntariness may afford a convenient explanation for the rule that money paid under a mistake of law cannot be recovered, but it is not an explanation in every case. Perhaps in the nature of things the cases may be relatively few, but it is obvious that a person may be caused by a mistake of law on his part to make a payment which he would not otherwise have made. The payment would not, in those circumstances, be voluntary.

In the present case, the full court below expressed the view that 'there is sufficient evidence from which one can infer that the appellants would have made no payment but that which they [405] regarded themselves as legally obliged to make pursuant to their contractual and security arrangements with the bank'.[110] Whether that is the appropriate inference to draw is another thing. It seems to me that the first question should be whether the appellants turned their minds to the question of their legal obligation at the time they made the relevant payments or whether they made those payments merely because the contract provided they should do so, that is to say, voluntarily and not because of any mistaken belief in the law. If the latter, then it is immaterial that they later formed the view, by reference to s 261 of the Income Tax Assessment Act, that they were not legally obliged to make the payments at the time they made them ...

Commentary

The joint judgment in this case held that a payment is made 'voluntarily in submission to a claim' in three circumstances (p 373):

(1) where the plaintiff chooses to pay the money despite knowledge or suspicion that there is no valid obligation to make the payment;

(2) where the plaintiff is prepared to assume the validity of the obligation rather than contest the claim for payment; or

(3) where the plaintiff is 'not concerned to query whether payment is legally required'.

As Brennan J points out (pp 396–97), the first proposition arguably does no more than confirm the requirement that the plaintiff must have been acting

---

110 *David Securities Pty Ltd v Commonwealth Bank of Australia* (1990), p 33.

under a causative mistake. Recent cases have in fact categorised payments as being 'voluntary' on the basis they were not made under a causative mistake.[111]

The second proposition has again been criticised by Brennan J (pp 397–98), and also by commentators[112] on the basis that it would apparently have the effect of denying relief except in those exceptional cases where the plaintiff has consciously considered the validity of a particular obligation and has reached a mistaken conclusion. It would unfairly deny relief to persons, such as many taxpayers, who assume the payment would not be demanded if it was not valid (p 398 *per* Brennan J).[113]

It is submitted that it is the third proposition that potentially founds a meaningful principle of 'voluntary submission'. A plaintiff should be treated as having voluntarily submitted to a claim in those exceptional cases where the plaintiff makes the payment in order to close the transaction and consciously waives any right to challenge the validity of the payment.[114] An example is where the plaintiff voluntarily elects to pay money in order to close the transaction rather than investigate the legal basis of the payment or institute litigation.[115]

DEFENCE OF HONEST CLAIM

David Securities Pty Ltd v Commonwealth Bank of Australia **(1992) 175 CLR 353 High Court of Australia**

The facts are stated at p 110.

Brennan J: ... [398] If it be desirable to introduce a principle to protect the finality of payments made under a mistake of law in satisfaction of what, to the mind of the payee, is an honest claim of right, it is not satisfactory to press into service the concept of voluntary payments. The principle should be dressed in modern attire rather than in an older garb that will not fit.

---

111 See in particular the decision of the Full Federal Court in *Roxborough v Rothmans of Pall Mall Australia Ltd* (1999). The High Court on appeal decided the case on a different ground: *Roxborough v Rothmans of Pall Mall Australia Ltd* (2001) (see extracts, pp 268 and 273). See also *Halgido Pty Ltd v DG Capital Company Ltd* (1996), pp 592–93.

112 Bryan, 'Mistaken payments and the law of unjust enrichment: *David Securities Pty Ltd v Commonwealth Bank of Australia*' (1993) 15 Syd LR 461 at 482; Liew, 'Mistaken payments – the right of recovery and the defences' (1995) 7 Bond LR 95 at 99; McInnes, 'Mistaken payments return to the High Court' (1996) Mon ULR 209 at 229.

113 See also Liew, 'Mistaken payments – the right of recovery and the defences' (1995) 7 Bond LR 95 at 99.

114 *Scottish Equitable plc v Derby* (2001) 3 All ER 818, p 825; Bryan, 'Mistaken payments and the law of unjust enrichment: *David Securities Pty Ltd v Commonwealth Bank of Australia*' (1993) 15 Syd LR 461 at 476–84; Burrows, *The Law of Restitution*, 1993, p 102; Goff and Jones, *The Law of Restitution*, 5th edn, 1998, pp 197–200. Compare *David Securities Pty Ltd v Commonwealth Bank of Australia* (1992), at 396–97 *per* Brennan J (see above extract).

115 *Kelly v Solari* (1841) (see extract, p 139). See also Liew, 'Mistaken payments – the right of recovery and the defences' (1995) 7 Bond LR 95 at 99. For a recent example of the application of voluntary submission principles, see *Riessen v State of South Australia* (2001).

The reason for introducing any limitation on restitution of payments made under a mistake of law should be identified: it is to achieve a degree of certainty in past transactions.[116] Unless some limiting principle is introduced, the finality of any payment would be as uncertain as the governing law. How should the limiting principle be stated? The *Restatement of the Law of Restitution*[117] proposes a rule of 'honest claim' in these terms:

> It is not essential to retention that the transferee demand performance; he is entitled to retain what he has received if, because of a mistake of law, he does not know when he learns of the transfer and for what it was given, that he was not entitled to it. On the other hand, if he has no substantial doubt as to the law and believes that the transfer is made because of the other's ignorance of the law, his non-disclosure is fraudulent and he is not entitled to retain what is given.

Whether the principle be stated positively ('an honest claim') or negatively ('does not know that he was not entitled'), it is right in my opinion to state it in terms of the state of mind of the payee at the time when he learns of the receipt of the payment. Then (or, at the latest, shortly thereafter) the payee acquires title to the money paid or property transferred and becomes enriched by the receipt.

The limiting principle will be applicable only in cases where the plaintiff has made a payment under a mistake of law and the defendant has no right to receive it. The principle will therefore be [399] invoked to rebut a *prima facie* right to restitution. Stated in terms of the defendant's state of mind, the onus of establishing the applicability of the principle must rest on the defendant. If the principle be seen as a defence to a claim in restitution for a payment made under a mistake of law, it is unnecessary to consider whether the payer has made the payment in submission to the payee's demand or not. Such a defence, focusing on the payee's state of mind, is best formulated in accordance with what Lord Mansfield said in *Bize v Dickason* (1786): 'where money is paid under a mistake, which there was no ground to claim in conscience, the party may recover it back again by this kind of action.' The protection which the principle should give to a payee who, on a true understanding of the governing law, has been unjustly enriched by the payment, should impose on the payee the onus of proving that, when he learnt of the payment, he had a 'ground to claim in conscience'. I would therefore state the principle thus:

> It is a defence to a claim for restitution of money paid or property transferred under a mistake of law that the defendant honestly believed, when he learnt of the payment or transfer, that he was entitled to receive and retain the money or property.

Three observations should be made about this formulation. First, it restores the distinction between mistake of fact and mistake of law which is no longer determinative of the question of unjust enrichment. Unless restitution for mistake of fact is to be curtailed, or restitution for mistake of law is to unsettle commercial transactions to an unacceptable extent, I see no formula which would eliminate the

---

116 See *Hydro Electric Commission of Nepean v Ontario Hydro* (1982) *per* Estey J.
117 American Law Institute, 1937, p 186.

147

distinction entirely, however unsatisfactory the distinction may be.[118] Secondly, the defence applies *pro tanto*; it does not apply to any part of the money or property which the defendant did not honestly believe himself to be entitled to receive and retain. Thirdly, if money paid under a mistake of law is not *received* in satisfaction of an honest claim of right, it may not be possible to raise a defence of change of position, assuming that that defence is available, in claims for restitution of money paid under a mistake of law.[119] This is a question which cannot be resolved in advance of a case in which the facts call for a resolution.

The defence of receipt in satisfaction of an honest claim of right is [400] necessarily subject to the operation of any relevant statute. Where the mistake under which the payment is made consists in the payer's ignorance of a statute which, in protection of a class of which the payer is a member, absolves the payer of the obligation to pay, the mistake of the payee who receives the payment honestly claiming it to be his due does not entitle the payee to retain it. If it were otherwise, an honest but mistaken claim by the payee would frustrate the operation of the statute. In the present case, s 261 does not prohibit the payment of the tax equivalent and it is therefore beside the point to inquire whether the parties are in *pari delicto*. Section 261, which is clearly a provision in protection of mortgagors, simply avoids an obligation on mortgagors to pay the tax equivalent. If, as Kitto J held in *South Australian Cold Stores Ltd v Electricity Trust of South Australia* (1965),[120] the payer is a member of a class protected by the statute, the payer is entitled to succeed in an action to recover the money paid under a supposed obligation nullified by the statute.[121] It follows that, if the tax equivalent was paid by the respective borrowers under the mistake that they were obliged to do so by the applicable loan agreement, they are entitled now to recover the money so paid ...

Commentary

Brennan J suggests that the plaintiff should be denied recovery of a payment made under a mistake of law where the defendant had an honest belief in an entitlement to receive and retain the enrichment. This suggested 'honest claim' defence has failed to attract significant judicial support,[122] and has been widely criticised by commentators on the basis that it would defeat a large number of claims, and would perpetuate the unsatisfactory distinction between mistakes of fact and mistakes of law.[123] It has been expressly rejected by two members of the House of Lords in the following decision.

---

118 Cf Goff and Jones, *The Law of Restitution*, 3rd edn, 1986, p 119, who suggest that 'the principle in *Bilbie v Lumley* (1802) should only preclude recovery of money which was paid in settlement of an honest claim'. The suggestion thus relates solely to payments made under a mistake of law.

119 See American Law Institute, *Restatement of the Law of Restitution*, 1937, p 13.

120 At pp 257–58: a case where the statute created an offence.

121 Cf *Kiriri Cotton Co Ltd v Dewani* (1960), pp 204–05.

122 Although Toohey and McHugh JJ apparently supported the defence in *Commissioner of State Revenue (Vic) v Royal Insurance Australia Ltd* (1994) (see extracts, pp 76 and 658).

123 Bryan, 'Mistaken payments and the law of unjust enrichment: *David Securities Pty Ltd v Commonwealth Bank of Australia*' (1993) 15 Syd LR 462, p 483; Butler, 'Restitution of overpaid taxes, windfall gains, and unjust enrichment: *Commissioner of State Revenue v Royal Insurance Ltd*' (1995) 18(2) UQLJ 318; McInnes, 'Mistaken payments return to the High Court' (1996) 22(2) Mon ULR 209, pp 232–33.

Kleinwort Benson Ltd v Lincoln City Council **[1999] 2 AC 349 House of Lords**

The facts are stated at p 126.

Lord Goff of Chieveley: ... [384] *Honest receipt*

This issue arises from a principle proposed by Brennan CJ (then Brennan J) in *David Securities Pty Ltd v Commonwealth Bank of Australia* (1992). It reads:

> It is a defence to a claim for restitution of money paid or property transferred under a mistake of law that the defendant honestly believed, when he learnt of the payment or transfer, that he was entitled to receive and retain the money or property.

This principle was expressly proposed in order to achieve a degree of certainty in past transactions. As Brennan J said: 'Unless some limiting principle is introduced, the finality of any payment would be as uncertain as the governing law.'

In this part of the law there has long been concern, among common law judges, about what is sometimes called the finality of transactions, and sometimes the security of receipts. This concern formed a significant part of the amalgam of concerns which led to the rule that money paid under a mistake of law was irrecoverable on that ground. Now that that rule has been abrogated throughout the common law world, attention has of course shifted to the formulation of appropriate defences to the right of recovery. The principle proposed by Brennan J is, I believe, the most far-reaching of the defences to the right of recovery that has yet been proposed.

Anything which falls from Brennan J is, of course, entitled to great respect. But I have to state at once that this proposal seems to have been stillborn. Of the judges who sat with Brennan J on the *David Securities* case, none supported this proposal. I know of no judicial support which the proposal has since received, nor of any support from any of the Law Commissions which have considered this part of the law. The reason for [385] this lack of support is, I believe, that the proposal is generally regarded as being wider than is necessary to meet the perceived mischief.

I start from the proposition that money paid under a mistake of law is recoverable on the ground that its receipt by the defendant will, *prima facie*, lead to his unjust enrichment, just as receipt of money paid under a mistake of fact will do so. There may of course be circumstances in which, despite the mistaken nature of the payment, it is not regarded as unjust for the defendant to retain the money so paid. One notable example is change of the defendant's position. Another is the somewhat undefined circumstance that the payment was made in settlement of an honest claim. Yet, Brennan J's proposed defence is so wide that, if it was accepted, these other defences would in practice cease to have any relevance in the case of money paid under a mistake of law. Moreover in many cases of this kind the mistake is shared by both parties, as for example in the case of the appeals now under consideration. In such cases, recovery by the plaintiff would automatically be barred by Brennan J's proposed defence. So sweeping is the effect of the defence that it is not perhaps surprising that it has not received support from others.

In my opinion, it would be most unwise for the common law, having recognised the right to recover money paid under a mistake of law on the ground of unjust enrichment, immediately to proceed to the recognition of so wide a defence as this which would exclude the right of recovery in a very large proportion of cases. The proper course is surely to identify particular sets of circumstances which, as a matter of principle or policy, may lead to the conclusion that recovery should not be allowed; and in so doing to draw on the experience of the past, looking for guidance in particular from the analogous case of money paid under a mistake of fact, but also drawing upon the accumulated wisdom to be found in the writings of scholars on the law of restitution. However, before so novel and far-reaching defence as the one now proposed can be recognised, a very strong case for it has to be made out; and I can discover no evidence of a need for so wide a defence as this. In particular, experience since the recognition of the right of recovery of money paid under a mistake of law in the common law world does not appear to have revealed any such need.

For these reasons, with all respect to Brennan J, I am unable to accept that the defence proposed by him forms part of the common law.

Lord Hope of Craighead: [413] [Brennan J in *David Securities Pty Ltd v Commonwealth Bank of Australia*] said that it should be a defence to a claim for money paid or property transferred under a mistake of law that the defendant honestly believed when he learned of the payment or transfer that he was entitled to receive and to retain the money or the property. I regret that, while I have derived much assistance from his judgment, I am unable to agree with him on this point. I have some difficulty in seeing why this defence, if there is merit in it as a means of preventing recovery where this would be unjust, should be confined to mistake of law cases. If an honest belief on the part of the payee can overcome the fact that it is *prima facie* unjust that the payer should not be able to recover what he paid under a mistake, why should this not be so in all cases? The reason, I think, is that in mistake of fact cases such a defence has never been recognised. To admit it now in such cases would be to run counter to many authorities. The defence seems to me to be based on expediency not on principle, and in any event to be too wide. But there are other objections. It does not sit easily with the defence of change of position. Indeed, in mistake of law cases, that defence would become unnecessary. The element of good faith would seem to be enough even though the defendant had not acted on the faith of the receipt. I think that this shows that it is lacking in principle. It would also tend to perpetuate the distinction between mistakes of fact and mistakes of law, [414] which is itself undesirable. The Law Commissions have not supported it. I would not favour the adoption of the defence as part of English law.

Commentary and question

What reasons did Lords Goff and Hope give for rejecting 'honest claim' as a defence to claims based on mistake of law?

The suggested 'honest claim' defence is contrary to the orthodox position that a defendant cannot defend a claim based on mistake merely on the basis that the defendant also shared in that mistake and *bona fide* believed in an entitlement to the money. This principle is illustrated clearly by the following case.

Air Canada v Ontario (Liquor Control Board) [1997] 2 SCR 581 Supreme Court of Canada

The appellant airlines provided alcohol to their passengers. As they believed they were required to do, they held licences to sell alcohol under the Ontario liquor licensing legislation which was administered by the Liquor Control Board of Ontario. As licence holders they were required to pay a 'gallonage fee' to the Board based on the volume of alcohol they purchased. Another airline, Wardair, discovered that the province of Ontario had no authority to require airlines to hold licences for the keeping of liquor intended to be consumed in flight, and, accordingly, that the provisions relating to the payment of gallonage fees were inapplicable to airlines. Apparently concerned that it would be liable to refund a considerable sum if the larger airlines discovered the true position, the Board reached a secret arrangement with Wardair that from 1 January 1984 that airline would no longer pay the gallonage fees. In 1989, Wardair merged with Canadian Airlines International. At that time, Canadian learned that Wardair did not hold a liquor licence in Ontario and had not paid gallonage fees after 1 January 1984. For obvious reasons, Canadian was interested in securing the same treatment for its own operations in Ontario. The Board, for its part, refused to concede that it had ever released Wardair from the obligation to pay the fees. In the event, Canadian agreed to continue paying gallonage fees, but only under protest. Canadian and another airline, Air Canada, commenced proceedings to recover the gallonage fees paid to the Board. The trial judge and the Ontario Court of Appeal ordered restitution of the gallonage fees paid after 1 January 1984 on the basis they were paid under a mistake of law. However, the fees paid prior to this date were held to be irrecoverable, as the Board was not aware of the error of law. The airlines appealed to the Supreme Court. The Board conceded before the Supreme Court that it was liable to make restitution of the gallonage fees paid after 1 January 1984, but the question was whether the Board was required to make restitution of the fees paid prior to this date.

Iacobucci J (delivering the judgment of the court): ... [597] The respondents concede that the Court of Appeal did not err in ordering restitution of the gallonage fees paid by the airlines after 1 January 1984 ...

The only real issue about restitution is whether the provincial authorities should be made to disgorge only gallonage fees paid after 1 January 1984, or whether they should be liable as well for the fees paid before that date.

In my view, the restriction of restitution to gallonage fees paid after 1 January 1984 is arbitrary. The trial judge and the Court of Appeal justified their choice of that date on the ground that it was then that Wardair brought the matter of the licence to the attention of the provincial authorities. The courts below concluded that before 1 January 1984, the parties were in *pari delicto*, and perhaps even that the airlines were more '*delictus*' than the provincial authorities. Both the trial judge and the Court of Appeal seem to have thought that the burden was on the airlines to discover that Ontario's liquor licensing laws were inapplicable to them.

This 'compromise' approach may seem to have a certain 'equitable' appeal, but in truth it has little to recommend it. Essentially, the position of the trial judge and the Court of Appeal is that a governmental agency may never be liable for amounts collected under an inapplicable law unless it can be shown that the agency knew that the law was inapplicable and nevertheless continued to apply it. But Canadian law has never required a showing of bad faith as a precondition to the recovery of moneys collected by a governmental agency under an inapplicable law. This court has said [in *Eadie v Township of Brantford* (1967)] that moneys paid under such a law may be recovered even if it appears that the governmental agent responsible for collecting them did not know that the law was inapplicable:

> In this case, the appellant, as a taxpayer and inhabitant of the defendant corporation, was dealing with the clerk treasurer of the corporation and that clerk treasurer was under a duty toward the appellant and other taxpayers of the municipality. When that clerk treasurer demands payment of a sum of money on the basis of an illegal bylaw *despite the fact that he does not know of its illegality*, he is not in *pari delicto* to the taxpayer who is required to pay that sum. [Emphasis added.]

In my view, the rule in *Eadie* is a sensible one. If the question is which of two parties should be responsible for guaranteeing the applicability of a law, and the choice is between the governmental agency charged with administering that law and the citizen who is subject to that law, surely the better choice is the governmental agency. I cannot see that it matters how sophisticated an actor the citizen is. Governments make laws and governments administer them. Citizens do not. The responsibility for taking care that the law is legal and applicable must rest with the party that makes and administers the law. And in any case, to make the apportionment of responsibility depend on [598] the sophistication of the actors would be to introduce a vague idea into an area of the law that is otherwise clear.

Therefore, I conclude that the trial judge and the Court of Appeal erred in restricting restitution to the gallonage fees collected after 1 January 1984. The provincial authorities should be made to restore all the moneys that they wrongfully took from the airlines ...

CHAPTER 6

NON-MONETARY BENEFITS
PROVIDED UNDER A MISTAKE

In this chapter a distinction is drawn between the mistaken provision of services and improvements to goods on the one hand, and the mistaken improvement to land on the other. This distinction is necessary because, as will be seen, quite different principles will apply in these two categories.

MISTAKEN PROVISION OF SERVICES AND IMPROVEMENT TO GOODS

Provided that a benefit can be established, a plaintiff who provides services acting under a causative mistake will be entitled to recover the reasonable value of the services provided.[1] This principle applies whether or not the services are pure services or result in an end product or an improvement to the defendant's goods. As with mistaken payments, the onus will be on the plaintiff to prove that the mistake was a cause of the provision of the services.[2] Alternatively, free acceptance will ground recovery if the defendant requested the services, or were aware they were being provided and failed to take a reasonable opportunity to reject the services.[3]

The plaintiff might face some difficulties in establishing an enrichment of the defendant where the services were not requested or accepted.[4] In that circumstance, the plaintiff must establish an incontrovertible benefit, in the form of a realisable end product or the saving of a necessary expense.[5] An incontrovertible benefit will be difficult to establish where the services are pure services which have not resulted in an end product or improvement to other goods of the plaintiff.

Greenwood v Bennett [1973] QB 195 English Court of Appeal

Bennett owned a Jaguar, worth between £400–£500, which he gave to Searle to perform repairs upon with a view to selling the car. Searle crashed the car causing extensive damage, and then sold it without Bennett's authority to Harper for £75, its market value in that condition. Harper restored the car to a good condition at a cost of £226. He then sold it to a finance company who let it on hire purchase to

---

1   *Greenwood v Bennett* (1973) (see following extract); Goff and Jones, *The Law of Restitution*, 5th edn, 1998, pp 246, 248.
2   *Rover International Ltd v Cannon Film Sales Ltd* (1989) (see extract, p 156).
3   See pp 281–82 for a general discussion of free acceptance as an unjust factor.
4   Where the services were requested or accepted, free acceptance establishes the benefit: *Angelopoulos v Sabatino* (1995) (see extract, p 418). See the discussion of free acceptance in the context of establishing benefit: pp 39–50.
5   For a discussion of the concept of incontrovertible benefit, see pp 51–66.

Prattle. The police repossessed the car from Prattle, and the matter ultimately became a contest between Bennett and Harper. Bennett was given possession of the car pursuant to a court order, and resold it for about £400 prior to the hearing in the Court of Appeal. Harper brought a claim against Bennett for the value of the work he had performed on the car.

Lord Denning MR: ... [201] To decide this case, I think it helpful to consider the legal position as if the police had not taken possession of the car, but it had remained in Mr Prattle's possession.

In the first place, if Mr Bennett's company had brought an action against Mr Harper for conversion of the car (relying on his purchase of it from Mr Searle for £75 as the act of conversion), then the damages would be £75 as its value at that time; whereas, if they had brought an action for conversion (relying on his sale of it to the finance company as the act of conversion) the damages would be its improved value at the time of sale, but the company would have to give credit for the work which Mr Harper had done on it: see *Munro v Willmott* (1949). So I suppose they would recover again about £75.

In the second place, if Mr Bennett's company had brought an action in detinue against Mr Prattle (whilst it was still in his possession) they could have recovered from him the value of the car at the time of judgment, that is, as improved by Mr Harper's work: see *Rosenthal v Alderton & Sons Ltd* (1946) and *General and Finance Facilities Ltd v Cooks Cars (Romford) Ltd* (1963), p 650 by Diplock LJ. But Mr Prattle would have a claim against the finance company (for breach of condition as to title), which the finance company could pass on to Mr Harper: and the damages recoverable by them from Mr Harper would be £450, the value of the car as he sold it to them. In those circumstances, I should think that justice would require that Mr Harper should be able to recover the cost of his work from Mr Bennett's company. Otherwise, you would get the very odd result that the company, by suing Mr Prattle in detinue, could – by this indirect means – recover from Mr Harper more than they could by suing him directly in conversion.

In the third place, if Mr Bennett's company had brought an action against Mr Prattle for specific delivery of the car, it is very unlikely that an order for specific delivery of the car would be made. But if it had been, no court would order its delivery unless compensation was made for the improvements. There is a valuable judgment by Lord Macnaghten in *Peruvian Guano Co v Dreyfus Brothers & Co* (1892), where he said:

> I am not aware of any authority upon the point, but I should doubt whether it was incumbent upon the court to order the defendant to return the goods *in specie* where the plaintiff refused to make a fair and just allowance ...

So, if this car were ordered to be returned to Mr Bennett's company, I am quite clear the court in equity would insist upon a condition that payment should be made to Mr Harper for the value of the improvements which he put on it.

Applying the principle stated by Lord Macnaghten, I should have thought that the county court judge here should have imposed a condition [202] on the plaintiffs. He should have required them to pay Mr Harper the £226 as a condition of being given delivery of the car.

But the judge did not impose such a condition. The plaintiffs have regained the car, and sold it. What then is to be done? It seems to me that we must order the plaintiffs to pay Mr Harper the £226; for that is the only way of putting the position right.

Upon what principle is this to be done? [Counsel for Mr Bennett] has referred us to the familiar cases which say that a man is not entitled to compensation for work done on the goods or property of another unless there is a contract express or implied, to pay for it. We all remember the saying of Pollock CB: 'One cleans another's shoes; what can the other do but put them on?': *Taylor v Laird* (1856). That is undoubtedly the law when the person who does the work knows, or ought to know, that the property does not belong to him. He takes the risk of not being paid for his work on it. But it is very different when he honestly believes himself to be the owner of the property and does the work in that belief. (That distinction is drawn in the mining cases such as *Wood v Morewood* (1841) and *Livingstone v Rawyards Coal Co* (1880).) Here we have an innocent purchaser who bought the car in good faith and without notice of any defect in the title to it. He did work on it to the value of £226. The law is hard enough on him when it makes him give up the car itself. It would be most unjust if the company could not only take the car from him, but also the value of the improvements he has done to it – without paying for them. There is a principle at hand to meet the case. It derives from the law of restitution. The plaintiffs should not be allowed unjustly to enrich themselves at his expense. The court will order the plaintiffs, if they recover the car, or its improved value, to recompense the innocent purchaser for the work he has done on it. No matter whether the plaintiffs recover it with the aid of the courts, or without it, the innocent purchaser will recover the value of the improvements he has done to it.

In my opinion, therefore, the judge ought not to have released the car to the plaintiffs except on condition that the plaintiffs paid Mr Harper the £226. But now that it has been released to them and they have sold it, we should order Mr Bennett's company to pay Mr Harper £226 in respect of the improvements he made to the car. I would allow the appeal, accordingly.

Phillimore LJ: I agree. This was a case in which I should have thought that in the ordinary way no order for specific restitution of the chattel would have been made, because this was an ordinary commercial article; but the judge has, in effect, dealt with it as if by an order of specific restitution in allowing Mr Bennett to take the car back. In those circumstances it seems to me perfectly clear that on equitable principles someone who has improved the car since it was originally converted and who is not himself a wrongdoer – and it is not suggested that Mr Harper was in any way a wrongdoer – should be credited with the value of the work which he had put into the car by way of improving it. It was not seriously disputed in this case that the £226 had improved the value of the car, making its value far above what it was; and I entirely agree with Lord Denning MR [203] that the judge having failed to allow Mr Harper's claim to be repaid his £226 as a condition of Mr Bennett recovering the motor car, the only course which this court can now take is to make an order that Mr Bennett should pay directly to Mr Harper that sum which indeed ought to have been a condition of Mr Bennett being allowed to take possession. I agree therefore that this appeal should succeed to that extent.

Cairns LJ: I agree. The main issue in this appeal is one on which there is no authority directly in point. The matter has been very well argued on both sides in this court. If the car had, before any proceedings were brought, reached the hands of Mr Bennett, it is difficult to see that Mr Harper could have had any claim against him for the expenditure that he was put to in making the repairs to it. If, on the other hand, the car had remained in the possession of Mr Prattle, and Mr Bennett had sued Mr Harper, then it appears to me that probably the action would have had to be in conversion, and that in assessing the damages for conversion a deduction would have to be made for the expenditure that Mr Harper had incurred. Alternatively, if there could have been an action for detinue against Mr Harper, then similarly, on the principles laid down in *Munro v Wilmott* (1949) and in the speech of Lord Macnaghten in *Peruvian Guano Co v Dreyfus Brothers & Co* (1892), Mr Harper's expenditure would have had to be allowed. It appears to me that in interpleader proceedings similar considerations come into play as those which would affect an action for detinue; and, an order for delivery of the car to Mr Bennett now having been made and carried out, it seems to me that the result must be that Mr Harper ought to receive from Mr Bennett the amount of his expenditure on the car. I agree, therefore, that the appeal should be allowed and that the order proposed ought to be made.

Questions

Do Phillimore and Cairns LJJ recognise a restitutionary claim in this situation? Does Lord Denning? Do the facts of this case fit an unjust enrichment analysis? Can enrichment be established?

Rover International Ltd v Cannon Film Sales Ltd [1989] 1 WLR 912
English Court of Appeal

The facts are stated at p 369.

Rover additionally claimed a *quantum meruit* for the distribution expenses incurred and for the reasonable value of the dubbing work performed.

Kerr LJ: ... [921] It had by [the time of the appeal] evidently become apparent to Cannon's legal advisers, in my view quite rightly, that Rover's claim for something by way of *quantum meruit* was irresistible in principle. In the face of the common mistaken belief held by both parties until about 25 July 1986 that the agreement was binding, subject only to the unfounded allegations of breaches made from the side of Cannon to which I have already referred, the task of the court, to put it broadly for the moment, was clearly to carry out a process of equitable restitution. Admittedly the responsibility for the invalidity of the agreement must rest on the Italian side since they should have ensured that Rover was incorporated before the agreement was executed. But while this might ground some claim for breach of warranty of authority against Mr Luigi de Rossi, who purported to sign on behalf of Rover, it is irrelevant for present purposes. So also is the fact that the repayment of the instalments sought to be recovered was made under a mistake of fact which Mr de Rossi and Mrs Karlin [of Rover] had the means of avoiding by using greater care: see the leading case of *Kelly v Solari* (1841), which decided that a genuine mistake is not vitiated by carelessness. In these circumstances, and perhaps also because [the trial judge] may not have appreciated that the entire gross receipts would now go to Cannon, counsel for the respondents made it clear that he did not seek to uphold the correctness of the judge's out-and-out rejection of a *quantum* *meruit* on the grounds stated by him.[6] The decision in *Re English and Colonial Produce Co Ltd* (1906) was clearly distinguishable, since it related solely to services purportedly rendered to a company before its incorporation. Counsel for the appellants rightly did not press any claim for a *quantum meruit* for anything done on the Italian side prior to 6 February 1986 when Rover were incorporated, and in any event virtually all Monitor's [Rover's associate company] services were rendered thereafter. In relation to these counsel for the respondents also abandoned any suggestion that he could support the judge's conclusion based on the absence of any requests by Cannon to Rover, and we did not have to consider whether anything in the nature of any express or implied request was indeed necessary to found a claim for a *quantum meruit* in circumstances like the present. I therefore say no more about these matters than that in my view counsel for the respondents was right to concede, as he did at an early stage of the appeal, that Rover were entitled to a *quantum meruit* for the services which generated the gross receipts for Cannon, and that this must include an element of reasonable remuneration.

...

Questions

Was the defendant enriched by the provision of the plaintiff's services? What was the mistake on which the plaintiff's claim was based? Was this mistake causative?

McKeown v Cavalier Yachts Pty Ltd (1998) 13 NSWLR 303
Supreme Court of New South Wales

The defendant commenced building a yacht for the plaintiff, acting under a mistake as to the price to be received for the yacht. When the defendant discovered the mistake it ceased work on the yacht. The plaintiff commenced proceedings in detinue for specific restitution of the partly completed yacht. Young J held that the plaintiff was entitled to specific restitution of the yacht, but only after making a fair allowance for the value of the improvements.

Young J: ... [313] The most authoritative treatment of this problem that I have been able to find is in Professor Birks' *An Introduction to the Law of Restitution*[7] and following. It appears clear that if the plaintiff sues for damages in respect of a chattel, and the defendant has improved the chattel, the defendant is entitled to compensation for the extent to which at the time at which the goods fall to be valued, the value of the goods is attributable to the improvement. However, where the plaintiff does not claim damages and where the added value of the chattel has not been realised by it being sold, one must ask oneself why the plaintiff should give compensation to the defendant for the enhanced value of his chattel. If it can be said that the plaintiff has given full and free acceptance to the work done by the second defendant then it is appropriate that the second defendant be compensated for its work. At first blush this looks like a case of free acceptance because the plaintiff knew that the work was going on and what happened to his laminated

---

6   *Rover International Ltd v Cannon Film Sales Ltd* (1987), pp 545–46.
7   Birks, *An Introduction to the Law of Restitution*, 1985, p 122.

hull was what he wanted to happen to it, that is, the hull to be built into a yacht. The problem, however, is that the financial deal between the plaintiff and Cavalier Yachts meant that the work could be done without further payment by the plaintiff except perhaps for sales tax ...

It would seem that in a case where the plaintiff expects X to do work on his chattel which will not mean any moneys having to be paid out of that person's purse and as things turn out, Y does the work, even though the work done is what the plaintiff expected, the acceptance of the work is 'not free enough to make the enrichment unjust'.[8] Accordingly, it seems to me that the test for compensation in this class of case is whether the work done conferred on the plaintiff an incontrovertible benefit. If it did, the plaintiff must pay compensation as a prerequisite to obtaining an order for specific recovery of the chattel and the measure of that compensation is the amount of incontrovertible benefit.

[Young J referred to the fact that the relevant cost price of the work was $4,409 and continued at p 314:]

This is the cost price of the work. What needs to be considered by the master is the increased value in the yacht as a result of the second defendant's work rather than the cost of providing such work which cost presumably includes profit margins.

...

Questions

Why was the plaintiff held not to have freely accepted the work, despite being aware of the fact that it was being provided? On what basis did Young J find a benefit to the plaintiff in the work? Was the yacht realised? What was the appropriate measure of relief according to Young J?

MISTAKEN IMPROVEMENT TO LAND

There is a paucity of authority dealing with the application of common law restitutionary principles to the situation where the plaintiff improves the defendant's land by mistake. The reason for the lack of authority is that these cases have traditionally been dealt with through the equitable doctrine of proprietary estoppel, not in restitution law.

The proprietary estoppel cases have consistently held that the plaintiff's mistake will not of itself justify relief: the plaintiff must establish that the defendant was aware the improvement was taking place and either acquiesced or encouraged the plaintiff to act.[9] The principles from the law of proprietary estoppel have heavily influenced the development of restitutionary jurisprudence in this area, so that the currently accepted position is that mistake

---

8   Birks, *An Introduction to the Law of Restitution*, 1985, p 116.
9   *Ramsden v Dyson* (1866); *Willmott v Barber* (1880); *Brand v Chris Building Co Pty Ltd* (1957) (see following extract), pp 628–29; *Inwards v Baker* (1965) (see extract, p 161), pp 36, 38; *Silovi Pty Ltd v Barbaro* (1988), p 472; *Strang Patrick Stevedoring Pty Ltd v The 'Sletter'* (1992), pp 521–24.

of itself will not ground recovery in restitution; rather the plaintiff must establish that the defendant knew of the mistake and acquiesced in or encouraged the provision of the services.[10] In restitutionary terms, the plaintiff must establish that the defendant requested or freely accepted the services.

Brand v Chris Building Co Pty Ltd [1957] VR 625 Supreme Court of Victoria

The defendant agreed with a Mr and Mrs Pulis to build for them a house on land either adjoining or in the immediate vicinity of the plaintiff's land. In October 1956, operating under a mistake which was induced by Mr Pulis pointing out the wrong piece of land to the managing director of the defendant, the defendant commenced construction of the house on land belonging to the plaintiff. The plaintiff was unaware of the building activity until November 1956, at which time he immediately took steps to inform the defendant of his rights. The plaintiff commenced an action claiming damages, a declaration that he was the owner of the house, and an injunction preventing the defendant from entering the land or demolishing the house. The defendant argued that the plaintiff's claims were barred by acquiescence.

Hudson J: ... [628] Those being the facts, it was urged on behalf of the defendant ... that the plaintiff should have knowledge imputed to him because he had had an opportunity of seeing the block and seeing what was going on. I think there is no foundation whatever for any such doctrine; I do not consider that the plaintiff should be saddled with knowledge which he did not have. I reject the argument presented along these lines. The position therefore is this, that the plaintiff as the owner is entitled to possession; the defendant under an honest mistake, which was not contributed to by the plaintiff, entered upon the land without any authority or licence of the plaintiff, became a trespasser and proceeded to build a house on it; and when the plaintiff found out, he took immediate steps to prevent the continuance of the trespass.

What does the law say about such a position? I think the correct statement of the position is as set out in *Halsbury's Laws of England*:[11] 'When A stands by while his right is being infringed by B, the following circumstances must as a general rule be present in order that the estoppel may be raised against A: (1) B must be mistaken as to his own legal rights; if he is aware that he is infringing the rights of another, he takes the risk of those rights being asserted; (2) B must expend money, or do some act, on the faith of his mistaken belief; otherwise, he does not suffer by A's subsequent assertion of his rights; (3) acquiescence is founded on contract with a knowledge of one's legal rights, and hence A must know of his own rights; (4) A must know of B's mistaken belief; with that knowledge it is inequitable for him to keep silence and allow B to proceed on his mistake; (5) A must encourage B in his expenditure of money or other act, either directly or by abstaining from asserting his legal right.'

---

10   *Brand v Chris Building Co Pty Ltd* (1957) (see following extract); *Cadorange Pty Ltd v Tanga Holdings Pty Ltd* (1990), pp 34–35; *Sunstar Fruit Pty Ltd v Cosmo* (1995), pp 225, 226–27; Goff and Jones, *The Law of Restitution*, 5th edn, 1998, pp 240–41; Birks, *An Introduction to the Law of Restitution*, rev edn, 1989, pp 291–93.

11   3rd edn, Vol 14, para 1179, p 639.

The authorities for these propositions regarding estoppel have been referred to in argument. Perhaps the most important is *Ramsden v Dyson* (1866), a case of high authority: there were others such as *Willmott v Barber* (1880) and the decision of our High Court in *Svenson v Payne* (1945). Those authorities, I think, amply support the propositions set out in *Halsbury* I have read, and in the absence of the requirements there set forth, the defence of acquiescence must fail. In my opinion, the last three requirements have not been satisfied. In other words, it has not been shewn that there was knowledge by the plaintiff of his own rights for the simple reason that he did not know his rights were being infringed. It follows that he could not know of the mistaken belief of the defendant. The plaintiff did not know what was going on, and therefore, there was nothing he could do until he found out on 30 November. Therefore, it is amply clear that the plea of acquiescence upon [629] which the defence and counterclaim are based fails. [Counsel for the defendant] in support of his argument for the defendant, relied on the maxim of equity: 'He who seeks equity must do equity.' This does not mean that in every action where a party seeks equitable relief that that relief will be refused if some injustice will be produced. The maxim must be applied having regard to the principles established by the cases. In cases such as the present, it must be shewn that the plaintiff was guilty of something in the nature of a fraud, and there is nothing of that kind here and I can find no ground which could raise an equity in favour of the defendant.

[Counsel for the defendant] also sought to call in aid the doctrine of unjust enrichment which has been the subject of much writing of recent years, but he was not able to point to any case where it had been applied in circumstances such as the present, and to apply it would be to fly in the face of the highest authority. It is quite impossible to apply it in the face of these authorities. I think, therefore, that the claim should succeed and the counterclaim must fail ...

Commentary

One reason for the courts' traditional insistence on free acceptance is that ordinarily the plaintiff will be unable to establish enrichment in its absence. However, one issue that arises for the future is whether the requirement of free acceptance will be strictly insisted upon where the enrichment can be established on the basis of an incontrovertible benefit. Admittedly, it might be difficult to establish an incontrovertible benefit in the situation where land has been improved, as the improvement will usually not be 'realisable'.[12] Nevertheless, there will be rare cases where the improvement has actually been realised by the defendant, in which case a clear incontrovertible benefit arises. Accordingly, it is at least arguable that where the enrichment can be established by relying on the principle of incontrovertible benefit, a requirement of free acceptance becomes redundant and the mistake of itself could constitute the unjust factor. The elements of the unjust enrichment claim can be established independently of free acceptance: incontrovertible benefit would establish the enrichment and mistake would constitute the unjust factor.

---

12 *Cadorange Pty Ltd v Tanga Holdings Pty Ltd* (1990), p 35; *Sunstar Fruit Pty Ltd v Cosmo* (1995), pp 225–26.

The law of restitution and the equitable doctrine of estoppel will often give quite different remedies. The objective of restitution is not to fulfil assumptions or expectations but rather to reverse the unjust enrichment of the defendant by awarding the plaintiff the reasonable value of the services provided. Accordingly, the law of restitution will be of no assistance to those plaintiffs who seek fulfilment of their assumption or expectation that they have, or will be granted, an interest in the property. Such plaintiffs must rely on the doctrine of estoppel.

Inwards v Baker [1965] 2 QB 29 English Court of Appeal

The appellant (defendant), Mr Jack Baker, was looking for land on which to build a house and his father suggested that he build the house on part of a piece of land owned by him. The appellant did build the house on his father's land, his father helping him with approximately half of the cost. The appellant moved into the house in 1931 and lived there to the date of the trial. The appellant's father died in 1951 and in his will left the land to the respondent, Miss Inwards. The trustees under the will (Miss Inwards' children) did not, for some time, take any steps to remove the appellant from the house, and visited him there periodically. However, in 1963 the trustees commenced ejectment proceedings against the appellant.

Denning LJ: ... [36] We have had the advantage of cases which were not cited to the county court judge cases in the last century, notably *Dillwyn v Llewelyn* (1862) and *Plimmer v Wellington Corporation* (1884). This latter was a decision of the Privy Council which expressly affirmed and approved the statement of the law made by Lord Kingsdown in *Ramsden v Dyson* (1866). It is quite plain from those authorities that if the owner of land requests [37] another, or indeed allows another, to expend money on the land under an expectation created or encouraged by the landlord that he will be able to remain there, that raises an equity in the licensee such as to entitle him to stay. He has a licence coupled with an equity. [Counsel for the plaintiffs] urged before us that the licensee could not stay indefinitely. The principle only applied, he said, when there was an expectation of some precise legal term. But it seems to me, from *Plimmer's* case (1884) in particular, that the equity arising from the expenditure on land need not fail 'merely on the ground that the interest to be secured has not been expressly indicated ... the court must look at the circumstances in each case to decide in what way the equity can be satisfied'.

So in this case, even though there is no binding contract to grant any particular interest to the licensee, nevertheless the court can look at the circumstances and see whether there is an equity arising out of the expenditure of money. All that is necessary is that the licensee should, at the request or with the encouragement of the landlord, have spent the money in the expectation of being allowed to stay there. If so, the court will not allow that expectation to be defeated where it would be inequitable so to do. In this case, it is quite plain that the father allowed an expectation to be created in the son's mind that this bungalow was to be his home. It was to be his home for his life or, at all events, his home as long as he wished it to remain his home. It seems to me that, in the light of that equity, the father could not in 1932 have turned to his son and said: 'You are to go. It is my land and my house.' Nor could he at any time thereafter so long as the son wanted it as his home.

[Counsel for the plaintiffs] put the case of a purchaser. He suggested that the father could sell the land to a purchaser who could get the son out. But I think that any purchaser who took with notice would clearly be bound by the equity. So here, too, the plaintiffs, the successors in title of the father, are clearly themselves bound by this equity. It is an equity well recognised in law. It arises from the expenditure of money by a person in actual occupation of land when he is led to believe that, as the result of that expenditure, he will be allowed to remain there. It is for the court to say in what way the equity can be satisfied. I am quite clear in this case that it can be satisfied by holding that the defendant can remain there as long as he desires to use it as his home ...

Danckwerts LJ: [38] I agree, and I will add only a few words. It seems to me that the claim of the defendant in respect of this property is amply covered by *Errington v Errington and Woods* (1952), *Dillwyn v Llewelyn* (1862) and *Plimmer v Wellington Corporation* (1884). Further, it seems to me to be supported by the observations of Lord Kingsdown in *Ramsden v Dyson* (1866). It is true that, in that case, Lord Kingsdown reached a result on the facts of the case which differed from that reached by the other members of the House of Lords, but Lord Kingsdown's observations which are relevant in the present case have received support since that case was decided; and, in particular, I would like to refer to the observations in the judgment of the Privy Council in *Plimmer v Wellington Corporation* (1884). It was said there at p 713: 'Their Lordships consider that this case falls within the principle stated by Lord Kingsdown as to expectations created or encouraged by the landlord, with the addition that in this case the landlord did more than encourage the expenditure, for he took the initiative in requesting it.'

There are the same circumstances in the present case. The defendant was induced to give up his project of building a bungalow on land belonging to somebody other than his father, in which case he would have become the owner or tenant of the land in question and thus have his own home. His father induced him to build on his, the father's, land and expenditure was incurred by the defendant for the purpose of the erection of the bungalow.

In my view, the case comes plainly within the proposition stated in the cases. It is not necessary, I think, to imply a promise. It seems to me that this is one of the cases of an equity created by estoppel, or equitable estoppel, as it is sometimes called, by which the person who has made the expenditure is induced by the expectation of obtaining protection, and equity protects him so that an injustice may not be perpetrated ...

Questions

What was the relief sought by the defendant in this case? Would this relief have been available in restitution? If a person in the defendant's position were to base his claim on restitution, would this claim be successful? If the restitutionary claim was successful, what would be the measure of relief provided?

CHAPTER 7

NECESSITOUS INTERVENTION

INTRODUCTION

'Necessitous intervention' refers to circumstances where the plaintiff intervenes in a situation of necessity or emergency to protect or preserve the person or goods of another. We are here concerned with situations where the plaintiff intervenes, not as a matter of legal obligation,[1] but as a matter of moral obligation or 'common humanity'.[2]

This chapter is concerned to identify the principles that govern the circumstances when a necessitous intervener can bring a claim for reimbursement of expenses incurred in intervening. Such a claim might be brought against the person who was the direct recipient of the necessitous intervention, or against a third party who had a superior legal or moral obligation to provide the service in question.[3] As we will see, there is no general principle allowing recovery of necessitous expenses: in order to recover the plaintiff must fit within one of the limited categories of case where such claims have been recognised.[4]

POLICY CONSIDERATIONS

The reluctance of the courts to allow claims by necessitous interveners stems from two main policy concerns. The first concern is that the recognition of claims might encourage officious behaviour, whereby interveners themselves create a situation of necessity in order to obtain recompense or to put the defendant in their debt.[5] The second concern is founded on the fact that the defendant has not requested the necessitous intervention, and in fact is often unaware that the intervention is taking place. The courts are resistant to forcing persons to pay for a benefit that they neither requested nor freely chose to accept.[6]

---

1   *Burns Philp & Co Ltd v Gillespie Bros Pty Ltd* (1947), p 175 (see extract, p 177); Mason and Carter, *Restitution Law in Australia*, 1995, p 234.

2   *The Great Northern Railway Company v Swaffield* (1874) (see extract, p 171). See also *Rogers v Price* (1829) (see extract, p 183).

3   For example, a plaintiff who has fulfilled the defendant's legal obligation to provide services to a third party will often seek reimbursement of expenses from the defendant rather than the third party: *Jenkins v Tucker* (1788) (see extract, p 182).

4   See below, pp 169–70.

5   *Nicholson v Chapman* (1793) (see following extract); *Wells v The Owners of the Gas Float Whitton No 2* (1897); *The Goring* (1987), p 708.

6   *Falcke v Scottish Imperial Insurance Company* (1886) (see extract, p 166).

Nicholson v Chapman (1793) 2 H Bl 254; 126 ER 536 Common Pleas

Some timber belonging to the plaintiff was placed in a dock on the banks of the Thames. The timber broke away from the dock by accident and floated to Putney where it was left at low tide within the grounds of a manor. The defendant, acting on the instructions of the bailiff of the manor, removed the timber in his wagon to a place of safety a short distance away. The plaintiff demanded the return of the timber, but the defendant refused unless he was given reasonable compensation for his services. The plaintiff commenced proceedings for *trover* (conversion) however the defendant claimed to have a lien over the timber representing the reasonable value of his services.

Eyre CJ: [257] The only difficulty that remained with any of us, after we had heard this case argued, was upon the question whether this transaction could be assimilated to salvage? The taking care of goods left by the tide upon the banks of a navigable river, communicating with the sea, may in a vulgar sense be said to be salvage; but it has none of the qualities of salvage, in respect of which the laws of all civilised nations, the laws of Oleron, and our own laws in particular, have provided that a recompense is due for the saving, and that our law has also provided that this recompense should be a lien upon the goods which have been saved, see *Sutton v Buck* (1810).

Such are the grounds upon which salvage stands; they are recognised by Lord Chief Justice Holt in the case of *Hartfort v Jones* (1698) which has been cited from Lord Raymond and Salkeld. But see how very unlike this salvage is to the case now under consideration. In a navigable river within the flux and reflux of the tide, but at a great distance from the sea, pieces of timber lie moored together in convenient places; carelessness, a slight accident, perhaps a mischievous boy, casts off the mooring rope, and the timber floats from the place where it was deposited, till the tide falls and leaves it again somewhere upon the banks of the river. Such an event as this, gives the owner [258] the trouble of employing a man, sometimes for an hour, and sometimes for a day, in looking after it till he finds it, and brings it back again to the place from whence it floated. If it happens to do any damage, the owner must pay for that damage; it will be imputable to him as carelessness, that his timber in floating from its moorings is found damage feasant; if that should happen to be the case. But this is not a case of damage feasance; the timber is found lying upon the banks of the river, and is taken into the possession, and under the care of the defendant, without any extraordinary exertions, without the least personal risk, and in truth, with very little trouble. It is therefore a case of mere finding, and taking care of the thing found (I am willing to agree) for the owner. This is a good office, and meritorious, at least in the moral sense of the word, and certainly intitles the party to some reasonable recompense from the bounty, if not from the justice of the owner; and of which, if it were refused, a court of justice would go as far as it could go, towards enforcing the payment.[7] So it would, if a horse had strayed, and was not taken as an estray by the lord under his manorial rights, but was taken up by some good natured man and taken care

---

7 It seems probable that in such a case, if any action could be maintained, it would be an action of *assumpsit* for work and labour, in which the court would imply a special instance and request, as well as a promise. On a *quantum meruit*, the reasonable extent of the recompense would come properly before a jury.

of by him, till at some trouble, and perhaps at some expense, he had found out the owner.[8] So it would be in every other case of finding that can be stated (the claim to the recompense differing in degree, but not in principle); which therefore reduces the merits of this case to this short question, whether every man who finds the property of another, which happens to have been lost or mislaid, and voluntarily puts himself to some trouble and expense to preserve the thing, and to find out the owner, has a lien upon it for the casual, fluctuating and uncertain amount of the recompense which he may reasonably deserve? It is enough to say that there is no instance of such a lien having been claimed and allowed; the case of the pointer dog, *Binstead v Buck* (1777), was a case in which it was claimed and disallowed, and it was thought too clear a case to bear an argument. Principles of public policy and commercial necessity support the lien in the case of salvage. Not only public policy and commercial necessity do not require that it should be established in this case, but very great inconvenience may be apprehended from it, if [259] it were to be established. The owners of this kind of property, and the owners of craft upon the river which lie in many places moored together in large numbers, would not only have common accidents from the carelessness of their servants to guard against, but also the wilful attempts of ill designing people to turn their floats and vessels adrift, in order that they might be paid for finding them. I mentioned in the course of the cause another great inconvenience, namely, the situation in which an owner seeking to recover his property in an action of *trover* will be placed, if he is at his peril to make a tender of a sufficient recompense, before he brings his action: such an owner must always pay too much, because he has no means of knowing exactly how much he ought to pay, and because he must tender enough. I know there are cases in which the owner of property must submit to this inconvenience; but the number of them ought not to be increased: perhaps it is better for the public that these voluntary acts of benevolence from one man to another, which are charities and moral duties, but not legal duties, should depend altogether for their reward upon the moral duty of gratitude. But at any rate, it is fitting that he who claims the reward in such case should take upon himself the burthen of proving the nature of service which he has performed, and the quantum of recompense which he demands, instead of throwing it upon the owner to estimate it for him, at the hazard of being non-suited in an action of *trover*.

Judgment for the plaintiff.

Questions

What conflicting policy considerations arise in claims for the value of necessitous services provided without a request? What special policy considerations arise in cases of salvage? Would the plaintiff's claim in the

---

8   It is however laid down, that a mere voluntary courtesy will not support an *assumpsit*. *Lampleigh v Braithwait* (1615); and see the 'Reporters' note' (1615) 3 Bos & Pul 251; 1 Saund 264 (n), 5th edn, Vol 1, p 93. According to the civil law the party is entitled to recover, see Wood's Institute 256, and see Bull NP 45. Whether the finder of goods is bound to take them into his possession to keep them safely, see *Isaack v Clark* (1615); *Mulgrave v Ogden* (1591).

principal case have been successful had he claimed a *quantum meruit* award rather than a lien?

Falcke v Scottish Imperial Insurance Company (1886) 34 Ch D 234
English Court of Appeal

Emanuel purchased a life insurance policy which he mortgaged to Falcke. Emanuel later went into bankruptcy, but by agreement the policy did not form part of his bankruptcy estate. Accordingly, Emanuel was the owner of the equity of redemption in the policy. In 1883 Emanuel, possibly in the mistaken belief he had purchased Falcke's interest in the policy, paid the annual premium in order to keep the policy on foot. Falcke died and his executrix sought to enforce her security. Emanuel claimed he had a lien on the policy to the amount of the premium paid by him which took priority over the interests of Falcke.

Cotton LJ: ... [241] Now let us see what the general law is. It is not disputed that if a stranger pays a premium on a policy that payment gives him no lien on the policy. A man by making a payment in respect of property belonging to another, if he does so without request, is not entitled to any lien or charge on that property for such payment. If he does work upon a house without request he gets no lien on the house for the work done. If the money has been paid or the work done at the request of the person entitled to the property, the person paying the money or doing the work has a right of action against the owner for the money paid or for the work done at his request. If here there had been circumstances to lead to the conclusion that there was a request by Falcke that this premium should be paid by Emanuel, then there would be a claim against Falcke or his representative for the money, and I do not say that there might not be a lien on the policy. But in my opinion there is no evidence upon which we should be justified in coming to the conclusion that there was any request expressed or implied by Falcke to Emanuel to pay this money. An express request is not suggested. Was there an implied request? I think that in a case of this sort, when money is paid in order to keep alive property which belongs to another, a request to make that payment might be implied from slight circumstances, but in my opinion there is no circumstance here in evidence from which such a request can be implied ...

[243] [W]hat was the position of Emanuel at the time? He was, in my opinion, owner of the ultimate equity of redemption. Does that give him a right to have this sum paid by him for premium repaid to him out of the moneys arising from the policy? In my opinion it does not. It would be strange indeed if a mortgagor expending money on the mortgaged property could establish a charge in respect of that expenditure in priority to the mortgage. It is true that here the mortgagor, the ultimate owner of the equity of redemption, was no longer personally liable to pay the sums charged on the policy and was not bound by the covenant to pay the premium, but he pays it as the owner of the equity of redemption entitled to the ultimate interest in the property, although not personally bound to pay the debt or provide for the premium. It must be considered, in my opinion, that he paid it not so as to get any claim in priority to the incumbrancer, but in order to retain the benefit of the interest which would come to him if the property proved sufficient to pay off the previous incumbrancers. In my opinion it would be utterly wrong to say that a mortgagor, the owner of the equity of redemption, can under those circumstances defeat the incumbrancers on the estate ...

Bowen LJ: [248] I am of the same opinion. The general principle is, beyond all question, that work and labour done or money expended by one man to preserve or benefit the property of another do not according to English law create any lien upon the property saved or benefited, nor, even if standing alone, create any obligation to repay the expenditure. Liabilities are not to be forced upon people behind their backs any more than you can confer a benefit upon a man against his will.

There is an exception to this proposition in the maritime law. I mention it because the word 'salvage' has been used from time to time throughout the argument, and some analogy is sought to be established between salvage and the right claimed by the Respondents. With regard to salvage, general average, and contribution, the maritime law differs from the common law. That has been so from the time of the Roman law downwards. The maritime law, for the purposes of public policy and for the advantage of trade, imposes in these cases a liability upon the thing saved, a liability which is a special consequence arising out of the character of mercantile enterprises, the nature of sea perils, [249] and the fact that the thing saved was saved under great stress and exceptional circumstances. No similar doctrine applies to things lost upon land, nor to anything except ships or goods in peril at sea.

With regard to ordinary goods upon which labour or money is expended with a view of saving them or benefiting the owner, there can, as it seems to me, according to the common law be only one principle upon which a claim for repayment can be based, and that is where you can find facts from which the law will imply a contract to repay or to give a lien. It is perfectly true that the inference of an understanding between the parties – which you may translate into other language by calling it an implied contract – is an inference which will unhesitatingly be drawn in cases where the circumstances plainly lead to the conclusion that the owner of the saved property knew that the other party was laying out his money in the expectation of being repaid. In other words, you must have circumstances from which the proper inference is that there was a request to perform the service. It comes to the same thing, but I abstain from using the word 'request' more than is necessary, for fear of plunging myself into all the archaic embarrassments connected with the cases about requests. But wherever you find that the owner of the property saved knew of the service being performed, you will have to ask yourself (and the question will become one of fact) whether under all the circumstances there was either what the law calls an implied contract for repayment or a contract which would give rise to a lien?

Now in the present case, how can it be said that Mr Falcke, whose representative is claiming the benefit of this policy, so conducted himself as to justify any inference of the kind on the part of Mr Emanuel? There is absolutely no fact from which any such inference, as it seems to me, can be drawn at common law.

But then it is said that though at the time there may have been no such implied contract, nevertheless, the subsequent attempt on the part of Mr Falcke's representatives to take the benefit of the preserved policy makes her, by virtue of something in the nature of adoption or ratification, liable to repay the money expended. There is nothing more vague than the way in which the word 'adoption' is used in arguments at law, and sometimes [250] ambiguous language used about adoption is imported into arguments about ratification. There is no such thing in law as adopting or ratifying anything except where there is the sanctioning of an act professedly done on your behalf in such a sense as to make you liable for it. A man can ratify that which purports to be done for him, but he cannot ratify a thing which purports to be done for somebody else. Ratification only takes effect in law from its being equivalent to a previous authority, and previous authority is an incident which only arises in the relation of principal and agent. There have been many attempts to make people liable by what is called adoption of a contract, or of some other act which never purported to be made or done on their behalf, and such attempts have failed. I may instance as a leading type of that class of cases the attempts that have been made of late to make companies liable for contracts entered into by promoters.

Now the first observation with regard to the attempt to make Mr Falcke's estate liable on the ground that his representative has taken the benefit of what Emanuel has done, is that what Emanuel did was not done for Falcke's estate. Still, if he or his representative took the benefit of it under such circumstances as raise the proper inference of a fresh contract to pay, that would be altogether a different matter. But when we come to examine the case there is not a single fact which raises the slightest presumption that there was any intention at anytime, either before Mr Falcke's death or afterwards, on the part of those who were negotiating with Mr Emanuel, to ask him to pay this sum of money. So much, therefore, for the idea of a lien or even of a right to be repaid this sum at common law.

Now in equity what is there here to give rise to any such right? The cases in equity were examined by Lord Justice Fry in *In re Leslie* (1883) and the general rule is the same in equity as at law. What have we here to take this case out of the general rule? Mr Emanuel was the owner of the equity of redemption. Does the mere fact that the owner of the equity of redemption paid premiums to keep alive the policy give him a right against the mortgagees to have the moneys which he so expended paid [251] in priority to their debt? He paid in his own interest; he did not pay in the interest of the mortgagees. There can be no question here of acquiescence. The mortgagor does not pay under a mistake of fact or any mistake as to his own title. The mortgagee does not stand by and allow him to pay under such a mistake, and as regards any notion that he was allowed to pay under the expectation that he would be repaid again, or would have a lien for the money upon the policy, I have examined that already in the first part of the observations I have been making. If there were any acquiescence of this last kind, it would be an acquiescence from which in common law you would draw the inference of a contract; but, as I said before, there is no fact that leads to that.

Then, what equity is there that can be relied upon? It is not even a case where the owner of the saved property requires the assistance of a court of equity, or the name of the person who has paid that money to get the property back. Here the simple question is whether there are any facts from which we can say that it is unjust or inequitable that Mr Falcke's representatives should be allowed to have that which is their own? If you state the case in that way the answer is obvious, that one cannot see anything of the kind.

Commentary and questions

This case involved a claim for a lien not a personal claim in restitution. Assuming that a personal claim had been brought, would the elements of an unjust enrichment claim be satisfied on these facts? Would there have been a valid defence to the claim? Why did the court refuse the claim on these facts?

It will only be in rare cases the defendant will have requested or accepted the necessitous intervention. Thus, in the absence of request or acceptance, the plaintiff will need to have recourse to the principle of incontrovertible benefit in order to establish an enrichment. The defendant's lack of freedom of choice is not relevant where the benefit is incontrovertible, as the premise of the concept of incontrovertible benefit is that the defendant would have had no choice but to incur the expense of the necessitous action had the plaintiff not intervened. As put by Gautreau:[9] 'The principle of freedom of choice is not the antithesis of freedom of choice. It is not in competition with the latter; rather, it exists when freedom of choice is absent.'

To establish an incontrovertible benefit the plaintiff will need to establish that the necessitous actions saved the defendant a legally or factually necessary expense.[10]

RECOGNISED CATEGORIES OF RELIEF FOR NECESSITOUS INTERVENTION

The law has not yet recognised a general right to restitutionary relief for necessitous intervention. However there are particular categories of case where recovery of necessitous expenses is permitted. The main categories are:

1 agency of necessity;

2 fulfilment of another's obligation;

3 provision of necessaries to mental incompetents; and

4 maritime salvage.[11]

There is also Canadian authority allowing medical practitioners to recover the cost of emergency services provided to unconscious patients,[12] however there is

---

9 Gautreau, 'When are enrichments unjust?' (1988–89) 10 Adv Q 258, p 271. See also McInnes, 'Incontrovertible benefits in the Supreme Court of Canada' (1994) 23 Can Bus LJ 122, p 128.

10 See the discussion above, pp 51–66.

11 The law relating to maritime salvage is voluminous and complex and is not included in this book. For a discussion of this area see Goff and Jones, *The Law of Restitution*, 5th edn, 1998, Chapter 18.

12 *Matheson v Smiley* (1932); *Soldiers Memorial Hospital v Sanford* (1934). The claim will be refused where the patient has expressly refused consent to the procedure: *Soldiers Memorial Hospital v Sanford* (1934).

as yet no Australian or English authority recognising recovery in this circumstance.[13]

The categories where reimbursement of necessitous expenses is permitted have been said to share certain common elements:[14]

1 the intervention must be both necessary and appropriate;

2 the plaintiff must be an appropriate person to intervene;

3 the intervention must be reasonable; and

4 the plaintiff must not be acting gratuitously.

It has been suggested by various academics that a general right of recovery for necessitous intervention can be formulated around these elements.[15] Nevertheless, no such general principal has yet been recognised by the courts, and plaintiffs wishing to recover necessitous expenses must currently fit their claim within one of the recognised categories of case identified above.

Agency of necessity

An agency of necessity can arise in situations where there is a pre-existing agency or bailment relationship between the plaintiff and defendant in relation to the defendant's goods, and an emergency situation arises which was unforeseen by either party and which makes it necessary for the plaintiff to take steps to preserve or dispose of the goods outside of the scope of the previous authority.[16]

The doctrine of 'agency of necessity' is applied in three different contexts. First, an 'agency of necessity' is used to confer on a person an authority to create contractual rights and obligations between the defendant and a third party which are directly enforceable by the third party against the defendant (and vice versa). Secondly, the doctrine is relied upon as a defence to a claim in tort or contract based on a wrongful dealing with the goods, such as conversion. Lastly, the doctrine is relied upon by persons seeking reimbursement of expenses incurred in taking steps that were reasonably necessary to preserve the defendant's goods. It is this third sense of 'agency of necessity' that is relevant to restitution law.

---

13 Mason and Carter, *Restitution Law in Australia*, 1995, pp 248–52; McInnes, 'Restitution and the rescue of life' (1994) 32 Alberta Law Rev 37, pp 46–48. And perhaps such claims will not regularly arise in practice as emergency treatment is usually provided in a public hospital.

14 *Re F (Mental Patient: Sterilisation)* (1990), p 75; Rose, 'Restitution for the rescuer' (1989) 9 OJLS 167, p 178ff; Mason and Carter, *Restitution Law in Australia*, 1995, pp 242–44; McInnes, 'Restitution and the rescue of life' (1994) 32 Alberta Law Rev 37, pp 53–62.

15 See, for example, Rose, 'Restitution for the rescuer' (1989) 9 OJLS 167, p 178ff; Muir, 'Unjust sacrifice and the officious intervener', in Finn (ed), *Essays on Restitution*, 1990, pp 311–14; McInnes, 'Restitution and the rescue of life' (1994) 32 Alberta Law Rev 37; Mason and Carter, *Restitution Law in Australia*, 1995, pp 242–45.

16 *Prager v Blatspiel, Stamp and Heacock Ltd* (1924) (see extract, p 173); *China Pacific SA v Food Corporation of India, The Winson* (1982), p 958 (see extract, p 179).

The weight of authority limits the doctrine of agency of necessity to cases where there is a pre-existing agency or bailment relationship: see in particular *Jebara v Ottoman Bank* (1927) (see extract, p 177) and *China Pacific SA v Food Corporation of India* (1982) (see extract, p 179). Insistence on a pre-existing agency or bailment relationship precludes a claim by a stranger who finds goods belonging to another and incurs expense in preserving the goods.[17] Thus, as the law currently stands, a finder of goods is unable to recover on the basis of an agency of necessity.[18] Nevertheless, there are some indications in the authorities, particularly in *Great Northern Railway Co v Swaffield* (1874) (see following extract) and *Burns Philp & Co Ltd v Gillespie Bros Pty Ltd* (1947) (see extract, p 177), that an agency of relationship can arise in the absence of a pre-existing legal relationship. If this were accepted, it could potentially open the way for a claim by a finder.

Great Northern Railway Company v Swaffield (1874) LR 9 Ex 132 Exchequer

The defendant sent a horse by the plaintiff's railway to himself. When the horse arrived late at night there was no one at the station to meet it on behalf of the defendant. The station master, who did not know the defendant's residence, directed the horse be taken to a livery stable near the station for safe custody. Soon afterwards the defendant's servant arrived to collect the horse and was referred to the stable keeper who refused to deliver the horse except on payment of reasonable charges. The next day the defendant demanded the return of the horse and the station master offered to pay the charges out of his own pocket and let the defendant take away the horse but the defendant declined and went away, leaving the horse at the livery stable. The plaintiff later renewed its offer to send the horse to the defendant without payment of any livery charges but the defendant again refused the offer. Some months later, the plaintiff paid the stable keeper his fees and sent the horse to the defendant, who accepted it. The plaintiff commenced proceedings to recover the livery charges.

Kelly CB: [136] I am clearly of opinion that the plaintiffs are entitled to recover. My Brother Pollock has referred to a class of cases which is identical with this in principle, where it has been held that a shipowner who, through some accidental circumstance, finds it necessary for the safety of the cargo to incur expenditure, is justified in doing so, and can maintain a claim for reimbursement against the owner of the cargo. That is exactly the present case. The plaintiffs were put into much the same position as the shipowner occupies under the circumstances I have described. They had no choice, unless they would leave the horse at the station or in the high road to his own danger and the danger of other people, but to place him in the care of a livery stable keeper, and as they are bound by their implied contract with the livery stable keeper to satisfy his charges, a right arises in them against the defendant to be reimbursed those charges which they have incurred for his benefit.

---

17 *China Pacific SA v Food Corporation of India, The Winson* (1982), p 961 (see extract, p 179); *Jebara v Ottoman Bank* (1927) (see extract, p 177).

18 For cases where claims by mere finders have been denied, see *Binstead v Buck* (1777); *Nicholson v Chapman* (1793) (see extract, p 164).

Piggot B: I am of the same opinion. I do not think we have to deal with any question of lien. We have only to see whether the plaintiffs necessarily incurred this expense in consequence of the defendant's conduct in not receiving the horse, and then whether, under these circumstances, the defendant is under an implied obligation to reimburse them. I am clearly of opinion that he is. The horse was necessarily put in the stable for a short time before the defendant's man arrived. I give no opinion on what then passed, whether the man was right, or whether the plaintiffs were right; I think it is not material. On the following day the defendant comes himself; and the basis of my judgment is, that at that time the station master offered, rather then the defendant should go away without the horse, to pay the charge out of his own pocket; but the defendant declared he would have nothing to do with it, and went away. That I [137] understand to be the substance of what was proved; and if that be so, it shews to me that there was a leaving of the horse by the defendant in the possession of the carriers, and a refusal to take it. Then what were the carriers to do? They were bound, from ordinary feelings of humanity, to keep the horse safely and feed him; and that became necessary in consequence of the defendant's own conduct in refusing to receive the animal at the end of the journey according to his contract. Then the defendant writes and claims the price of the horse; and then again, in answer to the plaintiffs' offer to deliver the horse without payment of the charges, he requires delivery at his farm and the payment of 30s; in point of fact, he again refuses the horse. Upon the whole, therefore, I come to the conclusion that, whoever was right on the night when the horse arrived, the defendant was wrong when, on the next day, he refused to receive him; that the expense was rightly incurred by the plaintiffs; and that there was, under these circumstances, an implied contract by the defendant entitling the plaintiff to recover the amount from him.

Pollock B: I am of the same opinion. If the case had rested on what took place on the night when the horse arrived, I should have thought the plaintiffs wrong, for this reason, that although a common carrier has by the common law of the realm a lien for the carriage, he has no lien in his capacity as warehouseman; and it was only for the warehousing or keeping of this horse that the plaintiffs could have made any charge against the defendant.

But the matter did not rest there; for it is the reasonable inference from what is stated in the case, that on the next day, when the defendant himself came, he could have had the horse without the payment of anything; but he declined to take it, and went away. Then comes the question, first, 'What was the duty of the plaintiffs as carriers, with regard to the horse?' and secondly: 'If they incurred any charges in carrying out that duty, could they recover them in any form of action against the owner of the horse?' Now, in my opinion it was the duty of the plaintiffs, as carriers, although the transit of the horse was at an end, to take such reasonable care of the horse as a reasonable owner would take of his own goods; and if they had turned him out on the highway, or allowed him [138] to go loose, they would have been in default. Therefore they did what it was their duty to do. Then comes the question: 'Can they recover any expenses thus incurred against the owner of the horse?' As far as I am aware, there is no decided case in English law in which an ordinary carrier of goods by land has been held entitled to recover this sort of charge against the consignee or consignor of goods. But in my opinion he is so entitled. It had been long debated whether a shipowner has such a right, and gradually, partly by custom and partly by some opinions of authority in this country, the right has come to be established. It was clearly held to exist in the case of *Notara v Henderson* (1872), where all the authorities on the subject are reviewed with very great care; and that case, with some others, was cited and acted upon by the Privy Council in the recent case of *Cargo ex Argos* (1873) ... It was there said at p 164 (after referring to the observations of Sir James Mansfield, CJ, in *Christy v Row* (1808)), 'The precise point does not seem to have been subsequently decided, but several cases have since arisen in which the nature and scope of the duty of the master, as agent of the merchant, have been examined and defined'. Then after citing the cases, the judgment proceeds: 'It results from them, that not merely is a power given, but a duty is cast on the master, in many cases of accident and emergency, to act for the safety of the cargo in such manner as may be best under the circumstances in which it may be placed; and that, as a correlative right, he is entitled to charge its owner with the expenses properly incurred in so doing.' That seems to me to be a sound rule of law. That the duty is imposed upon the carrier, I do not think any one has doubted; but if there were that duty without the correlative right, it would be a manifest injustice. Therefore, upon the whole of the circumstances, I have come to the conclusion that the claim of the company was a proper one ...

Amphlett B: [139] I am of the same opinion. It appears to me that this case, though trumpery in itself, involves important principles. I think it is perfectly clear that the railway company, when the horse arrived at the station, and no one was there to receive it, were not only entitled but were bound to take reasonable care of it. As a matter of common humanity, they could not have left the horse without food during the whole night, and if they had turned it out on to the road, they would not only have been responsible to the owner, but if any accident had happened to the general public they would have incurred liability to them. Therefore, as it appears to me, there was nothing that they could reasonably do except that which they did, namely, send it to the livery stable keeper to be taken care of ...

Even if the plaintiffs were in the wrong originally, of which I am by no means sure, in not giving up the horse on the night when it arrived, at any rate from the time when that was set right, it was the defendant who was in the wrong, and the company who were in the right. It appears [140] to me, therefore, quite clear that the company are entitled to recover the money which they have been obliged to pay, and have paid, to the livery stable keeper ...

Questions

Why did an agency of necessity arise on these facts according to Kelly CB and Pollock B? According to Piggot and Amphlett BB? Are the views of Piggot and Amphlett BB on the circumstances when an agency of necessity can arise broader than those of the other members of the court? In what sense?

Prager v Blatspiel, Stamp and Heacock Ltd [1924] 1 KB 566 King's Bench

The plaintiff lived in Bucharest and was the furrier to the Romanian court. The defendant was a firm of fur merchants based in London who for some years had acted as the agent for the plaintiff in the buying and dressing of skins. In 1915 and 1916 the defendant purchased for the plaintiff a large number of skins for a total cost of nearly £1,900. At the end of 1916 the German forces invaded Romania, technically making Romania an enemy nation. It was impossible for the defendant to send any goods to the plaintiff or to communicate with him in any way. The defendant sold off most of the skins to other persons, receiving about £400 in total. At the end of the war the plaintiff requested the defendant to send him the furs and, upon being told the furs had been sold, brought an action for conversion. The defendant admitted that it had no contractual right to sell the goods but argued that it had done so under an agency of necessity.

McCardie J: ... [568] Now the first question of law is this: Can the facts as I have outlined them afford a possible legal basis on which to rest an agency of necessity? The defendants say yes; the plaintiff says no. The doctrine of agency of necessity doubtless took its rise from marine adventure. Hence the numerous decisions set out in *Carver on Carriage by Sea*, 6th edn, s 294, and following sections. The substance of the matter as stated in that book is that in cases of necessity the master of a ship has power and it is his duty to sell the goods in order to save their value or some part of it: see s 297. In *Hawtayne v Bourne* (1841) Parke B expressed a view that [569] agency of necessity could not arise save in the case of a master of a ship and of the acceptor of a bill of exchange for the honour of the drawer. He added that: 'The authority of the master of a ship rests upon the peculiar character of his office.' In *Gwilliam v Twist* (1895) Lord Esher said: 'I am very much inclined to agree with the view taken by Eyre CJ in the case of *Nicholson v Chapman* (1793) and by Parke B in the case of *Hawtayne v Bourne* (1895), to the effect that this doctrine of authority by reason of necessity is confined to certain well known exceptional cases, such as those of the master of a ship or the acceptor of a bill of exchange for the honour of the drawer.' [McCardie J then referred to various authorities which extended agency of necessity principles beyond the two recognised categories of case, most importantly *Great Northern Railway Co v Swaffield* (1874) (see extract, p 171), and continued:]

The decisions I have already cited show that the *dictum* of Lord Esher in *Gwilliam v Twist* (1895) is not the law of today. Agency of necessity is not confined to shipmaster cases and to bills of exchange. I may next point out that in the well known judgment of the Court of Appeal in *De Bussche v* [570] *Alt* (1878) the court stated that unforeseen emergencies may arise which impose on an agent the necessity of employing a substitute, and the authority to do so which he would not otherwise possess. That case related to the sale of a ship in the East, and it shows an appreciation by the Court of Appeal in 1878 of a principle which, in its application, could not be confined to carriers or acceptors of bills of exchange. The object of the common law is to solve difficulties and adjust relations in social and commercial life. It must meet, so far as it can, sets of fact abnormal as well as usual. It must grow with the development of the nation. It must face and deal with changing or novel circumstances. Unless it can do that it fails in its function and declines in its dignity and value. An expanding society demands an expanding common law ... In my view there is nothing in the existing decisions which confines the agency of necessity to carriers whether by land or sea, or to the acceptors of bills of exchange. The basic principle I think is a broad and useful one. It lies at the root of the various classes of cases of which the carrier decisions are merely an illustration ...

[571] I see nothing which as a matter of strict law prevents the defendants here from seeking to rely on the doctrine of agency of necessity. In *Tetley v British Trade*

Corporation (1922) Bailhache J applied the doctrine of necessity to the case of an agent who, whilst in Russian Georgia, found himself, through violent events, unable to deal with goods in accordance with his instructions and equally unable to communicate with his principals. A like ruling has been given, on substantially similar facts, in other cases (unreported) in the King's Bench Division. Upon the first point I rule in the defendant's favour.

I must refer briefly to several other features of the doctrine of agency of necessity in a case where, as here, the agent has, without orders, sold the goods of his principal. In the first place, it is, of course, clear that agency of necessity does not arise if the agent can communicate with his principal. This is established by all the decisions: see *Carver on Carriage by Sea*, 6th edn, arts 295, 299; *Scrutton on Charterparties*, 11th edn, art 98; and *Springer v Great Western Rly* (1921). The basis of this requirement is, I take it, that if the principal's decision can be obtained the agent should seek it ere acting. In the present case it is admitted that the agents could not communicate with the principal. In the next place it is essential for the agent to prove that the sale was necessary. What does this mean? In *Cannan v Meaburn* (1823) Park J said: 'The master cannot sell except in a case of [572] inevitable necessity.' In *Australian Steam Navigation Co v Morse* (1872), however, Sir Montague Smith said: 'The word "necessity" when applied to mercantile affairs, where the judgment must, in the nature of things, be exercised, cannot of course mean an irresistible compelling power – what is meant by it in such cases is, the force of circumstances which determine the course a man ought to take' ... In substance I may say that the agent must prove an actual and definite commercial necessity for the sale. In the third place, I think that an alleged agent of necessity must satisfy the court that he was acting *bona fide* in the interests of the parties concerned.

[573] I can now state quite briefly my conclusions of fact after carefully weighing the whole of the evidence, the correspondence and arguments. I hold in the first place that there was no necessity to sell the goods ... The goods were not perishable like fruit or food. If furs are undressed they may deteriorate somewhat rapidly in the course of a year or two. But these furs were dressed, and not undressed. Dressed furs deteriorate very slowly. They lose somewhat in colour and suppleness year by year. The measure of deterioration depends on whether they are properly stored. If put into cold storage the deterioration is very little. Even if kept in an ordinary fur warehouse the deterioration is but slight, that is if care be used. The great bulk of the furs here were of the best quality. I see no adequate reason for the sale by the defendants, for I am satisfied that there was nothing to prevent the defendant from putting them into cold storage, and certainly nothing to prevent them from keeping them with proper care in their own warehouse. The expense of cold or other storage would have been but slight compared with the value of the furs. The plaintiff had given nearly £1,900 for them, and they steadily rose in value. The *contra* account of the defendants was less than £400. The margin therefore was of the most ample description. The defendants could and ought to have stored the goods till communication with Romania was restored ...

Commentary and questions

If the defendant had stored the furs for the duration of the war at its own expense, would this cost have been recoverable from the plaintiffs on the basis of the principles formulated by McCardie J?

It is possible to draw from this case a number of conditions that must be fulfilled before an agency of necessity will arise:

1   there must be no practicable opportunity for the plaintiff to obtain instructions from the principal;[19]

2   there must have been a necessity for the plaintiff to take steps to deal with the goods;[20]

3   the plaintiff must have been acting *bona fide* in the interests of both parties; and

4   the steps taken must have been reasonable in the circumstances.[21]

However, the House of Lords in *China Pacific SA v Food Corporation of India* (1982) (see extract, p 179) suggested that the courts might not always insist that these conditions be fulfilled in cases where the only claim is a restitutionary one for the reimbursement of expenses. In particular, the court suggested that an inability to communicate with the owners of the goods is not always a condition precedent to the recovery of expenses; it is sufficient if the owner failed to provide instructions when given a reasonable opportunity to do so.

The 'defence' of agency of necessity to a conversion claim was rejected in *Sachs v Miklos* (1948) for reasons similar to those in the principal case. In 1940 the defendants allowed the plaintiff to store furniture free of charge in their lodging house. The defendants subsequently needed the space taken up by the furniture in order to take in more lodgers and tried unsuccessfully to contact the plaintiff. The defendants then, being unable to contact the plaintiff, arranged for the furniture to be sold by auction, realising £15 for it. In 1946 the plaintiff sued the defendants for conversion of the furniture. The defendant argued that they had been acting under an agency of necessity. This defence was rejected on the basis that there was no emergency situation requiring the sale of the furniture: it was not perishable, nor was it exposed to the elements or to theft.

---

19   See also *Sims v Midland Railway* (1913) Scrutton J at 107, p 112; *Springer v Great Western Railway* (1921).

20   See also *Australasian Steam Navigation Co v Morse* (1872); *China Pacific SA v Food Corporation of India, The Winson* (1982), p 961 (see extract, p 179).

21   Although McCardie J did not expressly identify this element, it was implicit in his approach to the facts of the case.

Jebara v Ottoman Bank [1927] 2 KB 254 English Court of Appeal

The facts are not important.

Scrutton LJ: ... [270] [C]onsiderable difficulties arise on the question of agent of necessity in English law. Until recently it was treated as limited to certain classes of agents of whom masters of ships were the most prominent. High authorities had doubted whether it could be extended... Many of the authorities are collected in a recent judgment of McCardie J in *Prager v Blatspiel, Stamp and Heacock Ltd* (1924). He there finds the facts so as not to raise any question of action by an agent of necessity, but discusses what the law would be, if he had found the facts differently. He takes the view that judges should expand the common law to meet the needs of expanding society, and proceeds to expand the doctrine of agent of necessity without clearly defining the limits, if any, of its expansion. The difficulty may be seen by considering the case of the finder of perishable goods or chattels which need expenditure to preserve them. If the finder incurs such expenditure, can he recover it from the true owner when he finds him, as his 'agent of necessity'? Eyre CJ raises this difficulty in [*Nicholson v Chapman* (1793)], and cites *Binstead v Buck* (1777), the case of the pointer dog. The pointer dog was [271] lost, and his finder fed him for 20 weeks, and claimed the cost from his owner when he appeared, but the claim was treated as unarguable. The expansion desired by McCardie J becomes less difficult when the agent of necessity develops from an original and subsisting agency, and only applies itself to unforeseen events not provided for in the original contract, which is usually the case where a shipmaster is agent of necessity. But the position seems quite different where there is no pre-existing agency, as in the case of a finder of perishable chattels or animals, and still more difficult when there is a pre-existing agency, but it has become illegal and void by reason of war, and the same reason will apply to invalidate any implied agency of necessity ...

Questions

According to Scrutton LJ, what should be the scope of the doctrine of agency of necessity? Did his Honour consider that the doctrine could apply in the absence of a pre-existing legal relationship?

Burns Philp & Co Ltd v Gillespie Bros Pty Ltd (1947) 74 CLR 148
High Court of Australia

The defendant's ship was carrying a quantity of flour owned by the plaintiff from Australia to Singapore. The ship reached Batavia but had to turn back to Australia in order to avoid capture or destruction by the Japanese forces. One of the issues in the litigation arising out of this incident was whether the plaintiff was liable to pay freight in respect of the return voyage.

Latham CJ (dissenting): ... [174] It was argued that the master did not have in his mind the intention of acting as agent for the cargo-owners as his principals, and that therefore no claim can be made upon the basis of agency of necessity. Upon this contention I make two observations. In the first place the master gave evidence that in deciding to return to Australia without unloading the cargo he had regard to 'the safety of the ship, the cargo and the crew'. In the second place, though I agree that there was no evidence that he consciously and expressly decided to act as the agent of the plaintiff in returning to Australia, in my opinion this circumstance is not sufficient to exclude the application of the doctrine of agency of necessity. The master in acting as he did was acting in the interests of the ship and cargo. Doubtless he did not consciously determine to act as agent for each of the one [175] hundred or more consignors. But the phrase 'agent of necessity' is, in my opinion, only a convenient expression used in rationalising to some extent the rights and obligations which are created in certain circumstances of emergency. It is a 'shorthand' method of saying that such circumstances may create an authority to act in relation to the property of another person or to impose a liability upon him which would not exist in ordinary circumstances. Thus in some circumstances a wife may be an agent of necessity to pledge her husband's credit for necessaries. She may have no express authority to bind him, and the husband may even expressly repudiate her authority. But he cannot effectively do so. The authority is said to be irrevocable.[22] In such a case there is no express or implied agreement that the wife shall be the agent of the husband. The phrases of the law of agency are used to describe, not the means of constituting the relationship which enables the wife to create a liability in the husband, but the result which follows from the marital relationship in certain circumstances of necessity. The so called agency arises as what has been described an irrebuttable presumption of law.[23] Agency of necessity arises from action in circumstances of necessity and not from any real or presumed agreement between the person who becomes an 'agent of necessity' and the person in whose interest he has acted. In the case of masters of ships, the rule is, as stated by their Lordships in *Cargo ex Argos* (1873), that in circumstances where the cargo will be lost or destroyed unless some exceptional action is taken, there is not merely a power given but a duty is cast on the master to act for the safety of the cargo in such manner as may be best under the circumstances. If he does so act, then the shipowner is entitled to be paid a reasonable remuneration for the services rendered. This rule is part of 'the law of the ocean' (a phrase used in *Burton & Co v English* (1883), in relation to general average): it is based upon necessity, and is not part of the law of contract.

The master of a ship in a distant port may be faced with all kinds of emergencies. He may have to consider, for example, whether, in order to prevent loss of perishable goods he should sell them (*Acatos v Burns* (1878)) or whether in order to effect necessary repairs to the ship (*Hopper v Burness* (1876); *The Copenhagen* (1799); *The Gratitudine* (1801)), or to salvage the ship (*Hingston v Wendt* (1876)) [176] he should sell or hypothecate the cargo. In such a case, if possible, he should communicate with the owners of the cargo. But it may be absolutely necessary for him to act at once without waiting for instructions. Further, where the ship is a general ship, as is most frequently the case today, the instructions of the owners of cargo may differ, and some owners may give no instructions. It has not yet been decided that the master becomes legally paralysed in such a case, or that he can act to meet the emergency only on the footing that the shipowner will be liable in damages for breach of contract or for conversion of the cargo. In my opinion the real rule is that in circumstances of demonstrated emergency the master of a ship is entitled and, indeed, bound to adopt a reasonable and prudent course for the

---

22   See cases in *Halsbury's Laws of England*, 2nd edn, Vol 16, p 700.
23   See *Bowstead on Agency*, 8th edn, 1932, art 15, pp 31, 32.

purpose of securing the safety of ship and cargo. One element to be considered in determining whether he has adopted a prudent and reasonable course is whether it was practicable to communicate with owners of the cargo in order to obtain their views. But the responsibility for action must rest upon the master. This must be the rule, because he may receive varying instructions, which cannot all possibly be carried out. If, in such an emergency, he acts prudently and reasonably in bringing the cargo to a port in the country whence it was dispatched, then *Cargo ex Argos* (1873) shows that the shipowner is entitled to claim remuneration for the services so rendered to the owner of the cargo.

[Latham CJ concluded that the plaintiff was liable to pay for the backfreight.]

Commentary

The majority rejected the claim for the backfreight. The decision to return to Australia was as much for the purpose of protecting the security of the ship as to preserve the cargo. Accordingly, any benefit conferred on the cargo-owner was only incidental.[24]

Latham CJ emphasised that an agency of necessity is created by virtue of the existence of the emergency or necessitous circumstance, not as a result of an express or implied agreement. Latham CJ's approach supports the view that a pre-existing legal relationship between the parties is not necessary for the creation of an agency of necessity.

China Pacific SA v Food Corporation of India, The Winson [1982] AC 939
House of Lords

The *Winson* was carrying a full cargo of wheat from the United States to India when it was stranded on a reef in the South China Sea. China Pacific SA were professional salvors who signed a salvage agreement with the ship's managing agents in Hong Kong. During the salvage operation it was necessary to lighten the stranded vessel by offloading part of the cargo. Over a period of weeks from 10 February 1975 the salvors offloaded about 15,429 tonnes of wheat and carried it to Manila where they made arrangements for the storage of the wheat at their own expense. It was not until 25 February 1975 that the salvors' solicitors wrote to the cargo-owner's solicitors advising them that the salvage work was being carried on and requesting that the cargo-owner make arrangements to accept delivery of the cargo at Manila. The cargo-owner did not respond to that letter. On 24 April 1975 the shipowner abandoned the voyage and the cargo-owner subsequently accepted responsibility for storage charges incurred from that date. However, the cargo-owner refused to pay the storage charges incurred by the salvors between 10 February 1975 and 24 April 1975. The salvors commenced proceedings against the cargo-owner for recovery of the storage expenses incurred by them during this initial period.

Lord Diplock: ... [958] My Lords, with modern methods of communication and the presence of professional salvors within rapid reach of most parts of the principal maritime trade routes of the world, nearly all salvage of merchant ships and their

---

24 See also *J Gadsden v Strider 1 Ltd, The AES Express* (1990) (see extract, p 63).

cargoes nowadays is undertaken under a salvage contract in Lloyd's open form. The contract is one for the rendering of services; the services to be rendered are of the legal nature of salvage and this imports into the contractual relationship between the parties to the contract by necessary implication a number of mutual rights and obligations attaching to salvage of vessels and their cargo under common law, except in so far as such rights and obligations are inconsistent with express terms of the contract.

Lloyd's open form is expressed by cl 16 to be signed by the master 'as Agent for the vessel, her cargo and freight and the respective owners thereof and binds each (but not the one for the other or himself personally) to the due performance thereof'. The legal nature of the relationship between the master and the owner of the cargo aboard the vessel in signing the agreement on the latter's behalf is often, though not invariably, an agency of necessity. It arises only when salvage services by a third party are necessary for the preservation of the cargo. Whether one person is entitled to act as agent of necessity for another person is relevant to the question whether circumstances exist which in law have the effect of conferring on him authority to create contractual rights and obligations between that other person and a third party that are directly enforceable by each against the other. It would, I think, be an aid to clarity of legal thinking if the use of the expression 'agent of necessity' were confined to contexts in which this was the question to be determined and not extended, as it often is, to cases where the only relevant question is whether a person who without obtaining instructions from the owner of goods incurs expense in taking steps that are reasonably necessary for their preservation is in law entitled to recover from the owner of the goods the reasonable expenses incurred by him in taking those steps. Its use in this wider sense may, I think, have led to some confusion in the instant case, since where reimbursement is the only relevant question all of those conditions that must be fulfilled in order to entitle one person to act on behalf of another in creating direct contractual relationships between that other person and a third party may not necessarily apply.

[Lord Diplock held that the salvors were bailees of the cargo and accordingly owed a duty of care to the cargo-owner to take reasonable measures to preserve the salved wheat from deterioration and continued at p 960:]

My Lords, as I have already said, there is not any direct authority as to the existence of this correlative right to reimbursement of expenses in the specific case of a salvor who retains possession of cargo after the salvage services rendered by him to that cargo have ended; but Lloyd J discerned what he considered to be helpful analogous applications of the principle of the bailee's right to reimbursement in *Cargo ex Argos* (1973) from which I have taken the expression 'correlative right' and in *Great Northern Railway Co v Swaffield* (1874). Both these were cases of carriage of goods in which the carrier/bailee was left in possession of the goods after the carriage contracted for had terminated. Steps necessary for the preservation of the goods were taken by the bailee in default of any instructions from owner/bailor to do otherwise. To these [961] authorities I would add *Notara v Henderson* (1872), in which the bailee was held liable in damages for breach of his duty to take steps necessary for the preservation of the goods, and the Scots case of *Garriock v Walker* (1873), in which the bailee recovered the expenses incurred by him in taking such steps. Although in both these cases, which involved carriage of goods by sea, the steps for the prevention of deterioration of the cargo needed to be taken before the contract voyage was completed, the significance of the Scots case is that the cargo-owner was on the spot when the steps were taken by the carrier/bailee and did not acquiesce in them. Nevertheless, he took the benefit of them by taking delivery of the cargo thus preserved at the conclusion of the voyage.

In the instant case the cargo-owner was kept informed of the salvors' intention as to the storage of the salved wheat upon its arrival in Manila; it made no alternative proposals; it made no request to the salvors for delivery of any of the wheat after its arrival at Manila; and a request made by the salvors to the cargo-owner through their solicitors on 25 February 1975, after the arrival of the second of the six parcels, to take delivery of the parcels of salved wheat on arrival at Manila remained unanswered and uncomplied with until after notice of abandonment of the charter voyage had been received by the cargo-owner from the shipowner.

The failure of the cargo-owner as bailor to give any instructions to the salvors as its bailee although it was fully apprised of the need to store the salved wheat under cover on arrival at Manila if it was to be preserved from rapid deterioration, was, in the view of Lloyd J, sufficient to attract the application of the principle to which I have referred above and to entitle the salvors to recover from the cargo-owner their expenses in taking measures necessary for its preservation. For my part I think that in this he was right and the Court of Appeal, which took the contrary view, was wrong. It is, of course, true that in English law a mere stranger cannot compel an owner of goods to pay for a benefit bestowed on him against his will; but this latter principle does not apply where there is a pre-existing legal relationship between the owner of the goods and the bestower of the benefit, such as that of bailor and bailee, which imposes upon the bestower of the benefit a legal duty of care in respect of the preservation of the goods that is owed by him to their owner.

In the Court of Appeal Megaw LJ, as I understand his judgment, with which Bridge and Cumming-Bruce LJJ expressed agreement, was of opinion that, in order to entitle the salvors to reimbursement of the expenses incurred by them in storing the salvaged wheat at Manila up to 24 April 1975, they would have to show not only that, looked at objectively, the measures that they took were necessary to preserve it from rapid deterioration, but, in addition, that it was impossible for them to communicate with the cargo-owner to obtain from it such instructions (if any) as he might want to give. My Lords, it may be that this would have been so if the question in the instant case had been whether the depositaries could have sued the cargo-owner directly for their contractual storage charges on the ground that the cargo-owner was party as principal to the contracts of storage made on its behalf by the salvors [962] as its agents of necessity; for English law is economical in recognising situations that give rise to agency of necessity. In my view, inability to communicate with the owner of the goods is not a condition precedent to the bailee's own right to reimbursement of his expenses. The bailor's failure to give any instructions when apprised of the situation is sufficient ...

Commentary and questions

On what basis did Lord Diplock find that an agency of necessity arose on these facts, entitling the salvors to reimbursement of their expenses? Was there a pre-existing agency or bailment relationship between the parties vis à vis the goods? Why was the fact that the salvors could have further communicated with the owners of the goods before incurring the expense not fatal to their claim?

The principles laid down by Lord Diplock have been accepted in Australia by Carruthers J in *J Gadsden Pty Ltd v Strider 1 Ltd, The AES Express* (1990), pp 69–70 (see extract, p 63).

Fulfilment of another's obligation

A plaintiff who incurs expense in performing the legal duty of the defendant will be entitled to reimbursement where there was an important public interest in the duty being performed promptly. The burial cases below (*Jenkins v Tucker* (1788) and *Rogers v Price* (1829)) illustrate this principle. A further example is provided by *Simmons v Willmott* (1800) where a stranger who rendered medical treatment to an indigent was permitted recovery from a parish authority that was charged with the responsibility of caring for the indigent. Further, there is authority suggesting that a medical practitioner who renders urgent treatment to a child can recover remuneration from a parent, provided the parent's consent could not be obtained prior to treatment and there was not a more appropriate institution to provide the service.[25]

Jenkins v Tucker (1788) 1 H Bl 90; 126 ER 55 Common Pleas

The defendant was married to the plaintiff's daughter. The defendant went to Jamaica, leaving his wife and an infant child behind, and during his absence his wife died. The plaintiff brought a claim to recover the money he had paid for her funeral and to discharge the debts she had incurred in order to keep herself in a manner suitable to her husband's fortune.

Lord Loughborough: ... I think there was sufficient consideration to support this action for the funeral expenses, though there was neither request nor assent on the part of the defendant, for the plaintiff acted in discharge of a duty which the defendant was under a strict legal necessity of himself performing, and which common decency required at his hands; the money therefore which the plaintiff paid on this account, was paid to the use of the defendant. A father also seems to be the proper person to interfere in giving directions for his daughter's funeral in the absence of her husband. There are many cases of this sort, where a person having paid money for which another was under a legal obligation to pay, though without his knowledge or request, may maintain an action to recover back the money so paid: such as in the instance of goods being distrained by the commissioners of the land tax, if a neighbour should redeem the goods, and pay the tax for the owner, he might maintain an action for the money against the owner.

Gould J: ... It appears from this demurrer, that the defendant was possessed of a plantation in Jamaica, from the time he left his wife, till her death, which annually produced above 120 hogsheads of sugar, the value of which, at a moderate

---

25 *Greenspan v Slate* (1953) (NJ); Mason and Carter, *Restitution Law in Australia*, 1995, p 266.

estimation, amounted to a near £3,000 a year. He was therefore bound to support her in a manner suitable to his degree; and the expenses were such as were suitable to his degree and situation in life. The law takes notice of things suitable to the degree of the husband in the paraphernalia of the wife, and in other respects. In the present case, the demurrer admits that the money was expended on account of the wife and being for things suitable to the degree of the husband, the law raises a consideration, and implies a promise to pay it.

Heath J: The defendant was clearly liable to pay the expenses of his wife's funeral.

Wilson J: If the plaintiff in this case had declared as having himself buried the deceased, the husband clearly would have been liable; and as the case stands at present, the plaintiff having defrayed the expenses of the funeral, the husband is in justice equally liable to repay those expenses, and in him the law will imply an *assumpsit* for that purpose.

Commentary and questions

On what basis could it be argued that the husband in the principal case was enriched? What amount was recovered by the father?

A note to the English Reports states that the claim for the living expenses was not subsequently pursued.

Rogers v Price (1829) 3 Y & J 28; 148 ER 1080 Exchequer

The deceased died at his brother's home in Wales. His brother sent for the plaintiff, an undertaker, who arranged for the funeral. The plaintiff sued the defendant, the deceased's executor, for the value of the services and materials provided for the funeral.

Garrow B: ... [34] The simple question is, notwithstanding many ingenious views of the case which have been presented, who is answerable for the expenses of the funeral of this gentleman. In my opinion, the executor is liable. Suppose a person to be killed by accident at a distance from his home; what, in such a case, ought to be done? The common principles of decency and humanity, the common impulses of our nature, would direct every one, as a preliminary step, to provide a decent funeral, at the expense of the estate; and to do that which is immediately necessary upon the subject, in order to avoid what, if not provided against, may become an inconvenience to the public. Is it necessary in that or any other case to wait until it can be ascertained whether the deceased has left a will, or appointed an executor; or, even if the executor be known, can it, where the distance is great, be necessary to have communication with that executor before any step is taken in the performance of those last offices which require immediate attention? It is admitted here that the funeral was suitable to the degree of the deceased, and upon this record it must be taken that the defendant is executor with assets sufficient to defray this demand; I therefore think that, if the case had gone to the jury, they [35] would have found for the plaintiff ...

Hullock B: ... [36] If the executor had kept the body unburied, and the undertaker had come and said, I insist on burying it, he could not have recovered. But there is no evidence here that the person by whom this body was interred knew whether there was or was not an executor. It is the duty of the executor to dispose of the testator in the usual manner, viz by burying him. It is not that sort of duty which can be enforced by mandamus or other proceedings at law; but it is a duty which decency and the interest of society render incumbent upon the executor. The case of *Tugwell v Heyman* (1812) is precisely similar to the present, and I for one should have great difficulty in departing from an authority with which the feelings of all mankind must so fully concur. The instance alluded to, of the liability of parish officers in respect of casual poor, appears to me to be a [37] strong authority in support of the doctrine in the former case; because in like manner an implied contract may in this case be inferred, on the part of the executor, from the obligation imposed upon him with reference to his character and the estate of his testator.

Vaughan B: ... The discussion ... resolves itself into a mere question, whether an executor is liable to pay the funeral expenses of the testator, where he has assets and no unnecessary expense is incurred. I do not consider this as a duty of imperfect, but one of imperative obligation. It is not pretended that there was in this case any opportunity to consult the executor, who lived at a distance; and what under such circumstances could be done, if the defendant is not liable? ... [38] I consider the burial of the dead to be a clear obligation upon the executor, and think that he is liable for the expenses incurred, if in his absence that duty be performed for him by another.

Questions

On what basis could it be argued that the executor was enriched? How should the quantum of the enrichment be measured?

Provision of the necessities of life to an incompetent

A person who provides necessaries to a person who lacks capacity to contract (for example because of minority, mental illness or drunkenness) will be entitled to payment for the necessaries, provided that the conditions identified in the following case are met.

In re Rhodes (1890) 44 Ch D 94 English Court of Appeal

Eliza Rhodes, who was of unsound mind, was confined to a private asylum for over 25 years. The annual charges for the asylum were £140 per year, exceeding her income of under £96 per year. Her brother made up the deficiency out of his own funds until his death, after which his son (the appellant) did the same, with contributions from his brothers and sisters. After Eliza Rhodes's death, the appellant commenced proceedings against her executor claiming recovery of the moneys paid towards the asylum charges by himself and the other members of his family. None of the family members had made a claim against Eliza Rhodes's estate during her life, nor had they kept any account as to their particular contributions.

Cotton LJ ... [105] The question is, whether there can be an implied contract on the part of a lunatic not so found by inquisition to [106] repay out of her property sums expended for necessaries supplied to her. Now the term 'implied contract' is a most unfortunate expression, because there cannot be a contract by a lunatic. But whenever necessaries are supplied to a person who by reason of disability cannot himself contract, the law implies an obligation on the part of such person to pay for such necessaries out of his own property. It is asked, can there be an implied contract by a person who cannot himself contract in express terms? The answer is, that what the law implies on the part of such a person is an obligation, which has been improperly termed a contract, to repay money spent in supplying necessaries. I think that the expression 'implied contract' is erroneous and very unfortunate. In one case which was before the Court of Appeal, *In re Weaver* (1882), the question whether there could be what has been called an implied contract by a lunatic, was left undecided by the court, and one of the judges said that it was difficult to see how there could be what has been called an implied contract on the part of a lunatic if he was himself incompetent to make an express contract.

But we all agree with the view that I have thus expressed in order to prevent any doubt from arising in consequence of our having declined to settle the question in the case to which I have alluded.

But, then, although there may be an implied obligation on the part of the lunatic, the necessaries must be supplied under circumstances which would justify the court in implying an obligation to repay the money spent upon them.

I have no difficulty as to the question of the expenditure being for necessaries, for the law is well established that when the necessaries supplied are suitable to the position in life of the lunatic an implied obligation to pay for them out of his property will arise. But then the provision of money or necessaries must be made under circumstances which would justify the court in implying an obligation ... [106] [W]e must look to the facts of the case in order to see whether the payments for the lunatic were made with the intention of constituting thereby a debt against the lunatic's estate. [Cotton LJ concluded that the family members had no intention of claiming back their contributions as they had not kept accounts and, in the case of the appellant's brothers and sisters, had made no attempt to bring a claim themselves.]

Lindley LJ: ... The question we have to decide is whether a sum of £1,100 is payable as a debt out of the assets of the deceased lady. The claim is made on the ground that the money has been properly expended for necessaries. I think that the facts are in favour of [107] the money having been reasonably and properly expended for necessaries. Against that it is said that the lady might have been supported at an expense which her own income would been sufficient to meet; but, as in the case of a claim made for necessaries against the estate of an infant, the claimant is not always bound to shew that he sent the infant to the cheapest school that could be found, so, in this case, the fact that some cheaper place of residence might possibly have been found for this lady is not necessarily an answer to this claim, assuming that it can be made. The question whether an implied obligation arises in favour of a person who supplies a lunatic with necessaries is a question law, and in *In re Weaver* (1882) a doubt was expressed whether there is any obligation on the part of the lunatic to repay. I confess I cannot participate in that doubt. I think that that doubt has arisen from the unfortunate terminology of our law, owing to which the expression 'implied contract' has been used to denote not only a genuine contract established by inference, but also an obligation which does not arise from any real contract, but which can be enforced as if it had a contractual origin. Obligations of this class are called by civilians *obligationes quasi ex contractu*.

But that a lunatic's estate may be made liable for necessaries was treated as settled as long ago as *Manby v Scott* (1663) where three learned judges, after holding that an infant might be bound for necessaries provided for him, said, 'and what has been said of an infant is applicable to an idiot in case of housekeeping'.

I do not doubt that the cost of necessaries can be recovered against a lunatic's estate in a proper case.

Then we come to the question of fact. Now, in order to raise an obligation to repay, the money must have been expended with the intention on the part of the person providing it that it should be repaid. I think that that intention is not only not proved, but is expressly negatived in the present case. I do not believe that the brother ever intended to constitute himself a creditor of his sister so as to render her estate liable to repay [108] him. He was a kind and affectionate brother; but if he had had any such an intention, being a man of business, he would naturally have kept some kind of account between himself and his sister. There is no real ground for saying that he ever dreamt of repayment. Since his death his children maintained this lady by contribution, and, while there is no direct evidence to shew that the money contributed was a gift, there is still less evidence to shew any intention to be repaid.

Upon the facts, then, I come to the conclusion that the constitution of a debt between themselves and the lunatic was the last thing that the persons who made the payments contemplated.

Commentary

Birks[26] has criticised the focus in the principal case on intention to be repaid, pointing out that an intention to be repaid was not an essential requirement of the earlier burial cases of *Jenkins v Tucker* (1788) (see extract, p 182) and *Rogers v Price* (1829) (see extract, p 183). Muir,[27] on the other hand, agrees with the requirement of an intention to be repaid however distinguishes between the professional and the non-professional service provider. He contends that there should be a presumption of an intention to be repaid where the plaintiff is a professional performing professional services, but not where the plaintiff is a non-professional acting for altruistic reasons.

In addition to common law restitutionary rights, the sale of goods legislation in each jurisdiction provides that a reasonable price must be paid for goods to a person who is incompetent to contract.[28]

---

26 Birks, *An Introduction to the Law of Restitution*, rev edn, 1989, p 199.

27 Muir, 'Unjust sacrifice and the officious intervener', in Finn, *op cit*, fn 15, p 312. There is some judicial support for the reversal of the onus of proof in the case of the professional service provider: *per* Griffith CJ in *McLaughlin v Freehill* (1908).

28 Sale of Goods Act 1954 (ACT), s 7(3); Sale of Goods Act 1923 (NSW), s 7; Sale of Goods Act 1972 (NT), s 7; Sale of Goods Act 1896 (Qld), s 5; Sale of Goods Act 1895 (SA), s 2; Sale of Goods Act 1896 (Tas), s 7(2); Goods Act 1958 (Vic), s 7; Sale of Goods Act 1895 (WA), s 2. In New South Wales the sale of goods legislation does not apply to contracts for necessaries provided to minors, which are governed exclusively by the Minors (Property and Contracts) Act 1970 (NSW).

HYPOTHETICAL QUESTION

A Norwegian freighter encounters a sinking vessel just outside of the territorial waters of Australia. The freighter rescues the people on board the vessel, upon which it is discovered that they are refugees seeking asylum in Australia. The Australian government refuses to allow the freighter to sail into its territorial waters, and the freighter is forced to delay its voyage for a number of days until a solution can be found. The owners of the freighter incur considerable expense in feeding and sheltering the asylum seekers during their stay on board. On the basis of the principles recognised in this chapter, would the owners of the freighter have a good claim in restitution against the Australian government for recovery of the expenses incurred in providing for the asylum seekers?

CHAPTER 8

COMPULSORY DISCHARGE OF ANOTHER'S LEGAL OBLIGATIONS

UNREQUESTED DISCHARGE OF DEBT

The orthodox rule is that the unrequested payment of another's debt will not discharge the debt in the absence of ratification by the debtor, even if the payment was made under a mistake.[1] Accordingly, where P, without a request by D, pays a debt (or meets a legal liability) which D owes to T, P's payment will not, as a general rule, discharge D's debt. In these circumstances P will be unable to recover from D: D will not have been benefited by the payment as D will still be liable to T to meet the obligation.[2] If P is to recover the money at all it must be from T on the basis of a recognised unjust factor. However there are two exceptional cases where an unrequested and unratified payment will suffice to automatically discharge the debt of another, namely where the payment is made under legal compulsion or (more arguably)[3] as a matter of necessity.[4] Where P's payment is made under legal compulsion or (possibly) necessitous intervention, the payment will be effective to discharge D's debt, and P will be able to recover from D. This is because D has been benefited by the discharge of the debt owed to T as P's payment will have saved D a legally necessary expense.[5] P will be unable to recover from T, as T will set up the defence of discharge of debt in response to the claim.

The complex question of the circumstances when D's debt will be discharged by P's payment is discussed by various commentators.[6]

OVERVIEW OF LEGAL COMPULSION

A plaintiff who is compelled by law to make a payment that discharges a liability owed by the defendant to a third party can recover the payment from the defendant in restitution, provided certain conditions are met. The classic

---

1   *Belshaw v Bush* (1851); *Re Cleadon Trust Ltd* (1939); *City Bank of Sydney v McLaughlin* (1909); *Barclays Bank Ltd v Simms* (1980) (see extract, p 104); *Re Emanuel* (1997).

2   *Esso Petroleum Co Ltd v Hall Russell & Co Ltd* (1989), p 663; *Moule v Garrett* (1872) (see extract, p 193).

3   Birks and Beatson, 'Unrequested payment of another's debt' (1976) 92 LQR 188; Beatson, *The Use and Abuse of Unjust Enrichment*, 1991, pp 204–05; Burrows, *The Law of Restitution*, 1993, pp 222–30.

4   *Owen v Tate* (1976), pp 411–12 *per* Scarman LJ (see extract, p 199); *Zuhal K and Selin* (1987) (see extract, p 204).

5   *Halgido Pty Ltd v OK Capital Co Ltd* (1996), pp 543–44.

6   Birks and Beatson, *op cit*, fn 3; Friedmann, 'Payment of another's debt' (1983) 99 LQR 534; Muir, 'Unjust sacrifice and the officious intervener', in Finn (ed), *Essays on Restitution*, 1990, pp 329ff; Beatson, *op cit*, fn 3, Chapter 7; Burrows, *op cit*, fn 3, pp 222–23; Mason and Carter, *Restitution Law in Australia*, 1995, pp 214–16, 260–63.

statement of the principle is that of Cockburn CJ in *Moule v Garrett* (1872), p 104 (see extract, p 193):

> Where the plaintiff has been compelled by law to pay, or, being compellable by law, has paid money which the defendant was ultimately liable to pay, so that the latter obtains the benefit of the payment by the discharge of his liability; under such circumstances the defendant is held indebted to the plaintiff in the amount.

There are two broad categories of case where the plaintiff will be treated as having been compelled or compellable by law to make the payment:

(a) where the plaintiff and defendant are under a common liability to make the payment, but the plaintiff's liability is secondary to the defendant's liability ('personal liability');[7] and

(b) where the plaintiff is forced to pay a debt of the defendant in order to recover or protect property belonging to the plaintiff ('proprietary liability').[8]

The underlying principle in both categories is that the legal system has compelled the wrong person to pay the debt.[9]

The authorities have laid down two further conditions that must be fulfilled before the plaintiff can recoup money on the ground of legal compulsion:

(a) the plaintiff, in becoming exposed to the liability to make the payment, must not have acted officiously;[10] and

(b) the plaintiff's payment must have discharged a liability of the defendant.[11]

PERSONAL LIABILITY

The plaintiff was compelled or compellable by law to make the payment

A plaintiff will be held to have paid a debt under legal compulsion where it is a debt for which both the plaintiff and defendant were under a common liability to pay, however, as between them, the defendant was under a primary liability to pay. This principle is illustrated well by the following case.

---

7   *Moule v Garrett* (1872) (see extract, p 193); *Bonner v Tottenham and Edmonton Permanent Investment Building Society* (1899) (see extract, p 194); *Brook's Wharf & Bull Wharf v Goodman Bros* (1937), p 544 (see extract, p 191).

8   *Exall v Partridge* (1799) (see extract, p 209); *England v Marsden* (1866) (see extract, p 212); *Johnson v Royal Mail Steam Packet Company* (1867) (see extract, p 210); *Edmunds v Wallingford* (1885).

9   *Moule v Garrett* (1872) (see extract, p 193); *Brook's Wharf & Bull Wharf v Goodman Bros* (1937), p 544 (see extract, p 191); *Owen v Tate* (1976), p 407 (see extract, p 199); Mason and Carter, *Restitution Law in Australia*, 1995, pp 191, 212–13.

10 *England v Marsden* (1866) (see extract, p 212); *Owen v Tate* (1976) (see extract, p 199); *The Zuhal K and Selin* (1987) (see extract, p 204).

11 *Esso Petroleum Co Ltd v Hall Russell & Co Ltd, The Esso Bernica* (1989), p 663; *Receiver for the Metropolitan Police District v Croydon Corporation* (1957) (see extract, p 206); *Moule v Garrett* (1872) (see extract, p 193); *Edmunds v Wallingford* (1885). Contrast *Halgido Pty Ltd v DG Capital Company* (1996), pp 593–94.

Brook's Wharf & Bull Wharf Ltd v Goodman Bros [1937] 1 KB 534
English Court of Appeal

The defendant furriers imported from Russia a consignment of squirrel skins. Ten packages from the consignment were stored by the defendant in the bonded warehouse of the plaintiff and, through no negligence of the plaintiff, were stolen from the warehouse. Section 1 of the Import Duties Act 1932 (UK) imposed primary liability for customs duty on imported goods upon the defendant as importer. However, s 85 of that Act imposed liability upon the warehouse company to pay the customs duty on any goods which were improperly removed from its warehouse. The plaintiff paid the customs duty on the stolen packages in accordance with s 85, and then sought recovery of the duty paid from the defendant.

Lord Wright MR: [Lord Wright determined that the obligations of the plaintiffs to pay the customs duty were 'ancillary to and by way of security for' the payment of the duty by the importer and did not supersede the liability of the importer. His Honour continued at p 543:]

Under these circumstances the plaintiffs claim that they are entitled to recover from the defendants the amount which they have paid to the Customs in respect of duties due on the defendants' goods. They make their claim as for money paid to the defendants' use on the principle stated in *Leake on Contracts*. The passage in question is quoted in the Exchequer Chamber by Cockburn CJ, in *Moule v Garrett* (1872), and is in these terms: 'Where the plaintiff has been compelled by law to pay, or, being compellable by law, has paid money which the defendant was ultimately liable to pay, [544] so that the latter obtains the benefit of the payment by the discharge of his liability; under such circumstances the defendant is held indebted to the plaintiff in the amount.' This passage remains, with a slight verbal alteration, in the eighth edition of *Leake on Contracts* (p 46).

The principle has been applied in a great variety of circumstances. Its application does not depend on privity of contract. Thus, in *Moule v Garrett* (1872), which I have just cited, it was held that the original lessee who had been compelled to pay for breach of a repairing covenant was entitled to recover the amount he had so paid from a subsequent assignee of the lease, notwithstanding that there had been intermediate assignees. In that case the liability of the lessee depended on the terms of his covenant, but the breach of covenant was due to the default of the assignee, and the payment by the lessee under legal compulsion relieved the assignee of his liability.

That class of case was discussed by Vaughan Williams LJ, in *Bonner v Tottenham and Edmonton Permanent Investment Building Society* (1899), where *Moule v Garrett* (1872) was distinguished. The essence of the rule is that there is a liability for the same debt resting on the plaintiff and the defendant and the plaintiff has been legally compelled to pay, but the defendant gets the benefit of the payment, because his debt is discharged either entirely or *pro tanto*, whereas the defendant is primarily liable to pay as between himself and the plaintiff. The case is analogous to that of a payment by a surety which has the effect of discharging the principal's debt and which, therefore, gives a right of indemnity against the principal.

I need not refer to more than two of the numerous cases in which this principle has been applied. In *Pownal v Ferrand* (1827), an endorser of a bill had been compelled on default by the acceptor to make a payment on account to the holder. He sued the acceptor for the money so paid as money paid to his use. The money so paid was a part only [545] of the amount of the bill. He was held entitled to recover. Lord Tenterden CJ, said: 'I am of opinion that he is entitled to recover upon the general principle, that one man, who is compelled to pay money which another is bound by law to pay, is entitled to be reimbursed by the latter.' As an instance of money payable under a statute I may refer to *Dawson v Linton* (1822), where a tax was due from the landlord, but there was power to enforce payment by distress, if necessary, from the tenant. Abbott CJ, said: 'It is clear that this tax must ultimately fall on the landlord, and that the plaintiff has paid his money in discharge of it; he has therefore a right to call upon the landlord to repay it to him.'

These statements of the principle do not put the obligation on any ground of implied contract or of constructive or notional contract. The obligation is imposed by the court simply under the circumstances of the case and on what the court decides is just and reasonable, having regard to the relationship of the parties. It is a debt or obligation constituted by the act of the law, apart from any consent or intention of the parties or any privity of contract.

It is true that in the present case there was a contract of bailment between the plaintiffs and the defendants, but there is no suggestion that the obligation in question had ever been contemplated as between them or that they had ever thought about it. The court cannot say what they would have agreed if they had considered the matter when the goods were warehoused. All the court can say is what they ought as just and reasonable men to have decided as between themselves. The defendants would be unjustly benefited at the cost of the plaintiffs if the latter, who had received no extra consideration and made no express bargain, should be left out of pocket by having to discharge what was the defendants' debt.

I agree with the learned judge in holding that this principle applies to the present case. As I have explained, the duties were due from the importer. There is nothing in the machinery of the Customs Act which had removed this liability from him when the warehousemen paid the duties, as they were compelled to do under s 85. The payment relieved the importer of his obligation. The plaintiffs were no doubt liable to pay the Customs, but, as between themselves and the defendants, the primary liability rested on the defendants. The liability of the plaintiffs as warehousemen was analogous to that of a surety. It was imposed in order to facilitate the collection of duties in a case like the present, where there might always be a question as to who stood in the position of importer. The defendants as actual importers have obtained the benefit of the payment made by the plaintiffs and they are thus discharged from the duties which otherwise would have been payable by them ...

Commentary and questions

Were the plaintiff and defendant under a common liability to pay to Customs the duty on the skins? As between them, who was primarily liable to pay the customs duty?

Most of the cases involving the 'personal liability' form of legal compulsion can be grouped into three main categories: (a) breaches of lease covenants by an assignee; (b) actions by occupiers of property to abate a nuisance; and (c) payment of the principal debt by a guarantor.

(a) Breaches of lease covenants by an assignee

As the following case indicates, where an assignee of a lease breaches a covenant and the landlord of the premises recovers from the lessee a payment for the breach, the lessee can recover the sum paid from the assignee.

Moule v Garrett (1872) 7 Ex 101 Exchequer Chamber

The plaintiff was the lessee of premises under a lease which contained a covenant to keep the premises in good repair. The plaintiff assigned the lease to Bartley, who in turn assigned it to the defendants. Each of the assignments contained express covenants that the assignors would indemnify their respective assignee against all subsequent breaches. The defendants breached the covenant of good repair while in possession of the premises, in respect of which the landlord recovered damages from the plaintiff. The plaintiff sought recovery from the defendants of the amount paid to the landlord as damages.

Cockburn CJ: ... [103] [T]he premises which are the subject of the lease being in the possession of the defendants as ultimate assignees, they were the parties whose duty it was to perform the covenants which were to be performed upon and in respect of those premises. It was their immediate duty to keep [104] in repair, and by their default the lessee, though he had parted with the estate, became liable to make good to the lessor the conditions of the lease. The damage therefore arises through their default, and the general proposition applicable to such a case as the present is, that where one person is compelled to pay damages by the legal default of another, he is entitled to recover from the person by whose default the damage was occasioned the sum so paid. This doctrine, as applicable to cases like the present, is well stated by Mr Leake in his work on contracts, p 41: 'Where the plaintiff has been compelled by law to pay, or, being compellable by law, has paid money which the defendant was ultimately liable to pay, so that the latter obtains the benefit of the payment by the discharge of his liability; under such circumstances the defendant is held indebted to the plaintiff in the amount.'

Whether the liability is put on the ground of an implied contract, or of an obligation imposed by law, is a matter of indifference: it is such a duty as the law will enforce. The lessee has been compelled to make good an omission to repair, which has arisen entirely from the default of the defendants, and the defendants are therefore liable to reimburse him.

Willes J: I am of the same opinion, on the ground that where a party is liable at law by immediate privity of contract which contract also confers a benefit, and the obligation of the contract is common to him and to the defendant, but the whole benefit of the contract is taken by the defendant; the former is entitled to be indemnified by the latter in respect of the performance of the obligation.

Commentary and questions

Why was the plaintiff unable to bring a contractual claim against the defendant for reimbursement? How did Cockburn CJ formulate the legal compulsion principle? Were the plaintiff and defendant under a common liability to compensate the landlord for the breach of the covenant? As between them, who was primarily liable to the landlord?

The principal case was followed in *Re Healing Research Trustee Co Ltd* (1992) which concerned an assignment by A to B of an underlease of property owned by C. It was held that although the contract of assignment excluded A's statutory right of indemnity against B for unpaid rent, it did not exclude B's obligations at common law as set down in the principal case. Further, the statutory provisions conferring upon A a right of indemnity against B for non-observance of lease covenants did not intend to provide an exhaustive statutory regime and did not exclude the common law obligation.

Moule v Garrett was distinguished in the following case.

Bonner v Tottenham and Edmonton Permanent Investment Building Society [1899] 1 QB 161 English Court of Appeal

The plaintiff lessee assigned the remainder of the lease to Price who covenanted to pay the rent. Price mortgaged his interest in the premises to the defendants to secure advances made by them. The defendants covenanted with Price that if they entered into possession of the premises pursuant to the mortgage and received the profits from the premises they would pay the yearly rental specified in the lease. Price became bankrupt and the defendants entered into possession and received rents and profits, but did not pay the rent due under the lease. The landlord recovered the amount of unpaid rent from the plaintiff, and the plaintiff accordingly sought recovery from the defendants of the amount of the rent.

AL Smith LJ: ... [166] It is clear that no contract or privity of estate exists between the plaintiffs and the defendants, or between the original lessor, Moore, and the defendants; and, unless there be circumstances from which a request to pay can be implied, or, in other words, a contract can be implied between the defendants and the plaintiffs that the defendants would indemnify the plaintiffs if they paid to their landlord the rent accruing whilst they, the defendants, were in possession, there are no circumstances which will support an action by the plaintiffs against the defendants to recover the amount so paid. It is true that Moore could sue the plaintiffs, his lessees, upon their covenant with him in the lease. It is also true that the plaintiffs, the lessees, could sue their assignee, Price, upon his covenant with them. It is also true that Price could sue the defendants, his underlessees, upon their covenant with him. But how can the plaintiffs sue the defendants? I omit Price's trustee in bankruptcy, for he, in my opinion, does not affect this case. It is said that the case of *Moule v Garrett* (1872) shews that the plaintiffs can sue the defendants to recover what they have been compelled to pay to their lessor, and that this case falls within the principle of that case. Now what was the case of *Moule v Garrett* (1872) It was a case in which there had been two assignments of the term, the defendants being the second assignees thereof. First of all there was, as here, a lease from a lessor to the lessee, Moule, the plaintiff in the action, containing the usual covenants by a lessee. Moule afterwards assigned the term to Bartley, who afterwards assigned the term to the defendants, Garrett & Co, who then committed breaches of covenants in the lease. Moule, having been compelled under his covenant with his lessor to pay to him damages for these breaches committed by the defendants, Garrett & Co, the assignees of Bartley, sued Garrett & Co to recover the amount so paid by him, Moule, to his lessor. It was held that, in as much as both the plaintiff and the defendants were compellable to pay to the original lessor the damages accruing to him for the breaches [167] of covenant by the defendants whilst assignees of the term, the former by reason of his covenant with the original lessor and the latter by reason of their being assignees of the term and having committed the breaches whilst assignees, and in as much as the plaintiff had been compelled to pay damages to his lessor for these breaches of covenant by the defendants, for which the defendants were also compellable under privity of estate to pay to the lessor, they, the defendants, were liable to indemnify the plaintiff in respect of these payments of which the defendants had had the benefit. For, as Willes J puts it in *Roberts v Crowe* (1872) the lessee is liable for breaches of covenant committed by the assignee, but being only secondarily liable he has his remedy over against the person primarily liable – that is, the assignee. The *ratio decidendi* of *Moule v Garrett* (1872) is this: If A is compellable to pay B damages which C is also compellable to pay B, then A, having been compelled to pay B, can maintain an action against C for money so paid, for the circumstances raise an implied request by C to A to make such payment in his ease. In other words, A can call upon C to indemnify him. See the notes to *Lampleigh v Braithwait* (1615), and cases there cited. To raise this implied request, both A and C must, in my judgment, be compellable to pay B; otherwise, as it seems to me, the payment by A to B so far as regards C is a voluntary payment, which raises no implication of a request by C to A to pay. If Cockburn CJ, in his alternative reason in *Moule v Garrett* (1872) for holding the defendants liable meant this by the expression 'by the legal default of another', I agree; but, if it means by a default for which they were not compellable to pay in that case to the original lessor, I do not agree, and none of the other learned judges who decided that case adopted what Cockburn CJ then said, and, indeed, Willes J expressly points out that the obligation of the contract must be common to the plaintiff and the defendant, and that the whole benefit was taken by the defendants. In the present case the defendants are underlessees [168] of an assignee of the term, and are not liable at all to the original lessor for rent whenever it accrued, there being between them and the original lessor neither contract nor privity of estate, and there is no suggestion that there were goods upon the demised premises available for distress other than the goods of the mortgagor Price, even if this could have sufficed to maintain the action, about which I say nothing, for it is not before me. The above, in my judgment, is what was decided in *Moule v Garrett* (1872), and the present case, as it appears to me, is an attempt to stretch the decision of that case, and to say that the principle therein laid down applies equally to the case of an underlessee of an assignee who is not compellable to pay the original lessor as to the case of an assignee who is compellable to pay the original lessor. It will be seen upon looking at the case of *Penley v Watts* (1841) that Parke B deals with this exact point. He says: 'The lessee and his assignee are liable to precisely the same extent, and the assignee is a surety for the lessee, but that is not the case in a sub-lease.' And, again, in *Moule v Garrett* (1872), in the Exchequer Chamber, when it was suggested that the case of an underlessee of an assignee and an assignee of an assignee were the same, Blackburn J said: 'No, because the underlessee has never come under any obligation to the lessor, but here the defendant, by taking the same estate which the plaintiff had, has become liable to the same obligation,' and this is the foundation of the judgment of the Court of Exchequer delivered by Channell B, and the ground upon which the judgment was upheld in the Exchequer Chamber. The fact that in this case the defendants covenanted with Price, the assignee, that if they, the defendants, became mortgagees in possession they would pay the rent, gives Price a remedy against them subject to any setoff which may exist between him and them and does not give the present plaintiffs a right of action against them ...

Rigby LJ: ... [169] Now, *prima facie*, a sub-lessee of a lessee or assignee of a term comes under no liability to the original lessor either for payment of rent or performance of covenants in the original lease. This is true whether the sub-lease be by way of sale or by way of mortgage, and entry into possession of the sub-term does not make the sub-lessee liable to the lessor. But it is said that the present case is distinguishable from the ordinary case by the fact that the mortgagees expressly covenanted with their mortgagor (assignee of the lease) that, if they entered into possession, they would out of the rents and profits received by them (among other things) pay the rent, and that they have been, as they have, in possession during the whole time during which the rents recovered by the lessor against the plaintiffs, original lessees, have been accruing. The argument is that they are thus placed in the position of the defendants in *Moule v Garrett* (1872), who were held liable to repay to the plaintiff money which the latter had been compelled to pay to the original lessors for breach of covenant in the original lease. In that case the plaintiff, like the plaintiffs here, was an original lessee who had assigned the term before the breach on which he was sued; but the defendants were not, like the defendants here, holders of a sub-term, but were the actual holders at the time of the breach by puisne assignment of the whole of the original term, and in that capacity liable by privity of estate to the original lessors for the very damages which had been recovered by them against the original lessee, who in the action was [170] seeking to recover them over. Both plaintiff and defendants were under a direct obligation to pay the rent to the lessors; but the defendants reaped all the benefit of the payment. It was treated as plain that, as between the plaintiff and defendants, the liability of the defendants to the original lessors by privity of estate was in the nature of a primary liability, that of the plaintiff by privity of contract being secondary; and on this ground the plaintiff was held entitled to recover over against the defendants, as though he were in a manner surety for them for payment of their debt. Here there is no privity either of estate or contract between the defendants and either the original lessor or the plaintiffs in this action, so that there can be nothing analogous to the relation of principal and surety between them. The reasoning in *Moule v Garrett* (1872), therefore, has no application ...

Commentary

As this case indicates, the liability of the plaintiff and defendant to discharge the debt must be common to them. The rationale for this requirement is that, if the liability its common, the plaintiff's payment will discharge the defendant's liability and the defendant will have been enriched by the saving of a necessary expense. On the other hand if the liability is not common, the defendant's liability will not be discharged and the defendant, who remains liable to the third party to meet the obligation, is not enriched by the plaintiff's payment. This principle is further illustrated by *Esso Petroleum Co Ltd v Hall Russell & Co Ltd* (1989). Esso owned an oil tanker which was involved in an accident with a tug built by Hall Russell, spilling large quantities of bunker oil. Esso paid over £500,000 to crofters as compensation for damage to their sheep caused by oil on the foreshore. Esso sued Hall Russell in negligence in respect of the accident claiming, *inter alia*, reimbursement of the sums paid to the crofters. Esso could not proceed directly against Hall Russell on the basis of legal compulsion for, as Lord Goff recognised, Esso's payment to the crofters did not have the effect of discharging Hall Russell's liability to them. Accordingly, Esso's payment had not enriched Hall Russell.[12]

Despite what has been said above, there is some suggestion that Australian courts will not always insist that the liability be common. In *Halgido Pty Ltd v DG Capital Company Ltd* (1996) Halgido entered into a loan agreement with the defendant bank that contained a provision that Halgido was to pay additional amounts to the bank representing the amount of withholding tax payable on the interest of the loan. The High Court subsequently held in *David Securities Pty Ltd v Commonwealth Bank of Australia* (1992) (see extract, p 110) that provisions such as these were rendered void by s 261 of the Income Tax Assessment Act. Halgido commenced proceedings to recover the amounts of withholding tax from the bank on the ground, *inter alia*, of legal compulsion. This claim was allowed, despite the fact that the liability of Halgido and the bank to pay the withholding tax was a separate, not joint, liability. Tamberlin J held that it was sufficient that Halgido's payment *effectively* discharged the bank's obligation to pay the tax (pp 593–94):

> While it is true that Halgido had a liability distinct from that of the bank to pay an amount equal to the amount of the withholding tax, this is of no consequence, in my view, because the practical commercial result of the payment by Halgido is that Halgido paid an amount which effectively discharged the bank's debt to the Commissioner by providing a credit in favour of the bank. It would be unjust for the bank to retain this benefit, to which it had no entitlement under the credit agreement by reason of s 261 rendering cl 8(2) absolutely void. The bank has not persuaded me that it would not be unjust for the bank to retain the benefit of the payments by Halgido. Nor has the bank made good any defence based on change of position. This is not a case where it can be said that in making the payment Halgido somehow acted in an officious manner. The payment was clearly made under compulsion arising under the Act. Accordingly, I am of the view that ... Halgido was ... entitled to recover on the basis of its recoupment claim.[13]

(b) Abatement of nuisances by occupiers

There is a series of English authorities permitting an occupier of property who has been compelled under threat of penalty to meet the obligation of the owner to abate a nuisance to recoup the cost of abatement from the owner. The following case of *Gebhardt v Saunders* (1892) is one such authority.[14]

Gebhardt v Saunders [1892] 2 QB 452 Queen's Bench Division

The plaintiff was a tenant in a house belonging to the defendants. During the term of the tenancy it was discovered that water and sewage were collecting in the cellar due to a drain blockage, and the plaintiff gave notice of this problem to the

---

12 Nor was Esso permitted to subrogate itself to the crofters' claim against Hall Russell, as it had failed to secure a valid assignation of the crofters' claim.

13 See Mason and Carter, *Restitution Law in Australia*, 1995, para 631 and following.

14 See also *Andrew v St Olave's Board of Works* (1898); *Ellis v Bromley RDC* (1899); *Rhymney Iron Co v Gelligner District Council* (1917). For a more detailed discussion of these cases, see Goff and Jones, *The Law of Restitution*, 5th edn, 1998, pp 443–44.

defendants and to the relevant sanitary authority. It was impossible at this time to determine whether the nuisance was created by a structural defect or by improper use of the premises by the plaintiff. The authority served a notice at the premises directed to the owner or occupier requiring the nuisance to be abated immediately. If a structural defect was the cause of the nuisance the authority was bound to serve a notice upon the defendants as owners making them liable for the expenses of abating the nuisance, however no such notice was served by the authority. The plaintiff, who was liable for a penalty of £10 if the notice served at the premises was not complied with, paid for the necessary work to be done. The plaintiff then sought reimbursement from the defendants of the cost of the work when it was subsequently discovered that the nuisance was caused by a structural defect.

Day J: ... If two people are required to do certain work under a penalty in case of disobedience, and one does the work, and it turns out afterwards that the other ought to have done it, the expenses are properly money paid at the request of the person who was primarily liable, but who neglected to do the work ...

Charles J: ... [457] The first question is, was the plaintiff legally compellable to do this work? I think he was. It seems that there was in the plaintiff's house a drainage defect which, being latent, was one of which the sanitary authority may reasonably be held to be unable to find the author; they were, therefore, warranted in serving notice under s 4, sub-s 1, on the occupier or owner to abate the nuisance. Such a notice was served upon the plaintiff's premises, requiring the abatement of the nuisance forthwith. Did that notice impose upon the plaintiff the legal liability to obey it? Having regard to the provisions of sub-s 4, for the imposition of a penalty for default in compliance, I am clearly of the opinion that it did. It is contended, however, that the plaintiff was not legally liable to do the work, because in the result it turned out that the defects were structural. Now, there is no doubt that under the proviso in s 4, sub-s 3, where the defects are structural, notice is to be served on the owner; it turned out in the present case that they were structural: hence the defendants' contention. It is impossible, having regard to the language of sub-s 1, to assent to this argument; looking at that sub-section [458] it seems clear that, if on inspection the cause of the nuisance cannot be found, it is right to serve the notice on the occupier. This first question must, therefore, be answered in the affirmative.

The second question is whether the defendants were legally compellable to do the work. The jury found that the nuisance was caused by a structural defect; the moment that that defect was discovered the defendants were the proper persons to do the work, and were bound to do it. I think, therefore, that it having been proved that a nuisance existed, and that it arose from a structural defect in the drain, the defendants were legally compellable to set it right. In my opinion the ordinary principle of law is applicable to this case apart from the statute, the principle applicable to cases where one man has been legally compelled to expend money on what another man ought to have done, and, without having recourse to [statutory provisions] the plaintiff is entitled to recover from the defendants as having been legally compelled to incur expense in abating a nuisance which the defendants themselves ought to have abated ...

Questions

On what basis did the court hold that the plaintiff was legally compellable to abate the nuisance? Could the plaintiff and defendant be said to have been under a common liability to abate the nuisance? What other unjust factor(s) could potentially be available on these facts?

(c) Payment of principal debt by guarantor

A guarantor who the creditor calls upon to pay the debt of the borrower can, upon payment, seek recoupment from the borrower.[15] Although the guarantor and borrower are both liable to repay the debt, as between them the liability of the guarantor is secondary to that of the borrower.

The plaintiff must not have acted officiously

Claims based on legal compulsion will fail where claimants act officiously by voluntarily putting themselves into the position where they become compelled to make the payment. As the following case shows, plaintiffs will be refused relief where they voluntarily take on the liability in question in the absence of a request or circumstances of necessity.

Owen v Tate [1976] 1 QB 402 English Court of Appeal

The defendants obtained a loan of £350 from a bank. The loan was secured by a mortgage upon property belonging to Miss Lightfoot. Miss Lightfoot wanted a release of the mortgage, and in order to assist her the plaintiff, who was her former employer, voluntarily deposited an amount equivalent to the loan with the bank and signed a guarantee. In return, the bank discharged the mortgage upon Miss Lightfoot's property. The plaintiff had no connection with the loan transaction and did not consult the defendants prior to the giving of the guarantee. The defendants protested when they learnt of the plaintiff's action and made it clear this action was contrary to their wishes. Despite their objections, when the defendants failed to meet the repayments on the loan they requested that the bank apply the plaintiff's money to meet the repayments. The bank did so, and the plaintiff sued the defendants to recover the money.

Scarman LJ: ... [406] As I understand the law, there are two general rules, both of them well known. The first is conveniently set out in *Chitty on Contracts*[16] on which [counsel] for the defendants, naturally strongly relied. There it is said: 'If the payment is regarded by the law as voluntary, it cannot be recovered.' The editors then quote a passage from the judgment of Swinfen Eady J in *In re National Motor Mail-Coach Co Ltd* (1908). [407] I quote from that judgment one sentence. The judge said: 'If A voluntarily pays B's debt, B is under no obligation to repay A.' That is the first of the two general rules.

The second general rule which calls for consideration in this appeal was stated authoritatively by Lord Wright MR in *Brook's Wharf and Bull Wharf Ltd v Goodman Bros* (1937). The rule applied in that case was formulated by Lord Tenterden CJ in an earlier case *Pownal v Ferrand* (1827) in language which received the express approval of Lord Wright MR. I take Lord Tenterden's words from p 545 of the reports in the *Brook's Wharf* case. Lord Tenterden CJ said (p 443):

---

15 *Pownal v Ferrand* (1827); *Owen v Tate* (1976), pp 407, 412 (see following extract).
16 23rd edn, 1968, Vol 1, para 1736.

... one man, who is compelled to pay money which another is bound by law to pay, is entitled to be reimbursed by the latter ...

When one turns to the second general rule, namely, the rule that where a person is compelled by law to make a payment for which another is primarily liable he is entitled to be indemnified, notwithstanding the lack of any request or consent, one again finds that the law recognises exceptions. This rule has been subjected to very careful treatment in Goff and Jones, *The Law of Restitution*, 1966, p 207. The authors say, after stating the rule in general terms:

To succeed in his claim, however, the plaintiff must satisfy certain conditions. He must show: (1) that he has been compelled by law to make the payment; (2) that he did not officiously expose himself to the liability to make the payment; (3) that his payment discharged a *liability* of the defendant; and (4) that both he and the defendant were subject to a common demand by a third party, for which, as between the plaintiff and the defendant, the latter was primarily responsible.

In the present case we are very much concerned with the first two of those conditions: whether the plaintiff had been compelled by law to [408] make the payment, and whether he did or did not officiously expose himself to the liability to make the payment.

The editors (p 214) discuss the exceptions to the general rule which fall under their second condition, namely, the officious assumption of a liability to make the payment. If they are right – as I think they are, and as I think the cases show that they are – then there are exceptions to the second general rule; that is to say, the law does recognise that there may be exceptions, even when a man is legally liable to pay the debt of another, to the general rule that he has a right to an indemnity ...

We are, therefore, in this appeal faced with two recognised and well established general rules, each of which admits of exceptions. It is not necessary, therefore, in my judgment, to enter into the minutiae of factual analysis that [counsel] for the plaintiff invited us to undertake. In particular, he invited this court to answer the question raised *obiter* by Greene LJ in *In re A Debtor* (1937), the question being: at what stage in a transaction of guarantee does the guarantor become under an obligation to make the payment? The broad analysis of a guarantor situation suffices, and it is this: if, as in this case, there is no antecedent request, no consideration or consensual basis for the assumption of the obligation of a guarantor, he who assumes that obligation is a volunteer. That, of course, is not the end of the transaction. The time comes, or may come, and in this case did come, when the guarantor is called upon by the creditor to honour his guarantee. At that moment undoubtedly the guarantor, having entered into his guarantee, is under an obligation by law, or, in the words of the old cases, 'is compelled by law' to make the payment.

[Counsel for the plaintiff] invited this court to look exclusively at the situation as it existed when, in December 1970 or thereabouts, the plaintiff was called upon to pay. At that moment the plaintiff was undoubtedly compelled by law to make the payment. [Counsel for the defendants] invited us to look at the antecedent transaction and at the circumstances in which the plaintiff assumed the obligation of a guarantor. Of course, at that moment the plaintiff was, on the judge's findings, a pure volunteer.

For myself, I think the reconciliation (if that is what is needed) of the two general rules is easily achieved. I doubt whether it is necessary to consider in any case, and certainly I do not think it necessary to consider in this case, at what moment the volunteer guarantor becomes compellable at law to make the payment on behalf of the principal debtor. A right of indemnity is a right of restitution. It can arise, as the cases reveal, notwithstanding the absence of any consensual basis. [His Honour referred to the authorities, including *Exall v Partridge* (1799) (see extract, p 209) and *England v Marsden* (1866) (see extract, p 212) and continued at p 409:]

These cases, to my mind, amply support the proposition that a broad approach is needed to the question whether in circumstances such as these a right of indemnity arises, and that broad approach requires the court to look at all the circumstances of the case. It follows that the way in which the obligation came to be assumed is a relevant circumstance. If, for instance, the plaintiff has conferred a benefit upon the defendant behind his back in circumstances in which the beneficiary has no option but to accept the benefit, it is highly likely that the courts will say that there is no right of indemnity or reimbursement. But (to take the other extreme) if the plaintiff has made a payment in a situation not of his own choosing, but where the law imposes an obligation upon him to make the payment on behalf of the principal debtor, then clearly the right of indemnity does arise. Not every case will be so clear cut: the fundamental question is whether in the circumstances it was reasonably necessary in the interests of the volunteer or the person for whom the [410] payment was made, or both, that the payment should be made – whether in the circumstances it was 'just and reasonable' that a right of reimbursement should arise.

I think now one can see the importance to this case of Greene LJ's *dictum* [in *In re A Debtor* (1937)] on which [counsel for the plaintiff] so strongly relied. In this case it matters not when the obligation to make the payment arose. What is important to [counsel for the plaintiff's] case is that the *dictum* recognises that, even when an obligation is voluntarily assumed, the volunteer may be entitled at law to a right of indemnity.

Adopting this broad approach, I now come to consider in more detail than I have yet done the two phases of the transaction of guarantee which appear to me to be of critical importance. The first phase consists of the circumstances in which the plaintiff entered into the guarantee; the second phase consists of the circumstances in which the plaintiff made the payment.

It is enough to refer to the judge's findings of fact to know that the plaintiff assumed the obligation of a guarantor behind the back of the defendants, against their will, and despite their protest. At that moment he was interested, as the judge has found, not to confer a benefit on the defendants; he was interested to confer a benefit on Miss Lightfoot. Using the language of the old common law, I would say that the plaintiff was as absolute a volunteer as one could conceivably imagine anyone to be when assuming an obligation for the debt of another.

What of the second phase? [Counsel for the plaintiff,] rightly I think, relied strongly on two letters; and [counsel for the defendants], also rightly, I think, invited us to consider a third. I now turn to those letters. The first letter on which counsel for the plaintiff relied was a letter of 1 July 1970, addressed by the defendants' solicitors to the bank, who at the time held not only the plaintiff's signed guarantee, but the deposit of £350. [Counsel for the plaintiff] invited the court to read that letter as one in which the defendants were pressing the bank to clear their overdraft by recourse to the money deposited by the plaintiff: and there is no doubt that that is exactly what the defendants at that moment were doing. On 10 November they once more invited the bank to clear their overdraft by recourse to the plaintiff. [Counsel for the plaintiff] submits that if one looks at those two letters, and at the whole history of the case, one reaches this situation: that by the time those letters were written the defendants were well aware, although they had not known it at first, that the plaintiff had guaranteed their account up to the sum of £350 and had deposited this sum with the bank. The defendants' case, of course, is that this was an uncovenanted benefit, if benefit it was, and the fact that the plaintiff had conferred this benefit imposed on them no duty to indemnify him when he made the payment. But, says [counsel for the plaintiffs], if that is their position, they had a perfectly good opportunity in 1970 of telling the bank that on no account was it to have recourse to the plaintiff; that the plaintiff had interfered without their consent in their affairs, and that they proposed to deal with the matter of their overdraft without the support of the plaintiff's guarantee. No doubt had they either paid off the overdraft or made some suitable arrangements for securing it, the bank would not have had recourse to [411] the plaintiff. But they chose at that moment to encourage the bank to have recourse to the plaintiff.

[Counsel for the plaintiff] has, as one might expect, put his point in a number of different verbal ways: authority, ratification, adoption – all terms really borrowed from different transactions and different legal situations. But he is entitled to make the point under the general principle to which I have referred; he is entitled to rely on the circumstances of payment as part of the total circumstances of the case and to use them to support an argument that it would in all the circumstances be just and reasonable for the plaintiff to have his right of indemnity. But these letters have to be looked at in all the circumstances; and the circumstances, of course, include the earlier history. We learn from the third letter which was introduced before us by [counsel for the defendants], and to which I need not refer in terms, something of the earlier history. When the defendants learnt that the bank were proposing to release Miss Lightfoot's deeds because they had accepted a guarantee and a cash deposit, the defendants strongly objected. The bank, no doubt quite properly, did not tell the defendants that the guarantor was the plaintiff – who was, of course, a stranger to the Lightfoot and Tate transaction. When the Tates protested strongly, the bank replied that they were, as no doubt they were, entitled to disregard the protest, and were going to release, as in fact they did release, to Miss Lightfoot the deeds and rely upon the guarantee and deposit. At the time there was nothing to suggest to the defendants who the guarantor was, or that he was a stranger to the previous transaction. That being the case, must one read the subsequent letters to the bank to which I have referred as an adoption by the defendants of a benefit conferred upon them by the plaintiff? They never wished to lose the security of Miss Lightfoot's deeds. They lost it through circumstances outside their control and notwithstanding their protest. When the bank decided to call in the debt the defendants no longer had the security for the overdraft which was acceptable to them: they had to put up with a security which without their consent or authority had been substituted by the plaintiff for that which was, or had been, acceptable to them and agreed by them. I do not criticise the defendants, nor do I think they can be reasonably criticised, for making the best of the situation in which they then found themselves, a situation which they did not desire, and one which I doubt ever appeared to them as beneficial.

Looking, therefore, at the circumstances as a whole, and giving weight to both phases of the transaction, I come to the conclusion that the plaintiff has failed to make out a case that it would be just and reasonable in the circumstances to grant him a right to reimbursement. Initially he was a volunteer; he has, as I understand the findings of fact of the judge and as I read the documents in the case, established no facts, either initially when he assumed the obligation, or later when he was called upon to make the payment, such as to show that it was just and reasonable that he should have a right of indemnity. I think, therefore, that on the facts as found this appeal fails.

In my judgment, the true principle of the matter can be stated very shortly, without reference to volunteers or to the compulsions of the law, and I state it as follows. If without an antecedent request a person [412] assumes an obligation or makes a payment for the benefit of another, the law will, as a general rule, refuse him a right of indemnity. But if he can show that in the particular circumstances of the case there was some necessity for the obligation to be assumed, then the law will grant him a right of reimbursement if in all the circumstances it is just and reasonable to do so. In the present case the evidence is that the plaintiff acted not only behind the backs of the defendants initially, but in the interests of another, and despite their protest. When the moment came for him to honour the obligation thus assumed the defendants are not to be criticised, in my judgment, for having accepted the benefit of a transaction which they neither wanted nor sought ...

Stephenson LJ: ... On those facts I am driven to the conclusion that the plaintiff has not got a guarantor's ordinary right to be indemnified by the principal debtor, the defendants, against his liability to pay their debt. He voluntarily took upon himself the liability to pay their debt to the bank without any previous request from them, express or implied. He cannot, therefore, recover what he has paid: *In re National Motor Mail-Coach Co Ltd* (1908). He could have recovered if he had already been compellable by law to pay: *Moule v Garrett* (1872) and *Brook's Wharf and Bull Wharf Ltd v Goodman Bros* (1937). Nor can he recover because his apparently generous act – whether or not it is correctly described or unfairly denigrated as 'officious' – has enabled the creditor to discharge the debt at the request of the principal debtor. The subsequent request to the creditor cannot give rise to any antecedent request to the guarantor.

There may be cases where a guarantee given without any antecedent request by the debtor gives rise in law to an obligation by the debtor to repay the guarantor. Greene LJ in *In re A Debtor* (1937), p 166 and Pearson J in *Anson v Anson* (1953), pp 642–43 clearly [413] thought so. But I wish that they had indicated what those cases were. Perhaps they were cases of necessity as indicated by Goff and Jones, *The Law of Restitution*, 1966, p 214.

There may be cases where it is obviously unjust that the debtor should be enriched by accepting the benefit, though unasked and even unneeded, of a guarantor's payment of his debt without indemnifying his benefactor, and the court may be able to do justice by compelling the debtor to make restitution to the guarantor. I shall imitate the reticence of Greene LJ and Pearson J and give no instances. But I cannot see in the circumstances of loan and guarantee as far as they emerged at this trial any sufficient reason for imposing that obligation to indemnify on this debtor in favour of this guarantor ...

Ormrod LJ: ... This case demonstrates clearly, in my view, the wisdom of the common law approach to the volunteer, which may be cautious, and perhaps unkind, if not cynical, because looked at superficially this case could be said to be one in which the defendants had acquired a considerable benefit from the acts of the plaintiff and had given nothing in return. But a glance through the correspondence indicates that the transaction in this case is only a part of a much more complex series of transactions which have been going on between various people for some years. Speaking for myself, on the material which was before the county court judge – and I do not criticise that there was not more material – I find it quite impossible to sort out the rights and wrongs in this case, and certainly quite impossible to say whether or not the defendants in fact received a benefit by the plaintiff undertaking an obligation of guarantor which had previously been undertaken by Miss Lightfoot. It seems to me it is possible that the defendants' position was worsened, to use a general word, by the intrusion of the plaintiff rather than helped, and consequently I think it right to take a [414] cautious view towards volunteers in the sense that perhaps the old proverb about 'Greeks bearing gifts' may be applicable ...

Commentary and questions

Why did the claim fail in this case? Had the defendant requested the plaintiff to provide the guarantee? Was the provision of the guarantee 'reasonably necessary' in the circumstances? Do you think the case should have been decided differently on the basis that the defendants had freely accepted the plaintiff's provision of the guarantee?[17]

Commentators have been critical of this decision. Burrows[18] argues that the crucial fact was that the plaintiff was legally compelled under the guarantee to meet the defendant's obligations, and had not voluntarily chosen to do so. On this view, recovery should be allowed provided the legal compulsion was causative of the payment. Goff and Jones[19] and Watts[20] argue that a voluntary guarantor should be permitted to bring a claim against the debtor on the basis of the doctrine of subrogation.

The Zuhal K and Selin [1987] 1 Lloyd's Rep 151
Queen's Bench Division (Admiralty Court)

The *Selin*, which was owned by the defendants, carried a load of grapefruit from Turkey to Shoreham. Upon the *Selin*'s arrival at Shoreham it was discovered that the grapefruit was damaged and the ship was arrested by the cargo-owners when it reached a subsequent port. The defendants wanted the ship released from arrest and instructed Oceanus (a mutual underwriting association) to obtain its release by providing security. The cargo-owners were not willing to accept a letter of

---

17 See Birks and Beatson, 'Unrequested payment of another's debt' (1976) 92 LQR 188, pp 209–10; see also Mason and Carter, *Restitution Law in Australia*, 1995, pp 261–63.
18 Burrows, *The Law of Restitution*, 1993, pp 214–15; see also Birks, *An Introduction to the Law of Restitution*, rev edn, 1989, pp 311–12.
19 Goff and Jones, *The Law of Restitution*, 5th edn, 1998, p 446.
20 Watts (1989) LMCLQ 7. See also *Esso Petroleum Co Ltd v Hall Russell & Co Ltd, The Esso Bernica* (1984).

undertaking from Oceanus, being of the view that Oceanus might not be able to honour such an undertaking. Oceanus accordingly requested the plaintiffs, Home Insurance Co, to provide a bond guarantee for £30,000 to the cargo-owners in respect of the defendant's liability, which the plaintiffs duly did. The plaintiffs, acting under the bond, eventually settled the cargo-owners' claim against the defendants for £23,560, and sought to recover this amount from the defendants.

Sheen J: ... [156] The plaintiffs contend that if the bond was given by Home without any prior request by the defendants and the defendants did not subsequently adopt the guarantee and require payment of their debt to the cargo-owners by Home, they are nevertheless entitled to recover the sum of £23,560 from the defendants because they are able to show: (1) that they were compelled by law to make the payment; (2) that they did not officiously expose themselves to the liability to make the payment; (3) that their payment discharged a liability of the defendants. (See *The Law of Restitution* by Goff and Jones.)[21] The plaintiffs contend that these three elements are established. As to (1), Home were compelled to pay the cargo-owners by reason of the bond of guarantee. As to (2), Home did not officiously expose themselves to this liability because they were asked by Mr Pelling [of Oceanus] to undertake it. As to (3), it cannot be disputed that the defendants were under a liability to pay damages to the cargo-owners by virtue of the terms of settlement.

The only answer advanced by [counsel for the defendants] to the claim put in this way was that the transaction with Home was carried out for the benefit of Oceanus and was without the consent of the defendants. [Counsel for the defendants] submitted that the facts of this case are strikingly similar to the facts in *Owen v Tate* (1976). That was a bold submission. I have to confess that although counsel referred me to the judgments in *Owen v Tate* on several occasions during the course of their submissions it did not strike me that the facts of that case were similar to the facts of the case with which I am now concerned. It is, of course, true that when the facilities provided by Home were enlisted, the owners of *Selin* were unaware of the fact that their debt was being guaranteed by Home. But their agent who was seeking to secure the immediate release of their ship was well aware that Home was being asked to assist by providing a bond of guarantee. It was the only practicable way he could secure the immediate release of the ship. Any delay would have been very costly for the defendants. On p 409 of the report of *Owen v Tate* Lord Justice Scarman said:

> The fundamental question is whether in the circumstances it was reasonably necessary in the interests of the volunteer or the person for whom the payment was made, or both, that the payment should be made – whether in the circumstances it was 'just and reasonable' that a right of reimbursement should arise.

If that question is asked, there can be no doubt that it was reasonably necessary in the interests of the shipowners that the guarantee should be given. Pursuant to that guarantee payment had to be made. To my mind it is clearly just and reasonable that a right of reimbursement should arise ...

---

21 2nd edn, 1978, p 244.

Questions

Did Sheen J apply the reasoning in *Owen v Tate* (1976) (see extract, p 199)? On what basis did Sheen J consider this case was distinguishable from *Owen v Tate*?

The plaintiff must have discharged a *liability* of the defendant

As the following case illustrates, the plaintiff's payment must have discharged[22] the defendant's liability to a third party. In the absence of a discharge of liability, the defendant will not have been enriched by the payment.

Receiver for the Metropolitan Police District v Croydon Corporation
[1957] 2 QB 154 English Court of Appeal

Two police constables employed by different police authorities were injured in the performance of their duties by the negligence of the defendants and were incapacitated from work for several months. During the period of incapacity the respective police authorities paid the constables their full wage and allowance entitlements, as they were bound to do under statutory regulations. The constables commenced proceedings against the defendants for damages and one case was settled upon the defendants paying a sum of money and the other resulted in an award of damages. In neither action did the constables make a claim for lost wages. The police authorities brought an action against the defendants for recovery of the wages paid to the constables, claiming the defendants had been unjustly benefited by the payments as they reduced the liability of the defendants for damages.

Lord Goddard CJ: ... [161] It is said that the respective defendants have received a benefit by reason of the fact that the receiver and the county council paid the wages during the period of incapacity, and that therefore they, the defendants, have not had to pay damages as great as they would otherwise have had to pay. For example, in the case of an ordinary man who was in receipt of a weekly wage, and who was injured, the negligent defendant would have had to pay as part of the special damage the wages which the injured man had lost.

Slade J has treated the case as one which depends upon the doctrine of unjust enrichment. He has held that in as much as the defendants escaped paying these wages because of the payments made by the receiver, they have received a benefit and must now pay the receiver the amount of those wages. That seems to me to be a misconception, because I cannot see that the defendants have been in any way enriched. Indeed, the matter was dealt with by Earl Jowitt in his speech in *British Transport Commission v Gourley* (1956), p 202: '... it is, I think, if I may say so with the utmost respect, fallacious to consider the problem as though a benefit were being conferred on a wrongdoer by allowing him to abate the damages for which he would otherwise be liable. [162] The problem is rather for what damages is he liable? and, if we apply the dominant rule, we should answer: "He is liable for such damages as, by reason of his wrongdoing, the plaintiff has sustained."' It will

---

22 Contrast *Halgido Pty Ltd v DG Capital Company* (1996), pp 593–94 where it was held that a formal discharge of debt is not required, and that it would be sufficient that, where the creditor has been paid, it is practically unlikely that the creditor will sue the debtor. For a similar argument see Mason and Carter, *Restitution Law in Australia*, 1995, pp 214–16.

be remembered that in *Gourley's* case (1956) the question was whether, in compensating a man for loss of earnings, one was to take into account his gross earnings or his net earnings after tax; the latter was held to be the right measure.

In both these cases, the constables sustained certain damage for which they have been compensated. That damage, as I say, did not include wages, because they had already been paid their wages. What is the result of that? The receiver in the one case, and the county council in the other case, have not been called upon to pay anything which they would not otherwise have had to pay. Their obligation is to pay the police officers during the time when they are off duty through disablement, provided that the disablement arose in the course of their service. Therefore I cannot see that the receiver or the county council are any worse off than they would have been if these accidents had never taken place. It is their duty to pay a policeman so long as he is in their service.

Once that point is realised, it follows that the only loss which the police authorities have sustained is that they have had to pay the police officers, although they were deprived of their services. That loss is exactly the loss which was recoverable, and in certain limited cases is still recoverable, in an action *per quod servitium amisit*. The old action of *per quod* was given to a master because he was deprived of the services of his servant. [His Honour rejected the applicability of the action of *per quod* to police officers and continued at p 163:]

In order, therefore, to maintain this action, it must be shown that the legal liability rests on some other principle. The principle that is prayed in aid here is the principle that money which constitutes unjust enrichment of a person may be recovered in an action for money had and received, or money paid to the use of the person. In these cases both judges considered with great care the decision of this court in *Brook's Wharf and Bull Wharf Ltd v Goodman Bros* (1937) ...

To my mind, that case, and the large number of cases which were cited there and have been cited in this case, have no bearing on the matter which we have to decide. The obligation of the defendants here was to compensate the injured men, and to pay them the damage which they had sustained. If a man's employer has agreed to pay him wages, whether he is well or whether he is ill, it seems to me that that affords a benefit in one sense to a defendant, because he does not have to pay the damage which he would have had to pay if that agreement had not been made. That simply means that he does not have to compensate the plaintiff for an injury which he has not suffered. The obligation is, in the words of Earl Jowitt, simply to pay [164] 'such damages as, by reason of his [the defendant's] wrongdoing, the plaintiff has sustained' *British Transport Commission v Gourley* (1956), p 202. Having paid that, his obligation seems to me to be at an end ...

Morris LJ: ... It is said that the defendants have benefited. It seems to me that the answer to that is that they have not benefited. It is said that their obligation to Bowman was reduced *pro tanto*; again, it seems to me the answer to that is that their obligation has not been reduced at all. Their obligation was to pay what Bowman lost, and they have been adjudged to pay what they were liable to pay ...

The claim is put partly in reliance on the principles referred to in the *Brook's Wharf* case (1937). In his judgment in that case Lord Wright MR said this (at p 544): 'The essence of the rule is that there is a liability for the same debt resting on the plaintiff and the defendant and the plaintiff has been legally compelled to [167] pay, but the defendant gets the benefit of the payment, because his debt is discharged either entirely or *pro tanto*, whereas the defendant is primarily liable to pay as between himself and the plaintiff.' I agree, if I may say so, with [leading counsel for the plaintiffs] that it is never wise to take a passage out of a judgment, and to treat it as though it were a statutory enactment. Lord Wright is there merely stating the essence of the rule. But it does not seem to me that the plaintiff brings himself within that rule, because there was no liability on the defendants for the wages, for the reason that the policeman did not lose them ...

But [counsel for the plaintiffs], in inviting us not to take the words of Lord Wright as being an all inclusive statement of the legal principle, invites us to say that the law is adaptable, and that within its framework can be found a principle which entitles him to recover in this case. He has adopted as part of his argument a statement from Sir Percy Winfield's book, *The Law of Quasi-Contracts*, 1st edn, 1952, p 63. The passage reads: 'In spite of our endeavour to extract from the decided cases some broad general principle underlying the law as to compulsion in quasi-contract, the utmost we can do is to enlarge our conclusion that, where A, under what the law regards as compulsion, has paid money to B or to C in such circumstances that the law considers that its retention by B (where the payment was to B), or B's failure to recoup A (where the payment was to C) would constitute an unjust benefit to B at the expense of A, A can recover the amount of payment from B.' Again, it does not seem to me that [counsel for the plaintiffs] can bring himself within any such principle, for the whole basis of it is that there must be [168] some unjust benefit. I cannot see that there was any unjust benefit here received by the defendants when they have been held liable for all that they were in law liable to pay.

[Counsel for the plaintiffs] referred us to a number of cases in which he submitted that a basis of liability was that there had been the receipt of a benefit. He submitted that in the present case the defendants had received a benefit or advantage which it is unconscionable for them to retain, and he said that a benefit may or may not consist of a sum of money. I do not propose to refer to all the cases which were cited by [counsel for the plaintiffs] for it does not seem to me that they carry him in this case. Some of them were cases in which there were claims for funeral expenses brought against executors; another was a case in which it was held that there could be implied an obligation on the part of a lunatic to repay money necessarily spent on her. I very much doubt whether those cases, when analysed, really depend upon an application of any doctrine of receiving a benefit, but whether they do or not it seems to me that [counsel for the plaintiff's] submission here fails for the reason that it is not shown that the defendants received a benefit ...

Commentary and questions

The claim in this case failed because the only legal liability of the defendant was to compensate the officers for their loss, which could not include a sum for income lost which was not in fact lost. Do you agree with Burrows' criticism of this case as being 'over technical'?[23]

---

23 Burrows, *op cit*, fn 3, pp 217–18.

PROPRIETARY LIABILITY

Payment of a debt in order to protect or recover the plaintiff's goods

A plaintiff who pays the defendant's debt in order to recover the plaintiff's goods seized by a third party for non-payment of a debt by the defendant, will be entitled to recoup the amount of the debt from the defendant. The plaintiff's payment operates to discharge[24] the debt, despite the fact the plaintiff is not under a common liability with the defendant (or indeed under any legal liability at all) to make the payment.[25]

Exall v Partridge (1799) 8 Term Rep 308; 101 ER 1405 King's Bench

Exall left his carriage for repairs upon the premises of Partridge, a coach-maker, where it was lawfully seized by Partridge's landlord as distress for unpaid rent. Exall paid the arrears of rent to the landlord in order to recover his carriage. Exall then sought to recover that sum from Partridge and from two others who, to the knowledge of Exall, had assigned their interest in the lease to Partridge prior to Exall leaving his carriage on the premises.

Lord Kenyon CJ: [310] Some propositions have been stated, on the part of the plaintiff, to which I cannot assent. It has been said, that where one person is benefited by the payment of money by another, the law raised an *assumpsit* against the former; but that I deny: if that were so, and I owed a sum of money to a friend, and an enemy chose to pay that debt, the latter might convert himself into my debtor, *nolens volens*. Another proposition was, that the assignment from two of the defendants to the third, was not evidence against the plaintiff, because he was no party to it; that also I deny: it surely was evidence to shew in what relation the parties stood to this estate. I admit that where one person is surety for another, and compellable to pay the whole debt, and he is called upon to pay, it is money paid to the use of the principal debtor, and may be recovered in an action against him for money paid, even though the surety did not pay the debt by the desire of the principal: but none of those points affect the present question. As the plaintiff put his goods on the premises, knowing the interests of the defendants, and thereby placed himself in a situation where he was liable to pay this money, without the concurrence of two of the defendants, I thought at the trial that it was money paid to the use of the other defendants only; but on that point I have since doubted; and I rather think that the opinion I gave at the trial was not well founded.

---

24   Even if the plaintiff's payment does not effect a formal discharge of the defendant's debt, it will usually do so for all practical purposes: *Johnson v Royal Mail Steam Packet Company* (1867) (see extract, p 210).

25   *Exall v Partridge* (1799) (see following extract); Goff and Jones, *The Law of Restitution*, 5th edn, 1998, p 450.

Grose J: The question is, whether the payment made by the plaintiff, under these circumstances, were such a one from which the law will imply a promise by the three defendants to repay? I think it was. All the three defendants were originally liable to the landlord for the rent: there was an express covenant by all, from which neither of them was released. One of the defendants only being in the occupation of these premises, the plaintiff put his goods there, which the landlord distrained for rent, as he had a right to do; then, for the purpose [311] of getting back his goods, he paid the rent to the landlord, which all the three defendants were bound to pay. The plaintiff could not have relieved himself from the distress without paying the rent: it was not therefore a voluntary, but a compulsory payment. Under these circumstances, the law implies a promise by the three defendants to repay the plaintiff; and, on this short ground, I am of opinion that the action may be maintained.

Lawrence J: One of the propositions stated by the plaintiff's counsel certainly cannot be supported, that whoever is benefited by a payment made by another, is liable to an action of *assumpsit* by that other; for one person cannot, by a voluntary payment, raise an *assumpsit* against another: but here was a distress for rent, due from the three defendants; the notice of distress expressed the rent to be due from them all; the money was paid by the plaintiff in satisfaction of a demand on all, and it was paid by compulsion; therefore I am of opinion that this action may be maintained against the three defendants. The justice of the case indeed is, that the one who must ultimately pay this money, should alone be answerable here: but as all the three defendants were liable to the landlord for the rent in the first instance, and as by this payment made by the plaintiff, all the three were released from the demand of the rent, I think that this action may be supported against all of them.

Questions

What principle of legal compulsion was laid down in this case? Is the principle dependent on the plaintiff being under a legal liability to make the payment?

Johnson v Royal Mail Steam Packet Company (1867) LR 3 CP 38 Common Pleas

The plaintiffs were the mortgagees of a ship which was owned by the European and Australian Royal Mail Company and operated by the defendants. The plaintiffs served upon the defendants a notice under the mortgage requiring delivery up of the ship. When the ship was surrendered to the plaintiffs' agents at Sydney it was seized by officers of the Admiralty Court on behalf of the crew as lien for a large sum of wages which the defendants owed to the crew. The plaintiffs paid the wages in order to obtain possession of the ship, and then, *inter alia*, sought recovery from the defendants of the sum paid.

Willes J: ... [43] Now the mortgagees having had to pay sums of money for which the Royal Mail Company were liable in the first instance, which they ought, according to Maritime usage, and by their contract with the European and Australian Company, to have forthwith paid; what answer is set up by the Royal Mail Company against reimbursing the mortgagees who have paid their debt? Of course there is, upon the surface, that by the law of this country, differing, it is said, in that respect from the civil law, nobody can make himself the creditor of another by paying that other's debt against his will or without his consent; that is expressed by the common formula of the count for money paid for the defendant's use, *at his request*. That is the general rule, undoubtedly, but it is subject to this modification, that money paid to discharge the debt of another cannot be recovered unless it was paid at his request, *or under compulsion*, or *in respect of a liability imposed upon that other*. This is the modification of the rule relied upon by the plaintiff, and the question is, within which branch of the rule the present case falls?

It was argued on the part of the defendants that the non-payment [44] of the wages was a breach of contract only, and it was said the European and Australian Company may recover, because they have an agreement with the Royal Mail Company by which they have stipulated that the latter should pay those wages, so let them sue. They have, moreover, sued, and this court has held that the action was maintainable, and it was held, if one may use such an expression, *in terrorem* over the court, that if we decided that the mortgagees should recover in this action for the wages that they paid, the European and Australian Company may also recover in their action, and so that the same sum of money would be recovered by two different persons against the same defendants in respect of the same matter, which would be absurd. That difficulty, however, is not a practical one, because if the defendants pay the plaintiffs the European and Australian Company could only recover nominal damages in respect of the breach of that contract; they did not pay the wages in question; those were paid by the mortgagees, paid out of their moneys, and not out of the moneys of the European and Australian Company. It would be, therefore, a matter of nominal damages, simply founded upon the breach of contract, and by reason of the technical rule that any breach of contract, although not the cause of any damage, gives rise to a claim for nominal damages ... [T]he compulsion of law which entitles a person, paying the debt of another, to recover against that other as for money paid, is not such a compulsion of law as would avoid a contract, [45] like imprisonment. It has been decided in numerous cases that restraint of goods by reason of the non-payment of the debt due by one to another is sufficient compulsion of the law to entitle a person who has paid the debt in order to relieve his goods from such restraint to sustain a claim for money paid. This is a case which we have been compelled to consider very much upon its own circumstances, which are very peculiar, and may be difficult to be made a precedent, perhaps, in any future case. Perhaps the nearest case that could be put by way of illustration would be this. A lends B his horse for a limited period, which would imply that he must pay the expense of the horse's keep during the time he retains it. B goes to an inn and runs up a bill, which he does not pay, and the innkeeper detains the horse. In the meantime A has sold the horse out and out for its full price to C, and C is informed that the horse is at the inn, he proceeds there to take him away, but is told he cannot take him until he pays the bill, and he pays the bill accordingly and gets his horse; can C, who in order to get his horse is obliged to pay the debt of another, sue that other in an action for money paid? We are clearly of opinion that he could; and without heaping up authorities where it has been held, independent of contract, that a person occupying a property in respect of which there is a claim that ought to have been discharged by another, being compelled to pay, is entitled to reimbursement, we think that this is a case in which the mortgagees, by compulsion of law, have paid a debt for which the Royal Mail Company were liable, a ready money debt which they ought to have provided for on the arrival of the vessel at Sydney, and that, therefore, in respect to the claim for wages the plaintiffs are entitled to recover as on the count for the money paid.

Question

On what basis were the plaintiffs held to be entitled to recover?

The plaintiff must not have acted officiously

The plaintiff's claim will be defeated if the plaintiff officiously exposed the property to the risk of interference by leaving them on the defendant's property without authority.

England v Marsden (1866) LR 1 CP 529 Common Pleas

The plaintiff seized goods upon the defendant's premises pursuant to a bill of sale, but allowed the goods to remain upon the premises without any express request by the defendant. The defendant's landlord lawfully seized the goods as distress for unpaid rent and the plaintiff paid the arrears of rent in order to secure the release of the goods. The plaintiff sought to recover from the defendant the amount of the rent paid to the landlord.

Erle CJ: ... [531] The proposition which has been contended for on the part of the plaintiff is, that, where the owner of goods places them upon the premises of another, and rent becomes due, and the landlord [532] distrains the goods, and the owner pays the landlord's claim in order to release his goods, the payment so made is a payment made under compulsion of law, and may be recovered in an action against the tenant; and for this *Exall v Partridge* (1799) is relied on. There is, however, one great distinction between that case and this. There, Partridge was a coachmaker, and Exall at his request bailed his carriage with him. The landlord distrained it for rent, and Exall cleared it from that burthen by paying the sum claimed; and it was held that the action lay, because the carriage was left upon the defendant's premises at the defendant's request and for his benefit. Here, however, the plaintiff's goods were upon the defendant's premises for the benefit of the owner of the goods, and without any request of the defendant. The plaintiff having seized the goods under the bill of sale, they were his absolute property. He had a right to take them away; indeed it was his duty to take them away. He probably left them on the premises for his own purposes, in order that he might sell them to more advantage. At all events, they were not left there at the request or for the benefit of the defendant. It is to my mind precisely the same as if he had placed the goods upon the defendant's premises without the defendant's leave, and the landlord had come in and distrained them.

Byles J: I am of the same opinion. The case is clearly distinguishable from *Exall v Partridge*,[26] which has been recognised often. As I collect the facts, the payment was exclusively for the advantage of the plaintiff, and in no degree for that of the defendant. There is no evidence of any request on the defendant's part. The leaving the goods upon the premises was the plaintiff's own act, for his own advantage. There is nothing from which the law can imply a promise to pay.

Keating J: I am of the same opinion. The case of *Exall v Partridge* (1799), which is plainly distinguishable from this, is an illustration of the rule of law, that, where one man is compelled to pay a debt for which another is legally responsible, the

---

26 *Ibid.*

law will imply a promise by the latter to indemnify the former. But here the plaintiff was not compelled to pay the rent within the [533] meaning of that rule, because he voluntarily and for his own advantage allowed the goods to remain upon the premises whilst the rent was accruing. We do not, therefore, in any degree, impugn the rule which has been referred to.

Montague Smith J: I am of the same opinion. The facts obviously distinguish this case from *Exall v Partridge* (1799). The plaintiff by his own voluntary act, and without any request of the defendant, express or implied, placed his goods in a position to enable the landlord to seize them. He probably thought it would be more to his own advantage if he allowed the goods to remain upon the premises until a new tenant was obtained, in as much as they would in that case command a better price. He was not ignorant of the accruing claim of the landlord. The jury found that he had no express authority from the defendant to leave the goods on the premises. If the defendant had been asked, in all probability he would have declined to give such authority. This, moreover, is a very stale claim.

Commentary

The court refused the plaintiff's claim on the basis that the plaintiff had officiously exposed the goods to the risk of seizure by leaving them on the defendant's premises for his own convenience. In *Edmunds v Wallingford* (1885) the English Court of Appeal stated that *England v Marsden* should not be followed. The court in this latter case recognised that the plaintiff's claim should be refused where the goods are left without authority on the defendant's premises. However, this was not the situation in *England v Marsden*: the defendant had not objected to the goods remaining on the premises, and so must have tacitly authorised their presence.[27]

The plaintiff must have discharged a liability of the defendant

The plaintiff's payment must have discharged a liability the defendant owed to the third party, otherwise the defendant will not have been saved a legally necessary expense by the payment, and will not have been enriched.

HYPOTHETICAL QUESTION

A Minister in the Australian Commonwealth Government passes on the details of his government phone card to his son, John. John passes the card details onto two of his friends, Peter and Mary, who use the card to make personal calls in the amount of $30,000. There is a huge outcry when these events are made public, and the Minister comes under considerable political pressure to compensate the Commonwealth for the unlawful use of the card. The Minister eventually succumbs to this pressure and pays to the Government the sum of $30,000. On the basis of the principles discussed in this chapter, would the

---

27   See in particular *Ex p Bishop* (1885), p 417.

Minister have a good claim against Peter and Mary to recover the $30,000 from them?

CHAPTER 9

DURESS

OVERVIEW

Duress consists of illegitimate acts or threats against the person, property or economic interests of another. Payments made under duress will be recoverable on a restitutionary action, both in the circumstance where the payment was made pursuant to a contract that has been avoided for duress,[1] and also where the payment is a non-contractual payment.[2] Although many of the principles governing duress have been developed in cases where the duress led to the execution of a contract under which the payment was made, these principles equally apply to non-contractual payments.[3] In relation to contractual payments, the orthodox rule is that restitution is not permitted in the face of a subsisting contract.[4] Accordingly, the plaintiff should rescind the contract before bringing a claim in restitution.[5]

The plaintiff must establish that the duress caused the payment to be made.[6] Causation in this context will be satisfied where the duress was *one of the reasons* for the plaintiff making the payment.[7] The plaintiff does not have to satisfy the

---

1 See, for example, *Hawker Pacific Pty Ltd v Helicopter Charter Pty Ltd* (1991) (see extract, p 226); *Crescendo Management Pty Ltd v Westpac Banking Corporation* (1988), p 45 (see extract, p 246); *News Ltd v Australian Rugby League Ltd* (1996); *Pao On v Lau Yiu Long* (1980), p 636 (see extract, p 237); *Dimskal Shipping Co SA v International Transport Workers Federation (No 2), The Evia Luck* (1992) (see extract, p 248).

2 See, for example, *Astley v Reynolds* (1731); *Universal Tankships Inc of Monrovia v International Transport Workers Federation, The Universe Sentinel* (1983) (see extract, p 239).

3 Mason and Carter, *Restitution Law in Australia*, 1995, p 160.

4 This rule is discussed in Chapter 10, pp 265–66.

5 *Dimskal Shipping Co SA v International Transport Workers Federation (No 2), The Evia Luck* (1992), p 165 (see extract, p 248). Duress renders a contract voidable, so that the duress itself will be a ground for setting aside the contract: *Crescendo Management Pty Ltd v Westpac Banking Corporation* (1988), p 45 (see extract, p 246); *North Ocean Shipping Co Ltd v Hyundai Construction Co Ltd, The Atlantic Baron* (1979) (see extract, p 233); *Pao On v Lau Yiu Long* (1980), p 636 (see extract, p 237); *Universal Tankships Inc of Monrovia v International Transport Workers Federation, The Universe Sentinel* (1983), pp 383, 400 (see extract, p 239); *Dimskal Shipping Co SA v International Transport Workers Federation (No 2), The Evia Luck* (1992), p 165 (see extract, p 248).

6 If the payment was made pursuant to a contract between the parties, the duress must have caused the plaintiff to enter into the contract: *Crescendo Management Pty Ltd v Westpac Banking Corporation* (1988), p 46 (see extract, p 246); *Dimskal Shipping Co SA v International Transport Workers Federation (No 2), The Evia Luck* (1992), p 165 (see extract, p 248).

7 *Crescendo Management Pty Ltd v Westpac Banking Corporation* (1988), p 46 (see extract, p 246); *Barton v Armstrong* (1976), p 120 (see extract, p 219). A more stringent test requiring that the duress be a 'significant cause' has been suggested: *Dimskal Shipping Co SA v International Transport Workers Federation (No 2), The Evia Luck* (1992), p 165 (see extract, p 248). The two tests ('one of the reasons' and 'significant cause') were discussed by Cooper J in *Cockerill v Westpac Banking Corporation* (1996) (reversed *Westpac Banking Corporation v Cockerill* (1998)) without reference to the point however as the more stringent 'significant cause' test was satisfied on those facts, his Honour did not need to decide between the two.

'but for' test;[8] thus the claim will not be defeated by evidence that the plaintiff would have made the payment for reasons of a commercial or personal nature independent of the duress. Further, the onus of proof is reversed in duress cases, so that once the plaintiff establishes evidence of compulsion, the onus shifts to the defendant to disprove causation.[9]

It is a well established general principle that a payment made merely in order to avoid litigation will not be recoverable on the basis of duress.[10] The 'policy in favour of the finality of dispute resolution' (*David Securities Pty Ltd v Commonwealth Bank of Australia* (1992), p 375 (see extract, p 110)), requires that the payer should have contested the matter at the time the demand for payment was made. If the payer elects to pay the money rather than to contest the claim, the money is irrecoverable.[11] This principle was applied in the following case in order to deny recovery.

McKay v National Australia Bank Ltd (1998) 4 VR 677 Court of Appeal of Victoria

The appellants guaranteed a debt owed by their company, Caprid, to the bank, and secured the guarantee by a mortgage over certain of their properties, including their family home. The company's debt increased and the bank stated that unless the appellants sold at least one of their properties the bank would exercise its power of sale under the mortgage. The appellants sold their home and applied the proceeds in reduction of the company's debt. The guarantee was later found to have been unenforceable and the appellants commenced proceedings for recovery of the monies from the sale of their home on the ground they were paid under duress.

Winneke P: ... [686] Mr McKay submitted that, on the facts that he contended the judge should have found, his Honour was in error in failing to conclude that the bank's application of the proceeds was an involuntary payment by the appellants made under unlawful compulsion within the principles enunciated in *Mason v State of New South Wales* (1959).

But even accepting the appellant's case at its highest, namely that they were induced to apply the proceeds of the sale of their home at the bank's direction as the consequence of a demand made pursuant to an instrument which was not legally enforceable, I venture to suggest that the legal doctrine of involuntary payments made under compulsion or coercion has no application to the facts of this case. That doctrine, in my view, is limited to circumstances where a party has been wrongfully compelled to make a payment demanded of him by an authority which, *ex necessitate*, he cannot resist. Compulsion leading to involuntary payment within the meaning of this doctrine, as I understand it, can only occur where the

---

8   Contrast *Huyton v Peter Cremer* (1999), p 636.

9   *Crescendo Management Pty Ltd v Westpac Banking Corporation* (1988), p 46 (see extract, p 246); *Barton v Armstrong* (1976), p 120 (see extract, p 219).

10 *Werrin v Commonwealth* (1938), pp 157–60 (see extract, p 431); *Mason v New South Wales* (1959), pp 119; 126, 135, 144 (see extract, p 434); *David Securities Pty Ltd v Commonwealth Bank of Australia* (1992), pp 373–74, 404 (see extract, p 110); *Woolwich Equitable Building Society v Inland Revenue Commissioner* (1993), p 165 (see extract, p 456).

11 *Werrin v Commonwealth* (1938), pp 158–60 (see extract, p 431); *Mason v New South Wales* (1959), pp 126, 144; *Maskell v Horner* (1915) (see extract, p 222); *Woolwich Equitable Building Society v Inland Revenue Commissioners* (1993), p 165 (see extract, p 456).

demand for payment is made under threat of immediate and empowered distress or seizure of the party's property or person so that the party is coerced into making the payment as a matter of necessity.

It is a doctrine which appears to have developed alongside, or perhaps out of, a similar principle which applies to support the recovery by a party of payments made pursuant to a demand *colore officii sui* where a government or statutory office holder in the exercise of his office demands payment of money which he has no lawful right to demand or in an amount in excess of that which he is empowered to demand.[12]

However, the circumstances of this case, as I see them, are very different from those in which the doctrine has been applied. This is a case where the appellants, Caprid and the bank had, for a number of years been in a commercial relationship characterized by agreements which carried obligations and invested rights. At the end of the day, and on the facts which I am assuming, the bank made a demand of the appellants to repay the money owing by Caprid pursuant to an instrument which was later found to be unenforceable. It was within the power of the parties to the agreement upon whom the demand was made to resist that demand and to test its legitimacy. There will, ordinarily, be no compulsion of the sort which the law requires if payment cannot be enforced except through legal action which the person called upon to pay can resist. In other words, although the application of the doctrine must be determined according to the peculiar facts of each case, it will usually not be enough if the demand is made by one person in legal relationship with another, of that other, and the threat constituted by that demand is one that does not go beyond the threat of legal proceedings.[13]

[687] In the case of *Air India v Commonwealth* (1977), a case in which the plaintiff airline companies were seeking to recover excessive rental payments imposed by the Commonwealth, the Court of Appeal having traced the facts and authorities such as *Mason v State of New South Wales* said, at p 455:

> The authorities, and in particular *Mason's* case indicate that, in general, it must be established in order to show that a payment was made under compulsion that: (a) there was a fear that, if it were not paid, the payee would take some step, other than invoking legal process, which would cause harm to the payer; and (b) that this fear was reasonably caused and well-founded.

In that case the court went on to note that there was no express threat, 'and hence the submission that it was implicit in the relationship of the parties'.

The principles to which I have referred also would seem to have been adopted by Gobbo J in *Esso Australia Resources Ltd v Gas and Fuel Corporation of Victoria* (1993), pp 104–05. Because of certain arguments, however, which have been addressed to this court by Mr McKay suggesting that in this case the court might have resort to principles of unjust enrichment, I would also refer to and adopt certain comments made by Gobbo J in the *Esso* case where his Honour said, at p 105:

---

12 See *Morgan v Palmer* (1824); *Sargood Brothers v The Commonwealth* (1910) *per* O'Connor J; and *Mason v State of New South Wales* (1959), p 134 *per* Menzies J.

13 See *William Whitely (Ltd) v The King* (1909), p 745 *per* Walton J; *Werrin v The Commonwealth & Anor* (1938), pp 157–59 *per* Latham CJ; and *Mason v State of New South Wales* (1959), p 135 *per* Menzies J, p 144 *per* Windeyer J.

The primary issue of duress is ultimately to be addressed by reference to the principles to be elicited from *Mason's* case. Though there have been later cases where the High Court has had occasion to discuss questions of restitution and unjust enrichment, such as *Australia and New Zealand Banking Group v Westpac Banking Corporation* (1988) and *David Securities Pty Ltd v Commonwealth Bank of Australia* (1992), there was no discussion in those cases of the principles expounded in *Mason's* case and there was no reason why *Mason's* case should be treated as qualified in any way.

For these reasons I am of the view that there was no basis in this case for the application of the principles of involuntary payment through compulsion. However, and in any event, this was a case where his Honour has conclusively found that the appellants did not sell their house and allow the bank to apply the proceeds in reduction of Caprid's debt as a consequence of any compulsion imposed upon them by the bank's threats or demands. On the contrary he found affirmatively that the appellants willingly agreed to sell their house as a result of negotiations with the bank and did so after an exhaustive review of the evidence.

...

Tadgell JA: ... [690] When the relationship between the parties is that of debtor and creditor, a threat by the creditor to institute legal proceedings or to pursue another legal remedy in order to recover the debt could seldom be wrong in itself.[14]

The proper use of legal process does not constitute duress. Thus, the threat to institute a civil action in good faith cannot constitute duress.[15]

A *bona fide* threat by a secured creditor to exercise rights conferred by the security can scarcely be relevantly different from a *bona fide* threat to sue.

In this case the evidence entitled the learned judge to find, and indeed in my opinion he was constrained to find, that the ultimatum given by the respondent to the appellants and their company in March 1989 was that it, the respondent, would exercise its rights as secured creditor if a sale of at least one of the incumbered properties were not promptly made in order to reduce the company's debt. There was no direction given that any particular property be sold.

...

Batt JA: ... [691] [T]he appellants had the choice of either complying with the demand or, on the other hand, not complying and instead, defending any legal proceedings which the bank might thereafter take ... [I]t is the existence of that choice which makes inapplicable to this case the principle relied upon by the appellants, namely, that money paid under compulsion and not voluntarily is recoverable.

...

---

14 See Mason and Carter, *The Law of Restitution in Australia*, 1995, para 504.

15 Goff and Jones, *The Law of Restitution*, 4th edn, 1993 and the cases there cited; and see Mason and Carter, *ibid* and paras 519 and 527; *Mason v State of New South Wales* (1959); *Air India v The Commonwealth* (1971), p 455; and *Esso Australia Resources Ltd v Gas and Fuel Corporation of Victoria* (1993), p 105.

DURESS TO THE PERSON

Barton v Armstrong [1976] AC 104 Privy Council

Barton and Armstrong were engaged in a bitter struggle for the control of a company, Landmark Corporation Ltd, of which they were the major shareholders. After protracted negotiations, Barton entered into a deed with Armstrong agreeing to buy out Armstrong's interest in Landmark for almost twice its market value. Barton subsequently commenced proceedings against Armstrong seeking to set aside the deed on the basis that Armstrong had coerced him into executing it. Barton alleged that Armstrong had threatened to have him murdered, that Armstrong had in fact hired a criminal named Vojinovic to carry out the murder, and that Armstrong made various other threats of personal violence against him. The trial judge, Street J, found that Armstrong had threatened Barton, but found that these threats had not coerced Barton into signing the deed. Street J considered that Barton entered into the deed out of commercial necessity: he thought that Armstrong needed to be bought out if Landmark was to survive. The Court of Appeal of New South Wales dismissed Barton's appeal (Jacobs JA dissenting).

Lord Cross of Chelsea (delivering the majority judgment): ... [118] Their Lordships turn now to consider the question of law which provoked a difference of opinion in the Court of Appeal Division. It is hardly surprising that there is no direct authority on the point, for if A threatens B with death if he does not execute some document and B, who takes A's threats seriously, executes the document it can be only in the most unusual circumstances that there can be any doubt whether the threats operated to induce him to execute the document. But this is a most unusual case and the findings of fact made below do undoubtedly raise the question whether it was necessary for Barton in order to obtain relief to establish that he would not have executed the deed in question but for the threats. In answering this question in favour of Barton, Jacobs JA relied both on a number of old common law authorities on the subject of 'duress' and also – by way of analogy – on later decisions in equity with regard to the avoidance of deeds on the ground of fraud. Their Lordships do not think that the common law authorities are of any real assistance for it seems most unlikely that the authors of the statements relied on had the sort of problem which has arisen here in mind at all. On the other hand they think that the conclusion to which Jacobs JA came was right and that it is supported by the equity decisions. The scope of common law duress was very limited and at a comparatively early date equity began to grant relief in cases where the disposition in question had been procured by the exercise of pressure which the Chancellor considered to be illegitimate – although it did not amount to common law duress. There was a parallel development in the field of dispositions induced by fraud. At common law the only remedy available to the man defrauded was an action for deceit but equity in the same period in which it was building up the doctrine of 'undue influence' came to entertain proceedings to set aside dispositions which had been obtained by fraud.[16] There is an obvious analogy between setting aside a disposition for duress or undue influence and setting it aside for fraud. In each case – to quote the words of Holmes J in *Fairbanks v Snow* (1887) – 'the party has been subjected to an improper motive for action'.

---

16 See Holdsworth, *A History of English Law*, 1924, Vol 5, pp 328–29.

Again the similarity of the effect in law of *metus* and *dolus* in connection with dispositions of property is noted by Stair in his *Institutions of the Law of Scotland*.[17] Had Armstrong made a fraudulent misrepresentation to Barton for the purpose of inducing him to execute the deed of 17 January 1967, the answer to the problem which has arisen would have been clear. If it were established that Barton did not allow the representation to affect his judgment then he could not make it a ground for relief even though the representation was designed and known by Barton to be designed to affect his judgment. If, on the other hand, Barton relied on the misrepresentation Armstrong could not have defeated his claim to relief by showing that there were other more weighty causes which contributed to his decision to execute the deed, for in this field the court does not allow an examination into the relative importance of contributory causes.

'Once make out that there has been anything like deception, and no contract resting in any degree on that foundation can stand.'[18] Their Lordships think that the same rule should apply in cases of duress and that if Armstrong's threats were 'a' reason for Barton's executing the deed he is entitled to relief even though he might well have entered into the contract if Armstrong had uttered no threats to induce him to do so.

[Lord Cross reviewed the judgments below and continued at p 120:]

If Barton had to establish that he would not have made the agreement but for Armstrong's threats, then their Lordships would not dissent from the view that he had not made out his case. But no such onus lay on him. On the contrary it was for Armstrong to establish, if he could, that the threats which he was making and the unlawful pressure which he was exerting for the purpose of inducing Barton to sign the agreement and which Barton knew were being made and exerted for this purpose in fact contributed nothing to Barton's decision to sign. The judge has found that during the ten days or so before the documents were executed Barton was in genuine fear that Armstrong was planning to have him killed if the agreement was not signed. His state of mind was described by the judge as one of 'very real mental torment' and he believed that his fears would be at an end once the documents were executed. It is true that the judge was not satisfied that Vojinovic had been employed by Armstrong but if one man threatens another with unpleasant consequences if he does not act in a particular way, he must take the risk that the impact of his threats may be accentuated by extraneous circumstances for which he is not in fact responsible. It is true that on the facts as their Lordships assume them to have been Armstrong's threats may have been unnecessary; but it would be unrealistic to hold that they played no part in making Barton decide to execute the documents. The proper inference to be drawn from the facts found is, their Lordships think, that though it may be that Barton would have executed the documents even if Armstrong had made no threats and exerted no unlawful pressure to induce him to do so the threats and unlawful pressure in fact contributed to his decision to sign the documents and to recommend their execution by Landmark and the other parties to them ...

---

17   1832, Bk 4, title 40.25.

18   *Reynell v Sprye* (1852) *per* Lord Cranworth LJ; see also the other cases referred to in Cheshire and Fifoot, *Law of Contract*, 8th edn, 1972, pp 250–51.

Lord Wilberforce and Lord Simon of Glaisdale (dissenting): ... [121] The action is one to set aside an apparently complete and valid agreement on the ground of duress. The basis of the plaintiff's claim is, thus, that though there was apparent consent there was no true consent to the agreement: that the agreement was not voluntary.

This involves consideration of what the law regards as voluntary, or its opposite; for in life, including the life of commerce and finance, many acts are done under pressure, sometimes overwhelming pressure, so that one can say that the actor had no choice but to act. Absence of choice in this sense does not negate consent in law: for this the pressure must be one of a kind which the law does not regard as legitimate. Thus, out of the various means by which consent may be obtained – advice, persuasion, influence, inducement, representation, commercial pressure – the law has come to select some which it will not accept as a reason for voluntary action: fraud, abuse of relation of confidence, undue influence, duress or coercion. In this the law, under the influence of equity, has developed from the old common law conception of duress – threat to life and limb – and it has arrived at the modern generalisation expressed by Homes J – 'subjected to an improper motive for action'.[19]

In an action such as the present, then, the first step required of the plaintiff is to show that some illegitimate means of persuasion was used. That there were threats to Barton's life was found by the judge, though he did not accept Barton's evidence in important respects. We shall return to this point in detail later.

The next necessary step would be to establish the relationship between the illegitimate means used and the action taken. For the purposes of the present case (reserving our opinion as to cases which may arise in other contexts) we are prepared to accept, as the formula most favourable to the appellant, the test proposed by the majority, namely, that the illegitimate means used was *a* reason (not *the* reason, nor the *predominant* reason nor the *clinching* reason) why the complainant acted as he did. We are also prepared to accept that a decisive answer is not obtainable by asking the question whether the contract would have been made even if there had been no threats because, even if the answer to this question is affirmative, that does not prove that the contract was not made because of the threats.

[122] Assuming therefore that what has to be decided is whether the illegitimate means used was a reason why the complainant acted as he did, it follows that his reason for acting must (unless the case is one of automatism which this is not) be a conscious reason so that the complainant can give evidence of it: 'I acted because I was forced.' If his evidence is honest and accepted, that will normally conclude the issue. If, moreover, he gives evidence, it is necessary for the court to evaluate his evidence by testing it against his credibility and his actions.

[Lords Wilberforce and Simon considered that the issues before the court were issues of fact which were best decided by the trial judge, and would have dismissed the appeal.]

---

19 *Fairbanks v Snow* (1887), p 598.

Commentary and questions

Lords Wilberforce and Simon adopted a two step approach to the question of duress: (1) was the pressure complained of illegitimate; and (2) did the illegitimate pressure cause the plaintiff to enter the contract/make the payment? This general approach was subsequently approved of and applied to cases of economic duress by McHugh JA in *Crescendo Management Pty Ltd v Westpac Banking Corporation*.[20] It has also been adopted in England in *The Universe Sentinel* (1983) (see extract, p 239) and *The Evia Luck* (1992) (see extract, p 248).

According to Lord Cross, what test of causation is applicable where the conduct complained of involves illegitimate pressure? Which of the parties bears the onus of proof on the causation issue? Did Lords Wilberforce and Simon take the same approach to causation?

DURESS TO PROPERTY

Money is recoverable on the basis of duress to property where the plaintiff believes on reasonable grounds that the defendant would exercise an extra-curial power to harm the plaintiff's proprietary interests.[21]

Maskell v Horner [1915] 3 KB 106 English Court of Appeal

The plaintiff carried on the business of selling produce in the vicinity of Spitalfields Market for a period of 12 years. As soon as the plaintiff commenced business, the defendant, who was the owner of the market, demanded that the plaintiff pay tolls on goods sold, and threatened to seize the plaintiff's goods if he did not pay. On the first occasion of the threat the plaintiff refused to pay and the defendant seized the plaintiff's goods. The plaintiff, upon learning that other dealers outside the market paid the tolls, and acting upon the advice of solicitors, paid the tolls under protest. Whenever the plaintiff subsequently challenged the defendant's right to charge the tolls, or disputed the amount demanded, the defendant either actually seized, or threatened to seize, the plaintiff's goods. The plaintiff accordingly paid all the tolls demanded, though under protest. In separate litigation the tolls were held to be unlawfully demanded, and the plaintiff commenced an action to recover the tolls as money paid under a mistake or under duress of goods.

Lord Reading CJ: ... [Lord Reading CJ dismissed the claim based on mistake, finding that the plaintiff was not mistaken as to the unlawfulness of the plaintiff's demand. His Honour turned to consider the duress claim at p 118:] Upon the second head of claim the plaintiff asserts that he paid the money not voluntarily but under the pressure of actual or threatened seizure of his goods, and that he is therefore entitled to recover it as money had and received. If the facts proved support this assertion the plaintiff would, in my opinion, be entitled to succeed in this action.

---

20   (1988) (see extract, p 246). Although McHugh JA preferred Lord Cross's formulation of the test of causation.

21   *Mason v New South Wales* (1959) (see extract, p 434); *Air India v Commonwealth* (1977) (see extract, p 446). For further discussion, see Chapter 15, pp 429–48.

If a person with knowledge of the facts pays money, which he is not in law bound to pay, and in circumstances implying that he is paying it voluntarily to close the transaction he cannot recover it. Such a payment is in law like a gift, and the transaction cannot be reopened. If a person pays money, which he is not bound to pay, under the compulsion of urgent and pressing necessity or of seizure, actual or threatened, of his goods he can recover it as money had and received. The money is paid not under duress in the strict sense of the term, as that implied duress of person, but under the pressure of seizure or detention of goods which is analogous to that of duress. Payment under such pressure establishes that payment is not made voluntarily to close the transaction.[22] The payment is made for the purpose of averting a threatened evil and is made not with the intention of giving up a right but under immediate necessity and with the intention of preserving the right to dispute the legality of the demand.[23] There are numerous instances in the books of successful claims in this form of action to recover money paid to relieve goods from seizure. Other familiar instances are cases such as *Parker v Great Western Rly Co* (1844), where the money was paid to the railway company under protest in order to induce them to carry goods which they were refusing to carry except at [119] rates in excess of those they were legally entitled to demand. These payments were made throughout a period of twelve months, always accompanied by the assertion that they were made under protest, and it was held that the plaintiffs were entitled to recover the excess payments as money had and received, on the ground that the payments ere made under the compulsion of urgent and pressing necessity. That case was approved in *Great Western Rly Co v Sutton* (1869), when the judges were summoned to the House of Lords to give their opinion. Willes J, in stating his view of the law, said: 'When a man pays more than he is bound to do by law for the performance of a duty which the law says is owed to him for nothing, or for less than he has paid, there is a compulsion or concussion in respect of which he is entitled to recover the excess by *condictio indebiti*, or action for money had and received. This is every day's practice as to excess freight.' That is a clear and accurate statement in accordance with the views expressed by Blackburn J in the same case and adopted by the House of Lords. It treats such claims made in this form of action as matters of ordinary practice and beyond discussion.[24]

This principle of law is so well settled that it cannot be challenged, and I find nothing in *Brisbane v Dacres* (1813) to the contrary. Indeed the general proposition of law is not disputed; but it was contended, and the learned judge found, that the plaintiff had not brought himself within it, mainly because: (1) the payments were not accompanied by a declaration or assertion to the defendant that the plaintiff did not intend to give up his right to recover the money; and (2) the protests for a period of years had degenerated into a sort of grumbling acquiescence and were ineffective. I doubt whether Rowlatt J [the trial judge] intended to find that there must be anything in the shape of an express notice or declaration to the defendant of the plaintiff's intention to keep alive his right to recover. It is clear, and was indeed admitted at the Bar, that no express words are necessary and that the [120] circumstances attending the payments and the conduct of the plaintiff when making them may be a sufficient indication to the defendant that the payments were not made with the intention of closing the transactions. I do not now think that the mere fact of a payment under protest would be sufficient to entitle the

---

22   *Atlee v Backhouse* (1838) *per* Lord Abinger CB; p 650 *per* Parke B.
23   *Valpy v Manley* (1845) *per* Tindal CJ.
24   See also *per* Lord Chelmsford in *Lancashire and Yorkshire Rly Co v Gidlow* (1875).

plaintiff to succeed; but I think that it affords some evidence, when accompanied by other circumstances, that the payment was not voluntarily made to end the matter ...

[121] I come to the conclusion that the plaintiff never intended to depart, and never did depart, from the course taken by him at the commencement of the dispute. In order to preserve his right to recover, it is not, in my opinion, necessary that on every occasion there should be a refusal to pay by the plaintiff followed by seizure. It was not necessary to go through this form. The circumstances of these payments and the conduct of the plaintiff throughout the period of years satisfy me that he never made the payments voluntarily, that he never intended to give up his right to recover the sums paid, and that he only paid because he knew that a refusal to pay would be immediately followed by seizure of his goods, as in fact did happen whenever he disputed the defendant's right and refused to pay. The pressure of seizure was always present to his mind, and never ceased to operate upon it whenever demand for tolls was made. I am also satisfied that the circumstances of the payments and the conduct of the plaintiff were a sufficient indication to the defendant that the plaintiff did not intend to give up his right to recover. If any assertion or declaration of his intentions was necessary it was made to the defendant at the time and in the circumstances of the payments ...

One further point remains to be considered. Mr Sutton, on behalf of the defendant, contended that a payment of tolls under an actual or threatened seizure of goods should be treated like payment of a debt in an action or in consequence of a threat of action. There is no doubt that if a person pays in an action or under threat of action the money cannot be recovered by him, as the payment is made to avoid the litigation to determine the right to the money claimed. Such payment is not made to keep alive the right to recover it, in as much as the opportunity is thus afforded of contesting the demand, and payment in such [122] circumstances is a payment to close the transaction and not to keep it open. Even if the money is paid in the action accompanied by a declaration that it is paid without prejudice to the payer's right to recover it, the payment is a voluntary payment, and the transaction is closed.[25] It is argued that as unpaid tolls can be recovered by distress levied upon the goods of the person who fails to pay, the seizure is to be regarded like the issue of a writ, and therefore that a payment of tolls on seizure must be treated as a voluntary payment. I cannot agree with this contention. When goods are seized, the owner can only relieve them from seizure by payment. He has no opportunity of contesting the right to demand tolls from him except by allowing the seizure and detention of his goods to continue, or by making payment to protect them ...

Buckley LJ: ... [123] [T]he plaintiff is entitled, I think, to recover upon the ground that the payments which he made were not made voluntarily, but were made under the pressure of the defendant's threat to seize and sell his goods in default of payment and were made not without objection but under protest. [Counsel for the defendant] in his argument largely rested his case upon the judgment of Gibbs J in *Brisbane v Dacres* (1813), and contended that the learned judge meant to lay down as a general proposition that under circumstances such as those in the present case the party called upon to make payment has an option either (1) to litigate the question, or (2) to submit and pay, and that if he does the latter, the payment is by way of gift to the person to whom he pays and closes the

---

25   See *Brown v McKinally* (1795).

transaction between them. [Counsel for the defendant] argued that that proposition is true in law. In my opinion it is not the fact that there exist only those two alternatives of which the person called upon to make payment must elect one, and that if he elects to pay, his payment is by way of gift and is voluntary. To say that it is a gift and is voluntary seems to me to beg the question. He may submit (in the sense of making the payment) because the consequences to himself will be so disagreeable if he does not pay that he prefers to pay and prevent the seizure of his goods, but may at the same time reserve the right to contend that the [124] money has been obtained from him against his will. In *Atlee v Backhouse* (1838) Lord Abinger said that in cases where property has been unlawfully seized or unlawfully detained for the purpose of enforcing the payment of money not due, 'the party against whom the goods have been wrongfully seized or detained, is entitled, after payment of the money, to bring an action for money had and received,' and Parke B, referring to an argument by [counsel], which will be found at p 642 of the report, said:

> There is no doubt of the proposition laid down by [counsel], that if goods are wrongfully taken, and a sum of money is paid, simply for the purpose of obtaining possession of those goods again, without any agreement at all, especially if it be paid under protest, that money can be recovered back; not on the ground of duress, because I think that the law is clear, although there is some case in Viner's *Abridgement* to the contrary, that, in order to avoid a contract by reason of duress, it must be duress of a man's person, not of his goods; and it is so laid down in Sheppard's *Touchstone* – but the ground is, that it is not a voluntary payment. If my goods have been wrongfully detained, and I pay money simply to obtain them again, that being paid under a species of duress or constraint, may be recovered back *Atlee v Backhouse* (1838), p 650.

The same is true, I think, when payment is made not to release goods seized but to intercept a threat to seize them. When the defendant demanded payment of the plaintiff, the latter, if he refused payment, exposed himself to the seizure and sale, rightfully or wrongfully, of his goods. When he made payment to escape such seizure and sale, the payment was, I think, within Parke B's words, not a voluntary payment. Further, if there be added to the above facts the further fact that the party making the payment protests that the money is being wrongfully taken from him, a further factor is added which goes to show that the payment was not voluntary ...

Commentary

For application of these principles where the defendant is a public authority, see *Mason v New South Wales* (1959) (see extract, p 434) and *Air India v Commonwealth* (1977) (see extract, p 446).

Lord Reading CJ in the principal case lays down the proposition that a payment made merely in order to avoid litigation does not amount to duress. The plaintiff in such a case is often said to have voluntarily submitted to the claim. This principle has been affirmed in numerous subsequent cases.[26] However, the better view is that the law simply does not recognise, as a species

---

26   See, eg, *Werrin v The Commonwealth* (1938) (see extract, p 431); *Mason v New South Wales* (1959) (see extract, p 434); *David Securities Pty Ltd v Commonwealth Bank of Australia* (1992) (see extract, p 110); *McKay v National Australia Bank* (1998) (see extract, p 216).

of compulsion, a payment of money made in order to avoid litigating the matter. On this approach, the plaintiff's claim fails, not because she has voluntarily submitted, but because she has failed to establish an operative unjust factor.

Hawker Pacific Pty Ltd v Helicopter Charter Pty Ltd (1991) 22 NSWLR 298
Court of Appeal of New South Wales

The appellant agreed to repaint one of the helicopters belonging to the respondent and which the respondent used in its charter business. The agreed price for this work was $5,200. The appellant repainted the helicopter but the respondent was dissatisfied with the work and delivered the helicopter to the appellant for rectification. When the respondent's representatives went to the appellant's premises the next day to pick up the helicopter, they were asked to sign an agreement which provided for payment of $4,300 for the painting services and which released the appellant from any further liability in relation to the painting work. The respondent's representatives, aware that the helicopter was needed for a charter later that day, signed the agreement but the respondent subsequently commenced proceedings alleging that it had entered into the agreement under duress. There was no evidence of any express threat by the appellant to detain the helicopter unless the respondent signed the agreement. Nevertheless the trial judge, Brownie J, found that the respondent's representatives were justified in believing that signing the agreement was the only practical way of getting possession of the helicopter that day.

Priestley JA: ... [301] In the appeal, the appellant did not challenge the trial judge's primary findings of fact. The argument went to the complexion to be put on those findings. This submission needs to be measured against the legal principle concerning duress in commercial situations such as that in question. The general law on the subject was reviewed by Isaacs J in *Smith v William Charlick Ltd* (1924). In that case, the plaintiff sought to recover money paid to the defendant, by action for money had and received, in circumstances in which, the plaintiff claimed, the law implied a promise to repay by the defendant to the plaintiff. Isaacs J stated the law as follows (p 56):

> It is conceded that the only ground on which the promise to repay could be implied is 'compulsion'. The payment is said by the respondent not to have been 'voluntary' but 'forced' from it within the contemplation of the law. Leaving aside, for the present, the question whether in law the payment was 'forced' from the respondent by some undue advantage taken of its situation having regard to the Wheat Harvest legislation, the point is whether the board's insistence was what is regarded as 'compulsion' from the simple standpoint of common law. 'Compulsion' in relation to a payment of which refund is sought, and whether it is also variously called 'coercion', 'extortion', 'exaction', or 'force', includes every species of duress or conduct analogous to duress, [302] actual or threatened, exerted by or on behalf of the payee and applied to the person or the property or any right of the person who pays or, in some cases, of a person related to or in affinity with him. Such compulsion is a legal wrong, and the law provides a remedy by raising a fictional promise to repay.

This passage was adopted by Long Innes J as correct in *Nixon v Furphy* (1925). The full court adopted as correct the portion of the passage commencing '"compulsion" in relation to a payment ...' in *TA Sundell & Sons Pty Ltd v Emm Yannoulatos (Overseas) Pty Ltd* (1956), pp (SR) 328, (WN) 569–70. The court in the *TA Sundell* case[27] also noted in *TA Sundell & Sons Pty Ltd v Emm Yannoulatos (Overseas) Pty Ltd* (1956), p 328; p 570, that Isaacs J's formulation was in substance to the same effect as the opinion expressed by Fullagar J in *Re Hooper and Grass Contract* (1949). An interesting observation made by Fullagar J in that case was that 'the withholding of another's legal right' (which I take to be analogous to Isaacs J's 'duress ... applied to ... any right ...' of the opposing party) may be treated as 'practical compulsion', a term used in English cases decided since *Smith v William Charlick Ltd.*

Isaacs J's statement refers in terms only to situations where payment has been made under duress, not to contracts made under duress. I do not see why the underlying idea should not apply to both situations. That is, the sentence in his statement beginning '"compulsion" ... could just as well be written "compulsion" in relation to a contract which is sought to be set aside, includes every species of duress or conduct analogous to duress, actual or threatened, exerted by or on behalf of the promisee and applied to the person or the property or any right of the person who promises'. A similar conclusion was reached by Mocatta J in *North Ocean Shipping Co Ltd v Hyundai Construction Co Ltd* (1979), p 719 and by Lord Diplock in the House of Lords in *Universal Tankships Inc of Monrovia v International Transport Workers Federation* (1983), p 384. The course of authority in New South Wales seems to me to warrant the same conclusion.

Brownie J's finding seems to me to fall within the proposition stated by Isaacs J Brownie J said that the appellant's conduct on 5 March 1987, viewed objectively, amounted to a holding out to the respondent that the helicopter would not be released unless the respondent first promised to pay $4,300 to the defendant and signed the document of 5 March 1987: see p 14 of his reasons. In the language of Isaacs J, this represented a finding of conduct by the appellant analogous to threatened duress by the appellant applied to either or both the respondent's helicopter or the respondent's right to take its helicopter away from the appellant's premises ... The respondent was entitled to take away its helicopter from the appellant's premises on 5 March 1987. The appellant's conduct showed, and [the respondent] believed, that the appellant would not permit it to be taken away unless the respondent did what the appellant wanted. On Brownie J's findings, in my [303] opinion fully supported by the evidence, the respondent's need for the helicopter for business purposes that day was so urgent that recourse to legal proceedings for its recovery clearly would not have solved the company's practical problem.

The appellant's submission on this aspect of the case was that it was wrong to conclude from all the circumstances that its conduct was analogous to threatened duress to the helicopter or the right of the respondent to take away the helicopter. The chief points made in support of this general submission were that the threat that the appellant would not permit the respondent to take away the helicopter was never expressed, and that the respondent's subsequent behaviour showed

---

27 Roper CJ in equity, Hardie J and Manning AJ.

that it did not regard itself as having been threatened as was later alleged on its behalf.

On the first of these arguments, it does not seem to me to be sufficient for the appellant's purposes to show that no express threat was made. If circumstances for which the appellant was responsible conveyed the threat to the respondent, then the threat of duress would operate as forcefully as if it were put into words. Brownie J accepted that [the respondent's representatives] believed that the threat was being made; in light of the materials upon which Brownie J made this finding, it was not seriously open to challenge in this court, and was not challenged by the appellant. The appellant's submission was rather that the circumstances could not reasonably have given rise to the apprehension actually felt by the respondent's director and employee. However, in my opinion the circumstances were such as to make it reasonable for [the respondent] to believe that the appellant would withhold the helicopter from them unless the promise to pay were made ...

Clarke JA: ... [305] It is well settled that money paid in order to get possession of goods wrongfully detained, or to avoid their wrongful detention, may be recovered in an action for money had and received (*Astley v Reynolds* (1731); *Maskell v Horner* (1915), where Lord Reading CJ said that the money was recoverable because although it was not [306] paid under duress in the strict sense (not being duress of the person) it was paid under conditions analogous to duress; *Smith v William Charlick Ltd* (1924)).

On the other hand the traditional view, according to *Chitty on Contracts*, 26th edn, 1989, 'General principles' (para 505, pp 337–38), is that the unlawful detention, or threatened detention of a person's goods, is not duress which will at common law enable the owner of the goods to avoid an agreement obtained by it. *Skeate v Beale* (1841) is the authority cited in support of that view.

This distinction, if correct, leads to the absurd result that if A paid money under duress of goods he could recover the money paid but if he entered into a contract to pay money under similar duress he could not avoid the contract and would be obliged to pay the moneys due thereunder.

In my opinion the distinction is not supportable and to the extent that *Skeate* is authority for the so called traditional view it should not be followed. This is the view expressed in Goff and Jones, *The Law of Restitution*,[28] and by Kerr J in *The Siboen and The Sibotre* (1976) and accords with the authorities cited by Priestley JA ...

Commentary

The Court of Appeal rejects the distinction previously drawn in the context of duress of goods between contractual and non-contractual payments. This distinction, usually attributed to *Skeate v Beale* (1841), has also been rejected in England.[29]

---

28   2nd edn, 1978, p 170; see also Beatson, 'Duress as a vitiating factor in contract' (1974) 33 CLJ 97, p 108.

29   See *The Siboen and The Sibotre* (1976) (see extract, p 230); *The Atlantic Baron* (1979) (see extract, p 233).

ECONOMIC DURESS

A plaintiff will be able to recover money paid on the basis of economic duress. Although economic duress might take a number of forms, the most common form is where the defendant applies pressure on the plaintiff by threatening a breach of contract.[30]

As will be seen, the principles governing economic duress are controversial. However, in essence, a payment will be recoverable on this ground where it was paid because of the application of illegitimate pressure by the defendant in circumstances where the plaintiff had no reasonable alternative but to make the payment.[31]

TA Sundell & Sons Pty Ltd v Emm Yannoulatos (Overseas) Pty Ltd (1956) 56 SR (NSW) 323 Full Court of the Supreme Court of New South Wales

The plaintiff, Sundell, entered into a contract with the defendant to purchase a quantity of galvanised iron of French origin at £109 15s per ton. The plaintiff required the iron to fulfil other commitments, a fact known to the defendant. In accordance with the contract the plaintiff established a letter of credit in the defendant's favour to provide for payment of the price. Some months later the defendant wrote to the plaintiff stating that the French government had intervened to increase the price of zinc and that a price increase for the iron to be delivered to the plaintiff was 'inevitable'. The defendant indicated that the probable increase would be £27 per ton and requested an increase in the amount of the letter of credit to provide for this increase. The defendant made it clear that the plaintiff would lose the iron unless it agreed to increase its price. After some discussion the plaintiff agreed to the increased price and increased its letter of credit, but the defendant refused to accept an order at the increased price without prejudice to the plaintiff's rights. The plaintiff again later asserted that the increase in the letter of credit had been without prejudice to its rights. The plaintiff ultimately took delivery of the iron and the defendant collected the full amount under the letter of credit. The plaintiff commenced proceedings to recover the amount paid in excess of the price originally agreed on the grounds that the defendant had provided no consideration for the contract variation, or alternatively that the plaintiff had acted under duress.

The court: [The court upheld the claim by the plaintiff that the contract variation was not supported by consideration and so was of no effect. The court then turned to consider the duress claim at p 327.] The second question is within a comparatively narrow compass. We do not think we are doing an injustice to [counsel for the defendant's] comprehensive and able submissions by summarising them as follows: that the cases relating to the circumstances in which a payment will be said to be made 'under compulsion' are limited and should not be extended, and that these cases include instances where the payee has been

---

30 See, for example, *Occidental Worldwide Investment Corp v Skibs A/S Avanti, The Siboen and The Sibotre* (1976) (see extract, p 230); *North Ocean Shipping Co Ltd v Hyundai Constructions Co Ltd, The Atlantic Baron* (1979) (see extract, p 233).

31 See generally Nolan, 'Economic duress and the availability of a reasonable alternative (*Huyton v Peter Cremer*)' [2000] RLR 105 for a review of the relevant authorities.

under a statutory duty; where he has been in possession of the payer's goods; where he has held the legal title to land of which the payer was the equitable owner; and other cases where the 'compulsion' was exercised in relation to the property of the payer. But, so the argument went, the principle has never been applied [328] to a case where a compulsive threat has been made to refrain from performing merely a contractual duty as distinct from a threat to refrain from performing a statutory duty or a threat to interfere with a proprietary right of the payer. And it was said that to treat a threat to refrain from performing a contractual duty as a sufficient 'compulsion', would be to break new ground, and to extend the principle in this way would be contrary to the rule laid down by Lord Sumner in *Sinclair v Brougham* (1914) and adopted by Knox CJ in *Smith v William Charlick Ltd* (1924).

In the first place we are of opinion that the statements in the cases on which the [defendant] seeks to rely do not justify his contention. The authorities were reviewed by Long Innes J in *Nixon v Furphy* (1925) and his Honour said:

> 'Compulsion' in relation to a payment of which refund is sought ... includes every species of duress or conduct analogous to duress, actual or threatened, exerted by or on behalf of the payee and applied to the person or the property *or any right* of the person who pays or, in some cases, of a person related to or in affinity with him. ((1925), p 160))

This statement is, in substance, to the same effect as the opinion expressed by Fullagar J in *Re Hooper and Grass Contract* (1949). Furthermore, it was adopted by Rich J in *White Rose Flour Milling Co Pty Ltd v Australian Wheat Board* (1944) and applied to a similar type of case to that now under consideration.

[The court agreed with the findings of the trial judge that the payments had been made under compulsion.]

Question

According to this case, is the doctrine of duress limited to duress to the person or of goods?

Occidental Worldwide Investment Corp v Skibs A/S Avanti, The Siboen and The Sibotre [1976] 1 Lloyd's Rep 293 Queen's Bench

The defendants owned two oil/bulk ore carriers, the *Siboen* and the *Sibotre*, and in August 1970 agreed to let them out on charterparties to the plaintiff, which was a member of the Occidental group of companies. The agreed rate of hire was $4.40 per ton per month, which was the prevailing market rate. By the latter half of 1971 the financial position of the Occidental group had deteriorated and it was resolved to obtain a reduction in the charter hire payable to the defendants and other vessel owners. In March 1972 the plaintiff served cancellation notices upon the defendants, claiming that the charterparties were frustrated. There was no foundation for this claim. It was arranged that a meeting should take place in Paris between the plaintiff and the defendants. At that meeting the plaintiff's representatives gave the impression, proved to be false, that it was a company in a very unstable financial position, that it was dependent on its parent company for survival, and that its parent company was willing to let it go into liquidation unless the plaintiff could obtain a reduction in hire rates. The plaintiff knew that because of a slump in the charterparty market the defendants would have found it very difficult to find new charterers. The manager of the defendants, Mr Tschudi, agreed to vary the charterparty agreement to reduce the rate of hire to $4.10 per ton per month. An 'addenda' was accordingly entered into. In May 1973 the defendants claimed that they had been 'unlawfully forced' into agreeing to the variation and withdrew both ships. The plaintiff commenced proceedings claiming damages for wrongful withdrawal. The defendants counterclaimed that they were entitled to rescind the addenda as it had been obtained as a result of misrepresentations by the plaintiff, or alternatively had been entered into under duress. They also counterclaimed for the difference between the original rate of hire and that agreed to in the addenda up to the date of withdrawal of the vessels.

Kerr J: [Kerr J held that the plaintiff had given good consideration for the variation in the charterparty, and continued at p 334:] I then turn to [counsel for the defendants'] primary submission on duress. He agreed that for this purpose it had to be assumed that the charterers were in fact liable to go bankrupt if the various owners did not reduce their rates, without any misrepresentation having been made on this or any other subject. He submitted that the cancellation notices constituted threatened breaches of the charters, and with this I agree. He also submitted that if the charterers were liable to go bankrupt if the owners did not reduce their rates, then the owners would be left without any effective legal remedy in the face of these threatened breaches. He accordingly submitted that the defence of duress is made out whenever one party to a contract threatens to commit a breach [335] of it and the other party agrees to vary or cancel the contract under this threat because it has no effective legal remedy in respect of the threatened breach and has in this sense been compelled to agree. For good measure, though again I do not think that this makes any difference, he added that duress must *a fortiori* be a defence when the party threatening to break the contract is putting forward some justification for doing so without any *bona fides*.

I think that this submission is much too wide. On the other hand, [counsel for the plaintiff's] counter-submissions were in their turn in my view too narrow. These fell under two main heads. First, he submitted that English law only knows duress to the person and duress to goods, and that a case like the present falls into neither category, with the result that this defence must fail *in limine*. Secondly, he submitted that although money paid under duress to goods is recoverable, a contract can only be set aside for duress to the person but not in any other case of duress. He said that in every case in which a party enters into a contract otherwise than under duress to the person, any payment or forbearance pursuant to such contract is regarded as voluntary, whatever may have been the nature or degree of compulsion, short of violence to the person, which may have caused him to enter into the contract. He relied mainly on a line of authority in which *Skeate v Beale* (1841) is the leading case.

I do not think that English law is as limited as submitted by [counsel for the plaintiffs], though there are statements in some of the cases which support his submissions. For instance, if I should be compelled to sign a lease or some other contract for a nominal but legally sufficient consideration under an imminent threat of having my house burnt down or a valuable picture slashed, though without any threat of physical violence to anyone, I do not think that the law would uphold the agreement. I think that a plea of coercion or compulsion would be available in such cases. The latter is the term used in a line of Australian cases of strong persuasive authority to which I was referred: *Nixon v Furphy* (1925), *Re Hooper & Grass Contract* (1949), and *TA Sundell & Sons Pty Ltd v Emm Yannoulatos (Overseas) Pty Ltd* (1956). These judgments also state that the degree of compulsion or duress is not necessarily limited to cases of threats to the person or duress in relation to goods. Further, I think that there are indications in *Skeate v Beale* itself and in other cases that the true question is ultimately whether or not the agreement in question is to be regarded as having been concluded voluntarily; but it does not follow that every agreement concluded under some form of compulsion is *ipso facto* to be regarded as voluntary with the solitary exception of cases involving duress to the person. In *Wakefield v Newton* (1844), Lord Denman referred to cases such as *Skeate v Beale* as:

> ... that class where the parties have come to a voluntary settlement of their concerns, and have chosen to pay what is found due.

In *Kaufman v Gerson* (1904), the Court of Appeal refused to enforce a written contract signed by the defendant which was valid under French law because the consideration for the defendant's promise to pay sums of money to the plaintiff had been that the plaintiff would not prosecute the defendant's husband in France, he having apparently committed a criminal offence under French law. The reason for the refusal to enforce the contract was duress or coercion. The judge at first instance held the contract to be enforceable because there was no threat of physical violence. But this was reversed unanimously, and Sir Richard Henn Collins MR, significantly asked: 'What does it matter what particular form of coercion is used as long as the will is coerced?' The same approach is strongly supported by the judgments of Lord Denning, MR, and Lord Justice Danckwerts in *D & C Builders Ltd v Rees* (1966). The plaintiffs were owed about £480 by the defendant and were in desperate financial straits. They were in effect told that unless they settled for £300 they would get nothing, and when they unwillingly decided to accept the sum of £300 the defendant's wife insisted on their signing a receipt 'in completion of the account'. In the action they were nevertheless held entitled to recover the balance of £180. There were two grounds for the decision of Lord Denning and Lord Justice Danckwerts. First, that there was no consideration for the settlement, which was the only point dealt with in the concurring judgment of Lord Justice Winn, the third member of the court. Secondly, that there was no [336] 'true accord' because (in the words of Lord Denning, p 265) 'no person can insist on a settlement procured by intimidation'. It is true that in that case, and in all the three Australian cases, it was held that there had been no consideration for the settlement which the courts reopened. But I do not think that it would have made any difference if the defendants in these cases had also insisted on some purely nominal but legally sufficient consideration. If the contract is void the consideration would be recoverable in quasi-contract; if it is voidable equity could rescind the contract and order the return of the consideration. The anomaly of the position for which [counsel for the plaintiff] contends as a matter of principle is helpfully discussed in Goff and Jones, *The Law of Restitution* (p 150).

But even assuming, as I think, that our law is open to further development in relation to contracts concluded under some form of compulsion not amounting to duress to the person, the court must in every case at least be satisfied that the consent of the other party was overborne by compulsion so as to deprive him of any *animus contrahendi*. This would depend on the facts of each case. One relevant factor would be whether the party relying on duress made any protest at the time or shortly thereafter. Another would be to consider whether or not he treated the settlement as closing the transaction in question and as binding upon him, or whether he made it clear that he regarded the position as still open. All these considerations are mentioned in the Australian judgments, and the question whether or not there was any intention to close the transaction is also referred to in the judgments of Lord Reading CJ and Lord Justice Buckley in *Maskell v Horner* (1915). But the facts of the present case fall a long way short of the test which would in law be required to make good a defence of compulsion or duress. Believing the statements about the charterers' financial state to be true, as must for this purpose be assumed, Captain Tschudi made no protest about having to conclude the addenda, either at the Paris meeting on 26 March 1972, or at any time before the telex of 28 April 1973. He repeatedly said in his evidence that he regarded the agreement then reached as binding and sought to uphold it in the subsequent arbitration. He was acting under great pressure, but only commercial pressure, and not under anything which could in law be regarded as a coercion of his will so as to vitiate his consent. I therefore hold that the plea of duress fails.

[Kerr J upheld the claim for rescission based on misrepresentation, and on this basis the defendants were held entitled to receive hire at the original rate up until the time of withdrawal of the vessels.]

North Ocean Shipping Co Ltd v Hyundai Construction Co Ltd, The Atlantic Baron [1979] QB 705 Queen's Bench

Hyundai Construction operated a shipbuilding yard (the 'yard'). The yard agreed to build a tanker for North Ocean Shipping (the 'owners') for a fixed price in United States dollars, payment to be made in five instalments. The yard agreed to open a letter of credit to secure its obligations. The owners paid the first instalment, however the United States dollar was then devalued by 10%. The yard requested an increase of 10% on the remaining instalments but the owners, asserting there was no legal ground for claiming the increase, paid the second and third instalments without the additional 10%. The yard returned both instalments, and rejected the owners' suggestion of referring the matter to arbitration. The yard requested that the owners make a final decision on its demand for the increase by a stipulated date, failing which it would terminate the contract. The owners (unknown to the yard) were at the time negotiating a very lucrative agreement with Shell for the charter of the vessel and replied that they would make the additional payments. However the owners stated that they considered they were under no obligation to make the additional payments, and that they would do so 'without prejudice' to their rights. They requested that the yard arrange for a corresponding increase in its letter of credit, which it did. The owners remitted the remaining four instalments with the additional 10% and without protest. The yard delivered the tanker to the owners in November 1974. In July 1975 the owners commenced proceedings claiming the return of the extra 10% paid on the four instalments on the grounds that the yard provided no consideration for the agreement to make the extra payments, or alternatively that the agreement to vary had been entered into under duress.

Mocatta J: [Mocatta J held that the yard had provided consideration for the owners' agreement to pay the additional 10%, and then turned to consider the issue of duress at p 430:] I was referred to a number of cases decided overseas: *Nixon v Furphy* (1925), *Knutson v Bourkes Syndicate* (1941) and *Re Hooper and Grass Contract* (1949), all of which have a similarity to *Close v Phipps* (1844). Perhaps their greatest importance, however, is the quotation in the first mentioned from the judgment of Isaacs J in *Smith v William Charlick Ltd* (1924), where he said:

> It is conceded that the only ground on which the promise to repay could be implied is 'compulsion'. The payment is said by the respondent not to have been 'voluntary' but 'forced' from it within the contemplation of the law ... 'Compulsion' in relation to a payment of which refund is sought, and whether it is also variously called 'coercion', 'extortion', 'exaction' or 'force', includes every species of duress or conduct analogous to duress, actual or threatened, exacted by or on behalf of the payee and applied to the person or the property *or any right* of the person who pays ... Such compulsion is a legal wrong, and the law provides a remedy by raising a fictional promise to repay.

These cases do not, however, expressly deal with the position arising when the threat or compulsion result in a new or varied contract. This was, or something very like it, however, the position in *Sundell's* case (1956). In that case the plaintiff had originally entered into a contract to buy from the defendant a quantity of galvanised iron at £100 15s a ton and had established a letter of credit in favour of the defendant seller accordingly. The iron was to come from France and some months after the contract had been entered into the seller said that an increase in price of probably £27 was inevitable and requested that the letter of credit be increased, otherwise the plaintiff would not get his iron. Eventually the buyer on 17 April sent the seller a fresh order for the same quantity of iron at £140 per ton, but asking the seller to acknowledge that [431] the buyer should have the right to contend that the original contract required the seller to supply the iron at £109 15s a ton. The buyer amended and increased his letter of credit accordingly, but the seller in acknowledging the buyer's letter did not accept the terms laid down in it. Eventually the iron arrived before the argument had been resolved and full use was made of the increased letter of credit.

The buyer thereafter sued to recover the excess he had paid through the increased letter of credit as having been paid under 'practical compulsion'. The first point taken in answer to this was that the original contract was varied or superseded by a new contract made on 17 April and that accordingly the buyer was obliged thereunder to pay. This argument failed since the court found there was no consideration for the provision of the increased letter of credit. The second point argued was that a payment could not be said to have been made under 'practical compulsion' where a threat was made by the payee to withhold from the payer a contractual right as distinct from a right of possession of property, a statutory right or some proprietary right. This it was argued would be to break new ground and would be contrary to what was said by Lord Sumner in *Sinclair v Brougham* (1914) against extending the action for money had and received. These arguments were rejected by the court who cited the passage from the judgment of Isaacs J, set out above emphasising by italics the words 'or any right' of the person paying under compulsion. It would seem, therefore, that the Australian courts would be prepared to allow the recovery of excess money paid, even under a new contract, as the result of a threat to break an earlier contract, since the threat or compulsion would be applied to the original contractual right of the party subject to the compulsion or economic duress. This also seems to be the view in the United States, where this was one of the grounds of decision in *King Construction Co v WM Smith Electric Co* (1961). This view also accords with what was said in *D & C Builders Ltd v Rees* (1966), p 625 *per* Lord Denning MR: 'No person can insist on a settlement procured by intimidation.'

[Counsel for the owners] also relied on two English cases of the last century as showing that even when a contract has been entered into to pay an excess amount the remedy by way of a claim for money had and received is available. The first of these was *Hills v Street* (1828). There a broker was in possession of goods distrained for rent. The party distrained upon was anxious to have time to pay the rent and that the goods should not be sold. A written request was demanded by the broker and an undertaking to pay expenses given. Yet despite what appears to have been an agreement, the party distrained upon was held entitled to recover expenses charged by the broker. There was no voluntary payment. The second was *Tamvaco v Simpson* (1866), cited in Goff and Jones, *The Law of Restitution* (p 151) as being inconsistent with the so called rule based upon *Skeate v Beale* (1841). The case is, however, a difficult one to follow and draw conclusions from since the courts were limited to answering two questions on a case stated. Counsel for the owners further relied on the Chancery case of *Ormes v Beadel* (1860), reversed on appeal on the ground of affirmation or acquiescence, as showing that in equity a contract entered into under circumstances of acute economic pressure, increased by the refusal of an architect to pay a builder a sum which the court found was a fair and just demand for work done, would be set aside in equity.

[432] I may here usefully cite a further short passage from the valuable remarks of Kerr J in *The Siboen and The Sibotre* (1976), p 336, where after referring to three of the Australian cases I have cited he said:

> It is true that in that case, and in all the three Australian cases, it was held that there had been no consideration for the settlement which the courts reopened. But I do not think that it would have made any difference if the defendants in these cases had also insisted on some purely nominal but legally sufficient consideration. If the contract is void the consideration would be recoverable in quasi-contract; if it is voidable equity could rescind the contract and order the return of the consideration.

It is also interesting at this point to quote a few sentences from an article entitled 'Duress as a vitiating factor in contract', by Mr Beatson, Fellow of Merton College, Oxford (1974), p 108:

> It is submitted that there is no reason for making a distinction between actual payments and agreements to pay. If that is so there is nothing to prevent a court from finding that duress of goods is a ground upon which the validity of a contract can be impeached ... The law was accurately stated by the courts of South Carolina as early as 1975, when it was said that '... whenever *assumpsit* will lie for money extorted by duress of goods, a party may defend himself against any claim upon him for money to be paid in consequence of any contract made under similar circumstances'.

Before proceeding further it may be useful to summarise the conclusions I have so far reached. First, I do not take the view that the recovery of money paid under duress other than to the person is necessarily limited to duress to goods falling within one of the categories hitherto established by the English cases. I would respectfully follow and adopt the broad statement of principle laid down by Isaacs J cited earlier and frequently quoted and applied in the Australian cases. Secondly, from this it follows that the compulsion may take the form of 'economic duress' if the necessary facts are proved. A threat to break a contract may amount to such 'economic duress'. Thirdly, if there has been such a form of duress leading to a contract for consideration, I think that contract is a voidable one which can be avoided and the excess money paid under it recovered.

I think the facts found in this case do establish that the agreement to increase the price by 10% reached at the end of June 1973 was caused by what may be called 'economic duress'. The yard were adamant in insisting on the increased price without having any legal justification for so doing and the owners realised that the yard would not accept anything other than an unqualified agreement to the increase. The owners might have claimed damages in arbitration against the yard with all the inherent unavoidable uncertainties of litigation, but in view of the position of the yard vis à vis their relations with Shell it would be unreasonable to hold that this is the course they should have taken: see *Astley v Reynolds* (1731). The owners made a very reasonable offer of arbitration coupled with security for any award in the yard's favour that might be made, but this was refused. They then made their agreement, which can [433] truly I think be said to have been made under compulsion, by the telex of 28 June without prejudice to their rights. I do not consider the yard's ignorance of the Shell charter material. It may well be that had they known of it they would have been even more exigent.

If I am right in the conclusion reached with some doubt earlier that there was consideration for the 10% increase agreement reached at the end of June 1973, and it be right to regard this as having been reached under a kind of duress in the form of economic pressure, then what is said in *Chitty on Contracts*,[32] to which both counsel referred me, is relevant, namely that a contract entered into under duress is voidable and not void:

> ... consequently a person who has entered into a contract under duress, may either affirm or avoid such contract after the duress has ceased; and if he has so voluntarily acted under it with a full knowledge of all the circumstances he may be held bound on the ground of rectification, or if, after escaping from the duress, he takes no steps to set aside the transaction, he may be found to have affirmed it.

[Mocatta J concluded that the owners had affirmed the variation of the contract because of their failure to protest when making the four instalments and because of their delay in commencing proceedings, and so rejected the owners' claim.]

Commentary and questions

Mocatta J held that duress renders a contract voidable, not void. This view has been confirmed in a number of subsequent decisions.[33]

---

32 24th edn, 1977, Vol 1, para 442, p 207.
33 *Pao On v Lau Yiu Long* (1980) (see following extract); *The Universe Sentinel* (1983) (see extract, p 239); *Crescendo Management Pty Ltd v Westpac Banking Corporation* (1988) (see extract, p 246); *The Evia Luck* (1992) (see extract, p 248).

Halson[34] believes that a threat to break a contract as part of an attempt to renegotiate the contract in response to an unanticipated circumstance should not be classified as illegitimate pressure: '[T]he essential inquiry must always be whether the reduced profit was a result of unanticipated circumstances, caused by the materialisation of a risk not assigned by the contract.'[35] Does Halson's test provide a rationale for distinguishing between the (illegitimate) pressure in the principal case and the (legitimate) pressure in the case of *The Siboen and The Sibotre* (see extract, p 230)?

Pao On v Lau Yiu Long [1980] AC 614 Privy Council

The plaintiffs were the sole shareholders in a private company which owned a public building in Hong Kong. The defendants were the majority shareholders of a public company which wished to acquire the building. In February 1973 the plaintiffs agreed to sell their shares in the private company to the public company. No money was to pass under the agreement; rather the purchase price of the shares was to take the form of an issue to the plaintiffs of shares in the public company (the 'main agreement'). In order to preserve the share price of the public company the plaintiffs agreed at the defendants' request to retain 60% of their newly acquired shares in the public company until after 30 April 1974. In order to protect the plaintiffs against any loss from a possible fall in the value of the shares between their acquisition and 30 April 1974, the plaintiffs and defendants entered into a subsidiary agreement under which the defendants agreed to buy from the plaintiffs 60% of the allotted shares on or before 30 April 1974 at $2.50 per share (the 'subsidiary agreement'). It was confidently expected by all parties that the share price would increase. Prior to the completion of the main agreement the plaintiffs realised that, whilst the subsidiary agreement protected them against a fall in the share price of the public company, it did not, in respect of 60% of their holding, allow them to benefit from any rise in the share price above $2.50. The plaintiffs refused to complete the main agreement unless the defendants agreed to cancel the subsidiary agreement and replace it with a guarantee of indemnity. The defendants decided to accede to the plaintiffs' demands as they feared the delays of litigation and were concerned that the public would lose confidence in the company if the completion did not take place immediately. Accordingly the defendants signed a guarantee undertaking to indemnify the plaintiffs if the value of the shares fell below $2.50 per share on 30 April 1974. The share market slumped and the value of the shares held by the plaintiffs fell to $0.36. The plaintiffs sought to enforce the indemnity, however the defendants argued that there was no consideration for the indemnity or alternatively that their consent to the indemnity was vitiated by duress.

Lord Scarman: [Lord Scarman held that the contract of indemnity was supported by consideration and turned to consider the issue of duress at p 635:] Duress, whatever form it takes, is a coercion of the will so as to vitiate consent. Their Lordships agree with the observation of Kerr J in *Occidental Worldwide Investment Corporation v Skibs A/S Avanti* (1976), p 336 that in a contractual situation

---

34 Halson, 'Opportunism, economic duress and contractual modifications' (1991) 107 LQR 649.

35 *Ibid*, pp 661–62.

commercial pressure is not enough. There must be present some factor 'which could in law be regarded as a coercion of his will so as to vitiate his consent'. This conception is in line with what was said in this Board's decision in *Barton v Armstrong* (1976), p 121 by Lord Wilberforce and Lord Simon of Glaisdale – observations with which the majority judgment appears to be in agreement. In determining whether there was a coercion of will such that there was no true consent, it is material to inquire whether the person alleged to have been coerced did or did not protest; whether, at the time he was allegedly coerced into making the contract, he did or did not have an alternative course open to him such as an adequate legal remedy; whether he was independently advised; and whether after entering the contract he took steps to avoid it. All these matters are, as was recognised in *Maskell v Horner* (1915), relevant in determining whether he acted voluntarily or not.

In the present case there is unanimity amongst the judges below that there was no coercion of the first defendant's will. In the Court of Appeal the trial judges finding (already quoted) that the first defendant considered the matter thoroughly, chose to avoid litigation, and formed the opinion that the risk in giving the guarantee was more apparent than real was upheld. In short, there was commercial pressure, but no coercion. Even if this Board was disposed, which it is not, to take a different view, it would not substitute its opinion for that of the judges below on this question of fact.

It is, therefore, unnecessary for the Board to embark upon an inquiry into the question whether English law recognises a category of duress known as 'economic duress'. But, since the question has been fully argued in this appeal, their Lordships will indicate very briefly the view which they have formed. At common law money paid under economic compulsion could be recovered in an action for money had and received, *Astley v Reynolds* (1731). The compulsion had to be such that the party was deprived of 'his freedom of exercising his will', *Astley v Reynolds* (1731), p 916. It is doubtful, however, whether at common law any duress other than duress to the person sufficed to render a contract voidable.[36] American law[37] now recognises that a contract may be avoided on the [636] ground of economic duress. The commercial pressure alleged to constitute such duress must, however, be such that the victim must have entered the contract against his will, must have had no alternative course open to him, and must have been confronted with coercive acts by the party exerting the pressure.[38] American judges pay great attention to such evidential matters as the effectiveness of the alternative remedy available, the fact or absence of protest, the availability of independent advice, the benefit received, and the speed with which the victim has sought to avoid the contract. Recently two English judges have recognised that commercial pressure may constitute duress the pressure of which can render a contract voidable.[39] Both stressed that the pressure must be such that the victim's consent to the contract was not a voluntary act on his part. In their Lordship's view, there is nothing

---

36 See *Blackstone's Commentaries*, Bk 1, 12th edn, pp 130–31 and *Skeate v Beale* (1841).

37 *Williston on Contracts*, 3rd edn, 1970.

38 *Ibid*, Vol 13, s 1603.

39 *Occidental Worldwide Investment Corporation v Skibs A/S Avanti* (1976) *per* Kerr J; *North Ocean Shipping Co Ltd v Hyundai Construction Co Ltd* (1979) *per* Mocatta J.

contrary to principle in recognising economic duress as a factor which may render a contract voidable, provided always that the basis of such recognition is that it must amount to a coercion of will, which vitiates consent. It must be shown that the payment made or the contract entered into was not a voluntary act ...

Commentary and questions

Do all threats to commit an unlawful act amount to illegitimate pressure? Do all threats to commit a lawful act amount to legitimate pressure?

What facts did Lord Scarman rely upon in characterising the pressure as 'commercial' pressure rather than 'illegitimate' pressure? Are these factual elements likely to be present in most cases of attempted contractual renegotiation? Could it be said that the defendants in this case had not anticipated the devaluation of their shares?

Lord Scarman's judgment contains the classic exposition of the 'overborne will' approach to economic duress. The focus of this approach is on the effect of the illegitimate threat on the plaintiff. Duress will be established where the plaintiff's will has been coerced and the plaintiff has not truly consented to making the contract/payment. This approach has been rejected by McHugh JA in *Crescendo Management Pty Ltd v Westpac Banking Corporation* (1988) (see extract, p 246) and by the New South Wales Court of Appeal in *Equiticorp Finance Ltd (In Liq) v Bank of New Zealand* (1993) (see extract, p 254). McHugh JA in *Crescendo Management* recognised that the flaw of the overborne will theory is that the plaintiff usually fully intends making the contract/payment. The plaintiff has carefully weighed up the alternative courses of action and decided that submission to the defendant's demands is the lesser evil.[40] The overborne will theory has also been rejected in England.[41]

Universal Tankships Inc of Monrovia v International Transport Workers Federation, The Universe Sentinel [1983] 1 AC 366 House of Lords

The International Transport Workers' Federation (ITF) was undertaking a campaign to improve the wages and conditions of crews on ships flying flags of convenience. A ship registered in Liberia which was docked at Milford Haven was 'blacked' by the ITF in pursuance of this campaign. The ITF refused to let the ship sail unless the American shipowners complied with the ITF's demands, including payment of $80,000 back pay to the crew and a contribution of $6,480 to the ITF welfare fund. The owners acceded to the ITF's demands for fear of disastrous economic consequences if the ship was prevented from sailing, though later commenced proceedings to recover the back pay and the contribution to the welfare fund. The owners subsequently dropped the claim for repayment of the backpay, conceding that the ITF's actions in that regard were taken in furtherance of a valid industrial dispute within the relevant industrial relations legislation. The

---

40 Atiyah had previously launched a convincing attack upon the overborne will theory: see Atiyah, 'Economic duress and the overborne will' (1982) 98 LQR 197; Atiyah, 'Duress and the overborne will again' (1983) 99 LQR 353.

41 See *The Evia Luck* (1992) *per* Lord Goff (see extract, p 248).

ITF conceded before the House of Lords that its action of blacking the ship amounted to economic duress, but argued that to allow recovery of the $6,480 would be contrary to the policy in the industrial relations legislation which legitimised actions of trade unions taken in furtherance of a dispute about employment conditions. The House of Lords split on this policy question.

Lord Diplock: ... [383] My Lords, I turn to the second ground on which repayment of the $6,480 is claimed, which I will call the duress point. It is not disputed that the circumstances in which ITF demanded that the shipowners should enter into the special agreement and the typescript agreement and should pay the moneys of which the latter documents acknowledge receipt, amounted to economic duress upon the shipowners; that is to say, it is conceded that the financial consequences to the shipowners of the *Universe Sentinel* continuing to be rendered offhire under her time charter to Texaco, while the blacking continued, were so catastrophic as to amount to a coercion of the shipowners' will which vitiated their consent to those agreements and to the payments made by them to ITF. This concession makes it unnecessary for your Lordships to use the instant appeal as the occasion for a general consideration of the developing law of economic duress as a ground for treating contracts as voidable and obtaining restitution of money paid under economic duress as money had and received to the plaintiffs' use. That economic duress may constitute a ground for such redress was recognised, albeit *obiter*, by the Privy Council in *Pao On v Lau Yiu Long* (1980). The board in that case referred with approval to two judgments at first instance in the commercial court which recognised that commercial pressure may constitute duress: one by Kerr J in *Occidental Worldwide Investment Corporation v Skibs A/S Avanti* (1976), the other by Mocatta J in *North Ocean Shipping Co Ltd v Hyundai Construction Co Ltd* (1979), which traces the development of this branch of the law from its origin in the 18th and early 19th century cases.

It is, however, in my view crucial to the decision of the instant appeal to identify the rationale of this development [384] of the common law. It is not that the party seeking to avoid the contract which he has entered into with another party, or to recover money that he has paid to another party in response to a demand, did not know the nature or the precise terms of the contract at the time when he entered into it or did not understand the purpose for which the payment was demanded. The rationale is that his apparent consent was induced by pressure exercised upon him by that other party which the law does not regard as legitimate, with the consequence that the consent is treated in law as revocable unless approbated either expressly or by implication after the illegitimate pressure has ceased to operate on his mind. It is a rationale similar to that which underlies the avoidability of contracts entered into and the recovery of money exacted under colour of office, or under undue influence or in consequence of threats of physical duress.

Commercial pressure, in some degree, exists wherever one party to a commercial transaction is in a stronger bargaining position than the other party. It is not, however, in my view, necessary, nor would it be appropriate in the instant appeal, to enter into the general question of the kinds of circumstances, if any, in which commercial pressure, even though it amounts to a coercion of the will of a party in the weaker bargaining position, may be treated as legitimate and, accordingly, as not giving rise to any legal right of redress. In the instant appeal the economic duress complained of was exercised in the field of industrial relations to which very special considerations apply ...

The use of economic duress to induce another person to part with property or money is not a tort *per se*; the form that the duress takes may, or may not, be tortious. The remedy to which economic duress gives rise is not an action for damages but an action for restitution of property or money exacted under such duress and the avoidance of any contract that had been induced by it; but where the particular form taken by the economic duress used is itself a tort, the restitutional remedy for money had and received by the defendant to the plaintiff's use is one which the plaintiff is entitled to pursue as an alternative remedy to an action for damages in tort.

In extending into the field of industrial relations the common law concept of economic duress and the right to a restitutionary remedy for it which is currently in process of development by judicial decisions, this House would not, in my view, be exercising the restraint that is appropriate to such a process if it were so to develop the concept that, by the simple expedient of 'waiving the tort', a restitutionary remedy for money had and received is made enforceable in cases in which Parliament has, over so long a period of years, manifested its preference for a public policy that a particular kind of tortious act should be legitimised in the sense that I am using that expression.

It is only in this indirect way that the provisions of the Trade Union and Labour Relations Act 1974 are relevant to the duress point. The immunities from liability in tort provided by ss 13 and 14 are not directly applicable to the shipowners' cause of action for money had and received. Nevertheless, these sections, together with the definition of trade dispute in s 29, afford an indication, which your Lordships should respect, of where public policy requires that the line should be drawn between what kind of commercial pressure by a trade union upon an employer in the field of industrial relations ought to be treated as legitimised despite the fact that the will of the employer is thereby coerced, and what kind of commercial pressure in that field does amount to economic duress that entitles the employer victim to restitutionary remedies.

[Lord Diplock concluded that the restitutionary claim would not circumvent the policy of the industrial relations legislation as the dispute about the contribution to the fund did not have the requisite connection with employment conditions.]

Lord Scarman (dissenting): ... [400] It is, I think, already established law that economic pressure can in law amount to duress; and that duress, if proved, not only renders voidable a transaction into which a person has entered under compulsion but is actionable as a tort, if it causes damage or loss: *Barton v Armstrong* (1976) and *Pao On v Lau Yiu Long* (1980). The authorities upon which these two cases were based reveal two elements in the wrong of duress: (1) pressure amounting to compulsion of the will of the victim; and (2) the illegitimacy of the pressure exerted. There must be pressure, the practical effect of which is compulsion or the absence of choice. Compulsion is variously described in the authorities as coercion or the vitiation of consent. The classic case of duress is, however, not the lack of will to submit but the victim's intentional submission arising from the realisation that there is no other practical choice open to him. This is the thread of principle which links the early law of duress (threat to life or limb) with later developments when the law came also to recognise as duress first the threat to property and now the threat to a man's business or trade. The development is well traced in Goff and Jones, *The Law of Restitution*, 2nd edn, 1978, Chapter 9.

The absence of choice can be proved in various ways, for example, by protest, by the absence of independent advice, or by a declaration of intention to go to law to recover the money paid or the property transferred.[42] But none of these evidential matters goes to the essence of duress. The victim's silence will not assist the bully, if the lack of any practicable choice but to submit is proved. The present case is an excellent illustration. There was no protest at the time, but only a determination to do whatever was needed as rapidly as possible to release the ship. Yet nobody challenges the judge's finding that the owner acted under compulsion. He put it thus (1981), at p 143:

> It was a matter of the most urgent commercial necessity that the plaintiffs should regain the use of their vessel. They were advised that their prospects of obtaining an injunction were minimal, the vessel would not have been released unless the payment was made, and they sought recovery of the money with sufficient speed once the duress had terminated.

The real issue in the appeal is, therefore, as to the second element in the wrong duress: was the pressure applied by the ITF in the circumstances of this case one which the law recognises as legitimate? For, as Lord Wilberforce and Lord Simon of Glaisdale said in *Barton v Armstrong* (1976), p 121D: 'the pressure must be one of a kind which the law does not regard as legitimate.'

As the two noble and learned Lords remarked at p 121D, in life, including the life of commerce and finance, many acts are done 'under pressure, [401] sometimes overwhelming pressure': but they are not necessarily done under duress. That depends on whether the circumstances are such that the law regards the pressure as legitimate.

In determining what is legitimate two matters may have to be considered. The first is as to the nature of the pressure. In many cases this will be decisive, though not in every case. And so the second question may have to be considered, namely, the nature of the demand which the pressure is applied to support.

The origin of the doctrine of duress in threats to life or limb, or to property, suggests strongly that the law regards the threat of unlawful action as illegitimate, whatever the demand. Duress can, of course, exist even if the threat is one of lawful action: whether it does so depends upon the nature of the demand. Blackmail is often a demand supported by a threat to do what is lawful, eg, to report criminal conduct to the police. In many cases, therefore, 'What [one] has to justify is not the threat, but the demand ...'.[43]

The present is a case in which the nature of the demand determines whether the pressure threatened or applied, ie, the blacking, was lawful or unlawful. If it was unlawful, it is conceded that the owner acted under duress and can recover. If it was lawful, it is conceded that there was no duress and the sum sought by the owner is irrecoverable. The lawfulness or otherwise of the demand depends upon whether it was an act done in contemplation or furtherance of a trade dispute. If it

---

42 See *Maskell v Horner* (1915).
43 See *Thorne v Motor Trade Association* (1937), p 806 *per* Lord Atkin.

was, it would not be actionable in tort: s 13(1) of the Act. Although no question of tortious liability arises in this case and s 13(1) is not, therefore, directly in point, it is not possible, in my view, to say of acts which are protected by statute from suit in tort that they nevertheless can amount to duress. Parliament having enacted that such acts are not actionable in tort, it would be inconsistent with legislative policy to say that, when the remedy sought is not damages for tort but recovery of money paid, they become unlawful ...

Commentary and questions

What evidentiary factors were identified by Lord Scarman as assisting in the determination of economic duress?

Lord Scarman views the 'absence of a reasonable alternative' as an important determinant of duress, although others have doubted the utility of this requirement. An inquiry into the alternative courses of action open to the plaintiff provides no assistance in determining the crucial question: was the defendant's pressure legitimate (mere commercial pressure) or illegitimate? Moreover the only alternative usually open to the plaintiff will be to litigate, although considering the cost, delay and uncertainty of litigation, recourse to the courts will only rarely present to the plaintiff an alternative practical course of action.[44] Lastly, the 'no reasonable alternative' theory of duress fails to explain decisions such as *The Siboen and The Sibotre* (1976) (see extract, p 230) or *Pao On v Lau Yiu Long* (1980) (see extract, p 237) where the plaintiff's claim failed even though on the facts there would appear to have been no reasonable alternative to submitting to the defendant's demands.[45]

Lord Diplock emphasised that a claim for the recovery of money paid under duress is an independent action in restitution, not an action in restitution for wrongdoing. The conduct constituting the duress may or may not be tortious. A similar point was made by Lord Goff in *The Evia Luck* (1992) (see extract, p 248).

B & S Contracts and Design Ltd v Victor Green Publications Ltd [1984] ICR 419
English Court of Appeal

The defendant was staging a five day trade exhibition beginning on 23 April 1979. The plaintiff agreed with the defendant to erect stands for the exhibition for a price of £11,731.50. The plaintiff intended to use for the job some employees from an insolvent subsidiary company who had been given redundancy notices. After arriving at the exhibition centre on 12 April 1979 the workers refused to work until their demand for severance pay of £9,000 was met. The workers were not entitled to this severance pay. The plaintiff was having liquidity problems so Mr Barnes, a director of the defendant, offered to pay £4,500 of the contract price in advance. This was rejected by the plaintiff's financial director, Mr Fenech. Mr Fenech informed Mr Barnes that the contract would be cancelled unless the defendant paid £4,500 as an additional payment on the contract, not just as an advance. Mr

---

44 Burrows, *The Law of Restitution*, 1993, p 178. See also *The Atlantic Baron* (1979) *per* Mocatta J (see extract, p 233).

45 Burrows, *ibid*, pp 178–79.

Barnes paid the money to the plaintiff and the workers called off the strike (the plaintiff having paid them the other £4,500) and completed the work. The defendant then deducted £4,500 from the contract price before it was paid. The plaintiff commenced proceedings to recover the balance of £4,500 of the contract price, and the defendant counterclaimed for the same amount as money paid under duress.

Eveleigh J: ... [423] The matters that have to be established in order to substantiate a claim for the return of money on the ground that it was paid under duress have been stated in a number of different ways. We have been referred to a number of cases and indeed we have been taken through the history of the common law on duress, so thoroughly set out in the judgment of Mocatta J in *North Ocean Shipping Co Ltd v Hyundai Construction Co Ltd* (1979). It is not necessary to consider these cases: for the purpose of my judgment all I require to read is a passage from the speech of Lord Diplock in *Universal Tankships Inc of Monrovia v International Transport Workers Federation* (1982). He said, referring to the law on duress *Universal Tankships Inc of Monrovia v International Transport Workers Federation* (1982), pp 272–73:

> The rationale is that his apparent consent was induced by pressure exercised upon him by that other party which the law does not regard as legitimate, with the consequence that the consent is treated in law as revocable unless approbated either expressly or by implication after the illegitimate pressure has ceased to operate on his mind. It is a rationale similar to that which underlies the avoidability of contracts entered into and the recovery of money exacted under colour of office, or under undue influence or in consequence of threats of physical duress.

It is not necessary to consider precisely the meaning of the word 'legitimate' in that context. For the purpose of this case it is sufficient to say that if the claimant has been influenced against his will to pay money under the threat of unlawful damage to his economic interest he will be [424] entitled to claim that money back, and as I understand it that proposition was not dissented from.

In this case the plaintiffs say that there was no threat; that Mr Fenech was really stating the obvious, stating the factual situation, namely, that unless they could retain the workforce they would be unable to perform their contract. I have had some difficulty in deciding whether or not the evidence in this case did disclose a threat, but on a full reading of the evidence of Mr Fenech and Mr Barnes and the cross-examination of Mr Fenech I have come to the conclusion that the judge was right in the way in which he put it. There was here, as I understand the evidence, a veiled threat although there was no specific demand, and this conclusion is very much supported, as I see it, by Mr Barnes's reaction, which must have been apparent to Mr Fenech when Mr Barnes said, 'You have got me over a barrel'. On 18 April what was happening was this. Mr Fenech was in effect saying, 'We are not going on unless you are prepared to pay another £4,500 in addition to the contract price,' and it was clear at that stage that there was no other way for Mr Barnes to avoid the consequences that would ensue if the exhibition could not be held from his stands than by paying the £4,500 to secure the workforce ...

Griffiths LJ: [425] I agree. The law on economic pressure creating a situation which will be recognised as duress is in the course of development, and it is clear that many difficult decisions lie ahead of the courts. Many commercial contracts are varied during their currency because the parties are faced with changing circumstances during the performance of the contract, and it is certainly not on every occasion when one of the parties unwillingly agrees to a variation that the law would consider that he had acted by reason of duress. The cases will have to be examined in the light of their particular circumstances. But two recent decisions of the highest authority – the decision of the Privy Council in *Pao On v Lau Yiu Long* (1980) and *Universal Tankships Inc of Monrovia v International Transport Workers Federation* (1982) – establish that a threatened breach of contract may impose such economic pressure that the law will recognise that a payment made as a result of the threatened breach is recoverable on the grounds of duress.

The facts of this case appear to me to be as follows. The plaintiffs intended to break their contract, subject to the effect of the *force majeure* clause, by allowing their workforce to walk off the job in circumstances in which they could not possibly replace it with another workforce. The defendants offered to advance the sum of £4,500 on the contract price, which would have enabled the plaintiffs to pay the men a sufficient extra sum of money to induce them to remain on the job. The plaintiffs refused [426] this sum of money. There is no question that they refused to pay as a matter of principle. They refused to pay because they did not want to reduce the sum they would receive for the contract. They said to the defendants, 'If you will give us £4,500 we will complete the contract'. The defendants, faced with this demand, were in an impossible position. If they refused to hand over the sum of £4,500 they would not be able to erect the stands in this part of the exhibition, which would have clearly caused grave damage to their reputation and I would have thought might have exposed them to very heavy claims from the exhibitors who had leased space from them and hoped to use those stands in the ensuing exhibition. They seem to me to have been placed in the position envisaged by Lord Scarman in the Privy Council decision, *Pao On v Lau Yiu Long* (1980), in which they were faced with no alternative course of action but to pay the sum demanded of them. It was submitted to us that there was no overt demand, but it was implicit in negotiations between the parties that the plaintiffs were putting the defendants into a corner and it was quite apparent to the defendants, by reason of the plaintiffs' conduct, that unless they handed over £4,500 the plaintiffs would walk off the job. This is, in my view, a situation in which the judge was fully entitled to find in the circumstances of this case that there was duress. As the defendants' director said, he was over a barrel, he had no alternative but to pay; he had no chance of going to any other source of labour to erect the stands ...

Kerr LJ: ... [428] [T]he plaintiffs were clearly saying in effect, 'This contract will not be performed by us unless you pay an additional sum of £4,500.' This faced the defendants with a disastrous situation in which there was no way out for them, and in the face of this threat – which is what it was – they paid the £4,500. In the light of the authorities it is perhaps important to emphasise that there is no question in this case of the defendants having subsequently approbated this payment or failed to seek to avoid it, which in some cases (such as the *North Ocean Shipping Co Ltd v Hyundai Construction Co Ltd* (1979), a decision of Mocatta J, to which Eveleigh LJ has referred) would be fatal. In the present case the defendants took immediate action by deducting that £4,500 from the invoice price.

I also bear in mind that a threat to break a contract unless money is paid by the other party can, but by no means always will, constitute duress. It appears from the authorities that it will only constitute duress if the consequences of a refusal would be serious and immediate so that there is no reasonable alternative open, such as by legal redress, obtaining an injunction, etc. I think that this is implicit in the authorities to which we have been referred, of which the most recent one is *Universal Tankships Inc of Monrovia v International Transport Workers Federation* (1982). I would only refer to one passage from the speech of Lord Scarman, not because he states anything that differs from what was stated elsewhere, but because I wonder whether this passage may not contain a typographical error. Lord Scarman is reported (pp 288–89) as having said – and it applied to the facts of this case:

> The classic case of duress is, however, not the lack of will to submit but the victim's intentional submission arising from the realisation that there is no other practical choice open to him.

I wonder whether 'the lack of will to submit' should not have been 'the lack of will to resist' or 'the lack of will in submitting'. However that may be, there was no other practical choice open to the defendants in the present case, and accordingly I agree that this is a case where money has been paid under duress, which was accordingly recoverable by the defendants provided they acted promptly as they did, and which they have recovered by deducting it from the contract price. In these circumstances the plaintiffs' claim for this additional sum must fail.

Questions

What test of duress was adopted by the Court of Appeal? How was it applied to the facts of this case?

Crescendo Management Pty Ltd v Westpac Banking Corporation (1988) 19 NSWLR 40
Court of Appeal of New South Wales

Westpac was concerned about the level of debt owed by two companies of which Mr Hillbrink was a director. At about this time Mr and Mrs Hillbrink sold their family home and deposited the proceeds of sale with Westpac. Westpac refused to release the proceeds of sale unless Mr and Mrs Hillbrink executed certain documents which would secure the indebtedness of the two companies. Mr and Mrs Hillbrink, who needed the money to complete the purchase of another house, executed the documents. They later commenced proceedings to have the documents set aside as having been entered into under duress.

McHugh JA: ... [45] The rationale of the doctrine of economic duress is that the law will not give effect to an apparent consent which was induced by pressure exercised upon one party by another party when the law regards that pressure as illegitimate (see *Universal Tankships Inc of Monrovia v International Transport Workers Federation* (1983), p 384 *per* Lord Diplock). As his Lordship pointed out, the consequence is that the 'consent is treated in law as revocable unless approbated either expressly or by implication after the illegitimate pressure has ceased to operate on his mind' (p 384). In the same case Lord Scarman declared (p 400), that the authorities show that there are two elements in the realm of duress: (a) pressure amounting to compulsion of the will of the victim; and (b) the illegitimacy of the pressure exerted. 'There must be pressure,' said Lord Scarman 'the practical effect of which is compulsion or the absence of choice'.

The reference in *Universal Tankships Inc of Monrovia v International Transport Workers Federation* and other cases to compulsion 'of the will' of the victim is unfortunate. They appear to have overlooked that in *Director of Public Prosecutions for Northern Ireland v Lynch* (1975), a case concerned with duress as a defence to a criminal proceeding, the House of Lords rejected the notion that duress is concerned with overbearing the will of the accused. The Law Lords were unanimous in coming to the conclusion, perhaps best expressed (1975), p 695 in the speech of Lord Simon of Glaisdale 'that duress is not inconsistent with act and will, the will being deflected, not destroyed'. Indeed, if the true basis of duress is that the will is overborne, a contract entered into under duress should be void. Yet the accepted doctrine is that the contract is merely voidable.

In my opinion the overbearing of the will theory of duress should be rejected. A person who is the subject of duress usually knows only too well [46] what he is doing. But he chooses to submit to the demand or pressure rather than take an alternative course of action. The proper approach in my opinion is to ask whether any applied pressure induced the victim to enter into the contract and then ask whether that pressure went beyond what the law is prepared to countenance as legitimate? Pressure will be illegitimate if it consists of unlawful threats or amounts to unconscionable conduct. But the categories are not closed. Even overwhelming pressure, not amounting to unconscionable or unlawful conduct, however, will not necessarily constitute economic duress.

In their dissenting advice in *Barton v Armstrong* (1973), Lord Wilberforce and Lord Simon of Glaisdale pointed out (1973), p 634; (1976), p 121:

> ... in life, including the life of commerce and finance, many acts are done under pressure, sometimes overwhelming pressure, so that one can say that the actor had no choice but to act. Absence of choice in this sense does not negate consent in law: for this the pressure must be one of a kind which the law does not regard as illegitimate. Thus, out of the various means by which consent may be obtained – advice, persuasion, influence, inducement, representation, commercial pressure – the law has come to select some which it will not accept as a reason for voluntary action: fraud, abuse of relation of confidence, undue influence, duress or coercion.

In *Pao On v Lau Yiu Long* (1980), the Judicial Committee accepted (1973), p 635 that the observations of Lord Wilberforce and Lord Simon in *Barton v Armstrong* were consistent with the majority judgment in that case and represented the law relating to duress.

It is unnecessary, however, for the victim to prove that the illegitimate pressure was the sole reason for him entering into the contract. It is sufficient that the illegitimate pressure was one of the reasons for the person entering into the agreement. Once the evidence establishes that the pressure exerted on the victim was illegitimate, the onus lies on the person applying the pressure to show that it made no contribution to the victim entering into the agreement (1973), p 633; (1976), p 121 *per* Lord Cross.

[McHugh JA found that the pressure exerted by Westpac was unlawful, however, that it had been exerted after Mr and Mrs Hillbrink had executed the documents and so causation was not established.]

Commentary and questions

Samuels and Mahoney JJA agreed with McHugh JA on the causation point, but refrained from expressing a view on the conceptual basis of the doctrine of economic duress.

What test of causation did McHugh JA adopt? According to McHugh JA who bears the onus of proof with respected to causation?

Was McHugh JA suggesting that economic duress is an equitable doctrine?

According to McHugh JA, pressure will be illegitimate where it either consists of 'unlawful threats' or 'unconscionable conduct'. It is unlikely, however, that McHugh JA was suggesting that a threat to break a contract (in itself a threat of an unlawful act) will always amount to illegitimate pressure. The Australian courts may be moving towards the view that a threat to break a contract will only amount to duress where the defendant is acting unconscionably.[46] In determining whether the defendant's conduct in threatening a breach is unconscionable it might be useful to have regard to Birks's suggested test, namely whether the threat was 'intended to exploit the plaintiff's weakness rather than to solve financial or other problems of the defendant'.[47]

The principles advocated by McHugh JA have been cited with approval and applied in numerous Australian decisions.[48]

Dimskal Shipping Co SA v International Transport Workers Federation (No 2), The Evia Luck [1992] 2 AC 152 House of Lords

The facts are similar to *The Universe Sentinel* (1983) (see extract, p 239), but the vessel was flying a Panamanian flag, the events complained of took place in a Swedish port, and secondary boycotts no longer enjoyed immunity under the relevant industrial relations legislation. The owners paid $111,743 in response to the ITF's threat to black its ship and later commenced proceedings claiming restitution of this sum on the basis it had been paid under duress. The question before the House of Lords was whether the issue of economic duress was to be decided by English or Swedish law. It was conceded by the ITF that the blacking amounted to economic duress in English law.

Lord Goff of Chieveley: ... [165] It was common ground between the parties before your Lordships that the money in respect of which the owners claimed restitution was paid to the ITF under a contract, albeit a contract which the owners claim to have been voidable by them, and indeed to have been avoided by them,

---

46 *Equiticorp Finance Ltd (In Liq) v Bank of New Zealand* (1993) (see extract, p 254). Though cf *Westpac Banking Corp v Cockerill* (1998) (see extract, p 258).

47 Birks, *An Introduction to the Law of Restitution*, rev edn, 1989, p 183. This test, which finds some support in *D & C Builders Ltd v Rees* (1966), has also been adopted by Burrows, *op cit*, fn 44, p 181, though with some qualification.

48 *Equiticorp Finance Ltd (In Liq) v Bank of New Zealand* (1993) (see extract, p 254); *Hawker Pacific Pty Ltd v Helicopter Charter Pty Ltd* (1991) (see extract, p 226); *Scolio Pty Ltd v Cote* (1991), p 481; *Deemcope Pty Ltd v Cantown Pty Ltd*(1995); *Searle v Keayes* (1995), Federal Court of Australia *per* Tamberlin J; *Food Delivery Services Pty Ltd v ANZ Banking Group Limited* (1996); *News Limited v Australian Rugby League* (1996), pp 134–35. For an overview of the Australian decisions see Sindone, 'The doctrine of economic duress' (1996) 14 ABR 34, p 114.

on the ground of duress. It follows that, before the owners could establish any right to recover the money, they had first to avoid the relevant contract. Until this was done, the money in question was paid under a binding contract and so was irrecoverable in restitution. But once the contract was avoided, the money paid under it was recoverable in restitution, on the ground either of duress or possibly of failure of consideration. It was not, in my opinion, necessary for the owners, even if the duress relied upon by them was in fact tortious, to base their claim on waiver of tort,[49] nor have they done so. The present case is, however, concerned with the anterior question whether the pressure exerted by the ITF constituted duress enabling the owners to avoid the contract on that ground, as they claim to have been entitled to do.

We are here concerned with a case of economic duress. It was at one time thought that, at common law, the only form of duress which would entitle a party to avoid a contract on that ground was duress of the person. The origin for this view lay in the decision of the Court of Exchequer in *Skeate v Beale* (1841). However, since the decisions of Kerr J in *Occidental Worldwide Investment Corporation v Skibs A/S Avanti, The Siboen and The Sibotre* (1976), of Mocatta J in *North Ocean Shipping Co Ltd v Hyundai Construction Co Ltd* (1979), and of the Judicial Committee of the Privy Council in *Pao On v Lau Yiu Long* (1980), that limitation has been discarded; and it is now accepted that economic pressure may be sufficient to amount to duress for this purpose, provided at least that the economic pressure may be characterised as illegitimate and has constituted a significant cause inducing the plaintiff to enter into the relevant contract.[50] [166] It is sometimes suggested that the plaintiff's will must have been coerced so as to vitiate his consent. This approach has been the subject of criticism.[51] I myself, like McHugh JA, doubt whether it is helpful in this context to speak of the plaintiff's will having been coerced. It is not however necessary to explore the matter in the present case. Nor is it necessary to consider the broader question of what constitutes illegitimate economic pressure, for it is accepted that blacking or a threat of blacking, such as occurred in the present case, does constitute illegitimate economic pressure in English law, unless legitimised by statute. The question which has fallen for decision by your Lordships is whether, in considering the question whether the pressure should be treated as legitimised, the English courts should have regard to the law of Sweden (where the relevant pressure was exerted on the owners by the agents of the ITF) under which such pressure was lawful.

[Lord Goff concluded that the dispute should be resolved by English law as the proper law of the contract and accordingly that the contract was entered into under duress.]

---

49 See the note by McKendrick [1990] ILJ 195.

50 See *Barton v Armstrong* (1976), p 121 *per* Lord Wilberforce and Lord Simon of Glaisdale (referred to with approval in *Pao On v Lau Yiu Long* (1980), p 635 *per* Lord Scarman); and *Crescendo Management Pty Ltd v Westpac Banking Corporation* (1988), p 46 *per* McHugh JA.

51 See Beatson, *The Use and Abuse of Unjust Enrichment*, 1991, pp 113–17; and the notes by Professor Atiyah (1982) 98 LQR 197, pp 197–202, and by Professor Birks [1990] 3 LMCLQ 342, pp 342–51.

Commentary and questions

What test of causation did Lord Goff adopt in the principal case? Is this test the same as that adopted by McHugh JA in *Crescendo Management Pty Ltd v Westpac Banking Corporation* (1988)? (See extract, p 246.)

Lord Goff's statement of principles was adopted by Burchett J in *News Ltd v Australian Rugby League* (1996). News Ltd wished to establish a breakaway rugby league competition in opposition to the existing Australian Rugby League ('the league'). Certain rugby league clubs who became aligned with News Ltd argued that the league had applied economic duress to force the clubs to sign loyalty agreements, by threatening the clubs with expulsion from the league competition if they refused. Burchett J held that any pressure exerted on the clubs to sign the loyalty agreements was not illegitimate pressure. This was because the league had a legitimate interest in ensuring the competition did not become fragmented. In any event, if any improper pressure was exerted it was not a 'significant cause' of the clubs' decision to sign the loyalty agreements.

CTN Cash and Carry Ltd v Gallaher Ltd [1994] 4 All ER 714 English Court of Appeal

The plaintiff ran a 'cash and carry' business from warehouses in a number of towns. The plaintiff purchased its cigarettes from the defendant distributor, who was the sole distributor in England of certain popular brands. The defendant had arranged credit facilities for the plaintiff, which it had an absolute discretion to withdraw. The plaintiff placed an order with the defendant for a large consignment of cigarettes at a price of $17,000, but due to a mistake by the defendant, the cigarettes were delivered to the wrong warehouse. The defendant agreed to arrange for the transfer of the cigarettes but before this could occur the cigarettes were stolen. The defendant, *bona fide* believing that the cigarettes had been at the plaintiff's risk at the time of the theft, invoiced the plaintiff for the price of the stolen consignment. The plaintiff initially refused to pay but the defendant made it clear that it would withdraw the credit facilities for any future dealings if the plaintiff did not pay. The plaintiff paid the $17,000, making a commercial decision that it was the 'lesser of the two evils', however later commenced proceedings claiming repayment of the money as having been paid under duress. At the trial the defendant's counsel conceded that the risk in the stolen cigarettes had not passed to the plaintiff and so the defendant had no legal entitlement to be paid for them.

Steyn LJ: ... [717] The present dispute does not concern a protected relationship. It also does not arise in the context of dealings between a supplier and a consumer. The dispute arises out of arm's length commercial dealings between two trading companies. It is true that the defendants were the sole distributors of the popular brands of cigarettes. In a sense the defendants were in a monopoly position. The control of monopolies is, however, a matter for parliament. Moreover, the common law does not recognise the doctrine of inequality of bargaining power in commercial dealings.[52] The fact that the defendants were in a monopoly position cannot therefore by itself convert what is not otherwise duress into duress.

---

52 See *National Westminster Bank plc v Morgan* (1985).

[718] A second characteristic of the case is that the defendants were in law entitled to refuse to enter into any future contracts with the plaintiffs for any reason whatever or for no reason at all. Such a decision not to deal with the plaintiffs would have been financially damaging to the defendants, but it would have been lawful. *A fortiori*, it was lawful for the defendants, for any reason or for no reason, to insist that they would no longer grant credit to the plaintiffs. The defendants' demand for payment of the invoice, coupled with the threat to withdraw credit, was neither a breach of contract nor a tort.

A third, and critically important, characteristic of the case is the fact that the defendants *bona fide* thought that the goods were at the risk of the plaintiffs and that the plaintiffs owed the defendants the sum in question. The defendants exerted commercial pressure on the plaintiffs in order to obtain payment of a sum which they *bona fide* considered due to them. The defendants' motive in threatening withdrawal of credit facilities was commercial self-interest in obtaining a sum that they considered due to them.

Given the combination of these three features, I take the view that none of the cases cited to us assist the plaintiffs' case. [Counsel for the plaintiffs] accepted that there is no decision which is in material respects on all fours with the present case. It is therefore unnecessary to disinter all those cases and to identify the material distinctions between each of those decisions and the present case. But [counsel for the plaintiffs] rightly emphasised to us that the law must have a capacity for growth in this field. I entirely agree.

I also readily accept that the fact that the defendants have used lawful means does not by itself remove the case from the scope of the doctrine of economic duress. Professor Birks, in *An Introduction to the Law of Restitution*, 1989, p 177, lucidly explains:

> Can lawful pressures also count? This is a difficult question, because, if the answer is that they can, the only viable basis for discriminating between acceptable and unacceptable pressures is not positive law but social morality. In other words, the judges must say what pressures (though lawful outside the restitutionary context) are improper as contrary to prevailing standards. That makes the judges, not the law or the legislature, the arbiters of social evaluation. On the other hand, if the answer is that lawful pressures are always exempt, those who devise outrageous but technically lawful means of compulsion must always escape restitution until the legislature declares the abuse unlawful. It is tolerably clear that, at least where they can be confident of a general consensus in favour of their evaluation, the courts are willing to apply a standard of impropriety rather than technical unlawfulness.

And there are a number of cases where English courts have accepted that a threat may be illegitimate when coupled with a demand for payment even if the threat is one of lawful action.[53] On the other hand, Goff and Jones's *The Law of Restitution*[54] (p 240) observed that English courts have wisely not accepted any general

---

53   See *Thorne v Motor Trade Association* (1937), pp 160–61; 806–07; *Mutual Finance Ltd v John Wetton & Sons Ltd* (1937); and *Universal Tankships Inc of Monrovia v International Transport Workers' Federation* (1982), pp 76, 89; (1983), pp 384, 401.
54   3rd edn, 1986.

principle that a threat not to contract with another, except on certain terms, may amount to duress.

[719] We are being asked to extend the categories of duress of which the law will take cognisance. That is not necessarily objectionable, but it seems to me that an extension capable of covering the present case, involving 'lawful act duress' in a commercial context in pursuit of a *bona fide* claim, would be a radical one with far-reaching implications. It would introduce a substantial and undesirable element of uncertainty in the commercial bargaining process. Moreover, it will often enable *bona fide* settled accounts to be reopened when parties to commercial dealings fall out. The aim of our commercial law ought to be to encourage fair dealing between parties. But it is a mistake for the law to set its sights too highly when the critical inquiry is not whether the conduct is lawful but whether it is morally or socially unacceptable. That is the inquiry in which we are engaged. In my view there are policy considerations which militate against ruling that the defendants obtained payment of the disputed invoice by duress.

Outside the field of protected relationships, and in a purely commercial context, it might be a relatively rare case in which 'lawful act duress' can be established. And it might be particularly difficult to establish duress if the defendant *bona fide* considered that his demand was valid. In this complex and changing branch of the law I deliberately refrain from saying 'never'. But as the law stands, I am satisfied that the defendants' conduct in this case did not amount to duress.

It is an unattractive result, in as much as the defendants are allowed to retain a sum which at the trial they became aware was not in truth due to them. But in my view the law compels the result...

Sir Donald Nicholls VC: ... I agree, for the reasons given by Steyn LJ, that that claim must fail. When the defendant company insisted on payment, it did so in good faith. It believed the risk in the goods had passed to the plaintiff company, so it considered it was entitled to be paid for them. The defendant company took a tough line. It used its commercial muscle. But the feature underlying and dictating this attitude was a genuine belief on its part that it was owed the sum in question. It was entitled to be paid the price for the goods. So it took the line: the plaintiff company must pay in law what it owed, otherwise its credit would be suspended.

Further, there is no evidence that the defendant's belief was unreasonable. Indeed, we were told by the defendant's counsel that he had advised his client that on the risk point the defendant stood a good chance of success. I do not see how a payment demanded and made in those circumstances can be said to be vitiated by duress.

So that must be an end to this appeal. I confess to being a little troubled at the overall outcome. At a late stage of the trial the defendant's counsel accepted that the risk in the goods had not in law passed to the plaintiff. Hence, and this must follow, the defendant company was not, and never had been, entitled to be paid for the goods. The risk remained throughout on the [720] defendant. What also follows is that the basis on which the defendant had sought and insisted on payment was then shown to be false.

In those circumstances I confess to being a little surprised that a highly reputable tobacco manufacturer has, so far, not reconsidered the position. A claim for restitution based on wrongful retention of the money, once the risk point had been established, was not pursued before us, no doubt for good reasons. But on the sketchy facts before us, and I emphasise that we have heard argument only from the plaintiff, it does seem to me that *prima facie* it would be unconscionable for the defendant company to insist on retaining the money now. It demanded the money when under a mistaken belief as to its legal entitlement to be paid. It only made the demand because of its belief that it was entitled to be paid. The money was then paid to it by a plaintiff which, in practical terms, had no other option. In broad terms, in the end result the defendant may be said to have been unjustly enriched. Whether a new claim for restitution now, on the facts as they have since emerged, would succeed is not a matter I need pursue. I observe, as to that, only that the categories of unjust enrichment are not closed ...

Commentary and questions

What practical considerations did Steyn LJ take into account in denying recovery? Should the defendant's honest belief in an entitlement to make the demand be relevant to the determination of duress?

Do you agree with the suggestion by Sir Donald Nicholls that a restitutionary claim might have been brought for the return of the money on some ground other than duress?

The principal case reflects the policy view that courts should not be quick to make a finding of duress in the commercial context, in particular where the pressure complained of is the threat of a lawful act.[55] Modern Australian courts have been similarly reluctant to find duress in a commercial setting, evidenced by such decisions as *Equiticorp Finance Ltd (In Liq) v Bank of New Zealand* (1993) (see following extract) and *Deemcope Pty Ltd v Cantown Pty Ltd* (1995). In the latter case the plaintiff, who operated a real estate agency, purchased a commercial property from the defendant, who was an accountant. The plaintiff obtained approximately 10% of its valuation business from the defendant. The plaintiff alleged that the defendant threatened to withdraw its business from the plaintiff if it did not agree to purchase the property. Coldrey J held that, even if the defendant did make the threat that was alleged, this amounted to mere *commercial* pressure, not economic duress (1995), pp 55–56:

> In any event my conclusion is that any economic pressure applied to [the plaintiff] by the defendant did not amount to anything other than an unexceptional commercial circumstance and I am not satisfied that the plaintiff had no practical alternative but to enter into the contract. The conduct of the [defendant] was not illegitimate, in the sense that it consisted of any unlawful threats, nor did it amount to unconscionable conduct. Even accepting that the categories of economic duress are not closed the behaviour of the [defendant] in this case fell far short of conduct warranting relief.

---

55   Carter and Tolhurst, 'Restitution for duress' (1996) 9 JCL 220, p 221.

Equiticorp Finance Ltd (In Liq) v Bank of New Zealand **(1993) 32 NSWLR 50**
Court of Appeal of New South Wales

The plaintiffs, Equiticorp Finance Ltd and Equiticorp Financial Services Ltd, were members of the Equiticorp Group of companies of which Mr Hawkins was the chairman and major shareholder. One of the wholly owned subsidiaries within the Equiticorp Group (Uruz Pty Ltd) owed a substantial debt to the Bank of New Zealand. The date for the repayment of the debt was 30 June 1988 but the bank consented to an extension until 30 September 1988. Despite the bank's consent to an extension (which was not contractually binding) it later insisted that the Uruz debt be repaid on or before 28 July 1988, and insisted that the plaintiffs and another company in the Group use their liquidity reserves to discharge Uruz's debt by that date. Mr Hawkins, who was anxious to maintain the Group's credibility with the bank as well as the bank's support for the Group, transferred the plaintiffs' reserves to the bank in payment of the Uruz debt. The plaintiffs later went into liquidation and the liquidator commenced proceedings against the bank alleging a breach of fiduciary duty or alternatively duress. In connection with the duress claim, the plaintiffs alleged that the bank had applied illegitimate pressure upon Mr Hawkins in two main ways: (a) by insisting upon the repayment of the debt by 28 July despite the consent to an extension to 30 September; and (b) by threatening to spread a rumour that the Equiticorp Group was in financial difficulties. This latter allegation was withdrawn at trial after the trial judge, Giles J, found no evidence that such a threat had been made. Giles J also took the view that, despite the extension for repayment, both the plaintiffs and the bank had always acted on the basis that the debt would be discharged by 28 July unless the financial position of the Equiticorp Group improved. Giles J found that the bank had merely exercised commercial pressure for repayment which did not amount to duress.

Kirby P (dissenting on another issue): ... [106] In this already overlong opinion, I must deal with economic duress economically ... The test is one expressed by reference to somewhat unsatisfactory criteria. These ask: was the pressure exerted 'illegitimate' or 'unconscionable' in the circumstances? Or was it merely the kind of commercial pressure which operates in the economic marketplace and is said, by some, to be one of the most precious features of economic liberty? ...

[I]t was argued that Giles J had erred in excluding commercial pressure and in finding that this could not, by definition, amount to economic duress.

I see no error in Giles J's approach. It is true that, in *Crescendo Management Pty Ltd v Westpac Banking Corporation* (1988), p 46, McHugh JA offered only enigmatic guidance:

> The proper approach ... is to ask whether any applied pressure induced the victim to enter into the contract and then ask whether that pressure went beyond what the law is prepared to countenance as legitimate?

What precisely the law is prepared to countenance as 'legitimate' begs the question which needs to be answered in characterising particular conduct as impermissible economic duress (on the one hand) or the permissible (even necessary) operation of the market economy (on the other). There is no doubt that in some circumstances commercial pressure may constitute duress.[56]

---

56 See, eg, *Pao On v Lau Yiu Long* (1980).

The authors (Meagher, Gummow and Lehane) of *Equity, Doctrines and Remedies*[57] after reviewing the cases, came to the not unsurprising conclusion that attempts to circumscribe the jurisdiction of economic duress by 'attempts at exact verbal formulae' were bound to be unprofitable.[58]

Many (if not most) of the cases dealing with economic duress have concerned parties in seriously unequal economic bargaining positions. One of them effectively overbears the will of another in a way that strikes the decision maker as unconscionable. Such a case was *Williams v Bayley* (1866). Relief in such cases involves an arguably legitimate, if somewhat paternalistic, intervention of the law where the will of a party has been overborne or where what has occurred is so unconscionable as to call out for redress from the court. From one perspective, the relief offered can be seen as a defence of true *freedom* to contract and not an intervention by the courts to strike down contracts only achieved by duress.[59]

[107] There are various reasons why I approach this claim in the present case with reservation. These reasons include:

(a) the unsatisfactory and open ended *formulae* which have been offered in the cases. These do not seem to have been improved much over the past hundred years;

(b) the dangers of courts' substituting their opinions about agreements for those reached by parties, at least in circumstances such as the present where the parties are substantial corporations and where millions of dollars are involved;

(c) the overlap, in this jurisdiction, of the concepts involved in economic duress and those invoked by the Contracts Review Act 1980 whose applications are more sensibly limited and whose provisions more detailed and structured;

(d) the doctrine of economic duress may be better seen as an aspect of the doctrines of undue influence and unconscionability respectively. If relief, beyond statute, is appropriate, courts would be better able to provide such relief in a consistent and principled fashion under the rubric of undue influence and unconscionability rather than by pretending to economic expertise and judgment which they will generally lack: cf Phang;[60] and

(e) the doctrine renders the law uncertain and in an area where certainty is highly desirable. This is illustrated by the instant case. It invites judges (and lawyers advising clients) to substitute their opinions and decisions for those of commercial people who, almost always, will have a better grasp of detail of their relationships and a better appreciation of the economic forces which are at work.

For Bank of New Zealand, it was conceded that if Equiticorp Finance Ltd and Equiticorp Financial Services Ltd (Aust) were to succeed in their claim of a breach of trust and of the liability of Bank of New Zealand as constructive trustee for that

---

57 3rd edn, 1992.

58 See *ibid*, para 1216, pp 345–46.

59 See *Universal Tankships Inc of Monrovia v International Transport Workers Federation* (1983), p 383f: cf Halson, 'Opportunism, economic duress and contractual modifications' (1991) 107 LQR 649, p 656; Phang, 'Economic duress – uncertainty confirmed' (1992) 5 JCL 147; Phang, 'Whither economic duress? Reflections on two recent cases' (1990) 53 MLR 107.

60 (1990) 53 MLR 107, p 113.

breach of trust, the claim in economic duress would not advance the matter. This was the case, so it was said, because the illegitimacy of the conduct giving rise to the constructive trust would be the same. It would invoke the same remedies in equity. On the other hand, if Equiticorp Finance Ltd and Equiticorp Financial Services Ltd (Aust) failed to establish a constructive trust as against Bank of New Zealand, then they would fail, so it was applied in the claim of economic duress because the self-same considerations which underlined the constructive trust would deprive the suggested economic duress of the illegitimacy or offence to conscience required to attract relief.

In view of my conclusion that Equiticorp Finance Ltd and Equiticorp Financial Services Ltd (Aust) have made out the breaches of fiduciary duties alleged and the constructive trusts necessary to render Bank of New Zealand liable as a constructive trustee, it is unnecessary for me to explore the submissions of the appellants which sought to distinguish the considerations relevant to proving a breach of fiduciary duty and liability for that breach in a stranger to the duty (on the one hand) and unconscionable conduct amounting to economic duress (on the other). I am prepared to accept Bank of [108] New Zealand's concession that, the appellants having succeeded on their case of a constructive trust, economic duress would not in this case add any additional or different remedies.

But for the concession made for Bank of New Zealand I would myself have been inclined to question the application of relief for economic duress to a relationship such as existed here between Bank of New Zealand and the appellants. Equiticorp Finance Ltd and Equiticorp Financial Services Ltd (Aust) withdrew the suggestion that part of the economic duress was the threat by Bank of New Zealand to spread rumours about the liquidity (or even insolvency) of the companies of the Equiticorp Group. Giles J hit this contention on the head. It would scarcely have been to Bank of New Zealand's advantage to mortally damage the credit of customers which owed it extremely large sums. Specifically, there was no attempt on the part of the appellants to prove that the diversion of Equiticorp Finance Ltd and Equiticorp Financial Services Ltd (Aust)'s liquidity reserve caused or contributed to their ultimate insolvency.

I draw a distinction between the liability of Bank of New Zealand as constructive trustee for the breach of fiduciary duty on the part of those controlling Equiticorp Finance Ltd and Equiticorp Financial Services Ltd (Aust) (on the one hand) and the suggested liability of Bank of New Zealand for having exerted illegitimate unconscionable and uncommercial economic pressure (on the other). The former looks to the whole conduct of Bank of New Zealand over an extended period in its relationship with Equiticorp Finance Ltd and Equiticorp Financial Services Ltd (Aust). It does so in circumstances giving rise to the transfer of the liquidity reserves to the benefit of Equiticorp Tasman Ltd and then Bank of New Zealand (in discharge of the Uruz Pty Ltd facility). The latter's attention is concentrated upon the pressure which Bank of New Zealand exerted on Mr Hawkins to take the step he ultimately took, namely of authorising and instructing the use of the appellants' liquidity reserves. The former is not so narrowly confined. It is much more readily answered in favour of Equiticorp Finance Ltd and Equiticorp Financial Services Ltd (Aust). The latter is much more precisely focused.

Yet even if the theory of economic duress is no longer confined to overbearing the will of the party the subject of duress[61] the question posed for a court must be answered by reference to a much narrower spectrum of facts. It would be conceivable that Mr Hawkins in the end was able to, and should have, resisted the commercial pressure of Bank of New Zealand. That conclusion could be reached without in any way doubting the earlier determination (based on a much wider range of facts) that Bank of New Zealand was a constructive trustee for the breach of fiduciary duties of the directors of the appellants in the use of their liquidity reserves. Bank of New Zealand, after all, conceived, proposed and pressed forward with this idea despite initial resistance and hesitation from within the Equiticorp Group.

I would have been inclined to dismiss the claim of economic duress. But in the light of the concession made – and as no difference in remedies would seem to turn on the conclusion – I will refrain from stating a final opinion. Except that courts should be even more circumspect about extending the remedy of economic duress to cases of contracts between substantial businesses than they would be in other cases of equal bargaining power, where different considerations obtain.[62] The parties in this case had available to them legal and managerial advice of a high order. Each was accustomed to making large decisions affecting millions of dollars and the lives of thousands of people ...

Clarke and Cripps JJA: ... [149] We do not understand it to have been submitted that the learned trial judge misunderstood any of the principles he was required to apply under this ground. In *Crescendo Management Pty Ltd v Westpac Banking Corporation* (1988), pp 45–46, McHugh JA, in rejecting the overborne will theory of duress, said:

> A person who is the subject of duress usually knows only too well what he is doing. But he chooses to submit to the demand or pressure rather than take an alternative course of action. The proper approach in my opinion is to ask whether any applied pressure induced the victim to enter into the contract and then ask whether that pressure went beyond what the law is prepared to countenance as legitimate? Pressure will be [150] illegitimate if it consists of unlawful threats or amounts to unconscionable conduct. But the categories are not closed. Even overwhelming pressure, not amounting to unconscionable or unlawful conduct, however, will not necessarily constitute economic duress.

The unconscionable conduct alleged was the insistence by Bank of New Zealand that the Uruz Pty Ltd debt be repaid by 28 July 1988 notwithstanding that it had agreed to extend the repayment date to 30 September 1988 at a time when withdrawal of its support would destroy the Equiticorp Group's credibility. However, on one view all that the variation of the loan agreement did was to give the borrower until 30 September 1988 to discharge the liability unless Bank of New Zealand required its discharge earlier. It was also said that Bank of New Zealand applied pressure by insisting on the use of the liquidity reserves to repay Uruz Pty Ltd's debt conscious that this would be a breach of fiduciary duty. As the learned trial judge observed, the alternative way the appellants put the case was really

---

61 On which see *Crescendo Management Pty Ltd v Westpac Banking Corporation* (1988), p 45; and comment in Birks, 'The travails of duress' [1990] LMCLQ 342.

62 Cf *Austotel Pty Ltd v Franklins Self Serve Pty Ltd* (1989), p 584.

only another way of alleging breach of fiduciary duty. That finding has been criticised but, for the reasons given by Kirby P, we are of the opinion that no error was established.

Before the learned trial judge, it was submitted that there was an implied threat by Bank of New Zealand to start a rumour adverse to the Equiticorp Group to force early repayment. It was submitted that Bank of New Zealand threatened to let it be known that it would withdraw its support if the Equiticorp Group did not immediately repay the debt. For reasons given by the learned trial judge, that submission is rejected. Apart from anything else, it was not in the interests of Bank of New Zealand to have started such a rumour in the market place. Perhaps of more significance, however, is the denial by Mr Hawkins that the money was being paid under a threat. He said:

> I wouldn't put (it) in terms of a threat. The relationship between [representatives of the bank] and myself was not one of threat. It was one of knowing each other's position and discussing things out, and those two gentlemen were very, very human, so I knew what they meant when they talked to me. There wasn't a threat.

[Their Honours referred to Giles J's findings about the nature of the parties' understanding of the extension for repayment and continued at p 151:]

In our opinion, Giles J was correct in determining that the appellants had not established any illegitimate pressure of the kind to which McHugh JA referred in *Crescendo Management*. The defence having been rejected, it is unnecessary to consider what, if any, relief would follow had it been established. As Giles J observed, underlying the doctrine of restitution of money paid under duress is the 'unifying legal concept of unjust enrichment': *Pavey and Matthews Pty Ltd v Paul* (1987). Bank of New Zealand was owed a greater sum than the amount in the liquidity reserve. On the worst view of the matter from the perspective of Bank of New Zealand, Uruz Pty Ltd's debt was paid two months before it was due. Furthermore, Bank of New Zealand released security worth much more than the debt ...

Commentary and questions

In the view of Clarke and Cripps JJA was the Bank of New Zealand enriched by the early repayment of the debt? Did Clarke and Cripps JJA apply the doctrine of economic duress?

Did Kirby P reject the doctrine of economic duress? Why was his Honour critical of this doctrine? What standards would Kirby P apply to determine whether pressure is unlawful?

In the following case, the Full Court of the Federal Court expressed doubts as to the utility of unconscionability as a determinant of duress.

Westpac Banking Corp v Cockerill (1998) 152 ALR 267
Full Court of the Federal Court of Australia

The plaintiffs had signed a document releasing Westpac from any liability in connection with an offshore financial loan by Westpac to the plaintiffs or in connection with any currency dealings by Westpac involving the plaintiff. Cooper

J at first instance found that Westpac had exercised illegitimate pressure on the plaintiffs to sign the release document by threatening to appoint a receiver over their business and assets if they refused. Westpac appealed.

Kiefel J: ... [287] By 5 January 1988 the bank had decided, his Honour [the trial judge] found, to bring the applicants' loan on-shore and to offer them finance at concessional rates of interest in return for a release from liability from any action the applicants had or may have had against the bank in connection with the off shore loan. At that time, the only option available to the applicants, in his Honour's view, was negotiation of a rate of interest sufficiently low and for such a period as might enable the businesses to survive and avoid a sale of assets other than a certain building which the bank required to be sold. Proposals by the applicants were rejected by the bank. The rejection was accompanied by a threat that legal action would be commenced by the bank for recovery. His Honour appears to have been of the view that after this the applicants were in a position where they could do no more than make the best of a bad situation. His Honour found that the applicants signed the first concessional interest rate letter of 5 February 1988 (we need not discuss the factual complexity concerning the existence of two concessional interest rate letters) containing the release because they had no practical alternative. That was so, in his Honour's view:

> ... because of their parlous financial circumstances which, on the admissions made by Westpac for the purposes of determining this preliminary issue, was to the extent of a loss of $5,750,000, caused by the conduct of Westpac amounting to breach of contract and/or negligence and/or conduct in contravention of s 52 of the Trade Practices Act and by the unjust enrichment of Westpac wrongly charging and retaining withholding tax in connection with the offshore commercial loan.

The applicants, in his Honour's view, were then unable to obtain other finance; they were unable to litigate their rights; and although legal advice was clearly available to them, it could not have altered the situation which confronted them. They were unable to obtain interlocutory relief to restrain the appointment of a receiver and manager because they could not give any worthwhile undertaking as to damages. In this respect, his Honour was also unable to conclude that they would have been able to persuade a court as to the strength of their substantive claim for damages. The evidence, which did not extend to the applicants' substantive claim for damages, did not enable his Honour to form a view as to whether a court would have been persuaded to exercise any discretion to restrain the appointment. He was, however, able to conclude that the appointment of a receiver and manager would have had the effect of destroying the businesses.

...

[288] His Honour approached the question whether there had been 'economic' duress, in the manner suggested by McHugh JA in *Crescendo Management Pty Ltd v Westpac Banking Corp* (1988), pp 45–46, namely by enquiries, first, whether the pressure which had been applied was such that it operated as an inducement to enter into the contract; and, secondly, determining whether that pressure went beyond what the law is prepared to countenance as 'legitimate'. McHugh JA held that pressure would be illegitimate if it consisted of unlawful threats or amounted to unconscionable conduct. In *Barton v Armstrong* (1976), p 121 the Privy Council

had expressed a similar view, namely that there must be shown that some 'illegitimate means of persuasion' was used.

...

His Honour then turned to consider whether the pressure was illegitimate and concluded that it was, on an assessment of the conduct of the bank, the position in which the applicants were placed, and the resultant choices available to them. The fact that their financial state was 'parlous' was reiterated by his Honour. He held that the admissions made by the bank for the purpose of determination of the separate question that a loss to the extent of $5.75m had been caused by its conduct, permitted the conclusion that it had brought about that position. In those circumstances the applicants had no bargaining power. The 'huge disparity in bargaining position' between the applicants and the bank was, in his Honour's view, created by the bank and taken advantage of by it to obtain the releases in question, in circumstances where some of the bank officers concerned were of the view that, notwithstanding the refinancing, the applicants would default on the new loan. In his Honour's view, the bank's conduct went beyond driving a hard bargain in negotiating the price of a new loan. Rather, the bank used its dominant position which it had created by its conduct to protect it from further losses. His Honour went on:

> ... to exploit the applicants' position of financial dependency on Westpac, a situation created by the misconduct of Westpac in the manner alleged and admitted, to obtain a real and substantial benefit (the release) which ordinarily formed no part of a loan by a bank to its customer and was not necessary to secure its position as lender, in exchange for a benefit of doubtful worth to the applicants in their then parlous financial circumstances, was unconscionable in the sense used by McHugh JA in *Crescendo* and constituted illegitimate pressure ...

...

[289] His Honour discussed the question whether lawful pressure may qualify as 'illegitimate' pressure for the purpose of supporting a grant of relief at law on the ground of duress.

Cases to which his Honour referred in his reasons make clear that the answer is in the affirmative: *Universe Tankships Inc of Monrovia v International Transport Workers' Federation* (1983), pp 400–01; *Shivas v Bank of New Zealand* (1990), p 345; *Caratti v Deputy Commissioner of Taxation* (1993), p 457; *CTN Cash and Carry Ltd v Gallaher Ltd* (1994), pp 718–19. In the *CTN* case, Steyn LJ had referred to Professor Birks' observations that, while there were inherent difficulties in courts supplying notions of morality, nevertheless they appeared willing to apply, in the context of economic duress, 'a standard of impropriety rather than technical unlawfulness' (1994), p 718h. In *Barton v Armstrong* (1976), pp 118, 121, above, both the majority and minority judgments noted that the modern conception of duress, as applying where a person had been 'subjected to an improper motive for action', was a development under equity's influence, particularly, it might be added, through the equitable doctrine of undue influence. In *Williston on Contract*[63] it is said that both lawful and non-tortious conduct may be within the scope of the doctrine of duress,

---

63 3rd edn, vol 13, p 1606.

for what is required is that the pressure be wrongful.[64] In my view, his Honour was correct to hold that lawful pressure might operate as duress. The question which then arises is whether the pressure supposedly applied in this case was illegitimate.

In *Crescendo Management Pty Ltd v Westpac Banking Corp* McHugh JA, with whom Samuels and Mahoney JJA agreed, said (1988), p 46B:

> Pressure will be illegitimate if it consists of unlawful threats or amounts to unconscionable conduct. But the categories are not closed. Even overwhelming pressure, not amounting to unconscionable or unlawful conduct, however, will not necessarily constitute economic duress.

I do not think that his Honour was intending in this passage to refer to the equitable doctrine of unconscionable (see *Pao On v Lau Yiu Long* (1980)) dealing which is recognised as affording an independent ground on which a court exercising equitable jurisdiction can relieve from a contract.

The point of distinction which is relevant for present purposes is that duress, like undue influence, focuses upon the effect of pressure, upon the quality of the consent or assent of the pressured party, rather than the quality of the conduct of the party against which relief is sought – a distinction pointed to in *Commercial Bank of Australia Ltd v Amadio* (1983), p 474 and referred to by his Honour, the primary judge, in the present case. The cases, apart from *Crescendo Management*, which recognise the possibility of 'economic' duress, such as *Barton v Armstrong* and *Pao On v Lau Yiu Long*, [290] emphasise the feature that the pressure applied is so coercive of the will that consent is treated as vitiated. In *Smith v William Charlick Ltd* (1924) Isaacs J said at p 56:

> It is conceded that the only ground on which the promise to repay could be implied is 'compulsion'. The payment is said by the respondent not to have been 'voluntary' but 'forced' from it within the contemplation of the law. Leaving aside, for the present, the question whether in law the payment was 'forced' from the respondent by some undue advantage taken of its situation having regard to the Wheat Harvest legislation, the point is whether the Board's insistence was what is regarded as 'compulsion' from the simple standpoint of common law. 'Compulsion' in relation to a payment of which refund is sought, and whether it is also variously called 'coercion', 'extortion', 'exaction', or 'force', includes every species of duress or conduct analogous to duress, actual or threatened, exerted by or on behalf of the payee and applied to the person or the property or any right of the person who pays or, in some cases, of a person related to or in affinity with him. Such compulsion is a legal wrong, and the law provides a remedy by raising a fictional promise to repay. Apart from any additional feature presented by the relevant legislation, it is plain that a mere abstention from selling goods to a man except on condition of his making a stated payment cannot, in the absence of some special relation, answer the description of 'compulsion', however serious his situation arising from other circumstances may be ...

Although the conclusion in that case was that money had been paid as a result of commercial pressure not duress in the eye of the law, the passage set out above usefully emphasises that duress focuses attention on the quality of assent.

---

64 See also Mason and Carter, *Restitution Law in Australia*, 1995, paras 508, 519.

An approach which enquires whether, in all the circumstances, it is unconscientious to retain a benefit wrongfully procured might be thought to encompass the situation where improper pressure is brought to bear on one party, since it would have regard to that conduct and its relationship to the advantage obtained.[65] Relief will not be granted, however, only on the basis of an inequality, even a great inequality, of bargaining position. Relief may, however, be appropriate when the disparity was substantially brought about by the other party's antecedent conduct. The exploitation of the inequality could then be described as 'unconscientious'. *Amadio and Louth v Diprose*, in my opinion, may be viewed in this way. And, it seems to me, this was in large part the approach taken by his Honour.

It has been observed that the boundaries between common law duress, undue influence recognised in equity, and unconscionable pressure or 'equitable duress', are becoming blurred;[66] that the importance of common law duress and undue influence as distinct categories recognised in equity is diminishing;[67] and that the two jurisdictions may be said to be concerned, essentially, with exploitation or victimisation.[68] Nevertheless the distinction remains and, in the pleadings in the present case, resort was had to the common law doctrine, which necessitates a conclusion as to the quality and effect of both the threat made and the pressure applied.

His Honour the primary judge ultimately made the following declaration:

> [291] The matters pleaded in paragraph 22 of the amended defence do not operate to release Westpac from any claim or cause of action which the applicants had or may have had against Westpac arising out of or in connection with the off shore commercial loan or any foreign currency transaction which includes the causes of action sued on in proceedings number NH 29 of 1991.

I have referred above to the distinction to be drawn between the common law approach and that of equity[69] although on one view resort to the common law might not, in most cases be necessary. In this case however the applicants' reply relies on a case of duress at common law and not one of unconscionable dealing. In my respectful view, however, it was unconscionable dealing which his Honour found made out. This is to an extent confirmed by the applicants' reliance, on the appeal, on cases such as *Commonwealth v Verwayen* (1990) and *Louth v Diprose*, as supporting the conclusion reached by his Honour.

In the present case the focus of his Honour's findings was the position of disadvantage in which the applicants found themselves. At a number of places in the judgment, his Honour refers to their parlous financial circumstances, and

---

65   See *Muschinski v Dodds* (1985), pp 620–21; *Baumgartner v Baumgartner* (1987), pp 147–48; *Louth v Diprose* (1992), p 627.

66   See Dr Hardingham, 'Unconscionable dealing', in Finn (ed), *Essays in Equity*, 1985, pp 21–24.

67   Sir Anthony Mason, 'The place of equity and equitable remedies in the contemporary common law world' (1994) 110 LQR 238, p 249.

68   *Louth v Diprose* (1992), pp 627–29 *per* Brennan J; Duggan, 'Unconscientious dealing', in Parkinson, *The Principles of Equity*, 1996, p 122.

69   See *Blomley v Ryan* (1956), p 401; *Amadio* (1983), pp 461, 474; *Louth v Diprose* (1992), p 627.

states that it resulted from the admission made by the bank that it accepted it had brought those circumstances about. Given the way in which the matter was pleaded and the terms of the admission, it was always likely that difficulties would be encountered. His Honour referred, at an early point in the proceedings, to lack of clarity. This, however, was not resolved. The process undertaken by his Honour, against the background of what he described as some 'controversy' concerning the extent of the admission, was to construe the admission in light of the pleadings.

His Honour concluded that the admission made by the bank extended to embrace its liability in damages to the applicants as at February 1988 and that that liability arose by reason of its wrongful conduct in connection with the earlier off-shore commercial loan. I am, with respect, however, unable to agree that the case of duress pleaded by the applicants relied upon the bank's conduct in the negotiation of the earlier loan. The only pressure identified in the reply was said to arise from the representations themselves and the applicants' belief that they were liable to the bank and had no choice but to accede to the bank's demands as otherwise it was entitled to appoint receivers and managers. The case put forward was that the bank misrepresented that the applicants had no choice, whereas in truth they had, although they were not aware of it. That is a distinctly different case from that found by his Honour. Further, in my view, the bank's admission could not operate to widen the applicants' pleaded case of duress. The admission must be understood in the context of the case as pleaded by the applicants. So understood, it can be said to extend fairly to a case of misrepresentation operating as outlined above, but not one where antecedent background facts are to be taken and applied to achieve a different legal result.

On the hearing of the appeal, this court was not referred to any part of the hearing before his Honour which showed that, despite the pleadings, a case of unconscionability was conducted with the bank's consent. At most there had been some elliptical references to such a case by senior counsel for the applicants on the hearing, but it was not suggested to this court that the bank had so conducted itself as to acquiesce.

As the matter was pleaded, a case of duress could not in my view have been found by the trial judge. And, with respect, the facts as applied by his Honour [292] could not establish such a case. In most instances where duress is established the party coerced has had little choice. It is not, however, that inequality of bargaining position, or the reason for its creation, which is the essence of the action – it is the pressure brought to bear and its wrongfulness: 'There must be pressure the practical effect of which is compulsion or the absence of choice': *Universal Tankships Inc of Monrovia v International Transport Workers' Federation* (1983), p 400 *per* Lord Scarman, cited in *Crescendo Management* (1988), p 45.[70] Putting to one side the limitations imposed by the pleading referred to above, in my respectful opinion, neither the threats of appointment and sale nor the demand for release were themselves wrongful nor could they have operated as coercive. The critical matter was the applicants' lack of choice. The essence of the wrong identified by his Honour was in the creation of that position.

---

70   See also *North Ocean Shipping Co Ltd v Hyundai Construction Co Ltd* (1979), p 717.

...

[Northrop and Lindgren JJ agreed, although Lindgren J left open the question whether illegitimacy of pressure can be furnished by unconscionable conduct.]

Commentary and questions

On what basis did Kiefel J distinguish duress from unconscionable conduct? Did her Honour consider that unconscionability principles could be used as a determinant of duress? Why did Kiefel J overturn the finding of the trial judge on the issue of duress?

The commentators are divided on the virtues of unconscionability as a determinant of duress. Phang points out that the courts have consistently failed to provide objective criteria for differentiating between illegitimate pressure as opposed to mere commercial pressure,[71] and concludes that the doctrine of unconscionability provides a better basis for deciding these cases. Accordingly, he argues that the doctrine of economic duress should be subsumed under the equitable doctrine of unconscionability.[72] In a similar vein, McKeand argues that duress is a species of unconscionable conduct. He takes the view that pressure will be illegitimate where it consists of either unlawful threats or unconscionable conduct.[73] On the other hand, Mason and Carter are doubtful that the doctrine of unconscionability will provide much assistance in duress cases. Like Keifel J in *Cockerill* they point to the differing perspectives of unconscionability and duress, and they also express concern that the unconscionability principle confers a wide scope for judicial discretion.[74]

---

71 Phang, 'Economic duress: recent difficulties and possible alternatives' [1997] RLR 53. See also Phang, 'Whither economic duress? Reflections on two recent cases' (1990) 53 MLR 107; Phang, 'Economic duress – uncertainty confirmed' (1992) 5 JCL 147.

72 Phang, 'Economic duress: recent difficulties and possible alternatives' [1997] RLR 53, p 63.

73 McKeand, 'Economic duress – wearing the clothes of unconscionable conduct' (2001) 17 JCL 1, pp 9ff.

74 Mason and Carter, *Restitution Law in Australia*, 1995, p 184.

CHAPTER 10

INTRODUCTION TO INEFFECTIVE CONTRACTS

CATEGORIES OF INEFFECTIVE CONTRACT

A large number of claims in restitution law involve claims for the recovery of money paid or the reasonable value of non-monetary benefits conferred under a contract that is ineffective. These claims can be grouped into four main categories:[1]

(1) claims under contracts discharged for breach or repudiation (see Chapter 11);

(2) claims under contracts discharged for frustration (see Chapter 12);

(3) claims under contracts that are inherently ineffective due to being unenforceable, void or illegal (see Chapter 13); and

(4) claims for work done in the course of negotiations toward a contract that is never finalised (see Chapter 14).

These specific categories of claim are dealt with in subsequent chapters; the purpose of this chapter is to outline the principles that have common application to these categories.

THE REQUIREMENT THAT THE CONTRACT BE INEFFECTIVE

There is a large body of authority suggesting that a claim in restitution is only available where the contract under which the benefit was conferred is ineffective,[2] so that it will only be in rare situations that a restitutionary claim be permitted under a subsisting contract.[3] The usual rationale for this limitation on the availability of restitutionary relief is that restitution should not be allowed to reallocate the risks agreed to in the contract.[4]

---

1   A claim for restitution might also be brought under a contract that has been rescinded, as to which see Mason and Carter, *Restitution Law in Australia*, 1995, Chapter 13.

2   For money claims see *Foran v Wight* (1989), p 413; *Baltic Shipping Company v Dillon* (1993), p 385 (see extract, p 286); *Shephard v ANZ Banking Corporation Ltd* (1996), p 442; *Roxborough v Rothmans of Pall Mall Australia Ltd* (2001), p 382 *per* Kirby J (see extract, p 268). For services claims see *Pavey & Matthews Pty Ltd v Paul* (1987), Deane J at 256 (see extract, p 15); *Brooks Robinson Pty Ltd v Rothfield* (1951), p 409; *Update Constructions Pty Ltd v Rozelle Child Care Centre Ltd* (1990), p 275; *Independent Grocers Co-operative Ltd v Noble Lowndes Superannuation Consultants Ltd* (1993), pp 536–38; *Brenner v First Artists' Management Pty Ltd* (1993), p 257 (see extract, p 39).

3   Beatson, 'Restitution and contract: *non-cumul*?' (2000) 1 Theoretical Inquiries in Law 83, p 88.

4   *Ibid*, p 94. See also Bryan and Ellinghaus, 'Fault lines in the law of obligations: *Roxborough v Rothmans of Pall Mall Australia Ltd*' (2000) 22 Sydney Law Review 636, pp 662–63.

Nevertheless, there are recent indications that the courts will not always insist that the plaintiff demonstrate the contract is ineffective. In the High Court case of *Roxborough v Rothmans of Pall Mall Australia* (2001) (see extracts, pp 268 and 273) a majority of the court enabled the plaintiff to recover payments made under a consideration that had failed, despite the fact that the contract had not been terminated. The facts are discussed in detail at p 81, but in outline the claim was by retailers of tobacco products to recover a proportion of the contract price paid to their wholesaler representing unconstitutional licence fees. There was no suggestion of a breach of contract by the wholesaler, let alone termination by the retailers for that breach. Nevertheless, a majority of the court allowed the claim in restitution.[5] It has been suggested that the claim in this case was rightly permitted as the contract did not allocate the risk that the licence fees would be found to be unconstitutional, and thus the usual rationale for requiring discharge of the contract was not present.[6] An alternative explanation was advanced by Gyles J in the Full Court of the Federal Court, in a passage accepted by Callinan J in the High Court:[7]

> The contract has been executed in all respects save for the payment of the licence fee by the respondent. The licence fee is no longer payable. It cannot and will not be paid by the respondent. That is the end of the matter. Performance is no longer possible.[8]

It remains to be seen to what extent *Roxborough* heralds a more expansive approach of the courts to allowing restitution of benefits conferred under valid and subsisting contracts.

CLAIMS FOR MONEY

Historically, the common count for money had and received to the use of the plaintiff was used to recover payments made under ineffective contracts. One example of the situations where this count would lie was where the consideration for the payments had totally failed.[9] Total failure of consideration was adopted as an unjust factor when unjust enrichment was recognised as the basis for restitution law (*Fibrosa Spolka Akcyjna v Fairbairn Lawson Combe Barbour Ltd* (1943)) and remains the primary ground for recovery of payments of money made pursuant to ineffective contracts. This unjust factor applies to each of the

---

5   Though see Kirby J in *Roxborough v Rothmans of Pall Mall Australia Ltd* (2001), *op cit*, fn 2 p 382 (see extract, p 268), who insisted that a claim in restitution will not lie in the face of an effective contract.

6   Bryan and Ellinghaus, 'Fault lines in the law of obligations: *Roxborough v Rothmans of Pall Mall Australia Ltd*' (2000) *op cit*, fn 4.

7   (2001), pp 390–91. For academic endorsement of Gyles J's view, see Bryan and Ellinghaus, 'Fault lines in the law of obligations: *Roxborough v Rothmans of Pall Mall Australia Ltd*' (2000) *op cit*, fn 4, p 662.

8   *Roxborough v Rothmans of Pall Mall Australia Ltd* (1999), p 354. Gyles J was in dissent.

9   Bullen and Leake, *Precedents of Pleadings*, 3rd edn, 1868, pp 48–49; *Moses v Macferlan* (1760) (see extract, p 8); *Fibrosa Spolka Akcyjna v Fairbairn Lawson Combe Barbour Ltd* (1943), pp 47, 50, 57 (see extract, p 346); *Foran v Wight* (1989), pp 432, 459.

identified categories of ineffective contract, and is available even where the plaintiff is the party in breach.[10]

Mistake might also ground a claim in some cases, although it has been suggested that recovery on the basis of mistake should be limited to the situation where the mistake is one as to the validity of the contract pursuant to which the money is paid.[11]

The concept of total failure of consideration

The consideration for a payment will totally fail where the purpose for which the payment was made has totally failed: see *Roxborough v Rothmans of Pall Mall Australia Ltd* (2001), pp 340, 364–65 (see extracts, pp 268 and 273). Where the payment was made for the performance of a contractual obligation, consideration will totally fail where the defendant has failed to commence any part of the performance of the obligation.[12] In this regard, 'consideration' refers to the performance of the defendant's promise, not the promise itself.[13] Once the defendant has commenced performance of the contractual obligations for which the payment was made, consideration will not totally fail and the defendant will be entitled to retain the money.[14] This will be so even though the plaintiff has not received any benefit, as the test is not whether the defendant has conferred a benefit on the plaintiff, but whether the defendant has commenced performing the contractual obligations for which the money was paid.[15] Conversely, consideration will fail if the contractual performance has not been commenced, even though the plaintiff has received an incidental benefit from the defendant.[16]

10 See, for example, *Shaw v Ball* (1963) (see extract, p 310); *Hyundai Heavy Industries Co Ltd v Papadopoulos* (1980) (see extract, p 313); *Stocznia Gdanska SA v Latvian Shipping Co* (1998) (see extract, p 315). Although a payment will be irrecoverable where it is a deposit: *Howe v Smith* (1884) (see extract, p 303).

11 *Roxborough v Rothmans of Pall Mall Australia Ltd* (2001), pp 369–70 *per* Kirby J; Bryan and Ellinghaus, 'Fault lines in the law of obligations: *Roxborough v Rothmans of Pall Mall Australia Ltd*' (2000) *op cit*, fn 4, p 658. See also *Portman Building Society v Hamlyn Taylor Neck (A Firm)* (1998).

12 *Baltic Shipping Company v Dillon* (1993) (see extract, p 286). For recent Australian examples of failure of consideration, see *Heckenberg v Delaforce* (2000); *Ferryboat Ltd v Gray* (1990); *Arrow v Sportsworld Group Ltd* (1999); *Ocelota Ltd v Water Administration Ministerial Corporation* (2000).

13 *Baltic Shipping Company v Dillon* (1993), pp 350–51, 376–77, 389 (see extract, p 286); *Shaw v Ball* (1963), p 915 (see extract, p 310); *Heckenberg v Delaforce* (2000) pp 37–39; *Fibrosa Spolka Akcyjna v Fairbairn Lawson Combe Barbour Ltd* [(1943), pp 48, 72 (see extract, p 346).

14 *Baltic Shipping Company v Dillon* (1993) (see extract, p 286); *Hyundai Heavy Industries Co Ltd v Papadopoulos* (1980) (see extract, p 313); *Stocznia Gdanska SA v Latvian Shipping Co* (1998) (see extract, p 315).

15 This proposition is well illustrated by the cases involving contracts for the provision of work: see for example *Hyundai Heavy Industries Co Ltd v Papadopoulos* (1980) (see extract, p 313); *Stocznia Gdanska SA v Latvian Shipping Co* (1998) (see extract, p 315). See also *Heckenberg v Delaforce* (2000).

16 This proposition is well illustrated by the cases involving contracts for the sale of goods or land: *Rowland v Divall* (1923) (see extract, p 295); *Yeoman Credit Ltd v Apps* (1962) (see extract, p 296); *McDonald v Dennys Lascelles Ltd* (1933) (see extract, p 308).

Although failure to render contractual performance is the central example of failure of consideration, it is now settled that that principle should no longer be seen as being limited to contractual non-performance. In the following case the High Court held that the principle of failure of consideration extends beyond contractual non-performance to other situations where the basis on which the payment was made has failed. Thus 'failure of consideration' perhaps should be more accurately described as 'failure of the basis of the payment'.

Roxborough v Rothmans of Pall Mall Australia Ltd (2001) 185 ALR 335
High Court of Australia

The facts are stated at p 81.

Gleeson CJ, Gaudron and Hayne JJ: ... [340] Failure of consideration is not limited to non-performance of a contractual obligation, although it may include that. The authorities referred to by Deane J, in his discussion of the common law count for money had and received in *Muschinski v Dodds* (1985), pp 619–200, show that the concept embraces payment for a purpose which has failed as, for example, where a condition has not been fulfilled, or a contemplated state of affairs has disappeared.[17] Deane J, referring to 'the general equitable notions which find expression in the common law count', gave as an example 'a case where the substratum of a joint relationship or endeavour is removed without attributable blame and where the benefit of money or other property contributed by one party on the basis and for the purposes of the relationship or endeavour would otherwise be enjoyed by the other party in circumstances in which it was not specifically intended or specially provided that that other party should so enjoy it' (1985), pp 619–20. In the case of money paid pursuant to a contract, it would involve too narrow a view of those 'general equitable notions' to limit failure of consideration to failure of contractual performance. In the present case, the amount of the net total wholesale cost referable to the tax was, from one point of view, part of the money sum each appellant was obliged to pay to obtain delivery of the tobacco products. But there was more to it than that. The tax was a government imposition, in the form of a fee payable under a licensing scheme. The nature of the scheme was such that the licensed wholesaler, or, if not the wholesaler, then the licensed retailer, would pay the amount referable to particular tobacco products. The respondent, anticipating liability for the fee, required the appellants, when purchasing products by wholesale, to pay an amount equal to the fee. The appellants, in turn, had an interest in the respondent paying the fee to the revenue authorities, for they were thereby relieved of a corresponding liability. There was a purpose involved in the making of the requirement that the appellants pay the amounts described as 'tobacco licence fee', and in the compliance with that requirement. To describe those amounts as nothing more than an agreed part of the price (or, to use the language of the parties, cost) of the goods, is to ignore an important aspect of the facts.

...

---

17 See Birks, *An Introduction to the Law of Restitution*, 1985, p 223.

Gummow J: ... [364] The term 'failure of consideration' is used in the law to mean several things. The point was made as follows by Stoljar:[18]

First, a consideration fails because the defendant's promise is insufficient or illusory or formally void, the failure thus being an initial invalidity preventing a contract from being formed. Secondly, we say that the consideration fails where a promisor fails to perform; the failure is now simply a breach of contract, though usually a substantial or important breach. But, thirdly, failure of consideration has also a much older and specialised sense, one that describes a specific remedy when, upon the collapse of a bargain, the promisee seeks to recover money had and received by the promisor. Thus failure of consideration specifies not only a claim, but also the particular basis for that claim. [Footnotes omitted.]

It is the third meaning with which this litigation is concerned. But what is meant here by the term 'consideration'? It is important to appreciate that, although this often is the case, the 'bargain' referred to in describing failure of consideration need not be contractual in nature. For example, in *Martin v Andrews* (1856) the Court of Queen's Bench upheld a declaration for money had and received to recover conduct money tendered with a *subpoena ad test* where the case was settled before trial. Lord Campbell CJ said (1856), p 4:

The consideration has failed. The money is paid for the purpose of defraying the expences [sic] of the witness's journey: if there is no journey there is no expence [sic], and the consideration fails; and then an action lies for money had and received. There is indeed no express authority: but the general principles upon which that action is maintained are applicable.

The references to 'purpose' and to 'general principles' are significant.

In English law, the expression 'consideration' has various possible meanings. One is found in the principle referred to by Maitland[19] which treats 'valuable consideration' between members of the same family as a source of equitable rights of ownership. Another is the treatment in equity of a bare covenant by deed (where the presence of the seal would support an action at law for damages, *Cannon v Hartley* (1949), as insufficient to remove the covenants from the class of 'volunteers' in whose favour equitable remedies (for example, specific [365] performance) are unavailable.[20] Three other meanings were identified by Robert Walker LJ in *Guinness Mahon & Co Ltd v Kensington and Chelsea Royal London Borough Council* (1999). His Lordship said of the expression 'consideration' (1999), p 236:

Its primary meaning is the 'advantage conferred or detriment suffered', *Midland Bank Trust Co Ltd v Green* (1981), p 531, which is necessary to turn a promise not under seal into a binding contract. In the context of failure of consideration, however, it is, in the very well known words of Viscount Simon LC in *Fibrosa Spolka Akcyjna v Fairbairn Lawson Combe Barbour Ltd* (1943), p 48: 'generally speaking, not the promise which is referred to as the consideration, but the performance of the promise.' Then there is the older and looser, and potentially very confusing, usage of 'consideration' as equivalent to

18 'The doctrine of failure of consideration' (1959) 75 LQR 53.
19 *Lectures on Equity*, 1936, at p 33.
20 *Lewin on Trusts*, 17th edn, 2000, §10-06.

the Roman law '*causa*' reflected in the traditional conveyancing expression, 'in consideration of natural love and affection'.[21]

This is not the occasion to pursue the linkage between the last and the first of these meanings. Windeyer J said that '[i]n a very general way causa in modern civil law does resemble valuable consideration in English law'.[22] However that may be, the earlier reference by Lord Campbell CJ in *Martin v Andrews* to the purpose of a non-contractual payment indicates that the later emphasis by Viscount Simon LC in *Fibrosa* to the performance of a promise is an unsatisfactory explanation of all the cases where repayment is made for failure of consideration.

In the present case, there has been no failure in the performance by Rothmans of any promise it made. No question of repudiation by it of its contractual obligations arises. The question is that stated by Deane J in *Muschinski* set out earlier in these reasons. Is it unconscionable for Rothmans to enjoy the payments in respect of the tobacco licence fee, in circumstances in which it was not specifically intended or specially provided that Rothmans should so enjoy them? The answer should be in the affirmative. Here, 'failure of consideration' identifies the failure to sustain itself of the state of affairs contemplated as a basis for the payments the appellants seek to recover.[23]

...

Kirby J (dissenting): ... [382] The retailers ... claimed to recover under a 'unifying principle' of restitution for unjust enrichment at their expense.[24] They did so on the basis that, notwithstanding that consideration had not totally failed, some part of the [383] consideration could be separately identified, apportioned and then seen as having failed.[25] This submission should be rejected.

By their terms, the contracts between the wholesaler and the retailers left the obligation of the wholesaler to pay the tobacco licence fee to the government entirely out of account. It was unsurprising that this should have been so. At the time the contracts were agreed to, the obligation to pay the tobacco licence fees arose not by any contractual agreement at all but by the operation of statute law, namely pursuant to the duties purportedly imposed by the Act. As the majority in the Full Court explained (1999), p 200, the retailers could succeed in a claim for restitution on the ground of failure of consideration only if the wholesaler was bound to them by the promise to pay the amount identified as being for the licence fees and such a promise was wholly unperformed.

In light of the then understanding of the obligations of the Act, it borders on the surreal to suggest that the wholesaler 'promised' the retailers that it would pay the licence fees to the government, in default of which payment there would be a failure of consideration in respect of that part of the price paid. Not only does this hypothesis defy the express terms upon which the parties traded with each other. It also contradicts the historical fact that the obligation of the wholesaler to pay the

---

21 See Birks, *An Introduction to the Law of Restitution*, 1985, p 223.

22 *Smith v Jenkins* (1970), p 411.

23 *David Securities Pty Ltd v Commonwealth Bank of Australia* (1992), p 382; *Baltic Shipping Co v Dillon* (1993), p 389; *Goss v Chilcott* (1996), p 797.

24 Jones, 'Restitution: unjust enrichment as a unifying concept in Australia?' (1988–89) 1 JCL 8.

25 *David Securities* (1992) 175 CLR 353, at 382–83; *Goss v Chilcott* (1996), pp 797–98.

tax was an obligation imposed on the wholesaler not by private contract but by the terms of the Act.

I therefore agree with the Full Court that the basis for asserting a right to recover at common law was not established. The moneys were not had and received by the wholesaler to the use of the retailers. Properly analysed, they were had and received in discharge of a contractually stipulated price payable in full in exchange for the supply of specified goods which were duly delivered.

Commentary and question

The court refused to imply a term in the contract that Rothmans would pay over the amount representing the licence fees to the government (pp 341, 379–82). Nevertheless, on the view of the majority, the absence of such a contractual promise by Rothmans did not defeat the claim based on a total failure of consideration. It was sufficient that the purpose for which the payment was made (payment of the fees to the government) had failed, despite the fact this purpose had not become a term of the contract. Kirby J however would have refused recovery on the ground that there was no express or implied promise by Rothmans to pay the licence fees to the government. On this view, failure of consideration is equated with failure to perform an obligation specified in the contract. This narrow interpretation of total failure of consideration has been criticised.[26]

The appellant retailers limited their claim to licence fees that Rothmans had not paid over to the government. Based on the principles extracted above, do you think the retailers could have sustained a claim to recover the licence fees that Rothmans had in fact paid over to the government?

Contracts of sale vs contracts for work

Although the basis of the payment is one that will be determined on the facts of each case, and having regard to the terms of the particular contract,[27] previous authorities have established certain useful presumptions. In particular, the courts have drawn a distinction between simple contracts for the sale of goods or land, on the one hand, and contracts for the provision of work on the other.

In the case of contracts for the sale of goods or land, the consideration for payments made under those contracts towards the purchase price is the transfer of legal title; thus consideration will fail where the legal title is not transferred to

---

26 See the criticism of the Full Court of the Federal Court decision which had likewise adopted this narrow interpretation: Bryan, 'Where the constitutional basis for payment has failed (*Roxborough v Rothmans of Pall Mall Australia*)' [2000] 2 Restitution Law Review 218; Bryan and Ellinghaus, 'Fault lines in the law of obligations: *Roxborough v Rothmans of Pall Mall Australia Ltd*' (2000) *op cit*, fn 4; Erbacher, 'Recent developments in restitutionary recovery of contractual payments: *Roxborough v Rothmans of Pall Mall Australia Ltd*' (2000) 28 ABLR 226.

27 *Baltic Shipping Company v Dillon* (1993), pp 378–79, 386 (see extract, p 286) *Hyundai Heavy Industries v Papadopoulos* (1980), p 44 (see extract, p 313); *Stocznia Gdanska SA v Latvian Shipping Co* (1998), pp 895–96, 908 (see extract, p 315).

the plaintiff.[28] The fact the purchaser received interim possession of the goods or land will not prevent recovery on this ground, as interim possession is not the benefit that was contracted for.[29] This principle has also been applied to goods hired under a hire purchase agreement,[30] but not to a lease of premises[31] or to the sale of a business.[32]

In the case of contracts for work,[33] consideration is provided once the work is commenced.[34] Thus, consideration will not fail provided the defendant has commenced to perform the work, despite the fact the plaintiff might not have received any, or any substantial, benefit from the work.[35]

The requirement that the failure of consideration be total

The courts have consistently reaffirmed the requirement that the failure of consideration must be total: the payment will be irrecoverable if partial consideration has been provided.[36] However, there are two exceptional categories of case where the provision of partial consideration will not prevent recovery: (1) where the sum sought to be recovered is attributable to a severable obligation which the defendant has not yet commenced to perform; and (2) where it is easy for the plaintiff to make counter-restitution, such as where the contract involves solely an exchange of money payments.

(a) Severable obligations

The plaintiff will be entitled to recover a payment that is referable to a severable obligation that the defendant has not yet commenced to perform, despite the fact that the defendant has commenced performance of other obligations.[37] So, for example, assume the plaintiff contracts with the defendant to purchase a

---

28 *Rowland v Divall* (1923) (see extract, p 295); *Yeoman Credit Ltd v Apps* (1962) (see extract, p 296); *McDonald v Dennys Lascelles Ltd* (1933) (see extract, p 308).

29 *Rowland v Divall* (1923) (see extract, p 295) *McDonald v Dennys Lascelles Ltd* (1933) (see extract, p 308).

30 *AGC Corporation Ltd v Ross* (1983) (see extract, p 297); *Richards v Alliance Co Ltd* (1976); *Shoard v Palmer and General Credits Ltd* (1989); *Warman v Southern Counties Car Finance Corporation Ltd* (1949).

31 *Hunt v Silk* (1804) (see extract, p 300).

32 *Shaw v Ball* (1963) (see extract, p 310).

33 That is, contracts requiring the provision of substantial work prior to transferring any final product to the plaintiff.

34 *Hyundai Heavy Industries v Papadopoulos* (1980) (see extract, p 313); *Stocznia Gdanska SA v Latvian Shipping Co* (1998) (see extract, p 315); *Clowes (Development) UK Ltd v Mulchinook* (2001).

35 *Hyundai Heavy Industries v Papadopoulos* (1980) (see extract, p 313); *Stocznia Gdanska SA v Latvian Shipping Co* (1998) (see extract, p 315); *Clowes (Development) UK Ltd v Mulchinook* (2001).

36 *Fibrosa Spolka Akcyjna v Fairbairn Lawson Combe Barbour Ltd* (1943) (see extract, p 346); *Baltic Shipping Co v Dillon* (1993), p 375 (see extract, p 286); *Roxborough v Rothmans of Pall Mall Australia Ltd* (2001) (see extracts, pp 268 and 273); *Shaw v Ball* (1963) (see extract, p 310).

37 *Fibrosa Spolka Akcyjna v Fairbairn Lawson Combe Barbour Ltd* (1943), p 65 (see extract, p 346); explaining *Rugg v Minnett* (1809); *Goss v Chilcott* (1996) (see extract, p 356).

quantity of 50 computers of $2,000 each. The plaintiff pays the $100,000 in advance however the defendant delivers only 10 computers. The plaintiff should be entitled to recover the $80,000 that was attributable to the cost price of the computers that were not delivered. The correctness of this proposition has now been confirmed by the High Court in the following case.

Roxborough v Rothmans of Pall Mall Australia Ltd (2001) 185 ALR 335
High Court of Australia

The facts are stated at p 81.

Gleeson CJ, Gaudron and Hayne JJ: … [341] In a contract for the sale of goods, the total amount which the buyer is required to pay to the seller may be expressed as one indivisible sum, even though it is possible to identify components which were taken into account by the parties in arriving at a final agreed figure. The final figure itself may have been the result of negotiation, making it impossible to relate a cost component to any particular part of that figure. Or there may be other factors which prevent even a notional apportionment. But there are cases, of which the present is an example, where it is possible, both to identify that part of the final agreed sum which is attributable to a cost component, and to conclude that an alteration in circumstances, perhaps involving a failure to incur an expense, has resulted in a failure of a severable part of the consideration. Here, the buyers, the retailers, were required to bear, as a component of the total cost to them of the tobacco [342] products, a part of the licence fees which the seller, the wholesaler, was expected to incur at a future time, and which was referable to the products being sold. It was in the common interests of the parties that the fees, when so incurred, would be paid to the revenue authorities by the seller, and it was the common intention of the parties (and the revenue authorities) that the cost of the goods would include the fees. In the events that happened, the anticipated licence fees were not incurred by the seller. The state of affairs, which was within the contemplation of the parties as the basis of their dealings, concerning tax liability, altered. And it did so in circumstances which permitted, and required, severance of part of the total amount paid for the goods.

The case is not unlike that considered by the Court of Appeals of New York in *Wayne County Produce Co v Duffy-Mott Co Inc* (1927). A war tax of 10% was imposed on cider. A manufacturer sold a quantity of cider by wholesale, at a certain price per gallon, less a stated discount, plus the tax. The total amount was paid to the manufacturer, and the manufacturer remitted the tax to the government. Later, it was ruled that the particular product sold was not taxable, and the manufacturer recovered the tax from the government. The purchaser claimed to recover from the manufacturer that part of the amount paid for the cider which was referable to the tax. The Court of Appeals upheld the claim. Cardozo CJ, who delivered the reasons of the court, described the issue as being whether the money refunded to the manufacturer by the government was held 'to the use of the plaintiff' (1927), p 669. He went on to say:

> This is not a case where the item of the tax is absorbed in a total or composite price to be paid at all events … This is a case where the promise of the buyer is to pay a stated price, and to put the seller in funds for the payment of a tax besides. In such a case the failure of the tax reduces to an equivalent extent the obligation of the promise.

The same idea may be expressed by saying that, in the present case, the failure of the tax involved the failure of a severable part of the consideration for which the net total amounts shown on the invoices were paid.

Although an attempt was made by the appellants to invoke an implied agreement under which they could claim repayment of any unpaid tax, it was artificial and unconvincing. The parties made no agreement, express or implied, about what was to happen if the tax was held to be invalid. If there is here a right to enforce repayment upon the basis of a failure of consideration, it is because, in the circumstances, the law imposes upon the respondent an obligation to make just restitution for a benefit derived at the expense of the appellants.[38] If there had been a total failure of consideration, because, for example, there had been a prepayment for goods which were never delivered, the respondent's duty to make restitution would have been clear ...

[342] It accords with the basis of dealing, and contractual arrangements, between the appellants and the respondent to regard that part of the net total amount of each invoice referable to the 'tobacco licence fees' as a severable part of the consideration, which has failed. There is no conceptual objection to this. For the reasons already given, the tax component of the net total wholesale cost was treated as a distinct and separate element by the parties. It was externally imposed. It was not agreed by negotiation. It was not like the discounts, which might differ between retailers, just as the wholesale list price would vary from time to time in accordance with market conditions. To permit recovery of the tax component would not result in confusion between rights of compensation and restitution, or between enforcing a contract and claiming a right by reason of events which have occurred in relation to a contract.[39]

Gummow J: ... [365] At this stage attention is required to the notion that the failure relied upon be 'total'. The general rule, exemplified in *Baltic Shipping,* is that where there has been a partial failure in performance of a contractual promise there is no right to recover back a proportionate part of the money paid on an action for money had and received. One reason for this requirement that the failure be 'total' appears to be that, in cases in which the question has arisen, the plaintiff already will have a remedy in damages which will be governed by principles of compensation under which the plaintiff may recover no more than the loss sustained; to allow the plaintiff to claim restitution in respect of any breach, [366] particularly where the plaintiff had made a bad bargain by paying the defendant more than the defendant's performance was worth, would cut across the compensatory principle.[40]

Another reason for the general rule reflects the law's difficulty with apportionment in respect of an entire obligation, namely one in which the consideration for the payment of money is entire and indivisible. The rule is that the action will not be maintainable where 'the money payable is neither apportioned by the contract, nor capable of being apportioned by a jury'.[41] The 19th century cases whence that rule

---

38 *Pavey & Matthews Pty Ltd v Paul* (1987), p 257 *per* Deane J.
39 Cf *Fibrosa Spolka Akcyjna v Fairbairn Lawson Combe Barbour Ltd* (1943); *Baltic Shipping Co v Dillon* (1993).
40 Treitel, *The Law of Contract*, 10th edn, 1999, p 978.
41 *Steele v Tardiani* (1946), p 401. See also *Baltic Shipping Co v Dillon* (1993), pp 350, 374, 384, 393.

is derived were decided when fact finding was the function of juries not judges. They reflected an appreciation of the imperfections of that method of trial and also what today would be called a 'default rule' that the allocation of such gains and losses was properly the exclusive function of the terms of the parties' contract.[42]

Sir Guenter Treitel[43] suggests that the requirement of a 'total' failure of consideration should be restricted to those instances in which the reasons for it, indicated above, still have force. He continues:[44]

> It should, in other words, no longer apply where the payor has *no* remedy, or no satisfactory remedy, for breach (*eg* by way of action for damages[45]) in respect of the part left unperformed by the payee, or where there is in fact no difficulty in apportioning that part to the whole in respect of which the payor's advance payment had been made. [Original emphasis.]

In the present case, the appellants have no contractual remedy in respect of the retention of the moneys in question after the removal of the need for licence renewals as necessary conditions for the continuation of their businesses and that of Rothmans.

The circumstance that it is necessary for the appellants to pay the total of the invoiced amounts in order to obtain delivery and passing of title to the tobacco products supplied by Rothmans does not inevitably point to the conclusion that the sum designated in respect of 'tobacco licence fee' was referable solely to the delivery and transfer of property in the tobacco products sold by Rothmans. The parties contracted not only for the supply of the tobacco products but also, in the light of the provisions of s 41 of the Act, with respect to the renewal of the wholesaler's licence and the funding for that to take place. Whilst that is understood, the very form of the transactions indicates that the payments made by the appellants can be 'broken up'.[46]

...

Kirby J (dissenting): ... [382] The final ground upon which the retailers claimed relief was for restitution on the basis of a failure of consideration. The payments made by the retailers to the wholesaler were made in discharge of express contractual obligations agreed between them. The wholesaler discharged its part of such obligations by supplying the goods in question to the retailers. Those goods were supplied in accordance with an agreed price. That price, in each instance, subsumed, and included within it, various component parts, only one of which was that of the licence fees. No doubt it also included component parts for notional charges for acquisition of raw tobacco product, warehousing, packaging, processing, transport, overheads and the like. The separate appearance of the component for the tobacco licence fees on the wholesaler's invoices was doubtless

---

42 Kull, 'Mistake, frustration, and the windfall principle of contract remedies' (1991) 43 Hastings Law Journal 1, pp 30–31.

43 *The Law of Contract*, 10th edn, 1999, p 979.

44 *Ibid*.

45 Or, in the case of a loan of money, by way of action for the agreed sum.

46 See *David Securities Pty Ltd v Commonwealth Bank of Australia* (1992), p 383; *Goss v Chilcott* (1996), p 797; *Wayne County Produce Co v Duffy-Mott Co Inc* (1927).

convenient for accounting purposes. It permitted the ready aggregation of the licence fees then thought to be payable under the Act. But the legal obligation of the retailers to the wholesaler was to pay the price of the goods in full. This was a single aggregate amount referable to each occasion of supply.[47] Indeed, until such payment was 'made in full' to the wholesaler, the property in the goods supplied remained with the wholesaler. The retailers then agreed to hold such goods in a fiduciary capacity as bailee.[48]

In the foregoing circumstances, it is impossible to assert that there has been a total failure of consideration. The individual contracts between the wholesaler and the retailers were uncontestably valid. They were not ineffective. Nor were they terminated. Far from attempting to terminate the contracts for the supply of goods by the wholesaler, the retailers actually accepted the goods in every case. They onsold them to consumers, thereby recovering the component for licence fees about which they now complain. The law of restitution only rarely operates in the context of an effective contract.[49] The present, in my opinion, is not a case that falls within one of the recognised exceptions.

...

Callinan J: ... [390] The relevant sums paid by the appellants were shown as separate items ascribed to a particular component of the total sum payable. They answered [Lord Porter's description in] *Fibrosa Spolka Akcyjna v Fairbairn Lawson Combe Barbour Ltd* (1943) of separate parts of money payable for or on account of a divisible part of a contract (1943), p 77:

> Under that system money had and received to the plaintiff's use can undoubtedly be recovered in cases where the consideration has wholly failed, but unless the contract is divisible into separate parts it is the whole money, not part of it, which can be recovered. If a divisible part of the contract has wholly failed and part of the consideration can be attributed to that part, that portion of the money so paid can be recovered, but unless this be so there is no room for restitution under a claim in *indebitatus assumpsit*.

In the same case Viscount Simon LC explained the principle in this way (1943), pp 48–49:

> In English law, an enforceable contract may be formed by an exchange of a promise for a promise, or by the exchange of a promise for an act – I am excluding contracts under seal – and thus, in the law relating to the formation of contract, the promise to do a thing may often be the consideration, but when one is considering the law of failure of consideration and of the quasi-contractual right to recover money on that ground, it is, generally speaking, not the promise which is referred to as the consideration, but the performance of the promise. The money was paid to secure performance and, if performance fails the inducement which brought about the payment is not fulfilled.

---

47   Cl 6: see reasons of Callinan J.
48   Cl 10: see reasons of Callinan J.
49   *Pavey & Matthews Pty Ltd v Paul* (1987), p 256; Mason and Carter, *Restitution Law in Australia*, 1995, pp 83–84; cf Beatson, 'Restitution and contract: *non-cumul*?' (2000) 1 Theoretical Inquiries in Law 83, p 88.

If this were not so, there could never be any recovery of money, for failure of consideration, by the payer of the money in return for a promise of future performance, yet there are endless examples which show that money can be recovered, as for a complete failure of consideration, in cases where the promise was given but could not be fulfilled.[50] In this connexion the decision in *Rugg v Minett* (1809) is instructive. There the plaintiff had bought at auction a number of casks of oil. The contents of each cask were to be made up after the auction by the seller to the prescribed quantity so that the property in a cask did not pass to the plaintiff until this had been done. The plaintiff paid in advance a sum of money on account of his purchases generally, but a fire occurred after some of the casks had been filled up, while others had not. The plaintiff's action was to recover the money he had paid as money received by the defendants to the use of the plaintiffs. The Court of King's Bench ruled that this cause of action succeeded in respect of the casks which at the time of the fire had not been filled up to the prescribed quantity.

...

This is also a case of the kind referred to by Mason CJ, Deane, Toohey, Gaudron and McHugh JJ in *David Securities Pty Ltd v Commonwealth Bank of Australia* (1992), p 383 (footnote omitted):

> In cases where consideration can be apportioned or where counter-restitution is relatively simple, insistence on total failure of consideration can be misleading or confusing. In the present case, for instance, it is relatively simple to relate the additional amounts paid by the appellants to the supposed obligation under cl 8(b) of the loan agreements. The appellants were told that they were required to pay withholding tax and the payments that they made were predicated on the fact that, by doing so, they were discharging their obligation. Such an approach is no different in effect from the cases under the old statutes of usury whereby a borrower could recover from the lender the *excess interest* which the lender was prohibited from stipulating or receiving. [Original emphasis.]

Accordingly, I am of the opinion that the appellants have made out a case for the recovery of the money paid on the basis that relevantly there has been a total failure of consideration, that is to say, a failure in respect of a discrete, clearly identified component of the consideration.

...

Commentary and questions

On what basis did the majority hold that the claimed sums were severable from the remainder of the purchase price of the tobacco products? On what basis did Kirby J hold in dissent that severance could not take place?

According to Gummow J, what is the rationale for the requirement that the failure of consideration be total?

---

50   See the notes in Bullen and Leake, *Precedents of Pleadings*, 9th edn, 1935, p 263.

The approach in the principal case to causation was foreshadowed in *Goss v Chilcott* (1996) (see extract, p 356), where the Privy Council held that the obligation under a loan agreement to pay interest is severable from an obligation to repay the principal. In that case a finance company was entitled to recover the principal advanced under an unenforceable loan contract despite the fact that the borrowers had made two interest payments under the agreement, as no part of the principal had been repaid.

(b) Counter-restitution is easy

It has been suggested that the provision of partial consideration should not prevent recovery in cases where it would be a relatively simple matter for the plaintiff to make counter-restitution of the consideration received.[51] One of the leading proponents of this view is Peter Birks.

Movement towards partial failure?

Birks, P, 'No consideration: restitution after void contracts' (1993) 23 UWAL Rev 196, pp 210–13

Since the law of restitution began to be studied as a single category of our law, the requirement of 'total' failure has been made to answer to some rationale. What is the reasoning behind it? In the situation, not relevant on our facts, in which a plaintiff who has terminated a contract for breach would otherwise have a free choice between an action for breach and an action for unjust enrichment, the requirement of total failure may have been intuitively relied upon to create a near monopoly for the contractual action.[52] Outside that case, where there is no possibility of choice between different theories and measures of recovery, the only reason behind 'total' appears to be the same as is expressed in the requirement of counter-restitution: there cannot be restitution without counter-restitution, there cannot be taking back without giving back. If that is right, the requirement of total failure will be satisfied if the plaintiff can give back or allow for any partial benefit which he has received. This point is made very clearly by Professor Treitel:[53]

> If A employs B for a lump sum, paid in advance, to paint A's house, and B abandons the job before it is finished, A cannot recover back any part of the payment: his only remedy is in damages. The reason for the rule appears to be that the law cannot easily apportion the contract price to the amount of work actually done by B. Where the apportionment is in fact easy, the law will allow partial recovery: for example, a buyer who had paid in advance for 100 tons could get back half his money if only 50 tons were delivered.

51 *David Securities Pty Ltd v Commonwealth Bank of Australia* (1992), p 383 (see extract, p 646); *Heckenberg v Delaforce* (2000), para 41.

52 The old American case of *Bush v Canfield* (1818) vividly illustrates the potential for the conflict, as does *Boomer v Muir* (1933). On the legitimacy of two theories of recovery giving two very different measures of recovery, see Goff and Jones, *The Law of Restitution*, 3rd edn, 1986, p 455; Burrows, *The Law of Restitution*, 1993, p 265. Some systems insist on the matter being handled solely in contract, though it does not necessarily follow that the two measures of recovery are not then allowed to co-exist.

53 Treitel, *The Law of Contract*, 8th edn, 1991, p 927.

Following this line, the High Court of Australia has recently said: 'In cases where consideration can be apportioned or where counter-restitution is relatively simple, insistence on failure or total failure of consideration can be misleading or confusing.' And again: 'In circumstances where both parties have impliedly acknowledged that the consideration can be "broken up" or apportioned in this way, any rationale for adhering to the traditional rule requiring *total* failure of consideration disappears.'[54] Where, as in the swaps situation, the plaintiff has received money, there is no problem in making the necessary allowance ... It is a question in other cases how far the giving back may be done in money.[55]

... A dogmatic requirement of total failure, unconnected to the requirement of counter-restitution, would [in the case of contracts involving an exchange of money payments] be indefensible. Further, in so far as the cause of action based on mistake is not infrequently available as an alternative to failure of consideration, the explanation of 'total' failure in terms of counter-restitution eliminates the danger of a senseless asymmetry between two species of unjust enrichment. Again, even in regard to benefits less easily given back or impossible to give back, courts of equity have not been reluctant to make a money allowance for a partial benefit received.[56] And the Law Reform (Frustrated Contracts) Act 1943 (UK) threw over the requirement of total failure, requiring instead mutual restitution on the basis of a money valuation of non-money benefits.[57] That shows that valuation of incomplete performances, often difficult, is not regarded as impossible.

It requires to be emphasised that making allowances for incomplete performances received by the plaintiff raises questions at two separate levels, first where there are no difficulties in the valuation of that which the plaintiff has received or, simpler still, where what he has received can be given back exactly as received, and second where account of the incomplete performance which he has received can only be taken in money and there are difficulties of valuation. The interrupted swaps transactions do not involve problems on the second of these levels and they also do not involve any competition between remedies in contract and in unjust enrichment.

The better view nowadays is therefore likely to be that, even where a court decides that a benefit received by the plaintiff cannot be discounted, the receipt of an incomplete performance will not necessarily exclude restitution on the ground of failure of consideration. The most defensible position seems to be that the requirement of total failure will be satisfied if the partial benefit received by the plaintiff can to the satisfaction of the court be given back or allowed for in

---

54 *David Securities Pty Ltd v CBA* (1992), p 383 *per* Mason CJ, Deane, Toohey, Gaudron, McHugh JJ. In *Baltic Shipping Co v Dillon (The Mikhail Lermontov)* (1993) the court's treatment of failure of consideration was more mechanical but the issue was overshadowed by a competing claim for damages. See the excellent note by Barker, 'Restitution of passenger fare' [1993] LMCLQ 291.

55 See *Morris v Prefabrication Eng Co* (1947).

56 *Whincup v Hughes* (1871), p 61; cf *Atwood v Maude* (1868). See also *Towers v Barrett* (1786). And the Law Reform (Frustrated Contracts) Act 1943 (UK) threw over the requirement of total failure, requiring instead mutual restitution on the basis of a money valuation of non-money benefits; *BP Exploration Co (Libya) Ltd v Hunt (No 2)* (1982), pp 925–78, 986–92; cf Treitel, *op cit*, fn 53, p 927; McKendrick, 'Frustration, restitution and loss apportionment', in Burrows (ed), *Essays on the Law of Restitution*, 1991, pp 146, especially pp 159–65.

57 *BP Exploration Co (Libya) Ltd v Hunt (No 2)*, (1982), pp 978, 986–92; cf Treitel, *op cit*, fn 53, p 127; McKendrick, *ibid*, especially pp 159–65.

reduction of his own claim. Further, there will never be any problem in its being so given back or allowed if it consists solely in the receipt of money.

An objection will certainly be made that reinterpretation of the requirement of total failure of consideration as belonging to the principle which requires counter-restitution will be productive of sharp and unattractive distinctions on the line between incomplete and complete performances. There will be the case of 99% completion. Logic requires the line to be drawn between 99.999 and 100. It may be necessary to soften the line. *De minimis non curat lex* will do a certain amount. In cases of discharge by breach, where there is a potential choice between remedies in unjust enrichment and in contract, the line will be pulled back by the rule that an action in unjust enrichment can never be brought while the relations between the parties in regard to the value in question continue to be regulated by the contract.[58] In other cases, despite the absence of alternative remedies, it would not be impossible to develop a doctrine, mirroring the doctrine of substantial performance in contract, that a consideration which has been substantially fulfilled should not be regarded as having failed ...

Commentary

A 'counter-restitutionary' approach to failure of consideration has also been advocated by other commentators,[59] and has attained some judicial recognition. Where the transaction involves merely the exchange of monetary payments – loan contracts being the most obvious example – there are now indications in the case law that recovery will not be barred by partial repayment of the loan. The comments of the High Court in *David Securities Pty Ltd v Commonwealth Bank of Australia* (1992), p 383 (see extract, p 646)[60] on apportionment and counter-restitution which are quoted by Birks were followed by the Privy Council in *Goss v Chilcott* (1996) (see extract, p 356). That latter case involved a claim for the recovery of a loan advance on the basis of a total failure of consideration; the loan agreement being unenforceable. As no part of the principal had been repaid, Lord Goff, delivering the judgment of the Privy Council, held that the consideration had totally failed; the obligation to repay interest was a distinct obligation from the obligation to repay the principal. More importantly for present purposes, Lord Goff stated in *obiter* that partial repayment of the principal would not prevent recovery on a total failure of consideration. In such circumstances apportionment is an easy exercise: the court will simply set off the amount of the principal which has been paid back by the borrower against the amount which was advanced by the financial institution and which is being claimed back, and order the return of the balance

---

58   Goff and Jones, *The Law of Restitution*, 3rd edn, 1986, pp 31–32. The proposition may have to be more complex to cope with *Miles v Wakefield Metro DC* (1987); *Wiluszynski v Tower Hamlets LBC* (1987); Mead, 'Restitution within contract?' (1991) 11 LS 172.

59   See Burrows, *op cit*, fn 52, pp 259–61. Edelman, 'The new doctrine of partial failure of consideration' (1997) 15 ABR 299. Edelman, 'Restitution for a total failure of consideration: when a total failure is not a total failure' (1996) Newc LR 57; compare McKendrick, 'Total failure of consideration and counter-restitution: two issues or one?', in Birks (ed), *Laundering and Tracing*, 1995, pp 217ff.

60   Cf *Maguire v Makaronis* (1997), p 764.

of the loan. Counter-restitution is a simple matter. This approach is consistent with the principle that a borrower must make restitution of the outstanding loan amounts as a condition of rescinding a mortgage agreement.[61]

Birks' article was referred to by the English Court of Appeal in *Guinness Mahon & Co Ltd v Kensington and Chelsea Royal London Borough Council* (1998). This case involved a void swaps transaction which had been fully executed. The court rejected Birks' view that restitution of payments made under a fully completed contract should not be permitted.

CLAIMS FOR A NON-MONETARY BENEFIT

The primary basis of a claim in restitution for the value of work done under an ineffective contract is the defendant's acceptance of the benefit.[62] A mistake could also potentially provide the claim, at least where the mistake is as to the validity of the contract: see *Rover International Ltd v Cannon Film Sales Ltd* (1989) (see extract, p 156).

The concept of acceptance

The recipient of services under an ineffective contract will be held to have accepted the benefit of the services where the recipient:[63]

> ... as a reasonable person, should have realised that a person in the position of the provider of the services would expect to be paid for them and did not take a reasonable opportunity to reject those services.

The authorities suggest that there are two forms of acceptance: deemed (or 'constructive')[64] acceptance and actual acceptance.[65] The courts will deem the defendant to have accepted the plaintiff's services where the plaintiff provided the services in accordance with the defendant's contractual request for the benefit.[66] Thus, acceptance will be deemed where the plaintiff has fully performed the contract,[67] or has been prevented from full performance by the

---

61 *Maguire v Makaronis* (1997); *Bank of South Australia Ltd v Ferguson* (1998).

62 *Pavey & Matthews Pty Ltd v Paul* (1987), pp 227–28, 256–57 (see extract, p 15), *Horton v Jones (No 1)* (1934), p 367; *Horton v Jones (No 2)* (1939), p 320 (see extract, p 385); *Brenner v First Artists' Management* (1993), pp 257–61 (see extract, p 39); *Angelopoulos v Sabatino* (1995), pp 9–13 (see extract, p 418); *Bunbury-Harvey Regional Council v Giacci* (2000).

63 *Brenner v First Artists' Management* (1993), p 260 (see extract, p 39). This test of acceptance was endorsed in *Angelopoulos v Sabatino* (1995), pp 9–13 (see extract, p 418); see also *ABB Power Generation Ltd v Chapple* (2001), paras 20–21; *Lopresto v Sam* (2000), paras 21, 22.

64 See *Pavey & Matthews Pty Ltd v Paul* (1987), p 257.

65 Mason and Carter, *Restitution Law in Australia*, 1995, pp 302–04.

66 *Brenner v First Artists' Management* (1993), pp 257–60 (see extract, p 39).

67 *Pavey & Matthews Pty Ltd v Paul* (1987), p 257 (see extract, p 15); Mason and Carter, *op cit*, fn 65, pp 342–43.

defendant's breach.[68] On this deemed form of acceptance, recovery is in essence based on the contractual request for the services.

On the other hand, the courts will not allow recovery merely on the basis of the contractual request where the plaintiff is the party in breach who has partially performed an entire obligation.[69] Claims by a party in breach will be successful only in exceptional cases where an independent act of acceptance by the defendant of the plaintiff's incomplete performance can be established,[70] or alternatively where it can be shown that the defendant acquiesced in the incomplete performance, *Steele v Tardiani* (1946) (see extract, p 327). An 'independent act of acceptance' refers to an act of the defendant freely and voluntarily accepting the defective performance. An independent act of acceptance will rarely be present where the work has improved (or become absorbed into) other property of the defendant, as the defendant will have no real choice whether to accept or reject the work.[71]

Work performed outside of the contract

Reasonable remuneration will be awarded to a contracting party who performed additional work outside of the scope of the contract at the request of the defendant.[72] Reasonable remuneration will be awarded despite the fact the contract has not been discharged or repudiated (*Gigliotti Constructions Pty Ltd v Jalili* (1998)), and even though the contractual requirements for the doing of extra work have not been complied with.[73] This principle applies only where the work is additional to that which was necessary to be done to perform the contract. If the work was necessary to complete contractual obligations, the plaintiff's only claim will lie on the contract.[74]

NO CONTRACTUAL CEILING ON RECOVERY

The quantum of recovery for money paid or the value of services rendered is not limited to the contractual measure of damages or to the contract price. Thus,

---

68   *Brenner v First Artists' Management* (1993), pp 257–60 (see extract, p 39).

69   An 'entire obligation' is one where the contractual performance promised in return for payment of the money is entire and indivisible.

70   *Steele v Tardiani* (1946), pp 402–03 (see extract, p 327); *Nicholson v Burnett* (1922); *Sumpter v Hedges* (1898) (see extract, p 325).

71   *Munro v Butt* (1858); *Pattinson v Luckley* (1875); *Sumpter v Hedges* (1898) (see extract, p 325); *Steele v Tardiani* (1946), pp 402–03 (see extract, p 327).

72   *Liebe v Molloy* (1906) pp 353–55; *Update Constructions Pty Ltd v Rozelle Child Care Centre Ltd* (1990), pp 272–75; *Gigliotti Constructions Pty Ltd v Jalili* (1998); *ABB Power Generation Ltd v Chapple* (2001).

73   *Update Constructions Pty Ltd v Rozelle Child Care Centre Ltd* (1990), pp 274–75; *Gigliotti Constructions Pty Ltd v Jalili* (1998).

74   *Update Constructions Pty Ltd v Rozelle Child Care Centre Ltd* (1990), pp 274–75; *Gigliotti Constructions Pty Ltd v Jalili* (1998); *ABB Power Generation Ltd v Chapple* (2001).

the plaintiff is entitled to recover money paid on the basis of a total failure of consideration even though the amount recovered in restitution would exceed the measure of the plaintiff's expectation damages. An example is provided by *Bush v Canfield* (1818). The plaintiff agreed to buy flour from the defendant for a contract price of $14,000, prepaying $5,000. The defendant failed to deliver the flour, and the plaintiff terminated the contract and sought to recover the prepayment. The plaintiff was successful in recovering the full $5,000 even though the market price of the flour had dropped to $11,000 and thus the plaintiff's expectation damages amounted to only $2,000. This approach has been justified either on the basis that money is an incontrovertible benefit that cannot be subjectively devalued by reference to the contract terms,[75] or on the basis that to allow less than full recovery would confer a windfall on the breaching party.[76]

Similarly, the measure of recovery on a claim for the value of work done is not 'capped' by the contract price.[77] In *Renard Constructions (ME) Pty Ltd v Minister for Public Works* (1992) the New South Wales Court of Appeal awarded the plaintiff the reasonable value of construction services provided pursuant to a contract discharged for the defendant's repudiation, despite the fact the reasonable value of the services exceeded the contract price by more than $76,000. The court emphasised that the law of restitution is independent of the law of contract and that therefore restitutionary remedies should not be subordinated to contractual ones: pp 277–78. Although the commentators almost uniformly disagree with the result in this case,[78] there is significant judicial authority in support of it.[79]

---

75 Birks, 'In defence of free acceptance', in Burrows (ed), *Essays on the Law of Restitution*, 1991, pp 135–37; Burrows, *The Law of Restitution*, 1993, pp 265–66; McInnes, 'Contractual services, restitution and the avoidance of bad bargains' (1995) 23(3) ABLR 218.

76 Mason and Carter, *op cit*, fn 65, pp 562–63.

77 For contracts discharged for breach see: *Renard Constructions (ME) Pty Ltd v Minister for Public Works* (1992) (see extract, p 322); *Iezzi Constructions Pty Ltd v Watkins Pacific (Qld) Pty Ltd* (1995); *Slowey v Lodder* (1901) (approved (1904)); *Boomer v Muir* (1933). For unenforceable contracts see: *Pavey & Matthews Pty Ltd v Paul* (1987) p 257 (see extract, p 70); *Gino D'Alessandro Constructions Pty Ltd v Powis* (1987), pp 58–59. For void contracts see: *Stinchcombe v Thomas* (1957), p 513; *Rover International Ltd v Cannon Film Sales Ltd* (1989), pp 435–36 (see extract, p 387).

78 Birks, *op cit*, fn 75; Burrows, *op cit*, fn 75, pp 268–71; Mason and Carter, *op cit*, fn 65, pp 579–81; McInnes, *op cit*, fn 75. The academics' views are discussed in more detail in the next chapter: pp 323–24.

79 See the authorities set out in fn 77.

CHAPTER 11

CONTRACTS DISCHARGED FOR BREACH OR REPUDIATION

INTRODUCTION

A claim in restitution will not generally be permitted under a valid contract. As such, a plaintiff who is a party to a contract that has been breached or repudiated will usually be required to establish as a precondition to claiming restitutionary relief that the contract has been discharged for the breach or repudiation. However, following *Roxborough v Rothmans of Pall Mall Australia Ltd* (2001), it appears that restitution will be permitted where performance is, for all practical purposes, no longer possible despite the fact the contract has not been formally discharged.[1] This aspect of the case has been discussed in detail in Chapter 10, pp 265–66.

The primary claim for the recovery of money under a contract discharged for breach or repudiation is total failure of consideration, and the primary claim for the recovery of the value of services is acceptance: see generally Chapter 10. Different considerations will apply depending on whether the plaintiff is the innocent party or the party in breach. For money claims, both the innocent party and the party in breach will be able to rely on the doctrine of total failure of consideration. However where the claim is by a party in breach, the nature of the payment will need to be examined to determine whether it is a deposit (which will be irrecoverable even if there is a total failure of consideration) or a prepayment (which will be recoverable on a total failure of consideration).[2] For services claims, the requirements to prove an acceptance of the services vary significantly depending on whether the plaintiff is the innocent party or the party in breach.[3] For these reasons, cases in this chapter are grouped according to the status of the plaintiff.

The parties to a contract can contract out of restitutionary rights and liabilities in the event the contract is discharged.[4] The most common form of contracting out of restitutionary liability is an express forfeiture clause providing that instalments paid under a sale contract are to be forfeited if the purchaser defaults on the contract.[5] Likewise, a contractual regime that regulates in detail the recovery of benefits conferred will displace common law restitutionary rights and obligations.[6]

---

1 Callinan J, pp 390–91. See also Bryan and Ellinghaus, 'Fault lines in the law of obligations: *Roxborough v Rothmans of Pall Mall Australia Ltd*' (2000) 22 Sydney Law Review 636, p 662.

2 See below pp 286–320.

3 See above pp 281–82, and below pp 321–30.

4 *Sunstar Fruit Pty Ltd v Cosmo* (1995), p 227. Though clear words are necessary to displace restitutionary obligations: *Iezzi Constructions Pty Ltd v Watkins Pacific (QLD) Pty Ltd* (1995).

5 See below pp 317–20.

6 *Pan Ocean Shipping Ltd v Creditcorp Ltd, The 'Trident Beauty'* (1994), pp 473–74 (see extract, p 333).

RECOVERY OF MONEY: INNOCENT PARTY

Concept of failure of consideration

The principles governing failure of consideration were discussed in detail in Chapter 10. It will be recalled from that chapter that the consideration for a payment will totally fail where the purpose for which the payment was made has totally failed: see *Roxborough v Rothmans of Pall Mall Australia Ltd* (2001), pp 340, 364–65.

In the following decision the High Court discusses the principles that apply to a claim based on a failure by the defendant to perform his or her contractual obligations. The court confirms the requirement that the failure must be total: the claim will fail if the defendant has commenced performing any part of the contractual obligation for which the payment was made.

Baltic Shipping Co v Dillon (1993) 176 CLR 344 High Court of Australia

The respondent was a passenger on the appellant's cruise ship which had embarked on a fourteen day cruise around the South Pacific. The respondent had paid the cruise fare of $2,205 in advance. Ten days into the cruise the vessel struck a rock and sank, the respondent having been taken off the ship shortly before it sank. The appellant voluntarily refunded $787.50; the portion of the fare representing the remainder of the cruise which did not take place. The questions before the court were (1) whether the respondent was entitled to restitution of that portion of the fare attributable to the period of the cruise pre-shipwreck ($1,417) as money paid on a consideration which totally failed, and (2) whether restitution of the balance of the fare could be given in addition to an award of damages in contract for distress and disappointment.

Mason CJ: ... [350] *Is the fare recoverable on the ground of total failure of consideration or otherwise?*

...

In the context of the recovery of money paid on the footing that there has been a total failure of consideration, it is the performance [351] of the defendant's promise, not the promise itself, which is the relevant consideration, see *Fibrosa Spolka Akcyjna v Fairbairn Lawson Combe Barbour Ltd* (1943), p 480. In that context, the receipt and retention by the plaintiff of any part of the bargained for benefit will preclude recovery, unless the contract otherwise provides or the circumstances give rise to a fresh contract. So, in *Whincup v Hughes* (1871), the plaintiff apprenticed his son to a watchmaker for six years for a premium which was paid. The watchmaker died after one year. No part of the premium could be recovered. That was because there was not a total failure of consideration.[7] A qualification to this general rule, more apparent than real, has been introduced in the case of contracts where a seller is bound to vest title to chattels or goods in a buyer and the buyer seeks to recover the price paid when it turns out that title has not been passed. Even if the buyer has had the use and enjoyment of chattels or

---

7   See also *Hunt v Silk* (1804).

goods purportedly supplied under the contract for a limited time, the use and enjoyment of the chattels or goods has been held not to amount to the receipt of part of the contractual consideration. Where the buyer is entitled under the contract to good title and lawful possession but receives only unlawful possession, he or she does not receive any part of what he or she bargained for. And thus, it is held, there is a total failure of consideration.[8] As this court stated in *David Securities Pty Ltd v Commonwealth Bank* (1992), pp 381–83: 'the notion of total failure of consideration now looks to the benefit bargained for by the plaintiff rather than any benefit which might have been received in fact.'

...

I have come to the conclusion in the present case that the respondent is not entitled to recover the cruise fare on either of the grounds just discussed. The consequence of the respondent's enjoyment of the benefits provided under the contract during the first eight full days of the cruise is that the failure of consideration was partial, not total. I do not understand how, viewed from the perspective of failure of consideration, the enjoyment of those benefits was 'entirely negated by the catastrophe which occurred upon departure from Picton' (1989), to repeat the words of the primary judge.

Nor is there any acceptable foundation for holding that the advance payment of the cruise fare created in the appellant no more than a right to retain the payment conditional upon its complete performance of its entire obligations under the contract. As the contract called for performance by the appellant of its contractual obligations from the very commencement of the voyage and continuously thereafter, the advance payment should be regarded as the provision of consideration for each and every substantial benefit expected under the contract. It would not be reasonable to treat the appellant's right to retain the fare as conditional upon complete performance when the appellant is under a liability to provide substantial benefits to the respondent during the course of the voyage. After all, the return of the respondent to Sydney at the end of the voyage, though an important element in the performance of the appellant's obligations, was but one of many elements. In order to illustrate the magnitude of the step which the respondent asks the court to take, it is sufficient to pose two questions ... Would the respondent be entitled to a return of the fare if, owing to failure of the ship's engines, the ship was unable to proceed on the last leg of the cruise to Sydney and it became necessary to airlift the respondent to Sydney? Would the fare be recoverable if, owing to a hurricane, the ship was compelled to omit a visit to one of the scheduled ports of call? The answer in each case must be a resounding negative ...

Deane and Dawson JJ: ... [374] The fact that the promised consideration under a contract is 'entire' or 'entire and indivisible'[9] will, subject to any applicable provision of the contract, prevent recovery, *in an action in contract*, of part of the promised purchase price in circumstances where there has been a failure to provide part of that consideration. In such a case, the purchase price represents the contractual quid pro quo for the whole of the promised indivisible consideration and the promisee is not, in the absence of any applicable provision in the contract,

8   *Rowland v Divall* (1923); *Butterworth v Kingsway Motors Ltd* (1954).
9   See, eg, *Steele v Tardiani* (1946), p 401.

under a contractual obligation to accept or pay for part only thereof. If, in such a case, the promisee accepts the benefit of part only of the consideration, any enforceable obligation to pay for it must arise from some new contract or from the operation of principles of unjust enrichment in the particular circumstances.

[375] The present case is not, however, one in which a party who has provided part only of the promised consideration seeks to recover part of the agreed purchase price. In the present case, it is the promisee, Mrs Dillon, who seeks to recover the whole of a prepaid purchase price on the ground that the consideration for which it was paid has wholly failed. Mrs Dillon does not rely upon any provision of the contract between Baltic and herself under which Baltic was obliged to refund the whole of the fare in the events which happened. There was no such contractual provision. The basis of her claim is the obligation of restitution which the law *prima facie* imposes upon the recipient of a payment made under a contract which has become 'abortive for any reason not involving fault on the part of the plaintiff' in a case 'where the consideration, if entire, has entirely failed, or where, if it is severable, it has entirely failed as to the severable residue'.[10] Such a claim is not a claim on the contract.[11] Its historical antecedent in terms of forms of action is the old *indebitatus* count for money had and received to the use of the plaintiff.[12] Its modern substantive categorisation is as an action in unjust enrichment. In other words, the receipt of payment of money for a consideration which wholly fails 'is one of the categories of case in which the facts give rise to a *prima facie* obligation to make restitution ... to the person who has sustained the countervailing detriment' ...[13]

[376] The critical question on this aspect of the present case is whether the consideration for which Mrs Dillon paid the stipulated fare to Baltic wholly failed. That consideration was not, for the purposes of her action in unjust enrichment, the contractual promise which she received from Baltic ... *Prima facie*, where a simple promise of future performance is involved, the law of unjust enrichment looks to the future performance and not the bare promise as the relevant consideration.[14] Thus, the consideration for which Mrs Dillon paid the fare was the substance of Baltic's contractual promise, [377] namely, the actual provision of the components of the promised 14 day pleasure cruise upon the *Mikhail Lermontov*. If all that Mrs Dillon had relevantly received had been Baltic's bare promise, unperformed and unenforced, the consideration for the whole of the fare would have wholly failed. In fact, however, Baltic provided and Mrs Dillon accepted the accommodation, the sustenance, the entertainment and the transport

---

10 *Fibrosa Spolka Akcyjna v Fairbairn Lawson Combe Barbour Ltd* (1943), pp 64–65 *per* Lord Wright.

11 See *Pavey & Matthews Pty Ltd v Paul* (1987), pp 256–57; *Lipkin Gorman v Karpnale Ltd* (1991), pp 572, 578; and generally Birks, 'The independence of restitutionary causes of actions' (1990) 16 UQLQ 1, pp 19–20.

12 See, eg, *Moses v Macferlan* (1760); *Fibrosa, op cit*, fn 10, pp 62–64; Bullen and Leake, *Precedents of Pleadings*, 3rd edn, 1868, pp 44–50.

13 *Australia and New Zealand Banking Group Ltd v Westpac Banking Corporation* (1988), p 673.

14 See, eg, *Rowland v Divall* (1923); *Shaw v Ball* (1962), p 915; *Rover International Ltd v Cannon Film Ltd* (1989), pp 923–24, (1989) pp 433–34; Birks, *An Introduction to the Law of Restitution*, 1985, pp 222–23; Goff and Jones, *The Law of Restitution*, 3rd edn, 1986, pp 369–70; Beatson, *The Use and Abuse of Unjust Enrichment*, 1991, pp 3, 63.

involved in the first eight clear days of the 14 day cruise. We turn to consider the significance of that fact.

It is arguable that the promised consideration of the pleasure cruise was severable in the sense that, subject to the obligation to transport passengers back to Sydney, the fare could be apportioned or allocated on a day by day basis. As has been seen, however, the view that has prevailed in the courts below is that the consideration was entire and indivisible and it may be assumed, for the purposes of this appeal, that that view is correct. The fact that the promised consideration was entire and indivisible may be important in an action in unjust enrichment for restitution of money paid for a consideration that has failed. Thus, as the above extract from the speech of Lord Wright in *Fibrosa* indicates,[15] the weight of authority supports the approach that in such an action that fact will automatically preclude recovery of part of the purchase price in a case of partial failure of consideration[16] with the result that the innocent party is confined to suing in contract for the difference in value between what was promised and what was provided. (In many, and possibly most, cases, there will be no practical difference in the result in that the difference in value between what was promised and what was provided will be equivalent to that part of the purchase price which can be attributed to that which was not provided.) It is, however, unnecessary to consider that question here since it has not been argued that, if Mrs Dillon is not entitled to restitution of the full fare on the basis of a complete failure of consideration, the refund by Baltic of part of the fare was inadequate compensation for the failure to provide the final days of the cruise. Again, the fact that the consideration was entire and indivisible will *prima facie* entitle the promisee to reject a tender of only part of the consideration[17] and may, depending upon the circumstances, support a conclusion that part only of the consideration, if provided, was worthless and, [378] for the purposes of the law of unjust enrichment, no consideration at all.[18] Ordinarily, however, an entire and indivisible consideration will not wholly fail if part of it is tendered and accepted. If, for example, the customer of Sir George Jessel's shoemaker, having paid in advance, had accepted one shoe and worn it with a matching shoe from another pair, it could not be said that the consideration for the prepayment had wholly failed. On the other hand, if the customer, having paid in advance, had refused to accept the tender of a single shoe on the ground that the agreed consideration of a pair of shoes was entire and indivisible, the money which he had paid would have been recoverable for a total failure of consideration.

There can be circumstances in which there is, for relevant purposes, a complete failure of consideration under a contract of transportation notwithstanding that the carrier has provided sustenance, entertainment and carriage of the passenger during part of the stipulated journey. For example, the consideration for which the fare is paid under a contract for the transportation of a passenger by air from Sydney to London would, at least *prima facie*, wholly fail if, after dinner and the inflight film, the aircraft were forced to turn back due to negligent maintenance on the part of the carrier and if the passenger were disembarked at the starting point

---

15 *Fibrosa Spolka* (1943), pp 64–65 *per* Lord Wright; see also pp 56, 60, 77; and cf *The Commonwealth v Amann Aviation Pty Ltd* (1991), p 117.

16 See, generally, Goff and Jones, *op cit*, fn 14, pp 54–55, 369–71, 449–54, 458–65, 480–81.

17 See, eg, *Giles v Edwards* (1797).

18 See, eg, *Heywood v Wellers (A Firm)* (1976), pp 458–59.

in Sydney and informed that no alternative transportation would be provided. Thus, in *Heywood v Wellers*, Lord Denning MR regarded it as self-evident that, in some circumstances where part of a journey had been completed, money paid to the carrier or 'driver' was recoverable 'as of right' for the reason that it was 'money paid on a consideration which had wholly failed' (1976), p 458.

However, the promised consideration in the present case was not, as a matter of substance, the transportation of Mrs Dillon from Sydney to Sydney. As has been said, it was the provision of all that was involved in the promised pleasure cruise as a holiday experience. Even on the assumption that that promised consideration was entire and indivisible, it did not wholly fail. Baltic provided and Mrs Dillon accepted and enjoyed eight complete days of the cruise. It is true that Mrs Dillon would have been entitled to decline to board the ship or to accept only part of the promised consideration if it could have, and had, been known in advance that all that Baltic would in fact provide was eight days of cruising culminating in the sinking of the ship off New Zealand as a result of Baltic's breach of its contractual duty to take reasonable care. If, in [379] that necessarily hypothetical situation, Mrs Dillon had wisely decided to stay at home, the consideration for the fare would have failed completely and, subject to any applicable provisions of the contract between herself and Baltic,[19] she would have been entitled to succeed in an action in unjust enrichment for the recovery of the whole fare. In circumstances where Mrs Dillon accepted and enjoyed the major portion of the pleasure cruise, however, there was no complete failure of the consideration for which she paid the fare. The catastrophe of the shipwreck and its consequences undoubtedly outweighed the benefits of the first eight complete days. It did not, however, alter the fact that those benefits, which were of real value, had been provided, accepted and enjoyed ...

Gaudron J: ... In the present case, there can be no doubt that there was an obligation on the part of Baltic Shipping Co to take Mrs Dillon on a journey that began and ended in Sydney. That is an obligation that is either discharged or breached, depending on where the journey ends, and which may well be an entire obligation. And it is one which was satisfied by the arrangements made for Mrs Dillon's return to Sydney or, in any event, is one about which no complaint is made. But the contract was not merely a round trip journey contract; it was a contract for a 14 day pleasure cruise, beginning and ending in Sydney. It seems to me that, in that context and at least insofar as the duration of the cruise is concerned, there is no basis for treating the contract as an entire contract with the premature termination of the cruise constituting a total failure of consideration. And so far as the duration of the cruise is concerned, although it is something of a circular consideration, there are real difficulties in describing the events which happened as involving a total failure of consideration when, plainly enough, Mrs Dillon received the benefit of accommodation, sustenance and other facilities associated with the cruise until the ship went down ...

McHugh JJ: ... [389] *Conditional payments*

---

19   See, eg, *Fibrosa Spolka* (1943), p 67.

When a contractual payment is made conditionally upon the performance of a promise by the payee, the right to retain the moneys after discharge of the contract is dependent upon whether the promise has been performed. If the promise has not been performed, there has been a total failure of consideration by reason of the non-fulfilment of the condition, and the money is recoverable as money had and received to the use of the payer ...[20]

Furthermore, where the condition upon which the money was paid has failed, the payer is entitled to the return of the money advanced, even though that person has obtained some benefit from the contract. Work done or expense incurred by the payee or benefit enjoyed by the payer will not constitute consideration unless it constitutes a partial performance of the condition upon which the money was paid. Thus, the purchaser of a motor vehicle is entitled to the return of the full purchase price of the vehicle if the vendor has failed to make title even though the purchaser has had the use of the vehicle for a considerable period.[21] The seller cannot retain the purchase moneys because their retention is conditional upon the vendor making good his or her promise to transfer the title of the vehicle to the purchaser. Similarly, a solicitor who is paid money on account of costs to seek a court order cannot retain the [390] costs if he fails to take reasonable care to seek the order even though he has incurred expense or done work on the case, see *Heywood v Wellers (A Firm)* (1976).

Moreover, 'once it does appear that the condition for retaining the money has failed the fact that it failed in response to the payer's own breach does not matter'.[22] As Birks says,[23] this is the best explanation of the much discussed case of *Dies v British & International Mining & Finance Corporation* (1939) where a buyer in default was held entitled to recover instalments of the purchase price of guns and ammunition. Once the seller elected to accept the buyer's repudiation and terminate the contract, the consideration for the advance payment had wholly failed because the seller retained the guns and ammunition.

However, when a contractual payment is not subject to any condition or the condition for its retention has been fulfilled, discharge of the contract does not entitle the payer to the return of money advanced even though the payee is in breach of a promise going to the root of the contract. In such a case, the payer's remedy is for breach of contract for non-performance of the promise and not for restitution of the payment. In *McDonald v Dennys Lascelles Ltd* (1933), pp 476–77, Dixon J pointed out:

> When a party to a simple contract, upon a breach by the other contracting party of a condition of the contract, elects to treat the contract as no longer binding upon him, the contract is not rescinded as from the beginning. Both parties are discharged from the further performance of the contract, but rights are not divested or discharged which have already been *unconditionally* acquired. Rights and obligations which arise from the partial execution of the

---

20 *Fibrosa Spolka* (1943), p 65.
21 *Rowland v Divall* (1923); *Warman v Southern Counties Car Finance Corporation Ltd* (1949); *Butterworth v Kingsway Motors Ltd* (1954).
22 Birks, *op cit*, fn 14, p 238.
23 Birks, *op cit*, fn 14, pp 236–37.

contract and causes of action which have accrued from its breach alike continue unaffected. [Emphasis added.]

Thus in *Whincup v Hughes* (1871) the plaintiff, who had paid a premium to have his son apprenticed to a watchmaker for a term of six years, failed to recover the premium or any part of it when the watchmaker died during the second year of the apprenticeship. Bovill CJ said at p 82, that 'the person receiving the premium naturally assumes that it becomes his property to be dealt with as he pleases'. His Lordship said at p 81, that the 'general rule of law is, that where a contract has been in part performed no part of the money paid under such contract can be recovered back'.

[391] Whether or not a payment is the subject of a condition at the time a contract is discharged depends upon the express and implied terms of the contract. As a general rule, however, absent an indication to the contrary, a payment, made otherwise than to obtain the title to land or goods, should be regarded as having been made unconditionally, or no longer the subject of a condition, if the payee has performed work or services or incurred expense prior to the completion of the contract. If the payment has been made before the work has been performed or expense incurred, it should be regarded as becoming unconditional once work is performed or expense incurred. In that situation, the advance payment is ordinarily made in order to provide a fund from which the payee can meet the cost of performing the work or services or meeting the expenditure incurred or to be incurred before the completion of the contract. [McHugh J discussed *Hyundai Heavy Industries Co Ltd v Papadopoulos* (1980) (see extract, p 313) and continued:]

[392] In the present case, the termination of the cruise on the tenth day did not result in a total failure of consideration for the payment of the fare. If the fare had been payable at the end of the cruise, the consideration for the payment, for the purpose of the law of restitution, might possibly have been described as a 14 day cruise of the South Pacific. But the requirement that the fare be paid in advance makes it impossible, for the purpose of the law of restitution, to construe the consideration in that way.

The commercial purpose which is served by the advance payment of a fare for a cruise of the kind involved in this case is that it contributes to a fund which enables the shipowner to meet the cost of providing the benefits associated with the cruise without the necessity of using its working capital to meet the outgoings involved.[24] Much of that cost is incurred before the ship leaves port; almost all of the cost is incurred before the passenger finally disembarks. Furthermore, the passenger commences to enjoy the benefits of the cruise at or about the time of embarkation. The advance payment of such a fare cannot, therefore, be regarded as a security for the price of the services to be provided by the shipowner. Nor should it be regarded as a payment which is earned only upon completion of the cruise in accordance with the terms of the contract of carriage. Properly characterised, the advance payment of the fare is a reimbursement or prepayment of the cost of providing each of the benefits to be enjoyed by the passenger throughout the cruise.

The purpose of the advance payment would be negated if the shipowner's right to retain the fare was conditional upon an exact performance of its promise to carry

---

24 Cf *Scandinavian Trading Tanker Co AB v Flota Petrolera Ecuatoriana* (1983), pp 702–03.

the payee for the duration of the cruise. If that was the basis of the payment, the shipowner would be obliged to refund the fare if the contract was discharged by frustration even though the cruise was almost completed. The proper conclusion, therefore, is that once the passenger commences to enjoy the promised benefits, the right of the shipowner to retain the fare becomes unconditional. If the shipowner fails to fulfil its contractual promise after the passenger has commenced to enjoy the promised benefits, the passenger's remedy is an action for damages for breach of contract. The passenger cannot bring an action for restitution of the payment of the fare: once the passenger commences to receive the promised benefits, he or she receives consideration for the payment.

[393] Accordingly, once Baltic began to provide the promised benefits to Mrs Dillon, the right of that company to retain the fare became unconditional. The loss which she suffered, in paying for a cruise which was not completed, was recoverable in an action for breach of contract – not in an action for restitution ...

[Brennan and Toohey JJ relevantly agreed with Mason CJ.]

Commentary and questions

Why did the claim for recovery of the fare fail on these facts? According to the court, will a prepaid fare for transportation services always be irrecoverable? Does the receipt of a benefit under the contract always have the effect of preventing a total failure of consideration?

The High Court in the principal case defines failure of consideration as a failure of contractual performance. It has since been made clear however in the later decision of *Roxborough v Rothmans of Pall Mall Australia Ltd* (2001) that failure of consideration applies more broadly to other situations where the basis of the payment has failed due to a reason other than non-performance of contractual obligations. In that case, part of the contract price for tobacco products was referable to tobacco licence fees that the retailers paid to a wholesaler for the purpose that the wholesaler would pay over the fees to the New South Wales government in discharge of the parties' statutory obligation to pay those fees. The wholesaler did not pay the fees over to the Government due to a decision of the High Court that the tobacco licensing scheme was unconstitutional, and the retailers were entitled to recover the monies on the basis that the purpose for which they had been paid (payment over to the Government) was not fulfilled. Refer to Chapter 10 for extracts and further discussion of this case.

The reference in the judgment of Deane and Dawson JJ to Sir George Jessel's shoemaker is a reference to his well known example in *In re Hall & Barker* (1878): 'if a shoemaker agrees to make a pair of shoes, he cannot offer you one shoe, and ask you to pay one half the price.' The principle contained in this statement, namely that a party who fails to (substantially) perform an entire contractual obligation cannot recover the contract price, was reconfirmed by the High Court. Accordingly, there is a sharp distinction between an action to recover a prepaid contract price and an action to enforce an unpaid contract price: a customer who has prepaid the purchase price will be unable to recover it back if *any* part of the performance has been rendered, however will not be liable to pay an unpaid purchase price unless the service provider has at least substantially performed the contract. There is a need to reform both the entire contract doctrine and the total failure of consideration doctrine in order to remove this anomaly and to ensure justice between the parties.[25]

The analysis in the principal case of the basis of the total failure of consideration doctrine is disappointing. With the exception of Deane and Dawson JJ, the members of the court determine the question of recovery of the fare primarily from the point of view of contract construction rather than directly analysing the question from unjust enrichment principles.[26] Further, the case provided a potential vehicle for modifying the failure of consideration rule to one based upon restitution and counter-restitution, an approach which has gained increasing support in the case law and amongst commentators.[27] Despite the growing dissatisfaction with the traditional requirement of totality of failure, the court accepted its correctness without comment. The English courts have not been so reticent in reformulating the doctrine.[28]

The second issue in this case was whether a claimant could pursue both a claim for the recovery of money under a contract and a claim for damages for breach of that contract. See below, p 337 where this aspect of the decision is extracted.

Defects in title

There is a line of authorities establishing that the consideration for money paid to purchase goods or land is the transfer of legal title to the goods or land.[29] Accordingly, a purchaser who prepays part or all of the purchase price under a simple contract for the sale of goods or land will be entitled to recover the payment on a failure of consideration if the purchaser does not receive legal

---

25 The entire contract doctrine has traditionally been relied upon by courts to reject claims by parties in breach for the value of incomplete services, regardless of the value of those services.

26 Carter and Tolhurst, 'Restitution: payments made prior to discharge of contract' (1994) 7 JCL 273. For a discussion of the differences and comparative advantages between the construction approach and the restitutionary approach, see Beatson, *op cit*, fn 14, Chapter 3.

27 *David Securities Pty Ltd v Commonwealth Bank of Australia* (1992) p 383 (see extract, p 646); *Goss v Chilcott* (1996) (see extract, p 356); Birks, 'No consideration: restitution after void contracts' (1993) 23 UWAL Rev 196 (see extract, p 278); Carter, 'Discharged contracts: claims for restitution' (1997) 11(2) JCL 130. See also Edelman, 'The new doctrine of partial failure of consideration' (1997) 15 ABR 299. See further, pp 278–81.

28 See *Westdeutsche Landesbank Girozentrale v Council of the London Borough of Islington* (1996) (see extract, p 372) and *Goss v Chilcott* (1996) (see extract, p 356).

29 *AGC Corporation Ltd v Ross* (1983) (see extract, p 297); *Rowland v Divall* (1923) (see following extract); *Yeoman Credit Ltd v Apps* (1962) (see extract, p 296); *McDonald v Dennys Lascelles Ltd* (1933), pp 476–81 (see extract, p 308).

title. Interim possession of the goods, though possibly a valuable benefit, will not prevent consideration from totally failing.[30]

Rowland v Divall [1923] KB 500 English Court of Appeal

The plaintiff, a car dealer, bought a stolen motor car from the defendant and sold it on to a customer. The customer used it for several months after which the police took possession of the car. The plaintiff refunded the price of the car to the customer and then brought an action against the defendant to recover back the purchase price on the ground that the consideration had totally failed.

Bankes LJ: ... [503] [I]t cannot now be disputed that there was an implied condition on the part of the defendant that he had a right to sell the car, and unless something happened to change that condition into a warranty the plaintiff is entitled to rescind the contract and recover back the money. The Sale of Goods Act 1938 itself indicates in s 53 the circumstances in which a condition may be changed into a warranty: where the buyer elects, or is compelled, to treat any breach of a condition on the part of the seller as a breach of warranty: the buyer is not entitled to reject the goods, but his remedy is in damages. [Counsel for the defendant] contends that this is a case in which the buyer is compelled to treat the condition as a warranty within the meaning of that section, because, having had the use of the car for four months, he cannot put the seller *in statu quo* and therefore cannot now rescind, and he has referred to several authorities in support of that contention. But when those authorities are looked at I think it will be found that in all of them the buyer got some part of what he contracted for. In *Taylor v Hare* (1805) the question was as to the right of the plaintiff to recover back money which he had paid for the use of a patent which had turned out to be void. But there the court treated the parties, who had made a common mistake about the validity of the patent, as being in the nature of joint adventurers in the benefit of the patent; and Chambre J expressly pointed out that: 'The plaintiff has had the enjoyment of what he stipulated for.' The [504] language there used by Heath J, though it may have been correct as applied to the facts of that case, is much too wide to be applied to such a case as the present. In *Hunt v Silk* (1804) Lord Ellenborough went upon the ground that the plaintiff had received part of what he bargained for. He said: 'Where a contract is to be rescinded at all, it must be rescinded *in toto*, and the parties put *in statu quo*. But here was an intermediate occupation, a part execution of the agreement, which was incapable of being rescinded.' And *Lawes v Purser* (1856) proceeded on the same ground, that the defendant had derived benefit from the execution of the contract. But in the present case it cannot possibly be said that the plaintiff received any portion of what he had agreed to buy. It is true that a motor car was delivered to him, but the person who sold it to him had no right to sell it, and therefore he did not get what he paid for – namely, a car to which he would have title; and under those circumstances the use of the car by the purchaser seems to me quite immaterial for the purpose of considering whether the condition had been converted into a warranty ...

Scrutton LJ: ... No doubt the general rule is that a buyer cannot rescind a contract of sale and get back the purchase money unless he can restore the subject matter.

There are a large number of cases on the subject, some of which are not very easy to reconcile with others. Some of them make it highly probable that a certain degree of deterioration of the goods is not sufficient to take away the right to recover the purchase money. However I do not think it necessary to refer to them. It certainly seems to me that, in a case of rescission for the breach of the condition that the seller had a right to sell the goods, it cannot be that the buyer is deprived of this right to get back the purchase money because he cannot restore the goods which, from the nature of the transaction, are not the goods of the seller at all, and which the seller therefore has no right to under any circumstances. For these reasons I think that the plaintiff is entitled to recover the whole of the purchase money as for a total failure of consideration, and that the appeal must be allowed.

Atkin LJ: [506] I agree. It seems to me that in this case there has been a total failure of consideration, that is to say that the buyer has not got any part of that for which he paid the purchase money. He paid the money in order that he might get the property, and he has not got it. It is true that the seller delivered to him the *de facto* possession, but the seller had not got the right to possession and consequently could not give it to the buyer. Therefore the buyer, during the time that he had the car in his actual possession had no right to it, and was at all times liable to the true owner for its conversion ... Under those circumstances can it make any difference that the buyer has used the car before he found out that there was a breach of the condition? To my mind it makes no difference at all. The buyer accepted the car on the representation of the seller that he had a right to sell it, and inasmuch as the seller had no such right he is not entitled to say that the buyer has enjoyed a benefit under the contract. In fact the buyer has not received any part of that which he contracted to receive – namely, the property and right to possession – and, that being so, there has been a total failure of consideration. The plaintiff is entitled to recover the £334 which he paid.

Commentary

Although the transaction may have been void as title could not pass to the plaintiff (on the basis of the rule of personal property *nemo dat quod non habet*), the case was not decided on that basis, but as a claim for breach of an implied condition on the part of the seller that the seller possessed the right to sell the goods: see *Kwei Tek Chao v British Traders and Shippers Ltd* (1954).

The reasoning in *Rowland v Divall* has been applied in a number of English[31] and Australian[32] cases dealing with defects in title to chattels.

Yeoman Credit Ltd v Apps [1962] 2 QB 508 English Court of Appeal

By a hire purchase agreement the plaintiff finance company hired a second hand car to the defendant, who had an option to purchase the car if he met all the instalments. The plaintiff had bought the car from a dealer, Goodbody. The car

---

31 *Warman v Southern Counties Car Finance Corporation Ltd* (1949); *Butterworth v Kingsway Motors* (1954); *Barber v NWS Bank plc* (1996).

32 *Margolin v ER Wright Pty Ltd* (1959); *Australian Guarantee Corporation Ltd v Ross* (1983) (see extract, p 297); *Shoard v Palmer and General Credits Ltd* (1989); *Bridge Wholesale Acceptance Corporation (Australia) Ltd v Hartland and Hyde Pty Ltd* (1995).

was delivered to the defendant, but due to a number of latent defects, the car was in an 'unusable, unroadworthy and unsafe' condition. The defendant complained to the plaintiff a number of times about the car's condition, but he kept the car and paid three instalments as they fell due. When he failed to pay subsequent instalments the plaintiff terminated the hire purchase agreement and retook possession of the car. The plaintiff commenced proceedings claiming arrears of instalments and the defendant counterclaimed for recovery of the three instalments paid under the agreement on the basis the consideration for the payments had totally failed.

Holroyd Pearce LJ: ... [520] I cannot ... agree with the judge that there was a total failure of consideration. The defendant was plainly entitled to reject the car, to accept the plaintiff's repudiation of the contract by their delivery of such a car, and to rescind the contract. Had he done so, there would have been a total failure [521] of consideration, and he would have recovered the sums paid. But, as the judge found, he made no serious effort to return the car. He kept it for five or six months, and approbated the contract by paying three instalments. He intended (to quote his evidence) 'to keep the car, and hoped Goodbody would pay half the cost'. He tried to find out from the plaintiffs what he could do to make Goodbody carry out the work. In those circumstances he was at that stage continuing with the agreement while protesting against the state of the car which was due to a breach of condition by the plaintiffs. This is not a case like *Rowland v Divall* (1923) where title was lacking, and the defendant never had lawful possession. Here the defendant had the possession of the car and its use, such as it was. In evidence he said: 'That month I got a copy of the agreement. I had had the car by that time. I had been able to drive it – very poor.' Admittedly, the use was of little (if any) value, but in my view that use, coupled with possession, and his continuance of the hiring agreement with the intention of keeping the car and getting Goodbody to pay half the repairs, debars the defendant from saying that there was a total failure of consideration ...

Commentary

The principal case is to be contrasted with *Tradebanc International Pty Ltd v Balsdon* (1996)[33] where Tamberlin J allowed a claim on the basis of a failure of consideration where a computer software programme 'was for all practical purposes substantially useless' for the purpose for which it was commissioned.

Australian Guarantee Corporation Ltd v Ross [1983] 2 VR 319
Full Court of the Supreme Court of Victoria

A second hand car dealer, Duhig Ford Pty Ltd, bought a stolen vehicle in good faith. The plaintiff (respondent) subsequently entered into a hire purchase agreement with the defendant finance company (AGC) for the purchase of the vehicle, and took possession of it. Seven months later the police seized the vehicle and the plaintiff purported to rescind the hire purchase agreement and sought repayment of the instalments paid under it. Duhig Ford later obtained good title to

---

33 See also *Rogers v Parish (Scarborough) Ltd* (1987); *Bernstein v Pamson Motors (Golders Green) Ltd* (1987).

the vehicle. At the time the vehicle was seized the plaintiff had not yet exercised her option to purchase it by tendering the balance due to the defendant (AGC).

Young CJ: ... The question whether there was a total failure of consideration depends upon the nature of the rights sought to be conferred upon the hirer by the hire purchase agreement. In *Warman v Southern Counties Car Finance Corporation Ltd* (1949), p 582 and pp 712–13, Finnemore J said:

> A hire purchase agreement is, in law, an agreement in two parts. It is an agreement to rent a particular chattel for a certain length of time. If during the period or at the end of the period the hirer does not wish to buy the chattel he is not bound to do so. On the other hand, the essential part of the agreement is that the hirer has the option of purchase, and it is common knowledge – and I suppose, common sense – that when people enter into a hire purchase agreement they enter into it not so much for the purpose of hiring, but for the purpose of purchasing, by a certain method, by what is, in effect, deferred payments, and that is done by this special kind of agreement known as a hire purchase agreement, the whole object of which is to acquire the option to purchase the chattel when certain payments have been made.

It is not, however, possible or correct to treat a hire purchase agreement as though it were two separate agreements. This is because the consideration payable by the hirer is in part payment for the hire and in part instalments of the purchase price. The question is what rights were conferred upon the hirer by the agreement. They can be summarised I think by saying that they were rights to possession of the vehicle for the duration of the agreement or until the prior exercise of the option to purchase. AGC was not obliged to have a right to sell the vehicle until the option to purchase was exercised[34] but the agreement provided in cl 10 that until the exercise of the option the hirer should only be a bailee of the vehicle. The hirer is however a special sort of bailee for part of every payment which he makes is an instalment of the purchase price. Thus if it should turn out that the owner in unable to give to the hirer an indefeasible right to possession, indefeasible, that is to say, at the suit of a third party, the hirer cannot have had what he bargained for and there has been a total failure of consideration.

In *Karflex Ltd v Poole* (1933), pp 265–66, Goddard J (as he then was) left open the question whether a hirer who had enjoyed the use of property the subject of a hire purchase agreement, could recover all moneys paid as upon a total failure of consideration where the 'owner' failed to make title or whether he was obliged to give some allowance for the use of the property hired.

In *Rowland v Divall* (1923), the plaintiff bought a motor car from the defendant and used it for several months before he discovered that the defendant had no title to it. The plaintiff was compelled to surrender it to the true owner. The Court of Appeal held that the plaintiff could recover all that he had paid for the vehicle as upon a total failure of consideration. The court said that the plaintiff had not received any portion of what he had agreed to buy and thus there was a total failure of consideration notwithstanding that the plaintiff had had some use of the vehicle.

---

34   Hire Purchase Act 1959, ss 5(1)(b) and 11.

[324] Similarly in the present case I do not think that the plaintiff received any part of what she had agreed to take on hire purchase. The instalments she paid were part of the purchase price and when the vehicle was seized by the police and taken from her she was entitled to rescind the agreement and to recover all that she had paid. Finnemore J in *Warman's* case, from which I have already quoted, held that where a finance company had a defective title the hirer was entitled to recover the whole of the instalments paid as upon a total failure of consideration. It is true that that was a case of the owner's being unable to transfer title and it might be said that in the present case the time for transferring property in the vehicle had not arrived, but I think that the rights which the present plaintiff lost when the vehicle was seized by the police were just as fundamental to the hire purchase agreement as the loss suffered by the hirers in *Rowland v Divall* and *Warman's* case. I think that the decision in *Yeoman Credit Ltd v Apps* (1962), is clearly distinguishable. In that case the vehicle in question was found not to be fit for the purpose for which it was hired and that there had accordingly been a breach of an implied condition of the agreement giving the hirer a right to repudiate it. It was further held, however, that there had not been a total failure of consideration because the hirer had not rescinded the agreement. Instead he had retained the vehicle for several months and approbated the agreement by paying three instalments. See also *Richards v Alliance Co Ltd* (1976), p 100, where Hutley JA the dissenting member of the court, expressed his concurrence with the judgment of Finnemore J in *Warman's* case and added the pertinent comment from *Paton on Bailment in the Common Law*:[35] 'Why should the hire purchaser be forced to pay rent to the vendor for the use of a car belonging to a third party?'

I agree with Finnemore J that the real object of a hire purchase agreement is usually purchase and not hire and as AGC was unable to give the hirer the right to possession against the true owner for the whole of the period of the agreement, there was a total failure of consideration. It is nothing to the point that the occasion had not arisen for the transfer of the property when under s 5(1)(*b*) [of the Hire Purchase Act 1959 (Vic)] AGC would have been obliged to have a right to sell. It was essential to the agreement that the plaintiff have the right to exclude all comers from possession for the whole of the term of the agreement. The fact that she did not obtain such a right even at the outset means that there was more than a mere breach of the warranty of quiet possession implied by s 5(1)(*a*): there was in my opinion a total failure of consideration ...

Marks J: ... [332] [Counsel for AGC] submitted that the respondent was not entitled to rescind because she in fact had use of the Ford until its seizure by the police ... The question therefore is whether the use amounted to consideration under the agreement sounding against total failure ...

In my view, the agreement which is the subject of the present appeal may not involve title as such but it does ... include conditions for the transfer of possessory rights and an option to purchase which might be regarded as analogous to the ownership rights considered by the Court of Appeal in *Rowland v Divall*. This was the view also taken by Finnemore J in *Warman v Southern Counties Car Finance Corporation* (1949). That case also concerned a hire purchase agreement in respect of a motor vehicle to which the finance company had defective title ... Finnemore J

---

35 Page 323.

did not refer to *Rowland v Divall* but treated the problem as one he then had to decide for himself. He held that [333] notwithstanding the car having been used there had been a total failure of consideration. He said (1949), p 582 and pp 714–14:

> A hire purchase agreement is, in law, an agreement in two parts. It is an agreement to rent a particular chattel for a certain length of time. If during the period or at the end of the period the hirer does not wish to buy the chattel he is not bound to do so. On the other hand, the essential part of the agreement is that the hirer has the option of purchase, and ... the whole object ... is to acquire the option to purchase the chattel when certain payments have been made ... If he wanted to make an agreement merely to hire a car he would make it, but he enters into a hire purchase agreement because he wants to have the right to purchase the car; that is the whole basis of the agreement, the very foundation of it ...

In *Yeoman Credit Ltd v Apps* (1962), p 521; (1961), p 290, Holroyd Pearce LJ distinguished *Warman's* case from *Rowland v Divall* but observed: 'The defendant was plainly entitled to reject the car, to accept the plaintiff's repudiation of the contract by their delivery of such a car, and to rescind the contract. Had he done so, there would have been a total failure of consideration ...'

His Lordship found the distinguishing feature in the plaintiff having approbated the contract by paying instalments and retaining the use of the vehicle after knowledge of its defects. In *Richards v Alliance Acceptance* (1976), on which heavy reliance was placed by [counsel for AGC], Hutley JA expressed the opinion that the judgment of Finnemore J in *Warman's* case was correct and observed that no submission to the contrary had been put to the court. The other members of the Court of Appeal made no reference to *Warman's* case, their decision making its consideration irrelevant.

I agree in the reasoning to which I have referred. It leads to the conclusion that the mere use by the respondent of the Ford over the period before seizure does not alter the circumstance that there has been a total failure of consideration ...

Commentary and questions

On what basis did the court distinguish *Yeoman Credit Ltd v Apps* (1962) (see preceding extract)?

The principal case was followed in *Shoard v Palmer and General Credits Ltd* (1989).[36] It is clear, however, that where the finance company does have good title to the car, but subsequently repossesses the car for non-payment of hire instalments, the intermediate use of the car will prevent the consideration from failing totally.[37]

Hunt v Silk (1804) 5 East 449; 102 ER 1142 King's Bench

The defendant agreed to lease premises to the plaintiff, and agreed also to repair the premises and execute the lease within 10 days of the date of the lease agreement. The lease agreement further provided that the plaintiff would pay £10

---

36 See also *Barber v NWS Bank plc* (1996).
37 *Brooks v Bernstein* (1909); *Chatterton v Maclean* (1951); *Hyundai Heavy Industries v Papadopoulos* (1980), pp 1135–36, 1142, 1149 (see extract, p 313).

on the execution of the lease. The plaintiff took immediate possession of the premises and paid the £10, but the defendant failed to effect the repairs or execute the lease in the 10 day period. The plaintiff remained in possession of the premises for some days after the 10 day deadline elapsed but, when the defendant still failed to fulfil his obligations, left the premises and sought the return of the £10.

Lord Ellenborough CJ: [452] Without questioning the authority of the case cited [*Giles v Edwards* (1797)], which I admit to have been properly decided, there is this difference between that and the present; that there by the terms of the agreement the money was to be paid antecedent to the cording and delivery of the wood, and here it was not to be paid till the repairs were done and the lease executed. The plaintiff there had no opportunity by the terms of the contract of making his stand to see whether the agreement was performed by the other party before he paid his money, which the plaintiff in this case had: but instead of making his stand, as he might have done, on the defendant's non-performance of what he had undertaken to do, he waved his right, and voluntarily paid the money; giving the defendant credit for his future performance of the contract; and afterwards continued in possession notwithstanding the defendant's default. Now where a contract is to be rescinded at all, it must be rescinded *in toto*, and the parties put *in statu quo*. But here was an intermediate occupation, a part execution of the agreement, which was incapable of being rescinded. If the plaintiff might occupy the premises two days beyond the time when the repairs were to have been done and the lease executed, and yet rescind the contract, why might he not rescind it after a twelvemonth on the same account. This objection cannot be got rid of: the parties cannot be put *in statu quo*.

Lawrence J: In the case referred to [*Giles v Edwards*], where the contract was rescinded, both parties were put in the same situation they were in before. For the defendant must [453] at any rate have corded his wood before it was sold. But that cannot be done here where the plaintiff has had an intermediate occupation of the premises under the agreement. If indeed the £10 had been paid specifically for the repairs, and they had not been done within the time specified, on which the plaintiff had thrown up the premises, there might have been some ground for the plaintiff's argument that the consideration had wholly failed: but the money was paid generally on the agreement, and the plaintiff continued in possession after the 10 days, which can only be referred to the agreement.

Le Blanc J: The plaintiff voluntarily consented to go on upon the contract after the defendant had made the default of which he now wishes to avail himself in destruction of the contract. But the parties cannot be put in the same situation they were in, because the plaintiff has had an occupation of the premises under the agreement.

Commentary and question

It was decided in this case that advance rental payments are not recoverable upon a failure by the landlord to grant a legal leasehold interest in property where the tenant has had interim possession for even a short period of time.[38]

---

38 Although advance rental will be recoverable, despite a period of possession, where the rental is severable on a periodic basis: *Ocelota Ltd v Water Administration Ministerial Corporation* (2000), p 527.

On the other hand, where the parties have entered into a contract for the *sale* of land, temporary possession of the property will not prevent the consideration from failing: *McDonald v Dennys Lascelles Ltd* (1993) (see extract, p 308). This is because in the case of a sale of land contract the consideration for which the purchase price is paid is the transfer of legal title, not *de facto* possession. Do you agree that the lease of land situation can be meaningfully distinguished from a sale of land?

Damages ceiling?

The question has arisen whether the innocent party can recover moneys paid on the basis of a total failure of consideration where to do so would enable that party to avoid the consequences of having entered into a bad bargain. *Bush v Canfield* (1818) provides a good illustration of the issue. In that case the defendant agreed to deliver flour to the plaintiff for $14,000, the plaintiff prepaying $5,000. The market price fell to $11,000, though the defendant failed to deliver the flour. The plaintiff terminated and sued to recover the $5,000 prepayment. The claim was successful, despite the fact that the plaintiff's expectation damages amounted to only $2,000 (due to the fact the plaintiff suffered an expectation loss of $3,000 on the transaction).

There is widespread agreement amongst the commentators that *Bush v Canfield* is correct. These commentators argue that money is an incontrovertible benefit and as such is not liable to subjective devaluation by reference to the terms of the contract.[39] Mason and Carter[40] also agree that the full amount of the prepayment is recoverable, arguing that to allow less than full recovery would confer a windfall on the breaching party.

RECOVERY OF MONEY: PARTY IN BREACH

Introduction

A party in breach who has made a part payment (which is not a deposit) under a discharged contract will be able to recover the payments where there has been a total failure of consideration. The fact that it is the plaintiff's breach which has caused the consideration to fail should not be relevant: the concept of total failure of consideration is independent of fault.[41]

---

39 See McInnes, 'Contractual services, restitution and the avoidance of bad bargains' (1995) 23(3) ABLR 218, pp 221–22; Birks, 'In defence of free acceptance', in Burrows (ed), *Essays on the Law of Restitution*, 1991, pp 135–37; see also Burrows, *The Law of Restitution*, 1993, pp 265–66. See also pp 282–83.

40 Mason and Carter, *Restitution Law in Australia*, 1995, pp 562–63.

41 *Shaw v Ball* (1963) (see extract, p 310); *Baltic Shipping Co Ltd v Dillon* (1993), p 390 (see extract, p 286); Mason and Carter, *ibid*, pp 394–95; Birks, 'Restitution after ineffective contracts: issues for the 1990s' (1990) 2 JCL 227.

Deposits

As the following case demonstrates, a deposit is a guarantee of performance and will be irrecoverable even though the consideration for the payment has totally failed.

Howe v Smith (1884) 27 Ch D 89 English Court of Appeal

The plaintiff purchaser paid £500 under a contract for the sale of land. This sum was expressed in the contract to be 'a deposit, and in part payment of the purchase money'. The total purchase price was £12,500. The purchaser defaulted in paying the balance of the purchase price and the defendant vendor eventually resold the property. The purchaser brought an action for specific performance but this was refused by the court. The purchaser was given leave to bring a claim for the return of the £500.

Cotton LJ: ... [92] Now the claim for this return of the deposit of £500 is essentially a claim at common law, and one which has not arisen in equity except in bankruptcy cases, and that accounts for the little authority there is on the point. The first thing one must look at is the contract. The contract contains no clause at all as to what is to be done with the deposit if the contract is not performed ...

[94] In *Palmer v Temple* (1839), undoubtedly, the judges did say that independently of contract the vendor cannot on the default of the purchaser retain the deposit, and there are similar expressions in other cases. There is a similar expression of opinion in *Hinton v Sparkes* (1868), and I think similar expressions of opinion in other cases at common law. But that, as I understand the expression used by Lord St Leonards, in his book on vendors and purchasers, is not in accordance with his view; for he says there,[42] 'Where a purchaser is in default and the seller has not parted with the subject of the contract, it is clear that the purchaser could not recover the deposit; for he cannot, by his own default, acquire a right to rescind the contract'. Then he goes on and states his opinion that the mere resale of the estate after the purchaser's default cannot in any way affect the right of the vendor to retain the deposit.

Then we have a case of *Collins v Stimson* (1883) in which Baron Pollock refused to order the return of the deposit under circumstances somewhat different from this. What he says is this: 'According to the law of the vendor and purchaser the inference is that such a deposit is paid as a guarantee for the performance of the contract, and where the contract goes off by default of the purchaser, the vendor is entitled to retain the deposit.' That was the principle of his decision.

But the case does not quite stop there. There is a decision under somewhat different circumstances from the present case in *Depree v Bedborough* (1863), where there was a purchase under a sale by decree of the court. I will not refer further to that case, but it is in accordance with a subsequent decision of the Court of Appeal in *ex p Barrell* (1875), where the purchaser had become bankrupt, and the trustee in bankruptcy had disclaimed the contract under which he sought to recover the deposit. That was [95] refused. What Lord Justice James says is this (1875), p 514, 'The trustee in this case has no legal or equitable right to recover the deposit. The money was paid to the vendor as a guarantee that the contract should be

---

42   14th edn, p 40.

performed. The trustee refuses to perform the contract, and then says, Give me back the deposit. There is no ground for such a claim'.

There is a variance, no doubt, in the expressions of opinion, if not in the decisions, with reference to the return of the deposit, but I think that the judgment of Lord Justice James gives us the principle on which we should deal with the case. What is the deposit? The deposit, as I understand it, and using the words of Lord Justice James, is a guarantee that the contract shall be performed. If the sale goes on, of course, not only in accordance with the words of the contract, but in accordance with the intention of the parties in making the contract, it goes in part payment of the purchase money for which it is deposited; but if on the default of the purchaser the contract goes off, that is to say, if he repudiates the contract, then, according to Lord Justice James, he can have no right to recover the deposit.

I do not say that in all cases where this court would refuse specific performance, the vendor ought to be entitled to retain the deposit. It may well be that there may be circumstances which would justify this court in declining, and which would require the court, according to its ordinary rules, to refuse to order specific performance, in which it could not be said that the purchaser had repudiated the contract, or that he had entirely put an end to it so as to enable the vendor to retain the deposit. In order to enable the vendor so to act, in my opinion there must be acts on the part of the purchaser which not only amount to delay sufficient to deprive him of the equitable remedy of specific performance, but which would make his conduct amount to a repudiation on his part of the contract. In those circumstances, in my opinion, the rule is correctly laid down in Lord Justice James's judgment (of course the case there was stronger than the one we have to deal with) where the representatives of the purchaser had neither in law nor in equity the right to the return of the deposit ...

Bowen LJ: ... [97] The question as to the right of the purchaser to the return of the deposit money must, in each case, be a question of the conditions of the contract. In principle it ought to be so, because of course persons may make exactly what bargain they please as to what is to be done with the money deposited. We have to look to the documents to see what bargain was made. If any authority were wanted to prove that in each case it is a question of construction (I do not think it is wanted) it would be found in *Palmer v Temple* (1839), the case to which Lord Justice Cotton has referred, and which – whatever may be the value of the case as an authority on the construction of the contract in that case, as to which I agree with everything that has fallen from Lord Justice Cotton – adopts the principle that in each case we must consider what was the bargain. There is this observation (p 520): 'The ground on which we rest this opinion is, that in the absence of any specific provision, the question, whether the deposit is forfeited, depends on the intent of the parties to be collected from the whole instrument.'

In the present case we have in the first place, turning to the language of the instrument, a description of the manner in which the money is staked or deposited. It is a deposit, and it is to be both a deposit and in the nature of part payment, and there is further a special clause in the contract at which we ought to look to see if any light is thrown by it on the language of the provision that the money is deposited as a deposit.

We may however pass by that special clause, for I think it does not really deprive the deposit in this case of the character which it would bear if there were no special clause – because, in my opinion, that clause merely fixes the amount which the vendor is to receive in the event of his insisting on his rights under the [98] special clause. We have therefore to consider what in ordinary parlance, and as used in an ordinary contract of sale, is the meaning which business persons would attach to the term 'deposit'. Without going at length into the history, or accepting all that has been said or will be said by the other members of the court on that point, it comes shortly to this, that a deposit, if nothing more is said about it, is, according to the ordinary interpretation of business men, a security for the completion of the purchase. But in what sense is it a security for the completion of the purchase? It is quite certain that the purchaser cannot insist on abandoning his contract and yet recover the deposit, because that would be to enable him to take advantage of his own wrong. [Counsel for the purchaser] said the rule is different when the purchaser does not insist on abandoning his contract, but, on the contrary, is desirous, at the moment he appears before the court , of completing it, and therefore neither the principle nor the decisions apply – that this is not a case where the purchaser is receding from the contract, but on the contrary he is seeking to enforce it. It seems to me the answer to that argument is that although in terms in a case like the present the purchaser may appear to be insisting on his contract, in reality he has so conducted himself under it as to have refused, and has given the other side the right to say that he has refused, performance. He may look as if he wished to perform, but in reality he has put it out of his power to do so – he has, in the language of the Roman law, receded from his contract ...

[99] [I] think it is impossible, viewing the case from first to last, to doubt that [the purchaser] has so dealt with his bargain as to give the vendor a right to allege, if he chooses to say, that the contract is at an end, that the purchaser has receded from the bargain, and that the deposit money is liable to be retained by the vendor. Therefore the appeal fails.

Fry LJ: ... [102] [I] think we may conclude that the deposit in the present case is the earnest or *arrha* of our earlier writers; that the expression used in the present contract that the money is paid 'as a deposit and in part payment of the purchase money', relates to the two alternatives, and declares that in the event of the purchaser making default the money is to be forfeited, and that in the event of the purchase being completed the sum is to be taken in part payment.

[103] Such being my view of the nature of the deposit, it appears to me to be clear that the purchaser has lost all right to recover it if he has lost both his right to specific performance in equity and his right to sue for damages for its non-performance at law ...

Commentary

A sum of money paid under a sale of land contract that is nominated as a deposit might nevertheless be recoverable in equity in its jurisdiction to provide relief against forfeiture. A deposit will be recoverable under this equitable jurisdiction where it is penal in nature rather than a genuine pre-estimation of loss.[43] In most jurisdictions a deposit of 10% is customarily considered a

---

43 *Ward v Ellerton* (1927); *Smyth v Jessup* (1956), pp 232, 234; *Coates v Sarich* (1964), pp 15–16; *Tropical Traders Ltd v R&H Goonan (No 2)* (1965), p 176; *Yardley v Saunders* (1982), pp 236–37; *Delbridge v Low* (1990), p 331; *Workers Trust & Merchant Bank Ltd v Dojap Investments Ltd* (1993). It might also be necessary to show that it would be unconscionable for the defendant to retain the deposit: *Stockloser v Johnson* (1954), p 493 (see extract, p 318).

reasonable deposit,[44] so that a deposit significantly in excess of this amount runs the risk of being viewed as penal. The courts will determine whether a deposit exceeding 10% is penal by taking into account factors such as the proportion of the deposit to the contract price, the nature of the property, and the financial risk to the vendor on the transaction.[45]

If a deposit is ruled to be penal, it is the whole of the deposit that will be returned to the purchaser, not just the amount by which the deposit exceeds a reasonable amount: see *Workers Trust & Merchant Bank Ltd v Dojap Investments Ltd* (1993), p 582.

The equitable forfeiture rules have not yet been applied in Australia outside of the sale of land context, though there are *dicta* in the English case of *Stockloser v Johnson* (1954), pp 490–92 (see extract, p 318) that the forfeiture rules do extend to deposits paid under other sale contracts.

Part payments

A party in breach will be entitled to recover part payments for which there has been a total failure of consideration, provided the parties have not expressly agreed that the part payments should be forfeited.[46] The claim is not defeated by virtue of the fact that it was the plaintiff's non-performance that caused the consideration to fail.[47]

Rover International Ltd v Cannon Film Sales Ltd [1989] 1 WLR 912
English Court of Appeal

The Proper appeal

Proper Film Ltd entered into a licensing agreement with Thorn EMI for the exhibition of films on Italian television. Delivery of the films by Thorn EMI was to be not earlier than two years from the date of the first cinema release in Italy. The agreed licence fee was $1,800,000 which was to be paid in three instalments of $360,000, $540,000 and $900,000 respectively. Proper duly paid the first two instalments totalling $900,000. Cannon subsequently took over Thorn EMI. Relations between Proper and Cannon deteriorated and Proper considered that Cannon had evinced an intention not to be bound by the agreement and so joined

---

44 *Workers Trust & Merchant Bank Ltd v Dojap Investments Ltd* (1993); *Lexane Pty Ltd v Highfern Pty Ltd* (1985), p 455; *Freedom v AHR Constructions Pty Ltd* (1987), p 66; *Delbridge v Low* (1990), p 330.

45 For example, a larger deposit will be tolerated under a long term contract under which the purchaser is let into possession of the property, exposing the vendor to the risk of the property depreciating: *Re Hoobin, deceased* (1957). Thus, in *Coates v Sarich* (1964) relief against forfeiture of a 27% deposit was refused where the contract was for the sale of a farm and the purchaser was to be let into possession over a term of 15–16 years.

46 See below pp 317–20.

47 *Shaw v Ball* (1963) (see extract, p 310); *Baltic Shipping Co Ltd v Dillon* (1993), p 390 (see extract, p 286).

the Rover court action.[48] Proper treated the contract as still binding. While the court proceedings were pending the third instalment of $900,000 became due. When this was not paid by Proper, Cannon terminated the contract for the default of Proper in paying the instalment and counterclaimed against Proper for the payment of the instalment. The court approached the question on the basis that Cannon was not entitled to the instalment if, had it been paid, it would immediately have been recoverable by Proper as money paid for a consideration which has wholly failed.

Kerr LJ: ... [930] The relevant principles were stated by Dixon J in the High Court of Australia in *McDonald v Dennys Lascelles Ltd* (1933), pp 476–78. [Kerr LJ quoted from *McDonald v Dennys Lascelles Ltd* (1933) (for the relevant part of Dixon J's judgment, see extract, p 291) and continued:] [932] The issue in the present case, as I see it, is accordingly whether it falls on the side of cases such as *Dies v British and International Mining and Finance Corporation Ltd* (1939), or whether the terms of the contract and the facts lead to the conclusion that it is to be assimilated to the situation in *Hyundai Heavy Industries Co Ltd v Papadopoulos* (1980). Had Thorn EMI/Cannon provided any consideration under the contract for which the instalment of $900,000 was payable, or was this instalment payable merely as an advance for the obligations which Thorn EMI/Cannon had agreed to perform thereafter? When referring to the provision of consideration in this context, in the same way as in the context of a failure of consideration discussed earlier in the *Rover* appeal, one is not referring to the original promise to perform the contract. The question is whether there was any consideration in the nature of part performance for which the instalment was payable, as in the *Hyundai Heavy Industries Co Ltd v Papadopoulos* (1980), or whether the instalment was payable in advance of any performance which was required from Thorn EMI/Cannon.

In my view the present case falls clearly into the latter category and is indistinguishable in principle from the situations examined by Dixon J in *McDonald v Dennys Lascelles Ltd* (1933), and the decision in *Dies v British and International Mining and Finance Corporation Ltd*. It is true that *Dies* appears to have been a contract for the sale of unascertained goods whereas the present contract deals with specific films in relation to which Thorn EMI/Cannon had to possess or to acquire the necessary rights. It is also true that they were precluded from transferring these rights to anyone other than Proper. But that is not a situation whereby Thorn EMI/Cannon provided anything in the nature of part performance under the contract. It merely meant that they had to arrange matters so as to enable them to perform their contractual obligations at the time when these would become due. Thus, it is clear from *Palmer v Temple* (1839), and the judgment of Dixon J in *McDonald v Dennys Lascelles Ltd* (1933), that the principle that advance payments made on account of the price are recoverable applies even where the contract relates to a specific piece of land which the vendor must either acquire or retain in order to perform the contract. The fact that he is bound to the contract in that way does not alter the character of the payment being in the nature of an advance for a consideration to be provided in the future.

In the present case it is entirely clear, in my view, that this instalment was payable in advance of any consideration for the payment which fell to be provided from

---

48   For extracts of the *Rover* appeal, see p 369.

the side of Thorn EMI/Cannon. Indeed, when Proper declined to pay it, it was rightly pointed out on behalf of Cannon that nothing in the way of performance was as yet due from their side. This instalment would accordingly have been recoverable by Proper if it had been paid, and it is therefore irrecoverable by Cannon for the same reason. The only claim open to them would have been a claim for damages if they had shown that they had suffered any as the result of the termination of the contract ...

Question

Proper did not claim repayment of the $900,000 paid under the first and second instalments. On the basis of the reasoning of the Court of Appeal would those first two instalments have been recoverable if they had been claimed?

Contracts of sale

Where the contract is a simple contract of sale, the consideration for the purchase price will fail where legal title to the property is not transferred to the purchaser, even though it was the plaintiff's fault that the contract fell through. Thus, in *Dies v British and International Mining and Finance Corporation* (1939) the plaintiff was able to recover a prepayment of £100,000 on a contract to purchase rifles which the defendant terminated when the plaintiff refused to accept delivery of the rifles.[49] As the following case illustrates, the same principle applies to contracts for the sale of land.

McDonald v Dennys Lascelles Ltd (1933) 48 CLR 457 High Court of Australia

The registered proprietors of land entered into a contract to sell the land. The purchasers under the contract resold the land to a company (the 'sub-purchaser'); the purchase price being payable in instalments. The purchasers assigned to the respondent its interest in the contract of sale. The sub-purchaser was unable to meet an instalment which fell due under the contract of resale and the respondent agreed to postpone the date for payment of the instalment for a year on the condition that the appellants, who were directors of the sub-purchaser, guaranteed the payment of the instalment. At the expiry of the one year period, the sub-purchaser was still in default and the respondent and the sub-purchaser treated the contract as having come to an end. The respondent sued the appellants on the guarantee to recover the amount of the instalment. The liability of the appellants on the guarantee was dependent on whether the liability of the sub-purchaser to meet the instalment was extinguished when the contract was discharged.

Dixon J: ... [476] When a party to a simple contract, upon a breach by the other contracting party of a condition of the contract, elects to treat the contract as no longer binding upon him, the contract is not rescinded as from the beginning. Both parties [477] are discharged from the further performance of the contract, but rights are not divested or discharged which have already been unconditionally acquired. Rights and obligations which arise from the partial execution of the

---

49 Although Stable J doubted that a claim based on failure of consideration would be available to a party in breach, it has since been confirmed that it is so available, and that failure of consideration is the best explanation for the *Dies* case: *Baltic Shipping Co Ltd v Dillon* (1993), p 390 (see extract, p 286).

contract and causes of action which have accrued from its breach alike continue unaffected. When a contract is rescinded because of matters which affect its formation, as in the case of fraud, the parties are to be rehabilitated and restored, so far as may be, to the position they occupied before the contract was made. But when a contract, which is not void or voidable at law, or liable to be set aside in equity, is dissolved at the election of one party because the other has not observed an essential condition or has committed a breach going to its root, the contract is determined so far as it is executory only and the party in default is liable for damages for its breach.[50] It does not, however, necessarily follow from these principles that when, under an executory contract for the sale of property, the price or part of it is paid or payable in advance, the seller may both retain what he has received, or recover overdue instalments, and at the same time treat himself as relieved from the obligation of transferring the property to the buyer. When a contract stipulates for payment of part of the purchase money in advance, the purchaser relying only on the vendor's promise to give him a conveyance, the vendor is entitled to enforce payment before the time has arrived for conveying the land; yet his title to retain the money has been considered not to be absolute but conditional upon the subsequent completion of the contract. 'The very idea of payment falls to the ground when both have treated the bargain as at an end; and from that moment the vendor holds the money advanced to the use of the purchaser', see *Palmer v Temple* (1839). In *Laird v Pim* (1841), Parke B says, 'It is clear he cannot [478] have the land and its value too'; the case, however, was one in which conveyance and payment were contemporaneous conditions, see *Laird v Pim* (1841). It is now beyond question that instalments already paid may be recovered by a defaulting purchaser when the vendor elects to discharge the contract, see *Mayson v Clouet* (1924). Although the parties might by express agreement give the vendor an absolute right at law to retain the instalments in the event of the contract going off, yet in equity such a contract is considered to involve a forfeiture from which the purchaser is entitled to be relieved.[51] The view adopted in *In re Dagenham (Thames) Dock Co ex p Hulse* (1973) seems to have been that relief should be granted, not against the forfeiture of the instalments, but against the forfeiture of the estate under a contract which involved the retention of the purchase money ... [W]here there is no express agreement excluding the implication made at law, by which the instalments become repayable upon the discharge of the obligation to convey and the purchaser has a legal right to the return of the purchase money already paid which makes it needless to resort to equity and submit to equity as a condition of obtaining relief, the [471] vendor appears to be unable to deduct from the amount of the instalments the amount of his loss occasioned by the purchaser's abandonment of the contract. A vendor may, of course, counter-claim for damages in the action in which the purchaser seeks to recover the instalments ...

---

50 See *Boston Deep Sea Fishing and Ice Co v Ansell* (1888), p 365 *per* Bowen LJ; *Hirji Mulji v Cheong Yue Steamship Co* (1926), p 503 *per* Lord Sumner; *Cornwall v Henson* (1899); Salmond and Winfield, *Law of Contracts*, 1927, pp 284–89; Morison, *Principles of Rescission of Contracts*, 1916, pp 179, 180.

51 See the judgment of Long Innes J in *Pitt v Curotta* (1931), pp 480–82.

Commentary

The essence of this decision is that the sub-purchaser was not liable to pay the instalment for, if it had been paid, it would have been able to be recovered by the sub-purchaser on the basis that the consideration for the payment totally failed. This was so even though the sub-purchaser had been let into possession, a fact which was not adverted to in the judgments.[52] On the basis of this decision, the benefit bargained for in the case of a simple contract for the sale of land is the transfer of title, not temporary possession.[53] The position is different where the agreement is for the *lease* of property, in which case the temporary possession of the property would appear to constitute receipt of part of the agreed benefit,[54] or, as the following case indicates, where the contract is for the sale of a *business*.

Shaw v Ball (1963) 63 SR (NSW) 910 Full Court of the Supreme Court of New South Wales

The appellants agreed to sell to the respondent their motor garage business, including all goodwill, stock-in-trade, and plant and equipment. The appellants also agreed to transfer the unexpired portion of the lease to the respondent. The respondent entered into possession of the business and conducted it on his own behalf. About 16 months after the respondent took over the running of the business the appellants terminated the agreement for his default in paying instalments. The respondent sought recovery of the sums he had paid toward the purchase price on the ground, *inter alia*, that there had been a total failure of consideration. The respondent argued that the benefit bargained for was not mere possession, but rather the transfer of the legal title to the lease and all the assets of the business, and this had never been done.

Sugerman J: ... [914] In order that there should be a right to the recovery of moneys paid upon the ground that the consideration [915] for their payment has failed, it must appear that the failure of consideration was a total one. As to what is meant by a failure of consideration in the relevant sense – that is, failure in the performance of the promise given in return for the payment – and as to the necessity for its being total, it is sufficient to refer to *Fibrosa Spolka Akcyjna v Fairbairn Lawson Combe Barbour Ltd* (1943) and *The Julia* (1949). Although his Lordship's decision was ultimately reversed by the House of Lords, it is still useful in this connection to bear in mind the observation of Morris J, as he then was, in *The Julia* (1947) that: 'A claim so formulated prompts the two inquiries (a) for what consideration was the money paid, and (b) has such consideration wholly failed?' See *The Julia* (1947), p 120. Or, as applied to payments on account of the purchase money under a contract of sale, the question may be put as being whether the buyer has got any part of that for which he paid the purchase money.[55]

On behalf of the respondent, we have been referred to a number of decisions which are concerned with the recoverability of instalments of purchase money

---

52   *Shaw v Ball* (1963), p 916 (see following extract).

53   The same principle applies to contracts for the sale of goods: see above, pp 271–72; 294–302.

54   *Hunt v Silk* (1804) (see extract, p 300).

55   See *per* Atkin LJ, as he then was, in *Rowland v Divall* (1923), p 506, referred to by Lord McDermott in *The Julia* (1949), p 323.

paid pursuant to a contract for the sale of land where, the purchaser having made default under the contract, the seller rescinds and elects to treat it as at an end; see *Palmer v Temple* (1839), *Mayson v Clouet* (1924) and *McDonald v Dennys Lascelles Ltd* (1933), p 470 *per* Starke J; pp 477ff *per* Dixon J (as he then was). In the last mentioned case, Dixon J said:

> It does not, however, necessarily follow from these principles that when under an executory contract for the sale of property, the price or part of it is paid or payable in advance, the seller may both retain what he has received, or recover overdue instalments, and at the same time treat himself as relieved from the obligation of transferring the property to the buyer. When a contract stipulates for payment of part of the purchase money in advance, the purchaser relying only on the vendor's promise to give him a conveyance, the vendor is entitled to enforce payment before the time has arrived for conveying the land; yet his title to retain the money has been considered not to be absolute but conditional upon the subsequent completion of the contract (1933), p 477.

Then, after referring to *Palmer v Temple* (1839), and *Laird v Pim* (1841), his Honour said: 'It is now beyond question that instalments already paid may be recovered by a defaulting purchaser when the vendor elects to discharge the contract (*Mayson v Clouet* (1924))' (1933), p 478.

Dies v British & International Mining & Finance Corporation (1939) was relied upon for the application of the same principle to a prepayment on account of the price under a executory contract for the sale of goods. It is now possible to rely for this purpose upon the two decisions of the House of [916] Lords in the *Fibrosa* case (1943) and *The Julia* (1949), because since the overruling of *Chandler v Webster* (1904) by the first mentioned of these two cases the difference between frustration and rescission upon breach is not material in relevant respects – see *per* Lord Sumner in *Hirji Mulji v Cheong Yue Steamship Co* (1926), referred to by Lord Wright in the *Fibrosa* case (1943), p 65.

The present case, however, is not a case of an executory contract for the sale of land or of an executory contract for the sale of goods. It is a case of a contract for the sale of a business with all that carries with it, namely, the goodwill, the plant, the stock-in-trade and the lease of the premises in which the business is carried on. In directing attention to the answers to the questions which have been earlier stated, it is to be remembered that these several things were what the respondent was to receive in return for the moneys which he paid and promised to pay. Moreover, the respondent was to have and did have possession of the business forthwith. He enjoyed its goodwill. He carried on the trade and for that purpose was able to dispose of the stock as if it were his own. He was put in possession of the plant and was able to use it for the carrying on of the business for his own profit. Furthermore, in respect of all but the lease no further formality was necessary for the passing of property. For the passing of the property in the stock-in-trade and the movable plant of the business no more than a delivery of possession was required ... For the transfer of the goodwill no particular form was required; it passed as part of what was agreed to be sold under the contract for the sale of the business. All that remained was the assignment of the lease which the respondent refused to execute although more than once tendered to him for that purpose. But the conferment in this manner of a legal title to the leasehold was part only of the consideration in the relevant sense ...

In these circumstances it is, in my opinion, impossible to say that the moneys sought to be recovered in this action were moneys paid on a consideration which had totally failed – that the respondent had got no part of that for which he had paid these sums on account of purchase money – whatever view be taken on such of the facts of the case as were in dispute between the parties. The respondent received a part, and indeed a very substantial part, of that for which the consideration was paid. Our attention has been directed to several cases in which the purchaser, claiming recovery after rescission of instalments of purchase money paid, had under the contract of sale been let into possession in the meantime. Indeed, *McDonald v Dennys Lascelles Ltd* (1933) was itself a case of possession by the purchaser although the [917] circumstance is not adverted to in the judgments, possibly because the case turned upon another question and what was said as to the recovery of instalments paid by a defaulting purchaser was in strictness *obiter*. The result of the cases which I have referred to is perhaps not altogether conclusive, but I find it unnecessary to refer to them or to discuss them in the present context. For they were all cases of executory contracts for the sale of land, whereas the present was a case of a contract for the sale of a business. It may be that in an ordinary executory contract for the sale of land, or at any rate of a freehold, interim possession under the contract of sale is to be treated, at any rate in default of agreement on the point, as a merely incidental benefit or as something merely accessory or collateral, not forming part of the consideration for the payment of the moneys whose recovery is sought. I leave that question without any expression of opinion upon it. The position is, to my mind, otherwise where the contract is for the sale of a business – that is, of its goodwill, stock-in-trade, plant and leased premises ...

Commentary

Mcfarlan and Nagle JJ reached a similar conclusion. Mcfarlan J stated that:

> ... the result seems to me to be that the plaintiff, if he has not had the whole of that for which he has bargained he has at least had some and probably a substantial part. Whether what he has had be some or a substantial part, in my opinion the legal consequence is the same and he must fail in the action which he brought at law [(1963), p 925].

Contracts for work

Where the contract is a contract for the provision of work, rather than a simple contract of sale, the defendant provides consideration upon commencing performance of the work. Thus, in building contacts, payments will be irrecoverable on the basis of a failure of consideration once the defendant commences the building work, despite the fact that no part of the final product has been transferred to the plaintiff. This principle is well established by the two following House of Lords decisions: *Hyundai Heavy Industries Co Ltd v Papadopoulos* (1980) and *Stocznia Gdanska SA v Latvian Shipping Co* (1998) (see extract, p 315).[56]

---

56   See also *Clowes (Development) UK Ltd v Mulchinook* (2001). See further above, pp 271–72.

Hyundai Heavy Industries Co Ltd v Papadopoulos [1980] 1 WLR 1129 House of Lords

The respondents agreed to 'build, launch, equip and complete' a ship and 'deliver and sell' the ship to a buyer. The contract price was payable in instalments. The appellants guaranteed the payments of the buyer. The buyer defaulted in paying the second instalment and the respondents rescinded the contract and sued the appellants under the guarantee for the second instalment. No part of the ship was ever delivered to the buyer. A majority of the House of Lords held that the termination of the contract did not affect an accrued right to the payment of instalments of the purchase price, but there would be no liability to pay the instalment if the consideration for the payment had totally failed. Accordingly, the central issue became whether, had the instalment been paid, it would have been recoverable on the basis of a total failure of consideration.

Lord Fraser of Tullybelton: ... [1147] Counsel for the guarantors drew our attention to art 10(e) of the shipbuilding contract which is headed 'Refund' and which includes a provision that 'The payments made by the buyer to the builder prior to delivery of the vessel shall constitute *advances* to the builder' (my italics). That shows that such payments, which would of course have included the second instalment if it had been paid, are not earnests of ability to pay but advances of part of the price. But, said counsel, once the contract has been cancelled the price must cease to be payable; the purchaser can no longer be liable to pay the price for a vessel which the builder is no longer obliged to sell him, and which he said he has no intention of selling to him. The argument was supported by reference to a statement by Lord Denman CJ in *Palmer v Temple* (1839), where he said:

> But the very idea of payment falls to the ground when both [parties] have treated the bargain as at an end; and from that moment the vendor holds the money advanced to the use of the purchaser.

Palmer v Temple was a case where the plaintiff had contracted to purchase landed property and had paid a sum 'by way of deposit, and in part of £5,500', which was the purchase price, and had then failed to pay the balance of the price or to complete the contract. He was held to be entitled to recover his deposit, but the actual decision turned on the terms of the particular contract. In *Dies v British and International Mining and Finance Corporation Ltd* (1939), where a passage from Lord Denman's judgment in *Palmer v Temple* including the statement that I have quoted was relied on by Stable J (pp 740–42) the contract was again purely one of sale – in that case of rifles and ammunition. The vendor was a merchant or middle man who had intended to buy the goods from the manufacturer and to resell them to the purchaser at a profit. Stable J held that the purchaser who had paid a large sum as an advance of the purchase price, and who had then failed to complete payment or to take delivery of the goods, [1148] was entitled to recover his advance payment under deduction of an agreed sum of liquidated damages. Counsel for the guarantors in the instant case argued that if the buyer in the *Dies* case was entitled to recover an advance which had already been paid, then *a fortiori* the buyer in the instant case could not be liable to make an advance that was due but unpaid; if he did make it, said counsel, he would be entitled to immediate repayment of it.

I do not accept that argument. In my opinion the *Dies* case (1939) and *Palmer v Temple* (1839) are both distinguishable from the present case because in both these cases the contracts were simply contracts of sale which did not require the vendor to perform any work or incur any expense on the subjects of sale. But the contract in the instant case is not of that comparatively simple character. The obligations of the buyer were not confined to selling the vessel but included designing and building it and there were special provisions (art 2) that the contract price 'shall include payment for services in the inspection, tests, survey and classification of the vessel' and also 'all costs and expenses for designing and supplying all necessary drawings for the vessel in accordance with the specifications'. Accordingly the builder was obliged to carry out work and to incur expense, starting from the moment that the contract had been signed, including the wages of designers and workmen, fees for inspection and for cost of purchasing materials. It seems very likely that the increasing proportions of the contract price represented by the five instalments bore some relation to the anticipated rate of expenditure, but we have no information on which to make any nice comparison between the amount of expenses that the builder would have to bear from time to time, and the amounts of the instalments payable by the buyers. I do not think that such comparisons are necessary. It is enough that the builder was bound to incur considerable expense in carrying out his part of the contract long before the actual sale could take place. That no doubt is the explanation for the provision in art 10(b) of the shipbuilding contract that:

> ... all payments under the provisions of this article shall not be delayed or withheld by the buyer due to any dispute of whatever nature arising between the builder and the buyer hereto, unless the buyer shall have claimed to cancel the contract under the terms thereof ...

The importance evidently attached by the parties to maintaining the cash flow seems to support my view of the contract.

There was no evidence either way whether the builders had in fact carried out their obligations to start designing and building the vessel, but in my opinion we must assume, in the absence of evidence or even averment to the contrary, that they had carried out their part of the bargain up till the date of cancellation.

Much of the plausibility of the argument on behalf of the guarantors seemed to me to be derived from the assumption that the *contract* price was simply a *purchase* price. That is not so, and once that misconception has been removed I think it is clear that the shipbuilding contract has little similarity with a contract of sale and much more similarity, so far as the present issues are concerned, with contracts in which the party entitled to be paid had either performed work or [1149] provided services for which payment is due by the date of cancellation. In contracts of the latter class, which of course includes building and construction contracts, accrued rights to payment are not (in the absence of express provisions) destroyed by cancellation of the contract ...

[1150] In the instant case the buyer has not actually enjoyed any benefit from the work which the builder has performed, but it has been performed (or at least we must so assume, in the absence of evidence to the contrary) on the faith of the buyers' promise to pay the instalments on the due dates. The builder had acquired a vested right to the debt which was owed by the buyer at the date of cancellation and I see no reason for holding it to be cancelled ...

Commentary

McHugh J in *Baltic Shipping Co v Dillon* (1993) (see extract, p 286) relied on the principal case to support the view that an advance payment is usually made in order to provide a fund from which the payee can meet the cost of performing the services and reimburse expenses. Accordingly, an advance payment becomes unconditional once work is performed or expense incurred (p 391). Burrows is critical of this approach.[57] Burrows argues that in order to establish the provision of partial consideration it is necessary to show that the plaintiff received part of what was bargained for; detrimental reliance by the defendant is not sufficient. As no part of the ship was ever received by the buyer in the principal case the buyer could not be said to have been benefited by the partial performance of the contract and the consideration must have totally failed.

The correctness of the approach in the principal case has recently been affirmed by the House of Lords in the following case.

Stocznia Gdanska SA v Latvian Shipping Co [1998] 1 WLR 574 House of Lords

A shipbuilder brought a claim for payment of an instalment due under a shipbuilding contract discharged for non-payment of that instalment. The shipbuilding contract provided in art 2.01:

> The Seller shall design, build, complete and deliver the Vessel to the Purchaser after completion and satisfactory trials.

The contract was discharged prior to the purchaser receiving any part of the vessel. The court acted on the basis that the purchaser would not be required to pay the instalment if, had it been paid, the purchaser would have been able to recover it on the basis of a total failure of consideration.

Lord Goff of Chieveley ... [587] It was recognised by [Counsel] for the buyers that the second (keel-laying) instalments of the price payable in respect of vessels 1 and 2 accrued due under [the contract]. However he submitted that, after rescission of the contracts, an action by the yard for the recovery of the instalments must fail because, if paid, the instalments would immediately be recoverable by the buyers on the ground that they had been paid for a consideration which had wholly failed. It was [Counsel for the buyer's] submission that there would in such circumstances have been a total failure of consideration, because the buyers would have received nothing under the contract, no property in the vessel or any part of it having been transferred to them. The relevant question was: had the buyers received the benefit of any part of that which they had bargained for? The answer to that question must be in the negative, because any time or money spent by the yard in building the keels enured solely for the benefit of the yard, in whom the property remained. The situation was therefore different from that under an ordinary building contract, where the building as it is erected belongs to the building owner as the owner of the land on which it is being built.

---

57 Burrows, *The Law of Restitution*, 1993, p 256; see also Barker, 'Restitution of passenger fare' [1993] LMCLQ 291, p 293; cf Mason and Carter, *Restitution Law in Australia*, 1995, pp 406–07.

This submission was challenged by [counsel] for the yard, both on principle and authority. He relied in particular on the fact that, under the contracts in question, the yard was bound not merely to transfer the property in the vessels, when built, to the buyers. On the contrary it was bound to design, build, complete and deliver the vessels which were to be built in accordance with the agreed specification. The contracts were not therefore contracts of sale simpliciter, but 'contracts for work and materials', though they included an obligation to transfer the property in the finished product to the buyers. The contractual performance of the yard began with the translation of the agreed specification into a design which complied with its requirements, the next stage in the performance being the translation of the design into a completed vessel, subject of course to amendments to the design agreed by the parties in the course of construction. Only at a late moment would the title in the completed vessel pass to the buyers.

Before addressing the rival submissions of the parties, I pause to observe that these were both founded on the premise that the issue was [588] simply one of total failure of consideration. I am, of course, well aware of the continuing debate among scholars and law reformers as to the circumstances in which, and the basis on which, a party in breach of contract can recover a benefit conferred by him on the innocent party under the contract before it was terminated by reason of his breach, as to which see, for example, the admirable discussion by Professor Jack Beatson in *The Use and Abuse of Unjust Enrichment*, 1991, Chapter 3. However, I am content to approach this aspect of the case on the premise, common to both parties, that the issue is one of total failure of consideration since, as I understand it, this is consistent with the approach of the majority in *Hyundai Heavy Industries Co Ltd v Papadopoulos* (1980), which is directly in point on this aspect of the case.

I find myself to be in agreement with [counsel for the yard's] submission on this point. I start from the position that failure of consideration does not depend upon the question whether the promisee has or has not received anything under the contract like, for example, the property in the ships being built under contracts 1 and 2 in the present case. Indeed, if that were so, in cases in which the promisor undertakes to do work or render services which confer no direct benefit on the promisee, for example where he undertakes to paint the promisee's daughter's house, no consideration would ever be furnished for the promisee's payment. In truth, the test is not whether the promisee has received a specific benefit, but rather whether the promisor has performed any part of the contractual duties in respect of which the payment is due. The present case cannot, therefore, be approached by asking the simple question whether the property in the vessel or any part of it has passed to the buyers. That test would be apposite if the contract in question was a contract for the sale of goods (or indeed a contract for the sale of land) *simpliciter*, under which the consideration for the price would be the passing of the property in the goods (or land). However before that test can be regarded as appropriate, the anterior question has to be asked: is the contract in question simply a contract for the sale of a ship? Or is it rather a contract under which the design and construction of the vessel formed part of the yard's contractual duties, as well as the duty to transfer the finished object to the buyers? If it is the latter, the design and construction of the vessel form part of the consideration for which the price is to be paid, and the fact that the contract has been brought to an end before the property in the vessel or any part of it has passed to the buyers does not prevent the yard from asserting that there has been no total failure of consideration in respect of an instalment of the price which has been paid before the contract was terminated, or that an instalment which has then accrued due could not, if paid, be recoverable on that ground.

I am satisfied that the present case falls into the latter category. This was what the contracts provided in their terms. Moreover, consistently with those terms, payment of instalments of the price was geared to progress in the construction of the vessel. That this should be so is scarcely surprising in the case of a shipbuilding contract, under which the yard enters into major financial commitments at an early stage, in the placing of orders for machinery and materials, and in reserving and then occupying a berth for the construction of the vessel. Indeed if [counsel for buyer's] argument is right, it would follow that no consideration would have been furnished by the yard when instalments of the price fell due before the moment of delivery, notwithstanding all the heavy and irreversible financial commitments then undertaken by the yard.

[589] As authority for the construction of the contracts in question, [counsel for the yard] was able to invoke the decision of your Lordships' House in *Hyundai Heavy Industries Co Ltd v Papadopoulos* (1980), to which I have already referred, which was concerned with a shipbuilding contract in substantially the same form as that under consideration in the present case. [Lord Goff examined *Papadopoulos* and concluded that it directly governed the situation before him, and that he was not sufficiently persuaded to depart from it. Accordingly, the purchasers failed to establish that there had been a total failure of consideration for the instalment.]

[Lords Hoffman, Hope and Hutton agreed with Lord Goff.]

Commentary

The principal case and the previous case of *Hyundai Heavy Industries Co Ltd v Papadopoulos* (1980) illustrate that total failure of consideration is not only used as a ground of recovering money which has been paid, but also as a defence to a claim in contract for the recovery of an outstanding instalment.[58] The House of Lords recognise that there is no point in ordering payment of an outstanding sum if the defendant would immediately be able to recover it back on the basis of a total failure of consideration.

Relief against forfeiture of part payments

It is not uncommon, particularly in instalment sale of land contracts, for the parties to agree that the instalments paid will be forfeited to the vendor in the event the purchaser defaults on the contract. In this circumstance the instalments will be irrecoverable in restitution, despite the fact that the consideration for the payment has totally failed.[59] Nevertheless, the equitable rules against forfeiture might apply to provide relief where the amount forfeited is penal in nature, and where it would be unconscionable for the defendant to

---

58   See also *Rover International Ltd v Cannon Film Sales Ltd (the Proper appeal)* (1989) (see extract, p 306).

59   Mason and Carter, *Restitution Law in Australia*, 1995, p 409.

retain that amount.[60] Although in Australia the equitable rules against forfeiture are currently limited to the sale of land context, in the following English case the rules were applied to a contract for the sale of goods.

Stockloser v Johnson [1954] 1 QB 476 English Court of Appeal

The plaintiff agreed to purchase from the defendant plant and machinery for use in a quarry. The agreement provided for payment of the purchase price in instalments and contained a term that, upon default by the purchaser in paying the instalments, the defendant was entitled to retake possession of the plant and machinery and that the instalments paid were forfeited to the vendor.

Denning LJ: ... [488] There was acute contest as to the proper legal principles to apply in this case. On the one hand, [counsel for the plaintiff] urged us to hold that the buyer was entitled to recover the instalments at law. He said that the forfeiture clause should be ignored because it was of a penal character; and once it was ignored, it meant that the buyer was left with a simple right to repayment of his money on the lines of *Dies v British and International Mining and Finance Corporation* (1939), subject only to a cross-claim for damages. In asking us to ignore the forfeiture clause, [counsel for the plaintiff] relied on the familiar tests which are used to distinguish between penalties and liquidated damages, and said that these tests had been applied in cases for the repayment of money, citing *Barton v Capewell* (1893) and *Commissioner of Public Works v Hills* (1906). In neither of those cases, however, was the point argued or discussed, and I do not think they warrant [counsel for the plaintiff's] proposition. There is, I think, a plain distinction between penalty cases, strictly so called, and cases like the present.

It is this: when one party seeks to exact a penalty from the other, he is seeking to exact payment of an extravagant sum either by action at law or by appropriating to himself moneys belonging to the other party, as in *Commissioner of Public Works v Hills* (1906). The claimant invariably relies, like Shylock, on the letter of the contract to support his demand, but the courts decline to give him their aid because they will not assist him in [489] an act of oppression: see the valuable judgments of Somervell and Hodson LJJ in *Cooden Engineering Co v Stanford* (1953).

In the present case, however, the seller is not seeking to exact a penalty. He only wants to keep money which already belongs to him. The money was handed to him in part payment of the purchase price and, as soon as it was paid, it belonged to him absolutely. He did not obtain it by extortion or oppression or anything of that sort, and there is an express clause – a forfeiture clause, if you please – permitting him to keep it. It is not the case of a seller seeking to enforce a penalty, but a buyer seeking restitution of money paid. If the buyer is to recover it, he must, I think, have recourse to somewhat different principles from those applicable to penalties, strictly so called.

On the other hand, [counsel for the defendant] urged us to hold that the buyer could only recover the money if he was able and willing to perform the contract, and for this purpose he ought to pay or offer to pay the instalments which were in

---

60 *Stockloser v Johnson* (1954), pp 484–85, 491–92 (see following extract); *Legione v Hately* (1983); *Stern v McArthur* (1988), pp 526–27; *Pitt v Curotta* (1931); *Lexane Pty Ltd v Highfern Pty Ltd* (1985).

arrears and be willing to pay the future instalments as they became due; and he relied on *Mussen v Van Diemen's Land Co* (1938). I think that this contention goes too far in the opposite direction. If the buyer was seeking to re-establish the contract, he would of course have to pay up the arrears and to show himself willing to perform the contract in the future, just as a lessee, who has suffered a forfeiture, has to do when he seeks to re-establish the lease. So, also, if the buyer were seeking specific performance he would have to show himself able and willing to perform his part. But the buyer's object here is not to re-establish the contract. It is to get his money back, and to do this I do not think that it is necessary for him to go so far as to show that he is ready and willing to perform the contract.

I reject, therefore, the arguments of counsel at each extreme. It seems to me that the cases show the law to be this: (1) *When there is no forfeiture clause.* If money is handed over in part payment of the purchase price, and then the buyer makes default as to the balance, then, so long as the seller keeps the contract open and available for performance, the buyer cannot recover the money; but once the seller rescinds the contract or treats it as at an end owing to the buyer's default, then the buyer is entitled to recover his money by action at law, subject to a cross-claim by the seller for damages.[61] (2) *But when there is a forfeiture clause or the money is expressly paid as a deposit (which is equivalent to a forfeiture clause),* then the buyer who is in default cannot recover the money at law at all. He may, however, have a remedy in equity, for, despite the express stipulation in the contract, equity can relieve the buyer from forfeiture of the money and order the seller to repay it on such terms as the court thinks fit. That is, I think, shown clearly by the decision of the Privy Council in *Steedman v Drinkle* (1916), where the Board consisted of a strong three, Viscount Haldane, Lord Parker and Lord Sumner.

The difficulty is to know what are the circumstances which give rise to this equity ... Two things are necessary: first, the forfeiture clause must be of a penal nature, in this sense, that the sum forfeited must be out of all proportion to the damage, and, secondly, it must be unconscionable for the seller to retain the money. [Denning LJ referred to the facts of *Steedman v Drinkle* and continued at p 491:] The basis of the decision in *Steedman v Drinkle* (1916) was, I think, that the vendor had somewhat sharply exercised his right to rescind the contract and retake the land, and it was unconscionable for him also to forfeit the sums already paid. Equity could not specifically enforce the contract, but it could and would relieve against the forfeiture.

In the course of the argument before us Somervell LJ put an illustration which shows the necessity for this equity even though the buyer is not ready and willing to perform the contract. Suppose a buyer has agreed to buy a necklace by instalments, and the contract provides that, on default in payment of any one instalment, the seller is entitled to rescind the contract and forfeit the instalments already paid. The buyer pays 90% of the price but fails to pay the last instalment. He is not able to perform the contract because he simply cannot find the money. The seller thereupon rescinds the contract and retakes the necklace and resells it at

---

61 See *Palmer v Temple* (1839); *Mayson v Clouet* (1924); *Dies v British and International Co* (1939); *Williams on Vendor and Purchaser*, 4th edn, p 1006.

a higher price. Surely equity will relieve the buyer against forfeiture of the money on such terms as may be just.

Again, suppose that a vendor of property, in lieu of the usual 10% deposit, stipulates for an initial payment of 50% of the price as a deposit and a part payment; and later, when the purchaser fails to complete, the vendor resells the property at a profit and in addition claims to forfeit the 50% deposit. Surely the court will relieve against the forfeiture. The vendor cannot forestall this equity by describing an extravagant sum as a deposit, any more than he can recover a penalty by calling it liquidated damages.

[492] These illustrations convince me that in a proper case there is an equity of restitution which a party in default does not lose simply because he is not able and willing to perform the contract. Nay, that is the very reason why he needs the equity. The equity operates, not because of the plaintiff's default, but because it is in the particular case unconscionable for the seller to retain the money. In short, he ought not unjustly to enrich himself at the plaintiff's expense. This equity of restitution is to be tested, I think, not at the time of the contract, but by the conditions existing when it is invoked. Suppose, for instance, that in the instance of the necklace, the first instalment was only 5% of the price; and the buyer made default on the second instalment. There would be no equity by which he could ask for the first instalment to be repaid to him any more than he could claim repayment of a deposit. But it is very different after 90% has been paid. Again, delay may be very material. Thus, in *Mussen's* case (1938) the court was much influenced by the fact that the purchaser had allowed nearly six years to elapse before claiming restitution. He had already had a good deal of land conveyed to him and, during his six years delay, values had so greatly changed that it may be that he had had his money's worth. At any rate, it was not unconscionable for the defendant to retain the money.

Applying these principles to the present case, even if one regards the forfeiture clause as of a penal nature – as the judge did and I am prepared to do – nevertheless I do not think it was unconscionable for the seller to retain the money. The buyer seems to have gambled on the royalties being higher than they were. He thought they would go a long way to enable him to pay the instalments; but owing to bad weather they turned out to be smaller than he had hoped and he could not find the additional amount necessary to pay the instalments. The judge summarised the position neatly when he said that the purchaser 'is in the position of a gambler who has lost his stake and is now saying that it is for the court of equity to get it back for him'. He said, 'if it is a question of what is unconscionable, or, to use a word with a less legal flavour, unfair, I can see nothing whatever unfair in the defendant retaining the money'. With that finding of the judge I entirely agree and think that it disposes of the purchaser's claim to restitution ...

Questions

Why did Denning LJ hold that it would not be unconscionable for the seller to retain the instalments? According to Denning LJ do the same principles apply to penal deposits?

RECOVERY OF NON-MONETARY BENEFITS: INNOCENT PARTY

Liability

There are numerous Australian cases where the innocent party has been awarded reasonable remuneration for services upon discharge of the contract for the defendant's breach or repudiation.[62] The basis of the claim is the defendant's acceptance of the services; although in this context the courts appear to deem the defendant to have accepted the plaintiff's partial performance.[63] A defendant in breach is precluded from denying that a benefit was received,[64] and will be presumed to have accepted the partial performance on the basis that the plaintiff was prevented by the breach from rendering full performance. In practice, therefore, liability is based on the defendant's contractual request for the services.[65] It is not necessary for the plaintiff to establish that the defendant actually accepted, or acquiesced in, the incomplete performance.[66]

There is one possible qualification to the above principles. It has been suggested that a restitutionary claim will not be available to a plaintiff who has fully or substantially performed the contract. It is suggested that the plaintiff in that situation is limited to suing on the contract for the contract price.[67] This is the position in Canada,[68] although there is no significant judicial authority in Australia on this point.

Contractual ceiling?

Should the amount of the restitutionary award be limited to the price the plaintiff agreed to in the contract? The New South Wales Court of Appeal in the following case thought not.

---

62 *Brooks Robinson Pty Ltd v Rothfield* (1951) (building services); *Segur v Franklin* (1934) (services provided by arbitrator); *Renard Constructions (ME) Pty Ltd v Minister for Public Works* (1992) (construction services) (see extract, p 322); *Independent Grocers Co-Operative Ltd v Noble Lowndes Superannuation Consultants Ltd* (1993) (services provided by superannuation industry consultant); *Iezzi Constructions Pty Ltd v Currumbin Crest Development Pty Ltd* (1995) (construction services).

63 Mason and Carter, *Restitution Law in Australia*, 1995, pp 429ff.

64 *Brenner v First Artists' Management* (1993), pp 258–59 (see extract, p 39). See also *Planché v Colburn* (1831) (see extract, p 37); *Segur v Franklin* (1934), p 72; *Horton v Jones (No 2)* (1939), p 319 (see extract, p 385); *Iezzi Constructions Pty Ltd v Watkins Pacific (Qld) Pty Ltd* (1995), p 369.

65 *Brenner v First Artists' Management* (1993), pp 257–60 (see extract, p 39).

66 Contrast with a party in breach: see below pp 324–30.

67 Mason and Carter, *Restitution Law in Australia*, 1995, pp 425–29; Goff and Jones, *The Law of Restitution*, 5th edn, 1998, pp 516, 530.

68 *Morrison-Knudsen Co Ltd v British Columbia Hydro and Power Authority* (1978).

Renard Constructions (ME) Pty Ltd v Minister for Public Works (1992) 26 NSWLR 234
Court of Appeal of New South Wales

The plaintiff and defendant were parties to a building contract under which the plaintiff was to construct two pumping stations for the price of $208,950. The plaintiff commenced construction, but the project was hindered by numerous delays. Prior to full completion of the work the defendant repudiated the contract by wrongfully excluding the plaintiff from the site. The plaintiff discharged the contract and brought a claim for reasonable remuneration for the work done. The arbitrator made an award in favour of the plaintiff of $285,024.60; the amount representing the market value of the services provided by the plaintiff. This award was $76,074.60 greater than the contract price.

Meagher JA: ... [276] The second point [argued on behalf of the defendant] is that the amount of the arbitrator's award (particularly when aggregated with payments already made under the contract whilst it was on foot) exceeds the amount payable to the contractor under the contract, which latter amount must provide a 'ceiling' on any *quantum meruit* claim. This point should also, in my view, be rejected. In the first place, it is contrary to what authority exists on the question. The Court of Appeal in New Zealand, in *Slowey v Lodder* (1901) held that an innocent party who terminates a contract by acceptance of the defaulting [277] party's repudiation may sue on a *quantum meruit* for the value of work done before repudiation, and that the fact that a judgment on this basis exceeds the amount which would have been payable under the contract is irrelevant. That decision was affirmed on appeal to the Privy Council: see *Lodder v Slowey* (1904). In the United States, there is abundant authority to the same effect: see, eg, *Boomer v Muir* (1933), *United States v Zara Contracting Co* (1944), *Re Montgomery's Estate* (1936) and *Williston on Contracts*.[69] Certainly those United States authorities are tainted by the view that acceptance of a repudiation effects a rescission *ab initio*, a view regarded in Australia as heretical since *McDonald v Dennys Lascelles Ltd* (1933) and now recognised as such by the House of Lords in *Johnson v Agnew* (1980); but this reasoning on this point still remains unimpaired. Of these cases, *Boomer v Muir* is the most spectacular, because in that case a subcontractor on a construction project was awarded the sum of $258,000 as the fair value of the work he had performed for the defendant, even though only $20,000 remained as an outstanding debt due by the defendant under the contract. In so far as it is relevant, the decision of the Court of Appeal in England in *Rover International Ltd v Cannon Film Sales Ltd* (1989) – which has attracted the attention of Professor Birks (1990), Mr Beatson (1989) and Dr Carter[70] – is to the like effect. I say 'in so far as it is relevant' because it is a case dealing with a contract which was void *ab initio*, not a case of a contract terminated by the acceptance of a repudiation.

The cases to which I refer have been received with somewhat lukewarm enthusiasm by certain academic writers[71] on the apparent ground that they are 'anomalous'. But to my mind this criticism of them is superficial. They are right in principle as well as justified by authority. The law is clear enough that an innocent

---

69 3rd edn, 1970, Vol 12, s 1485, p 304.
70 Finn, *Essays on Restitution*, 1990, p 206.
71 See Goff and Jones, *The Law of Restitution*, 2nd edn, 1978, pp 379–80; Greig and Davis, *The Law of Contract*, 1987, pp 1286–87.

party who accepts the defaulting party's repudiation of a contract has the option of either suing for damages for breach of contract or suing on a *quantum meruit* for work done. An election presupposes a choice between different remedies, which presumably may lead to different results. The nature of these different remedies renders it highly likely that the results will be different. If the former remedy is chosen the innocent party is entitled to damages amounting to the loss of profit which he would have made if the contract had been performed rather than repudiated; it has nothing to do with reasonableness. If the latter remedy is chosen, he is entitled to a verdict representing the reasonable cost of the work he has done and the money he has expended; the profit he might have made does not enter into that exercise. There is nothing anomalous in the notion that two different remedies, proceeding on entirely different principles, might yield different results. Nor is there anything anomalous in the fact that either remedy may yield a higher monetary figure than the other. Nor is there anything anomalous in the prospect that a figure arrived at on a *quantum meruit* might exceed, or even far exceed, the profit which would have been made if the contract had been fully performed. Such a result would only be anomalous if there were some rule of law that the remuneration arrived at [278] contractually was the greatest possible remuneration available, or that it was a reasonable remuneration for all work requiring to be performed. There is no such rule of law. Nor can one say that as a matter of observable fact there is any such rule. The most one can say is that the amount contractually agreed is evidence of the reasonableness of the remuneration claimed on a *quantum meruit*; strong evidence perhaps, but certainly not conclusive evidence. On the other hand, it would be extremely anomalous if the defaulting party when sued on a *quantum meruit* could invoke the contract which he has repudiated in order to impose a ceiling on amounts otherwise recoverable.

[Priestley and Handley JJA relevantly agreed with Meagher JA.]

Commentary

The principal case has been followed by the Court of Appeal of Queensland in *Iezzi Constructions Pty Ltd v Watkins Pacific (Qld) Pty Ltd* (1995).[72] The commentators however are united in their disapproval of it, although are in disagreement about the appropriate principles to be applied. Birks[73] and Burrows[74] argue that a contract ceiling should not be imposed as the terms of a repudiated contract cannot *per se* restrict restitutionary recovery. However, they recognise that the contract price may operate as a *valuation ceiling* where the element of enrichment is established by free acceptance. In such circumstances the plaintiff must rely in evidence upon the terms of the contract in order to establish that the defendant freely accepted the services. The term as to contract

---

72 See also *Ward v Griffiths Bros Ltd* (1928); *Jennings Construction Ltd v QH and M Birt Pty Ltd* (1988); *Brenner v First Artists' Management Pty Ltd* (1993) (see extract, p 39); *Gino D'Alessandro Constructions Pty Ltd v Powis* (1987), pp 58–59.

73 Birks, 'In defence of free acceptance', in Burrows (ed), *Essays on the Law of Restitution*, 1991, pp 105, 135–37.

74 Burrows, 'Free acceptance and the law of restitution' (1988) 104 LQR 576, p 588; Burrows, *The Law of Restitution*, 1993, pp 268–71.

price will then be evidence that the defendant freely accepted the services on the basis that the contract price would mark the limit of her liability to pay for the services. However, the contract price would not operate as a valuation ceiling where the benefit is established on the basis of the test of incontrovertible benefit, as such benefit is by definition undeniable and is established without evidentiary recourse to the contractual terms.[75] The approach of Mason and Carter, although conceptually different, should in practice lead to similar results to that of Birks and Burrows. Mason and Carter[76] argue that in most cases the contract price should form a ceiling on the claim as to do otherwise would not only unjustifiably ignore the parties' contractual allocation of risk but would also ignore the fact that in most cases 'acceptance of benefit is found in the defendant's contractual receipt, rather than a genuine (free) acceptance'. They do however recognise that a contractual ceiling should not apply in the exceptional cases where the benefit is an incontrovertible one or was not part of the agreed return, or where acceptance is established by reference to conduct other than breach. Goff and Jones[77] take the most restrictive approach favouring a contractual ceiling which limits the measure of recovery to the contract price. This limit on recovery is thought to be necessary in order to protect the contractual expectations of both parties.

RECOVERY OF NON-MONETARY BENEFITS: PARTY IN BREACH

A plaintiff in breach will be unable to recover for the cost of partially performing an entire obligation.[78] Unlike claims by innocent parties,[79] claims by a party in breach will be successful only in exceptional cases where the claimant can establish an independent act of acceptance by the defendant of the incomplete performance,[80] or alternatively that the defendant acquiesced in the incomplete performance.[81] Liability will not be based on the fact of the contractual request for the work.

An 'independent act of acceptance' refers to an act of the defendant freely and voluntarily accepting the defective performance. This requires that the defendant must have had a reasonable opportunity to reject the incomplete

---

75 For a further explanation of this approach see McInnes, 'Contractual services, restitution and the avoidance of bad bargains' (1995) 23(3) ABLR 218.

76 Mason and Carter, *op cit*, fn 63, pp 580–81; see also Carter, 'Discharged contracts: claims for restitution' (1997) 11(2) JCL 130, pp 144–46.

77 Goff and Jones, *The Law of Restitution*, 5th edn, 1998, pp 530–34.

78 An 'entire obligation' is one where the contractual performance promised in return for payment of the money is entire and indivisible.

79 See above pp 321–24.

80 Mason and Carter, *Restitution Law in Australia*, 1995, pp 429ff; *Steele v Tardiani* (1946), pp 402–03 (see extract, p 327); *Nicholson v Burnett* (1922); *Sumpter v Hedges* (1898), p 676 (see following extract).

81 *Steele v Tardiani* (1946) (see extract, p 327).

performance, but chose to accept it.[82] As the following case establishes, an independent act of acceptance will rarely be present where the work has improved (or become absorbed into) other property of the defendant, as the defendant will have had no real choice whether to accept or reject the work.[83]

Sumpter v Hedges [1898] 1 QB 673 English Court of Appeal

The plaintiff, a builder, entered into a contract to build two houses and stables on the defendant's land for a lump sum of £565. The plaintiff did part of the work, amounting in value to about £333, and had received payment of part of the price. The plaintiff then abandoned the work as he had run out of money. The defendant finished the buildings himself, using certain materials which the plaintiff had left on the property. The trial judge gave judgment for the plaintiff for the value of the materials used by the defendant in completing the buildings but refused the plaintiff's claim for the value of the building work which he had done.

Smith LJ: [674] In this case the plaintiff, a builder, entered into a contract to build two houses and stables on the defendant's land for a lump sum. When the buildings were still in an unfinished state the plaintiff informed the defendant that he had no money, and was not going on with the work any more. The learned judge has found as a fact that he abandoned the contract. Under such circumstances, what is a building owner to do? He cannot keep the buildings on his land in an unfinished state forever. The law is that, where there is a contract to do work for a lump sum, until the work is completed the price of it cannot be recovered. Therefore the plaintiff could not recover on the original contract. It is suggested however that the plaintiff was entitled to recover for the work he did on a *quantum meruit*. But, in order that that may be so, there must be evidence of a fresh contract to pay for the work already done. With regard to that, the case of *Munro v Butt* (1858) appears to be exactly in point. That case decides that, unless the building owner does something from which a new contract can be inferred to pay for the work already done, the plaintiff in such a case as this cannot recover on a *quantum meruit*. In the case of *Lysaght v Pearson* (1879) to which we have been referred, the case of *Munro v Butt* (1858) does not appear to have been referred to. There the plaintiff had contracted to erect on the defendant's land two corrugated iron roofs. When he had completed one of them, he does not seem to have said that he [675] abandoned the contract, but merely that he would not go on unless the defendant paid him for what he had already done. The defendant thereupon proceeded to erect for himself the second roof. The Court of Appeal held that there was in that case something from which a new contract might be inferred to pay for the work done by the plaintiff. That is not this case. In the case of *Whitaker v Dunn* (1887) there was a contract to erect a laundry on defendant's land, and the laundry erected was not in accordance with the contract, but the official referee held that the plaintiff could recover on a *quantum meruit*. The case came before a Divisional Court, consisting of Lord Coleridge CJ and myself, and we said that the decision in *Munro v Butt* (1858) applied, and there being no circumstances to justify an

---

82 *Munro v Butt* (1858); *Pattinson v Luckley* (1875); *Sumpter v Hedges* (1898) (see following extract); *Steele v Tardiani* (1946), pp 402–03 (see extract, p 327).

83 See also *Munro v Butt* (1858); *Pattinson v Luckley* (1875).

interference of a fresh contract the plaintiff must fail. My brother Collins thinks that that case went to the Court of Appeal, and that he argued it there, and the court affirmed the decision of the Queen's Bench Division. I think the appeal must be dismissed.

Chitty LJ: I am of the same opinion. The plaintiff had contracted to erect certain buildings for a lump sum. When the work was only partly done, the plaintiff said that he could not go on with it, and the judge has found that he abandoned the contract. The position, therefore, was that the defendant found his land with unfinished buildings upon it, and he thereupon completed the work. That is no evidence from which the inference can be drawn that he entered into a fresh contract to pay for the work done by the plaintiff. If we held that the plaintiff could recover, we should in my opinion be overruling *Cutter v Powell* (1795), and a long series of cases in which it has been decided that there must in such a case be some evidence of a new contract to enable the plaintiff to recover on a *quantum meruit*. There was nothing new in the decision in *Pattinson v Luckley* (1875) but Bramwell B there pointed out with his usual clearness that in the case of a building erected upon land the mere fact that the defendant [676] remains in possession of his land is no evidence upon which an inference of a new contract can be founded. He says: 'In the case of goods sold and delivered, it is easy to shew a contract from the retention of the goods; but that is not so where work is done on real property.' I think the learned judge was quite right in holding that in this case there was no evidence from which a fresh contract to pay for the work done could be inferred.

Collins LJ: I agree. I think the case is really concluded by the finding of the learned judge to the effect that the plaintiff had abandoned the contract. If the plaintiff had merely broken his contract in some way so as not to give the defendant the right to treat him as having abandoned the contract, and the defendant had then proceeded to finish the work himself, the plaintiff might perhaps have been entitled to sue on a *quantum meruit* on the ground that the defendant had taken the benefit of the work done. But that is not the present case. There are cases in which, though the plaintiff has abandoned the performance of a contract, it is possible for him to raise the inference of a new contract to pay for the work done on a *quantum meruit* from the defendant's having taken the benefit of that work, but, in order that that may be done, the circumstances must be such as to give an option to the defendant to take or not to take the benefit of the work done. It is only where the circumstances are such as to give that option that there is any evidence on which to ground the inference of a new contract. Where, as in the case of work done on land, the circumstances are such as to give the defendant no option whether he will take the benefit of the work or not, then one must look to other facts than the mere taking the benefit of the work in order to ground the inference of a new contract. In this case I see no other facts on which such an inference can be founded. The mere fact that a defendant is in possession of what he cannot help keeping, or even has done work upon it, affords no ground for such an inference. He is not bound to keep unfinished a building which in an incomplete state would be a nuisance on his land. I am therefore of opinion that the plaintiff was not entitled to recover for the work which he had done. I feel clear that the case of *Whitaker v Dunn* (1887), to which reference has been made, was the case which as counsel I argued in the Court of Appeal, and in which the court dismissed the appeal on the ground that the case was concluded by *Munro v Butt* (1858).

Commentary and questions

On what basis did the court deny the plaintiff's claim for the reasonable value of the building services provided by him? Why did the court allow the claim for the reasonable value of the building materials the builder had left on site and which were used by the defendant in completing the building?

A claim by the party in breach will be successful in exceptional cases where the defendant had a free choice as to whether or not to accept the benefit. Accordingly, if the work results in a movable chattel that the defendant could freely choose to return, the act of retaining it and using it could amount to a free acceptance of the benefit of the chattel.[84] A claim will also be successful where the defendant acquiesced in the benefit of the incomplete performance by voluntarily dispensing with the need for exact performance. This proposition is established in the following case.

Steele v Tardiani (1946) 72 CLR 386 High Court of Australia

The defendant employed the three plaintiffs, Italians interned during the Second World War, to cut firewood at an agreed price per ton. The terms of the contract required the plaintiffs to cut the wood into lengths of six feet and widths of six inches, and to stack it and load it if necessary. The plaintiffs cut fifteen hundred tons of wood, but most of the wood was wider than the required six inches. The firewood cut by the plaintiffs was subsequently sold by the defendant. The plaintiffs sought remuneration for the work they had performed, both under the contract and on the basis of a *quantum meruit*. The claim under the contract failed. Although the contract was 'infinitely divisible', in relation to each piece of firewood the plaintiffs were under an entire obligation to cut the wood to the specified dimensions. The plaintiffs had failed to substantially comply with the specified dimensions and so were unable to claim on the contract for the contract price; however the claim on a *quantum meruit* was successful.

Dixon J: ... [402] To recover under a *quantum meruit* for wood split to substantially different widths from that required, the plaintiffs must show circumstances removing their right to remuneration from the exact conditions of the special contract. For, if no more appears, the fact of such a contract, open and, to that extent, unperformed, excludes any implied obligation on the part of the defendant to pay a fair and reasonable remuneration for the work done by the plaintiffs in cutting his timber to dimensions outside those allowed by the contract. It is not enough that the work has been beneficial to him by turning his standing timber into the more valuable form of firewood. 'It is a commonplace of the law that there can be no implied contract as to matters covered by an express contract until the express contract is displaced ... But where work is done outside the contract, and the benefit of the work is taken, a contract may be implied to pay for the work so done at the current rate of remuneration, and the terms of the express contract may remain binding in so far as they are not inconsistent with the implied contract': *per* Scrutton LJ, *Steven v Bromley & Son* (1919). But, 'taking the benefit of the work' means that the defendant has done so in the exercise of some choice that was actually open to him. As it is put in a recent treatise, 'An implicit promise to pay

---

84 *Munro v Butt* (1858); *Pattinson v Luckley* (1875); *Sumpter v Hedges* (1898).

connotes a benefit received by the promisor, but the receipt of the benefit is not in itself enough to raise the implication. No promise can be inferred unless it is open to the beneficiary either to accept or to reject the benefit of the work': *Law of Contract* by Cheshire and Fifoot.[85] The chief example of work of which the advantage must be received and in that sense accepted by the person for whom it is done, is that of the erection or repair of a building upon the land of the person benefiting, but not erected or repaired according to the conditions of the contract: see *Bullen and Leake*.[86] Of such a case, Lord Campbell CJ speaks as follows in *Munro v Butt* (1858): 'now, admitting that in the case of an independent chattel, a piece of furniture for example, to be made under a special contract, and some term, which in itself amounted to a condition precedent, being unperformed, if the party for whom it was to be made had yet [403] accepted it, an action might, upon obvious grounds, be maintained, either on the special contract with a dispensation of the conditions alleged, or an implied contract to pay for it according to its value; it does not seem to us that there are any grounds from which the same conclusion can possibly follow in respect of a building to be erected, or repairs done, or alterations made, to a building on a man's own land, from the mere fact of his taking possession.'

It is to be noticed that Lord Campbell referred to recovery in the case he contemplates on the special contract on the ground of dispensation with exact performance and to recovery upon a *quantum meruit* on a new contract implied or imputed. To these two positions he again referred, after describing the dilemma in which a building owner is placed by an incomplete execution of the contract. The Lord Chief Justice said (1858):

> How then does mere possession raise any inference of a waiver of the conditions precedent of the special contract, or of the entering into a new one? If indeed the defendant had done any thing, coupled with the taking possession, which had prevented the performance of the special contract, as if he had forbidden the surveyor from entering to inspect the work, or if, the failure in complete performance being very slight, the defendant had used any language, or done any act, from which acquiescence on his part might have been reasonably inferred, the case would have been very different.

No doubt the instances given by Lord Campbell, *scilicet* such things as conduct betokening actual acquiescence and acts calculated to prevent completion, were in the mind of Collins LJ in *Sumpter v Hedges* (1898) when he said: 'Where, as in the case of work done on land, the circumstances are such as to give the defendant no option whether he will take the benefit of the work or not, then one must look to other facts than the mere taking the benefit of the work in order to ground the inference of a new contract ... The mere fact that a defendant is in possession of what he cannot help keeping, or even has done work upon it, affords no grounds for such an inference.'

It is upon these principles that the defendant relies in support of his appeal against the decision by which he has been held liable to the plaintiffs for the value of the work done by them in cutting firewood to the quantity estimated, nearly all of it being in excess of the contract width or diameter. The defendant says that his trees

---

85   1st edn, 1945, pp 352, 353.
86   2nd edn, 1863, p 33; 3rd edn, 1868, p 41.

were cut upon his land and the firewood left lying there was his. What was he to do? By what step could he actively 'reject' the [404] advantage which the transmutation of his standing trees into firewood necessarily gave him, however unsuitable to his purpose might be the actual lengths and widths? Was he to allow the wood to rot on the ground? What practical choice had he except to make it clear to the plaintiffs that, to obtain payment, they must split the wood to the contract width, and, when they refused or failed to do so, to employ other labour for the purpose of reducing its width or 'diameter' so far as otherwise he was unable to dispose of the firewood. Why should he be precluded from selling his wood in the shape the plaintiffs wrongfully left it? It was his wood and why should his dealing with it imply a new contract with the plaintiffs?

If it were true that he made it clear to the plaintiffs before they departed that they must complete their contract by splitting the wood to the specified width, these considerations would indeed place him in a strong position. If his evidence were accepted, the plaintiffs would occupy the situation of a party who abandons a special contract to perform work on the property of another before completing the work and leaves that other party no effective choice in accepting or rejecting the benefit. But the defendant's evidence was not accepted by the judge at the trial, who, on the contrary, held that, as the timber cut, whether over six feet or not in length and whether over six inches or not in width, was sold by the defendant, he must pay a reasonable sum for that which he took and sold, even though it did not strictly comply with the terms of the original contract. What detailed facts the learned judge found on which to base this conclusion there is no express statement to show. But the rejection of the defendant's testimony generally is involved in other findings and I think that we must take it that the defendant did not base his refusal or failure to pay the plaintiffs on their failure to split the wood to the specified width, or, at all events, did not express to the plaintiffs his insistence or desire that they should so cut it. Indeed, even in his pleading, the defendant did not take the point as to diameter or width and it was only during cross-examination that it was developed as part of the defence.

On the other hand, there is evidence, which his Honour may have accepted, and which the learned judges of the full court certainly treated as representing fact, which would authorise a conclusion adverse to the defendant. Upon the evidence it would be open to conclude that the defendant considered that the plaintiffs were bound by the restrictions imposed upon them to go on working for him and that it was for this reason that he did pay them regularly, that he allowed them to continue cutting timber and splitting it to a [405] width of more than six inches and raised no objection, that notwithstanding this disconformity with the direction or stipulation he had originally given or made, he afterwards promised to pay for the wood cut if and when it was delivered to a buyer or buyers, that he suffered them to leave his employment without informing them that they must split the firewood again in order to reduce its diameter, if they were to be paid, he then having reason to suppose that they did not consider that he was insisting on this requirement and, indeed, that his reliance upon diameter or width was an afterthought. In such circumstances, it would be proper to treat the failure in complete performance as possessing little importance to the defendant and as acquiesced in by him, with the consequence that the subsequent sale of the firewood might rightly be regarded by the learned judge as a taking of the benefit of the work and so, as involving either a dispensation from precise performance or an implication at law of a new obligation to pay the value of the work done.

The actual finding made by the judge at the trial is general, but as it is consistent with his Honour's having proceeded on the foregoing views of the facts, which are open on the evidence, I do not think the defendant should succeed in his attack upon the conclusion that he is bound to pay a fair and reasonable rate of remuneration in respect of the timber actually cut, even though much of it exceeded the stipulated width ...

Commentary and questions

Was it enough according to Dixon J that the plaintiff's work had been beneficial to the defendant? What additional factor had to be established?

Latham CJ in the principal case stated the relevant principle in the following terms, quoting from *Bullen and Leake* (1946), p 393:

> Where work is done by one party under a special contract, but not according to its terms, the other may refuse to accept it (see *Ellis v Hameln* (1810)); but if he does accept it and takes the benefit of it, he may be sued for the value in this count [that is, the common *indebitatus* count for work done].[87]

THREE PARTY CASES

As the law currently stands, a plaintiff will be precluded from 'jumping the privity gap' and recovering a benefit from the defendant which the plaintiff conferred in the course of performing a contract with a third party. The usual reason given for refusing a claim in this circumstance is that it would subvert the contractual allocation of risks in the contracts between the plaintiff and the third party and the defendant and the third party.[88]

Christiani and Nielsen Pty Ltd v Goliath Portland Cement Co Ltd [1993] 2 Tas R 122
Full Court of the Supreme Court of Tasmania

The respondent ('Goliath') entered into a contract with the first defendant, McNally Australia Pty Ltd, for construction work. Pursuant to a request by Goliath, the appellant ('Christiani') entered into a subcontract with McNally under which it agreed to perform the construction work. Christiani performed its contractual obligations, but was not paid by McNally which went into liquidation. Goliath sued Christiani for negligence in doing the work and Christiani counterclaimed for the reasonable value of services and materials provided.

Zeeman J: ... [165] The circumstances in which the law will impose or impute an obligation or promise to make compensation for a benefit accepted in the absence

---

87 *Burn v Miller* (1813); *Farnsworth v Garrard* (1807).

88 *Christiani and Nielsen Pty Ltd v Goliath Portland Cement Pty Ltd* (1993), pp 168–69 (see following extract); *Pan Ocean Shipping Ltd v Creditcorp Ltd, The 'Trident Beauty'* (1994) (see extract, p 333); Davenport and Harris, *Unjust Enrichment*, 1997, p 112–16; Goff and Jones, *The Law of Restitution*, 5th edn, 1998, p 58; Burrows, 'Restitution from assignees' [1994] RLR 52, pp 55–56.

of contract was the subject of some incisive observations by Deane J (with whom Mason and Wilson JJ appear to have agreed) [in *Pavey & Matthews Pty Ltd v Paul*] (1987), pp 255, 256 (see extract, p 15)]:

> ... it is clear that the old common *indebitatus* count could be utilised to accommodate what should be seen as two distinct categories of claim: one to recover a debt arising under a genuine contract, whether express or implied; the other to recover a debt owing in circumstances where the law itself imposed or imputed an obligation or promise to make compensation for a benefit accepted. In the first category of case, the action was brought upon the genuine agreement regardless of whether it took the form of a special or a [166] common count.
>
> It follows from what has been said above that the cases in which a claimant has been held entitled to recover in respect of an executed consideration under an agreement upon which the Statute of Frauds precluded the bringing of an action should be seen as falling within the second and not the first category. In that second category of case, the tendency of common lawyers to speak in terms of implied contract rather than in terms of an obligation imposed by law (see, eg, *per* Salter J, *Scott v Pattison* (1923), pp 727–28) should be recognised as but a reflection of the influence of discarded fictions, buried forms of action and the conventional conviction that, if a common law claim could not properly be framed in tort, it must necessarily be dressed in the language of contract. That tendency should not be allowed to conceal the fact that, in that category of case, the action was not based upon a genuine agreement at all. Indeed, *if there was a valid and enforceable agreement governing the claimant's right to compensation, there would be neither occasion nor legal justification for the law to superimpose or impute an obligation or promise to pay a reasonable remuneration. The quasi-contractual obligation to pay fair and just compensation for a benefit which has been accepted will only arise in a case where there is no applicable genuine agreement or where such an agreement is frustrated, avoided or unenforceable.* In such a case, it is the very fact that there is no genuine agreement or that the genuine agreement is frustrated, avoided or unenforceable that provides the occasion for (and part of the circumstances giving rise to) the imposition by the law of the obligation to make restitution.
>
> To identify the basis of such actions as restitution and not genuine agreement is not to assert a judicial discretion to do whatever idiosyncratic notions of what is fair and just might dictate. The circumstances in which the common law imposes an enforceable obligation to pay compensation for a benefit accepted under an unenforceable agreement have been explored in the reported cases and in learned writings [167] and are unlikely to be greatly affected by the perception that the basis of such an obligation, when the common law imposes it, is preferably seen as lying in restitution rather than in the implication of a genuine agreement where in fact the unenforceable agreement left no room for one. [My emphasis.]

The parties sought to advance different constructions of the passage which I have emphasised. Counsel for Goliath submitted that the effect of what his Honour said was that if there is a valid and enforceable agreement governing the plaintiff's right to compensation, whether or not the defendant is a party to that agreement, then recovery is only possible pursuant to that agreement. Counsel for Christiani submitted that the passage ought not to be construed as going further than that where there is a valid and enforceable agreement between the plaintiff and the defendant then recovery by that plaintiff from that defendant is limited to that permitted by the contract, leaving unaffected the question as to whether such a plaintiff may have rights as against a third party with which he does not have a valid and enforceable agreement. In other words the question is whether the effect of what Deane J said is that, in order to maintain an action of the type presently under consideration, the absence of any relevant valid and enforceable agreement is a prerequisite. I consider that it is arguable that the construction advanced by counsel for Christiani is correct although it ought to be borne in mind that Deane J was dealing with law as it had developed through the cases rather than purporting to lay down some new principle. He was concerned with the basis of recovery in cases forming part of a well established category of cases rather than defining the limits of that category. The category is a well defined category. That category was referred to by Greer LJ in *Craven-Ellis v Canons Ltd* (1936), pp 413, 414 as being 'cases where the acts are purported to be done on the faith of an agreement which is supposed to be but is not a binding contract between the parties'.

[168] Whilst it may be arguable that there is nothing in *Pavey and Matthews Pty Ltd v Paul* (1987) which prevents recovery by Christiani, nothing that was said in that case is capable of forming the foundation for the claim by Christiani on a *quantum meruit*. By its pleadings, as I have construed them, Christiani sought to claim an entitlement to be paid what it claims is owing to it by the first defendant pursuant to the subcontract merely because Goliath requested that it do the work whereupon Christiani entered into the subcontract with the first defendant pursuant to which it was to do the work. One needs only to state the claim in those stark terms to immediately recognise that it is one which is not maintainable. Whilst it may be that Deane J did not have the present type of situation in mind when he referred to the concurrent existence of a valid and enforceable agreement, it may yet be said that the circumstances of the present case cannot possibly give rise to any 'occasion or legal justification for the law to superimpose or impute an obligation or promise to pay a reasonable remuneration' on the part of Goliath.

By entering into the subcontract, Christiani made a commercial decision that it was prepared to perform the subject matter of the subcontract and look to the first defendant for payment. That may have been a commercial decision which was wise or foolish. Regardless of the wisdom of that decision there is no occasion for the law to relieve Christiani of the consequences of the first defendant's inability to perform its side of the contract, if indeed it is unable to do so, by imposing upon Goliath the obligation to pay for work or materials for which the first defendant has failed to pay. Had Christiani wished to protect itself against the risk that it would not be paid by the first defendant then it could have sought to protect itself by asking that Goliath join in the subcontract in some appropriate way. Goliath might or might not have been prepared to accede to such a request. If it had done so then Christiani could have sought relief from Goliath on the [169] contract. If it had declined to do so then Christiani would have had to decide whether it would enter into the subcontract without such protection or not enter into the subcontract at all ...

[Crawford J agreed with Zeeman J.]

Commentary and questions

Was Goliath successful in its claim against Christiani? What reasons were given for the court's decision? Do you think the outcome of the decision could have been different had all relevant contracts been discharged?

This approach is supported by other Australian authorities[89] and by most academics.[90]

Pan Ocean Shipping Ltd v Creditcorp Ltd, The 'Trident Beauty' [1994] 1 WLR 161
House of Lords

Pan Ocean had entered into a time charterparty under which it chartered the *Trident Beauty* from its owners, Trident. The charter hire was at the rate of US$6,400 per day, payable 15 days in advance commencing on the day of the vessel's delivery. The charterparty contained various clauses providing for the vessel to be off hire in certain circumstances and the consequences which flowed from this. In particular, there was provision for 'any overpaid hire' to be 'returned at once' where the owner was in breach of contract by being unable to supply an operational vessel. The charterparty also provided that an adjustment was to be made to the next instalment of hire to reflect the period the vessel was off hire in the preceding period of hire. Trident assigned its right to the hire received from chartering the vessel 'free of all encumbrances and third party interests' to Creditcorp as part of a financing agreement. Pan Ocean was given written notice of this assignment and accordingly paid Creditcorp an advance payment to cover a period of hire. In fact, the vessel was off hire for the whole of the relevant period for repairs. Trident not being worth suing, Pan Ocean commenced an action in restitution against Creditcorp, the assignee of the payments. Pan Ocean claimed it was entitled to recover the payments from Creditcorp on the basis that the consideration for the payments had wholly failed.

Lord Goff of Chieveley: ... [163] To consider the question whether Pan Ocean is entitled to recover the money from Creditcorp on this ground, it is necessary first to turn to the time charter which governed the relationship between Trident and Pan Ocean. Under the charter the hire was, as normal, payable in advance – here 15 days in advance. Provision was made, also as normal, for the vessel to be off hire in certain specified circumstances. This is to be found in the usual off hire clause, cl 15 in the printed form. In addition, other circumstances were specified in some of the additional typed clauses, under which the vessel would or might be off hire (see cll 37, 56, 61, 74 and 79). In another typed clause (cl 59), there was provision for the hire to be reduced pro rata in certain circumstances. I should also record that, again as normal, the charter contained an arbitration clause (cl 17 of the printed form), providing for any dispute to be referred to arbitration in the manner there prescribed.

Now, given the circumstances that the charter hire was payable in advance and that the vessel might be off hire under one or other of the relevant clauses during a

---

89 *Winterton Constructions Pty Ltd v Hambros Australia Ltd* (1992); *Strang Patrick Stevedoring Pty Ltd v Owners of the MV Sletter* (1992).

90 Burrows, 'Restitution from assignees' [1994] RLR 52, pp 55–56; Mason and Carter, *Restitution Law in Australia*, 1995, pp 282–83. *Contra* Mead, 'Restitution within contract?' (1991) 11 LS 172.

period in respect of which hire had been paid, it was inevitable that, from time to time, there might have to be an adjustment of the hire so paid. Such adjustments are a normal feature of the administration of time charters. The usual practice is, I understand, for an adjustment to be made when the next instalment of hire falls due, by making a deduction from such instalment in respect of [164] hire previously paid in advance which has not been earned; in the present charter, provision is to be found to that effect in cl 29(f), one of the additional typed clauses. If the relevant period is the last hire period under the charter, such a deduction may not be possible. Any overpayment will then have to be repaid by the shipowner, and no doubt this will normally be taken care of in the final account drawn up at the end of the charter period.

Sometimes, the event which gives rise to the charterer being deprived of the services of the vessel, in whole or in part, which in its turn renders the vessel off hire under one of the applicable clauses, may constitute a breach of contract by the shipowner. If so, the charterer will have a claim for damages for breach of contract, which may embrace the amount of hire paid in advance in respect of the period during which the vessel was off hire. But this need not be so; and in any event the charter will usually make express provision for the repayment of hire which has been overpaid. In the present charter, such a provision is to be found in cl 18 of the printed form, which provides that 'any overpaid hire' is 'to be returned at once'. This provision gives rise to a contractual debt payable in the relevant circumstances by the shipowner to the charterer. But even in the absence of any such express contractual provision, advance hire which proves to have been paid in respect of a period during which the vessel was rendered off hire under a term of the contract must ordinarily be repaid, and if necessary a term will be implied into the contract to that effect. That such an implied obligation may arise is implicit in such early cases as *Tonnelier v Smith & Weatherall & Co* (1897) and *CA Stewart & Co v Phs Van Ommeren (London) Ltd* (1918). This will of course be dealt with in the ordinary case as a matter of administration of the time charter; if any dispute should persist, it will fall to be resolved by arbitration.

All this is important for present purposes, because it means that, as between shipowner and charterer, there is a contractual regime which legislates for the recovery of overpaid hire. It follows that, as a general rule, the law of restitution has no part to play in the matter; the existence of the agreed regime renders the imposition by the law of a remedy in restitution both unnecessary and inappropriate. Of course, if the contract is proved never to have been binding, or if the contract ceases to bind, different considerations may arise, as in the case of frustration (as to which, see *French Marine v Cie Napolitaine d'Eclairage et de Chauffage par le Gaz* (1921), and now the Law Reform (Frustrated Contracts) Act 1943). With such cases as these, we are not here concerned. Here, it is true, the contract was prematurely determined by the acceptance by Pan Ocean of Trident's repudiation of the contract. But, before the date of determination of the contract, Trident's obligation under cl 18 to repay the hire instalment in question had already accrued due; and accordingly that is the relevant obligation, as between Pan Ocean and Trident, for the purposes of the present case.

It follows that, in the present circumstances and indeed in most other similar circumstances, there is no basis for the charterer recovering overpaid hire from the shipowner in restitution on the ground of total failure of consideration. It is true that sometimes we find in the cases reference to there having been in such circumstances a failure of consideration (see, eg, *CA Stewart & Co v Phs Van Ommeren (London) Ltd* (1918)). But it should [165] not be inferred that such statements refer to a quasi-contractual, as opposed to a contractual, remedy. Consistently with this view, the remedy is not limited to the recovery of money paid for a consideration which has *wholly* failed. A contractual remedy is not, of course, so circumscribed and so, in *Stewart's* case itself, overpaid hire was recoverable where it was recognised that there had been a partial failure of consideration.[91]

It is against this background that we have to consider Pan Ocean's claim now made against Creditcorp for repayment of the hire instalment paid to it as assignee of the charter hire. First, although the benefit of the contract debt had been assigned to Creditcorp, with the effect that payment to Creditcorp by Pan Ocean constituted a good discharge of the debt, nevertheless the burden of the contract remained upon Trident. From this it follows that Trident remained contractually bound to repay to Pan Ocean any overpaid hire, notwithstanding that such hire had been paid not to Trident but to Creditcorp as assignee. [Counsel] for Pan Ocean accepted in argument that this was so; but he nevertheless maintained that Pan Ocean had alternative courses of action open to it – either to proceed against Trident in contract, or to proceed against Creditcorp in restitution. His argument proceeded on the basis that, in ordinary circumstances, a charterer has alternative remedies against the shipowner for the recovery of overpaid hire, either in contract or in restitution; and that here, since the hire had been paid to Creditcorp as assignee, Pan Ocean's remedy in restitution lay against Creditcorp in place of Trident. However, for the reasons I have already given, I am unable to accept this argument. This is because, in my opinion, Pan Ocean never had any remedy against Trident in restitution on the ground of failure of consideration in the present case, its only remedy against Trident lying under the contract ...

[166] I am of course well aware that writers on the law of restitution have been exploring the possibility that, in exceptional circumstances, a plaintiff may have a claim in restitution when he has conferred a benefit on the defendant in the course of performing an obligation to a third party.[92] But, quite apart from the fact that the existence of a remedy in restitution in such circumstances must still be regarded as a matter of debate, it is always recognised that serious difficulties arise if the law seeks to expand the law of restitution to redistribute risks for which provision has been made under an applicable contract. Moreover, it would in any event be unjust to do so in a case such as the present where the defendant, Creditcorp, is not the mere recipient of a windfall but is an assignee who has purchased from Trident the right to receive the contractual debt which the plaintiff, Pan Ocean, is now seeking to recover from Creditcorp in restitution despite the facts that the relevant contract imposes on the assignor (Trident) an obligation of repayment in the circumstances in question, and that there is nothing in the assignment which even contemplates, still less imposes, any additional

---

91   See *CA Stewart & Co v Phs Van Ommeren (London) Ltd* (1918), p 562 *per* RA Wright KC *arguendo*.

92   See, eg, Goff and Jones, *The Law of Restitution*, 4th edn, 1993, pp 55ff; and (for a particular example) Burrows, *The Law of Restitution*, 1993, pp 271–72.

obligation on the assignee (Creditcorp) to repay. This is the point which, as I understand it, concerned Neill LJ in the Court of Appeal, when he said that 'Creditcorp were in a position analogous to that of a *bona fide* purchaser for value' (1993), p 449.

Lord Woolf: ... [170] It is one thing to require the other party to the contract to repay if he does not provide the consideration which under the contract he was under obligation to supply, it is another to make the assignee, who was never intended to be under any obligation to supply the consideration, liable to make the repayment. It is conceded that there is no right to trace moneys which are paid to an assignee and there is never any question of their being any restriction on the assignee preventing him dealing with the money as his own. There is no justification for subjecting an assignee, because he has received a [171] payment in advance, to an obligation to make a repayment because of the non-performance of an event for which he has no responsibility ...

If Pan Ocean were entitled to recover from Creditcorp, the consequence would be that they would have two different parties instead of a single party from whom they could recover; on [counsel for Pan Ocean's] argument, against Trident under the contract and against Creditcorp for money had and received. It is equally possible to frame a different fundamental question. Why should Pan Ocean have two alternative parties to whom to look for a repayment [172] merely because Trident, as part of their own financial arrangements, have assigned their right to receive payment to a third party, Creditcorp? ...

[Lord Keith of Kinkel and Lord Slynn of Hadley agreed with Lord Woolf. Lord Lowry agreed with both Lord Goff of Chieveley and Lord Woolf.]

Commentary and questions

What were the two grounds put forward by Lord Woolf (the majority) for refusing restitution in this case? What was the primary ground upon which Lord Goff refused relief?

Burrows believes that the claim in restitution was rightly refused as to grant restitution in this situation would be to undermine the contract of assignment between Trident and Creditcorp:[93]

To take an analogous case, the reason an unpaid subcontractor performing work on a house under a contract with a head contractor cannot normally sue the owner in restitution is because this would undermine the contractual relationship between the head contractor and the owner. Similarly, if A sells a ship to B requiring B to pay the purchase price to C – as part of a contractual deal between A and C – B could not normally recover the price from C for failure of consideration in the event of non-delivery of the ship because this would undermine the contractual relationship between A and C. But restitution would be possible if the contract between the owner and the head contractor or between A and C were invalid (or non-existent). There was, of course, nothing invalid about the contract of assignment between Trident and Creditcorp and restitution was therefore correctly refused.

---

93   Burrows, 'Restitution from assignees' [1994] RLR 52, pp 55–56.

RELATIONSHIP BETWEEN RESTITUTION AND DAMAGES FOR BREACH OF CONTRACT

Baltic Shipping Co v Dillon (1993) 176 CLR 344 High Court of Australia

The facts are stated at p 286.

The courts below awarded both restitution of the balance of the fare and $5,000 as damages for disappointment and distress. The High Court affirmed the award of damages and addressed the issue whether, had the plaintiff been entitled to restitution of the fare, she could have recovered both the fare and damages for breach of contract.

Mason CJ: ... [354] In view of my conclusion that the respondent cannot succeed in her restitutionary claim for recoupment of the fare, there is no necessity for me to consider whether the two claims can be maintained. However, as the question has been argued, I should record my view of the question. There is authority to suggest that the claims are alternative and not cumulative.[94] But Lord Denning MR was clearly of the view that the claims may be concurrent. In _Heywood v Wellers (A Firm)_ (1976), p 458, he said:

> [The plaintiff] could recover the £175 as money paid on a consideration which had wholly failed. She was, therefore, entitled to recover it as of right. And she is entitled to recover as well damages for negligence. Take this instance. If you engage a driver to take you to the station to catch a train for a day trip to the sea, you pay him £2 – and then the car breaks down owing to his negligence. So that you miss your holiday. In that case you can recover not only your £2 back but also damages for the disappointment, upset and mental distress which you suffered.

Lord Denning was speaking of negligence in the sense of breach of [355] a contractual obligation of due care. He noted a qualification to the entitlement to maintain the two claims (1976), p 459:

> Some reduction should be made for the fact that if the [defendants] had done their duty ... it would have cost her something.

That reduction was accordingly made to the damages for breach of contract ...

And Treitel says in relation to claims for loss of bargain, reliance loss and restitution:[95]

> There is sometimes said to be an inconsistency between combining the various types of claim ... The true principle is not that there is any logical objection to combining the various types of claim, but that the plaintiff cannot combine them so as to recover more than once for the same loss ... The point has been well put by Corbin: '_full_ damages and _complete_ restitution ... will not both be given for the same breach of contract.'[96]

[359] ... [I]n my view, _Walstab v Spottiswoode_ (1846) and the earlier cases support the view expressed by Corbin and Treitel that full damages and complete restitution will not be given for the same breach of contract. There are several reasons. First,

---

94   Eg, _Walstab v Spottiswoode_ (1846) _per_ Pollock CB.

95   _Law of Contract_, 8th edn, 1991, p 834. However, elsewhere he appears to treat the claims as alternatives: pp 932–33.

96   _Corbin on Contracts_, p 1221. Emphasis added by Treitel.

restitution of the contractual consideration removes, at least notionally, the basis on which the plaintiff is entitled to call on the defendant to perform his or her contractual obligations. More particularly, the continued retention by the defendant is regarded, in the language of Lord Mansfield, as 'against conscience' or, in the modern terminology, as an unjust enrichment of the defendant because the condition upon which it was paid, namely, performance by the defendant may not have occurred.[97] But, equally, that performance, for deficiencies in which damages are sought, was conditional on payment by the plaintiff. Recovery of the money paid destroys performance of that condition. Secondly, the plaintiff will almost always be protected by an award of damages for breach of contract, which in appropriate cases will include an amount for substitute performance or an amount representing the plaintiff's reliance loss. It should be noted that nothing said here is inconsistent with *McRae v Commonwealth Disposals Commission* (1952).

I would therefore conclude that, even if the respondent had an entitlement to recover the cruise fare, Carruthers J and the majority of the Court of Appeal erred in allowing restitution of the balance of the fare along with damages for breach of contract ...

Brennan J: ... [372] Damages for breach of contract, the measure of which is governed by *Robinson v Harman* (1848)[98] are intended to restore the plaintiff to the same situation as if the contract had been performed. As Mason CJ and Dawson J said in *The Commonwealth v Amann Aviation Pty Ltd* (1991):

> The corollary of the principle in *Robinson v Harman* is that a plaintiff is not entitled, by the award of damages upon breach, to be placed in a superior position to that which he or she would have been in had the contract been performed.

As *Amann Aviation* shows, in assessing a plaintiff's damages for breach of contract, the cost to the plaintiff of performing his obligations under the contract must be taken into account. It follows that it was erroneous in the present case for the learned trial judge to award the plaintiff both an amount representing the fare and an amount of damages for disappointment and distress ...

Deane and Dawson JJ: ... [379] There is a further reason, which would appear not to have been raised in argument in the courts below, why Mrs Dillon's action for restitution of the fare paid to Baltic must fail. It is that she has sought and obtained an order against Baltic for compensatory damages for Baltic's failure to perform its contractual promises to her. In particular, she has received a refund of a proportionate part of the fare and has obtained and will retain the benefit of an award of damages for the disappointment and distress which she sustained by reason of Baltic's failure to provide her with the full pleasure cruise which it promised to provide. In these circumstances, Mrs Dillon has indirectly enforced, and indirectly obtained the benefit of, Baltic's contractual promises.

Ordinarily, as has been seen, 'when one is considering the law of failure of consideration and of the ... right to recover money on that ground, it is ... not the promise which is referred to as the consideration, but the performance of the promise'.[99] That statement has nothing to say, however, to the situation which

---

97   See *Fibrosa* (1943), pp 65–67 *per* Lord Wright.

98   See also *The Commonwealth v Amann Aviation Pty Ltd* (1991), pp 80, 98, 117, 134, 148, 161.

99   See, eg, *Fibrosa, op cit*, fn 97, p 48 *per* Viscount Simon LC.

exists when the promisee has sought and obtained an award of full compensatory damages for the failure to perform the promise. In that situation, the damages are awarded and received as full compensation for non-performance or breach of the promise and represent the indirect fruits of the promise. That being so, it would be quite wrong to say either that the only quid pro quo which has been obtained for the payment by the promisee is the bare promise or that the promise and the recovery of compensatory damages for its breach can realistically be seen as representing no consideration at all. In such a case, the promise has been indirectly enforced and the award of compensation has, as a matter of substance, been received in substitution for the promised consideration. In those [380] circumstances, the promisee, having received full compensation for non-performance of the promise, is not entitled to a refund of the price upon payment of which the performance of the promise was conditioned.[100] Were it otherwise, the promisee 'would have the equivalent' of performance of the contractual promise 'without having borne the expense' which he or she had agreed to pay for it ...[101]

Gaudron J: ... [387] In my view, Mrs Dillon's claim for damages, if successful, precludes a refund of the fare. The claim for damages is a claim to the full benefit of the contract, part of that benefit taking the form of money as compensation for its breach. If Mrs Dillon were to receive damages and a refund of her fare as well, she would, in effect, take the benefit of the contract without an obligation to give consideration for it ...

Commentary

There is disagreement about whether the plaintiff needs to make an election between the damages claim and the restitutionary claim where the claim is alternatively for contractual damages or for reasonable remuneration in restitution. The approach of the court (with the exception of Mason CJ) in the principal case appears to require that an election be made. There is also other Australian authority for this approach.[102] However these authorities tend to speak in terms of an election between alternative *remedies* and so fail to recognise that the competition is in reality one between distinct and concurrent *causes of action*. The better view, by analogy with the approach of Mason CJ in the principal case, is that in Australia it would be incorrect to regard the two claims as inconsistent and that a plaintiff should be allowed both, provided this does not amount to double recovery, although the position must be regarded as uncertain.[103] The position in England is similarly unsettled.[104]

---

100 See, eg, *Moses v Macferlan* (1760).

101 See *TC Industrial Plant Pty Ltd v Robert's Queensland Pty Ltd* (1963), p 293; (1964), p 1090.

102 *Renard Constructions Pty Ltd v Minister for Public Works* (1992), p 277 (see extract, p 322); *Martin Stern JR AIA v Hooker Corporation Ltd* (1990).

103 Mason and Carter, *Restitution Law in Australia*, 1995, p 579; Carter, 'Discharged contracts: claims for restitution' (1997) 11(2) JCL 130, pp 140–41; see also Treitel, *Remedies for Breach of Contract*, 1988, pp 98–100.

104 See Birks, 'Inconsistency between compensation and restitution' (1996) 112 LQR 375, p 378; Stevens, 'Election between alternative remedies' [1996] RLR 117.

CHAPTER 12

CONTRACTS DISCHARGED FOR FRUSTRATION

COMMON LAW

Traditional position: 'the loss lies where it falls'

Cutter v Powell **(1795) 6 Term Rep 320; 101 ER 573 King's Bench**

A master of a ship signed and delivered a promissory note to Cutter in Jamaica which stated: 'Ten days after the ship "Governor Parry" myself master, arrives at Liverpool, I promise to pay to Mr T Cutter the sum of thirty guineas (£31.50), provided he proceeds, continues and does his duty as second mate in the said ship from hence to the port of Liverpool.' The ship sailed from Jamaica on 2 August 1793 and Cutter served as second mate until 20 September when he died prior to the ship reaching Liverpool. The usual wages of a second mate on such a voyage was £4 per month, and the usual length of the voyage was eight weeks. Cutter's widow commenced proceedings to recover the value of the services.

Lord Kenyon Ch J: [324] I should be extremely sorry that in the decision of this case we should determine against what had been the received opinion in the mercantile world on contracts of this kind, because it is of great importance that the laws by which the contracts of so numerous and so useful a body of men as the sailors are supposed to be guided should not be overturned. Whether these kind of notes are much in use among the seamen, we are not sufficiently informed; and the instances now stated to us from Liverpool are too recent to form anything like usage. But it seems to me at present that the decision of this case may proceed on the particular words of this contract and the precise facts here stated, without touching marine contracts in general. That where the parties have come to an express contract none can be implied has prevailed so long as to be reduced to an axiom in the law. Here the defendant expressly promised to pay the intestate thirty guineas, provided he proceeded, continued and did his duty as second mate in the ship from Jamaica to Liverpool; and the accompanying circumstances disclosed in the case are that the common rate of wages is four pounds per month, when the party is paid in proportion to the time he serves: and that this voyage is generally performed in two months. Therefore if there had been no contract between these parties, all that the intestate could have recovered on a *quantum meruit* for the voyage would have been eight pounds, whereas here the defendant contracted to pay thirty guineas provided the mate continued to do his duty as mate during the whole voyage, in which case the latter would have received nearly four times as much as if he were paid for the number of months he served. He stipulated to receive the larger sum if the whole duty were performed, and nothing unless the whole of that duty were performed: it was a kind of insurance. On this particular contract my opinion is formed at present; at the same time I must say that if we were assured that these notes are in universal use, and that the commercial world have received and acted upon them in a different sense, I should give up my own opinion.

Ashurst J: ... We cannot collect that there is any custom prevailing among merchants on these contracts; and therefore we have nothing to guide us but the terms of the [325] contract itself. This is a written contract, and it speaks for itself. And as it is entire, and as the defendant's promise depends on a condition precedent to be performed by the other party, the condition must be performed before the other party is entitled to receive anything under it. It has been argued however that the plaintiff may now recover on a *quantum meruit*: but she has no right to desert the agreement; for wherever there is an express contract the parties must be guided by it; and one party cannot relinquish or abide by it as it may suit his advantage. Here the intestate was by the terms of his contract to perform a given duty before he could call upon the defendant to pay him anything; it was a condition precedent, without performing which the defendant is not liable. And that seems to me to conclude the question: the intestate did not perform the contract on his part; he was not indeed to blame for not doing it; but still as this was a condition precedent, and as he did not perform it, his representative is not entitled to recover.

Grose J: ... In this case the plaintiff must either recover on the particular stipulation between the parties, or on some general known rule of law, the latter of which has not been much relied on. I have looked into the laws of Oleron; and I have seen a late case on this subject in the Court of Common Pleas, *Chandler v Greaves* (1792). I have also inquired into the practice of the merchants in the city, and have been informed that these contracts are not considered as divisible, and that the seaman must perform the voyage, otherwise he is not entitled to his wages; though I must add that the result of my inquiries has not been perfectly satisfactory, and therefore I do not rely upon it. The laws of Oleron are extremely favourable to the seamen; so much so that if a sailor, who has agreed for a voyage, be taken ill and put on shore before the voyage is completed, he is nevertheless entitled to his whole wages after deducting what has been laid out for him. In the case of *Chandler v Greaves*, where the jury gave a verdict for the whole wages to the plaintiff who was put on shore on account of a broken leg, the court refused to grant a new trial, though I do not know the precise grounds on which the court proceeded. However in this case the agreement is conclusive; the defendant only engaged to pay the intestate on condition of his continuing to do his duty on board during the whole voyage; and the latter was to be entitled either to thirty guineas or to nothing, for such was [326] the contract between the parties. And when we recollect how large a price was to be given in the event of the mate continuing on board during the whole voyage instead of the small sum which is usually given per month, it may fairly be considered that the parties themselves understood that if the whole duty were performed, the mate was to receive the whole sum, and that he was not to receive anything unless he did continue on board during the whole voyage. That seems to me to be the situation in which the mate chose to put himself; and as the condition was not complied with, his representative cannot now recover anything. I believe however that in point of fact these notes are in common use, and perhaps it may be prudent not to determine this case until we have inquired whether or not there has been any decision upon them.

Commentary and questions

This case and the following case of *Appleby v Myers* (1867) were bedevilled by the doctrine of 'entire obligations'. The effect of this doctrine, as applied in the principal case and in *Appleby v Myers*, was that anything short of at least substantial performance of the frustrated contract would disentitle that party from recovering the pro rata contract price either on the contract or on a *quantum meruit* in restitution. The correctness of that principle from a restitutionary perspective must now be questioned in light of the High Court's decision in *Baltic Shipping Co v Dillon* (1993) (see extract, p 286) where it was held that the doctrine of entire obligations is a contractual doctrine which has no direct relevance for the law of restitution. On this view, the fact that an entire obligation was only partially performed will not *necessarily* lead to the rejection of a restitutionary claim, but will still be relevant when determining whether the defendant has been enriched by the plaintiff's work.

Would the application of unjust enrichment principles to the facts of *Cutter v Powell* give a different result? Would a restitutionary claim be excluded on these facts?

Appleby v Myers (1867) LR 2 CP 651 Exchequer Chamber

The plaintiffs agreed to construct machinery upon the defendant's premises and to keep it in repair for two years. The work was to be done in 10 separate stages, and it was agreed that the price would be paid only on completion of the work. After work on some of the stages was complete and while others were in the course of being completed, the premises, all the machinery thus far installed, and some of the plaintiffs' materials, were destroyed by an accidental fire. The plaintiff commenced proceedings to recover £419 for work done and materials supplied.

Blackburn J: ... [658] The whole question depends on the true construction of the contract between the parties ... [659] [E]ven on the supposition that the materials had become unalterably fixed to the defendant's premises, we do not think that, under such a contract as this, the plaintiffs could recover anything unless the whole work was completed. It is quite true that materials worked by one into the property of another become part of that property. This is equally true, whether it be fixed or movable property. Bricks built into a wall become part of the house; thread stitched into a coat which is under repair, or planks and nails and pitch worked into a ship [660] under repair, become part of the coat or the ship; and therefore, generally, and in the absence of something to shew a contrary intention, the bricklayer, or tailor, or shipwright, is to be paid for the work, and materials he has done and provided, although the whole work is not complete. It is not material whether in such a case the non-completion is because the shipwright did not choose to go on with the work, as was the case in *Roberts v Havelock* (1832), or because in consequence of a fire he could not go on with it, as in *Menetone v Athawes* (1746). But, though this is the *prima facie* contract between those who enter into contracts for doing work and supplying materials, there is nothing to render it either illegal or absurd in the workman to agree to complete the whole, and be paid when the whole is complete, and not till then: and we think that the plaintiffs in the present case had entered into such a contract. Had the accidental fire left the defendant's premises untouched, and only injured a part of the work which the plaintiffs had already done, we apprehend that it is clear the plaintiffs under such a contract as the present must have done that part over again, in order to fulfil their contract to complete the whole and 'put it to work for the sums above named respectively'. As it is, they are, according to the principle laid down in *Taylor v Caldwell* (1963), excused from completing the work; but they are not therefore entitled to any compensation for what they have done, but which has, without any fault of the defendant, perished. The case is in principle like that of a shipowner who has been excused from the performance of his contract to carry goods to their destination, because his ship has been disabled by one of the excepted perils, but who is not therefore entitled to any payment on account of the part performance of the voyage, unless there is something to justify the conclusion that there has been a fresh contract to pay freight pro rata.

On the argument, much reference was made to the civil law. The opinions of the great lawyers collected in the Digest afford us very great assistance in tracing out any question of doubtful principle; but they do not bind us: and we think that, on the principles of English law laid down in *Cutter v Powell* (1795), *Jesse v* [661] *Roy* (1834), *Munro v Butt* (1858), *Sinclair v Bowles* (1829), and other cases, the plaintiffs, having contracted to do an entire work for a specific sum, can recover nothing unless the work be done, or it can be shewn that it was the defendant's fault that the work was incomplete, or that there is something to justify the conclusion that the parties have entered into a fresh contract ...

Commentary and question

The essence of this case and the preceding case of *Cutter v Powell* (1795) is that in cases of frustration the loss should lie where it falls. This position has been adopted into Australian law in *Hirsch v The Zinc Corp Ltd* (1917) and *In re Continental C & G Rubber Co Pty Ltd* (1919) (see following extract). Although these cases have never been formally overruled, and thus still technically represent the law in Australia, it is clear that today courts will determine the question of recovery under a frustrated contract by reference to the principles of unjust enrichment. In *Pavey & Matthews Pty Ltd v Paul* (1987), p 256 (see extract, p 15) Deane J expressly recognised frustration as a ground for restitution.

Would the application of unjust enrichment principles to the facts of *Appleby v Myers* give a different result?

In re Continental C & G Rubber Company Pty Ltd (1919) 27 CLR 194
High Court of Australia

Continental (the 'company') contracted with W Anderson & Sons Pty Ltd (the 'contractors') for the contractors to build machinery and erect it on the company's land. Clause 22 of the contract provided for progress payments to be made to the contractors at the rate of 90% of the value of the machinery in progress, as certified by an engineer. The company made progress payments totalling £6,000 to the contractors however the contract became frustrated by the outbreak of war. The company became an enemy and in November 1914 a controller was appointed to manage the company. In June 1918 the minister for trade and customs ordered the controller to wind up the company. Nothing was done on the relevant contract since the date of the last progress payment on 22 December 1914, and no part of the machinery was ever delivered to the company. The questions relevantly before the High Court were whether the contractors were entitled to prove in the winding up of the company for compensation or damages for the services provided, and whether the company could recover any of the progress payments on the basis of a failure of consideration or mistake.

Knox CJ and Barton J: ... [201] (1) It is clear that under the contract the right of the contractors to payment of any money thereunder could only accrue upon a certificate having been given by the engineer (see cl 22 of general conditions). No certificate was ever given by the engineer except in respect of the sums which make up the £6,000 already paid. When it became, to the knowledge of the parties, impossible further to perform the contract, no right had accrued to the contractors under the contract to be paid any sum of money in addition to the £6,000 which has been paid to them. In these circumstances the ordinary rule applies, viz that where the further performance of a contract has become impossible, then, in the absence of special provisions in the contract, both parties are excused from further performance of the contract (see *Chandler v Webster* (1904); *Elliott v Crutchley* (1904)) and as regards further liability – ie, liability not then actually accrued and enforceable – the contract is at an end. This disposes of the claim of the contractors to prove in the liquidation.

(2) The grounds upon which it was suggested that the controller was entitled to recover from the contractors the whole or part of the £6,000 which had been paid to them were (a) total failure of consideration, and (b) that the payments made after the outbreak of war were made under mistake, and might be recovered as money received by the contractors for the use of the company.

As to (a) it is sufficient to say that the case is covered by the principle of the decisions in *Appleby v Myers* (1867) and *Civil Service Co-Operative Society v General Steam Navigation Co* (1903) ...

[Their Honours accordingly dismissed the claim based on failure of consideration. As to the mistake claim their Honours held that any mistake was a mistake of law which could not found recovery.]

Isaacs and Rich JJ: ... [203] The ... question is whether the company or the controller is entitled to recover back the progress payments and some excess payments intended as part payment of the machinery. We emphasise the facts adverted to, that no new implied contract is set up or could be validly made. The matter must rest upon the grounds [204] set up, namely, (1) mistake, and (2) failure of consideration. [Their Honours rejected the mistake claim on the basis it was founded upon a mistake of law and continued:] As to failure of consideration, it is based on the assumption that either the common law on the outbreak of war made the delivery impossible or the Statute, subsequently but retrospectively, did so. One answer to the 90% is that the 22nd clause disposes of the want of consideration, though leaving open the question of illegality of subsequent payment. But apart from that, the doctrine that, when the common law or a Statute annuls or declares void an agreement under which money is paid under a mistaken belief that there is a liability to pay it, it may be recovered back on failure of consideration, is unsound. Mistake as to the general law, not induced by the other party, must be endured by the party paying. In *Evanson v Crooks* (1911) Lord Sumner (then Hamilton J) said: 'Sums of money recovered as money had and received to a plaintiff's use, that is to say received *ex æquo bono*, a defendant ought to pay back whether the ground of it is that the sums were paid under a mistake of fact or whether the ground of it is that they were paid in view of a consideration which has wholly failed; and I think these different ways of stating the ground – which are merely differing circumstances – to support the cause of action for money had and received are not mutually independent of one another; but the action for money had and received can only be maintained where upon the whole view of the circumstances there is an obligation *ex æquo et bono* upon the defendant to repay the money, and a defendant is not under any obligation to repay the money *ex æquo et bono* where an Act of Parliament has said that the transaction shall be void.' The same learned Lord, in *Sinclair v Brougham* (1914), said there was no failure of consideration in that case, and the quotation he made from *In re Guardian Permanent Building Society* (1883) is much in point here ...

Question

Was there a total failure of consideration for the £6,000?

Modern position: restitution is available

In the following case, the House of Lords rejected the previous line of authorities that denied restitutionary relief under a frustrated contract.

Fibrosa Spolka Akcyjna v Fairbairn Lawson Combe Barbour Ltd [1943] AC 32
House of Lords

The respondent, an English company, agreed to sell machinery to the appellant, a Polish company, for the price of £4,800 of which one-third was to be paid with the order. The Polish company paid £1,000, but the contract was frustrated by the outbreak of the Second World War. No part of the machinery was ever delivered. The appellant commenced proceedings to recover the £1,000 on the basis the consideration for the payment had totally failed.

Viscount Simon LC: ... [45] The *locus classicus* for the view which has hitherto prevailed is to be found in the judgment of Sir Richard Collins MR in *Chandler v Webster* (1904). It was not a considered judgment, but it is hardly necessary to say that I approach this pronouncement of the then Master of the Rolls, with all the respect due to so distinguished a common lawyer. When his judgment is studied, however, one cannot but be impressed by the circumstance that he regarded the proposition that money in such cases could not be recovered back as flowing from the decision in *Taylor v Caldwell* (1863). *Taylor v Caldwell* however, was not a case in which any question arose whether money could be recovered back, for there had been no payment in advance, and there is nothing in the judgment of Blackburn J which, at any rate in terms, affirms the general proposition that 'the loss lies where it falls'. The application by Collins MR of *Taylor v Caldwell* to the actual problem with which he had to deal in *Chandler v Webster* (1904), deserves close examination. He said:

The plaintiff contends that he is entitled to recover the money which he has paid on the ground that there has been a total failure of [46] consideration. He says that the condition on which he paid the money was that the procession should take place, and that, as it did not take place, there has been a total failure of consideration. That contention does no doubt raise a question of some difficulty, and one which has perplexed the courts to a considerable extent in several cases. The principle on which it has been dealt with is that which was applied in *Taylor v Caldwell* (1863) (namely, that, where, from causes outside the volition of the parties, something which was the basis of, or essential to the fulfilment of, the contract has become impossible, so that, from the time when the fact of that impossibility has been ascertained, the contract can no further be performed by either party, it remains a perfectly good contract up to that point, and everything previously done in pursuance of it must be treated as rightly done, but the parties are both discharged from further performance of it). If the effect were that the contract were wiped out altogether, no doubt the result would be that the money paid under it would have to be repaid as on a failure of consideration. But that is not the effect of the doctrine; it only releases the parties from further performance of the contract. Therefore, the doctrine of failure of consideration does not apply.

It appears to me that the reasoning in this crucial passage is open to two criticisms: (a) The claim of a party, who has paid money under a contract, to get the money back, on the ground that the consideration for which he paid it has totally failed, is not based upon any provision contained in the contract, but arises because, in the circumstances which have happened, the law gives a remedy in quasi-contract to the party who has not got that for which he bargained. It is a claim to recover money to which the defendant has no further right because in the circumstances that have happened, the money must be regarded as received to the plaintiff's use. It is true that the effect of frustration is that, while the contract can no further be performed, 'it remains a perfectly good contract up to that point, and everything previously done in pursuance of it must be treated as rightly done'; but it by no means follows that the situation existing at the moment of frustration is one which leaves the party that has paid money and has not received the stipulated consideration without any remedy. To claim the return of money paid on the ground of [47] total failure of consideration is not to vary the terms of the contract in any way. The claim arises not because the right to be repaid is one of the stipulated conditions of the contract, but because, in the circumstances that have happened, the law gives the remedy. It is the failure to distinguish between (1) the action of *assumpsit* for money had and received in a case where the consideration has wholly failed, and (2) an action on the contract itself, which explains the mistake which I think has been made in applying English law to this subject matter. Thus, in *Blakeley v Muller & Co* (1903), Lord Alverstone CJ said: 'I agree that *Taylor v Caldwell* (1863) applies, but the consequence of that decision is that neither party here could have sued on the contract in respect of anything which was to be done under it after the procession had been abandoned.' That is true enough, but it does not follow that because the plaintiff cannot sue 'on the contract' he cannot sue *dehors* the contract for the recovery of a payment in respect of which consideration has failed. In the same case Wills J relied on *Appleby v Myers* (1867), where a contract was made for the erection by A of machinery upon the premises of B, to be paid for upon completion. There was no prepayment, and in the course of the work the premises were destroyed by fire. It was held that both parties were excused from further performance, and that no liability accrued on either side, but the liability referred to was liability under the contract, and the learned judge seems to have thought that no action to recover money in such circumstances as the present could be conceived of unless there was a term of the contract, express or implied, which so provided. Once it is realised that the action to recover money for a consideration that has wholly failed rests, not on a contractual bargain between the parties, but, as Lord Sumner said in *Sinclair v Brougham* (1914), 'upon a notional or imputed promise to repay', or (if it is preferred to omit reference to a fictitious promise) upon an obligation to repay arising from the circumstances, the difficulty in the way of holding that a prepayment made under a contract which has been frustrated can be recovered back appears to me to disappear. (b) There is, no doubt, a distinction between cases in which a contract is 'wiped out altogether', eg, because it is void as being illegal from the start, or as being due to fraud which the innocent party has [48] elected to treat as avoiding the contract, and cases in which intervening impossibility 'only releases the parties from further performance of the contract'. But does the distinction between these two classes of case justify the deduction of Collins MR that 'the doctrine of failure of consideration does not apply' where the contract remains a perfectly good contract up to the date of frustration? This conclusion seems to be derived from the view that, if the contract remains good and valid up to the moment of frustration, money which has already been paid under it cannot be regarded as having been paid for a consideration which has wholly failed. The party who has paid the money has had the advantage, whatever it may be worth, of the promise of the other party. That is true, but it is necessary to draw a distinction. In English law, an enforceable contract may be formed by an exchange of a promise for a promise, or by the exchange of a promise for an act (I am excluding contracts under seal) and thus, in the law relating to the formation of contract, the promise to do a thing may often be the consideration, but when one is considering the law of failure of consideration and of the quasi-contractual right to recover money on that ground, it is, generally speaking, not the promise which is referred to as the consideration, but the performance of the promise. The money was paid to secure performance and, if performance fails the inducement which brought about the payment is not fulfilled.

If this were not so, there could never be any recovery of money, for failure of consideration, by the payer of the money in return for a promise of future performance, yet there are endless examples which show that money can be recovered, as for a complete failure of consideration, in cases where the promise was given but could not be fulfilled: see the notes in Bullen and Leake's *Precedents of Pleading*, 9th edn, p 263. In this connection the decision in *Rugg v Minett* (1809) is instructive. There the plaintiff had bought at auction a number of casks of oil. The contents of each cask was to be made up after the auction by the seller to the prescribed quantity so that the property in a cask did not pass to the plaintiff until this had been done. The plaintiff paid in advance a sum of money on account of his purchases generally, but a fire occurred after some of the casks had been filled up, while the others had not. The plaintiff's action was to recover the money he had paid as money received by the [49] defendants to the use of the plaintiffs. The Court of King's Bench ruled that this cause of action succeeded in respect of the casks which at the time of the fire had not been filled up to the prescribed quantity.

A simple illustration of the same result is an agreement to buy a horse, the price to be paid down, but the horse not to be delivered and the property not to pass until the horse has been shod. If the horse dies before the shoeing, the price can unquestionably be recovered as for a total failure of consideration, notwithstanding that the promise to deliver was given. This is the case of a *contract de certo corpore* where the *certum corpus* perishes after the contract is made, but, as Vaughan Williams LJ's judgment in *Krell v Henry* (1903) explained, the same doctrine applies 'to cases where the event which renders the contract incapable of performance is the cessation or non-existence of an express condition or state of things, going to the root of the contract, and essential to its performance'. I can see no valid reason why the right to recover prepaid money should not equally arise on frustration arising from supervening circumstances as it arises on frustration from destruction of a particular subject matter. The conclusion is that the rule in *Chandler v Webster* is wrong, and that the appellants can recover their £1,000.

While this result obviates the harshness with which the previous view in some instances treated the party who had made a prepayment, it cannot be regarded as dealing fairly between the parties in all cases, and must sometimes have the result of leaving the recipient who has to return the money at a grave disadvantage. He may have incurred expenses in connection with the partial carrying out of the contract which are equivalent, or more than equivalent, to the money which he prudently stipulated should be prepaid, but which he now has to return for reasons which are no fault of his. He may have to repay the money, though he has executed almost the whole of the contractual work, which will be left on his hands. These results follow from the fact that the English common law does not undertake to apportion a prepaid sum in such circumstances (contrast the provision, now contained in s 40 of the Partnership Act 1890, for apportioning a premium if a partnership is prematurely dissolved). It must be for the legislature to decide whether provision should be made for an equitable apportionment of prepaid moneys which have to be returned by the recipient in view of the [50] frustration of the contract in respect of which they were paid ...

Lord Atkin: ... [50] A sells a horse to B for £50, delivery to be made in a month, the price to be paid forthwith, but the property not to pass till delivery, and B to pay A each week an agreed sum for keep of the horse during the month. The horse dies in a fortnight. A is excused from delivery and from taking delivery. B is bound to pay the sum due for the fortnight during which the horse was kept. But what is the position as to the £50, the price paid in advance? This is in simple terms the problem in the present case. The answer which I venture to think would occur to most people, whether laymen or lawyers, would be that the buyer ought to get his money back, having had nothing for [51] it, and the lawyer would support the claim by saying that it is money had and received to the use of the buyer, being money paid on a consideration which has wholly failed.

But that is not the answer which was given in similar circumstances in the coronation cases, and it is those decisions that come up for review in the present case ...

[Lord Atkin reviewed *Chandler v Webster* (1904) and continued at p 52:]

My Lords, the difficulty which this decision causes me is to understand how this great lawyer [Collins MR in *Chandler v Webster*] came to the conclusion that the claim for money paid on a consideration which wholly failed could only be made where the contract was wiped out altogether, and I have sought for some construction of his words which stopped short of that absolute statement, but I can find none. I know of no authority for the proposition. It is true that where a party is in a position to rescind a contract he may be able to sue for money which he has paid under the contract now rescinded, but there are numerous cases where there has been no question of rescission where such an action has lain. I may refer to *Giles v Edwards* (1797), where a contract to deliver wood was prevented by the defendant preventing performance by not loading all the wood; *Rugg v Minett* (1809), where the buyer had paid part of the purchase price on a sale of turpentine in casks, where the property in [53] some casks had passed while in seller's warehouse, but in some had not, and the purchaser was entitled to recover as money had and received the proportion properly attributable to the casks in which the property had not passed; *Nockels v Crosby* (1825), *Wilson v Church* (1879), *Johnson v Goslett* (1857), and *Ashpitel v Sercombe* (1850) in all of which the plaintiff had put up money for an adventure which was eventually abandoned by the promoters; *Devaux v Connolly* (1849), where there had been an overpayment in respect of goods delivered. In none of these cases was it suggested that the contract was 'wiped out altogether'. Indeed, in other cases where it is suggested that the contract was 'rescinded', all that is meant is that the party was entitled to treat himself as no longer bound to perform and to recover what he himself has paid.

With great respect, therefore, to the judgment in *Chandler v Webster* (1904), I do not agree with that part of it which refused to give effect to the plaintiff's claim for the return of the sum which he had paid on the ground of total failure of consideration ...

[54] That the result of the law may cause hardship when a contract is automatically stayed during performance and any further right to performance is denied to each party is incontrovertible. One party may have almost completed expensive work. He can get no compensation. The other [55] party may have paid the whole price, and, if he has received but a slender part of the consideration, he can get no compensation. At present it is plain that if no money has been paid on the contract there is no legal principle by which loss can be made good. What is being now decided is that the application of an old established principle of the common law does enable a man who has paid money and received nothing for it to recover the money so expended. At any rate, it can be said it leaves the man who has received the money and given nothing for it in no worse position than if he had received none. Many commercial contracts provide for various risks. It is always possible to provide for the risk of frustration, but what provision the parties may agree will probably take some time to negotiate. Meanwhile, by the application of a general doctrine which is independent of the special contract and only comes into play when further performance of the latter is precluded, the man who pays money in advance on a contract which is frustrated and receives nothing for his payment is entitled to recover it back. I think, therefore, that the appeal should be allowed.

Lord Russell of Killowen: ... [57] In his judgment in *Chandler v Webster* (1904), the Master of the Rolls states that the right to recover moneys paid for a consideration which has failed only arises where the contract is 'wiped out altogether', by which expression I understand him to mean is void *ab initio*. This is clearly a misapprehension on the part of the learned judge. The money was recoverable under the common *indebitatus* count, as money received for the use of the plaintiff.

The right so to recover money paid for a consideration that had failed did not depend on the contract being void *ab initio*. There are many such cases in the books in which the contract has not been void *ab initio*, but the money paid for a consideration which has failed has been held recoverable. Thus, as one example, money paid as a deposit on a contract of sale which has been defeated by the fulfilment of a condition is recoverable: *Wright v Newton* (1835). It was submitted by the respondents, but without argument, that money paid for a consideration which had failed was recoverable only when the failure was due to the fault of the other party to the contract, but, on the authorities, this submission is clearly ill founded. *Chandler v Webster* (1904) was accordingly, in my opinion, wrongly decided. The money paid was recoverable, as having been paid for a consideration which had failed. The rule that on frustration the loss lies where it falls cannot apply in respect of moneys paid in advance when the consideration moving from the payee for the payment has wholly failed, so as to deprive the payer of his right to recover moneys so paid as moneys received to his use, but, as I understand the grounds on which we are prepared to allow this appeal, the rule will, unless altered by legislation, apply in all other respects.

Lord Wright: [Lord Wright made the observations about the nature of the action for money had and received, which are extracted in Chapter 1, p 12, and continued at p 64:] Must, then, the court stay its hand in what would otherwise appear to be an ordinary case for the repayment of money paid in advance on account of the purchase price under a contract for the sale of goods merely because the contract has become impossible of performance and the consideration has failed for that reason? The defendant has the plaintiff's money. There was no intention to enrich him in the events which happened. No doubt when money is paid under a contract, it can only be claimed back as for failure of consideration where the contract is terminated as to the future. Characteristic instances are where it is dissolved by frustration or impossibility or by the contract becoming abortive for any reason not involving fault on the part of the plaintiff where the consideration, if entire, has entirely [65] failed, or where, if it is severable, it has entirely failed as to the severable residue, as in *Rugg v Minett* (1809). The claim for repayment is not based on the contract which is dissolved on the frustration but on the fact that the defendant has received the money and has on the events which have supervened no right to keep it. The same event which automatically renders performance of the consideration for the payment impossible, not only terminates the contract as to the future, but terminates the right of the payee to retain the money which he has received only on the terms of the contract performance ...

[72] [I] think it is clear both in English and Scots law that the failure of consideration which justifies repayment is a failure in the contract performance. What is meant is not consideration in the sense in which the word is used when it is said that in executory contracts the promise of one party is consideration for the promise of the other. No doubt in some cases the recipient of the payment may be exposed to hardship if he has to return the money though before the frustration he has incurred the bulk of the expense and is then left with things on his hands which become valueless to him when the contract fails, so that he gets nothing and has to return the prepayment. These and many other difficulties show that the English rule of recovering payment the consideration for which has failed works a rough justice. It was adopted in more primitive times and was based on the simple theory that a man who has paid in advance for something which he has never got

ought to have his money back. It is further imperfect because it depends on an entire consideration and a total failure. Courts of equity have evolved a fairer method of apportioning an entire consideration in cases where a premium has been paid for a partnership which has been ended before its time: Partnership Act 1890, s 40; contrary to the common law rule laid down in *Whincup v Hughes* (1871). Some day the legislature may intervene to remedy these defects ...

Commentary

Shortly after this decision, legislation was enacted in England providing for an adjustment of rights upon frustration.[1]

The status of *Fibrosa* in Australian law was uncertain for a long period of time. However, Mason CJ (Brennan and Toohey JJ concurring) approved the decision in *Baltic Shipping Co v Dillon* (1993) (see extract, p 286):

> [Fibrosa] correctly reflects the law in Australia and, to the extent that it is inconsistent, should be preferred to the decision of this court in *In re Continental C & G Rubber Co Pty Ltd*.

The other members of the court also referred to *Fibrosa* with approval.[2] And in *Pavey & Matthews Pty Ltd v Paul* (1987), p 256 Deane J held that a contract discharged for frustration can form the basis of a restitutionary claim. Thus, although *In re Continental* has never been formally overruled, it should no longer be viewed as good law in Australia.

The nature and operation of the doctrine of failure of consideration is dealt with elsewhere.[3] It is sufficient to restate here that traditionally the law has insisted that the failure of consideration be total. A partial failure is not sufficient, as illustrated in the case of *Whincup v Hughes* (1871). In this case Hughes had agreed to instruct George Whincup, the plaintiff's son, in the trade of watchmaker and jeweller. The plaintiff had paid to Hughes a premium of £25. George Whincup received instruction for almost a year, when Hughes died. It was held that the plaintiff could not recover a proportion of the premium as the consideration had only partially failed.

The members of the House of Lords in *Fibrosa* recognised that allowing recovery of an advance payment could operate harshly upon a defendant who has incurred expenses in carrying out work preparatory to the performance of the contract. The defence of change of position, which has been recognised only recently, should ameliorate this problem.[4] A defendant who incurs expenses in

---

1 Law Reform (Frustrated Contracts) Act 1943 (UK).
2 Pages 375, 377, 379 *per* Deane and Dawson JJ; p 385 *per* Gaudron J; p 389 *per* McHugh J.
3 See, in particular, Chapters 10 and 11.
4 McKendrick, 'Frustration, restitution, and loss apportionment', in Burrows (ed), *Essays on the Law of Restitution*, 1991, pp 151–52; Mason and Carter, *Restitution Law in Australia*, 1995, p 473.

reliance on the receipt of the part payment and in good faith will be entitled to raise the defence of change of position to the extent of the expenditure.

FRUSTRATED CONTRACTS LEGISLATION

Three Australian states (New South Wales, South Australia and Victoria) have enacted legislative schemes providing for an adjustment of the parties' rights following discharge by frustration.[5] The purpose of these legislative schemes is to reform the common law restitutionary rights of the parties. Certain types of contract are excluded from the operation of the legislation in each jurisdiction,[6] and in each jurisdiction the parties can expressly provide that the legislation is not to apply.

The object, basis of recovery and scope of the different pieces of legislation vary markedly, and a comparative analysis is outside the scope of this book.[7]

---

5   Frustrated Contracts Act 1978 (NSW); Frustrated Contracts Act 1988 (SA); Frustrated Contracts Act 1959 (Vic).

6   Eg, charterparties and most insurance contracts.

7   For such an analysis, see Stewart and Carter, 'Frustrated contracts and statutory adjustment: the case for a reappraisal' [1992] CLJ 66; Mason and Carter, *The Law of Restitution*, 1995, pp 487–93. For a recent analysis of the UK legislation, see Carter and Tolhurst, 'Gigs n' restitution – frustration and the statutory adjustment of payments and expenses' (1996) 10 JCL 264.

CHAPTER 13

UNENFORCEABLE, VOID AND ILLEGAL CONTRACTS

UNENFORCEABLE CONTRACTS

Introduction

A contract might be rendered unenforceable by statute (for example because it is not evidenced in writing) or by the common law (for example because of minority, mental illness or drunkenness). The unenforceability of the contract is not in itself the basis of a restitutionary claim; the claimant must establish one of the recognised unjust factors. The traditional unjust factors applied in this context are total failure of consideration for claims for the recovery of money and request and acceptance for claims for the recovery of non-monetary benefits. The unjust factor of mistake will also be relevant where the claimant paid the money or rendered the services on the erroneous assumption the contract was enforceable. This unjust factor has not traditionally been relied upon due to the mistake of law bar, now overturned. A claim based on mistake will be subject to the defence of the provision of good consideration. It is unsettled whether this defence applies pro rata, that is, only to the extent of the consideration given, or as a complete defence.[1] Also, the claim will be refused if permitting recovery would defeat the policy of the legislation or common law rule pursuant to which the contract is made unenforceable.[2]

There is authority suggesting that a claim in restitution will not be permitted under an executory unenforceable contract unless it is discharged for breach or repudiation, or rescinded.[3] However, it might be that a claim will be permitted in the absence of a formal discharge or rescission where performance is unlikely to be completed.[4]

---

1   Mason and Carter take the view that the defence serves to reduce the plaintiff's claim by the value of the consideration given: Mason and Carter, *Restitution Law in Australia*, 1995, p 855. However, this view may not be supported by the majority judgment in *David Securities Pty Ltd v Commonwealth Bank of Australia* (1992) (see extract, p 646), which approached the matter from the perspective of total failure of consideration.

2   *Pavey & Matthews Pty Ltd v Paul* (1987) (see extract, p 362). See below, pp 362–68 for further discussion.

3   *Pavey & Matthews Pty Ltd v Paul* (1987), p 257 (see extract, p 15); *Deposit and Investment Co Ltd v Kaye* (1963), pp 458–59; *Matthes v Carter* (1955); *Thomas v Brown* (1876).

4   *Roxborough v Rothmans of Pall Mall Australia* (2001). This aspect of the decision is discussed in Chapter 10, pp 265–66.

Recovery of money

Money paid under an unenforceable contract will be recoverable on the ground of a total failure of consideration.[5] Alternatively, the plaintiff could recover on the ground of mistake where he or she paid the money because of a mistaken assumption about the enforceability of the contract.[6]

The following case involved a claim for recovery of money paid under an unenforceable loan agreement on the basis that consideration for the payment had totally failed. The Privy Council makes some important comments about the requirement that the consideration be total.

Goss v Chilcott [1996] AC 788 Privy Council

A finance company advanced money to the defendants on a three month loan secured by a mortgage over the defendants' property. Interest was payable on three specified dates. The defendants agreed to lend the money to the second defendant's brother, Mr Haddon, who was a solicitor and director of the finance company, on the basis that he would repay the money and have the mortgage cancelled. The brother altered the mortgage instrument without the defendants' knowledge or authority in order to extend the time for repayment and to alter the interest date. He made only two payments which were appropriated in the finance company's books as interest payments. No part of the principal was repaid. The plaintiff (respondent), the liquidator of the finance company, brought an action seeking to enforce the contract of loan or alternatively restitution of the loan advance on the basis of a total failure of consideration. The House of Lords confirmed that the loan contract was unenforceable against the defendants due to the material alteration of the instrument by the defendant's brother who was acting as the agent of the finance company. The remaining issue was whether the advance could be recovered on the basis of a total failure of consideration.

Lord Goff of Chieveley: ... [796] As their Lordships have already recorded, [the trial judge] held that the company could not succeed on its claim in restitution, because he considered that there had been no total failure of consideration for the loan, the defendants having furnished consideration for it in the form of the mortgage instrument. With this conclusion, their Lordships are unable to agree.

The advance was in fact paid by the company to Haddon Marshall & Co, as solicitors, but, having regard to the terms on which they received it from the company, was retained by them in their trust account until after the defendants had executed the mortgage instrument. It was then [797] available to the defendants but was in fact received by Mr Haddon, as agreed between him and the defendants. In these circumstances the loan appears in fact to have been advanced to the defendants pursuant to the terms of the mortgage instrument, the consideration for the advance being expressed to be the personal covenants by the defendants to repay the advance upon those terms. Even if (which their Lordships doubt) the loan had been paid pursuant to a preceding oral agreement between the company and the defendants, it must have been paid in consideration for the

---

5   *Deposit & Investment Co v Kaye* (1963); *Goss v Chilcott* (1996) (see following extract).
6   *Marshall v Marshall* (1999), p 178 (see extract, p 394).

defendants' promise to repay it, though the ensuing loan contract would (as their Lordships have already indicated) have become merged in and superseded by the contract contained in the mortgage instrument.

But the consideration there referred to, necessarily implicit if not explicit in every loan contract, was the consideration necessary for the formation of the contract; and, as Viscount Simon LC observed in a much quoted passage in his speech in *Fibrosa Spolka Akcyjna v Fairbairn Lawson Combe Barbour Ltd* (1943), p 48:

> ... when one is considering the law of failure of consideration and of the quasi-contractual right to recover money on that ground, it is, generally speaking, not the promise which is referred to as the consideration, but the performance of the promise ... If this were not so, there could never be any recovery of money, for failure of consideration, by the payer of the money in return for a promise of future performance, yet there are endless examples which show that money can be recovered, as for a complete failure of consideration, in cases where the promise was given but could not be fulfilled.

Of course, in the case of a loan of money any failure by the borrower to repay the loan, in whole or in part, by the due date, will in ordinary circumstances give rise to a claim in contract for repayment of the part of the loan which is then due. There will generally be no need to have recourse to a remedy in restitution. But in the present case that course is, exceptionally, not open to the company, because the defendants have been discharged from their obligations under the mortgage instrument; and so the company has to seek recovery in restitution. Let it however be supposed that in the present case the defendants had been so discharged from liability at a time when they had paid nothing, by way of principal or interest, to the company. In such circumstances their Lordships can see no reason in principle why the company should not be able to recover the amount of the advance made by them to the defendants on the ground that the money had been paid for a consideration which had failed, viz the failure of the defendants to perform their contractual obligation to repay the loan, there being no suggestion of any illegality or other ground of policy which precluded recovery in restitution in such circumstances.

In the present case however, although no part of the principal sum had been repaid by the defendants, two instalments of interest had been paid; and the question arises whether these two payments of interest precluded recovery on the basis that in such circumstances the failure of consideration for the advance was not total. Their Lordships do not think so. The function of the interest payments was to pay for the use of the capital sum over the period for which the loan was outstanding, which [798] was separate and distinct from the obligation to repay the capital sum itself. In these circumstances it is, in their Lordships' opinion, both legitimate and appropriate for present purposes to consider the two separately. In the present case, since it is unknown when the mortgage instrument was altered, it cannot be known whether, in particular, the second interest instalment was due before the defendants were discharged from their obligations under the instrument. Let it be supposed however that both interest payments had fallen due before that event occurred. In such circumstances, there would have been no failure of consideration in respect of the interest payments rendering them recoverable by the defendants; but that would not affect the conclusion that there had been a total failure of consideration in respect of the capital sum, so that the latter would be recoverable by the company in full on that ground. Then let it be supposed instead that the second interest payment did not fall due until after the avoidance of the instrument. In such circumstances the consideration for that interest payment would have failed (at least if it was payable in advance), and it would *prima facie* be recoverable by the defendants on the ground of failure of consideration; but that would not affect the conclusion that the capital sum would be recoverable by the company also on that ground. In such a case, therefore, the capital sum would be recoverable by the lender, and the interest payment would be recoverable by the borrower; and doubtless judgment would, in the event, be given for the balance with interest at the appropriate rate: see *Westdeutsche Landesbank Girozentrale v Council of the London Borough of Islington* (1994). In either event, therefore, the amount of the loan would be recoverable on the ground of failure of consideration. In the present case, since no part of the capital sum had been repaid, the failure of consideration for the capital sum would plainly have been total. But even if part of the capital sum had been repaid, the law would not hesitate to hold that the balance of the loan outstanding would be recoverable on the ground of failure of consideration; for at least in those cases in which apportionment can be carried out without difficulty, the law will allow partial recovery on this ground: see *David Securities Pty Ltd v Commonwealth Bank of Australia* (1992), p 383.

[After rejecting the defences of change of position and ministerial receipt, the court continued at p 799:]

It remains to consider what order should be made on the appeal. *Prima facie*, the company is entitled to restitution in a sum equal to the amount of the advance, viz $30,000. The question of restitution in respect of the interest payments in theory depends upon whether one or both payments were made before the date when the contractual obligation of the defendants to repay the loan was discharged, ie, the date of the alteration of the instrument by Mr Haddon (a date which, as their Lordships have already recorded, is unknown). However the Court of Appeal, in giving judgment in favour of the company for the sum of $26,460.75, deducted both interest payments from the amount of the advance; and, since there is no cross-appeal by the company against the judgment on that point, their Lordships need not consider whether [800] the judgment should be varied in this respect ...

Commentary and questions

On what basis did Lord Goff hold that the principal was recoverable? According to his Lordship would the same result have followed if the borrowers had repaid part of the principal?

The approach of Lord Goff in the principal case to failure of consideration has been welcomed by most commentators.[7] However it is uncertain whether the counter-restitutionary approach will apply where the agreed return for the

---

7   Carter and Tolhurst, 'Restitution for failure of consideration' (1997) 11(2) JCL 162, p 171; Rickett, 'Restitution and contract' (1996) NZLJ 263, p 265; Watts, 'Restitution' [1996] NZLR 471.

payment is the provision of non-monetary benefits.[8] It has been suggested that where the plaintiff has received a non-monetary benefit, counter-restitution can be easily effected by the award of a *quantum meruit* or *quantum valebat*,[9] although there is no judicial authority on this point.

Lord Goff's approach to failure of consideration, based on restitution and counter-restitution, might at first glance be open to criticism as leading to the illogical position that if there is 99% completion by the defendant of the contract restitution is permitted, but not if there is 100% completion. This issue recently arose before the English Court of Appeal in *Guinness Mahon & Co Ltd v Kensington and Chelsea Royal London Borough Council* (1998). In that case, the court ordered restitution of the net balance of payments made under a void swaps contract, even though the contract was fully completed. The court held that the 'bargained for consideration' in such a case is not the payment of the money, but rather the *legal obligation to be paid the money*. On this view, the consideration totally fails regardless of whether the contract is partially or fully executed.

For further discussion of the counter-restitutionary approach to total failure of consideration, see Chapter 10, pp 278–80.

Recovery of non-monetary benefits

A plaintiff will be entitled to recover the value of work done under an unenforceable contract where the defendant has accepted the benefit of the plaintiff's performance.[10]

Deglman v Guaranty Trust [1954] 3 DLR 785 Supreme Court of Canada

The respondent, a student, lived for some time with his aunt. The respondent claimed that the aunt orally agreed that if he performed such services as she requested from time to time she would make adequate provision for him in her will and in particular she would leave him one of her houses. The respondent performed certain services at his aunt's request, involving taking her for drives and on car trips, doing odd jobs, running errands and attending to some of her personal needs. The aunt failed to leave the house to the respondent in her will nor to make any other provision for him. Any agreement between the respondent and his aunt was unenforceable under the Statute of Frauds due to the lack of writing. The respondent brought proceedings against the executor of his aunt's estate for specific performance of her promise to bequeath him the house or alternatively for the reasonable value of the services he had provided to her. The claim for specific performance was rejected by the court; however the *quantum meruit* claim was successful.

---

8   See generally Edelman, 'Restitution for a total failure of consideration: when a total failure is not a total failure' (1996) 1(3) Newc LR 57. See also Carter and Tolhurst, 'Restitution for failure of consideration' (1997) 11(2) JCL 162, pp 170–71.

9   Edelman, 'The new doctrine of partial failure of consideration' (1997) 15 ABR 299, pp 241–42.

10 *Pavey & Matthews Pty Ltd v Paul* (1987), pp 227–28, 255–56, 257, 263, 264 (see extract, p 15); *Lee Gleeson Pty Ltd v Stirling Estates Pty Ltd* (1991); *Nankuwarrin Yunti v Seeley Constructions Pty Ltd* (1998).

Cartwright J: ... [794] I agree with the conclusion of my brother Rand that the respondent is entitled to recover the value of these services from the respondent administrator. This right appears to me to be based, not on the contract, but on an obligation imposed by law.

In *Fibrosa Spolka Akcyjna v Fairbairn Lawson Combe Barbour Ltd* (1943), Lord Wright said (p 61):

It is clear that any civilised system of law is bound to provide remedies for cases of what has been called unjust enrichment or unjust benefit, that is to prevent a man from retaining the money of or some benefit derived from another which it is against conscience that he should keep. Such remedies in English law are generically different from remedies in contract or in tort, and are now recognised to fall within a third category of the common law which has been called quasi-contract or restitution.

And (p 62):

Lord Mansfield does not say that the law implies a promise. The law implies a debt or obligation which is a different thing. In fact, he denies that there is a contract; the obligation is as efficacious as if it were upon a contract. The obligation is a creation of the law, just as much as an obligation in tort. The obligation belongs to a third class, distinct from either contract or tort, though it resembles contract rather than tort.

Lord Wright's judgment appears to me to be in agreement with the view stated in *Williston on Contracts* referred to by my brother Rand.

In *Scott v Pattison* (1923), the plaintiff served the defendant under a contract of service not to be performed within one year which was held not to be enforceable by reason of the Statute of Frauds. It was held that he could nonetheless sue in *assumpsit* on an implied contract to pay him according to his deserts [795]. While I respectfully agree with the result arrived at in *Scott v Pattison* I do not think it is accurate to say that there was an implied promise. In my view it was correctly decided in *Britain v Rossiter* (1879), that where there is an express contract between the parties which turns out to be unenforceable by reason of the Statute of Frauds no other contract between the parties can be implied from the doing of acts in performance of the express but unenforceable contract. Brett LJ, after stating that the express contract although unenforceable was not void but continued to exist, said (p 27):

It seems to me impossible that a new contract can be implied from the doing of acts which were clearly done in performance of the first contract only, and to infer from them a fresh contract would be to draw an inference contrary to the fact. It is a proposition which cannot be disputed that no new contract can be implied from acts done under an express contract which is still subsisting; all that can be said is that no one can be charged upon the original contract because it is not in writing.

Cotton LJ (pp 129 and 130) and Thesiger LJ (p 133) expressed the same view.

In the case at bar all the acts for which the respondent asks to be paid under his alternative claim were clearly done in performance of the existing but unenforceable contract with the deceased that she would devise 548 Besserer Street to him, and to infer from them a fresh contract to pay the value of the services in money would be, in the words of Brett LJ quoted above, to draw an inference contrary to the fact.

In my opinion when the Statute of Frauds was pleaded the express contract was thereby rendered unenforceable, but the deceased having received the benefits of the full performance of the contract by the respondent, the law imposed upon her, and so on her estate, the obligation to pay the fair value of the services rendered to her ...

Commentary

The leading Australian case in this area is *Pavey & Matthews Pty Ltd v Paul* (1987) (see extracts, pp 15, 70 and 362), where a builder was successful in recovering the reasonable value of services and materials provided under an unenforceable contract. The basis of recovery was said to be the defendant's acceptance of the benefit of the work (pp 227–28, 255–56, 257, 263, 264).

The plaintiff in *Pavey & Matthews v Paul* had fully performed the contract, and thus the defendant was presumed to have accepted the benefit of the work performed in accordance with the contractual request.[11] The same principle applies where the plaintiff has been prevented from fully performing the unenforceable contract by the defendant's breach or repudiation: see *Gino D'Alessandro Constructions Pty Ltd v Powis* (1987), pp 58–59. In cases where the *plaintiff* is in breach of the unenforceable contract then, by analogy with the principles applying in the context of contracts discharged for breach,[12] the plaintiff should be denied a claim unless an independent act of acceptance of the plaintiff's performance can be established: *Gino D'Alessandro Constructions Pty Ltd v Powis* (1987), pp 58–59. However, this was not the approach taken in *Tea Tree Gully Builders v Martin* (1992). In that case a builder was awarded the value of building services provided under an agreement which was unenforceable by the builder due to the lack of a statutory licence. The claim was permitted despite the fact that the building work was incomplete and required rectification, Bollen J holding that the position of the defendant was adequately protected by an entitlement to set off damages for the defective performance:

> The result is that the respondent receives payment for work done and the appellant receives value by way of an award of damages for the consequences of fault and breach on the part of the respondents. Each party receives value.

This approach has the attraction of being just to both parties and has the support of Burrows.[13] However, it is contrary to the rule in *Sumpter v Hedges* (1898) (see extract, p 325) against allowing recovery by a party in breach unless an independent act of acceptance of the partial services can be shown. It has been argued that the effect of the decision in *Tea Tree Gully* is to put an unlicensed builder in a more advantageous position than a licensed one, which could not

---

11 See in particular the reference by Deane J to 'constructive' acceptance (1987) 162 CLR 221, p 257 (see extract, p 15).

12 See Chapter 11, pp 324–30.

13 Burrows, *The Law of Restitution*, 1993, pp 276–81.

have been the intention of the legislature, and which would be undesirable as a matter of policy.[14]

Policy considerations

A restitutionary claim for recovery of benefits conferred under an unenforceable contract will be refused where the claim would be contrary to the intent of the governing legislation. As the following case demonstrates, the courts will examine both the wording and intended object of the legislation to determine whether a restitutionary claim is defeated.

Pavey & Matthews Pty Ltd v Paul (1987) 162 CLR 221 High Court of Australia

The facts are stated at p 15.

Mason and Wilson JJ: ... [226] As a matter of ordinary legal usage the words 'enforceable' and 'unenforceable' may refer either to the judicial and curial remedies available for the enforcement of a contract or to all the remedies available for the enforcement of a contract, including such remedies as the contract itself may provide. Section 4 of the Statute of Frauds 1677 (UK) ('Statute of Frauds') and its successor s 128 of the Instruments Act 1928 (Vic), which was considered in *Turner v Bladin* (1951), provided for unenforceability of the first kind, whereas s 9 of the Money Lenders Act 1912 (WA), which was considered in *Mayfair Trading Co Pty Ltd v Dreyer* (1958), especially pp 448–49, provided for unenforceability of the second kind.

The language of s 4 of the Statute of Frauds and of its successors, which specifically provided that no action should be brought on a contract or agreement unless it complied with the prescribed requirements, naturally attracted an interpretation that excluded enforcement by judicial and curial remedies. The words 'enforceable' and 'unenforceable' did not appear in the relevant statutory provisions. Nevertheless, as a matter of history and tradition the effect of the provisions has always been said to make a non-conforming contract or agreement unenforceable in the sense already discussed. On the other hand, where a statutory provision provides that a security or a contract shall be unenforceable, it is natural, in the absence of some restraining context, to interpret the provision as giving rise to unenforceability in the wider sense mentioned above. So, in *Mayfair Trading* the court concluded that the injunction in s 9, which provided that if prescribed formalities were not observed no security should be 'enforceable', rendered the mortgagee's power of sale unenforceable.

The provisions of s 45 of the Act are apt to provide for unenforceability in the wider sense; they are different from the traditional Statute of Frauds formula. They should therefore be read [227] as entailing unenforceability of the contract, not only by means of legal proceedings, but also by means of any other remedy.

To say this is not to exclude the possibility that, in the context of the Act, the statutory concept of unenforceability extends to indirect, as well as direct, enforcement of the contract. The question then is whether the appellant's action on

14   Mason and Carter, *Restitution Law in Australia*, 1995, pp 281–82.

a *quantum meruit* amounts to a direct or an indirect enforcement of the oral contract.

[Their Honours made the observations which are extracted in Chapter 1, p 15, and continued at p 228:] In the present case the New South Wales Court of Appeal attributed a broader operation to s 45 by invoking the usual meaning of the expression 'to enforce', which is 'to compel observance of': see *R v Bates* (1982), p 895. The force of this approach to the problem is not to be underestimated because, as we have seen, the effect of the action on a *quantum meruit* is to enforce the plaintiff's claim in some circumstances in which an action on the contract would succeed, proof of the contract being an element in the quasi-contractual claim. However, it seems to us that in the context of a provision such as s 45 with its injunction that the contract shall not be 'enforceable', it is more appropriate to look to the more precise legal meanings that have been assigned to the term in comparable situations where a contract or a security is expressed to be unenforceable.

This is not a case in which other provisions of the Act throw textual light on what is meant by the word. It is therefore a matter of determining whether any assistance is to be gained from an examination of the policy and purpose of the statute. On one view the purpose of s 45 is to protect the building owner against spurious claims by a builder by preventing the enforcement by him of non-conforming contracts. This in substance was the view taken by the Court of Appeal in this case and in *Schwarstein v Watson* (1985). [229] That purpose includes the protection of the building owner against a claim by a builder on a written contract that fails to describe the building work sufficiently, even in a case where the builder has fully executed the contract on his part. But it would be going a very long way indeed to assert that the statutory protection extends to a case where the building owner requests and accepts the building work and declines to pay for it on the ground that the contract fails to comply with the statutory requirements. True it is that the informal contract, though not enforceable by the builder, is enforceable against him. But it is not to be supposed that it is enforceable against him on the footing that the building owner is under no liability to pay for building work upon which he insists and the performance of which he accepts. The consequences of the respondent's interpretation are so draconian that it is difficult to suppose that they were intended. An interpretation that serves the statutory purpose yet avoids a harsh and unjust operation is to be preferred.

And there is another view which may be taken of the statutory purpose which is more favourable to this interpretation. In *Gino D'Alessandro Constructions Pty Ltd v Powis* (1986) McPherson J pointed out that the function of s 75 of the Builders' Registration and Home Owners' Protection Act 1979 (Qld), a provision substantially similar to s 45 of the Act, was 'to ensure, so far as possible, that a degree of precision is introduced into house building contracts, so that it can be readily determined what is the work to be done and whether loss or damage has been suffered ... so as to attract the benefit of the insurance afforded by s 69' of the Queensland Act. Although there are differences between the Queensland and New South Wales statutes, and their respective schemes of compulsory insurance for the benefit of home owners, s 45 may nevertheless be seen as performing a function similar to that undertaken by s 75 in the Queensland Act. On this view of the purpose and function of s 45, a view which in our opinion has much to commend it, we would not be justified in ascribing to the section the far-reaching consequences urged by the respondent.

Unlike the Court of Appeal we do not see any compelling analogy between s 45 of the Act and the moneylending legislation considered by this court in *Mayfair Trading* and s 22 of the Moneylenders and Infants Loans Act 1941 (NSW) considered by Walsh J in *Deposit & Investment Co v Kaye* (1962). The relevant provisions in those cases explicitly rendered unenforceable contracts [230] executed by the moneylender. The statutes were directed at making unenforceable an obligation to repay money already lent and a security already given in respect of such an obligation. It was not possible to interpret these provisions so that they left on foot any quasi-contractual causes of action on the part of the lender. Request and receipt by the borrower of the money lent were integral elements in a situation in which the contract and all securities were expressed to be unenforceable. An additional feature of the moneylending cases is that the legislation was designed to protect borrowers by imposing onerous obligations on moneylenders to comply with the statutory requirements. The need to protect borrowers in this way was the outcome of oppressive conduct on the part of moneylenders. Section 45, seen in its setting and in conjunction with the insurance scheme established by the Act, stands on a different footing ...

Brennan J: ... [240] Although it is true to say that a plaintiff who has performed his obligations under an unwritten contract falling within the Statute of Frauds can sue to recover the amount due under the contract (whether a fixed sum or a reasonable amount), that proposition does not necessarily apply when the contract is affected by another statute enacted for a different purpose and couched in different terms. The question here is whether s 45 of the Builders Licensing Act goes further than the Statute of Frauds and precludes a registered builder from suing for the amount due for work done pursuant to an unwritten contract when he has completed the work (or, perhaps, when he has substantially completed the work: see [241] *H Dakin & Co Ltd v Lee* (1916); *Phillips v Ellinson Brothers Pty Ltd* (1941), pp 235, 246).

There is a difference in language and in purpose between s 4 of the Statute of Frauds and s 45 of the Builders Licensing Act. Section 4 of the Statute of Frauds prescribes that 'no action shall be brought whereby to charge any (person) upon' an agreement not in writing being an agreement of a kind therein specified. Section 45 of the Builders Licensing Act provides that a 'building contract' as therein prescribed which is not in writing 'is not enforceable' by the holder of a licence 'against the other party to the contract'. A general denial of enforceability against one party is a more extensive sterilisation of a contract than a denial of a right to enforce it by an action on the contract brought against that party. To make a contract unenforceable against a party is to give him a wider immunity than is given by preventing an action against him on the contract. A contract which is unenforceable cannot give rise to any legal remedy, whether curial or extra-curial: *Mayfair Trading Co Pty Ltd v Dreyer* (1958), pp 448–49 ...

[242] Section 45 was passed to protect the building owner. I respectfully agree with the view of Samuels JA in *Schwarstein v Watson* (1985), pp 140–41 (which his Honour adopted in the present case), that s 45 is designed 'to ensure that a written record was made of the work to be done and the rate to be charged; it being

notorious that disputes about both matters not infrequently arose requiring determination at tedious length'. Or, as McHugh JA said in this case (1985), p 132:

> Disputes between builders and home owners as to what work was agreed upon and what was to be its cost have plagued the building industry for many years. Section 45 represents a legislative attempt to overcome this problem by forcing licensed builders to obtain written contracts for building work before they are enforceable by builders. We must give effect to the legislative policy embodied in s 45, however harsh it may seem in an individual case ...

[243] [T]he submission that a licence holder can sue for remuneration due under his contract with the building owner when s 45 declares that the contract is not enforceable against the building owner seems contrary to the plain words of the statute. If s 45 were held not to bar such an action to recover a debt due under the contract the section would have had little, if any, practical effect on the litigation of building contracts where the holder of the licence had discharged his obligations to completion (or perhaps to substantial completion). If it were necessary to prove the discharge [244] of the licence holder's obligations under the unwritten contract in order to establish an enforceable debt recoverable by the plaintiff, litigation arising out of unwritten building contracts would focus on the work which had been agreed upon and the remuneration promised. The effect of s 45 would be to exacerbate the very problem, identified by Samuels and McHugh JJA, which s 45 was intended to overcome. In my opinion, s 45 precludes the arising of an enforceable debt. The contractual promise to pay is clearly unenforceable and there is no room, while the unenforceable contract is subsisting, for a quasi-contractual claim.

In Queensland a different view has been taken of a provision similar to s 45 in an Act which, in the opinion of the full court of the Supreme Court of Queensland, is designed not so much to protect the building owner as to provide the machinery for administering an insurance scheme: see *Gino D'Alessandro Constructions Pty Ltd v Powis and Another* (1986) Whether the different context of the Queensland provision is sufficient to warrant the operation attributed to its text may be doubted but that is not a question which we must now decide. In my opinion s 45, in its context in the Builders Licensing Act, precludes a licence holder from enforcing the obligations of a building owner under an unwritten contract between them to which that section applies whether or not the licence holder has executed the contract ...

Deane J: [Deane J made the observations about the basis of a claim for restitution of services which are extracted in Chapter 1, p 15, and continued at p 261:] [I]t was submitted on behalf of Mrs Paul that to allow recovery by the builder of what is fair and reasonable compensation for work done under a contract which is rendered unenforceable against her by s 45 of the Act would be contrary to the legislative intent to be discerned in the words of the section when read in the context of the Act. In support of that submission, reliance was placed on various decisions on the effect of provisions in moneylending legislation. I do not agree with this submission for reasons which I shall briefly state ...

The decisions on the moneylending legislation do not seem to me to be really in point. In the legislation involved in those cases, it was possible to argue, both by reference to the different words used and the quite different history of moneylending legislation, that it was the plain legislative intent that the moneylender should be precluded from recovering any compensation for the loan which had been made and received by the borrower. The relevant provisions went well beyond a mere statement that the agreement was to be unenforceable by the lender and were plainly directed towards imposing unenforceability in the ordinary case at a stage after the consideration had been fully executed by the lender, that is to say, after the money had been lent without an adequate memorandum in writing of the terms of the loan. Thus, the sub-section of the Nigerian Moneylenders Ordinance (s 19(4)) which was before the [262] Privy Council in *Kasumu v Baba-Egbe* (1956) expressly provided that a moneylender should not be entitled to enforce 'any' claim 'in respect of' any transaction in relation to which he had made default in complying with the requirement that he should enter certain particulars in a book. Section 9(1) of the Money Lenders Act 1912 (WA), which was before this court in *Mayfair Trading Co Pty Ltd v Dreyer* (1958), provided that no contract for the 'repayment by a borrower of money lent to him ... or for the payment by him of interest on money so lent, and no security given by the borrower ... in respect of any such contract' should be enforceable in the absence of the prescribed note or memorandum. In *Deposit & Investment Co Ltd v Kaye* (1962), p 460, Walsh J expressly drew attention to the fact that the form of the relevant provision did not simply say that 'the contract of loan is not to be enforceable' but provided that 'the borrower's obligations and the security for the performance of them shall not be enforceable'.

There is no apparent reason in justice why a builder who is precluded from enforcing an agreement should also be deprived of the ordinary common law right to bring proceedings on a common *indebitatus* count to recover fair and reasonable remuneration for work which he has actually done and which has been accepted by the building owner: cf *Johnsons Tyne Foundry Pty Ltd v Maffra Corporation* (1948), p 565. Nor, upon a consideration of the words of s 45 in their context in the Act, am I able to identify any legislative intent to deprive the builder of that ordinary common law right. The section does not make an agreement to which it applies illegal or void. Nor do its words disclose any legislative intent to penalise the builder beyond making the agreement itself unenforceable by him against the other party. It may be that the bringing of an action as on a common *indebitatus* count would conflict with the apparent legislative policy underlying s 45 if the claimant in such an action were entitled as of right to recover the amount which the building owner had agreed to pay under the unenforceable agreement. I am, however, unpersuaded that the bringing by a builder of an action on the common *indebitatus* count in which he can recover no more than what is fair and reasonable in the circumstances as compensation for the benefit of the work which he has actually done and which has been accepted by the building owner conflicts with any discernible legislative policy. Plainly enough, the survival of the ordinary common law right of the builder to recover, in an action [263] founded on restitution or unjust enrichment, reasonable remuneration for work done and accepted under a contract which is unenforceable by him does not frustrate the purpose of the section to provide protection for a building owner. The building owner remains entitled to enforce the contract. He cannot, however, be forced either to comply with its terms or to permit the builder to carry it to completion. All that he can be required to do is to pay reasonable compensation for work done of which he has received the benefit and for which in justice he is obligated to make such a payment by way of restitution. In relation to such work, he can rely on the contract, if it has not been rescinded, as to the amount of remuneration and the terms of payment. If the agreed remuneration exceeds what is reasonable in the circumstances, he can rely on the unenforceability of the contract with the result that he is liable to pay no more than what is fair and reasonable ...

Commentary and questions

What did the court identify to be the policy objective of s 45 of the Builders' Licensing Act? According to the majority, would a claim in restitution be contrary to this policy? Why did Brennan J dissent on this issue? Whose view do you prefer?

A number of later decisions have allowed *quantum meruit* claims by unlicensed builders on the authority of *Pavey's* case.[15] Legislative provisions preventing recovery of a 'fee or consideration' (*Nankuwarrin Yunti v Seeley Constructions Pty Ltd* (1998)), a 'fee or charge under any contract or engagement' (*Great City Pty Ltd v Kemayan Management Services (Australia) Pty Ltd* (1999)) or a 'remedy in respect of a breach' of contract (*Elkateb v Lawindi* (1997)) have been held, following *Pavey*, not to preclude a claim in restitution. However, *Pavey's* case was distinguished in *Sevastopoulos v Spanos* (1991), which involved a claim by a plaintiff builder for the reasonable value of services provided under a contract variation not in writing. Section 19(1) of the House Contracts Guarantee Act 1987 (Vic) provided:

> Subject to sub-section (2), if at any time after a domestic building work contract is entered into a variation is made to the contract, the builder is not entitled to recover in any court the cost of any work performed or materials supplied under the variation unless the variation is in writing and signed by the builder and the building owner personally or by an agent authorised to act on behalf of the builder or building owner.

The court held that the terms of the Act, prohibiting claims for 'the cost of any work performed or materials supplied', were much wider than the provision in *Pavey's* case, and specifically excluded any claim 'whether founded on contract or otherwise': p 202.[16] Further, the court recognised that it would be difficult to administer the system of builders' guarantees implemented by the Act unless building contracts and variations to them were in writing: pp 204–05. Lastly, the court pointed out that the effect of its decision to preclude recovery was less draconian than in *Pavey's* case as it would prevent builders from recovering only the cost of the variation, not the full cost of the work done: p 202.

Pavey's case has also been distinguished in cases dealing with statutory provisions that expressly prohibit the doing of the work for which remuneration

---

15 See, for example, *Lee Gleeson Pty Ltd v Stirling Estates Pty Ltd* (1991); *Nankuwarrin Yunti v Seeley Constructions Pty Ltd* (1998).

16 See also *FJ Richards Pty Ltd v Mills Pty Ltd* (1995) where a provision preventing recovery of 'remuneration' by an unlicensed real estate agent was said to prevent a *quantum meruit* claim.

is being sought.[17] These cases establish that recovery will be refused where the legislation not only renders the contract unenforceable, but also expressly prohibits the doing of the work which is the subject of the claim.

VOID CONTRACTS

Introduction

A void contract is one that never came into existence, for example because: (a) it is incomplete or uncertain; (b) a mistake vitiated the formation of the contract; (c) one of the parties lacked the authority to enter into the contract; or (d) the contract was *ultra vires* one of the parties.

The voidness of the contract does not of itself form the basis of a claim in restitution; the claimant must establish one of the recognised unjust factors. The traditional unjust factors applied in this context are total failure of consideration for claims for the recovery of money; and request and acceptance for claims for the recovery of non-monetary benefits. Mistake might alternatively be the relevant unjust factor where the claimant acted in conferring the benefit on the erroneous assumption that the contract was valid, and in Australia it is now irrelevant whether the mistake is classified as one of fact or law. It is unsettled whether the defence of provision of good consideration will apply where the mistake claim arises under a void contract. Mason and Carter[18] and Burrows[19] argue that the receipt of part of the bargained for performance under a void contract will not bar a claim based on mistake. Birks[20] however argues that a mistake claim cannot circumvent the failure of consideration doctrine, relying upon *National Mutual Life Association of Australasia Ltd v Walsh* (1987).

As with claims for restitution brought under unenforceable contracts, the claim will fail where the recognition of the claim would frustrate the policy of the legislation or common law rule rendering the contract void: for example, see *Guinness plc v Saunders* (1990).

Recovery of money

Money paid under a void contract can be recovered on the grounds of total failure of consideration or a mistake as to the validity of the contract.

---

17 *Marshall v Marshall* [1999] 1 Qd R 173 (see extract, p 394); *Zullo Enterprises Pty Ltd v Sutton* (1998) (see extract, p 395).

18 Mason and Carter, *Restitution Law in Australia*, 1995, p 331.

19 Burrows, *op cit*, fn 13, pp 127–28.

20 Birks, 'Restitution after ineffective contracts: issues for the 1990s' (1990) 2 JCL 227, p 236.

Total failure of consideration

As there can never be valid consideration provided under a void contract, the reference to 'consideration' should in this context be read as a reference to the *contemplated* consideration. Thus, in relation to claims under void contracts, consideration will totally fail where no part of the *contemplated* performance is rendered,[21] as illustrated by the following case.

Rover International Ltd v Cannon Film Sales Ltd [1989] 1 WLR 912
English Court of Appeal

Rover entered into a joint venture agreement with Thorn EMI under which Thorn EMI was to supply master prints of films to Rover and Rover was to arrange for the dubbing and distribution of the films to Italian cinemas. Rover advanced to Thorn EMI substantial payments in the nature of royalties, and in return Rover acquired the right to earn a substantial share of the gross receipts from exhibiting the films in Italy. Cannon subsequently took over Thorn EMI and was anxious to get out of the joint venture and so searched for a lawful means of terminating the agreement. After much of the dubbing work had been done by Rover, it was discovered that Rover had not been incorporated at the date of purporting to enter into the joint venture agreement, and accordingly the agreement was void. Legal proceedings were under way to determine whether Cannon could withdraw from the agreement on this basis. The parties entered into an escrow agreement which provided that all future royalty payments were to be paid into a joint solicitor's account pending the outcome of the trial. A few months later Cannon was given the excuse it needed to get out of the joint venture when Rover repudiated the contract by commencing the distribution of the film *Highlander* before the approved date. Cannon purported to terminate the agreement for that repudiation. Rover claimed, *inter alia*, the recovery of the advance royalty payments between the date of the incorporation of Rover and the date of the escrow agreement. The trial judge found that the joint venture agreement was at all times void *ab initio*.

Kerr LJ: ... [923] *Total failure of consideration*

The claim for repayment of the five instalments of the advance on this ground was rejected by the judge in the following terms (1987), p 546:

> As for the claim for money had and received, the answer is plain. The consideration, if there had been a contract, had not failed at all. Rover has had several films, including *Highlander*, and distributed them in Italy for payment no doubt of substantial sums. To allow it now to get back the moneys which it paid to Cannon would be grossly unjust. There is no claim in law here for moneys had and received to the use of Rover.

This passage strongly supports my impression that the judge did not have in mind the full financial consequences which would flow from his judgment. But that is of

---

21 *David Securities Pty Ltd v Commonwealth Bank of Australia* (1992), p 382 (see extract, p 646); Mason and Carter, *Restitution Law in Australia*, 1995, p 329. Contrast with *Guinness Mahon & Co Ltd v Kensington and Chelsea Royal London Borough Council* (1998), where it was suggested that 'consideration' under a void contract is the *legal* obligation to render the counter-performance.

no direct relevance at this juncture. The important point is that in my view the judge could not have expressed himself in this way if his attention had been directed to the correct approach in principle. The question whether there has been a total failure of consideration is not answered by considering whether there was any consideration sufficient to support a contract or purported contract. The test is whether or not the party claiming total failure of consideration has in fact received any part of the benefit bargained for under the contract or purported contract.

The relevant principles are set out in *Chitty on Contracts*[22] and the authorities there cited, to which we understand the judge was not referred. It is convenient to quote the following passages from the text:

> Where money has been paid under a transaction that is or becomes ineffective the payer may recover the money provided that the consideration for the payment has totally failed. Although the [924] principle is not confined to contracts most of the cases are concerned with ineffective contracts. In that context failure of consideration occurs where the payer has not enjoyed the benefit of any part of what he bargained for. Thus, the failure is judged from the payer's point of view and 'when one is considering the law of failure of consideration and of the quasi-contractual right to recover money on that ground, it is, generally speaking, not the promise which is referred to as the consideration, but the performance of the promise'. The failure has to be total ... Thus, any performance of the actual thing promised, *as determined by the contract*, is fatal to recovery under this heading. The role of the contractual specification means that it is not true to say that there can be a total failure of consideration only where the payer received no benefit at all in return for the payment. The concept of total failure of consideration can ignore real benefits received by the payer if they are not the benefit bargained for. [Chitty's emphasis.]

The quotation was taken from the speech of Viscount Simon LC in *Fibrosa Spolka Akcyjna v Fairbairn Lawson Combe Barbour Ltd* (1943), p 48. It is not necessary to refer to this or the other authorities cited in support of this passage, but I should refer to two authorities by way of illustration.

In *Rowland v Divall* (1923) the plaintiff bought a car from the defendants. He had the use of it for several months but then discovered that the seller had no title with the result that he had to surrender the car to the true owner. He sued for the return of the price on the ground that there had been a total failure of consideration. The defendant denied this, pointing out that the plaintiff had had the use of the car for a substantial time. This contention succeeded at first instance, leaving the plaintiff only with a claim for damages, but this court unanimously upheld the plaintiff's claim. The consideration for which he had bargained was lawful possession of the car and a good title to it, neither of which he got. Although the car had been delivered to him pursuant to the contract and he had had its use and enjoyment for a considerable time, there was a total failure of consideration because he had not got any part of what he had bargained for.

The decision of Finnemore J in *Warman v Southern Counties Car Finance Corp Ltd (WJ Ameris Car Sales, third party)* (1949) was to the same effect. The plaintiff was buying a car on hire purchase when he became aware that a third party was

---

22   25th edn, 1983, para 1964.

claiming to be the true owner of the car. But he nevertheless went on paying the remaining instalments and then the necessary nominal sum to exercise his option to purchase. When the true owner then claimed the car he surrendered it and sued the finance company for the return of everything he had paid. He succeeded on the ground that there had been a total failure of consideration. He had not bargained for having the use of the car without the option to purchase it.

The position of Rover in the present case is *a fortiori* to these cases. Admittedly, as the judge said, they had several films from the respondents. But the possession of the films was merely incidental to the performance of the contract in the sense that it enabled Rover/Monitor to render services in relation to the films by dubbing them, preparing them for release on the Italian market and releasing them. These were onerous incidents associated with the delivery of the films to them. And delivery [925] and possession were not what Rover had bargained for. The relevant bargain, at any rate for present purposes, was the opportunity to earn a substantial share of the gross receipts pursuant to cl 6 of the schedule to the agreement, with the certainty of at least breaking even by recouping their advance. Due to the invalidity of the agreement Rover got nothing of what they had bargained for, and there was clearly a total failure of consideration.

This equally disposes of counsel for the respondents' ingenious attempt to convert his concession of a *quantum meruit*, in particular the element of reasonable remuneration, into consideration in any relevant sense. Rover did not bargain for a *quantum meruit*, but for the benefits which might flow from cl 6 of the schedule. That is the short answer to this point. It follows that in my view Rover's claim for the repayment of the five instalments of the advance totalling US$312,500 succeeds on the basis of a total failure of consideration.

Commentary and questions

On what basis did the court find that the consideration for the payments had failed? Why did the court discount the fact that the defendant had delivered possession of several of the films to Rover?

Birks criticises the failure of the court in the principal case to make an allowance for the benefit which Rover enjoyed in using the films in order to make the dubbed copies. He argues that the principle of counter-restitution requires that allowance be made for factual benefits received, even if ancillary or collateral to the bargained for benefit.[23]

The principles governing recovery of money paid under a void contract on the basis of a total failure of consideration are further explored in the following case.

---

23 Birks, 'Restitution after ineffective contracts: issues for the 1990s' (1990) 2 JCL 227. For a general discussion of this case, see Beatson, 'Restitutionary remedies for void and ineffective contracts' (1989) 105 LQR 179; Beatson, 'What can restitution do for you?' (1989) 2 JCL 65.

Westdeutsche Landesbank Girozentrale v Council of the London Borough of Islington [1996] AC 669 House of Lords

In 1987 the parties entered into an interest rate swap agreement. A swap agreement is an agreement between two parties where each agrees to pay the other on a specified date an amount of 'interest' calculated on a notional principal sum. The amount payable by one of the parties is calculated in accordance with a fixed rate of interest whereas the other party's liability is based on a floating rate of interest. Usually, each of the parties do not pay the sums owing, but rather the sums are offset and the party owing the higher amount pays the difference. A variation of the interest rate swap agreement involved the making of an upfront payment by the fixed rate payer, which reduced the rate of interest payable by that party. It was this modified form of swap agreement which the parties entered into in this case, with Westdeutsche as the fixed rate payer and the council as the floating rate payer. Under the swap agreement Westdeutsche agreed to advance to the council an upfront payment of £2.5 million. In four successive half yearly payments between December 1987 and June 1989 the council made payments to Westdeutsche totalling £1,354,474.07. No further payments were made by the council in the light of a separate decision that local authorities had no capacity to enter into swap agreements, which were consequently void. Westdeutsche commenced proceedings to recover the balance of £1,145,525.93 which had not been repaid by the council under the void swap agreement. In its pleadings Westdeutsche claimed the net balance on the ground, *inter alia*, that the money had been paid for a consideration that had wholly failed. During the course of argument it appears that this ground mutated into a claim based upon the payment of money for an absence of consideration. Hobhouse J allowed a personal claim in restitution on this modified ground. His Honour also declared that the balance was held by the council on trust for Westdeutsche. The Court of Appeal upheld the decision of Hobhouse J. The sole issue facing the House of Lords on the appeal was whether the council had to pay compound interest on the money which it was to repay to Westdeutsche, but in the course of the judgments, statements were made in *obiter* by Lords Goff and Browne-Wilkinson about the nature of Westdeutsche's personal restitutionary claim.

Lord Goff of Chieveley (dissenting on the interest question): ... [681] Once the character of an interest swap transaction has been identified and understood, and it is appreciated that, because the transaction was beyond the powers of the council, it was void *ab initio*, the basic question is whether the law can restore the parties to the position they were in before they entered into the transaction. That is, of course, the function of the law of restitution. I feel bound to say that, in the present case, there ought to be no difficulty about that at all. This is because the case is concerned solely with money. All that has to be done is to order that each party should pay back the money it has received – or, more sensibly, to [682] strike a balance, and order that the party who has received most should repay the balance; and then to make an appropriate order for interest in respect of that balance. It should be as simple as that. And yet we find ourselves faced with a mass of difficult problems, and struggling to reconcile a number of difficult cases ...

Total failure of consideration

There has long been a desire among restitution lawyers to escape from the unfortunate effects of the so called rule that money is only recoverable at common law on the ground of failure of consideration where the failure is total, by reformulating the rule upon a more principled basis; and signs that this will in due course be done are appearing in judgments throughout the common law world, as appropriate cases arise for decision. It is fortunate, however that in the present case, thanks (I have no doubt) to the admirable researches of counsel, a line of authority was discovered which had escaped the attention of the scholars who work in this field. [683] This line of authority was concerned with contracts for annuities which were void if certain statutory formalities were not complied with. They were not therefore concerned with contracts void by reason of the incapacity of one of the parties. Even so, they were concerned with cases in which payments had been made, so to speak, both ways; and the courts had to decide whether they could, in such circumstances, do justice by restoring the parties to their previous positions. They did not hesitate to do so, by ascertaining the balance of the account between the parties, and ordering the repayment of the balance. Moreover, the form of action by which this was achieved was the old action for money had and received – what we nowadays call a personal claim in restitution at common law. With this precedent before him, Hobhouse J felt free to make a similar order in the present case; and in this he was self-evidently right.

The most serious problem which has remained in this connection is the theoretical question whether recovery can here be said to rest upon the ground of *failure* of consideration. Hobhouse J thought not. He considered that the true ground in these cases, where the contract is void, is to be found in the absence, rather than the failure, of consideration; and in this he was followed by the Court of Appeal. This had the effect that the courts below were not troubled by the question whether there had been a total failure of consideration.

The approach so adopted may have found its origin in the idea, to be derived from a well known passage in the speech of Viscount Simon LC in *Fibrosa Spolka Akcyjna v Fairbairn Lawson Combe Barbour Ltd* (1943), p 48, that a failure of consideration only occurs where there has been a failure of performance by the other party of his obligation under a contract which was initially binding. But the concept of failure of consideration need not be so narrowly confined. In particular it appears from the annuity cases themselves that the courts regarded them as cases of failure of consideration; and concern has been expressed by a number of restitution lawyers that the approach of Hobhouse J is contrary to principle and could, if accepted, lead to undesirable consequences.[24] However since there is before your Lordships no appeal from the decision that the bank was entitled to recover the balance of the payments so made in a personal claim in restitution, the precise identification of the ground of recovery was not explored in argument before the Appellate Committee. It would therefore be inappropriate to express any concluded view upon it. Even so, I think it right to record that there appears to me to be considerable force in the criticisms which have been expressed; and I shall, when considering the issues on this appeal, bear in mind the possibility that it may be right to regard the ground of recovery as failure of consideration ...

24 See Birks, 'No consideration: restitution after void contracts' (1993) 23 UWAL Rev 195; Swadling, 'Restitution for no consideration' [1994] RLR 73; and Burrows, 'Swaps and the friction between common law and equity' [1995] RLR 15.

[686] *Sinclair v Brougham*

The decision of this House in *Sinclair v Brougham* has loomed very large in both the judgments in the courts below and in the admirable arguments addressed to the Appellate Committee of this House. It has long been regarded as a controversial decision, and has been the subject of much consideration by scholars, especially those working in the field of restitution. I have however reached the conclusion that it is basically irrelevant to the decision of the present appeal.

It is first necessary to establish what the case was about. The Birkbeck Permanent Benefit Building Society decided to set up a banking business, known as the Birkbeck Bank. The banking business was however held to be *ultra vires* the objects of the building society; and there followed a spate of litigation concerned with solving the problems consequent upon that decision. *Sinclair v Brougham* was one of those cases.

The case has been analysed in lucid detail in the speech of my noble and learned friend, Lord Browne-Wilkinson, which I have read (in draft) with great respect. In its bare outline, it was concerned with the distribution of the assets of the society, which was insolvent. There were four classes of claimants. First, there were two classes of shareholders – the A shareholders (entitled to repayment of their investment on maturity) and the B shareholders (whose shares were permanent). Next, there was a numerous class of people who had deposited money at the bank, under contracts which were *ultra vires* and so void. Finally, there were the ordinary trade creditors of the society. By agreement, the A shareholders and the trade creditors were paid off first, leaving only the claims of the depositors and the B shareholders. There were sufficient assets to pay off the A shareholders, but not the depositors and certainly not both. The [687] question of how to reconcile their competing claims arose for consideration on a summons by the liquidator for directions.

The problem arose from the fact that the contracts under which the depositors deposited their money at the bank were *ultra vires* and so void. That prevented them from establishing a simple contractual right to be repaid, in which event they would have ranked with the ordinary trade creditors of the society in the liquidation. As it was, they claimed to be entitled to repayment in an action for money had and received – in the same way as the bank claimed repayment in the case now before your Lordships. But the House of Lords held that they were not entitled to claim on this ground. This was in substance because to allow such a claim would permit an indirect enforcement of the contract which the policy of the law had decreed should be void. In those days, of course, judges still spoke about the common law right to restitution in the language of implied contract, and so we find Lord Sumner saying in a much quoted passage (p 452):

> To hold otherwise would be indirectly to sanction an *ultra vires* borrowing. All these causes of action are common species of the genus *assumpsit*. All now rest, and long have rested, upon a notional or imputed promise to repay. The law cannot *de jure* impute promises to repay, whether for money had and received or otherwise, which, if made *de facto*, it would inexorably avoid.

This conclusion however created a serious problem because, if the depositors had no claim, then, in the words of Lord Dunedin (p 436):

> The appalling result in this very case would be that the society's shareholders, having got proceeds of the depositors money in the form of investments, so that each individual depositor is utterly unable to trace his money, are enriched to the extent of some 500%.

As a matter of practical justice, such a result was obviously unacceptable; and it was to achieve justice that the House had recourse to equity to provide the answer.

[Lord Goff then discussed the judgments in *Sinclair v Brougham* (see extract, p 3) and continued at p 688:]

For present purposes, I approach this case in the following way. First, it is clear that the problem which arose in *Sinclair v Brougham*, viz that a personal remedy in restitution was excluded on grounds of public policy, does not arise in the present case, which is not of course concerned with a borrowing contract. Second, I regard the decision in *Sinclair v Brougham* as being a response to that problem in the case of *ultra vires* borrowing contracts, and as not intended to create a principle of general application. From this it follows, in my opinion that *Sinclair v Brougham* is not relevant to the decision in the present case. In particular it cannot be relied upon as a precedent that a trust arises on the facts of the present case, justifying on that basis an award of compound interest against the council.

But I wish to add this. I do not in any event think that it would be right for your Lordships' House to exercise its power under the Practice Statement (*Practice Statement (Judicial Precedent)* (1966)) to depart from *Sinclair v Brougham*. I say this first because, in my opinion, any decision to do so would not be material to the disposal of the present appeal, and would therefore be *obiter*. But there is a second reason of substance why, in my opinion, that course should not be taken. I recognise that nowadays cases of incapacity are relatively rare, though the swaps litigation shows that they can still occur. Even so, the question could still arise whether, in the case of a borrowing contract rendered void because it was *ultra vires* the borrower, it would be contrary to public policy to allow a personal claim in restitution. Such a question has arisen in the past not only in relation to associations such as the Birkbeck Permanent Benefit Building Society, but also in relation to infants' contracts. Moreover there is a respectable body of opinion that, if such a case arose today, it should still be held that public policy would preclude a personal claim in restitution, though not of course by reference to an implied contract. That was the opinion expressed by Leggatt LJ in the Court of Appeal in the present case (1994), p 952E–F, as it had been by Hobhouse J; and the same view has been expressed by Professor Birks.[25] I myself incline to the opinion that a personal claim in restitution would not indirectly enforce the *ultra vires* contract, for such an action would be unaffected by any of the contractual terms governing the borrowing, and moreover would be subject (where appropriate) to any available restitutionary defences. If my present opinion were to prove to be correct then *Sinclair v Brougham* will fade into history. If not, then recourse can at least be had to *Sinclair v Brougham* as authority for the proposition that, in such circumstances, the lender should not be without a remedy. Indeed, I cannot think that English law, or equity, is so impoverished as to be incapable of providing relief in such circumstances. Lord Wright, who wrote in strong terms[26] endorsing

---

25 See Birks, *An Introduction to the Law of Restitution*, 1985, p 374.
26 See Wright [1938] CLJ 305.

the just result in *Sinclair v Brougham*, would turn in his grave at any such suggestion. Of course, it may be necessary to reinterpret the decision in that case to provide a more satisfactory basis for it: indeed one possible suggestion has been proposed by Professor Birks.[27] But for the present the case should in my opinion stand, though confined in the manner I have indicated, as an assertion that those who are caught in the trap of advancing money under *ultra vires* borrowing contracts will not be denied appropriate relief...

Lord Browne-Wilkinson: ... [710] The House of Lords [in *Sinclair v Brougham*] was unanimous in rejecting the claim by the *ultra vires* depositors to recover in quasi-contract on the basis of moneys had and received. In their view, the claim in quasi-contract was based on an implied contract. To imply a contract to repay would be to imply a contract to exactly the same effect as the express *ultra vires* contract of loan. Any such implied contract would itself be void as being *ultra vires*.

Subsequent developments in the law of restitution demonstrate that this reasoning is no longer sound. The common law restitutionary claim is based not on implied contract but on unjust enrichment: in the circumstances the law imposes an obligation to repay rather than implying an entirely fictitious agreement to repay: *Fibrosa v Fairbairn* (1943), pp 63–64 *per* Lord Wright; *Pavey & Matthews Pty Ltd v Paul* (1987), pp 583, 603; *Lipkin Gorman v Karpnale Ltd* [1991] 2 AC 548, 578c; *Woolwich Equitable Building Society v IRC* (1993). In my judgment, your Lordships should now unequivocally and finally reject the concept that the claim for moneys had and received is based on an implied contract. I would overrule *Sinclair v Brougham* on this point.

It follows that in *Sinclair v Brougham* the depositors should have had a personal claim to recover the moneys at law based on a total failure of consideration. The failure of consideration was *not* partial: the depositors had paid over their money in consideration of a promise to repay. That promise was *ultra vires* and void; therefore the consideration for the payment of the money wholly failed. So in the present swaps case (though the point is not one under appeal) I think the Court of Appeal were right to hold that the swap moneys were paid on a consideration that wholly failed. The essence of the swap agreement is that, over the whole term of [711] the agreement, each party thinks he will come out best: the consideration for one party making a payment is an obligation on the other party to make counter-payments over the whole term of the agreement.

If in *Sinclair v Brougham* the depositors had been held entitled to recover at law, their personal claim would have ranked *pari passu* with other ordinary unsecured creditors, in priority to the members of the society who could take nothing in the liquidation until all creditors had been paid.

[Lord Browne-Wilkinson then discussed the proprietary claim in *Sinclair v Brougham* and continued at p 713:]

As has been pointed out frequently over the 80 years since it was decided, *Sinclair v Brougham* is a bewildering authority: no single *ratio decidendi* can be detected; all the reasoning is open to serious objection; it was only intended to deal with cases where there were no trade creditors in competition and the reasoning is incapable of application where there are such creditors. In my view the decision as to rights *in rem* of *Sinclair v Brougham* should also be overruled. Although the case is one

---

27 See Birks, *op cit*, fn 25, pp 396ff.

where [714] property rights are involved such overruling should not in practice disturb long settled titles ...

If *Sinclair v Brougham*, in both its aspects, is overruled the law can be established in accordance with principle and commercial common sense: a claimant for restitution of moneys paid under an *ultra vires*, and therefore void, contract has a personal action at law to recover the moneys paid as on a total failure of consideration; he will not have an equitable proprietary claim which gives him either rights against third parties or priority in an insolvency; nor will he have a personal claim in equity, since the recipient is not a trustee ...

Commentary

Lord Goff does not name the line of annuity cases which he relied upon for the proposition that, where the contract is for payments both ways, the receipt of partial payment by the plaintiff does not prevent the consideration from totally failing. These cases were however identified in the courts below and include: *Shove v Webb* (1787); *Hicks v Hicks* (1802); *Cowper v Godmond* (1833). In *Goss v Chilcott* (1996) (see extract, p 356) Lord Goff confirmed that, where the contract involves an exchange of money payments, as with loan contracts, the net balance will be recoverable on the basis of a total failure of consideration.[28] The approach of Lord Browne-Wilkinson in the principal case to the identification of the bargained for counter-performance would usually give rise to the same result.

There is no clear majority in the principal case for overruling *Sinclair v Brougham* (1914) (see extract, p 3) on that aspect of the case concerning the personal claim. Nevertheless, the decision in *Sinclair v Brougham* as it related to the personal claim must be considered to be highly doubtful in England as a result of the above decision. The claim in restitution for the recovery of money payments is an independent obligation imposed by law on the basis that the consideration for the payments has wholly failed, and should no longer be viewed as indirectly enforcing a promise which cannot be directly enforced, *Pavey & Matthews Pty Ltd v Paul* (1987) 162 CLR 221 (see extract, p 362). However, the policy of the legislation or common law rule rendering the borrowing contract void would need to be carefully examined to determine whether the bringing of a restitutionary claim would frustrate that policy.

The principle of 'absence of consideration' was applied by the lower courts in the principal case as the ground for permitting restitution of the money. 'Absence of consideration' refers to the fact that, due to the voidness of the contract, the payments are unsupported by any consideration which is recognised at law; that is, there is no legal nexus between the contract and the payments. However the House of Lords ignored this suggested new unjust factor in favour of a sensible reformulation of the total failure of consideration doctrine. Lord Goff acknowledged that there is 'considerable force' in the arguments of academic writers, such as Birks,[29] that the doctrine of absence of

---

28 For further discussion, see above pp 278–80; 356–59.
29 Birks, 'No consideration: restitution after void contracts' [1993] 23 UWAL Rev 195.

consideration has no independent existence. The 'absence of consideration' unjust factor, if adopted, would result in *prima facie* recovery of payments made merely on the basis that the contract is void, without the additional requirement of proving an independent unjust factor. This would be contrary to the fundamental structure of restitution law. The absence of consideration unjust factor has been subject to severe criticism by commentators[30] and there has been no indication that it will be adopted into Australian law.

At the time of the decision in *Westdeutsche*, mistake of law had not yet been recognised in England as a ground of recovery. As will be seen in the next section, the House of Lords in *Kleinwort Benson Ltd v Lincoln City Council* (1999) has now overturned the mistake of law bar, and held that payments made under void swaps contracts are recoverable on the basis of mistake of law.

Mistake

Money paid under a void contract will be recoverable where the plaintiff pays the money under a mistake of fact or law.

Rover International Ltd v Cannon Film Sales Ltd [1989] 1 WLR 912
English Court of Appeal

The facts are stated at p 369.

Kerr LJ: ...

[925] *Mistake of fact*

In my view Rover are equally entitled to recover these instalments as having been paid to Cannon under a mistake of fact. As already mentioned, we concluded that this submission was open to Rover although it had only been touched on in argument below and was not referred to in the judgment. [Counsel for Cannon] submitted faintly that there was no evidence to prove that the instalments had in fact been paid under a mistake, but the facts speak for themselves. It is obvious that the payments would not have been made unless [representatives of Rover] had believed that there was a binding contract between Rover and Thorn EMI, and [counsel for Cannon] rightly did not suggest that this mistaken belief involved a mistake of law ...

Dillon LJ: ... [933] On the facts this is, in my judgment, a classic case of money paid under a mistake of fact. The instalments were paid because Rover mistakenly believed – as did Cannon – that there was a contract between them, and in order to satisfy Rover's obligations under that contract. It is impossible to suggest any other reason for the payments. *Prima facie*, therefore, Rover is entitled to recover the payments: see the very valuable explanation of the cases by Robert Goff J in

---

30 See Birks, *ibid*; Burrows, 'Swaps and the friction between common law and equity' [1995] RLR 15, pp 16–19; Swadling, 'Restitution for no consideration' [1994] RLR 73, pp 75–80. See also Kremer, 'Recovering money paid under void contracts: "absence of consideration" in failure of consideration' (2001) 17 JCL 37, where the author argues that the existing approach toward contracts based on 'unjust factors' is inappropriate and that recovery should be based on a 'right to retain' analysis.

Barclays Bank Ltd v WJ Simms, Son & Cooke (Southern) Ltd (1980), and especially the passage he there cites from the judgment of Parke B in *Kelly v Solari* (1841) ...

Even if, however, it is established that the five instalments were paid by Rover under a mistake of fact, it is nonetheless said for Cannon that Rover cannot now recover the money ... [I]t is said that any sum recoverable by Rover should be subject to a ceiling in that it should not exceed what Rover would have got under the agreement if the agreement had in truth initially been valid, ie, if Rover had been incorporated before the agreement was signed.

What lies behind this second point is that, on the findings of the judge which are not challenged, Rover was guilty in early October 1986 [934] of conduct in relation to the timing of the first theatre showing of the film *Highlander* which Cannon was entitled to treat, and elected to treat, as repudiatory of the agreement (or would have been entitled to treat as repudiatory etc if there ever had been the valid agreement the parties supposed there was). Had there been a valid agreement and had it come to an end at 13 October 1988 by the acceptance by Cannon of a repudiation on the part of Rover, Rover would not have been entitled to recover the five instalments. It is therefore said to be illogical if the money can be recovered by Rover just because it has transpired that, because of a mistake for which those interested in Rover bear prime responsibility, there never was any agreement at all.

For my part, I would reject this second, 'ceiling' argument. I venture to think that the argument involves a confusion of ideas. If the money is repayable because it was paid under a mistake of fact, that is because the mistake falsified the assumption on which the payment was made, viz that it was made under and to comply with a valid contract. It is thus irrelevant to consider what the position would have been if that assumption had not been falsified, and there had been a contract ...

Commentary

The plaintiff in this case was said to have been acting under a mistake of fact; namely a mistake as to the incorporated status of Rover. At the time of this decision, mistake of law was not a ground of recovery. However, the House of Lords eventually overturned the mistake of law bar in *Kleinwort Benson Ltd v Lincoln City Council* (1999) (see extract, p 126), a case that involved void interest rate swap agreements. The facts are stated in detail elsewhere (see p 126), however in brief the appellant Bank entered into interest rate swap agreements with four local authorities between 1982 and 1984. Each of the agreements were fully performed by the parties, and at the end of the term of the agreements the Bank was in the position where it had made net payments to the authorities. It was held that the appellant bank could recover the net amount paid under those agreements on the basis of a mistake of law. As seen by the following extracts from the decision, the court did not think that the fact the agreements were fully performed should bar recovery.

Kleinwort Benson Ltd v Lincoln City Council [1999] 2 AC 349 House of Lords

The facts are stated at p 126.

Lord Goff of Chieveley: ... [385] *Completed transactions*

This issue was added, by leave of your Lordships' House, to the issues set out in the order of Langley J. It arose from a footnote to an article by Professor Peter Birks entitled 'No consideration: restitution after void contracts' (1993).

...

[386] In this [footnote Birks] said (1993), at p 230:

> None the less there is one good argument against allowing restitution in this situation on the ground of this particular kind of mistake, namely the transferor's mistaken belief in his/her liability to make the transfer and the liability of the other to reciprocate. It is that after the execution of the supposed contract the force of this type of mistake is spent ... Therefore, even though it is true, as is admitted in the text above, that the mistake will have been causative at the time of the performance, that mistake cannot on this reasoning be relied upon when matters have progressed to the point at which it can clearly be seen that the only prejudice which it might have entailed never in fact eventuated.

The question for consideration on this issue is whether the thesis contained in the footnote is well founded.

... It is well established that the cause of action for the recovery of money paid under a mistake of fact accrues at the time of payment. As authority for this proposition it is usual to cite *Baker v Courage & Co* (1910) a decision of Hamilton J (later Lord Sumner) which, so far as I am aware, has never been questioned. So if an agreement such as those presently under consideration, under which a series of payments falls to be made, is held to have been void so that each payment has been made under a mistake of law, ie, the mistaken belief of the payer that he was liable to make the payment, the cause of action for the recovery of the money so paid will accrue, in respect of each payment, on the date when the payment was made. This will be true of each payment; and if the performance of the supposed contract is completed, it will be as true of the final payment as it will have been of all the previous payments. It follows that, if the argument in Professor Birks' footnote is correct, at the moment when the [387] final payment is made under such a contract, not only will the final payment itself be irrecoverable despite the fact that it was made under precisely the same mistake as the previous payments made by him, but the payer will somehow be divested of his accrued right to recover all those previous payments.

...

[I]t is in any event difficult to see how Professor Birks' proposal in his footnote can here be reconciled with the consequences of invalidity arising from the application of the *ultra vires* doctrine. As a result, following the decision of the House of Lords in *Hazell v Hammersmith and Fulham London Borough Council* (1992), it was ordered and declared that the items of account (irrespective whether they represented payments or receipts) appearing in the capital markets fund account of the local authority in that case (Hammersmith and Fulham London Borough Council) for the years under challenge were contrary to law.[31] Of the interest rate swap transactions entered into by the council, some were closed transactions, and a number were profitable, but no exceptions were made for these in the declarations so made. As [counsel] submitted on behalf of the bank, it is incompatible with the *ultra vires* rule that an *ultra vires* transaction should become binding on a local authority simply on the ground that it has been completed. Moreover the *ultra vires* rule is not optional; it applies whether the transaction in question proves to have been profitable or unprofitable. If the argument in Professor Birks' footnote is right, the result would be that effect would be given to a contract which public policy has declared to be void.

In my opinion, these points are unanswerable; and they are reinforced by further arguments advanced by Professor Burrows in his article entitled 'Swaps and the friction between common law and equity' (1995), pp 18–19. I would accordingly decide this issue in favour of the bank.

...

Lord Hope of Craighead: ... [415] *The completed swaps*

The reason why the swap contracts were held to be void was that they were *ultra vires* the local authorities. The purpose of the *ultra vires* doctrine is to protect the public, *Hazell v Hammersmith and Fulham London Borough Council* (1992), p 26 *per* Lord Templeman: So it is a legitimate criticism of [counsel's] argument for the local authorities that if, as he has contended, there is no claim for money had and received in the case of a completed swap the result will have been to give practical effect to a transaction which, on the doctrine of *ultra vires,* did not legally exist. All the items of account appearing within the capital markets fund account of the local authority in the *Hazell* case were held to be contrary to law, and the accounts were ordered to be rectified. This order extended to the swaps transactions which were entered into after July 1988 when the local authority was advised by the auditor that the transactions were of doubtful validity. It would be unsatisfactory if restitution were to be possible only in the case of the uncompleted transactions. That would leave any balance in favour of the local authorities without any item in the accounts which could properly be attached to it. It would not be possible for the bank to re-open the transactions as they are void. The grounds of decision in *Hazell* suggest that no distinction should be made between *ultra vires* transactions on the ground that in the one case they were completed and in the other they were not.

In my opinion the law of restitution should provide a remedy in these cases irrespective of the stage which the transactions had reached. In expressing his decision on the *Sandwell* case in *Westdeutsche Landesbank Girozentrale v Islington London BC* (1994), p 930, Hobhouse J said that it was irrelevant to the existence of a cause of action in connection with the payments made under the first *Sandwell* swap that the contract was fully performed. The Court of Appeal reached the same conclusion in *Guinness Mahon & Co Ltd v Kensington and Chelsea Royal London Borough Council* (1998). I agree with those decisions, and I have nothing to add to what my noble and learned friend Lord Goff has said about them. But restitution in those cases was not given on the ground of mistake, which is the ground [416]

---

31   (1992) at 43–44 *per* Lord Templeman, with whose opinion the other members of the Appellate Committee agreed.

on which the bank needs to succeed if they are to be successful in meeting the defence of limitation which has been raised by the local authorities.

Had it not been for what Professor Birks has said in footnote 137 at p 230 of his article 'No consideration: restitution after void contracts' (1993), I would not have thought that there was any difficulty about restitution on the ground of mistake in the case of the completed swaps. The assumption on which I proceed is that each payment was made on either side in the belief that the sum was legally due to the other party under the contract. The mistake was the same throughout the progress of the transaction. The right to recover each payment on the ground of mistake accrued when the sum was received by the payee. I do not think that it makes any difference whether there was a single payment or a series of payments or, where there was a series, whether the transaction was interrupted or had run its course. Each payment is to be looked at separately.

Professor Birks' argument is that after the execution of the proposed contract the force of this type of mistake is spent because the matter has proceeded to the point where the only prejudice which might be entailed – non-performance by the other party – never in fact eventuated. It was only the antecedent liability which was defective. But this seems to be inconsistent with the principle that the cause of action is complete when the payment is made and received by the payee. Brennan J in *David Securities v Commonwealth Bank of Australia* (1992), p 390 said that it is at that moment that it can be determined whether and to what extent the payee has been unjustly enriched. The argument also assumes, wrongly in my opinion, that the payer's mistake was that the payee was obliged to reciprocate. That is not the basis of the claim for restitution on the ground of mistake. The mistake which the payer made was in believing that he was obliged to make the payment because it was legally due to the payee. A further difficulty is that it produces a result which is one-sided and unjust. The local authorities, unlike Kleinwort Benson, can say that the transactions which they entered into were beyond their capacity. As their accounts must be rectified the transactions, although closed, must be re-opened to enable them to recover the money which they had no power to pay out. In a case where the bank was the net beneficiary it cannot retain the net benefit which it received in the form of *ultra vires* payments from the local authorities. It would be unjust if the bank was not to be able to recover its net loss in those cases where the balance lies the other way.

Professor Burrows has given convincing reasons for rejecting this argument.[32] I also am unpersuaded by Professor Birks on this point. In my opinion completed transactions are in the same position as transactions which were not completed when restitution is claimed on the ground of mistake.

...

Questions

What reasons did Lords Goff and Hope give for rejecting the argument that recovery should not be permitted under completed swaps agreements on the

---

32 Burrows, 'Swaps and the friction between common law and equity' [1995] RLR 15 pp 18–19.

basis of mistake? What effect did their Lordships give to the policy underlying the *ultra vires* rule in reaching their decision on this ground?

Recovery of non-monetary benefits

Non-monetary benefits conferred under a void contract will be recoverable where either acceptance or a causative mistake can be shown.

Craven-Ellis v Canons Ltd [1936] 2 KB 403 English Court of Appeal

On 31 December 1930 the plaintiff commenced, at the defendant's request, to provide his services as estate agent to the defendant company. No agreement for the provision of those services was initially in place. On 14 April 1931 the plaintiff was appointed managing director of the defendant by an agreement executed under the company's seal. The seal was affixed by resolution of unqualified directors and the agreement was accordingly void. The plaintiff sought to recover a *quantum meruit* for the value of his services.

Greer LJ: ... [409] The company, having had the full benefit of these services, decline to pay either under the agreement or on the basis of a *quantum meruit*. Their defence to the action is a purely technical defence, and if it succeeds the Messrs du Cros as the principal shareholders in the company, and the company, would be in the position of having received and accepted valuable services and refusing, for purely technical reasons, to pay for them.

As regards the services rendered between 31 December 1930 and 14 April 1931, there is, in my judgment, no defence to the claim. These services were rendered by the plaintiff not as managing director or as a director, but as an estate agent, and there was no contract in existence which could present any obstacle to a claim based on a *quantum meruit* for services rendered and accepted.

As regards the plaintiff's services after the date of the contract, I think the plaintiff is also entitled to succeed. The contract, having been made by directors who had no authority to make it with one of themselves who had notice of their want of authority was not binding on either party. It was, in fact, a nullity, and presents no obstacle to the implied promise to pay on a *quantum meruit* basis which arises from the performance of the services and the implied acceptance of the same by the company.

[410] It was contended by [counsel for the company] that, in as much as the services relied on were purported to be done by the plaintiff under what he and the directors thought was a binding contract, there could be no legal obligation on the defendants on a *quantum meruit* claim. The only one of the numerous authorities cited by [counsel] that appears to support his contention is the judgment of a Divisional Court in *In re Allison, Johnson & Foster Ltd ex p Birkenshaw* (1904). The court consisted of Lord Alverstone, Wills and Kennedy JJ, and the judgment was delivered by Kennedy J. In giving judgment that learned judge, expressing not merely his own opinion, but that of the other two judges, said (1904), p 330: 'There can be no implied contract for payment arising out of acceptance of the work done where the work was done upon an express request which turns out to be no request at all, but which down to the time when the whole of the work had been done was supposed by both parties to be valid and

operative.' This passage appears to involve the proposition that in all cases where parties suppose there is an agreement in existence and one of them has performed services, or delivered goods in pursuance of the supposititious agreement there cannot be any inference of any promise by the person accepting the services or the goods to pay on the basis of a *quantum meruit*. This would certainly be strictly logical if the inference of a promise to pay on a *quantum meruit* basis were an inference of fact based on the acceptance of the services or of the goods delivered under what was supposed to be an existing contract; but in my judgment the inference is not one of fact, but is an inference which a rule of law imposes on the parties where work has been done or goods have been delivered under what purports to be a binding contract, but is not so in fact.

In *Prickett v Badger* (1856) the question whether an obligation to pay on a *quantum meruit* basis depended upon an inference of fact from the conduct of the parties was negatived, and [411] such inference was stated to be one that the law imposed on the person accepting the services ... The decisions in *Clarke v Cuckfeld Union* (1852) and *Lawford v Billericay Rural District Council* (1903) are also authorities to the effect that the implied obligation to pay is an obligation imposed by law, and not an inference of fact, arising from the performance and acceptance of services. In the last mentioned case the work in respect of which the plaintiff sued was done in pursuance of express instructions given by the defendant council, but the contract purported to be so made was not binding on the defendants because no agreement had been executed under their seal. It was impossible to say as a matter of logical inference from the facts that by accepting the advantage of the plaintiff's work they had promised to pay him a reasonable sum therefore. Both parties assumed that there was a contract between them, and the acceptance of the work by the defendants could not in fact give rise to the inference of a promise to pay the reasonable value. For these reasons this case seems to me to show that the obligation is one which is imposed by law in all cases where the acts are purported to be done on the faith of an agreement which [412] is supposed to be but is not a binding contract between the parties. Vaughan Williams LJ in the course of his judgment referred to *Nicholson v Bradfield Union* (1866), and said that the ground of the decision in that case, as he understood it, was that the law raised an implied contract by the corporate body to pay for the goods in question in that case. In my judgment, the obligation to pay reasonable remuneration for the work done when there is no binding contract between the parties is imposed by a rule of law, and not by an inference of fact arising from the acceptance of services or goods. It is one of the cases referred to in books on contracts as obligations arising *quasi ex contractu*, of which a well known instance is a claim based on money had and received. Although I do not hold that the decision of the court in *Ex p Birkenshaw* (1904) was wrong, I think that the passage I read from the judgment is not a correct statement of the law.

I accordingly think that the defendants must pay on the basis of a *quantum meruit* not only for the services rendered after 31 December 1930, and before the date of the invalid agreement, but also for the services after that date. I think the appeal should be allowed, and judgment given for such a sum as shall be found to be due on the basis of a *quantum meruit* in respect of all services rendered by the plaintiff to the company until he was dismissed. The defendants seem to me to be in a dilemma. If the contract was an effective contract by the company, they would be bound to pay the remuneration in the contract. If, on the other hand, the contract was a nullity and not binding either on the plaintiff or the defendants, there would be nothing to prevent the inference which the law draws from the performance by the plaintiff of services to the company, and the company's acceptance of such services, which, if they had not been performed by the plaintiff, they would have had to get some other agent to carry out ...

Commentary

The application of the acceptance doctrine on these facts has been criticised. The directors were incapable of binding the defendant company and as such it could not be said that the *company* had freely accepted or requested the plaintiff's services.[33] Mason and Carter[34] however suggest that the concept of constructive acceptance could found recovery. Recovery could also possibly have been grounded on the plaintiff's mistake that the directors had the authority to enter into the management agreement.[35]

The principles relating to acceptance are discussed in more detail in Chapter 10, pp 281–82.

Horton v Jones (No 2) (1939) 39 SR (NSW) 305 Full Court of the Supreme Court of New South Wales

The plaintiff served as a housekeeper for Gordon Jones for a period of three years until his death. The plaintiff alleged that Jones had orally agreed to leave her his estate if she served him without wages for the rest of his life, however upon his death Jones left no part of his estate to the plaintiff. The plaintiff commenced proceedings against Jones's executors claiming damages for £30,000 for breach of the alleged agreement, or alternatively a *quantum meruit* for the services rendered to Jones at three guineas per week. The contract point went to the High Court (1935) where it was found by a majority that the alleged agreement was too uncertain to constitute a contract, and thus was void. The proceedings came back before the New South Wales Full Court on a procedural point and Jordan CJ took the opportunity to make some observations in *obiter* about the plaintiff's *quantum meruit* claim.

Jordan CJ: ... [319] No action will lie for a *quantum meruit* so long as there is in existence an enforceable express contract which provides for a special remuneration. Where there is or has been an express contract between the parties, the cases in which it has been held that an action for a *quantum meruit* may be maintained are the following: (1) If a person employs another to do work, or agrees to buy goods from him, nothing being said as to the wage or the price, the law implies a promise to pay a reasonable wage or a reasonable price, and an action may be maintained for a *quantum meruit* or a *quantum valebant*. In this case, the action is one to enforce an implied term of an express contract: cf Sale of Goods Act, 1923, s 13. (2) If one party to an express contract renders to the other some but

---

33   See Birks, '*Negotiorum gestio* and the common law' (1971) 24 CLP 110, pp 120–22; Goff and Jones, *The Law of Restitution*, 5th edn, 1998, pp 588–89.

34   Mason and Carter, *Restitution Law in Australia*, 1995, p 356.

35   Burrows, *The Law of Restitution*, 1993, p 307; Birks, *An Introduction to the Law of Restitution*, rev edn, 1989, p 119; Goff and Jones, *The Law of Restitution*, 5th edn, 1998, pp 588–89.

not all the services which have to be performed in order that he may be entitled to receive the remuneration stipulated for by the contract, and the other by his wrongful repudiation of the contract prevents him from earning the stipulated remuneration, the former may treat the contract as at an end and then sue for a *quantum meruit* for the services actually rendered: *Segur v Franklin* (1934), p 72. (3) If a person renders services to another under a contract which is unenforceable by reason of the absence of the written evidence required by the Statute of Frauds, and the other sets up the Statute as an answer to an action for the stipulated remuneration, it has been held that the former is entitled to recover a *quantum meruit*: *Scott v Pattison* (1924); cf (1925) 41 LQR 79.

Where there is no express contract between the parties: (1) if persons purport to enter into a special contract for services, but the special arrangement between them does not amount to a contract because the remuneration, although referred to, is not sufficiently defined to be ascertainable, and [320] if services are in fact afterwards rendered and accepted pursuant to the arrangement in circumstances which indicate that it is not intended by the parties that they are to be gratuitous, the law implies a contract of employment at a *quantum meruit*: *Way v Latilla* (1937), pp 763, 765; (2) if persons attempt to contract for services by a purported contract which is for some reason void in law, and services are rendered and accepted under the void contract, the law imposes on the party who has had the benefit of the services an obligation to pay a *quantum meruit*. This obligation is imposed by law, and does not depend on an inference of an implied promise: *Craven-Ellis v Canons Ltd* (1936), pp 409–12; cf (1939).

On the other hand, if the relation between the parties was never intended to be a business relation at all – if the services were rendered without any intention on either side of any charge being made for them, in the hope, on the part of the person who rendered them, that the recipient might be moved thereby to some *ex gratia* benevolence when making his will – no basis exists for a claim to a *quantum meruit*: *Te Ira Roa v Materi* (1919); *In Estate of Craig* (1895).

In the present case, the plaintiff, who addressed us in person, has assured us that her motives for associating with the deceased were entirely mercenary; and from the bitter dislike and contempt which she expressed for him we see no reason for doubting this assurance. It may be that, notwithstanding that the plaintiff's alleged promise to make a home for the deceased and to look after him for the rest of his life is too uncertain to admit of the alleged arrangement amounting to a contract, she will be able to prove that she in fact rendered to the deceased services which were of the kind described in the second count and were rendered and accepted in such circumstances as to warrant the inference that they were not understood by the deceased to be intended to be gratuitous. If so, than as at present advised we do not think that, having regard to the decision of the House of Lords in *Way v Latilla* (1937) there is anything in the reasons of the members of the High Court that would prevent the plaintiff from recovering the [321] amount which she assessed as the value of her services when she brought her present action, if the jury should think that they were worth so much.

Commentary

A similar set of circumstances arose in *Stinchcombe v Thomas* (1957). The plaintiff served as a housekeeper to Ernest Thomas for 12 years, relying on his promise that he would 'well reward' her in his will if she stayed with him until his death. During his lifetime Thomas paid the plaintiff only the sum of £1 per week. By his will he bequeathed property to the plaintiff which realised the sum of £100. The plaintiff commenced proceedings against Thomas's estate claiming damages for breach of the agreement to 'well reward' her, or alternatively a *quantum meruit* for the housekeeping services provided by her. The 'agreement' between herself and Thomas was held to be void for uncertainty, however the plaintiff was successful in her claim for a *quantum meruit*. Monahan J relied on the judgment of Greer LJ in *Craven-Ellis v Canons Ltd* (1936) (see extract, p 383) for the proposition that, p 512:

> [W]hen services are rendered and accepted on the footing that the parties supposed there was an actionable agreement in existence governing the situation, payment for such services may be recovered on the doctrine of *quantum meruit* if it turns out that what purported to be a binding contract was not so in fact. The inference of a promise to pay for the services in such a case was held to arise not as one of fact, but as one which a rule of law imposes on the parties where work has been done under what purports to be a binding contract, but is not so in fact ...

The *quantum meruit* awarded to the plaintiff in *Stinchcombe* was reduced to take into account the value of the property obtained under the will. Further, due to the operation of the Statute of Limitations, it was limited to the period of five and a half years preceding the death of the deceased.

Rover International Ltd v Cannon Film Sales Ltd [1989] 1 WLR 912
English Court of Appeal

The facts are stated at p 369.

Rover claimed a *quantum meruit* for the distribution expenses incurred and for the reasonable value of the dubbing work performed by it. The court allowed the *quantum meruit* on the basis that the services were provided under a mistake (see extract, p 156). It then turned to consider whether the contract price should form a cap on recovery.

Kerr LJ: ...

[926] However, this leaves one further major area of disagreement between the parties ... the so called 'ceiling' point. The question is whether the *quantum meruit* should in any event be limited to such amount, if any, as Rover would have been entitled to retain out of the gross receipts by 13 October 1986, when Cannon terminated the (purported) agreement pursuant to cll 16 and 17, the 'default' and 'termination' provisions. As already mentioned, Cannon's right to invoke these clauses on the ground of the unauthorised release of *Highlander* on 10 October was upheld below, and there has been no appeal against this part of the judgment.

[927] This raises an issue of principle of some general importance. Cannon submit that Rover would be unjustly enriched if they recovered more by way of a *quantum meruit* than what would have been their entitlement under the purported contract,

bearing in mind that it was their breach which led to its termination. They rely on the famous *dictum* of Lord Mansfield CJ in *Moses v Macferlan* (1760) that the defendant 'may defend himself by everything which shews that the plaintiff, *ex æquo et bono*, is *not entitled* to the whole of his demand, or to any part of it' (Lord Mansfield CJ's emphasis).

The problem only arises in cases where a contract has been rescinded by an 'innocent' party without a prior breach by the other party. Where there has been a prior breach, as in somewhat similar situations in which prepayments may be recoverable such as *Dies v British and International Mining and Finance Corp Ltd* (1939), to which I refer later in the context of the Proper contract, the 'innocent' party can of course sue for damages. But where the contract was void *ab initio* or has come to an end without breach, eg, by frustration, all remedies must necessarily lie in the area of restitution.

The contention on behalf of Cannon is at first sight attractive, that Rover's recovery of a *quantum meruit* should be subject to a 'ceiling' which would take account of their breach and the consequent right of Cannon, which was in fact invoked, to terminate under the 'default' clause, but for the fact that the contract had been void *ab initio*. However, on further consideration I have reached the clear conclusion that this would not be a correct analysis, for a number of reasons.

First, there are purely pragmatic reasons which militate against the justice of a superficially attractive solution on these lines. Thus, it is not simply a case of a contract which was void *ab initio* without the knowledge of either party and which was then broken by Rover. It was a case where the invalidity of the contract was discovered by Cannon, no doubt with considerable satisfaction, and relied on by them. If they had wished to do so they could have affirmed the contract, since the cause of its invalidity had no practical significance for the parties' bargain. But they chose to rely on the invalidity, and when they first invoked it there had been no breach on the side of Rover; merely unfounded allegations of breaches and other unattractive conduct from the side of Cannon. In these circumstances it does not appear unjust that Cannon cannot have the best of both worlds: reliance on the invalidity of the contract *ab initio* as well as on a subsequent breach on the part of Rover. Moreover, the suggested 'ceiling' would be unjust, since its operation would be one sided. The *quantum meruit* in favour of Rover would be limited, and indeed disappear entirely on the facts of this case, whereas the benefits of the restitutionary position in favour of Cannon would be without limit, since no 'ceiling' would be applicable to their entitlement to the gross receipts.

Secondly, I do not think that the contention in favour of a 'ceiling' is in accordance with principle. It would involve the application of provisions of a void contract to the assessment of a *quantum meruit* which only arises due to the non-existence of the supposed contract. Albeit on very different facts, a similar mixture between a contract and an extra-contractual *quantum meruit* was rightly rejected by Saville J in [928] *Greenmast Shipping Co SA v Jean Lion & Cie S, The Saronikos* (1986).

Moreover, as pointed out in Goff and Jones in *The Law of Restitution*,[36] there has been reluctance to accept the full breadth of Lord Mansfield CJ's *dictum*. As shown by this chapter, the concept of restitution in the face of what would otherwise be

---

36   3rd edn, 1986, p 691.

unjust enrichment has been limited by defences protecting the party from whom restitution is claimed not by considering the merits or demerits of the party which has made a payment under a mistake or for a consideration which has wholly failed.

Finally, if the imposition of a 'ceiling' in the present case were accepted, then the consequences could be far-reaching and undesirable in other situations which it would be impossible to distinguish in principle. It would then follow that an evaluation of the position of the parties to a void contract, or to one which becomes ineffective subsequently, could always be called for. We know that this is not the position in the case of frustrated contracts, which are governed by the Law Reform (Frustrated Contracts) Act 1943. It would cause many difficulties if the position were different in relation to contracts which are void *ab initio*. By analogy to Cannon's submission in the present case, in deciding on the equities of restitution the court could then always be called on to analyse or attempt to forecast the relative position of the parties under a contract with is *ex hypothesi* non-existent. This is not an attractive proposition, and I can see no justification for it in principle or on any authority.

I therefore conclude that Cannon must accept the primary basis on which they have succeeded, the invalidity of the contract *ab initio*, and that they cannot also rely on Rover's breach of this non-existent contract ...

Commentary

There is also a significant body of authority in the context of contracts discharged for breach and unenforceable contracts for the proposition that a claim for the value of services rendered under an ineffective contract should not be limited to the contract price.[37] This issue is discussed in more detail in Chapters 10, pp 282–83 and 11, pp 321–24.

ILLEGAL CONTRACTS

There is now a significant body of authority in Australia suggesting that a restitutionary claim will be permitted under a contract prohibited by statute, provided that the object of the governing legislation would not be defeated if the claim were permitted.[38] Before considering these cases, however, it is first necessary to set the background by examining the traditional approach of the courts to restitutionary claims under illegal contracts.

---

37 For contracts discharged for breach see: *Renard Constructions (ME) Pty Ltd v Minister for Public Works* (1992) (see extract, p 322); *Iezzi Constructions Pty Ltd v Watkins Pacific (Qld) Pty Ltd* (1995); *Jennings Constructions Pty Ltd v WH & M Birt Pty Ltd* (1988); *Slowey v Lodder* (1901); *Boomer v Muir* (1933) (DCA Cal). For unenforceable contracts see: *Pavey & Matthews Pty Ltd v Paul* (1987), p 257 (see extract, p 15); *Horton v Jones (No 1)* (1934), pp 368–69; *Gino D'Alessandro Constructions Pty Ltd v Powis* (1987), pp 58–59.

38 For a more detailed discussion of claims for restitution under contracts prohibited by statute see Vrisakis and Carter, 'Restitution of payments made under contracts prohibited by statute' (2000) 15 JCL 228. See also Enonchong, 'Illegal transactions: the future? (LCCP No 154)' [2000] RLR 82 for a discussion of the UK Law Commission's Report on illegality.

Traditional approach: the *Bowmakers* rule

In *Holman v Johnson* (1775) Lord Mansfield stated the influential proposition that no 'court will lend its aid to a man who founds his cause of action upon an immoral or an illegal act': p 343. This principle is embodied in the maxim: *ex turpi causa non oritur actio* (no cause of action will arise out of illegality). This principle was to lay the foundation of what became known as the '*Bowmakers* rule',[39] namely the rule that a plaintiff's claim would fail if the plaintiff had to rely on the illegal contract or illegal conduct in order to establish the claim. The effect of this rule was that a claim would be denied if the plaintiff needed to rely on the illegal contract or conduct in order to establish the elements of the cause of action, but the claim would not be denied if the plaintiff could establish a cause of action without reference to the illegal contract or conduct. The operation of this rule is illustrated by the following decision.

Parkinson v College of Ambulance Ltd [1925] 2 KB 1 King's Bench

Harrison, the secretary of the defendant charity, fraudulently represented to the plaintiff that the charity could arrange for the plaintiff to receive a knighthood if he made a donation. The plaintiff made a donation of £3,000 to the charity and Harrison undertook in return to arrange for the plaintiff to receive a knighthood. When the plaintiff did not receive the knighthood he commenced proceedings to recover back the donation.

Lush J: [Lush J held that a contract for the purchase of a title was contrary to public policy and illegal, and that the plaintiff knew that he was entering into an illegal contract. He then turned to consider whether the plaintiff could recover back the money.] [14] Now the first question to consider is this. The contract being against public policy, and being of the character that I have described, can the plaintiff still rely upon the fraud of Harrison and recover damages against him; and can he, as against the college, recover the £3,000 which the college has received through that fraud, as money had and received to his use? I am not prepared to hold – it is not necessary that I should decide the question – that in every case where a contract is against public policy, where one of the parties to it is defrauded by the other, he is prevented from recovering. It may be that whenever one party to a contract which is not improper in itself is unaware that it is illegal and is defrauded, the parties may not be in *pari delicto*. However that may be, I am of opinion that if the contract has any element of turpitude in it the parties are in *pari delicto* and no action for damages can be maintained by the party [15] defrauded. It is not correct to say, as was contended before me, that it is only if the contract is of a criminal nature that the plaintiff is precluded from recovering. The case of *Taylor v Chester* (1869) is an authority against this proposition. No criminal offence was committed there. And in *Fivaz v Nicholls* (1846) although a criminal offence was committed, the decision was not founded on that fact, but on the illegality and impropriety of the contract. It was also contended that fraud has the same effect as duress, and that it would be contrary to public policy to allow a party who has defrauded another to retain the fruits of his fraud. I cannot agree with that contention ... In the present case the

---

39   Named after *Bowmakers Ltd v Barnet Instruments Ltd* (1945).

plaintiff knew that he was entering into an illegal and improper contract. He was not deceived as to the legality of the contract he was making. How then can he say that he is excused? How can he say that he has suffered a loss through being defrauded into making a contract which he knew he ought never to have made? The answer is that he ought not to have made it. Where he was deceived was that he thought he would make a profit, derive a benefit from his unlawful act. He cannot be heard to say that. He has himself to blame for the loss that he has incurred. It is no [16] excuse to say that Harrison was more blameworthy than he, which is all that he really can say. That being the position, the plaintiff is in this difficulty. He cannot recover damages either against Harrison or the college, because he is disclosing or setting up a contract which is unlawful, and which he had no right to make. For the same reason he cannot recover the £3,000 from the college as money had and received. It is quite true that a principal cannot benefit by his agent's fraud, or a master by that of his servant. But the plaintiff is not in a position to rely on the fact that the college have benefited by their servant's fraud. He cannot reach that part of his case. He is precluded by the illegality from relying on it ...

Commentary

The High Court in *Nelson v Nelson* (1995) disapproved of the *Bowmakers* rule on the basis that it was unjust, capricious, and lacking foundation in public policy: see particularly pp 558, 595 and 609. The court held that the correct approach is to determine on a case by case basis whether the policy underlying the legislation or rule of public policy would preclude the relief sought.

Modern approach: consideration of legislative policy

There is a series of Australian cases permitting recovery of payments made under loan contracts that were unenforceable and illegal as being prescribed interests for which no approved deed was in place.[40] The approach adopted in these cases is that a restitutionary claim should be permitted for the recovery of benefits conferred under an illegal contract provided that such a claim would not be contrary to the policy of the governing legislation.

Hurst v Vestcorp Ltd (1988) 12 NSWLR 394 Court of Appeal of New South Wales

Filmco Ltd (renamed Vestcorp) lent money to a number of persons, including the appellants, to invest in film production in Australia. The loans and investments were made in accordance with a tax scheme formulated by an accountant. Filmco commenced proceedings against the appellants to recover the loan moneys and the appellants in defence alleged that the loan agreements were rendered illegal and unenforceable by the Companies Act 1961 as being prescribed interests for which no approved deed was in place. The Court of Appeal held that the loan agreements were illegal and unenforceable as being in breach of the Companies

---

40   *Hurst v Vestcorp Ltd* (1998) (see following extract); *Australian Breeders Co-operative Society Ltd v Jones* (1997); *Amadio Pty Ltd v Henderson* (1998).

Act 1961. The question then arose whether it should remit the matter to the trial judge to allow Filmco to bring an application for restitution of the amounts lent.

McHugh JA: ... [445] When, as the result of a breach of the law passed for the protection of certain persons, one or more contracts come into existence, the rationale of the illegality doctrine requires the invalidation only of a contract or part of a contract which defeats that protection. In many cases the unaffected contractual provision will be severable from the affected part. But in other cases, such as the present, severance may not be possible. Although a provision is outside the scope of the statute, it may be inextricably linked with the affected part of the contract or contracts. But it does not follow that the parties are without remedy in respect of executed transactions entered into under the unenforceable contract.

In some cases the doctrine of restitution will enable a party to recover compensation for a benefit accepted by the other party under the contract even though the contract is unenforceable. Recovery of compensation in these cases does not depend on the terms of the unenforceable contract. The right of recovery is based on an obligation or promise which the law itself imposes: *Pavey and Matthews Pty Ltd v Paul* (1987), pp 255–56. As the decision in that case shows, compensation may be payable in respect of work done and accepted under a contract even though a statute declares that the contract is unenforceable. Whether restitution is possible in respect of benefits accepted under a contract declared by statute to be unenforceable depends on the intention of the legislature That is to say, the question is whether the legislation evinces an intention not only to invalidate the contract but to preclude the recovery of compensation by way of restitution for benefits given and accepted under the unenforceable contract: cf *Pavey and Matthews v Paul* (p 263) *per* Deane J.

In the present case the contract of loan is invalid because it was made as the result of a breach of the Companies Act 1961, s 83. Nothing in s 83 and s 86 of the Act or the Act as a whole indicates that the legislature intended that a loan of money made to an investor who takes up an interest is not recoverable as a matter of restitution.

Although the contract of loan is unenforceable, the appellants have received and have had the benefits associated with the loans. With one exception, they have had the benefit of the tax deductions associated with the amounts of the loans. They have also been able to increase their interest in the films as the result of the loans. Yet the result of my judgment is that the contracts of loan are unenforceable. If appellants are not required to refund [446] the moneys which they borrowed, they will reap an unmerited benefit. That, of course, is often the result of the illegality doctrine. But the modern doctrine of restitution enables the court in appropriate cases to overcome these injustices.

Whether or not Filmco is entitled to recover compensation for the loans by way of restitution was not argued in this appeal or before [the trial judge]. This is understandable since Filmco was the defendant in an action which sought to declare the loan agreements invalid. But once the court declares the loan agreements are unenforceable, Filmco should be given the opportunity to raise the matter: see Supreme Court Act 1970, s 63. This should be done before [the trial judge].

Accordingly, the appeal should be allowed. The matter should be remitted to [the trial judge] to allow Filmco, if it wishes, to make any application for restitution and for his Honour to make such orders as are appropriate having regard to the reasons of this court ...

[Kirby P agreed with McHugh JA. Mahoney JA dissented on the basis that the money should not be recovered as a matter of policy.]

Commentary

McHugh JA failed to identify the legal basis of the claim, although it may have been mistake or failure of consideration.[41]

The principal case has been followed by the Full Court of the Federal Court in *Australian Breeders Co-operative Society Ltd v Jones* (1997) and by the Court of Appeal of Victoria in *Amadio Pty Ltd v Henderson* (1998). It was also referred to with approval by McHugh and Gummow JJ in *Fitzgerald v FJ Leonhardt Pty Ltd* (1997) in the following passage (p 231):

> [A]s was pointed out in *Hurst v Vestcorp Ltd* (1998), pp 445–46, what may now be classified as restitutionary remedies may be available to assist in the striking of a balance. For example, it was held long ago that where a borrower had paid interest in excess of the rate permitted by statute, whilst the debtor could not recover the whole back, an action would lie to recover the surplus.[42] The use of the *quantum meruit* in *Pavey & Matthews Pty Ltd v Paul* may be seen as another example.

The cases referred to so far involved contracts that were prohibited by statute; they were not cases where the *performance* of the contracts was prohibited by statutes. However, there is another set of cases dealing with claims for payment for the performance of a contract, where the performance was expressly prohibited by statute. More particularly, those cases involved claims for a *quantum meruit* where the statute expressly prohibited the doing of the work for which the remuneration was sought. The restitutionary claims were denied in this circumstance. The statutory provision under consideration in these cases was s 42 of the Queensland Building Services Authority Act 1991 which provides that:

> (1) A person must not carry out, or undertake to carry out, building work unless that person holds a contractor's licence of the appropriate class under this Act.
>
> ...
>
> (3) A person who carries out building work in contravention of this section is not entitled to any monetary or other consideration for doing so.

---

41 On the wider view of failure of consideration as exemplified by *Goss v Chilcott* (1996) (see extract, p 356).

42 *Smith v Bromley*, reported as a note to *Jones v Barkley* (1781); Stoljar, *The Law of Quasi-Contract*, 2nd edn, 1989, pp 228–29; Palmer, *The Law of Restitution*, 1978, vol 2, para 9.14.

This provision has been considered on two occasions by the Queensland Court of Appeal[43] which has held that the provision precludes claims in restitution by unlicensed contractors.

Marshall v Marshall [1999] 1 Qd R 173 Queensland Court of Appeal

The plaintiff commenced proceedings to recover money paid for building work by the defendant who the plaintiff later discovered did not hold a contractor's licence as required by s 42 of the Queensland Building Services Authority Act 1991. The plaintiff successfully recovered the money on the basis of a mistaken belief that the defendant was legally entitled to the money as a licensed builder. In the course of his judgment McPherson JA made certain observations about the availability to unlicensed contractors of a *quantum meruit*.

McPherson JA: ... [176] In my opinion, the effect of s 42(3) is to prevent an unlicensed builder, in proceedings of any kind, from recovering the price or any part if it payable under a contract for building work carried out in contravention of the section. Taken by itself, that might perhaps not prevent a builder from receiving money voluntarily paid by the other party. The terms of s 42(3) are, however, very wide. A person who carries out work in contravention of s 42 is 'not entitled' to any 'monetary consideration' for doing so. According to the ordinary meaning of those words, a person receives a 'monetary consideration' for carrying out work if he is paid for doing it. The sum of $51,000 paid by the plaintiff to the defendant satisfies that description. Counsel were unable to refer the court to authority bearing in any relevant way on the meaning of 'entitled' in a context like this. But s 42(3) expressly declares it to be money to which the recipient is 'not entitled', which can only mean that it is money to which he has in law no right or title. If that is so, there is no identifiable basis on which he can, as against the person who paid it, claim to keep or retain it or its equivalent.

There are several, and I consider, persuasive reasons for adopting such an interpretation of s 42. First, there is the history of the legislation. The corresponding provision of the Builders Registration and Home Owners Protection Act 1979, which was repealed by the current Act of 1991, was s 53(2)(d). It originally provided that a person who was not a registered builder should not be 'entitled to recover by action in a court a fee or charge under a contract to perform building construction for another ...'. In *Gino D'Alessandro Constructions Pty Ltd v Powis* (1987), it was held that, in that form, s 54(2)(d) did not prevent recovery, as a debt due and owing, for money for work done, or, as the High Court preferred to regard it, as restitution for unjust enrichment. See *Pavey & Matthews Pty Ltd v Paul* (1987). After that decision, s 53(2)(d) was revised by amending it to provide that a person not a registered builder should not:

> (d) be entitled to claim, sue for or otherwise recover ... any fee, charge, damages or other reward of whatever nature in respect [177] of the building construction performed or agreed to be performed.

However, in *Mostia Constructions Pty Ltd v Cox* (1994), White J held that, even in that form, s 53(2)(d) did not specifically preclude recovery of the amount of the

---

43   *Marshall v Marshall* (1999) (see following extract); *Zullo Enterprises Pty Ltd v Sutton* (1998) (see extract, p 395).

builder's outlays on labour and materials the benefit of which had been accepted by the party who had requested them.

Section 42 is thus the third attempt by the legislature to make its meaning clear. On this occasion it may be credited with having intended to cast the net as widely as possible. An unlicensed builder is, as s 42(3) now provides, not entitled to any monetary consideration for carrying out building work. A principal object of the legislation, both in its original and in its current form, is to prevent unlicensed builders from doing certain kinds of building work. Substandard workmanship and materials are, plainly enough, a principal target of the statutory prohibition: see s 3(a)(i). Preventing incompetent and unlicensed builders from doing building work, and penalising them if they do so, is one method of achieving that object. On occasions, however, even competent builders make mistakes and, having done so, sometimes become insolvent or for other reasons are not worth suing for the loss sustained. One object of the legislation was, as I suggested in *Gino D'Alessandro Constructions v Powis* (1987), pp 54–56, to establish and maintain the insurance scheme, which is now contained in Part 5 of the Act. It is funded by premiums paid by building contractors, from which claims by building owners or 'consumers' can be satisfied: cf *Pavey & Matthews Pty Ltd v Paul* (1987), p 229.

Under the statutory scheme, a building contractor must, before commencing residential construction work, pay to the Queensland Building Services Authority the appropriate insurance premium: s 68(1). When an insurance premium is paid in respect of residential construction work, a certificate of insurance issues: s 69(1). The insurance policy comes into force if a consumer (meaning a person for whom the building work is carried out) enters into a contract for the performance of residential construction work, in which event the contract is imprinted with a licensed contractor's licence card indorsed to show that the licensee may lawfully enter into contracts to carry out residential construction work: see s 69(2). It is true that s 69(2) applies whether or not an insurance premium has been paid or an insurance certificate has issued: s 69(3). It would nevertheless go far to diminish the funding available for the statutory insurance scheme if unlicensed builders were able to receive and retain money for doing residential construction work without complying with these provisions and with the licensing requirements of the Act. The insurance fund would be progressively depleted without receiving many of the premiums that were intended to form its source.

...

Commentary

The Court of Appeal subsequently endorsed McPherson JA's comments in the following case.

Zullo Enterprises Pty Ltd v Sutton unreported, 15 December 1998, Court of Appeal of Queensland

A builder commenced proceedings for a *quantum meruit* for work done. The builder did not possess the necessary licence as required by s 42 of the Queensland Building Services Authority Act 1991, and the issue before the court was the effect that s 42 had on the claim for restitution.

Pincus JA: … The most important point of distinction between the legal situation there considered [in *Pavey & Matthews v Paul*] and that which is before the court now is that here the restitutionary suit is to be one to recover a price for work the performance of which was prohibited by statute, done under a promise the making of which was prohibited by statute. We have not been referred to any appellate decision in which such a suit was held to be permissible on the basis of unjust enrichment. *Pavey & Matthews* was an action of a fairly familiar kind, where, suit on a contract not being available for want of formality, it was held that a restitutionary claim was nonetheless open.[44] The extension of *Pavey & Matthews* which we are invited to make here is into new territory, using a *quantum meruit* suit to recover for work the performance of which was prohibited by statute. According to *Restitution Law in Australia*,[45] by K Mason QC, S-G (as his Honour then was) and Professor JW Carter, where a transaction is both void and illegal 'claims for reasonable remuneration are almost invariably refused ...', and the authors, with reference to a case of the present kind, say:

> ... where a contract is illegal for failure to obtain a licence for building work, a *quantum meruit* claim, to recover reasonable remuneration has routinely been denied ... we must even today be sceptical of the restitutionary claim which is based on a request to do work expressed in an illegal contract, where acceptance of benefit takes place under the contract and the only reason for claiming in restitution is the illegality.[46]

The authors do not refer to, nor have I found, any reported instance in which such a claim has succeeded.

In summary, then, it is my opinion that for the reasons I have given, the word 'consideration' in s 42(3) of the Act should be given a construction covering a price recovered in a *quantum meruit* claim; further, I do not accept that the principle, of which the leading example is *Pavey & Matthews*, permitting such a claim to be made where a contract is unenforceable for want of formality should be extended to include also instances in which a statute prohibits both the contract and the doing of the work.

…

Question

According to Pincus JA, why was the claim before the court in this case distinguishable from the claim in *Pavey's* case?

---

44 See for other examples Burrows, *The Law of Restitution*, 1993, p 299.
45 Mason and Carter, *Restitution Law in Australia*, 1995, p 349.
46 *Ibid*, p 887.

CHAPTER 14

CONTRACTS WHICH FAIL TO MATERIALISE

INTRODUCTION

There are a number of cases involving claims in restitution by plaintiffs who, during the course of negotiating a contract with the defendant that is never finalised, provided services at the request of the defendant. These claims have sometimes been successful, despite the fact that it is difficult to identify an enrichment to the defendant by the receipt of the services,[1] and despite the fact that neither party intended that the work should be compensated for independently of the terms of a concluded contract.

It is usually helpful to distinguish between situations where the plaintiff has done work at the defendant's request which amounts to accelerated performance of the contract, and situations where the work done is preparatory to performance of the contract. In the former case, the existence of a request by the defendant will usually of itself be sufficient to found recovery, whereas in the latter case recovery depends on a range of interrelated factors, only one of which is a request for the services.

ACCELERATED PERFORMANCE

The plaintiff will be entitled to the reasonable value of work done at the defendant's request where the work amounts to accelerated performance of the anticipated contract; that is, where the work done is the very work which was contemplated to be done under the contract.

British Steel Corp v Cleveland Bridge and Engineering Co Ltd [1984] 1 All ER 504
Queen's Bench

The plaintiff, an iron and steel manufacturer, was approached by the defendant to produce a variety of cast steel nodes for a building project. The parties commenced negotiations for a contract but they were in dispute over material terms such as price and liability for late delivery. Meanwhile, the plaintiff went ahead with the manufacture and delivery of the nodes in stages. All of the nodes were eventually delivered, however the defendant complained that the plaintiff was late in delivering the nodes and failed to deliver them in the sequence requested by the defendant. The plaintiff claimed the value of the nodes on a *quantum meruit*. The defendant counterclaimed for damages for breach of contract for late delivery and delivery out of sequence. Robert Goff J found that no formal contract had been concluded.

---

1   The services provided will have become worthless to the defendant if the defendant changes its mind and no longer wishes to proceed with the project in question: see, for example, *Sabemo Pty Ltd v North Sydney Municipal Council* (1977) (see extract, p 408).

Robert Goff J: ... [511] In my judgment, the true analysis of the situation is simply this. Both parties confidently expected a formal contract to eventuate. In these circumstances, to expedite performance under that anticipated contract, one requested the other to commence the contract work, and the other complied with that request. If thereafter, as anticipated, a contract was entered into, the work done as requested will be treated as having been performed under that contract; if, contrary to their expectation, no contract was entered into, then the performance of the work is not referable to any contract the terms of which can be ascertained, and the law simply imposes an obligation on the party who made the request to pay a reasonable sum for such work as has been done pursuant to that request, such an obligation sounding in quasi contract or, as we now say, in restitution. Consistently with that solution, the party making the request may find himself liable to pay for work which he would not have had to pay for as such if the anticipated contract had come into existence, eg, preparatory work which will, if the contract is made, be allowed for in the price of the finished work (cf *William Lacey (Hounslow) Ltd v Davis* (1957)). This solution moreover accords with authority: see the decision in *William Lacey (Hounslow) Ltd v Davis*, the decision of the Court of Appeal in *Sanders & Forster Ltd v A Monk & Co Ltd* (1980), CA Transcript No 35 of 1980, though that decision rested in part on a concession, and the crisp *dictum* of Parker J in *OTM Ltd v Hydranautics* (1981), p 214, when he said of a letter of intent that 'its only effect would be to enable the defendants to recover on a *quantum meruit* for work done pursuant to the direction' contained in the letter ...

Commentary

If the benefit to the defendant had been reduced by the late and sequentially incorrect delivery of the nodes it may have been appropriate to adjust the amount of the *quantum meruit* to reflect the defendant's loss.[2] However, Goff J had found that the plaintiff had delivered the nodes within a reasonable time, and there was no evidence that the nodes were defective. Further, it appears from the facts that the defendant may not have clearly specified to the plaintiff in a timely manner its requirement as to the delivery sequence. In these circumstances it is arguable that a reduction of the restitutionary award was not justified.[3]

Another case in which there recovery was allowed for the cost of accelerated performance was *Peter Lind v Mersey Docks & Harbour Board* (1984). The plaintiff contractor completed a container freight terminal at the defendant's request. No contract was concluded as the parties failed to agree on a price and the court awarded a *quantum meruit*. The completed terminal was objectively valuable, and the request and acceptance prevented subjective devaluation.

---

2 Byrne, 'Benefits – for services rendered', in McInnes (ed), *Restitution: Developments in Unjust Enrichment*, 1996, Chapter 5, pp 107–08; Burrows, *The Law of Restitution*, 1993, p 297.

3 See Burrows, *The Law of Restitution*, 1993, p 296; Liew, 'Restitution and contract risk: commentary', in McInnes (ed), *Restitution: Developments in Unjust Enrichment*, 1996, Chapter 10, pp 177–78.

PREPARATORY PERFORMANCE

Where the work is preparatory to the performance of the contract – in the sense that it does not amount to performance of the contract, but rather is to put the plaintiff in the position to perform the contract – the defendant's request for the services will not of itself ground recovery. In this situation the courts weigh the fact of the request along with a number of other factors in deciding whether the cost of the preparatory work should be recoverable.[4] The factors, other than request, that are taken into account are:[5]

(1) **The reason for the failure of the contract negotiations**. One factor that has been said to be crucial in determining recovery is whether the contract negotiations fell through because of a unilateral decision to abandon the project, or because the parties genuinely failed to reach agreement on the material terms of the contract. For example, in *Sabemo Pty Ltd v North Sydney Municipal Council* (1977) (see extract, p 408) the critical factor in the decision to award restitution was that the contract fell though, not because the parties could not reach agreement, but because the defendant had decided to abandon the project.[6]

(2) **The parties' respective assumption of risk that the contract would not be finalised**. The courts regularly employ a risk analysis to determine whether the plaintiff should be entitled to the costs of the preparatory work, enquiring whether in all the circumstances the work was performed at the risk of the plaintiff or defendant.[7] A risk-oriented approach was explicitly adopted in *Brewer Street Investments Ltd v Barclays Woollen Co Ltd* (1954) (see the following extract), where Denning LJ said that the relevant test of recovery is: 'on whom in all the circumstances should the risk fall?': p 437.[8] The circumstances might indicate, for example, that the plaintiff was prepared to work on a contingency basis, and to take the risk that the negotiations would fail, because any resulting contract would be very lucrative.[9] The basis on which the contractual negotiations are conducted

---

4   *Sabemo Pty Ltd v North Sydney Municipal Council* (1977), pp 898, 900 (see extract, p 408); *Angelopoulos v Sabatino* (1995), pp 12–13 (see extract, p 418); *Countrywide Communications Ltd v ICL Pathway Ltd* (1999), QB [noted [2000] RLR 270] (see extract, p 424).

5   These four factors are stated in *Countrywide Communications Ltd v ICL Pathway Ltd* (1999), QB [noted [2000] RLR 270] (see extract, p 424).

6   The importance of this factor was also accepted in *Vivian Fraser & Associates Pty Ltd v Shipton* (1994), though its significance has not acquired universal support: see *Regalian Properties plc v London Docklands Development Corporation* (1995) (see extract, p 413); *POS Media Online Ltd v Queensland Investment Corporation* (2001), para 195.

7   *Hooker Corporation Ltd v Darling Harbour Authority* (1987); *Independent Grocers Co-operative Ltd v Noble Lowndes Superannuation Consultants Ltd* (1993), pp 561–62; *Vivian Fraser & Associates Pty Ltd v Shipton* (1994); *Brewer Street Investments Ltd v Barclays Woollen Co Ltd* (1954) (see extract, p 401); *Regalian Properties plc v London Docklands Development Corporation* (1995), p 231 (see extract, p 413); *Countrywide Communications Ltd v ICL Pathway Ltd* (1999) (see extract, p 424); *EASAT Antennas Ltd v Racal Defence Electronics Ltd* (2000).

8   See also Somervell LJ, p 434, Romer LJ, p 438.

9   *Independent Grocers Co-operative Ltd v Noble Lowndes Superannuation Consultants Ltd* (1993) per Duggon J, pp 561–62; *Vivian Fraser & Associates Pty Ltd v Shipton* (1994).

might also indicate that the plaintiff takes the risk that the contract will not eventuate, for example where the negotiations are expressly said to be 'subject to contract'. In that situation each party is free to withdraw from the negotiations at any time, and any work performed pending the finalising of the negotiations is done at the risk of the provider: *Regalian Properties plc v London Docklands Development Corporation* (1995) (see extract, p 413).

(3) **The extent to which the work falls outside the ambit of the anticipated contract**. The plaintiff is more likely to be able to recover the cost of pre-contractual work where it is performed for a purpose that is extraneous or collateral to the anticipated contract, rather than for the purpose of readying the plaintiff to commence performance of the contract. Thus, in *William Lacey (Hounslow) Ltd v Davis* (1957) (see extract, p 405),[10] a builder was held entitled to recover work that it would not ordinarily have performed without charge when tendering for a building contract, and which it undertook for a purpose collateral to the anticipated building contract.

(4) **Any benefit conferred on the defendant**. The courts have indicated that they would be more inclined to allow recovery where the defendant has acquired an objective benefit from the services,[11] 'since otherwise the abortive negotiations will leave the defendant with a windfall and the plaintiff out of pocket': see *Countrywide Communications Ltd v ICL Pathway Ltd* (1999) (see extract, p 424).

It will be seen from the anticipated contract cases that follow that some of them fit uneasily within a modern unjust enrichment framework, particularly with the requirement of an enrichment in the defendant's hands. Recovery has been permitted in cases such as *William Lacey (Hounslow) Ltd v Davis* (1957) (see extract, p 405) and *Sabemo Pty Ltd v North Sydney Municipal Council* (1977) (see extract, p 408) even though the preparatory work performed by the plaintiff became largely valueless to the defendant due to the defendant's decision not to go ahead with the project in question. The problem with identification of an enrichment is also well illustrated by the case of *Brewer Street Investments Ltd v Barclays Woollen Co Ltd* (1954) (see the following extract) where the cost of improvements made to the *plaintiff's* land was recoverable in restitution despite the fact the lease negotiations fell through and the defendant (the prospective tenant) never obtained the benefit of the improvements. In cases such as this, it can be difficult to identify in a meaningful sense an enrichment in the hands of the defendant which can be reversed.[12] Accordingly, it is often argued that the

---

10 See also *POS Media Online Ltd v Queensland Investment Corporation* (2001).

11 *Countrywide Communications Ltd v ICL Pathway Ltd* (1999) (see extract, p 424); *Vivian Fraser & Associates Pty Ltd v Shipton* (1994).

12 See Mason and Carter, *Restitution Law in Australia*, 1995, p 359 where the authors express the view that the *Brewer Street Investments* case is a case of recovery for reliance loss. See also Liew, 'Restitution and contract risk: commentary' in McInnes (ed), *Restitution: Developments in Unjust Enrichment*, 1996, Chapter 10; Mannolini, 'Restitution where an anticipated contracts fails to materialise' (1996) 59 MLR 111, p 113; cf McKendrick, 'Work done in anticipation of a contract which does not materialise', in Cornish *et al*, *Restitution: Past, Present and Future*, 1998, pp 172–80.

real basis of recovery in these cases is the plaintiff's detrimental reliance on the defendant's request, rather than the reversal of an unjust enrichment.[13] Various alternative bases of recovery for the anticipated contract cases have been suggested, including equitable estoppel[14] and 'unjust sacrifice'.[15] Nevertheless, attempts have been made to reconcile the anticipated contract cases with unjust enrichment principles. The most notable attempt is that by Justice Byrne in *Brenner v First Artists' Management Pty Ltd* (1993) (see extract, p 39), where his Honour held that enrichment can be established simply by reference to the defendant's request, on the assumption that the defendant would not have asked for the work unless he or she had seen some benefit in it. However, even his Honour has acknowledged that an approach to benefit based upon request is based upon a fiction in the sense that the benefit is based on the conduct of the defendant, rather than the identification of an objective benefit.[16] This fiction has been criticised.[17]

Brewer Street Investments Ltd v Barclays Woollen Co Ltd [1954] 1 QB 428
English Court of Appeal

The plaintiff and defendant were negotiating the lease of premises, owned by the plaintiff, to the defendant. The parties had reached agreement on the material terms, subject to contract. The defendant was anxious to enter the premises and the plaintiff agreed to make certain alterations to the premises which the defendant required. The defendant accepted responsibility for the cost of the alterations. The negotiations for the grant of a lease fell through as the parties could not reach an agreement over whether an option to purchase should be given. The plaintiff claimed reimbursement for the cost of the work done on the alterations.

Somervell LJ: [Somervell LJ rejected the defendant's claim that there was to be no liability for the cost of the alterations unless a lease was concluded or, alternatively, unless the plaintiff was willing to grant a lease on the terms of the original draft and continued at p 434:]

---

13 See *Countrywide Communications Ltd v ICL Pathway Ltd* (1999) (see extract, p 424) where the action was said to be in reality an action for 'a loss unfairly sustained by the plaintiff'. See also Stoljar, 'Unjust enrichment and unjust sacrifice' (1987) 50 MLR 603; Muir, 'Unjust sacrifice and the officious intervener', in Finn (ed), *Essays in Restitution*, 1990, Chapter 9; Wyvill, 'Enrichment, restitution and the collapsed negotiations cases' (1993) 11(2) ABR 93; Pegoraro, 'Recovery of benefits conferred pursuant to failed anticipated contracts – unjust enrichment, equitable estoppel or unjust sacrifice' (1993) 23 ABLR 117; Liew, 'Restitution and contract risk: commentary', in McInnes (ed), *Restitution: Developments in Unjust Enrichment*, 1996, Chapter 10.

14 Liew, 'Restitution and contract risk: commentary', in McInnes (ed), *Restitution: Developments in Unjust Enrichment*, 1996, Chapter 10.

15 Stoljar, 'Unjust enrichment and unjust sacrifice' (1987) 50 MLR 603; Muir, 'Unjust sacrifice and the officious intervener', in Finn (ed), *Essays in Restitution*, 1990, Chapter 9; Pegoraro, 'Recovery of benefits conferred pursuant to failed anticipated contracts – unjust enrichment, equitable estoppel or unjust sacrifice' (1993) 23 ABLR 117. The principle of unjust sacrifice is discussed further at p 428.

16 Byrne, 'Benefits – for services rendered', in McInnes (ed), *Restitution: Developments in Unjust Enrichment*, 1996, Chapter 6.

17 See *Countrywide Communications Ltd v ICL Pathway Ltd* (1999) (see extract, p 424). See also Wyvill, 'Enrichment, restitution and the collapsed negotiations cases' (1993) 11(2) ABR 93; Pegoraro, 'Recovery of benefits conferred pursuant to failed anticipated contracts – unjust enrichment, equitable estoppel or unjust sacrifice' (1993) 23 ABLR 117.

The only question of law, therefore, would be whether the events which have happened, by reason of some implication, entitle the defendants to put up a defence. The judge below clearly thought that if the matter had gone off because the plaintiffs had changed their mind or had found someone else who would pay more, the defendants would have such a defence. It is unnecessary to decide that point, though there seems to be a strong argument for that view. It is plain that the matter went off because of the defendants' own course of conduct in adhering to the condition that they should get an option when it had been made clear to them that the plaintiffs were not willing to grant an option. If [counsel for the defendants] is right in saying, in the alternative, that the lease went off through circumstances for which neither party can be regarded as responsible, that is in the ordinary course of negotiations and misunderstandings, I still think that that would not afford a good defence to this claim. I wish to guard the words which I use because an earlier case which came before this court shows that the area is somewhat difficult. Each case must be judged on its own circumstances. There might be a case in which the circumstances were such, and the benefits conferred on the landlord if the matter went off were such, that, even although it was not through the deliberate action of the landlord that the matter went off, the defendant still might have a defence. One should not seek to anticipate circumstances which may arise ...

Denning LJ: ... [435] This case raises questions of considerable interest. The landlords seek to recover from the prospective tenants the moneys which they have had to pay to their own contractors for the work done on the alterations before the negotiations for the lease broke down. The question is whether they can do so.

It is not easy to state the legal basis of the landlords' claim. The difficulty arises because, although the prospective tenants agreed to pay the cost of the alterations, nevertheless those alterations were never completed. The work was abandoned before it was finished. Once the negotiations for a lease broke down, both sides realised that the work must be stopped. It was a sensible thing to do, but it means that the landlords cannot sue for the price as on a completed contract. Nor can they sue the prospective tenants for damages for breach of contract, because the prospective tenants have not been guilty of a breach. Let me give an instance. One item of the work was a lift door to be made, fixed and installed for the lump sum of £48 10s. At the time when the work was abandoned, the lift door had been made in the provinces but it had not been transported to London, let alone fixed or installed. Nevertheless, the plaintiffs have had to pay to their contractors the full sum of £48 10s, presumably by way of damages, and they seek to recover it from the prospective tenants. They clearly cannot recover on a *quantum meruit* as ordinarily understood. The way they put their claim on this item and the others in the statement of claim is money paid on request. The prospective tenants, however, made no request in fact to the landlords to pay the money. Their request, if any, was to pay on completion of the work, and it was not completed. [436] In these circumstances, the proper way to formulate the claim is on a request implied in law, or, as I would prefer to put it in these days, on a claim in restitution.

It is clear on the facts that the parties proceeded on a fundamental assumption – that the lease would be granted – which has turned out to be wrong. The work done has been wasted. The question is: on whom is the loss to fall? The parties themselves did not envisage the situation which has emerged and did not provide for it; and we do not know what they would have provided if they had envisaged it. Only the law can resolve their rights and liabilities in the new situation, either by means of implying terms or, more simply, by asking on whom should the risk fall. That is how the court approached a similar question in *Jennings and Chapman Ltd v Woodman, Matthews & Co* (1952), and I think that we should approach the question in the same way.

Morris LJ gave a reserved judgment in which he put the matter in a way which appeals to me. He asked himself: what was the reason for the negotiations breaking down? If it was the landlords' fault, as, for instance, if they refused to go on with the lease for no reason at all, or because they demanded a higher rent than that which had been already agreed, then they should not be allowed to recover any part of the cost of the alterations. Even if the landlords derived no benefit from the work, they should not be allowed to recover the cost from the prospective tenants, seeing that it was by their fault that the prospective tenants were deprived of it.

On the other hand, if it was the prospective tenants' fault that the negotiations broke down, as, for instance, if they sought a lower rent than that which had been agreed upon, then the prospective tenants ought to pay the cost of the alterations up to the time they were stopped. After all, they did promise to pay for the work, and they should not be able to get out of their promise by their own fault, even though the alterations were not completed. It is a very old principle laid down by Sir Edward Coke that a man shall not be allowed to take advantage of a condition brought about by himself *Jennings and Chapman Ltd v Woodman, Matthews & Co* (1952).

I do not think, however, that in the present case it can be said that either party was really at fault. Neither party sought to alter the rent or any other point which had been agreed upon. They fell out on a point which had not been agreed at [437] all. From the very beginning the prospective tenants wanted an option to purchase, whereas the landlords were only ready to give them the first refusal. Each of them in the course of the negotiations sought on this point to get more favourable terms – the prospective tenants to get a firm option to purchase, the landlords to give a first refusal of little value – but their moves in the negotiations can hardly be considered a default by one or other. What, then, is the position when the negotiations go off without the default of either? On whom should the risk fall? In my opinion the prospective tenants ought to pay all the costs thrown away. The work was done to meet their special requirements and was *prima facie* for their benefit and not for the benefit of the landlords. If and in so far as the work is shown to have been of benefit to the landlords, credit should be given in such sum as may be just. Subject to such credit, the prospective tenants ought to pay the cost of the work, because they in the first place agreed to take responsibility for it; and when the matter goes off without the default of either side, they should pay the costs thrown away. There is no finding here that the work was of any benefit to the landlords, and in the circumstances the prospective tenants should, I think, pay the amount claimed.

[Counsel for the plaintiffs] argued that the test laid down in *Jennings and Chapman Ltd v Woodman, Matthews & Co* (1952) was wrong. It was not right, he said, to ask whose fault it was, or on whom should the risk fall, because each side had an absolute right to withdraw from the negotiations: and could not be said to be at fault in doing so. He referred to *Luxor (Eastbourne), Ltd v Cooper* (1941), and argued that, even if the landlord, for instance, demanded a higher rent and thus caused the negotiations to fall through, he could still recover the cost of the alterations. I do not think that that is right. Estate agents are employed on the footing that they get a large commission if a sale is completed, but nothing if it is not. They take the risk of the deal falling through. The cases on the subject are, therefore, illustrations of the same test: on whom in all the circumstances should the risk fall?

In the present case I think that the risk should fall on the prospective tenants and that they should pay the costs of the alterations ...

Romer LJ: ... [438] I agree. As has been pointed out by Somervell LJ, this case falls to be decided on its particular facts and circumstances. On those facts and circumstances I hope that I shall not be regarded as unsympathetic to the defendants if I say that in my opinion they have only themselves to blame for the judgment which was delivered against them. The truth of the matter is that they were in a great hurry to get into these premises because the lease of their own premises was running out, and because of that hurry they did things which in the normal course they would not have done.

... The defendants knew what the position was in regard to the lease. They knew that this formidable difference had already arisen between themselves and the plaintiffs with regard to the option. But they wanted to get on; they wanted work done; and I am satisfied that they were prepared to take the risk of the matter of the lease not coming eventually to a satisfactory conclusion ... Taking the whole of the circumstances, the dates, the urgency of the matter, the fact that the defendants themselves paid directly for part of the electrical work without any suggestion of their liability in that regard being conditional, I have no doubt but that in common phraseology they were 'taking the risk' for their own purposes in the hope that they would get the benefit of it if, as they hoped and thought, a lease was finally agreed and granted. As the negotiations failed, solely because the defendants right up to the end insisted on getting that which they had been told already the plaintiffs were unwilling to give, namely, an option, I cannot see how they can escape responsibility by seeking to put the blame on the shoulders of the plaintiffs. It may well be that if, [439] after this work had been done, the plaintiffs got the benefit of it, assuming it to be work which improved the value of the property, and had said 'We will not grant a lease at all', then the defendants would not have been without remedy. That was not the position in this case. The facts led to an entirely different result ...

Commentary

The court in the principal case adopted a risk analysis in determining whether the plaintiff should recover. A risk analysis was also adopted in a case with similar facts, *Jennings and Chapman Ltd v Woodman, Matthews & Co* (1952), though the opposite result was reached. This case also involved a plaintiff landlord altering his property at the request of a potential tenant and the collapse of the lease negotiations, however in this case recovery was denied. The lease negotiations fell through as the head lessee refused to give permission for the alterations to the premises. Unlike in the *Brewer Street* case, the risk fell on the plaintiff as it knew or should have known of the obligation to obtain the permission of the head lessee, however the defendant was not aware of this requirement.

In *Independent Grocers Co-operative Ltd v Noble Lowndes Superannuation Consultants Ltd* (1993) superannuation consultants performed services in connection with the creation of an industrial superannuation scheme. The scheme was abandoned after an industrial dispute over industry superannuation. The majority, applying the principal case, awarded a *quantum meruit* for the services provided. Duggan J dissented holding that the claimant had taken the risk that for one reason or another the project would fail. He found that the claimant consultants had agreed to do the work on a contingency basis, with the expectation of receiving substantial administration fees should the project proceed. The low establishment fee payable to the plaintiff in the event of the fund being instituted provided further support for this conclusion: pp 561–62.

The plaintiff will not ordinarily be taken to have assumed the risk of non-payment of work that is performed for a purpose collateral to the anticipated contract, as illustrated by the following case.

William Lacey (Hounslow) Ltd v Davis [1957] 1 WLR 932 Queen's Bench

The plaintiffs submitted to the defendant a tender for the reconstruction of premises owned by the defendant which had been damaged during the war and which the defendant proposed to rebuild. The plaintiffs' tender was the lowest and they were led to believe they would receive the contract. At the request of the defendant the plaintiffs prepared various estimates for the purpose of obtaining the necessary licences and for negotiating with the War Damage Commission, and in order to comply with amendments made to the plans by the defendant from time to time. The defendant subsequently sold the premises instead of proceeding with the reconstruction. The plaintiffs commenced proceedings seeking recovery of the cost of its services.

Barry J: [Barry J dismissed the claim based on breach of contract and continued at p 934:] In elaborating his argument [on the alternative claim, counsel for the plaintiffs] rightly conceded that if a builder is invited to tender for certain work, either in competition or otherwise, there is no implication that he will be paid for the work – sometimes a very considerable amount of work – involved in arriving at his price: he undertakes this work as a gamble, and its cost is part of the overhead expenses of his business which he hopes will be met out of the profits of such contracts as are made as a result of tenders which prove to be successful. This generally accepted usage may also – and I think does also – apply to amendments of the original tender necessitated by *bona fide* alterations in the specification and plans. If no contract ensues, the builder is, therefore, without a remedy. [Counsel for the plaintiffs], however, contends that no such principle applies if the builder's tender is sought and used not to ascertain the cost of erecting or reconstructing some genuinely contemplated building project, but for some extraneous or collateral purpose for which the building owner may require it. In such circumstances, [counsel for the plaintiffs] suggests that the builder is entitled to recover a reasonable payment for his work. It may also happen – as it certainly did happen in the present case – that when a builder is told that his tender is the lowest and led to believe that the building contract is to be given to him, he, the builder, is prepared to perform other incidental services at the request of the building owner without any intention of charging for them as such. He is not –

[counsel for the plaintiffs] suggests – rendering these services gratuitously, but is content to be recompensed for them out of the profit which he will make under the contract. If, without default on the builder's part, no contract supervenes, then, says [counsel for the plaintiffs], the law will imply a contract to pay a [935] reasonable sum for these services. His contention is that, for one or other of these two reasons, the defendants are under a legal obligation to pay for all the work itemised in the schedule.

[Counsel for the defendant's] answer can be put quite shortly. He does not deny that a considerable amount of work was done by the plaintiffs, but he says that it was all done – on [the plaintiffs'] own admission – in the expectation and hope that they would receive the building contract. They did not do so and, although the consequences to them are, of course, unfortunate, there can be no room for an implication that they were to be paid for services for which they never intended to charge. As an alternative, [counsel for the defendant] somewhat tentatively questioned the plaintiffs' allegation that their services were rendered at the defendant's request and, further, he suggested that even if requests for these services were in fact made by Day [a member of the firm of surveyors employed by the defendant], the latter had no authority from the defendant to make any such requests.

[His Honour examined the facts in detail and continued:] Now, on this evidence, I am quite satisfied that the whole of the work covered by the schedule fell right outside the work which a builder, by custom and usage, normally performs gratuitously, when invited to tender for the erection of a building. In the absence of any evidence called by the defendants, I can only find that the earlier estimates were given for work which it was never intended to execute. It is possible that, in the very latest stages, the defendant was intending to erect the type of building for which the plaintiffs were giving their quotation, but having obtained, without charge, an initial estimate for a purely notional building, Mr Davis could hardly expect the builders to go on giving free estimates when a state of reality was at last approached. The earlier estimates, as the correspondence shows, were in fact used, and used for some purpose, in the defendant's negotiations with the War Damage Commission and, as an apparent result of the plaintiffs' efforts, not only were the reconstruction plans approved, but a much higher 'permissible amount' was also agreed with the War Damage Commission. It is perhaps justifiable to surmise that these facts, especially the reconstruction plans and the increase in the permissible amount, had at least some influence upon the price of the damaged building which the defendant obtained when it was ultimately sold by him. The work itemised in the schedule which does not relate to estimation, as I think, falls even more clearly outside the type of work which any builder would be expected to do without charge when tendering for a building contract.

The plaintiffs are carrying on a business and, in normal circumstances, if asked to render services of this kind, the obvious inference would be that they ought to be paid for so doing. No one could expect a business firm to do this sort of work for nothing, and again, in normal circumstances, the law would imply a promise to pay on the part of the person who requested the services to be performed. [Counsel for the defendant], however, submits that no [936] such promise can be implied, in the circumstances of the present case. The existence, he submits, of a common expectation that a contract would ultimately come into being and that the plaintiffs' services would be rewarded by the profits of that contract leaves no room, in his submission, and, indeed, wholly negatives any suggestion, that the parties impliedly agreed that these services would be paid for in any other way.

This, at first sight, is a somewhat formidable argument which, if well founded, would wholly defeat the plaintiffs' alternative claim. If such were the law it would, I think, amount to a denial of justice to the plaintiffs in the present case, and legal propositions which have that apparent effect must always be scrutinised with some care. In truth, I think that [counsel's] proposition is founded on too narrow a view of the modern action for *quantum meruit*. In its early history it was no doubt a genuine action in contract, based on a real promise to pay, although that promise had not been expressed in words and the amount of the payment had not been agreed. Subsequent developments have, however, considerably widened the scope of this form of action, and in many cases the action is now founded upon what is known as quasi-contract, similar, in some ways, to the action for money had and received. In these quasi-contractual cases the court will look at the true facts and ascertain from them whether or not a promise to pay should be implied, irrespective of the actual views or intentions of the parties at the time when the work was done or the services rendered ...

[939] I am unable to see any valid distinction between work done which was to be paid for under the terms of a contract erroneously believed to be in existence, and work done which was to be paid for out of the proceeds of a contract which both parties erroneously believed was about to be made. In neither case was the work to be done gratuitously, and in both cases the party from whom payment was sought requested the work and obtained the benefit of it. In neither case did the parties actually intend to pay for the work otherwise than under the supposed contract, or as part of the total price which would become payable when the expected contract was made. In both cases, when the beliefs of the parties were falsified, the law implied an obligation – and, in this case, I think the law should imply an obligation – to pay a reasonable price for the services which had been obtained. I am, of course, fully aware that in different circumstances it might be held that work was done gratuitously merely in the hope that the building scheme would be carried out and that the person who did the work would obtain the contract. That, I am satisfied, is not the position here. In my judgment, the proper inference from the facts proved in this case is not that the work was done in the hope that the building might possibly be reconstructed and that the plaintiff company might obtain the contract, but that it was done under a mutual belief and understanding that the building was being reconstructed and that the plaintiff company were obtaining the contract. [His Honour examined at length the correspondence between the parties and continued at p 940:] It is abundantly plain from the correspondence that Mr Day requested the plaintiffs to do all this work. He never disguised the position from the defendant and I am perfectly satisfied that throughout the whole of his dealings with the plaintiffs he was acting within the scope of his authority.

I have, therefore, come to the conclusion that the defence to the alternative claim fails and that the court should imply a condition or imply a promise that the defendant should pay a reasonable sum to the plaintiffs for the whole of these services which were rendered by them. As to amount, I have considered the plaintiffs' charges as set out in the schedule with some care. On the rather scanty information available to me, I have come to the conclusion that, while some of the items may well be undercharged, certain of the larger items cannot be fully justified. The plaintiffs are entitled to a fair remuneration for the work which they have done ...

Commentary

Barry J makes it clear that costs incurred by a tenderer for the purposes of preparing the tender will not be recoverable. This is because, according to settled business practice, the tenderer is to bear the risk of the contract being awarded to someone else.[18] However, Barry J held that recovery will not be denied where the plaintiff performs work at the request of the defendant which exceeds what would normally be expected of a tenderer. More generally, the case is illustrative of the wider proposition that the cost of pre-contractual work is more likely to be recoverable where it was performed for a purpose collateral to the anticipated contract, rather than to place the plaintiff in a position to perform the contract.

It may be arguable that the defendant in the principal case received an incontrovertible benefit in this case in the form of the realisation of the value of costing estimates which enabled the defendant to negotiate for a higher level of compensation from the War Damage Commission, and which Barry J surmised would have had some influence on the price ultimately obtained for the building by the defendant. However the evidence on enrichment is scanty and this fact was not central to Barry J's decision. Jones has analysed the case as essentially a claim for reliance loss.[19]

Sabemo Pty Ltd v North Sydney Municipal Council [1977] 2 NSWLR 880
Supreme Court of New South Wales

The plaintiff was the successful tenderer for the development of a civic centre on land owned by the defendant council. The plaintiff carried out considerable work in developing three alternative schemes, the last of which satisfied the minister's planning requirements for the site. Most of the work done in developing the schemes was done at the request of the defendant. The defendant then decided to abandon the proposed scheme altogether, with no concluded agreement ever being reached between the parties. The plaintiff claimed reimbursement of $426,000, representing the cost of the work done by it for the defendant in connection with the proposed development.

Sheppard J: ... [Sheppard J reviewed the relevant authorities and continued at p 897:] In 1967 Lord Denning wrote a review of a work, *The Law of Restitution*, by Goff and Jones, 1966. His Lordship said (1967):

> When I started in the law, no one had ever heard of restitution. Some of us had heard of quasi-contract: but that was dismissed by Anson in 12 lines at the end of his book on contract. Every practitioner knew, however, about the money

---

18   See also *Magical Waters Fountains Ltd v City of Sarnia* (1992) (claim failed because the work was at the tender stage); *Brenner v First Artists' Management Pty Ltd* (1993), p 259 (see extract, p 39).

19   Jones, 'Anticipated contracts which do not materialise' (1980) 18 U of West Ont L Rev 447; Goff and Jones, *The Law of Restitution*, 5th edn, 1998, p 668. See also Wyvill, 'Enrichment, restitution and the collapsed negotiations cases' (1993) 11(2) ABR 93, pp 114–15.

counts. Money had and received, money paid, and *quantum meruit*. They were all based on a notional or imputed promise to repay. They had become ossified. The foremost judges of the time had declared that the law had been crystallised in the reported common law cases and we were not to go beyond them. Any attempt to introduce equity and good conscience was castigated as 'well meaning sloppiness of thought'. Under this influence we had to go back to the third edition of *Bullen and Leake* or to *Smith's Leading Cases* and try to find a parallel case in the old books. That was all that could be done. There was no principle to go by: only precedent. The change came with the speeches of Lord Atkin in *United Australia Ltd v Barclays Bank Ltd* (1941), p 29, and of Lord Wright in *Fibrosa Spolka Akcyjna v Fairbairn Lawson Combe Barbour Ltd* (1943), p 61. They swept away the fictitious promise which was the basis of the money counts, and restored the large generalisation of Lord Mansfield who would allow the recovery of money which the defendant 'is obliged by the ties of natural justice and equity to refund'. At length judges began to perceive that, beneath all the old cases, there was concealed a broad principle that no person should be allowed unjustly to enrich himself at the expense of another. This is the principle of 'unjust enrichment', which has given rise to a new category in the law. Contract and tort do not cover all causes of action. There is a third category which is conveniently called restitution.

What his Lordship said may perhaps be contrasted with what he wrote in 1939 when still at the Bar, in a note, shortly after *Craven-Ellis v Canons Ltd* (1936) was decided (1939).

I do not use what his Lordship wrote as necessarily reflecting the law concerning unjust enrichment. It may not have developed so far as he suggests, at least in this country. In any event this is not a case of unjust enrichment. The significance of the passage is to show the development in legal thought that has come about in the last forty years or so. Plainly there are cases not founded on contract, nor in tort, nor upon the application of any equitable doctrine or principle, where there may be recovery. It is not without interest to note the analogy drawn by Greer LJ in *Craven-Ellis v Canons Ltd* (1936), p 412. with the action for money had and received. That analogy was, of course, picked up by Barry J in the *William Lacey* case (1957), p 938, p 718. Of the action for money had and received *Bullen and Leake on Pleadings*,[20] says: 'This is the most comprehensive of all the common counts. It is applicable wherever the defendant has received money which in justice and equity belongs to the plaintiff, under circumstances which render the receipt of it a receipt by the defendant to the use of the plaintiff.' I should refer, however, to *Sinclair v Brougham* (1914) *per* Lord Sumner.

On this whole question general reference may be made to [898] *Salmond and Williams on Contracts*,[21] and to Goff and Jones on *Restitution*.[22]

It seems to me that the English authorities show that the significant change which has come about in the last forty years (it commenced no later than *Craven-Ellis v Canons Ltd* (1936)) is that it is now recognised that there are cases where an obligation to pay will be imposed (a promise to pay implied) notwithstanding that

---

20 3rd edn, p 44.
21 2nd edn, pp 23–25.
22 Goff and Jones, *The Law of Restitution*, 1966, Chapter 1, pp 3–33 and Chapter 23, pp 357–60.

the parties to a transaction, actual or proposed, did not intend, expressly or impliedly, that such an obligation should arise. The obligation is imposed by the law in the light of all the circumstances of the case. It may be true to say that not all the cases needed to have been decided on this basis. But the fact is that they were. The cases comprise *Craven-Ellis v Canons Ltd* (1936); *Upton-on-Severn Rural District Council v Powell* (1942); the *Jennings and Chapman* case (1953); the *Brewer Street* case (1954) and the *William Lacey* case (1957), all referred to above. The earlier Australian cases of *Sinclair v Rankin (No 2)* (1908) and *Magripilis v Baird* (1924) and the New Zealand case of *Watson v Watson* (1953) were decided upon ordinary contractual principles. No common intention could be presumed or implied; accordingly no recovery was permitted ...

[899] The question I must ask myself is whether, at this stage [900] of the development of the law in this country, it is right to say that, in some circumstances, in a case of this kind, there will be occasions when the law, irrespective of the common intention of the parties, will impose on one an obligation to pay the other for work done. After due reflection I have reached the conclusion, notwithstanding the weighty authority which the early Australian decisions have, that there is such a principle in existence. Upon the basis that I would reach that conclusion counsel for the defendant endeavoured to persuade me, nevertheless, that the principle was a narrow one, not having the wide application given it by Barry J in the *William Lacey* case (1957), p 939, p 719. He submitted that, if the work were work (which in the present case it plainly was) which was necessary to be done in the course of the parties' putting themselves in a position to contract, there could be no recovery, because the party spending the money (the plaintiff in this case) in such a situation had taken the risk. In other words in all such cases, applying the principles enunciated by the members of the Court of Appeal in the *Jennings and Chapman* case (1952) and in the *Brewer Street* case (1954), there could be no recovery, because the correct view of the situation was that both parties, until a contractual relationship came into existence, were taking a risk and loss up to that time should lie where it fell. That submission seems to me to go back to actual intention. It is, of course, a very important matter to be taken into account in determining the ultimate question of whether or not there should be recovery. But I cannot regard as correct a submission which brings about such an inflexible situation as would result, if it were accepted. In other words, the acceptance of the submission would mean that, no matter what the circumstances, there could be no recovery, if the parties did not originally contemplate a payment to the plaintiff for the work which was done.

In a judgment of this kind it would be most unwise, and in any event impossible, to fix the limitations which should circumscribe the extent of the right to recover. It is enough for me to say that I think that there is one circumstance here which leads to the conclusion that the plaintiff is entitled to succeed. That circumstance is the fact that the defendant deliberately decided to drop the proposal. It may have had good reasons for doing so, but they had nothing to do with the plaintiff, which, in good faith over a period exceeding three years, had worked assiduously towards the day when it would take a building lease of the land and erect thereon the civic centre which the defendant, during that long period, has so earnestly desired. In the *William Lacey* case (1957) too, the defendant made a unilateral decision not to go on, but to sell its land instead.

I realise that, in looking at the matter in this way, I am imputing a degree of fault to the defendant. To some this may seem to be, at least in English law, somewhat strange. It has long been the law that parties are free to negotiate such contract as they may choose to enter into. Until such contract comes about, they are in negotiation only. Each is at liberty, no matter how capricious his reason, to break off the negotiations at any time. If that occurs that is the end of the matter and, generally speaking, neither party will be under any liability to the other. But the concept that there can be fault in such a situation was adopted both by Somervell and Romer LJJ in the *Brewer Street* case (1954), pp 434, 438, 439 the latter, so it [901] seems to me, basing his judgment upon it. Denning LJ, at pp 435 and 437 did not in fact find fault in that case, but it would seem that he thought it could sometimes exist in negotiating situations, as distinct from contractual ones, although there had not in fact been fault in the case with which he was immediately concerned.

To my mind the defendant's decision to drop the proposal is the determining factor. If the transaction had gone off because the parties were unable to agree, then I think it would be correct, harking back to the expressions used by the judges in the *Jennings and Chapman* case (1952), pp 413–15 and in the *Brewer Street* case (1954), pp 436–38 to say that each party had taken a risk, in incurring the expenditure which it did, that the transaction might go off because of a *bona fide* failure to reach agreement on some point of substance in such a complex transaction. But I do not think it right to say that that risk should be so borne, when one party has taken it upon itself to change its mind about the entirety of the proposal.

As I have said, substantial and continuing work had been done over a period of three years or more. It seems to me to be unthinkable that the plaintiff would have been prepared to do what it did, if it had thought that the defendant might change its mind about proceeding with the proposal. It is true that the defendant is a council the members of which are elected from time to time, and that, therefore, it might not be expected necessarily to be as consistent in its approach to problems as a different sort of undertaking. But for more than three years its consistent policy had been to proceed with a scheme which would give it adequate accommodation for its various activities free from any obligation to pay rent therefore, and with the knowledge that, in due course of time when the lease expired, all would revert to it. It seems to me that, in those circumstances, the defendant is not entitled to have this problem considered differently than would be the case if it were an undertaking, public or private, the identity of whose members was not likely to undergo the same degree of change.

Much reliance was placed by counsel for the defendant upon the areas of disagreement which had emerged in the negotiations between the solicitors and to which I have earlier referred. It was not of course for him to demonstrate that the transaction would have gone off because of failure to agree upon one or more of those matters. As he rightly submitted, it was for the plaintiff to establish that, notwithstanding the areas of disagreement which there were, the transaction would have proceeded, but for the defendant's decision to drop it. I have given that submission much thought, but have reached the conclusion that I should be satisfied that the probabilities were that agreement would have been reached notwithstanding statements by the defendant's solicitors that indicate in respect of at least some of them an apparently uncompromising stand ...

[902] Finally, I should mention some submissions which were made concerning benefit. The principal of these was that, if the work were not work which was necessary to be done in the course of the parties' putting themselves in a position to contract, 'there could be a claim, but the determination of the success or failure of it would largely be influenced by the test, was there at the end benefit wholly or substantially to one party?'. I have already said that, in my opinion, the work was done in the course of the parties putting themselves in a position to contract. Thus the submission does not really arise for consideration. But, here and there throughout his submissions, there are to be found suggestions, by counsel for the defendant, that there could not in any event be recovery unless a benefit accrued to the defendant in respect of the work which was done and for which payment was claimed. An attempt was made to distinguish the *William Lacey* case (1957) from the present case on this basis. Reference was made to what was said by Barry J, at pp 935 and 716 respectively. His Lordship thought that the plaintiff's estimates and plans enabled the defendant to obtain a much higher 'permissible amount' for the purposes of the War Damage Commission. This in turn, in his Lordship's view, may well have enabled the defendant to obtain a higher price for the damaged building than might otherwise have been the case.

I do not regard those considerations as going to the root of his Lordship's decision in that case. No doubt they were additional factors to be taken into account in the plaintiff's favour. But the essence of the decision was that both parties proceeded upon the joint assumption that a contract for the building work would be let. The only reason that it did not come about was the defendant's decision not to proceed with the project, but to sell the building instead.

In my opinion, the better view of the correct application of the principle in question is that, where two parties proceed upon the joint assumption that a contract will be entered into between them, and one does work [903] beneficial for the project, and thus in the interests of the two parties, which work he would not be expected, in other circumstances, to do gratuitously, he will be entitled to compensation or restitution, if the other party unilaterally decides to abandon the project, not for any reason associated with *bona fide* disagreement concerning the terms of the contract to be entered into, but for reasons which, however valid, pertain only to his own position and do not relate at all to that of the other party. Perhaps counsel's submission could be put more strongly, if it were inverted. The proposition would then be that a claim of this kind will always fail, unless the work done is not work done to enable the parties to put themselves in a position to contract and, further, is work which is beneficial to the defendant. If that is the submission which is made, my view is that it should be rejected for the reasons I have already given.

It follows that the plaintiff is entitled to succeed ...

[Sheppard J held the matter over in order to allow the parties to make submissions on *quantum*. He indicated that he would not allow the plaintiff to recover certain items such as foreign travel and legal fees which he thought had been incurred at the sole risk of the plaintiff.]

Commentary and questions

Did Sheppard J view the case as one based on unjust enrichment? Did he consider that the Council had been enriched by the work done by *Sabemo?* Can you identify an objective benefit to *Sabemo?*

It has been suggested that equitable estoppel would have been the more appropriate ground of recovery in the principal case.[23] An estoppel will arise where the defendant has encouraged the plaintiff to assume a contract will be finalised, and, to the defendant's knowledge, the plaintiff detrimentally relies on that assumption by performing work and incurring expenses pending finalisation of the contract, in circumstances where it would be unconscionable to deny liability to pay for the work when the contract does not eventuate.[24] Where an estoppel action is made out, the court will award the minimum remedy necessary to remove the detriment,[25] which would often be an order for payment of the reasonable value of the services and reimbursement of expenses.[26]

Regalian Properties plc v London Docklands Development Corporation
[1995] 1 WLR 212 Chancery

The defendant ('LDDC') owned land which it wished to develop for housing. It accepted the plaintiff's tender for the development although the acceptance of the tender was expressed to be 'subject to contract' and certain other conditions. The plaintiff paid considerable fees to professional experts for the preparation of detailed architectural designs and the conduct of site investigations in connection with the development. Although the parties negotiated for over two years no formal contract was ever concluded as LDDC was experiencing difficulties in obtaining vacant possession of the site and the parties were ultimately unable to agree on a price due to fluctuations in the property market. The site was never developed. The plaintiff brought a claim in restitution claiming almost £3 million in professional fees paid in respect of the proposed development.

Rattee J: [Rattee J discussed *William Lacey (Hounslow) Ltd v Davis* (1957) (see extract, p 405) and *Sabemo Pty Ltd v North Sydney Municipal Council* (1977) (see extract, p 408) and continued at p 226:] Sheppard J [in *Sabemo*] described the principle he was applying (pp 902–03):

---

23 Liew, 'Restitution and contract risk: commentary', in McInnes (ed), *Restitution: Developments in Unjust Enrichment*, 1996, pp 171–72; Mason and Carter, *Restitution Law in Australia*, 1996, pp 358–59; Christensen, 'Recovery for work performed in anticipation of contract' (1993) 11 ABR 144. Although it is arguable that the facts of the case do not evidence sufficient unconscionability to attract the operation of the estoppel principle: Pegoraro, 'Recovery of benefits conferred pursuant to failed anticipated contracts – unjust enrichment, equitable estoppel or unjust sacrifice' (1993) 23 ABLR 117.

24 *Waltons Stores (Interstate) v Maher* (1988), pp 404, 406; 428–29; Liew, 'Restitution and contract risk: commentary', in McInnes (ed), *Restitution: Developments in Unjust Enrichment*, 1996, p 170.

25 *Waltons Stores (Interstate) v Maher* (1988), Brennan J at 423; *Commonwealth of Australia v Verwayen* (1990). Though see *Giumelli v Giumelli* (1999) where the High Court appeared to take the view that a successful plaintiff would *prima facie* be entitled to have the assumption fulfilled.

26 Liew, 'Restitution and contract risk: commentary', in McInnes (ed), *Restitution: Developments in Unjust Enrichment*, 1996, p 170.

In my opinion, the better view of the correct application of the principle in question is that, where two parties proceed upon the joint assumption that a contract will be entered into between them, and one does work beneficial for the project, and thus in the interests of [227] the two parties, which work he would not be expected, in other circumstances, to do gratuitously, he will be entitled to compensation or restitution, if the other party unilaterally decides to abandon the project, not for any reason associated with *bona fide* disagreement concerning the terms of the contract to be entered into, but for reasons which, however valid, pertain only to his own position and do not relate at all to that of the other party.

Sheppard J appears from other passages in his judgment to have considered that he was applying the decision in *William Lacey (Hounslow) Ltd v Davis* (1957). In my judgment, *Sabemo's* claim was distinguishable from that in *William Lacey (Hounslow) Ltd v Davis* on similar grounds to those on which I have already explained I think Regalian's claim in the present case is distinguishable – namely that in *William Lacey (Hounslow) Ltd v Davis* the work which was the subject matter of the claim was quite outside the ambit of the intended contract.

I will deal a little later in this judgment with the question whether the principle enunciated by Sheppard J in the *Sabemo* case (1977) should be held to apply in English law. Irrespective of the answer to that question in my judgment it would not apply to the facts of the present case, for the reason for the breakdown of negotiations between LDDC and Regalian was their inability to agree on an essential term of the intended contract, namely the price. It was not because one party 'unilaterally decided to abandon the project' in the words of Sheppard J in the *Sabemo* case.

In this context Regalian placed reliance on the letter of 8 July 1987 from Mr Ward, chief executive of LDDC, to [Regalian] ... in which Mr Ward said that 'the delay in our providing vacant possession will not create the situation under which we would seek to amend the terms of our disposal of the site to you'. Regalian submitted that in the end that was just what LDDC did try to do – namely increase the price because of the alleged change in market value during the period of delay in LDDC's obtaining vacant possession. I see some force in this submission, despite LDDC's response that in the interim Regalian itself had sought successfully to alter the terms of the deal to take account of the vacant possession problem. However, I cannot see that the submission helps Regalian's claim as formulated in this action, even if the principle enunciated by Sheppard J in the *Sabemo* case is to be applied, for it does not alter the fact that negotiations broke down because the parties could not ultimately agree on price. It may be that the letter of 8 July 1987 could have been relied on as giving rise to some sort of estoppel disentitling LDDC from seeking to renegotiate the price, but no such estoppel is relied on by Regalian for the obvious reason that presumably the result of such a plea, if successful, would be a contract between the parties at the price agreed subject to contract before LDDC tried to increase it and otherwise on the other terms agreed between the parties. This would be a result totally unwanted by Regalian, because in the light of market changes since mid-1988 such a contract would be financially very unattractive to Regalian.

The third authority particularly relied on by [counsel for the plaintiffs] is a decision of Judge Peter Bowsher QC sitting on official referees' business in *Marston*

Construction Co Ltd v Kigass Ltd (1979). In that case the defendant invited tenders for the rebuilding of a factory which had been burned down. The plaintiff tendered for the work. Its [228] tender was accepted. It was made clear by the defendant to the plaintiff that no contract for the rebuilding would be entered into unless and until the defendant had succeeded in obtaining from an insurance claim sufficient money to finance the rebuilding. Both the plaintiff and the defendant confidently expected that sufficient insurance moneys would be forthcoming and that, accordingly, a contract between them would result. In this confident expectation the plaintiff carried out substantial preparatory works the cost of which, if a contract had materialised, would have been included in the contract price. At one point the plaintiff sought an assurance from the defendant that the plaintiff's costs incurred before the expected contract was signed would be met by the defendant. No such assurance was forthcoming. The defendant's insurance claim did not produce sufficient to cover the cost of the proposed rebuilding and no contract was entered into between the parties. The plaintiff sought recompense for the preparatory works. Judge Bowsher QC referred to *William Lacey (Hounslow) Ltd v Davis* (1957) (p 126) and cited the passage (p 939) which I have already cited from the judgment of Barry J. He then referred to a *dictum* of Robert Goff J in *British Steel Corp v Cleveland Bridge and Engineering Co Ltd* (1984), p 511 to which I shall refer a little later in this judgment. Then Judge Bowsher QC said in *Marston Construction Co Ltd v Kigass Ltd* (1989), p 127:

> I find that the facts of the present case, although different in important respects are similar in kind to the facts in *William Lacey (Hounslow) Ltd v Davis* (1989), p 127. There was a request to do the work, though the request in respect of the bulk of the work was implied rather than express. It was contemplated that the work would be paid for out of the contemplated contract. Both parties believed that the contract was about to be made despite the fact that there was a very clear condition which had to be met by a third party if the contract was to be made. The defendants obtained the benefit of the work in my judgment, though [counsel] submitted that they did not.

Judge Bowsher QC expressed his conclusion in favour of the plaintiff in the following terms (p 129):

> The preliminary works requested were undoubtedly done for the benefit of the defendants and were only done for the benefit of the plaintiffs in the sense that they hoped to make a profit out of them. As a result of the works some progress was made towards getting consents and in the end the defendants had in the hands of their agent some designs and working drawings (though not a complete set) together with an implied licence to build to those drawings even though that licence be limited as I think (without having heard argument) to a licence to have the factory built by the plaintiffs. Whether the defendants decide ultimately to build a factory or to sell the land, they have a benefit which is realisable.

> *Conclusion.* I therefore conclude that there was no agreement as alleged in paras 5 to 8 of the statement of claim. I find that there was an express request made by the defendants to the plaintiffs to carry out a small quantity of design works and that there was an implied request to carry out preparatory works in general and that both the express and the implied requests gave rise to a right of payment of a reasonable sum.

[229] I have to say, with all respect for Judge Bowsher QC, that I find this a surprising decision, not least because, as I have recited from the his findings of fact, the plaintiff had earlier requested and been refused an assurance that it would be compensated for the preparatory work concerned. In this respect I agree with the critical commentary on Judge Bowsher's decision by the editor of the *Building Law Reports*.[27] However, whether the decision be right or wrong, I do not feel obliged to apply it in the present case, which is distinguishable on the facts in two particular respects. First, in the present case, unlike the *Marston Construction Co* case, even if a contract had materialised no part of any costs incurred or work done by Regalian in connection with the contract would have been paid for by LDDC. The only obligation on LDDC would have been to grant the building lease. Secondly, as I have already said, I am not satisfied in the present case that the preparatory works resulted in any benefit to LDDC.

I referred a little earlier to the citation by Judge Bowsher QC in the *Marston Construction Co* case of a *dictum* of Robert Goff J in *British Steel Corporation v Cleveland Bridge and Engineering Co Ltd* (1984), p 511. I should say a little more about that case. The defendant had successfully tendered for the fabrication of steelwork to be used in the construction of a building. It entered into negotiations with the plaintiff for a subcontract whereunder the plaintiff would supply certain steel nodes that would form part of the relevant steelwork. It was proposed that the subcontract would be in a standard form used by the defendant. The defendant requested the plaintiff to commence work on the steel nodes immediately 'pending the preparation and issuing to you of the official form of subcontract'. The intended formal contract was not entered into, because the parties failed to agree certain terms to go into it. The plaintiff produced and delivered to the defendant all but one of the steel nodes. The defendant refused to pay for them, and instead sought to recover from the plaintiff damages for late delivery of the nodes. The plaintiff sued for the value of the nodes it had supplied by way of *quantum meruit*. The defendant counterclaimed for damages for *inter alia* late delivery of the nodes, alleging that a binding contract came into being between the parties. Robert Goff J rejected the defendant's argument that a contract existed between the parties. He then considered the plaintiff's *quantum meruit* claim in these terms (p 511): 'In my judgment, the true analysis of the situation is simply this. Both parties confidently expected a formal contract to eventuate. In these circumstances, to expedite performance under that anticipated contract, one requested the other to commence the contract work, and the other complied with that request. If thereafter, as anticipated, a contract was entered into, the work done as requested will be treated as having been performed under that contract; if, contrary to their expectation, no contract was entered into, then the performance of the work is not referable to any contract the terms of which can be ascertained, and the law simply imposes an obligation on the party who made the request to pay a reasonable sum for such work as has been done pursuant to that request, such an obligation sounding in quasi-contract or, as we now say, in restitution. Consistently with [230] that solution, the party making the request may find himself liable to pay for work which he would not have had to pay for as such if the anticipated contract had come into existence, eg, preparatory work which will,

---

if the contract is made, be allowed for in the price of the finished work (cf *William Lacey (Hounslow) Ltd v Davis*) (1957).'

I do not consider that this decision lends any real support to Regalian's claim in the present case. I can well understand why Robert Goff J concluded that, where one party to an expected contract expressly requests the other to perform services or supply goods that would have been performable or suppliable under the expected contract when concluded, in advance of the contract, that party should have to pay a *quantum meruit* if the contract does not materialise. The present case is not analogous. The costs for which Regalian seeks reimbursement were incurred by it not by way of accelerated performance of the anticipated contract at the request of LDDC, but for the purpose of putting itself in a position to obtain and then perform the contract.

[Counsel for the plaintiffs] relied on the last part of the *dictum* of Robert Goff J (p 511) which I have cited, in which he pointed out that the application of the principle of restitution which he applied in that case can result in one party to an anticipated contract which does not materialise finding himself liable to pay the other party for preparatory work for which he would not have had to pay under the contract, because under the contract it would have been allowed for in the overall contract price. I do not think the judge had in mind (because he was not concerned with such a claim) that a landowner intending to contract to grant a building lease could find itself liable to pay the intending lessee developer for preparatory work done by the lessee for the purpose of putting itself in a position to obtain and perform the contract. I must return now to the statement of principle made by Sheppard J in the *Sabemo* case (1977), pp 900–01, 902–03, which I have cited earlier, for the essence of [counsel for the plaintiff's submissions] is that that principle should be applied in the present case ...

I have already said that the principle as so stated would not, in my judgment, apply in any event to the facts of this case, because the reason the contract did not materialise was that the parties could not agree on the price, and not that either party decided to abandon the project. However, in case I am wrong on this, I should say that in my respectful opinion the principle enunciated by Sheppard J in the passage I have [231] cited from his judgment is not established by any English authority. I appreciate that the English law of restitution should be flexible and capable of continuous development. However I see no good reason to extend it to apply some such principle as adopted by Sheppard J in the *Sabemo* case to facts such as those of the present case, where, however much the parties expect a contract between them to materialise, both enter negotiations expressly (whether by use of the words 'subject to contract' or otherwise) on terms that each party is free to withdraw from the negotiations at any time. Each party to such negotiations must be taken to know (as in my judgment Regalian did in the present case) that pending the conclusion of a binding contract any cost incurred by him in preparation for the intended contract will be incurred at his own risk, in the sense that he will have no recompense for those costs if no contract results. In other words, I accept in substance the submission made by [counsel for the defendants], to the effect that, by deliberate use of the words 'subject to contract' with the admitted intention that they should have their usual effect, LDDC and Regalian each accepted that in the event of no contract being entered into, any resultant loss should lie where it fell.

Regalian, under the leadership of Mr Goldstone, was a very experienced operator in the property development market. To his considerable credit Mr Goldstone did not pretend that he was not aware that LDDC, like any other party to negotiations 'subject to contract', was free to walk away from those negotiations, however little he expected it to do so. Regalian incurred the costs concerned in that knowledge. Though it is perhaps not strictly relevant, I see nothing inequitable in those circumstances in the loss resulting from the breakdown of negotiations lying where it fell, particularly bearing in mind that, in the light of the slump in the residential property market that followed the attempt by LDDC in May 1988 to renegotiate the price for the proposed building leases, Regalian has good reason to be thankful that it did not find itself having to take those leases on the terms previously proposed.

In my judgment, Regalian has failed to make good its claim based on the principles of restitution ...

Commentary and questions

How did Rattee J distinguish the case before him from *Sabemo v North Sydney Municipal Council* (1977) (see extract, p 408)? Did he approve of the 'fault based' analysis applied in *Sabemo*?

Rattee J distinguished *William Lacey (Hounslow) Ltd v Davis* (1957) (see extract, p 405) on the ground that there the work was performed for the collateral purpose of gaining the approval of the War Damage Commission, whereas in the principal case the work was done in order to perform the expected contract. This has been said to be a 'strained' distinction as at least some of the work in the principal case was directed towards obtaining approval to proceed from the planning authority, which happened to be the defendant.[28]

Angelopoulos v Sabatino (1995) 65 SASR 1 Full Court of the Supreme Court of South Australia

The first defendant, Mr Angelopoulos, was the controller of the second defendant, Ditara Pty Ltd, which owned the Britannia Hotel in Adelaide. The tenant operating the hotel went into liquidation and the plaintiffs, through their intermediary, Mr Constantino, commenced preliminary negotiations with Mr Angelopoulos and the tenant's liquidator with a view to becoming the new lessees of the hotel. Before the negotiations were concluded the liquidator suddenly stripped the hotel of most of its plant, equipment and stock. Mr Angelopoulos was anxious to get the hotel back into an operational state in time for the approaching Grand Prix and requested Mr Constantino to organise and oversee the necessary restoration work on the hotel. Mr Constantino hired contractors and casual workers to carry out the restoration work. The plaintiffs also carried out work on the hotel under the general supervision of Mr Constantino, there apparently being a general understanding between the plaintiffs, Mr Constantino and Mr Angelopoulos that they would all work together to bring the hotel back to an operational state. The plaintiffs also purchased and installed plant and equipment for the hotel for $57,000 which Mr

---

28 Steinepreis, 'Cancelled projects – who bears the risk for pre-contract expenses?' (1996) 12 BCL 303, p 307; see also Mannolini, 'Restitution where an anticipated contract fails to materialise' (1996) 59(11) MLR 111, pp 113, 115.

Angelopoulos had recommended to the plaintiffs as suitable for the hotel and reasonably priced. The plaintiffs expended their money and labour in the expectation they would receive favourable terms in a lease or rent relief. The hotel resumed trading at about the time of the Grand Prix, but the lease negotiations between the plaintiffs and Mr Angelopoulos broke down. Ditara granted a lease to a third party and sold to the third party a substantial amount of plant and equipment, including the plant and equipment which the plaintiffs had purchased and installed at the hotel. The plaintiffs sought compensation for their work and reimbursement of the expenditure on the plant and equipment.

Doyle CJ: ... [6] Counsel for the defendants founded the argument on appeal on the finding that there was no contract for the payment of the plaintiffs. It was then argued that the obligation to make restitution in the absence of an agreement, express or implied, was a quasi-contractual obligation which required of necessity a request that the work be performed and an expectation that it would be paid for. It was said that there was no such request and no such expectation, and accordingly the claim must fail. Reliance was placed by counsel on the decision of the High Court in *Pavey & Matthews Pty Ltd v Paul* (1987) and on the decision of a judge of the Supreme Court of Victoria in *Brenner v First Artists' Management Pty Ltd* (1993).

I cannot find anything in these cases to support the contention that a request, apparently as counsel would have it an explicit request, is an essential element to the success of a claim in a case such as the one before me. Quite apart from that, as I will explain later, it seems to me that in this case there was an implied request for the performance of the work. Moreover, it seems to me that far from supporting the case for the defendants *Pavey's* case is in fact the rock against which the defendants' argument founders ...

[7] It seems to me that the argument for the defendants in the present case harked back to the notion that a restitutionary claim for a *quantum meruit* was based upon a fictional promise to pay a reasonable amount, implied into a request to do work. Put a little differently, the argument for the defendants was that a restitutionary claim was based upon a contract which was implied as a matter of fact from the making of a request. But in my opinion *Pavey's* case has now made it clear that a restitutionary claim may be described as a claim 'to recover a debt owing in circumstances where the law itself imposed or imputed an obligation or promise to make compensation for a benefit accepted': Deane J (p 255); see also *Australia & New Zealand Banking Group Ltd v Westpac Banking Corporation* (1988), p 673. For this reason, the existence of a request in a case such as the present one, that work be performed, is not critical. [Doyle CJ discussed the judgments in *Pavey's* case and continued at p 9:] It seems to me that the decision of the majority in *Pavey's* case makes two important points which are relevant to the present case. First, that a claim in restitution is not founded upon an implied agreement, and while facts which might support an implied agreement may be relevant to a claim in restitution, it is not necessary to search for something akin to an agreement or request from which a promise to pay might be implied. Secondly, there is a significant emphasis in the judgments of the majority upon the notion of acceptance of a benefit from the performance by the claimant of an action which confers a benefit or enrichment upon the other person. However, to my mind it is equally clear from the majority judgments that the existing case law in this area has not been overturned. As Deane J pointed out, unjust enrichment is a 'unifying

legal concept' which explains the result reached in a variety of situations and not in itself a cause of action or a basis for recovery.

I am conscious of the fact that in *Pavey's* case the court was dealing with an express contract which could not be enforced in terms. In the present case we are dealing with an anticipated or hoped for contract which did not come into being. However, the decision in *Pavey's* case suggests that acceptance of a benefit is relevant as a basis for recovery in restitution. However, it is clear that more is involved than the simple fact of acceptance. The consideration of the [10] judgments in *Pavey's* case, and of other case law in this area, suggests that one must also consider the basis upon which the provider of the benefit acted, the choice which the recipient of the benefit had in deciding whether or not to accept the benefit and the conduct of the defendant, by which I mean the defendant's knowledge of what the plaintiffs were doing and the basis upon which they did it.

Finally, I should add that I recognise that caution is required in applying *Pavey's* case. Too sweeping an application of the notion of acceptance as a basis for a claim in restitution might unsettle aspects of the law of contract, the law of landlord and tenant (for example, relating to fixtures and fittings) and principles underlying the law of salvage, to mention just a few examples. In making this point I am conscious of significant academic writing in this area which writing, to my mind, demonstrates quite amply the need to integrate the decision in *Pavey's* case into the existing case law while at the same time giving proper force to the emphasis placed upon the notion of acceptance. I refer in passing to J Beatson, 'Unjust enrichment in the High Court of Australia' (see *Pavey's* case (1988)), AS Burrows, 'Contract, tort and restitution – a satisfactory division or not?' (see *Pavey's* case (1983)); Mason, 'Restitution in Australian law', in Finn (ed), *Essays on Restitution*, 1990; G Jones, 'Restitutionary claims for services rendered', *Pavey's* case (1977).

The decision in *Pavey's* case was considered by Byrne J in *Brenner v First Artists' Management Pty Ltd* (1993). In brief, the facts in *Brenner's* case were that the plaintiffs claimed remuneration on a contractual basis or alternatively on a *quantum meruit* for services performed under alleged management engagements. The judge found that there were no binding or enforceable contracts for management services because the parties had never reached the necessary degree of agreement on terms. He found that the claim succeeded in part on a *quantum meruit* basis. His Honour considered the decision in *Pavey's* case at some length. Referring to a case involving the application of the law of restitution or of unjust enrichment he said (p 257):

> In such a case, the gist of the claim is that the defendant has actually or constructively accepted the benefit of the plaintiffs' services in circumstances where it would be unjust for that party to do so without making restitution to the plaintiffs ... The circumstances in which the law considers it unjust to accept the benefit without payment are to be discerned from the principles to be extracted from the decided cases.

He went on to refer to a number of factors relevant generally and to the case before him. He went on to say (p 259):

> Indeed, where the services have been requested by the party to be charged, the main area of interest is likely to be whether the circumstances of the request are such as to give rise to a right of payment. This will involve proof that the services were not provided as a gift: *Pavey's* case (pp 227–28). Furthermore, it

will be necessary for the plaintiff to establish, where a certain event has not occurred, that the services were not provided on the basis that they were not to be paid for unless that event came to pass. In this category will fall cases where a tenderer carries out estimating or other work in response to an invitation to tender for a contract. It is understood in such cases that, in general, the tenderer takes the risk that the tender will be unsuccessful and that, as a consequence, the work will be unrewarded.

[11] A little later he said (pp 259–60):

It was submitted on behalf of the defendant that the test was whether each of the parties thought at the relevant time that the work would be recompensed. I think that the court is not concerned with the actual state of mind of the parties or of either of them: *Sabemo's* case [*Sabemo Pty Ltd v North Sydney Municipal Council* (1977) (see extract, p 408)], p 900. Moreover, the enquiry must in my view be principally directed to the position of the party to be charged, for the thread running through this area of law is the injustice of the enrichment of that party. In my opinion the appropriate enquiry is whether the recipient of the services, as a reasonable person, should have realised that a person in the position of the provider of the services would expect to be paid for them and did not take a reasonable opportunity to reject those services.[29]

He went on (p 261) to make the point that it must be shown that it was the defendant who accepted the services if it is the defendant from whom restitution is sought. If someone else obtained the benefit of the services then the claim was likely to fail. Likewise, it was a question of whether it was in the contemplation of the defendant as a reasonable man that the plaintiffs realised that he would be responsible for payment.

I respectfully agree with his Honour's approach as a matter of principle.

In an area of law such as this, one could range far and wide through cases decided in the past and through academic analysis of those decisions in the light of current theories of the law of restitution. But it seems to me that this case can be disposed of by focusing on the notion of acceptance and applying it in the light of principles to be derived from past case law, an application which is to be informed and enlivened by the understanding that the underlying principle is that of unjust enrichment.

There are two cases that I will mention which seem to me to illustrate the scope of the case law for recovery on these facts.

Watson v Watson (1953), which was referred to by the trial judge, involved a proposed partnership between two brothers who became plaintiff and defendant. The defendant invited the plaintiff to join him. They planned to do agricultural contracting and the cutting of firewood, but ultimately to build a sawmill and become partners in it. The brothers worked together building the mill, which was completed at least two years after it was begun. Although no partnership agreement ever eventuated, the plaintiff continued to work in the mill, supervising it when the defendant was away. The plaintiff received no wages but was given occasional payments if short of money. The plaintiff also purchased equipment for the mill. Gresson J held that the plaintiff was entitled to recover reasonable remuneration for his services and some equipment costs.

---

29   Jones, *Restitution in Public and Private Law*, 1991, p 108.

His Honour appears to have approached the question on the basis of an implied contract between the parties (pp 272–73). But the case is important as setting out a situation where the case law has permitted recovery on the basis of factors such as the provision of services on the basis of an assumption defeated by later events, and on the basis of the acceptance of those services, despite a different conceptual basis for the importance of these factors in the ultimate recovery. In my view, the case provides a useful guide to the state of the existing case law which must be integrated with the new concepts of acceptance and unjust enrichment.

[12] A second New Zealand case, which is explicitly based upon the principle of free acceptance, is *Van den Berg v Giles* (1979). This case involved a claim by a tenant against the owner of property. The tenant did extensive work on the house in which he lived, including the alteration of walls and the replacement of roofing and wiring. The tenant alleged that he had been told by the defendant that he would be able to purchase the house, and that he had proceeded to have the renovation work done on this basis.

The trial judge found that the plaintiff was entitled to restitution. His Honour found that (p 120):

> From the commencement of work on the property the defendant fully understood the need for it, the extent of it, and freely accepted it. I find on her part an active encouragement for it to have been carried out, and the deliberate creation of uncertainty about the possible sale of the house. I do not find on her part any request for the services, but a definite acquiescence and acceptance.

His Honour also found that there had been no expectation on the part of the plaintiff that the services would be paid for, the expected benefit being through purchase of the house; that the services were not officiously provided; and that the defendant did not take any of the opportunities that she had to reject the services.

His Honour's conclusion was that recovery would be permitted (p 121):

> I think the starting point for the plaintiff is to show that he performed services on the defendant's property which she, without demur and quite freely, accepted.

In my view, this case, which bears many factual similarities to the present one, was correctly decided. The combination of factors involved, including both encouragement and acceptance by the defendant, makes it impossible to dispute the finding that the enrichment of the defendant was unjust. It is interesting to note that a contemporaneous New Zealand case, *Avondale Printers & Stationers Pty Ltd v Haggie* (1979), denies that the decision in *Van den Berg* can properly be based on a general principle of unjust enrichment (p 149); but even so, Mahon J noted that, despite his disagreement with such a wide *ratio decidendi* for the case, 'No one could quarrel with the result of the litigation in *Van den Berg v Giles* ...' (p 149). When applying the principles laid down in *Pavey*'s case, I am fortified by the acceptance of a just result in this case, whatever differences might be expressed as to the principles underlying that result.

In my opinion the plaintiffs in the present case were entitled to succeed. This is a case in which the defendant accepted benefits (freely accepted, if the addition of that adverb adds anything) accruing to the defendant from the plaintiffs' performance of work. It is a case in which there has been an acceptance of a benefit under circumstances such that the law should, in my opinion, impose an obligation to make fair and just restitution. I now proceed to identify the circumstances which, in my opinion, give to the acceptance of the benefit the character necessary to support the claim. It is convenient at the same time to be a little more specific about what I mean by acceptance in the context of this case.

First, the plaintiffs did not intend to provide their services gratuitously. They expected a return, if only in the form of more favourable terms of lease. Secondly, the plaintiffs did not provide their services and supply the plant and [13] equipment entirely at their own initiative. They acted not only with the knowledge of Ditara, through its agents, but with the approval of Ditara. In my opinion there was more than passive acquiescence. It is not necessary for me to find that there was a request that the services be performed and the plant and equipment supplied, but were it necessary to do so I would be prepared to conclude that there was an implied request. Thirdly, the plaintiffs did not provide their services on the basis that there would be no payment unless a certain event came to pass. By proceeding as they did the plaintiffs incurred the risk that if a lease did not eventuate they would not be remunerated. But this was not a situation in which it was a common understanding that there would be no remuneration in the event of there being no lease. It was not a situation in which common business practice indicates the parties did intend or should as reasonable persons have realised that remuneration was conditional upon the grant of a lease. Fourthly, this was not a case in which the services were provided on a basis from which the plaintiffs chose to depart. It is not necessary to decide whether the failure to agree upon a lease was attributable to unreasonable conduct on the part of either party. It suffices to say that on the findings of his Honour the plaintiffs did not unilaterally or unreasonably terminate negotiations. Fifthly, the defendant Ditara benefited from what the plaintiffs did. Ditara either incurred less expense than it otherwise would have incurred in restoring the premises or alternatively had premises better fitted for letting out. Sixthly, that benefit was conferred at the expense of the plaintiffs. Seventh, Ditara by its agents approved of or agreed to the plaintiffs carrying out the work which they did. In addition, Ditara by its later sale of plant and equipment, including the plant and equipment installed by the plaintiffs (it being the case that some, at least, of that plant and equipment was readily removable), accepted the benefit of that part of the plaintiffs' work. Eighth, in my opinion the circumstances were such that Ditara by its agents must have known as a reasonable person that the plaintiffs expected to be remunerated for their services. Ninth, there is no argument advanced identifying any particular circumstance by virtue of which it is unjust to require Ditara to remunerate the plaintiffs. By this I mean that no matter such as change of position was advanced, nor, subject to the counterclaim, was it suggested that the work carried out was work which Ditara did not want done or which was of no use to Ditara.

In my opinion, for those reasons this is a case of acceptance (or free acceptance) by the defendant of a benefit conferred by the plaintiffs under circumstances such that the law should impose an obligation to make fair and just restitution. I consider that my decision is consistent with the basis upon which *Pavey's* case was decided, and consistent with the approach taken by previous case law in this area.

It is unwise and pointless, in my opinion, in a developing area of the law like this to attempt to identify specific facts which, when found, will invariably provide a basis for relief. That is why I have set out the facts upon which I rely in some detail

...

[Doyle CJ approved of the award made by the trial judge for the cost of the plant and equipment and the fair market value of the services.]

Commentary and questions

Had the defendant been enriched on these facts? What test(s) of enrichment does Doyle CJ rely upon in settling the issue of enrichment?

What factors did Doyle CJ take into account in determining that the plaintiffs' claim should succeed? What unjust factor grounded recovery? According to Doyle CJ had the plaintiffs assumed the risk of non-payment?

The principal case illustrates that the courts apply a composite of factors to determine whether the plaintiff should be remunerated for work done under a contract that fails to materialise. The factors taken into account by the courts are further discussed in the following decision.

Countrywide Communications Ltd v ICL Pathway Ltd
unreported, 21 October 1999, Queen's Bench[30]

Countrywide sought remuneration for public relations and communications services provided to ICL Pathway at its request. These services were provided as part of a bid by ICL Pathway to win a contract to supply another company with a computerised system for the payment of government benefits. ICL Pathway assured Countrywide that it would grant Countrywide a public relations sub-contract if the bid were successful. The bid was successful, however ICL Pathway awarded the public relations sub-contract to another firm.

Nicholas Strauss QC: ... I have found it impossible to formulate a clear general principle which satisfactorily governs the different factual situations which have arisen, let alone those which could easily arise in other cases. Perhaps, in the absence of any recognition in English law of a general duty of good faith in contractual negotiations, this is not surprising. Much of the difficulty is caused by attempting to categorise as an unjust enrichment of the defendant, for which an action in restitution is available, what is really a loss unfairly sustained by the plaintiff. There is a lot to be said for a broad principle enabling either to be recompensed, but no such principle is clearly established in English law. Undoubtedly the court may impose an obligation to pay for benefits resulting from services performed in the course of a contract which is expected to, but does not, come into existence. This is so, even though, in all cases, the defendant is *ex hypothesi* free to withdraw from the proposed contract, whether the negotiations were expressly made 'subject to contract' or not. Undoubtedly, such an obligation will be imposed only if justice requires it or, which comes to much the same thing, if it would be unconscionable for the plaintiff not to be recompensed.

Beyond that, I do not think that it is possible to go further than to say that, in deciding whether to impose an obligation and if so its extent, the court will take into account and give appropriate weight to a number of considerations which can be identified in the authorities. The first is whether the services were of a kind which would normally be given free of charge. Secondly, the terms in which the

---

30 Noted [2000] RLR 270.

request to perform the services was made may be important in establishing the extent of the risk (if any) which the plaintiffs may fairly be said to have taken that such services would in the end be unrecompensed. What may be important here is whether the parties are simply negotiating, expressly or impliedly 'subject to contract', or whether one party has given some kind of assurance or indication that he will not withdraw, or that he will not withdraw except in certain circumstances. Thirdly, the nature of the benefit which has resulted to the defendants is important, and in particular whether such benefit is real (either 'realised' or realisable') or a fiction, in the sense of Traynor CJ's *dictum* [in *Coleman Engineering Co v North American Aviation* 420 P 2d 713 (1966) where Traynor CJ said that it is a fiction to base benefit on the fact of a request]. Plainly, a court will at least be more inclined to impose an obligation to pay for a real benefit, since otherwise the abortive negotiations will leave the defendant with a windfall and the plaintiff out of pocket. However, the judgment of Denning LJ in the *Brewer Street* case suggests that the performance of services requested may of itself suffice amount to a benefit or enrichment. Fourthly, what may often be decisive are the circumstances in which the anticipated contract does not materialise and in particular whether they can be said to involve 'fault' on the part of the defendant, or (perhaps of more relevance) to be outside the scope of the risk undertaken by the plaintiff at the outset. I agree with the view of Rattee J [in *Regalian Properties plc v London Docklands Development Corporation* (1995) (see extract, p 413)] that the law should be flexible in this area, and the weight to be given to each of these factors may vary from case to case.

There is in my view considerable doubt whether an obligation can be imposed in a case in which the plaintiff has not provided a benefit of any kind, even of the 'fictional' kind discussed earlier of performing services at the request of the defendant albeit without enriching him in any real sense. Thus I doubt whether an obligation can be imposed on a contracting party to repay a plaintiff for expense incurred, reasonably or even necessarily, in anticipation of a contract which does not materialise, where this is not in the course of providing services requested by the defendant ...

Conclusions on quantum meruit *in this case*

I would regard it as most unjust if Countrywide were not appropriately recompensed for their work before and after the submission of the bid in March 1996. Put shortly, this is because (1) they were induced to provide their services free of charge by an assurance, ultimately dishonoured, that ICL Pathway would be prepared to negotiate a contract with them if the bid succeeded, and (2) their services provided ICL Pathway with a benefit for which (in the absence of such an assurance) they would otherwise have had to pay reasonable fees for time spent, namely advice and assistance in connection with the public relations and communications issues during the bid and subsequently.

As I have already found, the members of the consortium had a policy from the outset of seeking the services of potential sub-contractors during the bid process free, on the basis that they would be assured of being rewarded by a sub-contract if they gave their help until the final bid was submitted and if it succeeded. Such an assurance was given by [representatives of ICL Pathway] when ICL Pathway was formed. This is important for two reasons. In the first place, the formulation of this approach, and the giving of the assurance to Countrywide, suggest that the work which was to be expected from potential sub-contractors, and in particular from Countrywide, went beyond that which might be expected to be provided free by a sub-contractor who, if the bid succeeded, would merely be given a chance of bidding for the sub-contract. Secondly, such an assurance takes the case as far from a typical 'subject to contract' case, in which each party may be taken to have accepted the risk of withdrawal by the other and consequent waste of expenditure, as it could possibly be taken short of an actual contract. *Regalian* is clearly distinguishable on this ground.

As to the risk which Countrywide may be said to have accepted of unrecompensed work, clearly a degree of risk was accepted. Countrywide accepted the risk that their work would be unrewarded if it was found to be unsatisfactory at any time before a final bid was submitted, if the bid failed, or if negotiations failed with ICL Pathway for the sub-contract. As to the last, I think that it is most unlikely that this would have happened … It may be arguable that Countrywide also accepted other risks, for example that the consortium would decide not to proceed at all, or that [the benefits agency] would decide to do all the public relations/communication work themselves, and certainly they could not expected to be employed if their work was seriously defective at any stage. But Countrywide did not accept the risk that they would be dismissed, following a change of personnel within ICL Pathway, because their reputation was now not considered to be satisfactory. This is something which Countrywide were entitled to expect to be considered either by the consortium when they made their proposal in early 1995, or by ICL Pathway at the latest before the final tender was submitted. They cannot fairly be said to have taken the risk of being dismissed for this reason not only after the final tender had been submitted, but after having provided further help in preparation for the implementation of the work for a further two or three months.

On the question of benefit, the underlying position is not quite the same as in cases involving building contracts. Countrywide were not bidding for specific work. Rather, they were assisting ICL Pathway to formulate the correct approach to the public relations and communications work and to provide an estimate of costs for which allowance would be made in ICL Pathway's final tender. The details of the scope of the work, and of Countrywide's remuneration, were always going to be negotiated after the bid succeeded. From ICL Pathway's point of view, what they needed at this stage was advice and assistance, rather than a detailed final budget, and some of the work done before 21 March 1996 (for example attendance at meetings which were essentially so that Countrywide were up to date and in a position to advise on any issues which might arise suddenly), and all the work done after that date, was done principally to assist ICL Pathway, and not in the preparation of a bid or proposal for the sub-contract work. Indeed, all the work done between April 1995 and the submission of the final tender on 21 March 1996 can be said to have been done for a dual purpose. It was done to assist ICL Pathway in the formulation of their initial proposal and final tender, and therefore also, by enhancing the prospects of success of the latter, insofar as this depended upon its public relations content, to enhance the prospects of Countrywide being awarded the sub-contract. Countrywide's work was of value to ICL Pathway, not merely because they performed services at ICL Pathway's request, but because these services provided ICL Pathway with advice which they needed, and for which (in the absence of an assurance of the kind they gave), they would probably have had to pay either Countrywide or some other public relations consultant. Therefore, ICL Pathway was, in a real sense, enriched by Countrywide's work. The gain was realised, not merely realisable.

On the issue of benefit, this case is therefore distinguishable from *Regalian*, in which no benefit was conferred on the defendant. It is less easy to distinguish it from *Lacey* [*William Lacey (Hounslow) Ltd v Davis* (1957)]. It is true that Countrywide's work cannot be said to have conferred a benefit on ICL Pathway 'quite outside the ambit of the anticipated contract', which Rattee J said [in *Regalian*] was the basis on which *Lacey* was correctly decided. However, I do not understand Rattee J to have held that it was in all cases necessary that a benefit should have been conferred by the proposed contractor on the proposed employer which was 'outside the ambit' of the anticipated contract. Clearly, this was not true of the benefit conferred on the defendants in *British Steel Corp v Cleveland Bridge and Engineering Co Ltd* (1984). Indeed was it only partly true of the benefit conferred in *Lacey*. In that case, the work connected with the war damage claim, which was based upon a notional reconstruction of the building in its original state, was outside the ambit of the proposed building work. But the plaintiffs also recovered on a *quantum meruit* for revised estimates for the actual rebuilding, which was the subject matter of the anticipated contract.

Finally, with reference to the circumstances in which the anticipated contract failed to materialise, I have already found that the principal reasons for this were Ms Campopiano's [an employee of ICL Pathway] distrust of Countrywide, from her own experience and from what she had heard from within ICL, and the availability of another contractor, Financial Dynamics, in whom she did have trust. One could perhaps with some justice say that ICL Pathway ... was 'at fault' for not honouring the assurance which they had given. But I think that the more logical question to ask is whether Countrywide took the risk of ICL Pathway reaching this conclusion after all the preparatory work, and indeed some work towards the implementation of the project, had been done. Of course, in a sense, it follows from the very fact that no binding agreement was concluded that the plaintiffs did take this risk, but the effect of the authorities cited above is to require a broader view to be taken. Otherwise no claim of this kind could ever succeed. In my view, what happened was outside the various risks of working without recompense which Countrywide can fairly be said to have accepted. Therefore I think that it is unjust that ICL Pathway have enriched themselves by not paying for Countrywide's services. I would have held otherwise, if I had found that the, or even a, substantial reason for ICL Pathway's failure to offer Countrywide the sub-contract was a disagreement about terms. I would also have held otherwise, if the reason had been that Countrywide offered work which, in the circumstances in which it was offered, was seriously defective. However, they merely failed to provide work which was of sufficient excellence to overcome Ms Campopiano's predisposition to recommend Financial Dynamics. There was never much chance of their securing Ms Campopiano's support if Financial Dynamics were available.

...

Questions

What factors did the court rely upon in concluding that the plaintiff should be entitled to the reasonable value of the work done? Did the court find a benefit to the defendant in the work performed by the plaintiff? Did the court consider that a benefit could be founded merely on the basis of the request by the defendant for the services? Was the plaintiff found to have assumed the risk that the sub-contract would not be awarded to it?

UNJUST SACRIFICE

Stoljar and Muir have argued that recovery in pre-contractual expenditure cases such as *Brewer Street Investments Ltd v Barclays Woollen Co Ltd* (1954) (see extract, p 401), *William Lacey (Hounslow) Ltd v Davis* (1957) (see extract, p 405) and *Sabemo Pty Ltd v North Sydney Municipal Council* (1977) (see extract, p 408) cannot be based on unjust enrichment as it would create legal fictions to view the defendant as having benefited from the plaintiff's performance. They argue that cases such as these are better explained on the basis of 'unjust sacrifice'.[31] 'Unjust sacrifice' is said to form a discrete category in the law of obligations, concerned with compensating the plaintiff for losses incurred in reliance on a contract being concluded. 'A plaintiff makes an unjust sacrifice when he expends time or effort for the benefit of the defendant in circumstances in which the defendant should be obliged to pay the plaintiff for his intervention.'[32] This doctrine would ground recovery even though the defendant's conduct may not have been sufficiently unconscionable to attract the operation of equitable estoppel.[33]

---

31 Stoljar, 'Unjust enrichment and unjust sacrifice' (1987) 50 MLR 603; Muir, 'Unjust sacrifice and the officious intervener', in Finn (ed), *Essays in Restitution*, 1990, Chapter 9.

32 Muir, 'Unjust sacrifice and the officious intervener', in Finn (ed), *Essays in Restitution*, 1990, Chapter 9.

33 Pegoraro, 'Recovery of benefits conferred pursuant to failed anticipated contracts – unjust enrichment, equitable estoppel or unjust sacrifice' (1993) 23 ABLR 117; cf Birks, *Restitution – The Future*, 1992, pp 100–03; Burrows, *The Law of Restitution*, 1993, pp 5–6, 299.

CHAPTER 15

RESTITUTION AGAINST PUBLIC AUTHORITIES

INTRODUCTION

This chapter deals with claims against public authorities for recovery of unlawful exactions. The main grounds of recovery of an unlawful exaction are mistake,[1] duress (either actual duress or duress *colore officii*), or on the basis of the *Woolwich* principle. The '*Woolwich* principle' refers to the principle established in *Woolwich Equitable Building Society v Inland Revenue Commissioners* (1993) (see extract, p 456) where the House of Lords held that an exaction shown to be *ultra vires* the public authority is *prima facie* recoverable, without the need to show a mistake or duress. The High Court has yet to address the question whether the *Woolwich* principle is to be recognised for the purposes of Australian law. However a number of lower courts have acted on the basis that it does form part of our law,[2] and it seems likely that the High Court will adopt it for our law when the right opportunity arises.

The claim for recovery of an unlawful exaction will be denied where the governing legislation expressly or impliedly excludes common law restitutionary principles.[3]

PAYMENTS EXACTED UNDER DURESS

The nature of duress

An invalid exaction will be recoverable from a public authority on the basis of duress where:

(a) the payer apprehended that if he or she did not pay the unlawful exaction, the public authority would take some step, other than invoking legal process, which would cause harm to the payer; and (b) this apprehension was reasonably caused or well founded.[4]

---

1 See Chapter 5, 'Money Paid Under a Mistake'.

2 See, for example, *Melbourne Tramway and Omnibus Co Ltd v The Mayor of Melbourne* (1903); *Esso Australia Resources Ltd v Gas and Fuel Corporation of Victoria* (1993), pp 107–08; *Roxborough v Rothmans of Pall Mall Australia Ltd* (1999) (this case was appealed to the High Court on different grounds: see (2001) 185 ALR 335); *State Bank of New South Wales v Federal Commissioner of Taxation* (1995), p 658; *Federal Airports Corporation v Aerolineas Argentinas* (1997); *Lamesa Holdings BV v Federal Commissioner of Taxation* (1999).

3 See, for example, *Chippendale Printing Co Pty Ltd v Commissioner of Taxation* (1996); *Common Equity Housing Limited v Commissioner of State Revenue* (Vic) (1996). See pp 475–77 for further discussion.

4 *Air India v The Commonwealth* (1977), p 455 (see extract, p 446). See also *Mason v New South Wales* (1959), pp 117, 133, 146 (see extract, p 434).

The plaintiff must additionally establish that the duress was the cause of the payment, in the sense that it was one of the reasons why the payment was made.[5]

The usual form of duress claim brought against public authorities is duress of property, where the basis of the claim is that the plaintiff reasonably apprehended that the authority would exercise an extra-curial power to harm the plaintiff's proprietary interests, such as a statutory power to seize goods,[6] or a power of forfeiture conferred by a lease instrument.[7] Alternatively, payments will be recoverable on the basis of economic duress, where the public authority has made an illegitimate threat to break a contract with the plaintiff if the unlawful exaction is not paid.[8]

A mere refusal by the public authority to do future business with the plaintiff unless an unlawful exaction is paid is not duress: *Smith v William Charlick Ltd* (1924). Nor is duress established merely by proof that the payer felt compelled as a practical matter to meet the demand of the public authority, for example because of a concern about being perceived to be unable to meet financial obligations.[9] As Ralph Gibson J put it in the Court of Appeal in *Woolwich Equitable Building Society v Inland Revenue Commissioners* (1993), p 148: 'It is not enough to say that the payer had no commercial alternative to paying – the payee must do something wrong.'[10]

Lastly, a threat by the public authority to litigate unless the exaction is paid will not amount to duress. The authorities make it clear that a plaintiff cannot recover on the basis of duress where the only threat by the public authority is to commence proceedings to obtain the exaction and to recover a penalty for non-payment.[11] The plaintiff must establish that it had a reasonable apprehension that the authority would exercise an *extra-curial* means of harming the plaintiff's interests.[12] This principle was established in the following case.

Moore v Vestry of Fulham [1895] 1 QB 399 English Court of Appeal

The defendants issued a summons against the plaintiff to recover the plaintiff's proportion of the cost of certain street improvements alleged to be due by him. The plaintiff paid the money before the summons was heard, which was withdrawn.

---

5 *Crescendo Management Pty Ltd v Westpac Banking Corporation* (1988), p 46 (see extract, p 246); *Mckay v National Australia Bank Ltd* (1998) (see extract, p 216); *Barton v Armstrong* (1976), p 120 (see extract, p 219).

6 *Mason v New South Wales* (1959) (see extract, p 434).

7 *Air India v The Commonwealth* (1977) (see extract, p 446).

8 *White Rose Flour Milling Co Pty Ltd v Australian Wheat Board* (1944). See generally Chapter 9.

9 See *William Whiteley Ltd v R* (1910); *Woolwich Building Society v IRC* (1993), p 173; *Mason v New South Wales* (1959), p 144 (cf pp 125–26) (see extract, p 434).

10 Though in Canada the Supreme Court has taken the view that practical compulsion is sufficient to amount to duress: *Eadie v Township of Brantford* (1967).

11 *Werrin v Commonwealth* (1938) (see extract, p 431); *Mason v New South Wales* (1959), pp 119; 126, 135 (see extract, p 434); *William Whiteley Ltd v The King* (1909), p 745; *Maskell v Horner* (1915), pp 121–22; *Woolwich Equitable Building Society v Inland Revenue Commissioners* (1993), p 165 (see extract, p 456). See also *Riessen v State of South Australia* (2001).

12 *Mason v New South Wales* (1959) (see extract, p 434); *Qantas Airways Ltd v Commissioner of Taxation* (2001).

The plaintiff subsequently discovered that his property did not abut the street in question, and that he had not been liable to pay the charge demanded. He commenced proceedings to recover the charge on the basis it had been paid under compulsion. He was unsuccessful at first instance, and appealed to the Court of Appeal.

Lord Halsbury: [401] I am of the opinion that this appeal fails. The principle of law has not been quite accurately stated by counsel for the appellant, because the principle of law is not that money paid under a judgment, but that money paid under the pressure of legal process cannot be recovered. The principle is based upon this, [402] that when a person has had an opportunity of defending an action if he chose, but has thought proper to pay the money claimed by the action, the law will not allow him to try in a second action what he might have set up in the defence to the original action ... In the case upon which such reliance has been placed [*Caird v Moss* (1886)] my brother Lopes, in dealing with the case then before him, not unnaturally referred to the fact of the judgment still standing, and for this reason, because the money in that case was paid under a judgment founded on the construction of an agreement. Then an action was brought to rectify that agreement on the ground that such a construction was contrary to the intention of all the parties. My brother Lopes, without going into the merits of the case, practically says this: 'Why, this judgment stands now; you cannot reopen that question. You had full opportunity of commencing these proceedings while the former action was pending, and ought to have done so, and we cannot now interfere with that judgment. That judgment still stands.' ...

Lindley LJ: [403] I am also entirely of the same opinion. I think that the case is absolutely covered, not by one authority, but by a string of authorities, of which *Hamlet v Richardson* (1833) is as good a type as any. The money there was paid after a writ to recover it had been issued and served, and after an appearance had been entered. But what does that mean? It means this, that the defendant says in substance to his opponent, 'I do not intend to fight you. I will pay rather than fight.' If he chooses to take that course he cannot back out of it whether he discovers that he has made a mistake or does not ...

AL Smith LJ: I also think this appeal fails. This money was paid under threat or fear of a summons which had been taken out. That is a legal process. A summons had been taken out against the present appellant to compel him to pay this apportionment, and under that threat or fear he paid this money. A series of authorities from *Marriot v Hampton* (1797) to the present time has held that money paid under those circumstances [404] cannot be recovered back ...

Questions

What, according to the court, is the rationale for the principle that money paid under a threat of litigation is not subsequently recoverable on the basis of duress? If the facts of this case were to arise today, what other ground of recovery would have been open to the plaintiff?

Werrin v Commonwealth (1938) 59 CLR 150 High Court of Australia

The Commissioner of Taxation demanded the plaintiff pay sales tax on a transaction for the sale of secondhand goods. The plaintiff contended that the transaction was not a sale within the meaning of the Sales Tax Assessment Acts 1930 (Cth), though he reluctantly paid the sales tax demanded. It was subsequently decided by the High Court in separate litigation that sales tax was not payable in respect of sales of secondhand goods, and the plaintiff sought recovery of the tax paid as money paid under compulsion.

Latham CJ: ... [157] The commissioner defends the action upon the grounds that the payment was a voluntary payment made under a mistake of law but not under any mistake of fact ...

The general rule, as stated in *Leake on Contracts*, 6th edn, 1911, p 63, is that money paid voluntarily, that is to say, without compulsion or extortion or undue influence and with a knowledge of all the facts, cannot be recovered although paid without any consideration. In this case there was no force or fraud or fear, or duress of goods or of person. There was not even a threat of ordinary legal proceedings to recover the amount alleged to be due, though if there had been a threat of such proceedings I do not think that would have affected the matter. (See *Maskell v Horner* (1915) *per* Rowlatt J, at p 109, and *per* Reading LCJ, at pp 121, 122.) The present [158] is not a case where a person is entitled to the performance of a duty by a public officer and where the public officer insists upon receiving an additional payment as the price of performing his duty as in *Morgan v Palmer* (1824), or *Waterhouse v Keen* (1825), or *Steele v Williams* (1853), or *Payne v The Queen* (1901).

The case cannot, in my opinion, be distinguished from *William Whiteley (Ltd) v The King* (1909). In that case the plaintiff company sued for the recovery of amounts paid by way of duties demanded under the Inland Revenue Act 1869 which it had paid for several years in respect of certain male servants who were in its employment. The plaintiff had objected to pay and had paid only under protest, being told that in the opinion of the commissioner the duties were payable and that if they were not paid proceedings would be taken for penalties. At last, in the year 1906, the plaintiff refused to pay, and proceedings were taken which were ultimately decided in its favour. The plaintiff then claimed to recover the sums which it had paid in respect of duties for six prior years. Walton J ... examined the whole question and decided against the plaintiff. He said:

> There is no doubt as to the general rule stated in *Leake on Contracts* to which I have already referred, that money paid voluntarily – that is to say, without compulsion or extortion or undue influence, and, of course, I may add without any fraud on the part of the person to whom it is paid, and with knowledge of all the facts, though paid without any consideration, or in discharge of a claim not due, or a claim which might have been successfully resisted, cannot be recovered back. There is no doubt, and no question raised, that that is an accurate statement of the general rule. But, on the other hand, if the payment is not voluntary a different rule applies which may be stated, perhaps, as it is stated in *Leake on Contracts*, 5th edn, 1906, p 61, that money extorted by a person for doing what he is legally bound to do without payment, or for a duty which he fails to perform, may be [159] recovered back; as in the cases of illegal or excessive fees and payments extorted in the discharge of an office; and money paid under duress either of the person or of goods may be recovered back (pp 58–59). In all these cases the payment is not voluntary. The question which I have to decide here is whether the payments made during the years

which I have mentioned – from 1900–05 – were or were not voluntary payments. Was there any duress here? (See p 745.)

The only suggested evidence of duress or compulsion of any kind was that the commissioner had demanded the duties and had threatened to take proceedings for penalties if they were not paid. The learned judge had no doubt that the facts did not show any compulsion or duress or extortion *colore officii*. The principles laid down in this case are, in my opinion, precisely applicable to the present case and they show that the plaintiff cannot succeed.

In another very similar and more recent case, namely, *National Pari-Mutuel Association Ltd v The King* (1930), taxes had been paid by the plaintiff in the belief that they were properly payable. The House of Lords subsequently decided that tax was not payable in such a case as that of the plaintiff. The plaintiff failed in an action to recover moneys paid for the simple reason that the mistake which the plaintiff had made was one of law. In each of these cases the money was paid, as in the present case, to the Crown. In *Henderson v Folkestone Waterworks Co* (1885) money was paid under mistake of law to a water company and the same principles were applied; the money, having been paid voluntarily, could not be recovered.

The principle appears to me to be quite clear that if a person, instead of contesting a claim, elects to pay money in order to discharge it, he cannot thereafter, because he finds out that he might have successfully contested the claim, recover the money which he so paid merely on the ground that he made a mistake of law. The same principles have been applied to similar cases in New Zealand in *Julian v Auckland Corporation* (1927), and in Canada in *Cushen v Hamilton Corporation* (1982), as well as in the Victorian cases [160] which were cited in argument; I refer only to *Payne v The Queen* (1901) and *Kelly v The King* (1902). In my opinion these authorities are conclusive as against the plaintiff ...

McTiernan J: ... [168] The sums sued for, as the special case shows, were paid by the plaintiff upon the demand of the Commissioner of Taxation, who required the plaintiff to pay them as sales tax due by him in respect of the sale of secondhand goods although, as a decision of this court subsequently showed, secondhand goods were not within the scope of the Sales Tax Acts (*Deputy Federal Commissioner of Taxation (SA) v Ellis & Clarke Ltd* (1934)). The plaintiff was at liberty to refuse the demand. But he gave up his right to refuse to pay. The payment of the sum demanded has the character of a voluntary payment made by the plaintiff under a mistake of law about his liability to pay the sums. The decisions cited in the judgment of the Chief Justice, with whose reasons for answering the question in [169] the negative I agree, clearly show that the plaintiff cannot recover the money paid by him in these circumstances. It is also made clear that it is erroneous to regard the moneys sued for as moneys extorted from the plaintiff by the commissioner *colore officii*. In my opinion the plaintiff has no right of action to recover the moneys ...

Commentary

The other members of the court – Rich, Starke and Dixon JJ – did not need to consider the compulsion question as they concluded that the action was in any event barred by a statutory provision which had been enacted specifically to preclude persons from recovering sales tax paid on second hand goods prior to the change in the law.

Duress of property

An invalid exaction is recoverable on the ground of duress where the payer honestly and reasonably apprehended that the public authority would exercise an extra-curial power to injuriously affect the plaintiff's property. This principle was established in the following case.

Mason v New South Wales (1959) 102 CLR 108 High Court of Australia

The plaintiffs were interstate carriers of goods who were seeking repayment of sums of money paid as fees for permits issued under the State Transport (Co-Ordination) Act 1931 (the 'Act'). Pursuant to ss 12 and 28 of the Act it was an offence to carry goods for payment without a permit, and under s 36 a person who committed such an offence was subject to a penalty which was recoverable summarily. Section 47(2) of the Act provided:

> An authorised officer may seize any motor vehicle or any books, records, or papers in respect of which he suspects that an offence has been or is being committed by any person against this Act, and may detain the same pending investigation and legal proceedings.

The Privy Council ultimately decided in *Hughes and Vale Pty Ltd v State of New South Wales* (1955) that the Act was invalid in so far as it purported to apply to interstate trade and that accordingly the requirement of obtaining a permit was unconstitutional. The transport industry had anticipated this decision and the carrier's association in the meantime had advised carriers to pay the permit fees (or risk seizure of vehicles) but to pay them under protest. When buying the vehicle, the male plaintiff ('Mason') had been advised of the situation by the vendor and of the stance taken by the carrier's association. Prior to the Privy Council decision Mason obtained a permit for each of his interstate trips; on most occasions expressing a protest to the issuing clerks and on many occasions writing his protest on the cheque. Mason gave evidence that inspectors did regularly stop carriers and check for permits and that on a number of occasions he himself was stopped and asked to show his permit. According to his evidence the inspector told him that the consequence of not having a permit was that he would be prosecuted. Although Mason gave evidence that he had heard of one truck without a permit which had been stopped and was not permitted to proceed, there was no evidence that trucks without a permit had been seized, nor that the inspectors had made any express threat to Mason or to the other carriers to the effect that a truck would be seized if no permit had been obtained. The plaintiffs sought recovery of the permit fees as moneys paid under compulsion.

Dixon CJ: ... [115] The proofs are anything but exact or cogent or persuasive but no evidence was called in answer. The question is what inferences in favour of the plaintiffs may safely be drawn from these scanty materials. If it were not for the general circumstances which, so to speak, lie behind the specific facts proved in evidence I should have great hesitation in adopting any affirmative inference such as the plaintiffs would need in order to succeed if the matter had arisen between subject and subject. But as it is I think one may safely infer that had the plaintiffs attempted to carry goods between points in New South Wales and points in Victoria without a permit under s 22, being also without a licence under s 15, the vehicle would have been stopped and seized. It is necessary to bear in mind that since 1935 when the transport cases [which upheld the application of the Act to interstate carriage of goods] had been decided there had been a regular enforcement against inter-state carriers as well as other carriers of the provisions of the State Transport (Co-Ordination) Act. The resurgence some fifteen years later of the attempt to obtain a reconsideration of the old decisions meant no weakening of the administrative enforcement of the law. See for example the statement of facts in *Deacon v Grimshaw* (1955), pp 85, 86. The appeal to the Privy Council was obviously a thing in which the whole road transport industry took a lively interest. The question what should be done pending news of the result was one which obviously concerned State transport authorities as much as it did the carriers themselves. The plaintiffs made it plain enough that they paid for permits only under a sense of constraint and with the intention of making a claim [116] for a refund of the money if the decision of the Privy Council should uphold the contention that consistently with s 92 the State could not enforce its demand for the money. In all these circumstances I think that it is a proper inference that, in the case of each journey in question, the plaintiffs paid the money unwillingly and only because they apprehended on reasonable grounds that without the permit which could not otherwise be obtained officers acting under the authority of the State of New South Wales would or might stop the motor vehicle and refuse to allow it to proceed upon the journey. It may further be inferred that responsible officers of the government concerned with the administration of the Act were aware that it was on this basis that moneys were being paid by inter-state carriers; if not by all, at all events by a great number of them. So far as the male plaintiff went, the actual receiving clerks may be taken to know that his payments were made under protest. Doubtless there were occasions on which he failed to express his protest formally. But he had repeatedly stated his protest and he had made his position sufficiently clear. We are not in this case dealing with a claim against a public officer for the repayment of money he has exacted without authority nor with a claim against a corporate body which has so acted by its servants or agents. We are dealing with a claim against the Crown in right of the State ...

For myself I entertain some doubt whether the law to be applied in the present case is the law relating to the recovery by one subject from another of moneys paid by the former in consequence of a demand by the latter lacking lawful justification. The demand of the moneys amounted to, or at least formed part of, an infringement of the constitutional freedom of inter-state trade. It was made with the full authority of the State under the terms of a public general statute. There is, I think, no doubt now that s 92 does not directly confer private rights upon the individual. But it does protect him from the operation of any purported exercise of State [117] (and for that matter Commonwealth) legislative or executive authority incompatible with full freedom of inter-state trade commerce and intercourse. I have not been able completely to reconcile myself to the view that if the weight of a *de facto* governmental authority manifested in a money demand is not resisted although it is incompatible with s 92 the money belongs to the Crown unless the payment was the outcome of the actual threatened or apprehended withholding of something to which the payer was entitled or the actual threatened or apprehended impeding of him in the exercise of some right or liberty. But English authority seems now to say that moneys paid to the Crown as and for taxes cannot be recovered from the Crown upon its turning out that the moneys were not exigible notwithstanding that they were demanded by the Crown, unless the circumstances were such that they would be recoverable as between subject and subject, *exempla gratia* as involuntary payments or payments made under a mistake of fact. See *William Whiteley Ltd v The King* (1909); *National Pari-Mutuel Association Ltd v The King* (1930); and *Sebel Products Ltd v Commissioners of Customs and Excise* (1949) *per* Vaisey J, at p 413. See *per* Latham CJ in *Werrin v The Commonwealth* (1938), pp 157–60 and McTiernan J, at pp 168, 169.

However this may be, the plaintiffs must I think recover in the circumstances of the present case.

We are dealing with the assumed possession by the officers of government of what turned out to be a void authority. The moneys were paid over by the plaintiffs to avoid the apprehended consequence of a refusal to submit to the authority. It is enough if there be just and reasonable grounds for apprehending that unless payment be made an unlawful and injurious course will be taken by the defendant in violation of the plaintiffs' actual rights. The plaintiffs were not bound to wait until the illegality was committed in the exercise of the void authority. See *Valpy v Manley* (1845) *in arg per* Tindal LCJ, at pp 602, 603, 677 *per* Cresswell J, at pp 606, 678 and as to the compulsion of a void authority see *Newdigate v Davy* (1791).

On all the facts including the inferences the propriety of which has been discussed above the case is I think one in which a common count in money had and received would be sustained.

It follows that upon any view the plaintiffs are entitled to succeed. The amount for which they are entitled to judgment is £5,467.

McTiernan J (dissenting): ... [118] [The plaintiffs'] right to [119] recover back what they paid for the permits which were, in fact, issued to them depends upon whether the evidence proves that they paid under compulsion ... Mason, on all occasions when he drove into New South Wales or was about to drive back to Victoria, applied for permits covering the journeys to be travelled within the former State. On most occasions he paid under protest for the permits. What he generally said amounted to this: that he should not have to pay at all and that he expected that the pending case about the Transport Act would be successful and the money would be refunded to him. Other details of Mason's evidence were that inspectors asked drivers of motor vehicles carrying goods to show their permits and checked them. Mason gave evidence of a specific occasion when a vehicle was stopped by an inspector because the driver had no permit and of one occasion when the witness, himself, was asked to show his permit. According to Mason's evidence the inspector told him that the consequence of not having a permit would be that he would be prosecuted. This is the only evidence of any express threat. However, Mason did have a permit and the inspector's statement would appear to be gratuitous. The law does not regard money paid under a threat of legal proceedings as received to the use of the payer and hence recoverable by him. There is no evidence that Mason was forced to apply for a permit on any of the occasions in question or even that any officer of the defendant made any express demand for payment before Mason handed over the money. On the contrary, the evidence clearly proves that Mason, on his own initiative, carried out every detail of the procedure involved in obtaining a permit, from weighing [120] the loaded vehicle to paying the cheque for the fees payable on the issue of the permit. The only evidence of opposition on his part was that he paid under protest. Payment under protest is consistent with voluntary payment. 'I do not think that the mere fact of a payment under protest would be sufficient to entitle the plaintiff to succeed; but I think that it affords some evidence, when accompanied by other circumstances, that the payment was not voluntarily made to end the matter': see *Maskell v Horner* (1915) *per* Reading LCJ, at p 120. In *Union Pacific Railroad Co v Dodge County Commissioners* (1879), this was said: 'There are, no doubt, cases to be found in which the language of the court, if separated from the facts of the particular case under consideration, would seem to imply that a protest alone was sufficient to show that the payment was not voluntary; but on examination it will be found that the protest was used to give effect to the other attending circumstances (see pp 544 and 197 respectively).' There is no evidence here that any payment made under protest was attended by any circumstances that amounted to constraint or pressure to pay, so that it could be said that payment was made to end a deadlock and the protest was made to show that the payer did not regard the payment as closing the transaction. Therefore, I think that the protests provide no ground on which the plaintiffs can succeed. I think that it is clear from the general tenor of the protests which Mason made that he was merely reserving his right to claim back the money if the pending appeal to the Privy Council should succeed. The appeal was *Hughes and Vale Pty Ltd v State of New South Wales* (1954), p 120.

The evidence that inspectors were on duty on the roads to see if drivers had correct permits shows, of course, that the State was administering the Act. But such evidence no more proves that Mason paid under compulsion than does the evidence of the issuing of permits and the collection of fees for them. Presumably all the carriers knew that the Act was not a dead letter. If it matters that Mason was told by his predecessor in business about s 47(2), that he saw inspectors on the roads and had his permit checked, the result might be to put the plaintiffs in a better position to recover back the payments which Mason made for permits, than a carrier who had not had s 47(2) brought to his notice, or had never met an inspector on the roads. But would not that be a strange result? All carriers, as I have said, must be taken to have known that the State was administering the Act. If the fact that the State was [121] doing so proves that it was exacting money by duress, then no carrier could be held to have paid voluntarily. Obviously that would be too large an assumption to make. I think that it would be giving a false character to s 47(2) or to any other sanctions provided by the Act and to the mere fact that the Act was being administered, to say that these things constituted a threat or an intimidatory announcement. The material question is whether any officer of the defendant threatened to use the powers in s 47(2) against Mason if he did not obtain permits. There is no evidence that any officer ever made a threat to Mason to compel him to pay for a permit. Of course, if there were, it would be reasonable to conclude that thereafter Mason did not make any payment for a permit voluntarily. Proof that any other carrier's vehicle was stopped because its owner had no permit and that he thereafter paid involuntarily for a permit (if he did), does not prove that Mason (who had never had his vehicle seized or threatened with seizure) did not always pay voluntarily. Where a person complies with the law you cannot presume that he does so in fear of the possible consequences of disobeying it. Voluntary obedience to a law is compatible with knowledge that it contains drastic means of dealing with disobedience. All Mason's overt acts, except possibly his protests, tend to show that he voluntarily paid the sums of money expended on permits. I have stated my view as to the insufficiency of the protests as proof of compulsion. The protests are evidence of dissatisfaction, no doubt, but that is not enough. The inter-state carriers as a body decided in advance to pay under protest, and Mason was merely following that policy. There is no evidence that any officer constrained Mason by any action or threat of action pay for any permit, and that in order to secure the use of the motor vehicle Mason obtained a permit and protested in order to show that the transaction was not closed and that he reserved his rights to rip up the transaction and recover back what he paid. Mason knew before he embarked on the business of carrying goods between Victoria and New South Wales that it involved, as the law then stood, paying for permits. If he was not willing to pay for permits it was open to him to sue for an injunction *quia timet* to restrain the defendant from seizing his motor vehicle in the event of his not obtaining permits: see *Cam & Sons Pty Ltd v Chief Secretary of New South Wales* (1951). The evidence does not prove that Mason was constrained by any action or threat of action to apply for the permits. The reasonable inference, as I have already said, is that payment was his own free choice. The plaintiffs had profitable [122] orders or contracts for the carriage of goods to execute. They must be taken to have regarded the fees to be paid for permits as a normal expense of the business. Accordingly, they arranged to cover the fees as far as possible by the price they charged. They paid the charges for fees under business necessity to enable them to proceed with their orders and contracts for the carriage of goods inter-state. It is not a reasonable conclusion that having arranged to obtain from their customers money with which to pay for permits they were coerced into applying it to pay for permits. In my opinion, there is no evidence which satisfies me that Mason paid any of these sums of money under duress or compulsion of any kind. There is no evidence that he was subjected to any such constraint or pressure, and that in order to enable the inter-state carrying business to be carried on without interference his only reasonable alternative was to pay and to protest against payment in order to save the plaintiffs' rights.

[McTiernan J held that the position in this case was comparable with *Werrin v The Commonwealth* (1938) (see extract, p 431) and continued:]

[I]n my view, despite all the detail in Mason's evidence, it proves only that the sums of money in question were collected by the defendant upon the supposed authority of a statute when actually, according to the subsequent decision of the Privy Council, no authority existed. I think it is appropriate to quote here a passage from the judgment of Skerrett CJ in *Julian v Auckland Corporation* (1927), p 458: 'I decide it upon the simple proposition, which appears to be well established, that where money is paid at a time when [123] the law is in favour of the payee it cannot be recovered by reason of a subsequent judicial decision reversing the former understanding of the law: see *Henderson v Folkestone Waterworks Co* (1885).' A statement of Gibbs J in *Brisbane v Dacres* (1813) is important and relevant here:

> We must take this payment to have been made under a demand of right, and I think that where a man demands money of another as a matter of right, and that other, with a full knowledge of the facts upon which the demand is

founded, has paid a sum, he never can recover back the sum he has so voluntarily paid. It may be, that upon a further view he may form a different opinion of the law, and it may be, his subsequent opinion may be the correct one. If we were to hold otherwise, I think many inconveniences may arise; there are many doubtful questions of law: when they arise, the defendant has an option, either to litigate the question, or to submit to the demand, and pay the money. I think, that by submitting to the demand, he that pays the money gives it to the person to whom he pays it, and makes it his, and closes the transaction between them. He who receives it has a right to consider it as his without dispute: he spends it in confidence that it is his; and it would be most mischievous and unjust, if he who has acquiesced in the right by such voluntary payment, should be at liberty, at any time within the statute of limitations, to rip up the matter, and recover back the money. He who received it is not in the same condition: he has spent it in the confidence it was his, and perhaps has no means of repayment (pp 152, 153; p 645).

There is no satisfactory evidence that any of the sums was paid under any duress, express or implied. It is therefore not established that the defendant received any of these amounts to the use of the plaintiffs. I would dismiss the action.

Kitto J: ... [125] The question now is whether the plaintiffs are entitled to recover back the fees they paid in order to get permits.

This is a question to be resolved according to the same body of law as would govern the case if the parties were subject and subject: Judiciary Act, s 64. The general principle to be considered is that which Pollock called 'the common principle ... that if a man chooses to give away his money, or to take his chance whether he is giving it away or not, he cannot afterwards change his mind; but it is open to him to show ... that he really had no choice'.[13] The defendant says that the plaintiffs had ample choice. They might defy the State of New South Wales, entering its territory and using its roads in their inter-state journeys without regard to its statute, pinning their faith to s 92 as a guarantee that they would emerge scatheless from the enterprise. But when Pollock referred to a choice he was using the language of practical affairs. He meant a free choice, uninfluenced by compulsion of any sort. Hodges J expressed the conception in *Kelly v The King* (1902): 'The expression "voluntary payment" does not mean a payment which the petitioner or any other person wishes to make. In the case of many persons such payments never are voluntary in that sense. A "voluntary payment" means at most a payment made to get rid of a liability (ie, asserted by the payee though not sustainable in law), made with a free exercise of the will, where no advantage is taken of the position of the person or the situation of his property (p 532).'

An actual or threatened seizure or detention of the payer's property has often been the feature relied upon as showing that there really was no choice. But other circumstances may show it also. This is brought out very clearly by a consideration of two cases in the Supreme Court of the United States. In the earlier of the two, *Maxwell v Griswold* (1850) the court said: '... it can hardly be meant, in this class of cases, that, to make a payment involuntary, it should be by actual violence, or any physical duress. It suffices, if the payment is caused on the one part by an illegal demand, and made on the other part reluctantly and in consequence of that illegality, and without being able to regain possession of his property, [126] except

13 *Principles of Contract*, 13th edn, 1950, p 481.

by submitting to the payment (p 256; p 411).' But in *Robertson v Frank Bros Co* (1889) the court explained its decision in *Maxwell v Griswold* (1850) by saying: 'The ultimate fact, of which that (the inability to get possession of goods without making payment) was an ingredient in the particular case, was the moral duress not justified by law. When such duress is exerted under circumstances sufficient to influence the apprehensions and conduct of a prudent business man, payment of money wrongfully induced thereby ought not to be regarded as voluntary. But the circumstances of the case are always to be taken into consideration. When the duress has been exerted by one clothed with official authority, or exercising a public employment, less evidence of compulsion or pressure is required – as where an officer exacts illegal fees, or a common carrier excessive charges. But the principle is applicable in all cases according to the nature and exigency of each, *Robertson v Frank Bros Co* (1889).'

These observations, accurately reflecting, as I believe they do, the common law of England, seem to me to have special force in the case of a payment made to a government in order to obviate adverse consequences which a statute invalidly purports to provide as the alternative. The proposition need not be questioned that where an Act purports, invalidly, to require a payment to be made, leaving the liability to be enforced by means of an action in which the invalidity of the statute is an available defence, a person who might have relied upon that defence but has paid without raising it should not be held, just because he was obeying the *de facto* command of a legislature, to have made the payment involuntarily. But even in the case of such an Act, if there are superadded provisions which attach to non-payment consequences other than a bare liability to be sued, there can be no justification for refusing to have regard to those consequences and to consider whether the existence of the provisions creating them has placed the payer under such pressure that the payments have not in truth been voluntary. Holmes J observed in *Atchison, Topeka & Santa Fe Railway Co v O'Connor* (1911): '... when, as is common, the State has a more summary remedy, such as distress, and the party indicates by protest that he is yielding to what he cannot prevent, courts sometimes perhaps have been a little too slow to recognise the implied duress under which the payment is made ((1911) pp 285, 286; p 438).' There is no reason however why they should be slow [127] to see compulsion in the statute itself, whether it results from a provision for distraint or from any other provision facing people with a substantial prospect of harm if they do not pay, and whether or not in particular cases the making of a protest has underlined the fact that a payment constitutes a yielding to the pressure of such a prospect ...

[128] It is all very well to say in such a case that there was an alternative to payment, namely to carry on as if ss 12 and 28 had not been passed, resist the resulting prosecutions by pleading the invalidity of the Act, seek protection from the courts by injunction or otherwise in respect of a seizure, and appeal, if necessary to the Privy Council, against any unfavourable decision. But the critical question is not whether there was an alternative. It is whether the choice made between alternatives was made freely or under pressure. Holmes J summed the matter up in two sentences which follow the passage quoted above from his judgment in *Atchison, Topeka & Santa Fe Railway Co v O'Connor* (1911): 'But even if the State is driven to an action, if at the same time the citizen is put at a serious disadvantage in the assertion of his legal, in this case of his constitutional, rights, by defence in the suit, justice may require that he should be at liberty to avoid

those disadvantages by paying promptly and bringing suit on his side. He is entitled to assert his supposed [129] right on reasonably equal terms (p 286; p 438).' This seems to me to go to the core of the matter.

It is true that the plaintiffs in the present case need not have paid their fees. They might have discontinued their business, or, as I have said, they might have ignored the Act, risking the seizure of their vehicles and the detention of them 'pending investigations and legal proceedings', with the consequent disruption of their business and probable loss of customers, and risking, in respect of every operation of a vehicle in their business, a prosecution with its inevitable result, a conviction and the imposition of a penalty – the penalty, incidentally, being irrecoverable even if the Privy Council should one day give the decision for which the plaintiff hoped. But the loss to be anticipated from the adoption of either of these courses was so serious that any prudent person in their position must have felt strongly impelled to choose the lesser evil: to save his business and avoid the recurrent sanctions of the criminal law by paying the government to allow him the freedom which was his already by constitutional right. To describe the fees, when paid in these circumstances, as paid voluntarily – to describe the plaintiffs as taking their chance whether they were giving their money away or not – is surely impossible. How absurd it would be to say that they made their choice 'on reasonably equal terms'. What was their choice but a yielding to the superior power of the State?

I do not myself feel justified in attaching much weight to the tenuous evidence upon which we were invited to find that the plaintiffs made their payments because of apprehensions induced by words or conduct of State officials that vehicles would or might be seized and detained under s 47. My judgment rests upon the view that the plaintiffs had quite enough compulsion upon them from the terms of the Act itself, apart altogether from anything that may have been said or done by officers of government. Under that compulsion they parted with their money. What happened between them and their customers is irrelevant: it was still their money that they parted with, and there is nothing to account for their parting with it except the pressure they were under. In my opinion they are entitled by law to have it back.

Menzies J: ... [133] [I] think it proper to infer that the payments by the plaintiffs to the defendant were not made voluntarily. They were necessarily paid in order to obtain permits without which the plaintiffs, with cause, believed that their vehicles would be forced off the roads and that they could not carry on their business. That business they were entitled to carry on without obtaining permits or paying charges. Payments of this sort cannot be called voluntary. Furthermore, I am satisfied that the defendant was aware that the payments were made not because the plaintiffs grudgingly accepted liability nor because they preferred to pay rather than to litigate but substantially because they felt they had to pay in order to carry on the business which they were asserting that they were entitled to carry on without payment. They paid knowing that litigation was proceeding to determine whether the Act applied to inter-state trade and asserting the intention to recover the money if and when the Privy Council decided *Hughes and Vale Pty Ltd v State of New South Wales* (1955) as it did. In short, the money which the plaintiffs paid as charges was illegally demanded under colour of the Act and unwillingly paid in order that the plaintiffs might carry on a business which they rightly asserted was lawful and the defendant wrongly asserted was unlawful without permits for which the payments were prerequisite.

On these facts it seems to me that the case presents no legal difficulty. The payments were not voluntary and the compulsion under which they were made was something other than legal compulsion. To put it bluntly, the charges were unlawfully exacted. Cases such as *Morgan v Palmer* (1824); *Steele v Williams* (1853); *Hooper v Exeter Corporation* (1887) and *Great Western Railway Co v Sutton* (1869) show that money paid in such circumstances is recoverable. In *Sutton's* case (1869) Lord Chelmsford said: 'Now if the defendants were bound to charge the plaintiff for the carriage of his goods a less sum, and they refused to carry them except upon payment of a greater sum, as he was compelled to pay the amount demanded, and [134] could not otherwise have his goods carried, the case falls within the principle of several decided cases, in which it has been held that money which a party has been wrongfully compelled to pay under circumstances in which he was unable to resist the imposition, may be recovered back in an action for money had and received (p 263).' Again, in *Lancashire & Yorkshire Railway Co v Gidlow* (1875) Lord Chelmsford said: 'My Lords, there was a question raised here and argued, but, as my noble and learned friend said of another point, only faintly argued, that is, that the money for these terminal charges having been paid without objection, the plaintiff had no right to bring an action to recover it back. Now there can be no doubt that where a person pays money which he is not bound to pay, with a full knowledge of the facts, he cannot recover it back in an action for money had and received. But there has always been an exception made in cases where a party has paid money under compulsion. It has been decided that where a carrier refused to deliver goods until a payment was made by the person to whom the goods belonged, amounting to more than the carrier had a right to charge, the customer might in an action for money had and received recover back the money so paid. There can be no doubt whatever that the plaintiff here paid this money under; he was compelled to do it, or his coals would not have been carried by the company; and, therefore, that is the answer to that argument ... (p 527).'

[135] It may be that had nothing been proved beyond the mere existence of s 47 in the Act this would not have been enough to prove that the payments were involuntary but the findings I have made go a long way further. In *William Whiteley Ltd v The King* (1909) it was decided that duties wrongly demanded under the Revenue Act and paid were not recoverable because they were paid voluntarily and not under duress. The duress relied upon was that a revenue officer had told the taxpayer that if duties were not paid proceedings would be taken for penalties. As to this Walton J said that to the knowledge of the suppliant the Commissioners of Inland Revenue 'could take no action if the duties were not paid except by legal proceedings. They could not distrain' (p 745). This decision, which in *Werrin v The Commonwealth* (1938) was held to be indistinguishable, is clearly distinguishable here. The distinction is the simple one that in that case there was no compulsion beyond the threat of legal proceedings; in this case on my findings there is. Finally, in *Twyford v Manchester Corporation* (1946) the plaintiff failed in an attempt to recover moneys which the corporation had wrongly charged as fees for recutting monumental inscriptions in a cemetery but the basis

of the decision was that there was no duress in the sense that the plaintiff was led to apprehend exclusion from the cemetery unless the payments were made.

As Lowe J said in *Deacon v Transport Regulation Board* (1958) – a case like the present which arose under the Victorian legislation [136] corresponding with the Act but without a section corresponding with s 47 – the question whether any particular payment was made voluntarily or under compulsion is a question of fact and in this case my findings are, as were those of Lowe J in *Deacon's* case (1958), that the payments in question were made under compulsion ...

Windeyer J: ... [Windeyer J rejected the application of the *colore officii* doctrine to these facts (see extract, p 449) and continued at p 142:]

The plaintiffs are not to fail on their action, however, because the pleader has used inappropriate words to formulate their claim. But it is not just a matter of a wrong Latin label. The importance of the matter is that the plaintiffs cannot succeed simply because of the superior position of the defendant. They must go further and establish that there was, in a legal sense, compulsion by something actually done or threatened, something beyond the implication of duress arising from a demand by persons in authority, which suffices in a true *colore officii* case. Further the plaintiffs must establish that they actually paid because of this compulsion, and not voluntarily despite it. 'Voluntary payment' has a special meaning here. Clearly it does not import a payment by way of gift. And equally clearly it means more than payment willingly, in the [143] sense of without reluctance. One writer has said that, in this context, 'it is merely a shorthand way of saying that there is no approved ground on which restitution of benefits can be awarded' (Dawson, *Unjust Enrichment*). In most jurisdictions in the United States the difficulties of the question whether a payment is compulsory or voluntary have led to its being decided by the judge and not left to the jury (see Field, *The Effect of an Unconstitutional Statute*, Chapter 10, 'The recovery of unconstitutional taxes' reproducing an article in 45 Harvard Law Review 501). And in *Steele v Williams* (1853) the parties had agreed at the trial that this question was one for the judge. Yet it is, I think, ultimately a question of fact, as Lowe J said in *Deacon v Transport Regulation Board* (1958). Coleridge J in *Traherne v Gardner* (1856) said, 'we are in the character of jurymen' (p 951; p 731). Nevertheless it is a question for the resolution of which much citation of authority can be employed, as this and other cases have shown. In my view, a payment may be said to be voluntary, in this context and for present purposes, when the payer makes it deliberately with a knowledge of all relevant facts, and either being indifferent to whether or not he be liable in law, or knowing, or having reason to think, himself not liable, yet intending finally to close the transaction. And I respectfully agree with the criticism by Lowe J in *Deacon's* case (1958) of the statement attributed to Platt and Martin BB, in the headnote to *Steele v Williams* (1853). It seems plain that a man compelled by pressure *colore officii* or any other form of duress may yet say 'well I have really no option but to pay, nevertheless I will not dispute the matter further. I will pay to put an end to the question'.

Much was said in this case about the plaintiff's protests. A protest at the time of payment may of course 'afford some evidence, when accompanied by other circumstances, that the payment was not voluntarily made to end the matter' (*Maskell v Horner* (1915)). But there is no magic in a protest; for a protest may accompany a voluntary payment or be absent from one compelled. (See *Deacon v*

Transport Regulation Board (1958).) Moreover the word 'protest' is itself equivocal. It may mean the serious assertion of a right or it may mean no more than a statement that payment is grudgingly made. In some early cases a protest accompanying payment had more than an evidentiary importance. It was, and in some parts of the United States still is, a notice to the collector of a challenged levy that if he pays it over to the state he does so at his own risk. [144] In these cases the payer, by protesting before payment over, may preserve a right to sue the collecting officer personally – a matter of importance wherever a civil action cannot be brought against a state. (*Elliott v Swartwout* (1836); *Restatement of the Law of Restitution*, p 293.) The plaintiffs' protests do provide some evidence that their payments were not voluntary; but they do not prove that they were compelled by duress or coercion (cf *Twyford v Manchester Corporation* (1946)).

The plaintiffs pointed to the penal provisions of the Act. But the mere fact that the Act provided penalties for using the roads without a permit and made vehicles liable to seizure does not mean that anyone can recover from the Crown moneys he paid under the Act. The Crown is not to be assumed to have extorted money merely because the Parliament of New South Wales armed it with a power to do so. No doubt it is the duty of the Crown to enforce the will of Parliament; and, moreover, a statute may be well known to reflect the policy of the Government; but the mere appearance on the statute book of a measure providing for penalties and forfeitures does not mean that all moneys collected pursuant to the statute are extorted by the Crown. It is, in my view, necessary for the plaintiffs to do more than point to the provisions of the statute. They must show that the Crown by its servants was exercising, or threatening to exercise, powers under the statute in such a way as to constitute compulsion in law. A threat of proceedings for a pecuniary penalty does not make a payment made thereafter involuntary; for the payer might have defended the proceedings and relied upon the unlawfulness of the demand. (*William Whiteley Ltd v The King* (1909) and *Werrin v The Commonwealth* (1938), pp 158, 159.) But a payment made under pressing necessity to avoid a seizure of goods, or to obtain the release of goods unlawfully detained, or to prevent some interference with or withholding of a legal right, is compelled and not voluntary and is recoverable in an action for money had and received. *Shaw v Woodcock* (1827); *Hills v Street* (1828); *Great Western Railway Co v Sutton* (1960); *Maskell v Horner* (1915); *Nixon v Furphy* (1925); *White Rose Flour Milling Co Pty Ltd v Australian Wheat Board* (1944) and *In re Hooper & Grass' Contract* (1949) *per* Fullagar J, are examples of the application in different circumstances of the same general principle. There need be no actual interference with a legal right. [145] Money paid under the constraint of threats to interfere with a legal right is recoverable, *Valpy v Manley* (1845).

Payments made as the result of constraint are none the less involuntary because the law might have ultimately provided the payer with a remedy if he were prepared to suffer in the meantime. In *Astley v Reynolds* (1731) the court said, 'We think ... this is a payment by compulsion; the plaintiff might have such an immediate want of his goods, that an action of trover would not do his business' at p 916. And so generally in an action at law for the recovery of money illegally exacted by duress of property, a payment will be considered as made under compulsion notwithstanding that the plaintiff might have avoided having to make it by resorting to equity for an injunction, *Close v Phipps* (1844); *Kanhaya Lal v National Bank of India* (1913). In *Attorney General v Wilts United Dairies Ltd* (1922), where Atkin J, as he then was, said that if the defendants had actually paid they could have recovered the money in an action for money had and received, the illegal impost was, in effect, exacted as the price of a licence to buy milk which the defendants had a common law right to buy without a licence. And similarly in *Brocklebank Ltd v The King* (1924) a payment was illegally exacted as the condition of a licence to the plaintiffs to deal with their own property, which licence the plaintiffs ought to have been granted, if at all, without such payment.

In the American *Restatement of the Law of Restitution* there is a section (s 75) in the chapter headed 'Coercion' on 'void taxes and assessments'. A necessary condition for recovery is there stated to be that: 'the payor reasonably believed that if the payment was not made the means taken to enforce collection of the tax or assessment would subject him to serious risk of imprisonment or of the loss of possession of his things or of other substantial loss' (p 318). That I consider states the law applicable here.

The direct evidence adduced by the present plaintiffs to bring themselves within the above principles is somewhat scanty, and some matters are left to inference. There is not much direct evidence of any measures being taken by the authorities in New South Wales to enforce the statute and to compel road users to procure permits. The only actual threat to the plaintiffs which was proved may have amounted only to a threat of prosecution not of a seizure of the vehicle. Nevertheless, the proper inference from the admissible evidence as a whole is, I think, that the penal provisions of the Act, [146] including the provisions for the seizure of vehicles travelling without permits, were far from a dead letter. The Act, it appears, was being vigorously policed, and this was known to the plaintiffs. The proper conclusion in all the circumstances is that the plaintiffs paid the charges levied under the Act to ensure that they would not be denied the use of the roads, and that they paid under a reasonable apprehension, created by the defendant's servants, that, if they did not, by paying, obtain permits, the use of the roads would be denied them by seizure of their vehicle. There is present in this case much more than the circumstances which led Williams J in *McClintock v The Commonwealth* (1947), pp 39, 40 to his forceful statement that in that case there was compulsion. I think the plaintiffs are entitled to judgment for the amount they claim ...

[Fullagar and Taylor JJ agreed with the judgments of Menzies and Windeyer JJ.]

Commentary and questions

On what basis did Dixon CJ, Menzies and Windeyer JJ hold that the payments were recoverable on the basis of duress? How does Kitto J's reasoning differ from that of the other members in the majority? On what basis did McTiernan J dissent? Did McTiernan J disagree with the majority judges on the principles to be applied in these cases?

According to the majority in the principal case, is the fact the payer will be liable for penalties for non-payment relevant in determining whether the payment has been made under compulsion? Is a claim for restitution from a public authority governed by the same principles which apply where the claim is one between subject and subject?

According to the principal case, the plaintiff must provide sufficient evidence of an honest and reasonable apprehension that the authority would exercise its extra-curial power if the plaintiff did not pay the unlawful exaction. An express or implied threat by the public authority to exercise the extra-curial power will ordinarily provide the requisite evidence, however (as the result in the principal case shows) the existence of a threat is not crucial.[14] Likewise, a protest by the plaintiff at the time of payment might provide evidence that he or she reasonably apprehended that the extra-curial step would be taken, but it will not be determinative as 'there is no magic in a protest': *Mason v New South Wales* (1959), p 143.

The plaintiff's claim failed in the following case as the court was not satisfied that the evidence established an honest and reasonable apprehension that the authority would exercise its extra-curial power of forfeiture.

Air India v The Commonwealth [1977] 1 NSWLR 449
of Appeal of New South Wales

The plaintiffs were international airlines who leased terminal space at Sydney Airport from the Commonwealth Government. The Commonwealth increased the rent for the terminal space, purporting to act under the terms of the leases. The plaintiffs paid the extra rent under protest, and it was subsequently determined that the Commonwealth had failed to comply with the relevant terms of the leases concerning rent increases, and accordingly had no right to require the payment of the extra rent. The plaintiffs sought recovery of the extra rent on the ground that it had been paid under compulsion, claiming that they feared that, unless they paid the total rent, the Commonwealth would exercise its contractual right as lessor to forfeit the leases upon the rent being 14 days in arrears.

The court: ... [454] It is undoubted that, upon these facts, the only basis upon which the payers may recover back the excess payments is by their showing that the payments were not made voluntarily, ie, that they were made under some compulsion.

The plaintiffs claim, upon this appeal, that the meagre facts bearing on this issue entitle them to succeed. They found their argument upon such cases as *Morgan v Palmer* (1824) and *Steele v Williams* (1853) as supporting a proposition, applicable to the facts of this case, that where a demand is made, where the parties are in a 'hopelessly unequal position', and the payee has the power to work a forfeiture without recourse to ordinary litigious processes wherein the illegality of the increased rental could be pleaded and proved, any money paid is recoverable.

These two factors – inequality and an extra-curial remedy – are, so it was argued, sufficient proof that the payments made were involuntary – that they were made under compulsion.

It was part of this argument that there was no special rule relating to public officers.

Though there was no explicit threat, it was submitted that the superior position of the Commonwealth made its polite request for the payment of increased rent an

---

14 *Mason v New South Wales* (1959), pp 117, 133, 145–46; *Air India v The Commonwealth* (1977), p 455 (see following extract).

effective threat to pursue extra-curial and summary remedies, if its request went unheeded.

The superior position giving rise to 'hopeless inequality' was said to arise from the circumstance that the Commonwealth was a monopolistic operator of the airport, and that the leasing of space in a terminal building situated therein was essential to the conduct of the business of an international air carrier. It was also said that the fact that the lessor was the Crown was a significant factor.

In our opinion, these submissions result from an unwarranted compounding of the principles deriving from a special category of duress, namely, money exacted under colour of an office, with principles of general application in this field of the law.

In *Mason v The State of New South Wales* (1959) Windeyer J traced the development of the principles that money exacted *colore officii* is recoverable.

A compendious statement is found in *Sargood Brothers v The Commonwealth* (1910) where O'Connor J said:

> Where an officer of Government in the exercise of his office obtains payment of moneys as and for a charge which the law enables him to demand and enforce, such moneys may be recovered back from him if it should afterwards turn out that they were not legally payable even though no protest was made or question raised at the time of payment. Payments thus demanded *colore officii* are regarded by the law as being made under duress. The principle laid down in *Morgan v Palmer* (1824), *Steele v Williams* (1853), and adopted in *Hooper v Exeter Corporation* (1887), clearly establish that proposition.

This statement was quoted with approval by Menzies J and Windeyer J in *Mason v The State of New South Wales* (1959), pp 134, 141, 142.

There is no question in this case of an exaction made under colour of an office, any more than there was in *Mason's* case (1959). Though it is the Commonwealth of Australia which is the lessor, it did not withhold, in its official capacity, something which it was its duty to grant. The relevant [455] relationship was that of lessor and lessee. In a case where an unlawful demand is made by a public officer, under colour of his office, for that which he has a duty to provide free, or for a lesser sum, no more needs to be shown to establish compulsion. The demand and compliance suffice.

In other cases more must be shown.

The authorities, and in particular *Mason's* case (1959), indicate that in general it must be established in order to show that a payment was made under compulsion that: (a) there was a fear that, if it were not paid, the payee would take some step, other than invoking legal process, which would cause harm to the payer; and (b) that this fear was reasonably caused or well founded.

A threat to take the step in question could well fulfil both evidentiary requirements. In the instant case there was no express threat, and hence the submission that it was implicit in the relationship of the parties.

Let it be assumed that the fear deposed to in the affidavits existed, and that such fear should be construed as a fear that the defendant in fact would re-enter, without first taking any legal proceedings in which the validity of the increased charges or the proposed re-entry could be adjudicated upon. It nevertheless remained for the plaintiffs to show that it was a well founded belief that such an action, unlawful in the event, would be taken by the defendant and would have such serious consequences that the airlines had no real alternative but to pay, so that it may be said there was practical compulsion.

There was no evidence in the case other than that set out above as to the basis of any fear or belief entertained in the respective corporate minds. If it is to be found at all it is to be found only in the position and character of the parties.

Because it is not a case of exaction *colore officii*, a presumption of duress does not avail. Why then should a tribunal of fact determine that a fear that the Commonwealth would forfeit the lease was justly and reasonably held?

It hardly seems to be reasonable to fear that the Commonwealth would determine the leases of seven major international airlines servicing Sydney and Australia because of a rent dispute involving the construction of a lease document, when they could be held to their leases and sued to fruitful verdicts. Bringing about an almost empty and non-productive facility would hardly seem a likely course of action.

Whether the payments were made involuntarily was a question of fact for his Honour. In declining to be satisfied that the plaintiffs had established this, we are not persuaded that he was in error ...

Questions

Why did the court reject the duress claim? How did the court in the principal case formulate the duress principle? Did it limit the principle to threats to seize the plaintiff's property or to harm the plaintiff's proprietary interests?

PAYMENTS EXACTED *COLORE OFFICII*

A demand by a public authority for an unlawful payment for the performance of a duty or the proper exercise of a discretion will amount to duress *colore officii* (duress under colour of office). This principle applies where the plaintiff is required to pay an exaction in order to carry out an activity that the plaintiff is lawfully entitled to conduct without payment, or for a lesser amount than is being demanded by the authority.[15] A payment in response to a demand made under colour of office is presumed to have been made under duress. It is not necessary to show actual compulsion; the necessary compulsion is presumed to arise from the authority of the office.[16] The colour of office principle is concisely summarised by Skerrett CJ in *Julian v Mayor of Auckland* (1927) where he said the colour of office principle applies:

---

15 *Sargood Bros v The Commonwealth* (1910), pp 276, 301; *Mason v New South Wales* (1959), pp 118, 141–42 (see following extract); *Bell Bros Pty Ltd v Shire of Serpentine-Jarrahdale* (1969), pp 141, 145 (see extract, p 452). Where the official has charged an excessive fee, only the excess is recoverable: *Lovell v Simpson* (1800); *Dew v Parsons* (1819).

16 *Bell Bros Pty Ltd v Shire of Serpentine-Jarrahdale* (1969), p 145 (see extract, p 452); *Morgan v Palmer* (1824); *Sargood Bros v The Commonwealth* (1910).

Where the plaintiff is entitled to have some service performed or act done upon payment of a fee, and that service has been performed or the act done, accompanied by the demand of an illegal or illegally excessive fee. In such circumstances, the payment is held not to be voluntary, and the money recoverable as having been in substance exacted by the defendant *colore officii*.

Examples of official exactions recovered under this principle include invalid licence fees,[17] unlawful tolls[18] illegal fees charged to search official records,[19] and unlawfully excessive death duties.[20] A recent example of the operation of the *colore officii* principle is *Waikato Regional Airport Ltd v Attorney General* (2001). An unlawful demand by a government department to airport companies to reimburse the costs of border protection services provided by the department was held to be a demand *colore officii* and the sums paid pursuant to that demand were recoverable on this basis.

Mason v New South Wales (1959) 102 CLR 108 High Court of Australia

The facts are stated at p 434.

McTiernan J (dissenting): ... [118] The statement of claim contains an allegation that the amounts claimed were demanded by the defendant *colore officii*. I can see no support at all for that allegation. Extortion in the discharge of an office occurs where illegal or excessive fees are demanded by an officer for the performance of a duty to which the payer is entitled: see *Werrin v The Commonwealth* (1938), p 158. The plaintiffs had no right to the issue of a permit under the Act. It was beyond the constitutional power of the defendant to apply the provisions of the Act relating to permits to transportation among the States. Their right to [119] recover back what they paid for the permits which were, in fact, issued to them depends upon whether the evidence proves that they paid under compulsion ...

Windeyer J: ... A plaintiff's right to recover in an action for money had and received such as this depends upon proof that the moneys were paid by him involuntarily, that is, as the result of some extortion, coercion or compulsion in the legal sense. Exactions *colore officii* are a form of extortion.

The phrase 'colour of office' is an old one, carrying a stale odour of mediaeval complaints of corruption and abuse of power by officials. A fairly early example of its use is in the Statute 9 Hen VI, c 7, An Act for Restraining Extortion by the Sheriff of Herefordshire (1431). Extortion was a common law misdemeanour, defined by Coke as 'the taking of money by any officer, *by colour of his office*, either where none at all is due, or not so much is due, or where it is not yet due'. The indictment alleged that the prisoner had acted '*colore officii sui false, corrupte et extorsive*' (*R v Eyres* (1666) and *R v Clerk of the Peace of Cumberland* (1706)) or as in *Wentworth on Pleading*, 1797, Bk IV, p 147: '... by colour of his said office, unlawfully, unjustly and extorsively did exact, extort and receive ...'

The words *colore officii* thus came into the law in association with misdemeanour. In *Les Termes de la Ley*, Rastall says 'colour of office is always taken in the worst

---

17 *Bell Bros Pty Ltd v Shire of Serpentine-Jarrahdale* (1969) (see extract, p 452); *Morgan v Palmer* (1824).

18 *R v Roberts* (1692).

19 *Steele v Williams* (1853).

20 *Ochberg v Commissioner of Stamp Duties* (1943).

part'; and he contrasts the expression with *ratione officii* and *virtute officii* which he says are 'taken always in the best part'. He got his description of colour of office from Plowden's report of *Dive v Maningham* (1550) where Montague CJ in 1550 said: '... this word *colore officii sui* is always taken in *mala partes,* and signifies an act badly done under the countenance of an office, and it bears a dissembling visage of duty, and is properly called extortion. As if an officer will take more for his fees than he ought, this is done *colore officii sui,* but yet it is not part of his office, and it is called extortion, which [140] is no other than robbery, but it is more odious than robbery, for robbery is apparent, and always hath the countenance of vice, but extortion, being equally as great a vice as robbery, carries the mask of virtue, and is more difficult to be tried or discerned, and consequently more odious than robbery.'

Among early examples of extortion to be found in the reports are cases of sheriffs and coroners demanding fees for performing duties which they ought to have performed without payment (eg, *Empson v Bathurst* (1619)) a ferryman and a miller taking more by way of toll than custom allowed, and the farmer of a market making an unlawful demand for stallage. (*R v Roberts* (1692) and *R v Burdett* (1696).) Extortion by officials *colore officii* had thus been long known as a criminal offence when Lord Mansfield was giving generous scope to the action for money had and received, which in *Moses v Macfarlan* (1760) he said would lie 'for money got through imposition (express, or implied); or extortion; or oppression'. Examples of such actions soon multiplied. An early instance, interesting in the present context, is *Irving v Wilson* (1791) where the plaintiff's carts laden with goods on a journey from Scotland to Carlisle were stopped by a revenue collector, who demanded the plaintiff's permit, which not being with the first cart and immediately forthcoming, he seized all the carts with their cargoes and demanded money for their release. This the plaintiff paid and later recovered.

Yet, although all forms of extortion will ground an action for money had and received, all forms of extortion by officials are not properly described as being by colour of office. Extortion by colour of office occurs when a public officer demands and is paid money he is not entitled to, or more than he is entitled to, for the performance of his public duty. Examples of such exactions are overtolls paid to the keepers of toll-bridges and turnpikes, excessive fees demanded by sheriffs, poundkeepers, and so on. The parties were not on an equal footing; and generally the payer paid the sum demanded in ignorance that it was not due. In *Steele v Williams* (1853) the most frequently cited case on this topic, the defendant was a parish clerk who had demanded and received from the plaintiff's servant more than the statutory fee for permission to search the parish register. The amount asked for had been unprotestingly paid; and it was paid after the search was complete, so that there had been no [141] withholding of the right of search until payment was made. Baron Parke said: 'The defendant obtained the money by an improper exercise of his power as parish clerk; that is an illegal act, and therefore he must refund.' After saying also that 'in effect, the defendant told the plaintiff's clerk, that if he did not pay ... he should not be permitted to search', he added 'I by no means pledge myself to say that the defendant would not have been guilty of extortion ... without that species of duress, viz the refusal to allow the party to exercise his legal right, but *colore officii. Dew v Parsons* (1819) certainly goes to that extent', *Steele v Williams* (1853). In *Dew v Parsons* (1819) a sheriff had been paid more than he was entitled to have, the party paying being ignorant that it was not due. Similarly in *Hooper v Exeter Corporation* (1887), the plaintiff paid in ignorance that he was not liable for harbour dues. *Morgan v Palmer* (1824) is commonly cited along with *Steele v Williams* (1853) as an instance of money demanded *colore officii* being recoverable; and properly so, although, in relation to a technical requirement of notice of action, Bayley J said that the money was not there taken *colore officii*. In both cases the payment was made after the event had occurred for which it was paid. Neither was a case of duress by the actual withholding of a right until payment. The payment was made simply because it was demanded under colour of office. In *Morgan v Palmer* (1824) money was paid to the mayor of Yarmouth when the renewal of the plaintiff's publican's licence was announced. Similar fees had been regularly paid to the mayor for sixty-five years; and the defendant took the money in good faith, believing himself entitled to it by custom. This decision, and a statement of Collins J in *Shoppee v Nathan & Co* (1892) show that in an action for money had and received *colore officii* it is not necessary to show that the defendant acted in bad faith, as it is in criminal proceedings for similar extortions. Nevertheless the phrase bears an imputation of imposition by a person in authority upon another person ignorant of his rights.

In *Sargood's* case (1910), O'Connor J said: 'Where an officer of Government in the exercise of his office obtains payment of moneys as and for a charge which the law enables him to demand and enforce, such moneys may be recovered back from him if it should afterwards turn out that they were not legally payable even though no protest was made or question raised at the time of payment. [142] Payments thus demanded *colore officii* are regarded by the law as being made under duress, p 276.'

The present case is not one in which the plaintiffs seek to recover from an official. But no doubt an action could be brought against the State of New South Wales for the recovery of money which had been exacted under colour of his office by a servant of the Crown and paid into the State revenue, for petition of right was available in such circumstances: see *Brocklebank Ltd v The King* (1925). And, in my view, the State of New South Wales was properly made the defendant in this action, for money paid for permits was paid to persons who took it merely as the agents of the Crown to receive it and pay it into the Treasury. In these circumstances the servants of the Crown who were concerned could not, I think, properly be sued. (*Barton v Commissioner for Motor Transport* (1957); *Atlee v Backhouse* (1838); *Ochberg v Commissioner of Stamp Duties* (1943); cf *Marshal Shipping Co v Board of Trade* (1923).)

It cannot be said that here any official extorted or even demanded money by colour of his office. The charges imposed by a statute, which this court had declared to be valid but which it later transpired was unconstitutional, were simply collected by servants of the Crown in the course of their duty. The plaintiffs when they paid were not ignorant of the position. They knew their rights so far as they could be known before the Privy Council had spoken. They were not deluded or imposed on. They protested throughout that the charges were unlawful. All this is, I think, foreign to the concept of a payment exacted *colore officii*.

The plaintiffs are not to fail on their action, however, because the pleader has used inappropriate words to formulate their claim. But it is not just a matter of a wrong Latin label. The importance of the matter is that the plaintiffs cannot succeed simply because of the superior position of the defendant. They must go further and establish that there was, in a legal sense, compulsion by something actually done or threatened, something beyond the implication of duress arising from a demand by persons in authority, which suffices in a true *colore officii* case ...

Questions

On the basis of the principal case, to what unlawful exactions does the *colore officii* rule apply? Did the rule apply to the unconstitutional licence fees in this case? Why, or why not?

Bell Bros Pty Ltd v Shire of Serpentine-Jarrahdale (1969) 121 CLR 137
High Court of Australia

The bylaws of the defendant council prohibited quarrying activities in the council's district without a licence, and stipulated a licence fee. A person committing a breach of the bylaws was liable to a penalty not exceeding £20. The plaintiff made various payments to the council in order to secure a quarrying licence. The High Court decided in separate litigation that the council had no authority to charge fees for licences under the bylaws, and the plaintiff commenced proceedings to recover the licence fees on the basis, *inter alia*, that they were unlawfully demanded under colour of office. Both parties at all material times believed the council had the authority to charge the licence fee.

McTiernan J: ... [141] I am of opinion that it is enough in a case such as the present for the plaintiffs to show the relationship of the parties. This case falls squarely within the *dictum* of Abbott CJ in *Morgan v Palmer* (1824):

> It has been well argued that the payment having been voluntary, it cannot be recovered back in an action for money had and received. I agree that such a consequence would have followed had the parties been on equal terms. But if one party has the power of saying to the other, 'That which you require shall not be done except upon the conditions which I choose to impose', no person can contend that they stand upon anything like an equal footing,

to which Bayley J added:

> I entirely agree with the observations of my Lord Chief Justice, which shew, that the payment was by no means voluntary.

Lowe J said in *Deacon v Transport Regulation Board* (1958), p 460:

> Nor do I think that the statement attributed to Platt and Martin BB, in the headnote to *Steele v Williams* (1853) that money paid under illegal demand *colore officii* can never be voluntary is universally true. It finds a proper application where the payer is denied a right except on payment of the money demanded, as for instance in *Brocklebank Ltd v The King* (1925) and *Sargood Bros v The Commonwealth* (1910).

Those statements point to the feature which distinguishes this case from *Mason v The State of New South Wales* (1959).

The respondent shire in this case was validly empowered to license persons wishing to quarry. It was only the payments bylaw which was invalid.

In *Mason's* case (1959) however both the licensing and the payments enactments were held to be invalid as contrary to s 92 of the Constitution. A person could therefore legally disregard both enactments. In this case the appellants could not legally disregard the licensing bylaw. Applying the words of Lowe J the payments made to secure a licence in this case can never in law be voluntary and it is therefore irrelevant to attempt to show lack of protest, or acquiescence ...

Kitto J: ... [144] [The applicant] sued the respondent for moneys had and received, basing its claim upon alternative propositions: (1) that the payments had been unlawfully exacted by the respondent *colore officii;* and (2) that they had been paid by the applicant and received by the respondent under a mutual mistake of law and were recoverable by force of s 23 of the Law Reform (Property, Perpetuities and Succession) Act 1962 (WA). The trial judge and the full court rejected the claim, and the applicant now seeks special leave to appeal from the full court's judgment.

I need not discuss the second of the applicant's propositions, for in my opinion the claim should have succeeded upon the first. The contrary opinion of the learned judges of the Supreme Court resulted from a reading of the judgments delivered in this court in *Mason v The State of New South Wales* (1959) as involving that money which has been paid in order to obtain a licence which the payer needed, and which the recipient had power to grant but no authority to charge for, is not recoverable unless a conclusion be drawn from additional circumstances that the payment was involuntary. But the case was not of that kind, and the judgments do not support the proposition. A State, under legislation passed by its parliament, had taken fees for permits to carry goods on inter-state journeys, but the purported prohibition of carrying goods on such journeys without a permit was constitutionally invalid and consequently persons who had paid fees for permits could not rest their case for recovery on the ground that a need to obtain permits to make desired journeys had rendered payments of fees for such permits involuntary. It was argued against them that [145] having in truth no need of permits they yet had paid the fees, freely choosing to do so rather than to proceed on their inter-state journeys and resist any prosecution for not having permits. To answer that argument it was necessary for them to show circumstances of compulsion, and in order to do so they pointed to the existence of statutory provisions giving power to officials of the State to seize the vehicles of persons acting in breach of the purported prohibition, and to the conduct of such officials thereunder. The court considered that in the circumstances it was reasonable for them to apprehend, as they did, that seizure of their vehicles would follow any exercise of the right to make their journeys without permits, and the conclusion followed that they had not been on equal terms with the State, and that for that reason the payments had not been voluntary and were recoverable.

In a passage in the judgment of Dixon CJ which was relied upon in the Supreme Court in the present case, his Honour, p 117, accepted modern English authority as saying that 'moneys paid to the Crown as and for taxes cannot be recovered from the Crown upon its turning out that the moneys were not exigible notwithstanding that they were demanded by the Crown, unless the circumstances were such that they would be recoverable as between subject and subject, eg, as involuntary payments or payments made under a mistake of fact'. This may be agreed; and it follows that where moneys have been paid to the Crown, or to a body such as the respondent, for licences to pursue a course of conduct which is lawful without a licence, it is necessary to investigate the case further in order to ascertain whether or not there have been circumstances, eg, of compulsion or mistake, which give rise to a right of recovery. But where a person or body having power to grant or withhold a permission for another to pursue a course which he cannot lawfully pursue without that permission has used the power in order to exact a payment which he or it is not authorised to exact, the case is entirely different. The law holds that the involuntariness of the payment is established, because the parties were not on equal terms. As Abbott CJ said in *Morgan v Palmer* (1824):

> [I]f one party has the power of saying to the other, 'That which you require shall not be done except upon the conditions which I choose to impose', no person can contend that they stand upon anything like an equal footing.

[146] In the same case Littledale J said:

> I am of opinion that this defendant has no right to retain the money which was paid to him by the plaintiff. He had not any legal authority to make the charge ... The granting a licence was a public duty imposed by law, and for the execution of that he had no right to any payment ... Here, the plaintiff was merely passive, and submitted to pay the sum claimed, as he could not otherwise procure his licence.

These quotations exactly fit a case like the present. Portions of them were quoted with approval in *Brocklebank Ltd v The King* (1925), and that case is a clear authority in favour of the applicant here. The bylaws validly prohibited the applicant while unlicensed from carrying out the excavation work which it wished to carry out, and entrusted the respondent with a power to grant licences. The respondent, not being of opinion that the licences the applicant needed should be refused, and therefore being under a duty to grant them, demanded without lawful authority (though in good faith) that the applicant pay fees for the licences. The applicant, it is true, paid the fees without protest; but it had no real alternative, for save by submitting to the respondent's terms it could not get the licences and therefore could not lawfully proceed with its excavations. In my opinion this fact makes the case truly one of money exacted *colore officii*, and the money is recoverable. To adapt the language of Martin B in *Steele v Williams* (1853), it matters not whether the money was paid before or after the licences were granted. As Isaacs J said in *Sargood Bros v The Commonwealth* (1910):

> The right to recovery after a demand *colore officii* rests upon the assumption that the position occupied by the defendant creates virtual compulsion, where it conveys to the person paying the knowledge or belief that he has no means of escape from payment strictly so called if he wishes to avert injury to or deprivation of some right to which he is entitled without such payment ... The essence of the statement is the inability to obtain, otherwise than by absolute payment, those services which the recipient is bound to render without it.

In my opinion special leave to appeal should be granted and the appeal allowed.

Windeyer J: [147] I need not repeat the facts. As I see them they establish without any doubt that the moneys which the applicant paid to the shire as 'royalties' were paid as a result of extortion, as that word is used in this branch of the law. That conclusion follows, I consider, from the judgments in *Mason's* case (1959). Certainly I can see nothing in that case that should lead to any other conclusion. For myself I said there that 'a plaintiff's right to recover in an action for money had and received such as this depends upon proof that the moneys were paid by him involuntarily, that is, as the result of some extortion, coercion or compulsion in the legal sense. Exactions *colore officii* are a form of extortion'. It seemed to me that the payments there in question had not been made simply as the result of demands made *colore officii* in the strict sense. Rather they were made, I thought, as the result of fears based on the seeming authority of a statute. That case thus fell within the genus extortion by reason of coercion, not simply because it was an unlawful or excessive demand made by an official under colour of his office. The facts of this case are different. It resembles in essence a claim to recover moneys paid *colore officii*. Adopting, and adapting, Lord Kenyon's remark in *Cartwright v Rowley* (1799), concerning one of the early cases of this kind: the applicant here could not do without the licence 'so that the money was paid through necessity and the urgency of the case'. A long list of cases in which, before and after *Steele v Williams* (1853), the same principle was applied may be found in Messrs Goff and Jones's *The Law of Restitution*, 1966, p 153. This case falls squarely within that class. The case of *Hooper v Exeter Corporation* (1887) is a useful analogy.

I hesitate to use the phrase *colore officii* of this case, but only because that term was originally used to describe demands by an individual holder of an office rather than extortion by corporations. But the principle is the same. The words which express it are not material; and to question them may be pedantic since Lord Macmillan recognised the use of the phrase *colore officii* in *R & W Paul Ltd v Wheat Commission* (1937), p 161, of the defendant there, a body corporate ...

[Barwick CJ and Menzies J agreed with Kitto J.]

Commentary

Peter Birks has pointed out that the scope given to the *colore officii* principle in *Mason v New South Wales* and the principal case leads to absurd results. The absurdity is that if the whole enactment is *ultra vires*, actual compulsion must be established, but on the other hand if the enactment is within power but an excessive fee is charged, compulsion will be presumed (via the operation of the *colore officii* principle).[21] The current state of the law, where the greater the invalidity, the more that needs to be proved, is clearly unsatisfactory.

ULTRA VIRES DEMAND

Nature and ambit of the *ultra vires* demand ground of recovery

In the following case of *Woolwich Equitable Building Society v Inland Revenue Commissioners* (1993) the House of Lords recognised that a payment of an invalid tax or other levy pursuant to a demand by a public authority is *prima facie* recoverable. This ground of recovery is called '*ultra vires* demand' or simply the '*Woolwich* principle', and is complete without proof of mistake or duress.

---

21 Birks, 'Restitution from public authorities' (1980) 33 CLP 191, pp 196–97.

Woolwich Equitable Building Society v Inland Revenue Commissioners
[1993] 1 AC 70 House of Lords

Acting under the Income Tax (Building Societies) Regulations 1986, the revenue demanded payment by the plaintiff building society ('Woolwich') of nearly £57 million for payment of tax on interest and dividends paid to investors over a period of 5 months. Woolwich disputed the validity of the Regulations but, concerned about adverse publicity and possible liability to pay interest at a penal rate, ultimately paid in instalments the amount demanded. The payments were made without prejudice to Woolwich's rights. Woolwich applied for judicial review of the Regulations and commenced proceedings to recover the amounts paid as money had and received, together with interest. The trial judge who heard the judicial review proceedings held that the Regulations were *ultra vires* and void and the revenue repaid the capital sum with interest from the date of this judgment. However it refused to pay any interest in respect of the period between the dates of payment of the money and the date of judgment and Woolwich commenced proceedings to recover interest for this period, amounting to approximately £6.73 million. The success of this claim depended upon whether Woolwich acquired a *prima facie* right to recover back the unlawful taxes immediately upon payment of them.

Lord Keith of Kinkel (dissenting): ... [149] The primary submission for Woolwich was that a subject who makes a payment in response to an unlawful demand for tax, or any similar demand, at once acquires a right to recover the amount so paid as money had and received to the subject's use ...

[154] The argument for Woolwich starts with the general principle enunciated by Lord Wright in *Fibrosa Spolka Akcyjna v Fairbairn Lawson Combe Barbour Ltd* (1943), p 61:

> The claim was for money paid for a consideration which had failed. It is clear that any civilised system of law is bound to provide remedies for cases of what has been called unjust enrichment or unjust benefit, that is to prevent a man from retaining the money of or some benefit derived from another which it is against conscience that he should keep. Such remedies in English law are generically different from remedies in contract or in tort, and are now recognised to fall within a third category of the common law which has been called quasi-contract or restitution.

This general principle has, however, been circumscribed in various ways by decided cases, not least by the rule that money paid under a mistake of law is not recoverable, a rule which, though heavily criticised in academic writings and elsewhere, is in my opinion too deeply embedded in English jurisprudence to be uprooted judicially. There is a considerable tract of authority, both in England and in other jurisdictions, which must be examined in order to ascertain whether or not the circumstances of the present case fall within Lord Wright's principle.

[Lord Keith reviewed the United Kingdom authorities, canvassed below in Lord Goff's judgment, and continued at p 160:]

The foregoing review of the native authorities satisfies me that they afford no support for Woolwich's major proposition. The principle to be derived from them, in my opinion, is that payments not lawfully due cannot be recovered unless they were made as a result of some improper form of pressure. Such pressure may take the form of duress, as in *Maskell v Horner* (1915). It may alternatively take the form of withholding or threatening to withhold the performance of some public duty or the rendering of some public service unless a payment is [161] made which is not lawfully due or is greater than that which is lawfully due, as was the position in the *colore officii* cases. The mere fact that the payment has been made in response to a demand by a public authority does not emerge in any of the cases as constituting or forming part of the *ratio decidendi*. Many of the cases appear to turn on a consideration of whether the payment was voluntary or involuntary. In my opinion that simply involves that the payment was voluntary if no improper pressure was brought to bear, and involuntary if it was. In the present case no pressure to pay was put on Woolwich by the revenue. Woolwich paid because it calculated that it was in its commercial interest to do so. It could have resisted payment, and the revenue had no means other than the taking of legal proceedings which it might have used to enforce payment. The threat of legal proceedings is not improper pressure. There was no improper pressure by the revenue and in particular there was no duress.

To give effect to Woolwich's proposition would, in my opinion, amount to a very far-reaching exercise of judicial legislation. That would be particularly inappropriate having regard to the considerable number of instances which exist of parliament having legislated in various fields to define the circumstances under which payments of tax not lawfully due may be recovered, and also in what situations and on what terms interest on overpayments of tax may be paid ... It seems to me that formulation of the precise grounds on which overpayments of tax ought to be recoverable and of any exceptions to the right of recovery, may involve nice considerations of policy which are properly the province of parliament and are not suitable for consideration by the courts. In this connection the question of possible disruption of public finances must obviously be a very material one. Then it is noticeable that existing legislation is restrictive of the extent to which interest on overpaid tax (described as 'repayment supplement') may be recovered. A general right of recovery of overpaid tax could not incorporate any such restriction.

I would add that although in the course of argument some distinction was sought to be drawn between overpayment of tax under regulations later shown to be *ultra vires* and overpayment due to the erroneous interpretation of a statute, no such distinction can, in my view, properly be drawn. The distinction had particular reference to Art 4 of the [162] Bill of Rights (1688),[22] but I do not consider that this article has any relevance to the present case, being concerned, as it was, with the denial of the right of the executive to levy taxes without the consent of parliament.

[Lord Keith reviewed the Commonwealth authorities and concluded that they did not persuade him to adopt a contrary view.]

Lord Goff of Chieveley: ... [163] There can be no doubt that this appeal is one of considerable importance. It is certainly of importance to both parties – to the revenue, which is concerned to maintain the traditional position under which the repayment of overpaid tax is essentially a matter for its own discretion; and to Woolwich, which adopted a courageous and independent stance about the lawfulness of the underlying regulations, and now adopts a similar stance about

---

22   1 Will & Mary, sess 2, c 2.

the obligation of the revenue to repay tax exacted without lawful authority. In addition, of course, there is a substantial sum of money at stake. But the appeal is also of importance for the future of the law of restitution, since the decision of your Lordships' House could have a profound effect on the structure of this part of our law. It is a reflection of this fact that there have been cited to your Lordships not only the full range of English authorities, and also authorities from Commonwealth countries and the United States of America, but in addition a number of academic works of considerable importance. These include a most valuable consultation paper (Law Com No 120) published last year by the Law Commission, entitled *Restitution of Payments Made Under a Mistake of Law*, for which we owe much to Mr Jack Beatson and also, I understand, to Dr Sue Arrowsmith; and a series of articles by academic lawyers of distinction working in the field of restitution. I shall be referring to this academic material in due course. But I wish to record at once that, in [164] my opinion, it is of such importance that it has a powerful bearing on the consideration by your Lordships of the central question in the case.

My first task must be to review the relevant authorities. I am very conscious, however, that this task has already been performed in considerable detail, not only by Ralph Gibson and Glidewell LJJ in the Court of Appeal, but also by my noble and learned friends, Lord Keith of Kinkel and Lord Jauncey of Tullichettle. Rather than once again review the authorities in chronological order, therefore, I propose to encapsulate their effect in a number of propositions which can, I believe, be so stated as to reflect the law as it is presently understood with a reasonable degree of accuracy. The law as so stated has, I think, been so understood for most of this century, at least at the level of the Court of Appeal; but it has been the subject of increasing criticism by academic lawyers, and has been departed from in significant respects in some Commonwealth countries, both by legislation and by judicial development of the law. A central question in the present case is whether it is open to your Lordships' House to follow their judicial brethren overseas down the road of development of the law; and, if so, whether it would be appropriate to do so, and which is the precise path which it would then be appropriate to choose. But the answer to these fundamental questions must follow a review of the law as understood at present, which I would express in the following propositions.

Whereas money paid under a mistake of fact is generally recoverable, as a general rule money is not recoverable on the ground that it was paid under a mistake of law. This principle was established in *Bilbie v Lumley* (1802). It has, however, been the subject of much criticism, which has grown substantially during the second half of the present century. The principle has been adopted in most, if not all, Commonwealth countries; though in some it has now been modified or abandoned, either by statute or by judicial action. No such principle applies in civil law countries, and its adoption by the common law has been criticised by comparative lawyers as unnecessary and anomalous. This topic is the subject of the Consultation Paper No 120 published by the Law Commission last year, in which serious criticisms of the rule of non-recovery are rehearsed and developed, and proposals for its abolition are put forward for discussion.

But money paid under compulsion may be recoverable. In particular:

(a) Money paid as a result of actual or threatened duress to the person, or actual or threatened seizure of a person's goods, is recoverable. For an example of the latter, see *Maskell v Horner* (1915). Since these forms of compulsion are not directly relevant for present purposes, it is unnecessary to elaborate them; but I think it pertinent to observe that the concept of duress has in recent years been expanded to embrace economic duress.

(b) Money paid to a person in a public or quasi-public position to obtain the performance by him of a duty which he is bound to perform for nothing or for less than the sum demanded by him is recoverable to the extent that he is not entitled to it. Such payments are often described as having been demanded *colore officii*. There is much abstruse learning on the subject (see, in particular, the illuminating [165] discussion by Windeyer J in *Mason v The State of New South Wales* (1959), pp 139–42), but for present purposes it is not, I think, necessary for us to concern ourselves with this point of classification. Examples of influential early cases are *Morgan v Palmer* (1824) and *Steele v Williams* (1853); a later example of some significance is *TJ Brocklebank Ltd v R* (1925).

(c) Money paid to a person for the performance of a statutory duty, which he is bound to perform for a sum less than that charged by him, is also recoverable to the extent of the overcharge. A leading example of such a case is *Great Western Rly Co v Sutton* (1869); for a more recent Scottish case, also the subject of an appeal to this House, see *South of Scotland Electricity Board v British Oxygen Co Ltd* (1959).

(d) In cases of compulsion, a threat which constitutes the compulsion may be expressed or implied, a point perhaps overlooked in *Twyford v Manchester Corp* (1946).

(e) I would not think it right, especially bearing in mind the development of the concept of economic duress, to regard the categories of compulsion for present purposes as closed.

Where a sum has been paid which is not due, but it has not been paid under a mistake of fact or under compulsion ... it is generally not recoverable. Such a payment has often been called a voluntary payment. In particular, a payment is regarded as a voluntary payment and so as irrecoverable in the following circumstances:

The money has been paid under a mistake of law. See, eg, *Slater v Burnley Corp* (1888), and *National Pari-Mutuel Association Ltd v R* (1930).

The payer has the opportunity of contesting his liability in proceedings, but instead gives way and pays: see, eg, *Henderson v Folkestone Waterworks Co* (1885), and *Sargood Bros v Commonwealth* (1910), especially *per* Isaacs J (p 301). So where money has been paid under pressure of actual or threatened legal proceedings for its recovery, the payer cannot say that for that reason the money has been paid under compulsion and is therefore recoverable by him. If he chooses to give way and pay, rather than obtain the decision of the court on the question whether the money is due, his payment is regarded as voluntary and so is not recoverable: see, eg, *William Whiteley Ltd v R* (1909).

The money has otherwise been paid in such circumstances that the payment was made to close the transaction. Such would obviously be so in the case of a binding compromise; but even where there is no consideration for the payment, it may have been made to close the transaction and so be irrecoverable. Such a payment has been treated as a gift: see *Maskell v Horner* (1915) *per* Lord Reading CJ.

A payment may be made on such terms that it has been agreed, expressly or impliedly, by the recipient that, if it shall prove not to have been due, it will be repaid by him. In that event, of course, the money will be repayable. Such was held to be the case in *Sebel Products Ltd v Customs and Excise Comrs* (1949) (although the legal [166] basis on which Vaisey J there inferred the existence of such an agreement may be open to criticism). On the other hand, the mere fact that money is paid under protest will not give rise of itself to the inference of such an agreement; though it may form part of the evidence from which it may be inferred that the payee did not intend to close the transaction: see *Maskell v Horner* (1915) *per* Lord Reading CJ.

The principles which I have just stated had come to be broadly accepted, at the level of the Court of Appeal, at least by the early part of this century. But a formidable argument has been developed in recent years by leading academic lawyers that this stream of authority should be the subject of reinterpretation to reveal a different line of thought pointing to the conclusion that money paid to a public authority pursuant to an *ultra vires* demand should be repayable, without the necessity of establishing compulsion, on the simple ground that there was no consideration for the payment. I refer in particular to the powerful essay by Professor Peter Birks[23] entitled 'Restitution from the executive: a tercentenary footnote to the Bill of Rights'. I have little doubt that this essay by Professor Birks, which was foreshadowed by an influential lecture delivered by Professor WR Cornish in Kuala Lumpur in 1986 (the first Sultan Azlan Shah lecture),[24] provided the main inspiration for the argument of Woolwich, and the judgments of the majority of the Court of Appeal, in the present case.

I have a strong presentiment that, had the opportunity arisen, Lord Mansfield would have seized it to establish the law in this form. His broad culture, his knowledge and understanding at Roman law, his extraordinary gift for cutting through technicality to perceive and define principle, would surely have drawn him towards this result. Mr Gardiner, for Woolwich, relied on *Campbell v Hall* (1774) as authority that he did in fact reach that very conclusion. But that case was the subject of research by Mr Glick and his team [for the revenue], and was revealed (from the reports in Lofft 655 and in 20 St Tr 239) to be a *cause célèbre* in which the great issue (of immense public interest) related to the power to levy taxes in the island of Grenada following its capture from the French king, it being accepted by the Crown without argument that the relevant taxes, if not duly levied, must be repaid. Lord Mansfield's judgment in the case, adverse to the Crown, became known as the Magna Carta of the Colonies. The fact that the basis of recovery was not in issue, and indeed was overshadowed by the great question in the case, must detract from its importance in the present context; even so, the simple fact remains that recovery was stated to be founded on absence of consideration for the payment. Furthermore there are other cases in the late 18th and early 19th centuries, of which *Dew v Parsons* (1819) is a significant example, which supports this approach.

Later cases in the 19th century upon which Professor Birks places much reliance are *Steele v Williams* (1853), and *Hooper v Exeter Corp* (1887). In *Steele v Williams*, the

---

23 In Finn (ed), *Essays on Restitution*, 1990, pp 164–265.
24 (1987) 14 Jo Malaysian and Comparative Law 41.

judgment of Martin B was certainly on the basis that the money, having been the [167] subject of an *ultra vires* demand by a public officer, was as such recoverable. That approach seems also to have provided considerable attraction for Parke B; but although the point was left open by him, the case was decided by the majority (Parke and Platt BB) on the ground of compulsion. Both of them treated the case as one in which there was an implied threat by the defendant to deprive the plaintiff's clerk of his right to take extracts from the parish register for no charge; and both appear to have concluded that, in the circumstances, although that threat was made before the plaintiff's clerk obtained the extracts he needed, nevertheless it was causative of the payment which was therefore recoverable on the ground of compulsion. In *Hooper v Exeter Corp* Professor Birks is perhaps on stronger ground, although the basis on which the court proceeded is not altogether clear. The plaintiff sought to recover dues paid by him for landing stone for which, unknown to him, he was not liable because the stone was covered by an exemption. It was argued on his behalf that the payment was not voluntary, citing *Morgan v Palmer* (a case of compulsion). Reliance was also placed on the power of absolute and immediate distress in the statute. The court accepted the plaintiff's argument. Both Lord Coleridge CJ and Smith J relied on *Morgan v Palmer*; Smith J also invoked *Steele v Williams* without, however, referring to the judgment of Martin B. Neither referred to the power of immediate distress. The case, brief and obscure though it is, might well have provided a basis on which judges could later have built to develop a principle that money demanded *ultra vires* by a public authority was *prima facie* recoverable.

Professor Birks also places reliance on *Queens of the River Steamship Co Ltd v River Thames Conservators* (1899), and an *obiter dictum* of Atkin LJ in *AG v Wilts United Dairies Ltd* (1921). The former case, so far as it goes, is undoubtedly consistent with his thesis; but it is very briefly reported, without any indication of the arguments advanced or cases cited, and the conclusion is encapsulated in one brief sentence. The *dictum* of Atkin LJ is to the effect that such a payment is, if paid under protest, recoverable on the simple ground that it was a sum received by the public authority to the use of the citizen. However, the subsequent decision of the Court of Appeal in *TJ Brocklebank Ltd v R* (1925) shows that, in circumstances similar to those of the *Wilts United Dairies* case, recovery could be, and indeed there was, founded on compulsion and not on the simple fact that the money was paid pursuant to an *ultra vires* demand (see *per* Bankes LJ) (accepting the opinion of the trial judge, Avory J) *per* Scrutton LJ (p 67), and *per* Sargant LJ (p 72). So the question of the soundness of Atkins LJ's *dictum* did not arise for decision in that case. Even so, a similar approach to that of Atkin LJ is to be found in an *obiter dictum* of Dixon CJ in *Mason v The State of New South Wales* (1959), which was to the effect that he had not been able completely to reconcile himself to the view that, if the weight of a *de facto* governmental authority manifested in a money demand, the money belonged to the Crown [168] unless the payment was made under compulsion.

In all the circumstances, it is difficult to avoid the conclusion that in this country, at the level of the Court of Appeal (see, in particular, the decisions of that court in *T & J Brocklebank Ltd v R* and *National Pari-Mutuel Association Ltd v R*), the law had settled down in the form which I have indicated. I have little doubt that a major force in the moulding of the law in this form is to be found in the practitioners' text books of the time, notably *Bullen and Leake's Precedents of Pleading*, 3rd edn, 1868, p 50, and *Leake's Law of Contracts*, 5th edn, p 61; we can see this reflected in the form of the arguments advanced in the cases, and the manner in which the court reacted to submissions by counsel challenging the accepted view. I fear that the courts sorely missed assistance from academic lawyers specialising in this branch of the law; but the law faculties in our universities were only beginning to be established towards the end of the 19th century. It can, however, be said that the principle of justice, embodied in Martin B's judgment in *Steele v Williams* and perhaps also in *Hooper v Exeter Corporation*, and expressed in the *dicta* of Lord Atkin and Sir Owen Dixon, still calls for attention; and the central question in the present case is whether your Lordships' House, deriving their inspiration from the example of those two great judges, should rekindle that fading flame and reformulate the law in accordance with that principle. I am satisfied that, on the authorities, it is open to your Lordships' House to take that step. The crucial question is whether it is appropriate for your Lordships to do so ...

[171] I now turn to the submission of Woolwich that your Lordships' House should, despite the authorities to which I have referred, reformulate the law so as to establish that the subject who makes a payment in response to an unlawful demand of tax acquires forthwith a *prima facie* right in restitution to the repayment of the money. This is the real point which lies at the heart of the present appeal; in a sense everything which I have said so far has done no more than set the stage for its consideration.

The justice underlying Woolwich's submission is, I consider, plain to see. Take the present case. The revenue has made an unlawful demand for tax. The taxpayer is convinced that the demand is unlawful, and has to decide what to do. It is faced with the revenue, armed with the coercive power of the State, including what is in practice a power to charge interest which is penal in its effect. In addition, being a reputable society which alone among building societies is challenging the lawfulness of the demand, it understandably fears damage to its reputation if it does not pay. So it decides to pay first, asserting that it will challenge the lawfulness of the demand in litigation. Now, [172] Woolwich having won that litigation, the revenue asserts that it was never under any obligation to repay the money, and that it in fact repaid it only as a matter of grace. There being no applicable statute to regulate the position, the revenue has to maintain this position at common law.

Stated in this stark form, the revenue's position appears to me, as a matter of common justice, to be unsustainable; and the injustice is rendered worse by the fact that it involves, as Nolan J pointed out, the revenue having the benefit of a massive interest free loan as the fruit of its unlawful action. I turn then from the particular to the general. Take any tax or duty paid by the citizen pursuant to an unlawful demand. Common justice seems to require that tax to be repaid, unless special circumstances or some principle of policy require otherwise; *prima facie*, the taxpayer should be entitled to repayment as of right.

To the simple call of justice, there are a number of possible objections. The first is to be found in the structure of our law of restitution, as it developed during the 19th and early 20th centuries. That law might have developed so as to recognise a *condictio indebiti* – an action for the recovery of money on the ground that it was not due. But it did not do so. Instead, as we have seen, there developed common law actions for the recovery of money paid under a mistake of fact, and under certain forms of compulsion. What is now being sought is, in a sense, a reversal of that development, in a particular type of case; and it is said that it is too late to take that step. To that objection, however, there are two answers. The first is that the retention by the state of taxes unlawfully exacted is particularly obnoxious, because it is one of the most fundamental principles of our law – enshrined in a famous constitutional document, the Bill of Rights (1688) – that taxes should not be levied without the authority of parliament; and full effect can only be given to that principle if the return of taxes exacted under an unlawful demand can be enforced as a matter of right. The second is that, when the revenue makes a demand for tax, that demand is implicitly backed by the coercive powers of the state and may well entail (as in the present case) unpleasant economic and social consequences if the taxpayer does not pay. In any event, it seems strange to penalise the good citizen, whose natural instinct is to trust the revenue and pay taxes when they are demanded of him. The force of this answer is recognised in a much quoted passage from the judgment of Holmes J in *Atchison Topeka & Santa Fe Rly Co v O'Connor* (1912), when he said:

> ... when, as is common, the State has a more summary remedy, such as distress, and the party indicates by protest that he is yielding to what he cannot prevent, courts sometimes perhaps have been a little too slow to recognise the implied duress under which payment is made. But even if the State is driven to an action, if at the same time the citizen is put at a serious disadvantage in the assertion of his legal, in this case of his constitutional, rights, by defence in the suit, justice may require that he should be at liberty to avoid those [173] disadvantages by paying promptly and bringing suit on his side. He is entitled to assert his supposed right on reasonably equal terms.

This particular answer might, however, point at first sight to a development of the common law concept of compulsion, rather than recognition of the broad principle of justice for which Woolwich contends. This was what in fact occurred in the leading Australian case of *Mason v The State of New South Wales* (1959). It is impossible to summarise the effect of that complicated case in a few lines, but in practical terms the High Court of Australia found duress to exist in the possibility that the state might seize the plaintiff's property. A similar tendency to expand the concept of compulsion is to be discovered in the majority judgment of the Supreme Court of Canada in *Eadie v Township of Brantford* (1967) (though events of a more dramatic character have since occurred in that jurisdiction, to which I will refer in a moment). This type of approach has also been advocated by Mr Andrew Burrows in his interesting essay entitled 'Public authorities, *ultra vires* and restitution'.[25] We may expect that in any event the common law principles of compulsion, and indeed of mistake, will continue to develop in the future. But the difficulty with this approach for the present case is that Woolwich was in reality suffering from no mistake at all, so much so that it was prepared to back its conviction that the revenue was acting *ultra vires* by risking a very substantial amount of money in legal costs in establishing that fact; and, since the possibility of distraint by the revenue was very remote, the concept of compulsion would have to be stretched to the utmost to embrace the circumstances of such a case as this. It is for this reason that Woolwich's alternative claim founded on compulsion did not loom large in the argument, and is difficult to sustain. In the end, logic

---

25   See *Essays on the Law of Restitution*, 1991, pp 39ff.

appears to demand that the right of recovery should require neither mistake nor compulsion, and that the simple fact that the tax was exacted unlawfully should *prima facie* be enough to require its repayment.

There is, however, a second objection to the recognition of such a right of recovery. This is that for your Lordships' House to recognise such a principle would overstep the boundary which we traditionally set for ourselves, separating the legitimate development of the law by the judges from legislation. It was strongly urged by Mr Glick, in his powerful argument for the revenue, that we would indeed be trespassing beyond that boundary if we were to accept the argument of Woolwich. I feel bound however to say that, although I am well aware of the existence of the boundary, I am never quite sure where to find it. Its position seems to vary from case to case. Indeed, if it were to be as firmly and clearly drawn as some of our mentors would wish, I cannot help feeling that a number of leading cases in your Lordships' House would never have been decided the way they were. For example, the minority view would have prevailed in *Donoghue v Stevenson* (1932); our modern law of judicial review would have never developed from its old, ineffectual, origins; and Mareva injunctions would never have seen the light of day. Much seems to depend upon [174] the circumstances of the particular case. In the present case Mr Glick [for the revenue] was fully entitled to, and did, point to practical considerations to reinforce his argument. The first was that a case such as the present was so rare that it could not of itself call for a fundamental reformulation of the underlying principle – a point which I find unimpressive, when I consider that our task is essentially to do justice between the parties in the particular case before us. Second, however, he asserted that, if your Lordships' House were to accept Woolwich's argument, it would be impossible for us to set the appropriate limits to the application of the principle. An unbridled right to recover overpaid taxes and duties subject only to the usual six year time bar was, he suggested, unacceptable in modern society. Some limits had to be set to such claims; and the selection of such limits, being essentially a matter of policy, was one which the legislature alone is equipped to make.

My reaction to this submission of Mr Glick is to confess (to some extent) and yet to avoid. I agree that there appears to be a widely held view that some limit has to be placed on the recovery of taxes paid pursuant to an *ultra vires* demand. I would go further and accept that the armoury of common law defences, such as those which prevent recovery of money paid under a binding compromise or to avoid a threat of litigation, may be either inapposite or inadequate for the purpose; because it is possible to envisage, especially in modern taxation law which tends to be excessively complex, circumstances in which some very substantial sum of money may be held to have been exacted *ultra vires* from a very large number of taxpayers. It may well therefore be necessary to have recourse to other defences, such as for example short time limits within which such claims have to be advanced. An instructive example of this approach is to be found in German law, in which we find a general right of recovery which is subject to the principle that an administrative act is, even if in fact unlawful, treated as legally effective unless and until it is cancelled, either by the authority itself or by an administrative court. Furthermore a citizen can only enforce the cancellation by making a formal objection within one month of notification; and if that objection is rejected by the authority, the citizen must take legal action within another month. In addition, one citizen cannot benefit from the successful formal objection of another citizen; he must object in due time himself. Such draconian time limits as these may be too strong medicine for our taste; but the example of a general right of recovery subject to strict time limits imposed as a matter of policy is instructive for us as we seek to solve the problem in the present case.

At this stage of the argument, I find it helpful to turn to recent developments in Canada. First, in a notable dissenting judgment (with which Laskin CJC concurred) in *Nepean Hydro Electric Commission of Township of Nepean v Ontario Hydro* (1982), Dickson J subjected the rule against recovery of money paid under a mistake of law to a devastating analysis and concluded that the rule should be rejected. His preferred solution was that, as in cases of mistake of fact, money paid under a mistake of law should be recoverable if it would be unjust for the recipient to retain it. Next, in [175] the leading case of *Air Canada v British Columbia* (1989), the question arose whether money in the form of taxes paid under a statute held to be *ultra vires* was recoverable. It is impossible for me, for reasons of space, to do more than summarise the most relevant parts of the judgments of the Supreme Court of Canada. Of the seven judges who heard the appeal, four thought it necessary to consider whether the taxes paid were recoverable at common law. The leading judgment was delivered by La Forest J, with whom Lamer and L'Heureux-Dube JJ agreed. First, he decided (p 192) to follow Dickson J's lead, and to hold that the distinction between mistake of fact and mistake of law should play no part in the law of restitution. This did not, however, imply that recovery would follow in every case where a mistake had been shown to exist: 'If the defendant can show that the payment was made in settlement of an honest claim, or that he has changed his position as a result of the enrichment, then restitution will be denied.' However he went on to hold (p 193) that, where 'unconstitutional or *ultra vires* levies' are in issue, special considerations arose. These were twofold. First, if the plaintiff had passed on the relevant tax to others, the taxing authority could not be said to have been unjustly enriched at the plaintiff's expense, and he was not therefore entitled to recover. As La Forest J said (p 193): 'The law of restitution is not intended to provide windfalls to plaintiffs who have suffered no loss.' On that basis alone, he held that the plaintiff's claim in the case before the court must fail (pp 193–94). However he went on to hold that the claim failed on another ground, viz, that as a general rule there will, as a matter of policy, be no recovery of taxes paid pursuant to legislation which is unconstitutional or otherwise invalid. Basing himself on authority from the United States, La Forest J concluded that any other rule would at best be inefficient, and at worst could lead to financial chaos (pp 194–97). The rule against recovery should not, however, apply where a tax is exacted, not under unconstitutional legislation, but through a misapplication of the law. He added (p 198) that, in his opinion, if recovery in all cases is to be the general rule, then that was best achieved through the route of statutory reform.

Wilson J dissented. She did not think it necessary to consider whether the old rule baring recovery of money paid under mistake of law should be abolished, though had she thought it necessary to do so, she would have followed the approach of Dickson J. She considered (p 169) that money paid under unconstitutional legislation was generally recoverable:

> The taxpayer, assuming the validity of the statute as I believe it is entitled to do, considers itself obligated to pay. Citizens are expected to be law-abiding. They are expected to pay their taxes. Pay first and object later is the general

rule. The payments are made pursuant to a perceived obligation to pay which results from the combined presumption of constitutional validity of duly enacted legislation and the holding out of such validity by the legislature. In such circumstances I consider it quite unrealistic to expect the taxpayer to make its payments 'under protest'. Any taxpayer paying taxes exigible under a statute which it has no reason to [176] believe or suspect is other than valid should be viewed as having paid pursuant to the statutory obligation to do so.

Furthermore, she was unable to accept the view of La Forest J that the principle of recovery should be reversed for policy reasons. She spoke in forthright terms (p 169):

What is the policy that requires such a dramatic reversal of principle? Why should the individual taxpayer, as opposed to taxpayers as a whole, bear the burden of government's mistake? I would respectfully suggest that it is grossly unfair that X, who may not be (as in this case) a large corporate enterprise, should absorb the cost of government's unconstitutional act. If it is appropriate for the courts to adopt some kind of policy in order to protect government against itself (and I cannot say that the idea particularly appeals to me), it should be one that distributes the loss fairly across the public. The loss should not fall on the totally innocent taxpayer whose only fault is that it paid what the legislature improperly said was due.

She also rejected (p 169–70) the proposed defence of 'passing on'. Accordingly in her opinion the taxpayer should be entitled to succeed.

I cannot deny that I find the reasoning of Wilson J most attractive. Moreover I agree with her that, if there is to be a right to recovery in respect of taxes exacted unlawfully by the revenue, it is irrelevant to consider whether the old rule barring recovery of money paid under mistake of law should be abolished, for that rule can have no application where the remedy arises not from error on the part of the taxpayer, but from the unlawful nature of the demand by the revenue. Furthermore, like Wilson J, I very respectfully doubt the advisability of imposing special limits on recovery in the case of 'unconstitutional or *ultra vires* levies'. I shall revert a little later to the defence of passing on.

In all the circumstances, I do not consider that Mr Glick's argument, powerful though it is, is persuasive enough to deter me from recognising, in law, the force of the justice underlying *Woolwich's* case. Furthermore, there are particular reasons which impel me to that conclusion. The first is that this opportunity will never come again. If we do not take it now, it will be gone forever. The second is that I fear that, however compelling the principle of justice may be, it would never be sufficient to persuade a government to propose its legislative recognition by parliament; caution, otherwise known as the Treasury, would never allow this to happen. The third is that, turning Mr Glick's argument against him, the immediate practical impact of the recognition of the principle will be limited, for (unlike the present case) most cases will continue for the time being to be regulated by the various statutory regimes now in force. The fourth is that, if the principle is to be recognised, this is an almost ideal moment for that recognition to take place. This is because the Law Commission's Consultation Paper is now under active consideration, calling for a fundamental review of the law on this subject, including a fresh look at the various, often inconsistent, statutory regimes under which overpaid taxes and duties either may or must be repaid. The consultation may acquire a greater urgency and [177] sense of purpose if set against the background of a recognised right of recovery at common law. But in addition there is an immediate opportunity for the authorities concerned to reformulate, in collaboration with the Law Commission, the appropriate limits to recovery, on a coherent system of principles suitable for modern society, in terms which can (if it is thought right to do so) embrace the unusual circumstances of the present case. In this way, legislative bounds can be set to the common law principle, as Mr Glick insists that they should. Fifth, it is well established that, if the Crown pays money out of the consolidated fund without authority, such money is *ipso facto* recoverable if it can be traced (see *Auckland Harbour Board v R* (1924)). It is true that the claim in such a case can be distinguished as being proprietary in nature. But the comparison with the position of the citizen, on the law as it stands at present, is most unattractive ...

I would therefore hold that money paid by a citizen to a public authority in the form of taxes or other levies paid pursuant to an *ultra vires* demand by the authority is *prima facie* recoverable by the citizen as of right. As at present advised, I incline to the opinion that this principle should extend to embrace cases in which the tax or other levy has been wrongly exacted by the public authority not because the demand was *ultra vires* but for other reasons, for example because the authority has misconstrued a relevant statute or regulation. It is not, however, necessary to decide the point in the present case, and in any event cases of this kind are generally the subject of statutory regimes which legislate for the circumstances in which money so paid either must or may be repaid. Nor do I think it necessary to consider for the purposes of the present case to what extent the common law may provide the public authority with a defence to a claim for the repayment of money so paid; though for the reasons I have already given, I do not consider that the principle of recovery should be inapplicable simply because the citizen has paid the money under a mistake of law. It will be a matter for consideration whether the fact that the plaintiff has passed on the tax or levy so that the burden has fallen on another [178] should provide a defence to his claim. Although this is contemplated by the Court of Justice of the European Communities in *Amministrazione delle Finanze dello Stato v San Giorgio SA* (Case 199/82) (1983) it is evident from *Air Canada v British Columbia* that the point is not without its difficulties; and the availability of such a defence may depend on the nature of the tax or other levy. No doubt matters of this kind will in any event be the subject of consideration during the current consultations with the Law Commission ...

Lord Jauncey of Tullichettle (dissenting): ... [193] My Lords, I have no doubt that the weight of authority ... does not support the *Woolwich* principle. If this House were to apply such a principle it would involve going beyond what any of the authorities have decided, departing from such decisions as *Slater v Burnley Corporation*, *William Whiteley Ltd v The King* and *Twyford v Manchester Corporation* which have stood for many years and would involve making new law. For reasons to which I shall refer later I do not think that we should do that ...

Further support for the view that there does not exist a principle such as *Woolwich* contend for is to be found in statutory provisions for the recovery of imposts which should not have been paid. The Law Commission Consultation Paper (1991, Law Com No 120) 'Restitution of payments made under a mistake of law' sets out (paras 320–36, pp 74–83) a number of statutory provisions for the recovery of payments made to public authorities. These include such matters as value added tax, excise duty and car tax, income tax, corporation tax, capital gains tax, petroleum revenue tax, inheritance tax, stamp duty, social security contributions and community charges. I do not propose to refer to the various provisions in detail. If the *Woolwich* principle comprehends payments made under a mistake of law then such payments are also covered by the statutory provisions. If the principle does not comprehend such payments, as the majority of the Court of Appeal held to be the case, then there are other situations covered by the provisions which would also be within the ambit of the *Woolwich* principle. The importance of these statutory provisions appears to me to be that parliament has considered at various times and in various contexts the need for recovery of imposts paid but not due and has legislated in a manner which suggests that no such general principle as *Woolwich* contends for was thought to be in existence ...

[196] There is in theory a good deal to be said for the submission of Professor Birks in his *An Introduction to the Law of Restitution*, 1985, p 295, that a payer should be able to recover payments demanded *ultra vires* by a public authority on the sole ground that retention of such payment would infringe the principle of 'no taxation without parliament' enshrined in the Bill of Rights. However, it is clear that in practice some limitation would have to be imposed on any such principle. During the course of argument Mr Gardiner [for Woolwich] suggested certain alternative modifications to the *Woolwich* principle as initially enunciated by him. First and foremost he maintained that a mistake of law would be no defence to the application of the principle but as alternatives he submitted that the principle would be subject to the mistake of law defence or that the defence of mistake of law should be abrogated altogether. He also sought to draw a distinction between an unlawful demand made under an *ultra vires* instrument and one made under an *intra vires* instrument which was misconstrued or misapplied. A distinction which I consider to be without a difference. Public authorities are creatures of statute and can do no more than the statute permits them to do. A demand by such an authority under an *ultra vires* regulation is no more or no less unlawful than a demand under a valid regulation which does not apply to the situation in which the demand is made. I mention these matters because they show that to accept the *Woolwich* principle in one or other of its forms would appear to involve a choice of what the law should be rather than a decision as to what it is.

To apply the *Woolwich* principle as initially enunciated without limitation could cause very serious practical difficulties of administration and specifying appropriate limitations presents equal difficulties. For example, what, if any, knowledge if required on the part of a payer at the time of payment to entitle him to recovery at a later date? Or how long should any right to repayment last? Is it in the public interest that a public authority's finances should be disrupted by wholly unexpected claims for repayment years after the money in question has been received? These are all matters which would arise in any reform of the law to encompass some such principle as *Woolwich* contend for and are matters with which the legislature is best equipped to deal.

Lord Browne-Wilkinson: My Lords, in this case your Lordships are all agreed that, as the law at present stands, tax paid under protest in response to an *ultra vires* demand is not recoverable at common law. The authorities are fully analysed in the speeches of my noble and learned friends Lord Keith of Kinkel, Lord Jauncey of Tullichettle and Lord Goff of Chieveley and I agree with those analyses.

The issue which divides your Lordships is whether this House should now reinterpret the principles lying behind the authorities so as to give a right of recovery in such circumstances. On that issue, I agree with my noble and learned friend Lord Goff of Chieveley that, for the reasons he gives, it is appropriate to do so. Although as yet there is in English law no general rule giving the plaintiff a right of recovery from a defendant who has been unjustly [197] enriched at the plaintiff's expense, the concept of unjust enrichment lies at the heart of all the individual instances in which the law does give a right of recovery ...

In the present case, the concept of unjust enrichment suggests that the plaintiffs should have a remedy. The revenue demanded and received payment of the sum by way of tax alleged to be due under regulations subsequently held by your Lordships' House to be *ultra vires*, see *Woolwich Equitable Building Society v Inland Revenue Commissioners* (1990). The payment was made under protest. Yet the revenue maintains that it was under no legal obligation to repay the wrongly extracted tax and in consequence is not liable to pay interest on the sum held by it between the date it received the money and the date of the order of Nolan J. If the revenue is right, it will be enriched by the interest on money to which it had no right during that period. In my judgment, this is the paradigm of a case of unjust enrichment.

As in so many other fields of English law, the occasions on which recovery is permitted have been built up on a case by case basis. For present purposes there are in my judgment two streams of authority relating to moneys wrongly extracted by way of impost. One stream is founded on the concept that money paid under an *ultra vires* demand for a tax or other impost has been paid without consideration. The other stream is based on the notion that such payments have been made under compulsion, the relative positions and powers of the two parties being unequal.

The stream based on the concept of payment without consideration stems from what Lord Mansfield said in *Campbell v Hall* (1774) and is reflected in the decision in *Dew v Parsons* (1819). In *Steele v Williams* (1853) Martin B said that the payment in that case was not a voluntary payment but was 'more like the case of money paid without consideration'. In *Queens of the River Steamship Co Ltd v Conservators of the River Thames* (1899) Phillimore J founded his decision on the fact that there was no consideration for the payment. Although this stream seems subsequently to have run into the sand, I find the approach attractive: money paid on the footing that there is a legal demand is paid for a reason that does not exist if that demand is a nullity. There is in my view a close analogy to the right to recover money paid under a contract the consideration for which has wholly failed.

The other stream, based on compulsion, stems from *Morgan v Palmer* (1849) and the majority decision in *Steele v Williams*. [198] In their inception, these authorities were based on the fact that the payer and payee were not on an equal footing and it was this inequality which gave rise to the right to recovery. However, most of the cases which arose for decision were concerned with payments extracted *ultra vires* by persons who in virtue of their position could insist on the wrongful payment as a precondition to affording the payer his legal rights, ie, they were payments *colore officii*. In consequence, the courts came to limit the cases in which recovery of an *ultra vires* impost was allowed to cases where there had been an extraction *colore officii*. I can see no reason in principle to have restricted the original wide basis of recovery to this limited class of case. In my judgment, as a matter of principle the *colore officii* cases are merely examples of a wider principle, viz that where the parties are on an unequal footing so that money is paid by way of tax or other impost in pursuance of a demand by some public officer, these moneys are recoverable since the citizen is, in practice, unable to resist the payment save at the risk of breaking the law or exposing himself to penalties or other disadvantages.

In my view the principle is correctly expressed by Holmes J in *Atchison Topeka & Santa Fe Railway Co v O'Connor* (1912) where he said:

> It is reasonable that a man who denies the legality of a tax should have a clear and certain remedy. The rule being established that apart from special circumstances he cannot interfere by injunction with the State's collection of its revenues, an action at law to recover back what he has paid is the alternative left. Of course we are speaking of those cases where the State is not put to an action if the citizen refuses to pay. In these latter he can interpose his objections by way of defence, but when, as is common, the State has a more summary remedy, such as distress, and the party indicates by protest that he is yielding to what he cannot prevent, courts sometimes perhaps have been a little too slow to recognise the implied duress under which payment is made. But even if the State is driven to an action, if at the same time the citizen is put at a serious disadvantage in the assertion of his legal, and in this case of his constitutional, rights, by defence in the suit, justice may require that he should be at liberty to avoid those disadvantages by paying promptly and bringing suit on his side. He is entitled to assert his supposed right on reasonably equal terms.

In cases such as the present both the concept of want of consideration and payment under implied compulsion are in play. The money was demanded and paid for tax, yet no tax was due: there was a payment for no consideration. The money was demanded by the State from the citizen and the inequalities of the parties' respective positions is manifest even in the case of a major financial institution like Woolwich. There are, therefore, in my judgment sound reasons by way of analogy for establishing the law in the sense which Lord Goff proposes. I agree with him that the practical objections to taking this course are not sufficient to prevent this House from establishing the law in accordance [199] with both principle and justice ...

Lord Slynn of Hadley: ... [204] Although as I see it the facts do not fit easily into the existing category of duress or of claims *colore officii*, they shade into them. There is a common element of pressure which by analogy can be said to justify a claim for repayment.

If I felt compelled to hold that the taxpayer in this case could not recover I would share the no little regret expressed by my noble and learned friend, Lord Jauncey of Tullichettle. With great deference to him and to Lord Keith of Kinkel I do not, however, feel so constrained by authority, by statute or by principle.

I find it quite unacceptable in principle that the common law should have no remedy for a taxpayer who has paid large sums or any sum of money to the revenue when those sums have been demanded pursuant to an invalid regulation and retained free of interest pending a decision of the courts.

It is said that *William Whiteley Ltd v The King* (1909) and *Twyford v Manchester Corporation* (1946) are authorities to the contrary. I consider that they are cases where payments were made to close a transaction and are to be treated as cases of voluntary payments. If they were not, in my view they were wrongly decided and they should not influence your Lordships' decision.

Accordingly, I consider that Glidewell and Butler-Sloss LJJ [in the Court of Appeal] were right to conclude that money paid to the revenue pursuant to a demand which was *ultra vires* can be recovered as money had and received. The money was repayable immediately it was paid.

[205] I do not, however, agree that this principle cannot apply where there is a mistake of law. That is the situation where the relief is most likely to be needed and if it is excluded not much is left.

This is not a case where the demand was based on an erroneous interpretation of legislation by the revenue; my provisional view is that there is no distinction between such a case and a case like the present where the demand is based on an invalid regulation and is therefore *ultra vires*. That does not have to be decided in this case, nor is it necessary to consider what defences would be open to such a claim for recovery of the money paid if it lay ...

Commentary and questions

What reasons did the majority judges give for recognising *ultra vires* demand as a restitutionary ground of recovery? Is there a difference in emphasis between Lord Goff's judgment and the other majority judgments? What reasons did the minority judges give for refusing to recognise *ultra vires* demand as ground of recovery?

Australian cases have refused to apply the *ultra vires* demand principle to allow recovery of payments made under valid contracts, notwithstanding that the payments were attributable to an exaction later held to be invalid.[26] In the decision of the Full Court of the Federal Court in *Roxborough v Rothmans of Pall Mall Australia Ltd* (1999)[27] Hill and Lehane JJ rejected an argument that contractual payments could be recovered on the basis of the *ultra vires* demand principle (pp 342–43):

It was suggested that we should apply by analogy the principles recognised by the House of Lords in *Woolwich Equitable Building Society v Inland Revenue Commissioners* (1993). That case concerned recovery of a payment exacted under an unlawful demand for tax. It was submitted on behalf of the retailers that the injustice involved in a taxing authority retaining a payment unlawfully exacted is no greater in kind than, and no different in principle from, that which was said to be the injustice of Rothmans retaining the amounts paid by the retailers. But that, in our view, both ignores the effect of the contracts between Rothmans and the retailers and gives insufficient weight to considerations which the majority of the

---

26   *Esso Australia Resources Ltd v Gas & Fuel Corp of Victoria* (1993), Gobbo J at 108; *Roxborough v Rothmans of Pall Mall Australia Ltd* (1999) (this case was appealed to the High Court on different grounds: see (2001) 185 ALR 335).

27   For a statement of the facts of this case, see p 81.

House of Lords evidently regarded as crucial: particularly, that a public body, armed with the coercive powers of the state, exacted money unlawfully.[28]

The *ultra vires* demand ground of recovery applies to governmental levies other than taxes, such as customs duties and excise fees.[29] However, it might not apply to claims by local councils (on the basis they do not have the coercive powers of a taxing authority),[30] and it is doubtful whether it applies to charges by public utilities, or utilities that have been privatised or corporatised.[31] There is also some authority to the effect that the exaction will not be recoverable on the basis of this principle if the public authority gave good consideration for the payment. In *Waikato Regional Airport Ltd v Attorney General* (2001) Wild J held at p 712:[32]

> *Woolwich* appears not to apply to cases where consideration is present. It is concerned more with taxes and levies which are collected by a public authority as part of its general revenue and not for a direct or specific service.

In that case Wild J ordered recovery of unlawfully demanded border protection charges, however indicated that the authority would be entitled to retain a reasonable portion of the payments that could be said to be referable to the border protection services provided by the authority.

One question that has arisen is whether the principle is restricted to demands made under *ultra vires* legislation (as in *Woolwich* itself) or whether it extends to any demand for payment of an exaction which is unlawful for any reason, for example because of a mistaken interpretation of legislation. In *Woolwich* Lord Goff suggested, without deciding, that the principle would extend to the situation where the authority unlawfully demanded exactions as a result of misconstruing a statute. It has now been confirmed by the following English Court of Appeal case that the principle is sufficiently wide to cover this situation.

British Steel plc v Customs and Excise Commissioners [1997] 2 All ER 366
English Court of Appeal

The plaintiff manufacturing company paid excise duty on hydrocarbon oil used in its blast furnaces pursuant to demands by the commissioners under the

---

28 *Woolwich Equitable Building Society v Inland Revenue Commissioners* (1993), see pp 171, 172 *per* Lord Goff of Chieveley, p 198 *per* Lord Browne-Wilkinson and p 204 *per* Lord Slynn of Hadley.

29 *British Steel plc v Customs and Excise Commissioners* (1997) (see following extract); *British Sky Broadcasting Group plc v Commissioners for Customs and Excise* (2001); *Woolwich Equitable Building Society v Inland Revenue Commissioners* (1993), pp 177, 198.

30 *Norwich City Council v Stringer* (2000).

31 Burrows, *The Law of Restitution*, 1993, p 353; Beatson, 'Restitution of taxes, levies and other imposts: defining the extent of the *Woolwich* principle' (1993) 109 LQR 401, p 410ff; The Law Commission of England and Wales, Report No 227, *Restitution of payments made under a mistake of law* (London: HMSO, 1994), §6.43–6.45, 8.16–8.19.

32 *Ibid*, p 712. Wild J relied on various statements in *Woolwich* to the effect that unlawful demands are recoverable because they are paid for 'no consideration': see Lord Goff at p 166 and Lord Browne-Wilkinson at pp 197, 198.

Hydrocarbon Oil Duties Act 1979 (UK) (the Act). The plaintiff consistently asserted that it was exempted from paying the excise duty under s 9(1) of the Act on the basis that the oil was to be put by it to a 'qualifying use', however the commissioners consistently rejected this argument. The plaintiff commenced proceedings to recover the excise duties on the basis that they were unlawfully demanded and that it had a *prima facie* right to recover those duties on the basis of the principles laid down in *Woolwich*.

Sir Richard Scott VC: ... [374] If the demands by the commissioners for excise duty to be paid on the hydrocarbon oil to be delivered to British Steel's blast furnaces were unlawful demands, it would follow, in my opinion, from the decision of the House of Lords in *Woolwich Equitable Building Society v IRC* (1993), that whoever paid the duty would have a common law restitutionary right to repayment.

...

[375] In the *Woolwich* case the reason why the demands for tax were unlawful was because the relevant taxing provisions in the Regulations were *ultra vires* and void. But Lord Goff [said] this, at p 177:

> As at present advised, I incline to the opinion that this principle should extend to embrace cases in which the tax or other levy has been wrongly [376] exacted by the public authority not because the demand was *ultra vires*, but for other reasons, for example because the authority has misconstrued a relevant statute or regulation.

In the present case, it is contended that the commissioner's demand for excise duties was unlawful because the commissioners had made an error in deciding that the use of the oil in the British Steel blast furnaces was not a 'qualifying use' and, consequently, had wrongly refused to grant relief from duty under s 9(1). I have yet to examine whether that premise justifies a conclusion that the demands were unlawful; but, if it does, I can see no reason why the principle expressed by Lord Goff should not apply.

An unlawful demand for duty must, in a sense, always be an *ultra vires* demand. Whether the demand is based on *ultra vires* regulations, or on a mistaken view of the legal effect of valid regulations, or on a mistaken view of the facts of the case, it will, as it seems to me, be bound to be a demand outside the taxing power conferred by the empowering legislation. If, for any of these reasons, a demand for tax is an unlawful demand, it seems to me to follow from the speeches of the majority in the *Woolwich* case that the taxpayer would, *prima facie*, become entitled, on making payment pursuant to the unlawful demand, to a common law restitutionary right to repayment. The empowering legislation in question, or other legislation, might remove the taxpayer's common law right to repayment. That would depend on the construction of the Act or Acts in question.

In the present case, if the demands for excise duty were unlawful, the payer would, in my judgment, have a *prima facie* common law right to repayment.

Commentary

The *Woolwich* principle has also been said to apply to allow recovery of exactions that are unlawful because of an abuse of process: *British Sky Broadcasting Group plc v Commissioners for Customs and Excise* (2001).

Operation of the *Woolwich* principle in Australian law

The High Court is yet to address the question whether the *Woolwich* principle should be adopted into Australian law. However, the principle has been recognised on a number of occasions by the lower courts.[33] Also, there are High Court *dicta* supporting the recognition of a general right of recovery of invalid taxes, most notably[34] that of Dixon CJ in *Mason v New South Wales* (1959), p 117 (see extract, p 434) in the context of unconstitutional taxes:

> I have not been able completely to reconcile myself to the view that if the weight of a *de facto* governmental authority manifested in a money demand is not resisted although it is incompatible with s 92 [of the Constitution] the money belongs to the Crown unless the payment was the outcome of the actual threatened or apprehended withholding of something to which the payer was entitled or the actual threatened or apprehended impeding of him in the exercise of some right or liberty. But English authority seems now to say that moneys paid to the Crown as and for taxes cannot be recovered from the Crown upon its turning out that the moneys were not exigible notwithstanding that they were demanded by the Crown, unless the circumstances were such that they would be recoverable as between subject and subject, *exempli gratia* as involuntary payments or payments made under a mistake of fact.

The reasons given by the majority in *Woolwich* for the adoption of a *prima facie* right of recovery of invalid exactions demanded by a public authority are compelling and, generally speaking, equally valid for Australian law.[35] For example, the fundamental constitutional principle referred to in *Woolwich* that no taxes should be levied without the authority of Parliament also forms part of Australian constitutional law.[36] And the recognition in *Woolwich* that there is an inherent imbalance of power between a public authority and a citizen applies with equal force here. However, there are important differences between the

---

33 *Melbourne Tramway and Omnibus Co Ltd v The Mayor of Melbourne* (1903); *Esso Australia Resources Ltd v Gas and Fuel Corporation of Victoria* (1993), pp 107–08; *Roxborough v Rothmans of Pall Mall Australia Ltd* (1999) (this case was appealed to the High Court on different grounds: see (2001) 185 ALR 335); *State Bank of New South Wales v Federal Commissioner of Taxation* (1995), p 658; *Federal Airports Corporation v Aerolineas Argentinas* (1997); *Lamesa Holdings BV v Federal Commissioner of Taxation* (1999).

34 For another *dicta* statement to like effect see *Sargood Bros v The Commonwealth* (1910).

35 Contrast Fitzgerald, 'Ultra vires as an unjust factor in the law of unjust enrichment' (1993) 2(1) GLR 1. Fitzgerald argues that the invalidity of the exaction should not itself ground recovery, and that the ground of recovery should more aptly be described 'want of authority'.

36 This principle is embodied in Declaration 4 of the Bill of Rights 1688 (Imp) which is in force in Australia: see, for example, Imperial Acts Application Act 1969 (NSW), s 6. See also *Commissioner of Stamps v Telegraph Investment Company Pty Ltd* (1995), p 467.

constitutional systems of Australia and England which mean that it cannot be assumed automatically that the *Woolwich* principle is suitable for Australian law. The 'absolute legislative supremacy'[37] of the United Kingdom Parliament confers plenary power on it to legislate to extinguish rights of recovery where disruption to government finances is perceived to be a concern.[38] Thus, the majority in *Woolwich* pointed out that, if recovery of an exaction on the basis of the *Woolwich* principle would disrupt governmental finances, the Parliament could pass legislation preventing recovery: p 177. However, this means of preventing fiscal disruption is not always available to the Australian parliaments in the case of taxes found to be unconstitutional. As discussed below, legislation seeking to retrospectively validate a tax that is unconstitutional because it is beyond legislative power or because it contravenes a constitutional prohibition, will itself be struck down as unconstitutional.[39] Accordingly, if the *Woolwich* principle is adopted into Australian law, the courts will need to give consideration to fashioning defences to guard against disruption to public finances where taxes are found to be unconstitutional.[40]

DEFENCES TO CLAIMS AGAINST PUBLIC AUTHORITIES

Legislative bars or restrictions

The legislation under which a tax is imposed might expressly or impliedly exclude common law restitutionary principles. For example, restitutionary principles might be found to have been impliedly excluded by legislation that includes specific and detailed provisions for recovery of invalid taxes.[41] Where the legislation contains detailed provisions for recovery, restitution law cannot be used to enlarge the taxpayers' entitlements, for example by awarding

---

37 McKinley, 'Constitutional brokerage in Australia: constitutions and the doctrines of parliamentary supremacy and the rule of law' (1994) 22 FLR 194, p 196.

38 *Woolwich Equitable Building Society v Inland Revenue Commissioners* (1993), p 177 (see extract, p 456); Wells, 'Restitution from the Crown: private right and public interest' (1994) 16 Adel LR 191, pp 210–11.

39 *Antill Ranger & Co Pty Ltd v Commissioner for Motor Transport* (1956); *Barton v Commissioner for Motor Transport* (1957), pp 641, 662; *Mutual Pools & Staff Pty Ltd v The Commonwealth* (1994), pp 167, 175, 183, 206, 212–16; *Amax v Potash Ltd v Government of Saskatchewan* (1976).

40 Leading Australian commentators, Keith Mason and John Carter, conclude tentatively that the balance of justice favours recognition of the *Woolwich* principle, though point to the need to fashion appropriate defences to guard against massive disruption of public finances: Mason and Carter, *Restitution Law in Australia*, 1995, pp 753–56, 769–70.

41 *Commonwealth of Australia v SCI Operations Pty Ltd* (1998), pp 326–27 (see extract, p 686); *Malika Holdings Pty Ltd v Stretton* (2001); *Otto Australia Pty Ltd v Commissioner of Taxation* (1991), pp 480–81, 483; *A & G International Pty Ltd v Collector of Customs* (1995); *Chippendale Printing Co Pty Ltd v Commissioner of Taxation* (1996); *Amway of Australia Pty Ltd v Commonwealth of Australia* (1998), p 654.

interest.[42] In this regard, restitutionary claims for the recovery of overpaid sales tax have consistently been denied as the statutory refund regime in the Sales Tax Assessment Acts 1930 (Cth) is said to provide an exhaustive code of recovery.[43] The same conclusion has been reached regarding the statutory refund provision in the Customs Act 1901.[44]

A further legislative restriction on the recovery of invalid taxes is that shorter limitation periods for the recovery of invalid taxes have been enacted in each Australian jurisdiction. Depending on the jurisdiction, proceedings to recover invalid taxes must be commenced either six or 12 months from the date of the payment of the tax.[45] The Commonwealth has also enacted short limitation periods for the recovery of customs duty.[46] Further restrictions on the recovery of invalid imports exist in some jurisdictions. For example, invalid imports are irrecoverable in New South Wales where the ground of recovery arose because of a non-legislative change in the law.[47] And South Australia has enacted a statutory passing on defence in action for the recovery of taxes.[48]

Notwithstanding the above, the ability of Australian governments to exclude restitutionary principles is limited where the tax in question is unconstitutional because it is beyond legislative power or because it contravenes a constitutional prohibition such as s 92. Legislation which effectively prevents recovery of such unconstitutional taxes will itself be struck down as unconstitutional, for the courts will not allow governments to do indirectly what they could not do directly.[49] As said by Dickson J in *Amax Potash Ltd v Government of Saskatchewan* (1976): 'If a State cannot take by unconstitutional means it cannot retain by unconstitutional means' (p 12). Thus, in *Antill Ranger & Co Pty Ltd v Commissioner for Motor Transport* (1956) State legislation that attempted to

---

42 *Commonwealth of Australia v SCI Operations Pty Ltd* (1998), pp 306, 317, 326–27 (see extract, p 686); *A & G International Pty Ltd v Collector of Customs* (1995). See also *Qantas Airways Ltd v Commissioner of Taxation* (2001) (Taxation (Interest on Overpayments and Early Payments) Act 1983 (Cth) provides an exclusive code).

43 *Otto Australia Pty Ltd v Commissioner of Taxation* (1991), pp 480–81, 483; *Chippendale Printing Co Pty Ltd v Commissioner of Taxation* (1996); *Amway of Australia Pty Ltd Ltd v Commonwealth of Australia* (1998), p 654. The refund provisions of the Fringe Benefits Assessment Tax Act 1986 have also been held to be exhaustive: *Mt Gibson Manager Pty Ltd v Deputy Commissioner of Taxation* (1996).

44 *Comptroller-General of Customs v Kawasaki Motors Pty Ltd (No 2)* (1991), pp 247–53, 258–62; *Malika Holdings Pty Ltd v Stretton* (2001), p 230 *per* McHugh J.

45 Limitations of Actions Act 1958 (Vic), s 20A (12 months); Recovery of Imposts Act 1963 (NSW), s 2 (12 months); Limitation of Actions Act 1974 (Qld), s 10A (12 months); Limitation of Actions Act 1936 (SA), s 38 (six months); Limitation Act 1974 (Tas), s 25D (12 months); Limitation Act 1935 (WA), s 37A (12 months); Limitation Act 1985 (ACT), s 21A (six months); Limitation Act 1981, s 35D (six months).

46 Customs Act 1901 (Cth), s 167 (six months).

47 Recovery of Imports Act 1963 (CNSW), s 3.

48 Limitation of Actions Act 1936 (SA), s 38 (3a) and (3b).

49 *Antill Ranger & Co Pty Ltd v Commissioner for Motor Transport* (1956), pp 179–81; *Barton v Commissioner for Motor Transport* (1957), pp 641, 662; *Mutual Pools & Staff Pty Ltd v The Commonwealth* (1994), pp 167, 175, pp 183, 206, 212–16; *Amax v Potash Ltd v Government of Saskatchewan* (1976). On the other hand, legislation can validly prevent recovery of taxes that are unconstitutional merely because of a procedural irregularity: *Mutual Pools & Staff Pty Ltd v The Commonwealth* (1994).

abolish the right of interstate carriers to recover taxes paid under legislation contravening s 92 of the Constitution was struck down as unconstitutional. Likewise, the shorter limitations periods enacted for the recovery of taxes will be found to be unconstitutional where they have the 'real effect of depriving the plaintiff of practically effective redress'.[50] It is at least arguable that the limitation periods of six or 12 months from the date of payment (rather than the date the invalidity became known) do not allow 'practically effective redress'.[51]

General restitutionary defences

The general defences to restitutionary claims, such as voluntary submission to a claim,[52] or the defence of change of position,[53] will be available to public authorities. However, the latter defence will probably only apply in exceptional cases where the authority is able to identify a specific extraordinary expense which it incurred on the faith of the receipt of the particular payment of tax by the plaintiff.[54] Most taxes will be paid into consolidated revenue and the government will not be able to point to the specific expenditure of that tax. It will only be in the rare case where the government has levied the invalid exaction for a specific purpose and has paid it into, and disbursed it from, a specific purpose fund, that the government will potentially be able to argue that it has changed its position.[55]

It has been noted elsewhere[56] that the defence of passing on has not been accepted into Australian law.[57] Accordingly, public authorities cannot rely as a defence on the fact that the plaintiff has recouped the cost of the tax from its customers by increasing the price of its products.

Defence of disruption to public finances

Despite frequently voiced policy concerns about the potential for disruption to public finances should multiple claims arise for recovery of invalid taxes, Australian courts have shown a reluctance to adopt a special 'disruption to

---

50 *Barton v Commissioner for Motor Transport* (1957), p 660. See also *Antill Ranger & Co Pty Ltd v Commissioner for Motor Transport* (1956), pp 179–81; *Mutual Pools & Staff Pty Ltd v The Commonwealth* (1994), pp 167, 175, 183, 206, 212–16; *Amax v Potash Ltd v Government of Saskatchewan* (1976).

51 Glover, 'Restitutionary recovery of taxes after the *Royal Insurance* case: commentary', in McInnes (ed), *Restitution: Developments in Unjust Enrichment*, 1996, p 136. For a general discussion of the constitutional principles that apply in this area, see Brock, 'Restitution of invalid taxes – principles and policies' (2000) 5 Deakin Law Review 128.

52 See the discussion above pp 139–46.

53 See Chapter 18.

54 Burrows, *The Law of Restitution*, 1993, p 358; Virgo, 'The law of taxation is not an island – overpaid taxes and the law of restitution' [1993] British Tax Review 442, pp 458–60; Wells, 'Restitution from the Crown: private rights and public interest' (1994) 16 Adel LR 191, pp 199–200.

55 Mason and Carter, *Restitution Law in Australia*, 1995, pp 778–79; Hill, 'Restitution from public authorities and the Treasury's position' (1993) 56 MLR 856, p 864.

56 See Chapter 18, pp 658–66.

57 *Commissioner of State Revenue (Vic) v Royal Insurance Australia Ltd* (1994) (see extracts, pp 76 and 658); *Roxborough v Rothmans of Pall Mall Australia Ltd* (2001) (see extract, p 81).

finances' defence. In the following case the Supreme Court of Canada discusses at length the policy arguments that would need to be considered in determining whether or not such a defence should be adopted.

Air Canada v British Columbia (1989) 59 DLR (4th) 161 Supreme Court of Canada

The plaintiffs were airline companies which had paid tax on gasoline purchased in British Columbia pursuant to the Gasoline Tax Act 1948 (RSBC) (the 'Act'). As originally enacted, the provision in the Act imposing the tax was *ultra vires* and the plaintiffs brought proceedings to recover the taxes paid by them.

Wilson J (dissenting): ... [169] It is ... my view that payments made under unconstitutional legislation are not 'voluntary' in a sense which should prejudice the taxpayer. The taxpayer, assuming the validity of the statute as I believe it is entitled to do, considers itself obligated to pay. Citizens are expected to be law-abiding. They are expected to pay their taxes. Pay first and object later is the general rule. The payments are made pursuant to a perceived obligation to pay which results from the combined presumption of constitutional validity of duly enacted legislation and the holding out of such validity by the legislature. In such circumstances I consider it quite unrealistic to expect the taxpayer to make its payments 'under protest'. Any taxpayer paying taxes exigible under a statute which it has no reason to believe or suspect is other than valid should be viewed as having paid pursuant to the statutory obligation to do so.

Based on the foregoing reasoning I conclude that payments made under a statute subsequently found to be unconstitutional should be recoverable and I cannot, with respect, accept my colleague's [La Forest J's] proposition that the principle should be reversed *for policy reasons* in the case of payments made to governmental bodies. What is the policy that requires such a dramatic reversal of principle? Why should the individual taxpayer, as opposed to taxpayers as a whole, bear the burden of government's mistake? I would respectfully suggest that it is grossly unfair that X, who may not be (as in this case) a large corporate enterprise, should absorb the cost of government's unconstitutional act. If it is appropriate for the courts to adopt some kind of policy in order to protect government against itself (and I cannot say that the idea particularly appeals to me) it should be one which distributes the loss fairly across the public. The loss should not fall on the totally innocent taxpayer whose only fault is that it paid what the legislature improperly said was due. I find it quite ironic to describe such a person as 'asserting a right to disrupt the government by demanding a refund' or 'creating fiscal chaos' or 'requiring a new generation to pay for the expenditures of the old'. By refusing to adopt such a policy the courts are not 'visiting the sins of the fathers on the children'. The 'sin' in this case (if it can be so described) is that of government and only government and government has means available to it to protect against the consequences of it. It should not, in my opinion, be done by the courts and certainly not at the expense of individual taxpayers ...

La Forest J: ... [La Forest J rejected the traditional rule that money paid under a mistake of law is irrecoverable however said that 'special considerations' arise where the levy is unconstitutional. His Honour refused to allow recovery in this case on the basis that the airline companies had passed on the burden of the tax to their passengers, and continued at p 194:]

This alone is sufficient to deny the airlines' claim. However, even if the airlines could show that they bore the burden of the tax, I would still deny recovery. It is clear that the principles of unjust enrichment can operate against a government to ground restitutionary recovery, but in this kind of case, where the effect of an unconstitutional or *ultra vires* statute is in issue, I am of the opinion that special considerations operate to take this case out of the normal restitutionary framework, and require a rule responding to the specific underlying policy concerns in this area.

It is not without significance that an examination of the case law of the United States, Australia and New Zealand shows that generally there is no recovery of taxes paid pursuant to legislation which is unconstitutional or otherwise invalid.[58] While this rule has most often been stated in the traditional terms of mistake of law, which I have rejected, it is noteworthy that even in jurisdictions in the United States where the mistake of law rule is not followed (Connecticut and Kentucky), or has been abolished (New York), the courts have nevertheless held that a voluntary payment of taxes under an unconstitutional statute is not recoverable.[59]

What this suggests is that there are solid grounds of public policy for not according a general right of recovery in these circumstances, and that this prohibition exists quite independently of the law of restitution. This policy was forcefully stated by Logan J in the Kentucky Court of Appeals (where it will be remembered there is no general mistake of law doctrine) in *Coleman v Inland Gas Corp* (1929):

> ... all state governments have been slow indeed to open the doors of their treasuries and allow money to pass therefrom after it has once found lodgement within the governmental vaults. This is as it should be. The state is the sovereign and its affairs must be conducted for the best interest and welfare of the people. That calls for the expenditure of large sums of money for governmental affairs, and such sums of money can be obtained only through taxation. The state should determine the amount which it will spend by the probable income it will receive. When the income is collected it is allocated to different funds. The state uses the funds nearly always during the current year. It has been universally held, unless a contrary conclusion was forced by an ironclad statute, that no taxpayer should have the right to disrupt the government by demanding a refund of his money, whether paid legally or otherwise.

See also *Mercury Machine Importing Corp v City of New York* (1957), especially p 404. Similar sentiments were expressed by MacDonald JA in *Vancouver Growers Ltd v GH Snow Ltd* (1937). Such a rule is sensible. The only practical alternative as a general rule would be to impose a new tax to pay for the old, which is another way of saying that a new generation must pay for the expenditures of the old. At best it is simply inefficient.

A related concern, and one prevalent through many of the authorities and much of the academic literature is the fiscal chaos that would result if the general rule favoured recovery, particularly where a long standing taxation measure is involved. That this is not an unfounded concern can be seen by reference to one incident in the United States. A provision has been inserted in the United States

---

58 See Pannam, 'The recovery of unconstitutional taxes in Australia and in the United States' (1964) 42 Texas L Rev 779; Palmer, *The Law of Restitution*, Vol 3, p 248.

59 See Pannam, *ibid*, pp 793–94; Palmer, *ibid*, Vol 3, pp 248–49.

Internal Revenue Code removing the distinction between mistakes of fact and mistakes of law because of the harsh and unjust results that had occurred under the general rule. This, however, placed a severe strain on the United States Treasury when the Supreme Court in *United States v Butler* (1936), held unconstitutional the Agricultural Adjustment Act making almost one billion dollars in invalid taxes (a respectable amount now but overwhelming during the depression) repayable by the government. Faced with this situation, Congress immediately passed an Act which provided that no refunds for such taxes would be allowed unless the claimant could establish the burden of the tax. In view of *Amax Potash Ltd v Government of Saskatchewan* (1976), a province faced with a similar situation could not enact a similar measure.

To some extent the present case raises difficulties of a similar character. As Esson JA [in the Court of Appeal] remarked (p 390):

> It is instructive to consider what the consequences might be if Professor Hogg's thesis [which advocates general recovery of unconstitutional taxes] were to be applied to the Gasoline Tax Act. The tax imposed under it for decades before 1976 was a tax of broad general application. It has long been a major component of the provincial budget. Every operator of a vehicle contributed to the provincial coffers in this way. The total number of such [196] taxpayers must be in the millions. The amount involved in these three actions is 'only' something over six million dollars. In the modern scale of things, that will not have a major additional impact on the already sorry financial state of the province. A few more schoolrooms and a few more hospital wards may have to be closed and a few roads may go unrepaired; or perhaps the matter will be dealt with by a further increase in the deficit so that future generations will bear the burden. The blow will, however, be greater than that inflicted by these cases. We are told that other large taxpayers, including one of the national railways, commenced action before the period of limitation expired and await the outcome of these actions to decide whether to go ahead.

The situation would be much worse, of course, if the Statute of Limitations or laches could not be pleaded, a question Esson JA did not resolve and upon which it is unnecessary for me to embark.

Those who favour recovery of *ultra vires* taxes concede that an exception would be required where this would disrupt public finances; see John D McCamus, 'restitutionary recovery of moneys paid to public authority under a mistake of law: *ignorantia juris* in the Supreme Court of Canada', *Air Canada v British Columbia* (1983). But how would a court determine this? Among other complications is the fact that what can make recovery against the state impractical is the length of time during which an invalid tax has been collected. Equitable laches could be brought into service, but these ordinarily involve some discernible act of acquiescence to trigger their operation. The obvious remedy is a period of limitations, but it would be inappropriate for courts at this late date of legal development to define such periods which, to be effective, may have to differ from one type of tax to another.

Professor Birks has argued that the dominant value should be respect for the principle that there should be no taxation without parliamentary sanction, and so the general rule should favour recovery; see Peter Birks, *An Introduction to the Law of Restitution* (p 294). Even Professor Birks, however, concedes that 'Where there is a serious danger that public finances will be disrupted it may be necessary to limit or exclude a right to restitution' (p 298). I agree that the value he favours is worthy of protection, but in the context of taxes exacted through unconstitutional statutes in light of the other policies outlined above, I am not willing to give it the dominant status that Birks would accord it.

All in all, I have become persuaded that the rule should be against recovery of *ultra vires* taxes, at least in the case of unconstitutional statutes. It seems best to function from the basis of that rule with exceptions where the relationship between the state [197] and a particular taxpayer resulting in the collection of the tax are unjust or oppressive in the circumstances. However, this case does not call for departure from the general rule. The tax levied in this case, though unconstitutional, comes close to raising a mere technical issue. Had the statute been enacted in proper form there would have been no difficulty in exacting the tax as actually imposed. Though specific evidence was not led on this point, were recovery to be allowed, the airlines would receive a windfall, and fiscal chaos could well result. Many others could well bring suit, for this is a general tax applying to all purchases of gasoline in the province. It is true that many of these would not be in a position to establish their claims but it would be odd if this factor were taken into account since its general effect would be to favour the strong against the weak. Finally, there is not the element of discrimination, oppression or abuse of authority which would warrant recovery.

This rule against the recovery of unconstitutional and *ultra vires* levies is an exceptional rule, and should not be construed more widely than is necessary to fulfil the values which support it. Chief among these are the protection of the treasury, and a recognition of the reality that if the tax were refunded, modern government would be driven to the inefficient course of reimposing it either on the same, or on a new generation of taxpayers, to finance the operations of government. Though the drawing of lines is always difficult, I am persuaded that this rule should not apply where a tax is extracted from a taxpayer through a misapplication of the law. Thus, where an otherwise constitutional or *intra vires* statute or regulation is applied in error to a person to whom on its true construction it does not apply, the general principles of restitution for money paid under a mistake should be applied, and, subject to available defences and equitable considerations discussed earlier, the general rule should favour recovery. In exceptional cases public policy considerations may require a contrary holding, but those exceptional cases do not justify extending the general rule of non-recovery of unconstitutional or *ultra vires* levies. As Professor Palmer has noted:[60]

> The effect of restitution in dislocating the fiscal affairs of the governmental unit in such isolated instances of mistake is nothing like it would be where many payments have been made under a tax law which is unconstitutional or invalid for some other reason.

Commentary

The statements by La Forest J in the principal case were made in the context of his refusal to permit recovery of *ultra vires* taxes. Although, in Australia, recovery of *ultra vires* taxes is not *per se* excluded – provided an unjust factor can

---

60   *The Law of Restitution*, Vol 3, p 247.

be established – the same arguments and policy considerations which La Forest J refers to are applicable when considering whether a special governmental defence is necessary.

Mason CJ, in an *obiter* statement in *Commissioner of State Revenue (Vic) v Royal Insurance Australia Ltd* (p 68), disapproved of a special governmental defence based on disruption of public finances, preferring the majority view of Wilson J:

> The Commissioner did not argue that an exception from recovery should be acknowledged in order to protect public finances from disruption and the necessity of re-imposing taxes invalidly imposed. That proposition was accepted by La Forest J in *Air Canada v British Columbia* (1989), p 197 but it was repudiated by Wilson J, at p 169, in her dissenting judgment, for reasons which, to my mind, are compelling.[61] Those reasons centre upon the unfairness of requiring the innocent individual taxpayer, as opposed to taxpayers as a whole, to bear the burden of the government's mistake, see *Roxborough v Rothmans of Pall Mall Australia Ltd* (1999), p 169. Wilson J's exposition gives emphasis to the 'innocence' of the taxpayer and the 'mistake' of the government, factors which were present in *Air Canada*. These elements are not essential to the making out of a restitutionary claim for the recovery of money paid as and for tax as a result of a causative mistake and I do not see why the absence of these elements should justify the recognition of a vague and amorphous defence based on the notion of avoiding disruption of public finances. The remedy for any disruption of public finances occasioned by the recovery of money in conformity with the law of restitution lies in the hands of the legislature. It can determine who is to bear the burden of making up any shortfall in public funds.

Cornish has pointed out that such a defence:[62]

> ... would confer a discretion inherently difficult to exercise: and it seems to contain the imperative that, if governments are to exceed their taxing powers, this should be done on the grandest scale.

Despite initially being against imposing special limits upon recovery of unlawful exactions (see *Woolwich Equitable Building Society v Inland Revenue Commissioners* (p 174) (see extract, p 456), Lord Goff has now indicated that he would be in favour of adopting a special restriction on recovery of unlawful exactions in order to guard against a multitude of claims. In *Kleinwort Benson Ltd v Lincoln City Council* Lord Goff suggested that unlawful exactions should be irrecoverable where they were paid 'in accordance with a prevailing practice, or indeed under a settled understanding of the law': p 382. This aspect of his Honour's judgment is extracted below.

---

61 In *Woolwich Equitable Building Society v Inland Revenue Commissioners* (1993), p 176, Lord Goff of Chieveley found Wilson J's reasons on this point 'most attractive'.

62 Cornish, '"Colour of office": restitutionary redress against public authority' [1987] Jo Malaysian and Comparative Law 41, p 52.

Kleinwort Benson Ltd v Lincoln City Council **[1999] 2 AC 349 House of Lords**

The facts are stated at p 126.

Lord Goff of Chieveley: ... [381] At this point it is, in my opinion, appropriate to draw a distinction between, on the one hand, payments of taxes and other similar charges and, on the other hand, payments made under ordinary private transactions. The former category of cases was considered by your Lordships' House in *Woolwich Building Society v Inland Revenue Commissioners* in which it was held that at common law taxes exacted *ultra vires* were recoverable as of right, without the need to invoke a mistake of law by the payer ...

[382] Two observations may be made about the present situation ... The first observation is that, in our law of restitution, we now find two separate and distinct regimes in respect of the repayment of money paid under a mistake of law. These are: (1) cases concerned with repayment of taxes and other similar charges which, when exacted *ultra vires*, are recoverable as of right at common law on the principle in *Woolwich*, and otherwise are the subject of statutory regimes regulating recovery; and (2) other cases, which may broadly be described as concerned with repayment of money paid under private transactions, and which are governed by the common law. The second observation is that, in cases concerned with overpaid taxes, a case can be made in favour of a principle that payments made in accordance with a prevailing practice, or indeed under a settled understanding of the law, should be irrecoverable. If such a situation should arise with regard to overpayment of tax, it is possible that a large number of taxpayers may be affected; there is an element of public interest which may militate against repayment of tax paid in such circumstances; and, since *ex hypothesi* all citizens will have been treated alike, exclusion of recovery on public policy grounds may be more readily justifiable.

...

CHAPTER 16

RESTITUTION BY THE REVENUE

UNAUTHORISED PAYMENTS OUT OF CONSOLIDATED REVENUE

It is a fundamental constitutional principle that Parliament alone can authorise the disbursement of money from consolidated revenue.[1] This principle underpins the restitutionary ground of recovery known as the '*Auckland Harbour Board* principle'. In the case after which the principle was named, *Auckland Harbour Board v The King* (1924), the Privy Council famously uttered that:

> Any payment out of the consolidated fund made without Parliamentary authority is simply illegal and *ultra vires*, and may be recovered by the Government if it can, as here, be traced (p 327).

The *Auckland Harbour Board* principle has been accepted in a number of Australian cases.[2] It applies to payments which are *ultra vires* for any reason, for example because the payment was made under an *ultra vires* statute,[3] or the payment exceeded statutory authority,[4] or the payment exceeded the amount required to be paid under a contract with the Crown.[5] It is no defence to the claim that there is a parliamentary appropriation adequate to cover the disbursement.[6]

Australian authorities have consistently held that the defence of estoppel by representation cannot be relied upon to prevent recovery on the basis of the *Auckland Harbour Board* principle.[7] The injustice which this can cause is illustrated by the following case.

---

1   *Victoria v The Commonwealth* (1975); *Brown v West* (1990); *Northern Suburbs General Cemetery Reserve Trust v The Commonwealth* (1993). This principle is embodied in provisions in the Commonwealth and State Constitutions: see, for example, The Commonwealth Constitution, ss 81 and 83.

2   *Commonwealth v Thomson* (1962); *Commonwealth v Burns* (1971) (see extract, p 486); *Attorney General v Gray* (1977) (see extract, p 489); *Sandvik Australia Pty Ltd v The Commonwealth* (1989); *New South Wales v Bardolph* (1934), pp 471, 522; *Maguire v Simpson* (1977), p 388; *Brown v West* (1990), p 205; *Commonwealth v Crothall Hospital Services (Aust) Ltd* (1981) (see extract, p 496); *Formosa v Secretary, Department of Social Security* (1988); *Commonwealth v Hamilton* (1992) (see extract, p 493).

3   *Breckenridge Speedway Ltd v The Queen* (1970); Mason and Carter, *Restitution Law in Australia*, 1995, p 786.

4   *Commonwealth v Thomson* (1962); *Commonwealth v Burns* (1971) (see extract, p 486); *Attorney General v Gray* (1977) (see extract, p 489); *Sandvik Australia Pty Ltd v The Commonwealth* (1989); *Commonwealth v Ware* (1992).

5   *Commonwealth v Crothall Hospital Services (Aust) Ltd* (1981) (see extract, p 496).

6   *Attorney General v Gray* (1977), pp 412, 414 (see extract, p 489).

7   *Commonwealth v Burns* (1971) (see extract, p 486); *Attorney General v Gray* (1977) (see extract, p 489); *Commonwealth v Hamilton* (1992), pp 271–72 (see extract, p 493); *Formosa v Secretary, Department of Social Security* (1988), p 125.

Commonwealth of Australia v Burns [1971] VR 825 Supreme Court of Victoria

The defendant's father was entitled to a pension under the Repatriation Act 1920–65 (Cwlth) and the defendant, Mrs Burns, had been appointed to collect the pension on behalf of her father until his death in October 1960. In January 1961 payments of the pension to the defendant were resumed due to a mistake by an employee of the Repatriation Department. The defendant had no entitlement to the pension. Early in 1961 the defendant telephoned the department twice to enquire about the payments, and on the second occasion she was told in substance that the matter would have been looked into and she must be entitled to the pension. The defendant, believing that her father had been able to pass on his pension entitlement to her, spent most of the money. The department commenced an action seeking recovery of the payments.

Newton J: ... [827] I am ... satisfied that all the payments made to Mrs Burns were made without statutory or other lawful authority, and were also made by reason of a mistake on the part of the officers of the Repatriation Department who were concerned in the matter.

The primary contention on behalf of the Commonwealth was that it must inevitably follow from this conclusion that Mrs Burns is liable to the Commonwealth to repay the sum of $6,459. In my opinion, this contention is correct.

The payments made to Mrs Burns were made out of Consolidated Revenue: see s 113 of the Repatriation Act, and s 81 and s 83 of the Commonwealth of Australia Constitution. See too the relevant provisions of the Supply and Appropriation Acts relating to the period in question. In my opinion, the authorities establish that money paid out of Consolidated Revenue without statutory or other lawful authority is recoverable by the Crown from the recipient, at all events if paid without any consideration. And, in my opinion, the position is *a fortiori* where, as here, the payments are the result of a mistake. I consider that the principle, which I have just stated, is a special overriding principle applicable to public moneys in the sense of moneys of the Crown forming part of Consolidated Revenue; the principle is of wider scope than the principles relating to the recovery as between subject and subject of moneys paid under a mistake of fact or for a consideration which has failed. The principle is, in my view, based on public policy. In my statement of the principle I have used the words 'at all events if paid without any consideration', because special problems might arise with respect to unauthorised payments of public moneys in return for valuable consideration such as goods or services: cf *Re KL Tractors Ltd* (1961), especially pp 334–35. In the present case Mrs Burns gave no consideration for any of the payments which were made to her.

In *Auckland Harbour Board v The King* (1924), Viscount Haldane, speaking for the Privy Council, said (pp 326, 327):

> ... it has been a principle of the British Constitution now for more than two centuries, a principle which their Lordships understand to have been inherited in the Constitution of New Zealand with the same stringency, that no money

can be taken out of the consolidated fund into which the revenues of the State have been paid, excepting under a distinct authorisation from parliament itself. The days are long gone by in which the Crown, or its servants, apart from parliament, could give such an authorisation or ratify an improper payment. *Any payment out of the consolidated fund made without parliamentary authority is simply illegal and* ultra vires, *and may be recovered by the government if it can, as here, be traced* ... to invoke analogies of what might be held in a question between subject and subject is hardly relevant. (Italics are mine.)

[828] By the words 'if it can, as here, be traced' Viscount Haldane was, in my opinion, not referring to tracing in the equitable or proprietary sense, but to tracing the identity of the recipient of the money. The principle stated by his Lordship in the passage which I have set out was applied in the *Auckland Harbour Board Case* itself, notwithstanding that there was no evidence that the sum of £7,500 there in question was at any relevant time still identifiable in the hands of the recipient, the Auckland Harbour Board. And that case was stronger than the present case, because the sum of £7,500 had not been paid by mistake of fact. Reference may also be made to the report of counsel's argument (1924), p 320, where distinguished counsel for the Crown submitted that 'when a subject receives public money without authority he becomes a debtor to the Crown to that extent'. See also the report of the *Auckland Harbour Board* case in the Court of Appeal of New Zealand (1919).

The principle set out in the passage which I have cited from Viscount Haldane's judgment in the *Auckland Harbour Board* case has never since been questioned, so far as I have discovered. On the contrary it has been referred to in later cases without disapproval and has on occasion been applied. The principle was applied in *R v Toronto Terminals Railway Co* (1948) and in *Commonwealth of Australia v Thomson* (1962). The principle was referred to in *Attorney General v Great Southern and Western Railway Co of Ireland* (1925), p 772 *per* Viscount Haldane (where his Lordship makes no reference to 'tracing'), and also in *New South Wales v Bardolph* (1934).[8]

Since the conclusion of the hearing in the present case I have discovered that a similar principle is well recognised in the United States of America: see, for example, *Wisconsin Central Railroad Co v United States* (1896); *United States v Wurts* (1938), especially pp 415–16; *Dunne v City of Fall River* (1952), especially p 336; *Corbin on Contracts*;[9] and *American Law Reports Annotated*.[10]

Subject to two qualifications, to which I shall refer in a moment, it was not suggested that there was anything in the Commonwealth of Australia Constitution or in relevant Commonwealth legislation to exclude the application to the present case of the general principle formulated by Viscount Haldane in the *Auckland Harbour Board* case, *supra*, in the passage already set out. And in my opinion, the true position is that the application of the principle is confirmed by s 81, s 82 and s 83 of the Commonwealth of Australia Constitution: see too s 53, s 54 and s 56; and *Attorney General for Victoria v Commonwealth* (1945).

---

8   (1934), pp 470, 471 *per* Evatt J; and p 522 *per* McTiernan J. See also *Re KL Tractors Ltd* (1961), p 328 (*arguendo*) and p 335; *Halsbury's Laws of England*, 3rd edn, Vol 28, p 443, para 857; Vol 33, p 12, para 13, note (m); cf *Attorney General v Perry* (1734).

9   1960, Vol 3, p 758, s 617 and n 65.

10 (1929) 63 ALR, pp 1346–56.

The first of the two qualifications just mentioned is that it was submitted by [counsel] for Mrs Burns, that a sufficient authority for the payments which she received was to be found in the references to 'War and Repatriation Services' and to 'Repatriation Department' in the Schedules to Supply and Appropriation Acts passed by the Commonwealth parliament during the period in question. But Mrs Burns was never entitled to any repatriation pension or other payment, so that the payments which were in fact made to her were not an [829] application of the sums in question for War and Repatriation Services or for Repatriation Department services: cf the *Auckland Harbour Board* case (1919), and *R v Toronto Terminals Railway Co* (1948), pp 574, 575.

The second qualification is that it was submitted that the application of Viscount Haldane's principle was by implication excluded by s 120AA of the Repatriation Act, which was enacted by s 21 of the Repatriation Act 1963, and which provides as follows:

> 120AA Where, in consequence of a false statement or representation or of a failure or omission to comply with any provision of this Act or the regulations, an amount has been paid by way of pension, allowance or benefit that would not have been paid but for the false statement or representation or the failure or omission, the amount so paid is recoverable in a court of competent jurisdiction from the person to whom, or on whose account, the amount was paid, or from the estate of that person, as a debt due to the Commonwealth.

The right of recovery conferred upon the Commonwealth by this provision may perhaps be in some respects wider and in other respects narrower than those conferred at common law in accordance with the principle in the *Auckland Harbour Board* case. But however this may be, I consider that s 120AA does not exclude the latter principle. It does not in terms purport to exclude any common law rights to recover unauthorised payments, and no good reason appears why it should have been intended to exclude them. It is well established that 'a party is only bound to follow a remedy provided by Statute when his right is also created by Statute ... but where he has a common law right and a common law remedy, any further remedy provided by Statute is cumulative' *per* Hood J, in *Jones v Reed* (1890). This general rule will no doubt be excluded if a contrary intention sufficiently appears, but I find none in the case of s 120AA. See also *R v Henderson* (1896); *Ochberg v Commissioner of Stamp Duties* (1943), pp 190–91; and *Lowe v Dorling and Son* (1906) ...

On behalf of Mrs Burns it was finally submitted that the Commonwealth was estopped from alleging that the payments in question had been made to her without lawful authority. It was submitted that [830] the officer of the Repatriation Department with whom she had the second telephone conversation had represented to her that she was entitled to the payments, and that this representation was confirmed by the continuance of the payments. It was further submitted that Mrs Burns had spent the money now sought to be recovered in reliance upon the representation, so that a requirement that she repay the money would operate unjustly to her detriment: see, for example, *Holt v Markham* (1923), and *Grundt v Great Boulder Gold Mines Pty Ltd* (1939), especially pp 674–77 *per* Dixon J. But a sufficient answer to this submission is, in my view, to be found in the well established rule that a party cannot be assumed by the doctrine of estoppel to have lawfully done that which the law says that he shall not do: as earlier stated, nobody had, or could have had, any lawful authority to make the payments in question to Mrs Burns; see, for example, the *Auckland Harbour Board* case (1919); *Howell v Falmouth Board Construction Co Ltd* (1951), especially pp 845 and 849; *Attorney General for Ceylon v Silva* (1953), pp 479–81; *Maritime Electric Co Ltd v General Dairies Ltd* (1937); *Peart v Victorian Railways Commissioners* (1924), especially pp 429–30; *Attorney General v Municipal Council of Sydney* (1919); and Spencer Bower and Turner, *Estoppel by Representation*.[11] This rule is of wide application and can apply as between subject and subject, so that s 64 of the Judiciary Act, upon which [counsel for Mrs Burns] sought to rely in relation to the defence of estoppel, has no application. (It was not suggested that s 64 prevented the application of the principle in the *Auckland Harbour Board* case, and, in my view, it does not do so: cf *South Australia v Commonwealth* (1962), p 140 *per* Dixon CJ.) ...

Having regard to the conclusions which I have reached, it is unnecessary to consider whether the amount in question would be recoverable by the Commonwealth as money paid under a mistake of fact, which was in the end the only other basis upon which [counsel for the Commonwealth] sought to place the Commonwealth's claim: cf *Commonwealth of Australia v Kerr* (1919), (where the principle upon which I have decided the present case was not raised) ...

Commentary and questions

On what basis did the court grant the Commonwealth's claim? Was the claim founded upon a causative mistake?

Newton J in the principal case interprets the reference to tracing by Viscount Haldane in the *Auckland Harbour Board* case as a reference not to 'tracing in the equitable or proprietary sense but to tracing the identity of the recipient of the money'. Other Australian authorities have also consistently treated the claim as personal in nature. The position may be different in England however. Lord Goff in *Woolwich Equitable Building Society v Inland Revenue Commissioners* (1992), p 763 (see extract, p 456) interpreted Viscount Haldane's reference to tracing as meaning that a claim by the revenue for the recovery of unauthorised payments is proprietary in nature.

Attorney General v Gray [1977] 1 NSWLR 406
Court of Appeal of New South Wales

The defendant was a sculptor employed by the Department of Education on a casual basis to teach art. He was paid at the rate either of $22.94 or $20.28 per day, though for his level of academic qualifications he was in fact only entitled to be paid $18.01 per day. The excess aggregate amount paid to him totalled $911.55. The Attorney General sued on behalf of the New South Wales Government for this amount, claiming a right of recovery on the basis the money had been paid out of consolidated revenue without lawful authority or alternatively had been paid under a mistake of fact. The trial judge found that the money was paid under a mistake of fact but that the department, by reason of the conduct of its officers, was estopped from setting up such facts.

---

11 2nd edn, pp 131–34, para 140.

Glass JA: ... [411] On appeal to this court, counsel for the plaintiff has not sought to challenge the finding that an estoppel arose in favour of the defendant. Nor did he attempt to support the ground that the plaintiff was entitled to recover upon the basis of money paid under a mistake of fact. He acknowledged that to such a claim the unchallenged estoppel would operate as a complete defence: *Holt v Markham* (1923). But he sought to [412] maintain the title of the defendant to judgment upon two propositions: (1) that payments made by the department in excess of the sums properly due were illegally made and recoverable; and (2) that no estoppel could arise which involved the assumption that the plaintiff had lawfully done that which was contrary to law. The argument in support of the first proposition proceeded by the following stages. Section 14(1) and s 14A of the Public Service Act 1902 combine to provide that the salary payable to temporary employees such as the defendant was the salary determined from time to time by the Board. The Board had determined that the salary payable to him was to be calculated at the lower rate, namely $18.01 per day. Any payment made without parliamentary approval is illegal and recoverable: *Auckland Harbour Board v The King* (1924). Parliamentary approval is signified by means of an Appropriation Act which gives assent to the expenditure of moneys restricted to the purposes stated in the Act: *Commonwealth v Colonial Ammunition Co Ltd* (1924), pp 220–24; *Victoria v The Commonwealth* (1975), pp 174, 176, 183. The cheques by means of which the defendant was paid at the higher rate were drawn on the account of the Department of Education, and there was at all relevant times a fund of money appropriated for the payment of salaries of casual teachers. However, in order to determine whether or not a payment debited to funds appropriated in general terms was made with parliamentary authority it was necessary to consider the statutory law relevant to such payment. In the light of the provisions of the Public Service Act the payment made to the defendant was made without parliamentary authority. It was, therefore, illegal and could be recovered.

For the defendant it was argued that the payments were made with parliamentary approval, having regard to the decision in *New South Wales v Bardolph* (1934). I cannot agree. It was there held (1934), p 471, that an appropriation in general terms will provide sufficient parliamentary authority for the payment of money due under a contract validly made by government officers. But, in the absence of a valid contract providing for the payments made, the authority for them must be found in the general appropriation, as qualified by the provisions of the relevant law. It follows that the first proposition, and the title to recovery which it confers, has been established. I note that a similar argument was upheld in *Commonwealth v Burns* (1971) and *Commonwealth v Thomson* (1962). They related respectively to the recovery of pension payments and payments to a public servant in lieu of furlough, both of which were held to have been made without statutory authority.

The second proposition sought to overcome the estoppel which favoured the defendant. This arose, as his Honour held, because he had altered his position by spending the overpayments in reliance upon departmental representations that he was entitled to receive them. The plaintiff argued that the estoppel, although effective as regards the first ground of recovery based upon a mistake of fact, could not defeat the second. Estoppel could not operate, because it involved the assumption that the department had lawful authority to pay the defendant at the higher rate. There is no doubt that an estoppel cannot be allowed, if it prevents the representor from asserting the statutory illegality of the payment: [413] Spencer

Bower and Turner, *Estoppel by Representation*.[12] An electricity authority has been held not to be estopped by the mistaken representations in its accounts from claiming charges due to it, when it had a statutory duty to collect them and the defendant had a statutory duty to pay: *Maritime Electric Co Ltd v General Dairies Ltd* (1937). The general principle is that an estoppel cannot avail to release the plaintiff from an obligation to obey a statute enacted for the benefit of a section of the public (1937), p 620. I believe that it is for the benefit of the public to provide that temporary public servants shall not be paid salaries, except in accordance with the amounts determined by the Board. An estoppel, which would prevent the plaintiff from asserting that payments had been made in breach of that law, cannot be upheld. Consequently, I consider that the plaintiff's second proposition is also established.

The conclusion which follows from these two propositions is that public moneys which have been misapplied for want of sufficient appropriation are recoverable; and no defensive estoppels can be founded on the erroneous representations of functionaries. In that event it might be asked how did it come about that Colonel Markham: *Holt v Markham* (1923), and Major Skyring: *Skyring v Greenwood* (1825), could each, by means of an estoppel, defeat proceedings to recover the overpayments to them, as having been made under a mistake of fact. To conclude that the plaintiffs and their advisers overlooked an alternative ground of recovery, to which estoppel was unavailing, might encourage a pretence of antipodean superiority. But I think it is clear that the ground was not applicable. The plaintiffs were respectively described as Army agents and paymasters disbursing their own funds subject to recoupment from the Crown. They sued in their own names to recover sums which the Crown had disallowed in its accounts with them. The money they received was public money, but the payments they made were from private funds which did not attract the principle. Subject to one remaining consideration, I am of opinion that the plaintiff is entitled to succeed.

The outstanding question arises from the fact that the payments sued for constituted part only of the payments received by the defendant. They were the unauthorised excess, representing the difference, in each case, between the amount due at the lower rate, which was applicable, and the higher rate, which was not. The defendant who received the payments provided valuable consideration in the form of teaching services. His position in this respect differed from that of the defendants in *Commonwealth v Burns* (1971) and *Commonwealth v Thomson* (1962), who received unauthorised payments for which they gave no consideration of any kind. In the former case the following passage appears (1971), p 827: 'In my statement of the principle I have used the words "at all events if paid without any consideration", because special problems might arise with respect to unauthorised payments of public moneys in return for valuable consideration such as goods or services: cf *Re KL Tractors Ltd* (1961), pp 334–35.' In *Re KL Tractors Ltd* (1962), the Commonwealth had used funds properly appropriated by parliament to carry on the manufacture of gear boxes in a wartime ordinance factory. It was argued that the production [414] and sale of such goods in 1947 was beyond Commonwealth power. Assuming that the Commonwealth had exceeded its constitutional authority, the High Court held that the purchaser could not resist payment on that

12   2nd edn, p 132.

ground. With respect to his Honour, I do not find here any support for the view that public funds applied for purposes for which they have not been appropriated may nonetheless be irrecoverable, if given in exchange for valuable consideration. But I do think that the status of the defendant, as recipient of public moneys who gave value for them, does raise a difference which might be considered relevant in point of principle. There was parliamentary authority for part of the payment made to him. Is it proper to sever the unauthorised excess, and treat that as an illegal payment which is recoverable, or is it necessary to treat the whole payment as illegal? This was a factor which weighed with the trial judge. He considered that 'none of the payments made was unlawful, although each was for an amount which exceeded the proper amount. Each payment was for an executed consideration, namely the supply by the defendant of services, and each was paid out of a fund appropriated by parliament for the payment of teachers of a category which included the defendant'. Upon reflection I do not think that this approach is soundly based. The general appropriation cannot validate the payment made, if it exceeded limits imposed by statute. To the extent of the excess, public funds were misapplied. This was not only unauthorised but, in terms of the *Auckland Harbour Board* case (1924) constituted an illegal payment. If, in exchange for a valid consideration, several promises are given, some legal and one illegal, the latter may be severed and the balance of the contract enforced: *Kearney v Whitehaven Colliery Co* (1893). I would apply that solution here. The illegal excess was identifiable and may properly be severed. In my opinion, the plaintiff was entitled to succeed in an action to recover it ...

Commentary and questions

Was recovery restricted to the unauthorised excess payments? What rationale did Glass JA give for refusing to recognise estoppel as a defence to the claim? On what basis did Glass JA distinguish *Holt v Markham* (1923) (see extract, p 569) and *Skyring v Greenwood* (1825) (see extract, p 567) from the case before him?

The view expressed by Glass JA in the principal case and Newton J in *Commonwealth v Burns* (1971), (see extract, p 486) that a misrepresentation by a Crown employee could not ground an estoppel is well supported by other Australian authorities: see, for example, *The Commonwealth v Thomson* (1962) and *Formosa v Department of Social Security* (1988), p 125. Burrows[13] is critical of this approach to estoppel arguing that it carries the desire to protect public funds to 'unacceptable lengths'. Mason and Carter[14] however argue that it would be 'unlikely and inappropriate' that estoppel should be available as the rule in the *Auckland Harbour Board* case is premised upon the high constitutional principle that parliament alone may authorise the disbursement of money from the consolidated revenue fund. Mason and Carter also argue that the defence of change of position should not be available for the same reason.[15] However, it is at least arguable that the *pro tanto* nature of the defence strikes a fair balance

---

13 Burrows, *The Law of Restitution*, 1993, p 332.
14 Mason and Carter, *Restitution Law in Australia*, 1995, pp 784, 787.
15 Mason and Carter, *Restitution Law in Australia*, 1995, 787. The authors also argue that the requirement of detrimental reliance can never be met in this context, as reliance cannot properly be based on an illegal payment: *ibid*.

between the need on the one hand to protect parliamentary funds, and the need on the other hand to mitigate the harsh operation of the *Auckland Harbour Board* principle. The matter awaits judicial determination.

Glass JA in the principal case appeared to reject the argument that provision of good consideration is a defence to a claim based on the *Auckland Harbour Board* principle. On the other hand, Newton J in *Commonwealth v Burns* (1971) (see extract, p 486) suggested that payments made with consideration might fall outside of the principle: see p 827.

AUTHORISED PAYMENTS OUT OF CONSOLIDATED REVENUE

As the following case demonstrates, the statutory authority must be examined closely to determine if that authority has been exceeded.

Commonwealth of Australia v Hamilton [1992] 2 Qd R 257
Full Court of the Supreme Court of Queensland

The defendant applied for and was paid unemployment benefits during a period in which he was in employment. He had made false statements in order to satisfy officers of the Department of Social Security that he was unemployed throughout the relevant period. The Commonwealth commenced proceedings against the defendant to recover an amount representing the unemployment benefits received but not repaid by him. The relevant provisions of the Social Security Act 1947 (Cwlth) are set out in the judgment of McPherson ACJ.

McPherson ACJ: ... [262] T]he plaintiff in support of a right to judgment in its favour relied on the principle stated by the Privy Council in *Auckland Harbour Board v The King* (1924), and applied in a series of subsequent cases in Australia, including *Commonwealth v Burns* (1971); *Attorney General v Gray* (1977); and *Sandvik Australia Pty Ltd v Commonwealth* (1989). See also *Australian Alliance Assurance Co v Goodwyn* (1916).

[263] In *Auckland Harbour Board v The King* (1924), p 326 Viscount Haldane said:

> ... it has been a principle of the British Constitution now for more than two centuries ... that no money can be taken out of the consolidated fund into which the revenues of the State have been paid excepting under a distinct authorisation from parliament itself ... Any payment out of the consolidated fund made without parliamentary authority is simply illegal and *ultra vires*, and may be recovered by the government ...

In that case the principle was applied to the recovery of a sum the payment of which was under legislation passed in 1912 authorised to be effected only upon entry into a lease, which never took place. Acting on the same principle Newton J in *Commonwealth v Burns* (1971) held the plaintiff entitled to recover the amount received by the defendant of sums mistakenly paid to her by way of repatriation pension for the benefit of her father after he had died. Again, in *Attorney General v Gray* (1977), the plaintiff recovered from a State school teacher so much of the salary payments made to him at a rate that exceeded that at which he was entitled to be paid under statute.

In my opinion these cases are distinguishable from the present. In each of them the recipient of the payment out of consolidated funds failed to satisfy the statutory requirement which constituted the sole authority to make the payment or payments in question. In *Auckland Harbour Board v The King*, the statutory authority for payment was conditional upon the happening of an event that never took place. In *Commonwealth v Burns* the statutory qualification for payment of the pension is not precisely set out in the report of the case; but it is clear enough that the title of the defendant's father to receive it ceased at his death, and with it the authority to pay it either to him or to her on his behalf. In *Attorney General v Gray* the defendant did not possess the qualifications entitling him to payment at the rate appropriate under the relevant statutory provisions for teachers in a higher classification to which he did not belong. He was accordingly held liable to repay the excess.

Before the principle of the *Auckland Harbour Board* case can be invoked it is necessary to identify the precise terms of the statutory authority to pay, and to ask whether the terms of that authority were exceeded. It applies only when it can be seen that no such authority exists, as where its operation is made to depend on the fulfilment of a statutory condition that is not satisfied; or on the absence in the recipient of a particular statutory characteristic or qualification that would entitle him to payment; or on some other defect in the source of authority to pay. It is in events like those that money paid out of consolidated funds under parliamentary control will be recoverable according to this principle. As was recognised by Viscount Haldane in the passage set out above, and also by Gibbs CJ in *Maguire v Simpson* (1977), p 388, the rule is an application of the *ultra vires* doctrine, which means that the payment must be shown to have been made without or contrary to or in excess of the statutory authority to make it.

When one turns to that question in the present case, it is, as the learned judge of District Courts held, plain that payment of the subject unemployment benefits to the defendant was not unauthorised or outside or contrary to the relevant statutory authority. Section 238 of the Social Security Act 1947 (Cwlth) [264] provides that payment of benefits under the Act shall be made out of the Consolidated Revenue Fund, which is appropriated accordingly. Before the extensive renumbering of sections of the legislation undertaken in 1987, and at the time when the subject payments were made, the comparable provision of the Act was s 136, which was so far as material in identical terms. It identifies the public funds of the Commonwealth as the source from which payment is to be made, and it authorises money to be taken from that source for payment of benefits under the Act. The relevant benefit in this respect was unemployment benefit. Section 116(1) of the renumbered legislation now provides, so far as material, that a person:

> ... is qualified to receive an unemployment benefit if, and only if

> (a) ...

> (b) ...

> (c) the person satisfies the Secretary that –

>> (i) throughout the relevant period he was unemployed ...

Before being renumbered, the comparable statutory provision was s 107(1)(c), which was expressed in terms that are indistinguishable in substance from the current s 116(1)(c). The 'Secretary' referred to in both provisions means the Secretary to the Department, which, although not nominated in the Acts, is the Commonwealth Department of Social Security.

These provisions identify, by reference to criteria that are set out in the paragraphs of sub-s (1), the persons who are qualified to receive unemployment benefit under the Act. Expressly or by implication, they authorise payments from the money appropriated under s 238 (new) or s 136 (old) to persons so qualified. Both in the new s 116(1)(c) and the old s 107(1)(c), the critical words of qualification are 'satisfies the Secretary that ... he was unemployed ...'. As the learned trial judge rightly perceived, the title to make and receive payment of unemployment benefit under the Act is not dependent on the recipient having in fact the qualification of being unemployed but upon his satisfying the Secretary that he is unemployed, whether or not that is the fact. On that footing, the plaintiff cannot succeed in its claim to recover the amount of unemployment benefit paid to the defendant as a payment not authorised by parliamentary appropriation. Even if at the time the defendant received it he was not unemployed, he satisfied the Secretary that he was. No doubt it was an officer or officers of the department rather than the Secretary himself who was or were so satisfied; but that makes no difference for present purposes. The case is not within the principle laid down by Viscount Haldane in *Auckland Harbour Board v The King* or the other decisions that have applied it, because the payment or payments were made precisely in accordance with the statutory authority under the Act, and not contrary to or beyond it. The fact that the Secretary or his officers were deceived does not mean that he was not satisfied; but rather that he was, which is all that s 116(1)(c)(i) requires.

[McPherson ACJ went on to hold that the plaintiff could recover the payments by virtue of s 246 of the Social Security Act which provided a debt in the plaintiff's favour with respect to payments caused by false representations.]

Commentary

Shepherdson and Williams JJ relevantly agreed with McPherson ACJ. Williams J stated the position (p 272) as follows:

... this is not a case of money being paid out of consolidated revenue without the authorisation of parliament, but rather a case where a person has brought himself within the parliamentary authorisation by making fraudulently misleading statements.

A payment made in accordance with the exercise of a statutory discretion is not *ultra vires* and does not attract the operation of the *Auckland Harbour Board* principle: *Trimboli v Secretary to the Department of Social Security* (1988).

CONTRACTUAL PAYMENTS

As the following case demonstrates, the *Auckland Harbour Board* principle will not apply to make recoverable payments that are authorised under a valid contract entered into with the Crown.

Commonwealth v Crothall Hospital Services (Aust) Ltd (1981) 36 ALR 567
Federal Court of Australia

By a written agreement dated 1 November 1967 the respondent agreed with the Commonwealth to clean certain government buildings in Canberra. The agreement provided for a per annum contract price but contained clauses which provided a mechanism for varying the contract price due to variations in wages paid and areas cleaned. The Commonwealth met most of the claims submitted by the respondent during the period up to 27 November 1973, some of which incorporated increases in the weekly cost of cleaning due to increased award wages and variations in areas cleaned. These claims, some of which were accompanied by explanatory correspondence, were checked by the appropriate officers, certified as correct accounts, and paid. The respondent did not make a formal application for a variation in accordance with the relevant contractual terms. After 27 November 1973, the Commonwealth only partially met the respondent's claims for payment, alleging that it had not agreed to a variation of the contract price and that the respondent was entitled to payment only at the price originally agreed to. The Commonwealth deducted from its payments after 27 November 1973 an amount by which it claimed it had overpaid the respondent prior to this date, asserting that it was recoverable as being made without authority from consolidated revenue. The respondent claimed that the Commonwealth, by meeting the claims up to 27 November 1973, had accepted a variation of the contract. The respondent sued the Commonwealth for damages for a breach of contract, seeking recovery of the amount of the claims which the Commonwealth had refused to meet.

Ellicott J: [Ellicott J examined the evidence and concluded that the Commonwealth, through the conduct of its officers in investigating and verifying each claim, had agreed to vary the contract price in the manner sought by the respondent, even though this did not accord with the terms of the contract relating to variation. He continued at p 579:] The claims in this case were certified under the Act by the person said to be incurring the expense. In many instances this was Mr Simmonds a principal executive officer with the Department of Defence who was called to give evidence. He said in evidence that he had signed the forms as the person incurring the expenditure which he said was a formal delegation. As has been mentioned nowhere in his evidence did Mr Simmonds suggest that when he gave these certificates he was mistaken or misled. Nor did any other officer involved with this contract. The giving of the certificate under the Act is not a mere formality. It testifies both to the correctness of the account in regard to rates of charge as well as faithful performance of the services and in the absence of evidence to the contrary the assumption must be that the officer satisfied himself, from his own knowledge or from information placed before him by other officers, that what he was certifying was correct. In this case, when [580] variations of price and area were involved in particular claims, it can only be assumed that the certifying officer had satisfied himself that a decision had been made by the relevant officers to agree to the variations and to reflect this in the payments to be made for the services performed. When payments were made, therefore, they reflected not a mistaken belief on the part of the relevant officers but their agreement that the particular variations involved should be accepted whether based on increases in wages or changes in areas.

The only relevance of considering the evidence relating to these certificates and the actions of the officers leading up to their signature is to demonstrate that far from supporting a case that these payments were made by mistake it is completely inconsistent with it. Apart from this it is, in itself, of no ultimate significance to the question whether the contract price was varied.

What is important to this issue is not that the officers agreed but that the Commonwealth, when it received the claims and made unqualified payments in accordance therewith, was thereby in each case, agreeing to vary the contract by adopting the price shown thereon as the contract price for the work covered by the claims and for the future until varied again.

A variation to the original contract could only take place by agreement, that is, by offer and acceptance. Here the respondent offered to vary the contract by submitting claims specifying an increased contract price based either on increases in wages or changes in areas. The Commonwealth in each case, except when it was qualified, accepted that offer by making a payment in accordance with the claim. Its action in making this payment in each case was not only performance but constituted acceptance: cf *Brogden v Metropolitan Railway Company* (1988).

The Commonwealth relied strongly on the principle applied in such cases as *Auckland Harbour Board v The King* (1924); *Commonwealth v Burns* (1971); and *King v Toronto Terminals* (1948). These cases establish that where moneys are paid out of Consolidated Revenue without authority they may be recovered in an action by the government.

This could occur if a condition on which money was appropriated by statute had not been met at the time it was paid out or if money was paid out by mistake even though not recoverable under ordinary principles. The basis of the action is that there has been a payment out of the revenue fund without authority.

In relation to actions by the Commonwealth a question arises as to whether s 64 of the Judiciary Act has had the effect of destroying the Commonwealth's cause of action in such a case. This problem was mentioned by Gibbs J (as he then was) in *Maguire v Simpson* (1977), pp 387–88. I think the better view is that the section does not have this effect. However, having regard to my view that, in any event, the principle has no operation in this case, it is unnecessary to express a concluded view on the matter.

[581] Here, as I have indicated, there is nothing to support a claim that the payments were made by mistake. Nor were the moneys for cleaning services appropriated subject to conditions which were not fulfilled. Appropriations were made from time to time to meet the cost of cleaning the Defence Department's offices. But clearly enough where those cleaning services were provided pursuant to a contract the moneys so appropriated could be applied in meeting the accounts payable under that contract.

This is, of course, conceded by the Commonwealth, but it says that in the present case many payments were not authorised by the original contract and that they are therefore recoverable. This submission would, I think, have considerable weight were it not for the fact that subsequent to the original contract the parties, in my view, agreed to vary the original contract by varying the contract price payable thereunder from time to time and in the manner I have already analysed. The principles enunciated in the *Auckland Harbour Board* case do not in my view operate to exclude the application to contracts made by the Commonwealth of the ordinary rules of contract law. For instance they do not exclude the principle referred to earlier that payment may not only constitute performance but also acceptance of an offer. It was open to the Commonwealth if it wished, to qualify its payments of claims made by the respondent. Had it done so in an appropriate way the principles of the *Auckland Harbour Board* case would no doubt have applied. However, the payments relied upon were made without qualification.

In these circumstances I think the variations of the contract are a complete answer to the Commonwealth's claim. The Commonwealth was able to agree to vary the price payable for cleaning services and this it did and in so doing it provided lawful authority for the payment out of Consolidated Revenue of the moneys in question. The Commonwealth's claim for repayment therefore fails.

Commentary and questions

Why did the *Auckland Harbour Board* principle not apply in the principal case? According to Ellicott J, what is the effect of s 64 of the Judiciary Act 1903 (Cwlth) on the *Auckland Harbour Board* principle?

The *Auckland Harbour Board* principle will apply where the rates of payment are determined by statute, rather than the contract with the Crown: *Attorney General v Gray* (1977) (see extract, p 489).

CHAPTER 17

RESTITUTIONARY REMEDIES FOR WRONGS

INTRODUCTION

General

The commission of certain types of wrongs will entitle the plaintiff to elect between a compensatory remedy (damages) or a restitutionary remedy (disgorgement of gain). If the plaintiff elects a restitutionary remedy, the plaintiff's remedy will be calculated by reference to the gain acquired by the defendant from the commission of the wrong, rather than by reference to the loss suffered by the plaintiff.[1] Accordingly, a restitutionary remedy is concerned with disgorgement of the defendant's benefit rather than compensation for the plaintiff's loss. This remedy will obviously be advantageous where the plaintiff has not suffered a loss, where the loss suffered is less than the defendant's gain, and where the quantum of the loss is difficult to quantify.[2]

It is important to emphasise that the plaintiff's cause of action is not in restitution, but rather is based on the wrong itself.[3] Restitutionary principles, in particular the principle of unjust enrichment,[4] are relevant only at the remedial stage, to assist in the determination of the quantum of the remedy.[5] The principles relating to the award of restitutionary remedies should be, but tend not to be, or not in great detail, covered in textbooks and subjects covering the relevant area of wrongs. Instead, the principles relating to restitutionary remedies are usually covered in detail only in restitutionary textbooks and subjects, and for this reason are included in this book.

---

1   *Attorney General (UK) v Observer Ltd* (1990), p 286.
2   Mason and Carter, *Restitution Law in Australia*, 1995, p 625; Goff and Jones, *The Law of Restitution*, 5th edn, 1998, p 710.
3   It is sometimes suggested that the restitution for wrongdoing cases do in fact form part of the law of restitution: see, for example, *Commissioner of State Revenue (Vic) v Royal Insurance Australia Ltd* (1994), p 73; *Attorney General v Guardian Newspapers Ltd (No 2)* (1990), p 286 and *Portman Building Society v Hamlyn Taylor Neck (A Firm)* (1998), p 206; Friedmann, 'Restitution for wrongs: the basis of liability', in Cornish (ed), *Restitution: Past, Present and Future*, 1998, Chapter 9; Burrows, 'Quadrating restitution and unjust enrichment: a matter of principle?' [2000] RLR 257. However, this author prefers Peter Birks' view that the basis of the cause of action is the commission of the wrong, not unjust enrichment: Birks, 'Misnomer', in Cornish *et al*, *Restitution: Past, Present and Future*, 1998; cf McInnes, 'Restitution, unjust enrichment and the perfect quadration thesis' [1999] RLR 118.
4   *Hospitality Group Pty Ltd v Australian Rugby Union Ltd* (2001), para 172 *per* Emmett J; *Dart Industries v Décor Corporation Pty Ltd* (1993), pp 111, 116.
5   *Winterton Constructions Pty Ltd v Hambros Australia Ltd* (1991), p 374; *Kettle Chip Co Pty Ltd v Apand Pty Ltd* (1998), p 149; *Banque Financière de la Cité v Parc (Battersea) Ltd* (1998), p 740; Mason and Carter, *Restitution Law in Australia*, 1995, p 87.

Restitution-yielding wrongs

Not all wrongs have been recognised as being amenable to a restitutionary remedy. As a general rule, a restitutionary remedy is available only for those wrongs that interfere with an interest of a proprietary or possessory nature, or an interest analogous thereto.[6] Thus, a restitutionary remedy is available for the 'proprietary' torts such as detinue, conversion, trespass to land and passing off, however is not available for 'personal' torts such as defamation, battery and deceit.[7]

A restitutionary remedy has also been held to be available for a breach of a contractual term protective of a proprietary right,[8] as damages awarded under Lord Cairns' Act in lieu of an injunction,[9] and in other exceptional cases where the plaintiff has a 'legitimate interest' in depriving the defendant of the profit.[10]

An account of profits (clearly a gain-based remedy) is available for equitable wrongs such as a breach of fiduciary obligation and breach of confidence.[11] Although it has been acknowledged that principles of unjust enrichment might have a useful part to play in determining the liability to account for profits,[12] the remedy of an account of profits in Australia is firmly governed by equitable principles. As such, it was decided not to include that topic in this chapter. However, this chapter does address the question of recovery of bribes, as a cause of action in restitution has been said to be available to recover the amount of the bribe as an alternative to an account of profits in equity for a breach of a fiduciary obligation.[13]

ELECTION

The defendant's wrongful conduct might give rise in the alternative to a cause of action on the wrong, or a cause of action in restitution based on unjust enrichment. Further, if the defendant sues on the wrong, the defendant might be able to claim in the alternative a compensatory or a restitutionary remedy.

---

6   *Halifax Building Society v Thomas* (1996), pp 226, 227; *Surrey County Council v Bredero Homes Ltd* (1993), pp 710–11, 714–15 (see extract, p 531); Goff and Jones, *The Law of Restitution*, 5th edn, 1998, pp 709–10. For a radical proposal to realign causes of action and remedial responses, see McInnes, 'Disgorgement for wrongs: an experiment in alignment' [2000] RLR 516.

7   *Halifax Building Society v Thomas* (1996).

8   At least this is one interpretation of the decision in *Wrotham Park Estate Co Ltd v Parkside Homes Ltd* (1974) (see extract, p 537).

9   *Longtom Pty Ltd v Oberon Shire Council* (1996); *Rosser v Maritime Services Board* (1996). Compare *Surrey County Council v Bredero Homes Ltd* (1993), p 711 (see extract, p 531).

10   *Attorney General v Blake (Jonathan Cape Ltd Third Party)* (2001) (see extract, p 541).

11   For an argument that the equitable remedy of account of profits should be made available to common law wrongs, see Doyle and Wright, 'Restitutionary damages – the unnecessary remedy' (2001) 25 MULR 1.

12   *Warman International Ltd v Dwyer* (1995), p 561.

13   See below pp 550–63.

It used to be thought that a plaintiff who had alternative causes of action in restitution or in tort, and who commenced proceedings in restitution, had 'waived the tort'. This term, in so far as it implies that the plaintiff by commencing restitutionary proceedings waives any right to sue on the wrong, is misleading.[14] As will be seen from the following case, the general rule is that the plaintiff can sue in the alternative in restitution and on the wrong, and is not required to elect between these two causes of action until applying for judgment. The plaintiff will only lose this right of election where the plaintiff has done an unequivocal act choosing one cause of action over another.

United Australia Ltd v Barclays Bank Ltd [1941] AC 1 House of Lords

The appellant company received a cheque for £1,900 from one of its debtors. The appellant's company secretary, Emons, endorsed the cheque, without authority, to make it payable to the MFG Trust of which Emons was a director. MFG then endorsed the cheque and paid it into its account at the respondent bank. The respondent bank collected the proceeds of the cheque and credited the funds to MFG's account. The appellant issued a writ against MFG claiming the £1,900 as money lent or alternatively as money had and received. This claim was never pursued to judgment as MFG went into liquidation. Two years later the appellant commenced proceedings against the respondent bank for conversion, negligence, or alternatively for £1,900 as money had and received.

Viscount Simon LC: ... [9] The question to be decided in this appeal is whether the proceedings against MFG, carried on up to the point which they in fact reached, constitute a valid ground of defence for the respondent bank and so relieve it in the present action from a liability, which would otherwise certainly attach to it, to repay to the appellant company the sum of £1,900 of which they had been deprived and which they have not received from any other source.

The view taken by the courts below is that the appellant company, by bringing their action against MFG, elected to 'waive the tort' and thereby became irrevocably committed, even against a different defendant, to the view that Emons was, as he professed to be, duly authorised as the appellant company's agent to deal with the cheque as he did. If so, [10] the bank's dealing with the cheque was not tortious and the present action would fail ...

The House has now to decide whether the courts below are right in holding that the appellants are barred from recovering judgment against the bank because they previously instituted proceedings, on the basis of 'waiving the tort' against MFG, when those proceedings never produced any judgment [11] or satisfaction in the plaintiff's favour. This question may be conveniently dissected by first asking whether there would be any such bar even if the present action were an action in tort against MFG. If a remedy in tort would remain open against the same defendant, then there certainly cannot have been any conclusive election which could prevent an action against a different defendant who had previously not been sued at all.

The process known as 'waiving the tort' can be traced back to the latter half of the 17th century, when much accurate learning and refined analysis were addressed to

---

14   See further Mason and Carter, *Restitution Law in Australia*, 1995, pp 613–14.

determining what were the appropriate forms of action in which a claim could, or should, be embodied. Thus, in 1678, in the case of *Howard v Wood* (1679) the plaintiff brought his claim in *assumpsit* for fees due to him as steward of the Honour of Pomfret against a defendant who had received the fees under a subsequent grant of the office which was not valid. It was objected 'that this action will not lie for the money received by the defendant as money received for the plaintiff's use, because the defendant claimed title by another grant made to himself, and therefore received it to his own use; and that the plaintiff should have brought an action of trover for the money, or case, for disturbing him in his office'. To this the Court of King's Bench answered: 'That it might be hard perhaps to maintain it, if this were a new case, and the first of this nature; but they said two or three actions of this kind had been held before, and cited a case between Bradshaw and Porter of Grays Inn, for money received as judge of the Sheriff's Court of London to be so resolved; and therefore it would be hard now to adjudge the contrary.' In the previous year, 1677, a similar objection to the plaintiff proceeding in *assumpsit* to recover the profits of an office, which had wrongly been received by the defendant, was overruled by the Court of Exchequer in *Arris & Arris v Stukely* (1677), where the argument of the Solicitor General, Sir Francis Winnington, is thus reported: 'An *indebitatus assumpsit* would lie here; for [12] where one receives my rent, I may charge him as bailiff or receiver; or if any one receive my money without my order, though it is a tort yet an *indebitatus* will lie, because by reason of the money the law creates a promise; and the action is not grounded on the tort, but on the receipt of the profits in this case.'

Another example of the same objection being overruled is found in *Lamine v Dorrell* (1701), where an administrator of an estate sued in *assumpsit* to recover proceeds, which had been gathered in by a former administrator whose appointment had been revoked. In that case, Powell J said: 'It is clear the plaintiff might have maintained detinue or trover for the debentures, but when the act that is done is in its nature tortious, it is hard to turn that into a contract, and against the reason of *assumpsit*. But the plaintiff may dispense with the wrong, and suppose the sale made by his consent, and bring an action for the money they were sold for, as money received to his use. It has been carried thus far already.' And Holt CJ said: 'These actions have crept in by degrees,' and added, 'he could not see how it differed from an *indebitatus assumpsit* for the profits of an office by a rightful officer against a wrongful, as money had and received by the wrongful officer to the use of the rightful'.

It is not necessary in this connection to discuss the logical basis of the writ of *indebitatus assumpsit*; my noble and learned friend, Lord Wright,[15] has submitted it to searching analysis in his essay on the decision of this House, a quarter of a century ago in *Sinclair v Brougham* (1914). Suffice it to say that the device of 'waiving the tort' and suing in *assumpsit* soon spread. A learned author includes among torts which can be waived, conversion, trespass to land or goods, deceit, occasionally action upon the case, and the action for extorting money by threats.[16] An extreme instance is provided in *Lightly v Clouston* (1808), where the [13] defendant had wrongfully taken the plaintiff's apprentice into his employment,

---

15 *Legal Essays and Addresses by Lord Wright of Durley*, 1938, Cambridge: CUP, p 1.
16 *Winfield on the Province of the Law of Tort*, 1940, p 169.

and the plaintiff, instead of suing for seduction, successfully claimed in *assumpsit* against the defendant who had tortiously employed him. 'This case,' said Mansfield J 'approaches as nearly as possible to the case where goods are sold, and the money has found its way into the pocket of the defendant'. Six years later, Lord Ellenborough, in *Foster v Stewart* (1815), doubted whether this was not going too far. At any rate, it is clear that there are torts to which the process of waiver could not be applied; the tort of defamation, for example, or of assault, could not be dressed up into a claim in *assumpsit*.

Where 'waiving the tort' was possible, it was nothing more than a choice between possible remedies derived from a time when it was not permitted to combine them or to pursue them in the alternative, and when there were procedural advantages in selecting the form of *assumpsit*. For example, there were no pitfalls in drawing the declaration in *assumpsit*, and the cause of action did not drop with death; on the other hand, there were advantages for the defendant, too, for an action framed in *assumpsit* permitted the defendant to plead the general issue.[17]

Lamine v Dorrell (1701) contains the first judicial reference which I have been able to find to the effect of success in pursuing one form of action in barring proceedings under the other. For Holt J observes, 'If an action of *trover* should be brought by the plaintiff for these debentures after judgment in this *indebitatus assumpsit*, he may plead this recovery in bar of the action of trover, in the same manner as it would have been a good plea in bar for the defendant to have pleaded to the action of trover, that he sold the debentures, and paid to the plaintiff in satisfaction. But it may be a doubt if this recovery can be pleaded before execution'. It will be observed that Holt J does not say that the commencement of an action in one form bars the [14] possibility of recovery under another form of action; even against the same party, the bar only arises in his view, at earliest, on recovering judgment ...

Hitchin v Campbell (1772), which was treated [by the Court of Appeal] as having no bearing on the point now in issue, appears to me, on the contrary, to indicate clearly the distinction which it is all important to bear in mind. De Grey J, in delivering the judgment of the court, discusses the two questions whether the plaintiff by proceeding upon the tort bars himself from proceeding upon *assumpsit*, or whether, in order to create a bar, the first proceeding must not go as far as judgment, and he reaches the conclusion that one personal action not going to judgment is no bar to another being brought, but that if judgment is had on the merits, then it bars all other personal suits from the same cause of action ...

[15] This brings me to *Smith v Baker* (1873). Bovill J says:

> The law is clear that a person who is entitled to complain of a conversion of his property, but who prefers to waive the tort, may do so and bring his action for money had and received for the proceeds of goods wrongfully sold. The law implies, under such circumstances, a promise on the part of the tortfeasor that he will pay over the proceeds of the sale to the rightful owner. But if an action for money had and received is so brought, that is in point of law a conclusive election to waive the tort; and so the commencement of an action of trespass or *trover* is a conclusive election the other way. The principles which govern the subject are very well illustrated in the case of *Buckland v Johnson*

---

17 *Stephen's Principles of Pleading*, 2nd edn, p 197.

(1854), where it is held that the plaintiff having sued one of two joint tortfeasors in tort could not afterwards sue the other for money had and received.

Undoubtedly, my Lords, Bovill J, in this passage suggests that it is the bringing of the action which constitutes a conclusive election. But this is an isolated *dictum*, not at all necessary for the case with which Bovill J was dealing. The *dictum* was not affirmed by his colleagues ...

[17] This review of the authorities convinces me that the oft quoted *dictum* of Bovill J in *Smith v Baker* (1873) is wrong. There is, as far as I can discover, no reported case which has ever laid it down as matter of decision that when the plaintiff [18] 'waives the tort' and starts an action in *assumpsit*, he then and there debars himself from a future proceeding based on the tort. It would be very remarkable if it were so. 'The fallacy of the argument', as Lord Ellenborough said in *Hunter v Prinsep* (1808), 'appears to us to consist in attributing more effect to the mere form of this action than really belongs to it. In bringing an action for money had and received, instead of *trover*, the plaintiff does no more than waive any complaint, with a view to damages, of the tortious act by which the goods were converted into money; and takes to the neat proceeds of the sale as the value of the goods'. When the plaintiff 'waived the tort' and brought *assumpsit*, he did not thereby elect to be treated from that time forward on the basis that no tort had been committed; indeed, if it were to be understood that no tort had been committed, how could an action in *assumpsit* lie? It lies only because the acquisition of the defendant is wrongful and there is thus an obligation to make restitution.

The true proposition is well formulated in the Restatement of the Law of Restitution promulgated by the American Law Institute, p 525, as follows: 'A person upon whom a tort has been committed and who brings an action for the benefits received by the tortfeasor is sometimes said to "waive the tort". The election to bring an action of *assumpsit* is not, however, a waiver of tort but is the choice of one of two alternative remedies.' Contrast with this, instances of true waiver of rights, eg, waiver of forfeiture by receiving rent.

If, under the old forms of procedure, the mere bringing of an action while waiving the tort did not constitute a bar to a further action based on the tort, still less could such a result be held to follow after the Common Law Procedure Act 1852, and the Judicature Act 1875. For it is now possible to combine in a single writ a claim based on tort with a claim based on *assumpsit*, and it follows inevitably that the making of the one claim cannot amount to an election which bars the making of the other. No doubt, if [19] the plaintiff proved the necessary facts, he could be required to elect on which of his alternative causes of action he would take judgment, but that has nothing to do with the unfounded contention that election arises when the writ is issued. There is nothing conclusive about the form in which the writ is issued, or about the claims made in the statement of claim. A plaintiff may at any time before judgment be permitted to amend. The substance of the matter is that on certain facts he is claiming redress either in the form of compensation, ie, damages as for a tort, or in the form of restitution of money to which he is entitled, but which the defendant has wrongfully received. The same set of facts entitles the plaintiff to claim either form of redress. At some stage of the proceedings the plaintiff must elect which remedy he will have. There is, however, no reason of principle or convenience why that stage should be deemed to be reached until the plaintiff applies for judgment.

So far, I have been discussing what is the true proposition of law when the second action is brought against the same defendant. In the present case, however, the action which is said to be barred by former proceedings against MFG is not an action against MFG at all, but an action against Barclays Bank. I am quite unable to see why this second action should be barred by the plaintiffs' earlier proceedings against MFG. In the first place, the tort of conversion of which the bank was guilty is quite a separate tort from that done by MFG. MFG's tort consisted in taking the cheque away from the appellants without the appellants' authority; that tort would have equally existed if MFG, instead of getting the cheque cleared through the bank, had kept it in its own possession. The bank's tort, on the other hand, consisted in taking a cheque, which was the property of the appellants, and without their authority using it to collect money which rightly belonged to the appellants. MFG and the bank were not joint tortfeasors, for two persons are not joint tortfeasors because their independent acts cause the same damage ...

[21] To avoid misunderstanding, I must add that I do not think that the respondents in the present case would escape liability, even if judgment had been entered in the appellant company's earlier action against MFG. What would be necessary to constitute a bar, as Bayley J pointed out in *Morris v Robinson* (1824), would be that, as the result of such judgment or otherwise, the appellants should have received satisfaction ...

Lord Atkin: [Lord Atkin made the observations about the implied contract theory which are extracted in Chapter 1, p 7 and continued at p 29:]

Concurrently with the decisions as to waiver of tort there is to be found a supposed application of election: and the allegation is sometimes to be found that the plaintiff elected to waive the tort. It seems to me that in this respect it is essential to bear in mind the distinction between choosing one of two alternative remedies, and choosing one of two inconsistent rights. As far as remedies were concerned, from the oldest time the only restriction was on the choice between real and personal actions. If you chose the one you could not claim on the other. Real actions have long disappeared: and, subject to the difficulty of including two causes of action in one writ which has also now disappeared, there has not been and there certainly is not now any compulsion to choose between alternative remedies. You may put them in the same writ: or you may put one in first, and then amend and add or substitute another ...

[30] I therefore think that on a question of alternative remedies no question of election arises until one or other claim has been brought to judgment. Up to that stage the plaintiff may pursue both remedies together, or, pursuing one may amend and pursue the other: but he can take judgment only for the one, and his cause of action on both will then be merged in the one ...

[31] In the present case, therefore, I find that the plaintiffs were at no stage in the proceedings they took against MFG Trust called to make an election, and, if it were necessary so to hold, in fact made no election, to claim in contract and not to claim in tort: and the foundation of the defendant's defence disappears. But I think it necessary to add that even if the tort had been waived, or the plaintiff had made any final election against MFG Trust Ltd, I fail to see why that should have any effect upon their claims against the bank. If a thief steals the plaintiff's goods worth

£500 and sells them to a receiver for £50 who sells them to a fourth party for £400, if I find the thief and he hands over to me the £50 or I sue him for it and recover judgment I can no longer sue him for damages for the value of the goods, but why should that preclude me from suing the two receivers for damages. I shall not be misunderstood as imputing dishonesty in this case but the instance illustrates the point. I can see no justice in the contention: and I know of no authority in support of it ...

Commentary and questions

According to the House of Lords, was the appellant's claim in conversion against Barclays Bank barred by the appellant's prior claim in restitution against MFG? Would the position have been different had the prior claim in restitution been brought against Barclays Bank itself?

The principal case was concerned with alternative *causes of action* in restitution and in tort. However, it is apparent that the same principles apply where the plaintiff is entitled to pursue in the alternative a compensatory or a restitutionary *remedy*. Again, the rule is that the plaintiff is entitled to pursue these inconsistent remedies in the alternative and need not elect between them until applying for judgment.[18]

The principal case was followed by the Full Court of New South Wales in *Sutton Motors Pty Ltd v Campbell* (1956). Campbell left his truck with Sutton Motors to be sold. Four days later Campbell called at Sutton Motors' premises and withdrew the truck from sale, however Sutton Motors refused to return the truck, claiming that Campbell had empowered it to sell during a fixed period which had not expired. Sutton Motors sold the truck and Campbell commenced proceedings against them for detinue and also for money had and received in the sum of £1,300 (the alleged proceeds of sale of the truck). At the close of the evidence at the trial the judge directed a verdict for Sutton Motors on the money had and received claim. The detinue claim went to the jury which delivered a verdict for Campbell for the value of the vehicle and for special damages of £150. Sutton Motors appealed on the ground that Campbell had waived the tort and elected to rely upon contractual rights, and accordingly had lost the right to sue for detinue. The Full Court rejected this argument, holding that there had been no unequivocal act on behalf of Campbell which amounted to an election not to pursue the detinue claim. The plaintiff would be precluded from pursuing an alternative remedy or right only where there had been a true waiver, which is dependent upon intention. In this case it could not be inferred from Campbell's conduct that he had waived the right to claim a compensatory remedy in detinue.

---

18 *Ministry of Defence v Ashman* (1993), p 105 (see extract, p 521); Mason and Carter, *Restitution Law in Australia*, 1995, pp 638–39; *Tang Min Sit v Capacious Investments Ltd* (1996), p 521. In *JS Bloor (Measham) Ltd v Calcott* (2001), Chancery Division, Hart J held that the plaintiff in a trespass action has an election between a compensatory or a restitutionary remedy.

TORTS

Restitution-yielding torts

Not all torts are 'wrongs' for which a restitutionary remedy will be available. At present, a restitutionary remedy is available only for 'proprietary torts', that is, torts protecting against interference with proprietary or possessory rights.[19] Thus, those torts that are amenable to a restitutionary award are those involving intentional interference with goods (detinue, conversion and trespass to goods), trespass to land, and passing off. There is authority suggesting that a restitutionary remedy is available for nuisance (see *Carr-Saunders v Dick McNeill Associates Ltd* (1986), p 896), although there is also contrary authority: see *Stoke-on-Trent City Council v W & J Wass Ltd* (1988) (see extract, p 526). A restitutionary remedy is not currently available for 'personal' torts such as defamation, battery, or deceit.[20]

Nature and quantum of the restitutionary remedy

It will be seen from the cases extracted in this section that, with the exception of cases involving the conversion by sale of goods or minerals, the courts have not gone so far as to award an account of the actual profits earned by the defendant from the use of the property: see, in particular *Strand Electric and Engineering Co Ltd v Brisford Entertainments Ltd* (1952), p 252 (see extract, p 510). Rather, the courts have awarded a reasonable charge or fee for the use of the property. Thus, the defendant's gain in these cases has been measured negatively (by reference to the expenses saved by the defendant from not having to pay for usage of the property) rather than positively (by reference to the actual profits made by the defendant from the use of the property). By analogy with breach of confidence cases (see, in particular, *Peter Pan Manufacturing Corporation v Corsets Silhouette Ltd* (1964), p 109), a reasonable user charge is arguably the appropriate measure in cases where the defendant could lawfully have made the relevant profits had it paid for the use of the property.[21] However, an account of profits is arguably the more appropriate measure of recovery in cases where the defendant could not have earned the profits other than by the unlawful use of the property: see *Peter Pan Manufacturing Corporation v Corsets Silhouette Ltd* (1964), pp 108–09. However, the Full Court of the Federal Court in *Hospitality Group Pty Ltd v Australian Rugby Union Ltd* (2001) was sceptical about whether an account of profits could ever be awarded for a tort (para 162):

---

19 *Hospitality Group Pty Ltd v Australian Rugby Union Ltd* (2001), para 160.

20 *Halifax Building Society v Thomas* (1998) (deceit not a restitution-yielding wrong). For discussion of this case see Jaffey, 'Disgorgement and confiscation' [1996] RLR 92. It is uncertain whether the phrase 'loss or damage' in ss 82 and 87 of the Trade Practices Act 1974 (Cth) encompasses a restitutionary award of damages for misleading or deceptive conduct: *Re Munchies Management Pty Ltd and Others* (1988).

21 Law Commission of England and Wales, Report No 247, *Aggravated, Exemplary and Restitutionary Damages* (London: The Stationery Office, 1997), para 1.60.

However described, it is not possible to slot an account of profits into the general framework of remedies that are available in tort, when the account is not awarded to compensate the plaintiff for his actual or presumed loss. That is to say, under presently accepted principles, an injured plaintiff cannot claim a windfall to prevent a wrongdoer profiting from his wrong, except in those cases where exemplary damages are available and it is proper that illicit profits are taken into account in assessing the quantum of the award, as happened in *McMillan v Singh* (1984), p 125 and *John v MGN Ltd* (1997), p 619.

On this view, whilst the profits of the defendant can be taken into account in determining the quantum of an exemplary damages award, the profits cannot themselves be the subject of an award via an account of profits.

It is sometimes argued that the award of a reasonable hire charge in the proprietary torts cases is always compensatory; that is, that the defendant is compensating the plaintiff for the loss of a reasonable usage charge. This was the view taken of the proprietary torts cases by Lord Hobhouse in his dissenting judgment in *Attorney General v Blake (Jonathan Cape Ltd Third Party)* (2001), p 299. On the other hand Lord Nicholls, who wrote the leading judgment in *Blake*, reviewed the authorities in detail and concluded that the reasonable usage charge awarded cannot always be viewed as compensatory, and must sometimes be considered to have a restitutionary object. Their Lordships' conflicting statements on this point are extracted below.

Attorney General v Blake (Jonathan Cape Ltd Third Party) [2001] AC 268 House of Lords

The facts are stated at p 541.

Lords Nicholls of Birkenhead: ... [278] *Interference with rights of property*

So I turn to established, basic principles. I shall first set the scene by noting how the court approaches the question of financial recompense for interference with rights of property. As with breaches of contract, so with tort, the general principle regarding assessment of damages is that they are compensatory for loss or injury. The general rule is that, in the oft quoted words of Lord Blackburn, the measure of damages is to be, as far as possible, that amount of money which will put the injured party in the same position he would have been in had he not sustained the wrong: *Livingstone v Rawyards Coal Co* (1880). Damages are measured by the plaintiff's loss, not the defendant's gain. But the common law, pragmatic as ever, has long recognised that there are many commonplace situations where a strict application of this principle would not do justice between the parties. Then compensation for the wrong done to the plaintiff is measured by a different yardstick. A trespasser who enters another's land may cause the landowner no financial loss. In such a case damages are measured by the benefit received by the trespasser, namely, by his use of the land. The same principle is applied where the wrong consists of use of another's land for depositing waste, or by using a path across the land or using passages in an underground mine. In this type of case the damages recoverable will be, in short, the price a reasonable person would pay for the right of user: see *Whitwham v Westminster Brymbo Coal and Coke Co* (1892) and the 'wayleave' cases such as *Martin v Porter* (1839) and *Jegon v Vivian* (1871). A more recent example was the non-removal of a floating dock, in *Penarth Dock Engineering Co Ltd v Pounds* (1963).

The same principle is applied to the wrongful detention of goods. An instance is the much cited decision of the Court of Appeal in *Strand Electric and Engineering Co Ltd v Brisford Entertainments Ltd* (1952) concerning portable switchboards. But the principle has a distinguished ancestry. Earl of Halsbury LC famously asked in *The Mediana* (1900) that if a person took away a chair from his room and kept it for 12 months, could anybody say you had a right to diminish the damages by [279] showing that I did not usually sit in that chair, or that there were plenty of other chairs in the room? To the same effect was Lord Shaw's telling example in *Watson, Laidlaw & Co Ltd v Pott, Cassels, and Williamson* (1914). It bears repetition:

> If A, being a liveryman, keeps his horse standing idle in the stable, and B, against his wish or without his knowledge, rides or drives it out, it is no answer to A for B to say: 'Against what loss do you want to be restored? I restore the horse. There is no loss. The horse is none the worse; it is the better for the exercise.'

Lord Shaw prefaced this observation with a statement of general principle:

> ... wherever an abstraction or invasion of property has occurred, then, unless such abstraction or invasion were to be sanctioned by law, the law ought to yield a recompense under the category or principle ... either of price or of hire.

That was a patent infringement case. The House of Lords held that damages should be assessed on the footing of a royalty for every infringing article.

This principle is established and not controversial. More difficult is the alignment of this measure of damages within the basic compensatory measure. Recently there has been a move towards applying the label of restitution to awards of this character: see, for instance, *Ministry of Defence v Ashman* (1993), p 105 and *Ministry of Defence v Thompson* (1993). However that may be, these awards cannot be regarded as conforming to the strictly compensatory measure of damage for the injured person's loss unless loss is given a strained and artificial meaning. The reality is that the injured person's rights were invaded but, in financial terms, he suffered no loss. Nevertheless the common law has found a means to award him a sensibly calculated amount of money. Such awards are probably best regarded as an exception to the general rule.

...

Lord Hobhouse of Woodborough: ... [299] The examples given by my noble and learned friend are examples of compensatory damages. Lord Halsbury's dining-room chair is no different ... He would have lost the use of the chair and it, like other such amenity-value assets, can be assessed by reference to the sum which has been expended on its acquisition and/or maintenance or interest upon its capital value during the period of deprivation. The supposed problem arises from asking the wrong question not from receiving the wrong answer.

[Lords Goff and Browne-Wilkinson concurred with Lord Nicholls.]

Commentary

Although the examples given by Lord Nicholls in the principal case involved situations where no loss could be shown, it appears that the plaintiff is not restricted to claiming a restitutionary remedy only in situations where he or she has not suffered a loss. The plaintiff on a proprietary tort action can elect between a compensatory or restitutionary remedy, regardless of whether or not a loss is suffered: see *JS Bloor (Measham) Ltd v Calcott* (2001).

Intentional interference with goods

As the following case demonstrates, the courts will award a reasonable hiring charge for the wrongful detention of goods (at least where the goods were *used* by the defendant) despite the fact that the plaintiff has not suffered, or been proved to have suffered, a loss.

Strand Electric and Engineering Co Ltd v Brisford Entertainments Ltd
[1952] 2 QB 246 English Court of Appeal

The defendants were negotiating for the sale of a theatre and allowed the purchasers to go into possession prior to completion of the purchase. The purchasers hired portable switchboards from the plaintiffs for use in the theatre. The hiring out of portable switchboards was a normal part of the plaintiffs' business. The defendants subsequently took possession of the theatre and failed to return the switchboards to the plaintiffs despite a number of demands for their return made on the plaintiffs' behalf. The plaintiffs commenced proceedings against the defendants in detinue and the trial judge made an order for the return of the switchboards or their value, and damages of £200. The reasonable hiring charge for the switchboards over the period of detention was £400, however, the trial judge made an allowance for the possibility that, had the switchboards been returned to the plaintiffs, some of them might not have been on hire for the whole period of detention or might have been accidentally destroyed. The plaintiffs appealed against the making of the allowance. The Court of Appeal acted on the basis that the defendants had used the plaintiffs' switchboards.

Somervell LJ: ... [249] If this had been a case where the plaintiffs had been deprived of the use of their switchboards because they had been damaged by the negligence of the defendants the principles applied by the judge would, I think, have been right. It is, however, submitted that in a claim in detinue, and one in which the defendants have used a profit-earning chattel, they must pay by way of damages a fair sum for that user. They cannot, as wrongdoers, have [250] the use of the chattels for less than a fair price for their hire. Otherwise they would be benefiting by their own wrong.

It is curious that there is no authority on the point. [Somervell LJ referred to some earlier cases and continued at p 252:]

This is a claim in detinue. On the findings the defendants had for their own benefit the use of the plaintiffs' chattels. This is an incident which is not present in the damage by negligence cases. Why is not the plaintiffs' loss the value in the market of the user? The wrong is not the mere deprivation, as in negligence and possibly some detinue cases, but the user. I am, of course, not overlooking the fact that if the chattel has been damaged and depreciated this may be an item in a claim for special damage. There are no doubt some cases in which a wrongdoer may be called on to account for profits, but in considering the measure of damages as raised here I think the actual benefit which the defendants have obtained is irrelevant. The damages could not, in my view, be increased by showing that a defendant had made by his use of the chattels much more than the market rate of hire. Equally, they cannot be diminished by showing that he had made less.

It is curious, as I have said, that there is no authority on this point. The nearest analogy is a claim for mesne profits. The measure there is a reasonable sum in the nature of rent for the user during the period of the defendant's trespass. In other words, the defendant must pay what the plaintiff would have obtained if the defendant had lawfully been in possession. In principle the same measure should, I think, apply where a defendant has detained and used a chattel of the plaintiff which the plaintiff, as part of his business, hires out to users. I have added these latter words because I do not wish in this so far uncharted field to go beyond the facts of the case. We were referred to statements as to the law in the United States of America.[22] It would appear from the statements in these books that the principle may be more widely applied in the United States of America and would cover, for example, detention and use of a private motor car. I am not saying this is wrong. There may be no distinction in principle. The question had, however, better be left till it arises ...

Denning LJ: [253] In assessing damages, whether for a breach of contract or for a tort, the general rule is that the plaintiff recovers the loss he has suffered, no more and no less. This rule is, however, often departed from. Thus, in cases where the damage claimed is too remote in law, the plaintiff recovers less than his real loss: *Liesbosch Dredger (Owners) v Edison SS (Owners)* (1933). In other cases the plaintiff may get more than his real loss. Thus, where the damage suffered by the plaintiff is recouped or lessened owing to some reason with which the defendant is not concerned, the plaintiff gets full damages without any deduction on that account: *Slater v Hoyle & Smith* (1920); *Smiley v Townshend* (1950); *Haviland v Long*. Again, in cases where the defendant has obtained a benefit from his wrongdoing he is often made liable to account for it even though the plaintiff has lost nothing and suffered no damage: *Reading v Attorney General* (1951).

The question in this case is: what is the proper measure of damages for the wrongful detention of goods? Does it fall within the general rule that the plaintiff only recovers for the loss he has suffered, or within some other, and if so what, rule? It is strange that there is no authority upon this point in English law; but there is plenty on the analogous case of detention of land. The rule there is that a wrongdoer, who keeps the owner out of his land, must pay a fair rental value for it, even though the owner would not have been able to use it himself or to let it to anyone else. So also a wrongdoer who uses land for his own [254] purposes without the owner's consent, as, for instance, for a fair ground or as a wayleave, must pay a reasonable hire for it even though he has done no damage to the land at all: *Whitwham v Westminster Brymbo Coal Company* (1896). I see no reason why the same principle should not apply to detention of goods.

If a wrongdoer has made use of goods for his own purposes, then he must pay a reasonable hire for them, even though the owner has in fact suffered no loss. It may be that the owner would not have used the goods himself, or that he had a substitute readily available, which he used without extra cost to himself. Nevertheless, the owner is entitled to a reasonable hire. If the wrongdoer had asked the owner for permission to use the goods the owner would be entitled to

---

22 See *Sedgwick on Damages*, Vol 11, pp 1031 and 1045; *Corpus Juris Secundum*, col 26, p 1286.

ask for a reasonable remuneration as the price of his permission. The wrongdoer cannot be better off because he did not ask permission. He cannot be better off by doing wrong than he would be by doing right. He must therefore pay a reasonable hire. This will cover, of course, the wear and tear which is ordinarily included in a hiring charge: but for any further damage the wrongdoer must pay extra. I do not mean to suggest that an owner who has suffered greater loss will not be able to recover it. Suppose that a man used a car in his business, and owing to its detention he had to hire a substitute at an increased cost, he would clearly be able to recover the cost of the substitute. In such cases the plaintiff recovers his actual loss. I am not concerned with those cases.

I am here concerned with the cases where the owner has in fact suffered no loss, or less loss than is represented by a hiring charge. In such cases if the wrongdoer has in fact used the goods he must pay a reasonable hire for them. Nor do I mean to suggest that a wrongdoer who has merely detained the goods and not used them would have to pay a hiring charge. The damages for detention recoverable against a carrier or a warehouseman have never been measured by a hiring charge. They are measured by the loss actually sustained by the plaintiff, subject, of course, to questions of remoteness. They are like cases of injury to a ship or a car by negligence. If it is put out of action during repair the wrongdoer is only liable for the loss suffered by the plaintiff. (See the principles set out in *The Susquehanna* (1926), and many other cases.) The claim for a hiring charge is therefore not based on the loss to the plaintiff, but on the fact that the defendant has used the goods for his own [255] purposes. It is an action against him because he has had the benefit of the goods. It resembles, therefore, an action for restitution rather than an action of tort. But it is unnecessary to place it into any formal category. The plaintiffs are entitled to a hiring charge for the period of detention, and that is all that matters. I can imagine cases where an owner might be entitled to the profits made by a wrongdoer by the use of a chattel, but I do not think this is such a case ...

Romer LJ: ... [256] In my judgment, the three salient facts on which the assessment of damages in this case depends are, first, that the equipment of the plaintiffs which the defendants detained was profit-earning property; secondly, that the plaintiffs normally hired out the equipment in the course of their business; and, thirdly, that the defendants during the period of wrongful detention applied the property to the furtherance of their own ends ...

In the light, then, of these three established facts, the question is whether [counsel for the plaintiffs] is right in his proposition that if the use of an article has a recognised hiring value then such value constitutes the measure of damages recoverable by the owner from a defendant who, by wrongful detention, has the use of that article. Although, curiously enough, this question seems never to have come up for decision in our courts, I am of opinion that on principle [counsel's] proposition is sound. The fundamental aim in awarding damages is in general to compensate the party aggrieved. The inquiry is: what loss have the plaintiffs suffered by reason of the defendants' wrongful act? In determining the answer to this inquiry the question of quantifying the profit or benefit which the defendant has derived from his wrongful act does not arise; for there is no necessary relation between the plaintiffs' loss and the defendants' gain. It follows that in assessing the plaintiffs' loss in the present case one is not troubled by any need to evaluate the actual benefit which resulted to the defendants by having the plaintiffs' equipment at their disposal.

That element then being out of the way, the only substantial reason put forward by the defendants why the plaintiffs should not receive the full hiring value of the equipment during the period of detention is that the plaintiffs might not have been able to find [257] a hirer. In my judgment, however, a defendant who has wrongfully detained and profited from the property of someone else cannot avail himself of a hypothesis such as this. It does not lie in the mouth of such a defendant to suggest that the owner might not have found a hirer; for in using the property he showed that he wanted it and he cannot complain if it is assumed against him that he himself would have preferred to become the hirer rather than not have had the use of it at all. Apart from the minor matters which I mention later, it accordingly seems to me that the defendants are bound to pay the recognised hiring value for the property in question and that no sufficient answer has been made out to [counsel for the plaintiffs'] proposition which, in my judgment, has common sense to support it and no authority against it.

I say this because some reliance was placed by counsel for the defendants on the principles which have become established in assessing damages for negligence. (See, for example, *Admiralty Commissioners v SS Susquehanna* (1977), p 619.) These principles seem to me to have no relation to cases where a wrongdoer detains property of another and uses it for his own purposes; one can postulate, as I have already indicated, that such a wrongdoer would have preferred to pay for the use of the property rather than have gone without it, but no such assumption can be made where negligence and not improper user is involved.

I agree with [Somervell LJ] that in this comparatively virgin field it is better to confine our decision to the actual facts before us; and I express no opinion as to what the plaintiffs' rights would have been in the matter of damages had the property detained been of a non-profit earning character, or if, although profit earning, the plaintiffs had never applied it to remunerative purposes. The full hiring charge for the switchboards over the period of unlawful detention has been found to be just over £400, and it follows from what I have said that in the absence of other considerations that is the sum which, in my judgment, should be awarded as damages to the plaintiffs ...

Commentary

Only Denning LJ considered that the award of damages was restitutionary in nature; Somervell and Romer LJJ considered that they were awarding compensatory damages. It is submitted that Denning LJ is correct and that the damages awarded in this case are best described as restitutionary. The plaintiff had not proved that it would have hired out the switchboards for the whole period of detention, and thus had not proved the quantum of its loss. The failure by Somervell and Romer LJJ to insist upon proof of quantum of loss, indicates that the award was restitutionary rather than compensatory.

The following case is an even clearer example of an award of restitutionary damages, as the plaintiff had failed completely to adduce any evidence of loss whatsoever from the defendant's detention of the goods.

Gaba Formwork Contractors v Turner Corp (1991) 32 NSWLR 175
Supreme Court of New South Wales

The plaintiff commenced proceedings in detinue against the defendant claiming the return of formwork materials and an award of damages. The issue in these proceedings was whether the plaintiff was entitled to a hiring fee for the formwork materials despite the fact it had not established an available market in which it would have hired out the materials, nor any other form of loss as a result of the defendant's detention of the materials.

Giles J: ... [179] It was common ground that Gaba put no evidence before the referee to prove an available market for its formwork materials. In responding that proof was unnecessary, Gaba relied on *Strand Electric and Engineering Co Ltd v Brisford Entertainments Ltd*. Turner said that this decision was not good law because it offended the basic principle that damages are compensatory, whereby a plaintiff can recover only his actual (and thus proved) loss, and relied on *Butler v Egg and Egg Pulp Marketing Board* (1966) as demonstrating that this principle applies in actions for wrongful interference with goods.

[Giles J examined the judgments in *Strand Electric* (see extract, p 510) and continued at p 182:]

Fundamental to the reasons of each of their Lordships was that the defendant had used the goods for its own purposes. If the wrongdoer did not use the goods, for example by simply holding them as a warehouseman, the [183] position might be different (Somervell LJ) or would be different (Denning LJ); if the wrongdoer had disposed of the goods the hiring fee would cease (Denning LJ). The position in a claim for mesne profits in an action for trespass used as an analogy by Somervell LJ and Denning LJ (but not mentioned by Romer LJ) is established in *Whitwham v Westminster Brymbo Coal and Coke Co* (1896), *Penarth Dock Engineering Co Ltd v Pounds* (1963) and *Swordheath Properties Ltd v Tabet* (1979), and ultimately goes back to the wayleave cases: *Martin v Porter* (1839), *Jegon v Vivian* (1871), and *Phillips v Homfray* (1871).

In *Butler v Egg and Egg Pulp Marketing Board*, damages for the conversion of eggs were assessed not on the basis of the value of the eggs at the time of conversion but on the basis of the actual loss sustained by the plaintiff ...

[184] Turner submitted that the same rule would apply to prevent the plaintiff in an action in conversion from recovering more than 'the real damage he has sustained' as consequential loss, and to prevent the plaintiff in an action in detinue from recovering more than 'the real damage he has sustained' as damages for detention. It said that it followed that Gaba could not recover any hiring fee in the absence of proof that it had sustained 'real damage' because it could have hired out the formwork materials.

Butler v Egg and Egg Pulp Marketing Board was not a case where the defendants had used for their own purposes goods which the plaintiff would or might otherwise have hired out for reward. Is there an exception in that situation to the general principle that damages are compensatory for actual loss, and what is the foundation for any exception?

In England, *Strand Electric and Engineering Co Ltd v Brisford Entertainments Ltd* has been referred to by Thesiger J in *Sir Robert McAlpine and Sons Ltd v Minimax Ltd* (1970) and by Parker J in *Hillesden Securities Ltd v Ryiack Ltd* (1983). In *Sir Robert*

McAlpine and Sons Ltd v Minimax Ltd, the defendant had detained goods handed over for examination and had failed to show to the plaintiff the reports obtained on the examination. It was held that it had been obliged to show the reports to the plaintiff, and that the plaintiff was entitled to an order for delivery of the reports. The reasoning was that the reports were obtained by use of the plaintiff's property and were the equivalent to money had and received for the use of the plaintiff. The reference was to the judgment of Lord Denning, supplemented by the statement in *Mayne and McGregor on Damages*,[23] that a plaintiff could recover beyond his proved loss to the extent of the benefit conferred on the defendant by the defendant's use of the goods. In *Hillesden Securities Ltd v Ryjack Ltd*, the defendants had converted and used in the course of their business and for reward a car which the plaintiff had hired out. The car was returned after the commencement of the proceedings. It was held that the plaintiff was entitled to the hire charge to the date of return. There was no mention of whether or not that was the plaintiff's actual loss, and *Strand Electric and Engineering Co Ltd v Brisford Entertainments Ltd* (1983) was said, see p 963 and pp 187–88 respectively, to have held that in the case of conversion of a profit-earning chattel which a defendant has used for his own benefit the owner can recover by way of damages a hire charge plus either the return of the chattel or, if there has been a subsequent conversion by disposal, the value of the chattel at the date of such conversion.

In both cases it would seem that in the respect here under consideration *Strand Electric and Engineering Co Ltd v Brisford Entertainments Ltd* was regarded as good law. But its acceptance in Australia is less clear.

In *McKenna and Armistead Pty Ltd v Excavations Pty Ltd* (1957), the vendor of equipment failed to deliver it at the agreed time, and continued to use it for its own purposes. The trial [185] judge held that the purchaser was entitled to damages representing a reasonable hiring rate for the equipment from the date of sale for the period of the vendor's use, in reliance upon *Strand Electric and Engineering Co Ltd v Brisford Entertainments Ltd* (1957). In the Full Court it was held that this was in error, and that the purchaser's entitlement was to damages for delay in delivery and for any deterioration in the equipment. In the joint judgment of Street CJ, Owen J and Walsh J it was said at p 519:

> The case was not one in which the vendor had wrongfully deprived the owner of possession of his goods and instead had used them for its own purposes. In the *Strand Electric and Engineering Co's* case, the owner of income-earning goods had been wrongfully denied their possession. The defendant, while refusing to hand the goods over to the plaintiff who was entitled to their immediate possession, was using them for its own purposes and thereby preventing the plaintiff from using them in its own business. Whether on the facts of that particular case the amount awarded by the learned judge of first instance represented the true financial loss suffered by the plaintiff rather than the higher figure assessed by the Court of Appeal does not arise for consideration. The essential point was that the plaintiff, the owner of the goods, was wrongfully denied their possession, notwithstanding the fact that it had been demanded, and the plaintiff's damages were therefore to be assessed by considering what it could have earned by using the goods had it had them in its possession. In the present case the facts are very different ...

---

23   12th edn, 1961, p 619.

It appears that their Honours were at pains not to endorse the result in *Strand Electric and Engineering Co Ltd v Brisford Entertainments Ltd*, and treated it as a case in which the plaintiff's damages represented 'what it could have earned by using the goods had it had them in its possession'.

In *Yakamie Dairy Pty Ltd v Wood* (1976), the defendants had wrongfully depastured cattle upon land belonging to the plaintiff. The trial judge held that current rates for agistment fees during the relevant periods were not the proper measure of the plaintiff's loss. On appeal, the Full Court held that they were. Both Jackson CJ and Burt J accepted (p 58) the proposition that the plaintiff could claim by way of damages a reasonable remuneration for the use of its land 'as if it had been under an agreement', and Jackson CJ noted (p 58) that 'this approach to the measure of damages' had been approved by Denning LJ in *Strand Electric and Engineering Co Ltd v Brisford Entertainments Ltd*. Wallace J thought that (p 60) 'the parallel of agistment fees is not necessarily appropriate', and seems to have accepted (p 61) that the defendant 'should account to the plaintiff for the profits they have made in the use of his land and services' of which the evidence relating to agistment fees was an unsatisfactory but acceptable assessment ...

[186] In *Bilambil-Terranora Pty Ltd v Tweed Shire Council* (1980), the defendant had trespassed on the plaintiff's land and converted gravel taken from the land. There was evidence of a market for the gravel. Reynolds JA and Mahoney JA held that the measure of the plaintiff's damage in conversion was the market value of the gravel ...

[187] [T]he reasoning of Reynolds JA and Mahoney JA provides support for acceptance of *Strand Electric and Engineering Co Ltd v Brisford Entertainments Ltd*. Both thought it irrelevant that the plaintiff held its land for investment and had no intention of operating as a commercial vendor of gravel. In particular, Mahoney JA accepted that the approach to the assessment of damages should not allow a defendant to derive an advantage from his own wrong, and said at pp 494–95:

> The result of the adoption of this method of arriving at damages for loss of minerals may result, in a sense, in a plaintiff recovering more than it might otherwise have received in respect of the minerals. If the tort had not been committed, the likelihood may be that it would never have mined the minerals or received anything from them at all. But such a result is not unprecedented. Similar results may ensue where, eg, there is the waiver of a tort and the adoption of the advantageous act of the wrongdoer. Whether the law of unjust enrichment forms part of Australian law as such, the influences which inform it are not without effect in our law.

At the time of its decision *Strand Electric and Engineering Co Ltd v Brisford Entertainments Ltd* was noted without criticism, and is considered in, for example, *McGregor on Damages* and Ogus, *Law of Damages*, 1973, p 161, without any suggestion that it so departs from the basic principle of compensatory damages that it is not good law. In Goff and Jones, *The Law of Restitution*,[24] it is treated as a 'waiver of tort' case, meaning a case in which the plaintiff elects to sue in quasi-contract to recover the defendant's unjust benefit rather than sue in tort to recover damages. Somervell LJ expressly said that the benefit obtained by the defendant was irrelevant, and Denning LJ said that it was not a case of entitlement to the

---

24   3rd edn, 1986, pp 16, 25, 611.

profits made by the wrongdoer. Somervell LJ simply took an analogy from a claim to mesne profits. Denning LJ was moved by the consideration that the wrongdoer who used the goods could not be better off than if he had used them with permission, and his reference to restitution seems to have meant prevention of unjust enrichment by payment of a reasonable hiring fee rather than by accounting for profits.

Romer LJ purported to seek the loss suffered by the plaintiff, but recognised as proof of the loss a hiring fee payable by the defendant on the ground that the defendant's use of the goods showed that the plaintiff could have found a hirer in the market (or at least that the defendant could not say otherwise) – as is observed in *McGregor on Damages*,[25] an attempt 'to press the result into the straitjacket of loss to the plaintiff'. There is no [188] one foundation for the decision, and it does not seem to have been treated by those who decided it as a waiver of tort case.

In my view I should follow *Strand Electric and Engineering Co Ltd v Brisford Entertainments Ltd* so far as it applies to the facts before me. It has stood for nearly 40 years and, while confined to where the defendant has used for his own purposes goods which the plaintiff would or might otherwise have hired out for reward, has been generally accepted in that situation. It produces a just result, and that a degree of departure from the principle of compensatory damages applied in *Butler v Egg and Egg Pulp Marketing Board* is permissible in such circumstances is, I think, supported by the majority decision in *Bilambil-Terranora Pty Ltd v Tweed Shire Council*. In particular, that the influences which inform the law of unjust enrichment are not without effect in our law (to use the words of Mahoney JA in that case) has since been underlined by the recognition in the High Court that the basis of actions where the law imposes or imputes an obligation to make compensation for a benefit accepted is restitution: *Pavey and Matthews Pty Ltd v Paul* (1987); *Australia and New Zealand Banking Group Ltd v Westpac Banking Corporation* (1988). In England the House of Lords has recently embraced unjust enrichment as the source of the obligation to repay stolen money: *Lipkin Gorman v Karpnale Ltd* (1991).

Moreover, in other situations beyond the way leave and mesne profit cases damages have been measured by a reasonable fee: patent infringement (*Watson Laidlaw and Co Ltd v Pott Cassels and Williamson* (1914)); misuse of confidential information (*Seager v Copydex Ltd (No 2)* (1969)); breach of restrictive covenant (*Wrotham Park Estate Co v Parkside Homes Ltd* (1974)): see the discussion in Waddams, *The Law of Damages*, 1983, pp 544–49. With some influence from equity, where the circumstances require the common law has departed from the basic principle of compensatory damages.

On this basis, it would seem that Gaba is entitled to the hiring fee for the period to 17 May 1991, since although there is no express finding by the referee it may be inferred that the formwork materials were used by Turner or its sub-contractor the second defendant for its benefit during that period. At the least, therefore, Gaba's damages are $106,538.53 and interest. I do not feel able to make the same inference in the case of the unreturned materials for the period following 17 May 1991. They may have been retained and used by Turner or its sub-contractor; they may have been simply retained; or they may have been lost or disposed of. If they were

---

25   15th edn, 1988, p 845.

retained and used by Turner or its sub-contractor, Gaba is additionally entitled to a hiring fee for the unreturned materials to the date of judgment. If they were not, it is not so entitled in the absence of proof of actual loss ...

Commentary

Giles J is clearly correct in acting on the basis that he was making an award of restitutionary damages. The damages could not have been viewed as compensatory due to the lack of any evidence of an available market in which the goods could have been hired out, or of any other form of loss resulting from the defendant's detention.

Giles J suggested two limitations on recovery of restitutionary damages for wrongful detention of goods: first, that the defendant must actually have *used* the goods, and secondly that the goods were *income producing*, in the sense that the plaintiff was in the business of hiring out goods of that type for reward. The first limitation, that the defendant must have used the goods, was also put forward by Denning LJ in the previous case: *Strand Electric and Engineering Co Ltd v Brisford Entertainments Ltd* (1952). This limitation is arguably justified on the ground that a restitutionary remedy should not be awarded unless the defendant has gained from the detention of the property, in the sense that the defendant was saved the expense of having to hire those goods from a third party. The second limitation, that the plaintiff must have been in the business of hiring out the relevant goods for reward, has also been adopted in some other Australian authorities.[26] Although it is submitted that the nature of the plaintiff's business should be treated as irrelevant to a restitutionary damages award,[27] it nevertheless must be accepted that it is relevant on the current state of authorities.[28]

Trespass to land

As the following case demonstrates, a defendant who uses the plaintiff's land without consent will be liable to pay a reasonable charge for use, despite the fact that the plaintiff would not otherwise have used the property profitably, and has not established a loss.[29]

---

26 *McKenna and Armistead Pty Ltd v Excavations Pty Ltd* (1957); *Egan v State Transport Authority* (1982), p 529; *Roder Zelt-Und Hallenkonstruktionen GMBH v Rosedown Park Pty Ltd (In Liq)* (1995).

27 The nature of the plaintiff's business is only relevant if the objective is to assess the plaintiff's loss.

28 This limitation also apparently exists in England: see *Strand Electric and Engineering Co Ltd v Brisford Entertainments Ltd* (1952), p 252 *per* Somervell LJ, p 256–57 *per* Romer LJ (see extract, p 510); *Inverugie Investments Ltd v Hackett* (1995), p 845.

29 See also *Jegon v Vivian* (1871); *Whitwham v Westminster Brymbo Coal and Coke Co* (1968); *Yakamia Dairy Pty Ltd v Wood* (1976); *Swordheath Properties Ltd v Tabet* (1979); *LJP Investments Pty Ltd v Howard Chia Investments Pty Ltd* (1990) (see extract, p 519); *Ministry of Defence v Ashman* (1993) (see extract, p 521); *Ministry of Defence v Thompson* (1993); *Inverugie Investments Ltd v Hackett* (1995).

Penarth Dock Engineering Company v Pounds [1963] 1 Lloyd's Rep 359 Queen's Bench

The plaintiffs agreed to sell to the defendants a floating pontoon which occupied part of dock premises leased by the plaintiffs at Penarth Dock. Both parties were aware that it was the intention of the owner of the dock to close the dock as soon as possible. The defendants failed to comply with requests by the plaintiffs for the removal of the dock and the plaintiffs commenced proceedings claiming damages for breach of contract and trespass. Lord Denning MR upheld the plaintiffs claims and turned to consider the question of quantum of damages.

Lord Denning MR: ... [361] The question which remains is, what are the damages? True it is that the Penarth company themselves would not seem to have suffered any damage to speak of. They have not to pay any extra rent to the British Transport Commission. The dock is no use to them; they would not have made any money out of it. But, nevertheless, in a case of this kind, as I read the law, starting with *Whitwham v Westminster Brymbo Coal and Coke Company* (1896), on which I commented myself in the case of *Strand Electric and Engineering Company Ltd v Brisford Entertainments Ltd* (1952), pp 253–54, the test of the measure of damages is not what the plaintiffs have lost, but what benefit the defendant obtained by having the use of the berth; and he has been a trespasser, in my judgment, since 9 August 1962. What benefit has the defendant obtained by having the use of it for this time? If he had moved it elsewhere, he would have had to pay, on the evidence, £37 10s a week for a berth for a dock of this kind. But the damages are not put as high as that, and the damages are to be assessed in accordance with the law as I have stated it at the rate of £32 5s a week for a period commencing from 9 August 1962, which I would let run to 25 March 1963, because the dock has now been removed ...

Questions

Could the plaintiffs in the principal case establish that they had suffered a loss as a result of the trespass by the defendants? What was the measure of the damages award in this case? Could those damages be classified as compensatory damages?

LJP Investments Pty Ltd v Howard Chia Investments Pty Ltd (1990) 24 NSWLR 499
Supreme Court of New South Wales

Chia owned land adjoining residential premises owned by LJP. Chia wished to construct commercial premises on its land and sought permission from LJP to erect scaffolding which would encroach into the air space above LJP's land. LJP advised that it would give permission for the scaffolding only on terms including payment of a lump sum of about $30,000 plus a weekly payment of $570. Chia decided to erect the scaffolding without the permission of LJP, deliberately committing a trespass. The saving which Chia made by using the encroaching scaffolding rather than a non-trespassory method was assessed at $30,000 by LJP, and $15,000 by Chia.

Hodgson J: ... [507] It is convenient first to consider the question of what have been called 'restitutionary damages', that is, the damages equal to such sum as Chia should reasonably pay for the use which it made of LJP's land. [Counsel for Chia] submitted that the measure of damages was simply the market value of what was used. However, in my view, if what is used has peculiar value for a defendant, then damages under this head should reflect that value, rather than the general market value. For example, if a plaintiff is the last tenant in a development site, and is forcibly ejected and the building immediately demolished; and if the defendant acted on incorrect legal advice that he was entitled to do this, so that he may be able to escape exemplary damages; then I think the plaintiff's damages should not be limited to the general market value of the plaintiff's tenancy, but should reflect the price which the plaintiff and defendant would reasonably have negotiated, having regard to the plaintiff's position and the defendant's wish to develop the site.

If I were able to conclude, as [counsel for LJP] submits, that if Chia had refrained from trespassing, it would in fact have paid the amount LJP was demanding, then I think that would be the correct measure of damages. An inference that this is what would have happened, or alternatively further support for that as the correct measure of damages, could be provided if it appeared that Chia would have incurred comparable expense by alternative measures which were open to it.

In this case, it seems to me that the following factors are relevant. I think that Mr Wotton's [expert valuer for LJP] evidence does support a view that, in very general terms, Chia stood to gain something of the order of $200,000 by building right up to the boundary, rather than 1.5 m short of it. At the stage when the decision to trespass was made, the alternative open to Chia (if it had adverted to it) would have cost something approaching $15,000 more than the provision of encroaching scaffolding: in general terms, I think Chia's evidence on the comparative cost is to be preferred. However, Chia would have been left, as it has been in fact, with one unfinished external wall which [508] it otherwise would have been willing to pay $9,000 to finish: it seems to me that this is a further detriment resulting from not being able to use scaffolding. This means, I think, that the lower limit of the particular value to Chia of the air space in question is about $15,000. One may take the upper limit as being the sum demanded by the plaintiff, that is, $30,255 plus $570 per week, which works out at $37,380 for the period when the scaffolding was actually in place.

It is impossible to be certain which course Chia would have taken, if it had refrained from trespassing: Chia's own unlawful act in trespassing, plus the absence of any of Chia's decision makers from the witness box, have made such a decision highly problematic. I think in these circumstances, the court is justified in taking the course taken in *Armory v Delamire* (1722), and resolving the question of value against the party whose actions have made an accurate determination so problematic.

For those reasons, in my view, LJP is entitled to $37,380 restitutionary damages ...

Commentary and questions

Could the plaintiff in this case establish a loss? What measure of damages was awarded to the plaintiff? Could the damages awarded be viewed as compensatory in nature?

The cases dealt with so far have concerned trespasses by 'strangers'. However, it is clear that the principles discussed also apply to situations where the trespasser is a tenant who has held over after the expiry or termination of the lease without the consent of the landlord. The trespassing tenant will be liable to pay a reasonable rental for the period of trespass (often referred to as 'mesne profits'). In *Swordheath Properties v Tabet* (1979) the English Court of Appeal stated at p 242 that:

> It appears ... to be clear, both as a matter of principle and of authority, that in a case of this sort the plaintiff, when he has established that the defendant has remained on as a trespasser in residential property, is entitled, without bringing evidence that he could or would have let the property to someone else in the absence of the trespassing defendant, to have as damages for the trespass the value of the property as it would fairly be calculated; and, in the absence of anything special in the particular case it would be the ordinary letting value of the property that would determine the amount of damages.

As this passage indicates, there might exist special circumstances where the appropriate measure of recovery is something other than the ordinary (market) rental value of the property. As demonstrated by the following case, the benefit to the tenant of remaining in possession might in some circumstances be less than the market rental, in which case the tenant will be permitted to subjectively devalue the benefit below the market value.

Ministry of Defence v Ashman [1993] 2 EGLR 102 English Court of Appeal

The second defendant, Mr Ashman, was a flight sergeant in the Royal Air Force. In 1989 Mr Ashman moved with his wife (the first defendant) and their two children into a house owned by the plaintiff at 15 Perch Meadow, Halton. Upon moving into the house Mr Ashman signed a certificate acknowledging that he and his family would be required to vacate the house in various circumstances, including if he ceased living with his wife. The rental for the house was £95.41 per *month*. In February 1991 Mr Ashman moved out of the house leaving his wife and children behind. On 14 March 1991 Mr and Mrs Ashman were given notice to vacate the house by 16 May 1991. Mrs Ashman and the children did not move out as they had nowhere else to go. On 17 May 1991 the plaintiff served a seven day notice on Mrs Ashman which asserted the right to claim damages for trespass at £108.93 per *week*. The plaintiff subsequently commenced proceedings seeking possession and damages for trespass (mesne profits), and obtained an order for possession. In April 1992 Mrs Ashman accepted an offer of local authority accommodation at a rent of £33.44 per *week* and on 26 April 1992 she vacated the house. Evidence was given in the damages claim against Mr and Mrs Ashman that the open market value of the house was £108.93 per *week*, though the plaintiff produced no evidence that it would have let the property on the open market had it been vacant.

Kennedy LJ: [Kennedy LJ dismissed the argument that the plaintiff was estopped from claiming a market rental and continued at p 104:]

That leaves open the question of how the judge should have approached the problem of quantifying damages in this case. In my judgment it is helpful to start, as Megaw LJ did in *Swordheath Properties Ltd v Tabet* (1979), with the statement of principle to be found in *Halsbury's Laws of England*.[30] The paragraph begins:

---

30   4th edn, Vol 12, para 1170.

Particular rules have been evolved in cases of trespass to land. A plaintiff is entitled to nominal damages for trespass even if no damage or loss is caused; if damage or loss is caused, he is entitled to recover in respect of his loss according to general principles.

A little later there is a passage cited by Megaw LJ which reads:

Where the defendant has by trespass made use of the plaintiff's land the plaintiff is entitled to receive by way of damages such sum as should reasonably be paid for the use. It is immaterial that the plaintiff was not in fact thereby impeded or prevented from himself using his own land either because he did not wish to do so or for any other reason.

In further support of that passage Megaw LJ referred to *Penarth Dock Engineering Co Ltd v Pounds* (1963). There the defendant failed to recover a pontoon he had purchased from the plaintiff company which could not of itself point to any loss. Lord Denning MR said, at p 362:

The test of the measure of damages is not what the plaintiffs have lost, but what benefit the defendant obtained by having the use of the berth ... If he had moved it elsewhere, he would have had to pay on the evidence £37 10s a week for a berth for a dock of this kind.

Damages were claimed in that case at a lower rate. That rate was awarded. As Megaw LJ later explained, damages in the *Penarth Dock* case were calculated by reference to 'the proper value to the trespassers of use of the property'.

In the *Swordheath* case the Court of Appeal was able to apply that approach, which may be somewhat analogous to quasi-contractual restitution, to a claim by a landlord against occupants of residential property who had remained in unlawful possession. The landlord was held entitled to recover 'the proper letting value of the property' for the relevant period, that being in an ordinary case, in a free market, the value to the trespassers of its use.

But where, as in the present case, the property is not normally let on the open market, and the trespasser only remains in possession because she is in no position to move anywhere else, it seems to me that more assistance as to the proper value to Mrs Ashman of the use of the property might be gained by looking at what she would have had to pay for suitable local authority accommodation, had any been available, than by focusing on evidence given on behalf of the ministry as to market rent.

As [counsel for the plaintiff] in the course of his submissions pointed out, if an elderly widow living alone were to hold over possession of a mansion whilst attempting to arrange accommodation more suited to her needs, the court might conclude that the value to her of the use of the mansion was less than its rented value on the open market. Of course, even if that be the right approach, the figure Mrs Ashman paid to the local authority for her flat for the period from April 1992 would not necessarily be the right multiplicand from 16 May 1991 to 26 April 1992, because even if rents were stable in that period until her daughter married in March 1992 she would have needed accommodation with three bedrooms and there may be attributes of 15 Perch Meadows which can reasonably be said to have increased its value to her as long as she remained in occupation. If so, I am not aware of them. I do not exclude that possibility ...

Hoffmann LJ: [105] A person entitled to possession of land can make a claim against a person who has been in occupation without his consent on two alternative bases. The first is for the loss which he has suffered in consequence of the defendant's trespass. This is the normal measure of damages in the law of tort. The second is the value of the benefit which the occupier has received. This is a claim for restitution. The two bases of claim are mutually exclusive and the plaintiff must elect before judgment which of them he wishes to pursue. These principles are not only fair but, as Kennedy LJ demonstrated, well established by authority.

It is true that in the earlier cases it has not been expressly stated that a claim for mesne profit for trespass can be a claim for restitution. Nowadays I do not see why we should not call a spade a spade. In this case the Ministry of Defence elected for the restitutionary remedy. It adduced no evidence of what it would have done with the house if the Ashmans had vacated. In my judgment, such matters are irrelevant to a restitution claim. All that matters is the value of benefit which the defendant has received. For reasons given by Kennedy LJ I agree that the judge's finding that the ministry was estopped from claiming full value of benefit cannot be sustained.

That leaves only the question of how one values the benefit which Mr and Mrs Ashman received. In *Swordheath Properties v Tabe* (1979) Megaw LJ said, 'in the absence of anything special in the particular case' it will ordinarily be the rental value of the property in the open market. This the judge found to be £472 a month as against the concessionary licence fee of £95 a month, which Mr Ashman had previously been charged. As the only special feature found by the judge was the estoppel we have held to be unsustainable, the Ministry asks that we substitute a figure of £472 a month for that ordered by the judge.

In my judgment, however, the law of restitution is not so inflexible. The open market value will ordinarily be appropriate because the defendant has chosen to stay in the premises rather than pay for equivalent premises somewhere else. But such benefits may in special circumstances be subject to what Professor Birks, in his *Introduction to the Law of Restitution* has conveniently called *subjective devaluation*. This means that a benefit may not be worth as much to the particular defendant as to someone else. In particular, it may be worth less to a defendant who has not been free to reject it. Mr and Mrs Ashman would probably have never occupied the premises in the first place if they had to pay £472 a month instead of the concessionary licence fee of £95. Mrs Ashman would certainly not have stayed in the premises at the market rate if she had any choice in the matter. She stayed because she could not establish priority need to be rehoused by the local authority until the eviction order had been made against her. Once the necessary proceedings had been taken she was able to obtain local authority housing at £145 a month.

In my judgment, therefore, the special circumstances in this case are created by the combination of two factors. First, the fact that the Ashmans were occupying at a concessionary licence fee. Second, the fact that Mrs Ashman had, in practice, no choice but to stay in the premises until the local authority were willing to rehouse her. The first factor is important because I think if the Ashmans had voluntarily paid the ordinary market rate, they could not claim the premises had become less to them because they could not find anywhere else to go.

The second factor is important because I do not think the defendant can say the premises were worth less to him than suitable accommodation he could realistically obtain. In the circumstances of this case the value to Mrs Ashman was no more than she would have had to pay for suitable local authority housing, if she could have been immediately rehoused. Allowing subjective devaluation in circumstances like this case will not cause any injustice to the landlord. If he has suffered greater loss (for example, because there would have been a reletting at market value) it is always open to him to elect for the alternative tort measure of damages ...

Lloyd LJ: ... The plaintiffs claim is for possession of the premises and for the payment of mesne profits. There is no problem as to the claim for possession. As to mesne profits they are, as I understand it, simply damages for trespass recoverable against a tenant who holds over after the lawful termination of his tenancy. A claim for mesne profits is thus to be distinguished from an action for use and occupation where the tenant holds over with the consent of his landlord. The former action is grounded in tort, the latter in quasi-contract. So far as I know, it has never been held that in the former case the landlord has the option of waiving the tort and claiming restitution unless, of course, the landlord consents to the holding over, which is not suggested here. In the present case [counsel for the plaintiff] contends that he is entitled to ask for restitution and Kennedy and Hoffmann LJJ have so held.

There are two difficulties about that. In the first place the pleaded case is a claim for damages for trespass and nothing else. This is not surprising since the second notice to vacate given on 17 May 1991 makes clear that, if Mrs Ashman failed to comply with that notice, damages for trespass would be claimed against her. This is what the plaintiff has done. There has never been any application to amend the pleading so as to claim restitution in the alternative.

Secondly, it is very doubtful, as the law now stands, whether the restitutionary remedy is available in the case of wrongful occupation [106] of land. The reasons for this anomalous exception to the general rule are set out in *Goff and Jones on Restitution*.[31] Three reasons are discussed. The substantial reason is that it was so decided by the majority of this court in the case of *Phillips v Homfray* (1883). The editors of *Goff and Jones* express the view that *Phillips v Homfray* should be overruled and the dissenting judgment of Bagallay LJ preferred. But *Phillips v Homfray* was recently followed *obiter* by Lane J in the case of *Morris v Tarrant* (1971) and is, in any event, binding on us. We would be rash indeed to express a view about *Phillips v Homfray* without having heard full argument on both sides. We have not had that advantage in this case. So, with respect, it was not open to [counsel for the plaintiff] to elect in this case to claim restitution even if he had pleaded such a claim.

Where does that leave us? [Counsel for the plaintiff] told us that if the plaintiffs could not claim restitution, they could recover nothing at all since they had failed to prove any damage. I think that in that respect he did less than justice to his client's claim. It is true that the plaintiff did not prove that it had an alternative tenant who was waiting to move in. But that does not mean it cannot claim and recover damages. This was the very point decided in the case of *Swordheath*

---

31   3rd edn, p 607.

Properties v Tabet (1979). In that case Judge Solomon had held that, since the landlord had failed to adduce any evidence that they would have been able to relet the premises, they had failed to prove any damages. The Court of Appeal exposed the error.

Megaw LJ said at p 288:

> It appears to me to be clear, both as a matter of principle and of authority, that in a case of this sort the plaintiff, when he has established the defendant remained on as a trespasser in residential property, is entitled, without bringing evidence that he could or would have let the property to someone else in the absence of the trespassing defendant, to have as damages for the trespass the value of the property as it would fairly be calculated; and, in the absence of anything special in the particular case it would be the ordinary letting value of the property that would determine the amount of the damages.

I find nothing in that passage which suggests that Megaw LJ thought he was enforcing a restitutionary remedy. He was clearly awarding damages for trespass. The same is true of the case of *Penarth Dock Engineering Co Ltd v Pounds* (1963), the decision of Lord Denning MR at first instance. There is perhaps a whiff of restitution in the latter case, because of the statement that damages should be assessed by reference to the benefit to the defendant rather than loss to the plaintiff. But it was still a claim for damages and nothing else; and the reference to benefit in Lord Denning's judgment is perhaps explained by Lindley LJ's judgment in *Whitwham v Westminster Brymbo Coal & Coke Co* (1896). That was the case in which the plaintiff tipped soil on to the defendant's land. Lindley LJ said that the plaintiff had been injured in two respects. In the first place the value of its land had been diminished. In the second place it had lost the use of its land and the defendant had it for its own benefit. But both these aspects of the plaintiff's claim, it will be noted, were regarded as injuries to the plaintiff. That is why the editor of *McGregor on Damages*, at paras 15–18, does not regard this line of cases as an exception to the general rule stated by Lord Blackburn in *Livingstone v Rawyards Coal Co* (1880), but rather as special cases where the plaintiff can apparently recover more than his loss.

What then, is the measure of damages in a claim for mesne profits? In the vast majority of cases it will be at the same rate as the previous rent.[32] If the market has risen, the landlord may recover more: see *Clifton Securities v Huntley* (1948). Presumably, if the market has fallen, he will recover less. I see no difficulty in the landlord recovering damages at the market rate even though he has adduced no evidence that he would or could have relet the property. That is, as was held in *Swordheath*, the appropriate measure of damages in the normal case. But the question still remains whether the present case is indeed normal.

The judge obviously thought that it was. It is here, in my judgment, that he went wrong. The valuer, whose evidence the judge accepted, based his valuation on a similar type of house on a similar estate. But the reality is that the Ministry of Defence is not a normal landlord and Mr Ashman was not a normal tenant ...

There was some evidence in the present case that married quarters are occasionally let on the open market. But I am unwilling to accept on the evidence that that would be anything other than exceptional. The terms on which the

---

32 See *Halsbury's Laws of England*, 4th edn, Vol 27, para 255, n 3.

plaintiffs would have been likely to relet, if they had, are surely the same as the terms on which they had previously let to Mr Ashman. It is for the plaintiff to prove its damages. It does not have to adduce evidence that it would have let to another tenant, but it does have to show what the rent would have been if it had. They have failed to satisfy me that it would in practice have recovered any more than the artificially low level of rent applicable in the case of married quarters occupied by members of Her Majesty's Services. That, therefore, should be its measure of damages. It might, of course, have recovered more by way of liquidated damages if there had been a suitable provision in the certificate which Mr Ashman signed on 27 July 1989. But there was no such provision ...

[A]s Kennedy and Hoffmann have taken a different view, I am content to go along with the basis proposed by Kennedy LJ, that the damages should be based on the value of the benefit to Mrs Ashman. It may be that, in the end, it will not make much difference in terms of money.

Commentary and questions

What was the appropriate measure of mesne profits in the principal case according to Kennedy and Hoffmann LJJ? How did their Honours utilise the concept of subjective devaluation in order to reach this result? Could Mrs Ashman have been precluded from subjectively devaluing the benefit below the market rent on the basis she had freely accepted the benefit of the house, or had been incontrovertibly benefited by remaining there? What measure of mesne profits was preferred by Lloyd LJ?

There is nothing in this decision which would limit the principles recognised to tenants or licensees holding over, and as such they would be equally applicable to cases of trespass by a stranger.[33] This decision was followed in *Ministry of Defence v Thompson* (1993), a case with very similar facts.

Other proprietary torts

In the following case the English Court of Appeal held that restitutionary damages are not available for a nuisance.

Stoke-on-Trent City Council v W & J Wass Ltd [1988] 3 All ER 394
English Court of Appeal

For a number of years the plaintiff council had operated general retail markets on Wednesdays, Fridays and Saturdays pursuant to a statutory authority to operate markets within its area. The defendant began operating an unauthorised market within the council's area on a Thursday, at a time when the council had planned to open its own Thursday market. It was unlawful at common law to operate a rival same day market within six and two-third miles from a statutory market, however the defendant continued to operate its market despite warnings from the council that the market would infringe the council's common law proprietary rights. After

---

33   Cooke, 'Trespass, mesne profits and restitution' (1994) 110 LQR 420, p 427.

the Council commenced its own Thursday market it was successful in obtaining a permanent injunction restraining the defendant from operating its market. The trial judge also awarded damages to the council on the basis that, even though the council had not proved that it had suffered any loss to its Thursday market by the operation of the defendant's market, the council should receive compensation in the amount of the licence fee which it could have demanded from the defendant to operate the rival market. The defendant appealed, arguing that the council was entitled only to nominal damages as it could not establish a loss.

Nourse LJ: ... [397] The levying of an unlawful rival market is a tort. Whether it should properly be categorised as a nuisance or a trespass is probably not a question of importance. The better view must be that it is a nuisance. The general rule is that a successful plaintiff in an action in tort recovers damages equivalent to the loss which he has suffered, no more and no less. If he has suffered no loss, the most he can recover are nominal damages. A second general rule is that where the plaintiff has suffered loss to his property or some [398] proprietary right, he recovers damages equivalent to the diminution in value of the property or right. The authorities establish that both these rules are subject to exceptions. These must be closely examined, in order to see whether a further exception ought to be made in this case.

The first and best established exception is in trespass to land. It originated in the wayleave cases, where the defendant trespassed by carrying coals along an underground way through the plaintiff's mine. Although the value of his land had not been diminished by the trespass, the plaintiff recovered damages equivalent to what he would have received if he had been paid for a wayleave: see *Martin v Porter* (1839), *Jegon v Vivian* (1871), and *Phillips v Homfray Fothergill v Phillips*. The principle of those cases was applied in *Whitwham v Westminster Brymbo Coal and Coke Co* (1896), where for six years the defendants had trespassed by tipping refuse from their colliery onto part of the plaintiffs' land. The official referee found that the defendants had thereby rendered the whole of the land valueless for any but tipping purposes and he assessed its diminution in value at £200. But the plaintiffs contended that the proper measure was the reasonable value to the defendants of the land for tipping purposes and the official referee found that, on that footing, the damages were £963. It was held by Chitty J and this court that as to that part of the land which had been used for tipping the defendants must pay on the footing of the value of the land to them for tipping purposes, but without interest; and, as to the rest of the land, that they ought to pay on the footing of the diminished value of the land to the plaintiffs. That decision was applied by Lord Denning MR, sitting as a judge of the Queen's Bench Division, in *Penarth Dock Engineering Co Ltd v Pounds* (1963) and by this court in *Swordheath Properties v Tabet* (1979). In the latter case it was held that a defendant who had occupied residential premises as a trespasser was liable to pay damages calculated by reference to the ordinary letting value of the premises even where there was no evidence that the plaintiff could or would have let the premises to someone else. With the partial exception of *Whitwham's* case, all those were cases where the plaintiff had suffered no loss.

The second exception is in detinue. [Nourse LJ examined *Strand Electric and Engineering Co Ltd v Brisford Entertainments Ltd* (1952) (see extract, p 510) and concluded that the majority judgments in that case assumed that the plaintiffs had suffered loss through being unable to hire out the switchboards to other users. His Honour continued at p 399:]

The third exception is in infringement of patents ... In all such cases the plaintiff is readily proved or assumed to have suffered loss. I do not therefore think that they can, as a class, be regarded, like the trespass cases, as cases where the plaintiff has suffered no loss.

To these exceptions to the general rules in tort must be added the decision of Brightman J in *Wrotham Park Estate Co v Parkside Homes Ltd* (1974). [Nourse LJ discussed the *Wrotham Park* case (see extract, p 000) where the plaintiff was awarded as damages for breach of contract, the price which it would have required for relaxation of the restrictive covenant. Nourse LJ continued at p 400:]

The same approach [as in the *Wrotham Park* case] to the assessment of damages awarded in lieu of a final injunction was adopted by Graham J in *Bracewell v Appleby* (1975) (where the burden of an easement was wrongfully increased) and by Millett J in *Carr-Saunders v Dick McNeil Associates Ltd* (1986) (where a right to light was wrongfully obstructed). In each of those cases the plaintiff's claim lay in nuisance, of which tort damage is an essential ingredient. Indeed, it is clear that in each case the plaintiff had suffered loss and was therefore entitled to substantial damages.

As I understand these authorities, their broad effect is this. In cases of trespass to land and patent infringement and in some cases of detinue and nuisance the court will award damages in accordance with what Nicholls LJ has aptly termed 'the user principle'. On an analogous principle, in a case where there was a breach of a restrictive covenant the court has, in lieu of a permanent mandatory injunction to restore the breach, awarded damages equivalent to the sum which the plaintiffs might reasonably have demanded for a relaxation of the covenant. But it is only in the last-mentioned case and in the trespass cases that damages have been awarded in accordance with either principle without proof of loss to the plaintiff. In all the other cases, the plaintiff having established his loss, the real question has not been whether substantial damages should be awarded at all, but whether they should be assessed in accordance with the user principle or by reference to the diminution in value of the property or right. In other words, those other cases are exceptions to the second, but not to the first, of the general rules stated above.

Do the authorities support an award of damages in accordance with the user principle where an unlawful rival market has caused no loss to the market owner? In other words, is this case to be governed by the principle of the trespass cases and that of the *Wrotham* case?

The latter decision is in my opinion one which stands very much on its own. The conclusion of Brightman J may, I think, be more fully explained as follows. An injunction is frequently granted to enforce an express negative covenant, especially a restrictive covenant affecting land, without proof of loss to the plaintiff. Injunctions could therefore and would have been granted in that case but for the social and economic reasons against ordering the demolition of 14 houses. If injunctions had been granted, the loss to the defendant purchasers would have been enormous. If, on the other hand, injunctions were not granted and no damages were awarded, the purchasers would have been left in undisturbed possession of the correspondingly enormous fruits of their wrongdoing. Accordingly, if the plaintiffs had not been awarded substantial damages, justice manifestly would not have been done. If this analysis is correct, the practical result of the *Wrotham* decision was something akin to an award of exemplary damages for breach of contract, [401] albeit that their amount bore no relation to the loss which would have been suffered by the defendant purchasers if they had had to demolish their houses. In saying this, I do not wish to suggest that that case was wrongly decided. Indeed, I regard the result as having been entirely appropriate and I see no reason why it should not serve as a precedent for other cases of the same kind. I merely wish to emphasise that it stands a long way away from the present problem and does not assist in its solution.

On a superficial view, the trespass cases present a greater difficulty. In trespass the defendant makes an unlawful use of the plaintiff's land. Similarly, it can be said that in levying an unlawful rival market the defendant makes an unlawful use of the plaintiff's right to hold his own market which, at any rate in the case of a franchise market, is an incorporeal hereditament. Ought it to make all the difference that in the first case the unlawful use is a physical one? This is a formidable line of argument, but I think that it is unsound. If the wayleave cases are put on one side, it seems to me that the trespass cases really depend on the fact that the defendant's use of the plaintiff's land deprives the plaintiff of *any* opportunity of using it himself. And even on the assumption, which may be correct, that the broad view of Denning LJ in the *Strand Electric* case (1952), pp 800–01 and pp 253–56 respectively, is a correct view of the law, the same can be said of an unlawful detention of the plaintiff's chattel. On the other hand, an unlawful use of the plaintiff's right to hold his own market does not deprive him of the opportunity of holding one himself. Such indeed has been the state of affairs in the present case. If of course the plaintiff can show that he has thereby suffered loss, nobody would suggest that he ought not to receive substantial damages. But why should he receive them when he has been able to hold his own market and has suffered no loss from the defendant's?

It is characteristic of the development of the common law that the invention and increasingly extended application of the user principle should appear to have come about by accident rather than by design. Thus it seems from the interlocutory observations of the members of this court in *Whitwham's* case (1896) that they were initially resistant to the principle of the wayleave cases. But they saw in it a basis for the just decision of that case, and once it had been so decided the application of the principle to analogous states of affairs, for example the wrongful detention of chattels, seems to have been a perfectly natural development. However, in a process of development it is sometimes necessary to stand back from the authorities and to ask not simply where they have come to, but where, if a further extension is made, they may go next.

Although I would accept that there may be a logical difficulty in making a distinction between the present case and the wayleave cases, I think that if the user principle were to be applied here there would be an equal difficulty in distinguishing other cases of more common occurrence, particularly in nuisance. Suppose a case where a right to light or a right of way had been obstructed to the profit of the servient owner but at no loss to the dominant owner. It would be difficult, in the application of the user principle, to make a logical distinction between such an obstruction and the infringement of a right to hold a market. And yet the application of that principle to such cases would not only give a right to substantial damages where no loss had been suffered but would revolutionise the tort of nuisance by making it unnecessary to prove loss. Moreover, if the principle were to be applied in nuisance, why not in other torts where the defendant's wrong can work to his own profit, for example in defamation? As progenitors of the rule in trespass and some other areas, the wayleave cases have done good service. But just as their genus is peculiar, so ought their procreative powers to be exhausted.

These considerations have led me to conclude that the user principle ought not to be applied to the infringement of a right to hold a market where no loss has been suffered by the market owner. If loss caused by the diversion of custom from one market to the other had been proved, I would have agreed with Nicholls LJ that the general rule ought to apply, so that the council would have recovered damages equivalent to the diminution in value of its right through the loss of stallage, tolls and so forth. But I rest my decision in this case on the simple ground that where no loss has been suffered no substantial [402] damages of any kind can be recovered. Otherwise we would have to allow that the right to recover nominal damages for disturbance of a same-day market without proof of loss had become one to receive substantial damages on top. If we had to allow that, why not also in the case of an other-day market where no loss had been proved? It is possible that the English law of tort, more especially of the so called 'proprietary torts', will in due course make a more deliberate move towards recovery based not on loss suffered by the plaintiff but on the unjust enrichment of the defendant: see Goff and Jones, *The Law of Restitution*.[34] But I do not think that that process can begin in this case and I doubt whether it can begin at all at this level of decision ...

Commentary

Nourse LJ refused to award the plaintiff restitutionary damages on the basis that the defendant had not prevented the plaintiff from continuing to operate its market. His Honour adopted the view that restitutionary damages should be restricted to cases where the defendant has used the plaintiff's property, and by that use has prevented the plaintiff of any opportunity of using the property, such as in the trespass to land and detinue cases. On this view, restitutionary damages will never be available for an intangible interference with property. However a contrary view was taken by Millet J in *Carr Saunders v Dick McNeill Associates Ltd* (1986). In that case the defendants committed a nuisance by erecting extra storeys to their building which interfered with the plaintiff's light. Millet J said that, had there been evidence of the profit gained by the defendant as a result of the nuisance, he would have taken that into account when assessing damages (p 896).

---

34   3rd edn, 1986, pp 612–14.

BREACH OF CONTRACT

The orthodox view: no recovery

The orthodox rule is that restitutionary damages are not available for a breach of contract.[35] This rule was established in cases such as *Tito v Waddell (No 2)* (1977).[36] In that case the defendant was granted licences to mine phosphate on Ocean Island in the South Pacific. The defendant breached a covenant to replant the land as nearly as possible to its original state, the evidence being that this would involve the importation of soil from Australia and the construction of 80 miles of road. The plaintiffs were owners of various plots of land scattered throughout the islands who sought a variety of orders, including the cost of replanting. This cost could not be claimed as compensatory damages, as the evidence was that the plaintiffs had settled elsewhere and would never return and incur the cost of replanting themselves. Sir Robert Megarry VC refused to award the cost of replanting, stating at p 332 that:

> It is fundamental to all questions of damages that they are to compensate the plaintiff for his loss or injury by putting him as nearly as possible in the same position as he would have been in had he not suffered the wrong. The question is not one of making the defendant disgorge what he has saved by committing the wrong, but one of compensating the plaintiff.

This principle was confirmed in the subsequent decision.

Surrey County Council v Bredero Homes Ltd [1993] 1 WLR 1361
English Court of Appeal

The plaintiffs, Surrey County Council and the Mole Valley District Council, owned two adjoining parcels of land. The two councils decided to offer the entire site for development as a housing estate and the site was subsequently sold to the defendant developer for £1.5 million. The sale price was calculated by reference to the profits which the defendant was expected to make on the development. The defendant covenanted to comply with an existing planning permission which permitted the construction of 72 houses. The defendant later obtained a second planning permission from the Mole Valley District Council which allowed for 77 houses to be constructed. The defendant built 77 houses on the estate in accordance with the second planning permission, thus breaching the covenant, and all the houses were sold. At no time did the plaintiffs seek an injunction to prevent the defendant from building other than in accordance with the first planning permission. The plaintiffs commenced proceedings seeking the extra profit made by the defendant from the sale of the additional five houses, or in the alternative sought that part of the profit which would reflect the reasonable premium that the defendant should have paid them for a relaxation of the covenant. The plaintiffs accepted that they had not suffered any loss by reason of

---

35 *Surrey County Council v Bredero Homes Ltd* (1993) (see following extract); *Wenham v Ella* (1927); *Hospitality Group Pty Ltd v Australian Rugby Union Ltd* (2001).
36 See also *Occidental Worldwide Investment Corporation v Skibs A/S Avanti, The Siboen and The Sibotre* (1976) (see extract, p 230).

the defendant's breach as the extended development had not damaged any adjoining property owned or occupied by them.

Dillon LJ: ... [1365] Every student is taught that the basis of assessing damages for breach of contract is the rule in *Hadley v Baxendale* (1854), which is wholly concerned with the losses which can be compensated by damages. Such damages may, in an appropriate case, cover profit which the injured plaintiff has lost, but they do not cover an award, to a plaintiff who has himself suffered no loss, of the profit which the defendant has gained for himself by his breach of contract.

In the field of tort there are areas where the law is different and the plaintiff can recover in respect of the defendant's gain. Thus in the field of trespass it is well established that if one person has, without leave of another, been using that other's land for his own purposes he ought to pay for such user. Thus even if he had done no actual harm to the land he was charged for the user of the land. This was applied originally in wayleave cases where a person had without authority used his neighbour's land for passage: see, for instance, *Jegon v Vivian* (1871), and *Phillips v Homfray*. The same principle was applied where the defendant had trespassed by tipping spoil on the plaintiff's land – *Whitwham v Westminster Brymbo Coal and Coke Company* (1896). The same principle was applied to patent infringement by the House of Lords in *Watson Laidlaw & Co, Ltd v Pott Cassels and Williams* (1914). The infringer was ordered to pay by way of damages a royalty for every infringing article because the infringement damaged the plaintiff's property right, that is to say, his patent monopoly. So in a case of detinue the defendant was ordered to pay a hire for chattels he had detained: *Strand Electric and Engineering Co Ltd v Brisford Entertainments Ltd* (1952). Those cases do not apply in the present case as the defendant has made no use of any property of either plaintiff.

The cases have been taken still further in some fields of tort particularly concerned with intellectual property, where it is well established that the plaintiff can choose to have either damages or an account of profits made by the defendant by his wrongful acts: see, for instance, *Lever v Goodwin* (1887) *per* Cotton LJ. This is in line with the long established common law doctrine of waiving the tort. The liability in the present case is solely in contract and not in tort.

[Dillon LJ then examined *Wrotham Park Estate Co Ltd v Parkside Homes Ltd* (1974) (see extract, p 537), concluding that it was distinguishable from the present case as it had involved damages under Lord Cairns' Act. Dillon LJ continued at p 1367:]

I should however mention in passing that we were referred to a number of cases where the measure of damages chosen by Brightman J in the *Wrotham Park* case was applied by other judges, for instance, *Bracewell v Appleby* (1975), *Carr-Saunders v Dick McNeil Associates Ltd* (1986), and *Griffiths v Kingsley-Stubbs* (1986). All those were cases where the plaintiff's cause of action lay in tort, either trespass or nuisance, where the defendant had interfered with the plaintiff's property rights. The decisions and awards of damages are amply justified by the common law principles in tort of the wayleave cases and *Whitwham v Westminster Brymbo* (1896), already mentioned.

Given that the established basis of an award of damages in contract is compensation for the plaintiff's loss, as indicated above, I have difficulty in seeing how Sir William Goodhart's suggested common law principle of awarding the plaintiff who has suffered no loss the gain which the defendant has made by the breach of contract is intended to go. Is it to apply, for instance, to shipping contracts or contracts of employment or contracts for building works?

Sir William suggested, in his and Mr Weatherill's skeleton argument, that the conventional measure fails to do justice and a different measure should be applied where the following conditions are satisfied. (a) The breach is deliberate, in the sense that the defendant is deliberately doing an act which he knows or should know is plainly or arguably in breach of contract. (b) The defendant, as a result of the breach, has profited by making a gain or reducing a loss. (c) At the date of the breach it is clear or probable that damages under the conventional measure will either be nominal or much smaller than the profit to the defendant from the breach. (d) If the profit results from the avoidance of expenditure, the expenditure would not have been economically wasteful or grossly disproportionate to the benefit which would have resulted from it. He suggested in the skeleton argument that the underlying principle might be that the conventional measure of damages might be overridden in certain circumstances by the rule that no one should benefit from his deliberate wrongdoing.

In the course of his submissions Sir William limited his formulation and, while retaining conditions (a), (b) and (c), substituted for condition (d): 'Damages for loss of bargaining power can be awarded if, but only if, the party in breach could have been restrained by injunction from committing the breach of contract or compelled by specific performance [1368] to perform the contract. Where no such possibility existed there was no bargaining power in reality and no right to damages for loss of it. Hence damages for loss of bargaining power cannot be awarded where there is, for example, a contract for the sale of goods or generally a contract of employment.'

I find difficulty with that because in theory every time there is a breach of contract the injured party is deprived of his 'bargaining power' to negotiate for a financial consideration a variation of the contract which would enable the party who wants to depart from its terms to do what he wants to do. In addition it has been held in *Walford v Miles* (1992), that an agreement to negotiate is not an animal known to the law and a duty to negotiate in good faith is unworkable in practice, and so I find it difficult to see why loss of bargaining or negotiating power should become an established factor in the assessment of damages for breach of contract.

Beyond that, since we are looking for the measure of damages at common law for breach of contract, apart from Lord Cairns' Act, I do not see why that should vary depending on whether the party in breach could or could not have been restrained by injunction from committing the breach or compelled by specific performance to perform the contract. Injunctions and specific performance were not remedies in the common law courts and were granted by the court of chancery, which, before Lord Cairns' Act, had no power to award damages, just because the common law remedy of damages was not an adequate remedy ...

As I see it ... there never was in the present case, even before the writ was issued, any possibility of the court granting an injunction to restrain the defendant from implementing the later planning permission. The plaintiffs' only possible claim from the outset was for damages only, damages at common law. The plaintiffs have suffered no damage. Therefore on basic principles, as damages are awarded to compensate loss, the damages must be merely nominal.

Steyn LJ: [1368] I agree. The issue in this appeal was defined by Sir William Goodhart, appearing for the plaintiffs, as the correct measure of damages in a case where the following three circumstances are satisfied: (a) There has been a deliberate breach of contract; (b) the party in breach has made a profit from that breach; and (c) the innocent party is in financial terms in the same position as if the contract had been fully performed. It is an important issue with considerable implications for the shape of our law of obligations, and I therefore add a few remarks of my own.

Dillon LJ has reviewed the relevant case law. It would not be a useful exercise for me to try to navigate through those much travelled waters again. Instead, it seems to me that it may possibly be useful to consider the question from the point of view of the application of first principles.

An award of compensation for breach of contract serves to protect three separate interests. The starting principle is that the aggrieved party ought to be compensated for loss of his positive or expectation interests. In other words, the object is to put the aggrieved party in the same financial position as if the contract had been fully performed. But the law also protects the negative interest of the aggrieved party. If the aggrieved party is unable to establish the value of a loss of bargain he may seek compensation in respect of his reliance losses. The object of such an award is to compensate the aggrieved party for expenses incurred and losses suffered in reliance on the contract. These two complementary principles share one feature. Both are pure compensatory principles. If the aggrieved party has suffered no loss he is not entitled to be compensated by invoking these principles. The application of these principles to the present case would result in an award of nominal damages only.

There is, however, a third principle which protects the aggrieved party's restitutionary interest. The object of such an award is not to compensate the plaintiff for a loss, but to deprive the defendant of the benefit he gained by the breach of contract. The classic illustration is a claim for the return of goods sold and delivered where the buyer has repudiated his obligation to pay the price. It is not traditional to describe a claim for restitution following a breach of contract as damages. What matters is that a coherent law of obligations must inevitably extend its protection to cover certain restitutionary interests. How far that protection should extend is the essence of the problem before us. In my view *Wrotham Park Estate Co Ltd v Parkside Homes Ltd* (1974), is only defensible on the basis of the third or restitutionary principle: see *MacGregor on Damages*[37] and Professor Birks, *Civil Wrongs: A New World*.[38]

The plaintiffs' argument that the *Wrotham Park* case can be justified on the basis of a loss of bargaining opportunity is a fiction. The object of the award in the *Wrotham Park* case was not to compensate the plaintiffs for financial injury, but to deprive the defendants of an unjustly acquired gain. Whilst it must be acknowledged that the *Wrotham Park* case represented a new development, it seems to me that it was based on a principled legal theory, justice and sound policy. In the defendant's skeleton argument some doubt was cast, by way of alternative submission, on the correctness of the award of damages for breach of covenant in the *Wrotham Park*

---

37 15th edn, 1988, pp 12–13, para 18.
38 *Butterworths Lectures*, 1990–91, pp 55, 71.

case. In my respectful view, it was rightly decided and represents a useful development in our law. In *Tito v Waddell (No 2)* (1977), pp 335C–36C, Sir Robert Megarry VC interpreted the *Wrotham Park* case and *Bracewell v Appleby* (1975), which followed the *Wrotham Park* case, as cases of invasion of property rights. I respectfully agree. The *Wrotham Park* case is analogous to cases where [1370] a defendant has made use of the aggrieved party's property and thereby saved expense: see *Penarth Dock Engineering Co Ltd v Pounds* (1963). I readily accept that 'property' in this context must be interpreted in a wide sense. I would also not suggest that there is no scope for further development in this branch of the law.

But, in the present case, we are asked to extend considerably the availability of restitutionary remedies for breach of contract. I question the desirability of any such development. The acceptance of the plaintiff's primary or alternative submission, as outlined by Dillon LJ, will have a wide ranging impact on our commercial law. Even the alternative and narrower submission will, for example, cover charterparties and contracts of affreightment where the remedy of a negative injunction may be available. Moreover, so far as the narrower submission restricts the principle to cases where the remedies of specific performance and injunction would have been available, I must confess that that seems to me a bromide formula without any rationale in logic or commonsense. Given a breach of contract, why should the availability of a restitutionary remedy, as a matter of legal entitlement, be dependent on the availability of the wholly different and discretionary remedies of injunctions specific to performance? If there is merit in the argument I cannot see any sense in restricting a compensatory remedy which serves to protect restitutionary interests to cases where there would be separate remedies of specific performance and injunction, designed directly and indirectly to enforce payment.

For my part I would hold that if Sir William Goodhart's wider proposition fails the narrower one must equally fail. Both submissions hinge on the defendant's breach being deliberate. Sir William invoked the principle that a party is not entitled to take advantage of his own wrongdoing. Despite Sir William's disclaimer it seems to me that the acceptance of the propositions formulated by him will inevitably mean that the focus will be on the motive of the party who committed the breach of contract. That is contrary to the general approach of our law of contract and, in particular, to rules governing the assessment of damages.

In my view there are also other policy reasons which militate against adopting Sir William's primary or narrower submission. The introduction of restitutionary remedies to deprive cynical contract breakers of the fruits of their breaches of contract will lead to greater uncertainty in the assessment of damages in commercial and consumer disputes. It is of paramount importance that the way in which disputes are likely to be resolved by the courts must be readily predictable. Given the premise that the aggrieved party has suffered no loss, is such a dramatic extension of restitutionary remedies justified in order confer a windfall in each case on the aggrieved party? I think not. In any event such a widespread availability of restitutionary remedies will have a tendency to discourage economic activity in relevant situations. In a range of cases such liability would fall on underwriters who have insured relevant liability risks. Inevitably underwriters would have to be compensated for the new species of potential claims. Insurance premiums would have to go up. That, too, is a consequence which mitigates against the proposed extension. The recognition of the proposed extension will in my view not serve the public interest. It is sound policy to guard against extending the protection of the law of obligations too widely. For these substantive and policy reasons I regard it as undesirable that the range of restitutionary remedies should be extended in the way in which we have been invited to do so.

[1371] The present case involves no breach of fiduciary obligations. It is a case of breach of contract. The principles governing expectation or reliance losses cannot be invoked. Given the fact of the breach of contract the only question is whether restitution is an appropriate remedy for this wrong. The case does not involve any invasion of the plaintiffs' property interests even in the broadest sense of that word, nor is it closely analogous to the *Wrotham Park* position. I would therefore rule that no restitutionary remedy is available and there is certainly no other remedy available. I would dismiss the appeal.

[Rose LJ refused to award damages due to the failure of the plaintiffs to seek equitable relief and their delay in commencing proceedings.]

Commentary

The commentators are deeply divided over whether the current exclusionary rule is justifiable.[39] Some agree with the denial of restitution, for example because protection of the contract institution is sufficiently afforded by an award of expectation damages,[40] or because it is perceived that a restitutionary award would deter efficient breaches of contract.[41] At the opposite end of the spectrum, Goff and Jones[42] advocate that the courts should have a general discretion to award profits resulting from a breach, taking into account factors such as the nature of the contract, the nature of the breach, whether the breach is a deliberate one, and the laches of the innocent party. Other academics have suggested a more limited availability of restitutionary damages, including: (a) Birks[43] contends that recovery should be allowed where the breach was conducted deliberately and cynically in order to earn a profit; (b) Sir William Goodhart[44] (counsel for the plaintiffs in the principal case) argues that restitutionary damages should be generally available for a breach of contract except in three situations: where adequate substitute performance can be obtained, possibly where the contract is one of personal service, and where the party in breach can show that the breach occurred for reasons outside its

---

39   This deep division is reflected in the decision of the Law Commission (UK) to make no recommendations about restitution for a breach of contract: *op cit*, fn 21, para 1.47.

40   At least where the contract is not protective of a proprietary interest: Jackman, 'Restitution for wrongs' (1989) CLJ 302, pp 318–21. See also Jackman, *The Varieties of Restitution*, 1998, Chapter 7; Burrows, 'No restitutionary damages for breach of contract' [1993] LMCLQ 453.

41   See Posner, *Economic Analysis of Law*, 4th edn, 1992, p 107 and also Bishop, 'The choice of remedy for breach of contract' (1985) 14 JLS 289.

42   Goff and Jones, *op cit*, fn 2, pp 780–83. See also generally Jones, 'The recovery of benefits from a breach of contract' (1983) 99 LQR 443.

43   Birks, 'Restitutionary damages for breach of contract: *Snepp* and the fusion of law and equity' [1987] LMCLQ 421.

44   Sir William Goodhart, 'Restitutionary damages for breach of contract: the remedy that dare not speak its name' [1995] RLR 3, pp 10–11.

control; (c) Beatson[45] argues that restitution should depend upon whether specific relief is available; and (d) O'Dair[46] considers that restitution is justified to deter breach in cases where compensatory damages would be inadequate and where the duty to mitigate would not be eroded.

Steyn LJ gave various policy reasons for denying the availability of restitutionary damages in commercial cases, including that damages awards would become too unpredictable and insurance premiums would rise. Similar concerns were expressed by Lord Hobhouse in his dissenting judgment in *AG v Blake (Jonathan Cape Ltd Third Party)* (2001), p 299. It has been suggested that concerns such as these are overstated as in practice claims for restitutionary damages will rarely be brought. The amount of restitutionary damages will not usually exceed expectation damages as the plaintiff will have gone into the market to mitigate the loss.[47]

Exceptional cases

Wrotham Park Estate Co Ltd v Parkside Homes Ltd [1974] 1 WLR 798
Chancery Division

The defendant purchased land which formed part of the Wrotham Park Estate and commenced to build houses on the land in breach of a restrictive covenant to the effect that any development had to be in strict accordance with a lay-out plan approved by the estate owner. The purpose of the covenant was to preserve a green belt for the benefit of neighbouring inhabitants. The plaintiff (the estate owners) commenced proceedings seeking an injunction to restrain building on the land other than in accordance with the approved lay-out plan, and a mandatory injunction for the demolition of any buildings erected in breach of the covenant. No interlocutory relief was sought. The houses were completed and the purchasers moved in. Brightman J refused to grant a mandatory injunction as this would have involved an 'unpardonable waste of much needed houses'. He then considered whether damages should be awarded in lieu of an injunction under the Chancery Amendment Act 1858 (UK) (Lord Cairns' Act). The plaintiff conceded that the value of the estate had not been diminished as a result of the construction in breach of the covenant.

Brightman J: ... [812] I turn to the consideration of the quantum of damages. I was asked by the parties to assess the damages myself, should the question arise, rather than to direct an inquiry. The basic rule in contract is to measure damages by that sum of money which will put the plaintiff in the same position as he would have been in if the contract had not been broken. From that basis, the defendants argue that the damages are nil or purely nominal, because the value of the Wrotham Park estate as the plaintiffs concede is not diminished by one farthing in

---

45 Beatson, *The Use and Abuse of Unjust Enrichment*, 1991, pp 15–17. See also Waddams, 'Profits derived from breach of contract: damages or restitution?' (1997) 11 JCL 115.

46 O'Dair, 'Restitutionary damages for breach of contract and the theory of efficient breach: some reflections' (1993) 46(2) CLP 113.

47 Jones, 'The recovery of benefits gained from a breach of contract' (1983) 99 LQR 443; see also Goodhart, *op cit*, fn 44, p 10.

consequence of the construction of a road and the erection of 14 houses on the allotment site. If, therefore, the defendants submit, I refuse an injunction I ought to award no damages in lieu. That would seem, on the face of it, a result of questionable fairness on the facts of this case. Had the offending development been the erection of an advertisement hoarding in defiance of protest and writ, I apprehend (assuming my conclusions on other points to be correct) that the court would not have hesitated to grant a mandatory injunction for its removal. If, for social and economic reasons, the court does not see fit in the exercise of its discretion, to order demolition of the 14 houses, is it just that the plaintiffs should receive no compensation and that the defendants should be left in undisturbed possession of the fruits of their wrongdoing? Common sense would seem to demand a negative answer to this question. A comparable problem arose in wayleave cases where the defendant had trespassed by making use of the plaintiff's underground ways to the defendant's profit but without diminishing the value of the plaintiff's property. The plaintiff in [813] such cases received damages assessed by reference to a reasonable wayleave rent.

[Brightman J then referred to a number of authorities, including *Strand Electric and Engineering Co Ltd v Brisford Entertainments Ltd* (1952) (see extract, p 510) and *Penarth Dock Engineering Co Ltd v Pounds* (1963) (see extract, p 519), and continued at p 814:]

The facts of the cases I have mentioned are a long way from the facts of the case before me. Should I, as invited by the plaintiffs, apply a like principle to a case where the defendant Parkside, in defiance of protest and writ, has invaded the plaintiffs' rights in order to reap a financial profit for itself? In *Leeds Industrial Co-operative Society Ltd v Slack* (1924) Lord Sumner said:

> [815] no money awarded in substitution can be justly awarded, unless it is at any rate designed to be a preferable equivalent for an injunction and therefore an adequate substitute for it ...

This was said in a dissenting speech but his dissent did not arise in the context of that observation.

In the present case I am faced with the problem what damages ought to be awarded to the plaintiffs in the place of mandatory injunctions which would have restored the plaintiffs' rights. If the plaintiffs are merely given a nominal sum, or no sum, in substitution for injunctions, it seems to me that justice will manifestly not have been done.

As I have said, the general rule would be to measure damages by reference to that sum which would place the plaintiffs in the same position as if the covenant had not been broken. Parkside and the individual purchasers could have avoided breaking the covenant in two ways. One course would have been not to develop the allotment site. The other course would have been for Parkside to have sought from the plaintiffs a relaxation of the covenant. On the facts of this particular case the plaintiffs, rightly conscious of their obligations towards existing residents, would clearly not have granted any relaxation, but for present purposes I must assume that it could have been induced to do so. In my judgment a just substitute for a mandatory injunction would be such a sum of money as might reasonably have been demanded by the plaintiffs from Parkside as a *quid pro quo* for relaxing the covenant. The plaintiffs submitted that that sum should be a substantial proportion of the development value of the land. This is currently put at no less than £10,000 per plot, ie, £140,000 on the assumption that the plots are undeveloped. Mr Parker gave evidence that a half or a third of the development value was commonly demanded by a landowner whose property stood in the way of a development. I do not agree with that approach to damages in this type of case. I bear in mind the following factors:

(a) The lay-out covenant is not an asset which the estate owner ever contemplated he would have either the opportunity or the desire to turn to account. It has no commercial or even nuisance value. For it cannot be turned to account except to the detriment of the existing residents who are people the estate owner professes to protect.

(b) The breach of covenant which has actually taken place is over a very small area and the impact of this particular breach on the Wrotham Park estate is insignificant. The validity of the covenant over the rest of area 14 is unaffected.

I think that in a case such as the present a landowner faced with a request from a developer which, it must be assumed, he feels reluctantly obliged to grant, would have first asked the developer what profit he expected to make from his operations. With the benefit of foresight the developer would, in the present case, have said about £50,000 for that is the profit which Parkside concedes it made from the development. I think that the landowner would then reasonably have required a certain percentage of that anticipated profit as a price for the relaxation of the covenant, assuming, as I must, that he feels obliged to relax it. In assessing what would be a fair percentage I think that the court ought, on the particular facts of this case, to act with great moderation. For it is to be borne in mind that the plaintiffs were aware, before the auction took place, that the land was being offered for sale as freehold building land for 13 houses, [816] and they knew that they were not going to consent to any such development. They could have informed the Potters Bar Urban District Council of their attitude in advance of the auction, or could have given the like information to Parkside prior to completion of the contract for sale. In either event it seems highly unlikely that Parkside would have parted with its £90,000, at any rate unconditionally. I think that damages must be assessed in such a case on a basis which is fair and, in all the circumstances, in my judgment a sum equal to 5% of Parkside's anticipated profit is the most that is fair. I accordingly award the sum of £2,500 in substitution for mandatory injunctions ...

Commentary

There are three major explanations that have been put forward for the award of damages in *Wrotham Park*. The first suggested explanation is that the restrictive covenant was protective of a proprietary right, and thus the court was correct to award a reasonable charge for relaxation of the covenant by analogy with the torts cases involving wrongful interference with proprietary rights. This is the explanation of *Wrotham Park* that was favoured by Steyn LJ in *Surrey County Council v Bredero Homes Ltd* (1993), pp 1369–70 (see extract, p 531) and by Megarry VC in *Tito v Waddell (No 2)* (1977), p 335.[48]

---

48 It is also the explanation favoured by Jackman in *The Varieties of Restitution*, 1998, pp 128–29.

The second suggested explanation of *Wrotham Park* is based on the fact that the damages in that case were awarded under Lord Cairns' Act in substitution for an injunction, rather than at common law.[49] Australian authority supports the view that damages in equity under Lord Cairns' Act are assessed on different principles to common law damages, at least to the extent that damages under Lord Cairns' Act can include a reasonable sum for relaxation of a covenant in lieu of an injunction.[50]

The third explanation of *Wrotham Park* is that the damages awarded in that case were in fact compensatory.[51] In *Jaggard v Sawyer* (1995) the English Court of Appeal held that the award of damages in *Wrotham Park* was not restitutionary; rather that the award was designed to compensate the plaintiff for the loss of an opportunity to bargain for a relaxation of the covenant. Millett LJ in *Jaggard v Sawyer* expressed this view at p 355 as follows:

> It is plain from his judgment in the *Wrotham Park* case that Brightman J's approach was compensatory, not restitutionary. He sought to measure the damages by reference to what the plaintiff had lost, not by reference to what the defendant had gained. He did not award the plaintiff the profit which the defendant had made by the breach, but the amount which he judged the plaintiff might have obtained as the price of giving its consent. The amount of the profit which the defendant expected to make was a relevant factor in that assessment, but that was all.

This explanation of *Wrotham Park* is to be rejected. In *Bredero Homes* (1993) (see extract, p 531) Steyn LJ pointed out that it is fictional to classify the award of damages in *Wrotham Park* as compensatory. The evidence in *Wrotham Park* was that the plaintiff would never have agreed to relax the covenant, hence it is highly artificial to view the award as compensation for loss of an opportunity to bargain to relax a covenant when that opportunity would never have been taken up.[52]

The House of Lords addressed the question of the availability of a restitutionary remedy in breach of contract actions for the first time in the following case: *Attorney General v Blake (Jonathan Cape Ltd Third Party)* (2001).[53] As will be seen, Lord Nicholls (who wrote the leading judgment) held that courts do have a discretion to order an account of profits for a breach of contract in exceptional cases. Although his Lordship was reluctant to prescribe fixed rules as to when a court should exercise this discretion, he indicated that an

---

49   *AMEC Development Ltd v Jury's Hotel Management UK Ltd* (2000).

50   *Longtom Pty Ltd v Oberon Shire Council* (1996) 7 BPR 14,799; *Rosser v Maritime Services Board* (unrep) 17 September 1996, Supreme Court of New South Wales.

51   This is the explanation of *Wrotham Park* that was apparently accepted by Lord Hobhouse in his dissenting judgment in *Attorney General v Blake (Jonathan Cape Ltd Third Party)* (2001) (see following extract).

52   See also Burrows, *The Law of Restitution*, 1993, p 399; O'Dair, 'Remedies for breach of contract: a wrong turn' [1993] RLR 31, p 37; Goodhart, 'Restitutionary damages for breach of contract: the remedy that dare not speak its name' [1995] RLR 3, pp 7–8.

53   For an overview of the decision in *Blake* see Erbacher, 'An account of profits for a breach of contract (*Attorney General v Blake*)' (2001) 29 ABLR 73.

account of profits will not normally be awarded unless the existing remedies of compensatory damages, specific performance and injunction would not adequately remedy the defendant's breach. A further useful guide is whether the plaintiff 'had a legitimate interest in preventing the defendant's profit-making activity and, hence, in depriving him of his profit': *Attorney General v Blake (Jonathan Cape Ltd Third Party)* (2001), p 295 (see the following extract). On this approach, the plaintiff would be required to prove a special interest in preventing the defendant from profiting from the breach; that is, an interest over and above the usual interest in having the defendant perform the contract. It is arguable that this approach provides a fourth possible explanation of the *Wrotham Park* case. In that case the plaintiff did have a legitimate supererogatory interest, namely the superior proprietary interest protected by the restrictive covenant, and the usual contractual remedies were not adequate to fully remove the injustice to the plaintiff arising from the breach of the covenant.[54]

Attorney General v Blake (Jonathan Cape Ltd Third Party)
[2001] AC 268 House of Lords

The defendant (respondent) was a former member of the English intelligence organisation, the Security Intelligence Service (the 'SIS'). In 1961 the defendant was convicted of and imprisoned for spying for the Soviet Union, however he escaped in 1966 and moved to Moscow. In 1989 the defendant wrote an autobiography containing information acquired by him in the course of his duties as an SIS officer, and received substantial sums from the third party publisher for the book. The book was published without the knowledge of the SIS. The publication of the book was in breach of an undertaking that the defendant entered into upon commencing employment with the SIS not to publish any information that was gained by him in the course of his employment with the SIS. The Crown commenced an action seeking an order that it was entitled to payment of all profits received by the defendant from the publisher in connection with the book. The Crown conceded from the outset that the information divulged by the defendant was not confidential information, however it argued at first instance and on appeal to the Court of Appeal that the publication of the book amounted to a breach of a fiduciary obligation owed by the defendant to the Crown. This claim was rejected in both courts, although the Court of Appeal granted an injunction on public policy grounds. During the hearing before the Court of Appeal the court invited submissions from the Crown on whether it was entitled to restitutionary damages for breach of the undertaking. The Crown declined to argue the point (presumably believing the matter was settled by *Surrey County Council v Bredero Homes Ltd* (1993)). Nevertheless, the Court of Appeal tentatively expressed the view in obiter that a restitutionary remedy would be available for a breach of contract in two situations: where the defendant had 'skimped' on contractual performance to save money, and where the defendant obtained the profit by doing the very thing it had contracted not to do. On the appeal to the House of Lords, the Crown based its

---

54 See Erbacher, 'An account of profits for a breach of contract (*Attorney General v Blake*)' (2001) 29 ABLR 73, pp 76–77.

claim for the first time on an entitlement to an account of profits for the defendant's breach of the undertaking.

Lord Nicholls of Birkenhead: ... [283] The *Wrotham Park* case ... still shines rather as a solitary beacon, showing that in contract as well as tort damages are not always narrowly confined to recoupment of financial loss. In a suitable case damages for breach of contract may be measured by the benefit gained by the [284] wrongdoer from the breach. The defendant must make a reasonable payment in respect of the benefit he has gained. In the present case the Crown seeks to go further. The claim is for all the profits of Blake's book which the publisher has not yet paid him. This raises the question whether an account of profits can ever be given as a remedy for breach of contract. The researches of counsel have been unable to discover any case where the court has made such an order on a claim for breach of contract. In *Tito v Waddell (No 2)* (1977), p 332, a decision which has proved controversial, Sir Robert Megarry VC said that, as a matter of fundamental principle, the question of damages was 'not one of making the defendant disgorge' his gains, in that case what he had saved by committing the wrong, but 'one of compensating the plaintiff'. In *Occidental Worldwide Investment Corp v Skibs A/S Avanti* (1976), p 337, Kerr J summarily rejected a claim for an account of profits when ship owners withdrew ships on a rising market.

There is a light sprinkling of cases where courts have made orders having the same effect as an order for an account of profits, but the courts seem always to have attached a different label. A person who, in breach of contract, sells land twice over must surrender his profits on the second sale to the original buyer. Since courts regularly make orders for the specific performance of contracts for the sale of land, a seller of land is, to an extent, regarded as holding the land on trust for the buyer: *Lake v Baylis* (1974). In *Reid-Newfoundland Co v Anglo-American Telegraph Co Ltd* (1912) a railway company agreed not to transmit any commercial messages over a particular telegraph wire except for the benefit and account of the telegraph company. The Privy Council held that the railway company was liable to account as a trustee for the profits it wrongfully made from its use of the wire for commercial purposes. In *British Motor Trade Association v Gilbert* (1951) the plaintiff suffered no financial loss but the award of damages for breach of contract effectively stripped the wrongdoer of the profit he had made from his wrongful venture into the black market for new cars.

These cases illustrate that circumstances do arise when the just response to a breach of contract is that the wrongdoer should not be permitted to retain any profit from the breach. In these cases the courts have reached the desired result by straining existing concepts. Professor Peter Birks has deplored the 'failure of jurisprudence when the law is forced into this kind of abusive instrumentalism', see (1993), p 520. Some years ago Professor Dawson suggested there is no inherent reason why the technique of equity courts in land contracts should not be more widely employed, not by granting remedies as the by-product of a phantom 'trust' created by the contract, but as an alternative form of money judgment remedy. That well known ailment of lawyers, a hardening of the categories, ought not to be an obstacle.[55]

---

55   Dawson, 'Restitution or damages' (1959) 20 Ohio LJ 175.

My conclusion is that there seems to be no reason, in principle, why the court must in all circumstances rule out an account of profits as a remedy for breach of contract. I prefer to avoid the unhappy expression 'restitutionary damages'. Remedies are the law's response to a wrong (or, more precisely, to a cause of action). When, exceptionally, a just response to a breach of contract so requires, the court should be able to grant the discretionary [285] remedy of requiring a defendant to account to the plaintiff for the benefits he has received from his breach of contract. In the same way as a plaintiff's interest in performance of a contract may render it just and equitable for the court to make an order for specific performance or grant an injunction, so the plaintiff's interest in performance may make it just and equitable that the defendant should retain no benefit from his breach of contract.

The state of the authorities encourages me to reach this conclusion, rather than the reverse. The law recognises that damages are not always a sufficient remedy for breach of contract. This is the foundation of the court's jurisdiction to grant the remedies of specific performance and injunction. Even when awarding damages, the law does not adhere slavishly to the concept of compensation for financially measurable loss. When the circumstances require, damages are measured by reference to the benefit obtained by the wrongdoer. This applies to interference with property rights. Recently, the like approach has been adopted to breach of contract. Further, in certain circumstances an account of profits is ordered in preference to an award of damages. Sometimes the injured party is given the choice: either compensatory damages or an account of the wrongdoer's profits. Breach of confidence is an instance of this. If confidential information is wrongfully divulged in breach of a non-disclosure agreement, it would be nothing short of sophistry to say that an account of profits may be ordered in respect of the equitable wrong but not in respect of the breach of contract which governs the relationship between the parties. With the established authorities going thus far, I consider it would be only a modest step for the law to recognise openly that, exceptionally, an account of profits may be the most appropriate remedy for breach of contract. It is not as though this step would contradict some recognised principle applied consistently throughout the law to the grant or withholding of the remedy of an account of profits. No such principle is discernible.

The main argument against the availability of an account of profits as a remedy for breach of contract is that the circumstances where this remedy may be granted will be uncertain. This will have an unsettling effect on commercial contracts where certainty is important. I do not think these fears are well founded. I see no reason why, in practice, the availability of the remedy of an account of profits need disturb settled expectations in the commercial or consumer world. An account of profits will be appropriate only in exceptional circumstances. Normally the remedies of damages, specific performance and injunction, coupled with the characterisation of some contractual obligations as fiduciary, will provide an adequate response to a breach of contract. It will be only in exceptional cases, where those remedies are inadequate, that any question of accounting for profits will arise. No fixed rules can be prescribed. The court will have regard to all the circumstances, including the subject matter of the contract, the purpose of the contractual provision which has been breached, the circumstances in which the breach occurred, the consequences of the breach and the circumstances in which relief is being sought. A useful general guide, although not exhaustive, is whether the plaintiff had a legitimate interest in preventing the defendant's profit-making activity and, hence, in depriving him of his profit.

It would be difficult, and unwise, to attempt to be more specific. In the *Wrotham Park* case (1998) the Court of Appeal, Lord Woolf MR, suggested there are at least [286] two situations in which justice requires the award of restitutionary damages where compensatory damages would be inadequate, p 458. Lord Woolf MR was not there addressing the question of when an account of profits, in the conventional sense, should be available. But I should add that, so far as an account of profits is concerned, the suggested categorisation would not assist. The first suggested category was the case of 'skimped' performance, where the defendant fails to provide the full extent of services he has contracted to provide. He should be liable to pay back the amount of expenditure he saved by the breach. This is a much discussed problem. But a part refund of the price agreed for services would not fall within the scope of an account of profits as ordinarily understood. Nor does an account of profits seem to be needed in this context. The resolution of the problem of cases of skimped performance, where the plaintiff does not get what was agreed, may best be found elsewhere. If a shopkeeper supplies inferior and cheaper goods than those ordered and paid for, he has to refund the difference in price. That would be the outcome of a claim for damages for breach of contract. That would be so, irrespective of whether the goods in fact served the intended purpose. There must be scope for a similar approach, without any straining of principle, in cases where the defendant provided inferior and cheaper services than those contracted for.

The second suggested category was where the defendant has obtained his profit by doing the very thing he contracted not to do. This category is defined too widely to assist. The category is apt to embrace all express negative obligations. But something more is required than mere breach of such an obligation before an account of profits will be the appropriate remedy.

Lord Woolf MR, pp 457, 458 also suggested three facts which should not be a sufficient ground for departing from the normal basis on which damages are awarded: the fact that the breach was cynical and deliberate; the fact that the breach enabled the defendant to enter into a more profitable contract elsewhere; and the fact that by entering into a new and more profitable contract the defendant put it out of his power to perform his contract with the plaintiff. I agree that none of these facts would be, by itself, a good reason for ordering an account of profits.

The present case

The present case is exceptional. The context is employment as a member of the security and intelligence services. Secret information is the lifeblood of these services. In the 1950s Blake deliberately committed repeated breaches of his undertaking not to divulge official information gained as a result of his employment. He caused untold and immeasurable damage to the public interest he had committed himself to serve. In 1990 he published his autobiography, a further breach of his express undertaking. By this time the information disclosed was no longer confidential. In the ordinary course of commercial dealings the disclosure of non-confidential information might be regarded as venial. In the present case disclosure was also a criminal offence under the Official Secrets Acts, even though the information was no longer confidential ...

[287] When he joined the Secret Intelligence Service Blake expressly agreed in writing that he would not disclose official information, during or after his service, in book form or otherwise. He was employed on that basis. That was the basis on which he acquired official information. The Crown had and has a legitimate interest in preventing Blake profiting from the disclosure of official information, whether classified or not, while a member of the service and thereafter. Neither he, nor any other member of the service, should have a financial incentive to break his undertaking. It is of paramount importance that members of the service should have complete confidence in all their dealings with each other, and that those recruited as informers should have the like confidence. Undermining the willingness of prospective informers to co-operate with the services, or undermining the morale and trust between members of the services when engaged on secret and dangerous operations, would jeopardise the effectiveness of the service. An absolute rule against disclosure, visible to all, makes good sense.

In considering what would be a just response to a breach of Blake's undertaking the court has to take these considerations into account. The undertaking, if not a fiduciary obligation, was closely akin to a fiduciary obligation, where an account of profits is a standard remedy in the event of breach. Had the information which Blake has now disclosed still been confidential, an account of profits would have been ordered, almost as a matter of course. In the special circumstances of the intelligence services, the same conclusion should follow even though the information is no longer confidential. That would be a just response to the breach. I am reinforced in this view by noting that most of the profits from the book derive indirectly from the extremely serious and damaging breaches of the same undertaking committed by Blake in the 1950s. As already mentioned, but for his notoriety as an infamous spy his autobiography would not have commanded royalties of the magnitude Jonathan Cape agreed to pay.

As a footnote I observe that a similar conclusion, requiring the contract-breaker to disgorge his profits, was reached in the majority decision of the United States Supreme Court in *Snepp v United States* (1980). [288] The facts were strikingly similar. A former employee of the Central Intelligence Agency, whose conditions of employment included a promise not to divulge any information relating to the agency without pre-publication clearance, published a book about the agency's activities in Vietnam. None of the information was classified, but an agent's violation of his non-disclosure obligation impaired the agency's ability to function properly. The court considered and rejected various forms of relief. The actual damage was not quantifiable, nominal damages were a hollow alternative, and punitive damages after a jury trial would be speculative and unusual. Even if recovered they would bear no relation to either the government's irreparable loss or Snepp's unjust gain. The court considered that a remedy which required Snepp 'to disgorge the benefits of his faithlessness', was swift and sure, tailored to deter those who would place sensitive information at risk and, since the remedy reached only funds attributable to the breach, it could not saddle the former agent with exemplary damages out of all proportion to his gain. In order to achieve this result the court 'imposed' a constructive trust on Snepp's profits. In this country, affording the plaintiff the remedy of an account of profits is a different means to the same end.

...

Lord Steyn: ... [291] In the Court of Appeal in *Surrey County Council v Bredero Homes Ltd* (1993) I discussed some of the difficulties inherent in creating a general remedy for the recovery of restitutionary damages for breach of contract. On that occasion I remarked that it is not traditional to describe a claim for restitution following a breach of contract as damages. The terminology is however less important than the substance: under consideration are claims for the disgorgement of profits against a contract breaker. There has been a substantial academic debate on the merits of the actual decision in the *Bredero* case. Since this issue has not been directly debated in the present case I propose to express no view on it. But it is right to acknowledge that the academic comment has been critical of the decision in the *Bredero* case. I would, however, respectfully offer a comment on the valuable academic debate. On the one hand, there is no or virtually no support for a general action for disgorgement of profits made by a contract breaker by reason of his breach. On the other hand, there is significantly absent from the post-*Bredero* academic comment a reasoned statement of the particular circumstances when such a remedy should be available. That is not surprising because it is a notoriously a difficult subject. But the Court of Appeal has been bold. It is said that the remedy should be available in two situations, viz (1) in cases of 'skimped' performance (where the 'gain' would take the form of expense saved) and (2) 'where the defendant has obtained his profit by doing the very thing which he contracted not to do'. The second would cover the present case. But it potentially has wide application. Sir Guenter Treitel QC[56] has questioned the soundness of the observations of the Court of Appeal.[57] I am not at present willing to endorse the broad observations of the Court of Appeal. Exceptions to the general principle that there is no remedy for disgorgement of profits against a contract breaker are best hammered out on the anvil of concrete cases.

...

My Lords, it has been held at first instance and in the Court of Appeal that Blake is not a fiduciary. This is not an issue before the House. But, as my noble and learned friend Lord Nicholls of Birkenhead has observed, the [291] present case is closely analogous to that of fiduciaries: compare *Reading v Attorney General* (1951). If the information was still confidential, Blake would in my view have been liable as a fiduciary. That would be so despite the fact that he left the intelligence services many years ago. The distinctive feature of this case is, however, that Blake gave an undertaking not to divulge any information, confidential or otherwise, obtained by him during his work in the intelligence services. This obligation still applies to Blake. He was, therefore in regard to all information obtained by him in the intelligence services, confidential or not, in a very similar position to a fiduciary. The reason of the rule applying to fiduciaries applies to him. Secondly, I bear in mind that the enduring strength of the common law is that it has been developed on a case-by-case basis by judges for whom the attainment of practical justice was a major objective of their work. It is still one of the major moulding forces of judicial decision-making. These observations are almost banal: the public would be astonished if it was thought that judges did not conceive it as their prime duty to

---

56 *The Law of Contract*, 10th edn, 1999, pp 868–69.
57 See also the valuable comment by Janet O'Sullivan, 'Reflections on the role of restitutionary damages to protect contractual expectations' (to be published) and Hanoch Dagan, 'Restitutionary damages for breach of contract: an exercise in private law theory, theoretical inquiries in law' (2000) Vol 1 115.

do practical justice whenever possible. A recent example of this process at work is *White v Jones* (1995) where by a majority the House of Lords held that a solicitor who caused loss to a third party by negligence in the preparation of a will is liable in damages. Subordinating conceptual difficulties to the needs of practical justice a majority, and notably Lord Goff of Chieveley at pp 259–60H, upheld the claim. For my part practical justice strongly militates in favour of granting an order for disgorgement of profits against Blake. The decision of the United States Supreme Court in *Snepp v United States* (1980) is instructive. On very similar facts the Supreme Court imposed a constructive trust on the intelligence officer's profits. Our law is also mature enough to provide a remedy in such a case but does so by the route of the exceptional recognition of a claim for disgorgement of profits against the contract breaker. In my view therefore there is a valid claim vesting in the Attorney General against Blake for disgorgement of his gain.

...

Lord Hobhouse of Woodborough: ... [297] The Crown has to allege a breach of contract. This is not a claim to the performance of any obligation save in the sense used by Lord Diplock that contractual obligations are correctly understood as being the obligation to perform or pay damages for failing to do so – the primary and secondary [298] obligation: *Photo Production Ltd v Securicor Transport Ltd* (1980). The claim is for damages in order to put the plaintiff in the same position as if the contract had been performed. It is a *substitute* for performance. That is why it is necessarily compensatory. The error is to describe compensation as relating to a loss as if there has to be some identified physical or monetary loss to the plaintiff. In the vast majority of cases this error does not matter because the plaintiff's claim can be so described without distortion. But in a minority of cases the error does matter and cases of the breach of negative promises typically illustrate this category.

But, before coming to them, I would like to refer to *Ruxley Electronics and Construction Ltd v Forsyth* (1996). This was the case of the swimming pool. The defendant had contracted to build for the plaintiff a swimming pool of a specified depth. The pool was not of that depth. The defendant had broken his contract. The plaintiff was entitled to damages. The value of his property was affected either not at all or only marginally. The swimming pool was serviceable. But the plaintiff was entitled to a deeper pool. The *prima facie* measure of damages would have been the cost of increasing the depth of the pool to the stipulated depth – a considerable sum. But this sum was so disproportionate that the courts refused to award it. It would be unreasonable for the plaintiff to incur that expense. His damages must be assessed at a lower figure. The speech of Lord Mustill (1996), pp 359–61 is illuminating. The loss is a reasonable valuation of what the plaintiff ought to have had but did not get. It is not just the amount (if any) by which his property has a lower market value than that it would have had if the contract had been performed. In the present case, by 1989, Blake's undertaking had no remaining value to the Crown.

The question of negative covenants typically arise in relation to land and covenants not to build. A complication is that they usually involve a proprietary right of the plaintiff which he is *prima facie* entitled to enforce as such. Where the plaintiff has failed to obtain or failed to apply for an injunction, he has to be content with a remedy in damages. What has happened in such cases is that there has either actually or in effect been a compulsory purchase of the plaintiff's right of refusal. (The award of damages in tort for the conversion or detinue of goods is also an example of compulsory purchase as is demonstrated by the common law rule that the payment of the damages vests the title in the goods in the defendant.) What the plaintiff has lost is the sum which he could have exacted from the defendant as the price of his consent to the development. This is an example of compensatory damages. They are damages for breach. They do not involve any concept of restitution and so to describe them is an error. The error comes about because of the assumption that the only loss which the plaintiff can have suffered is a reduction in the value of the dominant tenement. It is for this reason that I agree with my noble and learned friend, Lord Nicholls, that the decision in *Wrotham Park Estate Co Ltd v Parkside Homes Ltd* (1974) is to be preferred to that in *Surrey County Council v Bredero Homes Ltd* (1993); see also *Jaggard v Sawyer* (1995). I would however add that the order proposed by your Lordships does not reflect this principle; it goes further. It does not award to the Crown damages for breach of contract assessed by reference to what would be the reasonable price to pay for permission to publish. It awards the Crown damages which equal the whole amount owed by [299] Jonathan Cape to Blake. That is a remedy based on proprietary principles when the necessary proprietary rights are absent.

The principle of compensation is both intellectually sound as the remedy for breach and provides the just answer. The examples discussed in my noble and learned friend's speech do not on the correct analysis disclose the supposed need to extend the boundaries of remedies for breach of contract. The reason why the Crown should not recover damages in the present case derives from the exceptional public law nature of the undertaking which Blake gave. If the relationship had been a commercial one it is probable that by 1989 the undertaking would be regarded as spent or no longer enforceable, but if still enforceable the breach of it would have supported compensatory damages on the 'compulsory purchase' basis.

...

I must also sound a further note of warning that if some more extensive principle of awarding non-compensatory damages for breach of contract is to be introduced into our commercial law the consequences will be very far reaching and disruptive. I do not believe that such is the intention of your Lordships but if others are tempted to try to extend the decision of the present exceptional case to commercial situations so as to introduce restitutionary rights beyond those presently recognised by the law of restitution, such a step will require very careful consideration before it is acceded to.

...

[Lords Goff and Browne-Wilkinson concurred with Lord Nicholls.]

Commentary and questions

According to Lord Nicholls, what are the principles that will determine whether an account of profits will be awarded for a breach of contract? What factors did Lord Nicholls rely upon in ordering an account of profits on the facts of this case? Why did Lord Steyn award the account of profits? On what basis did he consider that this case was distinguishable from *Surrey County Council v Bredero*

Homes (1993) (see extract, p 531)? What do you think is the status of *Bredero Homes* following *Attorney General v Blake*?

Lord Hobhouse's view in dissent was that restitutionary remedies are not needed, as principles of compensatory damages can be moulded to give appropriate and just relief in breach of contract cases involving skimped performance or a failure to comply with an undertaking (see extract, p 508). There is also academic support for this view.[58]

There is very little authority in Australia on the question of the availability of restitutionary remedies for a breach of contract,[59] and such authority that does exist is hostile to the idea of restitutionary damages. The Full Court of the Federal Court in *Hospitality Group Pty Ltd v Australian Rugby Union Ltd* (2001) said in *obiter*, at para 159:[60]

> Whether or not the law of contract is *'seriously defective'*[61] if the court is unable to award disgorgement damages,[62] the position in Australia is that the loss recoverable for breach of contract is limited to that laid down in *Robinson v Harman* (1848). That is, the aggrieved party is entitled only to compensation. If he has suffered no loss, he is not entitled to be compensated. In an appropriate case, the aggrieved party may be able to recover (by a claim in restitution) benefits that he has made available to the wrongdoer; for example, he may be able to recover the price paid under an incomplete contract or recover possession of goods sold but not paid for. Presently, however, it would be inconsistent with the current principles laid down by the High Court to confer a windfall on a plaintiff under the guise of damages for breach of contract.

Accordingly, it must be said that the general rule excluding a restitutionary remedy for a breach of contract still applies in Australia. When the courts in due course determine whether this exclusionary rule should be overturned, they will no doubt gain valuable assistance from the academic commentary on *Attorney General v Blake*.[63]

---

58 See in particular Mitchell, 'Remedial inadequacy in contract: the role of restitutionary damages' (1999) 15 JCL 133.

59 The most significant discussion of the availability of an account of profits for a breach of contract is by Deane J in *Hospital Products Ltd v US Surgical Corp* (1982) 156 CLR 41, p 125. Deane J held that a constructive trust could be imposed over profits earned as a result of a calculated and exploitative breach of contract.

60 *Per* Hill and Finkelstein JJ. Though Emmett J considered that an account of profits could be awarded for the tort of inducing a breach of contract: *ibid*, paras 169ff.

61 *Attorney General v Blake* (1998), p 457 *per* Lord Woolf MR.

62 The terminology proposed by Smith in 'Disgorgement of the profits of breach of contract: property, contract and "efficient breach"' (1994) 24 Canadian Business Law Journal 121.

63 See, for example, Phang and Lee, 'Rationalising restitutionary damages in contract law – an elusive or illusory quest?' (2001) 17 JCL 240; Edelman, 'Restitutionary damages and disgorgement damages for breach of contract' [2000] RLR 129; Jaffey, 'Disgorgement for breach of contract (*Attorney General v Blake*)' [2000] RLR 578.

BRIBES

Personal remedies

An employee or other agent who receives a bribe from a third party will be obliged to pay over the amount of the bribe to the employer or principal. This obligation can be enforced by two alternative but parallel actions: an action in restitution based on unjust enrichment, or an action in equity for a breach of fiduciary obligation.[64] As seen by the following case, the concept of a 'fiduciary' is applied expansively in this context to include employees or agents who would not otherwise be subject to fiduciary obligations.

Reading v Attorney General [1951] AC 507 House of Lords

The appellant was a sergeant in the Royal Army Medical Corps during the Second World War and was stationed in Cairo. The appellant accompanied a truck which was distributing black market alcohol, always wearing his uniform in order to avoid inspection of the truck by the police. He admitted that he had received about £20,000 from this activity. When he was arrested the military authorities confiscated £2,000 found in his possession. Upon his release from prison the appellant sought the recovery of the confiscated money. The issue before the court was whether the Crown had a valid entitlement to the money.

Lord Porter: ... [513] In these circumstances Denning J [the trial judge] held that the Crown was entitled to the money in question. It was, in his view, immaterial to consider whether the method of seizure was justified or not. Even if it was not, the Crown had a valid counterclaim, and, avoiding a circuity of action, could thus defeat the appellant's claim. 'The claim here is', he says ((1948), p 275), 'for restitution of moneys which, in justice, ought to be paid over'. It was suggested in argument that the learned judge founded his decision solely on the doctrine of unjust enrichment and that that doctrine was not recognised by the law of England. My Lords, the exact status of the law of unjust enrichment is not yet assured. It holds a predominant place in the law of Scotland [514] and, I think, of the United States, but I am content for the purposes of this case to accept the view that it forms no part of the law of England and that a right to restitution so described would be too widely stated.

But, indeed, this doctrine is not of the essence of Denning J's judgment. His reasoning is to be found in the passage which succeeds that quoted. He says:

> In my judgment, it is a principle of law that if a servant, in violation of his duty of honesty and good faith, takes advantage of his service to make a profit for himself, in this sense, that the assets of which he has control, or the facilities which he enjoys, or the position which he occupies, are the real cause of his obtaining the money as distinct from being the mere opportunity for getting it, that is to say, if they play the predominant part in his obtaining the money, then he is accountable for it to the master. It matters not that the master has not

---

64 *Boston Deep Sea Fishing and Ice Co v Ansell* (1888); *Reading v The King* (1949), p 237 (on appeal *Reading v Attorney General* (1951), Lord Porter pp 515, 517, 518) (see extract, p 550); *Mahesan v Malaysia Housing Society* (1979), p 380 (see extract, p 553).

lost any profit nor suffered any damage. Nor does it matter that the master could not have done the act himself. It is a case where the servant has unjustly enriched himself by virtue of his service without his master's sanction. It is money which the servant ought not to be allowed to keep, and the law says it shall be taken from him and given to his master, because he got it solely by reason of the position which he occupied as a servant of his master.

And again ((1948), p 276): 'The uniform of the Crown, and the position of the man as a servant of the Crown were the sole reasons why he was able to get this money, and that is sufficient to make him liable to hand it over to the Crown.' The learned judge, however, also says: 'This man Reading was not acting in the course of his employment: and there was no fiduciary relationship in respect of these long journeys nor, indeed, in respect of his uniform.' If this means, as I think it does, that the appellant was neither a trustee nor in possession of some profit-earning chattel and that it was contrary to his duty to escort unwarranted traffic or possibly any traffic through the streets of Cairo, it is true, but, in my view, irrelevant. He, nevertheless, was using his position as a sergeant in His Majesty's army, and the uniform to which his rank entitled him to obtain the money which he received. In my opinion, any official position, whether marked by a uniform or not, which enables the holder to earn money by its use gives his master a right to receive the money so earned even though it was earned by a criminal act. 'You have [515] earned', the master can say, 'money by the use of your position as my servant. It is not for you, who have gained this advantage, to set up your own wrong as a defence to my claim'.

Asquith LJ, in the Court of Appeal, points out ((1949), p 236) that there is a well established class of cases in which a master can recover whether or not he has suffered any detriment in fact, eg, those in which a servant or agent has realised a secret profit, commission or bribe in the course of his employment, and that the sum recoverable is the amount of such profit. It is perhaps sufficient to refer in this connection to *Boston Deep Sea Fishing & Ice Co v Ansell* (1888), and to quote the words of Bowen LJ:

> It is true, as Kekevich J says, that the money which is sought to be recovered must be money had and received by the agent for the principal's use; but the use which arises in such a case, and the reception to the use of the principal which arises in such a case, does not depend on any privity between the principal and the opposite party with whom the agent is employed to conduct business – it is not that the money ought to have gone into the principal's hands in the first instance; the use arises from the relation between the principal and the agent himself. It is because it is contrary to equity that the agent or the servant should retain money so received without the knowledge of his master. Then the law implies a use, that is to say, there is an implied contract, if you put it as a legal proposition – there is an equitable right, if you treat it as a matter of equity – as between the principal and agent that the agent should pay it over, which renders the agent liable to be sued for money had and received, and there is an equitable right in the master to receive it, and to take it out of the hands of the agent, which gives the principal a right to relief in equity.

But it is said that this right to recover is subject to two qualifications: (1) the sum obtained must have been obtained in the course of the servant's employment; and (2) there must exist in the matter in question a fiduciary relationship between employer and employee.

It is often convenient to speak of money obtained as received in the course of the servant's employment, but strictly speaking I do not think that expression accurately describes the position where a servant receives money by reason of his employment but [516] in dereliction of his duty. In *Attorney General v Goddard* (1929) the bribes given to Sergeant Goddard were received by reason of his employment, but not in the course of it, except in the sense that his employment afforded the opportunity by which the gain was made. Just as in the often quoted instance of a servant letting out his own services and the use of his master's horses for private gain, he is not acting in the course of his employment, he is taking advantage of the position which his employment gives him and for reward so gained he is answerable to his master none the less, as *Attorney General v Goddard* (1929) shows, though the obtaining of the money is a criminal act. It is true that the right of the master to demand payment of the money is often imputed to a promise implied from his relationship to the servant. I doubt whether it is necessary to raise such an implication in order to show that the money has been received to the master's use, but even if it were it may well be contended that there is no illegality in a servant promising to hand over to his master any sums he gains by use of his position. Nor would the master be affirming any criminal act committed by the servant in earning the sum claimed. He would only be saying that as between himself and the servant the servant could not set up his own wrong as a defence. Any third party's claim to the money would not be affected. In this aspect the making of the promise need not and should not in my view be referred to a point of time after the receipt of the bribe. It may well be ascribed to the time when the contract of employment was entered into.

As to the assertion that there must be a fiduciary relationship, the existence of such a connection is, in my opinion, not an additional necessity in order to substantiate the claim, but another ground for succeeding where a claim for money had and received would fail. In any case, I agree with Asquith LJ ((1949), p 236) in thinking that the words 'fiduciary relationship' in this setting are used in a wide and loose sense and include, *inter alia*, a case where the servant gains from his employment a position of authority which enables him to obtain the sum which he receives.

My Lords, the fact that the Crown in this case, or that any master, has lost no profits or suffered no damage is, of course, immaterial and the principle so well known that it is unnecessary to cite the cases illustrating and supporting it. It is the receipt and possession of the money that matters, not the loss or prejudice to the master ...

Lord Normand: ... [517] My Lords, I agree with the Court of Appeal with the single reservation that I have not found it necessary to consider whether the Crown would have been entitled to succeed in an action at law for money had and received. On that question I would have desired to hear further argument had it been necessary to decide it.

Though the relation of a member of His Majesty's forces to the Crown is not accurately described as that of a servant under a contract of service or as that of an agent under a contract of agency, the Court of Appeal has held that he owes to the Crown a duty as fully fiduciary as the duty of a servant to his master or of an agent to his principal, and in consequence that all profits and advantages gained by the use or abuse of his military status are to be for the benefit of the Crown. I respectfully think that these are unassailable propositions, and, further that the appellant cannot be allowed to propose as a defence to the Crown's claim his own criminal conduct either in accepting a bribe in breach of military discipline or in participating in an offence against the municipal law of Egypt.

Lord Oaksey: [517] My Lords, I agree with the judgment of the Court of Appeal except on one point. I do not think there is any difficulty in imputing to a servant an implied promise that he will account to his master for any moneys he may receive in the course of his master's business or by the use of his master's property or by the use of his position as his master's servant. There is nothing illegal in such a promise; on the contrary, in substance it is the basis for the equitable principle that an agent is accountable for profits made in the course of his agency without the knowledge and consent of his principal, and no less accountable if the profits arise out of corrupt transactions; an agent is bound to know the law, and, therefore, when he enters into a contract of agency he impliedly undertakes to be accountable for any such profits ...

Questions

Could the Crown establish that it would have made the profits represented by the bribe amounts? Was this relevant?

Mahesan v Malaysia Housing Society [1979] AC 374 Privy Council

The appellant was the purchasing agent of the respondent housing society. The appellant found land at a price of $456,000 which was suitable for the housing society's purposes but instead of buying it for the housing society he fraudulently arranged for one Manickam to buy it and then to resell it to the housing society for $944,000. Manickam realised a gross profit on the transaction of $488,000 of which he passed one quarter ($122,000) to the appellant. Manickam's resale expenses were $45,000, resulting in a net profit on the deal of $443,000. This amount also represented the housing society's loss as a consequence of the appellant's fraud. The housing society commenced proceedings against the appellant claiming both the amount of the bribe and damages for the loss suffered by it. The issue before the Privy Council was whether the society could recover from the appellant *both* the amount of the bribe and damages for its loss.

Lord Diplock: ... [379] The question of law which has caused their Lordships difficulty in this appeal is whether or not in civil proceedings the amount of the bribe can be recovered from the dishonest agent twice over. In allowing double recovery the Federal Court treated the question as governed in Malaysia by the common law and principles of equity in force in England in 1956 (the relevant date for the purpose of their acceptance as basic law in Malaysia). They did not consider that s 30 of the Prevention of Corruption Act 1961 made any relevant alteration to the civil liability of a bribed agent to his principal as it had been prior to the Act. They accordingly applied the principles stated in two judgments of the English Court of Appeal at the turn of the century: *Salford Corporation v Lever* (1891) and *Hovenden and Sons v Millhoff* (1900). On the face of them, the statements relied on by the Federal Court justify double recovery of the bribe from the agent who received it. They were, however, *obiter*. The actions in which they were made were actions by the principal against the giver of the bribe against whom there was no question of double recovery. They were not actions against the agent; and there does not appear to be any reported case of an action by a principal against his bribed agent in which double recovery of the amount of the bribe was obtained. In their Lordships' view, these *dicta*, notwithstanding the eminence of the judges by whom they were made, are in [380] conflict with basic principles of English law as they have been developed in the course of the present century. They call for re-examination in their historical setting.

By the early years of the 19th century it had become an established principle of equity that an agent who received any secret advantage for himself from the other party to a transaction in which the agent was acting for his principal was bound to account for it to his principal: *Fawcett v Whitehouse* (1829). The remedy was equitable, obtainable in the Court of Chancery, and there appears to be no reported case at common law for the recovery of a bribe by a principal from his agent before the Judicature Act 1875. No precedent for such a count is to be found in *Bullen and Leake's Precedents of Pleadings*. Nevertheless by 1888, Bowen LJ felt able to say that the bribe was recoverable at common law as money had and received by the agent to the use of the principal:

> ... the law implies a use, that is to say, there is an implied contract, if you put it as a legal proposition – there is an equitable right, if you treat it as a matter of equity – as between the principal and agent that the agent should pay it over, which renders the agent liable to be sued for money had and received, and there is an equitable right in the master to receive it, and to take it out of the hands of the agent, which gives the principal a right to relief in equity, see *Boston Deep Sea Fishing and Ice Co v Ansell* (1888).

This right of the principal to recover the amount of the bribe from the agent does not depend on his having incurred any loss as a result of his agent's conduct: *Reading v Attorney General* (1949). But the giving of the bribe was treated in equity as constructive fraud on the part of the giver and where it was given in connection with a contract between the principal and the briber the principal was entitled to rescission of the contract. This equitable right was additional to his right to recover the bribe from the agent.

[Lord Diplock examined the authority of *Salford Corporation v Lever* (1891) where it was held the principal could recover both the amount of the bribe from the agent and also damages for the loss from the agent and briber (who were jointly and severally liable). His Honour continued at p 381:]

The liability of the briber to the principal for damages for the loss sustained by him in consequence of entering into the contract in respect of which the bribe was given is a rational development from his former right in equity to rescission of the contract. The cause of action against the briber was stated by Lord Esher MR and Lopes LJ to be fraud, and, since the agent was necessarily party to the bribery, it follows that the tort was a joint tort of briber and agent for which either or both could be sued. But fraud is a tort for which the damages are limited to the actual loss sustained; and if the principal has recovered the bribe from the bribed agent the actual loss he has sustained in consequence of entering into the contract is reduced by that amount ...

[382] Although as a matter of decision *Salford Corporation v Lever* (1891) was concerned only with the liability of the briber, the *dicta* summarised in the headnote deal also with the liability of the agent. It was accurate to say that the principal had two distinct remedies against the agent, one for money had and

received and the other for the tort of fraud; but it was flying in the face of a long line of authority to say that these two remedies were not alternative but cumulative. The authorities to this effect are discussed at length in the speeches in *United Australia Ltd v Barclays Bank Ltd* (1941), a case in which the House of Lords confirmed the principle that where the same facts gave rise in law to two causes of action against a single defendant, one (formerly lying in *assumpsit*) for money had and received and the other for damages for tort, the plaintiff must elect between the remedies. It held, however, that such election was not irrevocable until judgment was recovered on one cause of action or the other. The House of Lords also held that where the same facts gave rise in law to a cause of action against one defendant for money had and received and to a separate cause of action for damages in tort against another defendant, judgment recovered against the first defendant did not prevent the plaintiff from suing the other defendant in a separate action: but that to the extent that the judgment was actually satisfied this constituted satisfaction *pro tanto* of the claim for damages in the cause of action against the second defendant. In so far as what was said in the *Salford* case conflicts with this, in their Lordships' opinion it can no longer be regarded as good law ... In the *Salford* case the principal's cause of action against the briber was described by the majority of the court as being fraud, as was his second cause of action against the agent. Damage is the gist of an action in fraud and any loss proved to have been sustained by the principal in consequence of entering into the contract in respect of which the bribe was given might be less or greater than the amount of the bribe. This would no doubt affect the principal's choice of whether to seek judgment against the agent for the amount of the bribe as money had and received or to seek damages for fraud against him, but as the law was laid down in the *Salford* case there would be no such right of election against the briber. The principal's only cause of action against him was for damages for fraud.

In subsequent cases, however, there developed differences of opinion between members of the Court of Appeal as to whether or not the principal had an alternative cause of action for money had and received against the briber too, as well as against the bribed agent. In *Grant v Gold Exploration and Development Syndicate Ltd* (1900) Collins LJ was of opinion that there was such a cause of action against the briber. Smith and Vaughan Williams LJJ doubted this and preferred to express their judgments as damages for fraud holding that the principal had proved a loss up to the amount of the bribes. However, in *Hovenden and Sons v Millhoff* (1900) Smith and Vaughan Williams LJJ recanted and a new chapter was opened in the law of civil remedies for bribery. The Court of Appeal (Smith, [383] Vaughan Williams, and Romer LJJ) allowed the appeal and entered judgment for the principal against the briber for the amount of the bribe. Romer LJ whose judgment was cited by the Federal Court in the instant case, laid down three rules which, if correct, would have the effect of making bribery a wrong committed by the principal which is *sui generis* and defies classification. The rules were: (first) that the motive of the briber in giving the bribe is not relevant; (secondly) that, there is an irrebuttable presumption that the agent was influenced by the bribe, and (thirdly):

> ... if the agent be a confidential buyer of goods for his principal from the briber, the court will assume as against the briber that the true price of the goods as between him and the purchaser must be taken to be less than the price paid to,

or charged by, the vendor by, at any rate, the amount or value of the bribe. If the purchaser alleges loss or damage beyond this, he must prove it.

These rules refer to three of the elements in the tort of fraud, the motive, the inducement, and the loss occasioned to the plaintiff, but go on to say that the existence of the first two elements and of the third up to the amount of the bribe are to be irrebuttably presumed. This is merely another way of saying that they form no part of the definition of bribery as a legal wrong. To the extent that it is said that there is an irrebuttable presumption of loss or damage to the amount of the value of the bribe, this is another way of saying that, unlike in the tort of fraud, actual loss or damage is *not* the gist of the action. But then to go on to say that actual loss in excess of the amount of the bribe can be recovered only if it is proved, is to produce a hybrid form of legal wrong of which actual damage *is* the gist of part only of a single cause of action.

Upon analysis, what these rules really describe is the right of a plaintiff who has alternative remedies against the briber: (1) to recover from him the amount of the bribe as money had and received; or (2) to recover, as damages for tort, the actual loss which he has sustained as a result of entering into the transaction in respect of which the bribe was given; but in accordance with the decision of the House of Lords in *United Australia Ltd v Barclays Bank Ltd* (1941) he need not elect between these alternatives before the time has come for judgment to be entered in his favour in one or other of them.

This extension to the briber of liability to account to the principal for the amount of the bribe as money had and received, whatever conceptual difficulties it may raise, is now and was by 1956 too well established in English law to be questioned. So both as against the briber and the agent bribed the principal has these alternative remedies: (1) for money had and received under which he can recover the amount of the bribe as money had and received; or (2) for damages for fraud, under which he can recover the amount of the actual loss sustained in consequence of his entering into the transaction in respect of which the bribe was given, but he cannot recover both ...

Commentary and questions

The Privy Council decided that the employer/principal has an action in restitution to recover the bribe. Are the bribes cases explained by the principle of unjust enrichment? Is the receipt of the bribe by the employee/agent 'at the expense of' the employer/principal? What unjust factor would apply to ground recovery?

In addition to an action in restitution to recover the amount of the bribe, the Privy Council recognised that the employer or principal could alternatively bring a cause of action in deceit to recover any loss suffered. The court also expressed the view that the employer or principal would have alternative causes of action against the *briber*: a cause of action in restitution to recover the amount of the bribe, and a cause of action in deceit to recover loss. Could an action in restitution against the briber be explained by the principle of unjust enrichment? Would the enrichment to the briber ordinarily correspond with the amount of the bribe? Is the receipt of the bribe by the employee/agent 'at the expense of' the employer/principal?

Proprietary remedies

The traditional rule, laid down in the following case of *Lister v Stubbs* (1890) is that the only liability of the recipient of a bribe is to personally account for the amount of the bribe. The courts consistently refused to impose a constructive trust over the bribe and its proceeds, thus allowing the recipient of the bribe to retain any profit made by the investment of the bribe.

Receipt of bribes – proprietary remedy

Lister & Co v Stubbs (1890) 45 Ch D 1 English Court of Appeal

The defendant was the purchasing officer of the plaintiff company which carried on the business of silk spinners, dyers and manufacturers. Over a period of about 10 years the defendant placed orders for large quantities of dye stuffs from the firm of Varley, and it was alleged that in return he had received from Varley the sum of about £5,541 in secret commissions. It was further alleged that the defendant had invested a large amount of the secret commissions in property. The plaintiff brought an action against the defendant to recover the amount of the secret commissions and sought to follow the commissions into the investments. It also sought an interlocutory injunction to restrain the defendant from dealing with the investments.

Cotton LJ: [12] The case here is this: the defendant, being in the confidential employment of the plaintiffs, made a corrupt bargain with persons who supplied the partnership with dye stuffs. The bargain was most manifestly corrupt; but does that make the money which the defendant received in pursuance of that bargain the money of the plaintiffs? Mr Justice Stirling, in the course of his judgment, referred to my decision in the case of *Metropolitan Bank v Heiron* (1880). I think that I took a correct view in my judgment in that case; and in my opinion this is not the money of the plaintiffs, so as to make the defendant a trustee of it for them, but it is money acquired in such a way that, according to all rules applicable to such a case, the plaintiffs, when they bring the action to a hearing, can get an order against the defendant for the payment of that money to them. That is to say, there is a debt due from the defendant to the plaintiffs in consequence of the corrupt bargain which he entered into; but the money which he has received under that bargain cannot, in the view which I take, be treated as being money of the plaintiffs, which was handed by them to the defendant to be paid to Messrs Varley in discharge of a debt due from the plaintiffs to Messrs Varley on the contract between them.

When the facts are ascertained, the plaintiffs will have the opportunity of setting aside the contract altogether and returning the stuffs, or, without setting aside the contract, of suing Messrs Varley for the money which they have fraudulently handed over to the defendant. But in my opinion the moneys which under this corrupt bargain were paid by Messrs Varley to the defendant cannot be said to be the money of the plaintiffs [13] before any judgment or decree in some such action has been made. I know of no case where, because it was highly probable that if the action were brought to a hearing the plaintiff could establish that a debt was due to him from the defendant, the defendant has been ordered to give security until that has been established by the judgment or decree. The plaintiff, if so advised, might apply for an immediate order under Order xiv, and then, if the defendant applied to defend, he could only do so on such terms as the judge might think reasonable. But in the present case that course has not been taken. In my opinion, however corrupt the bargain was, we cannot hold that, under the circumstances of this case, the money was the money of the plaintiffs ...

Lindley LJ: [14] If we were to accede to this application, I do not think that Stubbs could complain; but the question is, whether, having regard to the rules by which we are governed, we can properly make the order. I am clearly of opinion that we cannot. The real state of the case as between Lister & Co and Messrs Varley and Stubbs is this: Lister & Co, through their agent Stubbs, buy goods of Messrs Varley at certain prices, and pay for them. The ownership of the goods of course is in Lister & Co; the ownership of the money is in Messrs Varley. Then Messrs [15] Varley have entered into an arrangement with Stubbs, who ordered the goods to them, to give Stubbs a commission. That is what it comes to. What is the legal position between Messrs Varley and Stubbs? They owe him the money. He can recover it from them by an action, unless the illegality of the transaction afford them a defence; but the Appellants have asked us to go further, and to say that Messrs Varley were Stubbs' agents in getting his commission from Lister & Co. That appears to me to be an entire mistake. The relation between Messrs Varley and Stubbs is that of debtor and creditor – they pay him. Then comes the question, as between Lister & Co and Stubbs, whether Stubbs can keep the money he has received without accounting for it? Obviously not. I apprehend that he is liable to account for it the moment that he gets it. It is an obligation to pay and account to Messrs Lister & Co, with or without interest, as the case may be. I say nothing at all about that. But the relation between them is that of debtor and creditor; it is not that of trustee and *cestui que* trust. We are asked to hold that it is – which would involve consequences which, I confess, startle me. One consequence, of course, would be that, if Stubbs were to become bankrupt, this property acquired by him with the money paid to him by Messrs Varley would be withdrawn from the mass of his creditors and be handed over bodily to Lister & Co. Can that be right? Another consequence would be that, if the appellants are right, Lister & Co could compel Stubbs to account to them, not only for the money with interest, but for all the profits which he might have made by embarking in trade with it. Can that be right? It appears to me that those consequences shew that there is some flaw in the argument. If by logical reasoning from the premises conclusions are arrived at which are opposed to good sense, it is necessary to go back and look again at the premises and see if they are sound. I am satisfied that they are not sound – the unsoundness consisting in confounding ownership with obligation. It appears to me that the view taken of this case by Mr Justice Stirling was correct, and that we should be doing what I conceive to be very great mischief if we were to stretch a sound principle to the extent to which the Appellants ask us to stretch it, tempting as [16] it is to do so as between the plaintiffs and Stubbs. I think that the appeal ought to be dismissed.

Commentary

Although the principal case has some supporters,[65] it has been the subject of sustained criticism by the majority of commentators.[66] A particularly powerful criticism was made by Sir Peter Millett LJ, speaking extra-judicially. Millett LJ argued that a constructive trust should be recognised in bribes cases on the basis of the maxim 'equity regards as done that which ought to be done'. As the recipient of a bribe ought to have handed it over to the principal at the time of its receipt, the maxim treats the bribe as a legitimate payment intended for the principal, and hence as the principal's property, even before delivery. Millett LJ's reasoning was adopted by the Privy Council in *Attorney General for Hong Kong v Reid* (1994) (see following extract) which disapproved of the principal case.

The principal case has had a chequered history in Australian law. It was applied by the High Court in *Ardletham Options Ltd v Easdown* (1915), however has been more recently criticised by Hutley JA in the New South Wales Court of Appeal in *DPC Estates Pty Ltd v Grey & Consul Developments Pty Ltd* (1974), pp 470–71.[67] The Privy Council refused to apply *Lister v Stubbs* in the following decision.

Attorney General for Hong Kong v Reid [1994] 1 AC 324 Privy Council

The defendant worked as a solicitor in the Crown Prosecutor's office, ultimately being appointed Acting Director of Public Prosecutions. In the course of his career he accepted bribes as an inducement to obstruct the prosecution of certain criminals. His acceptance of the bribes was in breach of the fiduciary duty which he owed as a servant of the Crown. He was imprisoned and ordered to pay the Crown the sum of HK$12.4 million, being the value of his assets which could only have been derived from the bribes. The Attorney General registered caveats over three freehold properties owned by the defendant in New Zealand, two of which were held jointly with his wife and one of which was held in the name of his solicitor. The Attorney General applied to the High Court of New Zealand to renew the caveats however the application was refused on the basis the Crown had no equitable interest in the properties. The Court of Appeal of New Zealand dismissed the appeal.

Lord Templeman: ...[330] A bribe is a gift accepted by a fiduciary as an inducement to him to betray his trust. A secret benefit, which may or may not constitute a bribe, is a benefit which the fiduciary derives from trust property or obtains from knowledge which he acquires in the course of acting as a fiduciary. A fiduciary is not always accountable for a secret benefit but he is undoubtedly accountable for a secret benefit which consists of a bribe. In addition a person who

---

65   Birks, *An Introduction to the Law of Restitution*, rev edn, 1989, pp 387–89; Goode, 'Ownership and obligation in commercial transactions' (1987) 103 LQR 433; Burrows, *The Law of Restitution*, 1993, p 411.

66   See, eg, Finn, *Fiduciary Obligations*, 1977, para 513; Sir Anthony Mason, 'Themes and prospects', in Finn (ed), *Essays in Equity*, 1985, p 246; Millett, 'Bribes and secret commissions' [1993] RLR 7; Goff and Jones, *op cit*, fn 2, p 669.

67   Hutley JA considered that *Lister & Co v Stubbs* should be confined to its own special facts.

provides the bribe and the fiduciary who accepts the bribe may each be guilty of a criminal offence. In the present case the first respondent [Mr Reid] was clearly guilty of a criminal offence.

Bribery is an evil practice which threatens the foundations of any civilised society. In particular bribery of policemen and prosecutors [331] brings the administration of justice into disrepute. Where bribes are accepted by a trustee, servant, agent or other fiduciary, loss and damage are caused to the beneficiaries, master or principal whose interests have been betrayed. The amount of loss or damage resulting from the acceptance of a bribe may or may not be quantifiable. In the present case the amount of harm caused to the administration of justice in Hong Kong by the first respondent in return for bribes cannot be quantified.

When a bribe is offered and accepted in money or in kind, the money or property constituting the bribe belongs in law to the recipient. Money paid to the false fiduciary belongs to him. The legal estate in freehold property conveyed to the false fiduciary by way of bribe vests in him. Equity however, which acts *in personam*, insists that it is unconscionable for a fiduciary to obtain and retain a benefit in breach of duty. The provider of a bribe cannot recover it because he committed a criminal offence when he paid the bribe. The false fiduciary who received the bribe in breach of duty must pay and account for the bribe to the person to whom that duty was owed. In the present case, as soon as the first respondent received a bribe in breach of the duties he owed to the Government of Hong Kong, he became a debtor in equity to the Crown for the amount of that bribe. So much is admitted. But if the bribe consists of property which increases in value or if a cash bribe is invested advantageously, the false fiduciary will receive a benefit from his breach of duty unless he is accountable not only for the original amount or value of the bribe but also for the increased value of the property representing the bribe. As soon as the bribe was received it should have been paid or transferred *instanter* to the person who suffered from the breach of duty. Equity considers as done that which ought to have been done. As soon as the bribe was received, whether in cash or in kind, the false fiduciary held the bribe on a constructive trust for the person injured. Two objections have been raised to this analysis. First it is said that if the fiduciary is in equity a debtor to the person injured, he cannot also be a trustee of the bribe. But there is no reason why equity should not provide two remedies, so long as they do not result in double recovery. If the property representing the bribe exceeds the original bribe in value, the fiduciary cannot retain the benefit of the increase in value which he obtained solely as a result of his breach of duty. Secondly, it is said that if the false fiduciary holds property representing the bribe in trust for the person injured, and if the false fiduciary is or becomes insolvent, the unsecured creditors of the false fiduciary will be deprived of their right to share in the proceeds of that property. But the unsecured creditors cannot be in a better position than their debtor. The authorities show that property acquired by a trustee innocently but in breach of trust and the property from time to time representing the same belong in equity to the *cestui que* trust and not to the trustee personally whether he is solvent or insolvent. Property acquired by a trustee as a result of a criminal breach of trust and the property from time to time representing the same must also belong in equity to his *cestui que* trust and not to the trustee whether he is solvent or insolvent.

When a bribe is accepted by a fiduciary in breach of his duty then he holds that bribe in trust for the person to whom the duty was owed. If [332] the property representing the bribe decreases in value the fiduciary must pay the difference between that value and the initial amount of the bribe because he should not have accepted the bribe or incurred the risk of loss. If the property increases in value, the fiduciary is not entitled to any surplus in excess of the initial value of the bribe because he is not allowed by any means to make a profit out of a breach of duty.

[Lord Templeman referred to a number of authorities and then continued at p 335:]

It has always been assumed and asserted that the law on the subject of bribes was definitively settled by the decision of the Court of Appeal in *Lister & Co v Stubbs* (1890).

In that case the plaintiffs, Lister & Co, employed the defendant, Stubbs, as their servant to purchase goods for the firm. Stubbs, on behalf of the firm, bought goods from Varley & Co and received from Varley & Co bribes amounting to £5,541. The bribes were invested by Stubbs in freehold properties and investments. His masters, the firm Lister & Co, sought and failed to obtain an interlocutory injunction restraining Stubbs from disposing of these assets pending the trial of the [336] action in which they sought, *inter alia*, £5,541 and damages. In the Court of Appeal the first judgment was given by Cotton LJ, who had been party to the decision in *Metropolitan Bank v Heiron* (1880). He was powerfully supported by the judgment of Lindley LJ and by the equally powerful concurrence of Bowen LJ. In *Lister & Co v Stubbs* (1890), Cotton LJ said that the bribe could not be said to be the money of the plaintiffs. He seemed to be reluctant to grant an interlocutory judgment which would provide security for a debt before that debt had been established. Lindley LJ said that the relationship between the plaintiffs, Lister & Co, as masters and the defendant, Stubbs, as servant who had betrayed his trust and received a bribe:

> ... is that of debtor and creditor; it is not that of trustee and *cestui que* trust. We are asked to hold that it is – which would involve consequences which, I confess, startle me. One consequence, of course, would be that, if Stubbs were to become bankrupt, this property acquired by him with the money paid to him by Messrs Varley would be withdrawn from the mass of his creditors and be handed over bodily to Lister & Co. Can that be right? Another consequence would be that, if the appellants are right, Lister & Co could compel Stubbs to account to them, not only for the money with interest, but for all the profit which he might have made by embarking in trade with it. Can that be right?

For the reasons which have already been advanced, their Lordships would respectfully answer both these questions in the affirmative. If a trustee mistakenly invests moneys which he ought to pay over to his *cestui que* trust and then becomes bankrupt, the moneys together with any profit which has accrued from the investment are withdrawn from the unsecured creditors as soon as the mistake is discovered. *A fortiori*, if a trustee commits a crime by accepting a bribe which he ought to pay over to his *cestui que* trust, the bribe and any profit made therefrom should be withdrawn from the unsecured creditors as soon as the crime is discovered.

The decision in *Lister & Co v Stubbs* is not consistent with the principles that a fiduciary must not be allowed to benefit from his own breach of duty, that the fiduciary should account for the bribe as soon as he receives it and that equity regards as done that which ought to be done. From these principles it would appear to follow that the bribe and the property from time to time representing the bribe are held on a constructive trust for the person injured. A fiduciary remains personally liable for the amount of the bribe if, in the event, the value of the property then recovered by the injured person proved to be less than that amount.

The decisions of the Court of Appeal in *Metropolitan Bank v Heiron* (1880) and *Lister & Co v Stubbs* (1890) are inconsistent with earlier authorities which were not cited. Although over 100 years has passed since *Lister & Co v Stubbs*, no one can be allowed to say that he has ordered his affairs in reliance on the two decisions of the Court of Appeal now in question. Thus no harm can result if those decisions are not followed.

[337] The decision in *Lister & Co v Stubbs* was followed in *Powell & Thomas v Evans Jones & Co* (1905) and *Attorney General v Goddard* (1929). In *Regal (Hastings) Ltd v Gulliver* (1967) shares intended to be acquired by directors at par to avoid them giving a guarantee of the obligations under a lease were sold at a profit and the directors were held to be liable to the company for the proceeds of sale, applying *Keech v Sandford* (1726).

In *Reading v Attorney General* (1951), the Crown confiscated thousands of pounds paid to an army sergeant who had abused his official position to enable drugs to be imported. The Crown was allowed to keep the confiscated moneys to avoid circuity of action.

Finally in *Islamic Republic of Iran Shipping Lines v Denby* (1987) Leggatt J followed *Lister & Co v Stubbs* (1890), as indeed he was bound to do.

The authorities which followed *Lister & Co v Stubbs* do not cast any new light on that decision. Their Lordships are more impressed with the decision of Lai Kew Chai J in *Sumitomo Bank Ltd v Kartika Ratna Thahir* (1993). In that case General Thahir who was at one time general assistant to the president director of the Indonesian state enterprise named Pertamina, opened 17 bank accounts in Singapore and deposited DM54m in those accounts. The money was said to be bribes paid by two German contractors tendering for the construction of steel works in West Java. General Thahir having died, the moneys were claimed by his widow, by the estate of the deceased general and by Pertamina. After considering in detail all the relevant authorities Lai Kew Chai J determined robustly ((1993), p 810) that *Lister & Co v Stubbs* (1890) was wrong and that its 'undesirable and unjust consequences should not be imported and perpetuated as part of' the law of Singapore. Their Lordships are also much indebted for the fruits of research and the careful discussion of the present topic in the address entitled 'Bribes and Secret Commissions', delivered by Sir Peter Millett to a meeting of the Society of Public Teachers of Law at Oxford in 1993. The following passage elegantly sums up the views of Sir Peter Millett (*Sumitomo Bank Ltd v Kartika Ratna Thahir* (1993), p 20):

> [The fiduciary] must not place himself in a position where his interest may conflict with his duty. If he has done so, equity insists on treating him as having acted in accordance with his duty; he will not be allowed to say that he preferred his own interest to that of his principal. He must not obtain a profit for himself out of his fiduciary position. If he has done so, equity insists on treating him as having obtained it for his principal; he will not be allowed to say that he obtained it for himself. He must not accept a bribe. If he has done

so, equity insists on treating it as a legitimate payment intended for the benefit of the principal; he will not be allowed to say that it was a bribe.

The conclusions reached by Lai Kew Chai J in *Sumitomo Bank Ltd v Kartika Ratna Thahir* (1993) and the views expressed by Sir Peter Millett were influenced by the decision of the House of Lords [338] in *Phipps v Boardman* (1966) which demonstrates the strictness with which equity regards the conduct of a fiduciary and the extent to which equity is willing to impose a constructive trust on property obtained by a fiduciary by virtue of his office. In that case a solicitor acting for trustees rescued the interests of the trust in a private company by negotiating for a takeover bid in which he himself took an interest. He acted in good faith throughout and the information which the solicitor obtained about the company in the takeover bid could never have been used by the trustees. Nevertheless the solicitor was held to be a constructive trustee by a majority in the House of Lords because the solicitor obtained the information which satisfied him that the purchase of the shares in the takeover company would be a good investment and the opportunity of acquiring the shares as a result of acting for certain purposes on behalf of the trustees; see *per* Lord Cohen (1967), p 103. If a fiduciary acting honestly and in good faith and making a profit which his principal could not make for himself becomes a constructive trustee of that profit, then it seems to their Lordships that a fiduciary acting dishonestly and criminally who accepts a bribe and thereby causes loss and damage to his principal must also be a constructive trustee and must not be allowed by any means to make any profit from his wrongdoing ...

Commentary and questions

It is likely that the High Court would also refuse to follow *Lister v Stubbs* and would hold that the bribe and its proceeds were held on constructive trust,[68] though perhaps through a different process of reasoning than that used by the Privy Council in the principal case. As discussed in Chapter 19, a constructive trust will be imposed in Australia in those categories of case where it would be unconscionable for the defendant to retain the benefit.[69] Applying this criterion, it could confidently be predicted that a court would conclude that it would be unconscionable for the recipient of a bribe to retain any part of the bribe or its product.

Although the principal case has largely been welcomed by the commentators, Birks has expressed some serious reservations with the decision.[70] Birks, motivated by a concern about the effect of proprietary remedies on priorities in an insolvency, would prefer that the constructive trust be limited to those cases in which the plaintiff has a proprietary basis in the property in question which remains despite the transfer of possession to the defendant.

---

68 Mason and Carter, *Restitution Law in Australia*, 1995, p 678.

69 *Muschinski v Dodds* (1985) (see extract, p 688); *Baumgartner v Baumgartner* (1987).

70 Birks, 'Property in the profits of wrongdoing' (1994) 24 UWAL Rev 8.

CHAPTER 18

DEFENCES

INTRODUCTION

The defendant must establish a recognised defence in order to defend a *prima facie* liability to make restitution; the defendant is not absolved from liability merely by establishing that it would be 'unfair' to require the defendant to restore the benefit.[1]

This chapter covers general defences which are potentially available across a range of restitutionary claims. Some other defences which are closely related to particular claims are dealt with in the context of those claims. In particular, voluntary submission is included in Chapter 5 (Money Paid under a Mistake), Chapter 9 (Duress) and Chapter 15 (Restitution against Public Authorities); disruption to public finances is contained in Chapter 15 (Restitution against Public Authorities); and officiousness is included in Chapter 2 (Identification and Measurement of Enrichment), Chapter 7 (Necessitous Intervention) and Chapter 8 (Compulsory Discharge of Another's Legal Obligations).

The recognised defences covered in this chapter are:

- estoppel by representation;
- change of position;
- ministerial receipt;
- provision of consideration; and
- limitation of actions.

This chapter also discusses the suggested defence of passing on, although it should be noted that that defence has been rejected in Australia (see below, pp 658–66).

---

1   *Lipkin Gorman v Karpnale Ltd* (1991), p 578 (see extract, p 595); *David Securities Pty Ltd v Commonwealth Bank of Australia* (1992), p 379 (see extract, p 592).

ESTOPPEL BY REPRESENTATION

The nature of estoppel by representation

The common law defence of estoppel by representation is an available defence to restitutionary claims.[2] It can be raised where three elements are satisfied (see *Avon County Council v Howlett* (1983), p 605, and extract, p 571):

1 the plaintiff represented to the defendant that the defendant was entitled to keep the money;

2 the defendant, in good faith, acted to his or her detriment on the representation; and

3 the defendant was not primarily at fault in causing the mistaken payment to be made.

Estoppel by representation is a rule of evidence that prevents the plaintiff from reneging on a representation that the defendant is entitled to keep the money. Accordingly, unlike the *pro tanto* defence of change of position, the defence of estoppel provides a complete defence to a claim in restitution: *Avon County Council v Howlett* (1983) (see extract, p 571).

As the law currently stands, estoppel has not been superseded by the defence of change of position, despite suggestions in other jurisdictions that it should be.[3] Accordingly, estoppel is available as an alternative, and (where its conditions are satisfied) a generally more advantageous defence, to the defence of change of position.[4]

Element 1: A representation by the plaintiff that the money is the defendant's to keep

The defendant must show that the plaintiff made a collateral representation of fact that the defendant is entitled to the money; that is, a representation collateral to the payment of the money. A mere payment of money does not contain an inherent representation that the defendant is entitled to the money.[5] The rationale for this principle is explained in the following decision.

---

2 For examples of cases where this defence was successfully applied, see *Skyring v Greenwood* (1825) (see extract, p 567); *Deutsche Bank (London Agency) v Beriro and Co Ltd* (1895); *Holt v Markham* (1923) (see extract, p 569); *Avon County Council v Howlett* (1983) (see extract, p 571).

3 *RBC Dominion Securities Inc v Dawson* (1994), p 237; *Lipkin Gorman v Karpnale Ltd* (1991), p 579 (see extract, p 595); *Philip Collins Ltd v Davis* (2000), p 826 (see following extract).

4 *Scottish Equitable plc v Derby* (2001), pp 830–01 (see extract, p 580); *National Mutual Life Association of Australasia v Walsh* (1987), pp 596–97; *Australian Breeders Co-operative Society Ltd v Jones* (1997), p 542.

5 *Philip Collins Ltd v Davis* (2000), p 825 (see following extract); *RE Jones Ltd v Waring and Gillow Ltd* (1926), p 692; *Commonwealth of Australia v Webster* (1995).

Philip Collins Ltd v Davis [2000] 3 All ER 808 Chancery Division

The facts are stated at p 602.

Jonathan Parker: ... [825] *Estoppel by representation*

The defendants' case on this issue is that the mere making of each royalty payment represented that the payment was due; that the defendants relied on such representations to their detriment; and accordingly that the claimant is estopped from seeking repayment ...

In my judgment, however, the mere tendering of a payment under a contract does not, without more, amount to a representation that the payment is due, see *Lipkin Gorman (A Firm) v Karpnale Ltd* (1991), p 579. No reasonable person will assume that mistakes may not be made. The tender may well amount to a representation that the tenderer believes the sum tendered to be due, but that is a representation as to the tenderer's current state of mind and not as to the parties' rights under the contract ...

Commentary

One recognised exception to the requirement of a collateral representation arises where the plaintiff has breached a duty to make an accurate payment. As the following decision shows, where the plaintiff had a duty to make only the correct payment, there is a representation inherent in the payment that the defendant is entitled to the money.[6]

Skyring v Greenwood (1825) 4 B & C 282; 107 ER 1064 King's Bench

The paymasters of a military corps paid the members of the corps out of money received from the government. In 1821 the paymasters mistakenly rendered an incorrect account to Major Skyring which showed a higher amount than Major Skyring was entitled to. This error was made despite the fact that the paymasters had previously been advised by the government that persons in the position of Major Skyring were not entitled to that higher amount. Major Skyring's estate commenced proceedings against the paymasters to recover unpaid wages, but the paymasters claimed that they were entitled to deduct from the amount owing the amount which had been mistakenly credited to Major Skyring. The court dealt with this claim by considering whether the paymasters would have been able to bring a claim to recover the excessive amount had payment actually been made to Major Skyring. Major Skyring's estate argued that such a claim would have been successfully defended on the basis of estoppel.

Abbott CJ: ... [1067] The particular fact in this case upon which my judgment proceeds is, that the defendants were informed in 1816 that the Board of Ordnance would not allow these payments to persons in the situation of Major Skyring, but they never communicated to him that fact until 1821, having in the mean time given him credit for these allowances. I think it was their duty to communicate to the deceased the information which they had received from the Board of Ordnance; but they forbore to do so, and they suffered him to suppose during all

---

6   See also *United Overseas Bank v Jiwani* (1976), p 968 (see extract, p 576); Birks, *An Introduction to the Law of Restitution*, rev edn, 1989, p 404; Burrows, *The Law of Restitution*, 1993, p 434.

the intervening time that he was entitled to the increased allowance. It is of great importance to any man, and certainly not less to military men than others, that they should not be led to suppose that their annual income is greater than it really is. Every prudent man accommodates his mode of living to what he supposes to be his income; it therefore works a great prejudice to any man, if after having had credit given him in account for certain sums, and having been allowed to draw on his agent on the faith that those sums belonged to him, he may be called upon to pay them back. Here the defendants have not merely made an error in [290] account, but they have been guilty of a breach of duty, by not communicating to Major Skyring the instruction they received from the Board of Ordnance in 1816; and I think, therefore, that justice requires that they shall not be permitted either to recover back or retain by way of set-off the money which they had once allowed him in account.

Bayley J: This may be a case of hardship upon the defendants, but they have brought it upon themselves. This is an action for money had and received. If the defendants are entitled to set off the sum they claim, the action is not maintainable. From the years 1816–21 the defendants had given credit for certain sums, as if Major Skyring was entitled to them. I think they were guilty of a neglect of duty in not communicating to him the information they had received from the Board of Ordnance in 1816. Suppose that the balance of the account delivered in 1821 had been paid to Major Skyring, and that no subsequent pay had been received for his use by the defendants, and that they had brought an action to recover back the money paid. It would have been a good defence to that action to say that the defendants had voluntarily advanced money to the deceased when he asked no credit, and that they had told him that they had received the money for his use, and that on the faith of their representation he had drawn it out of their hands as his own money, and had been induced to spend it as such; and if they could not recover the money back, neither ought they now to be allowed to retain other moneys belonging to the deceased, upon the ground that they have paid or allowed him in account money which they had not in fact received to his [291] use, but which they suffered him to consider his own for a long period of time. I think they cannot now be permitted to say, that the money which they allowed him in account as money received by them to his use, was not money received to his use

...

Commentary

Despite the exception recognised in this case, the normal requirement is of a collateral factual representation by the plaintiff that the money is lawfully due to the defendant. The collateral representation is usually expressly made, in response to a query from the defendant about the accuracy of the payment.[7] However, as the following decision illustrates, the representation might be implied from the plaintiff's conduct and the surrounding circumstances.

---

7   See, for example, *Avon County Council v Howlett* (1983) (see extract, p 571); *Scottish Equitable plc v Derby* (2001) (see extract, p 580).

Holt v Markham [1923] 1 KB 504 King's Bench

The plaintiffs were the government's agents for paying gratuities to demobilised officers of the Royal Air Force. Upon the defendant's demobilisation from the Force's emergency list in September 1919 the plaintiffs paid to him a gratuity which was in excess of that which the defendant was entitled to as an officer on that list. The gratuity was paid partly in cash and partly in war savings certificates. In early February 1921 the plaintiffs wrote to the defendant demanding the return of the overpayment for a reason unconnected with the defendant being on the emergency list. The defendant quickly responded and satisfied the plaintiffs that their reason for demanding repayment was unfounded; the plaintiffs still attaching no importance to the fact the defendant was on the emergency list. The plaintiffs were later advised by the Air Ministry of the correct gratuity for an officer on that list and in April 1921 wrote to the defendant demanding the repayment of £431. In the meantime the defendant, having heard nothing from the plaintiff since his letter to them and assuming that the matter was concluded, had sold his war savings certificates and invested a substantial sum in a company which subsequently went into liquidation. The defendant refused to refund the overpayment and the plaintiffs commenced proceedings to recover it as money paid under mistake. The court concluded that there was no causative mistake (see extract, p 90) then turned to consider whether, had there been a *prima facie* claim, the defendant could have defended it by raising an estoppel.

Bankes LJ: ... [510] [I]t was also contended on behalf of the plaintiffs that it was inequitable for the defendant to retain the money. It was said that he knew all about his position, and that he received the money knowing that it was [511] largely in excess of what he was entitled to. All I can say is, if he did know it he knew more than [the plaintiffs] knew, or than the Admiralty or the Air Ministry knew. Indeed I am not certain myself that, if I had to apply these orders and fix the defendant's gratuity, I could even now say with certainty what was the exact amount that he was entitled to, having regard to the fact that after his appointment to the Air Force the authorities did not pay him the 25% bonus on his pay and consequently did not in fact treat him as being on the emergency list. I am satisfied that the defendant knew no more what his position was than any of the other persons concerned in the case. He was misled by the conduct of the plaintiffs into the belief that he might retain the money. I need not go into the authorities, but the judgment of Bayley J in *Skyring v Greenwood* (1925), to which we have been referred, is, I think, directly applicable to the present defendant's case, for it appears that for a considerable time he was left under the impression that, although there had been at one time a doubt about his title to the money, that doubt had been removed, and in consequence he parted with his war savings certificates. Having done that it seems to me that he altered his position for the worse, and consequently the plaintiffs are estopped from alleging that the payment was made under a mistake of fact ...

Warrington LJ: ... [512] [A]ssume that the payment was made under a mistake of fact. The question then arises whether the conduct of the plaintiffs was such as to render it inequitable to give effect to the relief which they claim. In my opinion it was. In a letter of 2 February 1921, the plaintiffs demanded the repayment of the difference between the £744 paid to the defendant and the £310 to which he was entitled, basing their claim on the fact that he was a retired officer on retired pay and came within art 497a. On 7 February he replied that that claim was mistaken as he was not a retired officer. From that date until 18 April he heard no more about the matter, and from that fact he was in my opinion entitled to conclude that his reply was regarded as satisfactory, and that he was at liberty to deal with the money as he pleased. The result was that he availed himself of that liberty and spent the whole or a large part of the gratuity which had been paid him, and he is not now in a position to repay it. The plaintiffs are in my opinion estopped from [513] asking that he should do so. On these grounds, first, that the plaintiffs have failed to establish that the money was paid under a mistake of fact, and secondly that, if it was, they are estopped from setting it up ...

Scrutton LJ: ... [514] I think this is a simple case of estoppel. The plaintiffs represented to the defendant that he was entitled to a certain sum of money and paid it, and after a lapse of time sufficient to enable any mistake to be rectified he acted upon that representation and spent the money. That is a case to which the ordinary rule of estoppel applies. In *Skyring v Greenwood* (1825), where the facts were very similar, Bayley J said: 'It would have been a good defence to that action to say that the defendants had voluntarily advanced money to the deceased when he asked no credit, and that they had told him that they had received the money for his use, and that on the faith of their representation he had drawn it out of their hands as his own money, and had been induced to spend it as such.' That view was acted upon by the Court of Appeal in the later case of *Deutsche Bank v* [516] *Beriro* (1895). There also money was paid by the plaintiffs under a mistake of fact, and the person to whom it was paid acted upon that payment and paid it over to another. It was held that the plaintiffs were estopped from recovering it back. In the present case the payment was made in September 1919, and it was not till February 1921, that there was any suggestion of a mistake having been made, and even then the suggestion was based on an entirely wrong ground. That was corrected by the defendant, and the matter was allowed to go on for another three months before the claim was made on the lines now put forward. That appears to me amply sufficient to bring the case within the principle that I have stated ...

Commentary and questions

It is a well established principle that estoppel is unavailable where the claim is for the recovery of money paid without authorisation out of consolidated revenue.[8] Estoppel is denied in this situation as a matter of public policy in order to prevent the undermining of high constitutional principles relating to appropriation of public moneys.[9] Should estoppel have been denied in the case of *Skyring v Greenwood* (1925) and in the principal case on the basis that the moneys had been paid without authority out of consolidated revenue?[10]

---

8   *Commonwealth v Burns* (1971) (see extract, p 486); *Attorney General v Gray* (1977) (see extract, p 489); *The Commonwealth v Thomson* (1962); *Formosa v Department of Social Security* (1988), p 125.

9   Mason and Carter, *Restitution Law in Australia*, 1995, pp 838, 839.

10   *See Attorney General v Gray* (1977), p 413 (see extract, p 489).

Element 2: Good faith detrimental reliance

The defendant must establish that he or she acted to her detriment in good faith in reliance on the representation. The defendant will be able to establish detrimental reliance by pointing to extraordinary expenditure of the money; that is, expenditure of the money on items that the defendant would not ordinarily have expended money on. In the estoppel context, examples of extraordinary expenditure have included making a bad investment as in *Holt v Markham* (1923) (see extract, p 569) and irrevocably paying over the money to a third party as in *RE Jones Ltd v Waring and Gillow Ltd* (1926). A general improvement in the defendant's standard of living will also suffice, as the courts do not require the defendant to identify and prove each specific item of extraordinary expenditure: see *Avon County Council v Howlett* (1983), p 620 (see the following extract).

The English Court of Appeal held in the following case that estoppel arises once the defendant shows that he or she detrimentally relied on the representation, despite the fact that the defendant cannot show detrimental reliance to the *full* extent of the overpayment. Thus, partial reliance, unless insignificant,[11] will be sufficient for estoppel purposes.

Avon County Council v Howlett [1983] 1 WLR 605 English Court of Appeal

The defendant was injured in the course of his employment as a teacher in one of the plaintiffs' schools and received sickness benefits. Due to a computer error the plaintiffs overpaid sickness benefits to the defendant in the amount of £1,007. The defendant and his wife made inquiries of the plaintiffs' officials and were informed that the payments were correct. The plaintiffs sought recovery of the money, but the defendant resisted the claim on the basis of estoppel. The defendant pleaded detrimental reliance to the extent of £546. The trial judge found as a matter of fact that the defendant had spent the full amount of the overpayment and invited the defendant to amend the defence, however the defendant wished to pursue a test case and refused to amend. Accordingly, the Court of Appeal was required to deal with the issue whether or not the defence of estoppel could operate *pro tanto*.

Slade LJ: ... [620] I now turn to the defence of estoppel. The following general propositions of law are to be found set out in Goff and Jones, *The Law of Restitution*, 2nd edn, 1978, pp 554–55 (though I do not quote them *verbatim*). A plaintiff will be estopped from asserting his claim to restitution if the following conditions are satisfied: (a) the plaintiff must generally have made a representation of fact which led the defendant to believe that he was entitled to treat the money as his own; (b) the defendant must have, *bona fide* and without notice of the plaintiff's claim, consequently changed his position; (c) the payment must not have been primarily caused by the fault of the defendant.

---

11   In the sense that it is very small in proportion to the total amount of the overpayment: *ibid*, pp 624–25.

In my opinion these propositions are entirely consistent both with the general principles which govern the doctrine of estoppel and with the authorities which have been cited to this court, illustrating the relevance of estoppel as a defence to claims to restitution. Examples of the more important of such authorities are *Skyring v Greenwood* (1825), *Holt v Markham* (1923) and *Lloyds Bank Ltd v Brooks* (1950).

In the present case it is common ground that the plaintiffs made representations to the defendant which led him to believe that he was entitled to treat the entirety of the overpaid moneys as his own. This was conceded by the plaintiffs at the trial, so that the judge did not find it necessary in his judgment to give any particulars at all of the relevant representations. Certain authorities suggest that a plea of estoppel can afford a good defence [621] to a claim for restitution only if the plaintiff owed a duty to the defendant to speak or act in a particular way.[12] However, this point causes no difficulty for the defendant in the present case since the plaintiffs, as the defendant's employers, in my opinion clearly owed him a duty not to misrepresent the amount of the pay to which he was entitled from time to time, unless the misrepresentations were caused by incorrect information given to them by the defendant. It has not been suggested that the misrepresentations were so caused or that the overpayments were brought about by the defendant's own fault.

The judge found as a fact that the defendant had, *bona fide* and without notice of the plaintiffs' claim, changed his position in reliance on the representations, by losing the claim for £86.11 social security benefit and expending the sum of £460.50 which I have already mentioned. In the circumstances and in accordance with the principles already stated, he was in my opinion clearly right to hold that the plaintiffs' claim was barred by estoppel to the extent of at least £546.61 and there is no challenge to this part of his decision. However, according to the defendant's case as specifically pleaded, the change of position which he has undergone in reliance on the plaintiffs' representations, has only deprived him of the opportunity to return £546.61 of the overpayment; it has not deprived him of the opportunity to return the outstanding balance of £460.39 which, so far as the pleading reveals, *may* be still in his possession.

The judge considered that the defence of estoppel was in effect capable of being applied *pro tanto*, in the sense that a payer who has overpaid a payee, even in circumstances where all of conditions (a), (b) and (c) above are satisfied, will be precluded from claiming restitution only to the extent that it would be inequitable to require the payee to repay the relevant sums or part of the relevant sums in question. The judge clearly regarded the doctrine of estoppel as being a flexible doctrine, as indeed Lord Denning MR so described it in *Amalgamated Investment & Property Co Ltd v Texas Commerce International Bank Ltd* (1982), p 122.

If I may respectfully say so, I feel some sympathy with the judge's point of view. I also initially found unattractive the submission, placed before and rejected by him, that, if the defendant be treated as having spent in reliance on the plaintiffs' representations some £546.61 of the £1,007 received, the plaintiffs could not recover the balance of £460.39, even if it were still sitting untouched in some

---

12 See, eg, *RE Jones Ltd v Waring and Gillow Ltd* (1926), p 693 *per* Lord Sumner; and *Lloyds Bank Ltd v Brooks* (1950), pp 168ff.

deposit account. At first sight such a conclusion would seem to leave the defendant unjustly enriched.

On further reflection, however, I think that references to broad concepts of justice or equity in a context such as the present may be somewhat misleading, as well as uncertain in their application. The conclusion of the judge in the present case really involves the proposition that, if the defendant is successfully to resist a claim for repayment of the entire sum of £1,007, the onus falls on him to prove specifically that the pecuniary amount of the prejudice suffered by him as a result of relying on the relevant representations made by the plaintiffs equals or exceeds that sum. For present purposes, however, one has to postulate a situation in which the defendant was perfectly entitled to conduct his business affairs on the assumption that the relevant representations were true, until he was told otherwise. Meantime, a defendant in the situation of the defendant in the present case may, in reliance on the representation, have either altered [622] his general mode of living or undertaken commitments or incurred expenditure or entered into other transactions which it may be very difficult for him subsequently to recall and identify retrospectively in complete detail; he may even have done so, while leaving some of the particular moneys paid to him by the plaintiff untouched. If the pecuniary amount of his prejudice has to be precisely quantified by a defendant in such circumstances, he may be faced with obvious difficulties of proof. Thus, though extreme hypothetical cases can be envisaged, and indeed were canvassed in argument, in which broad considerations of equity and justice might appear to require the barring of a plaintiff's claim only *pro tanto*, if this were legally possible, I would not expect many such cases to arise in practice. In any event I do not consider the present case to be one of them, even on the basis of the facts as pleaded. I prefer to approach it simply by what I regard as the established legal principles governing the doctrine of estoppel.

Estoppel by representation is a rule of evidence, the consequence of which is simply to preclude the representor from averring facts contrary to his own representation.[13] It follows that a party who, as a result of being able to rely on an estoppel, succeeds on a cause of action on which, without being able to rely on it, he would necessarily have failed may be able to recover more than the actual damage suffered by him as a result of the representation which gave rise to it. Thus if a bank's customer is estopped from asserting that a cheque with which he has been debited is a forgery, because of his failure to inform the bank in due time, so that it could have had recourse to the forger, the debit will stand for the whole amount and not merely that which could have been recovered from the forger: see *Ogilvie v West Australian Mortgage and Agency Corporation Ltd* (1896). In this case Lord Watson said:

> There are some *obiter dicta* favouring the suggestion that, in a case like the present, where the amount of the forged cheques is about £1,500, the estoppel against the customer ought to be restricted to the actual sum which the bank could have recovered from the forger. But these *dicta* seem to refer, not to the law as it was, but as it ought to be and, in any view of them, they are contrary to all authority and practice (p 270).

---

13 See Spencer, Bower and Turner, *Estoppel by Representation*, 3rd edn, 1977, p 112.

The decision of the Court of Appeal in *Greenwood v Martins Bank Ltd* (1932), affirmed by the House of Lords, is to the same effect.

So far as they go, the authorities suggest that, in cases where estoppel by representation is available as a defence to a claim for money had and received, the courts similarly do not treat the operation of the estoppel as being restricted to the precise amount of the detriment which the representee proves he has suffered in reliance on the representation. In *Skyring v Greenwood* (1825), the paymasters of a military corps had given credit in account to an officer for a period from January 1817 to November 1820, for certain increased pay. They had mistakenly supposed that this had been granted by a general order of 1806 to an officer of his situation. But in fact the paymasters had been informed in 1816 that the Board of Ordnance would not allow the increased payments to persons in the officer's situation. A statement of that account was delivered to the officer early in 1821, giving him credit for the increased pay to which they [623] supposed him to be entitled. After the officer's death in 1822, his personal representatives sought to recover the whole of the pay which had been credited to him. The defendants claimed the right to retain the overpaid sums. The Court of King's Bench rejected this claim, apparently without any inquiry as to the amount of the expenditure or financial commitments which the officer had incurred in reliance upon the erroneous credit. The basis of the court's decision is to be found in the following passage from the judgment of Abbot CJ:

> I think it was their duty to communicate to the deceased the information which they had received from the Board of Ordinance; but they forbore to do so, and they suffered him to suppose during all the intervening time that he was entitled to the increased allowances. It is of great importance to any man, and certainly not less to military men than others, that they should not be led to suppose that their annual income is greater than it really is. Every prudent man accommodates his mode of living to what he supposes to be his income; it therefore works a great prejudice to any man, if after having had credit given him in account for certain sums, and having been allowed to draw on his agent on the faith that those sums belonged to him, he may be called upon to pay them back (p 298).

In *Holt v Markham* (1923) the defendant was a demobilised officer of the Royal Air Force. His name was on a list called the emergency list. This meant that, under a certain military regulation, he was entitled to a gratuity at a lower rate than if he was not on that list. The plaintiffs acted as the government's agents for the payment of gratuities to demobilised officers. In ignorance of the fact that the defendant was on the emergency list, but also in forgetfulness of the regulation, and not appreciating the materiality of an officer being on that list, they paid the defendant his gratuity at the higher rate to which he would have been entitled if he had not been on it. Subsequently they sought to recover this sum. But by then the defendant, thinking this matter was concluded, had sold his holding of war savings certificates and invested a substantial sum in a company which subsequently went into liquidation. The Court of Appeal held that the plaintiffs' action failed on two grounds, first that the plaintiffs' mistake was one of law rather than of fact and second that, as their conduct had led the defendant to believe that he might treat the money as his own and he had altered his position in that belief, the plaintiffs were estopped from alleging that the money had been paid under a mistake. Scrutton LJ put the matter very simply:

> I think this is a simple case of estoppel. The plaintiffs represented to the defendant that he was entitled to a certain sum of money and paid it, and after a lapse of time sufficient to enable any mistake to be rectified he acted upon that representation and spent the money (p 514).

However, the facts as set out in the report of the case do not indicate that the defendant had necessarily spent the whole of his gratuity and Bankes and Warrington LJJ were careful not to suggest that they did. They clearly regarded it as immaterial whether or not he had. Thus Bankes LJ said:

> ... it appears that for a considerable time he was left under the impression that, although there had been at one time a doubt about his title to the money, that doubt had been removed, and in consequence he [624] parted with his war savings certificates. Having done that it seems to me that he altered his position for the worse, and consequently the plaintiffs are estopped from alleging that the payment was made under a mistake of fact (p 511).

Warrington LJ referred to the defendant as having spent 'the whole or a large part of the gratuity which had been paid him' (p 512).

If it were in every case possible for the doctrine of estoppel by representation to operate merely *pro tanto* in cases where it is being involved as a defence to an action for money had and received, I think that the Court of King's Bench in *Skyring v Greenwood* and the Court of Appeal in *Holt v Markham*, and indeed Lynskey J in *Lloyds Bank Ltd v Brooks* (1950), would have been bound to conduct a much more exact process of quantification of the alteration of the financial position of the recipients which had occurred by reason of the representations. The courts, however, in those cases, manifestly regarded any such process as irrelevant and inappropriate. All the relevant conditions for the operation of an estoppel being satisfied in those cases, the plea operated as a rule of evidence which precluded the payers from recovering any part of the money mistakenly overpaid or from retaining any part of the moneys mistakenly over credited.

I think that no authority has been cited, other than the judgment of the [trial] judge, which directly supports the proposition that estoppel is capable of operating merely *pro tanto* in a case such as the present, where it is otherwise capable of being invoked as a complete defence to an action for money had and received. For the reasons which I have given, I conclude that such a proposition is contrary to principle and authority. The authorities of Goff and Jones, *The Law of Restitution*, 2nd edn, 1978, do not assert any such proposition, but they do say:

> The effect of such an estoppel will generally be to defeat the claim altogether. But where the defendant's change of position has deprived him of the opportunity to return only part of the money he has received, to dismiss the plaintiff's claim in its entirety would enable the defendant to make a profit out of the transaction. This should not be allowed. In such circumstances the court may only give effect to the estoppel, subject to the defendant's undertaking to repay to the plaintiff any part of the sum received which he ought not to be entitled to keep (p 556).

The suggestion of an undertaking stems from the speech of Viscount Cave LC in *RE Jones Ltd v Waring & Gillow Ltd* (1926). In that case the majority of the House of

Lords held that the plaintiffs were entitled to recover certain moneys on the principle of *Kelly v Solari* (1841). Viscount Cave LC, who dissented and with whom Lord Atkinson agreed, considered that the plaintiffs were estopped from recovering the money. On the particular facts, however, the operation of an estoppel in this manner would have left the defendants with a profit. The defendants disclaimed any desire to make such a profit and offered an undertaking (in effect) to return it to the plaintiffs. Viscount Cave LC expressed the view that such undertaking should be recited in the order to be made on the appeal, but said that, subject to the undertaking, he would dismiss it (p 685).

I recognise that in some circumstances the doctrine of estoppel could be said to give rise to injustice if it operated so as to defeat in its entirety an action which would otherwise lie for money had and received. This might [625] be the case for example where the sums sought to be recovered were so large as to bear no relation to any detriment which the recipient could possibly have suffered. I would for my part prefer to leave open the question whether in such a case the court would have jurisdiction, in the exercise of its discretion, to exact an undertaking of the nature referred to by Viscount Cave LC, if it was not voluntarily proffered by the defendant.

On the particular facts of the present case as pleaded and proved, however, I could in any event see no sufficient ground for exacting any such undertaking from the defendant in the exercise of the court's discretion, even assuming that such discretion existed. The conditions for the operation of an estoppel have in my opinion all been satisfied. For the reasons which I have given, both on principle and in accordance with authority, I conclude that such estoppel bars the whole of the plaintiffs' claim ...

[Eveleigh LJ reached a similar conclusion. Cumming-Bruce LJ refused to decide the issue as it was not raised by the real facts.]

Commentary and questions

Did it matter that (as the case was conducted) the defendant had not spent the full amount of the overpayment? Does estoppel act as a complete, or a *pro tanto*, defence? What was the exceptional situation recognised where partial detrimental reliance would not be sufficient to found an estoppel? In what way had the defendant in this case detrimentally relied on the overpayment?

This decision has been followed in Australia on a number of occasions.[14]

The defendant in the principal case *bona fide* believed that he was entitled to the money. However, the good faith of the defendant was in issue in the following case, as was the requirement of *detrimental* reliance.

United Overseas Bank v Jiwani [1976] 1 WLR 964 Queen's Bench

The defendant, Mr Jiwani, operated a bank account with the plaintiff bank which at the relevant time had a credit balance of $10,000. Mr Jiwani drew a cheque upon the account for $20,000 which he intended to use, in conjunction with a bank loan,

---

14 See, for example, *National Mutual Life Association of Australasia v Walsh* (1987), p 596; *Commonwealth of Australia v Webster* (1995).

to purchase a hotel. A week later the sum of $11,000 was transferred to Mr Jiwani's account, but the bank mistakenly credited the amount twice. Mr Jiwani was advised of the (incorrect) balance of the account, and he also checked the balance by telephone and a visit in person to the bank. He then arranged for the bank to transfer another $11,000 to the hotel vendor, in addition to the $20,000 which had been paid on the cheque. When the bank discovered its mistake it commenced proceedings to recover the $11,000 however Mr Jiwani argued that they were estopped from pursuing the claim. MacKenna J found as a matter of fact that had the $11,000 not been available Mr Jiwani would have found the extra money needed for the purchase of the hotel, for example by borrowing a larger amount or by getting an extension of time to complete.

MacKenna J: ... [968] The question remains whether the defendant is liable to repay the plaintiffs the sum with which they credited him in error. In my opinion, which I base on the statement of the law in Goff and Jones, *The Law of Restitution,* 1966, pp 491, 492, he is liable unless he can show that the plaintiffs are estopped from claiming restitution, and there are three conditions to be satisfied by him if he is to make good this estoppel. First, he must show that either the plaintiffs were under a duty to give him accurate information about the state of this account and that in breach of this duty they gave him inaccurate information, or that in some other way there was a misrepresentation made to him about the state of the account for which the plaintiffs are responsible. Secondly, he must show that this inaccurate information misled him about the state of the account and caused him to believe that the plaintiffs were his debtors for a larger sum than was the case and to make the transfer to [the hotel vendor] in that mistaken belief. Thirdly, he must show that because of his mistaken belief he changed his position in a way which would make it inequitable to require him to repay the money. I have no doubt that the first of these requirements is satisfied. I shall assume for the moment that he has satisfied the second, returning to that matter a little later in this judgment. He has, I think, completely failed to establish the essential third condition.

[Counsel for the defendant] contended that if a bank's customer has spent the money with which he has been mistakenly credited, he cannot, in any case whatever, be required to repay it. If he has to show a detriment making it inequitable to require him to repay, he shows that detriment, it is argued, by proving that he has spent the money, irrespective of the purpose for which it was spent or of the effects of the expenditure, and that he will have to make it good, if at all, out of other moneys. To test [counsel for the defendant's] proposition I put the case to him of a customer who uses the overpayment to buy a gilt-edged security which can be immediately resold and which rises in value between the date of the purchase and the date when the mistake is discovered and he is called on to repay. [Counsel for the defendant] did not shrink from accepting the logical consequence of his argument. He said that in such a case the customer would be under no obligation to repay; he could treat his acquisition of the security as a windfall and let the bank whistle for its money. I do not believe that is the law.

Undoubtedly there are cases in which the customer who has spent the money in ignorance that he was being overpaid will not be required to repay. *Holt v Markham* (1923) was such a case. *Skyring v Greenwood* (1825), which *Holt's* case followed, was another. A third was *Lloyds Bank Ltd v Brooks* (1950). There was reason for believing in each of these cases that the defendant would have acted differently if he had not mistakenly believed that he was richer than he was, that because of his mistake, he had, to use Goff and Jones's words, altered his mode of living. There was the further fact in *Holt v Markham* (1923) that the defendant had invested part of the overpayment in a company which had since gone into liquidation.

There is in the present case, as I have already said, no reason for thinking that Mr Jiwani would have acted differently in the matter of the purchase or in any other way if the extra dollars had not been mistakenly made available to him. He would still have completed the purchase of the hotel by a further borrowing from Lloyds Bank or in some other way. The completion of the purchase, wherever he got the money to do it with, was in itself a benefit and is a continuing benefit, unlike the investment in *Holt's* case.

Other cases cited by [counsel for the defendant] are distinguishable in the same way. There was the case of the customer who had paid the money over to a third party which he was not bound to do if the money were not truly his own and who was unable to recover it from the third party on the discovery of the mistake, see *Deutsche Bank (London Agency) v Beriro and Co Ltd* (1895). That the customer in that case was not liable to repay the bank does not help [counsel for the defendant].

What I have said already is enough to show that there must be judgment in the plaintiffs' favour, but I have something to add on the second of the three requirements, namely that the bank's misstatement caused Mr Jiwani to believe that there had in fact been two transfers of $11,000 to the credit of his account.

[MacKenna J reviewed the evidence adduced on behalf of Mr Jiwani and concluded that he knew, or strongly suspected, the bank had made a mistake prior to expending the money. He concluded at p 970:]

For the reasons, first that Mr Jiwani has not satisfied me that he honestly believed that the two transfers had been made, and second that in any event, he has not proved that if he was misled by the plaintiffs he changed his position in such a way as would make it inequitable to require him to repay the money, I hold that this action succeeds ...

Commentary

The court doubted that the defendant was misled by the bank's representation into honestly believing that he was entitled to the money. It also refused the defence on the basis that a defendant does not act to his or her detriment by expending the money on the acquisition of a valuable asset that has maintained or risen in value; in that circumstance the enrichment has not been reduced, but merely changed form. There is also authority in the change of position context for the proposition that the defendant must return the second hand value of the asset, so that a change of position would be limited to any amount by which the goods have depreciated see *Lipkin Gorman v Karpnale Ltd* (1991), p 560 (see extract, p 595). However, there is no Australian authority directly addressing this point.

Element 3: The defendant is not primarily at fault

As the following case demonstrates, the plaintiff will not be estopped from recovering the amount of a mistaken overpayment where the overpayment came about because the defendant failed to comply with an obligation to advise the plaintiff about a material change of circumstances.

Larner v London County Council [1949] 2 KB 683 English Court of Appeal

The defendant local authority resolved to pay all their male employees who went to the second world war the difference between their war service pay and their civil pay until further order. The defendant was under no statutory obligation to make these payments. The resolution provided that each employee was responsible for advising the defendant immediately of any change arising in the amount of his war service pay so the defendant could make consequential adjustments in subsequent payments. The plaintiff was an employee of the defendant who enlisted in the Royal Air Force. He did not keep the defendant accurately informed of the changes in his service pay and the defendant consequently overpaid the plaintiff. Upon the plaintiff's return to the defendant's employment, the defendant commenced deducting money from his weekly wages in order to recoup the overpayments. The plaintiff commenced proceedings claiming the defendant was estopped from making the deductions and the defendant counterclaimed for recovery of the overpayments as money paid under a mistake of fact.

Denning LJ: [Denning LJ held that the moneys were *prima facie* recoverable as being paid under mistake and then turned to consider the question of the estoppel defence at p 688:]

It is next said, however, that [London County Council] should not be allowed to recover the money because the plaintiff changed his position for the worse before the council asked for the money. He spent the money on living expenses – or his wife spent it for him – and he spent it in a way which he would not otherwise have done. This defence of estoppel, as it is called – or more accurately, change of circumstances – must, however, not be extended beyond its proper bounds. Speaking generally, the fact that the recipient has spent the money beyond recall is no defence unless there was some fault, as, for instance, breach of duty on the part of the paymaster and none on [689] the part of the recipient. In both *Skyring v Greenwood and Cox* (1825) and *Holt v Markham* (1923) there was a breach of duty by the paymaster and none by the recipient, see *RE Jones Ltd v Waring and Gillow Ltd* (1926), p 693 *per* Lord Sumner. But if the recipient was himself at fault and the paymaster was not – as, for instance, if the mistake was due to an innocent misrepresentation or a breach of duty by the recipient – he clearly cannot escape liability by saying that he has spent the money. That is the position here. On the judge's findings, the London County Council was not at fault at all, but Mr Larner was. He did not keep them accurately informed of the various changes in his service pay. It does not lie in his mouth to say that, if he had done so, it would have made no difference. It might well have put them on inquiry and the mistake might not have been made at all. It would be strange, indeed, if those who neglected their duty were to be allowed to keep their gain.

The future of estoppel by representation

It has been said on a number of occasions that the 'all or nothing' nature of estoppel leads to unjust results, and that estoppel is no longer 'an appropriate concept'[15] to deal with claims of detrimental reliance. It is argued that the defence should be abolished in favour of the *pro tanto* change of position defence. Thus, in *Philip Collins Ltd v Davis* (2000), p 826 Jonathan Parker J said that the 'defence of estoppel by representation is no longer apt in restitutionary claims where the most flexible defence of change of position is in principle available'. And in *RBC Dominion Securities Inc v Dawson* (1994) the court refused to apply the estoppel defence on the basis that it can cause inequity to the payer. The defence of change of position was preferred as it 'most fairly balances the equities' (at p 237) of both parties. These sentiments have also been expressed by many commentators.[16] The English Court of Appeal discusses the precarious future of estoppel in the following cases, *Scottish Equitable plc v Derby* (2001) (see the following extract) and *National Westminster Bank plc v Somer International (UK) Ltd* (2002) (see extract, p 583).

Scottish Equitable plc v Derby [2001] 3 All ER 818 English Court of Appeal

The facts are stated at p 606.

Robert Walker LJ: ... [828] I have already quoted Lord Goff's observation in the *Lipkin Gorman* case (1991), p 579 that estoppel is not an appropriate [829] concept to deal with the problem, partly because of its 'all or nothing' operation. The same view has been widely expressed, both by academic writers and in the courts. The Newfoundland Court of Appeal (in the *RBC Dominion Securities* case (1994)) has flatly rejected it. Jonathan Parker J (in *Philip Collins v Davis* (2000), pp 825–26) has described it as no longer apt. In doing so he referred to the judgment now under appeal, in which the judge avoided a general statement of principle but (on the facts of this case) distinguished the *Avon CC* case (1983) and said at p 807:

> In my judgment, the justice of the situation is met by the extent to which the defence of change of position has succeeded and it would be wholly unjust and inappropriate in those circumstances to allow estoppel to operate so as to provide a complete defence to the whole of the overpayment.

In considering this part of the case the judge [at first instance] proceeded on the footing that Scottish Equitable had made to Mr Derby a representation that he really was entitled to the payment made to him in June 1995. It is not entirely clear whether the judge made a positive finding to that effect, or simply set out counsel's submission and assumed for the purposes of argument that it was correct; but on any view there was ample evidential material to justify such a finding.

---

15 *Lipkin Gorman v Karpnale Ltd* (1991), p 579 (see extract, p 595).
16 Goff and Jones, *The Law of Restitution*, 5th edn, 1998, p 829; Mason and Carter, *Restitution Law in Australia*, 1995, pp 844–45; Burrows, *The Law of Restitution*, 1993, pp 438–39.

The decision of this court in the *Avon CC* case was discussed at length both below and in this court and it calls for detailed mention ... [830] Slade LJ [in *Avon County Council v Howlett* (1983), pp 624–25] said:

> I recognise that in some circumstances the doctrine of estoppel could be said to give rise to injustice if it operated so as to defeat in its entirety an action which would otherwise lie for money had and received. This might be the case for example where the sums sought to be recovered were so large as to bear no relation to any detriment which the recipient could possibly have suffered.

Eveleigh LJ had made similar observations (1983), p 611. ... Harrison J [at first instance] treated the present case as 'just the sort of situation that the Court of Appeal must have had in mind in *Avon CC v Howlett* when expressing reservations about the ambit of that decision'.

I would be content to follow the judge in refraining from attempting any general statement of principle and treating this case as comfortably within the exception recognised by all three members of this court in *Avon CC v Howlett*. We cannot overrule that case but we can note that it was not seen, even by the court which decided it, as a wholly satisfactory authority, because of its fictional element.

I should record one further novel and ingenious argument addressed to us by [counsel for the insurance company]. That is that, since the *Lipkin Gorman* case, the defence of change of position pre-empts and disables the defence of estoppel by negativing detriment. Detriment must, it was correctly submitted, be judged at the time when the representor seeks to go back on his representation, since:

> ... the real detriment or harm from which the law seeks to give protection is that which would flow from the change of position if the assumption were deserted that led to it. So long as the assumption is adhered to, the party who altered his situation upon the faith of it cannot complain. His complaint is that when afterwards the other party makes a different state of affairs the basis of an assertion of right against him then, if it is allowed, his own original change of position will operate as a detriment.[17]

[831] The argument can be simply explained by an illustration in the form of a dialogue. A pays £1,000 to B, representing to him 'I have carefully checked all the figures and this is all yours'. B spends £250 on a party and puts £750 in the bank. A discovers that he has made a mistake and owed B nothing. He learns that B has spent £250 and he asks B to repay £750. B: 'You are estopped by your representation on which I have acted to my detriment.' A: 'You have not acted to your detriment. You have had a good party, and at my expense, because I cannot recover the £250 back from you.' The facts that B has spent £250 in an enjoyable way, and that A readily limits his claim to £750, put the argument in its most attractive form. But it seems to have some validity even if B had lost £250 on a bad investment, and A began by suing him for £1,000.

I find this argument not only ingenious but also convincing. If I prefer to base my conclusion primarily on the grounds relied on by the judge it is partly because the argument is novel and appears not to have been considered by any of the

---

17   See Dixon J in *Grundt v Great Boulder Pty Gold Mine*s (1938), pp 674–75, quoted in Spencer-Bower and Turner, *The Law Relating to Estoppel by Representation*, 3rd edn, 1977, pp 110–11.

distinguished commentators interested in this area of the law. But at present I do not see how the argument could be refuted.

Will estoppel by representation wither away as a defence to a claim for restitution of money paid under a mistake of fact? It can be predicted with some confidence that with the emergence of the defence of change of position, the court will no longer feel constrained to find that a representation has been made, in a borderline case, in order to avoid an unjust result. It can also be predicted, rather less confidently, that development of the law on a case by case basis will have the effect of enlarging rather than narrowing the exception recognised by this court in the *Avon CC* case. That process might be hastened (or simply overtaken) if the House of Lords were to move away from the evidential origin of estoppel by representation towards a more unified doctrine of estoppel, since proprietary estoppel is a highly flexible doctrine which, so far from operating as 'all or nothing', aims at 'the minimum equity to do justice': *Crabb v Avon District Council* (1976), p 198. Paul Key[18] has drawn attention to two decisions of the High Court of Australia[19] which he describes as a fundamental attack on the traditional perception of estoppel as a complete defence.

The remarks in the last four paragraphs are no more than tentative observations on points which were not fully argued, as not being necessary for the determination of the appeal. For the reasons given earlier in this judgment – which are essentially the reasons given by the judge in his admirable judgment – I would dismiss this appeal.

Commentary and questions

The defendant could establish detrimental reliance in the amount of approximately £9,600 of an overpayment totalling approximately £172,500. The court held that the detriment suffered was so small in proportion to the overpayment that the case fell within the exceptional situation recognised in *Avon County Council v Howlett* (1983), see in particular pp 624–25 (see extract, p 571) as one where an estoppel would not be recognised.

Robert Walker LJ agreed with an argument by counsel that 'the defence of change of position pre-empts and disables the defence of estoppel by negativing detriment'. What was the basis of this argument? Do you agree with it? What did Robert Walker LJ perceive to be the future of estoppel as a defence to a claim in restitution?

In the following case, *National Westminster Bank plc v Somer International (UK) Ltd*, the English Court of Appeal expressed the view that estoppel could and should be recognised as a defence operating *pro tanto*, however felt that it was not in a position to overrule *Avon County Council v Howlett* (1983). However, relying on certain statements in *Avon*, the Court held that estoppel should not act as a complete defence where it would be unconscionable to allow the defendant to retain the full enrichment.

---

18 Key, 'Excising estoppel by representation as a defence to restitution' [1995] CLJ 525, p 533.
19 *Waltons Stores (Interstate) v Maher* (1988); *Commonwealth of Australia v Verwayen* (1990).

National Westminster Bank plc v Somer International (UK) Ltd [2002] 1 All ER 198
English Court of Appeal

The Bank by mistake transferred a sum of US$76,708.57 into Somer's account. On the same day, the Bank advised Somer that the monies it had been waiting for had been paid into its account. Somer had been waiting for one of its customers, Mentor, to make a payment on its trading account, and Somer mistakenly believed that the money in the account had come from Mentor. On that basis, Somer shipped goods to a value of £13,180.57 to Mentor. The Bank subsequently discovered its mistake and demanded the repayment of the US$76,708.57. By this time, Mentor had ceased business and Somer was not able to recover the cost of the goods from it. Somer relied on the defence of estoppel on the basis that in shipping the goods to Mentor it had acted to its detriment on the Bank's representation.

Potter LJ: ... [211] It is unattractive that, in a case of monies paid over under a mistake of fact and sought to be recovered on the basis of unjust enrichment, the extent of the recovery should depend on whether or not, at the time of the transfer of the monies, the transferor represented by words or conduct that the transferee was entitled to such payment. When the mistake occurs, particularly in the context of a banker/customer relationship, whether or not an actual representation as to entitlement was made or can be spelt out is largely fortuitous and *ex hypothesi* the result of accident rather than deliberate conduct. It also seems clear that, [212] where there has been such a representation, the only substantial hurdle standing in the way of recovery, subject to an appropriate equitable adjustment in relation to the actual 'detriment' suffered, is the view that the historical origin and technical status of estoppel by representation as a rule of evidence dictates an 'all or nothing' solution the effect of which is that, once the representation has been acted on to the detriment of the transferee the contrary may not be asserted. This differs from the position in the case of so called 'equitable' or 'promissory' estoppel in respect of which a specific promise to waive or refrain from enforcing rights may be withdrawn on reasonable notice and, in 'proprietary' estoppel, where when giving effect to the interest or right in property which the party raising the estoppel asserts, the court assumes a wide discretion as to the terms on which such relief is granted. In this respect estoppel by representation also differs in nature from the defence of 'change of position' which is only permitted to prevail to the extent that it would be inequitable to require the transferee to return the money.

There is no doubt that the preponderance of legal authority and judicial *dicta* at the highest level favours the view that estoppel by representation is a rule of evidence rather than of substantive law: see *Low v Bouverie* (1891) *per* Bowen LJ: 'Estoppel is only a rule of evidence: you cannot found an action upon estoppel ... [It] ... is only important as being one step in the progress towards relief on the hypothesis that the defendant is estopped from denying the truth of something which he has said.' And see to similar effect *Nippon Menkwa Kabushiki Kaisha v Dawson's Bank Ltd* (1935) *per* Lord Russell of Killowen at p 150; see also *London Joint Stock Bank Ltd v MacMillan per* Viscount Haldane (1918): '... it is hardly a rule of what is called substantive law in the sense of declaring an immediate right or claim. It is rather a rule of evidence, capable not the less on that account of affecting gravely substantive rights.' Finally *per* Lord Wright in *Evans v Bartram* (1937), p 484: '...

estoppel is a rule of evidence that prevents the person estopped from denying the existence of a fact ...'

None the less, because of the decisive impact which estoppel by representation may have upon the outcome of any individual case, whether as a step on the way to establishing a cause of action, or as defeating a *prima facie* valid claim based on facts which (absent the representation) would entitle the claimant to recover, such estoppel undoubtedly gives rise to substantive legal consequences. As Lord Wright later observed in *Canada and Dominion Sugar Co Ltd v Canadian National (West Indies) Steamships Ltd* (1947), p 56:

> [213] Estoppel is a complex legal notion, involving a combination of several essential elements, the statement to be acted on, action on the face of it, resulting detriment to the actor. Estoppel is often described as a rule of evidence as, indeed, it may be so described. But the whole concept is more correctly viewed as a substantive rule of law.

It seems that the only judicial statement in unqualified form which classifies estoppel by representation as a rule of substantive law rather than a rule of evidence is the observation of Lord Denning MR in *Moorgate Mercantile Co Limited v Twitchings* (1976), p 241H:

> Estoppel is not a rule of evidence. It is not a cause of action. It is a principle of justice and of equity. It comes to this: when a man by his words or conduct, has led another to believe in a particular state of affairs, he will not be allowed to go back on it when it would be unjust or inequitable for him to do so.

In the light of the state of the authorities and the clear statement in *Avon CC v Howlett* on a matter integral to the court's decision, it does not seem to me that it is open to this court at least to depart from the traditional classification of estoppel by representation as a rule of evidence.

I would only add in this connection that there are various *dicta* in terms which support the view that a single purpose underlies all forms of estoppel on the basis that all aspects of the rules developed are examples of general principle applied so as to prevent A from refusing to recognise, or seeking unjustly to deny or avoid, an assumption or belief which he has induced, permitted or encouraged in B and on the basis of which B has acted or regulated his affairs: see for instance the *Moorgate Mercantile* case (1976), pp 241H–42G; see also the observations of Scarman LJ in *Crabb v Arun DC* (1976) in relation to the distinction between promissory and proprietary estoppel. However, various particular difficulties in the manner in which, and the limitations subject to which, the various types of estoppel have been developed, have so far prevented a rationalisation of this kind. As stated by Millett LJ in *First National Bank plc v Thompson*:

> [An attempt] to demonstrate that all estoppels other than estoppel by record are now subsumed in the single and all-embracing estoppel by representation and that they are all governed by the same requirements has never won general acceptance. Historically unsound, it has been repudiated by academic writers and is unsupported by authority.

Despite some advances in this direction made in Commonwealth jurisdictions, it seems to me that the position remains unchanged in this country to date. Thus, faced with an invitation to formulate a single general principle to cover two types of estoppel with which he was called upon to deal in *Republic of India v India Steamship Co Ltd* (1998), Lord Steyn observed:

> The question was debated whether estoppel by convention and estoppel by acquiescence are but aspects of one overarching principle. I do not underestimate the importance in the continuing development of the law of the search for simplicity. I, also, accept that at a high level of abstraction such an overarching principle could be formulated. But ... to restate the law in terms of an overarching principle might tend to blur the necessarily separate requirements, and distinct terrain of application, of the two kinds of estoppel.

That said, and accepting estoppel by representation to be a rule of evidence, which ordinarily requires that a more than *de minimis* degree of detriment is definitive of the transferee's right to retain the entirety of a mistaken payment, it is plain that the court in the *Avon CC* case, and subsequently in the *Scottish Equitable* case, considered that there yet remained scope for the operation of equity to alleviate the position on grounds of unfairness or unconscionability, although [214] the latter case it failed to elucidate that conclusion by reference to authority other than the *Avon CC* case which in turn quoted no authority to that effect. It seems to me that authority in the form of a clear statement as to the underlying principles being those of equity is nonetheless available, whatever the appropriate juridical classification of estoppel by representation ...

In *Jorden v Money* (1854) estoppel by representation was described by Lord Cranworth LC as a 'principle well known in the law, founded upon good faith and equity, a principle equally of law and of equity'.

Later he stated:

> The whole doctrine was very much considered at law, for it is a doctrine not confined to cases in equity, but one that prevails at law also; and there are, in fact, more cases upon the subject at law than in equity.

Thus, whether or not the *dicta* of Lord Denning MR in the *Moorgate Mercantile* case (see above) be correct in terms of classification, it is clear that the doctrine of estoppel by representation stems from and is governed by considerations of justice and equity. That being so, it is difficult to see why equity should, as between the parties, be impotent in an appropriate case or category of case to require a person relying upon the defence of estoppel by representation to rely upon it only to the extent of any detriment suffered.

In the *Avon CC* case the court cited three cases which suggested that, where estoppel by representation is raised as a defence to a claim for money had and received, the courts do not treat the operation of estoppel as being restricted to the precise amount of the detriment which the representee proves he has suffered in reliance on the representation: *Skyring v Greenwood* (1825); *Holt v Markham* (1923) and *Lloyds Bank Ltd v Brooks*[20] ...

[215] [T]he point is made that, albeit in *Skyring v Greenwood* and *Holt v Markham* there was no exact enquiry into the degree to which each defendant had altered his financial position, there was equally no judicial statement that estoppel by representation could not operate *pro tanto* in an appropriate case. In *Skyring v Greenwood*, indeed, it is not clear that there was evidence of any detrimental

---

20   6 Legal Decisions Affecting Bankers for the Arbitrators Award of 14 September 2000.

reliance, the court simply assuming that it had taken place. In *Holt v Markham* (1923), while it is clear from the judgment of Warrington LJ that not all the money had been spent, there is no indication whether the balance which remained was substantial and it is clear that, in addition to mere spending, the defendant had parted with his war savings certificates, p 511. It seems to me that those cases do no more than establish that the court will generally think it appropriate to treat the matter broadly and will not require the defendant to demonstrate in detail the precise degree or value of the detriment which he has suffered in circumstances where, as Slade LJ pointed out in *Avon County Council v Howlett* (1983), p 622 he may find it difficult subsequently to recall and identify retrospectively the nature and extent of commitments undertaken or expenditure incurred as a result of an alteration in his general mode of living. However, it is open to the court, acting on equitable principles, to take the view that some restitution is necessary, albeit the burden upon the defendant of proving the precise extent of his detriment should be a light one. In these circumstances, the court may well have broad regard to, without being bound to follow, the developing lines of the courts' approach in 'change of position' cases. However, the two defences will remain distinct, unless or until the House of Lords rules otherwise.

There may indeed be good reasons why this should be so and why the issue is not simply one of jurisprudential 'tidiness'. First, in considering the equities between the parties, there are plainly arguments for holding that the fact that a representation was made (albeit mistakenly) may in particular circumstances affect the court's view as to whether and how far, detriment having been established, it should order a restitutionary payment. Second, as pointed out by Fung and Ho in their article 'Change of position and estoppel',[21] the defence of 'change of position' only protects actual reduction of the transferee's assets following receipt. A transferee who, in reliance upon a receipt, forgoes a realistic and quantifiable opportunity to increase his assets is not apparently protected. It has also been held in *South Tyneside Metropolitan BC v Svenska International plc* (1995) following Hobhouse J in *Kleinwort Benson Limited v South Tyneside Metropolitan BC* (1994) that, in order to be successful, a change of position defence must be based on a change after the receipt of the mistaken payment, the facts of the *Lipkin Gorman* case having been exceptional. The *South Tyneside* decision has been the subject of some criticism.[22] However, assuming its correctness (and we have heard no submissions in that regard), it marks a further difference between the defence of 'change of position' and of estoppel in any case where a representation as to the entitlement of the payee has been communicated to him and relied on in anticipation of actual receipt.

Thus, the question to be decided on this appeal is whether, in the light the judge's findings that Somer had suffered detriment and/or changed its position only to the extent of £13,180.57, it should be obliged to repay the balance of the sum received from NatWest on the basis of the exception recognised in the *Avon CC* case. This was a case where the mistake of the bank would have been detected [216] early had Somer kept close account of its dealings with Mentor. Although the judge found that Mr Richardson [managing director of Somers] had continued to rely upon the information first communicated to him that the payment from

21   (2001) 117 LQR 14, p 17.
22   See Goff and Jones, *The Law of Restitution*, 5th edn, 1998, pp 822–24.

Mentor had now been received, NatWest shortly afterwards forwarded a credit advice which made the position clear at a time when Somer had forwarded goods worth only £5,221.99. The judge rejected the case for Somer that it had incurred any detriment other than despatch of goods worth £13,180.57 in reliance upon the representation, being satisfied that Somer's chance of pursuing Mentor successfully for payment was nil. In those circumstances, it seems to me that the judge was fully entitled to hold that the payment sought was of such a size that it bore no relation to the detriment which Somer could possibly have suffered and that it would be unconscionable for Somer to retain the balance over and above the value of the goods shipped.

...

Clarke LJ: I agree that this appeal should be dismissed for the reasons given by Peter Gibson and Potter LJJ, whose judgments I have seen in draft.

The decision in *Scottish Equitable plc v Derby*, and the argument in this case have again demonstrated some of the problems which surround the doctrine of estoppel by representation. In particular there are two problems which it seems to me should if possible be considered by the House of Lords in an appropriate case. The first is the extent, if at all, to which estoppel by representation can operate *pro tanto* and the second is the relationship between such an estoppel and the defence of change of position. I agree that it is not open to this court either to hold that there is no room for estoppel where the defence of change of position is available or to depart from *Avon CC v Howlett* (1983).

I do not wish to say anything about the defence of change of position, but only to consider briefly the principles which seem to me to apply to the application of the doctrine of estoppel by representation as matters stand at present and absent any definitive consideration by the House of Lords. I do so in part because this is an estoppel case on the facts and because it seems to me that, even if the House of Lords were to hold that there is no longer any room for the operation of estoppel where a defence of change of position is available, there are likely to remain cases where a defendant who has acted on a promise that he is to receive money will properly wish to plead an estoppel.

In order to consider the law as it stands at present, it seems to me that it is necessary to identify the propositions of law for which the *Avon CC* case is authority. To my mind it is authority for two propositions and there is a tension between them. The first is that estoppel by representation is a rule of evidence, the consequence of which is to preclude the representor from averring facts contrary to his own representation ...

[217] In the interesting article by Fung and Ho on 'Change of position and estoppel', *National Westminster Bank plc v Somer International (UK) Ltd* (2001) which is referred to by Potter LJ the authors criticise that approach and say (2001), p 19 that it is high time that estoppel was regarded as a substantive (as opposed to an evidential) defence and that it can operate *pro tanto* . There seems to me to be much to be said for that point of view, but I do not think that it is open to this court to develop the law in that way in the light of the decisions in the *Avon CC* case and the *Scottish Equitable* case. However, as I see it, much the same result has been achieved by an application of the second proposition to be derived from the *Avon CC* case.

All three members of the court in the *Avon CC* case recognised that the application of the first proposition might lead to injustice. So they concluded that there was or might be an exception to it, although they did not all express the exception in the same terms. Potter LJ has quoted the relevant passages from the judgments. Slade LJ gave as an example (1983), p 265A a case where the sums sought to be recovered were so large as to bear no relation to any detriment which the recipient could possibly have suffered. Cumming-Bruce LJ, who was particularly concerned by the hypothetical nature of the exercise upon which (as Peter Gibson LJ explains) the court was engaged, said (1983), p 608H that he did not consider the decision as authority for the proposition that where, on the facts, it would be clearly inequitable to allow a party to make a profit by pleading estoppel, the court will necessarily be powerless to prevent it.

Eveleigh LJ to my mind most clearly pointed the way to the future. He said, at (1983) pp 611H–12A:

> However, I am far from saying that whenever the recipient of money paid under a mistake of fact has been led to think that it is his, then he will be entitled to retain the whole by demonstrating that he has spent part of it. The payment may involve no representation, as where a debtor presents an account to a creditor. Then while there might have been a representation there may be circumstances which would render it unconscionable for the defendant to retain a balance in his hands. There may also be circumstances which would make it unfair to allow the plaintiff to recover.

Eveleigh LJ thus appears to have regarded a relevant test, if not the relevant test, as unconscionability.

The exception was further considered in the *Scottish Equitable* case, although the court did not attempt to formulate the nature of the exception. Robert Walker LJ, who gave the leading judgment, did not attempt a formulation of his own but was content to adopt the view of the judge that the case was 'just the sort of situation that the Court of Appeal must have had in mind in ... the *Avon CC* case when expressing reservations about the ambit of the decision'. He added that it can be predicted (albeit [218] with some reservation) that development of the law on a case by case basis will have the effect of enlarging rather than narrowing the exception.

It seems to me that the exception recognised in both the *Avon CC* case and the *Scottish Equitable* case can best be formulated as suggested by Cumming-Bruce and Eveleigh LJJ, namely that the estoppel should not operate in full where it would be clearly inequitable or unconscionable for the defendant to retain a balance in his hands. Whether it would or not of course depends upon all the circumstances of the particular case, which may include the nature of the representation and (as Peter Gibson LJ observes) will certainly include the steps taken by the recipient in reliance upon the representation.

I recognise that there is a tension between the first proposition in the *Avon CC* case and the exception because, as I see it, even after making all allowances in favour of the recipient, it will very often be unconscionable to permit him to keep the whole of the sums paid to him. However, I do not think that it is appropriate to allow a defendant to rely upon an estoppel, whether at common law or in equity, to achieve a result which can fairly be regarded as unconscionable. I am conscious of recent cases in which it has been said that it is not appropriate to try to identify a common principle applicable to all estoppels. However, I observe that in *Johnson v Gore Wood (A Firm)* (2001), which was admittedly not concerned with estoppel by representation, Lord Goff of Chieveley said:

> In the end, I am inclined to think that the many circumstances capable of giving rise to an estoppel cannot be accommodated within a single formula, and that it is unconscionability which provides the link between them.

This is perhaps an example of the principles of equity being employed to mitigate the rigours of the common law. However that may be, it seems to me to follow from the *Avon CC* case and the *Scottish Equitable* case that there are exceptions to the strict rule of evidence that an estoppel by representation cannot operate *pro tanto* and that those exceptions are or include cases where it would be unconscionable or wholly inequitable to permit the recipient of money to retain the whole of it.

I am not sure that this approach is markedly different from that described by Robert Walker LJ [in] his judgment in the *Scottish Equitable* case and referred to as a 'novel and ingenious point'. If, as Dixon J put it in *Grundt v Great Boulder Gold Mines Ltd* (1938), pp 674–75, and as Robert Walker LJ said was correct, detriment must be judged when the representee seeks to go back on his representation, the recipient will not have acted to his detriment if he is entitled to keep the part of the money that he has spent but not the rest. Provided that he is entitled to keep the amount spent, it is likely (subject to the circumstances of the particular case) to be unconscionable to allow him to keep the rest, in which event he should not in principle be entitled to do so. As I see it, the application of what may be called the unconscionability test does not involve the exercise of a discretion but provides a principled approach to the problem in a case of this kind.

For the reasons given by both Peter Gibson and Potter LJJ I agree that on the facts found by the judge it would be unconscionable and inequitable for Somer to be permitted to retain the balance paid to it in error by NatWest. It follows that I too would dismiss the appeal.

Peter Gibson LJ: ... [219] [Counsel for Somer] submits that the two defences are recognised as distinct and necessary parts of English law, estoppel being a defence of general availability apt to be invoked against the assertion of any kind of right, whereas the defence of change of position may be available in circumstances where the defence of estoppel could not be established, for example where there is no representation accompanying the mistaken payment. He relies on *Avon CC v Howlett* (1983) as authority binding this court that the operation of the defence of estoppel is not restricted to the precise amount which the recipient may prove he has suffered in reliance on the representation.

[Counsel] for the Bank submits that the defence of estoppel is no longer available in a case such as the present where the defence of change of position is available to the defendant. There are Canadian authorities which hold that estoppel is no longer an appropriate way of dealing with the problem, the defence of change of position most fairly balancing the equities (see *RBC Dominion Securities Inc v Dawson* (1994), a decision of the Newfoundland Court of Appeal, applied in *Empire Life Insurance Co v Neufeld Estate* (1998) a decision of Lowry J in the Supreme Court of British Columbia). In this country Jonathan Parker J in *Philip Collins Ltd v Davis* (2000), p 826 has suggested that a defence of estoppel is no longer apt in restitutionary claims where the defence of change of position is available. [Counsel for the bank] argues that we should not follow the *Avon CC* case on the basis that it cannot now stand with the decision of the House of Lords in the *Lipkin Gorman* case. Alternatively, he submits that the present case plainly falls within an exception recognised in the *Avon CC* case to the 'all or nothing' application of the estoppel defence.

The *Avon CC* case is a procedural oddity. The trial judge found as a fact that the defendant had spent all the money overpaid to him but decided the case on the artificial basis pleaded in the defence that he had only spent a little over half the money overpaid. The judge held that the payers were entitled to recover the balance, but they undertook not to execute the judgment without leave of the court. The defendant appealed, although, as Cumming-Bruce LJ put it, (1983), p 608, he had no practical reason for objecting to the order, and the appeal was brought in order to obtain the decision of this court upon a purely hypothetical question of detriment in its relevance to the law of estoppel. It was decided at a time when the defence of change of position was not recognised. But it was not expressly overruled by the House of Lords in the [220] *Lipkin Gorman* case. In Goff and Jones[23] it is said that 'the House of Lords may conclude that ... *Avon County Council v Howlett* cannot stand with *Lipkin Gorman (A Firm) v Karpnale Ltd* ... and should be overruled'. The caution of the editor should be noted: he is suggesting the possibility that the *Avon CC* case will be overruled by the House of Lords. I doubt if this court is free to treat the *Avon CC* case as overruled.

In my judgment in the present case this court should follow the approach adopted in *Scottish Equitable plc v Derby*, both by Harrison J at first instance (2000) and by this court on appeal from him, and should consider whether the circumstances are such that the case falls within the exception recognised as a possibility by each of the members of this court in the *Avon CC* case (1983), pp 608–09.[24] When Slade LJ posited the case where the sums sought to be recovered were so large as to bear no relation to any detriment which the recipient could possibly have suffered, he did so expressly by way of an example of circumstances where the doctrine of estoppel could be said to give rise to injustice were it to defeat in its entirety an action in restitution. The test is whether it would be unconscionable and inequitable for the recipient of the moneys mistakenly paid to retain the moneys having regard to what the recipient did in reliance on the representation made to him.

I fully accept that the court, when assessing detriment, should not apply too demanding a standard of proof because of the practical difficulties faced by a defendant conducting a business who has been led to believe that the moneys paid by mistake are his.[25] But in view of the clear findings of fact made by the judge as to the extent of the detriment suffered by Somer and in particular his outright rejection of the argument that Somer was induced to forgo the opportunity to pursue Mentor for payment, I am not able to accede to [counsel for Somer's] submission that this is a case where it would be unjust not to give full effect to the estoppel. On the contrary, the circumstances here, as found by the judge, are such that the disparity between the US $76,708.57 mistakenly credited to Somer and

---

23 Goff and Jones, *The Law of Restitution*, 5th edn, 1998, p 829.

24 *Per* Cumming-Bruce LJ, pp 611–12 *per* Eveleigh LJ and pp 624–25 *per* Slade LJ. See also *Chitty on Contracts*, 28th edn, 1999, para 30–113.

25 See the remarks of Slade LJ in *Howlett* at pp 621–22.

£13,180.57, being the value of the goods despatched by Somer in reliance on the bank's representation, makes it unconscionable and inequitable for Somer to retain the balance.

For these as well as the reasons given by Potter LJ I would dismiss the appeal ...

Commentary and questions

What reasons does the court give for concluding that estoppel could operate *pro tanto*? What reasons does Potter LJ give for suggesting that estoppel should remain as a defence distinct from change of position? How did the court formulate the exception recognised in *Avon County Council v Howlett* (1983)? (See extract, p 571.) How did the court apply the exception to the facts before them?

The court in the principal case and Robert Walker LJ in *Scottish Equitable plc v Derby* (2001) (see extract, p 580) both recognise that a more flexible approach to estoppel by representation can be achieved by aligning common law estoppel with equitable estoppel. In Australia, there is a movement towards one unified doctrine of estoppel, subsuming both common law and equitable estoppel: see in particular *Walton Stores (Interstate) Ltd v Maher* (1988) and *Commonwealth v Verwayen* (1990), pp 411, 440. Although that fusion process is not yet complete,[26] it has been suggested that the principles from equitable estoppel can be used to guide the application of common law forms of estoppel in the future. In particular, it is suggested that the influence of equitable estoppel could result in estoppel by representation being converted to a *pro tanto* defence. In *Waltons Stores* and *Verwayen* the High Court has emphasised that the appropriate relief for equitable estoppel is the 'the minimum equity to do justice';[27] that is, the minimum remedy needed to remove the detriment resulting from the unconscionable conduct.[28] A defence of estoppel by representation that operated *pro tanto* (only to the extent of the detriment suffered) would be consistent with this identified objective of modern estoppel.[29] The High Court is yet to address this issue however, and, in the meantime, the limits and operation of estoppel by representation in Australian law remain uncertain.[30]

---

26 The question of a unified doctrine of estoppel was left open in *Giumelli v Giumelli* (1999), pp 112–13.

27 *Walton Stores (Interstate) Ltd v Maher* (1988), p 404.

28 *Walton Stores (Interstate) Ltd v Maher* (1988), pp 404, 419, 423, 427; *Commonwealth of Australia v Verwayen* (1990), pp 411–12, 429, 442, 501; cf *Giumelli v Giumelli* (1999).

29 *Commonwealth of Australia v Verwayen* (1990), pp 411–13. See also Mason and Carter, *Restitution Law in Australia*, 1995, pp 844–45; Birks, 'Change of position: the nature of the defence and its relationship to other restitutionary defences', in McInnes (ed), *Restitution: Developments in Unjust Enrichment*, 1996, p 68; Key, 'Excising estoppel by representation as a defence to restitution' [1995] CLJ 525, pp 533–34; Liew, 'Mistaken payments – the right of recovery and the defences' (1995) 7 Bond LR 95, pp 116–17.

30 Meagher, Gummow and Lehane, *Equity Doctrines and Remedies*, 3rd edn, 1992, pp 409–11.

CHANGE OF POSITION

The nature of change of position[31]

The defence of change of position applies where the defendant in good faith acts to his or her detriment on the faith of the receipt. The defendant will have acted to his or her detriment on the faith of the receipt by incurring 'extraordinary expenditure', that is, expenditure that he or she would not have incurred in the ordinary course of things.[32] It follows that the defence will fail if the evidence establishes that the defendant would have spent the money on the item in question even had the overpayment not been made.

Unlike estoppel, which is a complete defence, the defence of change of position operates *pro tanto*; that is, only to the extent of the proven detrimental reliance.[33] The defendant must return any portion of the enrichment in relation to which the defendant has not changed position.

These principles were laid down in the following case.

David Securities Pty Ltd v Commonwealth Bank of Australia (1992) 175 CLR 353
High Court of Australia

The facts are stated at p 110.

Mason CJ, Deane, Toohey, Gaudron, McHugh JJ: ... [384] The respondent next submits that an order for restitution would be unjust because it has changed its position. The defence of change of position has not been expressly accepted in this country. In *Westpac Banking Corporation* (1988), the court referred to the displacement of *prima facie* liability by 'some adverse change of position by the recipient in good faith and in reliance on the payment', p 673. The issue did not, however, arise for decision in that case. In this country, conflicting views have been expressed. In *Bank of NSW v Murphett* (1983), Crockett J thought change of position was a defence. However, in *National Mutual Life Association v Walsh* (1987), pp 589–99, Clarke J concluded that the English Court of Appeal decision in *Baylis v Bishop of London* (1913) ruled out the acceptance of such a defence in the case before him. In England, there is strong authority in favour of acceptance of the defence, viz the judgment of Kerr LJ in *Rover International Ltd* (1989), p 925; p 434, *Barclays Bank* (1980), pp 695–96 and most importantly the recent decision of the House of Lords in *Lipkin Gorman v Karpnale Ltd* (1991), pp 558, 568, 578–80. In the last case, Lord Bridge of Harwich, Lord Ackner and Lord Goff of Chieveley held that English law should recognise the defence, although they declined to define its

---

31 For a comparative analysis of the change of position defence, see: Dorner, '"Change of position" and "Wegfall der Bereicherung"', in Swadling (ed), *The Limits of Restitutionary Claims: A Comparative Analysis*, 1997, Chapter 3; Hellwege, 'The scope of application of change of position in the law of unjust enrichment: a comparative study' [1999] RLR 92 and Jewell, 'The boundaries of change of position – a comparative study' [2000] RLR 1.

32 *David Securities Pty Ltd v Commonwealth Bank of Australia* (1992), pp 384 (see following extract). Note that it is not necessary that the money expended by the defendant is identical with the money received from the plaintiff: *Corporate Management Services v Abi Arraj* (2000).

33 *David Securities Pty Ltd v Commonwealth Bank of Australia* (1992), p 385 (see following extract); *Lipkin Gorman v Karpnale Ltd* [(1991), pp 579, 580–81 (see extract, p 595); *RBC Dominion Securities Inc v Dawson* (1994) (see extract, p 609).

scope. Text writers[34] such as Goff and Jones and Birks, also support the existence of the defence, particularly in view of the inflexibility of the related doctrine of estoppel, as evidenced by *Avon CC v Howlett* (1983) where the Court of Appeal held that estoppel could not operate *pro tanto*. And, in Canada, *Rural Municipality of Storthoaks v Mobil Oil Canada Ltd* (1975), and the United States,[35] the defence of change of position has been recognised. Section 125(1) of the Property Law Act 1969 (WA) and s 94B of the Judicature Act 1908 (NZ) also provide for this defence.

If we accept the principle that payments made under a mistake of law should be *prima facie* recoverable, in the same way as payments made under a mistake of fact, a defence of change of position is necessary to ensure that enrichment of the recipient of the payment is prevented only in circumstances where it would be *unjust*. This does not mean that the concept of unjust enrichment needs to shift the primary focus of its attention from the moment of enrichment. From the point of view of the person making the payment, what happens after he or she has mistakenly paid over the money is irrelevant, for it is at that moment that the defendant is unjustly enriched. However, the defence of change of position is relevant to the enrichment of the defendant precisely because its central element is that the defendant has acted to his or her detriment on the faith of the receipt.[36] In the jurisdictions in which it has been accepted (Canada and the United States), the defence operates in different ways but the common element in all cases is the requirement that the defendant point to expenditure or financial commitment which can be ascribed to the mistaken payment.[37] In Canada and in some United States decisions, the defendant has been required to point to specific expenditure being incurred because of the payment. Other cases in the United States, for example, *Moritz v Horsman* (1943), allow a wider scope to the defence, such that a defendant can rely upon it even though he or she cannot precisely identify the expenditure [386] caused by the mistaken payments. In no jurisdiction, however, can a defendant resort to the defence of change of position where he or she has simply spent the money received on ordinary living expenses.

The difficulty lying in the path of acceptance or detailed explication of the defence in this case is that the facts which might give rise to a plea of the defence and thus require a decision by this court were not adduced in the courts below. As mistake of law was only briefly raised by the appellants in the Federal Court, the respondent addressed no argument in support of the defence of change of position. Only in this court were submissions made by the parties on this issue. In its written outline of submissions, the respondent puts its case thus:

> In the present case, on the occasion of each rollover, the respondent changed its position by acceding to the appellants' request to 'rollover' a rollover which it would not have been bound to do, by the operation of clause 8(c). The respondent, thereby incurred a liability for withholding tax which it otherwise would not have incurred. If the respondent is now obliged to repay amounts to the appellants, it will be out of pocket.

---

34 Goff and Jones, *op cit*, fn 23, pp 46–47; Birks, *An Introduction to the Law of Restitution*, rev edn, 1989, pp 414–15; Beatson, *The Use and Abuse of Unjust Enrichment*, 1991, pp 155–60.

35 *Restatement of the Law of Restitution*, para 69(1).

36 Birks, *op cit*, fn 34, p 410.

37 *Rural Municipality of Storthoaks v Mobil Oil Canada Ltd* (1975), p 13; *Grand Lodge, AOUW of Minnesota v Towne* (1917), p 407.

Counsel for the respondent submits that an inference should be drawn that, having regard to the terms of the bargain, it would have exercised whatever contractual rights were open to it to ensure the performance of its bargain. The short answer to this submission is that there is simply an insufficient basis in the evidence for reaching this conclusion.

[Their Honours remitted the matter to the trial judge to consider this issue.]

Dawson J: ... [405] In *Australia and New Zealand Banking Group Ltd v Westpac Banking Corporation* this court recognised that the *prima facie* liability to restore money paid under a mistake may be displaced, but only in 'circumstances (eg, that the payment was made for good consideration such as the discharge of an existing debt or, arguably, that there has been some adverse change of position by the recipient in good faith and in reliance on the payment) which the law recognises would make an order for restitution unjust' (1988), p 673. No doubt the court regarded money paid voluntarily as money not paid under a mistake and hence as not giving rise to any *prima facie* liability to repay (cf Goff J's category 2(a)). The onus of proving the circumstances which displace *prima facie* liability must, of course, lie upon the recipient. The tentative acceptance of change of position as a defence to a claim for restitution may now I think be [406] stated more positively in the light of the decision of the House of Lords in *Lipkin Gorman v Karpnale Ltd* (1991). As Lord Goff of Chieveley observed in that case, it is basic to the concept of unjust enrichment that, (1991), p 579 'where an innocent defendant's position is so changed that he will suffer an injustice if called upon to repay or to repay in full, the injustice of requiring him so to pay outweighs the injustice of denying the plaintiff restitution'. Whilst unjust enrichment does not of itself constitute a cause of action, it provides a 'unifying legal concept' and serves to mark out the defences to claims in restitution ... See *Pavey & Matthews Pty Ltd v Paul* (1987), pp 256–57.

Commentary

The High Court was not attempting a definitive statement of the operation of the change of position defence (p 386) and it must be said that the court's discussion of change of position raises as many questions as it answers. It is not clear, for example, to what extent the change of position defence extends to other forms of detrimental reliance not involving expenditure or financial commitment. In *Palmer v Blue Circle Southern Cement Ltd* (1999) (see extract, p 614) it was held that the change of position defence could extend to a situation where the defendant had foregone an opportunity to obtain money from another source in reliance on the mistaken payment. However, the court in *David Securities* gave no indication whether this is correct.

It is also unclear whether the change of position defence as formulated by the High Court in the principal case could encompass situations where the enrichment is lost or reduced by a circumstance other than the incurring of an expenditure, for example because the enrichment is lost, stolen or destroyed.[38]

---

38 For discussion of the 'loss of enrichment' approach to change of position, see Nolan, 'Change of position', in Birks (ed), *Laundering and Tracing*, 1995, p 188; Key, 'Change of position' (1995) 58 MLR 505, pp 508, 511; Birks, 'Change of position: the nature of the defence and its relationship to other restitutionary defences', in McInnes (ed), *Restitution: Developments in Unjust Enrichment*, 1996.

The court in *David Securities* specifically excluded expenditure on 'ordinary living expenses' from the defence of change of position. It is submitted that the court should not be taken to mean by this statement that a general improvement in the defendant's standard of living does not qualify as a change of position.[39] It has been recognised in other cases that the defendant will have changed position by generally upgrading his or her lifestyle as a result of the receipt of the mistaken payment. The better interpretation of the High Court statement is that it refers to the fact that the defendant is unable to claim a change of position in relation to expenses that the defendant would have incurred anyway 'in the ordinary course of things': *Lipkin Gorman v Karpnale Ltd* (1991), p 580 *per* Lord Goff.

The change of position defence was recognised in England in the following decision of *Lipkin Gorman v Karpnale Ltd* (1991). As will be seen, the House of Lords in that case adopted a wider version of the defence than that accepted by the High Court in *David Securities*.

Lipkin Gorman v Karpnale Ltd [1991] 2 AC 548 House of Lords

Cass, a partner in the plaintiff firm of solicitors, misappropriated over a period of time the sum of £323,222 from the firm's client account. Cass paid back into the client account various sums totalling £100,313, leaving a net shortfall of £222,909. Cass used the misappropriated money to gamble at the defendant's club, which had no knowledge that the money was stolen. The total amount staked by Cass at the club was £561,014; comprised of the misappropriated money, some of Cass's own money, and some of Cass's winnings. Cass's total winnings amounted to £378,294 and the net sum won by the club from Cass's losing bets over the relevant period was £174,745. On the basis that £20,050 of the club's earnings had been derived from stakes of Cass's own money, the parties agreed that at least £154,695 of the club's gain had been derived from the money misappropriated from the client account. The House of Lords held that the plaintiff solicitors had a *prima facie* right to recover that sum of money in restitution. The club argued, however, that it had changed its position by paying out on the winning bets.

Lord Templeman: ... [559] In my opinion in a claim for money had and received by a thief, the plaintiff victim must show that money belonging to him was paid by the thief to the defendant and that the defendant was unjustly enriched and remained unjustly enriched. An innocent recipient of stolen money may not be enriched at all; if Cass had paid £20,000 derived from the solicitors to a car dealer for a motor car priced at £20,000, the car dealer would not have been enriched. The car dealer would have received £20,000 for a car worth £20,000. But an innocent recipient of stolen money will be enriched if the recipient has not given full consideration. If Cass had given £20,000 of the solicitors' money to a friend as a gift, the friend would have been enriched and unjustly enriched because a donee

---

39 Mason and Carter, *Restitution Law in Australia*, 1995, pp 846–47; Goff and Jones, *The Law of Restitution*, 5th edn, 1998, p 827. It has been decided in the estoppel context that a general upgrading by the defendant of his or her lifestyle will amount to detrimental reliance: *Avon County Council v Howlett* [1983] 1 WLR 605, p 620 (see extract, p 571).

of stolen money cannot in good conscience rely on the bounty of the thief to deny restitution to the victim of the theft. Complications arise if the donee innocently expends the stolen money in reliance on the validity of the gift before the donee receives notice of the victim's claim for restitution. Thus if the donee spent £20,000 in the purchase of a motor car which he would not have purchased but for the gift, it seems to me that the donee has altered his position on the faith of the gift and has only been unjustly enriched to the extent of the second hand value of the motor car at the date when the victim of the theft seeks restitution. If the donee spends the £20,000 in a trip round the world, which he would not have undertaken without the gift, it seems to me that the donee has altered his position on the faith of the gift and that he is not unjustly enriched when the victim of the theft seeks restitution. In the present case Cass stole and the club received £229,908.48 of the solicitors' money. If the club was in the same position as a donee, the club nevertheless in good faith allowed Cass to gamble with the solicitors' money and paid his winnings from time to time so that when the solicitors' sought restitution, the club only retained £154,695 derived from the solicitors. The question is whether the club which was enriched by £154,695 at the date when the solicitors sought restitution was unjustly enriched.

[His Honour decided that the only contract between the club and Cass was a gambling contract which was void under s 18 of the Gaming Act 1845 (UK) and continued at p 562:]

The club claims that even if the only consideration given by the club was a gambling consideration, nevertheless the club altered its position to its detriment because the club allowed Cass to gamble and the club paid his winnings. This is another way of relying on a void gaming contract justifying the retention of the solicitors' money. The club has not suffered any detriment. If the club pays £154,695 to the solicitors as a result of this appeal, the club will be in exactly the same position which would have obtained if Cass had not gambled away the solicitors' money. It is true that the club would have been in a better position if Cass had been gambling away his own money, but that plaintive observation does not entitle the club to retain the solicitors' money by which the club remains unjustly enriched to the extent of £154,695 ...

Lord Goff of Chieveley: ... [577] I turn then to the last point on which the respondents relied to defeat the solicitors' claim for the money. This was that the claim advanced by the solicitors was in the form of an action for money had and received, and that such a claim should only succeed where the defendant was unjustly enriched at the expense of the plaintiff. If it would be unjust or unfair to order restitution, the claim should fail. It [578] was for the court to consider the question of injustice or unfairness, on broad grounds. If the court thought that it would be unjust or unfair to hold the respondents liable to the solicitors, it should deny the solicitors recovery. [Counsel for the defendant] listed a number of reasons why, in his submission, it would be unfair to hold the respondents liable. These were: (1) the club acted throughout in good faith, ignorant of the fact that the money had been stolen by Cass; (2) although the gaming contracts entered into by the club with Cass were all void, nevertheless the club honoured all those contracts; (3) Cass was allowed to keep his winnings (to the extent that he did not gamble them away); (4) the gaming contracts were merely void not illegal; and (5) the solicitors' claim was no different in principle from a claim to recover against an innocent third party to whom the money was given and who no longer retained it.

I accept that the solicitors' claim in the present case is founded upon the unjust enrichment of the club, and can only succeed if, in accordance with the principles of the law of restitution, the club was indeed unjustly enriched at the expense of the solicitors. The claim for money had and received is not, as I have previously mentioned, founded upon any wrong committed by the club against the solicitors. But it does not, in my opinion, follow that the court has *carte blanche* to reject the solicitors' claim simply because it thinks it unfair or unjust in the circumstances to grant recovery. The recovery of money in restitution is not, as a general rule, a matter of discretion for the court. A claim to recover money at common law is made as a matter of right; and even though the underlying principle of recovery is the principle of unjust enrichment, nevertheless, where recovery is denied, it is denied on the basis of legal principle.

It is therefore necessary to consider whether [counsel for the defendant's] submission can be upheld on the basis of legal principle. In my opinion it is plain, from the nature of his submissions, that he is in fact seeking to invoke a principle of change of position, asserting that recovery should be denied because of the change in position of the respondents, who acted in good faith throughout.

Whether change of position is, or should be, recognised as a defence to claims in restitution is a subject which has been much debated in the books. It is however a matter on which there is a remarkable unanimity of view, the consensus being to the effect that such a defence should be recognised in English law. I myself am under no doubt that this is right.

Historically, despite broad statements of Lord Mansfield to the effect that an action for money had and received will only lie where it is inequitable for the defendant to retain the money,[40] the defence has received at most only partial recognition in English law. I refer to two groups of cases which can arguably be said to rest upon change of position: (1) where an agent can defeat a claim to restitution on the ground that, before learning of the plaintiff's claim, he has paid the money over to his principal or otherwise altered his position in relation to his principal on the faith of the payment; and (2) certain cases concerned with bills of exchange, in which money paid under forged bills has been held [579] irrecoverable on grounds which may, on one possible view, be rationalised in terms of change of position.[41] There has however been no general recognition of any defence of change of position as such; indeed any such defence is inconsistent with the decisions of the Exchequer Division in *Durrant v Ecclesiastical Commissioners for England and Wales* (1880), and of the Court of Appeal in *Baylis v Bishop of London* (1913). Instead, where change of position has been relied upon by the defendant, it has been usual to approach the problem as one of estoppel: see, eg, *RE Jones Ltd v Waring and Gillow Ltd* (1926), and *Avon County Council v Howlett* (1983). But it is difficult to see the justification for such a rationalisation. First, estoppel normally depends upon the existence of a representation by one party, in reliance upon which the representee has so changed his position that it is inequitable for the representor to

---

40   See in particular *Moses v Macferlan* (1760).

41   See, eg, *Price v Neal* (1762); and *London and River Plate Bank Ltd v Bank of Liverpool* (1896).

go back upon his representation. But, in cases of restitution, the requirement of a representation appears to be unnecessary. It is true that, in cases where the plaintiff has paid money directly to the defendant, it has been argued (though with difficulty) that the plaintiff has represented to the defendant that he is entitled to the money; but in a case such as the present, in which the money is paid to an innocent donee by a thief, the true owner has made no representation whatever to the defendant. Again, it was held by the Court of Appeal in *Avon County Council v Howlett* that estoppel cannot operate *pro tanto*, with the effect that if, for example, the defendant has innocently changed his position by disposing of part of the money, a defence of estoppel would provide him with a defence to the whole of the claim. Considerations such as these provide a strong indication that, in many cases, estoppel is not an appropriate concept to deal with the problem.

In these circumstances, it is right that we should ask ourselves: why do we feel that it would be unjust to allow restitution in cases such as these? The answer must be that, where an innocent defendant's position is so changed that he will suffer an injustice if called upon to repay or to repay in full, the injustice of requiring him so to repay outweighs the injustice of denying the plaintiff restitution. If the plaintiff pays money to the defendant under a mistake of fact, and the defendant then, acting in good faith, pays the money or part of it to charity, it is unjust to require the defendant to make restitution to the extent that he has so changed his position. Likewise, on facts such as those in the present case, if a thief steals my money and pays it to a third party who gives it away to charity, that third party should have a good defence to an action for money had and received. In other words, *bona fide* change of position should of itself be a good defence in such cases as these. The principle is widely recognised throughout the common law world. It is recognised in the United States of America;[42] it has been judicially recognised by the Supreme Court of Canada;[43] [580] it has been introduced by statute in New Zealand,[44] and in Western Australia,[45] and it has been judicially recognised by the Supreme Court of Victoria.[46] In the important case of *Australia and New Zealand Banking Group Ltd v Westpac Banking Corporation* (1988), there are strong indications that the High Court of Australia may be moving towards the same destination (1988), see especially pp 162, 168, *per curiam*. The time for its recognition in this country is, in my opinion, long overdue. I am most anxious that, in recognising this defence to actions of restitution, nothing should be said at this stage to inhibit the development of the defence on a case by case basis, in the usual way. It is, of course, plain that the defence is not open to one who has changed his position in bad faith, as where the defendant has paid away the money with knowledge of the facts entitling the plaintiff to restitution; and it is commonly accepted that the defence should not be open to a wrongdoer. These are matters which can, in due course, be considered in depth in cases where they arise for consideration. They do not arise in the present case. Here there is no doubt that the respondents have

---

42   See American Law Institute, *Restatement of the Law of Restitution,* 1937, section 142, pp 567–78; and Palmer, *The Law of Restitution,* 1978, Vol 3, para 16.8.

43   See *Rural Municipality of Storthoaks v Mobil Oil Canada Ltd* (1975).

44   Judicature Act 1908, s 94B (as amended).

45   See Western Australia Law Reform (Property, Perpetuities and Succession) Act 1962, s 24; and Western Australia Trustee Act 1962, s 65(8).

46   See *Bank of New South Wales v Murphett* (1983).

acted in good faith throughout, and the action is not founded upon any wrongdoing of the respondents. It is not however appropriate in the present case to attempt to identify all those actions in restitution to which change of position may be a defence. A prominent example will, no doubt, be found in those cases where the plaintiff is seeking repayment of money paid under a mistake of fact; but I can see no reason why the defence should not also be available in principle in a case such as the present, where the plaintiff's money has been paid by a thief to an innocent donee, and the plaintiff then seeks repayment from the donee in an action for money had and received. At present I do not wish to state the principle any less broadly than this: that the defence is available to a person whose position has so changed that it would be inequitable in all the circumstances to require him to make restitution, or alternatively to make restitution in full. I wish to stress however that the mere fact that the defendant has spent the money, in whole or in part, does not of itself render it inequitable that he should be called upon to repay, because the expenditure might in any event have been incurred by him in the ordinary course of things. I fear that the mistaken assumption that mere expenditure of money may be regarded as amounting to a change of position for present purposes has led in the past to opposition by some to recognition of a defence which in fact is likely to be available only on comparatively rare occasions. In this connection I have particularly in mind the speech of Lord Simonds in *Ministry of Health v Simpson* (1951), p 276.

I wish to add two further footnotes. The defence of change of position is akin to the defence of *bona fide* purchase; but we cannot simply say that *bona fide* purchase is a species of change of position. This is because change of position will only avail a defendant to [581] the extent that his position has been changed; whereas, where *bona fide* purchase is invoked, no inquiry is made (in most cases) into the adequacy of the consideration. Even so, the recognition of change of position as a defence should be doubly beneficial. It will enable a more generous approach to be taken to the recognition of the right to restitution, in the knowledge that the defence is, in appropriate cases, available; and while recognising the different functions of property at law and in equity, there may also in due course develop a more consistent approach to tracing claims, in which common defences are recognised as available to such claims, whether advanced at law or in equity.

I turn to the application of this principle to the present case. In doing so, I think it right to stress at the outset that the respondents, by running a casino at the club, were conducting a perfectly lawful business. There is nothing unlawful about accepting bets at a casino; the only relevant consequence of the transactions being gambling transactions is that they are void. In other words, the transactions as such give rise to no legal obligations. Neither the gambler, nor the casino, can go to court to enforce a gaming transaction. That is the legal position. But the practical or business position is that, if a casino does not pay winnings when they are due, it will simply go out of business. So the obligation in honour to pay winnings is an obligation which, in business terms, the casino has to comply with. It is also relevant to bear in mind that, in the present case, there is no question of Cass having gambled on credit. In each case, the money was put up front, not paid to discharge the balance of an account kept for gambling debts. It was because the money was paid over, that the casino accepted the bets at all.

In the course of argument before your Lordships, attention was focused upon the overall position of the respondents. From this it emerged, that, on the basis I have indicated (but excluding the banker's draft) at least £150,960 derived from money stolen by Cass from the solicitors was won by the club and lost by Cass. On this approach, the possibility arose that the effect of change of position should be to limit the amount recoverable by the solicitors to that sum. But there are difficulties in the way of this approach. Let us suppose that a gambler places two bets with a casino, using money stolen from a third party. The gambler wins the first bet and loses the second. So far as the winning bet is concerned, it is readily understandable that the casino should be able to say that it is not liable to the true owner for money had and received, on the ground that it has changed its position in good faith. But at first sight it is not easy to see how it can aggregate the two bets together and say that, by paying winnings on the first bet in excess of both, it should be able to deny liability in respect of the money received in respect of the second.

There are other ways in which the problem might be approached, the first narrower and the second broader than that which I have just described. The narrower approach is to limit the impact of the winnings to the winning bet itself, so that the amount of all other bets placed with the plaintiff's money would be recoverable by him regardless of the substantial winnings paid by the casino to the gambler on the winning [582] bet. On the broader approach, it could be said that, each time a bet is accepted by the casino, with the money up front, the casino, by accepting the bet, so changes its position in good faith that it would be inequitable to require it to pay the money back to the true owner. This would be because, by accepting the bet, the casino has committed itself, in business terms, to pay the gambler his winnings if successful. In such circumstances, the bookmaker could say that, acting in good faith, he had changed his position, by incurring the risk of having to pay a sum of money substantially larger than the amount of the stake. On this basis, it would be irrelevant whether the gambler won the bet or not, or, if he did win the bet, how much he won.

I must confess that I have not found the point an easy one. But in the end I have come to the conclusion that on the facts of the present case the first of these three solutions is appropriate. Let us suppose that only one bet was placed by a gambler at a casino with the plaintiff's money, and that he lost it. In that simple case, although it is true that the casino will have changed its position to the extent that it has incurred the risk, it will in the result have paid out nothing to the gambler, and so *prima facie* it would not be inequitable to require it to repay the amount of the bet to the plaintiff. The same would, of course, be equally true if the gambler placed a hundred bets with the plaintiff's money and lost them all; the plaintiff should be entitled to recover the amount of all the bets. This conclusion has the merit of consistency with the decision of the Court of King's Bench in *Clarke v Shee and Johnson* (1774). But then, let us suppose that the gambler has won one or more out of one hundred bets placed by him with the plaintiff's money at a casino over a certain period of time, and that the casino has paid him a substantial sum in winnings, equal, let us assume, to one half of the amount of all the bets. Given that it is not inequitable to require the casino to repay to the plaintiff the amount of the bets in full where no winnings have been paid, it would, in the circumstances I have just described, be inequitable, in my opinion, to require the casino to repay to the plaintiff more than one half of his money. The inequity, as I perceive it, arises from the nature of gambling itself. In gambling only an occasional bet is won, but when the gambler wins he will receive much more than the stake placed for his winning bet. True, there may be no immediate connection between the bets. They may be placed on different occasions, and each one is a separate gaming contract. But the point is that there has been a series of transactions under which all the bets have been placed by paying the plaintiff's money to the casino, and on each occasion the casino has incurred the risk that the gambler will win. It is the totality of the bets which yields, by the laws of chance, the occasional winning bet; and the occasional winning bet is therefore, in practical terms, the result of the casino changing its position by incurring the risk of losing on each occasion when a bet is placed with it by the gambler. So, when in such circumstances the plaintiff seeks to recover from the casino the amount of several bets placed with it by a gambler with his money, it would be inequitable to require the casino to repay in full without bringing into [583] account winnings paid by it to the gambler on any one or more of the bets so placed with it. The result may not be entirely logical; but it is surely just.

For these reasons, I would allow the solicitors' appeal in respect of the money ...

Commentary

The precise basis of the change of position defence as formulated by the House of Lords is unclear. For much of the discussion, Lord Goff is apparently advocating a balancing of the respective equities of the parties,[47] although elsewhere in his judgment he implies that the defence is reliance based, *Lipkin Gorman v Karpnale Ltd* (1991), p 579. A defence based on the balancing of competing equities is potentially much broader than a reliance based defence. For example, the 'competing equities' approach would more easily accommodate a situation where the enrichment is stolen or destroyed subsequent to receipt[48] and could leave the court with a residual discretion to allow the defence even though some or all of the enrichment remains in the hands of the defendant.[49]

Although the defence has usually arisen for consideration in mistake (or ignorance) claims, it potentially is available in any category of unjust enrichment claim. However, as recognised by Lord Goff in the principal case, an important limitation on the application of the defence is that it is not open to a wrongdoer: p 580.[50] Accordingly, the defence will be unavailable in circumstances where the unjust factor is established by reference to wrongful conduct of the defendant such as duress, at least where the conduct constituting the duress is

---

47 For discussion of the ambit of Lord Goff's formulation, see Goff and Jones, *The Law of Restitution*, 5th edn, 1998, pp 822–28.

48 Mason and Carter, *op cit*, fn 39, p 841; Burrows, *op cit*, fn 6, p 427; Goff and Jones, *ibid*, p 822.

49 An example of such a situation might be where the defendant suffers a causally unrelated supervening disaster, for example loses her job the day after receiving the money; see, generally, Birks, *op cit*, fn 38, pp 62–64; cf Burrows, *op cit*, fn 6, p 426.

50 *Equiticorp Industries Group Ltd (In Statutory Management) v The Crown* (1998); *Waikato Airport Ltd v Attorney General* (2001), p 715.

exploitative.[51] Further, it will be unavailable in a claim based on restitution for wrongdoing, unless, possibly, the operative wrong does not involve fault or a want of probity on the part of the defendant – for example, an innocent breach of fiduciary duty.[52]

Detrimental reliance by the incurring of an extraordinary expenditure

The core form of change of position referred to by the High Court in *David Securities Pty Ltd v Commonwealth Bank of Australia* (1992) (see extract, p 592) was where the defendant has acted to his or detriment by incurring an extraordinary expenditure or financial commitment. The following cases explore this notion of detrimental reliance in more depth.

Philip Collins Ltd v Davis [2000] 3 All ER 808 Chancery Division

The plaintiff company was a company incorporated by the well known singer, Phil Collins. In 1990 the plaintiff engaged the two defendants (Davis and Satterfield) to form part of his backing group on a world tour. Under their contracts the defendants were entitled to receive a royalty if live recordings of songs on which they performed were released on record for sale. In November 1990 an album was released containing 15 recordings of live performances; five of which the defendants had performed on. The plaintiff paid the defendants royalties in the mistaken belief that they had performed on all 15 tracks. In March 1997 the plaintiff discovered its mistake and informed the defendants that it intended to recoup the overpayments from future royalty payments. The defendants commenced proceedings relying, *inter alia*, on the defences of estoppel and change of position. A detailed examination of the evidence of the defendants regarding their acts of detrimental reliance on the overpayments is contained in the judgment.

Jonathan Parker J: ... [827] For obvious reasons, it would not be appropriate for me to attempt to set out an exhaustive list of the legal principles applicable to the defence of change of position, but four principles in particular seem to me to be called into play in the instant case.

In the first place, the evidential burden is on the defendant to make good the defence of change of position. However, in applying this principle it seems to me that the court should beware of applying too strict a standard. Depending on the circumstances, it may well be unrealistic to expect a defendant to produce conclusive evidence of change of position, given that when he changed his position he can have had no expectation that he might thereafter have to prove that he did so, and the reason why he did so, in a court of law.[53] In the second place, as Lord Goff stressed in the passage from his speech in the *Lipkin Gorman* case ... to amount to a change of position there must be something more than mere expenditure of the money sought to be recovered, 'because the expenditure might

---

51 Bryan, 'Change of position: commentary', in McInnes, *op cit*, fn 38, p 78.

52 See Nolan, *op cit*, fn 38, pp 153–54.

53 See the observations of Slade LJ in *Avon CC v Howlett* (1983), pp 621–22, and Goff and Jones, *The Law of Restitution*, 5th edn, 1998, p 827.

in any event have been incurred ... in the ordinary course of things'. In the third place, there must be a causal link between the change of position and the overpayment. In *South Tyneside Metropolitan BC v Svenska International plc* (1995), Clarke J, following Hobhouse J in *Kleinwort Benson Ltd v South Tyneside Metropolitan BC* (1994) held that, as a general principle, the change of position must have occurred after receipt of the overpayment, although in *Goff and Jones* the correctness of this decision is doubted. But whether or not a change of position may be anticipatory, it must (as I see it) have been made as a consequence of the receipt of, or (it may be) the prospect of receiving, the money sought to be recovered: in other words it must, on the evidence, be referable in some way to the payment of that money. In the fourth place, as Lord Goff also made clear in his speech in the *Lipkin Gorman* case, in contrast to the defence of estoppel the defence of change of position is not an 'all or nothing' defence: it is available only to the extent that the change of position renders recovery unjust.

With those basic principles in mind, I turn to the facts of the instant case.

At the outset, when considering the facts of the instant case, two matters are to be borne in mind. In the first place, the recovery which is sought relates only to the excess payments of royalty, since one-third of the sums actually paid was payable in any event. In consequence, any relevant change of position by the defendants must be referable to the receipt of such excess payments (or, it may be, the prospect of receiving such excess payments). In the second place, the fact [827] that the defendants are currently in financial difficulties is not in itself indicative of a relevant change of position on their part. Although that fact might have been relevant in considering whether to order repayment of the sums overpaid, the claimant is not seeking an order which requires the defendants to make any payment to the claimant: as I explained earlier, it seeks only to set off the overpayments against future royalties.

In their witness statements, which formed the basis of their oral evidence-in-chief, the defendants addressed the issue of change of position in unequivocal terms. Mr Davis said this in his witness statement:

> Until the royalty payments were stopped, I had adjusted my day to day life according to the regular payments I had received over such a long period, and had become both accustomed to and dependent upon them. I had a few savings. However, with many different projects underway including a clothing business and my solo career, these were soon exhausted. I had relied on the royalties both for my living expenses and to enable me to carry on working. My elderly mother in Chicago and three dependants as well as my household in Los Angeles had all been supported with these payments. I could no longer financially assist them – indeed, I have had to borrow money from family and friends. Most of this remains unpaid ... The unannounced withholding of funds has had a domino effect upon my life since most of my projects were predicated on the existence of these royalties.

Mr Satterfield said this in his witness statement:

> I was heavily reliant upon these royalty payments. Over the period until they were stopped, I would estimate that on average they represented 80–90% of my total income. I had, and have, no savings, and the money was used for the day to day living expenses of my family and myself. In particular, the payments were invaluable in assisting my wife with medical treatment ... I

sold my home in Chicago to assist with the care she required ... The cutting of the royalty payments could not have come at a worse time. In addition, the stopping of the payments dramatically affected my ability to work. There was still a reasonable demand for me. However, the nature of my work involves a great deal of travel, hotels, etc. There were engagements offered to me which I had to decline because I had no money. The effect is a vicious circle ...

Had those factual accounts been true and accurate, they would undoubtedly have provided a strong foundation for a complete defence on grounds of change of position; particularly so in the case of Mr Davis. No doubt the statements were drafted with that very consideration in mind. In the event, however, the passages in the defendants' witness statements dealing with the question of change of position turned out to be seriously exaggerated. I do not entirely blame the defendants for this. It may well be that they did not sufficiently appreciate the need for precision in the framing of their witness statements. But whatever the reason, the fact remains that the defendants' oral evidence, coupled with such documentary evidence as they were able to produce relating to their financial affairs (I referred earlier to the fact that documents were disclosed on a piecemeal basis during the course of the trial), not only failed to approach the degree of particularity reflected in their witness statements, but actually demonstrated that statements of fact made in the passages quoted above were not true.

[829] Thus, Mr Davis expressly accepted in cross-examination that there was no such 'domino effect' as is referred to in his witness statement. He also accepted that he was not 'dependent on' the royalty income. He frankly admitted that there is not, nor has there ever been, any reason why he cannot earn his living as a musician. It was also clear from his evidence that to the extent that he had not taken other jobs as a musician while the royalties were coming in, that was his choice. He acknowledged that at no stage did he have any savings to speak of, and that his present financial difficulties were due to some bad business decisions on his part. He was unable to point to any particular decision having been taken, or act done, whether by him or on his behalf, as being directly referable to the fact that he was in receipt of royalties calculated on a non-pro-rated basis. Rather, the true position (as revealed in cross-examination) was that he geared his expenditure to the level of his cash resources from time to time: he was content to enjoy the benefits of the royalty payments as and when they came in, and his outgoings increased accordingly. He was (as I find) fully aware at all material times that royalty income from a particular release tends to reduce over time to nil or a negligible sum. Consequently, he realised that his royalty income from the live album would not be maintained at the level of the payments received during the first year or so after its release. On the other hand, that realisation did not lead him to limit his outgoings to any significant extent.

So far as Mr Satterfield is concerned, I intend no criticism whatever of him when I describe him as having a somewhat relaxed and philosophical attitude to life in general, and in particular to financial and administrative matters. Like Mr Davis, Mr Satterfield accepted that there is nothing to prevent him continuing to earn his living as a musician, but, as he put it disarmingly in cross-examination, he earns money when he feels like it. He accepted that the assertion in his witness statement that he cannot work because he cannot afford the up-front hotel and travel costs is an overstatement. Further, it was apparent from his evidence, and I find, that such assets as he and his wife acquired post-1990 (including a number of properties in Chicago which his wife purchased with a view to refurbishment and letting) were not acquired in reliance on a future royalty stream but were purchased ad hoc, as and when they considered that they could afford it. At the conclusion of his cross-examination Mr Satterfield described his current financial position as follows (according to my note):

> I have no money left from my earnings. My lifestyle is hard to explain; you would not believe it. When I got the money in I spent it rather than saved it. A lot of the things I spent it on I am involved in now. I spent it for other people. I have done this throughout my career.

In general, whilst it would plainly not be accurate to describe the defendants as having been careful with their money, I am satisfied that in gauging how much they could spend from time to time they had regard to their current cash resources, the principal source of which (at least in the first two years after the release of the live album) was their royalty income.

On the basis of the defendants' oral evidence, coupled with such documentary evidence as they were able to produce, I am unable to find that any particular item of expenditure was directly referable to the overpayments of royalties. Their evidence was simply too vague and unspecific to justify such a finding. On the other hand, in the particular circumstances of the instant case the absence of such a finding is not, in my judgment, fatal to the defence of the change of position. Given that the approach of the defendants to their respective financial [830] affairs was, essentially, to gear their outgoings to their income from time to time (usually, it would seem, spending somewhat more than they received), and bearing in mind that the instant case involves not a single overpayment but a series of overpayments at periodic intervals over some six years, it is in my judgment open to the court to find, and I do find, that the overpayments caused a general change of position by the defendants in that they increased their level of outgoing by reference to the sums so paid. In particular, the fact that in the instant case the overpayments took the form of a series of periodical payments over an extended period seems to me to be significant in the context of a defence of change of position, in that it places the defendants in a stronger position to establish a general change of position such as I have described, consequent upon such overpayments.

Nor, on the evidence, can the defendants' increased level of expenditure be regarded as consisting exclusively of expenditure which (to use Lord Goff's words) 'might in any event have been incurred in the ordinary course of things'. I am satisfied that had the defendants been paid the correct sums by way of royalties their levels of expenditure would have been lower.

I accordingly conclude that each of the defendants has changed his position in consequence of the overpayments. The question then arises whether the defendants can rely on their change of position as a defence to the entirety of the claim, or only to some (and if so what) part of it.

In my judgment, the defence of change of position which I have found to be established cannot extend to the entirety of the claim, if only because had the correct amount of royalties been paid the defendants' level of outgoings might not have reduced proportionately. The defendants' propensity to overspend their income means that it is impossible to establish an exact correlation between their income and their outgoings.

So how far does the defence of change of position extend? I accept [counsel for the defendant's] submission that, on the particular facts of the instant case, the court should adopt a broad approach to this question; if only because, for reasons already given, the defendants' evidence as to their financial affairs does not admit of detailed analysis.

In all the circumstances as I have found them, I conclude that the defence of change of position extends to one-half of the overpayments: in other words, that (subject to the limitation issue) the claimant's recovery should be limited to US$72,575.61 and £14,685.12.

In my judgment that represents, on the evidence, a conservative assessment of extent to which the overpayments led to a change of position on the part of the defendants.

It is, however, to be observed that limiting the claim to half the overpayments will almost certainly have no practical effect, since on the evidence it is highly improbable, to put it no higher, that the defendants' future royalty entitlement from sales of the live album will amount to anything approaching that sum.

...

Commentary

The defendants argued successfully that they had changed their position by spending the money in maintaining a standard of lifestyle that they otherwise would not have been able to maintain. It was not fatal to the defence that they could not prove specific items of expenditure, because it would never have occurred to them that they would need to retain receipts. However, Jonathan Parker J recognised a change of position only in relation to one-half of the overpayments because he considered that the defendants had a propensity to live beyond their means, and thus would have incurred some of the same expenses even had they not received the overpayment.

Scottish Equitable plc v Derby [2001] 3 All ER 818
English Court of Appeal, Civil Division

In 1988 the defendant, Mr Derby, was made redundant. He invested his redundancy payment in a pension policy with the plaintiff life assurance company, Scottish Equitable. In 1989 Mr Derby decided to exercise an option to take early retirement benefits under his policy with Scottish Equitable, however through an administrative error the exercise of this option was not recorded in the computer records of the firm. In June 1995 Scottish Equitable sent Mr Derby a statement of his policy showing that his retirement benefits amounted to £201,938. Mr Derby checked this amount with Scottish Equitable, advising them that he was already receiving a pension from them, and he was assured that the figures quoted in the statement of retirement benefits were correct. Mr Derby then exercised an option to receive payment of those benefits. He received £51,333 in a tax-free lump sum, and £150,604 that he reinvested in a pension plan provided by Norwich Union. In fact, the amount of the fund as at June 1995 actually stood at only £29,486, which meant that Mr Derby had been overpaid by £172,451. Mr Derby's evidence was that he used £41,671 of the mistaken payment to reduce his mortgage, and spent the balance of approximately £9,600 in making modest improvements to his lifestyle.

Scottish Equitable realised its mistake in October 1996 and eventually commenced proceedings to recover the overpayment. Norwich Union subsequently unwound its policy and repaid the money to Scottish Equitable, leaving Mr Derby with the smaller pension that he would have received had it not been for the overpayment. In the proceedings, Mr Derby relied, *inter alia*, on the defences of estoppel and change of position. The trial judge rejected the defence of estoppel, and held that the change of position defence applied only to the extent of £9,600. The defendant appealed.

Robert Walker LJ: ... [825] *Change of position*

[827] [Lord Goff in *Lipkin Gorman Ltd v Karpnale* (1991)] noted the view, put forward by Andrew Burrows[54] that there is a narrow and a wide version of the defence of change of position, and that the wide view is to be preferred. The narrow view treats the defence as 'the same as estoppel minus the representation' (so that detrimental reliance is still a necessary ingredient). The wide view looks to a change of position, causally linked to the mistaken receipt, which makes it inequitable for the recipient to be required to make restitution. In many cases either test produces the same result, but the wide view extends protection to (for instance) an innocent recipient of a payment which is later stolen from him.[55]

In this court [counsel for Scottish Equitable] did not argue against the correctness of the wide view, provided that the need for a sufficient causal link is clearly recognised. The fact that the recipient may have suffered some misfortune (such as a breakdown in his health, or the loss of his job) is not a defence unless the misfortune is causally linked (at least on a 'but for' test) with the mistaken receipt. In my view [counsel for Scottish Equitable] was right to make that concession. Taking a wide view of the scope of the defence facilitates 'a more generous approach ... to the recognition of the right to restitution'.[56]

The criticisms of the judgment made by [counsel for Mr Derby] were directed, not so much to the principles of law enunciated by the judge, as to the way in which he applied those principles to the facts as he found them. Before considering those criticisms in detail I think it may be useful to note that when a person receives a mistaken overpayment there are, even on the narrow view as to the scope of the defence, a variety of conscious decisions which may be made by the recipient in reliance on the overpayment. Some are simply decisions about expenditure of the receipt: the payee may decide to spend it on an asset which maintains its value, or on luxury goods with little second-hand value, or on a world cruise. He may use it to pay off debts. He may give it away. Or he may make some decision which involves no immediate expenditure, but is nevertheless causally linked to the receipt. Voluntarily giving up his job, at an age when it would not be easy to get new employment, is the most obvious example. Entering into a long-term financial

---

54 *The Law of Restitution*, 1993, pp 425–28.

55 See Goff and Jones, *The Law of Restitution*, 5th edn, 1998, p 822, also favouring the wide view.

56 Lord Goff in *Lipkin Gorman*, p 581; and compare Lord Goff's observations in *Kleinwort Benson v Lincoln City Council* (1999), p 385A–F.

commitment (such as taking a flat at a high rent on a ten-year lease which would not be easy to dispose of) would be another example. The wide view adds further possibilities which do not depend on deliberate choices by the recipient.

[Counsel for Mr Derby] criticised the judge for looking simply at particular items of expenditure (the £9,662 which was conceded, the sum used to pay off the mortgage and the sum paid to the Norwich Union) and for paying insufficient attention to Mr Derby's decision to slow down his work, and his omission to take alternative steps to provide for the future of himself and his family. I would readily accept that the defence is not limited (as it is, apparently, in Canada and some states of the United States)[57] to specific identifiable items of expenditure. I would also accept that it may be right for the court not to apply too demanding a standard of proof when an honest defendant says that he has spent an overpayment by improving his lifestyle, but cannot [828] produce any detailed accounting: see the observations of Jonathan Parker J in *Philip Collins v Davis* (2000), p 827, with which I respectfully agree. The defendants in that case were professional musicians with a propensity to overspend their income, and Jonathan Parker J took a broad approach (2000), p 830.

In the present case, however, the judge made some clear findings of fact, set out ... above, to the effect that the improvements which Mr Derby was able to make in his family's lifestyle, between June 1995 and October 1996, were very modest and not irreversible, and that there was nothing that he could usefully have done to make provision for the future. [Counsel for Mr Derby] has submitted that that seriously understates the devastating effect which the demand for repayment has had on Mr Derby, with his annual income after tax being reduced at a stroke from a sum of the order of £20,000 to a sum of the order of £12,000 (these figures do not include Mrs Derby's earned income). It is easy to accept that Scottish Equitable's demand for repayment must have come as a bitter disappointment to Mr Derby, and it is impossible not to feel sympathy for him, beset as he now is by financial problems, matrimonial problems and health problems. But the court must proceed on the basis of principle, not sympathy, in order that the defence of change of position should not (as Burrows puts it at p 426) 'disintegrate into a case by case discretionary analysis of the justice of individual facts, far removed from principle'. [Counsel for Mr Derby] took the court to various passages in the transcript of Mr Derby's oral evidence but I am not persuaded that the judge erred in his findings of fact or that he failed to take advantage of seeing and hearing the witnesses.

[Counsel for Mr Derby] submitted that the payment-off of the mortgage was a change of position, but I cannot accept that submission. In general it is not a detriment to pay off a debt which will have to be paid off sooner or later: *RBC Dominion Securities v Dawson* (1994). It might be if there were a long-term loan on advantageous terms, but it was not suggested that that was the case here; and as the judge said (1994), p 803 the evidence was that the house was to be sold in the near future.

In relation to the Norwich Union policy it was argued below that Mrs Derby had certain rights or claims because of the impending divorce, and this argument is put

57   See *David Securities Pty v Commonwealth Bank of Australia* (1992), p 780, noted in Goff and Jones, *op cit*, fn 55, p 819.

608

forward again in paragraph 16 of the grounds of appeal and in oral argument. I found this argument rather surprising since it appears from the terms of the policy that Mrs Derby is named as a payee in respect of a reversionary annuity of £6,760 a year but that her right to the annuity ceases on divorce (although Mrs Derby may be able to take advantage of the new pension-sharing arrangements introduced by the Welfare Reform and Pensions Act 1999). However it was only by reference to the impending divorce that [counsel for Mr Derby] attacked the judge's conclusion that Mrs Derby's rights were no impediment to the unwinding of the policy to which Norwich Union is prepared to agree. Her potential rights on divorce do not depend on her having a power to veto the unwinding of the policy, nor do they have the effect of conferring such a power on her. They do not in my view assist Mr Derby's argument on change of position.

For these reasons the judge was in my view correct to accept the defence of change of position only in relation to the sum of £9,662.

...

[Keene and Simon Brown LJJ agreed with Robert Walker J.]

Commentary and questions

Did the court consider that the payment off the mortgage was a change of position? Did the court take into account the 'misfortunes' that had beset Mr Derby, in terms of his financial, matrimonial and health problems? Did the court accept Mr Derby's argument that, had it not been for the mistaken overpayment, he would have taken steps to make further provision for his future?

The court agreed with Jonathan Parker J in *Philip Collins Ltd v Davis* (2000) (see extract, p 602) that the defence of change of position is not limited to specifically identifiable items of expenditure. A defendant can rely on the defence where he or she has used the overpayment to make general lifestyle improvements and is unable to produce detailed accounting records of the expenditure of the money.

RBC Dominion Securities Inc v Dawson (1994) 111 DLR (4th) 230
Newfoundland Court of Appeal

The two respondents, Ms Dawson and Mr Dawson (brother and sister), bought shares in a company through the appellant stockbroker. Under an amalgamation plan they later became entitled to one share in another company, Eureka, for every five shares owned in the original company. The number of shares the respondents subsequently obtained in Eureka was overstated by mistake in the appellant's monthly statement to the respondents. Ms Dawson sought verification from one of the appellant's brokers of the facts contained in the statement and the broker confirmed the information, apparently on the basis of incorrect computer data. Both respondents then instructed the appellant to sell their shares in Eureka. Because of the mistake by the appellant Ms Dawson received $4,919.70 more than she was entitled to on the sale, and Mr Dawson received $3,206.70 more than he was entitled to. The respondents conceded that the overpayment was made due to a mistake of fact, however sought to defend the claim by relying on estoppel and change of position. Ms Dawson argued that she had detrimentally relied on the receipt of the overpayment by purchasing various items of household furnishings and Mr Dawson primarily relied on the early repayment of loans.

Cameron JA: [Cameron JA rejected estoppel as a defence to a restitutionary claim and then turned to consider the extent to which the respondents had changed their position.]

[238] The defence of estoppel being unavailable, the issue is whether the respondents established change of circumstances so as to limit their liability to the appellant and, if so, to what extent. The trial judge did not analyse each expenditure by the respondents in light of the requirements of the defence of change of circumstances, undoubtedly because he viewed such an examination as irrelevant once there was established sufficient detrimental change to bring into operation the defence of estoppel. However, before making a finding on the defence of estoppel, he found that the circumstances of the respondents 'were substantially changed as a result of the receipt of such moneys to the extent that it would be inequitable to direct that they repay same to the plaintiff'.

As the *Restatement of the Law of Restitution* noted, change of circumstances is not a defence if the change occurred after the recipient had knowledge of the facts entitling the other to restitution.

In *Rural Municipality of Storthoaks v Mobil Oil of Canada Ltd* (1975) the change of circumstances defence was denied because the money had been placed in general account and used to pay everyday expenses. There was 'no evidence of any special projects being undertaken or special financial commitments made because of the receipt of these payments, nor that the [defendant] altered its position in any way because these moneys were received. The mere fact that the moneys were spent does not, by itself, furnish an answer to the claim for repayment' (1975), p 13.

The clearest examples of change of circumstances are those cases where the defendant has spent the money and has nothing to show for it: the donation to charity which would not have otherwise been made; the investment in a business that has failed.

However, change of circumstances is not limited to those situations where the money is spent and there is nothing to show for it. In *Morgan Guaranty Trust Co of New York v Outerbridge* (1990), Osbourne J noted that the mere fact that the money had been spent was not, in itself, sufficient to amount to a change in position giving rise to an equitable defence to a claim for restitution. The change of circumstances was found on the basis of the defendant (a lawyer), on receipt of the money paid by mistake, having given up leverage (files) that would have been important in securing payment from a debtor.

The trial judge, on the evidence of Ms Dawson, found that most, if not all, of the money was spent prior to her receipt of the letter of 26 July 1990. With the exception of the table and chairs which [239] Ms Dawson clearly stated she purchased after the receipt of the letter, there is no basis upon which to overturn the trial judge's finding that the money had been spent prior to Ms Dawson learning of the mistake. The money was used: (1) refurbishing a dining room table and chairs ($990); (2) purchasing a video cassette recorder ($371); kitchen table and chairs ($150); Chesterfield ($300); floor lamp ($65); shades and drapes ($150–$200); and (3) purchasing clothing. Ms Dawson did not detail the cost of the clothing.

RBC argues that the nature of the items purchased was unspectacular, items one might reasonably expect to be acquired in the average household and probably would have been purchased by Ms Dawson at some time in the future when her income increased. With the exception of the Chesterfield, which Ms Dawson clearly stated she would have purchased anyway, there is no basis upon which to overturn the trial judge's finding of fact that Ms Dawson would not have made the purchases had she not received the windfall from the sale of the stocks.

What are the equities of the situation where the defendant may have an asset which has some value though perhaps not equivalent to the money spent? If it is an asset, like the Chesterfield, which the defendant would have purchased whether the mistake had been made or not, then clearly the defence of change of circumstances is not established to the extent of the money paid for that item. However, the more difficult questions arise with the refurbishing of the furniture and the purchase of items which would not have been bought except for the mistake but which continue to enrich the defendant.

The appellant submits that Ms Dawson has been enriched by the increase in value of her personal assets and should pay to the appellant an amount representing this enrichment. Of course, she has been enriched. These assets replace the money. That is not at issue. The question is should she now be called upon to return the money. The mere fact that she continues to benefit from the money does not defeat the defence of change of circumstances. Here, with one exception, the furniture acquisitions represent replacement of items Ms Dawson had in her possession when she would not have replaced the items except for the error. The trial judge found that Ms Dawson changed her standard of living when she would not have otherwise done so. The expenditures were not to meet ordinary expenses or pay existing debts. Equity favours Ms Dawson. Because of the actions of the appellant Ms Dawson exchanged less valuable items for more valuable items. Her position is not unlike the person who lives at a higher standard of [240] living because more money is available but would not have done so were it not for the windfall.

The onus is upon the defendant to establish the defence of change of circumstances. With one exception, Ms Dawson was unable to be precise about the purchase prices of the items she bought. The appellant argues that the respondents should have been required to submit receipts, dates of purchase and precise amounts rather than oral evidence and estimates. Certainly, the best evidence available should be provided to the court. However, to require that a private individual, who believed she was spending her own money, prove her expenditures as if she were claiming damages in an action for negligence would be most unfair. It was the plaintiff's error that put her in the funds in the first place and led her to believe the funds were hers to spend without having to account to anyone for her expenditures. The trial judge was not in error in these circumstances in accepting and giving weight to the oral evidence of the respondents. In the circumstances, the trial judge was not in error to be satisfied with reasonable approximations.

A corporation, municipality, trustee or other person who would as a matter of course keep accounts that are subject to audit might be expected to produce more detailed information.

On Ms Dawson's evidence, the amount paid for the Chesterfield ($300) was not an extraordinary payment and is not covered by the change of circumstances defence, nor are the table and chairs ($150) which were acquired after Ms Dawson knew of the mistake.

The second respondent Stephen Dawson spent his money: (1) repaying a Visa account ($1,720); (2) repaying loans to family members ($500); (3) on a fishing trip; and (4) on entertainment with friends who were visiting. In respect to the entertainment relevant expenses, including the fishing trip, the trial judge found Mr Dawson would not have made these expenditures were it not for the mistake of fact. With respect to these items, the defence of change of circumstances was established.

The trial judge found that Mr Dawson, who was at the time earning slightly less than $800 per month, had changed his position because he liquidated his Visa debt in a manner he would not have otherwise done had it not been for the mistake on the part of the appellant and therefore the payment of the Visa debt was not a payment made to meet ordinary expenses. The Visa debt and those to family members, which were incurred prior to the mistake, would have had to have been paid in any event and had Mr Dawson paid a debt when it had come due it would not have been considered a change of circumstances. Does the change in timing [241] make it so? It does not. The payment of debt in these circumstances cannot be said to be to Mr Dawson's detriment. Equitable principles would support the return of the money. With respect, I conclude the trial judge was in error in finding a change of circumstances as a result of payment of a debt already owed ...

Commentary

It is uncertain how Australian law will treat a defendant who has acquired a valuable asset with all or part of a mistaken payment.[58] In England, in *Lipkin Gorman v Karpnale Ltd* (1991) (see extract, p 595) Lord Templeman suggested that a defendant who purchased a car with a mistaken payment will be able to establish a change of position only as to the difference between the purchase price of the car and its second hand value: p 560.[59] Lord Templeman's approach is consistent with the approach taken in the estoppel context[60] and is also consistent with the loss of enrichment approach, for which there is some support in *David Securities Pty Ltd v Commonwealth Bank of Australia* (1992) (see extract, p 592). It is arguable that a defendant who acquires a valuable asset with the payment has not reduced or erased the enrichment, but merely converted it into another form.[61] Likewise, it is arguable that the defendant will not suffer *detriment* if required to realise the asset and return the proceeds of sale, provided at least that an allowance is made for any reasonable selling expenses and depreciation. However, problems may arise where the asset is not easily able to be realised.[62] In a situation, for example, where the defendant has used the money to build extensions on to the family home, a court may be reluctant to

---

58 In *Gertsch v Atsas* (1999) the court accepted the purchase of cars and improvements to a house as a relevant change of position as they were extraordinary expenditures.

59 Cf *Cheese v Thomas* (1994). See also Key, *op cit*, fn 38, pp 518–19.

60 *United Overseas Bank v Jiwani* (1976) (see extract, p 576).

61 Birks, *op cit*, fn 34, p 63; Key, *op cit*, fn 38, p 510; see also Burrows, *op cit*, fn 6, pp 428–29.

62 Bryan, 'Change of position: commentary', in McInnes, *op cit*, fn 29, pp 83–84.

force the defendant to sell the home in order to meet the court's judgment, at least in the absence of evidence that the defendant intended to sell in any event.[63] The principles relating to incontrovertible benefit may be of assistance here.[64]

Assume that D receives in good faith a payment of $10,000 that has been paid by P by mistake. On the basis of the principles enunciated in the preceding cases, consider whether D can establish a change of position in the following circumstances:

(a) D decides to move to a new apartment where the weekly rental is $100 more than D had previously been paying. D would not have been able to afford the extra rental but for the receipt of the mistaken payment;[65]

(b) D uses the money to buy shares in an insurance company which subsequently goes into liquidation;[66]

(c) D uses the money to buy shares in a major Australian bank which have increased considerably in value;[67]

(d) D uses the $10,000 to pay off her credit card debt;[68] and

(e) an acquaintance of D forges D's signature on a bank withdrawal slip and absconds with the whole $10,000.

Detrimental reliance by foregoing an income-generating opportunity

As noted above, the central example of change of position referred to by the High Court in *David Securities Pty Ltd v Commonwealth Bank of Australia* (1992) (see extract, p 592) was where the defendant has acted to his or her detriment by incurring an extraordinary expenditure or financial commitment. The question has arisen whether the defence is limited to this circumstance, or whether it is broad enough to encompass situations where the defendant has acted to his or her detriment on the faith of the receipt by foregoing an income-generating opportunity, for example by giving up paid employment or by foregoing an entitlement to receive income from another source. Australian authority suggests that the change of position defence would be available in this circumstance.

---

63 Liew, *op cit*, fn 29, p 113; cf Stoljar, *Law of Quasi-Contract*, 2nd edn, 1989, pp 43–44; Butler, 'Mistaken payments, change of position and restitution', in Finn (ed), *Essays on Restitution*, 1990, p 130.

64 Nolan, *op cit*, fn 38, pp 141–44.

65 See *Scottish Equitable plc v Derby* (2001) (see extract, p 606); *Philip Collins Ltd v Davis* (2000) (see extract, p 602).

66 See *Holt v Markham* (1923) (see extract, p 569).

67 See *Lipkin Gorman v Karpnale Ltd* (1991), p 560 *per* Lord Templeman (see extract, p 595); *United Overseas Bank v Jiwani* (1976) (see extract, p 576).

68 See *Scottish Equitable plc v Derby* (2001), p 828 (see extract, p 606); *RBC Dominion Securities v Dawson* (1994) (see extract, p 609).

Palmer v Blue Circle Southern Cement Ltd **(1999) 48 NSWLR 318**
Supreme Court of New South Wales

The respondent commenced proceedings to recover a sum of workers' compensation paid to the appellant pursuant to a court award in June 1983. In May 1998 that award was terminated with effect from September 1986. The respondent claimed to be entitled to recover the payments made between September 1986 and May 1988 (amounting to approximately $11,000) on the basis that they were paid under a mistake. The appellant sought to rely on the defence of change of position on the basis that he had suffered a detriment by not claiming social security benefits during that period; which benefits he would have been entitled to had he not been receiving the workers' compensation payments.

Bell J: ... [322] It is the appellant's contention that the magistrate erred in that he considered the finding that the award monies had been spent on ordinary living expenses was conclusive of the change of position defence. Having regard to his favourable factual findings as to the appellant's decision not to apply for social security benefits in reliance on the receipt of the award monies, it is an irresistible inference that the magistrate did not consider this alternative basis as admitting of a defence of change of position.

I was not referred to any authority which would support the proposition that a defence of change of position might be made out by evidence that the recipient of the subject monies had foregone his or her entitlement to make a claim on another source. [Counsel for the appellant] submitted that the broad statement of principle to be found in the judgment of the majority in *David Securities Pty Ltd* (1992), p 385 was a sufficient basis to found the defence:

> If we accept the principle that payments made under a mistake of law should be *prima facie* recoverable, in the same way as payments made under a mistake of fact, a defence of change of position is necessary to ensure that enrichment of the recipient of the payment is prevented only in circumstances where it would be *unjust*. This does not mean that the concept of unjust enrichment needs to shift the primary focus of its attention from the moment of enrichment. From the point of view of the person making the payment, what happens after he or she has mistakenly paid over the money is irrelevant, for it is at that moment that the defendant is unjustly enriched. However, the defence of change of position is relevant to the enrichment of the defendant precisely because its central element is that the defendant has acted to his or her detriment on the *faith of the receipt*.

[Counsel for the appellant] also relied on a passage in the judgment of Dawson J in *David Securities Pty Ltd* (1992), pp 405–06:]

> [323] The tentative acceptance of change of position as a defence to a claim for restitution may now I think be stated more positively in the light of the decision of the House of Lords in *Lipkin Gorman v Karpnale Ltd* (1991). As Lord Goff of Chieveley observed in that case, it is basic to the concept of unjust enrichment that 'where an innocent defendant's position is so changed that he will suffer an injustice if called upon to repay or to repay in full, the injustice of requiring him so to repay outweighs the injustice of denying the plaintiff restitution'. Whilst unjust enrichment does not of itself constitute a cause of action, it provides a 'unifying legal concept' and serves to mark out the defences to claims in restitution.

As [counsel for the appellant] submitted, the law with respect to restitution and the defence of change of position is in a developing state. In the passage immediately following the broad statement of principle for which he contends the majority make reference to the scope of the defence in Canada and the United States:

> [T]he defence operates in different ways but the common element in all cases is the requirement that the defendant point to expenditure or financial commitment which can be ascribed to the mistaken payment. In Canada and in some United States decisions, the defendant has been required to point to *specific* expenditure being incurred because of the payment. Other cases in the United States allow a wider scope to the defence, such that a defendant can rely upon it even though he or she cannot precisely identify the expenditure caused by the mistaken payments.

The appellant does not point to expenditure or financial commitment which might be ascribed to the award payments. He relies on the detriment that he made no claim to payment from the Department of Social Security. I have been able to locate few authorities which support the proposition that a detriment, other than the expenditure of the monies mistakenly paid (on items other than ordinary living expenses) constitutes a change of position for the purpose of the defence.

In *The Council of the City of Sydney v Burns Philp Trustee Company Ltd (In Liquidation)* (1992) Rogers CJ Com D considered the scope of the defence of change of position in the light of the decision in *David Securities Pty Ltd* which had just been handed down. In that case the provisions of a lease between the council as lessor and the trustee company as lessee provided that rent should be determined as a fixed percentage of the 'unimproved land value' of the premises. In the event that the concept of 'unimproved land value' was abandoned in the Valuation of Land Act 1916 a clause in the lease made provision for the parties to appoint a valuer to determine the valuation of the land. The concept of 'unimproved land value' was abandoned. The Valuer General thereafter issued assessments as to the 'land value' of the premises. Both parties to the lease acted for a number of years on the assumption that the latter was synonymous with 'unimproved land value'. Giles J in related proceedings found this assumption to be wrong. The trustee company brought a cross claim for recovery of overpayments of rent. Rogers CJ Com D accepted that the council had changed its position to its detriment by not obtaining a private valuation. This entitled the council to [324] defeat the *prima facie* right to restitution to the extent of the detriment suffered by reason of that change of position (1992), p 21.

In *Killham v Banque Nationale de Paris* (1994) Hedigan J considered that the defendant bank would have a defence to a claim in restitution against it arising out of its assignment of its security. His Honour said this (1994), p 50:

> Firstly, the assignment of the debenture itself constituted some alteration in position because the bank gave up its security. That security, in my judgment, must have at least realised, if exercised, the amount of the overpayment namely approximately $244,000 ... Its change of position in that respect was that instead of exercising its powers under the debenture, which I conclude would have enabled it to recover its debt, it would, if the plaintiff succeeded, be obliged to return the overpayment. In my judgment this constitutes a

change of position with detriment. It has never been argued by the plaintiff that the monies were not lawfully due to the bank.

It should be noted that his Honour's observations in this regard were *obiter*. In the event, the plaintiff's claim in that case failed.

In *Morgan Guaranty Trust Co of New York v Outerbridge* (1990), Osborne J in the Ontario High Court of Justice considered the change of position defence in a case in which the defendant's bank had mistakenly credited the sum of $150,000 to his account. The defendant was a solicitor. He believed that the sum had been paid into his account on behalf of a client. Acting on the strength of that belief he had handed over his files with respect to that client to new counsel believing that his account had been paid in full. Osborne J reviewed the authorities concerning the defence of change of position. In particular, he referred to the judgment of Goff J in *Barclays Bank Ltd v WJ Simms Son & Cooke (Southern) Ltd* (1979), p 535 together with a number of Canadian authorities and concluded (1979), p 551: 'if the defendant has changed his position so that it would be inequitable to require him to make restitution, then restitution will not be ordered.' His Honour went on to observe that the mere fact that the money or benefit conferred by the mistake has been spent is not sufficient to amount to a change in position, and in this respect he cited *Rural Municipality of Storthoaks v Mobil Oil Canada Ltd* (1975) and *Hydro Electric Commission of Township of Nepean v Ontario Hydro* (1982). His Honour accepted that the handing over of the defendant's files to new counsel had deprived him of the leverage that would have been immeasurably important in securing payment of the amount due to him on behalf of the client. In those circumstances his Honour was of the view that it would be inequitable for the defendant to be required to repay the monies to his bank.

I note that *Morgan Guaranty Trust Co of New York* was decided before *David Securities Pty Ltd* and was not referred by the majority in the course of a review of the Canadian authorities. As already noted, their Honours commented on the trend of Canadian and some United States decisions in which the defendant had been required to point to specific expenditure being incurred because of the payment.

In *David Securities Pty Ltd* the majority observed that it was not appropriate to give a detailed explication of the defence of change of position (1982), p 386. They noted that in *Lipkin Gorman v Karpnale Ltd* (1991) it was held [325] that English law should recognise the defence but, again, its scope had not been defined. In that case, Lord Bridge of Harwich observed (1991), p 558:

> I agree with my noble and learned friend, Lord Goff of Chieveley, that it is right for English law to recognise that a claim to restitution, based on the unjust enrichment of the defendant, may be met by the defence that the defendant has changed his position in good faith. I equally agree that in expressly acknowledging the availability of this defence for the first time it would be unwise to attempt to define its scope in abstract terms, but better to allow the law on the subject to develop on a case by case basis.

Lord Goff expressed the principle underlying the defence in this way (1991), p 579:

> In these circumstances, it is right that we should ask ourselves: why do we feel that it would be unjust to allow restitution in cases such as these? The answer must be that, where an innocent defendant's position is so changed that he will

suffer an injustice if called upon to repay or to repay in full, the injustice of requiring him so to repay outweighs the injustice of denying the plaintiff restitution.

I note that in Mason and Carter, *Restitution Law in Australia*[69] it is suggested that the broad statement of principle quoted above 'may be too flexible a view of the defence'.

I return to the principles which emerge from *David Securities Pty Ltd*. There is a *prima facie* right to recovery of monies mistakenly paid. The defence of change of position ensures that the enrichment of the recipient is prevented only in circumstances where it would be *unjust*. The central element of that defence is that the defendant acted to his or her detriment on the *faith of the receipt*. Such a defence is not made out where the defendant has simply spent the money received on ordinary living expenses.

In this case there was not one payment but rather over a period of some 87 weeks the appellant received periodic payments of $127. At the time of the receipt of each payment there was in existence a valid award of workers' compensation. On the faith of the receipt of those periodic payments throughout the period the appellant did not apply for or receive benefits to which on the magistrate's findings he was entitled.

The circumstance that the award payments were applied to meet the appellant's ordinary living expenses seems to me to overlook the detriment suffered by the appellant in not claiming social security benefits in reliance on the receipt of the workers compensation payments.

The defence of change of position assumes good faith on the part of the recipient. The magistrate's findings do not suggest this was an issue. Further, there is nothing to suggest that the weekly payments of $127 were in excess of the weekly payments which the appellant would otherwise have received in the way of Department of Social Security benefit payments.

I consider having regard to the magistrate's findings ... that the appellant has made out his defence of change of position within the broad statement of principle enunciated in *David Securities Pty Ltd*.

For these reasons I consider that the magistrate erred in law in concluding that the appellant had not established the defence of change of position.

Commentary

A broad approach was also taken to the defence of change of position in *Gertsch v Atsas* (1999) where Foster AJ approached the case 'in a broad fashion by weighing up the advantages and disadvantages accruing to [the defendant] from the receipt of the moneys and determining, thereby, whether she [was] in a position of nett detriment or nett advantage'. In particular, Foster AJ took into account the fact that, upon receipt of the mistaken payment, the defendant had given up paid employment in order to pursue a course of studies. The defendant had used nearly $70,000 of a $100,000 mistaken payment to pay off the mortgage on her home. Foster AJ held that the defendant had changed her

---

69   Mason and Carter, *Restitution Law in Australia*, 1995, para 2411.

position to the amount of $60,000 (in relation to the mortgage) as, if she had kept working for the relevant period, she would have reduced the mortgage debt to about $10,000 in any event. Thus, in respect of the payment of the mortgage, the plaintiff was entitled to claim a change of position to all but $10,000.[70]

The position in England is less certain. In *Scottish Equitable plc v Derby* (2001), p 826 (see extract, p 606)[71] the court suggested that the giving up of paid employment would amount to a change of position, however in *National Westminster Bank plc v Somer International (UK) Ltd* (2002) (see extract, p 583) Potter LJ stated that (p 215):[72]

> ... the defence of 'change of position' only protects actual reduction of the transferee's assets following receipt. A transferee who, in reliance upon a receipt, forgoes a realistic and quantifiable opportunity to increase his assets is not apparently protected.

It should be noted though that Potter LJ was concerned in that case with the defence of estoppel rather than change of position, and hence his comments were *obiter* only.

Anticipatory reliance

In *David Securities Pty Ltd v Commonwealth Bank of Australia* (1992), pp 385–86 (see extract, p 592) the High Court emphasised that the defendant must have changed position in reliance on the security of the receipt of the enrichment. This raises the question whether a defendant who changes position in *anticipation* of the receipt can rely upon the defence. There is conflicting authority on this question. In the following English case, *South Tyneside Metropolitan Borough Council v Svenska International plc* (1995) Clarke J refused to recognise the defendant's anticipatory reliance as a change of position.[73] However, in *Dextra Bank & Trust Company v Bank of Jamaica* (2001) (see extract, p 623), the Privy Council held that anticipatory reliance could amount to a change of position.

---

70 The application of a mistaken payment in discharge of a debt is not normally recognised as a change of position: see *Scottish Equitable plc v Derby* (2001), p 828 (see extract, p 606); *RBC Dominion Securities v Dawson* (1994) (see extract, p 609).

71 See also *Eastbourne BC v Foster* (2000).

72 Citing Fung and Ho, 'Change of position and estoppel' (2001) 117 LQR 14, p 17.

73 This decision was followed in *Hinckley & Bosworth Borough Council v Shaw* (2000).

South Tyneside Metropolitan Borough Council v Svenska International plc
[1995] 1 All ER 545 Queen's Bench Division (Commercial Court)

The plaintiff local authority entered into an interest rate swap agreement[74] with the defendant bank. Some payments were made both ways under the swap agreement however the House of Lords subsequently ruled in a separate decision that interest rate swap agreements entered into by local authorities were *ultra vires* and void. The local authority's payments exceeded the bank's payments by about £236,881, and the local authority sought restitution of this amount from the bank. Clarke J held that the net payment was recoverable by the local authority on the basis that there was no consideration for the local authority's payments. The bank, however, relied on the defence of change of position, arguing that it had entered into the swap agreement in good faith and had relied on the validity of the original swap agreement in entering into and maintaining hedging arrangements in order to limit the bank's risk on that agreement. The issue facing Clarke J was whether the defence of change of position extends to a situation where the alleged change occurs *before* the receipt of the money.

Clarke J: ... [564] In the context of a case such as this the defence is designed to protect the person who in good faith receives money which does not belong to him. If he thereafter alters his position in some way in which he would not have done if he had not received the money, as for example by buying the second hand car spoken of by Lord Templeman in *Lipkin Gorman* (1992), p 517; (1991), p 560, or if his position changes, as for example by the money being stolen as suggested above, it would not be just to require him to return the money to its owner.

[Counsel for the bank] submits that the same is or should be true where, as here, the money is accepted in good faith on the basis that the underlying transaction is valid. He gives a number of examples. One of them illustrates his point. A council employee who is about to retire is to be given a large bonus of say £10,000 which (unknown to either party) the council has no power to give. Then take two alternative cases. In the first, the employee spends £10,000 in his savings account on a holiday which he would not have taken but for the promised bonus, intending to replace the money in his savings account with the bonus. In the second, the employee receives the money and then spends it. In each case the invalidity of the bonus is only discovered after the payment has been made. [Counsel for the bank] submits that it makes no sense for the law to distinguish between those two cases. He adds a further variation. If the employee were paid by cheque and booked and paid for his holiday after receipt of the cheque but before the cheque was cleared he submits that it would be inequitable to deny him a defence.

There is obvious force in [counsel for the bank]'s submissions. However, [counsel for the local authority]'s response is that there is a distinction between the two cases. In the first, either [565] the employee is relying upon the implied promise or representation that the bonus will be paid and that it will be valid or he is acting

---

74 A swap agreement is an agreement between two parties where each agrees to pay the other on a specified date an amount of 'interest' calculated on a notional principal sum. The amount payable by one of the parties is calculated in accordance with a fixed rate of interest whereas the other party's liability is based on a floating rate of interest. Usually, each of the parties do not pay the sums owing, but rather the sums are offset and the party owing the higher amount pays the difference.

on the assumption to the same effect which is common to both parties. In the second, he is certainly relying upon substantially the same representation or assumption but he is also relying upon the fact of payment or, as Burrows puts it in *The Law of Restitution*[75] upon the security of the receipt. [Counsel for the local authority] submits that in so far as he relies upon the representation or assumption the only defence available to him would be one of estoppel. However, he submits that both in principle and on the authorities a plea of estoppel would fail. The reason is that the representation or promise that the transaction was valid and any assumption to the same effect would be void. Since, as the House of Lords held in *Hazell v Hammersmith and Fulham London BC* (1991) the transaction is *ultra vires* and void, it follows that any promise, representation or assumption to the contrary is also void. I accept that submission. It appears to me that in principle the one follows from the other. The submission is also in my judgment supported by the authorities.[76]

In my judgment in circumstances such as these the bank is not entitled to rely upon the underlying validity of the transaction either in support of a plea of estoppel or in support of a defence of change of position. That is because the transaction is *ultra vires* and void. It is for that reason that in a case of this kind, save perhaps in exceptional circumstances, the defence of change of position is in principle confined to changes which take place after receipt of the money. Otherwise the bank would in effect be relying upon the supposed validity of a void transaction ...

It does not however follow that the defence of change of position can never succeed where the alleged change occurs before the receipt of the money. I am conscious of the statement of Lord Goff that the defence should be developed on a case by case basis. Moreover, as [counsel for the bank] points out, the facts of *Lipkin Gorman* itself are an example of such a case.

That is because some of the bets placed by Cass were successful. Lord Goff considered three possible solutions: to allow the solicitors to recover the net amount received by the casino after taking account of all the winnings paid to Cass distributed over all the bets, to allow the solicitors to recover all the bets other than the winning bets or to allow them to recover nothing on the basis that the casino changed its position because it took a risk each time a bet was put on. The House of Lords chose the first of those possibilities.

[Counsel for the bank] submits that that decision is not consistent with a rule that only events occurring after receipt of the money by the defendant are relevant to the defence of change of position. That submission appears to me to be well founded in the light of Lord Goff's approach. Lord Goff held that in a case where a gambler wins the first bet but loses the second the amount of his winnings on the first bet should be deducted from the amount which he paid to the casino as his stake for the second bet. If there were a strict rule that only events since receipt of the money were relevant, the winnings on the first bet would not be a defence to a claim for the return of the second stake as money had and received. Yet the [566] House of Lords held that the casino was only liable to pay back the net amount

---

75 Burrows, *op cit*, fn 6, p 105.
76 See, eg, *Rhyl UDC v Rhyl Amusements Ltd* (1959); following *Ministry of Agriculture and Fisheries v Matthews* (1949). See also *Halsbury's Laws of England*, 4th edn, Vol 16, para 1043.

received from Cass overall regardless of which bets lost and which won and in what order. It is however plain that Lord Goff found this point difficult. He expressed his conclusion as follows (1992), p 536; (1991), pp 582–83:

> The inequity, as I perceive it, arises from the nature of gambling itself. In gambling only an occasional bet is won, but when the gambler wins he will receive much more than the stake placed for his winning bet. True, there may be no immediate connection between the bets. They may be placed on different occasions, and each one is a separate gaming contract. But the point is that there has been a series of transactions under which all the bets have been placed by paying the plaintiff's money to the casino, and on each occasion the casino has incurred the risk that the gambler will win. It is the totality of the bets which yields, by the laws of chance, the occasional winning bet; and the occasional winning bet is therefore, in practical terms, the result of the casino changing its position by incurring the risk of losing on each occasion when a bet is placed with it by the gambler. So, when, in such circumstances the plaintiff seeks to recover from the casino the amount of several bets placed with it by a gambler with his money, it would be inequitable to require the casino to repay in full without bringing into account winnings paid by it to the gambler on any one or more of the bets so placed with it. The result may not be entirely logical; but it is surely just.

It thus appears from that passage that Lord Goff recognised that a logical application of the principle would not have allowed the casino to rely upon earlier winning bets as a defence to a claim for the recovery of later bets, but that in the particular circumstances of the case it would have been inequitable to refuse to allow it to do so. That conclusion stemmed from Lord Goff's perception of the nature of gambling and in particular from his conclusion that there was a series of transactions entered into by Cass at the casino.

The highest that the point can be put in favour of the argument advanced by [counsel for the bank] is in my judgment that in the light of the actual decision in *Lipkin Gorman* there can be no rigid rule that events prior to receipt of the money or benefit are always irrelevant. Nevertheless, the earlier statements of principle in the speech of Lord Goff and in the statutes and authorities to which he refers support the conclusion that, save perhaps in exceptional circumstances, the defence of change of position is designed to protect a person who receives money in good faith and who thereafter changes his position in good faith so that it would be inequitable to require him to repay part or all of the money to its rightful owner.

But, however that may be as a matter of general principle, for the reasons which I have already given, there is in my judgment no justification for permitting the recipient to rely upon the understanding or supposition that a transaction is valid when in fact it is void. Moreover there is nothing in the decision or speeches in *Lipkin Gorman* to lead to any other conclusion ...

[567] In my judgment the position is that if a net payee can show that it has altered its position in good faith after receipt of money under a swap from the net payer it might in principle be entitled to rely upon the defence of change of position. What it cannot do is to rely upon the supposed validity of the transaction because the transaction is and has always been void ...

[568] *Application of defence to the facts*

[Counsel for the bank] has made it clear throughout his argument, both in his skeleton arguments and in his oral submissions, that the particular factors which the bank relies upon are that it entered into the swap in good faith, that it hedged (and continued to hedge) its position throughout and that (as he put it in his first skeleton), even if the hedging transactions could not themselves be regarded as a sufficient change of position, the supposed existence of the swap contracts, together with the supposed liability of the council to make payments on the due dates, continued until the matter was put beyond doubt by the decision of the House of Lords. In his second skeleton he submitted that it was of the essence of the bank's case that it relied upon the validity of the original swap contract in committing itself to its hedges and in maintaining its hedges day by day thereafter.

It follows from the conclusions of principle which I have stated above that that reliance does not afford the bank any defence of change of position since it involves relying, not upon the receipt of money, but upon the validity of a void transaction ...

The conclusion which I have reached also makes it unnecessary to reach a firm conclusion upon a further submission made by [counsel for the local authority], namely that the bank would not in any event be entitled to rely upon a change of position defence here because from the very beginning it took the risk that the swap would or might be void. I think that he makes that submission both on the basis that banks always take such risks and on the particular facts here because he says that the bank knew that there was such a risk when it entered into the swap in June 1988. I have already set out the relevant facts. Mr Clark [of the bank] knew that there was some risk but in common with others he reasonably regarded the risk as very small provided that reasonable precautions were taken. I am bound to say that I have some doubt whether it would be right to deny a council the right to recover net payments made to a commercial bank under a void contract where the bank knew that there was a risk that the transaction might be invalid, even if the risk was a very small one. However, in the light of the conclusions which I have already reached it is not necessary to give further consideration to this point and I shall not further lengthen this judgment by doing so ...

Commentary and questions

Why did Clarke J hold that the anticipatory reliance of the defendant did not amount to a change of position on these facts? What was the relevance to the decision of the fact that the contract under which payment was made was void? Did Clarke J consider that anticipatory reliance could *never* ground a successful change of position defence?

The principal case was followed in *Hinckley & Bosworth Borough Council v Shaw* (2000) where a local authority sought to recover redundancy payments that it had made to the defendant pursuant to an agreement that was beyond the power of the authority. An attempt by the defendant to rely on the defence of change of position was rejected on the basis that the defendant had changed his position: 'by virtue of his general financial position, which included reliance on the agreement ... rather than on any particular payments made under the unlawful parts of the agreement.' However, on a case with similar facts,

Eastbourne Borough Council v Foster (2000),[77] the court refused to follow *Hinckley*. The Court said the following about the defendant's change of position:

I believe that as each month from September 1998 went by a payment went into [the defendant's] account and that as month succeeded month he must have believed, with justification, that the payments would continue and could be relied on to do so. If at any stage he had been told the truth, that no further payment could lawfully be made because the agreement was void, what would he have done? It is not possible to predict this with any confidence, save to say he would certainly have done something. He could have hammered on the Council's door with at least a moral case for some form of reinstatement or non-enhanced redundancy payment. He could have looked for a job elsewhere. He could have considered the position of those who had advised him. The one thing he would not have done is nothing at all. Though the distinction is a fine one I believe it is right to say that in refraining from doing these things he was relying not on the expectation of future benefits under the agreement (such as the enhanced benefits due in September 1999) but on the stream of payments themselves.

Dextra Bank & Trust Company v Bank of Jamaica (unreported) 26 November 2001 Privy Council

Dextra Bank (Dextra) drew a cheque in favour of the Bank of Jamaica (BOJ) for US$2,999,000 intending to lend that sum to the BOJ on the security of a promissory note. In fact, both Dextra and the BOJ were the subject of a fraud by third parties, and the BOJ never had requested a loan. The fraudsters advised two authorised representatives of the BOJ that they were expecting a cheque drawn in favour of the BOJ in the amount of $US3 million, and asked that the representatives buy foreign currency in the names of third parties. The representatives of the BOJ purchased the foreign currency and paid it to the third parties, and did this before they had received the Dextra cheque. The Dextra cheque was subsequently received and banked by the BOJ. When it discovered the fraud, Dextra commenced proceedings against the BOJ to recover the amount of the cheque on the basis of conversion and mistake of fact. The BOJ raised the defence of change of position, however Dextra argued that this defence was not available as the BOJ had made the payments to the third parties before the Dextra cheque was received by it. Dextra argued that the payments of money in anticipation of the receipt of the cheque did not amount to a valid change of position. The Board rejected Dextra's claim based on a mistake of fact, but nevertheless went on to discuss in *obiter* the parties' arguments regarding the defence of change of position.

The Board: ... *Change of Position*

[T]heir Lordships propose to consider whether, against this background, the BOJ would, if necessary, have been able to rely on the defence of change of position. The submission of the BOJ has been that it would have been entitled to do so because the Dextra cheque was purchased by the BOJ's authorised agents on its behalf in good faith and the BOJ reimbursed their accounts in full, and that this rendered it inequitable for Dextra thereafter to recover the money so received by the BOJ as having been paid under a mistake of fact. Dextra has responded that the

---

77 There was an appeal to the Court of Appeal ([2001] EWCA Civ 1091 (unrep) 11 July 2001, English Court of Appeal), but not on the change of position point.

actions so relied on by the BOJ as constituting a change of position were performed by the BOJ before it received the benefit in question, and so amounted to what has been called 'anticipatory reliance' and as such could not amount to a change of position by the BOJ for the purposes of the law of restitution. Dextra's argument is that, for the act of the defendant to amount to a change of position, it must have been performed by the defendant in reliance on the plaintiff's payment, which cannot be the case if it was performed by him before he received the relevant benefit.

Anticipatory reliance

The question whether anticipatory reliance of the kind just described can amount to an effective change of position has been much debated in the books. Their Lordships have studied the relevant material with interest and profit, and have also been much assisted by the arguments of counsel.

Their Lordships start with the broad statement of principle by Lord Goff of Chieveley in *Lipkin Gorman v Karpnale Ltd* (1991), p 580:

> At present I do not wish to state the principle any less broadly than this: that the defence [of change of position] is available to a person whose position has so changed that it would be inequitable in all the circumstances to require him to make restitution, or alternatively to make restitution in full.

Their Lordships add that, although the actual decision in that case does not provide any precise guidance on the question now under consideration, since it was based upon the peculiar nature of gaming transactions, nevertheless the Appellate Committee in that case appears to have adopted a broad approach based on practical justice, and to have avoided technicality, see in particular (1991), pp 581–83 *per* Lord Goff of Chieveley.

The response by the BOJ to Dextra's argument has been that it is no less inequitable to require a defendant to make restitution in full when he has *bona fide* changed his position in the expectation of receiving a benefit which he is fact receives, than it is when he has done so after having received that benefit. Of course, in all these cases the defendant will *ex hypothesi* have received the benefit, because the context is an action by the plaintiff seeking restitution in respect of that benefit. For those who support the distinction, however, their reply appears to be that, whereas change of position on the faith of an actual receipt should be protected because of the importance of upholding the security of receipts, the same is not true of a change of position in reliance on an expected payment, which does not merit protection beyond that conferred by the law of contract (including promissory estoppel).

Their Lordships confess that they find that reply unconvincing. Here what is in issue is the justice or injustice of enforcing a restitutionary claim in respect of a benefit conferred. In that context, it is difficult to see what relevant distinction can be drawn between: (1) a case in which the defendant expends on some extraordinary expenditure all or part of a sum of money which he has received from the plaintiff; and (2) one in which the defendant incurs such expenditure in the expectation that he will receive the sum of money from the plaintiff, which he does in fact receive. Since *ex hypothesi* the defendant will in fact have received the expected payment, there is no question of the defendant using the defence of change of position to enforce, directly or indirectly, a claim to that money. It is surely no abuse of language to say, in the second case as in the first, that the defendant has incurred the expenditure in reliance on the plaintiff's payment or, as is sometimes said, on the faith of the payment. It is true that, in the second case, the defendant relied on the payment being made to him in the future (as well as relying on such payment, when made, being a valid payment); but, provided that his change of position was in good faith, it should provide, *pro tanto* at least, a good defence because it would be inequitable to require the defendant to make restitution, or to make restitution in full. In particular it does not, in their Lordships' opinion, assist to rationalise the defence of change of position as concerned to protect security of receipts and then to derive from that rationalisation a limitation on the defence. The defence should be regarded as founded on a principle of justice designed to protect the defendant from a claim to restitution in respect of a benefit received by him in circumstances in which it would be inequitable to pursue that claim, or to pursue it in full. In any event, since (as previously stated) the context of a restitutionary action requires that the expected payment has in any event been received by the defendant, giving effect to 'anticipatory reliance' in that context will indeed operate to protect the security of an actual receipt.

Before leaving this topic their Lordships think it right to refer to the decision of Clarke J in *South Tyneside BC v Svenska International* (1955). There the defendant bank had entered into *ultra vires* swap transactions with the plaintiff local authority, but the bank had also entered into hedging transactions which would substantially cancel out its potential liability to the local authority under the swap transactions. In the result the local authority was the net payer under the void swap transactions, and claimed repayment of the money so paid by it. The bank was held liable to make restitution, but claimed to be entitled to set off the losses incurred by it under the hedging transactions on the ground that it had changed its position in good faith in reliance on the validity of the original swap contract by committing itself to the hedging transactions and by maintaining them thereafter. The local authority submitted that the bank should not be entitled to set off those losses, because it changed its position before receiving the payments in question. Clarke J's conclusion on this point was as follows (1955), p 565d–g:

> In my judgment in circumstances such as these the bank is not entitled to rely upon the underlying validity of the transaction either in support of a plea of estoppel or in support of a defence of change of position. That is because the transaction is *ultra vires* and void. It is for that reason that in a case of this kind, save perhaps in exceptional circumstances, the defence of change of position is in principle confined to changes which take place after receipt of the money. Otherwise the bank would in effect be relying upon the supposed validity of a void transaction ... It does not however follow that the defence of change of position can never succeed where the alleged change occurs before receipt of the money ...

It follows that the exclusion of anticipatory reliance in that case depended on the exceptional facts of the case; though it is right to record that the decision of Clarke J has been the subject of criticism.[78]

---

78 See, eg, Goff and Jones, *The Law of Restitution*, 5th edn, 1998, pp 823–24.

Questions

What reasons did the court give for its conclusion that anticipatory reliance could amount to a change of position? Did the court agree with Clarke J in the *South Tyneside* case that to give effect to anticipatory reliance would be to allow the defendant to rely on the promise or representation that the enrichment would be received, rather than the *receipt* of the payment? Did the court disapprove of the decision in the *South Tyneside* case?

Good faith and reliance on the faith of the receipt

The defence of change of position is available only to those who have acted in good faith, in the sense of an honest belief in an entitlement to the enrichment.[79] Accordingly, the defence will not be available to a defendant who had knowledge of the facts entitling the plaintiff to restitution at the time of the change of position.

There is some judicial support for the view that constructive knowledge is sufficient to preclude good faith reliance. In *Mercedes-Benz (NSW) Pty Ltd v ANZ and National Mutual Royal Savings Bank Ltd* (1992), Palmer J held that a defendant who changes his or her position with knowledge of such facts as would reasonably raise a suspicion that the payment was made under a mistake or was induced by fraud, would not be acting in good faith. The factors that Palmer J said should be taken into account in determining whether the defendant had constructive notice of the mistake or fraud are:

> [F]irstly, whether there is any part of the payment transaction known to the recipient which, on its face, calls into question whether the payment is fraudulent or mistaken; and secondly, whether the recipient, in the light of the surrounding circumstances of the payment transaction known to him, is reasonably required to investigate, or is reasonably justified in failing to investigate, the questionable factor. Amongst the circumstances bearing upon the requirement to investigate a questionable factor raising suspicion of fraudulent or mistaken payment would be, for example, whether the payment was known or reasonably believed to be the subject of prior checking and authorisation by the payer, whether the payment was of an unusual or usual nature, whether it was a unique transaction or one of very many similar transactions occurring in the course of the recipient's ordinary business day, and, probably most importantly, whether the questionable factor was so unusual that one could say, at least, that it was more likely than not that there was a fundamental mistake involved.

The view of Palmer J that constructive notice will defeat the defence is also supported by the *dictum* of Clarke J in *South Tyneside MBC v Svenska International plc* (1995) (see extract, p 619), though academic opinion remains divided.[80]

---

79 *David Securities Pty Ltd v Commonwealth Bank of Australia* (1992), pp 385–86, 406 (see extract, p 592); *Lipkin Gorman v Karpnale Ltd* (1991), p 580 (see extract, p 595).

80 For the view that constructive notice suffices, see Birks, 'Change of position: the nature of the defence and its relationship to other restitutionary defences', in McInnes (ed), *Restitution: Developments in Unjust Enrichment*, 1996, p 58; Key, 'Change of position' (1995) 58 MLR 505, pp 514–5. For the contrary view, see Goff and Jones, *The Law of Restitution*, 5th edn, 1998, p 826.

In the following case, *State Bank of New South Wales v Swiss Bank Corp* (1995) the court went even further and held that a defendant will only be able to rely on the defence where the defendant's belief in the entitlement to the money was *induced by the plaintiff.*

State Bank of New South Wales v Swiss Bank Corp (1995) 39 NSWLR 350
Court of Appeal of New South Wales

Essington Ltd defaulted on a loan it had obtained from the defendant bank (State Bank of New South Wales) and Edwards, the managing director of Essington Ltd, advised State Bank of New South Wales that steps were being taken towards refinancing the loan. Edwards innocently met with a rogue called Sothirasan who offered to arrange a refinancing of the loan in return for a commission. Sothirasan then entered into a fraudulent arrangement with Singh, an employee of the plaintiff bank (Swiss Bank) whereby Singh caused the records of Swiss Bank to falsely show the receipt of $20 million on overnight deposit from State Bank of New South Wales, to be repaid the following day. The next day Swiss Bank duly transferred to State Bank of New South Wales the amount of $20 million by an electronic transfer. The Clearing House Inter Bank Payment System message accompanying the transfer did not contain any reference to Essington Ltd or to Essington Ltd's account number, or anything else to indicate that Essington Ltd was the intended recipient of the money. Although the money was paid into an account of State Bank of New South Wales which was mainly used for transactions for customers, the transfer appeared *ex facie* to be a bank to bank transaction. Nevertheless State Bank of New South Wales concluded that the money belonged to Essington Ltd and credited it to Essington Ltd's account. State Bank of New South Wales reached this conclusion because Edwards had informed West, an officer of State Bank of New South Wales, that an amount of $20 million would that day be received for the credit of Essington Ltd's account. The fraud was not discovered by Swiss Bank until a week later by which time State Bank of New South Wales had disbursed most of the money in accordance with the instructions of Essington Ltd. Swiss Bank commenced proceedings against State Bank of New South Wales to recover the money. The issue before the Court of Appeal was whether State Bank of New South Wales could rely upon the change of position defence, in particular whether it had acted on the faith of the receipt.

The court: ... [355] State Bank of New South Wales submitted that the central issue in the case was whether it adversely changed its position by paying away the funds believing in good faith that they belonged to Essington Ltd so that it would be unjust to require repayment to Swiss Bank, or whether it paid them away unreasonably, in contravention of proper banking practice and in disregard of the Clearing House Inter Bank Payment System rules so that the change of position defence was not available.

State Bank of New South Wales recognised that a finding of belief in good faith depended on its having, at the time of the receipt, information additional to that in the Clearing House Inter Bank Payment System message which led it to conclude that the money was for Essington Ltd's account. State Bank of New South Wales did not shirk this element in its case. The judge found that the Clearing House Inter Bank Payment System message showed that the payment was bank to bank, to State Bank of New South Wales as principal. State Bank of New South Wales challenged this conclusion on the ground that the message showed that the payment was to be credited to the TOS account which was mainly used for transactions for customers. We are content, without deciding upon this contention, to deal with State Bank of New South Wales's submissions on the basis that the payment it received was for the benefit of a customer.

State Bank of New South Wales submitted that it had paid away the funds believing in good faith that Essington Ltd was entitled to them. That 'good faith' must, in our opinion, be linked to the payee acting on the *faith of the receipt* (repeating the emphasis in *David Securities Pty Ltd v Commonwealth Bank of Australia* (1992), p 385). This is inherent in the passage where the italicised words appear. The court held that the critical moment for the payer is when payment is made, for it is then the unjust enrichment occurs. The critical moment for the payee is the moment of the change of position but that, in order to be relevant, must be on the faith of the receipt.

It seems to us that knowledge derived otherwise than from the payer cannot be relevant in deciding whether a change of position by the payee occurred on the faith of the receipt. This view is supported by the following considerations. [356] If the funds had been transmitted to State Bank of New South Wales without explanation it could not possibly have treated itself as entitled to use them for any purpose without further inquiry from Swiss Bank. Similarly if the amount had been transmitted with a message saying 'This is repayment of your overnight loan with interest' State Bank of New South Wales could only have sent the money back for it knew it had made no such loan. In either case State Bank of New South Wales could not have been acting on the faith of the receipt if it disbursed the funds to third parties. A bank which receives a mistaken payment and disburses it can only bring itself within the change of position defence if it shows that at the time of disbursement it knew or thought it knew more than the fact of receipt standing alone. This must be information which, if true, would entitle the payee to deal with the receipt as it did and that information must have come from the payer.

State Bank of New South Wales seeks to rely on information derived from Essington Ltd on whose instructions it paid the money away. Putting it slightly differently, State Bank of New South Wales's case is that the Clearing House Inter Bank Payment System message told it the money was for its TOS account, it took that to mean for a customer, and for reasons which had not come from Swiss Bank and were extraneous to the Clearing House Inter Bank Payment System message, it decided that Essington Ltd was the customer. This was a mistake brought about by the fraud of Messrs Sothirasan and Singh. The disbursement of Swiss Bank's money by State Bank of New South Wales was not on the faith of the receipt from Swiss Bank but on the faith of what Mr Edwards had told Mr West. It may be granted that State Bank of New South Wales was acting in good faith in the sense that it was not intending to defraud anyone, but the good faith it had to show was that it had 'acted to its detriment on the faith of the receipt' and in our opinion its own case shows that it did not do this.

Looked at on its own terms State Bank of New South Wales's submission has an element of the fantastic about it. It says that it received this very large payment with a message from Swiss Bank saying: 'Credit this to the account you keep for customers.' Nothing more than that. State Bank of New South Wales's case involves the propositions: (a) that it was for it to decide which customer should be credited; and (b) that it credited Essington Ltd because Essington Ltd asked it to do so. On the judge's findings what State Bank of New South Wales did was not dishonest but on any anybody's view it was not sensible and in our opinion it was not done on me faith of the receipt.

During the hearing of the appeal State Bank of New South Wales produced, in answer to a notice to produce which operated as a *subpoena*, the original Clearing House Inter Bank Payment System message annotated in the handwriting of Mr Nardella the officer at SBN New York who authorised the acceptance of the funds. State Bank of New South Wales had not previously been able to locate this document. Swiss Bank tendered this document which became Exhibit 1 in the appeal. Mr Nardella wrote on the Clearing House Inter Bank Payment System message 'Credit: Regular A/C F/O Essington Ltd A/C No 137–327 *per* Chris West 12/7/89' (meaning 7 December 1989). This notation demonstrates that the Clearing House Inter Bank Payment System message did not authorise the payment of the funds to Essington Ltd, and that State Bank of New South Wales was not acting on the faith of the message when it made that payment.

[357] This conclusion means that State Bank Of New South Wales fails on its main ground of appeal and makes it unnecessary to consider the challenge raised by State Bank of New South Wales to the judge's conclusion that the Clearing House Inter Bank Payment System message informed SBN New York that the money was being paid to State Bank of New South Wales as a principal.

What we have said also shows why we do not accept the contention by State Bank of New South Wales that the relevant question was: 'Did State Bank of New South Wales suspect that there was anything wrong with the Clearing House Inter Bank Payment System from Swiss Bank and refrain from making inquiry of Swiss Bank lest it discover that Swiss Bank did not intend to make that payment?' Certain authorities were cited in support of that submission but the short answer is supplied by the passage from *David Securities* upon which this judgment is founded. That makes it clear that the question this court must ask is whether State Bank of New South Wales changed its position on the faith of the receipt. If the answer to the question proposed by State Bank of New South Wales was 'yes', this would mean that the answer to what we regard as the correct question should be 'no'. However, it does not follow that if the answer to the question posed by State Bank of New South Wales were no that it would have disbursed the moneys on the faith of the receipt ...

Commentary

The court refused to allow the defence of change of position at least partly because it considered that the State Bank of New South Wales had acted unreasonably in crediting the money to its customer's account without first making further inquiries of Swiss Bank. In determining whether the defendant had acted unreasonably, the court looked solely to the information provided by the plaintiff, and discounted information derived from other sources.

It is arguable that the suggested limitation on the defence of change of position based on whether or not the defendant was induced by the plaintiff to believe in an entitlement to the money is unjustified. A representation by the plaintiff that the defendant is entitled to keep the money is a requirement for estoppel purposes, but not for the purposes of change of position.[81] Whilst inducement by the plaintiff, or lack thereof, might be one relevant factor in determining whether the defendant relied in good faith on the receipt, it should not be the determining factor. Despite considerable academic criticism of *State Bank of New South Wales v Swiss Bank Corp*,[82] it was followed by the Supreme Court of Queensland in the following decision.[83]

Port of Brisbane Corporation v ANZ Securities Ltd (unreported) 6 December 2001
Supreme Court of Queensland

Hinterdorfer, an accountant employed by the plaintiff for a number of years, embezzled $4.5 million of the plaintiff's money. Hinterdorfer incorporated a company, Windermere, in a tax haven jurisdiction. Stobie was a representative of Sovereign Trusts, an organization specialising in providing tax advice about tax havens. Hinterdorfer approached Stobie and authorised Sovereign Trust to act on behalf of Windermere in investing funds (to be embezzled from the plaintiff). Stobie approached the defendant, a licensed securities dealer, and indicated that he would like to trade some shares on behalf of his principal, Windermere. Windermere, through Hinterdorfer, appointed the defendant as trustee and authorised it to transact business on behalf of Windermere in its own name. Stobie later sent the defendant a fax reading:

> AUD 4 million should be credited to the ANZ Securities Ltd Trust Account by the end of today. Can you utilise these funds to purchase the following stock ... Commonwealth Bank receipts ... Westpac ... at market price ... Any surplus funds ... from these purchases are to be deposited into the V2 account. I will call you later today to confirm everything is acceptable.

The V2 account was a cash management account in Windermere's name that the defendant could operate. On the same day of the fax, Hinterdorfer fraudulently obtained a cheque payable to the defendant in the amount of $4.5 million drawn on the plaintiff's bank, and deposited it in the defendant's trust account. On the basis of the fax from Stobie, the defendant recorded the money as being held on behalf of Windermere. The defendant then dealt with the proceeds of the cheque in accordance with the instructions of Sovereign Trust, acting as principal for Windermere. These instructions were to remit the money overseas into bank

---

81 McInnes, 'The defence of change of position in the law of restitution' (1996) 24 ABLR 313, p 315.

82 Chambers, 'Change of position on the faith of the receipt' [1996] RLR 103, pp 107–08; McInnes, 'The defence of change of position in the law of restitution' (1996) 24 ABLR 313, p 315; Bryan, 'The liability of banks to make restitution for wrongful payments' (1998) 26 ABLR 93, p 98.

83 The South Australian Supreme Court has also accepted the correctness of the decision: *Orix Australia Corporation Ltd v M Wright Hotel Refrigeration Pty Ltd* (2000).

accounts owned and operated by Windermere. The fraud was later discovered and the plaintiff managed to recover about $2 million of the embezzled money. The plaintiff commenced proceedings to recover the balance, as well as interest, on the basis of mistake. The defendant relied on, *inter alia*, the change of position defence.

Chesterman J: ... The defence [of change of position] is not available to a defendant who has changed his position in bad faith, that is in spending the money with knowledge of the facts entitling the plaintiff to restitution, and it is only available to an innocent recipient of money, not one who has received it by wrongdoing. *Lipkin Gorman v Karpnale Ltd* (1991), p 580. A defendant acts in bad faith if he spends the money knowing that he is not entitled to it but 'snatched at the opportunity to use what he knew that he should return. That is a species of dishonesty'.[84]

...

There is no doubt the defendant acted in good faith. I accept the evidence of Mr Stewart [an employee of the defendant] that the defendant commenced buying and selling securities for Windermere utilising the moneys stolen from the plaintiff because he believed that the money had been lawfully credited to the defendant's trust account by or on behalf of Windermere. Mr Stewart had been told by Mr Stobie that $4.5m would be paid to the defendant's trust account on 20 August. On that day a deposit in that very amount was made. Mr Stewart assumed that it was Windermere's money.

There is also no doubt that the defendant was an innocent recipient of the money.

The plaintiff submits that the defendant did not change its position on the faith of the receipt. It relies upon *State Bank of New South Wales Limited v Swiss Bank Corporation* (1995) a decision of the Court of Appeal of the Supreme Court of New South Wales on facts which are relevantly indistinguishable from this case. The court held that a bank which receives a mistaken payment has not acted on the faith of the receipt if it disburses the money in a manner not authorised by the payer. In that case, as in this, the disbursement was made in reliance on information provided by a client. [Chesterman J discussed the *State Bank* case and then continued:]

The defendant seeks both to distinguish *State Bank* and to criticise it.

The distinction between *State Bank* and this case is said to be that the payer was not the plaintiff but Windermere, on whose instructions the defendant acted.

The submission is that when Hinterdorfer deposited the cheque at the ANZ bank in Brisbane he did so on behalf of Windermere. This characterisation of the act is said to follow from the fact that Hinterdorfer intended the money to go to Windermere and deposited it to an account which would result in the moneys being applied for Windermere's benefit. He had no authority from the plaintiff to deal with the moneys in such a way so he cannot have been acting on its behalf.

The submission continues:

---

84   See Birks, 'Change of position: the nature of the defence and its relationship to other restitutionary defences', in McInnes (ed), *Restitution: Developments in Unjust Enrichment*, 1996, p 58.

Hinterdorfer had no authority to make (the) deposit for the plaintiff and ... he or ... his company made the payment, although with stolen property ... the payment was just as much that of Windermere as it would have been with the use of cash stolen from the plaintiff or with the use of cash or a cheque obtained from an account into which funds stolen from the plaintiff had been placed.

I cannot accept this analysis of the facts, or the conclusion that Hinterdorfer was the payer.

The plaintiff's cheque, dishonestly obtained by Hinterdorfer, and the proceeds of it collected from the plaintiff's bank and deposited to the defendant's trust account, always remained the property of the plaintiff. O'Connor J pointed out in *Black v S Freedman & Co* (1910):

> Where money has been stolen, it is trust money in the hands of the thief, and he cannot divest it of that character. If he pays it over to another person, then it may be followed into that other person's hands.

Lord Templeman in Lipkin Gorman endorsed the proposition and noted its applicability 'to a claim for money had and received'.

No doubt Mr Hinterdorfer intended to deprive the plaintiff of its money by paying it into Windermere's account with the defendant. He was not authorised by the plaintiff to make the payment. But the money was never his. He may have been the instrument by which the payment was made, but he was not the payer. The plaintiff made the payment, unwittingly because of Mr Hinterdorfer's fraud, but it, not its dishonest servant, was the payer.

State Bank cannot be distinguished on this basis.

I should accept the decision as authoritative unless I think it is plainly wrong. I do not. There is much force in the remarks of the court (1995), p 356:

> Looked at on its own terms [*State Bank's*] submission has an element of the fantastic about it. It says that it received this very large payment with a message ... : 'Credit this to the account you keep for customers.' Nothing more than that. [*State Bank's*] case involves the propositions: (a) that it was for it to decide which customer should be credited; and (b) that it credited Essington Ltd because Essington Ltd asked it to do so. On the judge's findings what State Bank ... did was not dishonest but on anybody's view it was not sensible and in our opinion it was not done on the faith of the receipt.

Moreover the approach finds support in some older cases. *Perel v Australian Bank of Commerce* (1923) was in form an action in equity to redeem a mortgage. The real issue was whether the mortgagee bank could debit the mortgagors' account with the proceeds of cheques they had drawn in favour of the bank. The cheques were duly signed and were payable to the bank. A dishonest employee presented the cheques to the bank and persuaded a bank officer to give him in exchange a bank cheque payable to the employee's nominee. The funds were misappropriated. It was the proceeds of these cheques which were the disputed items in the account. Street CJ in Eq said (1923), pp 75–76:

> The cheques drawn in favour of the bank conveyed no information as to the wishes of the drawers. Cheques might be drawn in that form for more reasons than one, and without some further instructions the bank could not know what was required of it ... A cheque drawn in that way is merely a direction to the

bank to hold the amount for which it is drawn and to await further instructions as to its disposal. [Counsel] described the bank, not inaptly, as a trustee of the money in such a case. Then comes the question, for whom is it a trustee or to whom is it to look for instructions? I think that there can be only one answer. It must take its instructions from the drawers of the cheque ... There may be cases in which, either from the course of dealing or from other circumstances, a bank may safely assume that valid authority has been conferred on someone else by the drawer of a cheque to give instructions on his behalf, but a banker is not justified in parting with his customer's money without his instructions ...

There are passages to the same effect in *James v Oxley* (1938). Latham CJ said, at pp 443–44:

... a partner in the defendant firm, became aware that the defendants had £425 in their bank account which did not belong to them. He was content to accept the statement of Rees ... that it would be properly dealt with if it were paid out by cheques drawn in favour of the two named persons. The statement of Rees was false. Any inquiry which proceeded beyond Rees would have resulted in the discovery that the statement was false ... But the defendants, knowing that they had money belonging to some other person ... took the responsibility of dealing with it in such a way that Rees got it.

... The defendants were held liable because they dealt with the money otherwise than on the instructions of the persons entitled to it. It was pointed out that the only sure way of ascertaining who was entitled to the money was to ask the person who paid it into the defendant's account.

It is objected that these cases predate by many years the recognition of the defence of change of position to a claim for moneys had and received. I do not regard the cases, which were decided by very great judges, as obsolete. It is not to be supposed their Honours would have overlooked an obvious injustice if one in truth existed. All the cases require of a recipient of money, which is to be paid by it to a third party, is that he should ask the payer to identify the party.

The defendant points to academic criticism of *State Bank*. In *Lender Liability* by O'Donovan at 459 there is a complaint that the courts' 'interpretation of the change of position defence appears to require that the payee rely on a representation of the payer' which 'has no place in an enrichment-related defence'. It is asserted that the defence should be made out if the defendant acted in good faith and incurred a detriment after he had received the payment. It appears to be thought unfair that State Bank should have to repay the money when it was the victim of a sophisticated fraud.

I do not find this persuasive. The amount of money involved was very large indeed. It is surely not too much to require the recipient of such a sum to have a proper basis for deciding to whom it should be paid. If it did so there would have been no victim. The money would have gone back to Swiss Bank.

In 'Change of position on the faith of the receipt' by Chambers (1996), pp 107–08, the author criticises the statement in *State Bank* 'that knowledge derived otherwise than from the payer cannot be relevant in deciding whether a change of position by the payee occurred on the faith of the receipt'. He argues instead that the 'important issue must always be whether the defendant honestly and reasonably believes it was entitled to the mistaken payment. The source of that belief can only be relevant to the question whether that belief was honestly and reasonably held'. The requirement that a defendant act reasonably as well as honestly seems to introduce the consideration of whether the defendant acted carelessly in making the payment. The author, I think inconsistently, disputes this conclusion. He writes:

> There is no basis for denying the defence to *State Bank* because it acted carelessly ... where the defendant has acted honestly ... the enrichment is erased ...

I find it difficult to disagree with the court in *Swiss Bank* that it was not sensible to disburse the money to a customer merely because the customer claimed it and without inquiry of the only person who could authoritatively indicate for whom the money was intended. I also find it difficult to understand how a defendant can act reasonably and carelessly with respect to a payment.

Building upon Dr Chambers' article, Professor Bryan wrote:[85]

> ... there is a confusion [in *State Bank*] between the identification of the acts constituting the change of position, which must be in reliance on the validity of the money received, and the inquiry into the bank's good faith, where evidence from any reliable source ought to be admissible. If a question is raised as to whether a bank is entitled to credit a payment to a customer's account evidence derived from the customer ... will often be as relevant ... as anything said or done by the ... payer.

I cannot discern the confusion alleged to appear in the judgment. That aside, Professor Bryan appears to accept, at least implicitly, that the defence is not available unless an inquiry was made of a 'reliable source' as to how the money should be spent. There is acceptance of the view that carelessness in the recipient is fatal to the defence.

A similar criticism is made by Mr McInnes in 'The defence of change of position in the Law of Restitution'[86] where it is complained that:

> The insistence that the defendant's expenditure be based on information ... derived from the plaintiff is misguided. Effectively, the Court ... has introduced into the defence of change of position a requirement that the payee rely upon a representation by the payer ... Significantly, however, the defence of estoppel is distinguishable from the defence of change of position ...

The author also accepts that:

> ... the weight of caselaw and academic opinion appears to lean to the view that the law should not come to the aid of those who fail to reasonably assist themselves ...

I do not accept that the 'insistence' is 'misguided'. The payments in *State Bank*, and in this case, were ambiguous in the sense that the recipients knew the money was not intended for them and the payments did not indicate for whom they were intended. The State Bank, and the defendant here, could not act on the faith of the payment without ascertaining how the money should be dealt with. The only certain way to resolve the ambiguity was to ask the payer to identify the intended payee.

---

85 (1998) 26 Australian Business Law Review 93, p 98.
86 (1996) 24 Australian Business Law Review 313, p 315.

Professor Birks wrote in 'Change of position':[87]

> The real difficulty comes with the recipient who ought to have known but did not make the inquiries which a reasonable person would have made ... there is no very strong case for protecting the security of the receipts of those who fail to take reasonable precautions on their own account. It seems best to bar the defence ... wherever a defendant ought through reasonable inquiries to have discovered the defect in his entitlement. If this course is taken it will be necessary to bear in mind that in many contexts the standard of an inquiry ... may not be very exacting ... It would arguably be better ... if in commercial contexts the doctrine were kept under control, not by absolute exclusion, but by sensible application of the standard to everyday realities of commercial practice.

The comment was not directed at the particular situation which arises in this case, and which arose in *State Bank*, namely where a payment is made to a recipient who is to deal with the money on behalf of another, or to pay it over to that other and the circumstances of the payment do not identify the intended beneficiary. They appear to have particular application to the situation. Of the authors to whose work I have referred only Dr O'Donovan contends that honesty is the only precondition to the availability of the defence. The others (although Dr Chambers is ambiguous on the point) accept that the recipient of a mistaken payment must take reasonable care to ascertain how the money is to be applied. If this be correct the criticism of *State Bank* comes down to a quibble whether it was reasonable for the defendant to act upon Essington Ltd's claim to the money, or whether the exercise of reasonable care required it to ask the payer whether the money was intended for Essington Ltd.

There may be cases, as Street CJ pointed out in *Perel*, where the recipient of a payment may safely assume 'that valid authority has been conferred on someone else by the (payer) ... to give instructions on his behalf'.

This may be the same as saying that the defence should be available where the disbursement occurs in reliance on 'reliable' information from someone other than the payer. But the assumption will only be 'safe', the information can only be 'reliable' if it is reasonable in the circumstances so to regard it.

I am far from sure that this understanding of the defence emerges from *Lipkin Gorman* or *David Securities*. Nevertheless I turn to consider whether it was reasonable for the defendant to act on the basis of Mr Stobie's intimation that the deposit was for Windermere's benefit. [Chesterman J examined the evidence and concluded:]

I am satisfied that it was not reasonable for the defendant to act on Mr Stobie's intimation that the money was Windermere's. If the defence of change of position requires a recipient to act reasonably in spending the money paid to it, I am satisfied the defendant did not act reasonably. I would also hold that the defence is not available because, applying the ratio in *State Bank* the defendant did not act on the faith of the receipt because it did not inquire of the payer, the plaintiff, how the money should be disbursed. Accordingly, I find that the defendant's second ground for resisting the plaintiff's claim in restitution is not made out.

...

---

87 *Op cit*, fn 84, p 58.

Questions

According to Chesterman J, why should the defence of change of position be denied where the defendant has not made inquiries of the payer? Is it necessary, according to this decision, that the defendant have acted, not only honestly, but also reasonably in disbursing the payment?

Change of position and 'comparative fault'

In the United States and in New Zealand the courts undertake a 'comparative fault' analysis to determine the extent to which the defendant should be able to rely on a change of position defence. On this approach, the court examines the respective faults of both parties with a view to apportioning the loss between them.[88] The change of position defence will be denied completely where the defendant was more at fault than the plaintiff: see *Waikato Regional Airport v Attorney General* (2001), p 715. The Privy Council examined the 'comparative fault' approach in the following case, *Dextra Bank & Trust Company v Bank of Jamaica,* and concluded that it should not be accepted.

Dextra Bank & Trust Company v Bank of Jamaica (unreported) 26 November 2001
Privy Council

The facts are stated at p 623.

The Board: ... *The relevance of fault to the defence of change of position*

It was a further submission of *Dextra* that, in cases in which the defendant invokes the defence of change of position, it is necessary to balance the respective faults of the two parties, because the object of the defence is to balance the equity of the party deprived with that of the party enriched.

Their Lordships approach this submission as follows. First, they cannot help observing that the courts below appear to have formed the view that the fault of Dextra greatly outweighed the fault, if any, of the BOJ. If that is right, this submission will, if successful, do little to advance Dextra's case. Even so, their Lordships turn to consider the point as a matter of principle.

They take as their starting point the statement of the law in *Lipkin Gorman v Karpnale Ltd* (1991), where it was explained by Lord Goff of Chieveley that, for a defendant to be able to rely on his own conduct as giving rise to a change of position, he must have changed his position in good faith (1991), pp 579F–G and 580C. No mention was made by him of the relevance of fault. On the other hand Lord Goff was careful to state that 'nothing should be said at that stage to inhibit the development of the defence of change of position on a case by case basis, in the normal way' (1991), p 580C, which left it open to the courts to consider matters such as the relevance of fault on a subsequent occasion. Their Lordships make the initial comment that, if fault is to be taken into account at all, it would surely be unjust to take into account the fault of one party (the defendant) but to ignore fault

---

88 US Restatement of Restitution, para 142(2); *Thomas v Houston Corbett* (1969); *National Bank of New Zealand Ltd v Waitaki International Processing (NI) Ltd* (1999); *Waikato Regional Airport v Attorney General* (2001), p 715. See generally Grantham and Rickett, 'Change of position and balancing the equities' [1999] RLR 158.

on the part of the other (the plaintiff). The question therefore is whether it should be relevant to take into account the relative fault of the two parties.

In support of its submission, Dextra was able to invoke the law in two common law jurisdictions. First, in the United States of America, the Restatement of Restitution provides, in paragraph 142(2), that:

> Change of circumstances may be a defense or a partial defense if the conduct of the recipient was not tortious and he was no more at fault for his receipt, retention or dealing with the subject matter than was the claimant.

The Restatement of Restitution is a remarkable work, of which the Reporters were two much respected jurists, Professor Warren A Seavey and Professor Austin W Scott. It was however a pioneering work, and much water has flowed under the bridge since its publication in 1937. In particular another much respected American expert in the law of restitution, Professor JP Dawson, was later to express his regret at the inclusion in paragraph 142(2) of the provision relating to relative fault,[89] referred to by Professor Birks.[90] Professor Dawson's comment on the relevant part of paragraph 142(2) of the Restatement is as follows:

> The introduction of these complex themes would have been, I believe, a real disservice. Fortunately they have been disregarded in court decisions.

Second, in New Zealand a defence of change of position was introduced by statute, in s 94B of the Judicature Act 1908, introduced into that statute in 1958. The statutory provision requires the court to have regard to all possible implications in respect of other persons when considering whether to deny relief, on the ground of change of position, in an action for the recovery of money paid under a mistake of law or fact. That provision was considered by the Court of Appeal of New Zealand in *Thomas v Houston Corbett & Co* (1969) in which the Court held that it was entitled to look at the equities from both sides (1969), p 164, lines 13–14 *per* North P and, taking a number of matters into account including, it appears, matters going beyond 'fault or neglect in the strict sense' on the part of the respondents (1969), p 178, line 4 *per* McGregor J, held that the claim must be reduced. The quantum of the relief was treated as a matter of discretion on which opinions might differ (1969), p 178, line 26, also *per* McGregor J. More recently, in *National Bank of New Zealand Ltd v Waitaki International Processing (NI) Ltd* (1999) on which see the valuable note by Professor Grantham and Professor Rickett the Court of Appeal of New Zealand has given further consideration to s 94B. Following the decision of the Judicial Committee of the Privy Council in *Goss v Chilcott* (1996) the Court of Appeal concluded that s 94B did not exclude the operation of the common law defence of change of position, but went on to conclude that the common law defence was, like the defence under s 94B, an 'equitable' defence which required the court to undertake a 'balancing of the equities' by assessing the relative fault of the parties and apportioning the loss accordingly.

Their Lordships are however most reluctant to recognise the propriety of introducing the concept of relative fault into this branch of the common law, and indeed decline to do so. They regard good faith on the part of the recipient as a

---

89 (1981) 61 Boston UL Review 565, 571 *et seq*.

90 Birks, 'Change of position and surviving enrichment', in Swadling (ed), *The Limits of Restitutionary Claims: A Comparative Analysis*, 1997, p 41.

sufficient requirement in this context. In forming this view, they are much influenced by the fact that, in actions for the recovery of money paid under a mistake of fact, which provide the usual context in which the defence of change of position is invoked, it has been well settled for over 150 years that the plaintiff may recover 'however careless [he] may have been, in omitting to use due diligence': see *Kelly v Solari* (1841). It seems very strange that, in such circumstances, the defendant should find his conduct examined to ascertain whether he had been negligent, and still more so that the plaintiff's conduct should likewise be examined for the purposes of assessing the relative fault of the parties. Their Lordships find themselves to be in agreement with Professor Peter Birks who, in his article already cited on 'Change of position and surviving enrichment',[91] rejected the adoption of the criterion of relative fault in forthright language. In particular he stated (citing *Thomas v Houston Corbett & Co* (1969)) that the New Zealand courts have shown how hopelessly unstable the defence [of change of position] becomes when it is used to reflect relative fault. Certainly, in the case of *Thomas*, the reader has the impression of judges struggling manfully to control and to contain an alien concept.

For these reasons their Lordships are unable to accept the arguments advanced by Dextra in answer to the reliance by the BOJ on the defence of change of position.

...

Questions

What reasons did the court give for rejecting the 'comparative fault' approach to change of position? What arguments do you think might be raised in favour of the 'comparative fault' approach?

MINISTERIAL RECEIPT

An agent who receives an enrichment on behalf of a principal will be personally liable to return the money in restitution, unless the agent can establish a defence.[92] One defence that is specifically tailored to agents is the defence of ministerial receipt.[93] This defence is available to recipients who have received money as an agent on behalf of a disclosed[94] principal, and who pay over the

---

91 Birks 'Change of position and surviving enrichment', in Swadling (ed), *The Limits of Restitutionary Claims: A Comparative Analysis*, 1997, p 41.

92 *Australia and New Zealand Banking Group Ltd v Westpac Banking Corp* (1988), p 673 (see the following extract); *Bunge (Australia) Pty Ltd v Ying Sing* (1928); *Kleinwort, Sons & Co v Dunlop Rubber Co* (1907).

93 For a detailed examination of the defence see Bryan, 'The liability of banks to make restitution for wrongful payments' (1998) 26 ABLR 93, pp 99ff. In actual point of fact, the doctrine of ministerial receipt is not a defence, but a mechanism of determining the proper person to be sued: *Portman Building Society v Hamlyn Taylor Neck (A Firm)* (1998), p 207 (see extract, p 35).

94 The principle does not apply to an undisclosed principal: *Portman Building Society v Hamlyn Taylor Neck (A Firm)* (1998), p 207 (see extract, p 35).

enrichment to the principal without notice of the basis of the plaintiff's claim.[95] In this situation, the agent is treated as a 'mere conduit-pipe',[96] and the plaintiff must look to the principal for recovery.

The leading authority in Australia on ministerial receipt is *Australia & New Zealand Banking Group Ltd v Westpac Banking Corporation* (1988) (see the following extract) where the defence was applied to a bank that received a mistaken payment of money on account of a customer and applied the money in honouring cheques drawn on the account and in reducing the customer's overdraft.

Australia and New Zealand Banking Group Ltd v Westpac Banking Corp
(1988) 164 CLR 662 High Court of Australia

A meat company (Jakes) had an account with a branch of the Westpac Bank. At the relevant time the account was overdrawn in the amount of $67,000. A customer presented to ANZ a cheque in favour of Jakes for $14,000, but, by reason of a clerical error, ANZ credited Jakes's account with Westpac for $114,000. By the time ANZ notified Westpac of the error, Westpac had applied the money in reducing the overdraft and in honouring a number of Jakes's cheques. Jakes paid back only $2,500 of the $100,000 before going into liquidation. ANZ brought an action against Westpac to recover the overpayment, however Westpac sought to rely on the defence of ministerial receipt. Both parties acted on the basis of concessions made by Westpac that the reduction of the overdraft and the payment of certain cheques which could have been dishonoured by Westpac at the time it was notified of the mistake should be ignored for the purposes of determining whether the moneys had been applied. As a result of these concessions it was accepted by Westpac that it had not applied $17,021 of the overpayment and that it was liable to return this amount.

Mason CJ, Wilson, Deane, Toohey and Gaudron JJ: ... [673] The *prima facie* liability to make restitution is imposed by the law on the person who has been unjustly enriched. In the ordinary case of a payment of money, that person will be the payee. However, when the person to whom the payment is directly made receives it as an intermediary (eg, as agent for a designated principal), there may [674] be uncertainty about the identity of the actual recipient of the benefit at the moment of payment. If the circumstances are such that the intermediary is to be seen as being himself the initial recipient of the benefit, his *prima facie* liability will ordinarily be displaced when he has handed the money received on to the person for whom he received it. In such a case he has, in the event, not retained 'the benefit of the windfall' but been 'a mere conduit-pipe'[97] and 'the only remedy is to go against the principal'.[98] A more difficult case arises where the intermediary has not made a physical payment of money to, or on behalf of, the person for whom

---

95 *Australia and New Zealand Banking Group Ltd v Westpac Banking Corp* (1988), p 674 (see following extract); *East India Co v Tritton* (1824), p 289 [107 ER 738]; *Holland v Russell* (1861) (affirmed (1863) [122 ER 365]); *Gowers v Lloyds and National Provincial Foreign Bank Ltd* (1938).

96 *Continental Caoutchouc & Gutta Percha C v Kleinwort Sons and Co* (1904), cited in *Australia and New Zealand Banking Group Ltd v Westpac Banking Corp* (1988), p 674 (see following extract).

97 See *Continental Caoutchouc & Gutta Percha Co v Kleinwort, Sons, and Co* (1904) *per* Collins MR.

98 *Per* Greene MR, *Gowers v Lloyds and National Provincial Foreign Bank Ltd* (1938), p 773.

the payment was received but has made a credit entry in his books in favour of that person. In such cases, the question will arise whether the benefit of the payment made under fundamental mistake has been wholly or partly retained by the intermediary or effectively passed on to the third person.[99] In answering that question, the courts will pay regard to the substance rather than to the form of what has occurred. Thus, the cases indicate that a mere book entry which has not been communicated to the third party or which can be reversed without affecting the substance of transactions or relationships will ordinarily not suffice.[100] It must appear that the third party has effectively received the benefit of the payment with the consequence that the *prima facie* liability to make restitution has become his. It will subsequently be necessary to return to this aspect of the matter and consider whether the agent must also establish that he would sustain some overall detriment by reason of the mistaken payment if he were required to repay the amount to the payer and look to his principal for indemnity ...

[675] Westpac's concession to the effect that it bears the onus of displacing a *prima facie* liability to repay the amount of the overpayment makes it unnecessary to examine a question of some general importance which would otherwise arise. That question is whether the nature and scope of the business of a modern commercial bank in which both the lending and borrowing of money are activities to be pursued for profit and the fact that the receipt by a bank of a payment to the credit of a customer's account is ordinarily accompanied by the immediate application of the money on behalf of the customer (ie, by way of repayment of existing indebtedness or by way of loan to the bank) have the effect of qualifying the applicability to such a payment of any general rule that a person who receives a payment made under fundamental mistake of fact as an intermediary on behalf of another is under a *prima facie* liability to himself repay it. There is strong authority supporting the view, implicit in the concession, that a bank is, in such circumstances, in the same position as other agents.[101] Nonetheless, as Samuels JA pointed out in the Court of Appeal, it may be arguable that where a banker 'is subject to the anomalous responsibility exemplified in this case, it is for the party seeking repayment to establish the precise extent of its recovery'. That being so, we adopt Samuels JA's comment that 'the instant case should not be regarded as an authority for the contrary proposition'. Even accepting Westpac's concession for the purposes of the present case, however, the question remains whether it appears, on the evidence, that Westpac had, by the time it received [676] notice of ANZ's mistake, passed on the benefit of the overpayment to its principal (ie, Jakes) to the extent necessary if it is to be protected from liability to repay it.

[Their Honours examined the evidence and concluded that, on the basis of the concessions made by Westpac, the overpayment had been applied in accordance with Jakes's instructions except to the extent of $17,021. They continued at p 681:]

We turn to the consideration of [the] issue ... whether the fact that an agent has paid over money received by him as agent to, or on behalf of, his principal will of itself constitute a good defence to an action against him for recovery of money paid under a fundamental mistake.

---

99 *Continental Caoutchouc* (1904).

100 See, eg, *Buller v Harrison* (1777); *Cox v Prentice* (1815); *Colonial Bank v Exchange Bank of Yarmouth, Nova Scotia* (1886).

101 See, eg, *Kerrison v Glyn, Mills, Currie & Co* (1911); and *Admiralty Commissioners v National Provincial and Union Bank of England Ltd* (1922).

It was submitted on behalf of ANZ that the fact that Westpac had applied most of the overpayment in payments made on behalf of Jakes did not of itself constitute any defence in relation to the moneys so applied. The basis of that submission was the contention that the fact that an agent has applied funds received by him on behalf of a principal by payment to, or on behalf of, the principal does not, of itself, constitute a defence to an action for money paid under fundamental mistake of fact unless it appears that the agent would have suffered overall detriment if it had repaid the money at the time when it first received notice of the claim for repayment. The fact that Westpac had paid out most of the funds received on behalf of Jakes would not, so it was said, constitute such a detriment unless it appeared that Westpac would have been worse off by reason of the overpayment if it had, when it received notice of the mistake, repaid the $100,000 to ANZ, debited Jakes's account with that amount (on the basis that it was entitled to claim indemnity from Jakes), and dishonoured all of the cheques which it might then have dishonoured ...

There are several points at which this submission of ANZ is susceptible of legitimate criticism. For example, the proposition that a financial institution which makes profits by lending money at interest is better off whenever a corporate customer, which is not known to be insolvent, reduces its use of an overdraft facility which has been made available on commercial terms sounds somewhat strange in modern ears. The complete answer to the overall submission is, however, that its legal basis is mistaken for the reason that, on balance, both authority and principle support the conclusion that an agent who has received money on his principal's [682] behalf will, without more, have a good defence if, before learning that the money was paid under fundamental mistake, he has 'paid it to the principal or done something equivalent' thereto.[102] The rationale of such a general rule can be identified in terms of the law of agency and of notions of unjust enrichment. If money is paid to an agent on behalf of a principal and the agent receives it in his capacity as such and, without notice of any mistake or irregularity in the payment, applies the money for the purpose for which it was paid to him, he has applied it in accordance with the mandate of the payer who must look to the principal for recovery.[103] In those circumstances, the benefit of the payment has been effectively passed on to the principal who will be *prima facie* liable to make restitution if the payment was made under a fundamental mistake of fact. If the matter needs to be expressed in terms of detriment or change of position, the payment by the agent to the principal of the money which he has received on the principal's behalf, of itself constitutes the relevant detriment or change of position. In that regard, no relevant distinction can be drawn between payment to the principal or payment to another or others on behalf of the principal.[104]

[Their Honours then referred to various United Kingdom authorities, holding that they did not support ANZ's submission that the defendant must establish detriment, and concluded at p 684:]

---

102 See *Rahimtoola v Nizam of Hyderabad* (1958), pp 396, 406; Goff and Jones, *op cit*, fn 80, p 707.
103 See *Fitzpatrick v M'Glone* (1897) *per* Palles CB; and *Holland v Russell* (1861) *per* Cockburn CJ.
104 See *Gowers v Lloyds and National Provincial Foreign Bank Ltd* (1938), pp 773G–73H.

It follows that Westpac has a good defence to ANZ's claim to the extent that it had, on behalf of Jakes, paid out the proceeds of the telegraphic transfer before it first received notice of ANZ's mistake. Acting on the basis of the concessions made by Westpac in ANZ's favour, Westpac had, by that time, irretrievably paid out $82,978.32 of the overpayment of $100,000 in honouring cheques drawn on it by ANZ ...

Commentary and questions

Did the court consider that a bank should bear the onus of displacing a *prima facie* liability to repay money paid by mistake to a customer's account? Did the court consider that a bank is always enriched when it applies a mistaken payment in reduction of an overdraft facility?

The court recognises that the defence of ministerial receipt is only available to an agent who has effectively paid over the enrichment to the principal.[105] A 'mere book entry which has not been communicated to the third party or which can be reversed without affecting the substance of transactions or relationships will ordinarily not suffice'.[106] However, the defence will apply if the agent, on the strength of the book entry, has settled the account[107] or allowed the principal new credit.[108]

It is unclear whether ministerial receipt is simply a particular instance of the change of position defence. There is significant academic opinion that it is.[109] Burrows[110] and Swadling[111] argue, however, that ministerial receipt is independent of change of position, primarily on the basis that detriment is essential to change of position, whereas the principal case held that detriment is not relevant to ministerial receipt. However, it has been suggested that the change of position defence is not exclusively linked to detrimental reliance and could encompass a causally related outflow of enrichment.[112] The payment over of the money by the agent would clearly amount to a causally related outflow of enrichment and accordingly could, on this view, amount to a relevant change of position.[113]

---

105 *Australia and New Zealand Banking Group Ltd v Westpac Banking Corp* (1988), p 674. See also *Buller v Harrison* (1771); *Cox v Prentice* (1815); *Continental Caoutchouc & Gutta Percha C v Kleinwort Sons and Co* (1904); *Scottish Metropolitan Assurance Co Ltd v P Samuel & Co Ltd* (1923).

106 *Australia and New Zealand Banking Group Ltd v Westpac Banking Corp* (1988), p 674. See also *Buller v Harrison* (1771); *Cox v Prentice* (1815); *Colonial Bank v Exchange Bank of Yarmouth, Novia Scotia* (1886); *Scottish Metropolitan Assurance Co Ltd v P Samuel & Co Ltd* (1923).

107 *Holland v Russell* (1861) (affirmed (1863)).

108 *Bunge (Australia) Pty Ltd v Ying Sing* (1928); *Buller v Harrison* (1771).

109 Birks, *op cit*, fn 6, p 67; McInnes, 'The defence of change of position in the law of restitution' (1996) 24(4) ABLR 313, p 316.

110 Burrows, *op cit*, fn 6, pp 484–86.

111 Swadling, 'The nature of ministerial receipt', in Birks, *op cit*, fn 6, p 256.

112 Birks, *op cit*, fn 6, p 67; Bryan, 'The liability of banks to make restitution for wrongful payments' (1998) 26 ABLR 93, p 98.

113 Birks, *op cit*, fn 6, p 67; Bryan, 'The liability of banks to make restitution for wrongful payments' (1998) 26 ABLR 93, p 98.

In the following case the English Court of Appeal rejected an argument that ministerial receipt is a species of change of position.

Portman Building Society v Hamlyn Taylor Neck (A Firm) [1998] 4 All ER 202
English Court of Appeal

The facts are stated at p 35.

Millett LJ: ... [207] The general rule is that money paid (eg by mistake) to an agent who has accounted to his principal without notice of the claim cannot be recovered from the agent but only from the principal. The society submits that the agent's defence in such a case is a particular species of the change of position defence and does not avail the agent who has notice, actual or constructive, of the mistake which founds the plaintiff's claim.

I myself do not regard the agent's defence in such a case as a particular instance of the change of position defence, nor is it generally so regarded. At common law the agent recipient is regarded as a mere conduit for the money, which is treated as paid to the principal, not to the agent. The doctrine is therefore not so much a defence as a means of identifying the proper party to be sued. It does not, for example, avail the agent of an undisclosed principal; though today such an agent would be able to rely on a change of position defence.

The true rule is that where the plaintiff has paid money under (for example) a mistake to the agent of a third party, he may sue the principal whether or not the agent has accounted to him, for in contemplation of law the payment is made to the principal and not to his agent. If the agent still retains the money, however, the plaintiff may elect to sue either the principal or the agent, and the agent remains liable if he pays the money over to his principal after notice of the claim. If he wishes to protect himself, he should interplead. But once the agent has paid the money to his principal or to his order without notice of the claim, the plaintiff must sue the principal.

But all this is by the way, because the doctrine is concerned with the receipt of money by an agent from a third party and his subsequent payment of the money [208] to his own principal without the authority of the third party. Where the agent remains liable, it is not because a change of position defence is not available. It is because neither he nor his own principal was entitled to retain the money as against the third party who made the payment. The agent is liable to make restitution to the third party because he knew that his principal was no more entitled to the money than he was himself, *Ex p Edwards* (1884).

But in the present case, while the society's mandate remained unrevoked, the firm was entitled and bound to deal with the money in accordance with the mandate. In the present case there is no third party plaintiff. The firm was the agent of the society. It received the payment from its principal, held it to the order of its principal and applied it in accordance with its principal's instructions. The firm's defence is not that it has paid the money away to a third party but that it has dealt with it in accordance with the society's instructions, and thereby obtained a good discharge.

...

Commentary and questions

Why was the defence of ministerial receipt held not to apply on the facts of this case? According to Millett LJ, who is the payer entitled to sue when the agent has not paid over the money to the principal?

If ministerial receipt is not a species of change of position as suggested by Millett LJ in the principal case, an explanation of the basis of the defence is urgently required. Various explanations have been suggested,[114] the most common being that the receipt of the agent is the receipt of the principal so that the agent is not enriched by the receipt. This is not, however, a satisfactory explanation of the defence as it fails to explain why the defence is limited to the situation where the money has actually been paid over to the principal. The proper basis of the defence, if it is independent of change of position, requires explanation by the courts.[115]

In the following case it was held that the defence of ministerial receipt is not available to a recipient who receives the money as a trustee.

Port of Brisbane Corporation v ANZ Securities Ltd (unreported) 6 December 2001
Supreme Court of Queensland

The facts are stated at p 630.

Chesterman J: ... *Receipt as trustee*

The first argument arises from the fact that the money was paid into the defendant's trust account. That fact alone constitute the moneys trust moneys. They were to be held by the defendant on trust, putting to one side for the moment the question of the terms of the trust and the identity of the beneficiary. At no time did the defendant have a beneficial interest in the money which it held as bare trustee. The submission is, in effect, that the money was never paid *to the defendant* but to the beneficiary of the trust. Reliance was placed upon the cases in which an agent who receives money which becomes the subject of a restitutionary claim pays it to his principal before notice of the claim. In such cases the agent is not liable to repay the money to the plaintiff. In *Australia and New Zealand Banking Group Limited v Westpac Banking Corporation* (1987–88), p 682 the High Court said:

> If money is paid to an agent on behalf of a principal and the agent receives it in his capacity as such and, without notice of any mistake or irregularity in the payment, applies the money for the purpose for which it was paid to him, he has applied it in accordance with the mandate of the payer who must look to the principal for recovery ... In those circumstances, the benefit of the payment has been effectively passed on to the principal who will be *prima facie* liable to make restitution ...

See also *Gowers v Lloyds and National Provincial Foreign Banks Ltd* (1938).

---

114 The various explanations of the defence are discussed in Swadling, 'The nature of ministerial receipt', in Birks (ed), *Laundering and Tracing*, 1995, pp 253–60.

115 Swadling has suggested that the defence is based on an estoppel, arguing that the defence arises where the plaintiff makes the payment to a known agent and mandates that the money be paid over to the principal. The plaintiff would then be estopped from denying the agent's right to pay over: Swadling, 'The nature of ministerial receipt', in Birks (ed), *Laundering and Tracing*, 1995, pp 257–59.

It is noteworthy that the statement of principle makes it clear that the agent is liable to repay the money if he retains it, or has notice of the plaintiff's claim before paying the money to his principal or otherwise expending it on his principal's behalf. In such a case the agent could say what the defendant says, that he was not unjustly enriched because the money was never to benefit him: it was inevitably to be paid to the principal and could never confer a benefit on the agent. He is, nevertheless, liable to make restitution except in the special case postulated.

If the defendant's contention were right it would have the consequence that the money would have been irrecoverable by the plaintiff had it remained in the trust account. As long as the defendant was the bare trustee of the money it could say it had not been unjustly enriched because it had not been enriched at all.

I cannot accept this as a correct statement of the law. As between plaintiff and defendant the defendant was enriched. The plaintiff's money was in its account, if not its pocket. It cannot matter that as between the defendant and a third party the defendant may not be entitled to the benefit of the money.

The defendant cited no authority to support its submission. The absence of authority was said to be due to the emergent nature of the law of restitution which has not yet had to grapple with the situation of money paid to a trustee. I doubt this, and doubt even more that the defendant's proposal is a sensible way for the law to develop ...

The proposition is, I think, inconsistent with *James v Oxley* (1938) in which the defendant was a firm of solicitors into whose trust account was paid a cheque for £425. The money was obtained as a result of an employee misrepresenting to the plaintiff the purpose for which it was wanted. The employee, by further misrepresentation to the firm, obtained from it two cheques aggregating the amount of the first cheque. The proceeds were stolen. The plaintiff, the payer of the first cheque, recovered the money from the defendants in an action for money had and received. The solicitors were relevantly in the same position as the defendant here. The money was paid to them as trustees. Latham CJ said (1938), p 444:

> But the defendants, knowing that they had money belonging to some other person ... took the responsibility of dealing with it in such a way that Rees got it. They had no authority from the plaintiffs to do so. The result is that they have not duly accounted for moneys belonging to the plaintiffs which were in their possession. The position would have been exactly the same if the defendants had never paid the money out of their account to any person.

The High Court declared in *Westpac* (1987–88), p 673 that:

> ... receipt of a payment ... is one of the categories of case in which the facts give rise to a *prima facie* obligation to make restitution ...

There is an air of unreality about the defendant's submission. Later in these reasons I conclude that on receipt of the money the defendant held the sum on a resulting trust for the plaintiff. As the only beneficiary, and being absolutely entitled to the trust estate, the plaintiff could call for the immediate payment of the money to it. The law would be odd indeed if in equity the defendant must pay the money over but at law be entitled to retain it because the money was held on a trust, and one for the plaintiff at that.

To an extent one can sympathise with the notion which underlies the argument. In the ordinary case, if a recipient of money paid by mistake spends it he obtains some benefit, even if it be the purchase of transient pleasure. The position of the trustee is different. If it parts with the money it does so to benefit someone else and obtains no advantage for itself. The consequence is not, in my opinion, that payment has not been made to the trustee so that it has not been 'enriched'. If the trustee is to be excused from the obligation to repay, it must be on the basis that it changed position on receipt of the money so as to make it unjust to insist upon repayment.

...

Commentary

What reasons did Chesterman J give for denying the defence to a trustee? According to Chesterman J, does it make any difference whether or not the trustee has paid over the money to the beneficiary?

PROVISION OF CONSIDERATION

General

It is a defence to a restitutionary claim that the defendant has provided good consideration for the enrichment, for example by way of the provision of services. However, a mere executory consideration, in the sense of a promise to confer a benefit, is probably not 'good consideration' for these purposes. Nor, as the following decision illustrates, is a void consideration; that is, consideration provided under a void contract.

***David Securities Pty Ltd v Commonwealth Bank of Australia* (1992) 175 CLR 353**
High Court of Australia

The facts are stated at p 110.

Mason CJ, Deane, Toohey and Gaudron JJ: ... [379] The two 'defences' upon which the respondent relies in this court are, first, that the payments by the appellants were made for good consideration and, secondly, that in reliance upon receipt of the payments the respondent, in good faith, changed its position to its detriment. In the context of a mistake case, these 'defences' [380] were included in the well known formulation of Goff J in *Barclays Bank* (1980). His Lordship stated, at p 695:

> (1) If a person pays money to another under a mistake of fact which causes him to make the payment, he is *prima facie* entitled to recover it as money paid under a mistake of fact. (2) His claim may however fail if: (a) the payer intends that the payee shall have the money at all events, whether the fact be true or false, or is deemed in law so to intend; or (b) the payment is made for good consideration, in particular if the money is paid to discharge, and does discharge, a debt owed to the payee (or a principal on whose behalf he is authorised to receive the payment) by the payer or by a third party by whom

he is authorised to discharge the debt; or (c) the payee has changed his position in good faith, or is deemed in law to have done so.

The respondent argues that this is a case where the appellants, having accepted the benefit of performance by the respondent, now seek to recover part of the consideration promised for that performance, namely, the payments made referable to withholding tax. This argument and the respondent's attempt to analyse the facts on the broader basis of unjust enrichment rather than mistake specifically, already discussed, echo the view expressed by some writers that 'the true basal principle which enables recovery of money paid under a mistake, whether of fact or law, is "failure of consideration"'.[116] It is unnecessary in the present context to assess the merits of this argument because, as we have stated, the more traditional approach, exemplified by the judgment of Goff J in *Barclays Bank* and the decision of this court in *Westpac Banking Corporation*, specifically provides for the 'defence' of valuable consideration.

The respondent submits that it agreed to lend money to the appellants at the rate named in the loan agreements because of the appellants' agreement to pay the additional amounts pursuant to cl 8(b). If it had known that these additional amounts were not payable, the respondent argues, it would have negotiated a different interest rate to ensure that its net return reached the required level. By not being charged this higher interest, the appellants have received consideration for the bargain. In the circumstances, they should not be allowed to take advantage of the chance to recover some of the money they had agreed to pay.

The difficulty in evaluating this argument lies in the fact that it [381] depends primarily upon an assessment of the intention and purpose of the appellants at the time of entering the loan agreements and paying the additional amounts pursuant to cl 8(b). By stating that the appellants contracted to pay the additional amounts without adverting to the question of whether they could legally be forced to pay, the respondent effectively submits that the appellants voluntarily submitted to payment. This entails the conclusion that the appellants either cannot truly be said to have made a mistake, as they knew what they were agreeing to ... or waived inquiry into the issue and paid the additional amounts with the intention to effect an absolute transfer.

It is necessary to examine closely the terms of the loan agreement and the course of events preceding its signing in order to discover what the payer gave and expected to receive by way of consideration. It is only by doing this that it can be ascertained whether the payment of the additional amounts was absolute or conditional. If the payment was conditional, it was subject to the original or continued existence of a particular subject matter, such as an existing or future indebtedness or other obligation owed to the payee.[117] In this case, the evidence suggests that the appellants agreed to pay and actually paid the amounts representing withholding tax because the respondent represented that the withholding tax on interest payments must be met by the appellants. Such representations may have caused the appellants to believe that cl 8(b) took its form because of a general obligation on borrowers to pay the particular tax. When the matter is looked at in this light, it

---

116 Butler, 'Mistaken payments, change of position and restitution', in Finn (ed), *Essays on Restitution*, 1990, p 88; see also Matthews, 'Money paid under mistake of fact' [1980] 130 NLJ 587; *National Mutual Life Association v Walsh* (1987), pp 595–96.

117 *Porter v Latec Finance (Qld) Pty Ltd* (1964), p 205.

can be argued that the appellants agreed to pay the nominated interest rate as the price of the loan and further agreed to pay the additional amounts with which the Dee Why branch, as agent of the appellants, discharged what the appellants considered to be their own tax liability. However, the true situation was, of course, that the liability for payment of withholding tax fell upon the lender and that s 261 avoided any attempt to pass this burden on to a borrower in circumstances such as the present. The appellants thus had no indebtedness in respect of withholding tax, the discharge of which could form consideration for the payments under cl 8(b). Those payments were therefore not made for good consideration within the terms of the defence outlined in *Barclays Bank* and *Westpac Banking Corporation*.

The respondent, taking a different view of the contractual arrangements, asserts that all its pre-contractual statements concerning payment of withholding tax simply took the form of a [382] contractual offer, which the appellants were at liberty to accept or to reject. Viewed from the angle of contract formation between equal and experienced parties, this is undoubtedly true. But we are not concerned in this case with what a hypothetical, experienced commercial person believed he or she was contracting for; in order to decide whether the appellants in this case have received consideration for payment of the additional moneys, we must ask what these particular appellants, in all the circumstances, thought they were receiving as consideration. In this context, consideration means the matter considered in forming the decision to do the act, 'the state of affairs contemplated as the basis or reason for the payment'.[118] And, as we have stated, the 'state of affairs' existing in the appellants' minds was that the withholding tax was their liability.

So, in the context of failure of consideration, the failure is judged from the perspective of the payer. In *Rover International Ltd v Cannon Film Ltd* (1989), p 923,[119] Kerr LJ stated:

> The question whether there has been a total failure of consideration is not answered by considering whether there was any consideration sufficient to support a contract or purported contract. The test is whether or not the party claiming total failure of consideration has in fact received any part of the benefit bargained for under the contract or purported contract.

On the other hand, there has been an insistence that the failure of consideration be *total*. The law has traditionally not allowed recovery of money if the person who made the payment has received any part of the 'benefit' provided for in the contract.[120] However, as the passage already quoted from *Rover International Ltd* demonstrates, the notion of total failure of consideration now looks to the benefit bargained for by the plaintiff rather than any benefit which might have been received in fact. Thus, in *Rowland v Divall* (1923), the plaintiff succeeded in an action for repayment of the purchase price of a car he had bought from the defendant, unaware that the car had been stolen before it came into the defendant's possession. The defendant resisted the claim with the argument that the plaintiff could not prove total failure of consideration because he had used the

---

118 Birks, *An Introduction to the Law of Restitution*, rev edn, 1989, p 223.
119 See also *Fibrosa Spolka Akcyjna v Fairbairn Lawson Combe Barbour Ltd* (1943), p 48 *per* Viscount Simon LC.
120 *Hunt v Silk* (1804); *Whincup v Hughes* (1871).

car for several months. The Court of Appeal, however, [383] dismissed this argument on the ground that the plaintiff had not received 'any part of that which he contracted to receive – namely, the property and right to possession' (1923), p 507.

Similarly, in *Rover International Ltd* itself, the plaintiff succeeded in its claim for restitution of payments made to the defendant even though the defendant had performed some of its obligations under the contract. The plaintiff was to dub and distribute films provided to it by the defendant and receive a share of the box office receipts as its payment. The plaintiff was also required to make substantial payments to the defendant in advance of recovering its share of the receipts. The defendant supplied the films to the plaintiff and the plaintiff made the pre-payments before breaching the contract. The plaintiff was then able to recover the pre-payments on the basis that the delivery and possession of the films were not what the plaintiff had bargained for; the 'relevant bargain' was the opportunity to earn a substantial share of the gross receipts.

In cases where consideration can be apportioned or where counter-restitution is relatively simple, insistence on total failure of consideration can be misleading or confusing. In the present case, for instance, it is relatively simple to relate the additional amounts paid by the appellants to the supposed obligation under cl 8(b) of the loan agreements. The appellants were told that they were required to pay withholding tax and the payments that they made were predicated on the fact that, by so doing, they were discharging their obligation. Such an approach is no different in effect from the cases under the old statutes of usury whereby a borrower could recover from the lender the *excess interest* which the lender was prohibited from stipulating or receiving.[121]

In this case, the bank must prove that the appellants are not entitled to restitution because they have received consideration for the *payments which they seek to recover*. It does not avail the bank to argue that the appellants were provided with the loan moneys agreed. Indeed, the severability of the loan agreement into its relevant parts would seem to be accepted by the bank for it submitted that the appellants' consideration for agreeing to pay the additional amounts under cl 8(b) was the bank's agreement not to charge a higher interest rate. In circumstances where both parties have impliedly acknowledged that the consideration can be 'broken up' or apportioned in this way, any rationale for adhering to the traditional rule requiring *total* failure of consideration disappears.

[Their Honours then turned to consider the change of position defence. For the relevant extract, see p 592.]

Commentary and questions

On what basis did the bank argue that it had provided good consideration for the mistaken payment? Was this argument successful?

The court indicated that the correct approach to determining whether the defence of good consideration is made out is to inquire whether the defendant commenced the performance that was bargained for by the plaintiff. This

---

121 Eg, *Bosanquett v Dashwood* (1734).

approach has been criticised by commentators,[122] who point out that the principles determining whether a total failure of consideration has occurred for the purpose of establishing a *prima facie* claim have no relevance where the question is whether the defendant has a good defence for having provided something of value in exchange for the enrichment received.

Mason and Carter take the view that the defence of good consideration serves to reduce the claim *pro tanto* by the value of the consideration given,[123] however this view may not be supported by the joint judgment in the principal case. Their Honours approached the matter from the perspective of total failure of consideration, an all-or-nothing approach.[124] Although this approach has been criticised,[125] it appears their Honours were concerned to ensure that plaintiffs seeking the recovery of money under an ineffective contract could not use the mistake rule in order to circumvent the considerable body of jurisprudence underlying the total failure of consideration principle. There is other authority supporting the view that the defence is a complete one.[126]

There are three particular applications of the more general defence of good consideration: compromise, discharge of debt and *bona fide* purchase.

Compromise

A plaintiff who has paid money to the defendant pursuant to a contract of compromise to settle a claim, cannot subsequently recover the money on the basis of mistake where it is subsequently discovered that the claim was without foundation.[127] In *David Securities Pty Ltd v Commonwealth Bank of Australia* (1992), p 395 Brennan J emphasised that the mistake of law doctrine cannot be used to set aside a contract of compromise:

> When a claim is settled by accord and satisfaction, a payment made in satisfaction is made in discharge of an obligation created by the accord: it is unaffected by any mistake as to the validity of the claim compromised. Accordingly, a person who makes a payment pursuant to a contract of compromise, in the mistaken belief that she is legally liable to the payee, will be unable to recover the compromise payment upon discovering the mistake. The payee will have provided good

---

122 Birks, 'Modernising the law of restitution' (1993) 109 LQR 164 at 167; Mason and Carter, *Restitution Law in Australia*, 1995, pp 862–63; Liew, 'Mistaken payments – the right of recovery and the defences' (1996) 7 Bond Law Review 95, pp 107–08.

123 Mason and Carter, *Restitution Law in Australia*, 1995, pp 855, 862.

124 At least where counter-restitution or severance is not a simple matter.

125 Birks, 'Modernising the law of restitution' (1993) 109 LQR 164 at 167; Mason and Carter, *Restitution Law in Australia*, 1995, p 863; Liew, 'Mistaken payments – the right of recovery and the defences' (1996) 7 Bond Law Review 95, pp 107–08.

126 In *National Mutual Life Association of Australia Ltd v Walsh* (1987), Clarke J treated the defence as a complete defence (pp 595–96). See also *Killham v Banque Nationale de Paris* (1994) where Hedigan J considered the extent of the value given for the purpose of applying the defence of change of position, but not the defence of good consideration.

127 *Wigan v Edwards* (1973); *Da Costa v Firth* (1766); *Callisher v Bischoffsheim* (1870); *Kleinwort Benson Ltd v Lincoln City Council* (1998), pp 564–65; *Hydro Electric Commission of Township of Nepean v Ontario Hydro* (1982), p 218.

consideration by agreeing not to pursue the claim. The payer will be able to recover the money only if the contract of compromise is vitiated, for example because of fraud, duress, or undue influence.

Two cases illustrate this principle. In *Prudential Assurance Co Ltd v Breedon Pty Ltd* (1994) the insured under a life insurance policy was entitled to surrender the policy and receive 'cash surrender value', less the amount of any debts owed to the insurer. The insured opted to surrender the policy and the insurer paid an amount as surrender value. It was subsequently discovered by the insurer that it had miscalculated the amount to which the insured was entitled, and it sought to recover the overpayment on the basis that it had been paid under a mistake of fact. The claim was unsuccessful as the Full Court of Victoria held that the parties had concluded a new and binding contract upon the cancellation of the policy, and that in return for the receipt of the surrender value the insured had given good consideration by agreeing that all claims under the policy were fully discharged and satisfied. *Prudential Assurance* was followed in *CIC Insurance Ltd v Tancredi* (1995). This case involved an attempt by an insurer to recover money paid in settlement of a claim on the basis of mistake of fact. The insurer had paid out on a motor vehicle insurance claim, unaware that the insured was driving with a blood alcohol level over the prescribed legal limit. Pursuant to the settlement the insured signed a release which contained a condition that the policy was discharged. Nathan J accepted that the insurer had paid the money under a causative mistake of fact, however held that the insured could make out the defence of provision of good consideration on the basis of the principles laid down in *Prudential Assurance*.

Discharge of debt

The defendant is entitled to raise as a defence the fact that the plaintiff's payment discharged a debt owed to the defendant. The discharge of the debt constitutes good consideration, as the defendant has lost the right to sue upon the debt. As the following case illustrates, the defence arises even though the debt that is discharged was owed by a third party, not by the plaintiff.

Aiken v Short (1856) 1 H & N 210; 156 ER 1180 Exchequer

The facts are stated at p 97.

Pollock CB: ... [214] The bank had paid the money in one sense without any consideration, but the defendant had a perfect right to receive the money from Carter, and the bankers paid for him. They should have taken care not to have paid over the money to get a valueless security, but the defendant has nothing to do with their mistake. Suppose it was announced that there was to be a dividend on the estate of a trader, and persons to whom he was indebted went to an office and received instalments of the debts due to them, could the party paying recover back the money if it turned out that he was wrong in supposing that he had funds in hand? The money was, in fact, paid by the bank, as the agents of Carter.

Platt B: ... The action for money had and received lies only for money which the defendant ought to refund *ex æquo et bono*. Was there any obligation here to refund? There was a debt due to Short, secured by a bond and a supposed equitable charge by way of collateral security. The property on which Short had the charge was conveyed by Carter to the bank. [215] Short having died, the defendant, his executrix, applied to George Carter for payment of the debt due to her husband, the testator. Carter referred her to the bank, who paid the debt, and the bond was satisfied. The money which the defendant got from her debtor was actually due to her, and there can be no obligation to refund it.

Commentary

The principal case was followed by a majority of the High Court of Australia in *Porter v Latec Finance (Qld) Pty Ltd* (1964). HH Gill was the owner of certain property. His son, LH Gill, borrowed money from Porter by fraudulently impersonating his father, and purported to give a mortgage over the land to Porter by forging his father's signature. Subsequently LH Gill approached Latec Finance for a new loan and this loan was also secured by a forged mortgage over the father's property. The moneys advanced by Latec were paid to Porter by Latec's solicitors to enable the discharge of the first mortgage. Upon discovering the fraud by LH Gill, Latec sought recovery of the advance from Porter. This claim was dismissed by a bare majority of the court on the basis that the payment by Latec's solicitors was made on behalf of LH Gill rather than Latec itself. Accordingly, the payment by Latec operated to discharge the debt owed by LH Gill to Porter, giving Porter a valid defence of discharge of debt.[128]

Platemaster Pty Ltd v M&T Investments Pty Ltd [1973] VR 93
Supreme Court of Victoria

The plaintiff commenced an action against the defendant for a *quantum meruit*. In those proceedings the defendant raised a counter-claim and a set-off arising out of a different transaction, claiming the recovery of money paid under a mistake of fact. The relevant payment was made by the defendant to the plaintiff for the reconditioning of a piece of machinery which it was subsequently discovered belonged to a different company, Space Equipment Co. The reconditioning had taken place on the orders of Walker, the managing director of the defendant. The defendant argued that it would not have paid for the reconditioning had it not believed that it owned the machinery. The defendant acted as the marketing agent for Space Equipment Co, and had sold the relevant piece of machinery to that company.

Gowans J: ... [96] At the outset it is necessary to remember that the circumstances of money being paid under a mistake of fact is merely an element in the cause of action for money had and received to the use of the party making the payment. The payment must be made in such circumstances as to give rise in law to a promise or obligation to repay. The view of Lord Mansfield in *Moses v Macferlan* (1760), that the action lies for money which *ex æquo et bono* the defendant ought to refund has been regarded as too sweeping, but his *dictum* that it does not lie for

---

128 See *Ngamwasusiri v Murray* (1993).

money paid to a person who has a claim to be paid even though the claim is statute barred or otherwise unenforceable by rules of procedural law, has not so far as I am aware been challenged, and it would not be consistent with that *dictum* or with principle that a payment could be recovered by reason of a mistake of fact when it had been made in satisfaction of a debt due and owing.[129] That would lead to a circuity of action which the law does not tolerate.

As Hamilton, LJ, said in *Baylis v Bishop of London* (1913), approved by Atkinson J in *Transvaal v Delagoa Investment Co Ltd* (1944): 'The question is whether it is conscientious for the defendant to keep the money, not whether it is fair for the plaintiff to ask it back.'

It seems to me then that the first inquiry must be as to whether there was a debt actually due by the defendant to the plaintiff in respect of which the payment was made. That depends (apart from ratification) on whether the order for the work was given by a person having authority on behalf of the defendant to give it.

There is no proof whatever that the defendant's managing director had no authority to request the plaintiff to do the work. For all that appears Walker could have been authorised to give the order by a resolution of the board of directors of the defendant company. But in any case I think it is quite clear that it would be within the implied authority of a managing director of a company to give an order for the reconditioning of a machine in respect of which his company was the marketing agent even though it did belong to someone else who was its selling principal, where it was considered necessary to recondition the machine in order to put it in a saleable condition. The evidence as to the relationship between the firm and the company, the condition of the machine, the activities of the defendant's officers, the notations on the invoice, and the fact of payment is ample to justify the necessary inferences to support the view of the matter just expressed. It is said that there is nothing to show that Walker in giving the order for the work purported to act on behalf of the defendant company and not for himself or Space Equipment Co. This inverts the onus of proof. But in any event the subsequent acts of the defendant's officers in relation to the work and the act of Walker in passing the invoice and that of Wilson in signing the cheque justify an inference that Walker was purporting to act for the defendant company.

My conclusion is that this evidence shows that the defendant had incurred a debt to the plaintiff, as set out in the invoice, and by the cheque the defendant paid that debt. It was money to which the plaintiff was entitled. On this view of the matter, the moneys paid could not be recovered even if there were a mistake of fact by the defendant which was of a relevant character ...

Commentary

The defence of discharge of debt was also applied in *Griffiths v Commonwealth Bank of Australia* (1994). The applicant borrowed money from the Commonwealth Bank (the 'bank') which was secured by a mortgage over property and a deposit of $100,000 with the bank. The applicant authorised the bank to set off any amount of the deposit against the debt. Subsequently, the

---

129 See *Aiken v Short* (1856); *Krebs v World Finance Co Ltd* (1958).

bank, overlooking a stop order on the deposit, transferred it at the applicant's request to a bank in New Zealand (the 'NZ bank'). The applicant subsequently defaulted on the loan and the property was sold. The NZ bank repaid the deposit to the bank at the bank's request in return for an indemnity. The applicant commenced proceedings seeking damages from the bank for intentional interference with the applicant's contractual relations with the NZ bank. The bank pleaded justification in its defence on the basis that it was entitled to the money as it had paid the money to the NZ bank under a mistake of fact. Lee J held that even if a *prima facie* case of mistake could be established the applicant had a valid defence to a restitutionary claim by the bank. The applicant had provided good consideration for the payment of the money to the NZ bank, namely the release of the bank from its indebtedness to her on the deposit. The fact that the bank would not have elected to pay the money had it not mistakenly overlooked the stop order did not prevent consideration arising by a corresponding reduction of the bank's indebtedness: pp 123–24.

Bona fide **purchase**

The *bona fide* purchaser defence operates to clear title to property of the plaintiff acquired by the defendant from a third party. The defence applies where the defendant gave valuable consideration for the acquisition of the property, and took the property without notice of the plaintiff's interest. It is most prominent in equity, however, as the following case shows, it is also available on a common law tracing claim.

Lipkin Gorman v Karpnale Ltd [1991] 2 AC 548 House of Lords

The facts are stated at p 595.

> **Lord Goff of Chieveley**: ... [574] There is no doubt that the respondents received the money in good faith; but, as I have already recorded, there was an acute difference of [575] opinion among the members of the Court of Appeal whether the respondents gave consideration for it. Parker LJ was of opinion that they did so, for two reasons: (1) the club supplied chips in exchange for the money. The contract under which the chips were supplied was a separate contract, independent of the contracts under which bets were placed at the club; and the contract for the chips was not avoided as a contract by way of gaming and wagering under s 18 of the Gaming Act 1845; (2) although the actual gaming contracts were void under the Act, nevertheless Cass in fact obtained in exchange for the money the chance of winning and of then being paid and so received valuable consideration from the club. May LJ agreed with the first of these two reasons. Nicholls LJ disagreed with both.
>
> I have to say at once that I am unable to accept the alternative basis upon which Parker LJ held that consideration was given for the money, viz that each time Cass placed a bet at the casino, he obtained in exchange the chance of winning and thus of being paid. In my opinion, when Cass placed a bet, he received nothing in return which constituted valuable consideration. The contract of gaming was void; in other words, it was binding in honour only. Cass knew, of course, that, if he

won his bet, the club would pay him his winnings. But he had no legal right to claim them. He simply had a confident expectation that, in fact, the club would pay; indeed, if the club did not fulfil its obligations binding in honour upon it, it would very soon go out of business. But it does not follow that, when Cass placed the bet, he received anything that the law recognises as valuable consideration. In my opinion he did not do so. Indeed, to hold that consideration had been given for the money on this basis would, in my opinion, be inconsistent with *Clarke v Shee and Johnson* (1774). Even when a winning bet has been paid, the gambler does not receive valuable consideration for his money. All that he receives is, in law, a gift from the club.

However, the first basis upon which Parker and May LJJ decided the point is more difficult. To that I now turn. In common sense terms, those who gambled at the club were not gambling for chips: they were gambling for money. As Davies LJ said in *CHT Ltd v Ward* (1965), p 79:

> People do not game in order to win chips; they game in order to win money. The chips are not money or money's worth; they are mere counters or symbols used for the convenience of all concerned in the gaming.

The convenience is manifest, especially from the point of view of the club. The club has the gambler's money up front, and large sums of cash are not floating around at the gaming tables. The chips are simply a convenient mechanism for facilitating gambling with money. The property in the chips as such remains in the club, so that there is no question of a gambler buying the chips from the club when he obtains them for cash. [576]

But this broad approach does not solve the problem, which is essentially one of analysis. I think it best to approach the problem by taking a situation unaffected by the impact of the Gaming Acts.

Suppose that a large department store decides, for reasons of security, that all transactions in the store are to be effected by the customers using chips instead of money. On entering the store, or later, the customer goes to the cash desk and obtains chips to the amount he needs in exchange for cash or a cheque. When he buys goods, he presents chips for his purchase. Before he leaves the store, he presents his remaining chips, and receives cash in return. The example may be unrealistic, but in legal terms it is reasonably straightforward. A contract is made when the customer obtains his chips under which the store agrees that, if goods are purchased by the customer, the store will accept chips to the equivalent value of the price, and further that it will redeem for cash any chips returned to it before the customer leaves the store. If a customer offers to buy a certain item of goods at the store, and the girl behind the counter accepts his offer but then refuses to accept the customer's chips, the store will be in breach of the contract for chips. Likewise if, before he leaves the store, the customer hands in some or all of his chips at the cash desk, and the girl at the cash desk refuses to redeem them, the store will be in breach of the contract for chips.

Each time that a customer buys goods, he enters into a contract of sale, under which the customer purchases goods at the store. This is a contract for the sale of goods; it is not a contract of exchange, under which goods are exchanged for chips, but a contract of sale, under which goods are bought for a price, ie, for a money consideration. This is because, when the customer surrenders chips of the appropriate denomination, the store appropriates part of the money deposited with it towards the purchase. This does not however alter the fact that an independent contract is made for the chips when the customer originally obtains them at the cash desk. Indeed that contract is not dependent upon any contract of sale being entered into; the customer could walk around the store and buy nothing, and then be entitled to redeem his chips in full under the terms of his contract with the store.

But the question remains: when the customer hands over his cash at the cash desk, and receives his chips, does the store give valuable consideration for the money so received by it? In common sense terms, the answer is no. For, in substance and in reality, there is simply a gratuitous deposit of the money with the store, with liberty to the customer to draw upon that deposit to pay for any goods he buys at the store. The chips are no more than the mechanism by which that result is achieved without any cash being handed over at the sales counter, and by which the customer can claim repayment of any balance remaining of his deposit. If a technical approach is adopted, it might be said that, since the property in the money passes to the store as depositee, it then gives consideration for the money in the form of a chose in action created by its promise to repay a like sum, subject to draw-down in respect of goods purchased at the store. I however prefer the common sense approach. Nobody would say that the store has purchased the [577] money by promising to repay it: the promise to repay is simply the means of giving effect to the gratuitous deposit of the money with the store. It follows that, by receiving the money in these circumstances, the store does not for present purposes give valuable consideration for it. Otherwise a bank with which money was deposited by an innocent donee from a thief could claim to be a *bona fide* purchaser of the money simply by virtue of the fact of the deposit.

Let me next take the case of gambling at a casino. Of course, if gaming contracts were not void under English law by virtue of s 18 of the Gaming Act 1845, the result would be exactly the same. There would be a contract in respect of the chips, under which the money was deposited with the casino; and then separate contracts would be made when each bet was placed, at which point of time part or all of the money so deposited would be appropriated to the bets.

However, contracts by way of gaming or wagering are void in English law. What is the effect of this? It is obvious that each time a bet is placed by the gambler, the agreement under which the bet is placed is an agreement by way of gaming or wagering, and so is rendered null and void. It follows, as I have said, that the casino, by accepting the bet, does not thereby give valuable consideration for the money which has been wagered by the gambler, because the casino is under no legal obligation to honour the bet. Of course, the gambler cannot recover the money from the casino on the ground of failure of consideration; for he has relied upon the casino to honour the wager – he has in law given the money to the casino, trusting that the casino will fulfil the obligation binding in honour upon it and pay him if he wins his bet – though if the casino does so its payment to the gambler will likewise be in law a gift. But suppose it is not the gambler but the true owner of the money (from whom the gambler has perhaps, as in the present case, stolen the money) who is claiming it from the casino. What then? In those circumstances the casino cannot, in my opinion, say that it has given valuable consideration for the money, whether or not the gambler's bet is successful. It has given no consideration if the bet is unsuccessful, because its promise to pay on a successful bet is void; nor has it done so if the gambler's bet is successful and the casino has paid him his winnings, because that payment is in law a gift to the gambler by the casino.

For these reasons I conclude, in agreement with Nicholls LJ, that the respondents did not give valuable consideration for the money ...

Commentary and questions

On what basis did the casino argue that it had provided good consideration for the appellant's money? Was this argument accepted?

The defence of *bona fide* purchase is applied primarily in proprietary claims, however it will also be applied to personal restitutionary claims to ensure the personal claim does not subvert the operation of the rule in proprietary actions. As Birks points out, a defendant would feel little joy in being told that she has title to the enrichment, but must nevertheless pay over its value to the plaintiff on a personal restitutionary claim:[130]

> The reason why *bona fide* purchase extinguishes personal as well as proprietary claims is that, if it did not, its work in relation to proprietary claims would be wholly subverted. It is no good telling a person that he gets good title to the thing or money in question if you then tell him that he must pay over its value. That is obvious. To the extent that a system decides to clear title in favour of a *bona fide* purchaser it must also and to the same extent protect that purchaser from claims in unjust enrichment. What was given with one hand would otherwise be taken with the other.

It has been suggested that the defence of *bona fide* purchase is 'simply the paradigm change of position defence'.[131] However Lord Goff in the principal case treated the two defences as distinct, recognising that the defences operate differently.[132] In particular, the defence of *bona fide* purchase is complete upon the provision of value, and no inquiry is made into the amount of value provided.[133] On the other hand, the defence of change of position defeats the claim only to the extent of the defendant's detrimental reliance.[134]

---

130 Birks, 'Change of position: the nature of the defence and its relationship to other restitutionary defences', in McInnes (ed), *Restitution: Developments in Unjust Enrichment*, 1996, p 65. For a general discussion of the defence as it applies to claims in restitution, see Swadling, 'Restitution and *bona fide* purchase', in Swadling (ed), *The Limits of Restitutionary Claims: A Comparative Analysis*, 1997, Chapter 4; Barker, '*Bona fide* purchase as a defence to unjust enrichment claims: a concise restatement' [1999] 7 RLR 75.

131 Millett, 'Tracing the proceeds of fraud' (1991) 107 LQR 71, p 82.

132 Lord Goff pp 580–81. See also Lord Templeman, p 559. The weight of academic opinion is in agreement: Mason and Carter, *Restitution Law in Australia*, 1995, pp 865–66; Nolan, 'Change of position', in Birks (ed), *Laundering and Tracing*, 1995, p 186; Birks, 'Change of position and surviving enrichment', in Swadling (ed), *The Limits of Restitutionary Claims: A Comparative Analysis*, 1997, pp 56–57; Goff and Jones, *The Law of Restitution*, 5th edn, 1998, p 845.

133 *Basset v Nosworthy* (1673); *Midland Bank Ltd v Green* (1981); *Lipkin Gorman v Karpnale Ltd* (1991), Lord Goff pp 580–81.

134 *David Securities Pty Ltd v Commonwealth Bank of Australia* (1992) pp 384–86 (see extract, p 592); *Lipkin Gorman v Karpnale Ltd* (1991), pp 580–81 (see extract, p 595).

PASSING ON

Defendants have in the past attempted to raise a defence of 'passing on', arguing that the plaintiff's claim in restitution should be denied where the plaintiff has recouped the enrichment from third parties. However, the High Court has consistently rejected 'passing on' as a defence in Australian restitution law.[135]

Commissioner of State Revenue (Vic) v Royal Insurance Australia Ltd [1994] 182 CLR 51
High Court of Australia

The facts are stated at p 120.

Mason CJ: ... [69] *Is passing on a good defence to a restitutionary claim?*

Whether a passing on 'defence' should be recognised must be considered at two levels: the levels of public law and restitutionary law. There is the fundamental principle of public law that no tax can be levied by the executive government without parliamentary authority, a principle which traces back to the Bill of Rights (1688) (Imp).[136] In accordance with that principle, the Crown cannot assert an entitlement to retain money paid by way of causative mistake as and for tax that is not payable in the absence of circumstances which disentitle the payer from recovery. It would be subversive of an important constitutional value if this court were to endorse a principle of law which, in the absence of such circumstances, authorised the retention by the executive of payments which it lacked authority to receive and which were paid as a result of causative mistake.

From the perspective of the law of restitution, there is some support for the view that, if the payer has passed on the burden of a tax which is found not to be payable, the payer will not be entitled to recover payments made to the public authority as and for tax. The suggestion is that, in these circumstances, the defendant's enrichment is not at the expense of the plaintiff. In *Air Canada v British Columbia* (1989), the [70] plaintiff airlines had passed on an unconstitutional gasoline tax in the form of fares charged to their passengers. Four justices considered the question whether the airlines could recover the payments which they had made as and for the tax. La Forest J (with whom Lamer and L'Heureux-Dubé JJ concurred) decided that question against the airlines. La Forest J cited ((1989), p 193) the comments of Professor Palmer in his work *The Law of Restitution*:[137]

> There is no doubt that if the tax authority retains a payment to which it was not entitled it has been unjustly enriched. It has not been enriched at the taxpayer's expense, however, if he has shifted the economic burden of the tax to others. Unless restitution for their benefit can be worked out, it seems preferable to leave the enrichment with the tax authority instead of putting the judicial machinery in motion for the purpose of shifting the same enrichment to the taxpayer.

---

135 In South Australia the defence has been incorporated in legislation in the case of claims to recover invalid imports: Limitation of Actions Act 1936 (SA), s 38 (3a) and (3b).

136 (1688) 1 Will and Mar, Sess 2, c 2: 'That levying Money for or to the Use of the Crowne by pretence of Prerogative without Grant of Parlyament for longer time or in other manner than the same is or shall be granted is Illegal.'

137 1986 Supp, p 255.

La Forest J expressed his agreement with the comment and went on to say ((1989), pp 193–94):

> The law of restitution is not intended to provide windfalls to plaintiffs who have suffered no loss. Its function is to ensure that where a plaintiff has been deprived of wealth that is either in his possession or would have accrued for his benefit, it is restored to him. The measure of restitutionary recovery is the gain the province made at the airlines' expense.

Wilson J did not agree, concluding that to deny recovery in such a situation would be tantamount to allowing the legislature to impose illegal burdens and would be inconsistent with restitutionary principles ((1989), pp 169–70). The levying of an unconstitutional tax is an imposition of an illegal burden, but there was no such imposition in the present case.

The approach taken by La Forest J in *Air Canada* accords with that adopted in the United States in *Shannon v Hughes and Co* (1937). There, the plaintiff failed to recover payments of an unconstitutional tax on its ice cream operations because it had passed on the tax to its customers and had shifted to them the burden of the imposition. The court invoked Lord Mansfield's proposition in *Moses v Macferlan* (1760) that, in the common law action for money had and received, the defendant 'may defend himself by every thing which shews that the plaintiff, *ex æquo et bono*, is not intitled to the whole [71] of his demand, or to any part of it'. In *Shannon v Hughes and Co* (1937), the court concluded that to hold otherwise would result in unjust enrichment of the plaintiff, despite the fact that the imposition of the tax and its passing on to customers caused the plaintiff's ice cream sales to drop sharply and the plaintiff's profits to collapse. By denying relief on the ground that the plaintiff would unjustly be enriched by a windfall, the court left the plaintiff without a remedy even though it had suffered significant loss and damage.

The argument that a plaintiff who passes on a tax or charge will receive a windfall or will unjustly be enriched if recovery from a public authority is permitted rests at bottom upon the economic view that the plaintiff should not recover if the burden of the imposition of the tax or charge has been shifted to third parties. In the context of the law of restitution, this economic view encounters major difficulties. The first is that to deny recovery when the plaintiff shifts the burden of the imposition of the tax or charge to third parties will often leave a plaintiff who suffers loss or damage without a remedy. That consequence suggests that, if the economic argument is to be converted into a legal proposition, the proposition must be that the plaintiff's recovery should be limited to compensation for loss or damage sustained. The third is that an inquiry into and a determination of the loss or damage sustained by a plaintiff who passes on a tax or charge is a very complex undertaking. And, finally, it has long been thought that, despite Lord Mansfield's statement in *Moses v Macferlan*, the basis of restitutionary relief is not compensation for loss or damage sustained but restoration to the plaintiff of what has been taken or received from the plaintiff without justification.[138]

Shannon v Hughes and Co illustrates the first problem. Because passing on the tax or charge increases the price or cost of the goods or service to the customer or consumer it may have an adverse economic impact upon demand and, accordingly, upon the profitability of the plaintiff's activities. That means that

---

138 *Mason v The State of New South Wales* (1959), p 146 *per* Windeyer J.

passing on should not be accepted as a universal defence to a restitutionary claim unless it is related and limited to denying recovery except for loss or damage sustained. And that requires a consideration of practical and legal objections inherent in the third and fourth objections mentioned above.

In the United States, the Supreme Court has rejected the passing [72] on defence in the context of treble damages claims under anti-trust laws by plaintiffs who have passed on overpayments to their customers.[139] Though the context is different, the reasons given for that rejection are relevant to the present case. They include the difficulty of determining the economic impact upon the plaintiff's business of passing on the overpayment (*Hanover Shoe* (1968), pp 492–93), the practical problems which availability of the defence would generate involving 'massive evidence and complicated theories' (1968), p 493 to demonstrate the occurrence or non-occurrence of passing on. Further, the defence would probably apply all the way down the chain of distribution to the ultimate consumer who would have little interest to sue ((1968), p 494). In *Illinois Brick Co v Illinois* (1977), the Supreme Court confirmed these grounds of objection and pointed to the problems of multiple litigation if both direct and indirect purchasers could sue for anti-trust damages. The court also noted that economic theories rely upon assumptions that do not operate in the real world, thereby making the proof of passing on extremely difficult ((1977), pp 741–42).

A similar approach was taken in the opinion of Advocate General Mancini in *Amministrazione delle Finanze dello Stato v San Giorgio SA* (1985). San Giorgio was required to pay health inspection charges under an Italian decree and regulations. They were held to be invalid. An Italian court ordered repayment to San Giorgio, notwithstanding another law which denied recovery when the charge is presumed to have been passed on. The Advocate General considered that the nature of a free market is such that one cannot isolate any portion of the price and link it causally to a particular cost ((1985), p 673). However, the European Court concluded ((1985), pp 688–89):

> Community law does not prevent a national legal system from disallowing the repayment of charges which have been unduly levied where to do so would entail unjust enrichment of the recipients. There is nothing in Community law therefore to prevent courts from taking account, under their national law, of the fact that the unduly levied charges have been incorporated in the price of the goods and thus passed on to the purchasers.

The court has also decided that it is inconsistent with Community [73] law for a State to impose on a taxpayer the burden of establishing that unduly paid charges have not been passed on.[140] Thus, in European law it is accepted that the defence of passing on, though difficult to establish, does not infringe Community law when made available by the statute of a Member State.

The United States and European decisions demonstrate that any acceptance of the defence of passing on is fraught with both practical and theoretical difficulties.[141]

---

139 *Hanover Shoe Inc v United Shoe Machinery Corp* (1968); *Illinois Brick Co v Illinois* (1977); see also *McKesson Corporation v Division of Alcoholic Beverages and Tobacco* (1990), pp 42–43.

140 *Les Fils de Jules Bianco SA v Directeur Générale des Douanes* (1989).

141 See also Rudden and Bishop, 'Gritz and Quellmehl: pass it on' (1981) 6 ELR 253, especially pp 253–56.

Indeed, the difficulties are so great that, in my view, the defence should not succeed unless it is established that the defendant's enrichment is not at the expense of the plaintiff but at the expense of some other person or persons.[142] In that event, the plaintiff fails, not because it has passed on the tax or charge, but because the defendant has been enriched by receiving moneys which belonged to or proceeded from someone other than the plaintiff. Take, for example, the case where there is an overpayment of a tax levied on someone other than the plaintiff who collects the tax and pays it to the public authority. In such a case, the plaintiff should not recover unless it is established that the plaintiff will distribute the proceeds to the true taxpayers.

Historically, as I have already noted, the basis of restitutionary relief in English law was not compensation for loss or damage but restoration of what had been taken or received. The requirement that the defendant be unjustly enriched 'at the expense of' the plaintiff can mean that the enrichment is 'by doing wrong to' or 'by subtraction from' the plaintiff.[143] Hence, a plaintiff can succeed by showing that he or she was the victim of a wrong which enriched the defendant – this is not such a case – or that the defendant was enriched by receiving the plaintiff's money or property.

When the plaintiff succeeds in a restitutionary claim, the court [74] awards the plaintiff the monetary equivalent of what the defendant has taken or received, except in those cases in which the plaintiff is entitled to specific proprietary relief. Because the object of restitutionary relief is to divest the defendant of what the defendant is not entitled to retain, the court does not assess the amount of its award by reference to the actual loss which the plaintiff has sustained. That is what Windeyer J was saying in *Mason v The State of New South Wales* (1959), p 146 when he rejected the notion that impoverishment of the plaintiff is a correlative of the defendant's unjust enrichment.[144]

Windeyer J did not regard the fact that the plaintiffs had 'passed on' to their customers the amounts unlawfully charged for permits as a reason for denying recovery. His Honour said ((1959), p 146):[145]

> If the defendant be improperly enriched on what legal principle can it claim to retain its ill gotten gains merely because the plaintiffs have not, it is said, been correspondingly impoverished? The concept of impoverishment as a correlative of enrichment may have some place in some fields of continental

---

142 There is limited support from the textwriters for the view that passing on is not a defence: see Birks, *Restitution – The Future*, 1992, p 75, n 55; Burrows, *op cit*, fn 6, pp 475–76 (though he favours a mitigation of loss defence in some cases where it is established that the charge has been passed on); but others consider it is a defence: see Palmer, *The Law of Restitution*, 1986 Supp, p 255; see also Goff and Jones, *The Law of Restitution*, 4th edn, 1993, p 553, where it is suggested that 'the burden should, in principle, be on the defendant to show that the plaintiff has suffered no loss'. In *Woolwich*, Lord Goff of Chieveley commented: 'The point is not without its difficulties; and the availability of the defence may depend upon the nature of the tax': [1993] AC 70, p 178.

143 Birks, *An Introduction to the Law of Restitution*, rev edn, 1989, pp 23–24.

144 But cf *Air Canada v British Columbia* (1989), pp 193–94 *per* La Forest J (with whom Lamer and L'Heureux-Dubé JJ concurred); Wilson J *contra*. See also Beatson, 'Restitution of taxes, levies and other imposts: defining the extent of the *Woolwich* principle' (1993) 109 LQR 401, pp 427–28; Law Commission (UK), *Restitution of Payments Made Under a Mistake of Law*, 1991, Consultation Paper No 120, paras 3.83–3.85.

145 See also p 136 *per* Menzies J.

law. It is foreign to our law. Even if there were any equity in favour of third parties attaching to the fruits of any judgment the plaintiffs might recover ... this circumstance would be quite irrelevant to the present proceedings. Certainly it would not enable the defendant to refuse to return moneys which it was not in law entitled to collect and which *ex hypothesi* it got by extortion.

Windeyer J was directing his remarks to a case in which, as in *Air Canada*, the State was asserting its entitlement to payment of the charge. In the present case, there never was a demand or claim by the State or the Commissioner that tax was payable in respect of premiums received under the relevant policies. Here overpayment occurred simply because Royal made a mistake in the process of self-assessment. But I do not consider that this difference touches the question whether passing on the tax or duty is relevant to restitutionary recovery. Once it is accepted that causative mistake of law is a basis for recovery, the making of an unlawful demand for [75] payment, though material to the making of a causative mistake, is no longer of critical importance.

Restitutionary relief, as it has developed to this point in our law, does not seek to provide compensation for loss. Instead, it operates to restore to the plaintiff what has been transferred from the plaintiff to the defendant whereby the defendant has been unjustly enriched. As in the action for money had and received, the defendant comes under an obligation to account to the plaintiff for money which the defendant has received for the use of the plaintiff. The subtraction from the plaintiff's wealth enables one to say that the defendant's unjust enrichment has been 'at the expense of the plaintiff',[146] notwithstanding that the plaintiff may recoup the outgoing by means of transactions with third parties.

On this approach, it would not matter that the plaintiff is or will be over-compensated because he or she has passed on the tax or charge to someone else. And it seems that there is no recorded instance of a court engaging in the daunting exercise of working out the actual loss sustained by the plaintiff and restricting the amount of an award to that measure.

[Mason CJ held that if the tax is specifically recouped from customers as a separately charged item, the plaintiff must hold any sum recovered upon a constructive trust for its customers. This aspect of Mason CJ's judgment is extracted at p 76. Mason CJ continued at p 78:]

If, however, the plaintiff did not become the constructive trustee of the moneys by separately charging them as tax to the patrons, I do not see why the plaintiff's claim should be defeated simply because the plaintiff has recouped the outgoing from others. As between the plaintiff and the defendant, the plaintiff having paid away *its* money by mistake in circumstances in which the defendant has no title to retain the moneys, the plaintiff has the superior claim. The plaintiff's inability to distribute the proceeds to those who recoup the plaintiff was, in my view, an immaterial consideration, as Windeyer J suggested it was in *Mason v The State of New South Wales*. There was in that case the additional element of an unlawful demand but the absence of that element does not mean that, in the situation under consideration, unjust enrichment was otherwise than at the plaintiff's expense.

In the present case, that reasoning leads me to the conclusion that the Commissioner would have no defence to a restitutionary claim by Royal to recover

---

146 Birks, *op cit*, fn 6, pp 23–24.

the mistaken payments of duty. Even if it had been established that Royal charged the tax as a separate item to its policy holders so that it was a constructive trustee of the moneys representing that separate charge when it made the payments to the Commissioner, it would have been entitled to recover from the Commissioner, provided that it satisfied the court that it will account to its policy holders. The courts below, unlike [79] Judge Learned Hand in *123 East Fifty-Fourth Street*, did not draw an inference that the tax was charged as a separate item to the policy holders. And, in any event, it has not been suggested that the court should draw such an inference ...

Brennan J: ... [90] *The windfall gain defence*

The fact that Royal had passed on to its policy holders the burden of the payments made to the Commissioner does not mean that Royal did not pay its own money to the Commissioner. The passing on of the burden of the payments made does not affect the situation that, as between the Commissioner and Royal, the former was enriched at the expense of the latter. It may be that, if Royal recovers the overpayments it made, the policy holders will be entitled themselves to claim a refund from Royal[147] of so much of the overpayments made by Royal to the Commissioner as represents the amount paid to Royal by the policy holder.[148] However that may be, no defence of 'passing on' is available to defeat a claim for moneys paid by A acting on his own behalf to B where B has been [91] unjustly enriched by the payment and the moneys paid had been A's moneys ...[149]

[Toohey and McHugh JJ agreed with Brennan J, thus constituting a majority of the court.]

Commentary and questions

What are the legal arguments for and against the recognition of a passing on defence? What does Mason CJ recognise to be the practical difficulties with applying this defence? Are there other jurisdictions in which the defence of passing on has been accepted?

A majority of the High Court in *Roxborough v Rothmans of Pall Mall Australia Ltd* (2001) (see extract, p 81) followed the *Royal Insurance* case and rejected passing on as a defence to a claim in restitution. That case involved a claim by one private citizen against another, however it was held that this was not a sufficient basis to distinguish the *Royal Insurance* case (pp 343–44):

It is impossible to explain ... that decision, upon the ground that there is some constitutional reason for treating restitutionary claims against governments differently from claims against private citizens. It may be that the same principle applies with even greater force in the case of claims against governments, but *Royal Insurance* stands as clear authority against the respondent's argument on this

---

147 *Mutual Pools and Staff Pty Ltd v The Commonwealth* (1994), pp 177, 191.

148 This was the effect of s 99(8) and (9) of the Act in relation to the particular refunds which the comptroller was directed to make to insurers under s 99. The original sub-sections inserted by the Accident Compensation Act were amended by the Stamps and Business Franchise (Tobacco) (Amendment) Act 1985: s 11(3)(a) and (b).

149 *Mason v The State of New South Wales* (1959), pp 136, 146; see also *Woolwich Building Society v Inland Revenue Commissioners* (1993), pp 177–78; and *Air Canada v British Columbia* (1989), pp 169–70 *per* Wilson J (dissenting).

question. We see no reason to depart from that recent decision of this Court; and every reason in principle to support it.

In contrast, Justice Kirby in his dissenting judgment held that, where the claim is between *private parties*, as in the principal case, the courts are entitled to take into account the fact that the plaintiff has recouped the cost of the tax from its customers. This aspect of Kirby J's judgment is extracted below.

Roxborough v Rothmans of Pall Mall Australia Ltd (2001) 185 ALR 335
High Court of Australia

The facts are stated at p 81.

Kirby J: ...[375] In *Commissioner of State Revenue (Vic) v Royal Insurance Australia Ltd* (1994), the defendant commissioner raised an objection that he had not been enriched 'at the expense of' the plaintiff taxpayer which was claiming reimbursement.[150] This objection was rejected by Brennan J ((1994), pp 90–91, 103) (with whom Toohey and McHugh JJ concurred). His Honour held that the passing on of the burden of the payments by Royal Insurance did not 'affect the situation that, as between the Commissioner and Royal [Insurance], the former was enriched at the expense of the latter'. Upon this analysis, the search was not for the 'ultimate' burden of the unlawful tax. It was enough to demonstrate that the 'immediate' expense fell upon the plaintiff.[151]

As the opinion of three justices of this court, the foregoing reasoning in *Royal Insurance* must be accorded respect. However, I do not consider that it constitutes a statement of general principle by the court binding on me in the circumstances of this case. Once again, the issue before the court in *Royal Insurance* was one of recovery from a state party, which presents different considerations of legal policy and principle, as I shall shortly show. As well, the fourth member of the majority in that case, Mason CJ, expressed himself in language that, with respect, I find more convincing and relevant to the circumstances of the present case. Moreover, the legal principle for which *Royal Insurance* primarily stands involves the interpretation of a recovery provision in the applicable Victorian statute.[152] It does not concern the general rules governing the private rights *inter se* of parties to a contract the terms of which are subsequently said to be affected by a court decision holding that certain statutory fees are constitutionally invalid.

Whereas in *Royal Insurance* (1994) Mason CJ dismissed the commissioner's claim that to allow the plaintiff recovery would result in a form of unjust enrichment of the plaintiff, his Honour distinguished between the operation of 'passing on' in the context of public law and in the law of restitution. So far as the former was concerned, Mason CJ said at p 69:

> It would be subversive of an important constitutional value if this court were to endorse a principle of law which ... authorized the retention by the

---

150 According to the generally accepted analysis, a successful restitutionary claim requires proof of: (1) enrichment of the defendant; (2) gained at the plaintiff's expense; (3) as a result of an unjust factor; (4) in the absence of a recognised defence.

151 See McInnes, '"Passing on" in the law of restitution: a re-consideration' (1997) 19 Sydney Law Review 179, p 181.

152 Stamps Act 1958 (Vic), s 111(1).

executive of payments which it lacked authority to receive and which were paid as a result of causative mistake.

Like Mason CJ, I would accept that point of distinction. As I have shown, it is also one that is recognised in United States and European judicial authority. [376] Ultimately, it derives its justification from the way in which the constitutional context shapes the applicable legal rules. But, as to the law of restitution outside the context of public law, Mason CJ noted that an accurate determination of the effects of an attempt to pass on an expense to others could be 'a very complex undertaking' ((1994), p 71). Sometimes a taxpayer will indeed have been able to effect a transmission of its statutory obligation to consumers. As Professor Birks has pointed out, its capacity to do so will depend upon many factors, including the 'elasticity of demand' for its product.[153] This too is a consideration addressed in recent United States authority and in academic commentary on the application of the law of restitution in this context.[154]

It can therefore safely be said that, in Australia, no general legal 'defence' to recovery of a tax found to have been unlawful is established merely by proof that the taxpayer has 'passed on' the tax in question to unknown and unidentifiable consumers. There are special reasons, in proceedings for recovery from a state authority, as to why such a 'defence' may not apply. In every case the suggested 'passing on', so far as it is said to be relevant, should be subjected to factual analysis. However, where, as in the present case, the demand for recovery is addressed not to a government or government party but to a private corporation the 'important constitutional value' (*Royal Insurance* (1994), p 69) of upholding recovery of the unlawful tax from the State is absent. In such a case, in my view, Australian law (as in the law of the United States, Canada and the European Union) is free to, and does, take into account the fact (if it be established) that the plaintiff taxpayer, seeking recovery, has already passed on the tax in question to third party consumers and has not done, or will not do, anything to reimburse those consumers but instead seeks only to make a private gain for itself. In such a case the fact of 'passing on' is certainly relevant. In a given case, it may mean that the taxpayer has, in fact, suffered no loss and is entitled to no legal recovery. [Kirby J went on to reject the various grounds of recovery claimed by the defendants (see extracts, pp 268, 273 and 696), and continued at p 383:]

Restitution arose as a remedy 'to avoid unjust results in specific cases'.[155] By no means does the present case involve an unjust result. The retailers rejected any obligation to reimburse their consumers, who carry the ultimate burden of the licence fees. There has been no unjust enrichment of anyone at the expense of the retailers.

...

---

153 Birks, *Restitution – The Future*, 1992, p 126.

154 Eg, Bryan, 'Mistaken payments and the law of unjust enrichment: *David Securities Pty Ltd v Commonwealth Bank of Australia*' (1993), p 471; cf Rose, 'Passing on', in Birks (ed), *Laundering and Tracing*, 1995, 261, p 284; see *Royal Insurance* (1994), p 73 *per* Mason CJ.

155 Laycock, 'The scope and significance of restitution' (1989) 67 Texas Law Review 1277, p 1278.

Commentary and question

On what basis did his Honour distinguish between claims against the State, on the one hand, and claims against a private citizen on the other?

Kirby J treated the defendants' unwillingness to give a refund to customers as being particularly important to the constructive trust claim. His Honour refused to recognise a constructive trust on the basis that the defendants could not seek the aid of equity where they were not themselves willing to act equitably by refunding the money to their customers. This aspect of his Honour's judgment is extracted at p 696.

LIMITATION OF ACTIONS

General

In each Australian jurisdiction the limitation period for claims in restitution is the same as that prescribed for claims in contract. This is achieved variously by references to 'quasi-contract',[156] contracts 'implied by law',[157] or 'implied contract'.[158] For claims other than claims against the government for the recovery of taxes and other imposts, the prescribed limitation period in each jurisdiction is six years except in the Northern Territory where it is three years.[159] In the case of claims against the government for the recovery of unlawful exactions, provisions in each jurisdiction prescribe special shortened limitations periods of either six or 12 months.[160] These provisions are discussed elsewhere (see above, pp 475–77).

The general rule is that the limitation period runs from the date of accrual of the cause of action.[161] There is an abundance of authority in the mistake context that, at common law, the cause of action accrues at the date of the payment.[162] On the other hand, there is a scarcity of authority on the date of the accrual of

---

156 Limitation Act 1969 (NSW), s 14(1)(a); Limitation Act 1981 (NT), s 12(1)(a); Limitation of Actions Act 1974 (QLD), s 10(1)(a).

157 Limitation Act 1974 (Tas), s 4(1)(a); Limitations of Actions Act 1958 (Vic), s 5(1)(a); Limitation Act 1935 (WA), s 38(1)(c)(v).

158 Limitation of Actions Act 1936 (SA), s 35(a). In the ACT a six year limitation period is prescribed for all claims unless otherwise provided: Limitation Act 1985 (ACT), s 11.

159 Limitation Act 1981 (NT), s 12(1)(b).

160 Limitations of Actions Act 1958 (Vic), s 20A (12 months); Recovery of Imposts Act 1963 (NSW), s 2 (12 months); Limitation of Actions Act 1974 (QLD), s 10A (12 months); Limitation of Actions Act 1936 (SA), s 38 (6 months); Limitation Act 1974 (Tas), s 25D (12 months); Limitation Act 1935 (WA), s 37A (12 months); Limitation Act 1985 (ACT), s 21A (6 months); Limitation Act 1981, s 35D (6 months); Customs Act 1901 (Cth), s 167.

161 *Torrens Aloha Pty Ltd v Citibank NA* (1997) (see extract, p 670).

162 *Torrens Aloha, ibid; Baker v Courage & Co Ltd* (1910); *Maskell v Horner* (1915); *Fuller v Happy Shopper Markets Ltd* (2001).

the cause of action for claims other than mistake. However, by analogy with mistake, it would be expected that the general rule is that the cause of action accrues at the date the enrichment is received.[163] This rule is not absolute,[164] and has been varied by legislation with respect to claims based on fraud or mistake.

Mistake and fraud

Limitations legislation in each jurisdiction, with the exception of South Australia and Western Australia, prescribe an extended limitation period where the action is based on the fraud of the defendant or is a claim for 'relief from the consequences of a mistake'.[165] Representative of these provisions[166] is s 27 of the Limitations of Actions Act 1958 (Vic).

Limitations of Actions Act 1958 (Vic), s 27

27 Postponement of limitation periods in case of fraud or mistake

Where, in the case of any action for which a period of limitation is prescribed by this Act –

(a) the action is based upon the fraud of the defendant or his agent or of any person through whom he claims or his agent; or

(b) the right of action is concealed by the fraud of any such person as aforesaid; or

(c) the action is for relief from the consequences of a mistake –

the period of limitation shall not begin to run until the plaintiff has discovered the fraud or the mistake, as the case may be, or could with reasonable diligence have discovered it.

Commentary

The effect of this provision is that in the case of claims based on mistake or fraud the limitation period of six years does not begin to run until the fraud or mistake 'could with reasonable diligence have [been] discovered'.

In the following case, the House of Lords considered the applicability of the UK equivalent of s 27 to a claim based on mistake of law where the payment was considered legally due according to the state of the law at the time it was paid, however some years later the law was changed by judicial decision and the payment was held not to have been due.

---

163 The leading textbooks adopt this general rule: Burrows, *The Law of Restitution*, 1993, pp 443–44; Mason and Carter, *Restitution Law in Australia*, 1995, p 923; Goff and Jones, *The Law of Restitution*, 5th edn, 1998, p 848.

164 See the discussion below of benefits conferred under ineffective contracts.

165 Limitation Act 1985 (ACT), s 34(1); Limitation Act 1969 (NSW), s 56(1); Limitation Act 1981 (NT), s 43(1); Limitation of Actions Act 1974 (QLD), s 38; Limitation Act 1974 (Tas), s 32; Limitations of Actions Act 1958 (Vic), s 27(c).

166 Although the wording in each jurisdiction is different they all have the same general effect: Mason and Carter, *Restitution Law in Australia*, 1995, p 939.

Kleinwort Benson Ltd v Lincoln City Council [1999] 2 AC 349 House of Lords

The facts are stated at p 126.

Lord Goff of Chieveley: ... [387] *Does s 32(1)(c) of the Limitation Act 1980 apply to mistakes of law*:

Section 32(1) of the Limitation Act 1980 provides as follows:

(1) Subject to subsections (3) and (4A) below, where in the case of any action for which a period of limitation is prescribed by this Act either –

(a) the action is based upon the fraud of the defendant; or

(b) any fact relevant to the plaintiff's right of action has been deliberately concealed from him by the defendant; or

(c) the action is for relief from the consequences of a mistake;

the period of limitation shall not begin to run until the plaintiff has discovered the fraud, [388] concealment or mistake (as the case may be) or could with reasonable diligence have discovered it.

The question which arises under this issue is whether the actions brought by the bank for the recovery on the ground of mistake of law of money paid to the local authorities under void interest swaps agreements are actions for relief from the consequences of a mistake within s 32(1)(c).

...

The submission of the bank was that their actions for the recovery on the ground of mistake of law of money paid under void interest swap agreements were actions for relief from the consequences of a mistake within s 32(1)(c) of the Act of 1980. In support of this submission, they relied, first, on *In re Diplock; Diplock v Wintle* (1948), pp 515–16, in which the Court of Appeal stated that s 26 of the Act of 1939 [the precursor to s 32(1)(c)] would operate to postpone the running of time in the case of an action at common law to recover money paid under a mistake of fact, and would likewise apply to an analogous claim in equity to recover money paid under a mistake of law. Second, they relied on the judgment of Pearson J in *Phillips-Higgins v Harper* (1954), p 418 in which he stated with reference to s 26 of the Act of 1939 that the essential question was whether the action was for relief from the consequences of a mistake, a familiar example of which was an action for the recovery of money paid in consequence of a mistake. On this basis, it was submitted, the bank's causes of action in the present cases fell clearly within s 32(1)(c) of the Act of 1980.

In answer to this submission, the submission of the local authorities was twofold. First, they submitted that there was no mistake on the part of the bank; but I have already explained that I am satisfied that they indeed paid the money in question under a mistake of law. Second, they submitted that s 32(1)(c) does not on its true construction apply to mistakes of law. In this connection they relied in particular on the fact that the mistake of law rule was in full force in 1939, when the provision was first enacted; and they further submitted that the words of the sub-section, which referred to a mistake being 'discovered', showed that the legislature was referring to mistakes of fact rather than mistakes of law of which it would not be apt to refer to such a mistake being 'discovered', still less 'discovered with reasonable diligence'. In my opinion, however, this verbal argument founders on the fact that the pre-existing equitable rule applied to all mistakes, whether they were [389] mistakes of fact or mistakes of law: see, eg, *Earl Beauchamp v Winn* (1873) and the *dicta* from *In re Diplock* to which I have already referred.

I recognise that the effect of s 32(1)(c) is that the cause of action in a case such as the present may be extended for an indefinite period of time. I realise that this consequence may not have been fully appreciated at the time when this provision was enacted, and further that the recognition of the right at common law to recover money on the ground that it was paid under a mistake of law may call for legislative reform to provide for some time limit to the right of recovery in such cases. The Law Commission may think it desirable, as a result of the decision in the present case, to give consideration to this question indeed they may think it wise to do so as a matter of some urgency. If they do so, they may find it helpful to have regard to the position under other systems of law, notably Scottish and German law. On the section as it stands, however, I can see no answer to the submission of the bank that their claims in the present case, founded upon a mistake of law, fall within the sub-section ...

Lord Hope of Craighead: ... [416] *Limitation*

The bank's purpose in claiming restitution of the ground of mistake has been to pre-empt the limitation defence by the local authorities. The final question is whether, on the assumption that restitution on the ground of mistake is available, the bank can take the benefit of the postponement [417] provision in s 32(1)(c) of the Limitation Act 1980. The answer to it depends on whether the action is one for relief from the consequences of a mistake within the meaning of that subsection.

There is no difficulty about the language. The word 'mistake' appears in the sub-section without qualification. There is nothing in the words used in it which restricts its application to a mistake of fact. The origin of the section suggests that the absence of restriction was intentional. In its 5th Interim Report (*Statutes of Limitation*)[167] the Law Revision Committee recommended that the equitable rule of postponement should prevail in all cases where relief was sought from the consequences of a mistake, and that time should only run from the moment when the mistake was discovered or could with reasonable diligence have been discovered. This recommendation was put into effect in s 26(c) of the Limitation Act 1939, of which s 32(1)(c) is a re-enactment. In *In re Diplock* (1948), p 515 the Court of Appeal said that s 26(c) of the 1939 Act would operate to postpone the running of time in the case of an action to recover money paid under a mistake of fact.

But the distinction between mistake of fact and mistake of law as a ground for recovery is not absolute. Relief is available where the mistake of law relates to private rights: *Earl Beauchamp v Winn* (1873). Private agreements made under a mistake of law may be set aside, and relief will be given in respect of payments made under such agreements. Other examples may be given where a cause of action for relief will be available although the mistake was one of law. In *Reg v Tower Hamlets London Borough Council ex p Chetnik Developments Ltd* (1988), pp 874H–77C Lord Bridge referred to a substantial line of authority showing circumstances in which the court would not permit the mistake of law rule to be invoked. These include payments made under an error of law to or by a trustee in bankruptcy as an officer of the court: *Ex p James; In re Condon*. It is hard to see why

---

167 (1936) (Cmd 5334), pp 31–32, para 23.

in those cases the equitable rule which allows for the postponement of the limitation period should not apply, to the effect that time will not run until the claimant knew of the mistake or ought with reasonable diligence to have known of it. If the postponement can apply in these examples of mistake of law, I think that it ought to apply to mistakes of law generally.

The objection may be made that time may run on for a very long time before a mistake of law could have been discovered with reasonable diligence, especially where a judicial decision is needed to establish the mistake. It may also be said that in some cases a mistake of law may have affected a very large number of transactions, and that the potential for uncertainty is very great. But I do not think that any concerns which may exist on this ground provide a sound reason for declining to give effect to the section according to its terms. The defence of change of position will be available, and difficulties of proof are likely to increase with the passage of time. I think that the risk of widespread injustice remains to be demonstrated. If the risk is too great that is a matter for the legislature ...

[418] In my opinion the bank will be entitled to the benefit of s 32(1)(c) of the Act of 1980 if they can show that the payments which they seek to recover were made under a mistake of law.

...

Commentary and questions

According to the court, when does time begin to run in relation to claims based on a mistake of law? What are the practical and policy objections to this approach? How does the court deal with these objections?

There are no equivalent extension provisions in South Australia or Western Australia. Therefore in those jurisdictions the common law rule will apply, namely that the limitation period runs from the date the payment was received, not the date the mistake was discovered.[168] This principle is discussed in the following case.

Torrens Aloha Pty Ltd v Citibank NA **(1997) 144 ALR 89**
Full Court of the Federal Court of Australia

The issue before the court was whether the limitation period for a claim based on mistake of law did not begin to run until the decision of the High Court of Australia in *David Securities Pty Ltd v Commonwealth Bank of Australia* (1992) (see extract, p 110) recognising for the first time that a mistake of law could ground recovery.

Sackville J: ... [101] In my opinion, the fact that judicial law-making operates retrospectively does not mean that a person is or should be free to rely on the novel principle or doctrine to establish rights in relation to events or transactions occurring in the distant past, free from the constraints that would otherwise be imposed by statutes of limitations. The authorities do not support any such contention.

---

168 *David Securities Pty Ltd v Commonwealth Bank of Australia* (1992), p 389; *Torrens Aloha Pty Ltd v Citibank NA* (1997); *Baker v Courage & Co Ltd* (1910); *Re Mason* (1929), p 9; *Fuller v Happy Shopper Markets Ltd* (2001).

The classic formulation of a 'cause of action' is that of Brett J in *Cooke v Gill* (1873):

> '... cause of action' has been held from the earliest time to mean every fact which is material to be proved to entitle the plaintiff to succeed – every fact which the defendant would have a right to traverse.

This formulation was adopted by Lord Esher MR in *Read v Brown* (1888).[169] In *Do Carmo v Ford Excavations Pty Ltd* (1984), p 245, Wilson J said that the:

> ... concept of a 'cause of action' would seem to be clear. It is simply the fact or combination of facts which gives rise to a right to sue. In an action for negligence, it consists of the wrongful act or omission and the consequent damage ... Knowledge of the legal implications of the known facts is not an additional fact which forms part of a cause of action. Indeed, a person may be well appraised of all of the facts which need to be proved to establish a cause of action but for want of taking legal advice may not know that those facts give rise to a right to relief.

See also *Carter v Egg and Egg Pulp Marketing Board* (Vic) (1942), p 600 *per* Williams J.

There is nothing in these formulations which suggests that a cause of action does not accrue until the courts acknowledge the existence of the right to sue. The statements focus on the facts which a plaintiff must establish. Knowledge of the right to sue is not an essential ingredient of a cause of action. It would seem to follow that recognition of the right to sue by the courts is also not an essential [102] ingredient. If it were otherwise, many cases would have been decided differently.

...

This conclusion is consistent with the principles governing the accrual of a cause of action to recover money paid by mistake. In a common law action for the recovery of money paid under a mistake of fact, the rule was that time ran from the date of payment of the money and not the date of discovery of the mistake.[170] Where equitable remedies were sought, the relevant statute of limitation was applied by analogy, but lapse of time was no bar for such relief until the mistake was discovered or ought reasonably to have been discovered.[171]

Section 26 of the Limitation Act (UK) resolved the conflict between law and equity by providing that, where there is a cause of action for relief from the consequences of mistake, time does not begin to run until the person having the cause of action discovers, or could with reasonable diligence have discovered, the mistake. That provision was ultimately adopted in New South Wales by s 56(1) of the Limitation Act, implementing the recommendation of the New South Wales Law Reform Commission Report on *Limitation of Actions*.[172] Section 56(1), like its United Kingdom counterpart and the pre-existing rules of equity, addresses the circumstances in which the commencement of the limitation period should be postponed. In a case where the plaintiff seeks relief from the consequences of mistake, the period is postponed only until the plaintiff discovers or could with reasonable diligence have discovered the mistake – that is the mistake giving rise

---

169 See also *Trower and Sons Ltd v Ripstein* (1944), p 263 *per* Lord Wright.

170 *Baker v Courage & Co* (1910); *In re Mason* (1929), p 9 *per* Lord Hanworth MR.

171 *Brooksbank v Smith* (1836); *Denys v Shuckburgh* (1840); *Preston and Newsom on Limitation of Action*, 3rd edn, 1953, pp 253–55.

172 LRC, 1967, para 271.

to the cause of action. (It is not necessary to consider the precise significance of the words 'relief from the consequences of a mistake'.)[173]

Neither the rule of equity nor the language of s 56(1) of the Limitation Act is apt to postpone the commencement of the limitation period until the courts recognise a novel cause of action for recovery of payments made under a mistake. The authorities to which I have referred suggest strongly that a cause of action for recovery of moneys paid under a mistake of law accrues on the date of payment. Indeed, this was the view taken by Brennan J in his concurring judgment in *David Securities* (1992). His Honour said this at p 399 (see extract, p 110):

> If under a mistake, money is paid to and unjustly enriches a payee, *the payer's right to recover the amount paid accrues at the moment when the payee received the money.* [Emphasis added.]

At the very least, the authorities provide no support for the contention that the cause of action does not accrue until the courts acknowledge that the facts alleged give rise to a cause of action.

...

[Foster and Lehane JJ concurred.]

Questions

According to the court, when does the limitation period begin to run at common law in relation to mistake claims? Did the New South Wales equivalent of s 27 of the Limitations of Actions Act 1958 (Vic) have the effect that the limitation period did not begin to run until the right to recover on the basis of a mistake of law was recognised in *David Securities*? Is the court's approach to these special limitation provisions consistent with the approach taken by the House of Lords in *Kleinwort Benson Ltd v Lincoln City Council* (1999) (see extract, p 668)?

Compulsion

Where the claim is based on duress, legal compulsion, necessitous intervention or pursuant to an *ultra vires* demand, the limitation period runs from the date the enrichment was conferred.[174] There is admittedly little judicial authority on this point, however it is the view taken in the leading textbooks,[175] and is supported by analogy with mistake.

Benefits conferred under ineffective contracts

The general rule is that a claim in restitution is not available where the benefit under which the contract was conferred is still effective (see the discussion in

---

173 Cf *Phillip-Higgins v Harper* (1954), affirmed (1954); Mason and Carter, *Restitution Law in Australia*, 1995, para 2741.

174 *Maskell v Horner* (1915) (see extract, p 222).

175 Mason and Carter, *Restitution Law in Australia*, 1995, p 925; Goff and Jones, *The Law of Restitution*, 5th edn, 1998, pp 852–54; Burrows, *The Law of Restitution*, 1993, pp 442–43. Mason and Carter analogise with *Woolwich Equitable Building Society v Inland Revenue Commissioners* (1993) (see extract, p 456) where interest was awarded from the date of the payment, not the date the payment was known to be *ultra vires*.

Chapter 10, pp 265–66). Accordingly, where the contract is valid, it must first be discharged or rescinded before a claim in restitution will lie. It follows that discharge or rescission of the contract is a condition to bringing a claim in restitution, and as such the better view is that the cause of action does not accrue until such time as the discharge or rescission takes place.[176] This was the view taken in the following case.

Shephard v ANZ Banking Corp Ltd (1997) 41 NSWLR 431
New South Wales Court of Appeal

The issue before the court was whether a claim based on a total failure of consideration was a 'debt' for the purposes of issuing a statutory demand for repayment of the debt under s 556 of the Companies (New South Wales) Code.

Giles JA: ... [434] A debt might have been incurred for the purposes of s 556(1) notwithstanding that it was a contingent debt, in the sense of the undertaking of a conditional but unavoidable obligation to pay a definite sum of money at a future time. So in *Hawkins v Bank of China* giving a guarantee of payment of an existing debt was held to be the incurring of a debt, and in *Commissioner of State Taxation v Pollack* (1994) employing an employee in respect of whom pay-roll tax must be paid was held to be the incurring of a debt although the amount could only be ascertained in the future ...

[435] The contingent obligations were of a very different kind from the contingent debt in *Hawkins v Bank of China*. They depended upon failure by Holdings to perform within a reasonable time, upon the customers' elections to terminate the contracts rather than to keep them on foot, and upon the circumstances being such that in the absence of restitution there would be unjust enrichment and no defence such as a change of position. The first contingency was up to a point within [the defendant's] control, though not inevitably so. The second contingency was not, but was a necessary event for recovery of the deposits because the restitutionary remedy was not available until the contract had been discharged. If the circumstances called for a remedy to prevent unjust enrichment, the restitutionary obligation was imposed by law rather than by agreement of the parties, and arose at the time the consideration for which the deposits were paid failed, that is, when the contracts were validly terminated for non-performance.[177]

...

Abadee AJA: ... [442] [R]eturning to what might be regarded as the core submission of the respondents, it is that a customer has a restitutionary remedy if he or she terminates future performance of the contract and seeks recovery of the money paid under it. This remedy does not arise under the contract, and arises only when the contract has been so terminated by election. The basis of the remedy is that in the absence of the customer receiving the agreed performance or its equivalent in unliquidated damages, the law recognises it as unjust that the company continue to retain the purchase moneys received at the expense of the

---

176 Mason and Carter, *Restitution Law in Australia*, 1995, pp 925–27; contrast Goff and Jones, *The Law of Restitution*, 5th edn, 1998, p 854. For cases dealing with rescission see *Commonwealth Homes and Investment Co Ltd v Smith* (1937), pp 463, 466; cf p 458; *Lakshmijit v Sherani* (1974), p 616.

177 See *David Securities Pty Ltd v Commonwealth Bank of Australia* (1992), p 389.

customer. The law then imposes the restitutionary obligation on the company. The restitutionary obligation is 'incurred', if at all, only at that time. Thus, in this case no restitutionary obligation and hence no debt was incurred at any of the stages asserted by the appellant.

Commentary

This case was followed and applied in *Arrow Asset Management Pty Ltd v Sportsworld Group plc* (1999).

There are recent indications that the courts will not always insist that the plaintiff demonstrate that the contract has been discharged or rescinded before allowing a restitutionary claim. In the High Court case of *Roxborough v Rothmans of Pall Mall Australia* (2001) a majority of the court enabled the plaintiff to recover payments made under a consideration that had failed, despite the fact that the contract had not been terminated (see extracts, pp 268 and 273). This raises the question of when the limitation period will commence where the court has held that formal discharge of the contract is not necessary. Perhaps in this situation an analogy can be drawn with unenforceable or void contracts (which are inherently ineffective and therefore do need to be discharged or rescinded). It has been suggested in that context that the limitation period for claims based on total failure of consideration commences at the date of the failure of the condition,[178] and that the limitation period for claims based on the acceptance of the work commences at the date the work was done and accepted.[179]

---

178 *Reed International Books Australia Pty Ltd (t/a Butterworths v King & Prior Pty Ltd)* (1993); *Guardian Ocean Cargoes Ltd v Banco de Brazil SA (Nos 1 and 3)* (1994), p 160.

179 Mason and Carter, *Restitution Law in Australia*, 1995, p 924.

CHAPTER 19

REMEDIES

OVERVIEW OF AVAILABLE REMEDIES

The objective of restitutionary remedies is to reverse the unjust enrichment of the defendant. In most cases the plaintiff will seek a personal remedy; that is, a remedy imposing a personal obligation on the defendant to make restitution to the plaintiff. Two main personal remedies are available: an order that money be repaid to the plaintiff, and an order that the reasonable value of goods or services be paid to the plaintiff. However in some circumstances, particularly where the defendant is insolvent, the plaintiff will seek equitable proprietary relief; that is, an order that the plaintiff has a proprietary interest in certain property being held by the defendant. The three main forms of equitable proprietary relief are the constructive trust, resulting trust, and equitable lien.

PERSONAL CLAIMS

General

Most claims in restitution are personal, where the plaintiff seeks the imposition of a personal obligation on the defendant to make restitution to the plaintiff. The claim is for the recovery of the value of the enrichment, not for the enforcement of a trust or recovery of specific money or property.[1] Hence, it is irrelevant on a personal claim in restitution that the money or property can no longer specifically be identified in the hands of the recipient or be traced into other specific property.[2]

Interest on personal claims

A plaintiff who is successful in obtaining restitution might seek an award of interest on the sum recovered. The courts have jurisdiction pursuant to statute, equity and the common law to award interest on a sum recovered in restitution.

---

1 *Australia and New Zealand Banking Group Ltd v Westpac Banking Corporation* (1988), p 673; *Lipkin Gorman v Karpnale Ltd* (1991), p 572.
2 *Ibid.*

Statutory interest

There are statutory provisions conferring jurisdiction on Federal Courts and State and Territory Supreme Courts to award interest.[3] Representative of these provisions is s 51A of the Federal Court of Australia Act 1976 (Cth):

(1) In any proceedings for the recovery of any money (including any debt or damages or the value of any goods) in respect of a cause of action that arises after the commencement of this section, the Court or a Judge shall, upon application, unless good cause is show to the contrary either:

(a) order that there be included in the sum for which judgment is given interest at such rate as the Court or the Judge as the case may be, thinks fit on the whole or any part of the money or any part of the period between the date when the cause of action arose and the date as of which judgment is entered; or

(b) without proceeding to calculate interest in accordance with paragraph (a), order that there be included in the sum for which judgment is given a lump sum in lieu of any such interest.

(2) Sub-section (1) does not:

(a) authorize the giving of interest upon interest or of a sum in lieu of such interest; or

...

(d) limit the operation of any enactment or rule of law which, apart from this section, provides for the award of interest

...

An award of interest made under a statutory interest provision such as s 51A is discretionary, both as to whether an award is made and the quantum of the award. The statutory interest provisions do not comprise an exhaustive code, so that interest can be sought in the alternative at common law and in equity.[4] In fact, there are two significant limitations on the statutory interest provisions that might make it more advantageous for the plaintiff to seek equitable or common law interest rather than statutory interest. First, statutory interest provisions preclude an award of compound interest.[5] Secondly, the statutory provisions have no application where the moneys are repaid prior to commencing proceedings, as statutory interest can only be claimed in the same proceedings

---

3   Judiciary Act 1903 (Cth), s 77MA; Federal Court of Australia Act 1976 (Cth), s 51A; Supreme Court Act 1933 (ACT), s 69; Supreme Court Act 1970 (NSW), s 94; Supreme Court Act 1979 (NT), s 84; Common Law Practice Act 1867 (Qld), s 72; Supreme Court Act 1935 (SA), s 30C; Supreme Court Civil Procedure Act 1932 (Tas), s 34; Supreme Court Act 1986 (Vic), s 58; Supreme Court Act 1935 (WA), s 32.

4   *Hungerfords v Walker* (1989), pp 134, 148; *National Australia Bank Ltd v Budget Stationery Supplies Ltd* (1997) (see extract, p 683). Contrast the position in England: *President of India v La Pintada Compania Navigacion SA* (1985), p 130; *Westdeutsche Landesbank Girozentrale v Islington London Borough Council* (1996), pp 717, 719, 740–41 (see extract, p 681).

5   Most of the statutory provisions effect this by precluding 'interest upon interest'.

as the claim for the principal debt.[6] Some of the earlier decisions also concluded that statutory interest cannot be awarded where the principal claim is paid or settled after proceedings are commenced, but prior to judgment,[7] however it now seems settled that these cases should no longer be treated as correct.

State Bank of New South Wales v Commissioner of Taxation (1995) 62 FCR 371
New South Wales Supreme Court

The applicant paid certain sums of money into a Commonwealth government bank account pending determination of a dispute regarding liability for sales tax. The Commonwealth refunded part of that money. The applicant commenced proceedings to recover the remainder of the money, together with interest. The Commonwealth refunded the rest of the money prior to judgment being given. The applicant continued the proceedings in order to recover interest on the sum of money that had not been repaid until after the commencement of proceedings.

Wilcox J: … [385] It will be noted that the power to award interest [under s 51A of the Federal Court of Australia Act 1976 (Cth)] is confined to interest on the 'money' in respect of which the proceeding is brought. In the present case, the bulk of the money ($420,161.86) was repaid before the institution of the action. The proceeding was not brought in respect of any part of that money. It follows, as counsel for the applicant accept, that s 51A(1) does not authorise the court to award interest on that sum. However, the sum of $148,068.35 remained unpaid when the proceeding was instituted and, by an amendment to the statement of claim, it was claimed in this proceeding. Counsel for the applicant argue that, notwithstanding that it was paid before trial, it is correct to regard this proceeding as being, amongst other things, one for recovery of that money; accordingly, s 51A empowers the court to award interest on that sum between the date when the cause of action arose and the date of payment.

Counsel for the respondents dispute this interpretation of s 51A(1). They say that it only authorises the court to award interest on moneys that the court orders to be paid; so the court may not award interest on moneys the subject of the proceeding that are paid before judgment. They say this interpretation of s 51A(1) is compelled by the word 'included' in para (a); interest may be a component of the judgment sum, not the judgment sum itself.

In support they cite a decision of Hewson J in the Admiralty Division of the English High Court of Judicature, *Hepworth SS Medina Princess (Owners), The Medina Princess* (1962), p 19:

> It is quite unnecessary in a claim for damages or in respect of a debt to claim for interest, but it seems to me that this court has no power to order, and there is no discretion in the matter of ordering, interest to be paid unless it has given judgment in respect of the damages or debt. The words of the section are 'shall be included in the sum for which judgment is given'. This court has given no judgment in respect of any sum and, so far as I can see, is not empowered to

---

6   *Commonwealth of Australia v SCI Operations Pty Ltd* (1998), p 306 *per* Gaudron J (see extract, p 678); *State Bank of New South Wales Limited v Commissioner of Taxation* (1995) (see the following extract); *National Australia Bank Ltd v Budget Stationery Supplies Ltd* (1997) (see extract, p 683); *Matthew v TM Sutton Ltd* (1994), p 461.

7   *The 'Medina Princess'* (1962), p 21; *President of India v La Pintada Cia Navigacion SA* (1985), p 121.

award interest upon sums which have already been paid and which have not been the subject of its judgment.

I do not think this court should adopt that view of the significance of the word 'included'. It is not clear to me that it would be followed even in England today. In *Woolwich Equitable Building Society v Inland Revenue Commissioners* (1993) the only order was for payment of interest; the capital sums had long since been repaid. Apparently, nobody saw any problem about that, notwithstanding that s 35A of the Supreme Court Act uses the same formula: 'included in any sum for which judgment is given simple interest ...'. In any event, whatever the position in England, s 51A(1) is a facultative provision intended to confer power on the court to do justice between parties in relation to pre-judgment interest; a matter of some importance in these days of high interest rates and extensive delays in finalising litigation. The sub-section should be interpreted as widely as its language allows. While it is true that an item 'included' in another item will usually constitute only part of the latter item, this is not necessarily so. The point may be illustrated by a sporting example. Take a batsman who has the misfortune to score 'ducks' in his first three innings in a season, then scores 50 runs in the fourth. If a computation was then made of the team members' aggregates, his 50 runs would be 'included' in his aggregate, notwithstanding that it constituted all the runs in the aggregate. Similarly, runs scored by a batsman off the opening ball of an innings are immediately 'included' in the team's innings score.

In my opinion, as a matter of interpretation, s 51A(1) is available in this case.

...

Questions

According to Wilcox J, would statutory interest have been recoverable on the amount repaid by the Commonwealth prior to the applicant commencing proceedings? According to his Honour, was statutory interest recoverable on the sum repaid by the Commonwealth after the applicant commenced proceedings, but before judgment?

Commonwealth of Australia v SCI Operations (1997) 192 CLR 285
High Court of Australia

Between 1987 and 1992 the applicants imported PET resin for use in the production of plastic bottles. In September 1987 it sought an order that customs duty was payable on the PET resin at a concessional rate, however this was rejected. In June 1994 the Comptroller General of Customs eventually made an order applying a concessional rate of customs duty for the importation of PET resin for one period, and made them duty free for another period. The result was that the applicants had overpaid customs duty, and they commenced proceedings to recover the amount of the overpayments, together with interest. Later on the same day that the proceedings were commenced, the Commonwealth refunded the overpaid duty to the applicants, but without interest. The applicants continued the court proceedings in order to recover interest, both on the basis of s 51A of the Federal Court of Australia Act 1976 (Cth) and on the basis of a free standing right to interest based on restitutionary principles. The following extract deals with the claim to statutory interest, and the issue whether statutory interest can be awarded where the principal amount sought had been repaid by the defendant prior to judgment.

Gaudron J: ... [300] *Section 51A: interest where moneys paid before judgment*

In essence, the Commonwealth's first argument is that s 51A(1) does not authorise the payment of interest where the moneys claimed in legal proceedings are paid in full prior to judgment. It was put that it was held by Hewson J in *The 'Medina Princess'* (1962) that a provision which is not relevantly distinguishable from s 51A(1)(a), namely, s 3(1) of the Law Reform (Miscellaneous Provisions) Act 1934 (UK),[8] had no application in that situation and that, properly construed, s 51A(1) is also inapplicable.

In *The 'Medina Princess'*, the moneys claimed were, in fact, paid prior to judgment. However, Hewson J did not base his decision on that aspect of the matter but, rather, on the view that the court had no power 'to award interest upon a motion when it [had] not given judgment upon the principal sum claimed' (1962), p 21. The decision in that case was subsequently criticised in *Tehno-Impex v Gebr Van Weelde Scheepvaartkantoor BV* (1981), pp 665, 675–76, 181. Later, in *President of India v La Pintada Compania Navigacion SA* (1985), p 121, Lord Brandon of Oakbrook expressed the view that *The 'Medina Princess'* was correctly decided, his Lordship apparently treating it as having decided that the provision in [301] question in that case did not confer power to award interest on debts paid prior to judgment.

In my view, neither the language of s 51A(1) nor the decision in *The 'Medina Princess'* dictates the conclusion that interest cannot be awarded on moneys paid prior to judgment. In this last regard, it may be noted that, in discussion as to costs in *The 'Medina Princess'*, Hewson J made this observation (1962), p 23: 'I have not said that [the plaintiffs] were not entitled to interest. I said that this method of asking for it does not appeal to me.' More significantly, however, the power conferred by s 51A(1), being a power conferred on a court, is not to be construed as subject to limitations which its terms do not require.[9]

Sub-section (1) of s 51A does not specify that interest may be included in a judgment for a sum of money claimed in legal proceedings. Rather, it provides that it may be included 'in the sum for which judgment is given'. Clearly, s 51A(1) requires that there be a 'sum for which judgment is given' before interest can be included. But that does not mean that interest cannot be awarded if payment of the moneys claimed in the proceedings is made prior to judgment. The mere payment of a debt or other money sum claimed in legal proceedings does not deprive a court of power to enter judgment for the costs of those proceedings. And judgment may be entered for costs in a fixed sum. In that event, there is, in terms of s 51A(1),

---

8   Subject to provisos which are not presently relevant, that section provided:

In any proceedings tried in any court of record for the recovery of any debt or damages, the court may, if it thinks fit, order that there shall be included in the sum for which judgment is given interest at such rate as it thinks fit on the whole or any part of the debt or damages for the whole or any part of the period between the date when the cause of action arose and the date of the judgment.

9   See *Owners of 'Shin Kobe Maru' v Empire Shipping Co Inc* (1994), p 421. See also *FAI General Insurance Co Ltd v Southern Cross Exploration NL* (1988), pp 283–84 *per* Wilson J, 290 *per* Gaudron J; *Knight v FP Special Assets Ltd* (1992), pp 185 *per* Mason CJ and Deane J, 202–03 *per* Dawson J, 205 *per* Gaudron J; *David Grant & Co Pty Ltd v Westpac Banking Corporation* (1995), pp 275–76 *per* Gummow J; *Emanuele v Australian Securities Commission* (1997), p 729 *per* Gaudron J; 144 ALR 359, p 376; *Hyman v Rose* (1912), p 631 *per* Earl Loreburn LC.

a 'sum for which judgment is given' and, in my view, there may be included in that sum interest pursuant to para (a), or, a lump sum in lieu of interest pursuant to para (b).

...

Questions

According to Gaudron J, is statutory interest recoverable on sums repaid by the defendant prior to the plaintiff commencing proceedings? According to her Honour, is statutory interest recoverable on sums repaid after the plaintiff commences proceedings, but before judgment?

Interest in equity

Equity will award interest on a range of restitutionary claims. The award of interest is independent of the claim for the principal debt and so can be awarded even though the defendant repaid the principal sum before the proceedings were commenced.[10]

Equity can award both simple and compound interest. The circumstances when equity will award simple interest are discussed by McHugh and Gummow JJ in the following decision.

Commonwealth of Australia v SCI Operations (1997) 192 CLR 285
High Court of Australia

The facts are stated above.

McHugh and Gummow JJ: ... [316] It is true that in the administration of its remedies, equity followed a different path to the common law with respect to the award of interest. In cases of money obtained and retained by fraud and money withheld or misapplied by a trustee or fiduciary, the decree might require payment of compound interest[11] ...

In other instances, equitable relief might involve the payment of simple interest. As an element in the relief administered upon rescission of a contract under which the plaintiff had paid over moneys to the defendant, the order might require the defendant to make the repayment with interest calculated from the date of the initial payment.[12] Relief against forfeiture by a vendor of payments under an instalment or terms contract might require repayment with interest from the dates the respective instalments were paid.[13] An account of profits would carry interest.[14] Conversely, a party seeking equitable relief may be obliged to do equity by the payment or [317] repayment of moneys with interest.[15] A purchaser who, after the date fixed for completion, seeks specific performance will be treated in

---

10 *Matthew v TM Sutton Ltd* (1994).
11 See *Hungerfords v Walker* (1989), p 148.
12 An example is the orders made in *Alati v Kruger* (1955), pp 229–30.
13 *Pitt v Curotta* (1931), p 483.
14 See *Warman International Ltd v Dwyer* (1995), p 570.
15 See, for example, the orders in *Nelson v Nelson* (1995), pp 618–19; *Maguire v Makaronis* (1997), p 500.

equity as having been in possession from the completion date and, in general, will be required to offer the vendor interest on the purchase price from that date.[16]

Commentary and question

In what circumstances will equity award simple interest?

McHugh and Gummow JJ recognise that the courts of equity have jurisdiction to award compound interest in two categories of case: where money is wrongfully obtained and retained by fraud, and where money is wrongfully withheld by a trustee or fiduciary.[17] These are the two traditional cases were equity conferred upon the courts a discretion to award compound interest. Ordinarily, compound interest is awarded in these two categories of case where the defendant has used the money in trade or commerce and so has earned, or has the capacity to earn, compound interest.

It is not clear whether the power to award of compound interest is limited to the two identified situations of fraud and misapplication of property by a trustee or fiduciary,[18] or whether these are merely two specific instances in which compound interest might be awarded.[19] In the leading authority, *Westdeutsche Landesbank Girozentrale v Islington Borough Council* (1996) (see the following extract), the majority of the House of Lords took the narrower view.[20] The majority rejected the argument that equity in its auxiliary jurisdiction could award compound interest on a personal claim in restitution for the recovery of money paid under a void swaps contract. However, Lords Goff and Woolf in dissent considered that equity could award compound interest on a successful claim in restitution where such an award was necessary to achieve full restitution of the enrichment received by the defendant. Lord Goff's judgment on this point is extracted below.

Westdeutsche Landesbank Girozentrale v Islington Borough Council [1996] AC 669
House of Lords

The facts are stated at p 372.

Lord Goff: ... [696] The question which arises in the present case is whether, in the exercise of equity's auxiliary jurisdiction, the equitable jurisdiction to award compound interest may be exercised to enable a plaintiff to obtain full justice in a personal action of restitution at common law.

---

16 *Esdaile v Stephenson* (1822); *Harvela Ltd v Royal Trust Co* (1986), pp 236–37. See also Davis, 'Interest as compensation', in Finn (ed), *Essays on Damages*, 1992, 129, pp 138–39.

17 See also *Hungerfords v Walker* (1989), p 148; *President of India v La Pintada Cia Navigacion SA* (1985) p 116; *Westdeutsche Landesbank Girozentrale v Islington London Borough Council* (1996), pp 702, 718, 738.

18 For statements that it is so limited see *President of India v La Pintada Cia Navigacion SA* (1985), p 116; *Westdeutsche Landesbank Girozentrale v Islington London Borough Council* (1996), pp 702, 718, 738.

19 For statements to this effect see *Hungerfords v Walker* (1989), p 148; *JAD International Pty Ltd v International Trucks Australia Ltd* (1994), p 392; *Westdeutsche Landesbank Girozentrale v Islington London Borough Council* (1996) (see following extract).

20 *Westdeutsche Landesbank Girozentrale v Islington London Borough Council* (1996), pp 702, 718, 738.

I start with the position that the common law remedy is, in a case such as the present, plainly inadequate, in that there is no power to award compound interest at common law and that without that power the common law remedy is incomplete. The situation is therefore no different from that in which, in the absence of jurisdiction at common law to order discovery, equity stepped in to enable justice to be done in common law actions by ordering the defendant to make discovery on oath. The only difference between the two cases is that, whereas the equitable jurisdiction to order discovery in aid of common law actions was recognised many years ago, the possibility of the equitable jurisdiction to award compound interest being exercised in aid of common law actions was not addressed until the present case. Fortunately, however, judges or equity have always been ready to address new problems. and to create new doctrines, where justice so requires. As Sir George Jessel MR said in a famous passage in his judgment in *In re Hallett's Estate; Knatchbull v Hallett* (1880):

> I intentionally say modern rules, because it must not be forgotten that the rules of Courts of Equity are not, like the rules to the Common Law, supposed to have been established from time immemorial. It is perfectly well known that they have been established from time to time – altered, improved, and refined from time to time. In many cases we know the names of the Chancellors who invented them. No doubt they were invented for the purpose of securing the better administration of justice, but still they were invented.

I therefore ask myself whether there is any reason why the equitable jurisdiction to award compound interest should not be exercised in a case such as the present. I can see none. Take, for example, the case of fraud. It is well established that the equitable jurisdiction may be exercised in cases of fraud. Indeed it is plain that, on the same facts, there may be a remedy both at law and in equity to recover money obtained by fraud: see *Johnson v The King* (1904) *per* Lord Mcnaghten. Is it to be said that, if the plaintiff decides to proceed in equity, compound interest may be awarded: but that if he chooses to proceed in an action at law, no such auxiliary relief will be available to him? I find it difficult to believe that, at the end of the 20th century, our law should be so hidebound by forms of action as to be compelled to reach such a conclusion.

For these reasons I conclude that the equitable jurisdiction to award compound interest may be exercised in the case of personal claims at [697] common law, as it is in equity. Furthermore I am satisfied that, in particular, the equitable jurisdiction may, where appropriate, be exercised in the case of a personal claim in restitution.
...

I recognise that, in so holding, the courts would be breaking new ground, and would be extending the equitable jurisdiction to a field where ir has not hitherto been exercised. But that cannot of itself be enough to prevent what I see to be a thoroughly desirable extension of the jurisdiction, consistent with its underlying basis that it exists to meet the demands of justice. An action of restitution appears to me to provide an almost classic case in which the jurisdiction should be available to enable the courts to do full justice. Claims in restitution are founded upon a principle of justice, being designed to prevent the unjust enrichment of the defendant, see *Lipkin Gorman v Karpnale Ltd* (1991). Long ago, in *Moses v Macferlan* (1760) Lord Mansfield said that the gist of the action for money had and received is that 'the defendant, upon the circumstances of the case, is obliged by the ties of natural justice and equity to refund the money'. It would be strange indeed if the courts lacked jurisdiction in such a case to ensure that justice could be fully achieved by means of an award of compound interest, where it is appropriate to make such an award, despite the fact that the jurisdiction to award such interest is itself said to rest upon the demands of justice. I am glad not to be forced to hold that English law is so inadequate as to be incapable of achieving such a result. In my opinion the jurisdiction should now be made available, as justice requires, in cases of restitution, to ensure that full justice can be done. The seed is there, but the growth has hitherto been confined within a small area. That growth should now be permitted to spread naturally elsewhere within this newly recognised branch of the law. No genetic engineering is required, only that the warm sun of judicial creativity should exercise its benign influence rather than remain hidden behind the dark clouds of legal history.

...

Commentary

The High Court has not yet directly addressed the question of the scope of the equitable jurisdiction to award compound interest. However, as will be seen in the next section, the Australian courts have shown a preference for expanding the common law jurisdiction to award interest by moving toward recognition of an independent restitutionary right to interest, rather than expanding the equitable jurisdiction.

Interest at common law

National Australia Bank Ltd v Budget Stationery Supplies Ltd [1997] NSWSC CA 41 (unreported) 23 April 1997, Court of Appeal of New South Wales

A loan agreement entered into by the parties was found to be void for uncertainty. Budget repaid the principal, however the bank commenced proceedings to recover interest on the principal on the basis of a general right to recover interest in restitution.

Mason P: ... The common law's attitude to interest on debts is confused and largely negative.

London, Chatham & Dover Railway Co v South Eastern Railway Co (1893) is frequently cited as authority for the proposition that damages are not payable for late payment of a debt. (For present purposes, I include both contractual and restitutionary obligations to pay a money sum as falling within the concept of 'debt'.) It is generally stated that interest will only be added if there is express agreement, an implied agreement arising from a course of dealing between the parties, or clear custom.[21] In *London, Chatham*, the House of Lords felt reluctantly constrained by what was recognised to be an unsatisfactory stream of earlier authority supporting these propositions. It cited earlier cases supporting such a view and offering as the rationale the difficulty of juries assessing interest as part of damages, see *Page v Newman* (1829). The limited statutory redress obtained by

---

21   See, eg, *Halsbury's Laws of England*, 4th edn; Vol 32, 'Money', para 108.

Lord Tenterden's Act of 1833[22] was viewed as confirming the torpor of the common law. To this day, one may find many statements citing *London, Chatham* as fixing the common law and stating a universal proposition against the award of interest (by way of damages or otherwise), save in the exceptional situations to which I have already referred.[23]

But there have always been streams of cases of undoubted authority which simply walked around any such general principle. Some involve restitutionary obligations, although this does not appear to be the basis upon which the '*London, Chatham* principle' was bypassed. Thus, interest at common law has been awarded for money had and received, where the facts would have supported an equitable claim for account, see *Bayne v Stephens* (1908); where restitution follows the reversal on appeal of a previously satisfied judgment;[24] where damages are awarded under the rule in *Bain v Fothergill* (1874);[25] and where a contract has been discharged for breach, repudiation or in exercise of a contractual right.[26] One might be pardoned for thinking that this litany of 'exceptions' to the *London, Chatham* principle goes a long way towards eating up the general rule. In all of these cases, interest was awarded at common law and computed from the date of receipt of moneys ordered to be repaid, even where (in cases unlike the present) the restitutionary cause of action leading to the obligation to repay the 'principal' may have arisen later. Thus, it is well established that where a contract is terminated for breach by the vendor, the purchaser will recover the deposit together with interest from the date of original payment, even though termination does not operate *ab initio*.[27]

Passing *London, Chatham* like ships in the night, these cases proceeded upon the obvious principle that, when A retains money owned by or owing to B over a period of time, A derives a benefit (at B's expense) usually measurable by what A would have had to pay in the market to borrow that sum for that period. Since this benefit is derived without justification and at the expense of the person to whom the principal sum was due, we should now recognise it as an unjust enrichment. It stands independently of, but appurtenant upon the obligation to pay, the 'principal' sum. The independent nature of the restitutionary entitlement to interest is evidenced by historical recognition of a distinct *indebitatus* count for

---

22 Civil Procedure Act 1833 (UK), s 28. The Act required a written demand claiming interest. The New South Wales counterpart became s 140 of the Common Law Procedure Act 1899, which remained until the enactment of s 94 of the Supreme Court Act 1970.

23 See, eg, *Bayne v Stephens* (1908); *Marine Board of Launceston v Minister for the Navy* (1945), pp 525, 529; *Mathew v TM Sutton Ltd* (1994). For a recent statement see *Andjelic v Marsland* (1996), p 36 *per* McHugh and Gummow JJ. Contrast *Hungerfords v Walker* (1988), p 138 where Mason CJ and Wilson J pointedly described *London, Chatham* as stating the common law 'in England'.

24 *Rodger v The Comptoir d'Escompte de Paris* (1871); *Commonwealth v McCormack* (1984); *National Australia Bank Ltd v Bond Brewing Holdings Ltd* (1991), p 597. In New South Wales the practice is to award such interest at the rates payable on judgments unless special circumstances exist: see *Production Spray Painting & Panel Beating Pty Ltd v Newnham (No 2)* (1991); *Haig v Minister Administering the National Parks and Wildlife Act 1974 (No 3)* (1996).

25 See *Day v Singleton* (1899); *Ashok Trading Pty Ltd v Kintay Pty Ltd* (1983).

26 See, eg, *Elder's Trustee and Executor Co Ltd v Commonwealth Homes and Investment Co Ltd* (1941) 65 CLR 603; *Lexane Pty Ltd v Highfern Pty Ltd* [1985] 1 Qd R 446, pp 461–62.

27 See, eg, *Sandeman v Wilson* (1880); *Delbridge v Low* (1990), p 335.

interest.[28] A 19th century authority on an unrelated topic pointed aptly to this conclusion in stating: 'As interest may be considered as the "mesne profits" of money in the same way as rent is of land, it is not, perhaps, too much to consider it amenable to the same rules as regulate the repayment of mesne profits of land.'[29]

The justice of the claim to interest was recognised in *London, Chatham* itself, where Lord Herschell LC acknowledged that 'the party who is wrongfully withholding the money from the other ought not in justice to benefit by having the money in his possession and enjoying the use of it' (1893).[30] Unfortunately, the Lord Chancellor and the other Law Lords felt constrained in *London, Chatham* from giving effect to the injustice they recognised, citing *Page v Newman* and the negative implication deriving from the limited intervention of Parliament in Lord Tenterden's Act of 1833. The Lord Chancellor thus recognised the unjust enrichment, but felt practically powerless to remedy it. In my view we should not feel similar restraint in the light of developments stemming in Australia from *Pavey & Matthews Pty Ltd v Paul* (1992). The particular categories of cases involving awards of interest at common law to which I have referred strongly support such a development. No longer are we troubled about juries being confused by having to compute interest in these matters. And the notion that the existence of a limited statutory remedy to award interest should restrain the incremental and principled development of the common law in this area (though still current in the United Kingdom)[31] has been repudiated in Australia.[32]

In *State Bank of New South Wales Ltd v Federal Commissioner of Taxation* (1995), pp 659–61, Wilcox J referred to some of these developments. He held that 'in ordering a payment of money by way of restitution, a court has power to include something by way of interest, where this is necessary to do justice between the parties' (1995), p 660. Indeed he went further and awarded interest with respect to a discrete sum that had been 'retained' but repaid before proceedings were instituted (1995), pp 656, 663. In *SCI Operations Pty Ltd v Commonwealth* (1996), Beaumont and Einfeld JJ indicated concurrence with Wilcox J in *State Bank*. I would do likewise.

It follows that, absent the misleading and deceptive conduct of the Bank, I would have held that the Bank was entitled to recover interest at common law with respect to the periods during which Budget had 'the use of' the $300,000 advanced under the void contract. I reserve for an occasion when the court has had the benefit of full argument consideration whether the majority of the House of Lords in *Westdeutsche Landesbank Girozentrale* (1996) (Lord Goff and Lord Woolf dissenting) were correct in rejecting the availability of compound interest. Nothing turns on this point in the present case ...

[Mason P refused to award interest to the bank on these facts, as the bank had engaged in misleading or deceptive conduct regarding the repayment of the loan.]

---

28 See *Nordenstrom v Pitt* (1845); *Norman v Federal Commissioner of Taxation* (1963), p 38; *South Australia v Commonwealth* (1992), p 253.

29 Clode, *Law and Practice of Petition of Right*, 1887, p 96.

30 See also *Marine Board of Launceston*, p 525 *per* Latham CJ.

31 See *President of India v La Pintada Compania Navigacion SA* (1985), p 130; *Westdeutsche Landesbank Girozentrale v Islington London Borough Council* (1996), pp 717, 718–19, 740–01.

32 See *Hungerfords v Walker* (1988), pp 147–48.

Commentary and questions

Mason P recognises that the courts traditionally awarded interest at common law only in a limited number of cases. However, his Honour held that the courts have a general power to award interest when ordering the repayment of money in restitution to ensure that the defendant does not retain a benefit from the use of the money. What reasons did his Honour give for recognising an independent restitutionary right to interest? Is it relevant that the defendant had repaid the principal sum prior to the commencement of proceedings by the plaintiff?

There are other Australian cases in which an independent restitutionary cause of action for the recovery of interest has been recognised.[33] Nevertheless, McHugh and Gummow JJ in *dicta* in *Commonwealth of Australia v SCI Operations* (1997) doubted whether an independent restitutionary right to interest is established on the current state of authorities.

If an independent restitutionary action for interest does exist, the courts will nevertheless refuse to award interest on the basis of this principle where the legislation under which the principal sum was paid contain detailed refund provisions which evince an intention to exclude the restitutionary right to interest. This is illustrated in the following case.

Commonwealth of Australia v SCI Operations (1997) 192 CLR 285
High Court of Australia

The facts are stated above. The Customs Regulations contained detailed provisions for the refund of overpaid customs duty.

Gaudron J: ... [306] [I]t is not in dispute that, the tariff concession order not having then been made, customs duty was payable at non-concessional rates on the goods which later became the subject of that order when those goods were entered for home consumption. The only right with respect to the moneys paid at that time is the right conferred by the refund provisions. And the refund provisions confer a right to a refund but not a right to interest on the amount refunded.

The right conferred by the refund provisions is a statutory right which has no counterpart in the general law. Being a right based wholly in statute, it can neither be cut down nor enlarged by resort to the general law or to restitutionary principles. More precisely, those principles cannot convert a statutory right to obtain a refund of money into a right to obtain a refund with interest. There is, thus, no substance in the claim that [the applicants] were entitled to a judgment for interest by reason of restitutionary principles.

...

---

33 *Star v O'Brien* (1996) 40 NSWLR 695; *SCI Operations v Commonwealth of Australia* 1996) 69 FCR 346, pp 377–78 (on appeal *Commonwealth of Australia v SCI Operations Pty Ltd* (1998) 192 CLR 285). For academic discussion of an independent restitutionary right to interest see: Edelman, 'Claims to compound interest Pt I' (1997) 27 ABLR 211; Edelman, 'Claims to compound interest Pt II: extending compound interest claims for wrongdoing' (2000) 28 ABLR 115; Ridge, 'Just feel-good words? Recent Australian developments towards a restitutionary cause of action for pre-judgment interest' (2000) 28 ABLR 275.

EQUITABLE PROPRIETARY REMEDIES

There are three equitable proprietary remedies that are potentially available in cases where a right to restitution arises: the constructive trust, the resulting trust, and the equitable lien. These proprietary remedies confer two main advantages over a personal remedy:

1   priority over unsecured creditors in an insolvency; and

2   the ability to take advantage of an increase in the value of the product of the enrichment.[34]

It is not intended that the following discussion of these equitable remedies be taken as a definitive statement as to the circumstances in which they will be awarded. That task is best left to texts on equity. Rather, the focus in this book will be on the availability of those equitable proprietary remedies in restitutionary claims; that is, where the facts of the case give rise to an independent action in restitution. As will be seen, however, the exact circumstances where the equitable proprietary remedies are available on a restitutionary claim remains uncertain and controversial.[35]

Constructive trusts

The Australian courts have consistently refused to adopt the Canadian and American form of remedial constructive trust based on unjust enrichment. In those jurisdictions, the constructive trust is a purely remedial device that the court can award at its discretion across the spectrum of civil obligations whenever the defendant retains property of which the plaintiff has been unjustly deprived.[36] However, in Australia the constructive trust is a creature of equity. Although the reversal of an unjust enrichment is an important objective of the constructive trust, unjust enrichment principles do not form the basis of that trust. Rather, as the following case demonstrates, the constructive trust is imposed in certain recognised categories of case where it would be unconscionable for the defendant to retain full beneficial interest in property.

---

34   Though it is unclear whether an equitable lien can be claimed over an increase in the value of the property: see below p 713.

35   For recent academic discussions of the role of equitable proprietary remedies in restitution claims see, for example, Birks, 'Trusts raised to reverse unjust enrichment: the *Westdeutsche* case' [1996] RLR 3, pp 13–15; McCormack, 'Proprietary claims and insolvency in the wake of *Westdeutsche*' (1996) JBL 48; Chambers, *Resulting Trusts*, 1998; Millett, 'Restitution and constructive trusts', in Cornish *et al* (eds), *Restitution: Past, Present and Future*, 1998, Chapter 13; Oakley, 'Restitution and constructive trusts: a commentary', in Cornish *et al* (eds), *Restitution: Past, Present and Future*, 1998, Chapter 14; Burrows, 'Proprietary restitution: unmasking unjust enrichment' (2001) 117 LQR 412; Evans, 'Rethinking tracing and the law of restitution' [1999] 115 LQR 469; Evans, 'Defending discretionary remedialism' (2001) 23 Sydney Law Review 463.

36   *Sorochan v Sorochan* (1986); *LAC Minerals Ltd v International Corona Resources Ltd* (1989); *Soulos v Korkontzilas* (1997).

Muschinski v Dodds (1985) 160 CLR 583 High Court of Australia

A *de facto* couple, Mrs Muschinski and Mr Dodds, who had lived together for three years, decided to buy a property at Picton. The purchase price for the property was provided by Mrs Muschinski however she agreed to include Mr Dodds' name on the title if he undertook to renovate a cottage on the land and pay for the erection of a prefabricated house. The land was accordingly transferred to them as tenants in common in equal shares. The parties separated without the cottage having been renovated or the house erected. Mrs Muschinski commenced proceedings claiming to be entitled to the whole beneficial interest in the property.

Deane J: ... [611] There was no express or implied agreement, arrangement or understanding between the parties that they should hold their legal interests upon trust for themselves in shares corresponding to their respective contributions. To the contrary, the evidence leads inexorably to the conclusion – expressed in concurrent findings of fact in the courts below – that it was their shared intention that, from the time of purchase, each should have a full one half beneficial, as well as legal, interest in the property. Mrs Muschinski's intention was that her own and Mr Dodds' interest or, to use her word, 'status' in the whole venture should be equal: it should be a 'joint venture', a 'partnership'... Nor, upon a proper assessment of the evidence, is there room for a finding of an express or implied contract between Mrs Muschinski and Mr Dodds to the effect that, if things fell apart in respect of both their personal relationship and their planned development of the land, they would hold the property either upon trust to repay their respective contributions and then for themselves equally or upon trust for themselves in shares according to their respective contributions. There is no suggestion at all of any express contract to that effect and no adequate foundation for the implication of one. As the learned trial judge found, it was not the intention of either of them that Mr Dodds' equal beneficial interest should be acquired by [612] stages as he contributed towards the planned joint endeavour. Their planned future association and joint activity provided the occasion for, and the explanation of, the arrangement between them. That arrangement was however to the effect that Mr Dodds' beneficial interest in the property should be immediate and unconditional. It was not qualified to provide for the uncontemplated double contingency that their personal relationship would fail and that the proposed venture involving the development and joint use of the land would crumble under the yoke of inauspicious stars.

In these circumstances, there is no occasion for recourse to the presumption of the law of equity that, where two or more persons advance the purchase price of property in different shares, the person or persons to whom the legal title is transferred holds or hold the property upon resulting trust in favour of those who provided the purchase price in the shares in which they provided it: *Calverley v Green* (1984), p 121; p 500. That presumption performs much the same function as a civil onus of proof. General statements to the effect that it is not lightly to be rebutted should not, in my respectful view, now be accepted as good law (1984), pp 120, 122; pp 499, 503. That is not, of course, to deny that the facts which call the presumption into operation may, in the circumstances of a particular case, also lead to such a strong inference of an intended trust that convincing evidence would be necessary to rebut it: cf *Wirth v Wirth* (1956), pp 241–42. Even in such a case however, the presumption operates by reference to the presumed intention of the party whose contribution exceeds his or her proportionate share; it cannot prevail over the actual intention of that party as established by the overall evidence, including the evidence of the parties' respective contributions.

It follows that no relief is available to Mrs Muschinski on the grounds of breach of express or implied agreement or of express or implied trust. The question remains whether the circumstances of the case are such as to entitle her to claim relief on some other ground. In particular, the question arises whether she is entitled to claim relief by way of declaration of, or order imposing, a constructive trust. It was submitted on behalf of Mrs Muschinski that she was entitled to a declaration of constructive trust based on broad notions of fairness and unjust enrichment.

The nature and function of the constructive trust have been the subject of considerable discussion throughout the common law world for several decades.[37] [613] At times, disputing factions have tended to polarise the discussion by reference to competing rallying points of 'remedy' and 'institution'. The perceived dichotomy between those two catchwords has, however, largely been the consequence of lack of definition. In a broad sense, the constructive trust is both an institution and a remedy of the law of equity. As a remedy, it can only properly be understood in the context of the history and the persisting distinctness of the principles of equity that enlighten and control the common law. The use or trust of equity, like equity itself, was essentially remedial in its origins. In its basic form it was imposed, as a personal obligation attaching to property, to enforce the equitable principle that a legal owner should not be permitted to use his common law rights as owner to abuse or subvert the intention which underlay his acquisition and possession of those rights. This was consistent with the traditional concern of equity with substance rather than form. In time, the relationships in which the trust was recognised and enforced to protect actual or presumed intention became standardised and were accepted into conveyancing practice (particularly in relation to settlements) and property law as the equitable institutions of the express and implied (including resulting) trust. Like express and implied trusts, the constructive trust developed as a remedial relationship superimposed upon common law rights by order of the Chancery Court. It differs from those other forms of trust, however, in that it arises regardless of intention.

---

37 See particularly Pound, 'Equitable remedies' (1919–20) 33 Harv LR 420, pp 420–23; Scott, 'Constructive trusts' (1955) 71 LQR 39; Maudsley, 'Proprietary remedies for the recovery of money' (1959) 75 LQR 234; Waters, *The Constructive Trust*, 1964; Goff and Jones, *The Law of Restitution*, 2nd edn, 1978, especially Chapters 1 and 2; Oakley, *Constructive Trusts*, 1978; Wade, 'Trusts, the matrimonial home and *de facto* spouses' (1978–80) 6 U Tas LR 97; Davies, 'Informal arrangements affecting land' (1976–79) 8 Syd LR 578; *Underhill's Law Relating to Trusts and Trustees*, 13th edn, 1979, Chapter 7; Dewar, 'The development of the remedial constructive trust' (1982) 60 Can Bar Rev 265; Pettit, *Equity and the Law of Trusts*, 5th edn, 1984, p v and Chapter 10; Hanbury and Maudsley, *Modern Equity*, 12th edn, 1985, Chapter 12.

For that reason, it was not as well suited to development as a conveyancing device or as an instrument of property law. Indeed, whereas the rationale of the institutions of express and implied trust is now usually identified by reference to intention, the rationale of the constructive trust must still be found essentially in its remedial function which it has predominantly retained.[38] The constructive trust shares, however, [614] some of the institutionalised features of express and implied trust. It demands the staple ingredients of those trusts: subject matter, trustee, beneficiary (or, conceivably, purpose), and personal obligation attaching to the property.[39] When established or imposed, it is a relationship governed by a coherent body of traditional and statute law. Viewed in its modern context, the constructive trust can properly be described as a remedial institution which equity imposes regardless of actual or presumed agreement or intention (and subsequently protects) to preclude the retention or assertion of beneficial ownership of property to the extent that such retention or assertion would be contrary to equitable principle.

There is, however, a more limited sense in which there is some superficial plausibility in the notions of 'institution' and 'remedy' as competing characterisations of the constructive trust. If 'institution' is understood as connoting a relationship which arises and exists under the law independently of any order of a court and 'remedy' is defined as referring to the actual establishment of a relationship by such an order, the catchwords of 'institution' and 'remedy' do serve the function of highlighting a conceptual problem that persists about the true nature of a constructive trust. Even in this more limited sense however, any perceived dichotomy between the two notions tends to prove ephemeral upon closer examination. Equity acts consistently and in accordance with principle. The old maxim that equity regards as done that which ought to be done is as applicable to enforce equitable obligations as it is to create them and, notwithstanding that the constructive trust is remedial in both origin and nature, there does not need to have been a curial declaration or order before equity will recognise the prior existence of a constructive trust.[40] Where an equity court would retrospectively impose a constructive trust by way of equitable remedy, its availability as such a remedy provides the basis for, and governs the content of, its existence *inter partes* independently of any formal order declaring or enforcing it. In this more limited sense, the constructive trust is also properly seen as both 'remedy' and 'institution'. Indeed, for the student of equity, there can be no true dichotomy between the two notions.

The acknowledgment of the institutional character of the constructive trust does not involve a denial of its continued flexibility as a remedy: cf *Wirth v Wirth* (1956), p 238. The institutional character of the trust has never completely obliterated its remedial origins even in [615] the case of the more traditional forms of express and implied trust. This is *a fortiori* in the case of constructive trust where, as has been mentioned, the remedial character remains predominant in that the trust itself

---

38   Waters, 1964, *ibid*, pp 37–39.
39   Cf Sir Frederick Jordan, *Chapters on Equity in New South Wales*, 6th edn, 1947, pp 17–18.
40   Cf Scott, *The Law of Trusts*, 3rd edn, 1967, Vol 5, para 462.4.

either represents, or reflects the availability of, equitable relief in the particular circumstances. Indeed, in this country at least, the constructive trust has not outgrown its formative stages as an equitable remedy and should still be seen as constituting an *in personam* remedy attaching to property which may be moulded and adjusted to give effect to the application and interplay of equitable principles in the circumstances of the particular case. In particular, where competing common law or equitable claims are or may be involved, a declaration of constructive trust by way of remedy can properly be so framed that the consequences of its imposition are operative only from the date of judgment or formal court order or from some other specified date. The fact that the constructive trust remains predominantly remedial does not, however, mean that it represents a medium for the indulgence of idiosyncratic notions of fairness and justice. As an equitable remedy, it is available only when warranted by established equitable principles or by the legitimate processes of legal reasoning, by analogy, induction and deduction, from the starting point of a proper understanding of the conceptual foundation of such principles.[41] Viewed as a remedy, the function of the constructive trust is not to render superfluous, but to reflect and enforce, the principles of the law of equity.

Thus it is that there is no place in the law of this country for the notion of 'a constructive trust of a new model' which, '(b)y whatever name it is described ... is ... imposed by law whenever justice and good conscience' (in the sense of 'fairness' or what 'was fair') 'require it': *per* Lord Denning MR, *Eves v Eves* (1975), pp 1341, 1342; 771, 772 and *Hussey v Palmer* (1972), pp 1289–90; 747. Under the law of this country – as, I [616] venture to think, under the present law of England cf *Burns v Burns* (1984) – proprietary rights fall to be governed by principles of law and not by some mix of judicial discretion (cf *Wirth v Wirth* (1956), pp 232, 247 subjective views about which party 'ought to win'[42] and 'the formless void of individual moral opinion': cf *Carly v Farrelly* (1975), p 367; *Avondale Printers & Stationers Ltd v Haggie* (1979), p 154). Long before Lord Seldon's anachronism identifying the Chancellor's foot as the measure of Chancery relief, undefined notions of 'justice' and what was 'fair' had given way in the law of equity to the rule of ordered principle which is of the essence of any coherent system of rational law. The mere fact that it would be unjust or unfair in a situation of discord for the owner of a legal estate to assert his ownership against another provides, of itself, no mandate for a judicial declaration that the ownership in whole or in part lies, in equity, in that other.[43] Such equitable relief by way of constructive trust will only properly be available if applicable principles of the law of equity require that the person in whom the ownership of property is vested should hold it to the use or for the benefit of another. That is not to say that general notions of fairness and justice

---

41 Cf generally Sir Frank Kitto, 'Foreword', in Meagher, Gummow and Lehane (eds), *Equity: Doctrines and Remedies*, 1st edn, 1975; 2nd edn, 1984, pp v–vii; and see also, eg, *Re Diplock* (1948), pp 481–82; *Pettitt v Pettitt* (1970), pp 793, 801, 809, 825; *Cowcher v Cowcher* (1972), p 430; p 948; *Jacobs's Law of Trusts in Australia*, 4th edn, 1977; Meagher *et al, ibid*, paras 1301–02, 1325–29; *Allen v Snyder* (1977), pp 689, 702ff; Oakley, *op cit*, fn 37, pp 1–10; Pettitt, *Equity and the Law of Trusts*, 5th edn, 1984, pp 4–6.

42 Cf Maudsley, 'Constructive trusts' (1977) 28 NILQ 123, especially pp 123, 137, 139–40.

43 Cf *Hepworth v Hepworth* (1963), pp 317–18.

have become irrelevant to the content and application of equity. They remain relevant to the traditional equitable notion of unconscionable conduct which persists as an operative component of some fundamental rules or principles of modern equity: cf, eg, *Legione v Hateley* (1983), p 444; *Commercial Bank of Australia Ltd v Amadio* (1983), pp 461–64, 474–75.

The principal operation of the constructive trust in the law of this country has been in the area of breach of fiduciary duty. Some text writers have expressed the view that the constructive trust is confined to cases where some pre-existing fiduciary relationship can be identified.[44] Neither principle nor authority requires however that it be confined to that or any other category or categories of case.[45] Once its predominantly remedial character is accepted, [617] there is no reason to deny the availability of the constructive trust in any case where some principle of the law of equity calls for the imposition upon the legal owner of property, regardless of actual or presumed agreement or intention, of the obligation to hold or apply the property for the benefit of another.[46] In the United States of America, a general doctrine of unjust enrichment has long been recognised as providing an acceptable basis in principle for the imposition of a constructive trust.[47] It may well be that the development of the law of this country on a case by case basis will eventually lead to the identification of some overall concept of unjust enrichment as an established principle constituting the basis of decision of past and future cases. Whatever may be the position in relation to the law of other common law countries (cf, as to Canada, *Pettkus v Becker* (1980) and, as to New Zealand, *Hayward v Giordani* (1983), p 148) however, no such general principle is as yet established, as a basis of decision as distinct from an informative generic label for purposes of classification, in Australian law. The most that can be said at the present time is that 'unjust enrichment' is a term commonly used to identify the notion underlying a variety of distinct categories of case in which the law has recognised an obligation on the part of a defendant to account for a benefit derived at the expense of a plaintiff (cf Goff and Jones).[48] It therefore becomes necessary to consider whether there is any narrower and more specific basis on which, independently of the actual intention of the parties, Mrs Muschinski can claim to be entitled to relief by way of constructive trust in the particular circumstances of the present case ...

[618] Both common law and equity recognise that, where money or other property is paid or applied on the basis of some consensual joint relationship or endeavour which fails without attributable blame, it will often be inappropriate simply to draw a line leaving assets and liabilities to be owned and borne according to where they may *prima facie* lie, as a matter of law, at the time of the failure. Where there are express or implied contractual provisions specially dealing with the

---

44 See, eg, *Lewin on Trusts*, 16th edn, 1964, p 141.
45 Cf generally Professor Austin, 'Constructive trusts', in Finn (ed), *Essays in Equity*, 1985, especially pp 196–201; Waters, *The Constructive Trust*, 1964, pp 28ff.
46 Cf Hanbury and Maudsley, *Modern Equity*, 12th edn, 1985, p 301; Pettit, *Equity and the Law of Trusts*, 5th edn, 1984, p 55.
47 See, eg, Scott, *Law of Trusts*, 3rd edn, 1967, Vol 5, para 461.
48 *The Law of Restitution*, 2nd edn, 1978, p 1115.

consequences of failure of the joint relationship or endeavour, they will ordinarily apply in law and equity to regulate the rights and duties of the parties between themselves and the *prima facie* legal position will accordingly prevail. Where, however, there are no applicable contractual provisions or the only applicable provisions were not framed to meet the contingency of premature failure of the enterprise or relationship, other rules or principles will commonly be called into play. If, in the last mentioned case, the relevant relationship is merely contractual and the contract has been frustrated without fault on either side, the present tendency of the common law is that contributions made should be refunded at least if there has been a complete failure of consideration in performance (cf *Fibrosa Spolka Akcyjna v Fairbairn Lawson Combe Barbour Ltd* (1943); *Denny, Mott and Dickson Ltd v James B Fraser and Co Ltd* (1944), p 275; and, generally, Treitel, *The Law of Contract*[49]). If the relevant relationship is a partnership, the *prima facie* rule of equity on premature dissolution is, as in the case of an ordinary dissolution, that the parties are, after the discharge of partnership debts, entitled to be repaid their respective capital contributions. More importantly for present purposes, if a premium has been paid by a fixed term partner who is not to be held responsible for the premature dissolution, an equity court will order a refund or partial refund of the premium to the extent that its retention by the other partner would be unconscionable ...

[619] That more general principle of equity can also be readily related to the general equitable notions which find expression in the common law count for money had and received (cf *Moses v Macferlan* (1760); *J and S Holdings Pty Ltd v NRMA Insurance Ltd* (1982), p 120) and to the rationale of the particular rule of contract law to which reference has been made (cf *Fibrosa* (1943), pp 61ff, especially p 72). Like most of the traditional doctrines of equity, it [620] operates upon legal entitlement to prevent a person from asserting or exercising a legal right in circumstances where the particular assertion or exercise of it would constitute unconscionable conduct (cf Story, *Commentaries on Equity Jurisprudence*;[50] *Legione v Hateley* (1983), p 444). The circumstances giving rise to the operation of the principle were broadly identified by Lord Cairns LC, speaking for the Court of Appeal in Chancery, in *Atwood v Maude* (1868), p 375: where 'the case is one in which, using the words of Lord Cottenham in *Hirst v Tolson* (1850), a payment has been made by anticipation of something afterwards to be enjoyed (and) where ... circumstances arise so that future enjoyment is denied'. Those circumstances can be more precisely defined by saying that the principle operates in a case where the substratum of a joint relationship or endeavour is removed without attributable blame and where the benefit of money or other property contributed by one party on the basis and for the purposes of the relationship or endeavour would otherwise be enjoyed by the other party in circumstances in which it was not specifically intended or specially provided that that other party should so enjoy it. The content of the principle is that, in such a case, equity will not permit that other party to assert or retain the benefit of the relevant property to the extent that it

---

49 6th edn, 1983, pp 695ff.
50 12th edn, 1877, Vol 2, para 1316.

would be unconscionable for him so to do (cf *Atwood v Maude* (1868), and *per* Jessel MR, *Lyon v Tweddell* (1881)).

The circumstances of the present case provide the necessary context for the operation of that general principle of the law of equity. Mrs Muschinski's payment of the purchase price of the Picton property, which was transferred into the joint names of Mr Dodds and herself, was made on the basis and for the purposes of their planned venture with respect to the land. The substratum of that planned joint endeavour was removed without attributable blame. Mr Dodds is left as a half owner of the property in circumstances (ie, the collapse of the joint endeavour) to which the parties did not advert and in which it was not specifically intended or specially provided that Mr Dodds should enjoy such a benefit at Mrs Muschinski's expense. In these circumstances, the operation of the relevant principle is to preclude Mr Dodds from asserting or retaining, against Mrs Muschinski, his one half ownership of the property to the extent that it would be unconscionable for him so to [621] do. In assessing whether or to what extent such an assertion or retention of legal entitlement by Mr Dodds would constitute unconscionable conduct, one is not left at large to indulge random notions of what is fair and just as a matter of abstract morality. Notions of what is fair and just are relevant but only in the confined context of determining whether conduct should, by reference to legitimate processes of legal reasoning, be characterised as unconscionable for the purposes of a specific principle of equity whose rationale and operation is to prevent wrongful and undue advantage being taken by one party of a benefit derived at the expense of the other party in the special circumstances of the unforeseen and premature collapse of a joint relationship or endeavour ...

[623] There remains the question whether there should be a declaration that the Picton property is held by the parties upon constructive trust. In my view, there should. That property was acquired, in pursuance of the consensual arrangement between the parties, to be held and developed in accordance with arrangement. The contributions which each party is entitled to have repaid to her or him were made for, or in connection with, its purchase or development. The collapse of the commercial venture and the failure of the personal relationship jointly combined to lead to a situation in which each party is entitled to insist upon realisation of the asset, repayment of her or his contribution and distribution of any surplus. In these circumstances, the appropriate order to give effect to the rights and obligations of the parties is an order declaring that the Picton property is held by them upon constructive trust. Lest the legitimate claims of third parties be adversely affected, the constructive trust should be imposed only from the date of publication of reasons for judgment of this court ...

Commentary

The principles laid down by Deane J in this case were unanimously accepted by the High Court in *Baumgartner v Baumgartner* (1987).

Deane J concludes that the constructive trust is a 'remedial institution', in the sense that it possesses both institutional and remedial features. The constructive trust is 'institutional' in the sense that it arises automatically by operation of law upon proof of a set of circumstances where a constructive trust is recognised as being applicable, and is independent of any formal order or decree of the court. The categories of case where it will arise are those where it would be unconscionable for the defendant to retain the full beneficial interest in the property. The constructive trust also possesses certain remedial features. The trust is imposed as a personal obligation attaching to property, to enforce the equitable principle that a legal owner should not be allowed to deal with the property in a manner inconsistent with the beneficiary's interest. The remedial nature of the constructive trust means that it can be moulded and adjusted to fit the justice of the particular case and to protect third parties. Thus, Deane J postponed the date of the commencement of the trust in the principal case in order to protect third parties. Further, as recognised in the later case of *Giumelli v Giumelli* (1999), the court can refuse to recognise the constructive trust where there is another sufficient remedy available (p 113):

> Before a constructive trust is imposed, the court should first decide whether, having regard to the issues in the litigation, there is an appropriate equitable remedy which falls short of the imposition of a trust.[51]

It should be clear from the foregoing discussion of the nature of the Australian constructive trust that it will only be available in those restitutionary cases where the circumstances upon which the restitutionary claim is based render it unconscionable for the defendant to retain the property. So, for example, there is some authority suggesting that a constructive trust will be imposed over moneys paid under mistake where the defendant receives the money with the knowledge that it is paid under mistake,[52] or retains the money with that knowledge.[53] The trust should be imposed from the moment of receipt, or from the moment of acquisition of the knowledge, respectively.[54] Further, it is well recognised that a thief holds stolen money on a constructive trust for the owner of the money.[55] It is also arguable that a constructive trust should be available in cases where the defendant has knowingly acquiesced in or encouraged the plaintiff's mistaken improvement of the defendant's land,[56] and where the defendant is the recipient of a bribe.[57]

---

51 *Bathurst City Council v PWC Properties Pty Ltd* (1988), pp 584–85; *Napier v Hunter* (1993), pp 738, 744–45, 752.

52 *Westdeutsche Landesbank Girozentrale v Council of the London Borough of Islington* (1996), p 715 (see extract, p 703); *Friends Provident v Hillier Parker May & Rowden* (1996), pp 137–38; *Port of Brisbane Corporation v ANZ Securities Ltd* (2001). See also *Woolworths Ltd v Richmond Growth Pty Ltd* (1996).

53 *Westdeutsche Landesbank Girozentrale v Council of the London Borough of Islington* (1996), p 715 (see extract, p 703). See also *Opus Productions Pty Ltd v Popwing Pty Ltd T/A Kevin Jacobsen Productions* (1994).

54 *Westdeutsche Landesbank Girozentrale v Council of the London Borough of Islington* (1996), p 715 (see extract, p 703).

55 *Zobory v Federal Commissioner of Taxation* (1995); *Bankers Trust Co v Shapiro* (1980); *Westdeutsche Landesbank Girozentrale v Council of the London Borough of Islington* (1996), pp 714, 715 (see extract, p 703).

56 *Cadorange Pty Ltd (In Liq) v Tanga Holdings Pty Ltd* (1990), pp 35–40.

57 See the discussion above pp 550–63.

Another situation where it has been suggested that a constructive trust should be imposed is where a plaintiff taxpayer recovers taxes on a restitutionary claim, in circumstances where the taxpayer had separately charge the tax to its customers. This type of constructive trust, which was first suggested by Mason CJ in *Commissioner of State Revenue (Vic) v Royal Insurance Australia Ltd* (1994) (see extract, p 76) is discussed by Kirby J in the following case.

Roxborough v Rothmans of Pall Mall Australia Ltd (2001) 185 ALR 335
High Court of Australia

The facts are stated at p 81.

Kirby J: ... [377] In *Commissioner of State Revenue (Vic) v Royal Insurance Australia Ltd* (1994), Mason CJ recognised that a constructive trust for consumers might be imposed where the consumers had been separately levied with a tax and had paid the tax on the basis that an equivalent sum would be forwarded to the revenue (1994), p 78. His Honour contemplated that such a plaintiff, when seeking restitution from the revenue, might be required to satisfy a court, in the form of an 'undertaking or other means, that it will distribute the moneys to the patrons from whom they were collected, thereby recognizing their beneficial ownership of those moneys' (1994), p 78.

In *Mutual Pools & Staff Pty Ltd v The Commonwealth* (1994), pp 177, 191, Brennan, Deane and Gaudron JJ suggested, without deciding, that a taxpayer, to whom a refund of an invalidly imposed tax was paid, in circumstances where the burden had already been passed on to a third party, could be bound, by the law of restitution, to refund to that third party the amount received from the revenue, or the amount recouped from the third party, whichever was the less.

The source of this notion (whether explained in terms of the law of trusts or of restitution) is often traced to the influential dissenting opinion of Learned Hand J in *123 East Fifty-Fourth Street Inc v United States* (1946). That opinion was referred to by Mason CJ in *Royal Insurance*, with general approval (1994), pp 75–79. Learned Hand J was of the opinion that recovery by the taxpayer in that case would be dependent upon its giving an undertaking that the moneys recovered would be refunded to their beneficial owners. The approach adopted by Learned Hand J in *123 East Fifty-Fourth Street* has been followed in many cases in the United States.[58]

In *123 East Fifty-Fourth Street*, a restaurant was informed by State revenue authorities that it was liable to pay a cabaret tax. In consequence, the establishment increased the prices charged to customers. It separately itemised the component attributed to the tax in the customers' bills. Later, it was held that the restaurant was not a 'cabaret'. Accordingly, it was not subject to the tax. The issue was whether the invalidly levied tax could be recovered by the restaurant from the revenue, although the restaurant had already transferred the cost of the tax to its customers.

A majority of the Second Circuit Court of Appeals upheld the restaurant's claim for recovery on the basis of restitution. They did so on the footing that, as between the restaurant and the government, the former was entitled to the amounts

---

58   Eg, *Decorative Carpets Inc v State Board of Equalization* (1962), p 638.

illegally collected. The payments made by customers had become the property of the restaurant from which property it had paid its own moneys to the [378] government *123 East Fifty-Fourth Street Inc v United States* (1946), pp 68–70 *per* Chase J, Swan J concurring. However, in his dissent Learned Hand J concluded that there was no entitlement for the restaurant patrons to assert a legally recognisable interest in the judgment moneys. The tax having been passed on to the customers in the form of itemised bills, the only foundation for recovery by the taxpayer was the imposition of a constructive trust upon the payments made. Learned Hand J said at pp 70–71:

> [T]he [restaurant] collected the money under what the guests must have understood to be a statement that it was obliged to pay it as a tax, and that [as] it meant to do so, the money was charged with a constructive trust certainly so long as it remained in the [restaurant's] hands ...

> When the [restaurant], having taken the money charged with the constructive trust, paid it to the [revenue], a claim against the [revenue] at once arose in [the restaurant's] favor, based upon the [revenue's] unlawful exaction. That claim was ... a substitute for the money whose payment created it ... and, if a constructive trust attached to the money, the same trust attached to the claim.

In the opinion of Learned Hand J, the restaurant was entitled to relief of this kind in equity but only if it established that the individual customers were identifiable in a manner that would facilitate refunds to them. As this had not been proved on the facts, his Honour was of the view that the provision of equitable relief should be denied.[59]

At the core of the foregoing reasons is a basic principle of equity. Relief is denied to those who come to a court seeking equitable intervention without themselves indicating a willingness to do equity. For reasons of constitutional principle, the unwillingness or inability of a plaintiff to make a refund to consumers from any sum recovered by it from a government party might give way to the importance of requiring the government to disgorge moneys unlawfully collected. However, no such consideration applies to the invocation by a private party of equitable relief against another private party. In such a case there is every reason to insist that, before any such equitable relief is granted, the party claiming relief should have demonstrated a willingness to refund the whole, or some proper part, of its recovery to those who, in the language of the Supreme Court of the United States, are the 'actual sufferers' and the 'real parties in interest': *Jefferson Electric* (1934), p 402. Without such a commitment, such a plaintiff is not 'entitled in justice and good conscience to such relief' (1934), p 402. So much follows from the equitable nature of the relief claimed (1934), pp 402–03.

I will assume that, conformably with applicable Australian law, a constructive trust of some kind might be imposed upon the wholesaler in proceedings such as the present, so as to make it liable as a constructive trustee for having failed to carry out the purpose for which the moneys had been received by it from the retailers.[60] However, this would not avail the retailers in the [379] present case.

---

59 See also *Benzoline Motor Fuel Co v Bollinger* (1933); *Indian Motorcycle Co v United States* (1935) where similar conditions were imposed.

60 *Muschinski v Dodds* (1985) p 613; *Baumgartner v Baumgartner* (1987); cf O'Connor, 'Happy partners or strange bedfellows: the blending of remedial and institutional features in the evolving constructive trust' (1996) 20 Melbourne University Law Review 735.

That is so because the retailers made it absolutely clear that they did not offer, and would not submit to, any obligation to reimburse the consumers who had purchased the tobacco products from them at prices assumed to include the component referable to the licence fees held to be unconstitutional. In other circumstances, upon different evidence, it might be possible, in a case between a wholesaler and a retailer, affected by an unconstitutional tax, for the retailer to establish that it had suffered some losses itself. The retailer might have done so notwithstanding recoupment from consumers. In such a case, equitable relief might indeed be granted. But the present was not such a case. No such claim was made, still less proved.

The onus of securing equitable intervention in the present proceedings rested squarely on the retailers. The provision of equitable relief was within the discretion of the Federal Court. That court found, uncontroversially, that the arrangements between the parties, and the scheme of the Act, envisaged that the cost of licence fees would be (as it was) passed on to consumers. In the case of tobacco products, the court could readily infer that demand for them was relatively inelastic. Such an inference arises from common knowledge about the qualities of the product and the consequent dependence of consumers upon its supply to fulfil their needs. Certainly, the retailers produced no evidence to show that they had been unable to pass the whole, or any part, of the cost of the tobacco licence fees on to their customers. The Federal Court found that the opposite was the case *Roxborough* (1999), p 199.

In such circumstances, the Full Court was correct to hold that equity's intervention, by way of a constructive trust, would only be warranted if the retailers could establish that the wholesaler's retention of the sums paid, pursuant to contract, was unconscionable (1999), pp 206–07. But if the retailers refused to provide, or submit to a requirement for, reimbursement to their customers, the result was that, as between the wholesaler and the retailers, the retention of the sums paid was not unconscionable. No 'seminal equitable notions of good conscience', *Australia and New Zealand Banking Group Ltd v Westpac Banking Corporation* (1988), p 673, were activated by the proved facts. On the contrary, there was nothing in the circumstances to establish a higher claim in conscience to the component for licence fees as between any of the parties. And where 'the equities are equal ... legal title should prevail', see *123 East Fifty-Fourth Street* (1946), p 71, absent any consideration of a constitutional or public law character supporting the entitlement to recovery. It follows that the constructive trust case was correctly dismissed.

...

Commentary and questions

In what circumstances did Kirby J suggest that a constructive trust could be imposed in circumstances where the plaintiff has recovered a mistaken payment of tax? Does Kirby J make clear the basis of such a constructive trust? Why did he refuse to recognise a constructive trust on the facts before him?

The courts have consistently cautioned against the indiscriminate adoption of equitable proprietary remedies into commercial transactions. Thus, in *Westdeutsche Landesbank Girozentrale v Islington London Borough Council* (1996) (see extract, p 703) Lord Goff saw no reason why a party who had an opportunity to request a security when negotiating a contract, but failed to do so, should be granted priority over other unsecured creditors: p 684.[61] Lord Browne-Wilkinson in the same case was concerned that imposition of proprietary remedies in commercial transactions would introduce 'a new area of unmanageable risk ... into commercial dealings': p 705. Imposition of a trust would create a form of 'off balance sheet liabilities' of which creditors dealing with the defendant would be unaware.

The court in the following case discusses some of the objections in principle and policy to the imposition of constructive trusts in commercial dealings wherever there is an unjust enrichment.

Stephenson Nominees Pty Ltd v Official Receiver (1987) 76 ALR 485
Full Court of the Federal Court of Australia

The facts are not relevant.

Gummow J: ... [502] [A]s the law stands in Australia (a) there is no general principle requiring restitution in cases of unjust enrichment of the defendant at the expense of the plaintiff and (b) even if there were, it would not necessarily follow that the constructive trust was the appropriate remedy to express that right to restitution. This follows from *Muschinski v Dodds* (1985), particularly from what was said by Deane J (with the concurrence of Mason J (as he then was)), pp 614–18; see also the warning by Gibbs CJ (with the concurrence of Wilson and Dawson JJ) against too readily confounding ownership (ie, by dint of constructive trust) with obligation (eg, in account, [503] a personal remedy), in *Daly v The Sydney Stock Exchange Limited* (1986), pp 379–80.

Care is called for against over emphasising the role of the constructive trust in this area. Whilst the constructive trust may readily, in many cases, be seen as a restitutionary remedy for an unjust enrichment at the expense of the plaintiff, this by no means always will be the case. The constructive trust may be imposed as a cautionary or deterrent remedy even where there has been no unjust enrichment at the expense of the plaintiff. For example, leading cases have made it plain that it is no answer to the application to company directors of the rule forbidding fiduciaries placing their interest in conflict with their duty, that the profits they have made are of a kind the company itself could not have obtained or that no loss to the company is caused by their gain: *Furs Limited v Tomkies* (1936), p 592; *Regal (Hastings) Ltd v Gulliver* (1967). Relief by way of constructive trust may be available in these cases even though the profit or benefit obtained by the fiduciary was not one the obtaining of which was an incident of his duty to the plaintiff: *Hospital Products Limited v United States Surgical Corporation* (1984), pp 107–09. In such situations the constructive trust operates not to restore to the company that of which it was deprived by the conduct complained of, but to enforce observance of the fiduciary duty not to prefer personal interest to duty to the plaintiff. As Professor Birks has observed, it is difficult, in the situations revealed in these and

---

61   See also *Re Goldcorp Exchange Ltd* (1995).

other cases, to treat a constructive trust remedy as necessarily operating to prevent unjust enrichment at the expense of the plaintiff.[62]

Nor, even if it be established that in Australian law, unlike English law as expounded by Lord Diplock in *Orakpo v Manson Investments Ltd* (1978), p 104 there is a general doctrine of unjust enrichment, it by no means will follow that the constructive trust with its proprietary character will always or necessarily be the appropriate remedy. It would, for example, be quite wrong to assume that in the United States the law of restitution is concerned principally with proprietary remedies in the nature of a constructive trust. 'Restitution' is used as a term identifying a range of remedies linked by a perceived common character. Australian decisions such as *Sabemo Pty Ltd v North Sydney Municipal Council* (1977), and *Pavey & Matthews Pty Ltd v Paul* (1987), although based immediately in quasi-contract, apparently would be classed in the United States as cases of restitution, although no constructive trust was involved. The leading American treatise on the subject, Professor Palmer's four volume work, *The Law of Restitution* contains the following (section 1.3, p 16):

> The recognition of constructive trust as a remedy aimed at preventing unjust enrichment has been accompanied by a growing recognition of its connection with quasi-contract, a legal remedy with the same general aim ... It is important to recognise the connection between the two remedies; but as long as distinctions between law and equity persist, it needs to be recognised that 'quasi-contract' and 'constructive trust' are not interchangeable terms ...

> It is a striking fact nonetheless that judges often seem to find it easier to reach and rectify an unjust enrichment by describing the recipient of the enrichment as a constructive trustee, even though the judgment entered is [504] one for money and can be obtained at law, in quasi-contract. The constructive trust idea stirs the judicial imagination in ways that *assumpsit*, *quantum meruit*, and the other terms associated with quasi-contract have never quite succeeded in duplicating.

Deane J spoke to like effect in *Pavey and Matthews Pty Ltd v Paul* (1987), pp 165–66.[63] In the standard United States student text by Leavell, Love and Nelson, *Equitable Remedies and Restitution*, 3rd edn, 1980, the subject of restitution is introduced by describing it (p 495) as 'an abstraction that describes a variety of remedies' including such legal remedies as quasi-contract and such equitable remedies as constructive trust, equitable lien and accounting.

Further, as I have earlier indicated, it will be apparent that the security given by an equitable lien or charge affords a proprietary remedy; it would be wrong to treat the constructive trust as the only proprietary remedy in this field: *Hewett v Court* (1983) pp 645–46, 662–69; *Calverley v Green* (1984), p 263; *Muschinski v Dodds* (1985), p 598; *Morris v Morris* (1982), p 64; *In re Hallett's Estate* (1880), pp 709, 717. The equitable lien is not confined in its operation to cases where the parties are in

---

62 Birks, *An Introduction to the Law of Restitution*, 1985, pp 88–89.
63 See also Palmer, *The Law of Restitution*, 1982 Supp, Vol 1, p 6; *Scott on Trusts*, 3rd edn, section 462; and 1983 Supp, section 666; and Stoljar, 'Unjust enrichment and unjust sacrifice' (1987) 50 MLR 603, pp 604–05, 609–10.

contractual relations (as with vendor and purchaser). It has been described as an equitable remedy, created by the court, regardless of the intent of the parties, as a remedial device to protect a party against some inequitable loss.[64] The lien may attach to incorporeal as well as corporeal property: *Dansk Rekylriffel Syndikat Aktieselskab v Snell* (1908).

In an earlier passage in his work (section 1.1), Professor Palmer writes:

> Today, anything like a whole view of the law of restitution must take into account both law and equity, and both are therefore within the scope of this book. At law the principal remedy is quasi-contract, leading to a money judgment, but replevin of goods is sometimes a form of restitution. In equity the principal remedy is constructive trust; but equitable lien, subrogation, and accounting are techniques frequently used to prevent unjust enrichment. It would be a major advance if courts, having identified an enrichment felt to be unjust, were free to choose the form of relief that seems fairest and most appropriate to the circumstances. This *is* the largely hidden tendency of modern decisions, but our legal system has not yet reached the point of giving it explicit recognition. In the application of equitable relief it may be necessary to consider whether the legal remedy is adequate, and this is not quite the same as determining which remedy is most appropriate.

The last sentence quoted above may be read with those passages in the judgment of Gibbs CJ in *Daly v The Sydney Stock Exchange Limited* (1986), pp 377–80, where his Honour, in dealing with a claim for a constructive trust where a fiduciary, in breach of duty, had taken moneys on loan from a client, considered whether the client's legal remedies were adequate to meet the case. Gibbs CJ said (p 379): [505] 'In deciding whether or not the money should be held to have been subject to a constructive trust it is not unimportant that the ordinary legal remedy of a creditor would have been adequate to prevent the firm from being benefited at the expense of the appellant ...'

Further, a serious difficulty with any general legal principle of restitution for unjust enrichment lies in isolating the criteria which indicate in a given case whether a personal or proprietary remedy (constructive trust or equitable lien or charge) is appropriate.

It has recently been said (by Professor Klippert in *Unjust Enrichment*, 1983, p 196):

> One of the great advantages of constructive trust is that it gives the plaintiff a claim over the defendant's assets that takes precedence over the claim of general creditors. But this very advantage creates a problem, because it means that the remedy cannot be made available to just anyone. For example, it would be unfair if contractual claimants were always granted a lower priority than any claimants in unjust enrichment. All unsecured creditors would seek to claim unjust enrichment and thus in effect become secured creditors.

---

64 McClintock, *Equity*, 2nd edn, section 118; see also Pomeroy, *Equity Jurisprudence*, sections 1238–41; note 'Equitable liens' (1931) 31 Col L Rev 1335.

In the well known work by Lord Goff and Professor Jones, *The Law of Restitution*, 3rd edn, p 78, the learned authors say only: 'In our view the question whether a restitutionary proprietary claim should be granted should depend on whether it is just, in the particular circumstances of the case, to impose a constructive trust on, or an equitable lien over, particular assets, or to allow subrogation to a lien over such assets.'

In United States law, it has been suggested that a proprietary remedy should apply only against a fiduciary or a 'conscious wrongdoer' in the sense of one to whose conduct moral blame attaches: *Restatement on Restitution*, 1937, section 202; Palmer, *The Law of Restitution*, section 2.14.

Reference was made by Gibbs CJ (in *Daly v The Sydney Stock Exchange Limited* (1986), p 379) to the effect of the constructive trust in withdrawing assets from the general body of creditors; this generally will be so unless the beneficiary of that trust himself holds his rights for the benefit of a fund he administers, for example, on insolvency (as would be the position of the Official Receiver in the present case). However, in general the result may be seen, as the Chief Justice observed, as unjust to the general creditors of the constructive trustee unless there is given further explanation of the *raison d'être* of the trust ...

Questions

What reasons does Gummow J give for exercising caution in using proprietary remedies in unjust enrichment claims? What non-restitutionary functions are performed by a constructive trust?

Resulting trusts

A resulting trust arises by operation of law where legal title to property is transferred to another but the beneficial title does not pass to the recipient. The beneficial title reverts to the transferor and the recipient holds the beneficial title on a resulting trust for the transferor.

As the following case illustrates, a resulting trust will rarely arise on a restitutionary claim, as full beneficial and equitable title will, as a general rule, pass to the recipient upon payment or transfer.[65] The fact that the transferor's intention to pay the money or transfer the property is vitiated (for example by mistake or compulsion) will not prevent full legal and beneficial title passing to the recipient.

---

65   See also Millett, 'Restitution and constructive trusts', in Cornish *et al* (eds), *Restitution: Past, Present and Future*, 1998, Chapter 13; Oakley, 'Restitution and constructive trusts: a commentary', in Cornish *et al* (eds), *Restitution: Past, Present and Future*, 1998, Chapter 14.

Westdeutsche Landesbank Girozentrale v Council of the London Borough of Islington
[1996] AC 669 House of Lords

The facts are stated at p 372.

The issue before the House of Lords was whether the Council was liable to pay compound interest on the balance of the loan moneys recovered by the bank. This question depended upon whether the Council held the money as a trustee.

Lord Goff of Chieveley (dissenting on the interest question): ... [Lord Goff made the observations about the nature of the bank's personal claim in restitution which are extracted at p 372. He continued, at p 683:]

A proprietary claim in restitution

I have already stated that restitution in these cases can be achieved by means of a personal claim in restitution. The question has however arisen [684] whether the bank should also have the benefit of an equitable proprietary claim in the form of a resulting trust. The immediate reaction must be – why should it? Take the present case. The parties have entered into commercial transaction. The transaction has, for technical reasons, been held to be void from the beginning. Each party is entitled to recover its money, with the result that the balance must be repaid. But why should the plaintiff bank be given the additional benefits which flow from a proprietary claim, for example the benefit of achieving priority in the event of the defendant's insolvency? After all, it has entered into a commercial transaction, and so taken the risk of the defendant's insolvency, just like the defendant's other creditors who have contracted with it, not to mention other creditors to whom the defendant may be liable to pay damages in tort.

I feel bound to say that I would not at first sight have thought that an equitable proprietary claim in the form of a trust should be made available to the bank in the present case, but for two things. The first is the decision of this House in *Sinclair v Brougham* (1914) which appears to provide authority that a resulting trust may indeed arise in a case such as the present. The second is that on the authorities there is an equitable jurisdiction to award the plaintiff compound interest in cases where the defendant is a trustee. It is the combination of those two factors which has provided the foundation for the principal arguments advanced on behalf of the bank in support of its submission that it was entitled to an award of compound interest. I shall have to consider the question of availability of an equitable proprietary claim, and the effect of *Sinclair v Brougham*, in some depth ...

[685] *Equitable proprietary claims*

I now turn to consider the question whether an equitable proprietary claim was available to the bank in the present case.

Ever since the law of restitution began, about the middle of this century, to be studied in depth, the role of equitable proprietary claims in the law of restitution has been found to be a matter of great difficulty. The legitimate ambition of restitution lawyers has been to establish a coherent law of restitution, founded upon the principle of unjust enrichment; and since certain equitable institutions, notably the constructive trust and the resulting trust, have been perceived to have the function of reversing unjust enrichment, they have sought to embrace those institutions within the law of restitution, if necessary moulding them to make them fit for that purpose. Equity lawyers, on the other hand, have displayed anxiety that in this process the equitable principles underlying these institutions may become illegitimately distorted; and though equity lawyers in this country are nowadays much more sympathetic than they have been in the past towards the need to develop a coherent law of restitution, and of identifying the proper role of the trust within that rubric of the law, they remain concerned that the trust concept should not be distorted, and also that the practical consequences of its imposition should be fully appreciated. There is therefore some tension between the aims and perceptions of these two groups of lawyers, which has manifested itself in relation to the matters under consideration in the present case.

In the present case, however, it is not the function of your Lordships' House to write the agenda for the law of restitution, nor even to identify the role of equitable proprietary claims in that part of the law. The judicial process is neither designed for, nor properly directed towards, such objectives. The function of your Lordships' House is simply to decide the questions at issue before it in the present case; and the particular question now under consideration is whether, where money has been paid by a party to a contract which is *ultra vires* the other party and so void *ab initio*, he has the benefit of an equitable proprietary claim in respect of the money so paid. Moreover the manner in which this question has arisen before this House renders it by no means easy to address. First of all, the point was not debated in any depth in the courts below, because they understood that they were bound by *Sinclair v Brougham* to hold that such a claim was here available. But second, the point has arisen only indirectly in this case, since it is relevant only to the question whether the court here has power to make an award of compound interest. It is a truism that, in deciding a question of law in any particular case, the courts are much influenced by considerations of practical justice, and especially by the results which would flow from the recognition of a particular claim on the facts of the case before the court. Here, however, an award of compound interest provides no such guidance, because it is no more than a consequence which is said to flow, for no more than historical reasons, from the availability of an equitable proprietary claim. It therefore provides no guidance on the question whether such a claim should here be available.

[686] In these circumstances I regard it as particularly desirable that your Lordships should, so far as possible, restrict the inquiry to the actual questions at issue in this appeal, and not be tempted into formulating general principles of a broader nature. If restitution lawyers are hoping to find in your Lordships' speeches broad statements of principle which may definitively establish the future shape of this part of the law, I fear that they may be disappointed. I also regard it as important that your Lordships should, in the traditional manner, pay particular regard to the practical consequences which may flow from the decision of the House.

With these observations by way of preamble, I turn to the question of the availability of an equitable proprietary claim in a case such as the present. The argument advanced on behalf of the bank was that the money paid by them under the void contract was received by the Council subject to a resulting trust. This approach was consistent with that of Dillon LJ in the Court of Appeal. It is also consistent with the approach of Viscount Haldane LC (with whom Lord Atkinson agreed) in *Sinclair v Brougham* (1914).

I have already expressed the opinion that, at first sight, it is surprising that an equitable proprietary claim should be available in a case such as the present. However before I examine the question as a matter of principle, I propose first to consider whether *Sinclair v Brougham* supports the argument now advanced on behalf of the bank.

[Lord Goff examined *Sinclair v Brougham* and concluded that a resulting trust was recognised in that case because of the need to do justice to the depositors who were precluded from bringing a personal claim for the return of their money. His Lordship considered that *Sinclair v Brougham* should be confined to its own special facts and continued at p 689:]

The availability of an equitable proprietary claim in the present case

Having put *Sinclair v Brougham* on one side as providing no authority that a resulting trust should be imposed in the facts of the present case, I turn to the question whether, as a matter of principle, such a trust should be imposed, the bank's submission being that such a trust arose at the time when the sum of £2.5 million was received by the Council from the bank.

As my noble and learned friend Lord Browne-Wilkinson observes, it is plain that the present case falls within neither of the situations which are traditionally regarded as giving rise to a resulting trust: viz: (1) voluntary payments by A to B, or for the purchase of property in the name of B or in his and A's joint names, where there is no presumption of advancement or evidence of intention to make an out and out gift; or (2) property transferred to B on an express trust which does not exhaust the whole beneficial interest. The question therefore arises whether resulting trusts should be extended beyond such cases to apply in the present case, which I shall treat as a case where money has been paid for a consideration which fails.

In a most interesting and challenging paper published in *Equity: Contemporary Legal Developments*, 1992, Goldstein (ed), Professor Birks has argued for a wider role for the resulting trust in the field of restitution, and specifically for its availability in cases of mistake and failure of consideration. His thesis is avowedly experimental, written to test the temperature of the water. I feel bound to respond that the temperature of the water must be regarded as decidedly cold: see, eg, Professor Burrows (1995) and WJ Swadling (1996).

In the first place, as Lord Browne-Wilkinson points out, to impose a resulting trust in such cases is inconsistent with the traditional principles of trust law. For on receipt of the money by the payee it is to be presumed that (as in the present case) the identity of the money is immediately lost by mixing with other assets of the payee, and at that time the payee has no knowledge of the facts giving rise to the failure of consideration. By the time that those facts come to light, and the conscience of the payee may thereby be affected, there will therefore be no identifiable fund to which a trust can attach. But there are other difficulties. First, there is no general rule that the property in money paid under a void contract does not pass to the payee: and it is difficult to escape the conclusion that, as a [690] general rule, the beneficial interest to the money likewise passes to the payee. This must certainly be the case where the consideration for the payment fails after the payment is made, as in cases of frustration or breach of contract: and there appears to be no good reason why the same should not apply in cases where, as in the present case, the contract under which the payment is made is void *ab initio* and the consideration for the payment therefore fails at the time of payment. It is true that the doctrine of mistake might be invoked where the mistake is fundamental in the orthodox sense of that word. But that is not the position in the present case; moreover the mistake in the present case must be classified as a mistake of law which, as the law at present stands, creates its own special problems. No doubt that much criticised doctrine will fall to be reconsidered when an appropriate case occurs; but I cannot think that the present is such a case, since not only has the point not been argued but (as will appear) it is my opinion that there is any event jurisdiction to award compound interest in the present case. For all of these reasons I conclude, in agreement with my noble and learned friend, that there is no basis for holding that a resulting trust arises in cases where money has been paid under a contract which is *ultra vires* and therefore void *ab initio*. This conclusion has the effect that all the practical problems which would flow from the imposition of a resulting trust in a case such as the present, in particular the imposition upon the recipient of the normal duties of trustee, do not arise. The dramatic consequences which would occur are detailed by Professor Burrows in his article, 'Swaps and the friction between common law and equity' (1995), p 27: the duty to account for profits accruing from the trust property; the inability of the payee to rely upon the defence of change of position; the absence of any limitation period; and so on. Professor Burrows even goes so far as to conclude that the action for money had and received would be rendered otiose in such cases and indeed in all cases where the payer seeks restitution of mistaken payments. However, if no resulting trust arises, it also follows that the payer in a case such as the present cannot achieve priority over the payee's general creditors in the event of his insolvency – a conclusion which appears to me to be just.

For all these reasons I conclude that there is no basis for imposing a resulting trust in the present case, and I therefore reject the bank's submission that it was here entitled to proceed by way of an equitable proprietary claim. I need only add that, in reaching that conclusion, I do not find it necessary to review the decision of Goulding J in *Chase Manhattan Bank NA v Israel British Bank (London) Ltd* (1981).

Lord Browne-Wilkinson: ... [703] *The breadth of the submission*

Although the actual question in issue on the appeal is a narrow one, on the arguments presented it is necessary to consider fundamental principles of trust law. Does the recipient of money under a contract subsequently found to be void for mistake or as being *ultra vires* hold the moneys received on trust even where he had no knowledge at any relevant time that the contract was void? If he does hold on trust, such trust must arise at the date of receipt or, at the latest, at the date the legal title of the payer is extinguished by mixing moneys in a bank account: in the present case it does not matter at which of those dates the legal title was extinguished. If there is a trust two consequences follow: (a) the recipient will be personally liable, regardless of fault, for any subsequent payment away of the moneys to third parties even though, at the date of such payment, the 'trustee' was still ignorant of the existence of any trust;[66] (b) as from the date of the establishment of the trust (ie, receipt or mixing of the moneys by the 'trustee') the original payer will have an equitable proprietary interest in the moneys so long as they are traceable into whomsoever's hands they come other than a purchaser for value of the legal interest without notice. Therefore, although in the present case the only question directly in issue is the personal liability of the local authority as a trustee, it is not possible to hold the local authority liable without imposing a trust which, in other cases, will create property rights affecting third parties because moneys received under a void contract are 'trust property'.

The practical consequences of the bank's argument

Before considering the legal merits of the submission, it is important to appreciate the practical consequences which ensue if the bank's arguments are correct. Those who suggest that a resulting trust should arise in these circumstances accept that the creation of an equitable proprietary interest under the trust can have unfortunate, and adverse, effects if the original recipient of the moneys becomes insolvent: the moneys, if traceable in the hands of the recipient, are trust moneys and not available for the creditors of the recipient. However, the creation of an equitable proprietary interest in moneys received under a void contract is capable of having adverse effects quite apart from insolvency. The proprietary interest under the unknown trust will, quite apart from [704] insolvency, be enforceable against any recipient of the property other than the purchaser for value of a legal interest without notice.

Take the following example. T (the transferor) has entered into a commercial contract with R1 (the first recipient). Both parties believe the contract to be valid but it is in fact void. Pursuant to that contract: (i) T pays £1 million to R1 who pays it into a mixed bank account; (ii) T transfers 100 shares in X company to R1. who is registered as a shareholder. Thereafter R1 deals with the money and shares as follows; (iii) R1 pays £50,000 out of the mixed account to R2 otherwise than for value; R2 then becomes insolvent, having trade creditors who have paid for goods not delivered at the time of the insolvency; (iv) R1 charges the shares in X company to R3 by way of equitable security for a loan from R3.

If the bank's arguments are correct, R1 holds the £1 million on trust for T once the money has become mixed in R1's bank account. Similarly R1 [28] becomes the legal owner of the shares in X company as from the date of his registration as a shareholder but holds such shares on a resulting trust for T. T therefore has an equitable proprietary interest in the moneys in the mixed account and in the shares.

T's equitable interest will enjoy absolute priority as against the creditors in the insolvency of R2 (who was not a purchaser for value) provided that the £50,000 can be traced in the assets of R2 at the date of its insolvency ... So far as the shares in the X company are concerned, T can trace his equitable interest into the shares

66   See Burrows, 'Swaps and the friction between common law and equity' [1995] RLR 15.

and will take in priority to R3, whose equitable charge to secure his loan even though granted for value will *pro tanto* be defeated.

All this will have occurred when no one was aware, or could have been aware, of the supposed trust because no one knew that the contract was void.

I can see no moral or legal justification for giving such priority to the right of T to obtain restitution over third parties who have themselves not been enriched, in any real sense, at T's expense and indeed have had no dealings with T. T paid over his money and transferred the shares under a supposed valid contract. If the contract had been valid, he would have had purely personal rights against R1. Why should he be better off because the contract is void?

My Lords, wise judges have often warned against the wholesale importation into commercial law of equitable principles inconsistent with the certainty and speed which are essential requirements for the orderly conduct of business affairs: see *Barnes v Addy* (1874); *Scandinavian Trading Tanker Co AB v Flota Petrolera Ecuatoriana* (1983), pp 703–04. If the bank's arguments are [705] correct, a businessman who has entered into transactions relating to or dependent upon property rights could find that assets which apparently belong to one person in fact belong to another; that there are 'off-balance-sheet' liabilities of which he cannot be aware; that these property rights and liabilities arise from circumstances unknown not only to himself but also to anyone else who has been involved in the transactions. A new area of unmanageable risk will be introduced into commercial dealings. If the due application of equitable principles forced a conclusion leading to these results, your Lordships would be presented with a formidable task in reconciling legal principle with commercial common sense. But in my judgment no such conflict occurs. The resulting trust for which the bank contends is inconsistent not only with the law as it stands but with any principled development of it ...

[707] *Resulting trust*

This is not a case where the bank had any equitable interest which pre-dated receipt by the local authority of the upfront payment. Therefore, in order to show that the local authority became a trustee, the bank must demonstrate circumstances which raised a trust for the first time either at the date on which the local authority received the money or at the date on which payment into the mixed account was made. Counsel for the bank specifically disavowed any claim based on a constructive trust. This was plainly right because the local authority had no relevant knowledge sufficient to raise a constructive trust at any time before the moneys, upon the bank account going into overdraft, became untraceable. Once there ceased to be an identifiable trust fund, the local authority could not become a trustee: *In re Goldcorp Exchange Ltd* (1993). Therefore, as the argument for the bank recognised, the only possible trust which could be established was a resulting trust arising from the circumstances in which the local authority received the upfront payment.

[708] Under existing law a resulting trust arises in two sets of circumstances: (A) where A makes a voluntary payment to B or pays (wholly or in part) for the purchase of property which is vested either in B alone or in the joint names of A and B, there is a presumption that A did not intend to make a gift to B: the money or property is held on trust for A (if he is the sole provider of the money) or in the case of a joint purchase by A and B in shares proportionate to their contributions. It is important to stress that this is only a *presumption*, which presumption is easily rebutted either by the counter-presumption of advancement or by direct evidence of A's intention to make an outright transfer: see Underhill and Hayton;[67] *Vandervell v Inland Revenue Commissioners* (1967), p 312ff; *In re Vandervell's Trusts (No 2)* (1974), p 288ff. (B) Where A transfers property to B *on express trusts*, but the trusts declared do not exhaust the whole beneficial interest (1974), p 288ff.[68] Both types of resulting trust are traditionally regarded as examples of trusts giving effect to the common intention of the parties. A resulting trust is not imposed by law against the intentions of the trustee (as is a constructive trust) but gives effect to his presumed intention. Megarry J in *In re Vandervell's Trusts (No 2)* suggests that a resulting trust of type (B) does not depend on intention but operates automatically. I am not convinced that this is right. If the settlor has expressly, or by necessary implication, abandoned any beneficial interest in the trust property, there is in my view no resulting trust: the undisposed-of equitable interest vests in the Crown as *bona vacantia*: see *In re West Sussex Constabulary's Widows, Children and Benevolent (1930) Fund Trusts* (1971).

Applying these conventional principles of resulting trust to the present case, the bank's claim must fail. There was no transfer of money to the local authority on express trusts: therefore a resulting trust of type (B) above could not arise. As to type (A) above, any presumption or resulting trust is rebutted since it is demonstrated that the bank paid, and the local authority received, the upfront payment with the intention that the moneys so paid should become the absolute property of the local authority. It is true that the parties were under a misapprehension that the payment was made in pursuance of a valid contract. But that does not alter the actual intentions of the parties at the date the payment was made or the moneys were mixed in the bank account. As the article by William Swadling[69] demonstrates the presumption of resulting trust is rebutted by evidence of any intention inconsistent with such a trust, not only by evidence of an intention to make a gift.

Professor Birks,[70] whilst accepting that the principles I have stated represent 'a very conservative form' of definition of a resulting trust (p 360), argues from restitutionary principles that the definition should be extended so as to cover a perceived gap in the law of 'subtractive unjust enrichment' (p 368) so as to give a plaintiff a proprietary remedy when he has transferred value under a mistake or

---

67   Underhill and Hayton, *Law of Trusts and Trustees*, 15th edn, 1995, pp 317ff.
68   See also *Barclays Bank v Quistclose Investments Ltd* (1970).
69   Swadling, 'A new role for resulting trusts' (1992) 16 LS 133.
70   Birks, 'Restitution and resulting trusts', in Goldstein (ed), *Equity: Contemporary Legal Developments*, 1992, pp 355, 360.

under a contract the consideration for which wholly fails. He suggests that [709] a resulting trust should arise wherever the money is paid under a mistake (because such mistake vitiates the actual intention) or when money is paid on a condition which is not subsequently satisfied.

As one would expect, the argument is tightly reasoned but I am not persuaded. The search for a perceived need to strengthen the remedies of a plaintiff claiming in restitution involves, to my mind, a distortion of trust principles. First, the argument elides rights in property (which is the only proper subject matter of a trust) into rights in 'the value transferred': see p 361. A trust can only arise where there is defined trust property: it is therefore not consistent with trust principles to say that a person is a trustee of property which cannot be defined. Second, Professor Birks's approach appears to assume (for example in the case of a transfer of value made under a contract the consideration for which subsequently fails) that the recipient will be deemed to have been a trustee from the date of his original receipt or money, ie, the trust arises at a time when the 'trustee' does not, and cannot, know that there is going to be a total failure of consideration. This result is incompatible with the basic premise on which all trust law is built, viz that the conscience of the trustee is affected. Unless and until the trustee is aware of the factors which give rise to the supposed trust, there is nothing which can affect his conscience. Thus neither in the case of a subsequent failure of consideration nor in the case of a payment under a contract subsequently found to be void for mistake or failure of condition will there be circumstances, at the date of receipt, which can impinge on the conscience of the recipient, thereby making him a trustee. Thirdly, Professor Birks has to impose on his wider view an arbitrary and admittedly unprincipled modification so as to ensure that a resulting trust does not arise when there has only been a failure to perform a contract, as opposed to total failure of consideration: see pp 356–59 and 362. Such arbitrary exclusion is designed to preserve the rights of creditors in the insolvency of the recipient. The fact that it is necessary to exclude artificially one type of case which would logically fall within the wider concept casts doubt on the validity of the concept.

If adopted, Professor Birks's wider concepts would give rise to all the practical consequences and injustices to which I have referred. I do not think it right to make an unprincipled alteration to the law of property (ie, the law of trusts) so as to produce in the law of unjust enrichment the injustices to third parties which I have mentioned and the consequential commercial uncertainty which any extension of proprietary interests in personal property is bound to produce.

[Lord Browne-Wilkinson discussed *Sinclair v Brougham* and continued at p 713:]

As has been pointed out frequently over the 80 years since it was decided, *Sinclair v Brougham* is a bewildering authority: no single *ratio decidendi* can be detected; all the reasoning is open to serious objection; it was only intended to deal with cases where there were no trade creditors in competition and the reasoning is incapable of application where there are such creditors. In my view the decision as to rights *in rem* of *Sinclair v Brougham* should also be overruled. Although the case is one where [714] property rights are involved such overruling should not in practice disturb long settled titles ...

If *Sinclair v Brougham,* in both its aspects, is overruled the law can be established in accordance with principle and commercial common sense: a claimant for restitution of moneys paid under an *ultra vires,* and therefore void, contract has a personal action at law to recover the moneys paid as on a total failure of consideration; he will not have an equitable proprietary claim which gives him either rights against third parties or priority in an insolvency; nor will he have a personal claim in equity, since the recipient is not a trustee.

Chase Manhattan Bank NA v Israel-British Bank (London) Ltd (1981)

In that case Chase Manhattan, a New York bank, had by mistake paid the same sum twice to the credit of the defendant, a London bank. Shortly thereafter, the defendant bank went into insolvent liquidation. The question was whether Chase Manhattan had a claim *in rem* against the assets of the defendant bank to recover the second payment.

Goulding J was asked to assume that the moneys paid under a mistake were capable of being traced in the assets of the recipient bank: he was only concerned with the question whether there was a proprietary base on which the tracing remedy could be founded: p 116B. He held that, where money was paid under a mistake, the receipt of such money without more constituted the recipient a trustee: he said that the payer 'retains an equitable property in it and the conscience of [the recipient] is subjected to a fiduciary duty to respect his proprietary right': p 119.

It will be apparent from what I have already said that I cannot agree with this reasoning. First, it is based on a concept of retaining an equitable property in money where, prior to the payment to the recipient bank, there was no existing equitable interest. Further, I cannot understand how the recipient's 'conscience' can be affected at a time when he is not aware of any mistake. Finally, the judge found that the law of England and that of New York were in substance the same. I find this a surprising conclusion since the New York law of constructive trusts has for a long time been influenced by the concept of a *remedial* constructive trust, whereas hitherto English law has for the most part only recognised an institutional constructive trust: see *Metall & Rohstoff v Donaldson Inc* (1990), pp 478–80. In the present context, that distinction is of fundamental importance. Under an institutional constructive trust, the trust arises by operation of law as from the date of the circumstances which give rise to it: the function of the court is merely to declare that such trust has arisen in the past. The consequences that flow from such trust having arisen (including the possibly unfair consequences to third parties who in the interim have received the trust property) are also determined by rules of law, not under a discretion. A remedial constructive trust, as I understand it, is different. It is a judicial remedy giving rise to an enforceable equitable obligation: the extent to which it operates retrospectively to the prejudice of third parties lies in the [715] discretion of the court. Thus for the law of New York to hold that there is a remedial constructive trust where a payment has been made under a void contract gives rise to different consequences from holding that an institutional constructive trust arises in English law.

However, although I do not accept the reasoning of Goulding J, *Chase Manhattan* may well have been rightly decided. The defendant bank knew of the mistake made by the paying bank within two days of the receipt of the moneys: see p 115A. The judge treated this fact as irrelevant (p 114F) but in my judgment it may well provide a proper foundation for the decision. Although the mere receipt of the moneys, in ignorance of the mistake, gives rise to no trust, the retention of the moneys after the recipient bank learned of the mistake may well have given rise to a constructive trust ...[71]

[716] *Restitution and equitable rights*

Those concerned with developing the law of restitution are anxious to ensure that, in certain circumstances, the plaintiff should have the right to recover property which he has unjustly lost. For that purpose they have sought to develop the law of resulting trusts so as to give the plaintiff a proprietary interest. For the reasons that I have given in my view such development is not based on sound principle and in the name of unjust enrichment is capable of producing most unjust results. The law of resulting trusts would confer on the plaintiff a right to recover property from, or at the expense of, those who have not been unjustly enriched at his expense at all, eg, the lender whose debt is secured by a floating charge and all other third parties who have purchased an equitable interest only, albeit in all innocence and for value.

Although the resulting trust is an unsuitable basis for developing proprietary restitutionary remedies, the remedial constructive trust, if introduced into English law, may provide a more satisfactory road forward. The court by way of remedy might impose a constructive trust on a defendant who knowingly retains property of which the plaintiff has been unjustly deprived. Since the remedy can be tailored to the circumstances of the particular case, innocent third parties would not be prejudiced and restitutionary defences, such as change of position, are capable of being given effect. However, whether English law should follow the United States and Canada by adopting the remedial constructive trust will have to be decided in some future case when the point is directly in issue ...

Commentary

The members of the House of Lords were unanimous in rejecting the bank's argument that the Council was liable to account to it as a trustee. The court rejected the bank's argument that the council held the money on a resulting trust, holding that full legal and beneficial title to the money passed upon payment. The fact that the money was paid under a void contract and on a consideration that had totally failed, did not prevent full title from passing. All of the members of the court disapproved of the earlier decision of *Sinclair v Brougham* (1914) (see extract, p 3), either expressly overruling it, or confining it to its own facts.

---

71 See *Snell's Equity*, 29th edn, 1990, p 193; Pettit, *Equity and the Law of Trusts*, 7th edn, p 168; *Metall and Rohstoff v Donaldson Inc* (1990), pp 473–74.

It follows from this decision that a resulting trust will only be available in restitutionary claims in the rare case where beneficial title to money or property does not pass, for example because the payment or transfer is *ultra vires* the transferor,[72] is illegal,[73] or is vitiated by a mistake that is 'fundamental'.[74] Further, there is authority suggesting that a resulting trust will be imposed where the money was paid 'to the defendant to be held by it on trusts which were not specified and for a beneficiary who was not identified'.[75]

A prior decision of the Privy Council had also held that proprietary remedies are not available merely on the basis that there has been a total failure of consideration: *Re Goldcorp Exchange Ltd* (1995). In that case investors paid for gold which was to be kept for them and insured, however no gold was ever appropriated to them. Although they could establish a total failure of consideration, the investors were denied proprietary relief. As soon as they paid over their money both the legal and beneficial title passed to the company, and accordingly they were unable to trace their money into the surviving assets of the company.

Equitable liens

An equitable lien will be imposed over property where the defendant has used the plaintiff's money to improve property, and it would be unconscionable for the defendant to retain the benefit of the improvements without compensating the plaintiff.[76] Also, an equitable lien will be imposed over property where the plaintiff mistakenly improves the defendant's property, to the knowledge of and with the acquiescence of the defendant.[77]

It is not clear whether the quantum of the equitable lien is limited to the amount actually expended by the plaintiff, or whether the plaintiff is entitled to a share of the property proportionate to the plaintiff's contribution (thus enabling the plaintiff to take advantage of an increase in the value of the property). Although the former view is the more traditional view, there is Australian authority for the latter view.[78]

---

72 Millett, 'Restitution and constructive trusts', in Cornish *et al* (eds), *Restitution: Past, Present and Future*, 1998, pp 210–11, 215.

73 *Ibid*, pp 211, 215.

74 *Westdeutsche Landesbank Girozentrale v Council of the London Borough of Islington* (1996), p 690; *Ilich v R* (1987), pp 126-27, 139–40.

75 *Port of Brisbane Corporation v ANZ Securities Ltd* (2001), para 72.

76 *Morris v Morris* (1982); *Jackson v Crosby (No 2)* (1979); *Cadorange Pty Ltd (In Liq) v Tanga Holdings Pty Ltd* (1990), pp 35–40; *Chalmers v Pardoe* (1963); *Hewett v Court* (1983), p 668; *Morris v Morris* (1982);

77 *Giumelli v Giumelli* (1999), pp 119–20; *Morris v Morris* (1982); *Jackson v Crosby (No 2)* (1979); *In re Whitehead, Whitehead v Whitehead* (1988).

78 *Scott v Scott* (1962) 109 CLR 649; *Hagan v Waterhouse* (1991) 34 NSWLR 308, pp 335–36. See also *Foskett v McKeown* [1998] 2 WLR 298, p 310; Burrows, *The Law of Restitution*, 1993, p 35.

BIBLIOGRAPHY

Books

American Law Institute, *Restatement of the Law of Restitution: Quasi-Contract and Constructive Trusts*, 1937, St Paul: American Law Institute Publishers

Beatson, J, *The Use and Abuse of Unjust Enrichment*, 1991, Oxford: Clarendon Press

Birks, P, *An Introduction to the Law of Restitution*, rev edn, 1989, Oxford: Clarendon Press

Birks, P, *Restitution – The Future*, 1992, Sydney: The Federation Press

Burrows, A, *The Law of Restitution*, 1993, London: Butterworths

Burrows, A and McKendrick, E, *Cases and Materials on the Law of Restitution*, 1997, Oxford: OUP

Davenport, P and Harris, C, *Unjust Enrichment*, 1997, Sydney: The Federation Press

Dietrich, J, *Restitution: A New Perspective*, 1998, Sydney: The Federation Press

Ellinger, EP and Lemnicka, E, *Modern Banking Law*, 1994, Oxford: Clarendon Press

Finn, P, *Fiduciary Obligations*, 1977, Sydney: Lawbook Co

Jackman, *The Varieties of Restitution*, 1998, Sydney: The Federation Press

Jones, G, *Restitution in Public and Private Law*, 1991, London: Sweet & Maxwell

Goff (Lord Goff of Cheiveley) and Jones, G, *The Law of Restitution*, 5th edn, 1998, London: Sweet & Maxwell

Mason, K and Carter, JW, *Restitution Law in Australia*, 1995, Sydney: Butterworths

McInnes, M (ed), *Restitution: Developments in Unjust Enrichment*, 1996, Sydney: Lawbook Co

Meagher, R, Gummow, W and Lehane, J, *Equity Doctrines and Remedies*, 3rd edn, 1992, Sydney: Butterworths

Palmer, G, *The Law of Restitution*, 1978 (1986 supp), Boston: Little, Brown

Posner, R, *Economic Analysis of Law*, 4th edn, 1992, Boston: Little, Brown

Treitel, G, *Remedies for Breach of Contract*, 1988, Oxford: Clarendon Press

Book chapters

Arrowsmith, S, 'Mistake and the role of the submission to an honest claim', in Burrows, A (ed), *Essays on the Law of Restitution*, 1991, Oxford: Clarendon Press

Barker, K, 'After change of position: good faith exchange in the modern law of restitution', in Birks, P (ed), *Laundering and Tracing*, 1995, Oxford: Clarendon Press

Birks, P, 'Restitution from the executive', in Finn, P (ed), *Essays on Restitution*, 1990, Sydney: Lawbook Co

Birks, P, 'In defence of free acceptance', in Burrows, A (ed), *Essays on the Law of Restitution*, 1991, Oxford: Clarendon Press

Birks, P, 'Change of position: the nature of the defence and its relationship to other restitutionary defences', in McInnes, M (ed), *Restitution: Developments in Unjust Enrichment*, 1996, Sydney: Lawbook Co

Birks, P, 'Change of position and surviving enrichment', in Swadling, W (ed), *The Limits of Restitutionary Claims: A Comparative Analysis*, 1997, London: The British Institute of International and Comparative Law

Birks, P, 'Misnomer', in Cornish, WR *et al* (eds), *Restitution: Past, Present and Future*, 1998, Oxford: Hart Publishing

Bryan, M, 'Change of position: commentary', in McInnes, M (ed), *Restitution: Developments in Unjust Enrichment*, 1996, Sydney: Lawbook Co

Burrows, A, 'Public authorities, *ultra vires* and restitution', in Burrows, A (ed), *Essays on the Law of Restitution*, 1991, Oxford: Clarendon Press

Butler, P, 'Mistaken payments, change of position and restitution', in Finn, P (ed), *Essays on Restitution*, 1990, Sydney: Lawbook Co

Byrne, D, 'Benefits – for services rendered', in McInnes, M (ed), *Restitution: Developments in Unjust Enrichment*, 1996, Sydney: Lawbook Co

Carter, JW, 'Restitution and contract risk', in McInnes, M (ed), *Restitution: Developments in Unjust Enrichment*, 1996, Sydney: Lawbook Co

Dorner, M, '"Change of position" and "Wegfall der Bereicherung"', in Swadling, W (ed), *The Limits of Restitutionary Claims: A Comparative Analysis*, 1997, London: The British Institute of International and Comparative Law

Finn, P, 'Equitable doctrine and discretion in remedies', in Cornish, WR *et al* (eds), *Restitution: Past, Present and Future*, 1998, Oxford: Hart Publishing

Friedmann, D, 'Restitution for wrongs: the basis of liability', in Cornish, WR *et al* (eds), *Restitution: Past, Present and Future*, 1998, Oxford: Hart Publishing

Garner, M, 'Benefits – for services rendered: commentary', in McInnes, M (ed), *Restitution: Developments in Unjust Enrichment*, 1996, Sydney: Lawbook Co

Glover, J, 'Equity and restitution', in Parkinson, P (ed), *The Principles of Equity*, 1996, Sydney: Lawbook Co

Glover, J, 'Restitutionary recovery of taxes after the *Royal Insurance* case: commentary', in McInnes, M (ed), *Restitution: Developments in Unjust Enrichment*, 1996, Sydney: Lawbook Co

Gummow, W, 'Unjust enrichment, restitution and proprietary remedies', in Finn, P (ed), *Essays on Restitution*, 1990, Sydney: Lawbook Co

Jones, G, 'The law of restitution in the past and the future', in Burrows, A (ed), *Essays on the Law of Restitution*, 1991, Oxford: Clarendon Press

Liew, KL, 'Restitution and contract risk: commentary', in McInnes, M (ed), *Restitution: Developments in Unjust Enrichment*, 1996, Sydney: Lawbook Co

Mason, A, 'Themes and prospects', in Finn, P (ed), *Essays in Equity*, 1985, Sydney: Lawbook Co

Mason, K, 'Restitution in Australian law', in Finn, P (ed), *Essays on Restitution*, 1990, Sydney: Lawbook Co

McCamus, J, 'Unjust enrichment: its role and its limits', in Waters, D (ed), *Equities, Fiduciaries and Trusts*, 1993, Scarborough, Ont: Carswell

McKendrick, E, 'Frustration, restitution and loss apportionment', in Burrows, A (ed), *Essays on the Law of Restitution*, 1991, Oxford: Clarendon Press

McKendrick, E, 'Total failure of consideration and counter-restitution: two issues or one?', in Birks, P (ed), *Laundering and Tracing*, 1995, Oxford: Clarendon Press

McKendrick, E, 'Work done in anticipation of a contract which does not materialise', in Cornish, WR *et al* (eds), *Restitution: Past, Present and Future*, 1998, Oxford: Hart Publishing

McInnes, M, 'The structures and challenges of unjust enrichment', in McInnes, M (ed), *Restitution: Developments in Unjust Enrichment*, 1996, Sydney: Lawbook Co

Merralls, JD, 'Restitutionary recovery of taxes after the *Royal Insurance* case', in McInnes, M (ed), *Restitution: Developments in Unjust Enrichment*, 1996, Sydney: Lawbook Co

Millett, P, 'Restitution and constructive trusts', in Cornish, WR *et al* (eds), *Restitution: Past, Present and Future*, 1998, Oxford: Hart Publishing

Muir, G, 'Unjust sacrifice and the officious intervener', in Finn, P (ed), *Essays on Restitution*, 1990, Sydney: Lawbook Co

Nolan, R, 'Change of position', in Birks, P (ed), *Laundering and Tracing*, 1995, Oxford: Clarendon Press

Oakley, AJ, 'Restitution and constructive trusts: a commentary', in Cornish, WR *et al* (eds), *Restitution: Past, Present and Future*, 1998, Oxford: Hart Publishing

Rose, F, 'Passing on', in Birks, P (ed), *Laundering and Tracing*, 1995, Oxford: Clarendon Press

Sutton, R, 'What should be done for mistaken improvers?', in Finn, P (ed), *Essays on Restitution*, 1990, Sydney: Lawbook Co

Swadling, W, 'The nature of ministerial receipt', in Birks, P (ed), *Laundering and Tracing*, 1995, Oxford: Clarendon Press

Swadling, W, 'Restitution and *bona fide* purchase', in Swadling, W (ed), *The Limits of Restitutionary Claims: A Comparative Analysis*, 1997, London: The British Institute of International and Comparative Law

Virgo, G, 'What is the law of restitution about?', in Cornish, WR *et al* (eds), *Restitution: Past, Present and Future*, 1998, Oxford: Hart Publishing

Journal articles

Atiyah, P, 'Economic duress and the overborne will' (1982) 98 LQR 197

Atiyah, P, 'Duress and overborne will again' (1983) 99 LQR 353

Barker, K, 'Restitution of passenger fare' [1993] LMCLQ 291

Barker, K, '*Bona fide* purchase as a defence to unjust enrichment claims: a concise restatement' [1999] 7 RLR 75

Beatson, J, 'Unjust enrichment in the High Court of Australia' (1988) 104 LQR 13

Beatson, J, 'What can restitution do for you?' (1989) 2 JCL 65

Beatson, J, 'Restitutionary remedies for void and ineffective contracts' (1989) 105 LQR 179

Beatson, J, 'Restitution of taxes, levies and other imposts: defining the extent of the *Woolwich* principle' (1993) 109 LQR 401

Beatson, J, 'Restitution and contract: *non-cumul*?' (2000) 1 Theoretical Inquiries in Law 83

Birks, P, '*Negotiorum gestio* and the common law' (1971) 24 CLP 110

Birks, P, 'Restitution from public authorities' (1980) 33 CLP 191

Birks, P, 'English and Roman learning in *Moses v Macferlan*' (1984) 37 CLP 1

Birks, P, 'Restitutionary damages for breach of contract: *Snepp* and the fusion of law and equity' [1987] LMCLQ 421

Birks, P, 'Misdirected funds: restitution from the recipient' [1989] LMCLQ 296

Birks, P, 'The travails of duress' [1990] LMCLQ 342

Birks, P, 'Restitution after ineffective contracts: issues for the 1990s' (1990) 2 JCL 227

Birks, P, 'The English recognition of unjust enrichment' [1991] LMCLQ 473

Birks, P, 'No consideration: restitution after void contracts' (1993) 23 UWAL Rev 196

Birks, P, 'Restitution: dynamics of the modern law' (1993) 46 CLP 157

Birks, P, 'Modernising the law of restitution' (1993) 109 LQR 164

Birks, P, 'Property in the profits of wrongdoing' (1994) 24 UWAL Rev 8

Birks, P, 'Inconsistency between compensation and restitution' (1996) 112 LQR 375

Birks, P, 'Equity in the modern law: an exercise in taxonomy' (1996) 26 UWAL Rev 1

Birks, P, 'Trusts raised to reverse unjust enrichment: the *Westdeutsche* case' [1996] RLR 3

Birks, P, 'The "law of restitution" at the end of an epoch' (1999) 28 UWALR 1

Birks, P and Beatson, J, 'Unrequested payment of another's debt' (1976) 92 LQR 188

Bishop, W, 'The choice of remedy for breach of contract' (1985) 14 Journal of Legal Studies 289

Brock, M, 'Restitution of invalid taxes – principles and policies' (2000) 5 DLR 128

Bryan, M, 'Mistaken payments and the law of unjust enrichment: *David Securities Pty Ltd v Commonwealth Bank of Australia*' (1993) 15 Syd LR 462

Bryan, M, 'The acceptance world: *Angelopoulos v Sabatino*' [1997] LMCLQ 337

Bryan, M, 'Where the constitutional basis for payment has failed' [2000] 2 RLR 218

Bryan, M, 'The liability of banks to make restitution for wrongful payments' (1998) 26 ABLR 93

Bryan, M and Ellinghaus, MP, 'Fault lines in the law of obligations: *Roxborough v Rothmans of Pall Mall Australia Ltd*' (2000) 22 Syd LR 636

Burrows, A, 'Free acceptance and the law of restitution' (1988) 104 LQR 576

Burrows, A, 'No restitutionary damages for breach of contract' [1993] LMCLQ 453

Burrows, A, 'Restitution from assignees' [1994] RLR 52

Burrows, A, 'Understanding the law of restitution: a map through the thicket' (1995) 18 UQLJ 149

Burrows, A, 'Swaps and the friction between common law and equity' [1995] RLR 15

Burrows, A, 'Quadrating restitution and unjust enrichment: a matter of principle?' [2000] RLR 257

Burrows, A, 'Proprietary restitution: unmasking unjust enrichment' (2001) 117 LQR 412

Butler, P, 'Restitution of overpaid taxes, windfall gains and unjust enrichment: *Commissioner of State Revenue v Royal Insurance Ltd*' (1995) 18(2) UQLJ 318

Butler, P, 'Illegally tainted transfers and resulting trusts: *Nelson v Nelson*' (1996) 19 UQLJ 150

Byrne, D, 'Restitution for work done in anticipation of contract' (1997) 13 BCL 4

Byrne, M, 'Restitution and equity' (1995) 11 QUTLJ 169

Carter, JW, 'Discharged contracts: claims for restitution' (1997) 11(2) JCL 130

Carter, JW and Furmston, M, 'Good faith and fairness in the negotiation of contracts' (1994) 8 JCL 1 and 93

Carter, JW and Tolhurst, G, 'Restitution: payments made prior to discharge of contract' (1994) 7 JCL 273

Carter, JW and Tolhurst, G, 'Restitution for duress' (1996) 9 JCL 220

Carter, JW and Tolhurst, G, 'Gigs n' restitution – frustration and the statutory adjustment of payments and expenses' (1996) 10 JCL 264

Carter, JW and Tolhurst, G, 'Restitution for failure of consideration' (1997) 11(2) JCL 162

Cavanagh, S, 'Unenforceable contracts – *indebitatus assumpsit* and unjust enrichment: *Pavey & Matthews Pty Ltd v Paul*' [1987] 2 CLQ 9

Chambers, R, '*Westdeutsche Landesbank Girozentrale v Islington LBC*' [1996] MULR 1192

Chambers, R, 'Change of position on the faith of the receipt' [1996] RLR 103

Christensen, S, 'Recovery for work performed in anticipation of contract' (1993) 11 ABR 144

Cohen, N, 'The quiet revolution in the enforcement of illegal contracts' [1994] LMCLQ 163

Cooke, E, 'Trespass, *mesne* profits and restitution' (1994) 110 LQR 420

Cooper, G, 'The Statute of Frauds and actions in restitution and debt' [1989] 19 UWAL Rev 56

Cornish, W, '"Colour of office": restitutionary redress against public authority' [1987] Jo Malaysian and Comparative Law 41

Dietrich, J, 'A welcome retreat on unjust enrichment?: *Warman International Ltd v Dwyer*' (1996) 16 Queensland Lawyer 147

Dixon, Sir Owen, 'Concerning judicial method' (1956) 26 ALJ 468

Dow, S, 'Restitution of payments on cheques with forged drawers' signatures: loss allocation under English law' [1996] RLR 27

Doyle, S and Wright, D, 'Restitutionary damages – the unnecessary remedy' (2001) 25 MULR 1

Edelman, J, 'Restitution for a total failure of consideration: when a total failure is not a total failure' (1996) 1(3) Newc LR 57

Edelman, J, 'The new doctrine of partial failure of consideration' (1997) 15 ABR 299

Edelman, J, 'Claims to compound interest Part I' (1997) 27 ABLR 211

Edelman, J, 'Restitutionary damages and disgorgement damages for breach of contract' [2000] RLR 129

Edelman, J, 'Claims to compound interest Part II: extending compound interest claims for wrongdoing' (2000) 28 ABLR 115

Edgell, C, 'Privity of contract in Australia: the beginning of the end?' [1989] LMCLQ 139

Enonchong, N, 'Illegality: the fading flame of public policy' (1994) 14 OJLS 295

Enonchong, N, 'Illegal transactions: the future? (LCCP No 154)' [2000] RLR 82

Erbacher, S, 'Recent developments in restitutionary recovery of contractual payments: *Roxborough v Rothmans of Pall Mall Australia Ltd*' (2000) 28 ABLR 226

Erbacher, S, 'An account of profits for a breach of contract (*Attorney General v Blake*)' (2001) 29 ABLR 73

Evans, S, 'Rethinking tracing and the law of restitution' [1999] 115 LQR 469

Evans, S, 'Defending discretionary remedialism' (2001) 23 Syd LR 463

Fitzgerald, B, '*Ultra vires* as an unjust factor in the law of unjust enrichment' (1993) 2(1) GLR 1

Fitzgerald, B, 'Tracing at law, the exchange product theory and ignorance as an unjust factor in the law of unjust enrichment' (1994) 13 U Tas Law Rev 116

Friedmann, D, 'Payment of another's debt' (1983) 99 LQR 534

Fuller, L and Perdue, W, 'The reliance interest in contract damages' (1936–37) 46 Yale LJ 52

Fung, E and Ho, L, 'Change of position and estoppel' (2001) 117 LQR 14

Garner, M, 'The role of subjective benefit in the law of unjust enrichment' (1990) 10 OJLS 42

Gautreau, JRM, 'When are enrichments unjust?' (1988–89) 10 Adv Q 258

Goode, R, 'The bank's right to recover money paid on a stopped cheque' (1981) 97 LQR 254

Goode, R, 'Ownership and obligation in commercial transactions' (1987) 103 LQR 433

Goodhart, W, 'Restitutionary damages for breach of contract: the remedy that dare not speak its name' [1995] RLR 3

Grantham, R and Rickett, C, 'Change of position and balancing the equities' [1999] RLR 158

Halson, R, 'Opportunism, economic duress and contractual modifications' (1991) 107 LQR 649

Hastie, P, 'Restitution and remedy in intellectual property law' (1996) 14 ABR 6

Hedley, S, 'Unjust enrichment as the basis of restitution – an overworked concept' (1985) 5 LS 56

Hedley, S, 'Unjust enrichment' (1995) CLJ 578

Hellwege, P, 'The scope of application of change of position in the law of unjust enrichment: a comparative study' [1999] RLR 92

Hill, T, 'Restitution from public authorities and the Treasury's position' (1993) 56 MLR 856

Hope, E, 'Officiousness' (1929) 15 Cornell Law Quarterly 25

Hudson, A, 'Assessing mistake of law in derivative transactions: *Kleinwort Benson* and the local authority swaps cases' (1999) 14(3) JIBL 96

Ibbetson, D, 'Implied contracts and restitution: history in the High Court of Australia' (1988) 8 OJLS 312

Jackman, I, 'Contract rights and liabilities of third parties' (1989) 63 ALJ 638

Jackman, I, 'Restitution for wrongs' (1989) CLJ 302

Jaffey, P, 'Disgorgement and confiscation' [1996] RLR 92

Jaffey, P, 'Restitution, reliance and *quantum meruit* (*Countrywide Communications v ICL Pathway*)' [2000] RLR 270

Jaffey, P, 'Disgorgement for breach of contract (*Attorney General v Blake*)' [2000] RLR 578

Jewell, M, 'The boundaries of change of position – a comparative study' [2000] RLR 1

Jones, G, 'Restitution of benefits obtained in breach of another's confidence' (1970) 86 LQR 463

Jones, G, 'Anticipated contracts which do not materialise' (1980) 18 U of West Ont Law Rev 447

Jones, G, 'The recovery of benefits from a breach of contract' (1983) 99 LQR 443

Jones, G, 'Restitution: unjust enrichment as a unifying concept in Australia?' (1988–89) 1 JCL 8

Key, P, 'Excising estoppel by representation as a defence to restitution' [1995] CLJ 525

Key, P, 'Change of position' (1995) 58 MLR 505

Kremer, B, 'Recovering money paid under void contracts: "absence of consideration" in failure of consideration' (2001) 17 JCL 37

Liew, KL, 'Recovery of moneys paid under a mistake of law: the Australian approach' (1994) 6(2) Corp and Bus LJ 3

Liew, KL, 'Mistaken payments – the right of recovery and the defences' (1995) 7 Bond LR 95

Mannolini, J, 'Restitution where an anticipated contract fails to materialise' (1996) 59(11) MLR 111

Matthews, P, 'Money paid under mistake of fact' (1980) 130 NLJ 587

McCormack, G, 'Proprietary claims and insolvency in the wake of *Westdeutsche*' [1996] JBL 48

McInnes, M, 'Case comment: *David Securities v Commonwealth Bank of Australia*' (1994) 22 ABLR 437

McInnes, M, 'Incontroverible benefits in the Supreme Court of Canada' (1994) 23 Can Bus LJ 122

McInnes, M, 'Restitution and the rescue of life' (1994) 32 Alberta Law Rev 37

McInnes, M, 'The plaintiff's expense in restitution: difficulties in the High Court' (1995) 23 ABLR 472

McInnes, M, 'Contractual services, restitution and the avoidance of bad bargains' (1995) 23(3) ALBR 218

McInnes, M, 'Contract and restitution' (1996) 24(3) ABLR 238

McInnes, M, 'Mistaken payments return to the High Court' (1996) 22(2) Mon ULR 209

McInnes, M, 'Bases for restitution: a call for clarity with unjust factors' (1996) 10 JCL 73

McInnes, M, 'The defence of change of position in the law of restitution' (1996) 24 ABLR 313

McInnes, M, '"Passing on" in the law of restitution: a re-consideration' (1997) 19 Syd LR 179

McInnes, M, 'Restitution, unjust enrichment and the perfect quadration thesis' [1999] RLR 118

McInnes, M, 'Disgorgement for wrongs: an experiment in alignment' [2000] RLR 516

McKeand, R, 'Economic duress – wearing the clothes of unconscionable conduct' (2001) 17 JCL 1

McKinley, D, 'Constitutional brokerage in Australia: constitutions and the doctrines of parliamentary supremacy and the rule of law' (1994) 22 FLR 194

Mead, G, 'Restitution within contract?' (1991) 11 LS 172

Miller, D, 'Restitutionary and exemplary damages for copyright infringment' (1996) 14 ABR 143

Millett, P, 'Tracing the proceeds of fraud' (1991) 107 LQR 71

Millett, P, 'Bribes and secret commissions' [1993] RLR 7

Mitchell, C, 'Remedial inadequacy in contract: the role of restitutionary damages' (1999) 15 JCL 133

Nicholson, K, 'Recovery of money paid under a mistake of fact' (1986) 60 ALJ 459

Nolan, D, 'Economic duress and the availability of a reasonable alternative (*Huyton v Peter Cremer)*' [2000] RLR 105

O'Connor, P, 'Happy partners or strange bedfellows: the blending of remedial and institutional features in the evolving constructive trust' (1996) 20 MULR 735

O'Dair, R, 'Restitutionary damages for breach of contract and the theory of efficient breach: some reflections' (1993) 46(2) CLP 113

O'Dair, R, 'Remedies for breach of contract: a wrong turn' [1993] RLR 31

Pegoraro, E, 'Recovery of benefits conferred pursuant to failed anticipated contracts – unjust enrichment, equitable estoppel or unjust sacrifice' (1993) 23 ABLR 117

Perillo, J, 'Restitution in a contractual context' (1973) 73 Col LR 1208

Perell, P, '*Kleinwort Benson v Lincoln CC* and mistake of law and unjust enrichment – the House of Lords starts down a new path' (1999) 21 Adv Q 495

Phang, A, 'Whither economic duress? Reflections on two recent cases' (1990) 53 MLR 107

Phang, A, 'Economic duress – uncertainty confirmed' (1992) 5 JCL 147

Phang, A, 'Economic duress: recent difficulties and possible alternatives' [1997] RLR 53

Phang, A and Lee, PW, 'Rationalising restitutionary damages in contract law – an elusive or illusory quest?' (2001) 17 JCL 240

Proksch, L, 'Restitution and privity' (1994) 68 ALJ 188

Rickett, C, 'Restitution and contract' (1996) NZLJ 263

Ridge, P, 'Just feel-good words? Recent Australian developments towards a restitutionary cause of action for pre-judgment interest' (2000) 28 ABLR 275

Rose, F, 'Restitution for the rescuer' (1989) 9 OJLS 167

Sharpe, R and Waddams, S, 'Damages for lost opportunity to bargain' (1982) 2 OJLS 290

Simester, A, 'Unjust free acceptance' [1997] LMCLQ 103

Sindone, M, 'The doctrine of economic duress' (1996) 14 ABR 34

Smith, L, 'Three-party restitution: a critique of Birks' theory of interceptive subtraction' (1991) 11 OJLS 481

Smith, L, 'Restitution for mistake of law (*Kleinwort Benson v Lincoln CC)*' [1999] RLR 148

Soh, K, 'Privity of contract and restitution' (1989) 105 LQR 4

Steinepreis, G, 'Cancelled projects – who bears the risk for pre-contract expenses?' (1996) 12 BCL 303

Stevens, J, 'Election between alternative remedies' [1996] RLR 117

Stewart, A and Carter, JW, 'Frustrated contracts and statutory adjustment: the case for a reappraisal' [1992] CLJ 66

Stoljar, S, 'Unjust enrichment and unjust sacrifice' (1987) 50 MLR 603

Stowe, H, 'The unruly horse has bolted: *Tinsley v Milligan*' (1994) 57 MLR 441

Sutton, 'Unjust enrichment' (1981) 5 Otago LR 187

Swadling, W, 'Restitution for no consideration' [1994] RLR 73

Tapsell, K, 'The negligence juggernaut and unjust enrichment' (1997) 16 ABR 70

Virgo, G, 'The law of taxation is not an island – overpaid taxes and the law of restitution' [1993] British Tax Review 442

Virgo, G, 'Striking the balance in the law of restitution' [1995] LMCLQ 362

Vrisakis, A and Carter, JW, 'Restitution of payments made under contracts prohibited by statute' (2000) 15 JCL 228

Waddams, S, 'Profits derived from breach of contract: damages or restitution' (1997) 11 JCL 115

Watts, P, 'Restitution' [1996] NZLR 471

Wells, B, 'Restitution from the Crown: private rights and public interest' (1994) 16 Adel LR 191

Wyvill, A, 'Enrichment, restitution and the collapsed negotiations cases' (1993) 11(2) ABR 93

Reports

The Law Commission of England and Wales, Report No 227, *Restitution of Payments Made Under a Mistake of Law*, 1994, London

The Law Commission of England and Wales, Report No 247, *Aggravated, Exemplary and Restitutionary Damages*, 1997, London

INDEX